Java™ Swing

Related titles from O'Reilly

Ant: The Definitive Guide

Building Java™ Enterprise Applications

Database Programming with JDBC and Java™

Developing JavaBeans™

Enterprise JavaBeans™

J2ME™ in a Nutshell

Java™ 2D Graphics

Java™ and SOAP

Java™ & XML

Java™ and XML Data Binding

Java™ and XSLT

Java™ Cookbook

Java™ Cryptography

Java™ Distributed Computing

Java™ Enterprise in a Nutshell

Java™ Examples in a Nutshell

Java™ Foundation Classes in a Nutshell

Java™ I/O

Java™ in a Nutshell

Java™ Internationalization

Java™ Message Service

Java™ Network Programming

Java™ NIO

Java™ Performance Tuning

Java™ Programming with Oracle JDBC

Java™ Programming with Oracle SQLJ

Java™ RMI

Java™ Security

JavaServer™ Pages

JavaServer™ Pages Pocket Reference

Java™ Servlet Programming

Java™ Threads

Java™ Web Services

JXTA™ in a Nutshell

Learning Java™

Learning Wireless Java™

Also available

The Java™ Enterprise CD Bookshelf

SECOND EDITION

Java™ Swing

Marc Loy, Robert Eckstein, Dave Wood,
James Elliott, and Brian Cole

O'REILLY®

Beijing · Cambridge · Farnham · Köln · Paris · Sebastopol · Taipei · Tokyo

Java™ Swing, Second Edition

by Marc Loy, Robert Eckstein, Dave Wood, James Elliott, and Brian Cole

Published by O'Reilly Media, Inc., 1005 Gravenstein Highway North, Sebastopol, CA 95472.

O'Reilly Media, Inc. books may be purchased for educational, business, or sales promotional use. On-line editions are also available for most titles (*safari.oreilly.com*). For more information contact our corporate/institutional sales department: (800) 998-9938 or *corporate@oreilly.com*.

Editors:	Mike Loukides and Debra Cameron
Production Editor:	Matt Hutchinson
Cover Designer:	Hanna Dyer
Interior Designer:	David Futato

Printing History:

September 1998:	First Edition.
November 2002:	Second Edition.

ISBN-10: 0-596-00408-7
ISBN-13: 978-0-596-00408-8
[M]

Table of Contents

Preface

When Java was first released, its user interface facilities were a significant weakness. The Abstract Window Toolkit (AWT) was part of the JDK from the beginning, but it really wasn't sufficient to support a complex user interface. It supported everything you could do in an HTML form and provided free-standing frames, menus, and a few other objects, but you'd be hard-pressed to implement an application as complex as Quicken or Lotus Notes. AWT also had its share of portability problems; it relied heavily on the runtime platform's native user interface components, and it wasn't always possible to hide differences in the way these components behaved.

JDK 1.1 fixed a number of problems—most notably, it introduced a new event model that was much more efficient and easier to use—but it didn't make any major additions to the basic components. We got a ScrollPane and a PopupMenu, but that was about it. Furthermore, AWT still relied on the native components and therefore continued to have portability problems.

In April 1997, Sun's Java group (then called JavaSoft) announced the Java Foundation Classes, or JFC, which supersedes (and includes) AWT. A major part of the JFC was a set of much more complete, flexible, and portable user interface components called "Swing." (The JFC also includes a comprehensive facility for 2D graphics, printing, and Drag and Drop.) With Swing, you can design interfaces with tree components, tables, tabbed dialogs, tooltips, and a growing set of other features that computer users are accustomed to.

In addition to the new components, Swing made three major improvements to the AWT. First, Swing doesn't rely on the runtime platform's native components. It's written entirely in Java and creates its own components. This approach solved most of the portability problems since components don't inherit weird behaviors from the runtime environment or do they work against its grain. Second, because Swing is in complete control of the components, it's in control of the way components look on the screen and gives you more control over how your applications look. You can choose between several pre-built "look-and-feels" (L&Fs), or you can create your own if you want your software to show your personal style (more appropriate for games than for daily productivity software, of course). This feature is called "Pluggable Look-and-Feel," or PLAF. Third, Swing makes a very clear distinction between the data a component displays (the "model") and the actual display (the "view"). While the fine points of this distinction are appreciated mostly by computer scientists, it has important implications for all developers. This separation means that components are extremely flexible. It's easy to adapt components to display new kinds of data that their original design didn't anticipate or to change the way a component looks without getting tangled up in assumptions about the data it represents.

The first official release of Swing, for use with JDK 1.1, took place in the spring of 1998. Swing (and the rest of JFC) was built into Java 2 and revolutionized Java user interface development. The Swing components continue to evolve with Java, and Java 2 SDK 1.4 is the best version yet. This book shows you how to join the revolution.

What This Book Covers

This book gives a complete introduction to the entire Swing component set. Of course, it shows you how to use all of the components: how to display them on the screen, register for events, and get information from them. You'd expect that in any Swing book. This book goes much further. It goes into detail about the model-delegate architecture behind the components and discusses all of the data models. Understanding the models is essential when you're working on an application that requires something significantly different from the components' default behavior. For example, if you need a component that displays a different data type or one that structures data in some nonstandard way, you'll need to work with the data models. This book also discusses how to write "accessible" user interfaces and how to create your own look-and-feel.

There are a few topics this book doesn't cover, despite its girth. We assume you know the Java language. For Swing, it's particularly important to have a good grasp of inner classes (both named and anonymous), which are used by Swing itself and in our examples. We assume that you understand the JDK 1.1 event model, Java's mechanism for communicating between asynchronous threads. Swing introduced many new event types, all of which are discussed in this book, but we provide only an overview of the event mechanism as a whole. We also assume that you understand the older AWT components, particularly the Component and Container classes, which are superclasses of the Swing's JComponent. We assume that you understand the AWT layout managers, all of which are usable within Swing applications. If you are new to Java, or would like a review, you can find a complete discussion of these topics in the *Java AWT Reference* by John Zukowski[*] or a solid introduction in *Learning Java* by

---

[*] PDFs for the *Java AWT Reference* are available at this book's web site, *http://www.oreilly.com/catalog/jswing2*.

Pat Niemeyer and Jonathan Knudsen (both published by O'Reilly). We do not assume that you know anything about other JFC topics, like Java 2D—check out *Java 2D* by Jonathan Knudsen for that; all the drawing and font manipulation in this book can be done with AWT. (We do cover the JFC Accessibility API, which is supported by every Swing component, as well as the drag-and-drop facility, since this functionality is a requirement for modern user interfaces.)

The major Swing classes fall into the following packages:

`javax.accessibility`
   Classes that support accessibility for people who have difficulty using standard user interfaces. Covered in Chapter 25.

`javax.swing`
   The bulk of the Swing components. Covered in Chapters 3–14 and 27–28.

`javax.swing.border`
   Classes for drawing fancy borders around components. Covered in Chapter 13.

`javax.swing.colorchooser`
   Classes providing support for the `JColorChooser` component. Covered in Chapter 12.

`javax.swing.event`
   Swing events. Covered throughout the book.

`javax.swing.filechooser`
   Classes providing support for the `JFileChooser` component. Covered in Chapter 12.

`javax.swing.plaf`
   Classes supporting the PLAF, including classes that implement the Metal and Multi L&Fs. (Implementations of the Windows and Motif L&Fs are packaged under `com.sun.java.swing.plaf`, and the Macintosh Aqua L&F is under `com.apple.mrj.swing`.) Covered in Chapter 26.

`javax.swing.table`
   Classes providing support for the `JTable` component (`JTable` itself is in `javax.swing`). Covered in Chapters 15 and 16.

`javax.swing.text`
   Classes providing support for the text components (such as `JTextField`; the components themselves are in the `javax.swing` package). Covered in Chapters 19–23.

`javax.swing.text.html` and `javax.swing.text.rtf`
   "Editor kits" for working with HTML and Microsoft RTF documents. Covered in Chapter 23. The `text.html` package has a subpackage, `parser`, which includes tools for parsing HTML.

`javax.swing.tree`

    Classes providing support for the `JTree` component (`JTree` itself is in `javax.swing`). Covered in Chapter 17.

`javax.swing.undo`

    Classes that implement undoable operations. Covered in Chapter 18.

What's New in This Edition?

This second edition covers the latest developments in the Java 2 Standard Edition SDK 1.3 and 1.4. We've tried to highlight the changes from 1.2 in case you have to work with older releases for compatibility or political reasons.

For brevity's sake, we refer to Java versions by their SDK version number, describing this or that feature as having been introduced in SDK 1.3 or 1.4. Earlier versions were called Java Development Kits, so in those cases we refer to JDK 1.1 or 1.2.

This new edition incorporated your feedback from the first edition! The first edition was too heavy on the documentation side for many readers. The Javadoc for the Swing packages continues to improve, and more and more people are familiar with the patterns of Java classes and methods. With those two facts in mind, we try to focus on the parts of the API that are interesting and useful rather than just including them because they exist. We added many new examples and improved the existing examples. This book is a true and thorough revision of the first edition, not a mere update.

As a quick reference to some of the changes you'll find in the 1.3 and 1.4 releases of the SDK, Table P-1 and Table P-2 list any significant changes to components and briefly describe those changes. We detail these changes throughout the book as we discuss the particular components.

Table P-1. Swing changes in the Java 2 SDK 1.3

Component or feature	In chapter	Description of changes or additions
`JTree`	17	Several new properties were added, including the click count to start editing and the selection path.
`JTable`	15	Improved general performance and cell rendering. `AbstractCellEditor` is now the parent class of the `DefaultCellEditor` used by tables.
`JSplitPane`	11	A new `resizeWeight` property was added, and the `dividerLocationProperty` is now bound.
`JFileChooser`	12	You can now remove the Ok and Cancel buttons. A new property, `acceptAllFileFilterUsed`, was added.
`JCheckBox`	5	Added new `borderPaintedFlat` property.
`DefaultButtonModel`	5	Added new `getGroup()` method.

Table P-1. Swing changes in the Java 2 SDK 1.3 (continued)

Component or feature	In chapter	Description of changes or additions
JInternalFrame	9	Several fixes and newly public classes and methods. Internal frames are now invisible by default, and the default close operation is now DISPOSE_ON_CLOSE.
JTabbedPane	11	Added new toolTipTextAt indexed property.
Text components	19-23	Several fixes applied. Several improvements in general HTML support via the HTMLEditorKit and related classes. (XHTML documents are still not supported.)
JViewport	11	New scrollMode property added.
JComponent	3	New print methods added: printComponent( ), printBorder( ), printChildren( ).
InputVerifier	20	New class added.
Keyboard binding	3, B	New keyboard binding mechanism added. New classes, InputMap and ActionMap, replace Keymap functionality.
Borders	13	New LineBorder constructor to support rounded corners added.
Actions	3, 5, 14	AbstractAction class was updated, and new constructors for JCheckBox, JRadioButton, JToggleButton, JMenu, JMenuItem, JCheckBoxMenuItem, and JRadioButtonMenuItem that use Action were added.
JToolBar	14	Support for titling undocked toolbars added.
JPopupMenu	14	Added new popupTrigger boolean property.
JFrame	11	Added new EXIT_ON_CLOSE constant for use with the defaultCloseOperation property.
ListenerList	27	Added getListeners( ) method to several model classes, including AbstractDocument, AbstractTableModel, AbstractListModel, DefaultButtonModel, DefaultTreeModel, and DefaultListSelectionModel.

Table P-2. Swing changes in the Java 2 SDK 1.4

Component or feature	In chapter	Description of changes or additions
JProgressBar	6	Added support for indeterminate progress bars.
JSpinner	7	Added new spinner class.
JFormattedTextField	20	Added new formatted text field class that validates user input.
Focus	3, 28	A new focus model and methodology was introduced. Several of the old-style focus methods and classes were deprecated as of 1.4.1.

Table P-2. Swing changes in the Java 2 SDK 1.4 (continued)

Component or feature	In chapter	Description of changes or additions
Drag and Drop	24	New architecture introduced, and `dragEnabled` and `transferHandler` properties added to several components.
Box	11	Now descends from `JComponent`.
JButton	5	More control over mnemonic underline location granted.
JComboBox	7	Added `PopupMenuListener` and support for cell size prototyping.
JFileChooser	12	Added support for modifying the properties of the Open button (such as its text and tooltip). Also added support for selecting multiple files. (The multiple file selection mode was introduced in the 1.2 release but was not implemented until 1.4.)
JInternalFrame	9	Long titles are now truncated, and the title bar is rendered with a gradient.
Text components	19–23	Tooltip support was improved. HTML support, including accessibility in documents, was improved (XHTML is still not supported). New `replace( )` method added to `AbstractDocument`.
JOptionPane	10	New input dialog methods added.
JPopupMenu	14	Now properly supports key bindings.
JTabbedPane	11	Introduced scrollable tabs for panes with a large number of tabs. Mnemonic support for accessing tabs was also added.
JTree	17	Null roots are now allowed, and first-letter keyboard navigation was added.
JList	7	Items can now be arranged horizontally, and first-letter keyboard navigation was added.
SwingConstants	27	New constants, NEXT and PREVIOUS, were added.
SwingUtilities	27	New methods added, including `calculateInnerArea( )` and `applyComponentOrientation( )`
LookAndFeel	3, 26, B	General support for auditory cues was added. Access to Windows desktop properties was also added.
JComponent	3	`requestFocus( )` and `requestFocusInWindow( )` methods are now public.
MouseWheelEvent MouseWheelListener	11	New event and listener for mouse wheels added.
JRootPane	10	Look-and-feel can now supply window decoration.
JScrollBar	6	Now properly overrides `setUI( )`.
JScrollPane	11	Now supports mouse wheel events. (This support can be turned off.)
RepaintManager	28	New method to return a `VolatileImage`.
SpringLayout	11	New class (and supporting classes) added.

On the Web Site

The web site for this book, *http://www.oreilly.com/catalog/jswing2/,* offers some important materials you'll want to know about. All the examples in this book can be found there, as well as free utilities, PDFs of John Zukowski's *Java AWT Reference* (foundational for understanding Swing), and selected material from the first edition for those of you working with older SDKs.

The examples are available as a JAR file, a ZIP archive, and a compressed TAR archive. The files named *swing* were tested against J2SE SDK 1.4 for this edition. The files named *swing-1e* were tested against JDK 1.2 for the first edition of the book. The files named *swing-old* were written with the beta releases of Swing and use the com.java.swing hierarchies.

We also include a few free utilities on the site that you may want to check out:

macmetrics.jar
> Lee Ann Rucker's MacMetrics theme. See "Mac OS X and the Default Look-and-Feel" in Chapter 26 for details on this helpful tool that enables developers without access to Mac OS X to see how their applications' interfaces will look on that platform.

oraswing.jar
> Our very own utilities bundle with documentation, including:

> *eel.jar*
>> The Every Event Listener utility for debugging events from the various Swing and AWT components.

> *relativelayout.jar*
>> A nifty XML-based layout manager.

> *mapper.jar*
>> A quick helper for discovering the InputMap and ActionMap entries (both bound and unbound) for any given component. This is the utility we used to build Appendix B.

We may add other utilities as we receive feedback from readers, so be sure to check the README file on the site!

We owe a debt of gratitude to John Zukowski and O'Reilly & Associates, who have graciously allowed the classic *Java AWT Reference* to be placed online at our site. You can download PDFs of the entire book.

The web site also includes some expanded material that we couldn't shoehorn into this edition of the book. For those of you still working with JDK 1.2, we've included a PDF containing the "Keyboard Actions" section from Chapter 3 of the first edition—the approach changed markedly with SDK 1.3. Regardless of your version of

Java, if you're planning on extending the `HTMLEditorKit`, you should check out the expanded material online. We cover the basics of this editor kit in Chapter 23, but for those of you who want to dig in deep, you should download PDFs of the two chapters devoted to this topic..

Conventions

This book follows certain conventions for font usage, property tables, and class diagrams. Understanding these conventions up-front makes it easier to use this book.

This book uses the following font conventions:

Italic
> Used for filenames, file extensions, URLs, application names, emphasis, and new terms when they are first introduced

`Constant width`
> Used for Java class names, functions, variables, components, properties, data types, events, and snippets of code that appear in text

`Constant width bold`
> Used for commands you enter at the command line and to highlight new code inserted in a running example

`Constant width italic`
> Used to annotate output

 This icon designates a note, which is an important aside to the nearby text.

 This icon designates a warning relating to the nearby text.

Properties Tables

Swing components are all JavaBeans. Properties provide a powerful way to work with JavaBeans, so we use tables throughout the book to present lists of properties. Table P-3 is an example from the hypothetical `JFoo` class that shows how we use these tables.

Table P-3. Properties of the fictional JFoo class

Property	Data type	get	is	set	Default value
opaque[b, o, 1.4]	boolean	•	•	•	true

[b]bound, [o]overridden, [1.4]since 1.4

See also properties from the JComponent class (Table 3-6).

Properties tables tell you the data type; whether it has is, get, and set methods; and its default value, if any. Footnotes to the properties tables tell you, among other things, whether a property is bound, protected, indexed, and/or overridden. We use "overridden" to mean both actual overridden methods in the case of a concrete parent class and implemented methods in the case of an abstract parent class or an interface. If it is a recent addition, the version of the SDK that added the property is noted (assume 1.2 if there is no footnote).

Table P-3 indicates that a JFoo object has a read/write bound property named opaque with the data type boolean. The property was introduced in the 1.4 release of the SDK. This property has accessor methods with the signatures:

```
public boolean getOpaque( );
public boolean isOpaque( );
public void setOpaque(boolean opaque);
```

These methods aren't listed separately when we discuss the class's other methods. Because opaque is a bound property, changing its value generates a PropertyChange-Event. The overridden footnote indicates that the opaque property is also inherited (or possibly implemented for the first time); it is listed here because the JFoo class has altered the property in some way—e.g., the default value was changed, accessor methods were added, or new behavior when accessing or modifying the value was specified. A cross-reference following the table says that JFoo has inherited properties from the JComponent class; see the discussion of that class for details on these properties.

We've listed default values for properties wherever applicable. (Properties of interfaces, for example, will not have any values listed.) To save space, we omit the new operator in these tables.

One more note about bound properties. The Swing developers introduced some confusion into the notion of a "bound property" by adding a new lightweight event, ChangeEvent, which is a stateless version of PropertyChangeEvent. In these tables, we adhere strictly to the JavaBeans definition of a bound property: modifying a bound property generates a PropertyChangeEvent.

Class Diagrams

The class diagrams that appear throughout the book are similar to those in *Learning Java* and other Java books from O'Reilly. Solid lines indicate inheritance relationships; dotted lines indicate interface relationships. In Figure P-1, ClassA extends AbstractClass, which implements InterfaceX. There are two interface relationships that we don't show in this way. All Swing classes implement Serializable, and showing this relationship explicitly would clutter the diagram; just assume that any Swing class implements Serializable, unless stated otherwise in the text. Many Swing classes implement the Accessible interface; rather than cluttering the diagrams, we show that a class implements Accessible with an A icon.

We also use the class diagrams to show information about relations between classes. In Figure P-1, the long, dashed arrow indicates that ClassA uses ClassB. The label on the arrow indicates the nature of the relationship; other common relations are "contains" and "creates." *1..** indicates the multiplicity of the relationship. Here, an instance of ClassA uses one or more instances of ClassB. Other multiplicities are *1* (exactly one instance), *0..** (any number of instances), and *0..1* (zero or one instance).

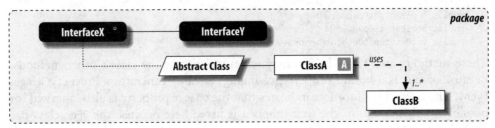

Figure P-1. Class diagram notation

How to Contact Us

Along with O'Reilly, we have verified the information in this book to the best of our abilities, but you may find that features have changed (or even that we have made mistakes!). Please let us know about any errors you find, as well as your suggestions for future editions, by writing to:

O'Reilly & Associates, Inc.
1005 Gravenstein Highway North
Sebastopol, CA 95472
(800) 998-9938 (U.S. and Canada)
(707) 829-0515 (international/local)
(707) 829-0104 (fax)

You can also contact O'Reilly by email. To be put on the mailing list or request a catalog, send a message to:

info@oreilly.com

We have a web page for this book, where we list errata, examples, and any additional information. You can access this page at:

http://www.oreilly.com/catalog/jswing2/

To ask technical questions or comment on the book, send email to:

bookquestions@oreilly.com

For more information about O'Reilly books, conferences, Resource Centers, and the O'Reilly Network, see O'Reilly's web site at:

http://www.oreilly.com/

Acknowledgments

We're particularly indebted to our technical reviewers for this second edition: Christian Hessler, John Pyeatt, Maciek Smuga-Otto, and Dave Wood.

Marc Loy

I'll start off the mutual admiration society by thanking my cohorts Jim and Brian. They came to the table after we lost Dave and Bob (from the first edition) to other books, and well, life in general. This update would not have been possible without them. Our editor Deb Cameron has the patience and diligence of some very patient and diligent god. I continue to be amazed by the support and insight I receive from my colleagues Tom Berry, Damian Moshak, and Brooks Graham. Gratitude for the inspiration to keep writing (even if it is technical) goes to Amy Hammond, my sister and confidante. A special thanks to Kathy Godeken for an early push in the right direction. Words are not enough to thank my partner Ron, so I'll not waste the space.

Brian Cole

Thanks to my family for putting up with me as an author. This goes tenfold for my partner, Beth, for that and more. Thanks to Deb, who was very understanding about deadlines, and especially to Marc and Jim, who were always willing to lend a hand despite deadlines of their own. Thanks to my employers and coworkers, who were willing to accommodate my schedule. Finally, thanks to the anonymous programmer who discovered that running java with `-Dsun.java2d.noddraw=true` fixes the appalling 1.3 drawing problems common on Win32 systems equipped with some popular types of video cards. You saved me a lot of time.

James Elliott

Any list of thanks has to start with my parents for fostering my interest in computing even when we were living in countries that made that a major challenge, and with my partner Joe for putting up with it today when it has flowered into a major obsession. I'd also like to acknowledge my Madison employer, Berbee, for giving me an opportunity to delve deeply into Java and build skills as an architect of reusable APIs; for letting me stay clear of the proprietary, platform-specific tar pit that is engulfing so much of the programming world; for surrounding me with such incredible colleagues; and for being supportive when I wanted to help with this book. Of course, I have Marc to thank for getting me involved in this crazy adventure in the first place, and Deb for helping make sense of it.

I wanted to be sure this edition gave good advice about how to work with Swing on Mac OS X, Apple's excellent, Unix-based environment for Java development, so I asked for some help. Lee Ann Rucker (who should also be thanked for her heroic work of single-handedly implementing the new Mac OS Look-and-Feel while on loan from Sun to Apple) shared some great ideas and approaches to writing solid, cross-platform Java applications, including the MacMetrics theme described in Chapter 26. Count me among the many people wishing Sun or Apple would put her back on the Mac Java team! Eric Albert, another frequent source of insight on Apple's Java-Dev mailing list, gave me more suggestions and pointed me to his excellent chapter in *Early Adopter Mac OS X Java* (Wrox Press). Finally, Matt Drance at Apple's Developer Technical Support sent me an early (and helpful) version of his technical note on how to make Java applications as Mac-friendly as possible. There are many others to whom I'm indebted, but I've already used more than my fair share of space, so the rest of you know who you are!

We all want to thank the many members of O'Reilly's production department, who put in lots of work under a tight schedule.

CHAPTER 1

Introducing Swing

Welcome to Swing! By now, you're probably wondering what Swing is and how you can use it to spice up your Java applications. Or perhaps you're curious as to how the Swing components fit into the overall Java strategy. Then again, maybe you just want to see what all the hype is about. Well, you've come to the right place; this book is all about Swing and its components. So let's dive right in and answer the first question that you're probably asking right now, which is...

What Is Swing?

If you poke around the Java home page (*http://java.sun.com/*), you'll find Swing described as a set of customizable graphical components whose look-and-feel (L&F) can be dictated at runtime. In reality, however, Swing is much more than this. Swing is the next-generation GUI toolkit that Sun Microsystems created to enable enterprise development in Java. By *enterprise development*, we mean that programmers can use Swing to create large-scale Java applications with a wide array of powerful components. In addition, you can easily extend or modify these components to control their appearance and behavior.

Swing is not an acronym. The name represents the collaborative choice of its designers when the project was kicked off in late 1996. Swing is actually part of a larger family of Java products known as the Java Foundation Classes (JFC), which incorporate many of the features of Netscape's Internet Foundation Classes (IFC) as well as design aspects from IBM's Taligent division and Lighthouse Design. Swing has been in active development since the beta period of the Java Development Kit (JDK) 1.1, circa spring of 1997. The Swing APIs entered beta in the latter half of 1997 and were initially released in March 1998. When released, the Swing 1.0 libraries contained nearly 250 classes and 80 interfaces. Growth has continued since then: at press time, Swing 1.4 contains 85 public interfaces and 451 public classes.

Although Swing was developed separately from the core Java Development Kit, it does require at least JDK 1.1.5 to run. Swing builds on the event model introduced in the 1.1 series of JDKs; you cannot use the Swing libraries with the older JDK 1.0.2. In addition, you must have a Java 1.1–enabled browser to support Swing applets. The Java 2 SDK 1.4 release includes many updated Swing classes and a few new features. Swing is fully integrated into both the developer's kit and the runtime environment of all Java 2 releases (SDK 1.2 and higher), including the Java Plug-In.

What Are the Java Foundation Classes?

The FC is a suite of libraries designed to assist programmers in creating enterprise applications with Java. The Swing API is only one of five libraries that make up the JFC. The JFC also consists of the Abstract Window Toolkit (AWT), the Accessibility API, the 2D API, and enhanced support for Drag and Drop capabilities. While the Swing API is the primary focus of this book, here is a brief introduction to the other elements in the JFC:

AWT

The Abstract Window Toolkit is the basic GUI toolkit shipped with all versions of the Java Development Kit. While Swing does not reuse any of the older AWT components, it does build on the lightweight component facilities introduced in AWT 1.1.

Accessibility

The accessibility package provides assistance to users who have trouble with traditional user interfaces. Accessibility tools can be used in conjunction with devices such as audible text readers or braille keyboards to allow direct access to the Swing components. Accessibility is split into two parts: the Accessibility API, which is shipped with the Swing distribution, and the Accessibility Utilities API, which is distributed separately. All Swing components support accessibility, so this book dedicates an entire chapter (Chapter 25) to accessibility design and use.

2D API

The 2D API contains classes for implementing various painting styles, complex shapes, fonts, and colors. This Java package is loosely based on APIs that were licensed from IBM's Taligent division. The 2D API classes are not part of Swing, so they are not covered in this book.

Drag and Drop

Drag and Drop (DnD) is one of the more common metaphors used in graphical interfaces today. The user is allowed to click and "hold" a GUI object, moving it to another window or frame in the desktop with predictable results. The DnD API allows users to implement droppable elements that transfer information between Java applications and native applications. Although DnD is not part of

Swing, it is crucial to a commercial-quality application. We tackle this topic in Chapter 24.

Figure 1-1 enumerates the various components of the Java Foundation Classes. Because part of the Accessibility API is shipped with the Swing distribution, we show it overlapping Swing.

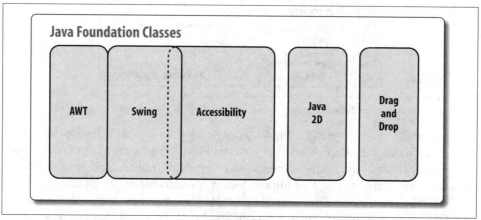

Figure 1-1. The five APIs of the JFC

Is Swing a Replacement for AWT?

No. Swing is actually built on top of the core AWT libraries. Because Swing does not contain any platform-specific (native) code, you can deploy the Swing distribution on any platform that implements the Java 1.1.5 or above virtual machine. In fact, if you have JDK 1.2 or higher on your platform, then the Swing classes are already available, and there's nothing further to download. If you use a JDK version prior to 1.2, you can download the entire set of Swing libraries as a set of Java Archive (JAR) files from the Swing home page, *http://java.sun.com/products/jfc*. In either case, it is generally a good idea to visit this URL for any extra packages or L&Fs that may be distributed separately from the core Swing libraries.

Figure 1-2 shows the relationship between Swing, AWT, and the Java Development Kit in the 1.1 and higher JDKs. In JDK 1.1, the Swing classes must be downloaded separately and included as an archive file on the classpath (*swingall.jar*).* JDK 1.2 (and higher) comes with a Swing distribution.

---

* The standalone Swing distributions contain several other JAR files. *swingall.jar* is everything (except the contents of *multi.jar*) wrapped into one lump and is all you normally need to know about. For completeness, the other JAR files are: *swing.jar*, which contains everything but the individual L&F packages; *motif.jar*, which contains the Motif (Unix) L&F; *windows.jar*, which contains the Windows L&F; *multi.jar*, which contains a special L&F that allows additional (often nonvisual) L&Fss to be used in conjunction with the primary L&F; and *beaninfo.jar*, which contains special classes used by GUI development tools.

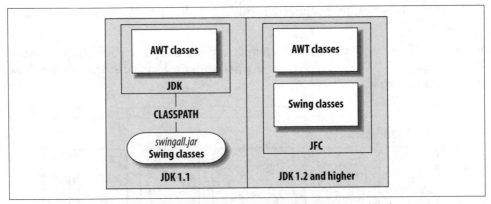

Figure 1-2. Relationships between Swing, AWT, and the JDK in the 1.1 and higher SDKs

Swing contains many more graphical components than its immediate predecessor, AWT 1.1. Many are components that were scribbled on programmer wishlists since Java first debuted—including tables, trees, internal frames, and a plethora of advanced text components. In addition, Swing contains many design advances over AWT. For example, Swing introduced an Action class that makes it easier to coordinate GUI components with their functionality. You'll also find that a much cleaner design prevails throughout Swing; this cuts down on the number of unexpected surprises that you're likely to face while coding.

Swing depends extensively on the event-handling mechanism of AWT 1.1, although it does not define a comparatively large amount of events for itself. Each Swing component also contains a variable number of exportable properties. This combination of properties and events in the design was no accident. Each of the Swing components, like the AWT 1.1 components before them, adhere to the popular JavaBeans specification. As you might have guessed, this means that you can import all of the Swing components into various GUI builder tools, which is useful for powerful visual programming.

Rethinking the AWT

To understand why Swing exists, it helps to understand the market forces that drive Java as a whole. The Java Programming Language was developed in 1993 and 1994, largely under the guidance of James Gosling and Bill Joy at Sun Microsystems, Inc. When Sun released the Java Development Kit on the Internet, it ignited a firestorm of excitement that swept through the computing industry. At first, developers primarily experimented with Java for *applets*, mini-programs embedded in web browsers. However, as Java matured over the course of the next two years, many developers began using Java to develop full-scale applications.

Or at least they tried. As developers ported Java to more and more platforms, its weak points started to show. The language was robust and scalable, extremely powerful as a networking tool, and served well as an easy-to-learn successor to the more established C++. The primary criticism, however, was that it was an interpreted language, which means that by definition it executed code slower than its native, compiled equivalents. Consequently, many developers flocked to just-in-time (JIT) compilers—highly optimized interpreters—to speed up their large-scale applications. This solved many problems, but one weak point that continually received scathing criticism was the graphical widgets that Java was built on: the Abstract Window Toolkit (AWT). The primary issue here was that AWT provided only the minimal amount of functionality necessary to create a windowing application. For enterprise applications, it quickly became clear that programmers needed something bigger.

After nearly a year of intense scrutiny, the AWT classes were ready for a change. From Java 1.0 to Java 1.1, the AWT reimplemented its event model from a "chain" design to an "event subscriber" design. This meant that instead of propagating events through a predefined hierarchy of components, interested classes simply registered with other components to receive noteworthy events. Because events typically involve only the sender and receiver, this eliminated much of the overhead in propagating them. When component events were triggered, an event object was passed only to those classes interested in receiving them.

Sun developers also began to see that relying on native widgets for the AWT components was proving to be troublesome. Similar components looked and behaved differently on many platforms, and coding for the ever-expanding differences of each platform became a maintenance nightmare. In addition, reusing the component widgets for each platform limited the abilities of the components and proved to be expensive on system memory.

Clearly, Sun knew that AWT wasn't enough. It wasn't that the AWT classes didn't work; they simply didn't provide the functionality necessary for full-scale enterprise applications. At the 1997 JavaOne Conference in San Francisco, JavaSoft announced the Java Foundation Classes. Key to the design of the JFC was that the new Swing components would be written entirely in Java and have a consistent L&F across platforms. This allowed Swing and the JFC to be used on any platform that supported Java 1.1 or later; all the user had to do was to include the appropriate JAR files on the CLASSPATH to make each of the components available for use. Since JDK 1.2, Swing has been part of the standard Java distribution; no special action is needed to use Swing components.

Swing Features

Swing provides many features for writing large-scale applications in Java. Here is an overview of some of the more popular features.

Pluggable Look-and-Feels

One of the most exciting aspects of the Swing classes is the ability to dictate the L&F of each of the components, even resetting the L&F at runtime. L&Fs have become an important issue in GUI development over the past 10 years. Many users are familiar with the Motif style of user interface, which was common in Windows 3.1 and is still in wide use on Unix platforms. Microsoft created a more optimized L&F in their Windows 95/98/NT/2000 operating systems. In addition, the Macintosh computer system has its own carefully designed L&F, which most Apple users feel comfortable with.

Swing is capable of emulating several L&Fs and currently supports the Windows, Unix Motif, and "native" Java Metal L&Fs. Mac OS X comes with full support for its own L&F based on Apple's Aqua Human Interface Guidelines, although you can still access Metal if you prefer. In addition, Swing allows the user to switch L&Fs at runtime without having to close the application. This way, a user can experiment to see which L&F is best for her with instantaneous feedback. (In practice, nobody really does this, but it's still pretty cool from a geeky point of view.) And, if you're feeling really ambitious as a developer (perhaps a game developer), you can create your own L&F for each one of the Swing components!

The Metal L&F combines some of the best graphical elements in today's L&Fs and even adds a few surprises of its own. Figure 1-3 shows an example of several L&Fs that you can use with Swing, including the Metal L&F. All Swing L&Fs are built from a set of base classes called the Basic L&F. However, though we may refer to the Basic L&F from time to time, you can't use it on its own. If you're lucky enough to be developing applications in the Mac OS X environment, you'll be familiar with the L&F shown in Figure 1-4.

Lightweight Components

Most Swing components are lightweight. In the purest sense, this means that components are not dependent on native peers to render themselves. Instead, they use simplified graphics primitives to paint themselves on the screen and can even allow portions to be transparent.

The ability to create lightweight components first emerged in JDK 1.1, although the majority of AWT components did not take advantage of it. Prior to that, Java programmers had no choice but to subclass java.awt.Canvas or java.awt.Panel if they wished to create their own components. With both classes, Java allocated an opaque peer object from the underlying operating system to represent the component, forcing each component to behave as if it were its own window, thereby taking on a rectangular, solid shape. Hence, these components earned the name "heavyweight" because they frequently held extra baggage at the native level that Java did not use.

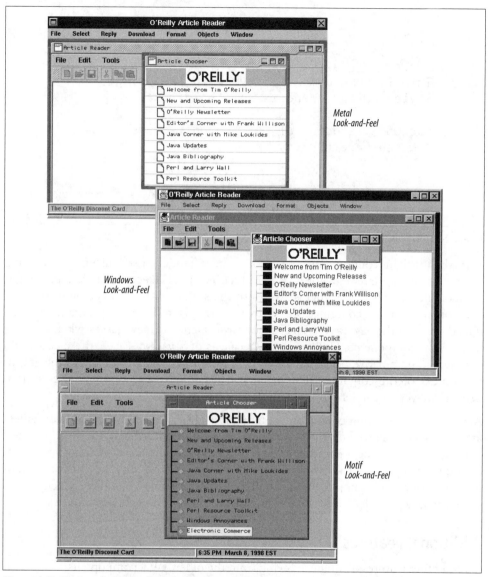

Figure 1-3. Various L&Fs in the Java Swing environment

Heavyweight components were unwieldy for two reasons:

- Equivalent components on different platforms don't necessarily act alike. A list component on one platform, for example, may work differently than a list component on another. Trying to coordinate and manage the differences between components was a formidable task.

- The L&F of each component was tied to the host operating system and could not be changed.

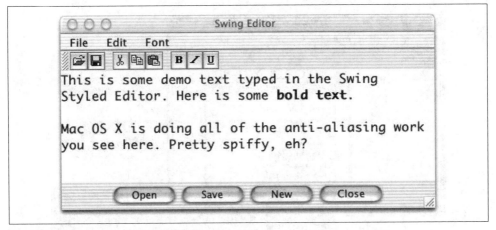

Figure 1-4. The new Mac L&F in OS X

With lightweight components, each component renders itself using the drawing primitives of the Graphics object (e.g., drawLine( ), fillRect( ), etc.). Lightweight components always render themselves onto the surface of the heavyweight top-level component they are contained in. With the arrival of JDK 1.1, programmers can directly extend the java.awt.Component or java.awt.Container classes when creating lightweight components. Unlike java.awt.Canvas or java.awt.Panel, these classes do not depend on a native peer and allow the developer to render quickly to the graphics context of the container. This results in faster, less memory-intensive components than were previously available in Java.

Almost all of the Swing components are lightweight; only a few top-level containers are not. This design allows programmers to draw (and redraw) the L&F of their application at runtime, instead of tying it to the L&F of the host operating system. In addition, the design of the Swing components supports easy modification of component behavior. For example, you can tell almost any Swing component whether you wish it to accept or decline focus and how it should handle keyboard input.

Additional Features

Several other features distinguish Swing from the older AWT components:

- Swing has wide variety of new components, such as tables, trees, sliders, spinners, progress bars, internal frames, and text components.

- Swing components support the replacement of their insets with an arbitrary number of nested borders.

- Swing components can have *tooltips* placed over them. A tooltip is a textual pop up that momentarily appears when the mouse cursor rests inside the component's painting region. Tooltips can be used to give more information about the component in question.

- You can arbitrarily bind keyboard events to components, defining how they react to various keystrokes under given conditions.
- There is additional debugging support for rendering your own lightweight Swing components.

We discuss each of these features in greater detail as we move through the next three chapters.

How Can I Use Swing?

Not everyone uses Swing for the same reasons. In fact, the Swing libraries have many levels of use, with varying levels of prerequisite knowledge. Here are some potential uses:

- Use the Swing components as they are to build your own enterprise applications.
- Create your own Swing components—or extend those that already exist.
- Override or create a new L&F for one or more of the Swing components.

The first approach is what the vast majority of Swing programmers use. Here, using Swing components is just like using the AWT components. A familiar set of components, containers, and layout managers are all available in the Swing packages to help you get your application up and running quickly. If you're adept at AWT programming, you probably need only a cursory introduction to each component to get started. You will we need to get into broader issues only if you use some of the larger and newer component families, such as tables and text. If you are planning to use each component as a JavaBean for visual programming, you also fall into this category.

Creating your own component, or extending an existing one, requires a deeper understanding of Swing. This includes a firm understanding of Swing architecture, events, and lower-level classes. Also, if you decide to subclass a Swing component, the responsibilities of that component must be adopted and handled accordingly—otherwise, your new component may perform erratically.

Finally, you may wish to change the L&F of one or more Swing components. This is arguably the most complex of the three routes that you can take—it requires a thorough knowledge of the design, architectural fundamentals, and graphical primitives of each lightweight component. In addition, you need to understand how Swing's UIManager and UIDefaults classes work together to "set" each component's L&F.

This book strives to help you with each of these issues. Because we anticipate that the vast majority of readers are in the first category, we spend a great deal of time reviewing each component's properties and methods, as well as providing source code for various scenarios that use these components. We try to document and illustrate the useful parts of the components. The online documentation (called Javadoc) has matured along with the rest of Java; the current stuff is always there first.

Programming your own L&F can get pretty complex; in fact, the source code for an entire L&F would far exceed the size of this book. However, we don't want to leave you in the dark. If you are an experienced Swing programmer already, and you're looking for a concise introduction on how to get started, see Chapter 26. This chapter provides details on working with L&Fs as well as examples of how to code your own L&F for both simple and complex Swing components.

Swing Packages and Classes

Here is a short description of each package in the Swing libraries:

javax.accessibility
> Contains classes and interfaces that can be used to allow *assistive technologies* to interact with Swing components. Assistive technologies cover a broad range of items, from audible text readers to screen magnification. Although the accessibility classes are technically not part of Swing, they are used extensively throughout the Swing components. We discuss the accessibility package in greater detail in Chapter 25.

javax.swing
> Contains the core Swing components, including most of the model interfaces and support classes.

javax.swing.border
> Contains the definitions for the abstract border class as well as eight predefined borders. Borders are not components; instead, they are special graphical elements that Swing treats as properties and places around components in place of their insets. If you wish to create your own border, you can subclass one of the existing borders in this package, or you can code a new one from scratch.

javax.swing.colorchooser
> Contains support for the JColorChooser component, discussed in Chapter 12.

javax.swing.event
> Defines several new listeners and events that Swing components use to communicate asynchronous information between classes. To create your own events, you can subclass various events in this package or write your own event class.

javax.swing.filechooser
> Contains support for the JFileChooser component, discussed in Chapter 12.

javax.swing.plaf
> Defines the unique elements that make up the pluggable L&F for each Swing component. Its various subpackages are devoted to rendering the individual L&Fs for each component on a platform-by-platform basis. (Concrete implementations of the Windows and Motif L&Fs are in subpackages of com.sun. java.swing.plaf, and the Mac OS L&F is under com.apple.mrj.swing.)

`javax.swing.table`

Provides models and views for the table component, which allows you to arrange various information in a grid format with an appearance similar to a spreadsheet. Using the lower-level classes, you can manipulate how tables are viewed and selected, as well as how they display their information in each cell.

`javax.swing.text`

Provides scores of text-based classes and interfaces supporting a common design known as *document/view*. The text classes are among the more advanced Swing classes to learn, so we devote several chapters (19–23) to both the design fundamentals and the implementation of text applications.

`javax.swing.text.html`

Used specifically for reading and formatting HTML text through an ancillary editor kit.

`javax.swing.text.html.parser`

Contains support for parsing HTML.

`javax.swing.text.rtf`

Used specifically for reading and formatting Rich Text Format (RTF) text through an ancillary editor kit.

`javax.swing.tree`

Defines models and views for a hierarchal tree component, which may represent a file structure or a series of properties.

`javax.swing.undo`

Contains the necessary functionality for implementing undoable functions.

By far the most widely used package is `javax.swing`. In fact, almost all the Swing components, as well as several utility classes, are located inside this package. The only exceptions are borders and support classes for the trees, tables, and text-based components. Because the latter components are much more extensible and often have many more classes to work with, these classes have been divided into separate packages.

Class Hierarchy

Figure 1-5 shows a detailed overview of the Swing class hierarchy as it appears in the 1.4 SDK. At first glance, the class hierarchy looks very similar to AWT. Each Swing component with an AWT equivalent shares the same name, except that the Swing class is preceded by a capital J. In most cases, if a Swing component supersedes an AWT component, it can be used as a drop-in replacement.

Upon closer inspection, however, you will discover that there are welcome differences between the Swing and AWT components. For example, the menu components, including `JMenuBar`, are now descendants of the same base component as the others: `JComponent`. This is a change from the older AWT menu classes. Both the

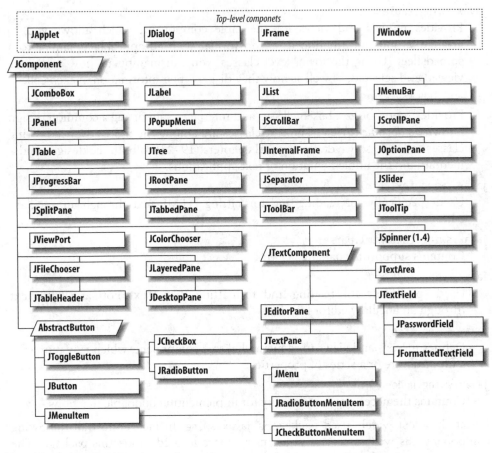

Figure 1-5. The Swing component hierarchy

AWT 1.0 and 1.1 menu classes inherited their own high-level component, MenuComponent, which severely limited their capabilities. In addition, this design prevented menu bars from being positioned with layout managers inside containers; instead, Java simply attached menu bars to the top of frames.

Also, note that Swing has redesigned the button hierarchy. It now includes a JToggleButton class, used in dual-state components. For example, if you click on a toggle button while in the released position, the button switches to the pressed state and remains in that state. When it is clicked again, the button returns to the released state. Note that JToggleButton outlines behavior seen in radio buttons and checkboxes. Hence, these classes inherit from JToggleButton in the new Swing design. Also note the addition of the JRadioButton and JRadioButtonMenuItem classes in Swing. Until now, Java forced developers to use the AWT checkbox equivalent to mimic radio buttons.

You might have noticed an increase in the number of frames and panes in Swing. For example, consider internal frames. Swing supports placing frames inside other frames—this is commonly referred to as a multiple document interface (MDI) in the Microsoft Windows world. You can assign these internal frames arbitrary vertical layers; these layers determine which internal frame appears on top. In fact, even the simplest frame, JFrame, embraces the concept of layers by including support for layered panes on which you can position different elements of your application. These topics are discussed in more detail in Chapters 9 and 11.

There are many other design enhancements in Swing—too many, in fact, to discuss here. However, before we go on, we should discuss one of the fundamental designs behind every Swing component: the model-view-controller architecture.

The Model-View-Controller Architecture

Swing uses the *model-view-controller architecture* (MVC) as the fundamental design behind each of its components. Essentially, MVC breaks GUI components into three elements. Each of these elements plays a crucial role in how the component behaves.

Model

The model encompasses the state data for each component. There are different models for different types of components. For example, the model of a scrollbar component might contain information about the current position of its adjustable "thumb," its minimum and maximum values, and the thumb's width (relative to the range of values). A menu, on the other hand, may simply contain a list of the menu items the user can select from. This information remains the same no matter how the component is painted on the screen; model data is always independent of the component's visual representation.

View

The view refers to how you see the component on the screen. For a good example of how views can differ, look at an application window on two different GUI platforms. Almost all window frames have a title bar spanning the top of the window. However, the title bar may have a close box on the left side (like the Mac OS platform), or it may have the close box on the right side (as in the Windows platform). These are examples of different types of views for the same window object.

Controller

The controller is the portion of the user interface that dictates how the component interacts with events. Events come in many forms—e.g., a mouse click, gaining or losing focus, a keyboard event that triggers a specific menu command, or even a directive to repaint part of the screen. The controller decides how each component reacts to the event—if it reacts at all.

Figure 1-6 shows how the model, view, and controller work together to create a scrollbar component. The scrollbar uses the information in the model to determine how far into the scrollbar to render the thumb and how wide the thumb should be. Note that the model specifies this information relative to the minimum and the maximum. It does not give the position or width of the thumb in screen pixels—the view calculates that. The view determines exactly where and how to draw the scrollbar, given the proportions offered by the model. The view knows whether it is a horizontal or vertical scrollbar, and it knows exactly how to shadow the end buttons and the thumb. Finally, the controller is responsible for handling mouse events on the component. The controller knows, for example, that dragging the thumb is a legitimate action for a scrollbar, within the limits defined by the endpoints, and that pushing on the end buttons is acceptable as well. The result is a fully functional MVC scrollbar.

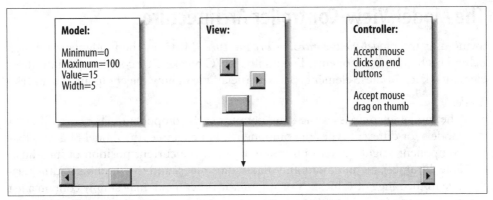

Figure 1-6. The three elements of a model-view-controller architecture

MVC Interaction

With MVC, each of the three elements—the model, the view, and the controller—requires the services of another element to keep itself continually updated. Let's continue discussing the scrollbar component.

We already know that the view cannot render the scrollbar correctly without obtaining information from the model first. In this case, the scrollbar does not know where to draw its "thumb" unless it can obtain its current position and width relative to the minimum and maximum. Likewise, the view determines if the component is the recipient of user events, such as mouse clicks. (For example, the view knows the exact width of the thumb; it can tell whether a click occurred over the thumb or just outside of it.) The view passes these events on to the controller, which decides how to handle them. Based on the controller's decisions, the values in the model may need to be altered. If the user drags the scrollbar thumb, the controller reacts by incrementing the thumb's position in the model. At that point, the whole cycle repeats. The three elements, therefore, communicate their data as shown in Figure 1-7.

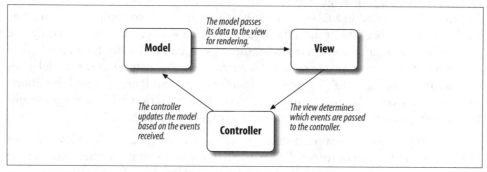

Figure 1-7. Communication through the model-view-controller architecture

MVC in Swing

Swing actually uses a simplified variant of the MVC design called the *model-delegate*. This design combines the view and the controller object into a single element, the *UI delegate*, which draws the component to the screen and handles GUI events. Bundling graphics capabilities and event handling is somewhat easy in Java, since much of the event handling is taken care of in AWT. As you might expect, the communication between the model and the UI delegate then becomes a two-way street, as shown in Figure 1-8.

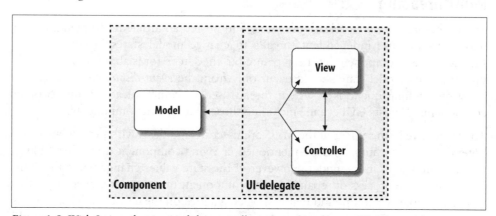

Figure 1-8. With Swing, the view and the controller are combined into a UI-delegate object

So let's review: each Swing component contains a model and a UI delegate. The model is responsible for maintaining information about the component's state. The UI delegate is responsible for maintaining information about how to draw the component on the screen. In addition, the UI delegate (in conjunction with AWT) reacts to various events that propagate through the component.

Note that the separation of the model and the UI delegate in the MVC design is extremely advantageous. One unique aspect of the MVC architecture is the ability to tie multiple views to a single model. For example, if you want to display the same data in a pie chart and in a table, you can base the views of two components on a single data model. That way, if the data needs to be changed, you can do so in only one place—the views update themselves accordingly (Chapter 16 has an example that does exactly this). In the same manner, separating the delegate from the model gives the user the added benefit of choosing what a component looks like without affecting any of its data. By using this approach, in conjunction with the lightweight design, Swing can provide each component with its own pluggable L&F.

By now, you should have a solid understanding of how MVC works. However, we won't yet spoil the fun of using MVC. Chapters 2 and 3 go into further detail about how you can use MVC to your advantage in even the simplest of applications.

Working with Swing

Our introduction to Swing wouldn't be complete unless we briefly mentioned some caveats of the Swing libraries. There are two pertinent areas: multithreading and lightweight versus heavyweight components. Being aware of these issues will help you make informed decisions while working with Swing. Chapter 28 gives you in-depth guidance in these difficult areas.

Multithreading

Shortly before the initial release of Swing, Sun posted an article recommending that developers not use independent threads to change model states in components.* Instead, once a component has been painted to the screen (or is about to be painted), updates to its model state should occur only from the *event-dispatching queue*. The event-dispatching queue is a system thread used to communicate events to other components. It posts GUI events, including those that repaint components.

The issue here is an artifact of the MVC architecture and deals with performance and potential race conditions. As we mentioned, a Swing component draws itself based on the state values in its model. However, if the state values change while the component is in the process of repainting, the component may repaint incorrectly—this is unacceptable. To compound matters, placing a lock on the entire model, as well as on some of the critical component data, or even cloning the data in question, could seriously hamper performance for each refresh. The only feasible solution, therefore, is to place state changes in serial with refreshes. This ensures that modifications in

---

* Hans Muller and Kathy Walrath, "Threads and Swing," The Swing Connection, *http://java.sun.com/products/jfc/tsc/swingdoc-archive/threads.html*.

component state do not occur at the same time Swing is repainting any components and prevents race conditions.

The Z-Order Caveat: Lightweight and Heavyweight Components

One of the most frequent issues to come out of lightweight/heavyweight component use is the idea of depth, or *z-order*—that is, a well-defined method for how elements are stacked on the screen. Because of z-order, it is not advisable to mix lightweight and heavyweight components in Swing.

To see why, remember that heavyweight components depend on peer objects used at the operating system level. However, with Swing, only the top-level components are heavyweight: JApplet, JFrame, JDialog, and JWindow. Also, recall that heavyweight components are always "opaque"—they have a rectangular shape and are nontransparent. This is because the host operating system typically allocates the entire painting region to the component, clearing it first.

The remaining components are lightweight. So here is the crux of the dilemma: when a lightweight component is placed inside a heavyweight container, it shares (and actually borrows) the graphics context of the heavyweight component. The lightweight component must always draw itself on the same plane as the heavyweight component that contains it; as a result, it shares the z-order of the heavyweight component. In addition, lightweight components are bound to the clipping region of the top-level window or dialog that contains them. In effect, lightweight components are all "drawings" on the canvas of a heavyweight component. The drawings cannot go beyond the boundaries of the canvas and can always be covered by another canvas. Heavyweight components, however, are free from this restriction. Therefore, they always appear on top of the lightweight components—whether that is the intent or not.

Heavyweight components have other ramifications in Swing as well. They do not work well in scrollpanes, where they can extend beyond the clipping boundaries; they also don't work in front of lightweight menus and menu bars (unless certain precautions are taken) or inside internal frames. Some Swing classes, however, offer an interesting approach to this problem. These classes allow you to specify whether the component draws itself using a lightweight or a heavyweight window. Hence, with a bit of judicious programming, you can keep your components correctly rendered—no matter where they are located.

The Swing Set Demo

If you're in a hurry to see all the components Swing has to offer, be sure to check out the Swing Set demonstration. The demonstration is extremely easy to set up. If you have the 1.3 or 1.4 SDK, the demonstration is included. If you have 1.2, you must first download and extract the demo classes and add them to your classpath. Then follow these steps:

1. Change the directory to the *demo/jfc/SwingSet2* directory. (For the 1.2 release, the directory is *demo/jfc/SwingSet*.)

2. Run the SwingSet2 (or SwingSet for 1.2) jar file:

```
% java -jar SwingSet2.jar
```

You should immediately see a splash screen indicating that the Swing Set demo is loading. When it finishes, a window appears, similar to the one in Figure 1-9.

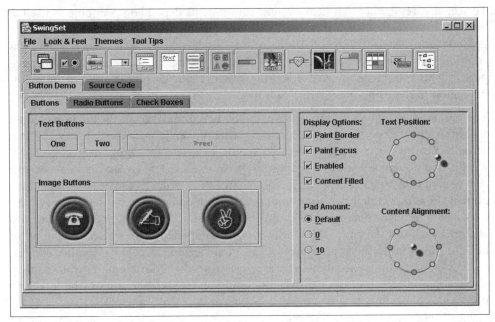

Figure 1-9. The Swing Set demo

This demo contains a series of tabs that demonstrate almost all of the components in the Swing libraries. Be sure to check out the internal frames demo and the Metal L&F. In addition, some of the Swing creators have added "Easter eggs" throughout the Swing Set demo. See if you can find some!

Reading This Book

We're well aware that most readers don't read the Preface. You have our permission to skip it, provided that you look at the Conventions section. That section is particularly important because in this book we experiment with a few new techniques for explaining the Swing classes. As we said earlier, everything in Swing is a JavaBean.

This means that much of an object's behavior is controlled by a set of properties, which are manipulated by accessor methods. For example, the property color is accessed by the getColor( ) (to find out the color) and setColor( ) (to change the color) methods. If a property has a boolean value, the get method is often replaced by an is method; for example, the visible property would have the isVisible( ) and setVisible( ) methods.

We found the idea of properties very powerful in helping us understand Swing. Therefore, rather than listing all of a class's accessor methods, we decided to present a table for each class, listing the class's properties and showing the property's data type, which accessor methods are present, whether the property is "bound" (i.e., changing the property generates a PropertyChangeEvent), when it was introduced (1.2 is the default; 1.3 and 1.4 are marked where appropriate), and the property's default value. This approach certainly saves paper (you didn't really want a 2,000-page book, did you?) and should make it easier to understand what a component does and how it is structured. Furthermore, if you're not already in the habit of thinking in terms of the JavaBeans architecture, you should get in the habit. It's a very powerful tool for understanding component design.

The conventions we use in the property tables—plus some other conventions that we use in class diagrams—are explained in the Preface. So you may ignore the rest of the Preface as long as you familiarize yourself with the conventions we're using.

The next chapter helps AWT developers get a jump on Swing by presenting a simple application; those without AWT experience may just want to skim the chapter. In Chapter 3, we continue our discussion by presenting some of the fundamental classes of Swing and discribing how you can use the features inherent in each of these classes to shorten your overall development time. Don't stop now—the best is yet to come!

CHAPTER 2

Jump-Starting a Swing Application

Now that you have an overview of Swing, let's look at a few Swing components you can put into your applications right now. This chapter shows you how to add images to buttons and how to create a rudimentary Swing application using internal frames. We won't belabor the theory and background. You'll find everything we talk about now (and tons more we don't discuss here) presented in later chapters in much greater detail. We just want to show you some of the fun stuff right away.

This chapter, and only this chapter, assumes that you have prior experience with AWT and AWT-based programs that you'd like to upgrade to use lightweight Swing components. If you are new to Java, this may not be the case; you are probably interested in learning Swing without the need to upgrade AWT applications. You can either skim this chapter or skip ahead to Chapter 3, which lays a foundation for the rest of your work in Swing.

If you want to see how easily Swing components can be dropped into existing AWT applications, though, read on.

Upgrading Your AWT Programs

One of the benefits of object-oriented languages is that you can upgrade pieces of a program without rewriting the rest. While practice is never as simple as theory, with Swing it's close. You can use most of the Swing components as drop-in replacements for AWT components with ease. The components sport many fancy new features worth exploiting, but they still maintain the functionality of the AWT components you're familiar with. As a general rule, you can stick a "J" in front of your favorite AWT component and put the new class to work as a Swing component. Constructors for components such as `JButton`, `JTextField`, and `JList` can be used with the same arguments and generate the same events as `Button`, `TextField`, and `List`. Some Swing containers, like `JFrame`, take a bit of extra work, but not much.

Graphical buttons are essential to modern user interfaces. Nice monitors and cheap hardware have made icons almost a necessity. The AWT package in Java does not directly support image buttons. You could write an extension to support them easily enough, but why bother when Swing's JButton class provides a standard way to add image buttons?

A Simple AWT Application

You probably have some programs lying around that use regular AWT buttons that you'd love to replace with image buttons, but you don't have the time or, honestly, the necessity to produce your own image button class. Let's look at a simple application that demonstrates an upgrade path you can use on your own programs.

First, let's look at the code for this very simple application:

```
// ToolbarFrame1.java
// A simple frame containing a "toolbar" made up of several java.awt.Button
// objects. We'll be converting the Buttons to JButtons in the ToolbarFrame2.java
// file.
//
import java.awt.*;
import java.awt.event.*;

public class ToolbarFrame1 extends Frame {

  Button cutButton, copyButton, pasteButton;
  public ToolbarFrame1() {
    super("Toolbar Example (AWT)");
    setSize(450, 250);
    addWindowListener(new WindowAdapter() {
      public void windowClosing(WindowEvent e) {
        System.exit(0);
      }
    });

    ActionListener printListener = new ActionListener() {
      public void actionPerformed(ActionEvent ae) {
        System.out.println(ae.getActionCommand());
      }
    };

    Panel toolbar = new Panel();
    toolbar.setLayout(new FlowLayout(FlowLayout.LEFT));

    cutButton = new Button("Cut");
    cutButton.addActionListener(printListener);
    toolbar.add(cutButton);

    copyButton = new Button("Copy");
    copyButton.addActionListener(printListener);
    toolbar.add(copyButton);
```

```
        pasteButton = new Button("Paste");
        pasteButton.addActionListener(printListener);
        toolbar.add(pasteButton);

        // The "preferred" BorderLayout add call
        add(toolbar, BorderLayout.NORTH);
    }

    public static void main(String args[]) {
        ToolbarFrame1 tf1 = new ToolbarFrame1();
        tf1.setVisible(true);
    }
}
```

Our application has the very simple interface that is in Figure 2-1.

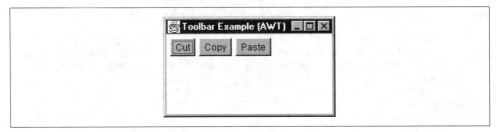

Figure 2-1. A simple application using three java.awt.Button objects

These buttons don't really do anything except report that they've been pressed. A standard 1.1-style handler for action events reports button presses to standard output. It's not exciting, but it lets us demonstrate that Swing buttons work the same way as AWT buttons. If you examine the code you'll notice that we had to register a window listener to tell when the user is trying to close the window, and explicitly exit the program in response. Once you update your programs to use Swing's JFrame rather than AWT's Frame (as we will for the final example in this chapter), you get this capability "for free" with JFrame's defaultCloseOperation property, described in Table 8-8.

Including Your First Swing Component

The first step in adding a Swing component to your application is preparing the Swing package for use. As long as you have installed SDK 1.2 or later, you don't have to take any special steps to use the Swing classes. If you're preparing an application to run with JDK 1.1, you'll need to put the *swingall.jar* file on the CLASSPATH so that the Swing components are available during compilation and at runtime.

In your source code, you include the Swing package by adding an import statement:

```
import javax.swing.*;
```

Now you're ready to replace your Button objects with JButton objects. We'll also set up the application to take advantage of Swing's L&F capabilities; we've put another row of buttons at the bottom of the frame that let you select one of the standard L&Fs:

```java
// ToolbarFrame2.java
// The Swing-ified button example
//
import java.awt.*;
import java.awt.event.*;
import javax.swing.*;

public class ToolbarFrame2 extends Frame {

  // This time, let's use JButtons!
  JButton cutButton, copyButton, pasteButton;
  JButton javaButton, macButton, motifButton, winButton;

  public ToolbarFrame2() {
    super("Toolbar Example (Swing)");
    setSize(450, 250);

    addWindowListener(new WindowAdapter() {
      public void windowClosing(WindowEvent e) {
        System.exit(0);
      }
    });

    ActionListener printListener = new ActionListener() {
      public void actionPerformed(ActionEvent ae) {
        System.out.println(ae.getActionCommand());
      }
    };

    // JPanel works similarly to Panel, so we'll use it.
    JPanel toolbar = new JPanel();
    toolbar.setLayout(new FlowLayout(FlowLayout.LEFT));

    cutButton = new JButton("Cut");
    cutButton.addActionListener(printListener);
    toolbar.add(cutButton);

    copyButton = new JButton("Copy");
    copyButton.addActionListener(printListener);
    toolbar.add(copyButton);

    pasteButton = new JButton("Paste");
    pasteButton.addActionListener(printListener);
    toolbar.add(pasteButton);

    add(toolbar, BorderLayout.NORTH);
```

```
    // Add the L&F controls.
    JPanel lnfPanel = new JPanel();
    LnFListener lnfListener = new LnFListener(this);
    macButton = new JButton("Mac");
    macButton.addActionListener(lnfListener);
    lnfPanel.add(macButton);
    javaButton = new JButton("Metal");
    javaButton.addActionListener(lnfListener);
    lnfPanel.add(javaButton);
    motifButton = new JButton("Motif");
    motifButton.addActionListener(lnfListener);
    lnfPanel.add(motifButton);
    winButton = new JButton("Windows");
    winButton.addActionListener(lnfListener);
    lnfPanel.add(winButton);
    add(lnfPanel, BorderLayout.SOUTH);
  }

  public static void main(String args[]) {
    ToolbarFrame2 tf2 = new ToolbarFrame2();
    tf2.setVisible(true);
  }
}
```

As you can see in Figure 2-2, the application is more or less the same. All we did was change Button to JButton and add four more JButtons for L&F selection. We update the application's L&F in the LnFListener class, which gets its events from the simple Swing buttons at the bottom of the application. Apart from figuring out which button was pressed, we must also force the L&F to change. That's pretty simple. The first step is setting the new L&F using the UIManager.setLookAndFeel() method. (This is the method that needs the correct name for the L&F we want.) Once the L&F is set, we want to make the change visible immediately, so we update the L&F for all of the components using the SwingUtilities.updateComponentTreeUI() method:

```
// LnFListener.java
// A listener that can change the L&F of a frame based on the actionCommand of an
// ActionEvent object. Supported L&Fs are: Mac, Metal, Motif, and Windows. Not all
// L&Fs will be available on a given machine. Notably, the Mac and Windows L&Fs work
// only on their specific platforms.
import java.awt.*;
import java.awt.event.*;
import javax.swing.*;

public class LnFListener implements ActionListener {
  Frame frame;

  public LnFListener(Frame f) {
    frame = f;
  }

  public void actionPerformed(ActionEvent e) {
    String lnfName = null;
```

```
    if (e.getActionCommand().equals("Mac")) {
      lnfName = "com.apple.mrj.swing.MacLookAndFeel";
    } else if (e.getActionCommand().equals("Metal")) {
      lnfName = "javax.swing.plaf.metal.MetalLookAndFeel";
    } else if (e.getActionCommand().equals("Motif")) {
      lnfName = "com.sun.java.swing.plaf.motif.MotifLookAndFeel";
    } else if (e.getActionCommand().equals("Windows")) {
      lnfName = "com.sun.java.swing.plaf.windows.WindowsLookAndFeel";
    } else {
      System.err.println("Unrecognized L&F request action: " +
        e.getActionCommand());
      return;
    }
    try {
      UIManager.setLookAndFeel(lnfName);
      SwingUtilities.updateComponentTreeUI(frame);
    }
    catch (UnsupportedLookAndFeelException ex1) {
      System.err.println("Unsupported LookAndFeel: " + lnfName);
    }
    catch (ClassNotFoundException ex2) {
      System.err.println("LookAndFeel class not found: " + lnfName);
    }
    catch (InstantiationException ex3) {
      System.err.println("Could not load LookAndFeel: " + lnfName);
    }
    catch (IllegalAccessException ex4) {
      System.err.println("Cannot use LookAndFeel: " + lnfName);
    }
  }
}
```

With the JButton objects in place we get the application shown in Figure 2-2.

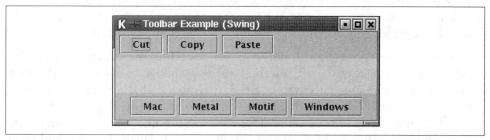

Figure 2-2. The same application with JButtons for Cut, Copy, and Paste (in the Metal L&F)

When we run the new version of the application, we still get ActionEvent objects from pressing the buttons, and the events are still delivered to the actionPerformed() method. OK, big deal. Now we have buttons that work just like before and don't look particularly great. So what? Well, for one thing, we can now take advantage of the new UI management capabilities of Swing components. Swing provides L&Fs that we can use with any of its components. If you press the Mac, Metal, Motif, or

Windows button in this application, it switches from the current L&F to the appropriate version (if it's available on your system). Figure 2-3 shows the effect.

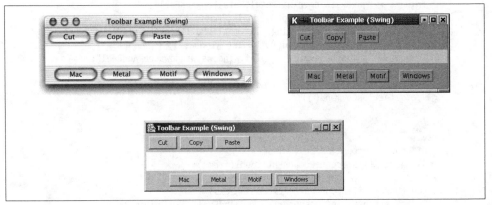

Figure 2-3. JButtons using the Mac (left), Motif (right), and Windows (bottom) L&Fs

Now we've got a bunch of JButtons. We're still using the old AWT Panel and Frame objects as containers for our applications. You can change them easily, too. Changing Panel to JPanel is as simple as updating the buttons: just do a global replace, and you're done. Updating Frame is a little more complex. Once you've replaced Frame with JFrame, you must also look at the calls to add( ) that put things in the JFrame. A JFrame has something in it called a "content pane"; when we add something to a JFrame, we usually want to add it to this content pane:

```
getContentPane( ).add(something);    // Formerly just add(something)
```

With these changes, the JFrame and JPanel also change their appearance when you change the application's L&F. It may not be noticeable. But you'll also get the other new features that Swing gives you. We'll stick with the old Frame and Panel for now, but we'll use JFrame and JPanel later in this chapter and throughout the book.

This is all very nice, but it's still not what we came for. We weren't interested in making minor changes in the way our buttons look, though that's a nice side effect. So let's get to those images! First, we need to create what the Swing components refer to as an Icon. You can get the details on icons in Chapter 4, but for now, just think of them as nicely self-contained images we can use inside just about any of the Swing components that can display normal text (such as labels, buttons, and menu items). We'll start out by adding an image to the text we're currently displaying in each button. We can use all of the graphics formats Java supports (GIF, JPEG, and others) with icons, including transparent and animated GIF-89a images. Here's the code to add images to each of our buttons:

```
cutButton = new JButton("Cut", new ImageIcon("cut.gif"));
cutButton.addActionListener(this);
toolbar.add(cutButton);
```

```
copyButton = new JButton("Copy", new ImageIcon("copy.gif"));
copyButton.addActionListener(this);
toolbar.add(copyButton);

pasteButton = new JButton("Paste", new ImageIcon("paste.gif"));
pasteButton.addActionListener(this);
toolbar.add(pasteButton);
```

This creates buttons with little icons to the left of the text. Any L&F can display the images. Figure 2-4 shows the result.

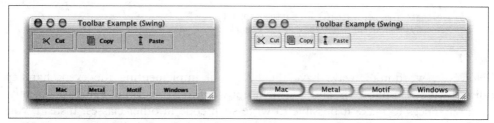

Figure 2-4. Icon and text buttons in the Metal (left) and Mac (right) L&Fs

Adding the icons hasn't changed anything. In particular, our action event handlers are exactly the same as they were with normal AWT buttons. But you probably see a problem developing. Our handler uses the buttons' text labels to decide which button was pressed. That's not a problem since our buttons still display some text. What happens if we throw that text out? How can we tell which button was pressed? First, let's look at the code to create an image-only button:

```
copyButton = new JButton(new ImageIcon("copy.gif"));
copyButton.addActionListener(this);
toolbar.add(copyButton);
```

If we do this for every button, the application looks like Figure 2-5.

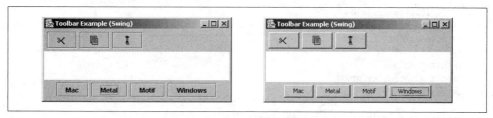

Figure 2-5. Icon-only JButtons in the Metal (left) and Windows (right) L&Fs

Now let's look back at the event handler we use:

```
public void actionPerformed(ActionEvent e) {
    System.out.println(e.getActionCommand());
}
```

This doesn't do much. Normally, you would need to distinguish between the various buttons or other components that report to this handler. Since we implement the

ActionListener interface directly in the application class, we can use the simple route of checking the source of the event against the buttons we know we have. For example, we could differentiate the Cut, Copy, and Paste buttons like this:

```
public void actionPerformed(ActionEvent ae) {
    if (ae.getSource() == cutButton) {
    System.out.println("Got Cut event");
    }
    else if (ae.getSource() == copyButton) {
        System.out.println("Got Copy event");
    }
    else if (ae.getSource() == pasteButton) {
        System.out.println("Got Paste event");
    }
}
```

However, we don't always have the luxury of implementing the event handler directly in our application, and we might not want to pass around a huge list of button references to make it possible to write such code in other classes. Instead, you can use the actionCommand property of the Button class to distinguish your buttons from one another. The JButton class also implements this property, so we can just call setActionCommand() for each of the buttons and pass in a unique string that we can check in the actionPerformed() method—regardless of which class that method sits in. Using the actionCommand property to distinguish a component works for components whose appearance might be changing for any of a variety of reasons. (For example, you might be writing an international application in which the text on the button changes depending on the user's native language.)

Now, this is not the only or even best way to handle events from our buttons, but it's a slightly more portable version of our simple application. Later, we'll look at the new Action interface to better support this type of event handling in a more object-oriented manner. For now, this code is easy to understand, even if it is a bit clunky.

```
// ToolbarFrame3.java
// The Swing-ified button example. The buttons in this toolbar all carry images
// but no text.
//
import java.awt.*;
import java.awt.event.*;
import javax.swing.*;

public class ToolbarFrame3 extends Frame {

  JButton cutButton, copyButton, pasteButton;
  JButton javaButton, macButton, motifButton, winButton;

  public ToolbarFrame3() {
    super("Toolbar Example (Swing no text)");
    setSize(450, 250);
```

```
addWindowListener(new WindowAdapter() {
  public void windowClosing(WindowEvent e) {
    System.exit(0);
  }
});

// JPanel works much like Panel does, so we'll use it.
JPanel toolbar = new JPanel();
toolbar.setLayout(new FlowLayout(FlowLayout.LEFT));

CCPHandler handler = new CCPHandler();

cutButton = new JButton(new ImageIcon("cut.gif"));
cutButton.setActionCommand(CCPHandler.CUT);
cutButton.addActionListener(handler);
toolbar.add(cutButton);

copyButton = new JButton(new ImageIcon("copy.gif"));
copyButton.setActionCommand(CCPHandler.COPY);
copyButton.addActionListener(handler);
toolbar.add(copyButton);

pasteButton = new JButton(new ImageIcon("paste.gif"));
pasteButton.setActionCommand(CCPHandler.PASTE);
pasteButton.addActionListener(handler);
toolbar.add(pasteButton);

add(toolbar, BorderLayout.NORTH);

// Add the L&F controls.
JPanel lnfPanel = new JPanel();
LnFListener lnfListener = new LnFListener(this);
macButton = new JButton("Mac");
macButton.addActionListener(lnfListener);
lnfPanel.add(macButton);
javaButton = new JButton("Metal");
javaButton.addActionListener(lnfListener);
lnfPanel.add(javaButton);
motifButton = new JButton("Motif");
motifButton.addActionListener(lnfListener);
lnfPanel.add(motifButton);
winButton = new JButton("Windows");
winButton.addActionListener(lnfListener);
lnfPanel.add(winButton);
add(lnfPanel, BorderLayout.SOUTH);
}

public static void main(String args[]) {
  ToolbarFrame3 tf3 = new ToolbarFrame3();
  tf3.setVisible(true);
}
}
```

Here's the new event handler for this simple application. Notice that we set up some constants for the different actions we plan to take. We can now use these constants in the setActionCommand( ) call of any application whenever we're setting up Cut, Copy, or Paste buttons—regardless of what we display on the screen for the buttons. We can now easily tell which action to take in the actionPerformed( ) method. However, you may still need to pass a reference to objects that contain the buttons because you will most likely need to take a real action when the user presses a button. We'll look at such a program a bit later in the chapter.

```java
// CCPHandler.java
// A Cut, Copy, and Paste event handler. Nothing too fancy, just define some
// constants that can be used to set the actionCommands on buttons.
//
import java.awt.event.*;

public class CCPHandler implements ActionListener {

  public final static String CUT   = "cut";
  public final static String COPY  = "copy";
  public final static String PASTE = "paste";

  public void actionPerformed(ActionEvent e) {
    String command = e.getActionCommand( );
    if (command == CUT) { // We can do this since we're comparing constants.
      System.out.println("Got Cut event");
    }
    else if (command == COPY) {
      System.out.println("Got Copy event");
    }
    else if (command == PASTE) {
      System.out.println("Got Paste event");
    }
  }
}
```

Finally, we should point out that although CCPHandler illustrates another way of handling button events, the Action mechanism introduced at the end of this chapter, and discussed in depth at the start of Chapter 3, is more powerful, object-oriented, and far more commonly used.

Beyond Buttons

Buttons are very useful, but even with great images forming the buttons, they still lack a certain glamour—every application has buttons. For the next example, let's take a look at JInternalFrame, which allows you to create free-standing frames with menus, title bars, and everything else a Frame needs right inside your application.

What Is an Internal Frame?

Before we start coding, here's a brief rundown of the features of an internal frame:

- Same functions as a normal Frame object, but confined to the visible area of the container it is placed in
- Can be iconified (icon stays inside main application frame)
- Can be maximized (frame consumes entire main application frame area)
- Can be closed using the standard controls for application windows
- Can be placed in a "layer," which dictates how the frame displays itself relative to other internal frames (a frame in layer 1 can never hide a frame in layer 2)

To be honest, in practice, standalone frames are often more useful than internal frames. You'll want to know about both; we have chapters dedicated to each of these topics (Chapters 8 and 9, respectively).

Figure 2-6 shows a simple internal frame using the Metal L&F.

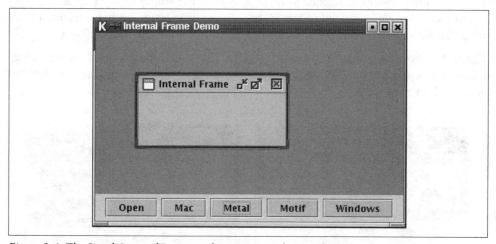

Figure 2-6. The SimpleInternalFrame application using the Metal L&F

For this first example, we'll add an empty internal frame to an application. Once that's working, we'll expand the simple frame to create a couple of different types of internal frames and create the framework for a simple application.

One of the prerequisites for using internal frames is that you need a window capable of managing them. The Swing package provides the JDesktopPane class for this purpose. You'll see the details of the JDesktopPane in Chapter 9, but for now, here's how to get one started:

```
// Set up the layered pane.
JDesktopPane desktop = new JDesktopPane();
add(desktop, BorderLayout.CENTER);
```

With the desktop in place, you can create a new internal frame and show it. The JInternalFrame constructor takes five arguments that tailor the look and functionality of the frame:

```
public JInternalFrame(String title,
                      boolean resizable,
                      boolean closable,
                      boolean maximizable,
                      boolean iconifiable);
```

We'll turn on every feature for the example. The following makes the internal frame visible:

```
internalFrame = new JInternalFrame("Internal Frame", true, true, true, true);
internalFrame.setBounds(50, 50, 200, 100);
desktop.add(internalFrame, new Integer(1));
```

The desktop.add( ) call does the real work here. You supply the internal frame and the "layer" your frame belongs in. Layers are Integer objects. The values determine the order of your layers and what shows on top of what. For example, frames in layer 2 always show on top of frames in layer 1, even if the frame in layer 1 has the keyboard focus. But you do need to remember to give your frame both a size and a location. The internal frames have default preferred and minimum sizes of 0 × 0.

Figure 2-7 shows how the JInternalFrame class also takes advantage of Swing's pluggable L&F feature. You can switch the appearance of the frames, just like you did with the buttons.

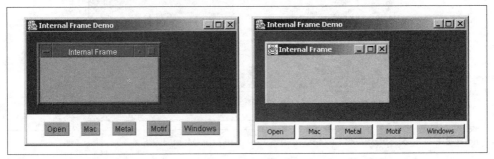

Figure 2-7. The SimpleInternalFrame in the Motif (left) and Windows (right) L&Fs

You can even iconify these frames. They turn into an "iconified box" appropriate for the current L&F. Figure 2-8 shows an iconified frame.

Here's the complete application with an open button and an internal frame. When you click the button, it pops up the internal frame. You can use the button in the upper-right corner of the frame to close it (providing you're using either the Metal or the Windows L&F). You can use the other buttons in the main frame to adjust the L&F of the internal frame:

```
// SimpleInternalFrame.java
// A quick demonstration of setting up an internal frame in an application
//
```

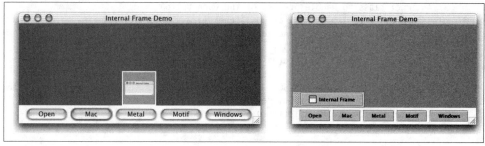

Figure 2-8. An iconified internal frame in the Mac (left) and Metal (right) L&Fs

```java
import java.awt.*;
import java.awt.event.*;
import javax.swing.*;

public class SimpleInternalFrame extends Frame {

    JButton openButton, macButton, javaButton, motifButton, winButton;
    JLayeredPane desktop;
    JInternalFrame internalFrame;

    public SimpleInternalFrame() {
        super("Internal Frame Demo");
        setSize(500,400);
        openButton = new JButton("Open");
        macButton = new JButton("Mac");
        javaButton = new JButton("Metal");
        motifButton = new JButton("Motif");
        winButton = new JButton("Windows");
        Panel p = new Panel();
        p.add(openButton);
        p.add(macButton);
        p.add(javaButton);
        p.add(motifButton);
        p.add(winButton);
        add(p, BorderLayout.SOUTH);
        addWindowListener(new WindowAdapter() {
            public void windowClosing(WindowEvent e) {
                System.exit(0);
            }
        });
        openButton.addActionListener(new OpenListener());
        LnFListener lnf = new LnFListener(this);
        macButton.addActionListener(lnf);
        javaButton.addActionListener(lnf);
        motifButton.addActionListener(lnf);
        winButton.addActionListener(lnf);

        // Set up the layered pane.
        desktop = new JDesktopPane();
        desktop.setOpaque(true);
        add(desktop, BorderLayout.CENTER);
    }
```

```
        // An inner class to handle presses of the Open button
        class OpenListener implements ActionListener {
          public void actionPerformed(ActionEvent e) {
            if ((internalFrame == null) || (internalFrame.isClosed())) {
              internalFrame = new JInternalFrame("Internal Frame",
                                            true, true, true, true);
              internalFrame.setBounds(50, 50, 200, 100);
              desktop.add(internalFrame, new Integer(1));
              internalFrame.setVisible(true);
            }
          }
        }
      }

      public static void main(String args[]) {
        SimpleInternalFrame sif = new SimpleInternalFrame( );
        sif.setVisible(true);
      }
    }
```

The internal frame examples use the same L&F listener and basic window monitor
as the JButton example. You'll notice some nasty flickering when you move the internal frame around. That's because we put it inside a Frame, not a JFrame. In our next
example, the problem disappears.

A Bigger Application

Now that you've seen how to create internal frames and played around with them a
bit, let's tackle a slightly larger problem. We want to build an application that can
pop up internal frames that you can actually use. This starter application is a web
site manager that shows us a list of HTML pages at a site and, for any of those pages,
allows us to pop up the page in a separate frame and edit it. We'll keep the main list
of HTML pages in one "site" frame that contains a simple list box.

Once you have a site built up with a couple of pages, you can click on any entry in
the list, and if the file exists, we'll create a new "page" frame and load the file into a
JTextArea object for you to edit. You can modify the text and save the file using the
File menu in the page frame.

As a bonus, we'll put those cut, copy, and paste icons to use as well. You can manipulate text in any of the open page frames. The icons work as Action objects by looking at the selected text and insertion point of the active frame. (We alluded to the
Action class after our last Toolbar example. We'll demonstrate it here and discuss it
thoroughly at the start of the next chapter.) If the active frame is a site frame, nothing happens.

You could certainly add a lot of features to this application and make it a real working program, but we don't want to get mired down in details just yet. (If you want to
get really fancy, you could look at some of the editor kits discussed in Chapter 23

and build yourself a real HTML editor.) Figure 2-9 shows the finished application with a couple of open frames.

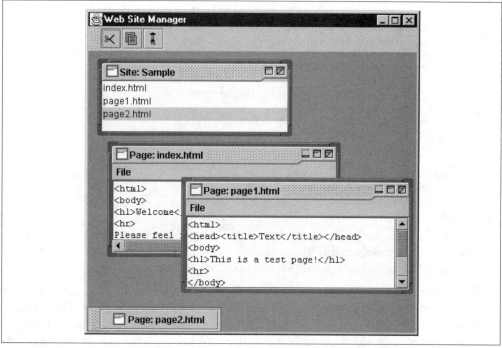

Figure 2-9. The SiteManager application running on a platform where Metal is the default L&F

We break the code for this application into three separate classes to make discussing it more manageable. The first class handles the real application frame. The constructor handles all of the interface setup work. It sets up the toolbar, as well as the Cut, Copy, and Paste buttons. It uses the default L&F for the platform on which it is run. (You could certainly attach the LnFListener, if you wanted to.) Here's the source code:

```
// SiteManager.java
//
import java.awt.*;
import java.io.*;
import java.util.*;
import java.awt.event.*;
import javax.swing.*;

public class SiteManager extends JFrame {

  JLayeredPane desktop;
  Vector popups = new Vector();

  public SiteManager() {
    super("Web Site Manager");
```

```
        setSize(450, 250);
        setDefaultCloseOperation(EXIT_ON_CLOSE);
        Container contentPane = getContentPane();

        JToolBar jtb = new JToolBar();
        jtb.add(new CutAction(this));
        jtb.add(new CopyAction(this));
        jtb.add(new PasteAction(this));
        contentPane.add(jtb, BorderLayout.NORTH);

        // Add our LayeredPane object for the internal frames.
        desktop = new JDesktopPane();
        contentPane.add(desktop, BorderLayout.CENTER);
        addSiteFrame("Sample");
    }

    public static void main(String args[]) {
        SiteManager mgr = new SiteManager();
        mgr.setVisible(true);
    }
```

Notice that since we're finally using Swing's JFrame rather than an AWT Frame, we can replace the cumbersome WindowAdapter, which handles user close requests, with a single call to setDefaultCloseOperation(EXIT_ON_CLOSE).

Now for the creation of the site and page frames. The SiteFrame class and PageFrame class, discussed later in this chapter, extend the JInternalFrame class. These classes handle all of the hard work in getting the frames to look and act correctly. Here, we just need to make the internal frame visible and keep a reference to the frame. By keeping the popups vector around, we could eventually add Save All, Close Site, and other options. For now we just use it to help find the current frame.

```
    // Methods to create our internal frames
    public void addSiteFrame(String name) {
        SiteFrame sf = new SiteFrame(name, this);
        popups.addElement(sf);
        desktop.add(sf, new Integer(2));  // Keep sites on top for now.
        sf.setVisible(true);
    }

    public void addPageFrame(String name) {
        PageFrame pf = new PageFrame(name, this);
        desktop.add(pf, new Integer(1));
        pf.setVisible(true);
        pf.setIconifiable(true);
        popups.addElement(pf);
    }

    public JInternalFrame getCurrentFrame() {
        for (int i = 0; i < popups.size(); i++) {
            JInternalFrame currentFrame = (JInternalFrame)popups.elementAt(i);
            if (currentFrame.isSelected()) {
                return currentFrame;
```

```
        }
      }
      return null;
    }
  }
```

The getCurrentFrame( ) method runs through a list of all the frames currently open in the site manager and returns the active frame. (Yes, this is a bit inefficient, but we're ignoring that for right now.)

Notice that we're using a JToolBar object in our example. This is a great shortcut if you just want a few buttons along the top (or side or bottom) of your application. A JToolBar can contain almost any kind of component, though it's most often used for buttons. We don't add buttons directly; instead, we add Action objects, which are automatically converted into buttons when placed in a toolbar. The Action interface encapsulates an icon and an actionPerformed( ) method so that you don't have to do lengthy if/else-if testing. When you add an Action to the toolbar, the toolbar displays the Action's icon, and when you click on the icon, the Action's actionPerformed( ) method is called automatically. Here's the code for the CopyAction class:

```
// CopyAction.java
// A simple Action that copies text from a PageFrame object
//
import java.awt.event.ActionEvent;
import javax.swing.*;

public class CopyAction extends AbstractAction {
  SiteManager manager;

  public CopyAction(SiteManager sm) {
    super("", new ImageIcon("copy.gif"));
    manager = sm;
  }

  public void actionPerformed(ActionEvent ae) {
    JInternalFrame currentFrame = manager.getCurrentFrame( );
    if (currentFrame == null) { return; }
    // Can't cut or paste sites
    if (currentFrame instanceof SiteFrame) { return; }
    ((PageFrame)currentFrame).copyText( );
  }
}
```

The cut and paste action classes work in a similar fashion. (We won't show them here.) Swing provides a large number of pre-built Actions, so you may not even need to write your own. We'll discuss several in Chapter 23. Appendix B lists all the Actions that are provided by Swing's components as well as the key bindings (if any) with which they can be triggered.

Next we need a way to create the site frames. We can set up a separate class that extends the JInternalFrame class and contains the functionality appropriate for the site manager. Namely, we must be able to list available pages in the site and open any of those pages for editing.

We can create a frame that has a listbox as its primary component. This won't be a fancy manager, but it will do what we want. The nice thing about internal frames, from the frame's point of view, is that they look just like regular frames. You can use the constructor to add all of the graphical interface elements and put in event listeners. The only difference with internal frames is that they need to be added to an appropriate desktop pane, but again, that's not a difference we can see here in the code for the individual frames. You can change existing standalone Frame classes to JInternalFrame classes with very little effort:

```java
// SiteFrame.java
// A simple extension of the JInternalFrame class that contains a list object.
// Elements of the list represent HTML pages for a web site.
//
import java.awt.*;
import javax.swing.*;
import javax.swing.event.*;

public class SiteFrame extends JInternalFrame {

    JList nameList;
    SiteManager parent;
    // Hardcode the pages of our "site" to keep things simple.
    String[] pages = {"index.html", "page1.html", "page2.html"};

    public SiteFrame(String name, SiteManager sm) {
        super("Site: " + name, true, true, true);
        parent = sm;
        setBounds(50,50,250,100);

        nameList = new JList(pages);
        nameList.setSelectionMode(ListSelectionModel.SINGLE_SELECTION);
        nameList.addListSelectionListener(new ListSelectionListener() {
            public void valueChanged(ListSelectionEvent lse) {
                // We know this is the list, so pop up the page.
                if (!lse.getValueIsAdjusting()) {
                    parent.addPageFrame((String)nameList.getSelectedValue());
                }
            }
        });
        Container contentPane = getContentPane();
        contentPane.add(nameList, BorderLayout.CENTER);
    }
}
```

In the valueChanged( ) method for the ListSelectionListener, we handle the basic functions of the page list. Single-clicking on an entry in the list creates a new PageFrame object for that file. If the file doesn't exist, you get a blank text area for creating the page from scratch. Note that very little error checking is going on here. But

---

you probably have already discovered that robust error checking just gets in the way of having fun, and that's all we're really trying to accomplish with this application.

Now you have the site frame going. The new page frame needs to be able to open the file (if it exists) and display the file for editing. The Cut, Copy, and Paste buttons from our earlier example allow you to move text around in a file and between open files in the application.

Like the site frame, we'll create a subclass of `JInternalFrame` for our page frame. We can use the constructor for the interface work again, and then allow the text area to manage all of the text display and editing work:

```
// PageFrame.java
// A simple extension of the JInternalFrame class that contains a text area
// and a local menu to save changes to simple HTML text.
//
import java.awt.*;
import java.io.*;
import java.awt.event.*;
import javax.swing.*;

public class PageFrame extends JInternalFrame {

  SiteManager parent;
  String filename;
  JTextArea ta;

  public PageFrame(String name, SiteManager sm) {
    super("Page: " + name, true, true, true, true);
    parent = sm;
    setBounds(50,50,300,150);

    // Use the JFrame's content pane to store our desktop.
    Container contentPane = getContentPane( );

    // Create a text area to display the contents of our file and put it in a
    // scrollable pane so we can get to all of it.
    ta = new JTextArea( );
    JScrollPane jsp = new JScrollPane(ta);
    contentPane.add(jsp, BorderLayout.CENTER);

    // Add a "File->Save" option to the menu bar for this frame.
    JMenuBar jmb = new JMenuBar( );
    JMenu fileMenu = new JMenu("File");
    JMenuItem saveItem = new JMenuItem("Save");
    saveItem.addActionListener(new ActionListener( ) {
      public void actionPerformed(ActionEvent ae) { saveContent( ); }
    });
    fileMenu.add(saveItem);
    jmb.add(fileMenu);
    setJMenuBar(jmb);
```

```
    // Now get the content, based on the filename that was passed in.
    filename = name;
    loadContent();
  }
}
```

Here, we need to add some load and save routines to the `PageFrame` class for the text areas. You'll learn more about the `read()` and `write()` methods in Chapter 19, but for now, we'll just use them since they provide such a convenient way to read and write text files:

```
public void loadContent() {
  try {
    FileReader fr = new FileReader(filename);
    ta.read(fr, null);
    fr.close();
  }
  catch (Exception e) { System.err.println("Could not load page: "+filename); }
}

public void saveContent() {
  try {
    FileWriter fw = new FileWriter(filename);
    ta.write(fw);
    fw.close();
  }
  catch(Exception e) { System.err.println("Could not save page: "+filename); }
}
```

To make the cut and paste operations simpler, we'll put in some public access methods to manipulate the text. All three of these routines are built to function regardless of the clipboard implementation you use. We'll use the system clipboard (via some convenience methods found in `JTextComponent`) for this example, but you could just as easily use your own clipboard, or eventually, Drag and Drop text.

```
public void cutText() { ta.cut(); }
public void copyText() { ta.copy(); }
public void pasteText() { ta.paste(); }
```

Now you can start the program and bring up the individual HTML files by selecting them from the list. Each file has its own internal frame that you can move around, resize, iconify, maximize, and close. You can cut, copy, and paste text between files. You can save edits using menus attached to each pop-up frame. You can even detach the toolbar and let it "float." All this for about 250 lines of code!

Well, now that we've had a bit of fun, it's time to move on to the details. The next chapter plunges into the world of Swing with the `JComponent` class. Good luck, and have fun!

CHAPTER 3

Swing Component Basics

The previous chapter showed how easy it is to create some impressive programs with Swing components. Now it's time to dig in a little deeper. We begin this chapter by presenting an overview of a few key (but lower-level) helper classes such as Action, GraphicsContext, ChangeEvent, and PropertyChangeEvent, as well as the HeadlessException exception. We spend the remainder of the chapter introducing the JComponent class, the heart and soul of all Swing components.

Understanding Actions

Actions are a popular addition to Swing. An action allows a programmer to bundle a commonly used procedure and its bound properties (such as its name and an image to represent it) into a single class. This construct comes in handy if an application needs to call upon a particular function from multiple sources. For example, let's say that a Swing programmer creates an action that saves data to disk. The application could then invoke this action from both the Save menu item on the File menu and the Save button on a toolbar. Both components reference the same action object, which saves the data. If the Save function is disabled for some reason, this property can be set in the action as well. The menu and toolbar objects are automatically notified that they can no longer save any data, and they can relay that information to the user.

Actions and Containers

Swing containers, such as JMenu, JPopupMenu, and JToolBar, can each accept action objects with their add( ) methods. When an action is added, these containers automatically create a GUI component, which the add( ) method then returns to you for customization. For example, a JMenu or a JPopupMenu creates and returns a JMenuItem from an Action while a JToolBar creates and returns a JButton. The action is then paired with the newly created GUI component in two ways: the GUI component registers as a PropertyChangeListener for any property changes that might occur in the action object, while the action object registers as an ActionListener on the GUI component. Figure 3-1 shows the interactions between a menu item or toolbar and an Action.

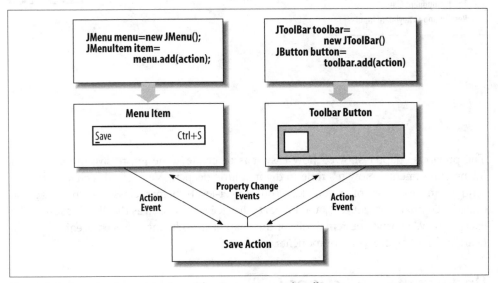

Figure 3-1. An action in conjunction with a Swing item and toolbar

Essentially, this means that if the menu item or button is selected by the user, the functionality inside the action is invoked. On the other hand, if the action is disabled, it sends a PropertyChangeEvent to both the menu item and the toolbar, causing them to disable and turn gray. Similarly, if the action's icon or name is changed, the menu and toolbar are automatically updated.

The Action Interface

An action is defined by the interface it implements, in this case javax.swing.Action. Action extends the ActionListener interface from AWT; this forces concrete classes that implement Action to provide an actionPerformed( ) method. The programmer uses the actionPerformed( ) method to implement whatever behavior is desired. For example, if you are creating a Save action, you should put the code that saves the data inside of your actionPerformed( ) method.

When the action is added to an accepting container such as JMenu, JPopupMenu, or JToolBar, the container automatically registers the action as an ActionListener of the GUI component it creates. Consequently, if the GUI component is selected by the user, it simply invokes the actionPerformed( ) method of the action to do its job.

The `Action` interface defines five constants (shown in Table 3-2), which serve as keys for storing standardized `Action` properties. The method of storage varies from implementer to implementer, but a `Hashtable` is common. These properties store information such as the name of the action, its description, and a representative icon. Also, the `Action` interface defines a boolean property that indicates whether the action is enabled or disabled. Recall that the GUI component created for the action registers itself as a `PropertyChangeListener`. Hence, if any of these properties are modified, the GUI component is notified and can react accordingly.

Table 3-1. String-based key constants for the Action interface

Constant	Meaning
DEFAULT	Default setting
NAME	Name of the action
SHORT_DESCRIPTION	Short text description of what the action does
LONG_DESCRIPTION	Long text description of what the action does
SMALL_ICON	Represents a small icon; typically used in a toolbar

Property

The `Action` interface defines the property shown in Table 3-2.

Table 3-2. Action property

Property	Data type	get	is	set	Default value
enabled	boolean		•	•	

See also `java.awt.event.ActionListener`.

The `enabled` property defines whether anyone can invoke the action. When this property changes, the action should fire a `PropertyChangeEvent` describing the change.

Note that the properties whose keys appear in Table 3-1 are not also shown here. These *are* really properties because changing one should fire a `PropertyChangeEvent`. However, because they do not use standard accessors, they do not fit the true Java-Beans property model, so we have omitted them from Table 3-2.

Methods

public abstract Object getValue(String key)
public abstract void putValue(String key, Object value)
> Store various keyed properties for the action. A string-based key is used to index the values. Several string constants representing the keys are shown in Table 3-1. When putValue( ) is called with any property, and the value passed in is different than

what was there previously, the implementing object must fire a `PropertyChangeEvent` describing the change to all registered listeners.

public abstract void actionPerformed(ActionEvent e)

This method is required by the `ActionListener` interface (it does not actually exist in the `Action` interface). Any concrete class that implements the `Action` interface must provide an `actionPerformed()` method that performs whatever task the action is supposed to accomplish.

Events

Objects implementing the `Action` interface must fire a `PropertyChangeEvent` when any keyed property is changed, or when the action is enabled or disabled. Containers that accept actions typically listen for these `PropertyChangeEvent` notifications so they can update their own properties or appearances.

public abstract void addPropertyChangeListener(PropertyChangeListener listener)
public abstract void removePropertyChangeListener(PropertyChangeListener listener)

Add or remove the specified `PropertyChangeListener` from the event listener list.

The AbstractAction Class

The `AbstractAction` class is an abstract implementation of the `Action` interface. `AbstractAction` provides the default functionality for almost all methods in the `Action` interface. You can extend this class to create your own specific actions. If you do so, the only method for which you must provide an implementation is the `actionPerformed()` method, which provides the functionality for the action. Here is a simple example:

```
class MyAction extends AbstractAction {

    public MyAction(String text, Icon icon) {
        super(text,icon);
    }
    public void actionPerformed(ActionEvent e) {
        System.out.println("Action [" + e.getActionCommand() + "]!");
    }
}
```

Here, we simply print the action command sent with the `ActionEvent`. You can add more features based on the contents of the `ActionEvent`.

Properties

The `AbstractAction` class stores its keyed properties in a `Hashtable` object. Beyond that, the `AbstractAction` object contains a few properties, as shown in Table 3-3. The `enabled` property defines whether the application can invoke the action. When this property changes, `AbstractAction` fires a `PropertyChangeEvent`. The mutator for this

---

property, setEnabled( ), is synchronized. If you want a list of the current property listeners, use the propertyChangeListeners property.

Table 3-3. AbstractAction properties

Property	Data type	get	is	set	Default value
enabled[b]	boolean		•	•	true
keys[b, 1.3]	Object[]			•	null
propertyChangeListeners[1.4]	PropertyChangeListener[]			•	Empty array

[1.3]since 1.3, [1.4]since 1.4, [b]bound

Events

The AbstractAction class fires a PropertyChangeEvent when any property in the hashtable is changed or when the action is enabled or disabled.

public void addPropertyChangeListener(PropertyChangeListener listener)
public void removePropertyChangeListener(PropertyChangeListener listener)
   Add or remove the specified PropertyChangeListener from the event listener list.

Constructors

public AbstractAction( )
public AbstractAction(String name)
public AbstractAction(String name, Icon icon)
   The constructors for the AbstractAction object can be used to set the name and icon hashtable properties of the action under the NAME or SMALL_ICON keys, respectively.

Methods

public Object getValue(String key)
public void putValue(String key, Object value)
   These methods store or retrieve various elements in a private Hashtable. A string-based key is used to index the Hashtable values. See the Action interface earlier in the chapter for an enumeration of common string-based keys.

Using an Action

This example creates an Action for both a menu item and a toolbar, displaying both components and allowing the user to click on either one. When the components are clicked, the actionPerformed( ) method of the action is called. Don't worry if you don't understand all the methods behind the toolbar or the menu; these classes are discussed later. For now, it is important to see that selecting either one performs the action.

```java
// ActionExample.java
//
import java.awt.*;
import java.awt.event.*;
import javax.swing.*;
import javax.swing.border.*;

public class ActionExample extends JPanel {

    public JMenuBar menuBar;
    public JToolBar toolBar;

    public ActionExample() {
        super(true);

        // Create a menu bar and give it a bevel border.
        menuBar = new JMenuBar();
        menuBar.setBorder(new BevelBorder(BevelBorder.RAISED));

        // Create a menu and add it to the menu bar.
        JMenu menu = new JMenu("Menu");
        menuBar.add(menu);

        // Create a toolbar and give it an etched border.
        toolBar = new JToolBar();
        toolBar.setBorder(new EtchedBorder());

        // Instantiate a sample action with the NAME property of "Download" and the
        // appropriate SMALL_ICON property.
        SampleAction exampleAction = new SampleAction("Download",
                                        new ImageIcon("action.gif"));

        // Finally, add the sample action to the menu and the toolbar. These methods
        // are no longer preferred:
        //     menu.add(exampleAction);
        //     toolBar.add(exampleAction);
        // Instead, you should create actual menu items and buttons:
        JMenuItem exampleItem = new JMenuItem(exampleAction);
        JButton exampleButton = new JButton(exampleAction);
        menu.add(exampleItem);
        toolBar.add(exampleButton);
    }

    class SampleAction extends AbstractAction {
        // This is our sample action. It must have an actionPerformed() method, which
        // is called when the action should be invoked.
        public SampleAction(String text, Icon icon) {
            super(text,icon);
        }

        public void actionPerformed(ActionEvent e) {
            System.out.println("Action [" + e.getActionCommand() + "] performed!");
        }
    }
}
```

```
    public static void main(String s[]) {
        ActionExample example = new ActionExample();
        JFrame frame = new JFrame("Action Example");
        frame.setDefaultCloseOperation(JFrame.EXIT_ON_CLOSE);
        frame.setJMenuBar(example.menuBar);
        frame.getContentPane().add(example.toolBar, BorderLayout.NORTH);
        frame.setSize(200,200);
        frame.setVisible(true);
    }
}
```

The preceding example creates a toolbar with a single button and a menu with a single menu item. Both are generated from the `SampleAction` class and are shown in Figure 3-2.

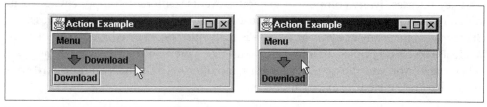

Figure 3-2. An action in a menu and in a toolbar

Selecting the menu item or clicking on the toolbar button a few times both yield the same results on the console:

```
Action [Download] performed!
Action [Download] performed!
Action [Download] performed!
```

Now for something interesting. You can add the following line to the constructor to disable the action:

```
exampleAction.setEnabled(false);
```

With this line, the `PropertyChangeEvent` propagates to listeners in the menu item and in the toolbar button, causing both components to turn gray and become disabled. Figure 3-3 shows what happens when an action is disabled.

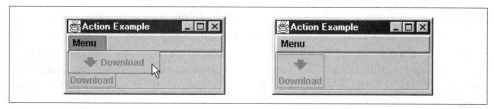

Figure 3-3. A disabled action in a menu and in a toolbar

Of course, you can enable the menu item and toolbar button again at any time with the following line of code:

```
exampleAction.setEnabled(true);
```

Upon execution, the property change again propagates, re-enabling both components simultaneously.

Actions also play a critical role in supporting key bindings within components (see "Keyboard Events" later in this chapter).

Graphical Interface Events

Whenever you interact with your application's user interface, the application receives an event from the windowing system to let it know that something happened. Some events come from the mouse, such as mouse clicks, mouse movements, and mouse drags. Other events come from the keyboard, such as key presses and key releases. Every component generates events. Different components generate different events as dictated by their purpose (and their L&F). For example, pressing a JButton generates an ActionEvent (which is really just a converted mouse event). The ActionEvent class bundles up interesting stuff like which button the event came from, when the button was pressed, whether any modifier keys (such as Shift or Ctrl) were pressed at the time of the event, and so on.

While the event-dispatching and -handling mechanism is grounded in the world of AWT (and beyond the scope of this book), we do want you to know what events the various Swing components generate—and when. The *what* of the events is discussed in conjunction with each of the components. As we introduce components like JTextField, JButton, and JTable, we show the events that they fire and the methods you use to attach listeners and catch the events.

The *when* of the events is a bit more difficult to describe. Rather than attempt to list every possible scenario for every component, we've built a small utility: EEL, the Every Event Listener. The EEL class implements every listener interface from the java.awt.event and javax.swing.event packages. It has a variety of logging mechanisms to show you the events coming from your components. You attach an EEL instance to a component (or to multiple components) using the component's add...Listener( ) method(s). You can choose to have the events sent to a file, to your console, or to an onscreen text area.

This discussion really is beyond the scope of the book. So we're posting this utility and its documentation on the web site for this book (*http://www.oreilly.com/catalog/jswing2*). Feel free to download it and use it to play with individual components or to debug an entire application. That's one of the beauties of delegation event handling: you can attach EEL to an existing component without breaking its normal interactions with the application.

Graphics Environments

SDK 1.4 recognizes a great deal of information about its environment. You can retrieve that information for your own code through the GraphicsEnvironment, GraphicsDevice, and GraphicsConfiguration classes from the java.awt package. While they aren't part of Swing proper, these classes are definitely useful for Swing applications, especially those that take full advantage of their environment.

To sum up these classes, a system keeps a local GraphicsEnvironment object that describes the devices on the system with an array of GraphicsDevice objects. Each GraphicsDevice contains (or at least may contain) multiple configurations of device capabilities (such as pixel formats or which visual screen you're on) bundled up in an array of GraphicsConfiguration objects.

> The GraphicsConfiguration class should not be confused with the DisplayMode class (although it's easy to do so). The display mode is something with which most savvy computer users will be familiar. On a system that supports multisync monitors, the DisplayMode class encapsulates the width, height, color-depth, and refresh rate information for a given mode. The GraphicsConfiguration class stores things like square versus rectangular pixels. GraphicsConfiguration could even be used for devices such as printers. The configuration information is highly dependent on the native platform and thus varies widely from system to system. In any given system, both configurations and modes can be found through the available GraphicsDevice objects.

If you're curious about the various graphics configurations on your system, try out this little program, *GuiScreens.java*. It prints information on all devices and configurations. For each configuration, it also pops up a JFrame using that configuration.

```java
// GuiScreens.java
//
import java.awt.*;
import javax.swing.*;

public class GuiScreens {
  public static void main(String[] args) {
    Rectangle virtualBounds = new Rectangle();
    GraphicsEnvironment ge = GraphicsEnvironment.getLocalGraphicsEnvironment();
    GraphicsDevice[] gs = ge.getScreenDevices();
    JFrame frame[][] = new JFrame[gs.length][];
    for (int j = 0; j < gs.length; j++) {
      GraphicsDevice gd = gs[j];
      System.out.println("Device " + j + ": " + gd);
      GraphicsConfiguration[] gc = gd.getConfigurations();
      frame[j] = new JFrame[gc.length];

      for (int i=0; i < gc.length; i++) {
        System.out.println("  Configuration " + i + ": " + gc[i]);
```

```
        System.out.println("     Bounds: " + gc[i].getBounds());
        virtualBounds = virtualBounds.union(gc[i].getBounds());
        frame[j][i] = new JFrame("Config: " + i, gc[i]);
        frame[j][i].setBounds(50, 50, 400, 100);
        frame[j][i].setLocation(
          (int)gc[i].getBounds().getX() + 50,
          (int)gc[i].getBounds().getY() + 50);
        frame[j][i].getContentPane().add(new JTextArea("Config:\n" + gc[i]));
        frame[j][i].setDefaultCloseOperation( WindowConstants.EXIT_ON_CLOSE );
        frame[j][i].setVisible(true);
      }
      System.out.println("Overall bounds: " + virtualBounds);
    }
  }
}
```

Here's the text output from a Solaris system running CDE with one monitor:

```
Device 0: X11GraphicsDevice[screen=0]
  Configuration 0: X11GraphicsConfig[dev=X11GraphicsDevice[screen=0],vis=0x22]
    Bounds: java.awt.Rectangle[x=0,y=0,width=1152,height=900]
  Configuration 1: X11GraphicsConfig[dev=X11GraphicsDevice[screen=0],vis=0x26]
    Bounds: java.awt.Rectangle[x=0,y=0,width=1152,height=900]
  Configuration 2: X11GraphicsConfig[dev=X11GraphicsDevice[screen=0],vis=0x25]
    Bounds: java.awt.Rectangle[x=0,y=0,width=1152,height=900]
  Configuration 3: X11GraphicsConfig[dev=X11GraphicsDevice[screen=0],vis=0x24]
    Bounds: java.awt.Rectangle[x=0,y=0,width=1152,height=900]
  Configuration 4: X11GraphicsConfig[dev=X11GraphicsDevice[screen=0],vis=0x27]
    Bounds: java.awt.Rectangle[x=0,y=0,width=1152,height=900]
Overall bounds: java.awt.Rectangle[x=0,y=0,width=1152,height=900]
```

And here's the output from an OS X system with two monitors:

```
Device 0: sun.awt.MacGraphicsDevice@4dd8d9
  Configuration 0: com.apple.mrj.internal.awt.graphics.MacGraphicsConfig@303297
    Bounds: java.awt.Rectangle[x=0,y=0,width=1280,height=1024]
Device 1: sun.awt.MacGraphicsDevice@5c08c3
  Configuration 0: com.apple.mrj.internal.awt.graphics.MacGraphicsConfig@435a72
    Bounds: java.awt.Rectangle[x=1280,y=-52,width=1152,height=870]
Overall bounds: java.awt.Rectangle[x=0,y=-52,width=2432,height=1076]
```

Headless Modes

One other variation on the graphics environment is "headless" operation. This mode of running without any monitor shows up quite often on back-end systems. Java servlets trying to use the AWT, 2D, and Swing classes to draw dynamic graphs for a web page are a classic example of applications that need a graphics environment on a machine that might not have any graphics displays. You can detect such a case with the GraphicsEnvironment.isHeadless() call.

If an environment is headless, there are certain calls that cannot be made. These calls tend to create onscreen components such as frames or dialogs—no good without a head—or otherwise attempt to interact with the (nonexistent) local user. Table 3-4 shows the documented Swing components that generate a `HeadlessException` when called. Since `HeadlessException` is an unchecked exception (i.e., a descendant of `RuntimeException`), it is not always documented in the Javadoc for a method or in its throws clause (in the source code). The best practice that has evolved for writing Javadoc for such exceptions requires that the Javadoc mention the exception (with an `@throws` entry), but that the `throws` clause in the actual method signature *omit* it. This leads to a visual indication that it is an unchecked exception. Not all code has adopted this best practice, of course.

Table 3-4. Swing components that throw HeadlessException

Component	Method(s)
JApplet	Constructors
JColorChooser	showDialog( ); setDragEnabled( ); createDialog( ); constructors
JDialog	Constructors
JFileChooser	createDialog( ); showDialog( ); showOpenDialog( ); showSaveDialog( ); setDragenabled( )
JFrame	Constructors
JList	setDragEnabled( )
JOptionPane	All show dialog methods; createDialog( ); getFrameForComponent( ); getWindowForComponent( ); getRootFrame( )
JTable	setDragEnabled( )
JTree	setDragEnabled( )
JWindow	Constructors
SwingUtilities	getSharedOwnerFrame( )

Sending Change Events in Swing

Swing uses two different change event classes. The first is the standard `java.beans.PropertyChangeEvent` class. This class passes a reference to the object, sending the change notification as well as the property name, its old value, and its new value. The second, `javax.swing.event.ChangeEvent`, is a lighter version that passes only a reference to the sending object—in other words, the name of the property that changed, as well as the old and new values, are omitted.

Since the `ChangeEvent` class is not part of the JavaBeans specifications, properties that use this event are not "bound" according to the Java-Beans standard. In order to prevent confusion, properties that use a `ChangeEvent` to notify listeners of property changes have not been marked as bound in our property tables.

Because the `ChangeEvent` includes only a reference to the event originator, which never changes, you can always define a single `ChangeEvent` and reuse it over and over when firing events from your component.

The ChangeEvent Class

The ChangeEvent is a stripped-down version of the java.beans.PropertyChangeEvent class. This class has no methods or properties, only a constructor. This simplicity makes it a popular class for developers wanting to fire off their own events. Recipients get a reference to the source of the event but then must query the source directly to find out what just happened. It's great for quick notifications or instances in which the state of the source component is so complex it's hard to predict which pieces of information the recipient will need, but it shouldn't be used simply to save the component author a little time at the expense of runtime inefficiency if the recipient always needs to look up information that could have been part of a PropertyChangeEvent.

Constructor

public ChangeEvent(Object source)
> The constructor for the ChangeEvent class. It takes only a single object, which represents the entity sending the event.

The ChangeListener Interface

Objects that intend to receive change events must implement the javax.swing.event. ChangeListener interface. They can then register to receive ChangeEvent objects from a publisher class. The ChangeListener interface consists of only one method.

Method

public abstract void stateChanged(ChangeEvent e)
> Implemented in a listener object to receive ChangeEvent notifications.

The JComponent Class

JComponent is an abstract class that almost all Swing components extend; it provides much of the underlying functionality common throughout the Swing component library. Just as the java.awt.Component class serves as the guiding framework for most of the AWT components, the javax.swing.JComponent class serves an identical role for the Swing components. We should note that the JComponent class extends java.awt.Container (which in turn extends java.awt.Component), so it is accurate to say that Swing components carry with them a great deal of AWT functionality as well.

Because JComponent extends Container, many Swing components can serve as containers for other AWT and Swing components. These components may be added using the traditional add( ) method of Container. In addition, they can be positioned with any Java layout manager while inside the container. The terminology remains the same as well: components that are added to a container are said to be its *children*; the container is the *parent* of those components. Following the analogy, any component that is higher in the tree is said to be its *ancestor*, while any component that is lower is said to be its *descendant*.

Recall that Swing components are considered "lightweight." In other words, they do not rely on corresponding peer objects within the operating system to render themselves. As we mentioned in Chapter 1, lightweight components draw themselves using the standard features of the abstract Graphics object, which not only decreases the amount of memory each component uses but allows components to have transparent portions and take on nonrectangular shapes. And, of course, lightweight components are free of a dedicated L&F.

It's not out of the question to say that a potential benefit of using lightweight components is a decrease in testing time. This is because the functionality necessary to implement lightweight components in the Java virtual machine is significantly less than that of heavyweight components. Heavyweight components must be individually mapped to their own native peers. On the other hand, one needs to implement only a single lightweight peer on each operating system for all the Swing components to work correctly. Hence, there is a far greater chance that lightweight components will execute as expected on any operating system and not require rounds of testing for each platform.

 Because all Swing components extend Container, you should be careful that you don't add( ) to Swing components that aren't *truly* containers. The results range from amusing to destructive.

In JDK 1.2, JComponent reuses some of the functionality of the java.awt.Graphics2D class. This consists primarily of responsibilities for component painting and debugging.

Inherited Properties

Swing components carry with them several properties that can be accessed through JComponent but otherwise originate with AWT. Before we go any further, we should review those properties of java.awt.Container and java.awt.Component that can be used to configure all Swing components. This discussion is relatively brief; if you need a more thorough explanation of these AWT classes, see *Java AWT Reference* by John Zukowski (O'Reilly), which can be downloaded from this book's web site, *http://www.oreilly.com/catalog/jswing2/*. Table 3-5 lists the properties that JComponent inherits from its AWT superclasses.

Table 3-5. Properties inherited from the AWT Component and Container classes

Property	Data type	get	is	set	Default value (if applicable)
background	Color	•		•	
colorModel	ColorModel	•			
component[i]	Component	•			
componentCount	int	•			
components	Component[]	•			
cursor	Cursor	•		•	Cursor.DEFAULT_CURSOR
enabled	boolean		•	•	true
font	Font	•		•	
foreground	Color	•		•	
insets	Insets	•			Insets(0,0,0,0)
layout	LayoutManager	•		•	BorderLayout()
locale	Locale	•		•	
location	Point	•		•	
locationOnScreen	Point	•		•	
name	String	•		•	""
parent	Container	•		•	null
size	Dimension	•		•	
showing	boolean		•		true
valid	boolean	•			
visible	boolean	•		•	true

[i]indexed

Let's discuss these properties briefly. The background and foreground properties indicate which colors the component uses to paint itself. We should mention that with Swing the background property is disabled if the component is transparent (not opaque). The read-only colorModel property returns the current model used to translate colors to pixel values; generally, the user does not need to access this property. The font property lets you get or set the font used for displaying text in the component.

The indexed component property maintains a list of all the components inside the container. You can tell how many there are with the integer componentCount property. If you want to access all of them through a Component array, retrieve the components property. The insets property specifies the current insets of the container, while the layout property indicates which layout manager is managing the components of the container. Technically, this means that you can use any component as a container. Don't be misled; if a component doesn't seem like a reasonable container, it probably can't be used as one. (Don't, for example, try to add a JButton to a `JScrollBar`.) A number of components use these properties for internal, specialized layout managers and components.

The `locale` property specifies the internationalization locale for the application. The `location` property indicates the *x,y* coordinates of the component's upper-left corner in the container's coordinate space. If you want to see the location of the component's upper-left corner in screen coordinates, use the read-only `locationOnScreen` property.

The `name` property gives this component a string-based name that components can display if they choose. The `parent` property references the container that is acting as this component's parent, or `null` if there is none. The `size` property specifies the component's current height and width in pixels.

The `showing` property indicates whether the component is currently showing on the screen, while the `visible` property tells if the component is marked to be drawn on the screen. There's an odd, nonintuitive relationship between `visible` and `showing`. A component that is visible isn't necessarily showing. "Visible" means that a component is capable of being displayed; "showing" means that the component is actually displayed (though it may be obscured by something else). Most containers (`JPanel`, `JFrame`, etc.) are invisible by default; most other components (`JButton`, etc.) are visible by default. So if you add a `JButton` to an invisible `JFrame`, for example, the button is visible but not showing. It can be displayed but happens to be in a container that isn't currently displayed.

Finally, if the `valid` property is `false`, the component needs to be resized or moved by the component's layout manager. If it is `true`, the component is ready to be displayed.

Common Methods

Here are some other frequently called methods for working with Swing components:

public Component add(Component comp)
public Component add(Component comp, int index)
public void add(Component comp, Object constraints)
public void add(Component comp, Object constraints, int index)
> Add a component to the container, given the optional constraints and the current index.

public void remove(int index)
public void remove(Component comp)
public void removeAll( )
> Remove the appropriate component from the container. The final method empties the entire container.

public void pack( )
> This method of `java.awt.Window` resizes the window to encompass the preferred size of all the contained components, as placed by the current layout manager.

It's a good idea to call pack( ) after you've added components to a top-level container with a layout manager, such as JFrame, JDialog, and JWindow.

public void validate( )
public void invalidate( )

The invalidate( ) method is typically called on a Container to indicate that its children need to be laid out, or on a Component to indicate that it needs to be re-rendered. This method is often called automatically. However, certain changes to a Component (such as changing the size of a button by changing its label or font) do not cause it to be invalidated. In such cases, invalidate( ) must be called on the Component to mark it as invalid, and validate( ) must be called on its Container. The validate( ) method is typically called to validate, lay out, and repaint a Container. Calling this method is especially important when you add or remove Components in a Container that is already displayed.

Swing improves the validate( )/invalidate( ) situation a bit by calling invalidate( ) in response to many property changes, saving you from having to make the call. Unfortunately, there are still situations (such as changing a JButton's font) that do not trigger an automatic invalidate( ) call, so you'll still have to explicitly call invalidate( ) in these cases.

The key things to take away from these methods are:

- You may need to call invalidate( ) if you make changes to the appearance of a displayed component.
- You must call validate( ) on Containers that have been invalidated (typically by the addition or invalidation of a child).

As a result of deprecation and the movement toward JavaBeans accessors, AWT has some methods with multiple names. For example, show( ) and setVisible(true) are essentially the same. It is always better to use the JavaBeans-style name—setVisible( ) in this case—when working with Swing; the newer name is less confusing for people familiar with the JavaBeans conventions.

JComponent Properties

Now to the heart of the matter. JComponent has many properties of its own and overrides (or otherwise modifies) the behavior of many of its inherited properties. This is where the new and interesting stuff happens. Table 3-6 shows a summary of JComponent's properties.

Table 3-6. JComponent properties

Property	Data type	get	is	set	Default value
UI[b, p]	ComponentUI			•	
UIClassID	String	•			"ComponentUI"
accessibleContext	AccessibleContext	•			null
actionMap[1.3]	ActionMap	•		•	
alignmentX[o]	float	•		•	
alignmentY[o]	float	•		•	
ancestorListeners[1.4]	AncestorListener[]	•			
autoscrolls	boolean	•		•	false
border[b]	Border	•		•	null
bounds[o]	Rectangle	•		•	
debugGraphicsOptions	int	•		•	DebugGraphics.NONE_OPTION
defaultLocales[1.4]	Locale	•		•	
doubleBuffered	boolean		•	•	false
enabled[b,o]	boolean		•	•	true
focusCycleRoot	boolean		•		false
focusTraversable[d]	boolean		•		true
graphics[o]	Graphics	•			
height	int	•			bounds.height
inputMap[f, 1.3]; also indexed get	InputMap	•		•	
inputVerifier[b, 1.3]	InputVerifier	•		•	
insets[o]	Insets	•		•	
location[o]	Point	•		•	Point(bounds.x, bounds.y)
managingFocus[d]	boolean		•		false
maximumSize[b, o]	Dimension	•		•	
minimumSize[b, o]	Dimension	•		•	
nextFocusableComponent[d]	Component	•		•	
opaque[b]	boolean		•	•	false
optimizedDrawingEnabled	boolean		•		true
paintingTile	boolean		•		
preferredSize[b, o]	Dimension	•		•	
propertyChangeListeners (also string indexed version)	PropertyChangeListener[]	•			

[1.3]since 1.3, [1.4]since 1.4, [b]bound, [d]deprecated, [f]final, [i]indexed, [o]overridden, [p]protected, [s]static

See also java.awt.Container and java.awt.Component (Table 3-5).

Table 3-6. JComponent properties (continued)

Property	Data type	get	is	set	Default value
registeredKeyStrokes	KeyStroke[]	•			
requestFocusEnabled	boolean		•	•	true
rootPane	JRootPane	•			
size°	Dimension	•		•	Dimension (bounds.height, bounds.width)
toolTipText	String	•		•	null
topLevelAncestor	Container	•			
transferHandler[b,1.4]	TransferHandler	•		•	null
validateRoot	boolean		•		false
verifyInputWhenFocusTarget[b, 1.3]	boolean	•		•	
vetoableChangeListeners[1.4]	VetoableChangeListener[]				
visible°	boolean		•	•	true
visibleRect	Rectangle	•			
width°	int	•			bounds.width
x°	int	•			bounds.x
y°	int	•			bounds.y

[1.3]since 1.3, [1.4]since 1.4, [b]bound, [d]deprecated, [f]final, [i]indexed, [o]overridden, [p]protected, [s]static

See also java.awt.Container and java.awt.Component (Table 3-5).

New properties in the 1.3 and 1.4 SDKs

The properties added in 1.3 and 1.4 focus on three areas. The InputMap and ActionMap classes were added in 1.3 to improve the handling of keyboard events. (These classes are discussed in "Keyboard Events" later in this chapter.) SDK 1.4 added some convenience support for accessing event handlers such as property and vetoable property change listeners. The transferHandler property was also added in 1.4—a big step up in the usability of Drag and Drop (DnD). You can learn more about that property in Chapter 24, which is devoted to DnD functionality.

Finally, the inputVerifier and verifyInputWhenFocusTarget properties were added in 1.3 to offer applications an easy and reliable way to check a user's text input for validity. Text components with attached InputVerifiers will call the verifier's shouldYieldFocus() method when they're about to lose input focus, providing an opportunity to give the user feedback and keep focus if the input isn't valid. Any Components, such as Cancel buttons, that should remain usable even when there is invalid input in some text field, can be configured to work properly by setting their verifyInputWhenFocusTarget property to false. These capabilities are discussed in greater depth in Chapter 20.

UI Delegates and UIClassIDs

As we mentioned in Chapter 1, all Swing components use a modified MVC architecture. Each Swing component is responsible for maintaining two unique objects: a model and a UI delegate. The object representing the model handles the state information specific to the component while the UI delegate determines how the component paints itself based on the model's state information.

Note that there is no property for a model in JComponent. You typically access the model property at the level of a JComponent subclass. This is because each Swing component defines its own data model, which is unique from that of all other components. The UI delegate property, on the other hand, can be handled at the JComponent level because the methods for rendering lightweight components are always the same. These methods (e.g., installUI( ), uninstallUI( ), setUI( ), paint( )) can be traced back to the abstract class javax.swing.plaf.ComponentUI, which serves as the superclass for all UI delegates.

JComponent contains a reference to the current UI delegate for the object. JComponent allows a subclass to alter the component's UI delegate with the protected setUI( ) method; this method effectively resets the L&F of the component. The UI therefore acts like a write-only property, but we hesitate to call it a property because its mutator isn't public. Invoking setUI( ) by itself, however, does not change the display. A call to updateUI( ) is also required, which forces the component to redraw itself. If you are looking to change the entire L&F of the application, it is better to change it universally with the setLookAndFeel( ) method of UIManager than to change it one component at a time. See Chapter 2 for a simple example of how to work with various L&Fs.

Each Swing component maintains a read-only string constant, UIClassID, that identifies the type of UI delegate that it uses. Most Swing components override the accessor getUIClassID( ) and return a string constant, typically the letters "UI" appended to the name of the component (without the "J"). This string is then used by Swing's UI manager to match the component with a UI delegate for the current L&F. For example, a JButton object has a UIClassID string of ButtonUI. If the current L&F is Metal, the UIManager can figure out that the MetalButtonUI is the correct UI-delegate class to use. See Chapter 26 for more information about the UIManager and how to change L&Fs.

Invalidating and Repainting

Sometimes entire components need to be drawn to the screen. At other times, only parts of components can (or should) be drawn. For example, if an internal frame is dragged across the container, the entire internal frame is redrawn along the way until it reaches its destination. However, only the parts of the container uncovered by the internal frame need to be repainted. We typically do not repaint the entire component, as this would be an unnecessary waste of processing time. (See Figure 3-4.)

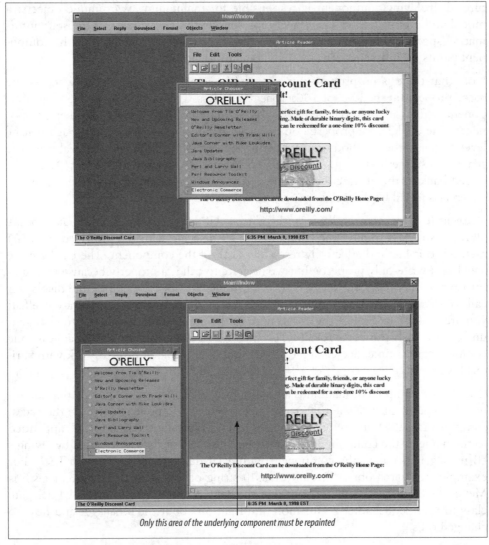

Only this area of the underlying component must be repainted

Figure 3-4. Performing repaints for components in Java

Swing uses a *repaint manager* to repaint lightweight components. The repaint manager maintains a queue of rectangular areas that need to be repainted; it calls these areas "dirty regions." Sometimes the rectangles are the size of entire components; at other times they are smaller. The repaint manager processes repaint requests as they are added to the queue, updating dirty regions as quickly as possible while preserving the visual order of the components. In AWT, the Component class contains an overloaded repaint( ) method that allows you to repaint only a subrectangle of the component. The same is true with JComponent. If only part of a component needs to be repainted, the repaint manager invokes an overloaded version of the repaint( ) method that takes a Rectangle parameter.

JComponent contains two repaint( ) methods that add specified rectangles directly to the dirty region. Like AWT, you should call these methods instead of invoking the paint( ) method directly, which bypasses the RepaintManager. The RepaintManager class is discussed in more detail in Chapter 28.

The paint( ) method and opaqueness

Because JComponent is the direct subclass of the AWT Container class, it is the official recipient of repaint requests through its paint( ) method. As you might guess, JComponent must delegate this request by passing it to the paint( ) method of the UI-delegate object. The responsibility, however, does not end there. JComponent is actually responsible for painting *three* items: the component itself, any borders associated with the component, and any children that it contains.

The order is intentional. Components drawn last are always on top; hence, child components always paint over their parents. JComponent contains three protected methods that it uses to complete this functionality:

- protected void paintComponent(Graphics g)
- protected void paintBorder(Graphics g)
- protected void paintChildren(Graphics g)

Because of the complexity involved in painting and repainting Swing components, you should always try to override these three methods while creating your own components. Also, do not try to override paint( ) unless you call super.paint( ).

SDK 1.4 introduced a series of methods relating to printing rather than painting. Calling the print( ) or printAll( ) methods (both public and available since 1.2) now results in calls to printComponent( ), printBorder( ), and printChildren( ) in that order.

When painting or printing JComponent subclasses, the Graphics object passed to these methods is actually a Graphics2D object. You can cast it as such if you want to take advantage of the increased functionality available in the 2D packages. Check out Jonathan Knudsen's *Java 2D Graphics* (O'Reilly) for more detailed information.

The boolean property opaque dictates the transparency of each Swing object.* If this property is set to false, the component's background color is transparent. This means that any areas left untouched by the component's rendering allow graphics in

---

* In JDK 1.2, the isOpaque( ) method is defined in java.awt.Component.

the background to show through. If the property is set to `true`, the rectangular painting region is completely filled with the component's background color before it is rendered. Incidentally, transparency was not possible before lightweight components. Native peer objects in Java 1.0 always drew their component on a solid rectangle; anything that was behind the component was erased. Figure 3-5 shows the difference between an opaque and a transparent (nonopaque) label, both with a dark background color. The label on the left is transparent, so its background color is ignored; the label's text appears on top of the container's relatively light background.

Figure 3-5. Transparency and opaqueness

`JComponent` can optimize its repainting time if none of its children overlap; this is because the repaint manager does not have to compute the hidden and visible areas for each child component before rendering them. Some containers, such as `JSplitPane`, are designed so that overlap between child components is impossible, so this optimization works nicely. Other containers, such as `JLayeredPane`, have support for child components that can overlap. `JComponent` contains a property that Swing frequently calls upon to see if it can optimize component drawing: `optimizedDrawingEnabled`. In `JComponent`, this property is set to `true` by default. If overlap occurs in a subclass of `JComponent`, the subclass should override the `isOptimizedDrawingEnabled()` accessor and return `false`. This prevents the repaint manager from using the optimized drawing process when rendering the container's children.

`JComponent` contains a boolean read-only property (`paintingTile`) that indicates whether the component is currently in the process of painting a *tile*, which is a child component that does not overlap any other children. The `isPaintingTile()` method returns `true` until all tiles have been painted.

The `visibleRect` property is a `Rectangle` that indicates the intersection of the component's visible rectangles with the visible rectangles of all of its ancestors. Why the intersection? Remember that you can have a contained object that is clipped by its parent. For example, you can move an internal frame so that a portion of it falls outside the parent window's clipping region. Therefore, the visible portion (the portion that is actually drawn to the screen) consists only of the intersection of the parent's visible portion and the child's visible portion. You typically do not need to access this property.

The validateRoot property is false by default. If it is set to true, it designates this component as the root component in a validation tree. Recall that each time a component in a container is invalidated, its container is invalidated as well, along with all of its children. This causes an invalidation to move all the way up the component hierarchy, stopping only when it reaches a component for which isValidateRoot() returns true. Currently, the only components that set this property to true are JRootPane (which is used by all the Swing top-level components), JScrollPane, and JTextField.

The topLevelAncestor property contains a reference to the top-level window that contains this component, usually a JWindow or JApplet. The rootPane property contains the low-level JRootPane for this component; JRootPane is covered in more detail in Chapter 8.

Finally, JComponent contains a property called autoscrolls, which indicates whether a component is capable of supporting autoscrolling. This property is false by default. If the property is true, an Autoscroller object has been set over this component. The Autoscroller object monitors mouse events on the target component. If the mouse is dragged outside the component, the autoscroller forces the target component to scroll itself. Autoscrolling is typically used in containers such as JViewport.

Position, Size, and Alignment

You can set and retrieve a Swing component's current position and size on the screen through the bounds property, or more precisely, through the location and size properties of JComponent. The location property is defined as a Point in the parent's coordinate space where the upper-left corner of the component's bounding box resides. The size property is a Dimension that specifies the current width and height of the component. The bounds property is a Rectangle object that gives the same information: it bundles both the location and the size properties. Figure 3-6 shows how Swing measures the size and location of a component.

Unlike the AWT Component class, the getBounds() accessor in JComponent can take a preinstantiated Rectangle object:

```
Rectangle myRect = new Rectangle();
myRect = component.getBounds(myRect);
```

If a Rectangle is supplied, the getBounds() method alters each of the fields in the passed-in Rectangle to reflect the component's current size and position, returning a copy of it. If the reference passed in is a null, the method instantiates a new Rectangle object, sets its values, and returns it. You can use the former approach to reduce the number of garbage rectangles created and discarded over multiple calls to getBounds(), which increases the efficiency of your application.

The setBounds() method alters the component's size and position. This method also takes a Rectangle object. If the new settings are different from the previous settings,

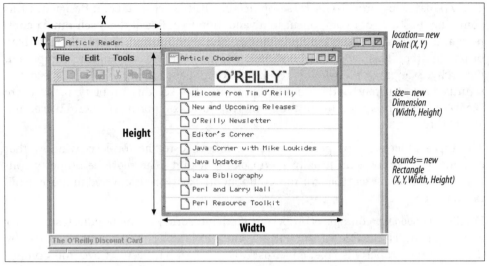

Figure 3-6. Working with the bounds, size, and location properties

the component is moved, typically resized, and invalidated. If the component has a parent, it is invalidated as well. Be warned that various layout managers may override any changes you attempt to make to the bounds property. Invalidating a component with a call to setBounds( ) may force the layout manager to recompute and reset the bounds of the component in relation to the other components, resolving it to the same size as before.

Here is a short example that shows how to retrieve the current position and size of any Swing component:

```
JFrame frame = new JFrame("Test Frame");
frame.setBounds(20,20,200,200);
frame.setVisible(true);

Rectangle r = new Rectangle( );
r = frame.getBounds(r);
System.out.println("X      = " + r.x( ));
System.out.println("Y      = " + r.y( ));
System.out.println("Width  = " + r.width( ));
System.out.println("Height = " + r.height( ));
```

There is a shorthand approach for retrieving each of the bounds properties. JComponent contains four methods that directly access them: getX( ), getY( ), getWidth( ), and getHeight( ). You can use these accessors directly instead of instantiating a Rectangle object on the heap with a call to getBounds( ). Consequently, you can replace the last six lines with the following four:

```
System.out.println("X      = " + frame.getX( ));
System.out.println("Y      = " + frame.getY( ));
System.out.println("Width  = " + frame.getWidth( ));
System.out.println("Height = " + frame.getHeight( ));
```

In addition, if it is just the size or location you are concerned with, you can use the getSize( ) and getLocation( ) accessors to set or retrieve the size or location. Size is specified as a Dimension while location is given as a Point. Like getBounds( ), the getLocation( ) accessor also allows the programmer to pass in a preinstantiated Point object. If one is passed in, the method alters the coordinates of the Point instead of instantiating a new object.

```
Point myPoint = new Point( );
myPoint = component.getLocation(myPoint);
```

You can still use the setSize( ) and setLocation( ) methods of java.awt.Component if you prefer to code with those as well. Again, note that when altering the size of the component, the layout manager may override the new value and reset it to its previous value, thus ignoring your new size values.

The three well-known AWT sizing properties, minimumSize, preferredSize, and maximumSize, are accessible through JComponent. minimumSize indicates the smallest size for the component when it is in a container. preferredSize contains the size at which the container's layout manager should strive to draw the component. maximumSize indicates the largest size the component should be when displayed in a container. If none of these properties are set by the user, they are always calculated by the component's UI delegate or directly by the layout manager of the container, in that order. The methods setMinimumSize( ), setPreferredSize, and setMaximumSize( ) allow you to change these properties without subclassing.

Finally, JComponent contains two read/write properties that help interested layout managers align the component in a container: alignmentX and alignmentY. Both of these properties contain floating-point values between 0.0 and 1.0; the numbers determine the position of the component relative to any siblings. A number closer to 0 indicates that the component should be positioned closer to the left or top side, respectively. A perfect 0.5 indicates that the component should be placed at the center, while a number nearing 1 indicates that the component should be positioned closer to the right or bottom. Currently, the only layout managers that use these properties are the BoxLayout and OverlayLayout managers; all AWT 1.1 layout managers ignore these properties and position their children by other means. We discuss these managers further in Chapter 11.

Adding Borders

It's easy to add borders to Swing components, a feature AWT lacks. The JComponent border property accepts objects that implement the javax.swing.border.Border interface. Figure 3-7 shows a component with a border.

Swing currently provides several styles of borders, including an empty border. Each one extends the javax.swing.border.Border interface. In addition, you can surround a Swing component with multiple borders through the use of the CompoundBorder

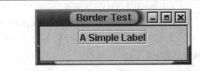

Figure 3-7. Simple borders in Swing

class. This class allows you to combine any two borders into a single border by specifying an outer and inner border. Because CompoundBorder accepts other compound borders, you can recursively layer as many borders as you like into a single border.

Using borders is extremely easy. For example, one of Swing's border styles is an etched border. Here is how you might create a border similar to the one in Figure 3-7:

```
JLabel label = new JLabel("A Simple Label");
label.setBorder(BorderFactory.createEtchedBorder( ));
```

One important characteristic of Swing is that if a border property is set on a component, the border overrides the component's insets property. Swing allows the programmer to specify an empty border, so you can still pad the component with extra space as well as provide a border if you use a CompoundBorder. If the border property is null, the default insets are used for the component instead. Borders are covered in more detail in Chapter 13.

Working with Tooltips

JComponent also provides Swing components with support for *tooltips*. Tooltips are small windows of text that pop up when the user rests the mouse over the target component. They typically supplement the meaning of an icon or button, but they can also provide the user with instructions or important information about the underlying component. The tooltip usually disappears after a designated amount of time (four seconds by default) or if the mouse is moved outside of the component's bounds.

Simple string-based tooltips can be automatically set or retrieved using the toolTipText property of JComponent, as shown here:

```
JButton button = new JButton("Press Me!"); // JButton extends JComponent.
button.setToolTipText("Go Ahead!");
System.out.println(button.getToolTipText( ));
```

Figure 3-8 shows what a tooltip looks like on the screen.

JComponent does not manage tooltips by itself; it gets help from the ToolTipManager class. The ToolTipManager continually scans for mouse events on components that have tooltips. When the mouse passes into a component with a tooltip set, the ToolTipManager begins a timer. If the mouse has not left the component's region in 0.75

Figure 3-8. A tooltip for a component

seconds, a tooltip is drawn at a preset location near the component. If the mouse has moved out of a region for longer than 0.5 seconds, the tooltip is removed from the screen.

With the default setToolTipText( ) and getToolTipText( ) methods, JComponent handles the creation of an appropriate tooltip. If you want to get more creative, however, Swing provides a separate object for tooltips: JToolTip. With it, you can completely redefine the characteristics of a tooltip by declaring your own JToolTip object and overriding the createToolTip( ) method of JComponent to return it to the ToolTipManager on demand.

We cover the JToolTip object and the ToolTipManager in more detail in Chapter 27.

Client Properties

Swing components can maintain a special table of properties called "client properties." This provides specialized properties that can be meaningful in components only in certain instances. For example, let's assume that a specific L&F uses a client property to store information about how a component should display itself when that L&F is activated. As you might guess, this client property would be meaningless when another L&F is activated. Using the client properties approach allows various L&Fs to expand their component properties without deluging the Swing source base with L&F-specific data.

The name "client properties" is somewhat confusing because client properties are distinct from JavaBeans-style properties. Obviously, there's a big difference: unlike JavaBeans properties, you can create new client properties without subclassing; you can even create new client properties at runtime. These two methods in JComponent store and retrieve client properties:

```
myComponent.putClientProperty("aClientProperty", Boolean.TRUE);
Boolean result = (Boolean)getClientProperty("aClientProperty");
```

Because we are using a hashtable, the properties must be objects and not primitive data types; we must use the Boolean object instead of simply setting true or false.

Double Buffering

The JComponent class allows all Swing components to take advantage of *double buffering*. The idea behind double buffering is that it takes longer for a component to render its individual parts on screen than it does for a rectangular-area copy to take place. If the former occurs over multiple screen refreshes, the human eye is likely to catch the component in the process of being drawn, and it may appear to flicker. With the latter, the screen is usually updated as fast as the monitor can refresh itself.*

When double buffering is activated in Swing, all component rendering performed by the repaint manager is done in an offscreen buffer. Upon completion, the contents of the offscreen buffer are quickly copied (not redrawn) on the screen at the component's position. You can request double buffering for a particular component by accessing the boolean doubleBuffered property of JComponent. Passing in true to the setDoubleBuffered( ) method enables double buffering; false shuts it off:

```
JButton button = new JButton("Test Button");
button.setDoubleBuffered(true);    // Turns on double buffering
```

You can use the isDoubleBuffered( ) method to check if double buffering is currently enabled on a Swing component. The component level setting is only a request, and Swing double buffering may be completely disabled at the level of the repaint manager (for example, when running under an operating system like Mac OS X, double buffering is always performed by the window manager, so doing it again in Swing would simply throw away processor cycles for no benefit). See "The Repaint-Manager Class" in Chapter 28 for more details and for information about how you can use graphics-accelerated "volatile images" in SDK 1.4 to further speed up Swing double buffering.

With double buffering, transparency is maintained in nonopaque components because the graphics underneath the component are copied into the buffer before any offscreen rendering takes place. However, there is a slight penalty for double buffering nonopaque components because Swing performs two area copies instead of one: one to copy the context in which the component is drawn to the offscreen buffer before drawing, and one to copy this context plus the rendered component back to the screen.

Buffers also chew up a great deal of memory, so the repaint manager tries to avoid using more than one offscreen buffer at a time. For example, if an offscreen buffer has been set for both a container and one of its children, the buffer for the parent container is used for both components.

---

* Area copies are always faster because they are performed by the operating system or even the graphics card of the computer. At this level, they are commonly referred to as "bit-block transfers," or BitBLTs.

Serialization

Objects that extend JComponent are serializable; that is, the object's data at any point can be written out, or *serialized*, onto an output stream, which might send it over a network or save it in a file.* The serialized output can later be *deserialized* back into memory, where the object continues to operate from its original state. Object serialization gives Java programmers a powerful and convenient way to store and retrieve object data, as opposed to saving or transmitting state data in custom-made storage files. Serialization also provides the ability to transfer active components quickly from one virtual machine to another, which can be useful in remote method invocation (RMI) and other forms of distributed computing.

You can serialize components in Swing as you normally would in Java by passing a reference to the object into the writeObject( ) method of an ObjectOutputStream object. In the event that the serialized object contains a reference to another object, the serialization algorithm recursively calls writeObject( ) on that object as well, continuing until all objects in the class hierarchy are serialized. The resulting *object graph* is then written out to the output stream. Conversely, you can deserialize a component back in by using the readObject( ) method of an ObjectInputStream, which reverses the entire process.

Serialization in its current form is suited primarily for short-term uses such as RMI and interprocess communication. The binary file produced by serialization is guaranteed to be readable only by another virtual machine of the same revision. If you want to store components for long-term (archival) use, you can use the XMLEncoder to dump the public properties (as defined by the JavaBeans spec) to an XML file. See the java.beans.XMLEncoder class for more details.

The DebugGraphics Class

Lightweight components are rendered entirely in Java, as opposed to offloading their work to a native heavyweight peer. The abstract Graphics class outlines platform-independent implementations for line-drawing, image-painting, and area-copying and filling that a lightweight peer can call upon to draw itself. If you create your own component, or extend an existing one, a Graphics object is often passed to the UI delegate's paint( ) method to help with the drawing.

Sometimes the way you intend a component to be painted, however, isn't how it appears on the screen. Debugging painting problems can prove to be troublesome, especially when dealing with transparency, opaqueness, and double buffering. JComponent, however, can generate a special version of the Graphics object, called

---

* The only exceptions to this are fields marked with the transient keyword.

DebugGraphics, which it can pass to a UI delegate's paint( ) method. This object can take a set of user-configurable debugging options that modify how a component is drawn to the screen.

If you wish to activate debugging for the component's graphics, you can pass one or more debugging flags (see Table 3-7) into JComponent's setDebugGraphicsOptions( ) method.

Table 3-7. Constants for DebugGraphics options

DebugGraphics constant	Description
DebugGraphics.FLASH_OPTION	Causes each graphics primitive to flash a configurable number of times as it is being rendered.
DebugGraphics.LOG_OPTION	Prints a text message to the screen as each graphics primitive is drawn.
DebugGraphics.BUFFERED_OPTION	Raises a window that shows the drawing that is taking place in the offscreen buffer. This is useful in the event that the double-buffered feature has been activated.
DebugGraphics.NONE_OPTION	Disables all debug graphics options.

The debug options outlined in Table 3-7 are bits in a binary mask; you can set more than one at the same time by using the bitwise OR (|) operator, as shown here:

```
JButton myButton = new JButton("Hello");  // JButton extends JComponent.
myButton.setDebugGraphicsOptions(DebugGraphics.FLASH_OPTION
                            | DebugGraphics.LOG_OPTION);
```

When any of the debug graphics options are set, the getComponentGraphics( ) method of JComponent returns a DebugGraphics object instead of a normal Graphics object. As we mentioned earlier, the same type of object is passed to the UI delegate of the component. When a component draws itself, it calls upon the functionality of the DebugGraphics object to perform the task, just as it would with a typical Graphics object. The drawing primitives are then slowed or logged so that the user can help identify any problems.

Focus and Focus Cycle Methods

The term *focus* refers to the active component on the screen. We typically think of the active component as the frame or window that is the current recipient of mouse and keyboard events. Other components, such as buttons and text fields, can have the focus as well. Visual cues, like a colored title bar or a dashed outline, often help us determine where the current focus resides.

When we click on another component with the mouse, the focus is typically shifted, and that component is now responsible for consuming mouse and keyboard events. You can also *traverse* the focus by pressing the Tab key to move forward or the Tab and the Shift key together to move backward. This causes the focus to cycle from one component to the next, eventually completing a loop and returning to its original position. This loop is called the *focus cycle*.

A group of components within a single container can define a focus cycle of its own. If the container has its own focus cycle, the focus repeatedly traverses through all of its children that accept the focus. The focus cycle is typically determined by the location of components in the container, although you can create your own focus traversal policy if you require different behavior. With the default focus policy, the component closest to the top-left corner of the container always receives focus first. The focus then moves from left to right across the components, and from top to bottom. Figure 3-9 shows how the default focus cycle shifts focus between components in a container.

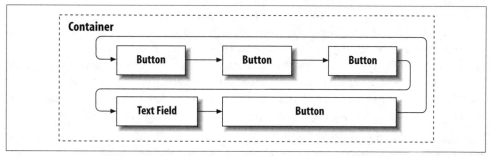

Figure 3-9. The default container focus traversal policy

If a container has a focus cycle of its own, it should override the Container method isFocusCycleRoot( ) and return true. If the method returns true, then the container is known as the *root container* of the focus cycle.

With SDK 1.2 or 1.3, you can explicitly name the component that should receive the focus after a given JComponent by setting its nextFocusableComponent property. In addition, focus can be programmatically requested through the JComponent method requestFocus( ), which the focus manager can call to shift the focus to this component. This is often done when the user selects the object (i.e., presses a JButton). If you don't want your component to be able to respond to requestFocus( ) calls, you can set the requestFocusEnabled property of JComponent to false.

With SDK 1.4, this method of managing focus was replaced by the more flexible FocusTraversalPolicy class as part of a major overhaul of the whole focus system. This class allows you to define a focus policy to manage a container. (In this case, "focus policy" simply means an algorithm to figure out which component follows, and which one precedes, the current component in the focus cycle.) One advantage of moving to policy-based management is that generic policies can be developed for containers—no more need to hook up individual components.

There is an important distinction here: setting the requestFocusEnabled property to false does not mean that the focus cannot be *traversed* onto your component; it simply means that it cannot be programmatically requested. JComponent provides a similar property, focusable,* that you can enable or disable to specify whether a component ever receives focus at all.

We discuss the concept of focus in detail in Chapter 28.

Keyboard Events

Swing components can be programmed to trigger various actions when certain keystrokes occur. For example, components automatically handle focus-related keyboard events. The default focus mechanism watches for Tab and Shift-Tab keystrokes, adjusting the focus and consuming the keystrokes. If the focus mechanism does not know how to handle a keystroke, and no registered low-level KeyListeners have consumed it, JComponent checks to see whether the processComponentKeyEvent( ) method consumes it. The default implementation does nothing, the idea being that you can override it in a subclass if you want to react to a keystroke in your own way. You're not likely to want to use that approach, though, because it's much less flexible than what happens next: if nothing has consumed the key event, JComponent checks to see if a *keyboard action* has been registered for that keystroke. A set of maps provide a convenient way to translate key events to appropriate component-related actions.

Translation to an action starts by converting the key event to the KeyStroke that represents it. This is used as a key to check the component's InputMap for a corresponding action name (the InputMap could return any kind of object, but convention dictates that it be a String corresponding to a logical action name). The result of this lookup, if not null, is used in turn as a key to look in the component's ActionMap for an Action to perform. Assuming that a non-null Action was found, its actionPerformed method is invoked (as described in "The Action Interface" earlier in this chapter).

It might seem like overkill to use a two-map lookup like this. Wouldn't it be simpler to just put the Actions directly in the InputMap? It turns out there are a couple of good reasons for the second layer. Although a given type of component generally supports a well-defined set of logical operations, the specific Action classes that implement them often vary depending on the L&F in use. Similarly, the keys that are used to invoke the actions vary between L&Fs, which leads to a complex coupling between the component and the L&F-specific UI delegate. Separating the two concepts into two maps provides an easy-to-understand translation between KeyStrokes and logical event names, and from event names to specific Action implementations. It also

---

* Prior to SDK 1.4, the focusTraversable property (now deprecated) was used instead; setting this property to false allowed the component to receive focus programmatically but not through traversal.

---

means that InputMaps are nicely self-documenting; it's easy to turn them into a human-readable table that shows the functions assigned to various keys.*

InputMaps and ActionMaps are also designed to be easy to share between components (or even similar component types). They have a parent property that is checked if a binding isn't found, so common functionality can be placed in a shared parent map, and component-specific definitions added to a local map on an as-needed basis; the text components make extensive use of this capability. JComponent makes this easy by providing newly initialized components with empty InputMaps and ActionMaps whose parents are the (likely shared) map provided by the UI. So, as a developer, you never need to worry about the possible existence of shared maps; you can just start adding your custom mappings and rely on Swing to provide the rest.

Before showing you the details of how to register keyboard actions, there is one more complication to clarify. The process outlined here described a single InputMap used to translate keystrokes to action names. In fact, components have three separate InputMaps to address the fact that there are different situations under which a component might be asked to respond to a keyboard event. The most obvious case, which probably sprang to mind, is when the component itself is the owner of the keyboard focus. Components can also have a chance to respond to key events if they don't have focus in two other cases. First, a component may respond if it is an ancestor of (contains) the focused component. Think of a ScrollPane, in which the Page Up and Page Down keys remain functional even though you're working with the *contents* of the pane rather than the pane itself. Second, a component may respond if it is simply inside a window that is focused (this is how button mnemonics work). In order to create the proper InputMap, the methods to manipulate them offer a condition parameter whose legal values are shown in Table 3-8.

Table 3-8. Constants for InputMap selection

Constant	Description
WHEN_FOCUSED	The InputMap used when the component has the focus
WHEN_IN_FOCUSED_WINDOW	The InputMap used when the component resides in a container that has the focus
WHEN_ANCESTOR_OF_FOCUSED_COMPONENT	The InputMap used when the component is the ancestor of (contains) the component that currently has the focus

---

* For more details about the design goals of this key-binding mechanism, which was introduced in SDK 1.3, see *http://java.sun.com/products/jfc/tsc/special_report/kestrel/keybindings.html*, which also describes the limitations of the previous mechanism. If you are still working with a pre-1.3 version of Swing, you can find the first edition's version of this section, which discusses how to use the old key-binding mechanism, on this book's web site, *http://www.oreilly.com/catalog/jswing2/*.

You obtain a component's input map through one of the following two methods (these were mentioned in Table 3-6, but bear repeating in this context):

public InputMap getInputMap(int condition)
>   Return the input map to be used under the specified condition.

public InputMap getInputMap()
>   A convenience method that calls getInputMap(WHEN_FOCUSED), which is the most commonly used condition.

Looking up the action map is simpler since there's only one method:

public ActionMap getActionMap()
>   Return the action map associated with the component.

A brief example illustrates how to perform the common task of assigning an event to a component using this binding mechanism. Suppose we wanted to extend the example program in "Using an Action" to perform a download whenever the F8 key is pressed. One way we could do this is by adding the following lines to the end of the ActionExample constructor:

```
exampleButon.getActionMap( ).put("download", exampleAction);
exampleButton.getInputMap(WHEN_IN_FOCUSED_WINDOW).put(
   KeyStroke.getKeyStroke("F8"), "download");
```

The first line binds the logical action name download to our sample download action within the button's action map. The second line causes the F8 key to trigger this logical action whenever the button's window has the focus, even if the button itself does not. This two-step registration process in which both an InputMap and the ActionMap are retrieved and modified is very common when working with custom actions because of the two-stage, key-mapping process. If you're simply changing or adding bindings for a standard keystroke or action, you need to work with only one of the maps.

To remove a binding you've set, both types of maps provide a remove method that takes a KeyStroke object that will be removed from the mapping. The clear method removes all mappings. Neither of these methods affect inherited mappings. In fact, if you added a keystroke that overrode an inherited mapping, removing that keystroke restores the inherited mapping. If you actually want to block an inherited mapping without providing a new action, register a mapping to the action "none", which convention mandates never has an Action bound to it.

There are corresponding methods for setting the map properties themselves, of course. These are used far less commonly, but do provide a way to eliminate the inherited parent maps provided by the L&F's UI delegate:

public void setInputMap(int condition)
public void setActionMap(ActionMap actionMap)
> Replace the corresponding map completely, eliminating any inherited mappings. Passing a null argument causes the component to have no bindings at all.

Note that if you replace the mappings this way, there's no way to get back the previously inherited mappings unless you keep a reference to the original maps yourself. (See Appendix B for a list of default bindings.)

Accessibility

As we mentioned in Chapter 1, Swing components support accessibility options. Accessibility options are constructed for users who have trouble with traditional user interfaces and include support for alternative input and output devices and actions. There are several parts to accessibility (covered in detail in Chapter 25). JComponent implements the methods required by the Accessible interface, though it does not implement the interface itself.

The accessibleContext property holds an AccessibleContext object that is the focal point of communication between the component and auxiliary accessibility tools. There's a different default context for each kind of JComponent. For more information, see Chapter 25.

Events

Table 3-9 shows the events fired by JComponent (not counting the many events it inherits from the AWT classes).

Table 3-9. JComponent events

Event	Description
PropertyChangeEvent	A change has occurred in JComponent.
VetoablePropertyChangeEvent	A change has occurred in JComponent that can be vetoed by interested listeners.
AncestorEvent	An ancestor of a JComponent has moved or changed its visible state.

Event methods

The 1.3 SDK added an access method for general event listeners:

public EventListener[] getListeners(Class listenerType)
> This method pulls listeners from a protected listListener field based on the specified type. All the various addListener( ) methods for JComponent add their listeners to this list. Subclasses can add their own listeners to the listListener field. See Chapter 27 for more information on event listener lists.

The following methods may move to java.awt.Component in the future:

public void firePropertyChange(String propertyName, byte oldValue, byte newValue)
public void firePropertyChange(String propertyName, char oldValue, char newValue)
public void firePropertyChange(String propertyName, short oldValue, short newValue)
public void firePropertyChange(String propertyName, int oldValue, int newValue)
public void firePropertyChange(String propertyName, long oldValue, long newValue)
public void firePropertyChange(String propertyName, float oldValue, float newValue)
public void firePropertyChange(String propertyName, double oldValue, double newValue)
public void firePropertyChange(String propertyName, boolean oldValue, boolean newValue)

> Fire a PropertyChangeEvent to all registered listeners if newValue differs from oldValue. There are overloaded versions of this method for each primitive data type.

public void addPropertyChangeListener(PropertyChangeListener listener)
public void removePropertyChangeListener(PropertyChangeListener listener)

> Add or remove a PropertyChangeListener to the event registration list.

public void addVetoableChangeListener(VetoableChangeListener listener)
public void removeVetoableChangeListener(VetoableChangeListener listener)

> Add or remove a VetoableChangeListener to the event registration list. A VetoableChangeListener is allowed to veto any property changes that occur inside a component. If only one veto occurs, the property is not changed.

public void addAncestorListener(AncestorListener listener)
public void removeAncestorListener(AncestorListener listener)

> Add or remove an AncestorListener to the event registration list. All registered objects are notified if any of the components' ancestors change position or are made visible or invisible.

JComponent also inherits all the event listener registration methods from its AWT superclasses, Container and Component. From Component, it inherits the methods to add or remove a ComponentListener, FocusListener, KeyListener, MouseListener, or MouseMotionListener. From Container, it inherits the methods to add or remove a ContainerListener. We won't describe all the listener interfaces here; for more information, see *Java AWT Reference* by John Zukowski (O'Reilly). However, you should note that Swing supports only the event model established in JDK 1.1. To receive an event, you must always register as a listener with the JComponent that generates the event—events are never propagated through the containment hierarchy, as they were in JDK 1.0.

Constructor

public JComponent()

> Initialize a simple JComponent and set the layout manager to null.

Graphics Methods

protected Graphics getComponentGraphics(Graphics g)

Accept a graphics context and modify its foreground color and font to match the current defaults. If the debug graphics option has been activated, the method returns a special graphics object that the programmer can configure for debugging component drawing with the color and font modifications.

public void update(Graphics g)

Equivalent to paint(g). This is significantly different from the update( ) method of Component, which first cleared the component's background. In Swing, clearing the component is handled by ComponentUI, based on whether the component is opaque.

public boolean contains(int x, int y)

Return true if the coordinates passed in are inside the bounding box of the component, false otherwise. The method always asks the UI delegate first, giving it an opportunity to define the bounding box as it sees fit. If the UI delegate does not exist for this component, or cannot define the bounding box, the standard component contains( ) method is invoked.

public Insets getInsets (Insets insets)

Copy the JComponent's insets into the given Insets object and return a reference to this object.

public void paint(Graphics g)

The primary method that the AWT subsystem calls upon for components to draw themselves if they are not obscured. This method delegates most of its work to the protected methods paintComponent( ), paintBorder( ), and paintChildren( ), which it calls in that order. Because this method performs its own internal calculations, it is generally not a good idea to override it in a subclass; if you want to redefine how a component draws itself, override paintComponent( ) instead.

public void reshape(int x, int y, int w, int h)

Reset the bounds property of the component.

protected void paintComponent(Graphics g)

Draw the component using the graphics context provided. Unless overridden, it simply turns around and calls the paint( ) method of the delegate. If there is no delegate, the method does nothing.

protected void paintChildren(Graphics g)

Cycle through each of the component's children, invoking the paint( ) method on each one.

protected void paintBorder(Graphics g)

Paint the border (or borders) outlined by the border property of JComponent. Note that if a border is defined, JComponent ignores its own insets and uses the border instead.

public void repaint(long tm, int x, int y, int width, int height)
public void repaint(Rectangle r)

> Place a request to repaint the specified region on the repaint manager's update queue. The initial variable tm of the first repaint( ) method is no longer used and can be ignored. Because the redrawing queue knows the correct order to draw various component layers, it is widely preferred that you call these methods, instead of directly invoking paint( ).

public void paintImmediately(int x, int y, int w, int h)
public void paintImmediately(Rectangle r)

> Force an immediate repaint of the specified region in the component. This method is invoked by the repaint manager when it is time for the component to draw itself; the programmer should not call this method. This method may move to java.awt.Component in the future.

public void revalidate( )

> Add the current component to the repaint manager's revalidation queue, which is located on the system event queue.

public void computeVisibleRect(Rectangle visibleRect)

> Calculate a Rectangle that represents the intersection of the component's own visible rectangle and each of its ancestors. The result is placed in the visibleRect property and is used to determine how much of a component is drawn on the screen.

Focus Methods

public void requestFocus( )

> Shift the focus to this component if the requestFocusEnabled property is true.

public boolean requestDefaultFocus( )

> Shift the focus to a default component, typically the first focus-traversable component in the current container. If the method is unable to find such a component, it returns false. This method was deprecated in SDK 1.4. (You should generally move your focus-related code to FocusTraversalPolicy implementations.)

public void grabFocus( )

> Used by focus managers to shift the focus to this component, regardless of the state of the requestFocusEnabled property. Because of this, it is generally better to use requestFocus( ) instead of this method.

public boolean hasFocus( )

> Return true if this component currently has the focus. This method is defined in java.awt.Component in JDK 1.2.

Tooltip Methods

public String getToolTipText(MouseEvent event)
> Retrieve the text used for the component's tooltip, given the appropriate mouse event. JComponent always returns the current toolTipText property. However, you can override this method in your own component if you want to return different strings based on various mouse events.

public Point getToolTipLocation(MouseEvent event)
> This method currently returns null. You can override it in your own component to specify the local component coordinates where its tooltip should be displayed. If the method returns null, Swing chooses a location for you.

public JToolTip createToolTip( )
> Return a new instance of JToolTip by default. If you want to extend the JToolTip class with a tooltip of your own, you can override this method in your components, forcing it to return the new class to the tooltip manager.

Client Properties Methods

public final Object getClientProperty(Object key)
> Search the client property list for the Object specified under the appropriate key. It returns null if no object is found.

public final void putClientProperty(Object key, Object value)
> Insert the specified client property value under the appropriate key. If the value passed in is null, the property is cleared from the list.

Miscellaneous Methods

protected void setUI(ComponentUI u)
> Install u as the UI delegate for the component, effectively changing the component's L&F. This change doesn't appear onscreen until updateUI( ) is called.

public void updateUI( )
> Called by the current UIManager to notify the component that its L&F has changed, and that the UI delegate should repaint itself.

public void scrollRectToVisible(Rectangle aRect)
> Call similar methods up the component hierarchy. You can override this method at any level if you want to explicitly handle scrolling updates.

public static boolean isLightweightComponent(Component c)
> A convenience method that returns a boolean indicating whether the component passed is a lightweight component. If it is, the method returns true. Otherwise, it returns false. This method may move to java.awt.Component in the future.

Responding to Keyboard Input

Swing provides a flexible framework for keyboard-based control, which can be used by any component. The rest of the chapter explains this mechanism.

The InputMap Class

InputMap maps keystrokes to logical action names. When the user types a key combination, it's looked up in the input map of the focused component (and perhaps other components in the active window, as described earlier). If a match is found, the resulting object is used as a key in the corresponding component's ActionMap to look up the concrete Action class to be invoked. The platform-specific L&F implementations provide InputMaps consistent with the key-binding conventions for their platforms.

When looking for values in an InputMap, a java.awt.KeyStroke is always used as the key. KeyStroke is a simple, immutable class that represents a particular keyboard action (including any modifier keys). KeyStrokes are intended to be unique (that is, if two KeyStroke variables represent the same action, they should reference the same KeyStroke instance). To ensure uniqueness, you can't create KeyStrokes directly; you must obtain them through the static getKeyStroke() factory methods in the KeyStroke class.

Although the result of looking up a KeyStroke in an InputMap is an arbitrary object, and any object can be used as a key for looking up an action in an ActionMap, in practice the values are Strings. By convention, their content is a descriptive name for the action to be performed (such as copy, print, save, or the like). This allows InputMaps to be largely self-documenting (it's easy to print their contents as a "cheat sheet" showing the keys that invoke particular commands) and also improves the readability of code that requests actions programmatically. The most common way this string is obtained is by calling getName() on the Action to be added to the map.

InputMaps can be chained together so that common functionality can be shared in a basic InputMap; specialized components can add custom keystrokes to their own InputMap and delegate the common cases to the shared map via the parent property.

Property

The single property defined by InputMap is shown in Table 3-10. The parent property establishes a fallback InputMap that is consulted if a key mapping is not found in the current map, much as the inheritance chain is followed when looking up the members of Java classes. If you create a cycle in the parent chain (for example, by setting two InputMaps to be parents of each other), many of the method calls crash with a StackOverflowError.

Table 3-10. InputMap property

Property	Data type	get	is	set	Default value
parent	InputMap	•		•	null

Constructor

public InputMap()

The default constructor is the only constructor available. It creates an empty InputMap with no parent.

Methods

public KeyStroke[] allKeys()

Return an array of all KeyStrokes defined in the InputMap, either directly or anywhere along the parent chain. If there are no mappings, this method returns either an empty array or null, depending on the history of the InputMap(s). Each key appears only once even if it overrides another on the parent chain.

public void clear()

Remove all keystroke mappings from this InputMap (does not affect any mappings in the parent chain).

public Object get(KeyStroke keyStroke)

Look up the specified keyStroke in the InputMap (and the parent chain), returning a value that represents the logical action that should be taken in response. If no match is found, returns null. The result is generally used immediately to look up an Action in the ActionMap of the component that owns this InputMap. Convention dictates that the values returned are Strings describing the nature of the action to perform.

public KeyStroke[] keys

Return an array of KeyStrokes locally defined in this InputMap. That is to say, it does *not* follow the parent chain. If there are no mappings, this returns either an empty array or null, depending on the history of the InputMap.

public void put(KeyStroke keyStroke, Object actionMapKey)

Define a new mapping for the specified keyStroke. Future calls to the get() method return actionMapKey as the logical action associated with keyStroke. As suggested by the parameter name, actionMapKey is intended to be used to look up an Action in an ActionMap. By convention, it should be a String whose value is descriptive of the action. (Appendix B lists the standard ActionMap keys supported by Swing components; your own classes can use these or define their own as appropriate.) Passing a null actionMapKey has the same effect as calling remove(keyStroke).

public void remove(KeyStroke keyStroke)

Remove the mapping defined for the specified keyStroke from this InputMap. Looking up that keyStroke in the future returns a value that is determined by the parent chain (which is *not* affected by this method). If you want to "block" a mapping in a shared InputMap that is part of your parent chain, define a mapping for that KeyStroke to the string none. By convention, there is never an Action associated with none in any ActionMap, so its presence in your InputMap causes the parent check to be skipped without allowing any action to take place.

public int size( )

Return the number of mappings defined in this InputMap (not counting any that might be defined in the parent chain). For a new or newly cleared InputMap, this returns 0.

The ActionMap Class

ActionMap is responsible for mapping logical action names to concrete Action instances that carry them out. When the user types a key combination, it's looked up in the InputMap of a component, and the result is looked up as a key in the corresponding ActionMap.

Although any object can be used as a key in an ActionMap, in practice they are Strings. By convention, their content is a descriptive name for the action to be performed (such as copy, print, save, or the like), often obtained by calling getName( ) on the corresponding Action.

ActionMaps can be chained together so that common functionality can be shared in a basic ActionMap; specialized components can add unique actions to their own ActionMap and delegate the common cases to the shared map through the parent property.

A component's ActionMap can also be used to configure auditory cues to be played at appropriate points by the component, as described in Chapter 26.

Property

The single property defined by ActionMap is shown in Table 3-11. The parent property establishes a fallback ActionMap that is consulted if an action name is not found in the current map, much as the inheritance chain is followed when looking up the members of Java classes. If you create a cycle in the parent chain (for example, by setting two ActionMaps to be parents of each other), many of the method calls crash with a StackOverflowError.

Table 3-11. ActionMap property

Property	Data type	get	is	set	Default value
parent	ActionMap	•		•	null

Constructor

public ActionMap()

The default constructor is the only constructor available. It creates an empty ActionMap with no parent.

Methods

public Object[] allKeys()

Return an array of all logical action names defined in the ActionMap, either directly or anywhere along the parent chain. If there are no mappings, this method returns either an empty array or null, depending on the history of the ActionMap(s). Each key appears only once even if it overrides another on the parent chain.

public void clear()

Remove all action mappings from the local ActionMap (does not affect any in the parent chain).

public Action get(Object key)

Look up the specified action name in the ActionMap (and the parent chain), returning the corresponding Action to be executed. If no match is found, returns null. The keys are often obtained by looking up a KeyStroke in an InputMap.

public Object[] keys

Return an array of the logical action names locally defined in this ActionMap. That is to say, it does *not* follow the parent chain. If there are no mappings, this returns either an empty array or null, depending on the history of the ActionMap.

public void put(Object key, Action action)

Define a new mapping for the specified action. Future calls to the get( ) method return it as the Action associated with the logical name key. By convention, key should be a String whose value is descriptive of the action. Appendix B lists the standard ActionMap keys supported by Swing components; your own classes can use these as well, or define their own, as appropriate. Passing a null key has the same effect as calling remove(action).

public void remove(Object Key)

Remove the mapping defined for the specified key from this ActionMap. Looking up that logical action name in the future returns a value determined by the parent chain (which is *not* affected by this method).

public int size()

Return the number of mappings defined in this ActionMap (not counting any that might be defined in the parent chain). For a new or newly cleared ActionMap, this method returns 0.

## CHAPTER 4

Labels and Icons

We'll begin our look at the Swing components with the JLabel class. In addition, we'll look at Swing's Icon interface and an implementation of this interface called ImageIcon. With just these few constructs, you'll begin to see how Swing aids in the sophisticated UI development in Java.

Labels

Swing allows you to create labels that can contain text, images, or both. We'll begin this chapter with a look at the JLabel class.

The JLabel class allows you to add basic, noninteractive labels to a user interface. Because of its inherent simplicity, there is no model class for JLabel. Figure 4-1 shows a class diagram for JLabel. We'll get into the two relationships to Icon a little later.

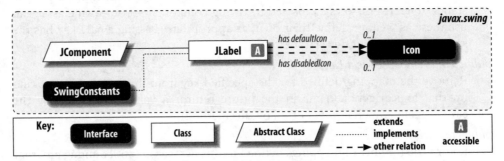

Figure 4-1. JLabel class diagram

JLabel objects may consist of both text and graphics (icons), but for simple text-only labels, the interface with JLabel is very similar to that of java.awt.Label. The code to create and display a very simple text label looks like this:

```
// SimpleJLabelExample.java
//
import javax.swing.*;

public class SimpleJLabelExample {
  public static void main(String[] args) {
    JLabel label = new JLabel("A Very Simple Text Label");

    JFrame frame = new JFrame();
    frame.setDefaultCloseOperation(JFrame.EXIT_ON_CLOSE);
    frame.getContentPane().add(label); // Adds to CENTER
    frame.pack();
    frame.setVisible(true);
  }
}
```

Running this simple program produces the display shown in Figure 4-2.

Figure 4-2. A simple JLabel

Properties

The JLabel class contains the properties shown in Table 4-1. The icon and disabledIcon properties specify the icon to be displayed by default and when the label is disabled, respectively. If an icon is specified without a disabledIcon, a disabledIcon is automatically created by converting the default icon to grayscale. The font property is shown in this table only because the setFont() method is overridden to call repaint() after calling super.setFont().

Table 4-1. JLabel properties

Property	Data type	get	is	set	Default value
UI	LabelUI	•		•	From L&F
UIClassID[o]	String				"LabelUI"
accessibleContext[o]	AccessibleContext	•			JLabel.AccessibleJLabel
disabledIcon[b]	Icon	•		•	null
displayedMnemonic[b]	int	•		•	KeyEvent.VK_UNDEFINED
displayedMnemonicIndex[1.4, b]	int				-1
font[o]	Font	•		•	From L&F
horizontalAlignment[b]	int	•		•	LEADING[1.3]

[1.3]since 1.3, [1.4]since 1.4, [b]bound, [o]overridden

See also properties from the JComponent class (Table 3-6).

Table 4-1. JLabel properties (continued)

Property	Data type	get	is	set	Default value
horizontalTextPosition[b]	int	•		•	TRAILING[1.3]
icon[b]	Icon	•		•	null
iconTextGap[b]	int	•		•	4
labelFor[b]	Component	•		•	null
text[b]	String	•		•	null
verticalAlignment[b]	int	•		•	CENTER
verticalTextPosition[b]	int	•		•	CENTER

[1.3]since 1.3, [1.4]since 1.4, [b]bound, [o]overridden

See also properties from the JComponent class (Table 3-6).

displayedMnemonic indicates the character to be used as an accelerator key, which typically means that an occurrence of this character is decorated with an underline in the label text. displayedMnemonicIndex is the index of the character that receives the decoration; it is set automatically to the first occurrence of the displayedMnemonic character in the label text. You can override this behavior by setting displayedMnemonicIndex to another index, or to -1 to force no decoration. (L&Fs are not technically required to honor the displayedMnemonicIndex property, but most of them do.)

> The displayedMnemonic property is int because its value is intended to be one of the VK_ "virtual keycode" constants defined in java.awt.KeyEvent (see Table 27-6). However, a setDisplayedMnemonic() method, which takes a char is also defined. It's usually easier to call setDisplayedMnemonic('a') than it is to call setDisplayedMnemonic(KeyEvent.VK_A). If you use the char version, it doesn't matter if you specify an uppercase or lowercase character.

If the labelFor property has been set, the referenced component gains focus when the mnemonic is pressed in conjunction with the Alt key.* One common use of this feature is to apply mnemonics to labels appearing next to text fields, allowing the fields to gain focus when the shortcut key is pressed. We'll see an example of this strategy later in this section.

The horizontalAlignment and verticalAlignment properties are used to specify the alignment of the label's content (text and icon) within its interior. If a label is sized to be just large enough for its content (as FlowLayout does), setting these properties makes no difference. The values for these properties are defined in SwingConstants

---

* This is actually up to the L&F, but the Basic L&F implements it this way, and none of the other Swing L&Fs change this behavior. On the Macintosh, the Option key is used for Alt; newer keyboards have both labels.

and must be LEADING, TRAILING, LEFT, RIGHT, or CENTER for horizontalAlignment, and TOP, BOTTOM, or CENTER for verticalAlignment. The LEADING and TRAILING constants were introduced in SDK 1.3 to accommodate locales in which text does not flow left-to-right. In the default locale, LEADING acts the same as LEFT, and TRAILING acts the same as RIGHT. In right-to-left locales, they are reversed. Prior to the introduction of these values, horizontalAlignment defaulted to LEFT, and horizontalTextPosition defaulted to RIGHT.

horizontalTextPosition, verticalTextPosition, and iconTextGap are meaningful only if both icon and text are defined. They designate the position of the label's text relative to its icon. Like the alignment properties, the valid values for the text position properties are LEFT, RIGHT, TOP, BOTTOM, and CENTER. (We'll cover these properties in more detail in the sections that follow.) The iconTextGap property reflects the space (in pixels) between the label's icon and text. Note that JLabel implements SwingConstants, so you can refer to the constant values listed in this paragraph as either SwingConstants.XYZ or JLabel.XYZ—whichever you prefer.

The UI property holds a reference to the LabelUI object used to render the label.

displayedMnemonic and labelFor properties

The following example shows how the displayedMnemonic and labelFor properties can be used to direct focus to a component based on the mnemonic assigned to a label. All we do here is create three labels and three text fields, assigning one field to each label:

```
// MnemonicLabels.java
//
import javax.swing.*;
import java.awt.*;

// Shows how displayedMnemonic and labelFor properties work together
public class MnemonicLabels {
  public static void main(String[] args) {

    JTextField firstField = new JTextField(10);
    JTextField middleField = new JTextField(10);
    JTextField lastField = new JTextField(10);

    // Create labels and mnemonics.
    JLabel firstLabel = new JLabel("First Name", JLabel.RIGHT);
    firstLabel.setDisplayedMnemonic('F');
    firstLabel.setLabelFor(firstField);

    JLabel middleLabel = new JLabel("Middle Initial", JLabel.RIGHT);
    middleLabel.setDisplayedMnemonic('I');
    middleLabel.setDisplayedMnemonicIndex(7); // Requires 1.4
    middleLabel.setLabelFor(middleField);
```

```
        JLabel lastLabel = new JLabel("Last Name", JLabel.RIGHT);
        lastLabel.setDisplayedMnemonic('L');
        lastLabel.setLabelFor(lastField);

        // Layout and display
        JPanel p = new JPanel( );
        p.setLayout(new GridLayout(3, 2, 5, 5));
        p.add(firstLabel);
        p.add(firstField);
        p.add(middleLabel);
        p.add(middleField);
        p.add(lastLabel);
        p.add(lastField);

        JFrame f = new JFrame("MnemonicLabels");
        f.setDefaultCloseOperation(JFrame.EXIT_ON_CLOSE);
        f.setContentPane(p);
        f.pack( );
        f.setVisible(true);
    }
}
```

When executed, this example produces the display shown in Figure 4-3. The first letter in each label is underlined, based on the assigned mnemonic. Pressing Alt-F, Alt-I, or Alt-L causes focus to shift to the corresponding text field.

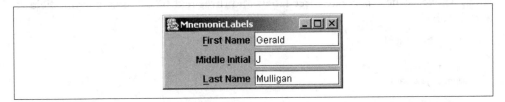

Figure 4-3. JLabels with mnemonics

Note that calling `middleLabel.setDisplayedMnemonicIndex(7)` is incompatible with SDKs prior to 1.4, so remove that line of code if you want the program to run on older SDKs without throwing a `NoSuchMethodError`. Doing so will decorate the lowercase "i" in "Middle" instead of the uppercase "I" in "Initial," though.

Alignment

The following example shows the effects of JLabel horizontal and vertical alignment:

```
// AlignmentExample.java
//
import javax.swing.*;
import java.awt.*;

public class AlignmentExample {
  public static void main(String[] args) {
```

```
    // Create the labels and set alignment.
    JLabel label1 = new JLabel("BottomRight", SwingConstants.RIGHT);
    JLabel label2 = new JLabel("CenterLeft", SwingConstants.LEFT);
    JLabel label3 = new JLabel("TopCenter", SwingConstants.CENTER);
    label1.setVerticalAlignment(SwingConstants.BOTTOM);
    label2.setVerticalAlignment(SwingConstants.CENTER);
    label3.setVerticalAlignment(SwingConstants.TOP);

    // Add borders to the labels (more on Borders later in the book).
    label1.setBorder(BorderFactory.createLineBorder(Color.black));
    label2.setBorder(BorderFactory.createLineBorder(Color.black));
    label3.setBorder(BorderFactory.createLineBorder(Color.black));

    // Put it all together.
    JFrame frame = new JFrame("AlignmentExample");
    frame.setDefaultCloseOperation(JFrame.EXIT_ON_CLOSE);
    JPanel p = new JPanel(new GridLayout(3, 1, 8, 8));
    p.add(label1);
    p.add(label2);
    p.add(label3);
    p.setBorder(BorderFactory.createEmptyBorder(8, 8, 8, 8));
    frame.setContentPane(p);
    frame.setSize(200,200);
    frame.setVisible(true);
  }
}
```

Figure 4-4 shows the result of running this program.

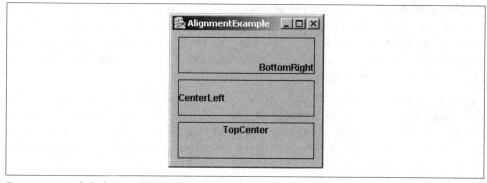

Figure 4-4. JLabel alignment

If you're familiar with pre-Swing java.awt.Labels, you'll appreciate the ability to specify a vertical alignment; the java.awt.Label class sets only horizontal alignment. (A java.awt.Label's horizontal alignment can be set via an argument to its constructors. Because the JLabel constructors are modeled after those of java.awt.Label, the JLabel class provides the same type of flexibility and has constructors that support specifying the horizontal position of the label. In contrast, the vertical position of a JLabel can be set only through the setVerticalAlignment( ) method.)

Working with Images

JLabels make it very simple to add graphics to your user interface. Images used in JLabels (and also in other Swing components, such as buttons) are of type javax.swing.Icon, an interface described in detail in the next section.

These two lines of code show how simple it is to create a label containing an image:

```
ImageIcon icon = new ImageIcon("images/smile.gif");
JLabel label = new JLabel(icon);
```

For labels that contain both graphics and text, Swing provides considerable flexibility with respect to the relative location of the text and image. The text for the label may be displayed at any one of nine locations relative to the image. These locations are specified via the setVerticalTextPosition( ) and setHorizontalTextPosition( ) methods, which take values from the SwingConstants class discussed earlier. Note the distinction between the label's text position and its alignment; text position reflects the position of the text relative to the image while alignment specifies the location of the label's contents (image and text) relative to the borders of the label.

Another useful feature of the JLabel class is the ability to enable and disable the label by "graying out" the label and text. By default, a call to JLabel.setEnabled(false) switches the image to an automatically generated grayscale version of the original image and alters the text rendering in some (L&F-specific) way. However, the grayscale image is used only if no disabled icon has been set. The setDisabledIcon( ) method can be used to set an alternate image for the disabled label.

Additionally, the spacing between the image and the text can be specified by a call to setIconTextGap( ), which takes a single parameter specifying the number of pixels between the image and the icon. This setting has no effect if both the horizontal and vertical text positions are set to SwingConstants.CENTER since, in this case, the text is placed directly over the image.

Figure 4-5 shows a group of labels with text and images, with the text at each of the nine locations relative to the image. Labels 0 and 1 are disabled, the first one using the default disabled image and the second one using an explicitly specified alternate image. Labels 2 and 3 show nondefault text gap settings. Here's the source code that produces these labels:

```
// ImageLabelExample.java
//
import javax.swing.*;
import java.awt.*;

public class ImageLabelExample {

    private static Icon icon = new ImageIcon("images/smile.gif");

    public static void main(String[] args) {
      JLabel[] labels= new JLabel[9];
```

Figure 4-5. JLabel text position and properties

```
labels[0] = makeLabel(JLabel.TOP, JLabel.LEFT);
labels[1] = makeLabel(JLabel.TOP, JLabel.CENTER);
labels[2] = makeLabel(JLabel.TOP, JLabel.RIGHT);
labels[3] = makeLabel(JLabel.CENTER, JLabel.LEFT);
labels[4] = makeLabel(JLabel.CENTER, JLabel.CENTER);
labels[5] = makeLabel(JLabel.CENTER, JLabel.RIGHT);
labels[6] = makeLabel(JLabel.BOTTOM, JLabel.LEFT);
labels[7] = makeLabel(JLabel.BOTTOM, JLabel.CENTER);
labels[8] = makeLabel(JLabel.BOTTOM, JLabel.RIGHT);

// Disable label 0.
labels[0].setEnabled(false);

// Disable label 1 with a disabled icon.
labels[1].setDisabledIcon(new ImageIcon("images/no.gif"));
labels[1].setEnabled(false);

// Change text gap on labels 2 and 3.
labels[2].setIconTextGap(15);
labels[3].setIconTextGap(0);

// Add the labels to a frame and display it.
JFrame frame = new JFrame( );
frame.setDefaultCloseOperation(JFrame.EXIT_ON_CLOSE);
Container c = frame.getContentPane( );
c.setLayout(new FlowLayout(FlowLayout.CENTER, 3, 3));
for (int i=0;i<9;i++)
  c.add(labels[i]);
frame.setSize(350,150);
frame.setVisible(true);
}

protected static JLabel makeLabel(int vert, int horiz) {
  JLabel l = new JLabel("Smile", icon, SwingConstants.CENTER);
  l.setVerticalTextPosition(vert);
  l.setHorizontalTextPosition(horiz);
  l.setBorder(BorderFactory.createLineBorder(Color.black));
  return l;
}
}
```

Don't worry if you don't understand everything we did in this example. We'll explain icons in more detail in this chapter and will get to borders and frames later in the book. For now, just concentrate on the various properties we set on the different labels and compare the code to the display it produced in Figure 4-5.

Events

The only events explicitly fired by `JLabel` are `PropertyChangeEvents`.

Constant

`JLabel` defines a single constant, shown in Table 4-2. A client property set with this constant as a key is used by `JComponent.AccessibleJComponent` to derive a name for components that haven't explicitly set one. If the component has a defined `LABELED_BY_PROPERTY`, the text from the `JLabel` referenced by the property value is used as the accessible name of the component.

Table 4-2. JLabel constant

Constant	Type	Description
LABELED_BY_PROPERTY	String	Client property key used as a back-pointer by the `labelFor` property

Constructors

JLabel()
> Create a label with no text or icon.

JLabel(Icon image)
JLabel(Icon image, int horizontalAlignment)
> Create labels displaying the given icon. The horizontal alignment defaults to CENTER. If specified, it must be one of the following values taken from SwingConstants: LEADING, TRAILING, LEFT, RIGHT, or CENTER.

JLabel(String text)
JLabel(String text, int horizontalAlignment)
> Create labels displaying the supplied text. If specified, the horizontal alignment must be one of the following values taken from SwingConstants: LEADING, TRAILING, LEFT, RIGHT, or CENTER.

JLabel(String text, Icon image, int horizontalAlignment)
> Create a label with an image, text, and specified horizontal alignment. The horizontal alignment must be one of the following values taken from SwingConstants: LEADING, TRAILING, LEFT, RIGHT, or CENTER.

Public Method

public void setDisplayedMnemonic(char mnemonic)

> A convenient way to set the mnemonic property by passing in a char (instead of the property's actual type, int). The character is converted to the equivalent integer "virtual keycode" (defined in the java.awt.KeyEvent class) and passed to the other setDisplayedMnemonic( ) method.

Support for HTML

The use of HTML is supported by most Swing components. For example, it is possible to use HTML markup to create multiline and multifont labels:

```
JLabel label = new JLabel("<html>line 1<p><font color=blue size=+2>"
                  + "big blue</font> line 2<p>line 3</html>");
```

There are a number of things to watch out for when taking advantage of Swing's HTML support:

- The text is interpreted as HTML only if the first six characters are <html> (case doesn't matter).
- The font of components using HTML may not match that of components that don't.
- Bad HTML may throw RuntimeExceptions, so test your code thoroughly. (Older SDKs are especially fragile in this respect. SDK 1.2 can't even handle an unknown tag.)
- There is no good way to determine if a particular component supports HTML programmatically.
- XHTML-style self-closing tags (such as <br />) insert a spurious > character into the output, at least as of SDK 1.4.1.
- SDKs prior to 1.3 are unable to size properly in the presence of <br> tags, so for maximum compatibility use <p> tags instead. Newer SDKs treat the two tags identically.

HTML support keeps improving with each release of Swing, but serious bugs remain. Slightly older releases are riddled with bugs in their HTML implementations. (Versions 1.1 and earlier don't support HTML at all. The JLabel would be displayed as 77 characters of verbatim text, just like the java.awt.Label in Figure 4-6.)

As of SDK 1.4.1 the following components support HTML text:[*] JLabel, JButton, JToggleButton, JCheckBox, JRadioButton, JMenu, JMenuItem, JCheckBoxMenuItem,

---

[*] The list for 1.3 is the same, but with several more sizing problems. 1.2 does not support HTML with JToggleButton, JCheckBox, or JRadioButton.

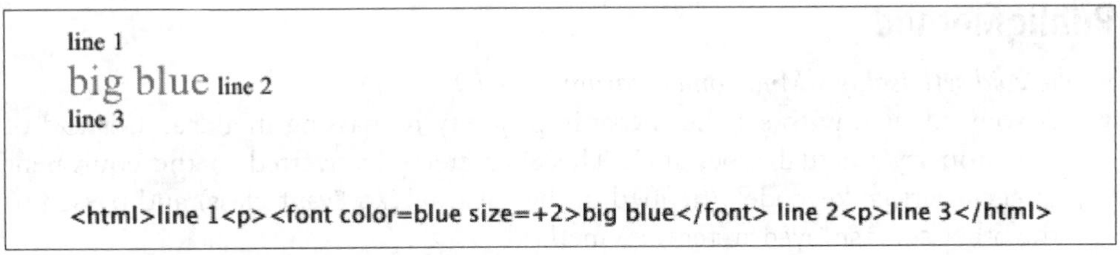

```
line 1
big blue line 2
line 3


<html>line 1<p> <font color=blue size=+2>big blue</font> line 2<p>line 3</html>
```

Figure 4-6. A JLabel and a java.awt.Label displaying the same text

JRadioButtonMenuItem, JComboBox, JList, the tabs of JTabbedPane, JTable,* JTree, and JToolTip. (And, of course, JEditorPane was designed to support HTML from day one.)

Icons

Swing introduces the concept of an icon for use in a variety of components. The Icon interface and ImageIcon class make dealing with simple images extremely easy.

The Icon interface is very simple, specifying just three methods used to determine the size of the Icon and display it. Implementations of this interface are free to store and display the image in any way, providing a great deal of flexibility. In other words, icons don't have to be bitmaps or GIF images, but are free to render themselves any way they choose. As we'll see later, an icon can simply draw on the component if that's more efficient. The examples at the end of this section show a couple of different ways the interface might be implemented.

Properties

The Icon interface defines the properties listed in Table 4-3. The iconHeight and iconWidth properties specify the size of the Icon in pixels.

Table 4-3. Icon properties

Property	Data type	get	is	set	Default value
iconHeight	int	•			
iconWidth	int	•			

* HTML works in table rows and in the table header, but as of SDK 1.4.1, neither is automatically resized if the HTML needs more vertical space than a single line of plain text. You might have to manually resize them.

Method

public void paintIcon(Component c, Graphics g, int x, int y)

Paint the `Icon` at the specified location on the given `Graphics`. For efficiency reasons, the `Graphics` object will (probably) not be clipped, so be sure not to draw "outside the lines." You must make sure to keep your horizontal position between x and x + `getIconWidth( )` - 1, and your vertical position between y and y + `getIconHeight( )` - 1 while painting. The `Component` is provided to allow its properties (such as foreground or background color) to be used when painting or so it can be used as an image observer (see "The ImageIcon Class" later in this chapter).

Implementing Your Own Icons

Here's a class that implements the `Icon` interface and uses ovals as simple icons:

```
// OvalIcon.java
//
import javax.swing.*;
import java.awt.*;

// A simple icon implementation that draws ovals
public class OvalIcon implements Icon {

  private int width, height;

  public OvalIcon(int w, int h) {
    width = w;
    height = h;
  }

  public void paintIcon(Component c, Graphics g, int x, int y) {
    g.drawOval(x, y, width-1, height-1);
  }

  public int getIconWidth( ) { return width; }
  public int getIconHeight( ) { return height; }
}
```

A simple class that creates a few labels shows how it works:

```
// TestOval.java
//
import javax.swing.*;
import java.awt.*;

public class TestOval {
  public static void main(String[] args) {
    JFrame f = new JFrame( );
    f.setDefaultCloseOperation(JFrame.EXIT_ON_CLOSE);
```

```
    JLabel label1 = new JLabel(new OvalIcon(20,50));
    JLabel label2 = new JLabel(new OvalIcon(50,20));
    JLabel label3 = new JLabel("Round!", new OvalIcon(60,60), SwingConstants.CENTER);
    label3.setHorizontalTextPosition(SwingConstants.CENTER);

    Container c = f.getContentPane();
    c.setLayout(new FlowLayout());
    c.add(label1);
    c.add(label2);
    c.add(label3);
    f.pack();
    f.setVisible(true);
  }
}
```

Running this test program produces the display shown in Figure 4-7.

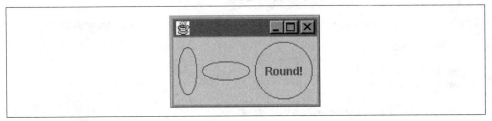

Figure 4-7. OvalIcon labels

Dynamic Icons

Icons are under no obligation to paint themselves the same way every time they are displayed. It's perfectly reasonable (and often quite useful) to have an icon that uses some sort of state information to determine how to display itself. In the next example, we create two sliders (JSlider is explained in detail in Chapter 6) that can be used to change the width and height of a dynamic icon:

```
// DynamicIconExample.java
//
import javax.swing.*;
import javax.swing.event.*;
import java.awt.*;

// Example of an icon that changes form.
public class DynamicIconExample {
  public static void main(String[] args) {

    // Create a couple of sliders to control the icon size.
    final JSlider width = new JSlider(JSlider.HORIZONTAL, 1, 150, 75);
    final JSlider height = new JSlider(JSlider.VERTICAL, 1, 150, 75);
```

```
// A little icon class that uses the current slider values
class DynamicIcon implements Icon {
  public int getIconWidth() { return width.getValue(); }
  public int getIconHeight() { return height.getValue(); }

  public void paintIcon(Component c, Graphics g, int x, int y) {
    g.fill3DRect(x, y, getIconWidth(), getIconHeight(), true);
  }
};
Icon icon = new DynamicIcon();
final JLabel dynamicLabel = new JLabel(icon);

// A listener to repaint the icon when sliders are adjusted
class Updater implements ChangeListener {
  public void stateChanged(ChangeEvent ev) {
    dynamicLabel.repaint();
  }
};
Updater updater = new Updater();

width.addChangeListener(updater);
height.addChangeListener(updater);

// Lay it all out.
JFrame f = new JFrame();
f.setDefaultCloseOperation(JFrame.EXIT_ON_CLOSE);

Container c = f.getContentPane();
c.setLayout(new BorderLayout());
c.add(width, BorderLayout.NORTH);
c.add(height, BorderLayout.WEST);
c.add(dynamicLabel, BorderLayout.CENTER);
f.setSize(210,210);
f.setVisible(true);
  }
}
```

Figure 4-8 shows the dynamic icon in its initial state, and then after we've moved the sliders around a bit.

The important thing to notice is that the DynamicIcon class does not actually store any information. In this case, we made the Icon class an inner class, giving it direct access to the sliders. Whenever the icon is told to paint itself, it gets its width and height from the values of the sliders. You could also choose to make your Icon class an event listener and have it update itself according to changes in certain events. The options here are wide open.

No matter how your icon gets its data, you need to make sure that any time you want to change the way it looks, you trigger a repaint of the icon. In this example, we've done this by listening to change events from the sliders and calling repaint() on the label that's holding the icon whenever one of the sliders changes.

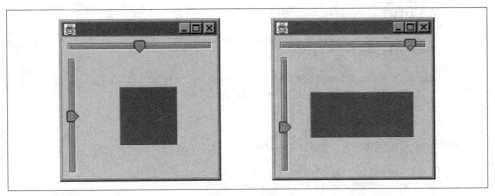

Figure 4-8. A dynamic icon's size is controlled by the sliders

The ImageIcon Class

Swing provides a concrete implementation of the Icon interface that is considerably more useful than our OvalIcon class. ImageIcon uses a java.awt.Image object to store and display any graphic and provides synchronous image loading (i.e., the Image is loaded completely before returning), making ImageIcons very powerful and easy to use. You can even use an ImageIcon to display an animated GIF89a, making the ubiquitous "animation applet" as simple as this:

```
// AnimationApplet.java
//
import javax.swing.*;

// A simple animation applet
public class AnimationApplet extends JApplet {
  public void init() {
    ImageIcon icon = new ImageIcon("images/rolling.gif");  // Animated gif
    getContentPane( ).add(new JLabel(icon));
  }
}
```

All we did here was load an animated GIF in the init( ) method and then add it to the applet. For more information on JApplet, see Chapter 8.

ImageIcon currently supports the JPEG, GIF (including animation and transparency), PNG, and XBM image formats. TIFF support should be coming soon. SVG might be supported eventually.

Properties

The ImageIcon class defines the properties listed in Table 4-4. The description property allows an arbitrary description of the image to be specified. One possible use of this property might be to give a blind user an audio description of the image.

Table 4-4. ImageIcon properties

Property	Data type	get	is	set	Default value
description	String	•		•	null
iconHeight°	int	•			-1
iconWidth°	int	•			-1
image	Image	•		•	null
imageLoadStatus	int	•			0
imageObserver	ImageObserver	•		•	null

°overridden

The iconHeight and iconWidth properties default to -1 if no image is loaded by the constructor, while the image property simply contains the Image object rendered by the icon. ImageLoadStatus indicates the success or failure of the image load process using the constants defined in java.awt.MediaTracker (ABORTED, ERRORED, or COMPLETE). The default for this property is 0, which does not map to any of these constants.

The imageObserver property contains the ImageObserver that should receive notifications of changes to the image. If this property is null (as it is by default), the component containing the icon will be treated as the image observer when the image is painted.

Figure 4-9 shows a class diagram for ImageIcon and the classes related to it.

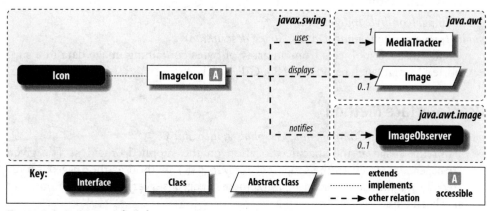

Figure 4-9. ImageIcon class diagram

Serialization

Like most Swing classes, ImageIcon implements Serializable. The keen observer may see a problem with this: the java.awt.Image class used by ImageIcon is *not* serializable. By default, this would keep ImageIcon objects from serializing properly. The good news is that ImageIcon implements its own readObject( ) and writeObject( ) methods so that the pixel representation of the image is stored and retrieved correctly.

Constructors

ImageIcon( )
> Create an uninitialized ImageIcon.

ImageIcon(Image image)
ImageIcon(Image image, String description)
> Create ImageIcon objects from an existing image. A textual description of the image may be provided. If no description is provided, an attempt is made to retrieve the "comment" property from the input Image. If this is a non-null string, it is used as the description.

ImageIcon(String filename)
ImageIcon(String filename, String description)
> Create ImageIcon objects from the contents of the specified JPEG, PNG, GIF, or XBM file. The image is guaranteed to be completely loaded (unless an error occurs) when the constructor returns.

ImageIcon(URL location)
ImageIcon(URL location, String description)
> Create ImageIcon objects from the contents of the specified java.net.URL. The image is guaranteed to be completely loaded (unless an error occurs) when the constructor returns.

public ImageIcon(byte imageData[])
public ImageIcon(byte imageData[], String description)
> Create ImageIcon objects from an array of bytes containing image data in a supported format, such as JPEG, PNG, GIF, or XBM.

User Interface Method

public void paintIcon(Component c, Graphics g, int x, int y)
> Paint the Image at the specified location on the supplied Graphics. The given Component is passed to the Graphics's drawImage( ) method as the ImageObserver (recall that java.awt.Component implements ImageObserver) if no image observer has been explicitly set.

CHAPTER 5

Buttons

Buttons are simple UI components used to generate events when the user presses them. Swing buttons can display icons, text, or both. In this section, we'll introduce the ButtonModel interface and DefaultButtonModel class (which define the state of the button). Next, we'll look at the AbstractButton class (which defines much of the functionality for all button types). Finally, we'll look at four concrete subclasses of AbstractButton and see how they can be grouped together using a ButtonGroup.

Figure 5-1 shows the class hierarchy, with significant relationships between the button-related Swing classes. As we discussed in the introductory chapters, each button (AbstractButton) keeps a reference to a ButtonModel, which represents its state.

The JMenuItem class shown here (and its subclasses, not shown) is not covered in this chapter; see Chapter 14 for details.

The ButtonModel Interface

The state of any Swing button is maintained by a ButtonModel object. This interface defines methods for reading and writing a model's properties and for adding and removing various types of event listeners.

Properties

The properties for the ButtonModel interface are listed in Table 5-1. The actionCommand property specifies the name of the command to be sent as part of the ActionEvent that is fired when the button is pressed. This can be used by event handlers that are listening to multiple buttons to determine which button is pressed.

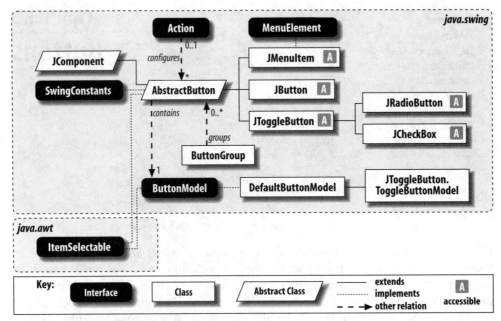

Figure 5-1. Button class diagram

Table 5-1. ButtonModel properties

Property	Data type	get	is	set	Default value
actionCommand	String	•		•	
armed	boolean		•	•	
enabled	boolean		•	•	
group	ButtonGroup			•	
mnemonic	int	•		•	
pressed	boolean		•	•	
rollover	boolean		•	•	
selected	boolean		•	•	

See also java.awt.ItemSelectable.

If no actionCommand is specified, an ActionEvent takes the button's text for its command string, so it is usually not necessary to specify an explicit actionCommand. You may find it useful to do so for buttons that have icons but no text or for multiple buttons with the same text. actionCommand properties can also be handy for internationalization. For example, if you need to change a button's text from "Hot" to "Caliente", you won't have to change any event-handling code if you set the actionCommand to "Hot".

The group property refers to the `ButtonGroup` that contains the button (if any). `mnemonic` contains the key that can be pressed in conjunction with a L&F-specific modifier key in order to produce the same effect as clicking the button with the mouse. The modifier key is currently the Alt* key for all Swing L&Fs.

 The type of the `mnemonic` property is int because its value is intended to be one of the `VK_` "virtual keycode" constants defined in `java.awt.KeyEvent` (see Table 27-6). However, a `setMnemonic( )` method that takes a char is defined in `AbstractButton`. It's usually easier to call `setMnemonic('a')` than it is to call `setMnemonic(KeyEvent.VK_A)` unless you are working with the model directly. If you use the char version, it doesn't matter if you specify an uppercase or lowercase character.

The other properties are boolean flags that reflect certain aspects of the button's state. The properties are:

armed
> Indicates whether releasing the button causes an action to be performed. This becomes false if the cursor is moved away from the button while the mouse button is still being held down.

enabled
> Indicates whether the button is currently enabled. A button must be enabled to be pressed.

pressed
> Indicates whether the button is currently being pressed (meaning that the button is being held down).

rollover
> Indicates whether the mouse cursor is currently over the button. This allows an alternate image to be displayed.

selected
> Indicates whether the button is currently selected. This is used only by `JToggleButton` and its subclasses. This property toggles between true and false each time the button is clicked.

Events

Objects implementing the `ButtonModel` interface fire action events, change events, and item events, as shown in Table 5-2.

---

* On the Macintosh, the Option key is used for Alt. Newer Mac keyboards have both labels.

Table 5-2. ButtonModel events

Event	Description
ActionEvent	The button is pressed.
ChangeEvent	A change has occurred in one or more properties of the button model.
ItemEvent	The button is toggled on or off.

The `ButtonModel` interface contains the following standard methods for maintaining event subscribers:

```
public void addActionListener(ActionListener l)
public void removeActionListener(ActionListener l)
public void addItemListener(ItemListener l)
public void removeItemListener(ItemListener l)
public void addChangeListener(ChangeListener l)
public void removeChangeListener(ChangeListener l)
```

The DefaultButtonModel Class

Swing provides an implementation of the `ButtonModel` interface called `DefaultButtonModel`. This class is used directly by the `AbstractButton` class and indirectly by the other button classes. `JToggleButton` defines an inner class extending `DefaultButtonModel` that it and its descendants use to manage their state data.

Properties

The `DefaultButtonModel` class gets most of its properties from `ButtonModel`. The default values set by this class are shown in Table 5-3.

Table 5-3. DefaultButtonModel properties

Property	Data type	get	is	set	Default value
actionCommand°	String	•		•	null
armed°	boolean		•	•	false
enabled°	boolean		•	•	true
group°,*	ButtonGroup	•		•	null
mnemonic°	int	•		•	KeyEvent.VK_UNDEFINED
pressed°	boolean		•	•	false
rollover°	boolean		•	•	false
selected°	boolean		•	•	false
selectedObjects	Object[]	•			null

°overridden, *getter was introduced in SDK 1.3

The only property here that does not come from the `ButtonModel` interface is the `selectedObjects` property. `DefaultButtonModel` provides a `getSelectedObjects()` method because it is mandated by the `ItemSelectable` interface, but it always returns `null`. SDK 1.3 added the `getGroup()` method.

Events

The events fired by `DefaultButtonModel` are those required by `ButtonModel` and listed in Table 5-2. An `ActionEvent` is fired when the button is pressed, an `ItemEvent` is fired when the button's state is changed, and a `ChangeEvent` is fired when a change has occurred to the button's properties.

This class implements the following standard methods:

```
public void addActionListener(ActionListener l)
public void removeActionListener(ActionListener l)
public ActionListener[] getActionListeners() (added in SDK 1.3)
public void addItemListener(ItemListener l)
public void removeItemListener(ItemListener l)
public ItemListener[] getItemListeners() (added in SDK 1.3)
public void addChangeListener(ChangeListener l)
public void removeChangeListener(ChangeListener l)
public ChangeListener[] getChangeListeners() (added in SDK 1.3)
public EventListener[] getListeners(Class listenerType) (added in SDK 1.4)
```

Note that the `ButtonModel` properties are not technically "bound properties" as defined by the JavaBeans specification because the lighter-weight `ChangeEvent` is sent when they change, rather than the standard `PropertyChangeEvent`.

Constants

`DefaultButtonModel` uses the constants shown in Table 5-4 to store internal state.

Table 5-4. DefaultButtonModel constants

Constant	Type
ARMED	int
ENABLED	int
PRESSED	int
ROLLOVER	int
SELECTED	int

Constructor

public DefaultButtonModel( )

Instantiates a new model. The model's properties are shown in Table 5-3.

The AbstractButton Class

AbstractButton is an abstract base class for all button components (JButton, JToggleButton, JCheckBox, JRadioButton, and JMenuItem and its subclasses). Since it provides functionality common to all types of buttons, we'll cover it here before getting to the concrete button classes.

AbstractButton provides much of the functionality associated with the interaction between the various concrete button classes and their ButtonModel objects. As we mentioned earlier, buttons in Swing can be made up of an image (Icon), text, or both. The relative positions of the text and icon are specified exactly as they are with the JLabel class.

Image buttons may specify as many as seven different images, allowing the button to be displayed differently depending on its current state. The seven icons are described in Table 5-5, with the other properties defined by AbstractButton.

Properties

The AbstractButton class defines the properties shown in Table 5-5.

Table 5-5. AbstractButton properties

Property	Data type	get	is	set	Default value
action[1.3]	Action	•		•	null
actionCommand	String	•		•	null
borderPainted[b]	boolean		•	•	true
contentAreaFilled[b]	boolean		•	•	true
disabledIcon[b]	Icon	•		•	null
disabledSelectedIcon[b]	Icon	•		•	null
displayedMnemonicIndex[1.4]	int	•		•	-1
enabled[o]	boolean		•	•	true
focusPainted[b]	boolean		•	•	true
horizontalAlignment[b]	int	•		•	CENTER
horizontalTextPosition[b]	int	•		•	TRAILING[1.4]
icon[b]	Icon	•		•	null

[1.3]since 1.3, [1.4]since 1.4, [b]bound, [d]deprecated, [o]overridden

See also properties from the JComponent class (Table 3-6).

Table 5-5. AbstractButton properties (continued)

Property	Data type	get	is	set	Default value
iconTextGap[1.4]	int	•		•	4
label[d]	String	•		•	Same as text
margin[b]	Insets	•		•	null
mnemonic[b]	int	•		•	KeyEvent.VK_UNDEFINED
model[b]	ButtonModel	•		•	null
multiClickThreshhold[1.4]	long	•		•	0
pressedIcon[b]	Icon	•		•	null
rolloverEnabled[b]	boolean		•	•	false
rolloverIcon	Icon	•		•	null
rolloverSelectedIcon[b]	Icon	•		•	null
selected	boolean		•	•	false
selectedIcon[b]	Icon	•		•	null
selectedObjects	Object[]	•			null
text[b]	String	•		•	""
UI[b]	ButtonUI	•		•	From L&F
verticalAlignment[b]	int	•		•	CENTER
verticalTextPosition[b]	int	•		•	CENTER

[1.3]since 1.3, [1.4]since 1.4, [b]bound, [d]deprecated, [o]overridden

See also properties from the JComponent class (Table 3-6).

There are seven different icons available for a button. Each is shown when the button is in a certain state:[*]

icon

> The default icon for the button, or null for no icon.

disabledIcon

> The icon shown when the button is disabled. If none is specified, a grayscale version of the default icon is generated automatically.

selectedIcon

> The icon shown when the button is selected.

disabledSelectedIcon

> The icon shown when the button is selected and also disabled. If none is specified, a grayscale version of the selected icon is generated. If no selected icon is set, it uses the value returned by getDisabledIcon( ).

---

[*] Prior to SDK 1.4, disabledSelectedIcon and rolloverSelectedIcon were ignored by the Swing L&Fs.

pressedIcon
> The icon shown while the button is being pressed.

rolloverIcon
> The icon shown (if rolloverEnabled is true) when the cursor is moved over the unselected button.

rolloverSelectedIcon
> The icon shown (if rolloverEnabled is true) when the cursor is moved over the selected button.

The text property contains the text, if any, displayed on the button (note that this property replaces the deprecated label property). The model property is the ButtonModel containing the state information for the button.

Setting the action property does a lot of work in one step. The newly attached Action receives any ActionEvents fired by the button, and the previous Action (if any) is deregistered. The button almost completely resets its properties based on the Action (see the configurePropertiesFromAction( ) method and Table 5-8). Furthermore, the button registers a PropertyChangeListener on the Action so it can automatically update itself when changes are made to the Action in the future.

The horizontalAlignment and verticalAlignment properties specify where the button's content (text, icon, or both) should be drawn within the button's borders. These properties are significant only when the button is larger than the default size. horizontalTextPosition and verticalTextPosition specify the location of the text relative to the icon, and iconTextGap specifies the amount of space (in pixels) separating the text and the icon. These are meaningful only if both an icon and text have been specified.*

The multiClickThreshhold property is the length of time (in milliseconds) during which multiple mouse clicks are coalesced into a single ActionEvent. A value of 0 (the default) indicates that each click generates an ActionEvent no matter how quickly it follows its predecessor.

The margin property specifies the distance between the button's borders and its contents (text, icon, or both). However, it's up to the border implementation to take advantage of the value of this property. The Swing L&Fs define borders that take the value of margin into account, but if you replace a button's border with one of your own, be aware that the margin space is not used unless you access it explicitly in your border code. borderPainted indicates whether a border (recall from Chapter 3 that border is inherited from JComponent) should be painted around the button. This property is meaningful only if the button actually has a border (it does by default).

---

* See "Labels" in Chapter 4 for an example of the alignment and text position properties.

The `contentAreaFilled` property indicates whether the rectangular content area of the button should be filled. This should be set to `false` if you want to define an image-only button. Note that this is preferable to calling `setOpaque(false)` because the value of the opaque property for buttons is set by the L&F. `focusPainted` indicates whether something special (such as a dashed line inside the button's border) should be painted to show that the button has focus.

Finally, the `rolloverEnabled` property indicates whether moving the cursor over the button should cause the `rolloverIcon` or `rolloverSelectedIcon` to be displayed. Calling `setRolloverIcon( )` causes this property to be set to true.

The `actionCommand`, `mnemonic`, and `selected` properties are taken directly from the `AbstractButton`'s `ButtonModel` object. The `displayedMnemonicIndex` property behaves the same way it does in `JLabel` (see "Labels" in Chapter 4). `AbstractButton` adds its own implementation of `setEnabled( )`, inherited from `java.awt.Component`, which updates the enabled property of its `ButtonModel`.

`UI` holds the `ButtonUI` used to render the button.

Events

`AbstractButton` fires the events required by the `ButtonModel` interface (see Table 5-6). An `ActionEvent` is fired when the button is pressed, an `ItemEvent` is fired when the button's state is changed, and a `ChangeEvent` is fired when a change has occurred to the button's properties.

Table 5-6. AbstractButton events

Event	Description
ActionEvent	The button is pressed.
ChangeEvent	A change has occurred in one or more properties of the button's model.
ItemEvent	The button is toggled on or off.

All of these events are generated by the button's model. `AbstractButton` registers with the model as a listener for each type of event and refires any events fired by the model to any registered listeners. The following standard listener management methods are implemented in this class:

```
public void addActionListener(ActionListener l)
public void removeActionListener(ActionListener l)
public ActionListener[] getActionListeners( ) (Added in SDK 1.4)
public void addItemListener(ItemListener l)
public void removeItemListener(ItemListener l)
public ItemListener[] getItemListeners( ) (Added in SDK 1.4)
public void addChangeListener(ChangeListener l)
```

```
public void removeChangeListener(ChangeListener l)
public ChangeListener[] getChangeListeners( ) (Added in SDK 1.4)
```

Constants

The constants shown in Table 5-7 are defined by AbstractButton for use in
PropertyChangeEvents. Some PropertyChangeEvents generated by AbstractButton use
strings other than these. There's no constant defined to indicate that the action
property has changed, so the setAction( ) method fires a PropertyChangeEvent with
the string "action". Accessibility-related change events use strings defined in the
AccessibleContext class.

Table 5-7. AbstractButton constants

Constant	Type	Description
BORDER_PAINTED_CHANGED_PROPERTY	String	borderPainted property has changed
CONTENT_AREA_FILLED_CHANGED_PROPERTY	String	contentAreaFilled property has changed
DISABLED_ICON_CHANGED_PROPERTY	String	disabledIcon property has changed
DISABLED_SELECTED_ICON_CHANGED_PROPERTY	String	disabledSelectedIcon property has changed
FOCUS_PAINTED_CHANGED_PROPERTY	String	focusPainted property has changed
HORIZONTAL_ALIGNMENT_CHANGED_PROPERTY	String	horizontalAlignment property has changed
HORIZONTAL_TEXT_POSITION_CHANGED_PROPERTY	String	horizontalTextPosition property has changed
ICON_CHANGED_PROPERTY	String	icon property has changed
MARGIN_CHANGED_PROPERTY	String	margin property has changed
MNEMONIC_CHANGED_PROPERTY	String	mnemonic property has changed
MODEL_CHANGED_PROPERTY	String	model property has changed
PRESSED_ICON_CHANGED_PROPERTY	String	pressedIcon property has changed
ROLLOVER_ENABLED_CHANGED_PROPERTY	String	rolloverEnabled property has changed
ROLLOVER_ICON_CHANGED_PROPERTY	String	rolloverIcon property has changed
ROLLOVER_SELECTED_ICON_CHANGED_PROPERTY	String	rolloverSelectedIcon property has changed
SELECTED_ICON_CHANGED_PROPERTY	String	selectedIcon property has changed
TEXT_CHANGED_PROPERTY	String	text property has changed
VERTICAL_ALIGNMENT_CHANGED_PROPERTY	String	verticalAlignment property has changed
VERTICAL_TEXT_POSITION_CHANGED_PROPERTY	String	verticalTextPosition property has changed

Public Methods

public void doClick(int pressTime)

Programmatically simulate a user pressing the button for a specified number of milliseconds. Calling this method has the same effect as pressing the button—the button even appears to be pressed.

public void doClick( )

This version of doClick( ) calls the first version with a value of 68 milliseconds.

public void setMnemonic(char mnemonic)

This method provides a convenient way to set the mnemonic property by passing in a char (as opposed to the property's actual type, int). The character is converted to the equivalent integer "virtual keycode" (defined in the java.awt.KeyEvent class) and passed to the other setMnemonic( ) method.

Action Configuration Methods

These protected methods do most of the work to support Actions. Subclasses that wish to alter the way they behave with Actions should override these methods. (These methods were added in SDK 1.3.)

protected PropertyChangeListener createActionPropertyChangeListener(Action a)

Return a PropertyChangeListener that will be responsible for reconfiguring the button in response to changes in the button's action.

protected void configurePropertiesFromAction(Action a)

The values of several properties are pulled from the given Action and applied to this button. The specific properties are listed in Table 5-8, though the concrete subclasses of AbstractButton can and do add and remove from this list.

Table 5-8. Properties set by configurePropertiesFromAction( )

Button property	Value taken from Action	Value if Action is null
text	a.getValue(NAME)	null
icon	a.getValue(SMALL_ICON)	null
mnemonic	a.getValue(MNEMONIC_KEY)	KeyEvent.VK_UNDEFINED
toolTipText	a.getValue(SHORT_DESCRIPTION)	null
actionCommand	a.getValue(ACTION_COMMAND_KEY)	null
enabled	a.isEnabled( )	true

The JButton Class

JButton is the simplest of the button types, adding very little to what is provided by the AbstractButton class. JButtons are buttons that are not toggled on and off but instead act as push buttons, which invoke some action when clicked. Figure 5-2 shows what these buttons look like in four of the Swing L&Fs.

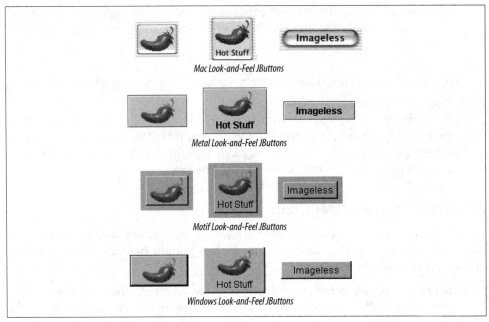

Figure 5-2. JButtons in four L&Fs

Properties

The JButton class inherits most of its properties and default values from its super-classes. The exceptions to this are shown in Table 5-9. The model property is set to a new instance of DefaultButtonModel when a JButton is created.

Table 5-9. JButton properties

Property	Data type	get	is	set	Default value
accessibleContext°	AccessibleContext	•			JButton.AccessibleJButton()
defaultButton	boolean		•		false
defaultCapable	boolean		•	•	true
model°	ButtonModel	•		•	DefaultButtonModel()
UIClassID°	String	•			"ButtonUI"

°overridden

See also properties from AbstractButton (Table 5-5).

The defaultButton property indicates whether the button is activated by default when some event occurs within the JRootPane containing the button. Typically, the event that would trigger the button would be an Enter key press, but this is actually up to the L&F implementation.

The defaultButton property cannot be set directly. Instead, it is set by telling the JRootPane which button should be the default. (We'll cover JRootPane in Chapter 8—at this point, it's enough to know that the Swing containers JApplet, JDialog, JFrame, and JWindow all use a JRootPane as their primary content container.) If the button is inside one of these Swing containers, this property may be true.

The other new property, defaultCapable, indicates whether the button may be set as a root pane's default button. A button may be treated only as the default button if this property is set to true.

Using the Default Button

Here's a quick example showing how the default button property can be used:

```
// DefaultButtonExample.java
//
import javax.swing.*;
import java.awt.*;

// Example using defaultButton and JRootPane.setDefaultButton()
public class DefaultButtonExample {
  public static void main(String[] args) {

    // Create some buttons.
    JButton ok = new JButton("OK");
    JButton cancel = new JButton("Cancel");
    JPanel buttonPanel = new JPanel();
    buttonPanel.add(ok);
    buttonPanel.add(cancel);

    JLabel msg = new JLabel("Is this OK?", JLabel.CENTER);

    // Create a frame, get its root pane, and set the OK button as the default. This
    // button is pressed if we press the Enter key while the frame has focus.
    JFrame f = new JFrame();
    f.setDefaultCloseOperation(JFrame.EXIT_ON_CLOSE);
    JRootPane root = f.getRootPane();
    root.setDefaultButton(ok);

    // Layout and display
    Container content = f.getContentPane();
    content.add(msg, BorderLayout.CENTER);
    content.add(buttonPanel, BorderLayout.SOUTH);
    f.setSize(200,100);
    f.setVisible(true);
  }
}
```

The first thing we do here is create two buttons and a label. We then create a JFrame and get its "root pane." Next, we call this pane's setDefaultButton( ) method, passing in a reference to the OK button. When this program runs, the OK button is drawn with a different border around it, as shown with the Metal L&F in Figure 5-3. More importantly, when we press Enter while the frame has focus, the OK button is pressed automatically.

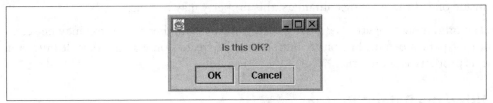

Figure 5-3. Default button

Events

JButton does not define any new events, but it's important to understand which of the events defined by its superclasses are fired when the button is pressed. The most important thing to know about JButton events is that JButtons fire ActionEvents when they are clicked. This type of event is sent after the button is released, and only if the button is still armed (meaning that the cursor is still over the button). The following example creates event listeners for action, change, and item events to show which events are fired when we press the button:

```
// JButtonEvents.java
//
import javax.swing.*;
import javax.swing.event.*;
import java.awt.*;
import java.awt.event.*;

public class JButtonEvents {
  public static void main(String[] args) {
    JButton jb = new JButton("Press Me");

    jb.addActionListener(new ActionListener( ) {
      public void actionPerformed(ActionEvent ev) {
        System.out.println("ActionEvent!");
      }
    });
    jb.addItemListener(new ItemListener( ) {
      public void itemStateChanged(ItemEvent ev) {
        System.out.println("ItemEvent!");
      }
    });
    jb.addChangeListener(new ChangeListener( ) {
      public void stateChanged(ChangeEvent ev) {
        System.out.println("ChangeEvent!");
```

```
            }
        });
        JFrame f = new JFrame( );
        f.setDefaultCloseOperation(JFrame.EXIT_ON_CLOSE);
        f.getContentPane( ).add(jb);
        f.pack( );
        f.setVisible(true);
    }
}
```

Running this program and pressing the button produces the following output:

```
ChangeEvent!
ChangeEvent!
```

When the button is released, the following additional output is produced:

```
ActionEvent!
ChangeEvent!
```

The initial change events are fired, indicating that the button is *armed* and *pressed*. When the button is released, the action event is fired, along with another change event to indicate that the button is no longer pressed.

Pressing the button a second time results in only a single change event, followed by the action event and change event when the button is released. This is because the button's armed property is still set to true after the button is clicked. This property is set to false again only if you hold the mouse button down and then move the cursor away from the button. If the button is released while the pointer is no longer over the button, no ActionEvent is fired.

In practice, you are typically interested only in the ActionEvents fired by a JButton.

Constructors

public JButton( )
> Create a button with no image or text.

public JButton(Action a)
> Create a button with property values taken from the specified Action (see Table 5-8), register the Action to receive ActionEvents fired by the button, and register the button as a ChangeListener of the Action. The button adapts to any future changes made to the Action. This is equivalent to instantiating a JButton with the default constructor and then calling its setAction( ) method. (This constructor was introduced with SDK 1.3.)

public JButton(Icon icon)
> Create a button displaying the specified icon.

public JButton(String text)
> Create a button displaying the specified text.

public JButton(String text, Icon icon)
> Create a button displaying the specified text and icon.

Using Actions

The following example creates four `Action` objects and uses them to create buttons (and to create menu items, just to show how easy it is). Each button (and menu) takes its `text`, icon, `mnemonic`, `toolTip`, and enabled status from the `Action`. If an `Action` changes one or more of these, the button (and menu) reflects the change automatically. Figure 5-4 shows an example of this: both the button and the menu item change from "Go to channel 9" in their enabled state to "Go to channel 2" in their disabled state when the user clicks on (or invokes via the mnemonic with Alt-S)* the Set 'Go to' channel button.

Figure 5-4. ActionExample before and after clicking on the Set 'Go to' channel button

```
// ActionExample.java
//
import javax.swing.*;
import java.awt.*;
import java.awt.event.*;

public class ActionExample extends JFrame {
```

---

* As we noted earlier, the use of the Alt key is actually up to the L&F, but currently, the Swing L&Fs that support button mnemonics use Alt. The Mac L&F does not, so if you run this program on a Mac, the buttons do not display any underlines, and pressing the key combinations has no effect.

```java
    public static final int MIN_CHANNEL = 2;
    public static final int MAX_CHANNEL = 13;

    private int currentChannel = MIN_CHANNEL;
    private int favoriteChannel = 9;
    private JLabel channelLabel = new JLabel();

    private Action upAction = new UpAction();
    private Action downAction = new DownAction();
    private GotoFavoriteAction gotoFavoriteAction = new GotoFavoriteAction();
    private Action setFavoriteAction = new SetFavoriteAction();

    public class UpAction extends AbstractAction {
      public UpAction() {
        putValue(NAME, "Channel Up");
        putValue(SMALL_ICON, new ImageIcon("images/up.gif"));
        putValue(SHORT_DESCRIPTION, "Increment the channel number");
        putValue(MNEMONIC_KEY, new Integer(KeyEvent.VK_U));
      }
      public void actionPerformed(ActionEvent ae) {
        setChannel(currentChannel+1);
      }
    }

    public class DownAction extends AbstractAction {
      public DownAction() {
        putValue(NAME, "Channel Down");
        putValue(SMALL_ICON, new ImageIcon("images/down.gif"));
        putValue(SHORT_DESCRIPTION, "Decrement the channel number");
        putValue(MNEMONIC_KEY, new Integer(KeyEvent.VK_D));
      }
      public void actionPerformed(ActionEvent ae) {
        setChannel(currentChannel-1);
      }
    }

    public class GotoFavoriteAction extends AbstractAction {
      public GotoFavoriteAction() {
        putValue(SMALL_ICON, new ImageIcon("images/fav.gif"));
        putValue(MNEMONIC_KEY, new Integer(KeyEvent.VK_G));
        updateProperties();
      }
      public void updateProperties() {
        putValue(NAME, "Go to channel "+favoriteChannel);
        putValue(SHORT_DESCRIPTION, "Change the channel to "+favoriteChannel);
      }
      public void actionPerformed(ActionEvent ae) {
        setChannel(favoriteChannel);
      }
    }
```

```java
public class SetFavoriteAction extends AbstractAction {
  public SetFavoriteAction( ) {
    putValue(NAME, "Set 'Go to' channel");
    putValue(SMALL_ICON, new ImageIcon("images/set.gif"));
    putValue(SHORT_DESCRIPTION, "Make current channel the Favorite channel");
    putValue(MNEMONIC_KEY, new Integer(KeyEvent.VK_S));
  }
  public void actionPerformed(ActionEvent ae) {
    favoriteChannel = currentChannel;
    gotoFavoriteAction.updateProperties( );
    setEnabled(false);
    gotoFavoriteAction.setEnabled(false);
  }
}

public ActionExample( ) {
  super("ActionExample");

  setChannel(currentChannel); // Enable/disable the Actions as appropriate.

  channelLabel.setHorizontalAlignment(JLabel.CENTER);
  channelLabel.setFont(new Font("Serif", Font.PLAIN, 32));

  getContentPane( ).add(channelLabel, BorderLayout.NORTH);

  JPanel buttonPanel = new JPanel(new GridLayout(2, 2, 16, 6));
  buttonPanel.setBorder(BorderFactory.createEmptyBorder(6, 16, 16, 16));
  getContentPane( ).add(buttonPanel, BorderLayout.CENTER);
  buttonPanel.add(new JButton(upAction));
  buttonPanel.add(new JButton(gotoFavoriteAction));
  buttonPanel.add(new JButton(downAction));
  buttonPanel.add(new JButton(setFavoriteAction));

  JMenuBar mb = new JMenuBar( );
  JMenu menu = new JMenu("Channel");
  menu.add(new JMenuItem(upAction));
  menu.add(new JMenuItem(downAction));
  menu.addSeparator( );
  menu.add(new JMenuItem(gotoFavoriteAction));
  menu.add(new JMenuItem(setFavoriteAction));
  mb.add(menu);
  setJMenuBar(mb);
}

public void setChannel(int chan) {
  currentChannel = chan;
  channelLabel.setText("Now tuned to channel: "+currentChannel);
  // Enable/disable the Actions as appropriate.
  downAction.setEnabled(currentChannel > MIN_CHANNEL);
  upAction.setEnabled(currentChannel < MAX_CHANNEL);
```

```
      gotoFavoriteAction.setEnabled(currentChannel != favoriteChannel);
      setFavoriteAction.setEnabled(currentChannel != favoriteChannel);
  }

  public static void main(String argv[]) {
    JFrame f = new ActionExample( );
    f.setSize(400, 180);
    f.setDefaultCloseOperation(JFrame.EXIT_ON_CLOSE);
    f.setVisible(true);
  }
}
```

Fancy Buttons

While looking at AbstractButton, we learned that quite a few things can be done
with Swing buttons to make them more visually interesting. In this example, we'll
see how we can spice up a user interface by adding rollover and selected icons to our
buttons. We'll also take away the button borders, focus painting, and fill content
area to give our display a nice clean look.

```
// FancyButton.java
//
import javax.swing.*;
import java.awt.*;

public class FancyButton extends JButton {
  // Create a JButton that does not show focus, does not paint a border, and displays
  // different icons when rolled over and pressed.
  public FancyButton(Icon icon, Icon pressed, Icon rollover) {
    super(icon);
    setFocusPainted(false);
    setRolloverEnabled(true);
    setRolloverIcon(rollover);
    setPressedIcon(pressed);
    setBorderPainted(false);
    setContentAreaFilled(false);
  }

  // A simple test program
  public static void main(String[] args) {

    FancyButton b1 = new FancyButton(
      new ImageIcon("images/redcube.gif"),
      new ImageIcon("images/redpaw.gif"),
      new ImageIcon("images/reddiamond.gif"));
    FancyButton b2 = new FancyButton(
      new ImageIcon("images/bluecube.gif"),
      new ImageIcon("images/bluepaw.gif"),
      new ImageIcon("images/bluediamond.gif"));
    JFrame f = new JFrame( );
    f.setDefaultCloseOperation(JFrame.EXIT_ON_CLOSE);
    Container c = f.getContentPane( );
```

```
        c.setLayout(new FlowLayout( ));
        c.add(b1);
        c.add(b2);
        f.pack( );
        f.setVisible(true);
      }
    }
```

Figure 5-5 shows our new button class with the different states of the buttons. Of course, this is just one fancy button implementation. You can create your own special button classes using some or all of the features shown in FancyButton, as well as other features, such as adding icons for other button states.

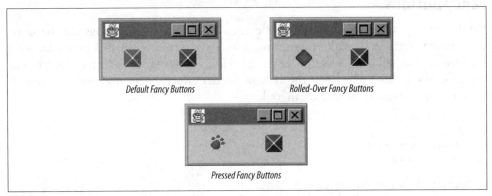

Figure 5-5. Buttons using "rollover" and "pressed" icons

The JToggleButton Class

JToggleButton is an extension of AbstractButton and is used to represent buttons that can be toggled on and off (as opposed to buttons like JButton which, when pushed, "pop back up"). It should be noted that while the subclasses of JToggleButton (JCheckBox and JRadioButton) are the kinds of JToggleButtons most commonly used, JToggleButton is not an abstract class. When used directly, it typically (though this is ultimately up to the L&F) has the appearance of a JButton that does not pop back up when pressed (see Figure 5-6).

Properties

The JToggleButton class inherits all of its properties and most of its default values from its superclass. The exceptions are shown in Table 5-10. The model property is set to a new instance of ToggleButtonModel when a JToggleButton is created. ToggleButtonModel (described in the next section) is a public inner class that extends DefaultButtonModel.

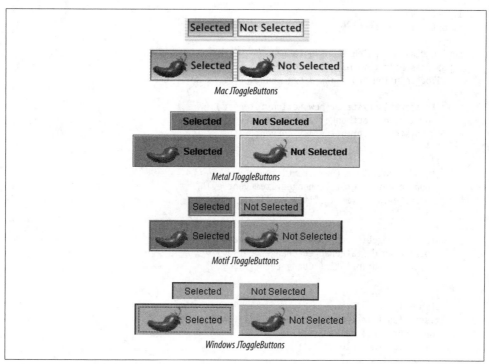

Figure 5-6. JToggleButtons in four L&Fs

Table 5-10. JToggleButton properties

Property	Data type	get	is	set	Default value
accessibleContext[o]	AccessibleContext	•			JToggleButton. AccessibleJToggleButton( )
model[o]	ButtonModel	•		•	ToggleButtonModel( )
UIClassID[o]	String	•			"ToggleButtonUI"

[o]overridden

See also properties from AbstractButton (Table 5-5).

Events

Like JButton, JToggleButton defines no new events. However, the events fired by JToggleButtons are slightly different than those fired by JButton. Let's look at these events by running a simple program like the one used in the JButton event section. This time, we'll create a JToggleButton instead of a JButton:

```
// JToggleButtonEvents.java
//
import javax.swing.*;
import javax.swing.event.*;
```

```
import java.awt.*;
import java.awt.event.*;

public class JToggleButtonEvents {
  public static void main(String[] args) {
    JToggleButton jtb = new JToggleButton("Press Me");

    jtb.addActionListener(new ActionListener( ) {
      public void actionPerformed(ActionEvent ev) {
        System.out.println("ActionEvent!");
      }
    });
    jtb.addItemListener(new ItemListener( ) {
      public void itemStateChanged(ItemEvent ev) {
        System.out.println("ItemEvent!");
      }
    });
    jtb.addChangeListener(new ChangeListener( ) {
      public void stateChanged(ChangeEvent ev) {
        System.out.println("ChangeEvent!");
      }
    });
    JFrame f = new JFrame( );
    f.setDefaultCloseOperation(JFrame.EXIT_ON_CLOSE);
    Container c = f.getContentPane( );
    c.setLayout(new FlowLayout( ));
    c.add(jtb);
    f.pack( );
    f.setVisible(true);
  }
}
```

When we run this program and press the button, we get the following output:

```
ChangeEvent!
ChangeEvent!
```

After releasing the button, we see:

```
ChangeEvent!
ItemEvent!
ChangeEvent!
ActionEvent!
```

As in our JButton example, the first two events are fired to indicate that the button is *armed* and *pressed*. When the button is released, we get another change event indicating that the button has now been *selected*. Additionally, toggle buttons fire an ItemEvent to indicate button selection. The final two events match those of JButton, indicating that the button is no longer being pressed and that an action (button press) has occurred.

Subsequent button presses result in one less ChangeEvent (just like we saw with JButton) because the button remains armed after it is pressed. (Depending on the L&F, there may also be additional ChangeEvents.)

Constructors

public JToggleButton()
> Create a button that has no text or icon and is not selected.

public JToggleButton(Action a)
> Create a button with property values taken from the specified `Action` (see Table 5-8), register the `Action` to receive `ActionEvents` fired by the button, and register the button as a `ChangeListener` of the `Action`. The button adapts to any future changes made to the `Action`. This is equivalent to instantiating a `JToggleButton` with the default constructor and then calling its `setAction()` method. (This constructor was introduced with SDK 1.3.)

public JToggleButton(Icon icon)
public JToggleButton(Icon icon, boolean selected)
> Create a button that displays the specified icon. If included, the boolean parameter determines the initial selection state of the button.

public JToggleButton(String text)
public JToggleButton(String text, boolean selected)
> Create a button that displays the specified text. If included, the boolean parameter determines the initial selection state of the button.

public JToggleButton(String text, Icon icon)
public JToggleButton(String test, Icon icon, boolean selected)
> Create a button that displays the specified text and icon. If included, the boolean parameter determines the initial selection state of the button.

The JToggleButton.ToggleButtonModel Class

As we mentioned earlier, `JToggleButton` does not use the `DefaultButtonModel` class as its model. `ToggleButtonModel`, a public static inner class that extends `DefaultButtonModel`, is used instead.

Properties

`ToggleButtonModel` modifies the methods for working with the properties listed in Table 5-11. New implementations of `isSelected()` and `setSelected()` use the button's `ButtonGroup` (if defined) to keep track of which button is selected, ensuring that even if multiple selected buttons are added to a group, only the first one is considered selected (since the group keeps track of the "officially" selected button). In addition, the setPressed( ) method is redefined to call setSelected( ) when the button is released (if it is armed)

Table 5-11. JToggleButton.ToggleButtonModel properties

Property	Data type	get	is	set	Default value
pressed[o]	boolean		•	•	false
selected[o]	boolean		•	•	false

[o]overridden

See also properties from DefaultButtonModel (Table 5-3).

The JCheckBox Class

The JCheckBox[*] class is shown in various L&Fs in Figure 5-7. JCheckBox is a subclass of JToggleButton and is typically used to allow the user to turn a given feature on or off or to make multiple selections from a set of choices. A JCheckBox is usually rendered by showing a small box into which a "check" is placed when selected (as shown in Figure 5-7). If you specify an icon for the checkbox, this icon replaces the default box. Therefore, if you specify an icon, you should always also supply a selected icon—otherwise, there is no way to tell if a checkbox is selected.

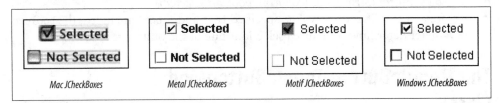

Figure 5-7. JCheckBoxes in four L&Fs

Properties

The JCheckBox class inherits most of its properties from its superclasses. The exceptions are shown in Table 5-12. By default, no border is painted on JCheckBoxes, and their horizontalAlignment is to the leading edge (which means to the left in the default locale, in which text reads left to right).[†] Setting the borderPaintedFlat property to true is a hint to the L&F that the checkbox should be drawn more plainly than usual. (This is used primarily by cell renderers for tables and trees.)

---

[*] Note that the java.awt.Checkbox class differs in capitalization from javax.swing.JCheckBox.

[†] This locale sensitivity was introduced in SDK 1.4; previously, checkboxes were always aligned to the left.

Table 5-12. JCheckBox properties

Property	Data type	get	is	set	Default value
accessibleContext[o]	AccessibleContext	•			AccessibleJCheckBox
borderPainted[o]	boolean		•	•	false
borderPaintedFlat[1.3, b]	boolean		•	•	false
horizontalAlignment[o]	int	•		•	LEADING[1.4]
UIClassID[o]	String	•			"CheckBoxUI"

[1.3]since 1.3, [1.4]since 1.4, [b]bound, [o]overridden

See also properties from `JToggleButton` (Table 5-10).

Events

See the discussion of `JToggleButton` (`JCheckBox`'s superclass) events.

Constant

`JToggleButton` adds one constant for use in `PropertyChangeEvents` to the list defined by `AbstractButton` (see Table 5-13).

Table 5-13. JToggleButton constant

Constant	Type	Description
BORDER_PAINTED_FLAT_CHANGED_PROPERTY	String	borderPaintedFlat property has changed

See also the constants defined by `AbstractButton` in Table 5-7.

Constructors

public JCheckBox( )
> Create a checkbox that has no text or icon and is not selected.

public JCheckBox(Action a)
> Create a checkbox with property values taken from the specified `Action`, register the `Action` to receive `ActionEvents` fired by the checkbox, and register the checkbox as a `ChangeListener` of the `Action`. The checkbox adapts to any future changes made to the `Action`. The properties set are the ones listed in Table 5-8, except that the `SMALL_ICON` is not honored since `JCheckBox` uses its `icon` property to show its state. (This constructor was introduced with SDK 1.3.)

public JCheckBox(Icon icon)
public JCheckBox(Icon icon, boolean selected)
> Create a checkbox that displays the specified icon. If included, the `selected` parameter determines the initial selection state of the button.

public JCheckBox(String text)
public JCheckBox(String text, boolean selected)
> Create a checkbox that displays the specified text. If included, the selected parameter determines the initial selection state of the button.

public JCheckBox(String text, Icon icon)
public JCheckBox(String text, Icon icon, boolean selected)
> Create a checkbox that displays the specified text and icon. If included, the selected parameter determines the initial selection state of the button.

The JRadioButton Class

JRadioButton is a subclass of JToggleButton, typically used with other JRadioButtons, that allows users to make a single selection from a set of options (Figure 5-8). Because radio buttons form a set of choices, JRadioButtons are usually used in groups, managed by a ButtonGroup (described in the next section). If you specify an icon for the radio button, you should also specify a selected icon so it will be visually apparent if a button is selected.

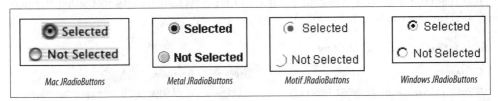

| Mac JRadioButtons | Metal JRadioButtons | Motif JRadioButtons | Windows JRadioButtons |

Figure 5-8. JRadioButtons in four L&Fs

Properties

The JRadioButton class inherits all its properties and most of its default values from its superclass. The only exceptions are shown in Table 5-14. By default, no border is painted on JRadioButtons, and their horizontalAlignment is set to the leading edge (to the left in the default locale, in which text reads left to right).[*]

Table 5-14. JRadioButton properties

Property	Data type	get	is	set	Default value
accessibleContext°	AccessibleContext	•			JRadioButton. AccessibleJRadioButton()
borderPainted°	boolean		•	•	false

1.4since 1.4, °overridden
See also properties from JToggleButton (Table 5-10).

---

[*] This locale sensitivity was introduced in SDK 1.4; previously, radio buttons were always aligned to the left.

Table 5-14. JRadioButton properties (continued)

Property	Data type	get	is	set	Default value
horizontalAlignment°	int	•		•	LEADING[1.4]
UIClassID°	String	•			"RadioButtonUI"

[1.4]since 1.4, °overridden

See also properties from JToggleButton (Table 5-10).

Events

See the discussion of JToggleButton (JRadioButton's superclass) events.

Constructors

public JRadioButton( )
> Create a button that has no text or icon and is not selected.

public JRadioButton(Action a)
> Create a button with property values taken from the specified Action, register the Action to receive ActionEvents fired by the button, and register the button as a ChangeListener of the Action. The button adapts to any future changes made to the Action. The properties set are the ones listed in Table 5-8, except that the SMALL_ICON is not honored since JRadioButton uses its icon property to show its state. (This constructor was introduced with SDK 1.3.)

public JRadioButton(Icon icon)
public JRadioButton(Icon icon, boolean selected)
> Create a button that displays the specified icon. If included, the boolean parameter determines the initial selection state of the button.

public JRadioButton(String text)
public JRadioButton(String text, boolean selected)
> Create a button that displays the specified text. If included, the boolean parameter determines the initial selection state of the button.

public JRadioButton(String text, Icon icon)
public JRadioButton(String text, Icon icon, boolean selected)
> Create a button that displays the specified text and icon. If included, the boolean parameter determines the initial selection state of the button.

Opaque JRadioButtons and JCheckBoxes

Typically, JRadioButtons and JCheckBoxes should be left transparent (not opaque) with their contentAreaFilled property set to false. These components usually fill only some of their allocated space, and making them opaque or filled causes an awkward-looking rectangle to be painted behind them, as shown in Figure 5-9.

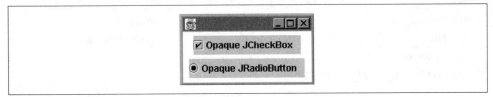

Figure 5-9. Opaque JCheckBox and JRadioButton

The ButtonGroup Class

The ButtonGroup class allows buttons to be logically grouped, guaranteeing that no more than one button in the group is selected at any given time. In fact, once one of the buttons is selected, the ButtonGroup ensures that exactly one button remains selected at all times. Note that this allows for an initial state (in which no button is selected) that can never be reached again once a selection is made, except programmatically.

As mentioned earlier, ButtonGroups typically hold JRadioButtons (or JRadioButtonMenuItems, discussed in Chapter 14), but this is purely a convention and is not enforced by ButtonGroup. ButtonGroup's add( ) method takes objects of type AbstractButton, so any button type may be added—even a mix of types. Of course, adding a JButton to a ButtonGroup would not be very useful since JButtons do not have selected and deselected states. In fact, JButtons added to ButtonGroups have no effect on the state of the other buttons if they are pressed.

ButtonGroup objects do not have any visual appearance; they simply provide a logical grouping of a set of buttons. You must add buttons in a ButtonGroup to a Container and lay them out as though no ButtonGroup were being used.

It's worth noting that some methods in the ButtonGroup class deal with AbstractButton objects and some deal with ButtonModel objects. The add( ), remove( ), and getElements( ) methods all use AbstractButton, while the getSelection( ), isSelected( ), and setSelected( ) methods use ButtonModel objects.

Properties

ButtonGroup defines the properties listed in Table 5-15. The buttonCount property is the number of buttons in the group. The elements property is an Enumeration of the AbstractButton objects contained by the group. The selection property contains the ButtonModel of the currently selected button.

Table 5-15. ButtonGroup properties

Property	Data type	get	is	set	Default value
buttonCount	int	•			0
elements	Enumeration	•			Empty
selection	ButtonModel	•			null

Voting with a Button Group

The following example demonstrates the use of a ButtonGroup to ensure that only a single selection is made from a list of choices. Listeners are added to the buttons to show which events are fired each time a new button is selected.

```
// SimpleButtonGroupExample.java
//
import javax.swing.*;
import java.awt.*;
import java.awt.event.*;

// A ButtonGroup voting booth
public class SimpleButtonGroupExample {

  public static void main(String[] args) {
    // Some choices
    JRadioButton choice1, choice2, choice3;
    choice1 = new JRadioButton("Bach: Well Tempered Clavier, Book I");
    choice1.setActionCommand("bach1");
    choice2 = new JRadioButton("Bach: Well Tempered Clavier, Book II");
    choice2.setActionCommand("bach2");
    choice3 = new JRadioButton("Shostakovich: 24 Preludes and Fugues");
    choice3.setActionCommand("shostakovich");

    // A group that ensures we vote for only one
    final ButtonGroup group = new ButtonGroup();
    group.add(choice1);
    group.add(choice2);
    group.add(choice3);

    // A simple ActionListener, showing each selection using the ButtonModel
    class VoteActionListener implements ActionListener {
      public void actionPerformed(ActionEvent ev) {
        String choice = group.getSelection().getActionCommand();
        System.out.println("ACTION Choice Selected: " + choice);
      }
    }
```

```
// A simple ItemListener, showing each selection and deselection
class VoteItemListener implements ItemListener {
  public void itemStateChanged(ItemEvent ev) {
    boolean selected = (ev.getStateChange( ) == ItemEvent.SELECTED);
    AbstractButton button = (AbstractButton)ev.getItemSelectable( );
    System.out.println("ITEM Choice Selected: " + selected +
                        ", Selection: " + button.getActionCommand( ));
  }
}

// Add listeners to each button.
ActionListener alisten = new VoteActionListener( );
choice1.addActionListener(alisten);
choice2.addActionListener(alisten);
choice3.addActionListener(alisten);

ItemListener ilisten = new VoteItemListener( );
choice1.addItemListener(ilisten);
choice2.addItemListener(ilisten);
choice3.addItemListener(ilisten);

// Throw everything together.
JFrame frame = new JFrame( );
frame.setDefaultCloseOperation(JFrame.EXIT_ON_CLOSE);
Container c = frame.getContentPane( );
c.setLayout(new GridLayout(0, 1));
c.add(new JLabel("Vote for your favorite prelude & fugue cycle"));
c.add(choice1);
c.add(choice2);
c.add(choice3);
frame.pack( );
frame.setVisible(true);
  }
}
```

We first create three radio buttons and add them to a button group. Then, we define an ActionListener and an ItemListener to print out some information each time a selection is made. We add both listeners to each button. The rest of the code is just layout.

When executed, the initial selection of a radio button produces the following output:

```
ITEM Choice Selected: true, Selection: shostakovich
ACTION Choice Selected: shostakovich
```

Changing the selection causes two item events to be fired, showing which button was toggled off and which was toggled on:

```
ITEM Choice Selected: false, Selection: shostakovich
ITEM Choice Selected: true, Selection: bach1
ACTION Choice Selected: bach1
```

Constructor

public ButtonGroup()
> Create an empty group.

Methods

public void add(AbstractButton b)
> Add a button to the group. If there is no selected button in the group, and the supplied button is selected, it becomes the group's selection. (Conversely, if there is already a selected button, adding a selected button does not change the selection; Swing adds the button to the group but if necessary deselects it first.)

public void remove(AbstractButton b)
> Remove a button from the group. If the removed button was the currently selected button, the group's selection is set to null.

public void setSelected(ButtonModel m, boolean b)
> Select the given button if the boolean parameter is true. If there was a previously selected button in the group, it is deselected. Calling this method with a false argument has no effect.

public boolean isSelected(ButtonModel m)
> This method indicates whether the given button is the group's currently selected button.

## CHAPTER 6

Bounded-Range Components

This chapter groups several Swing components together by the model that drives them: the *bounded-range model*. Bounded-range components in Swing include JSlider, JProgressBar, and JScrollBar. In addition, we discuss two classes that use progress bars: ProgressMonitor and ProgressMonitorInputStream. These classes display status dialogs using a JOptionPane that you can assign to a variety of tasks.

The Bounded-Range Model

Components that use the bounded-range model typically consist of an integer value that is constrained within two integer boundaries. The lower boundary, the *minimum*, should always be less than or equal to the model's current *value*. In addition, the model's value should always be less than the upper boundary, the *maximum*. The model's value can cover more than one unit; this size is referred to as its *extent*. With bounded range, the user is allowed to adjust the value of the model according to the rules of the component. If the value violates any of the rules, the model can adjust the values accordingly.

The javax.swing.BoundedRangeModel interface outlines the data model for such an object. Objects implementing the BoundedRangeModel interface must contain an adjustable integer value, an extent, a minimum, and a maximum. Swing contains three bounded-range components: JScrollBar, JSlider, and JProgressBar. These components are shown in Figure 6-1.

Properties

Table 6-1 shows the properties of the BoundedRangeModel interface.

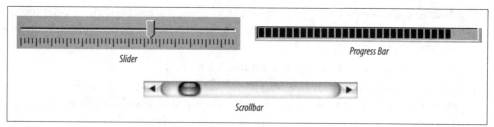

Figure 6-1. Bounded-range components in Swing

Table 6-1. BoundedRangeModel properties

Property	Data type	get	is	set	Default value
extent	int	•		•	
maximum	int	•		•	
minimum	int	•		•	
value	int	•		•	
valueIsAdjusting	boolean	•		•	

The minimum, maximum, and value properties form the actual bounded range. The extent property can give the value its own subrange. Extents can be used in situations where the model's value exceeds a single unit; they can also be changed dynamically. For example, the sliding "thumbs" of many scrollbars resize themselves based on the percentage of total information displayed in the window. If you wish to emulate this behavior with Swing, you could declare a bounded-range scrollbar and set the extent property to grow or shrink as necessary.

Figure 6-2 illustrates a bounded range with the following properties:

```
minimum = 1; maximum = 24; value = 9; extent = 3
```

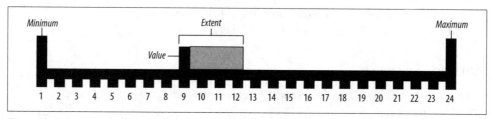

Figure 6-2. Properties of the BoundedRangeModel interface

Extents always define a range greater than the model's value, never less. If you do not want the value to have a subrange, you can set the extent to 0.

Here are some rules to remember when working with bounded ranges:

- If the user sets a new value that is outside the bounded range, the value is set to the closest boundary (minimum or maximum).

- If the user sets a new value so that extent exceeds the maximum, the model resets the value to the amount of the maximum minus the extent—thus preserving the width of the extent.
- If the user sets extent to a negative number, it is reset to 0.
- If the user sets extent large enough to exceed the maximum, the model resets extent to be the remaining width, if any, between the model's current value and its maximum.
- If the user resets the minimum or maximum so that the model's value now falls outside the bounded range, the value is adjusted to become the boundary closest to its original value.
- If a user resets a minimum so that it exceeds the maximum, the maximum and the value are reset to the new minimum. Conversely, if a new maximum is less than the current minimum, the minimum and value are adjusted to be the new maximum. In both cases, extent is reset to 0.
- If the user resets a minimum or maximum so that extent goes beyond the maximum, extent is decreased so it does not exceed the maximum.

Finally, the valueIsAdjusting property is a boolean that indicates that the model is undergoing changes. JSlider, for example, toggles this property to true while the user is dragging the thumb. This alerts any ChangeEvent listeners on the component that this event is probably one in a series, and they may choose not to react immediately.

Events

Objects implementing the BoundedRangeModel interface must fire a ChangeEvent when the model modifies its minimum, maximum, value, or extent properties. The BoundedRangeModel interface contains the standard methods for maintaining a list of ChangeEvent subscribers.

public abstract void addChangeListener(ChangeListener 1)
public abstract void removeChangeListener(ChangeListener 1)
   Add or remove a ChangeListener for receiving events when a property changes.

Method

public abstract void setRangeProperties(int value, int extent, int min, int max,
   boolean adjusting)
   Typically, one event is generated per property change. However, if you wish to make multiple changes without triggering events, you can call the setRangeProperties() method to change all five properties at once. This method generates a single ChangeEvent per call. For example:

```
setRangeProperties(40, 4, 32, 212, false); // Generates a single change event
```

The DefaultBoundedRangeModel Class

Swing provides a standard implementation of the BoundedRangeModel interface with the DefaultBoundedRangeModel class. This class provides the minimum functionality necessary to correctly implement the bounded-range model. Programmers are free to use and extend this class as they see fit.

Properties

The properties of the DefaultBoundedRangeModel class are identical to the properties of the interface it implements; it provides default values but doesn't otherwise add or change properties, as shown in Table 6-2. See the BoundedRangeModel interface earlier in this chapter for a description of the rules this component follows when the values of its properties are changed.

Table 6-2. DefaultBoundedRangeModel properties

Property	Data type	get	is	set	Default value
changeListeners[1.4]	ChangeListener[]	•			Empty array
extent[o]	int	•		•	0
maximum[o]	int	•		•	100
minimum[o]	int	•		•	0
value[o]	int	•		•	0
valueIsAdjusting[o]	boolean	•		•	false

[1.4]since 1.4, [o]overridden

Events

As specified by the bounded-range interface, the DefaultBoundedRangeModel fires a ChangeEvent when the model modifies its minimum, maximum, value, or extent properties.

public void addChangeListener(ChangeListener l)
public void removeChangeListener(ChangeListener l)
> Add or remove a change listener from the list of objects that receive a ChangeEvent when a property changes.

public EventListener[] getListeners(Class listenerType)
> This method was introduced in SDK 1.3 as a way of learning about the registered listeners. The changeListeners property added in 1.4 is a more convenient way to get the same information.

Constructors

public DefaultBoundedRangeModel()
> The default constructor for this class. It initializes a bounded-range model with a minimum of 0, a maximum of 100, and a value and extent of 0.

public DefaultBoundedRangeModel(int value, int extent, int minimum, int maximum)
> Initialize the bounded-range model with the specified values.

Working with the bounded-range model

Here is a program that helps to demonstrate some of the features of the `DefaultBoundedRangeModel` class and the bounded-range interface. We intentionally try to confuse the model to show how it reacts to inappropriate property values.

```java
//  Bounded.java
//
import java.awt.*;
import java.awt.event.*;
import java.util.*;
import javax.swing.*;
import javax.swing.event.*;

public class Bounded {
    public Bounded() {
        try {
            DefaultBoundedRangeModel model = new DefaultBoundedRangeModel( );
            ChangeListener myListener = new MyChangeListener( );
            model.addChangeListener(myListener);

            System.out.println(model.toString( ));
            System.out.println("Now setting minimum to 50 ...");
            model.setMinimum(50);
            System.out.println(model.toString( ));
            System.out.println("Now setting maximum to 40 ...");
            model.setMaximum(40);
            System.out.println(model.toString( ));
            System.out.println("Now setting maximum to 50 ...");
            model.setMaximum(50);
            System.out.println(model.toString( ));
            System.out.println("Now setting extent to 30 ...");
            model.setExtent(30);
            System.out.println(model.toString( ));

            System.out.println("Now setting several properties ...");
            if (!model.getValueIsAdjusting( )) {
                model.setValueIsAdjusting(true);
                System.out.println(model.toString( ));
                model.setMinimum(0);
                model.setMaximum(100);
                model.setExtent(20);
                model.setValueIsAdjusting(false);
            }
```

```
        System.out.println(model.toString());
    } catch (Exception e) { e.printStackTrace(); }
}

class MyChangeListener implements ChangeListener {
    public void stateChanged(ChangeEvent e) {
        System.out.println("A ChangeEvent has been fired!");
    }
}

public static void main(String args[]) { new Bounded(); }
}
```

Let's go through the output step by step. The first step is to define a DefaultBoundedRangeModel and attach a ChangeListener to it. After doing so, we print the default values of the model:

```
DefaultBoundedRangeModel[value=0, extent=0, min=0, max=100, adj=false]
```

Here, we set the minimum to 50 and the maximum to a value smaller than the minimum, 40. Looks like trouble ahead...

```
Now setting minimum to 50...
A ChangeEvent has been fired!
DefaultBoundedRangeModel[value=50, extent=0, min=50, max=100, adj=false]
Now setting maximum to 40 (smaller than min)...
A ChangeEvent has been fired!
DefaultBoundedRangeModel[value=40, extent=0, min=40, max=40, adj=false]
```

There are two things to note here. First, by resetting the minimum to 50, we let the value property fall outside the bounded range. The model compensated by raising the value to match the new minimum. Second, we threw a monkey wrench into the model by setting the maximum less than the minimum. However, the bounded-range model adjusted the minimum and the value accordingly to match the newly specified maximum.

Now let's try a different tactic:

```
Now setting maximum to 50...
A ChangeEvent has been fired!
DefaultBoundedRangeModel[value=40, extent=0, min=40, max=50, adj=false]
Now setting extent to 30 (greater than max)...
A ChangeEvent has been fired!
DefaultBoundedRangeModel[value=40, extent=10, min=40, max=50, adj=false]
```

Here, we see what happens when we try to set an extent with a subrange greater than the current maximum—the model shortens the extent so that it falls within the bounded range. The same thing occurs if we reset the value of the extent's subrange so that it violates the maximum.

Finally, we activate the valueIsAdjusting property to notify any listeners that this is one in a series of changes, and the listener does not need to react immediately:

```
Now setting several properties...
A ChangeEvent has been fired!
```

```
DefaultBoundedRangeModel[value=40, extent=10, min=40, max=50, adj=true]
A ChangeEvent has been fired!
A ChangeEvent has been fired!
A ChangeEvent has been fired!
A ChangeEvent has been fired!
DefaultBoundedRangeModel[value=40, extent=20, min=0, max=100, adj=false]
```

The JScrollBar Class

JScrollBar is the Swing implementation of a scrollbar. The JScrollBar class is shown in various L&Fs in Figure 6-3.

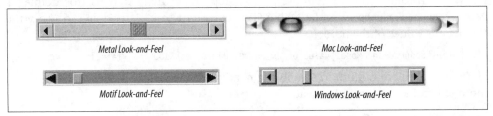

Figure 6-3. Scrollbars in several L&Fs

To program with a scrollbar, it is important to understand its anatomy. Scrollbars are composed of a rectangular tab, called a *slider* or *thumb*, located between two arrow buttons. The arrow buttons on either end increment or decrement the slider's position by an adjustable number of units, generally one. In addition, clicking in the area between the thumb and the end buttons (often called the *paging area*) moves the slider one *block*, or 10 units by default. The user can modify the value of the scrollbar in one of three ways: by dragging the thumb in either direction, by pushing on either of the arrow buttons, or by clicking in the paging area.

Scrollbars can have one of two orientations: horizontal or vertical. Figure 6-4 provides an illustration of a horizontal scrollbar. JScrollBar uses the bounded-range model to represent the scrollbar's data. The assignment of each bounded-range property is also shown in Figure 6-5. The minimum and maximum of the scrollbar fall on the interior edges of the arrow buttons. The scrollbar's value is defined as the left (or top) edge of the slider. Finally, the extent of the scrollbar defines the width of the thumb in relation to the total range. (The older Adjustable interface from the java.awt package referred to the extent as the "visible amount.") Note that horizontal scrollbars increment to the right and vertical scrollbars increment downward.

Properties

Table 6-3 shows the properties of the JScrollBar component. Most of these properties come from the java.awt.Adjustable interface. The orientation property gives the direction of the scrollbar, either JScrollBar.HORIZONTAL or JScrollBar.VERTICAL. The unitIncrement property represents the integer amount by which the bounded-range

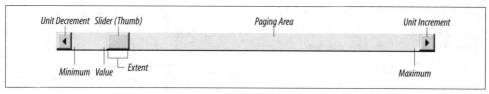

Figure 6-4. Anatomy of a horizontal scrollbar

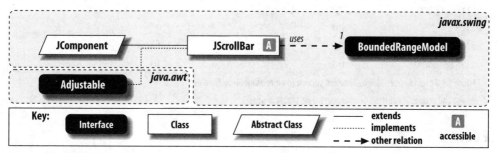

Figure 6-5. JScrollBar class diagram

value changes when the user clicks on either of the arrow buttons. The blockIncrement property represents the integer amount by which the scrollbar value changes when the user clicks in either of the paging areas. The enabled property indicates whether the scrollbar can generate or respond to events. The minimum, maximum, value, and valueIsAdjusting properties match the equivalent properties in the BoundedRangeModel of the scrollbar. The visibleAmount property matches the extent property in the model; it indicates the thickness of the thumb. The minimumSize and maximumSize properties allow the scrollbar to behave appropriately when it is resized.

Table 6-3. JScrollBar properties

Property	Data type	get	is	set	Default value
accessibleContext[o]	AccessibleContext	•			JScrollBarAccessibleJ-ScrollBar()
adjustment-Listeners[1.4]	Adjustment-Listener[]	•			Empty array
blockIncrement[b, o, *]	int	•		•	10
enabled[o]	boolean			•	true
maximum[o]	int	•		•	100
maximumSize[o]	Dimension	•			
minimum[o]	int	•		•	0
minimumSize[o]	Dimension	•			
model[b]	BoundedRangeModel	•		•	DefaultBoundedRangeModel()

[1.4]since 1.4, [b]bound, [o]overridden, [*]indexed version (on direction) also available

See also the properties of the JComponent class (Table 3-6).

Table 6-3. JScrollBar properties (continued)

Property	Data type	get	is	set	Default value
orientation[b, o]	int	•		•	JScrollBar.VERTICAL
UI[b, o]	ScrollBarUI	•		•	From L&F
UIClassID[o]	String	•			"ScrollBarUI"
unitIncrement[b, o, *]	int	•		•	1
value[o]	int	•		•	0
valueIsAdjusting	boolean	•		•	false
visibleAmount[o]	int	•		•	10

[1.4]since 1.4, [b]bound, [o]overridden, [*]indexed version (on direction) also available

See also the properties of the JComponent class (Table 3-6).

Events

JScrollBar objects trigger java.awt.event.AdjustmentEvents whenever the component undergoes a change. Recall, however, that the bounded-range model generates a ChangeEvent when one of its properties changes. It becomes the responsibility of the JScrollBar class to convert change events to adjustment events and pass them on to registered listeners. Figure 6-6 shows the sequence of events between the component, model, and delegate when the user drags the scrollbar. JScrollBar also generates a PropertyChangeEvent when any of its bound properties change.

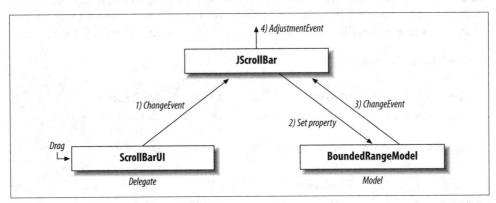

Figure 6-6. Chain of events after the user drags the scrollbar

Because JScrollBar was meant as a drop-in replacement for the AWT scrollbar, the older event system has been preserved to maintain consistency with the AWT 1.1 Adjustable interface. However, with Swing, the majority of cases in which you would have used a scrollbar have been taken care of with the JScrollPane class. You rarely need a standalone JScrollBar. (See Chapter 11 for more information on JScrollPane.)

The following methods are defined in the JScrollBar class:

public void addAdjustmentListener(AdjustmentListener l)
public void removeAdjustmentListener(AdjustmentListener l)
    Add or remove a specific listener for AdjustmentEvents from the scrollbar.

Constructors

public JScrollBar( )
public JScrollBar(int orientation)
public JScrollBar(int orientation, int value, int extent, int minimum, int maximum)
    Set the initial values of the scrollbar. If either of the first two constructors is invoked, the scrollbar initializes itself using the default values shown in Table 6-3. The orientation must be either JScrollBar.HORIZONTAL or JScrollBar.VERTICAL, or else the constructor throws a runtime IllegalArgumentException. If desired, the last four parameters in the third constructor can be used to initialize the scrollbar's bounded-range model to new values.

Miscellaneous

public int getUnitIncrement(int direction)
public int getBlockIncrement(int direction)
    Convenience methods that return the scrollbar unit and block increments for a particular direction. The direction is -1 for down and left, and 1 for up and right. These methods are typically invoked by the UI delegate to determine how far to increment in a particular direction. Subclasses can override these methods to specify the units to increment in either direction, based on the content represented. For example, if a scrollbar was attached to a word-processing document, the variable-sized text in the document could result in different unit increments at any particular time for a vertical scrollbar.

public void setValues(int newValue, int newExtent, int newMinimum, int newMaximum)
    This method maps to the setRangeValues( ) method in the BoundedRangeModel interface.

Handling Events from a Scrollbar

The following program demonstrates how to monitor events generated by a pair of scrollbars:

```
// ScrollBarExample.java
//
import java.awt.*;
import java.awt.event.*;
import javax.swing.*;
```

```
public class ScrollBarExample extends JPanel {

    JLabel label;

    public ScrollBarExample() {
        super(true);
        label=new JLabel();
        setLayout(new BorderLayout());

        JScrollBar hbar=new JScrollBar(JScrollBar.HORIZONTAL, 30, 20, 0, 300);
        JScrollBar vbar=new JScrollBar(JScrollBar.VERTICAL, 30, 40, 0, 300);

        hbar.setUnitIncrement(2);
        hbar.setBlockIncrement(1);

        hbar.addAdjustmentListener(new MyAdjustmentListener());
        vbar.addAdjustmentListener(new MyAdjustmentListener());

        add(hbar, BorderLayout.SOUTH);
        add(vbar, BorderLayout.EAST);
        add(label, BorderLayout.CENTER);
    }

    class MyAdjustmentListener implements AdjustmentListener {
        public void adjustmentValueChanged(AdjustmentEvent e) {
            label.setText("    New Value is " + e.getValue() + "        ");
            repaint();
        }
    }

    public static void main(String s[]) {
        JFrame frame = new JFrame("Scroll Bar Example");
        frame.setDefaultCloseOperation(JFrame.EXIT_ON_CLOSE);
        frame.setContentPane(new ScrollBarExample());
        frame.setSize(200,200);
        frame.setVisible(true);
    }
}
```

The code is relatively easy to follow. The application creates a single panel and adds two scrollbars, one on the right side and one on the bottom. It then listens for any adjustments in either scrollbar and paints the scrollbar's new value in the middle of the panel. Figure 6-7 shows the result.

The JSlider Class

The JSlider class represents a graphical slider. Like scrollbars, sliders can have either a horizontal or vertical orientation. With sliders, however, you can enhance their appearance with tick marks and labels. The class hierarchy is illustrated in Figure 6-8. In most instances, a slider is preferable to a standalone scrollbar. Sliders

Figure 6-7. A simple scrollbar example

represent a selection of one value from a bounded range. Scrollbars represent a range of values within a bounded range and are best used in things like the JScrollPane.

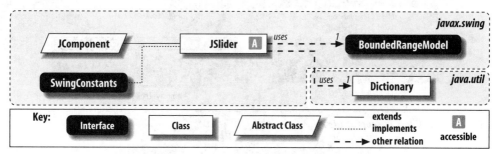

Figure 6-8. JSlider class diagram

The JSlider class allows you to set the spacing of two types of tick marks: major and minor. Major tick marks are longer than minor tick marks and are generally used at wider intervals. Figure 6-9 shows various sliders that can be composed in Swing.

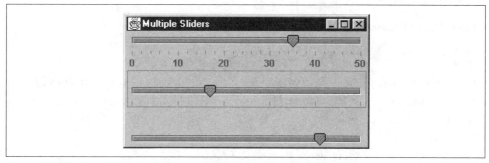

Figure 6-9. Various sliders in Swing

The setPaintTicks() method sets a boolean, which is used to activate or deactivate the slider's tick marks. In some L&Fs, the slider changes from a rectangular shape to a pointer when tick marks are activated. This is often done to give the user a more accurate representation of where the slider falls.

You can create a `Dictionary` of `Component` objects to annotate the slider. Each entry in the `Dictionary` consists of two fields: an `Integer` key, which supplies the index to draw the various components, followed by the component itself. If you do not wish to create your own label components, you can use the `createStandardLabels()` method to create a series of `JLabel` objects for you. In addition, if you set the `paintLabels` property to `true` and give a positive value to the `majorTickSpacing` property, a set of labels that matches the major tick marks is automatically created. Figure 6-10 shows what a `JSlider` looks like in four L&Fs.

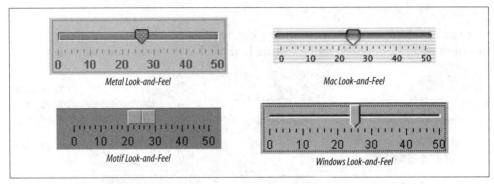

Figure 6-10. Sliders in several L&Fs

Properties

Table 6-4 shows the properties of the `JSlider` component. The slider object has several properties in addition to those of its data model. The `orientation` property determines which way the slider moves. It can be one of two values: `JSlider.HORIZONTAL` or `JSlider.VERTICAL`.

Table 6-4. JSlider properties

Property	Data type	get	is	set	Default value
accessibleContext[o]	AccessibleContext	•			JSlider.AccessibleJSlider()
changeListeners[1.4]	ChangeListener[]	•			Empty array
extent	int	•		•	0
inverted[b]	boolean	•		•	false
labelTable[b]	Dictionary	•		•	null
majorTickSpacing[b]	int	•		•	10

[1.4]since 1.4, [b]bound, [o]overridden

See also properties from the `JComponent` class (Table 3-6).

Table 6-4. JSlider properties (continued)

Property	Data type	get	is	set	Default value
maximum[b]	int	•		•	100
minimum[b]	int	•		•	0
minorTickSpacing[b]	int	•		•	2
model[b]	BoundedRangeModel	•		•	DefaultBoundedRangeModel
orientation[b]	int	•		•	JSlider.HORIZONTAL
paintLabels[b]	boolean	•		•	false
paintTicks[b]	boolean	•		•	false
paintTrack[b]	boolean	•		•	true
snapToTicks[b]	boolean	•		•	true
UI[b]	SliderUI	•		•	From L&F
UIClassID[o]	String	•			"SliderUI"
value	int	•		•	50
valueIsAdjusting	boolean	•		•	false

[1.4]since 1.4, [b]bound, [o]overridden

See also properties from the JComponent class (Table 3-6).

The labelTable is a Dictionary of slider values and JLabel objects. The labels in this dictionary are used to label the slider; they can be explicitly set by the user or generated automatically by calling createStandardLabels( ), which we'll discuss later. The paintLabels property is a boolean that determines whether to paint the textual labels associated with the slider. If paintLabels is set to true, the JLabel objects in the labelTable are painted at the appropriate locations in the slider.

The paintTicks property is a boolean; it decides if the major and minor tick marks are drawn. If it is true, both types of tick marks are drawn (unless their spacing is set to 0—see the last paragraph in this section). The snapToTicks property indicates whether the slider adjusts its value to the nearest tick. The paintTrack property controls whether the "track" on the slider is painted. If the inverted property is false, then the table increments from left to right or from bottom to top; if the property is true, the table increments from right to left or from top to bottom. All tick marks and labels are shifted accordingly.

The minimum, maximum, value, and valueIsAdjusting properties match the equivalent properties in the BoundedRangeModel of the slider. The extent property is slightly different from the model; it tells how much the slider increments up or down when L&F-specific keys are pressed (generally, PageUp and PageDown).

The majorTickSpacing and minorTickSpacing properties decide the repetition rate of the tick marks. In the event that both a major and minor tick mark occupy the same position, the major wins out. Neither property should ever be less than zero. If you want to prevent either type of tick mark from being drawn, give it a spacing value of 0.

Client properties

The JSlider object contains one client property that works only with the Metal L&F: JSlider.isFilled. When this client property is set to true, as shown in Figure 6-11, the result is a slider component that fills itself only on its descending half:

```
JSlider slider = new JSlider();
slider.putClientProperty("JSlider.isFilled", Boolean.TRUE);
```

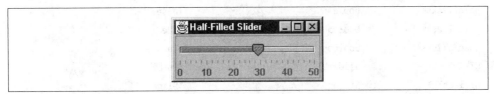

Figure 6-11. JSlider with the isFilled client property set (Metal L&F)

Events

JSlider triggers a ChangeEvent whenever the user modifies any of its properties. It also generates a PropertyChangeEvent whenever any of its properties change.

public void addChangeListener(ChangeListener l)
public void removeChangeListener(ChangeListener l)
 Add or remove a specific listener from receiving property change events generated by the JSlider object.

Constructors

public JSlider()
public JSlider(int orientation)
public JSlider(int min, int max)
public JSlider(int min, int max, int value)
public JSlider(int orientation, int minimum, int maximum, int value)
public JSlider(BoundedRangeModel brm)
 Set the initial values of the slider. The orientation must be either JSlider.HORIZONTAL
 or JSlider.VERTICAL. If anything else is passed in, the JSlider object throws a runtime
 IllegalArgumentException. The remaining parameters are used to initialize the slider's
 bounded-range model. If the parameters are not given, they are initialized to the
 default values in Table 6-4. The final constructor accepts a bounded-range model
 object to initialize the slider.

Labels

public Hashtable createStandardLabels(int increment)
public Hashtable createStandardLabels(int increment, int start)

Utility functions that create a hashtable of numeric labels, starting at the value specified by start (or the minimum if omitted), and incrementing by the value specified by increment. The resulting Hashtable can be placed in the labelTable property, and its labels are drawn on the slider if the drawLabels property is set to true.

Miscellaneous

public void updateUI()

Signal that a new L&F has been set using the setUI( ) accessor. Invoking this method forces the slider component to reset its view using the new UI delegate.

Creating a Slider

The following program shows how to create a full-featured slider:

```
// SliderExample.java
//
import java.awt.*;
import java.awt.event.*;
import javax.swing.*;
import javax.swing.border.*;

public class SliderExample extends JPanel {

    public SliderExample() {

        super(true);
        this.setLayout(new BorderLayout());
        JSlider slider = new JSlider(JSlider.HORIZONTAL, 0, 50, 25);

        slider.setMinorTickSpacing(2);
        slider.setMajorTickSpacing(10);
        slider.setPaintTicks(true);
        slider.setPaintLabels(true);

        // We'll use just the standard numeric labels for now.
        slider.setLabelTable(slider.createStandardLabels(10));

        add(slider, BorderLayout.CENTER);
    }

    public static void main(String s[]) {
        JFrame frame = new JFrame("Slider Example");
        frame.setDefaultCloseOperation(JFrame.EXIT_ON_CLOSE);
        frame.setContentPane(new SliderExample());
```

```
        frame.pack();
        frame.setVisible(true);
    }
}
```

This code yields the slider shown in Figure 6-12.

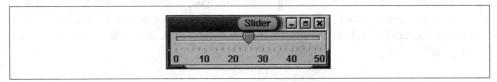

Figure 6-12. Swing slider

The JProgressBar Class

Swing makes it easy to create progress bars. Applications typically use progress bars to report the status of time-consuming jobs, such as software installation or large amounts of copying. The bars themselves are simply rectangles of an arbitrary length, a percentage of which is filled based on the model's value. Swing progress bars come in two flavors: horizontal and vertical. If the orientation is horizontal, the bar fills from left to right. If the bar is vertical, it fills from bottom to top. SDK 1.4 added the ability to show indeterminate progress (progress when you don't know the total). The class hierarchy is illustrated in Figure 6-13.

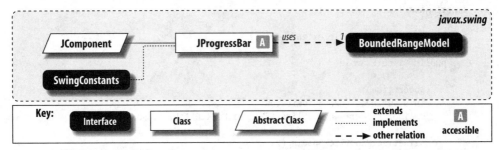

Figure 6-13. JProgressBar class diagram

Different L&Fs can contain different filling styles. Metal, for example, uses a solid fill, while the Windows L&F uses an LCD style, which means that the bar indicates progress by filling itself with dark, adjacent rectangles instead of with a fluid line (at the opposite extreme, the Mac's is so fluid that it even contains moving ripples). The JProgressBar class also contains a boolean property that specifies whether the progress bar draws a dark border around itself. You can override this default border by setting the border property of the JComponent. Figure 6-14 shows a Swing progress bar with the different L&Fs.

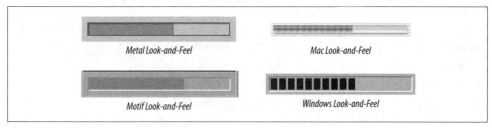

Figure 6-14. Progress bars in various L&Fs

Properties

The basic properties of the JProgressBar object are listed in Table 6-5. The orientation property determines which way the progress bar lies; it must be either JProgressBar.HORIZONTAL or JProgressBar.VERTICAL. The minimum, maximum, and value properties mirror those in the bounded-range model. If you don't really know the maximum, you can set the indeterminate value to true. That setting causes the progress bar to show an animation indicating that you don't know when the operation completes. (Some L&Fs might not support this feature.) The boolean borderPainted indicates whether the component's border should appear around the progress bar. Borders are routinely combined with progress bars—they not only tell the user where its boundaries lie, but also help to set off the progress bar from other components. An important note about the JProgressBar class: there are no methods to access the extent variable of its bounded-range model. This property is irrelevant in the progress bar component.

Table 6-5. JProgressBar properties

Property	Data type	get	is	set	Default value
accessible-Context[o]	AccessibleContext	•			JProgressBarAccessibleJProgressBar()
borderPainted[b]	boolean		•	•	true
changeListeners[1.4]	ChangeListener[]	•			Empty array
indeterminate[b, 1.4]	boolean		•	•	false
maximum	int	•		•	100
minimum	int	•		•	0
model	BoundedRangeModel	•		•	DefaultBoundedRangeModel()
orientation[b]	int	•		•	JProgressBar.HORIZONTAL
percentComplete	double	•	•		

[1.4]since 1.4, [b]bound, [o]overridden

See also properties from the JComponent class (Table 3-6).

Table 6-5. JProgressBar properties (continued)

Property	Data type	get	.is	set	Default value
string[b]	String	•		•	null
stringPainted[b]	boolean	•		•	false
UI[b]	progressBarUI	•		•	From L&F
UIClassID[o]	String	•			"ProgressBarUI"
value[b]	int	•		•	0

[1.4]since 1.4, [b]bound, [o]overridden

See also properties from the JComponent class (Table 3-6).

Three properties control whether a string is painted onto the progress bar. stringPainted is true if the string should appear. The string property is the actual string that will be painted. If it is null, the progress bar displays the value of percentComplete, converted to a percentage between 0 and 100 (e.g., "35%"). Regardless of the string property setting, percentComplete holds the completion value as a number between 0.0 and 1.0.

Events

JProgressBar triggers a ChangeEvent whenever the user modifies any of its properties and a PropertyChangeEvent when a bound property changes.

public void addChangeListener(ChangeListener l)
public void removeChangeListener(ChangeListener l)
   Add or remove a specific listener for ChangeEvent notifications from the component.

Constructors

public JProgressBar( )
   Create a horizontal progress bar with a lowered border. The DefaultBoundedRangeModel is used as the data model for the progress bar.

public JProgressBar(BoundedRangeModel model)
public JProgressBar(int orient, int min, int max)
public JProgressBar(int min, int max)
public JProgressBar(int orient)
   These constructors create progress bars with initial values specified by their arguments. In the first of these constructors, model supplies the initial values and serves as the data model of the progress bar.

Working with Progress Bars

Like the other bounded-range components, progress bars are easy to work with. This example displays a simple progress bar that fills from left to right by updating itself every 0.1 seconds:

```
//  ProgressBarExample.java
//
import java.awt.*;
import java.awt.event.*;
import javax.swing.*;

public class ProgressBarExample extends JPanel {

  JProgressBar pbar;
  static final int MY_MINIMUM=0;
  static final int MY_MAXIMUM=100;

  public ProgressBarExample() {
     pbar = new JProgressBar();
     pbar.setMinimum(MY_MINIMUM);
     pbar.setMaximum(MY_MAXIMUM);
     add(pbar);
  }

  public void updateBar(int newValue) {
    pbar.setValue(newValue);
  }

  public static void main(String args[]) {

     final ProgressBarExample it = new ProgressBarExample();

     JFrame frame = new JFrame("Progress Bar Example");
     frame.setDefaultCloseOperation(JFrame.EXIT_ON_CLOSE);
     frame.setContentPane(it);
     frame.pack();
     frame.setVisible(true);

     for (int i = MY_MINIMUM; i <= MY_MAXIMUM; i++) {
       final int percent=i;
       try {
       SwingUtilities.invokeLater(new Runnable() {
           public void run() {
              it.updateBar(percent);
           }
       });
       java.lang.Thread.sleep(100);
       } catch (InterruptedException e) {;}
     }
  }
}
```

We used SwingUtilities.invokeLater( ) here because we are updating the user interface from within our own thread (rather than from the event-handling thread). For more information on working with multiple threads in Swing, see Chapter 28.

Monitoring Progress

By themselves, progress bars are pretty boring. Swing, however, combines progress bars with the dialog capabilities of JOptionPane to create the ProgressMonitor and ProgressMonitorInputStream classes. You can use ProgressMonitor to report on the current progress of a potentially long task. You can use ProgressMonitorInputStream to automatically monitor the amount of data that has been read in with an InputStream. With both, you can define various strings to be posted in the progress monitor dialogs to offer a better explanation of the task at hand.

The ProgressMonitor Class

The ProgressMonitor class is a generic progress dialog box that can be used for practically anything. There are two string descriptions that can be set on a ProgressMonitor dialog box. The first is a static component that can never change; it appears on the top of the dialog and is set in the constructor. The second is a variable string-based property that can be reset at any time. It appears below the static string, slightly above the progress bar. Figure 6-15 shows the structure for this class.

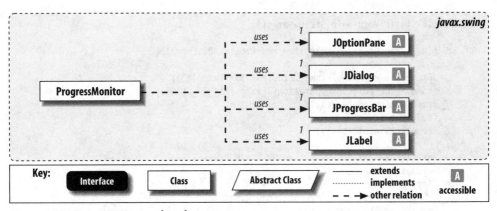

Figure 6-15. ProgressMonitor class diagram

Once instantiated, the ProgressMonitor dialog (shown in Figure 6-16) does not pop up immediately. The dialog waits a configurable amount of time before deciding whether the task at hand is long enough to warrant the dialog. If it is, the dialog is displayed. When the current value of the progress bar is greater than or equal to the maximum, as specified in the constructor, the progress monitor dialog closes. If you need to close the progress monitor early, you can call the close( ) method. The user can close this dialog as well by pressing OK or Cancel; you can test the canceled property to see if the user wanted to cancel the operation or simply did not care to watch the progress.

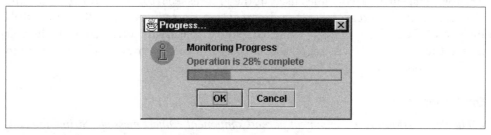

Figure 6-16. The ProgressMonitor dialog

 The `ProgressMonitor` class does not fire any events indicating that it is complete or that the operation was canceled. You should test the `isCancelled( )` method each time you call `setProgress( )` to see if the user has canceled the dialog.

Properties

Table 6-6 shows the properties for the `ProgressMonitor` class. The canceled property is a boolean that indicates whether the progress monitor has been canceled. This is useful if you need to determine whether the user dismissed the dialog halfway through. The `minimum` and `maximum` properties define the range of the progress bar; the `progress` property is analogous to the progress bar's current value. The `note` property is a string that can be updated as the progress monitor works; it serves to indicate what the progress monitor is currently doing.

Table 6-6. ProgressMonitor properties

Property	Data type	get	is	set	Default value
canceled	boolean		•		false
maximum	int	•		•	100
millisToDecideToPopup	int	•		•	500
millisToPopup	int	•		•	2000
minimum	int	•		•	0
note	String	•		•	
progress	int	•		•	0

As we said, the progress monitor dialog does not pop up immediately. Instead, it waits `millisToDecideToPopup` milliseconds before estimating how long the current progress might take. If it appears that it will take longer than `millisToPopup` milliseconds, a progress monitor dialog pops up.

UIManager properties. Two values used in the `ProgressMonitor` are extracted from the UIManager settings. `ProgressMonitor.progressText` (introduced in SDK 1.3) controls the text of the dialog's title bar while `OptionPane.cancelButtonText` controls the text on the Cancel button. See `ProgressMonitorExample` below for an example of how to set these properties.

Constructor

public ProgressMonitor(Component parentComponent, Object message, String note, int min, int max)
> Create a `ProgressMonitor` dialog box, placed above the component specified as `parentComponent`. The dialog contains a static `message` that is constant throughout the life of the dialog (see `JOptionPane` in Chapter 10 for a discussion of valid values) and a note that changes during the life of the dialog. If the `note` value is initially `null`, the note cannot be updated throughout the life of the dialog. The min and max values specify the minimum and maximum of the progress bar.

Miscellaneous

public void close()
> Force the `ProgressMonitor` to shut down, even if it did not complete all of its tasks.

Using a progress monitor

The following example shows a `ProgressMonitor` in action. With it, we simulate updating the dialog with a timer that fires off events every 0.5 seconds. We use the `invokeLater()` method to place the update on the system event queue. The `run()` method of the `Update` inner class simply increments the progress bar's `progress` property, updates the text on the progress bar, and updates the counter. The result is shown in Figure 6-16.

```
// ProgressMonitorExample.java
//
import java.awt.*;
import java.awt.event.*;
import javax.swing.*;

public class ProgressMonitorExample extends JFrame implements ActionListener {

    static ProgressMonitor pbar;
    static int counter = 0;

    public ProgressMonitorExample() {
        super("Progress Monitor Demo");
```

```
        setSize(250,100);
        setDefaultCloseOperation(JFrame.EXIT_ON_CLOSE);

        pbar = new ProgressMonitor(null, "Monitoring Progress",
                "Initializing . . .", 0, 100);

        // Fire a timer every once in a while to update the progress.
        Timer timer = new Timer(500, this);
        timer.start();
        setVisible(true);
    }

    public static void main(String args[]) {
        UIManager.put("ProgressMonitor.progressText", "This is progress?");
        UIManager.put("OptionPane.cancelButtonText", "Go Away");
        new ProgressMonitorExample();
    }

    public void actionPerformed(ActionEvent e) {
        // Invoked by the timer every 0.5 seconds. Simply place
        // the progress monitor update on the event queue.
        SwingUtilities.invokeLater(new Update());
    }

    class Update implements Runnable {
        public void run() {
            if (pbar.isCanceled()) {
                pbar.close();
                System.exit(1);
            }
            pbar.setProgress(counter);
            pbar.setNote("Operation is "+counter+"% complete");
            counter += 2;
        }
    }
}
```

The ProgressMonitorInputStream

The ProgressMonitorInputStream is a stream filter that allows the programmer to monitor the amount of data read from an input stream. It contains a ProgressMonitor object that the user can access to see how the reading of the input stream is progressing. Figure 6-17 shows the class diagram for this filter.

For the most part, the ProgressMonitorInputStream class contains many of the methods found in java.io.InputStream. Like all FilterInputStream objects, you can tie this class together with other filters for better control over the input. Figure 6-18 shows the progress monitor dialog associated with a typical ProgressMonitorInputStream.

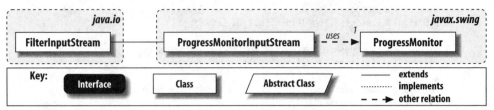

Figure 6-17. JProgressMonitorInputStream class diagram

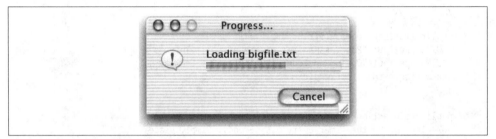

Figure 6-18. The ProgressMonitorInputStream dialog

Property

Table 6-7 shows the only property of the `ProgressMonitorInputStream`. `progressMonitor` contains the progress monitor defined inside this object. The read-only accessor allows you to change the progress or the note string, as well as close the dialog.

Table 6-7. ProgressMonitorInputStream property

Property	Data type	get	is	set	Default value
progressMonitor	ProgressMonitor	•			ProgressMonitor()

When it's created, the `ProgressMonitorInputStream` attempts to read the amount of data available and updates the progress monitor's progress property as bytes are read from the stream. This can lead to strange results if you wrap a `ProgressMonitorInputStream` around some other input stream for which the amount of data waiting to be read isn't well-defined—for example, a `PipedInputStream`. It's a good idea to read small amounts of data from a `ProgressMonitorInputStream` at a time. This way, the dialog has a chance to update its progress frequently. Finally, as with any blocking request, try not to perform a `read( )` while on the event dispatching queue. That way, if the call blocks for an inordinate amount of time, you won't drag down any repainting requests and give the illusion that your application has crashed.

Constructor

public ProgressMonitorInputStream(Component parentComponent, Object message, InputStream in)

Create a `ProgressMonitorInputStream` dialog box, placed above the `parentComponent`. The dialog contains a static `message` that is constant throughout the life of the dialog (see `JOptionPane` in Chapter 10 for a discussion of valid values). The constructor also takes a reference to the target input stream.

InputStream methods

public int read( ) throws IOException

Read a single byte and update the progress monitor.

public int read(byte b[]) throws IOException
public int read(byte b[], int off, int len) throws IOException

Read an array of bytes and update the progress monitor.

public long skip(long n) throws IOException

Skip a series of bytes and update the progress monitor.

public void close( ) throws IOException

Close the input stream and the progress monitor.

public void reset( ) throws IOException

Reset the current reading position back to the beginning and update the progress monitor.

Using a ProgressMonitorInputStream

Here is a simple example that demonstrates using a `ProgressMonitorInputStream` class to monitor the progress of loading a file. You can specify the name of the file on the command line as follows:

```
% java ProgressMonitorInputExample myfile
```

This program reads in the file a little at a time, dumping the results to the screen. If the file is not found, an error dialog is displayed. Note that we specifically don't try to buffer the input—we want "bad" performance to make sure the monitor dialog has time to pop up. (Still, you may need to load a fairly large file.) If you run the program, be sure to load a text file (not a binary file). Here is the source code:

```
// ProgressMonitorInputExample.java
//
import java.io.*;
import java.awt.*;
import javax.swing.*;

public class ProgressMonitorInputExample {

    public ProgressMonitorInputExample(String filename) {
        ProgressMonitorInputStream monitor;
```

```
        try {
            monitor = new ProgressMonitorInputStream(
                null, "Loading "+filename, new FileInputStream(filename));
            while (monitor.available( ) > 0) {
                byte[] data = new byte[38];
                monitor.read(data);
                System.out.write(data);
            }
        } catch (FileNotFoundException e) {
            JOptionPane.showMessageDialog(null, "Unable to find file: "
                + filename, "Error", JOptionPane.ERROR_MESSAGE);
        } catch (IOException e) {;}
    }

    public static void main(String args[]) {
        new ProgressMonitorInputExample(args[0]);
    }
}
```

## CHAPTER 7

Lists, Combo Boxes, and Spinners

This chapter deals with three similar components: lists, combo boxes, and spinners. All three present a catalog of choices to the user. A list allows the user to make single or multiple selections. A combo box permits only a single selection but can be combined with a text field that allows the user to type in a value as well. From a design standpoint, both lists and combo boxes share similar characteristics, and both can be extended in ways that many Swing components cannot. SDK 1.4 introduced spinners, which are compact components that allow you to click or "spin" through a set of choices one at a time.

Lists

A *list* is a graphical component that presents the user with choices. Lists typically display several items at a time, allowing the user to make either a single selection or multiple selections. In the event that the inventory of the list exceeds the space available to the component, the list is often coupled with a scrollpane to allow navigation through the entire set of choices.

The Swing JList component allows elements to be any Java class capable of being rendered—which is to say anything at all because you can supply your own renderer. This offers a wide range of flexibility; list components can be as simple or as complex as the programmer's needs dictate.

Let's get our feet wet with a simple list. The following example uses the Swing list class, JList, to create a single-selection list composed only of strings. Figure 7-1 shows the result.

```
// SimpleList.java
//
import java.awt.*;
import java.awt.event.*;
import javax.swing.*;
```

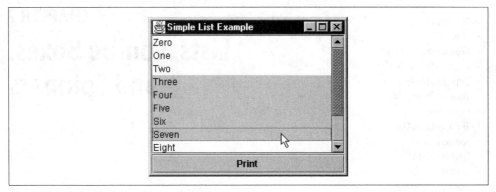

Figure 7-1. A simple Swing list

```java
public class SimpleList extends JPanel {
    String label[] = { "Zero","One","Two","Three","Four","Five","Six",
                        "Seven","Eight","Nine","Ten","Eleven" };
    JList list;

    public SimpleList( ) {
        this.setLayout(new BorderLayout( ));
        list = new JList(label);
        JScrollPane pane = new JScrollPane(list);
        JButton button = new JButton("Print");
        button.addActionListener(new PrintListener( ));

        add(pane, BorderLayout.CENTER);
        add(button, BorderLayout.SOUTH);
    }

    public static void main(String s[]) {
        JFrame frame = new JFrame("Simple List Example");
        frame.setDefaultCloseOperation(JFrame.EXIT_ON_CLOSE);
        frame.setContentPane(new SimpleList( ));
        frame.setSize(250, 200);
        frame.setVisible(true);
    }

    // An inner class to respond to clicks of the Print button
    class PrintListener implements ActionListener {
        public void actionPerformed(ActionEvent e) {
            int selected[] = list.getSelectedIndices( );
            System.out.println("Selected Elements:  ");

            for (int i=0; i < selected.length; i++) {
                String element =
                    (String)list.getModel( ).getElementAt(selected[i]);
                System.out.println("  " + element);
            }
        }
    }
}
```

Take a close look at the source. The first thing you might notice is that we embedded the Swing list inside the viewport of a scrollpane object. The Swing JList class itself does not support scrolling through its data. Instead, it hands off the responsibility to the JScrollPane class. This is a significant design change from its predecessor, java.awt.List, which automatically managed a scrollbar for you. However, making a list the view of a scrollpane object fits better into the overall modular philosophy of Swing. The clear separation of function allows developers to reuse a customized scrollbar (or scrollpane) with their own lists instead of simply accepting a default provided with the list component. It also enables autoscrolling support, so you can drag the mouse above or below the list, and its contents scroll automatically.

Try selecting multiple numbers (you can do this in most L&Fs by holding down the Shift key while clicking). Note that by using Shift you can select only one *range*, or continuous set of numbers, at a time. If you select a number beyond the current selection range, the range is extended to cover everything in between. The first number selected (i.e., the one you didn't have to hold Shift down for) becomes the initial endpoint for the range. This endpoint is called the *anchor*. The most recent selection (which is outlined) forms the second endpoint. This element is called the *lead*. Together, the anchor and the lead form a range of selections in the list, as shown in Figure 7-2.

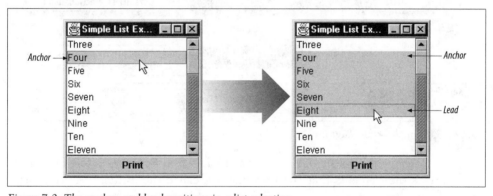

Figure 7-2. The anchor and lead positions in a list selection

When the user presses the button, an actionPerformed( ) method is called. This method reports all the items that are currently selected in the list:

```
Selected Elements:
   Four
   Five
   Six
   Seven
   Eight
```

There is also a way to make discontiguous selections (so you could select Four, Six, and Eight through Ten, for example). This is done by holding down a different modifier key: on Unix and Windows this is typically the Control key while on the Macintosh the Command (Apple) key is used. As usual, these differences are managed by the L&F. Since 1.3, the default behavior for a list is to support both ranges and discontiguous selections. Prior versions allowed only a single range. All versions let you override the default.

If you are using SDK 1.4 or later, you can also select elements in the list by typing the first characters in their label.

Anatomy of a Swing List

Now that we've seen the basics, let's take a closer look at JList. Figure 7-3 shows a high-level class diagram for Swing's list classes. In particular, note the three interfaces in the middle.

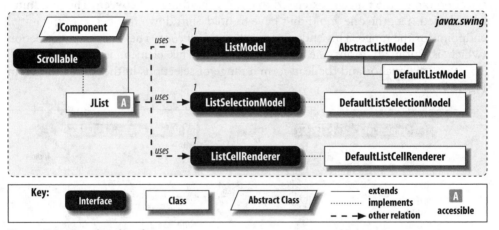

Figure 7-3. Swing list class diagram

Each list component consists of three parts, as shown in Figure 7-4. The first of the three parts is the elements that comprise the list, called the *list data*. As you might guess, the list data is assigned to a model—an object implementing the ListModel interface represents the list data. By default, JList uses the DefaultListModel class, an implementation of ListModel that stores a collection of data objects in a Vector. If you want a model more specific to your needs, the most convenient way to do it is to extend the AbstractListModel class and add your specific functionality to the basic housekeeping it provides.

The second element is a model as well; however, this one represents the user's *selections*. The model interface for selection data is the ListSelectionModel. Like the list data model, it also has a standard implementation: DefaultListSelectionModel. With the default JList, for example, you can select several ranges simultaneously. However,

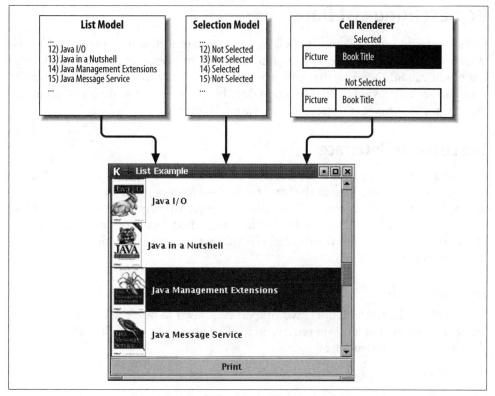

Figure 7-4. The three parts of a Swing list

you can also program the DefaultListSelectionModel to allow only one element to be selected at a given time.

The final piece is called a *cell renderer*. A cell renderer defines how each cell displays its data in the list, including when the cell is selected. Why an entire class for rendering list elements? As we mentioned previously, list data is not constrained to strings. Icons and animations can be displayed in place of or next to descriptive text. In many Swing components, a cell renderer is a common way to render complex data, or any data in a way that's specific to your application. If you write one carefully, it can be reused in several locations.

Where to Go from Here?

The following sections outline the various models and support classes that make up a Swing list. If you simply want to get to know the Swing JList class, you can skip ahead to "The JList Class," where we create a graphical list of some O'Reilly Java books. On the other hand, if you want to learn more about the data and selection models of the JList, then read on!

Representing List Data

Swing uses one interface and two classes to maintain a model of the list elements. When programming with lists, you often find that you can reuse these classes without modification. Occasionally, you may find it necessary to extend or even rewrite these classes to provide special functionality. In either case, it's important to examine all three in detail. Let's start with the easiest: ListModel.

The ListModel Interface

ListModel is a simple interface for accessing the data of the list. It has four methods: one method to retrieve data in the list, one method to obtain the total size of the list, and two methods to register and unregister change listeners on the list data. Note that the ListModel interface itself contains a method only for retrieving the list elements—not for setting them. Methods that set list values are defined in classes that implement this interface.

Properties

The ListModel interface defines two properties, shown in Table 7-1. elementAt is an indexed property that lets you retrieve individual objects from the list; size tells you the total number of elements.

Table 7-1. ListModel properties

Property	Data type	get	is	set	Default value
elementAt[i]	Object	•			
size	int	•			

[i]indexed

Events

The ListModel interface also contains the standard addListDataListener() and removeListDataListener() event subscription methods. These methods accept listeners that notify when the contents of the list have changed. A ListDataEvent should be generated when elements in the list are added, removed, or modified. ListDataEvent and the ListDataListener interface are discussed later in this chapter.

public abstract void addListDataListener(ListDataListener l)
public abstract void removeListDataListener(ListDataListener l)

   Add or remove a specific listener for ListDataEvent notifications.

The AbstractListModel Class

The `AbstractListModel` class is a skeletal framework to simplify the life of programmers who want to implement the `ListModel` interface. It provides the required `addListDataListener( )` and `removeListDataListener( )` event registration methods. It also provides three protected methods that subclasses can use to fire `ListDataEvent` objects. These methods are triggered when an addition, subtraction, or modification to the list data has taken place. Note that a `ListDataEvent` is not the same as a `PropertyChangeEvent`, which is more general in nature. (`ListDataEvent` is covered later in this chapter.)

Methods

protected void fireContentsChanged(Object source, int index1, int index2)
> Called by subclasses to trigger a `ListDataEvent`, which indicates that a modification has occurred in the list elements between `index1` and `index2`. `index2` can be less than `index1`. The source parameter provides a reference to the `ListModel` that signaled the change.

protected void fireIntervalAdded(Object source, int index1, int index2)
> Called by subclasses to trigger a `ListDataEvent`, which indicates that the list elements between `index1` and `index2` (inclusive) have been added to the list. Assuming that `index2` is the greater index, the element previously at `index1` in the list is now element `index2+1`. All subsequent elements are shifted as well. `index2` can be less than `index1`. The source parameter provides a reference to the `ListModel` that signaled the change.

protected void fireIntervalRemoved(Object source, int index1, int index2)
> Called by subclasses to trigger a `ListDataEvent`, which indicates to a listener that the list elements from `index1` to `index2` have been removed from the list. Assuming that `index2` is the larger index, the element previously at `index2+1` now becomes `index1`, and all greater elements are shifted down accordingly. `index2` can be less than `index1`. The source parameter provides a reference to the `ListModel` that signaled the change.

Although the `AbstractListModel` class completes the event framework defined by the list model interface, it does not implement the remaining two methods of the `ListModel` interface: `getSize( )` and `getElementAt( )`. Instead, it defines these as abstract (making the entire class abstract), leaving the actual implementation choices of the list storage to a subclass, such as `DefaultListModel`. Providing an abstract class that takes care of the mundane tasks required by an interface is characteristic of the useful *Skeletal Implementation* design pattern found throughout Java's Collections classes.[*]

---

[*] For a detailed discussion of this approach and its benefits, see "Item 16: Prefer interfaces to abstract classes" in Joshua Bloch's *Effective Java Programming Language Guide* (Addison-Wesley).

SDK 1.3 introduced a method to get the list of registered event listeners:

public EventListener[] getListeners(Class listenerType)
> You need to pass in the type of listener you're interested in, which is generally the ListDataListener.class, and you need to cast the result to that specific type.

SDK 1.4 introduced a simpler way to do the same thing:

public ListDataListener[] getListDataListeners()
> Return an array of all the list data listeners that have been registered.

The DefaultListModel Class

Swing provides a default implementation of the ListModel interface called DefaultListModel. This class is based on the java.util.Vector class, a resizable array of objects that has been around since the early days of Java (the comments keep saying that there are plans to replace this with a more modern Collection-based implementation, but it hasn't happened yet). A majority of the methods of the DefaultListModel class are identical to those of Vector, with the added (and necessary) feature that those methods fire a ListDataEvent each time the vector changes. DefaultListModel extends AbstractListModel to take advantage of its listener-list management features.

Properties

The DefaultListModel class has three properties, shown in Table 7-2. The size property indicates how many elements are currently stored in the list. You can use the setSize( ) method to alter the size of the list. If the new size is larger than the previous size, the additional elements are populated with null references, and the method fires a ListDataEvent describing the range that was added. If the new size is smaller, the list is truncated, and the method fires a ListDataEvent describing the range that was removed.

Table 7-2. DefaultListModel properties

Property	Data type	get	is	set	Default value
elementAt[i]	Object	•		•	
empty	boolean		•		true
size	int	•		•	0

[i]indexed

The empty property is a boolean that indicates whether the list has no elements. elementAt is an indexed property that you can use to access the list elements. If you set a new element using the setElementAt( ) method, the method fires a ListDataEvent describing the element that was changed.

Constructor

public DefaultListModel()

> Create an empty vector to be used as the list model.

Methods

public void copyInto(Object anArray[])

> Copy all of the objects in the list into the array `anArray`, which must be large enough to hold the contents of the model.

public void trimToSize()

> Collapse the capacity of the list to match its current size, removing any empty storage.

public void ensureCapacity(int minCapacity)

> Tell the list to make sure that its capacity is at least `minCapacity`.

public int capacity()

> Return the current capacity of the list. The capacity is the number of objects the list can hold without reallocating for more space.

public int size()

> Return the number of elements currently contained in the list. It is equivalent to `getSize()`.

public Enumeration elements()

> Return an `Enumeration` that iterates over each of the elements in the list.

public boolean contains(Object elem)

> Return an indication of whether the object `elem` is currently contained in the list.

public int indexOf(Object elem)

> Return the first index at which the object `elem` can be found in the list, or `-1` if the object is not contained in the list.

public int indexOf(Object elem, int index)

> Return the first index at which the object `elem` can be found in the list, beginning its search at the element specified by `index` and moving forward through the list. The method returns `-1` if the object is not contained in the list at or beyond `index`.

public int lastIndexOf(Object elem)

> Return the last index at which the object `elem` can be found in the list. The method returns `-1` if the object is not contained in the list.

public int lastIndexOf(Object elem, int index)

> Return the last index at which the object `elem` can be found in the list, searching backwards from the element specified by `index` to the front of the list. The method returns `-1` if the object is not contained in the list at or before `index`.

public Object elementAt(int index)

Return a reference to the object at the specified index. It is equivalent to `getElementAt(index)`.

public Object firstElement( )

Return a reference to the first object in the list.

public Object lastElement( )

Return a reference to the last object in the list.

public void removeElementAt(int index)

Remove the element at the specified index. The method then fires off a `ListDataEvent` to all registered listeners, describing the element that was removed.

public void insertElementAt(Object obj, int index)

Insert the object `obj` into the list at the given index, incrementing the index of the element previously at that index and any elements above it. (That is, it adds `obj` before the element at index.) The total size of the list is increased by one. The method then fires off a `ListDataEvent` to all registered listeners, describing the element that was inserted.

public void addElement(Object obj)

Add the object `obj` to the end of the list and fire off a `ListDataEvent` to all registered listeners, describing the element that was appended.

public boolean removeElement(Object obj)

Attempt to remove the first occurrence of the object `obj` from the list, returning true if successful and `false` if no such object existed in the list. If the method is successful, the indices of all later elements are decremented, and the size of the list is reduced by one. The method then fires off a `ListDataEvent` to all registered listeners, describing the element that was removed.

public void removeAllElements( )

Remove all the elements from the list. It then fires off a `ListDataEvent`, indicating that the entire range was removed.

public String toString( )

Provide a comma-separated list of each element currently in the list.

public Object[] toArray( )

Return the contents of the list as an array of type `Object`. It is functionally equivalent to the `copyInto( )` method, except that it allocates an array of the appropriate size and returns it.

public Object get(int index)

Equivalent to `getElementAt(index)`.

public Object set(int index, Object element)

Equivalent to `setElementAt(element, index)`.

public void add(int index, Object element)

Equivalent to `insertElementAt(element, index)`.

public Object remove(int index)

    Equivalent to `removeElementAt(index)`.

public void clear()

    Equivalent to `removeAllElements()`.

public void removeRange(int fromIndex, int toIndex)

    Remove all elements between the first and second index (including the boundary elements) from the list. The method fires a `ListDataEvent` describing the interval that was removed.

A JList with changing contents

Here's a simple program that dynamically adds and removes elements from a `JList`. To do so, we work with the `DefaultListModel` that keeps track of the list's contents.

```
// ListModelExample.java
//
import java.awt.*;
import java.awt.event.*;
import javax.swing.*;

public class ListModelExample extends JPanel {

    JList list;
    DefaultListModel model;
    int counter = 15;

    public ListModelExample() {
        setLayout(new BorderLayout());
        model = new DefaultListModel();
        list = new JList(model);
        JScrollPane pane = new JScrollPane(list);
        JButton addButton = new JButton("Add Element");
        JButton removeButton = new JButton("Remove Element");
        for (int i = 0; i < 15; i++)
            model.addElement("Element " + i);

        addButton.addActionListener(new ActionListener() {
            public void actionPerformed(ActionEvent e) {
                model.addElement("Element " + counter);
                counter++;
            }
        });
        removeButton.addActionListener(new ActionListener() {
            public void actionPerformed(ActionEvent e) {
            if (model.getSize() > 0)
                model.removeElementAt(0);
            }
        });

        add(pane, BorderLayout.NORTH);
        add(addButton, BorderLayout.WEST);
```

```
            add(removeButton, BorderLayout.EAST);
    }

    public static void main(String s[]) {
        JFrame frame = new JFrame("List Model Example");
        frame.setDefaultCloseOperation(JFrame.EXIT_ON_CLOSE);
        frame.setContentPane(new ListModelExample());
        frame.setSize(260, 200);
        frame.setVisible(true);
    }
}
```

The result is shown in Figure 7-5.

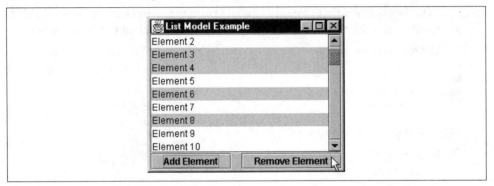

Figure 7-5. Dynamically adding and removing elements from a list

This example demonstrates a few important concepts. First, we instantiated our own `DefaultListModel` instead of using the default provided with the `JList`. If we hadn't done this, we wouldn't have been able to add anything to the list since the `ListModel` interface doesn't provide any methods to add or remove items. Working with your own instantiation is generally easier when you need to make runtime changes to any model—again, assigning new models is a benefit of the MVC architecture in Swing.

We've provided two ways for changing the list's contents: the Add Element button and the Remove Element button at the bottom. Clicking on Add Element calls our `actionPerformed( )` method and appends an element to the end of the list. Clicking on Remove Element calls the same method and deletes an element from the front of the list. After either button is pressed, the `JList` is notified of the change in the model and updates itself automatically. If you watch carefully, you can see the scrollbar thumb grow or shrink as the list size changes.

Try selecting some elements, then click on the Remove Element button a couple of times. Note that the list model and selection models communicate: as the top element is removed and the others move up, the selection moves too, in order to keep the same elements selected even though their indices have changed. This is an example of objects collaborating through event listeners, which you'll find throughout Swing.

There is one little bug, though.* The selection model's lead and anchor positions are not updated when elements are moved around. Although there's no visible evidence of this, you can prove it by running the program, clicking on Element 3, clicking Remove Element twice, then Shift-clicking on Element 7. You'd expect to see the range from Element 3 (which you last selected, and which was selected before your Shift-click) to Element 7 become highlighted. Instead, you end up with just the range from Element 5 (which is now positioned where you clicked before removing any elements) through Element 7 as the new selection.

ListDataEvent

ListDataEvent is an extension of java.util.EventObject that holds information about a change in the list data model. The event describes the nature of the change as well as the bounding indices of the elements involved. However, it does not send the actual elements. Listeners must query the source of the event if they're interested in the new contents of the affected elements.

There are three types of changes that can occur to the list data: elements can be altered, inserted, or removed from the list. Note that the indices passed in form a closed interval (i.e., both indices are included in the affected range). If a ListDataEvent claiming that list elements have been altered is received, the bounding indices typically describe the smallest range of data elements that have changed. If elements have been removed, the indices describe the range of elements that have been deleted. If elements have been added, the indices describe the new elements that have been inserted into the list.

Properties

The ListDataEvent contains four properties, each with its own accessor, as shown in Table 7-3. The source property indicates the object that is firing the event. The type property represents the type of change that has occurred, represented by one of the constants in Table 7-4. The index0 and index1 properties outline the range of affected elements. index0 does not need to be less than index1 for the ListDataEvent to be valid.

Table 7-3. ListDataEvent properties

Property	Data type	get	is	set	Default value
index0	int	•			
index1	int	•			

---

* Perhaps by the time you read this, the bug will have been fixed, but it was reported against version 1.2.2 and was still present in 1.4.1 as this book went to press.

Table 7-3. ListDataEvent properties (continued)

Property	Data type	get	is	set	Default value
source[o]	Object	•			
type	int	•			

[o]overridden

Constants

Table 7-4 lists the event type constants used by the ListDataEvent.

Table 7-4. Constants for ListDataEvent

Constant	Data type	Description
CONTENTS_CHANGED	int	The elements between the two indices (inclusive) have been altered.
INTERVAL_ADDED	int	The elements now between the two indices (inclusive) have just been inserted into the list.
INTERVAL_REMOVED	int	The elements previously between the two indices (inclusive) have now been removed from the list.

Constructor

public ListDataEvent(Object source, int type, int index0, int index1)

Take a reference to the object that is firing this event, as well as the event type and bounding indices.

Method

public String toString()

SDK 1.4 added a toString method that provides useful debugging information about the contents of the event, which is suitable for logging. The String returned includes the values of all the event's properties other than source.

The ListDataListener Interface

The ListDataListener interface, which is the conduit for receiving the ListDataEvent objects, contains three methods. Each method receives a different ListDataEvent type that can be generated. This interface must be implemented by any listener object that wishes to be notified of changes to the list model.

Methods

public abstract void intervalAdded(ListDataEvent e)
> Called after the range of elements specified in the `ListDataEvent` has been added to the list. The specified interval includes both endpoints. Listeners may want to query the source of the event for the contents of the new interval.

public abstract void intervalRemoved(ListDataEvent e)
> Called after the range of elements specified in the `ListDataEvent` has been deleted. The specified interval includes both endpoints.

public abstract void contentsChanged(ListDataEvent e)
> Called when the range of elements specified in the `ListDataEvent` has been altered. The specified interval includes both endpoints, although not all elements are guaranteed to have changed. Listeners may want to query the source of the event for the contents of the range.

Handling Selections

The `JList` class in Swing depends on a second model, this one to monitor the elements that have been selected by the user. As with the list data model, the programmer is given many places in which standard behavior can be altered or replaced when dealing with selections. Swing uses a simple interface for models that handle list selections (`ListSelectionModel`) and provides a default implementation (`DefaultList-SelectionModel`).

The ListSelectionModel Interface

The `ListSelectionModel` interface outlines the methods necessary for managing list selections. Selections are represented by a series of ranges, where each range is defined by its endpoints. For example, if the elements One, Two, Three, Six, Seven, and Nine were selected in the opening example of the chapter, the list selection model would contain three entries that specified the ranges {1,3}, {6,7}, and {9,9}. All selection indices are zero-based, and the ranges are closed, meaning both endpoint indices are included within the selection. If only one element is present in a range, such as with Nine, both endpoints are identical.

Properties

Table 7-5 shows the properties of the `ListSelectionModel` interface. The first four properties of the list selection model can be used to retrieve various indices that are currently selected in the list. The `anchorSelectionIndex` and `leadSelectionIndex` properties represent the anchor and lead indices of the most recent range of selections, as illustrated in Figure 7-2. The `maxSelectionIndex` and `minSelectionIndex` properties return the largest and smallest selected index in the entire list, respectively.

Table 7-5. ListSelectionModel properties

Property	Data type	get	is	set	Default value
anchorSelectionIndex	int	•		•	
leadSelectionIndex	int	•		•	
maxSelectionIndex	int	•			
minSelectionIndex	int	•			
selectionEmpty	boolean		•		
selectionMode	int	•		•	
valueIsAdjusting	boolean	•		•	

The selectionMode property defines the type of selections that the user may make in the list. This property can take one of three constants representing a single selection, a single range of selections, or multiple ranges of selections. The default (since SDK 1.3) is multiple ranges of selections. (The selectionMode constants are outlined in greater detail in Table 7-6.) The selectionEmpty property is a boolean indicating whether there are any selections. If there are no selections anywhere in the list, the property is set to true.

Setting the valueIsAdjusting property to true indicates that the object is sending a series of selection change events. For example, when the user is dragging the mouse across the list, the object can set this property to true, which indicates that the selection change events are part of a series. When the series has been completed, the property should be set to false. The receiver may wish to delay action until all events have been received.

In versions prior to 1.4, discontiguous selection events generated by clicking while holding down Ctrl (or Command, depending on the L&F) set the valueIsAdjusting property to true, without ever sending a closing event with the property equal to false. Unless you're using SDK 1.4 or later, it is safest to pay attention to this property only for lists that support a single selection.

Constants

The constants shown in Table 7-6 are used in conjunction with the selectionMode property of the ListSelectionModel interface.

Table 7-6. Constants for the ListSelectionModel interface

Constant	Data type	Description
MULTIPLE_INTERVAL_SELECTION	int	The user can make selections of several ranges at a time.
SINGLE_INTERVAL_SELECTION	int	The user can select only one range of items at a time.
SINGLE_SELECTION	int	The user can select only one item at a time.

Methods

public abstract void addSelectionInterval(int index1, int index2)

Add a group of list elements, ranging from index1 to index2 (including both end-points), to the selection list. If the current selection mode supports only single selections, the method selects only the element at index2. This method must trigger a ListSelectionEvent describing the resulting change.

public abstract void removeSelectionInterval(int index1, int index2)

Remove the group of list elements from index1 to index2 (including both end-points) from the selection list, whether the elements are selected or not. This method must trigger a ListSelectionEvent describing any changes it makes.

public abstract void clearSelection()

Clear all selections from the data model. This method must trigger a ListSelectionEvent, indicating that the entire selection has been cleared.

public abstract void insertIndexInterval(int index, int length, boolean before)

Synchronize the selection list after an addition to the list data. If before is true, this method inserts length elements into the selection list starting before index. If before is false, the method inserts length elements after index. All added elements are unselected. The indices of any selected elements following them will be updated. If the changes do affect the selection, the method must trigger a ListSelectionEvent reflecting the changes to the selection list.

public abstract void removeIndexInterval(int index1, int index2)

Synchronize the selection list after a deletion in the list data. This method removes the indices between index1 and index2 from the selection model and renumbers entries that come later in the list. If the changes do affect the selection, the method must trigger a ListSelectionEvent reflecting the changes to the selection list.

public abstract boolean isSelectedIndex(int index)

Is true if the specified index is currently selected.

public abstract void setSelectionInterval(int index1, int index2)

Clear all selections and reset the selection to cover the range between index1 and index2. If the selection mode allows only a single selection, the element referenced by index2 is selected. This method must trigger a ListSelectionEvent describing the change, if there is one.

While reading through the above interface, you may have been puzzled to find no way to get a list of all selected items. Even though you'd expect this to be a responsibility of the selection model, you must instead get this information from the JList itself.

Events

The ListSelectionModel interface declares the addListSelectionListener() and removeListSelectionListener() event subscription methods for notifying other objects of selection changes. These selection changes come in the form of ListSelectionEvent objects.

public void addListSelectionListener(ListSelectionListener l)
public void removeListSelectionListener(ListSelectionListener l)

> Add or remove a listener interested in receiving list selection events. The listener objects are notified each time a change to the list selection occurs.

The DefaultListSelectionModel Class

Swing provides a default implementation of the list selection interface called DefaultListSelectionModel. This class implements accessors for each of the ListSelectionModel properties and maintains an EventListenerList of change listeners. If you thought about how to implement all the behavior specified by the ListSelectionModel interface while reading about it on the last few pages, you probably realized that the code for all this is quite complex and tedious. We're glad Sun provides a default implementation!

The DefaultListSelectionModel can chain ListSelectionEvent objects in a series to notify listeners of a change in the selection list. This is common, for example, when the user is dragging the mouse across the list. In this case, a series of selection change events can be fired off with a valueIsAdjusting property set to true, which indicates that this event is only one of many. The listener may wish to delay any activity until all the events are received. When the chain of selections is complete, an event is sent with the valueIsAdjusting property set to false, which tells the listener that the series has completed. (Relying on this final event prior to SDK 1.4 is safe only for lists that don't support selection ranges.)

Properties

Table 7-7 lists the properties of the DefaultListSelectionModel. Almost all the properties are implementations of the properties defined by the ListSelectionModel interface. The only new property, leadAnchorNotificationEnabled, designates whether the class fires change events over leadSelectionIndex and anchorSelectionIndex each time it fires a series of notification events. (Recall that the anchor selection is at the beginning of the selection range while the lead selection is the most recent addition to the selection range.) If the property is false, only the elements selected or deselected since the last change are included in the series.

Table 7-7. DefaultListSelectionModel properties

Property	Data type	get	is	set	Default value
anchorSelectionIndex	int	•		•	-1
leadAnchorNotificationEnabled	boolean		•	•	true

Table 7-7. DefaultListSelectionModel properties (continued)

Property	Data type	get	is	set	Default value
leadSelectionIndex	int	•		•	-1
maxSelectionIndex	int	•			-1
minSelectionIndex	int	•			Integer.MAX_VALUE
selectionEmpty	boolean		•		true
selectionMode	int	•		•	MULTIPLE_INTERVAL_SELECTION
valueIsAdjusting	boolean	•		•	false

Events

The DefaultListSelectionModel uses the ListSelectionEvent to signal that the list selection has changed. The event notifies interested listeners of a modification to the selection data and tells which elements were affected.

public void addListSelectionListener(listSelectionListener 1)
public void removeListSelectionListener(listSelectionListener 1)
> Add or remove a listener from the list of objects interested in receiving ListSelectionEvents.

public EventListener[] getListeners(Class listenerType)
> You need to pass in the type of listener you're interested in (generally ListSelectionListener.class) and cast the result to that specific type (available since SDK 1.3).

public ListSelectionListener[] getListSelectionListeners()
> Return an array of all the list selection listeners that have been registered (available since SDK 1.4).

Constructor

public DefaultListSelectionModel()
> The default constructor. It initializes a list selection model that can be used by a JList or JComboBox component.

Method

public Object clone() throws CloneNotSupportedException
> Return a clone of the current selection model. You should be aware that the event listener list is not cloned. This sort of problem is a small part of why the entire clone mechanism has fallen out of favor in Java.

Working with the ListSelectionModel

The following example is a modified version of our earlier list example. This one has its own ListSelectionListener that reports each list selection event as it occurs.

```
// SimpleList2.java
//
import java.awt.*;
import java.awt.event.*;
import javax.swing.*;
import javax.swing.event.*;

public class SimpleList2 extends JPanel {

    String label[] = { "Zero","One","Two","Three","Four","Five","Six",
                        "Seven","Eight","Nine","Ten","Eleven" };
    JList list;

    public SimpleList2() {
        setLayout(new BorderLayout());

        list = new JList(label);
        JButton button = new JButton("Print");
        JScrollPane pane = new JScrollPane(list);

        DefaultListSelectionModel m = new DefaultListSelectionModel();
        m.setSelectionMode(ListSelectionModel.SINGLE_SELECTION);
        m.setLeadAnchorNotificationEnabled(false);
        list.setSelectionModel(m);

        list.addListSelectionListener(new ListSelectionListener() {
            public void valueChanged(ListSelectionEvent e) {
                System.out.println(e.toString());
            }
        });
        button.addActionListener(new PrintListener());

        add(pane, BorderLayout.NORTH);
        add(button, BorderLayout.SOUTH);
    }

    public static void main(String s[]) {
        JFrame frame = new JFrame("List Example");
        frame.setDefaultCloseOperation(JFrame.EXIT_ON_CLOSE);
        frame.setContentPane(new SimpleList2());
        frame.pack();
        frame.setVisible(true);
    }

    // An inner class to respond to clicks of the Print button
    class PrintListener implements ActionListener {
        public void actionPerformed(ActionEvent e) {
            int selected[] = list.getSelectedIndices();
            System.out.println("Selected Elements:  ");
```

```
            for (int i=0; i < selected.length; i++) {
                String element =
                    (String)list.getModel().getElementAt(selected[i]);
                System.out.println("   " + element);
            }
        }
    }
}
```

Try running this code and selecting a couple of items in the list. If you drag the mouse from item 0 to item 5, you get the following output (the detailed contents of the JList have been omitted for readability since they don't change from line to line):

```
javax.swing.event.ListSelectionEvent[ source=javax.swing.JList[...] firstIndex= 0
lastIndex= 1 isAdjusting= true ]
javax.swing.event.ListSelectionEvent[ source=javax.swing.JList[...] firstIndex= 1
lastIndex= 2 isAdjusting= true ]
javax.swing.event.ListSelectionEvent[ source=javax.swing.JList[...] firstIndex= 2
lastIndex= 3 isAdjusting= true ]
javax.swing.event.ListSelectionEvent[ source=javax.swing.JList[...] firstIndex= 3
lastIndex= 4 isAdjusting= true ]
javax.swing.event.ListSelectionEvent[ source=javax.swing.JList[...] firstIndex= 4
lastIndex= 5 isAdjusting= true ]
javax.swing.event.ListSelectionEvent[ source=javax.swing.JList[...] firstIndex= 0
lastIndex= 5 isAdjusting= false ]
```

Each entry describes a change in selection. The first five entries recognize that a change of selection has occurred between one element and the next as the mouse was dragged. In this case, the former was deselected, and the latter was selected. However, note that the isAdjusting property was true, indicating that this is potentially one in a series of changes. When the mouse button is released, the list knows that the drag has stopped and fires a ListSelectionEvent with the isAdjusting property set to false, repeating the last changed index.

ListSelectionEvent

Much like the ListDataEvent, the ListSelectionEvent specifies a change by highlighting those elements in the selection list that have altered. Note that a ListSelectionEvent does not indicate the new selection state of the list element, only that some change has occurred. You should not assume that the new state is the opposite of the previous state; always check with the event source to see what the current selection state really is.

Properties

There are four properties in the ListSelectionEvent, as shown in Table 7-8.

Table 7-8. ListSelectionEvent properties

Property	Data type	get	is	set	Default value
firstIndex	int	•			
lastIndex	int	•			
source⁰	Object	•			
valueIsAdjusting	boolean	•			

⁰overridden

Constructor

public ListSelectionEvent(Object source, int firstIndex, int lastIndex,
boolean isAdjusting)
> This constructor takes a reference to the object that is firing the event, as well as the bounding indices and a boolean indicating whether the event is expected to be followed by another. Note that firstIndex should always be less than or equal to lastIndex.

Methods

public String toString( )
> Provide human-readable string output of the event properties for debugging.

ListSelectionListener

The ListSelectionListener interface, as the means of receiving ListSelectionEvents, consists of only one method: valueChanged( ). This method must be implemented by any listener object interested in changes to the list selection model.

public abstract void valueChanged(ListSelectionEvent e)
> Notify the listener that one or more selection elements have changed.

Listening for ListSelectionEvents

Here is a brief example that demonstrates how to use ListSelectionListener and the ListSelectionEvent. The example creates a series of checkboxes that accurately mirror the current selections in the list by listening for selection events. Some results from playing with the program are shown in Figure 7-6.

```
//  SelectionMonitor.java
//
import java.awt.*;
import java.awt.event.*;
import javax.swing.*;
import javax.swing.event.*;

public class SelectionMonitor extends JPanel {
```

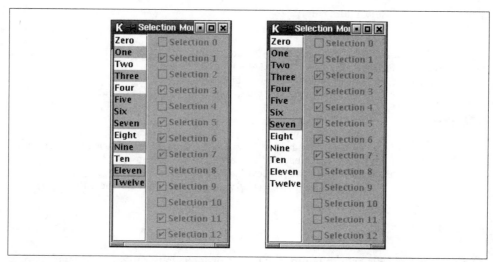

Figure 7-6. Monitoring list selection events

```java
String label[] = { "Zero","One","Two","Three","Four","Five","Six",
                   "Seven","Eight","Nine","Ten","Eleven","Twelve" };
JCheckBox checks[] = new JCheckBox[label.length];
JList list;

public SelectionMonitor( ) {
    setLayout(new BorderLayout( ));

    list = new JList(label);
    JScrollPane pane = new JScrollPane(list);

    // Format the list and the buttons in a vertical box.
    Box rightBox = new Box(BoxLayout.Y_AXIS);
    Box leftBox = new Box(BoxLayout.Y_AXIS);

    // Monitor all list selections.
    list.addListSelectionListener(new RadioUpdater( ));

    for(int i=0; i < label.length; i++) {
        checks[i] = new JCheckBox("Selection " + i);
        checks[i].setEnabled(false);
        rightBox.add(checks[i]);
    }
    leftBox.add(pane);
    add(rightBox, BorderLayout.EAST);
    add(leftBox, BorderLayout.WEST);
}

public static void main(String s[]) {
    JFrame frame = new JFrame("Selection Monitor");
    frame.setDefaultCloseOperation(JFrame.EXIT_ON_CLOSE);
    frame.setContentPane(new SelectionMonitor( ));
    frame.pack( );
```

```
            frame.setVisible(true);
    }

    // Inner class that responds to selection events to update the buttons
    class RadioUpdater implements ListSelectionListener {
        public void valueChanged(ListSelectionEvent e) {
            // If either of these are true, the event can be ignored.
            if ((!e.getValueIsAdjusting()) || (e.getFirstIndex() == -1))
                return;

            // Change the radio button to match the current selection state for each
            // list item that reported a change.
            for (int i = e.getFirstIndex(); i <= e.getLastIndex(); i++) {
                checks[i].setSelected(((JList)e.getSource()).isSelectedIndex(i));
            }
        }
    }
}
```

If you're running this example under SDK 1.4 or later, experiment with Swing's new support for keyboard-driven selection. Try typing the first letter, or few letters, of some of the list elements, and watch the selection jump around. Notice that if you type te, the selection starts by selecting Two and then jumps to Ten, but neither event reports an isAdjusting value of true. This feature is examined in more depth in the discussion of the getNextMatch( ) method.

Remember that a ListSelectionEvent does not inform you of the new selection state of an element that has changed. You might be tempted to conclude that if you receive a ListSelectionEvent, the selection state for the target element would simply be the opposite of what it was before. This is not true. The selection state *cannot* be determined from the ListSelectionEvent; it must be determined by querying the event source.

Displaying Cell Elements

Swing gives the programmer the option to specify how each element in the list (called a *cell*) should be displayed on the screen. The list itself maintains a reference to a *cell renderer*. Cell renderers are common in Swing components, including lists and combo boxes. Essentially, a cell renderer is a component whose paint( ) method is called each time the component needs to draw or redraw an element. To create a cell renderer, you need only to register a class that implements the ListCellRenderer interface. This registration can be done with the setCellRenderer( ) method of JList or JComboBox:

```
JList list = new JList();
list.setCellRenderer(new myCellRenderer());
```

The ListCellRenderer Interface

The ListCellRenderer interface must be implemented by cell renderers for lists and combo boxes. It has only one method.

public abstract Component getListCellRendererComponent(JList list, Object value,
  int index, boolean isSelected, boolean cellHasFocus)

This method must return a Component that can be used to draw the cell given the five variables passed in. The JList argument is a reference to the list itself. value is the object within the list data that will be drawn in this cell. The index of the cell in the list is given by the argument index. isSelected tells the renderer if the cell is currently selected, and cellHasFocus tells the renderer if the cell currently has the input focus.

 Occasionally, Swing calls this method with an index of -1, which is, of course, not a valid list index, and implementations must be able to return a valid renderer anyway. Situations in which you'd encounter this include combo boxes that are drawing user-entered custom values (since they're not present in the associated list, they have no index) and during UI layout, when the size of a typical list element is needed even if the list doesn't contain any values.

It may be necessary to set the preferred size of the component returned by the cell renderer before returning it so that the requesting list knows how large to paint the component. This can be done by calling the setPreferredSize() method on the component.

Implementing a Cell Renderer

Here are some classes we'll use with the Java Books example later in this chapter, including a BookEntry class that contains composite information stored in a book list and a custom renderer that draws each cell in a list of O'Reilly books by placing its title side-by-side with a small icon of its cover:

```
// BookEntry.java
import javax.swing.ImageIcon;

public class BookEntry {
    private final String title;
    private final String imagePath;
    private ImageIcon image;

    public BookEntry(String title, String imagePath) {
        this.title = title;
        this.imagePath = imagePath;
    }
```

```java
    public String getTitle( ) { return title; }

    public ImageIcon getImage( ) {
        if (image == null) {
            image = new ImageIcon(imagePath);
        }
        return image;
    }

    // Override standard toString method to give a useful result.
    public String toString( ) { return title; }
}

// BookCellRenderer.java
import javax.swing.*;
import java.awt.*;

public class BookCellRenderer extends JLabel implements ListCellRenderer {
    private static final Color HIGHLIGHT_COLOR = new Color(0, 0, 128);

    public BookCellRenderer( ) {
        setOpaque(true);
        setIconTextGap(12);
    }

    public Component getListCellRendererComponent(
        JList list,
        Object value,
        int index,
        boolean isSelected,
        boolean cellHasFocus)
    {
        BookEntry entry = (BookEntry)value;
        setText(entry.getTitle( ));
        setIcon(entry.getImage( ));
        if(isSelected) {
            setBackground(HIGHLIGHT_COLOR);
            setForeground(Color.white);
        } else {
            setBackground(Color.white);
            setForeground(Color.black);
        }
        return this;
    }
}
```

Notice that each call to getListCellRendererComponent( ) returns the same instance. This is very important for performance. Creating a new instance each time the method is called would place needless strain on the system. Even if you need to return slightly different renderers under different circumstances, maintain a static pool of these distinct instances and reuse them.

Our custom cell renderer displays images similar to those in Figure 7-7. Before we put the O'Reilly books example together, however, we need to discuss the central list class in Swing: JList. We'll do that after a brief detour for DefaultListCellRenderer.

Figure 7-7. The ListCellRenderer results

The DefaultListCellRenderer Class

Swing contains a default list cell renderer class used by JList whenever the programmer does not explicitly set a cell renderer. This class, DefaultListCellRenderer, implements the ListCellRenderer interface.

public Component getListCellRendererComponent(JList list, Object value, int index, boolean isSelected, boolean cellHasFocus)

> This method returns a Component used to draw a default list cell. If isSelected is true, then the cell is drawn with the selectedBackground and selectedForeground properties defined in the list variable. If the cell is not selected, it uses the standard background and foreground colors of the list component. If the cell has focus, a UI-specific border (typically a 1-pixel LineBorder) is placed around the component. The cell renderer can handle both text and icons. If the value is text, the default font of the list is used.

The JList Class

The JList class is the generic Swing implementation of a list component. In the default selection mode, you can make multiple selections by clicking with the mouse while holding down the modifier key defined by the current L&F (generally Shift for a single, contiguous range and Ctrl or Command for noncontiguous selections). The JList class does not provide scrolling capabilities, but it can be set as the viewport of a JScrollPane to support scrolling. Figure 7-8 shows the JList component in four different L&Fs.

Properties

The JList class essentially combines the features of the data model, the selection model, and the cell renderer into a single Swing component. The properties of the JList class are shown in Table 7-9.

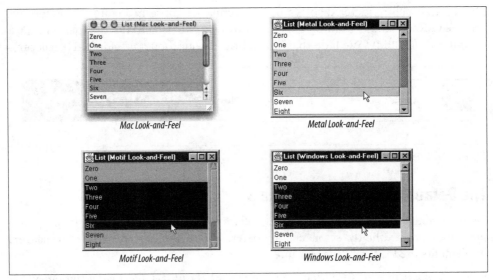

Mac Look-and-Feel

Metal Look-and-Feel

Motif Look-and-Feel

Windows Look-and-Feel

Figure 7-8. The JList component in four L&Fs

Table 7-9. JList properties

Property	Data type	get	is	set	Default value
accessibleContext[o]	AccessibleContext	•			JList.AccessibleJList
anchorSelectionIndex	int	•			
cellRenderer[b]	ListCellRenderer	•		•	From L&F
dragEnabled[1.4]	boolean	•		•	false
firstVisibleIndex	int	•			
fixedCellHeight[b]	int	•		•	-1
fixedCellWidth[b]	int	•		•	-1
lastVisibleIndex	int	•			
layoutOrientation[1.4, b]	int	•		•	VERTICAL
leadSelectionIndex	int	•			
maxSelectionIndex	int	•			
minSelectionIndex	int	•			
model[b]	ListModel	•	•		
opaque[o]	boolean		•	•	true
preferredScrollableViewportSize[o]	Dimension	•			
prototypeCellValue[b]	Object	•		•	null
scrollableTracksViewportHeight[o]	boolean	•			

[1.4]since 1.4, [b]bound, [i]indexed, [o]overridden

See also properties from JComponent (Table 3-6).

Table 7-9. JList properties (continued)

Property	Data type	get	is	set	Default value
scrollableTracksViewportWidth°	boolean	•			
selectedIndex	int	•		•	-1
selectedIndex^i	boolean		•		
selectedIndices	int[]	•		•	
selectedValue	Object	•			
selectedValues	Object[]	•			
selectionBackground^b	Color	•		•	null
selectionEmpty	boolean		•		true
selectionForeground^b	Color	•		•	null
selectionMode	int	•		•	MULTIPLE_INTERVAL_SELECTION
selectionModel^b	ListSelectionModel	•		•	DefaultListSelectionModel
UI^b	ListUI	•		•	From L&F
UIClassID°	String	•			"ListUI"
valueIsAdjusting	boolean	•		•	false
visibleRowCount	int	•		•	8

[1.4]since 1.4, [b]bound, [i]indexed, [o]overridden

See also properties from JComponent (Table 3-6).

The model property contains an object that implements the ListModel interface; this object holds the element data of the list. If you don't supply a model (or the data from which to build a model) when you construct the JList, a useless default is created that contains zero entries (and cannot be added to). The selectionModel property contains an object that implements the ListSelectionModel interface; this object manages the current selections in the list. Both interfaces were covered earlier in the chapter.

The selectionMode mirrors the selectionMode property of the ListSelectionModel. This property indicates how many ranges can be selected at a time. The selectionForeground and selectionBackground properties set the foreground and background colors of the selected cells. The opaque property is always set to true to indicate that the JList is opaque.

The firstVisibleIndex property represents the topmost, leftmost (assuming a Western componentOrientation) element that is at least partially visible in the list's "window," while the lastVisibleIndex property represents the bottommost, rightmost (again, depending on the componentOrientation and layoutOrientation properties) element that is at least partially visible. visibleRowCount indicates the number of elements currently visible in the list. You can set this property to ensure that the list shows no more than a certain number of elements at a time.

The next series of properties mirrors those in the ListSelectionModel. The anchorSelectionIndex and leadSelectionIndex give the anchor and lead positions for the most recent selection. The minSelectionIndex and maxSelectionIndex give the smallest and largest indices of all selected components. selectedIndex gives the first selected index in the list (or -1 if there is none) while selectedIndices holds an ordered integer array of all current selections. There is also an indexed selectedIndex property that indicates whether a specific index is selected. The selectedValue property lets you retrieve the first selected object, and selectedValues lets you retrieve an array that contains all the selected objects. Finally, the selectionEmpty property is a boolean that tells whether there are any elements currently selected.

The fixedCellHeight and fixedCellWidth properties allow the user to explicitly set a fixed height in pixels for the cells in the list. The prototypeCellValue is a reference to an object that the list can use to calculate the minimum width of every cell in the list; you can use this property to define the size needed for each cell. This keeps the list from having to compute the size by checking each item in the list and can greatly speed up drawing. For example, you might set this property to the string "mmmmm" to ensure that each cell could contain five characters. The preferredScrollableViewportSize property indicates the Dimension necessary to support the visibleRowCount property. The valueIsAdjusting property is used to indicate that a series of ListSelectionEvent objects is being generated by the selection model, such as when a drag is occurring.

The scrollableTracksViewportWidth and scrollableTracksViewportHeight properties report whether the JList is resized to match the size of the viewport containing it. They are true if the preferred size of the JList is smaller than the viewport (in the appropriate direction), allowing a JList to stretch. They are false if the JList is larger than the viewport. The standard JScrollPane's scrollbars become active when these properties become false.

SDK 1.4 introduced two new properties: dragEnabled and layoutOrientation. dragEnabled can be set to true to turn on the new automatic Drag and Drop support. For this to work, the L&F must support Drag and Drop, and you need to set the component's transferHandler, as discussed in Chapter 24. (Note that even though you'd expect to use "isDragEnabled" to retrieve the value of a boolean property, JList defines getDragEnabled instead.) Lists can now have more than one column. The layoutOrientation property controls this and determines in what order the cells should "flow" when there is more than one column. Its value must be one of the constants defined in Table 7-10. To support internationalization, layoutOrientation interacts with JComponent's componentOrientation property to determine cell layout.

Constants

Table 7-10 shows constants for the layoutOrientation property. These constants determine the layout of list elements.

Table 7-10. JList layoutOrientation constants

Constant	Data type	Description
VERTICAL	int	Indicates the default layout, a single column of cells
VERTICAL_WRAP	int	Indicates a multi-column layout with cells flowing vertically, then horizontally
HORIZONTAL_WRAP	int	Indicates a multi-column layout with cells flowing horizontally, then vertically

Constructors

public JList( )

> Create an empty JList. Nothing can be added to this list without changing the model.

public JList(ListModel model)

> Create a JList using the specified data model.

public JList(Object[] objects)

> Create a JList using the array of objects passed in to populate a default data model.

public JList(Vector vector)

> Create a JList using a Vector of objects passed in to populate a default data model.

Miscellaneous

public void ensureIndexIsVisible(int index)

> Automatically scroll the viewport associated with the list until the element specified by index is visible.

public Rectangle getCellBounds(int index1, int index2)

> Return a Rectangle object that outlines the area covered by the range of list elements. In the event that the range is invalid, the method returns null.

public int getNextMatch(String prefix, int startIndex,
javax.swing.text.Position.Bias bias)

> Starting with SDK 1.4, users can select items within lists by typing the first letter (or letters) of the contents of the cell that they'd like to select. This method was introduced to support that capability, but it can also be used from code. The arguments specify the textual prefix to be searched for, the index from which searching should begin (when the method is invoked in response to a user keypress, this will be the index selected last), and the direction in which searching should occur, which must be one of Position.Bias.Forward or Position.Bias.Backward. (Despite

the unconventional capitalization, these are constants. In fact, they form a type-safe enumeration.)[*]

public String getToolTipText(MouseEvent event)
> Since SDK 1.4, JList overrides this method to allow the tooltips of the underlying cells' renderers to appear when the mouse is held over a list cell. Note that if you call setToolTipText(null) on the list itself, you disable this feature from that point on.

public Point indexToLocation(int index)
> Return a point representing the upper-left corner of the list element in local coordinates. In the event that the element is not currently displayed on the screen, or does not exist, the method returns null.

public int locationToIndex(Point p)
> Return the index of the list element that contains the graphical point p.

Selection Model

public void setSelectionInterval(int index0, int index1)
> Reset the selection interval to the inclusive range specified by the two indices passed in.

public void setSelectedValue(Object obj, boolean shouldScroll)
> Set the list element that matches the reference obj as the only selection in the list. If shouldScroll is true, the list automatically scrolls to ensure that the element is visible.

public void addSelectionInterval(int index0, int index1)
> Add the interval specified by the two indices passed in to the current selection.

public void removeSelectionInterval(int index0, int index1)
> Remove the interval specified by the two indices passed in from the current selection.

public void clearSelection( )
> Clear the entire selection.

Scrolling

The following methods are used for internal configuration purposes. Along with the getPreferredScrollableViewportSize( ), getScrollableTracksViewportHeight( ), and getScrollableTracksViewportWidth( ) methods (accessors for three of the properties listed in Table 7-9), these methods implement the Scrollable interface. Scrollable

---

[*] If you're not familiar with this extremely useful Java pattern, learning about it is worth the price of Joshua Bloch's outstanding *Effective Java Programming Language Guide* (Addison-Wesley).

allows a JScrollPane to be more intelligent about scrolling. You would rarely call these methods.

public int getScrollableBlockIncrement(Rectangle visibleRect, int orientation,
    int direction)

> If the orientation is vertical, this method returns the height of the visibleRect rectangle. If the orientation is horizontal, this method returns the width. The direction variable is not used.

public int getScrollableUnitIncrement(Rectangle visibleRect, int orientation,
    int direction)

> Return the number of pixels it takes to expose the next element in the list. If direction is positive, it is assumed that the user is scrolling downwards, and the method returns the height of the first element that is visible or partially visible on the list. If the direction is negative, it is assumed that the user is scrolling upwards, and the method returns the height of the last element that is visible or partially visible on the list.

Data Model

public void setListData(Object[] objects)

> Create a ListDataModel from the array of objects passed in and resets the current data model of the JList to reference it.

public void setListData(Vector vector)

> Create a ListDataModel from the vector of objects passed in and resets the current data model of the JList to reference it.

User Interface

public void updateUI( )

> A new L&F has been selected by the user. Invoking this method forces the component to reset its UI delegate.

Events

The JList component fires a ListSelectionEvent when any of its selections change. These methods mirror the ListSelectionEvents that are fired directly from the selection model and are used to notify any selection listeners that have registered directly with the JList itself. The source of the event is always the JList object.

public void addListSelectionListener(ListSelectionListener)
public void removeListSelectionListener(ListSelectionListener)

> Add or remove a selection listener from the event registration list.

public ListSelectionListener[] getListSelectionListeners( )

> Available since SDK 1.4, this method returns the list of registered listeners.

The Java Books Example

Here is the code for the list displaying some O'Reilly Java books. It uses the BookEntry and BookCellRenderer classes.

```java
// ListExample.java
//
import java.awt.*;
import java.awt.event.*;
import javax.swing.*;

public class ListExample extends JPanel {

    private BookEntry books[] = {
        new BookEntry("Ant: The Definitive Guide", "covers/ant.gif"),
        new BookEntry("Database Programming with JDBC and Java",
                      "covers/jdbc.gif"),
        new BookEntry("Developing Java Beans", "covers/beans.gif"),
        new BookEntry("Developing JSP Custom Tag Libraries", "covers/jsptl.gif"),
        new BookEntry("Java 2D Graphics", "covers/java2d.gif"),
        new BookEntry("Java and XML", "covers/jxml.gif"),
        new BookEntry("Java and XSLT", "covers/jxslt.gif"),
        new BookEntry("Java and SOAP", "covers/jsoap.gif"),
        new BookEntry("Java and XML Data Binding", "covers/jxmldb.gif"),
        new BookEntry("Java Cookbook", "covers/jcook.gif"),
        new BookEntry("Java Cryptography", "covers/jcrypto.gif"),
        new BookEntry("Java Distributed Computing", "covers/jdist.gif"),
        new BookEntry("Java I/O", "covers/javaio.gif"),
        new BookEntry("Java in a Nutshell", "covers/javanut.gif"),
        new BookEntry("Java Management Extensions", "covers/jmx.gif"),
        new BookEntry("Java Message Service", "covers/jms.gif"),
        new BookEntry("Java Network Programming", "covers/jnetp.gif"),
        new BookEntry("Java Performance Tuning", "covers/jperf.gif"),
        new BookEntry("Java RMI", "covers/jrmi.gif"),
        new BookEntry("Java Security", "covers/jsec.gif"),
        new BookEntry("JavaServer Pages", "covers/jsp.gif"),
        new BookEntry("Java Servlet Programming", "covers/servlet.gif"),
        new BookEntry("Java Swing", "covers/swing.gif"),
        new BookEntry("Java Threads", "covers/jthread.gif"),
        new BookEntry("Java Web Services", "covers/jws.gif"),
        new BookEntry("Learning Java", "covers/learnj.gif")
    };

    private JList booklist = new JList(books);

    public ListExample() {
        setLayout(new BorderLayout());
        JButton button = new JButton("Print");
        button.addActionListener(new PrintListener());

        booklist = new JList(books);
        booklist.setCellRenderer(new BookCellRenderer());
        booklist.setVisibleRowCount(4);
        JScrollPane pane = new JScrollPane(booklist);
```

```
        add(pane, BorderLayout.NORTH);
        add(button, BorderLayout.SOUTH);
    }

    public static void main(String s[]) {
        JFrame frame = new JFrame("List Example");
        frame.setDefaultCloseOperation(JFrame.EXIT_ON_CLOSE);
        frame.setContentPane(new ListExample());
        frame.pack();
        frame.setVisible(true);
    }

    // An inner class to respond to clicks of the Print button
    class PrintListener implements ActionListener {
        public void actionPerformed(ActionEvent e) {
            int selected[] = booklist.getSelectedIndices();
            System.out.println("Selected Elements:  ");

            for (int i=0; i < selected.length; i++) {
                BookEntry element =
                  (BookEntry)booklist.getModel().getElementAt(selected[i]);
                System.out.println("  " + element.getTitle());
            }
        }
    }
}
```

The code to create the list is relatively short. The list is instantiated with an array of entries that encapsulate the titles and images. In our constructor, we inform the JList to use our example cell renderer to display each of the books in the list. Finally, we add the list to a JScrollPane object to allow support for scrolling. The result appears in Figure 7-9.

We added a Print button that extracts and prints the titles of all selected books. Using custom classes to encapsulate multi-part information is a major benefit of object-oriented code, and, as this example illustrates, JList makes it pretty easy to work with and display such composite building blocks.

Combo Boxes

A combo box component is actually a combination of a Swing list (embedded in a pop-up window) and a text field. Because combo boxes contain a list, many of the classes discussed in the first part of this chapter are used here as well. Unlike lists, a combo box allows the user only one selection at a time, which is usually copied into an editable component at the top, such as a text field. The user can also manually enter a selection (which does not need to be on the list). Figure 7-10 shows a high-level class diagram for Swing's combo box classes.

Like lists, the combo box component uses a data model to track its list data; the model is called ComboBoxModel.

Figure 7-9. A complete JList with a custom cell renderer

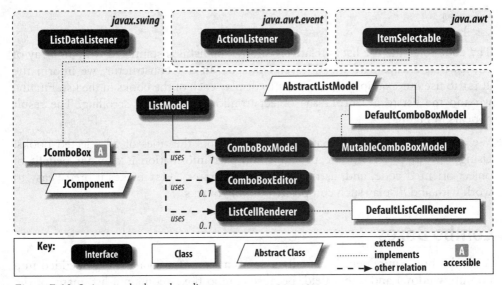

Figure 7-10. Swing combo box class diagram

The ComboBoxModel Interface

The ComboBoxModel interface extends the ListModel interface and is used as the primary model for combo box data. It adds two methods to the interface, setSelectedItem( ) and getSelectedItem( ), thus eliminating the need for a separate selection model. Since a JComboBox allows only one selected item at a time, the selection "model" is trivial and is collapsed into these two methods.

Because the data of the ComboBoxModel is stored in an internal list, the ComboBoxModel also reuses the ListDataEvent to report changes in the model state. However, with the addition of methods to monitor the current selection, the model is now obligated to report changes in the selection as well, which it does by firing a modification ListDataEvent with both endpoints as -1. Again, you should always query the event source to determine the resulting change in the elements.

You can create your own ComboBoxModel or use the default provided with the JComboBox class. The default model is an inner class of JComboBox. If you need to create your own, it is (as before) a good idea to extend the AbstractListModel class and go from there.

Property

Table 7-11 shows the property defined by the ComboBoxModel interface. The selected-Item property lets you set or retrieve the currently selected object.

Table 7-11. ComboBoxModel property

Property	Data type	get	is	set	Default value
selectedItem	Object	•		•	

See also properties of the ListModel interface (Table 7-1).

Events

The ComboBoxModel interface reuses the ListDataEvent to indicate that the selection or the contents of the list has changed. No new event-related methods are added to the ComboBoxModel interface.

The MutableComboBoxModel Interface

In addition to the ComboBoxModel, which supports unchanging lists of choices, Swing defines MutableComboBoxModel. This model, which extends the ComboBoxModel interface, adds four new methods to support changes to the list:

public abstract void addElement(Object obj)
    Add a specific element to the data model.

public abstract void removeElement(Object obj)
    Remove a specific element from the data model.

public abstract void insertElementAt(Object obj, int index)
    Insert a specific element at the given index.

public abstract void removeElementAt(int index)
    Delete a specific element from the list.

A data model that implements the MutableComboBoxModel interface also implements ComboBoxModel and ListModel, which gives the model the ability to add, remove, and retrieve elements; set a selection; and support change listeners.

The DefaultComboBoxModel Class

If you're getting lost with all these interfaces, don't despair: Swing provides a DefaultComboBoxModel that implements each of these interfaces. This probably works in almost any situation where you'd want to use a combo box.

Table 7-12 shows the properties of the DefaultComboBoxModel class. The indexed elementAt property allows you to retrieve any particular element in the list. The selectedItem property points to the currently selected item in the model. Note that the setSelectedItem( ) method fires a modification ListDataEvent, specifying both endpoints of the "change" as -1 to indicate that the selection has changed. Finally, the read-only size property lets you find out the number of elements in the vector.

Table 7-12. DefaultComboBoxModel properties

Property	Data type	get	is	set	Default value
elementAt	Object	•			null
selectedItem⁰	Object	•		•	null
size	int	•			0

⁰overridden

Constructors

public DefaultComboBoxModel( )
public DefaultComboBoxModel(Object items[])
public DefaultComboBoxModel(Vector v)
   Create a default combo box model, perhaps using an array or vector to initialize the data model. In the first case, an empty model is created. In the second, the objects in the items variable are copied into a new model. In the third case, an existing vector is installed into the model.

Methods

public void addElement(Object obj)
   Add a specific element to the data model, firing a ListDataEvent that describes the addition.

public void removeElement(Object obj)
   Remove a specific element from the data model, firing a ListDataEvent that describes the removal.

public void removeAllElements( )

Remove all elements from the data model, firing a `ListDataEvent` that describes the removal.

public void insertElementAt(Object obj, int index)

Insert an element at the specified index, firing a `ListDataEvent` that describes the insertion.

public void removeElementAt(int index)

Delete a specific element from the list, firing a `ListDataEvent` that describes the removal.

public int getIndexOf(Object obj)

Return the index of the object referenced by the variable `obj`, or `-1` if it's not found.

Event

The `DefaultComboBoxModel` interface reuses the `ListDataEvent` to indicate that the contents of the model or its selection have changed. See Table 7-13.

Table 7-13. DefaultComboBoxModel event

Event	Description
ListDataEvent	Indicates that a change in the contents of the combo box model has occurred (which includes the current selection)

Because it extends `AbstractListModel`, `DefaultComboBoxModel` provides all the listener-registration methods described earlier in this chapter: `addListDataListener( )`, `removeListDataListener( )`, `getListeners( )` (since SDK 1.3), and `getListDataListeners( )` (since SDK 1.4).

ComboBoxEditor

`ComboBoxEditor` is an interface that defines a component used for editing in the combo box. By default, `JComboBox` uses a text field for its editor. However, you can create your own combo box editor by implementing the methods of this interface.

Creating your own combo box editor takes a bit of imagination. You might notice that the methods are heavily biased toward text editing. This is not a coincidence since most of the editable components in Swing deal with text. However, there is nothing to prevent you from mixing various components together, including some of your own invention, and using the editor interface to specify how they react.

Properties

The `ComboBoxEditor` interface defines the two properties shown in Table 7-14. The `editorComponent` can be used to edit the contents of a field in the combo box. The getEditorComponent( ) accessor is typically called once, when the combo box is first displayed. You would implement this method to return the component you want to use for editing.

Table 7-14. ComboBoxEditor properties

Property	Data type	get	is	set	Default value
editorComponent	Component	•			
item	Object	•		•	

The item property is the object being edited. The setItem( ) mutator lets the editor know which item is being edited; it is called after the user selects an item from the list or completes an edit (e.g., by pressing Enter in a text field). The getItem( ) accessor returns the item currently being edited.

Events

The ComboBoxEditor interface uses an ActionListener to indicate that the user has finished modifying the item in the ComboBoxEditor. For example, the default text editor of the combo box component fires this event after the user finishes typing in the text box and presses Enter. After the editing has been completed, the combo box generally calls setItem( ) to ensure that the results are set correctly in the editor.

public abstract void addActionListener(ActionListener l)
public abstract void removeActionListener(ActionListener l)
> Add or remove a specific listener interested in receiving ActionEvents concerning the item currently being edited.

Method

public abstract void selectAll( )
> Select all content within the editable region.

Implementing a Custom Editor

The following example shows a simple custom editor for a combo box:

```
//  ComboBoxEditorExample.java
//
import java.awt.*;
import java.awt.event.*;
import java.util.*;
import javax.swing.*;
import javax.swing.border.*;

public class ComboBoxEditorExample implements ComboBoxEditor
{
```

```
Map map;
ImagePanel panel;
ImageIcon questionIcon;

public ComboBoxEditorExample(Map m, BookEntry defaultChoice) {
    map = m;
    panel = new ImagePanel(defaultChoice);
    questionIcon = new ImageIcon("question.gif");
}

public void setItem(Object anObject)
{
    if (anObject != null) {
        panel.setText(anObject.toString( ));
        BookEntry entry = (BookEntry)map.get(anObject.toString( ));
        if (entry != null)
            panel.setIcon(entry.getImage( ));
        else
            panel.setIcon(questionIcon);
    }
}

public Component getEditorComponent( ) { return panel; }
public Object getItem( ) { return panel.getText( ); }
public void selectAll( ) { panel.selectAll( ); }

public void addActionListener(ActionListener l) {
    panel.addActionListener(l);
}

public void removeActionListener(ActionListener l) {
    panel.removeActionListener(l);
}

// We create our own inner class to set and repaint the image and text.
class ImagePanel extends JPanel {

    JLabel imageIconLabel;
    JTextField textField;

    public ImagePanel(BookEntry initialEntry) {
        setLayout(new BorderLayout( ));

        imageIconLabel = new JLabel(initialEntry.getImage( ));
        imageIconLabel.setBorder(new BevelBorder(BevelBorder.RAISED));

        textField = new JTextField(initialEntry.getTitle( ));
        textField.setColumns(45);
        textField.setBorder(new BevelBorder(BevelBorder.LOWERED));

        add(imageIconLabel, BorderLayout.WEST);
        add(textField, BorderLayout.EAST);
    }
```

```
        public void setText(String s) { textField.setText(s); }
        public String getText() { return (textField.getText()); }

        public void setIcon(Icon i) {
            imageIconLabel.setIcon(i);
            repaint();
        }

        public void selectAll() { textField.selectAll(); }

        public void addActionListener(ActionListener l) {
            textField.addActionListener(l);
        }
        public void removeActionListener(ActionListener l) {
            textField.removeActionListener(l);
        }
    }
}
```

This example is tightly coupled with the example for the JComboBox class (later in the chapter). However, the source is not hard to understand. When the combo box is initialized, Swing calls getEditorComponent( ) to position and paint the combo box editor at the top of the JComboBox component. This is our inner class, and essentially consists of a JPanel with both the name of a book and its cover image.

The user is allowed to interact freely with the text field. Whenever the user selects a list element or completes an edit in the text field, the setItem( ) method is called to update the book icon. If an icon cannot be found for the text, a question mark is displayed. Whenever the editor needs to retrieve the currently edited object, it makes a call to getItem( ). Note that our addActionListener( ) and removeActionListener( ) methods pass the listener to the JTextField defined in the editor.

The JComboBox Class

JComboBox combines a button or editable field and a drop-down list. It is very similar to the AWT Choice component and even implements the ItemSelectable interface for backward compatibility. By default, the JComboBox component provides a single text edit field adjacent to a small button with a downward arrow. When the button is pressed, a pop-up list of choices is displayed, one of which can be selected by the user. If a selection is made, the choice is copied into the edit field, and the pop up disappears. If there was a previous selection, it is erased. You can also remove the pop up by pressing Tab (or Esc, depending on the L&F) while the combo box has the focus. Figure 7-11 shows combo boxes as they appear in four different L&Fs.

The text field in the JComboBox component can be either editable or not editable. This state is controlled by the editable property. If the text field is editable, the user is allowed to type information into the text box (which may not correspond to anything

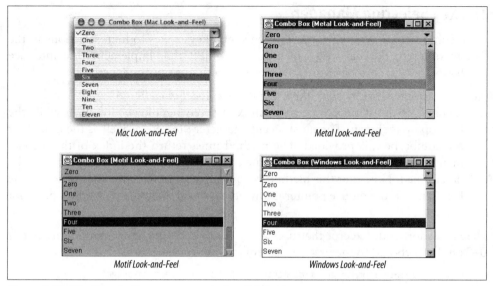

Mac Look-and-Feel

Metal Look-and-Feel

Motif Look-and-Feel

Windows Look-and-Feel

Figure 7-11. The JComboBox component in four L&Fs

in the list), as well as make selections from the list. If the component is not editable, the user can only make selections from the list.

Unless you specify a set of objects in the constructor, the combo box comes up empty. You can use the addItem( ) method to add objects to the combo box list. Conversely, the removeItem( ) and removeItemAt( ) methods remove a specified object from the list. You also have the ability to insert objects at specific locations in the combo box list with the insertItemAt( ) method. If you wish to retrieve the current number of objects in the list, use the getItemCount( ) method, and if you wish to retrieve an object at a specific index, use the getItemAt( ) method.

Note that the list component inside the JComboBox is not part of the component itself but rather part of its UI delegate. Hence, there is no property to access the list component directly. However, you should be able to get any information you need through the component properties or the ComboBoxModel.

As with regular pop-up menus, you have the ability to specify whether the pop up in the JComboBox component should be drawn as a lightweight or a heavyweight component. Lightweight components require less memory and computing resources. However, if you are using any heavyweight components, you should consider forcing the combo box to use a heavyweight pop up, or else the pop up could be obscured behind your heavyweight components. This can be done by setting the lightWeightPopupEnabled property to false. If the property is set to true, the combo box uses a lightweight pop up when appropriate.

Combo boxes use the same ListCellRenderer as the JList component (discussed earlier in this chapter) to paint selected and nonselected items in its list.

The Key Selection Manager

With combo boxes, you have the ability to map keystrokes to item selections in the list. In order to do this, you can create an object that implements the interface JComboBox.KeySelectionManager. This interface contains only one method:

public int selectionForKey(char aKey, ComboBoxModel model)

Invoked by the JComboBox component after receiving a keyboard event while the list pop up is shown. The most recent character pressed, as well as the model for the combo box, is provided. The method must return the index of the list element that should be highlighted in the combo box, or -1 if a selection cannot be determined. Note that this method is equivalent to moving the mouse across the list; hence, if the mouse pointer is anywhere inside the list, this method does not work.

Here is a short code excerpt that uses a key selection manager to map the numerals 0–9 on the keyboard to the first 10 elements in the combo box list:

```
class myKeySelectionManager implements JComboBox.KeySelectionManager
{
    public int selectionForKey(char aKey, ComboBoxModel aModel) {
        if ((aKey >= '0') && (aKey <= '9'))
            return (aKey - '0');
        else
            return -1;
    }
}
```

You can install the key selection manager using the setKeySelectionManager( ) method of JComboBox:

```
myComboBox.setKeySelectionManager(new myKeySelectionManager( ));
```

If you do not install your own, a default key selection manager selects items in the list whose first character matches what you've typed on the keyboard. (This is not as sophisticated as what JList now supports, in that only the first character is ever considered, but the interface was defined prior to JList's keyboard navigation capability.)

Properties

Table 7-15 shows the properties that can be found in the JComboBox component. As we mentioned earlier, the editable property defines whether the text field of the combo box allows text to be entered manually. The lightWeightPopupEnabled property allows you to specify whether JComboBox should use a lightweight component to draw the list pop up. The popupVisible property controls whether the pop up associated with the combo box is visible. The maximumRowCount property represents the total number of list elements that can be displayed in the pop up. If the list contains more than maximumRowCount, a scrollbar provides access to the rest of the items.

Table 7-15. JComboBox properties

Property	Data type	get	is	set	Default value
accessibleContext	AccessibleContext	•			JComboBox.AccessibleJComboBox( )
action[1.3, b]	Action	•		•	null
actionCommand	String	•		•	"comboBoxChanged"
editable[b]	boolean		•	•	false
editor[b]	ComboBoxEditor	•		•	ComboBoxEditor( )
enabled[b, o]	boolean			•	true
itemAt[i]	Object	•			null
itemCount	int	•			0
keySelectionManager	JComboBox.KeySelectionManager	•		•	JComboBox.DefaultKeySelectionManager( )
lightWeightPopupEnabled[b]	boolean		•	•	true
maximumRowCount[b]	int	•		•	8
model[b]	ComboBoxModel	•		•	JComboBox.DefaultComboBoxModel( )
opaque[o]	boolean		•	•	true
popupVisible	boolean		•	•	
prototypeDisplayValue[1.4, b]	Object	•		•	null
renderer[b]	ListCellRenderer	•		•	
selectedIndex	int	•		•	-1
selectedItem	Object	•		•	null
selectedObjects	Object[]	•			null
UI[b]	ComboBoxUI	•		•	From L&F
UIClassID[o]	String	•			"ComboBoxUI"

[1.3]since 1.3, [1.4]since 1.4, [b]bound, [i]indexed, [o]overridden

See also properties from the JComponent class (Table 3-6).

Some properties mimic those in JList. The selectedItem property represents the object currently selected in the combo box. If you call the setSelectedItem( ) method with an object that does not exist, the first object in the list is selected instead. The selectedIndex property gives the index of the selected item, or -1 if there is none. The selectedObjects property holds an array of size 1—the object currently selected. The getSelectedObjects( ) method is present to provide backward compatibility with the AWT Choice component. The read-only itemCount property tells how many elements are currently in the combo box's list.

The enabled property overrides that of the java.awt.Component class. If the property is set to false, the method prevents the user from selecting items from the list and typing text into the text field or editor. The opaque property is always true to indicate that the component uses all of its drawing region.

The actionCommand property is coupled to an ActionEvent that is fired when the user makes a selection inside the list. The actionCommand typically contains a string-based representation of the selected item. SDK 1.3 introduced the more powerful action property, which allows you to tie the combo box to an Action object so that its enabled state and tooltip text are automatically updated if the Action is changed.

Finally, the prototypeDisplayValue property, added in SDK 1.4, allows you to greatly speed up the display of the combo box. If you set this property, the combo box uses the prototype object you supply when trying to calculate its size in the layout. If you don't set this, it has no choice but to iterate over all the contents of its data model and find the biggest size among them, which takes much longer. (Of course, if you're supplying a prototype, it's your responsibility to make sure it's the right size for the entire list.)

Events

Combo boxes fire both an ItemEvent and an ActionEvent when the selection in the list has changed. The ItemEvent is fired when there is a change in the current selection of the list, from any source. The ActionEvent is fired when the user explicitly makes a selection; it is coupled with the actionCommand property. (Note that the actionCommand does not by default tell you the item that was selected.) The ItemEvent and its listener list maintain backward compatibility with the ItemSelectable interface of AWT 1.1.

public void addItemListener(ItemListener aListener)
public void removeItemListener(ItemListener aListener)
> Add or remove an ItemListener from the list. These methods maintain backward compatibility with the ItemSelectable interface of AWT 1.1.

public ItemListener[] getItemListeners()
> Return the currently registered item listeners (introduced in SDK 1.4).

public void addActionListener(ActionListener l)
public void removeActionListener(ActionListener l)
> Add or remove an ActionListener for ActionEvents sent when the user makes a selection.

public ActionListener[] getActionListeners()
> Return the currently registered action listeners (added in SDK 1.4).

In developing real applications, many developers wanted to have the contents of a combo box react to the current state of the application (items might be added or removed depending on the modes or documents that the user had active). The most convenient way to achieve such context-sensitivity is to update the content of the combo box right before it is displayed. Unfortunately, there was no public API for doing this, so some developers chose to dive into the details of the actual L&F-specific UI delegate implementations and hook their applications into the "guts" of Swing. Starting with SDK 1.4, the Swing API provides an official, public way to update your combo box before its list pops up for the user. You can now express interest in being notified before the combo box shows a pop-up menu by registering a PopupMenuListener. (Note that if the L&F does not use a pop-up menu to implement the list portion of the combo box, you may not receive any notifications. So far, all standard L&Fs do use pop-up menus and do fire these events).

public void addPopupMenuListener(PopupMenuListener aListener)
public void removePopupMenuListener(PopupMenuListener aListener)
public PopupMenuListener[] getPopupMenuListeners()
  These methods provide the familiar set of event-notification support for learning about the imminent display of the pop-up menu associated with a combo box, starting with SDK 1.4. See "The PopupMenuListener Interface" and "The Popup-MenuEvent Class" in Chapter 14 for details about the events you can receive.

Constructors

public JComboBox(ComboBoxModel aModel)
  This constructor initializes its items from an existing ComboBoxModel.

public JComboBox(Object items[])
  Create a JComboBox using the items specified in the array.

public JComboBox(Vector items)
  Create a JComboBox using the items specified in the Vector passed in.

public JComboBox()
  Create an empty JComboBox using the DefaultComboBoxModel as its data model.

Methods

public void updateUI()
  Called by the UIManager when the L&F of the component has changed.

public void showPopup()
  Raise the popup that contains the combo box list.

public void hidePopup()
  Close the popup that contains the combo box list.

public void configureEditor(ComboBoxEditor anEditor, Object anItem)
  Initialize the specified ComboBoxEditor with the object passed in.

List methods

These methods require that the combo box use a `MutableComboBoxModel`; otherwise, an exception is thrown:

public void addItem(Object anObject)
> Add a specific object to the end of the list.

public void insertItemAt(Object anObject, int index)
> Insert an object into the list after the specified index.

public void removeItem(Object anObject)
> Remove the specified object from the list after the specified index.

public void removeItemAt(int anIndex)
> Remove an object from the list at the specified index.

public void removeAllItems( )
> Remove all items from the list.

Key selection

protected JComboBox.KeySelectionManager createDefaultKeySelectionManager( )
> Return a new instance of the default key selection manager. This selection manager matches keystrokes against the first character of each item in the list starting with the first item below the selected item (if there is one).

public boolean selectWithKeyChar(char keyChar)
> Attempt to select a list item that corresponds to the character passed in. If the method is successful, it returns `true`. If there is no list item that corresponds to that character, the method returns `false`.

Internal methods

Because the `JComboBox` uses a number of other components to build its interface (often a text field, a pop-up menu, and a list), it implements several methods needed to interact with these constituent components. These methods must be public so the components can call them, but they are *not* intended to be invoked by you or me. But if you are tempted to use one of these anyway, be aware that since the previous publication of this book, a number of such methods have been removed, and your code would have broken had you relied on them.

public void processKeyEvent(KeyEvent e)
> Override processKeyEvent( ) in `JComponent`. This method calls `hidePopup( )` if the user presses the Tab key. It should not be invoked by the programmer.

public void actionPerformed(ActionEvent e)
> Monitor internal action events from the embedded list component. Although it is public, you should not invoke or overridde this method.

public void contentsChanged(ListDataEvent e)

Monitor model events from the list component. Although it is public, you should not invoke or overridde this method.

public void firePopupMenuWillBecomeVisible( )
public void firePopupMenuWillBecomeInvisible( )
public void firePopupMenuCanceled( )

These methods help the combo box track the state of its pop-up menu. They should not be called by the programmer.

Java Books Revisited

Here is the list of some O'Reilly Java books implemented as a combo box. We use our new combo box editor to allow the user to see which book is selected.

```
// EditableComboBox.java
//
import java.awt.*;
import java.awt.event.*;
import java.util.*;
import javax.swing.*;

public class EditableComboBox extends JPanel {

    private BookEntry books[] = {
      // Include same book information as in ListExample above.
    };

    Map bookMap = new HashMap( );

    public EditableComboBox( ) {
      // Build a mapping from book titles to their entries.
      for (int i = 0 ; i < books.length; i++) {
        bookMap.put(books[i].getTitle( ), books[i]);
      }

      setLayout(new BorderLayout( ));

      JComboBox bookCombo = new JComboBox(books);
      bookCombo.setEditable(true);
      bookCombo.setEditor(
        new ComboBoxEditorExample(bookMap, books[0]));
      bookCombo.setMaximumRowCount(4);
      bookCombo.addActionListener(new ActionListener( ) {
          public void actionPerformed(ActionEvent e) {
              System.out.println("You chose " + ((JComboBox)e.getSource( )).
                                            getSelectedItem( )  + "!");
          }
      });
      bookCombo.setActionCommand("Hello");
      add(bookCombo, BorderLayout.CENTER);
    }
```

```
public static void main(String s[]) {
    JFrame frame = new JFrame("Combo Box Example");
    frame.setDefaultCloseOperation(JFrame.EXIT_ON_CLOSE);
    frame.setContentPane(new EditableComboBox());
    frame.pack();
    frame.setVisible(true);
}
}
```

The code to initialize the combo box is relatively simple. After the combo box is instantiated, we set the editable property to true and inform the combo box of our custom editor. Finally, we set the maximumRowCount property to 4, ensuring that the user cannot see more than four books in the list at a time. If the user types in a book that cannot be found in our list, the example displays a question mark instead of a cover. Whenever a selection is made, the results are printed on the screen. Figure 7-12 shows the result.

Figure 7-12. A custom JComboBox component

Spinners

You might be wondering just what a spinner is. It's a new 1.4 component similar to the JComboBox, but it shows only one item. It includes up and down arrows to "scroll" through its set of values. A JFormattedTextField is used to edit and render those values. Spinners are quite flexible. They work nicely with a set of choices (such as the months of the year) as well as with unbounded ranges such as a set of integers. Figure 7-13 shows several examples of spinners in different L&Fs. The Mac L&F is missing from this figure because the SDK 1.4 was not available on OS X at the time we went to press.

The classes involved in spinners are shown in Figure 7-14.

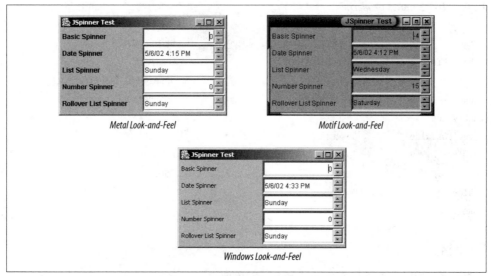

Figure 7-13. Various JSpinner instances in three L&Fs

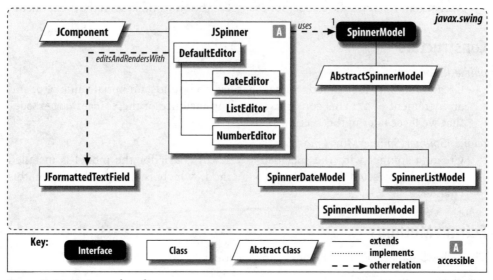

Figure 7-14. JSpinner class diagram

Properties

JSpinner has several properties related to the values it displays (see Table 7-16). Most of the properties are easy to understand from their names alone. The currently selected value is available through the read/write value property.

Table 7-16. JSpinner properties

Property	Data type	get	is	set	Default value
changeListeners	ChangeListener[]	•			Empty array
editor[b]	JComponent	•		•	JPspinner.NumberEditor( )
model[b]	SpinnerModel	•		•	SpinnerNumberModel( )
nextValue	Object	•			
previousValue	Object	•			
UI	SpinnerUI	•			L&F-dependent
UIClassID	String	•			"SpinnerUI"
value	Object	•		•	

[b]bound

Events

public void addChangeListener(ChangeListener l)
public void removeChangeListener(ChangeListener l)
 Add or remove a specific listener for ChangeEvent notifications from the component.

Constructors

public JSpinner( )
 Create a spinner for numeric values that has no bounds, an initial value of 0, and an increment of 1. (This constructor uses an instance of the SpinnerNumberModel that we'll see later in this section.)

public JSpinner(SpinnerModel model)
 Create a spinner with the specified model. An editor for the model is installed using the protected createEditor( ) method, which is discussed later in this chapter.

Editing Methods

The following methods may be of use to developers:

public void commitEdit( )
 Commit the current value to the spinner model. With a JFormattedTextField as your editor, you can commit the value you typed by pressing the Enter key. The model then stores the value internally. If you type in an invalid value (bad date, not a number, etc.), the editor does not accept the change, and you have to continue editing. You can also cancel the edit using the Esc key.

 Your model might also reject the value you tried to commit. For example, you might type in a perfectly valid date, but that date is outside the range of dates the model expects. In this case, `JFormattedTextField` does not complain, but the value is still unacceptable.

protected JComponent createEditor(SpinnerModel model)

Create an editor appropriate for the specified model. "Appropriate" currently means a `JFormattedTextField` with a format designed for dates, numbers, or `String` representations of elements in a list. If `model` is not an instance of one of the known models, a default editor (which uses a `String` representation of the value) is used. To install your own editor based on a model, you'll have to subclass `JSpinner` and override this method. (You could always call `setEditor( )` for one of the editors.)

Simple Spinners

The code for the spinner examples in Figure 7-13 is shown below. Notice that we use various model constructors to build the different spinners. The spinner models are discussed in the next section.

```
// SpinnerTest.java
//
import javax.swing.*;
import javax.swing.event.*;
import java.awt.*;

public class SpinnerTest extends JFrame {

  public SpinnerTest( ) {
    super("JSpinner Test");
    setSize(300,180);
    setDefaultCloseOperation(EXIT_ON_CLOSE);

    Container c = getContentPane( );
    c.setLayout(new GridLayout(0,2));

    c.add(new JLabel(" Basic Spinner"));
    c.add(new JSpinner( ));

    c.add(new JLabel(" Date Spinner"));
    c.add(new JSpinner(new SpinnerDateModel( )));

    String weekdays[] = new String[] { "Sunday", "Monday", "Tuesday",
        "Wednesday", "Thursday", "Friday", "Saturday" };
    c.add(new JLabel(" List Spinner"));
    c.add(new JSpinner(new SpinnerListModel(weekdays)));

    c.add(new JLabel(" Number Spinner"));
    c.add(new JSpinner(new SpinnerNumberModel(0, 0, 100, 5)));

    c.add(new JLabel(" Rollover List Spinner"));
    c.add(new JSpinner(new RolloverSpinnerListModel(weekdays)));
```

```
      setVisible(true);
   }

   public static void main(String args[]) {
      new SpinnerTest();
   }
}
```

Spinner Models

The `javax.swing` package includes several pre-built models for many common data types suited to spinners. Figure 7-15 shows the hierarchy of these models.

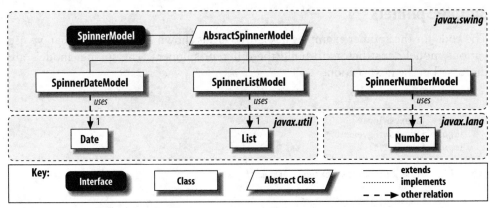

Figure 7-15. SpinnerModel class diagram

The SpinnerModel Interface

The `SpinnerModel` interface includes methods required to successfully store and retrieve spinner data. It includes a read/write value and next and previous properties, and it forces implementing models (such as `AbstractSpinnerModel`) to support a `ChangeListener`.

Properties

Not surprisingly, the properties for `SpinnerModel` are centered on the value being shown in the spinner. Notice in Table 7-17 that the model stores only the current value and the next/previous values. The actual list (or other object) behind these values is not part of the model.

Table 7-17. SpinnerModel properties

Property	Data type	get	is	set	Default value
nextValue	Object	•			
previousValue	Object	•			
value	Object	•		•	

Events

Any changes to the selected value should be reported through ChangeEvent objects.

public void addChangeListener(ChangeListener l)
public void removeChangeListener(ChangeListener l)
    Add or remove a specific listener for ChangeEvent notifications from the component.

The AbstractSpinnerModel Class

The AbstractSpinnerModel class implements the event parts of the SpinnerModel. Implementations of addChangeListener( ), removeChangeListener( ), and getChange-Listeners( ) are all present. Two expected methods, fireStateChange( ) and get-Listeners( ), have been added. All the other models subclass AbstractSpinnerModel, as shown in Figure 7-15.

The SpinnerDateModel

If you're retrieving dates from users, a date spinner can make the input process much simpler. You can supply minimum and maximum dates along with an increment value (to increment by day, week, month, year, etc.).

Properties

Table 7-18 shows the properties for SpinnerDateModel. Apart from the properties inherited from AbstractSpinnerModel, start and end properties have been added to make it possible to work within a bounded range of dates. Either of these properties can be set to null to indicate that you do not want a minimum or maximum. The calendarField property determines the increment/decrement step size and uses constants defined in the java.util.Calendar class. The valid step sizes are shown in Table 7-19. The date property is a convenience property that allows you to retrieve the current value of the spinner as a Date object.

Table 7-18. SpinnerDateModel properties

Property	Data type	get	is	set	Default value
calendarField	int	•		•	Calendar.DAY_OF_MONTH
date	java.util.Date	•			Current date
end	Comparable	•		•	null (no end)
nextValue°	Object	•			
previousValue°	Object	•			
start	Comparable	•		•	null (no start)
value°	Object	•		•	

°overridden

Table 7-19. Calendar constants for SpinnerDateModel

Calendar.AM_PM	Calendar.MILLISECOND
Calendar.DAY_OF_MONTH	Calendar.MINUTE
Calendar.DAY_OF_WEEK	Calendar.MONTH
Calendar.DAY_OF_WEEK_IN_MONTH	Calendar.SECOND
Calendar.DAY_OF_YEAR	Calendar.WEEK_OF_MONTH
Calendar.ERA	Calendar.WEEK_OF_YEAR
Calendar.HOUR	Calendar.YEAR
Calendar.HOUR_OF_DAY	

Constructors

public SpinnerDateModel( )

> This constructor creates a date model with no start or end point that uses the current date for the current value. The spin increment/decrement value is one day.

public SpinnerDateModel(Date value, Comparable start, Comparable end, int calendarField)

> This constructor builds a model with the specified current value, start, and end points, and an increment of calendarField. Note that start and end can be null to indicate that no minimum or maximum dates are applicable.

The SpinnerListModel Class

This model allows you to spin through the (String representation of) items in a List (or an array—which gets turned into a List). When you hit the start or the end, trying to go past them results in a null next or previous value that effectively stops the spinner from spinning; in other words, you can't go past the bounds of the array.

The Javadoc makes a point worth repeating here: the model stores only a reference to the list of items, not a copy. If the list changes, it's up to the programmer to deal with the consequences. The benefit, of course, is that the items shown by the spinner stay in near-perfect sync with the list. We say near-perfect because if you're sitting on the item that changed, it won't show up until you spin away and spin back.

Properties

The only new property added to SpinnerListModel is, not surprisingly, the list itself. See Table 7-20.

Table 7-20. SpinnerListModel properties

Property	Data type	get	is	set	Default value
list	java.util.List	•		•	List with one entry: "empty"
nextValue[o]	Object	•			
previousValue[o]	Object	•			
value[o]	Object	•		•	

[o]overridden

Constructors

Three constructors exist for creating new SpinnerListModel objects:

public SpinnerListModel( )

This constructor creates a spinner with an effectively empty list. (The list is built by calling the Object array version of the constructor with a one-element String array containing the word empty.)

public SpinnerListModel(List values)
public SpinnerListModel(Object[] values)

These constructors build SpinnerListModel objects associated with the specified values. Note that only a reference to values is kept in the model, so you can update the content somewhat dynamically. In the case of the Object array version, the list returned from the list property is a private inner class from the java.util.Arrays class that does not override the default add( ) behavior (which simply throws an UnsupportedOperationException). To be honest, you really should rethink using a JSpinner on dynamic lists—or at least make your own model that pays proper attention to changing contents.

The SpinnerNumberModel Class

The number model allows you to spin numbers (both integers and decimals). The range can be bounded, or you can selectively leave off the minimum, maximum, or both. While you normally use Number objects to fill the model, special case constructors exist for the very common `int` and `double` types. For those types, you specify the starting position, the minimum and maximum, and the step size. (Note that for `doubles`, the step size is also a `double`, so you can increment by 0.1, 0.05, 2.5, etc.)

Properties

Table 7-21 shows the properties for the number model. Beyond the standard properties, minimum and maximum properties are added to provide a range for the spinner. As with the `SpinnerDateModel`, either of these values can be `null` to indicate that no limit exists. The `stepSize` property allows you to specify the increment/decrement value for the spinner. The `number` property is a convenience property that allows you to retrieve the current value as a `Number` object.

Table 7-21. SpinnerNumberModel properties

Property	Data type	get	is	set	Default value
maximum	Comparable	•		•	null (no max)
minimum	Comparable	•		•	null (no min)
nextValue°	Object	•			
number	Number	•			Integer(0)
previousValue°	Object	•			
stepSize	Number	•		•	Integer(1)
value°	Object	•		•	Integer(0)

°overridden

Constructors

public SpinnerNumberModel()
> Construct a `SpinnerNumberModel` with no `minimum` or `maximum` value, a `stepSize` equal to one, and an initial value of 0.

public SpinnerNumberModel(int value, int minimum, int maximum, int stepSize)
public SpinnerNumberModel(double value, double minimum, double maximum, double stepSize)
public SpinnerNumberModel(Number value, Comparable minimum, Comparable maximum, Number stepSize)
> Build number models with a starting point of value, the specified `minimum` and `maximum` points, and the given `stepSize`. The `int` and `double` constructors are for convenience only. If you need an open `minimum` or `maximum`, you'll have to use the `Number`/`Comparable` version.

A Custom Model: Rollover Lists

As an example of how simple it can be to extend the functionality of these spinner models, here's a `RolloverListModel` that you can use. Like the `SpinnerListModel`, it takes a list, but rather than return `null` if you try to go past the end (or the beginning, for that matter), it "rolls over" to the beginning (or the end). Here's the source code for this model:

```
// RolloverSpinnerListModel.java
//

import javax.swing.*;
import java.util.List;

public class RolloverSpinnerListModel extends SpinnerListModel {

  public RolloverSpinnerListModel(Object[] items) { super(items); }
  public RolloverSpinnerListModel(List items) { super(items); }

  public Object getNextValue( ) {
    Object nv = super.getNextValue( );
    if (nv != null) {
      return nv;
    }
    return getList( ).get(0);
  }

  public Object getPreviousValue( ) {
    Object pv = super.getPreviousValue( );
    if (pv != null) {
      return pv;
    }
    List l = getList( );
    return l.get(l.size( ) - 1);
  }
}
```

This model is used for the last spinner shown in Figure 7-13. In that example, we use the weekdays array for both a standard list model and this rollover list model. You'll have to play with the spinner to get the effect—static screen shots just don't do it justice.

Spinner Editors

You probably noticed that the JSpinner class also includes several inner classes. These inner classes provide basic editors (and renderers) for spinners for each of the major model types. While you'll typically rely on the editor picked by your spinner when you create it, you can override that decision if you like. Here's a simple example of a modified DateEditor. This spinner displays an mm/yy date, and the step size is one month. Figure 7-16 shows such a spinner.

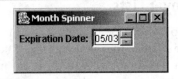

Figure 7-16. A customized DateEditor used in a JSpinner

Here's the source code that built this editor:

```java
// MonthSpinner.java
//
import javax.swing.*;
import javax.swing.event.*;
import java.awt.*;
import java.util.*;

public class MonthSpinner extends JFrame {

  public MonthSpinner( ) {
    super("Month Spinner");
    setSize(200,100);
    setDefaultCloseOperation(EXIT_ON_CLOSE);

    Container c = getContentPane( );
    c.setLayout(new FlowLayout(FlowLayout.LEFT, 4,4));

    c.add(new JLabel("Expiration Date:"));
    Date today = new Date( );
    // Start the spinner today, but don't set a min or max date.
    // The increment should be a month.
    JSpinner s = new JSpinner(new SpinnerDateModel(today,
               null, null, Calendar.MONTH));
    JSpinner.DateEditor de = new JSpinner.DateEditor(s, "MM/yy");
    s.setEditor(de);
    c.add(s);

    setVisible(true);
  }
  public static void main(String args[]) {
    new MonthSpinner( );
  }
}
```

DefaultEditor

All of the other inner class editors descend from the DefaultEditor class, as shown in Figure 7-14. That's exactly why you would use this class: it's a starting point for creating other simple editors. It's based on a single JFormattedTextField.

Constructors

This editor takes a single constructor:

public JSpinner.DefaultEditor(JSpinner spinner)
> Build an editor for the given spinner. This constructor registers itself as a listener to spinner's change events and displays the current value of spinner's model.

Properties

The DefaultEditor has two read-only properties, which are shown in Table 7-22.

Table 7-22. JSpinner.DefaultEditor properties

Property	Data type	get	is	set	Default value
spinner	JSpinner	•			
textField	JFormattedTextField	•			

Editing methods

public void commitEdit( ) throws ParseException
> Send the current value in the editor to the model for the spinner.

public void dismiss(JSpinner spinner)
> Disconnect the editor from the specified spinner. (This should be the same spinner as the one passed to the constructor.) By default, this simply detaches the editor from spinner's ChangeListener list. For example, if you want to cancel your edits, you dismiss( ) the spinner.

DateEditor

As you can see in the previous example, the DateEditor inner class provides simple display and edit functionality for dates. The supported formats follow those in the java.text.SimpleDateFormat class.

Note that the editor is just looking for valid date formats. You can set up a SpinnerDateModel that increments dates on a week-by-week basis, e.g., every Sunday. If you type in a date that should be a Monday, the DateEditor allows it, and the default model sets the new date. Now when you use the spinner's up/down buttons, you'll bounce forward and backward on Mondays—not Sundays. Check out the ListEditor discussion for an example of stopping the user from editing spinner values by hand.

Constructors

public JSpinner.DateEditor(JSpinner spinner)

> Create a standard editor (a formatted text field) for dates using the model from the given spinner. The format of the date (in the U.S. English locale) is M/d/yy h:mm a (for example, 4/13/07 3:14 PM).

public JSpinner.DateEditor(JSpinner spinner, String dateFormatPattern)

> Create a standard editor for dates using the model from the specified spinner. The dateFormatPattern determines how dates are shown as well as how they can be entered by a user. The pattern must match the specifications of the java.text.SimpleDateFormat class. Table 7-23 shows some of the more common elements you might use in such a pattern.

Table 7-23. SimpleDateFormat common formats

Code	Description	Example usage
d	Day in month	d -> "7", "17"; dd -> "07", "17"
E	Day in week	E -> "Monday"; EEE -> "Mon"
M	Month in year	M -> "4", "12"; MM -> "04", "12"; MMM -> "Apr", "Dec"; MMMM -> "April", "December"
y	Year	yy -> "02", "99"; yyyy -> "2002", "1999"
h	Hours (1–12)	h -> "5", "10"; hh -> "05", "10"
m	Minutes (0–59)	mm -> "15", "32"
a	A.M./P.M. marker	a -> "AM", "PM"

Properties

Two read-only properties exist for the DateEditor. These are shown in Table 7-24.

Table 7-24. JSpinner.DateEditor properties

Property	Data type	get	is	set	Default value
format	SimpleDateFormat	•			"M/d/yy h:mm a"
model	SpinnerDateModel	•			

ListEditor

This simple editor works on spinners with a SpinnerListModel installed. Its primary function is to make sure typed values match up with values in the actual model. If you start typing in a list spinner, the text field tries to auto-complete. If you type a value that does not exist in the model, the typed value is discarded when you press Enter.

This editor works only on strings. If your list is numeric (like denominations of paper money) or composed of arbitrary objects, they will be represented and edited as strings. For non-String objects, then, typing values into the spinner is a futile exercise. Even if you type the representation of a valid object, the List underneath it will not recognize the value. (The editor handed over a String, but the List is composed of Number objects, so how can they be equivalent?) In cases such as this, you should either build your own editor or, more simply, disable the editing features of the spinner to restrict the user to the up/down buttons:

```
Integer[] bills = new Integer[] { new Integer(1), new Integer(2), new Integer(5),
                                  new Integer(10), new Integer(20) };
JSpinner spinner = new JSpinner(new SpinnerListModel(bills));
((JSpinner.DefaultEditor)spinner.getEditor()).getTextField().setEditable(false);
```

For the record, this code snippet happily removes the editing capacity from any spinner—not just those built on the ListSpinnerModel.

Constructor

public JSpinner.ListEditor(JSpinner spinner)
> Create an editor for spinner and register for change events coming from the spinner.

Property

As you can see in Table 7-25, the spinner's model is the only property for the ListEditor inner class.

Table 7-25. JSpinner.ListEditor property

Property	Data type	get	is	set	Default value
model	SpinnerListModel	•			

NumberEditor

The NumberEditor closely resembles the DateEditor. It creates a formatted text field for the display and input of numeric data and can use a custom formatter to alter the syntax of acceptable information.

Constructors

public JSpinner.NumberEditor(JSpinner spinner)
> Create a standard editor (a formatted text field) for decimal numbers using the model from the given spinner. The format of the number (in the U.S. English locale) is #,##0.### (for example, 6,789.125).

public JSpinner.NumberEditor(JSpinner spinner, String decimalFormatPattern)

Create a standard editor for numbers using the model from the specified spinner. The decimalFormatPattern determines how numbers are shown as well as how they can be entered by a user. The pattern must match the specifications of the java.text.DecimalFormat class. Table 7-26 shows some of the more common elements you might use in such a pattern. Note that the pattern is localized. If your locale uses "," for the decimal separator, that's precisely what appears on the screen. The code you enter should follow the (nonlocalized!) syntax in the DecimalFormat class.

Table 7-26. DecimalFormat common formats

Code	Description	Example usage
#	Digit, zeros don't show	# -> "4", "123456"
0	Digit, zeros show as zeros	0.00 -> "3.14", "250.00"
,	Grouping separator	#,##0 -> "25", "1,250", "3,141,593"
.	Decimal separator	0.# -> "25", "3.1"
-	A (required) minus sign	-#.0## -> "-25.0", "-1.414"
;	Positive and negative pattern separator	#;(#) -> "25", "(32)"

Properties

The NumberEditor has two read-only properties (see Table 7-27). Note that these are the same properties the DateEditor has.

Table 7-27. JSpinner.NumberEditor properties

Property	Data type	get	is	set	Default value
format	DecimalFormat	•			"#,##0.###"
model	SpinnerNumberModel	•			

A Custom Editor

"Custom editor" is a bit of a misnomer in this case. While we will install our own editor for a JSpinner, it doesn't allow editing. What we're really after is the rendering facilities that are provided by the editor component. This example does lay out the pieces of the custom editor that make it interesting if you need to build an editor that is not based on JFormattedTextField.

One of the most obvious things missing from JFormattedTextField is the ability to display graphics. We'll build a simple "editor" that displays Icon objects. Figure 7-17 is a quick look at the spinner in action.

The code to build a custom editor is not too difficult if you can base your editor on existing components. Our IconEditor class is based on JLabel. The most important

Figure 7-17. Our IconEditor used in a JSpinner (before and after pressing the up arrow)

step in making the editor render the proper image is registering a ChangeListener with the spinner. (Recall that the spinner fires a ChangeEvent any time the user alters the current value.) Here's the code for IconEditor:

```java
//IconEditor.java
//
import javax.swing.*;
import javax.swing.event.*;

public class IconEditor extends JLabel implements ChangeListener {

  JSpinner spinner;
  Icon icon;

  public IconEditor(JSpinner s) {
    super((Icon)s.getValue(), CENTER);
    icon = (Icon)s.getValue();
    spinner = s;
    spinner.addChangeListener(this);
  }

  public void stateChanged(ChangeEvent ce) {
    icon = (Icon)spinner.getValue();
    setIcon(icon);
  }

  public JSpinner getSpinner() { return spinner; }
  public Icon getIcon() { return icon; }
}
```

Of course, actual editors that let you modify the value of the spinner without using the up/down buttons require quite a bit more code. But you do have a reference to the spinner for this editor. Once you have a valid value in your custom editor, you just call spinner.setValue( ) to pass the value back to the spinner's model. (The commitEdit( ) method of JSpinner works only on subclasses of JSpinner.DefaultEditor.)

To put your editor into play with a particular spinner, you just call setEditor( ) for the spinner. Here's the code that sets up the simple example shown in Figure 7-17.

```java
// IconSpinner.java
//
import javax.swing.*;
import java.awt.*;

public class IconSpinner extends JFrame {
```

```
public IconSpinner( ) {
  super("JSpinner Icon Test");
  setSize(300,80);
  setDefaultCloseOperation(EXIT_ON_CLOSE);

  Container c = getContentPane( );
  c.setLayout(new GridLayout(0,2));

  Icon nums[] = new Icon[] {
    new ImageIcon("1.gif"),
    new ImageIcon("2.gif"),
    new ImageIcon("3.gif"),
    new ImageIcon("4.gif"),
    new ImageIcon("5.gif"),
    new ImageIcon("6.gif")
  };
  JSpinner s1 = new JSpinner(new SpinnerListModel(nums));
  s1.setEditor(new IconEditor(s1));
  c.add(new JLabel(" Icon Spinner"));
  c.add(s1);

  setVisible(true);
}

public static void main(String args[]) {
  new IconSpinner( );
}
}
```

Notice we didn't have to build a new model for our icons. We certainly could, but
the SpinnerListModel does exactly what we need—except for rendering the icons.
(Try it once without the setEditor( ) line. You should get a standard text field with
the name of the image file displayed.) We just set the editor to a new instance of our
IconEditor class and we're off and rolling.

CHAPTER 8
Swing Containers

In this chapter, we'll take a look at a number of components Swing provides for grouping other components together. In AWT, such components extended java.awt.Container and included Panel, Window, Frame, and Dialog. With Swing, you get a whole new set of options, providing greater flexibility and power.

A Simple Container

Not everything in this chapter is more complex than its AWT counterpart. As proof of this claim, we'll start the chapter with a look at the JPanel class, a very simple Swing container.

The JPanel Class

JPanel is an extension of JComponent (which, remember, extends java.awt.Container) used for grouping together other components. It gets most of its implementation from its superclasses. Typically, using JPanel amounts to instantiating it, setting a layout manager (this can be set in the constructor and defaults to a FlowLayout), and adding components to it using the add( ) methods inherited from Container.

Properties

JPanel does not define any new properties. Table 8-1 shows the default values that differ from those provided by JComponent.

Table 8-1. JPanel properties

Property	Data type	get	is	set	Default value
accessibleContext[o]	AccessibleContext	•			JPanel.AccessibleJPanel()
doubleBuffered[o]	boolean		•	•	true
layout[o]	LayoutManager	•		•	FlowLayout()
opaque[o, b]	boolean	•	•		true
UI[1.4]	PaneUI	•		•	From L&F
UIClassID	String	•			"PanelUI"

[1.4]since 1.4, [b]bound, [o]overridden

See also properties from the JComponent class (Table 3-6).

The doubleBuffered and opaque properties default to true, while the layoutManager defaults to a new FlowLayout.

Constructors

public JPanel( )
> Create a new panel with a FlowLayout and double buffering.

public JPanel(boolean isDoubleBuffered)
> Create a new panel with a FlowLayout. Double buffering is enabled if isDoubleBuffered is true.

public JPanel(LayoutManager layout)
> Create a new panel with the specified layout manager and double buffering.

public JPanel(LayoutManager layout, boolean isDoubleBuffered)
> This constructor (called by all the others) creates a new panel with the specified layout manager and double-buffering policy.

Opacity

Here's a simple program showing what it means for a JPanel to be opaque. All we do is create a few JPanels. Inside the first JPanel, we place another JPanel, which is opaque. In the second, we place a transparent (nonopaque) JPanel. In both cases, we set the background of the outer panel to white and the background of the inner panel to black. We'll place a JButton inside each inner panel to give it some size. Figure 8-1 shows the result.

On the left, we see the black panel inside the white one. But on the right, since the inner panel is not opaque, its black background is never painted, and the background of the outer panel shows through. Here's the code:

```
// OpaqueExample.java
//
import javax.swing.*;
import java.awt.*;
```

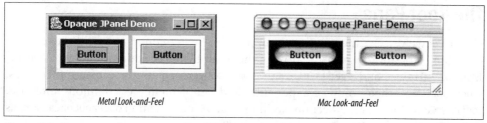

Metal Look-and-Feel   Mac Look-and-Feel

Figure 8-1. Opaque and nonopaque JPanels (in Metal and Mac L&Fs)

```java
public class OpaqueExample extends JFrame {

  public OpaqueExample( ) {
    super("Opaque JPanel Demo");
    setSize(400, 200);
    setDefaultCloseOperation(EXIT_ON_CLOSE);

    // Create two JPanels (opaque), one containing another opaque JPanel and the
    // other containing a nonopaque JPanel.
    JPanel opaque = createNested(true);
    JPanel notOpaque = createNested(false);

    // Throw it all together.
    getContentPane( ).setLayout(new FlowLayout( ));
    getContentPane( ).add(opaque);
    getContentPane( ).add(notOpaque);
    }

  public static void main(String[] args) {
    OpaqueExample oe = new OpaqueExample( );
    oe.setVisible(true);
  }

  // Create a JPanel containing another JPanel. The inner JPanel's opacity is set
  // according to the parameter. A JButton is placed inside the inner JPanel to give
  // it some content.
  public JPanel createNested(boolean opaque) {
    JPanel outer = new JPanel(new FlowLayout( ));
    JPanel inner = new JPanel(new FlowLayout( ));
    outer.setBackground(Color.white);
    inner.setBackground(Color.black);

    inner.setOpaque(opaque);
    inner.setBorder(BorderFactory.createLineBorder(Color.gray));

    inner.add(new JButton("Button"));
    outer.add(inner);

    return outer;
  }
}
```

The Root Pane

Now that we've seen the simplest example of a Swing container, we'll move on to something a bit more powerful. Most of the other Swing containers (JFrame, JApplet, JWindow, JDialog, and even JInternalFrame) contain an instance of another class, JRootPane, as their only component, and implement a common interface, RootPaneContainer. In this section, we'll look at JRootPane and RootPaneContainer, as well as another class JRootPane uses, JLayeredPane.

Before jumping into the descriptions of these classes, let's take a look at how the classes and interfaces that make up the Swing root containers fit together. Figure 8-2 shows that JApplet, JFrame, JDialog, and JWindow do not extend JComponent as the other Swing components do. Instead, they extend their AWT counterparts, serving as top-level user interface windows. This implies that these components (unlike the lightweight Swing components) have native AWT peer objects.

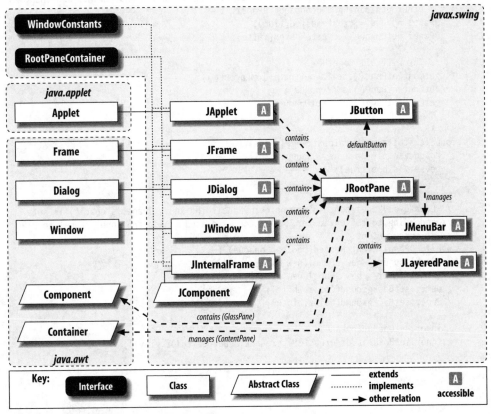

Figure 8-2. Swing "root" container class diagram

Notice that these Swing containers (as well as JInternalFrame) implement a common interface, RootPaneContainer. This interface gives access to the JRootPane's properties. Furthermore, each of the five containers uses a JRootPane as the "true" container of child components managed by the container. This class is discussed later in this chapter.

The JRootPane Class

JRootPane is a special container that extends JComponent and is used by many of the other Swing containers. It's quite different from most containers you're probably used to using. The first thing to understand about JRootPane is that it contains a fixed set of components: a Component called the glass pane and a JLayeredPane called, logically enough, the layered pane. Furthermore, the layered pane contains two more components: a JMenuBar and a Container called the content pane.* Figure 8-3 shows a schematic view of the makeup of a JRootPane.

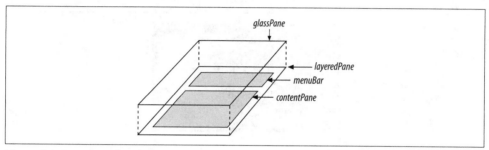

Figure 8-3. JRootPane breakout

Attempts to add additional components to a JRootPane are ignored by its custom layout manager (a protected inner class called RootLayout).† Instead, children of the root pane should be added to its content pane. In fact, for most uses of JRootPane, all you need to do is get the content pane and add your components to it. Here's a simple example (using a JFrame) that adds a single button to the content pane.

```
// RootExample.java
//
import javax.swing.*;
import java.awt.*;

public class RootExample {
  public static void main(String[] args) {
```

---

* In general, JLayeredPanes can contain any components they wish. This is why Figure 8-2 does not show JLayeredPane containing the menu bar and content pane. In the case of the JRootPane, a JLayeredPane is used to hold these two specific components.

† It is possible to change the layout manager for JRootPane to one of your own choosing, but it would be responsible for handling all details of laying out the pane. Using any of the other AWT or Swing layouts will not work properly.

```
        JFrame f = new JFrame();
        f.setDefaultCloseOperation(JFrame.EXIT_ON_CLOSE);
        JRootPane root = f.getRootPane();           // XXX Pay attention to these
        Container content = root.getContentPane(); // XXX lines. They are
        content.add(new JButton("Hello"));          // XXX explained below.
        f.pack();
        f.setVisible(true);
    }
}
```

This may seem like a lot of complexity just to add something to a frame. Thankfully, (as we'll see in the next section) each of the containers that use JRootPane implement the RootPaneContainer interface, which provides direct access to each of the root's subcomponents. This allows the three lines marked with "XXX" to be replaced with:

```
    f.getContentPane().add(new JButton("Hello"));
```

In the next example, we'll see how to add a menu to a root pane, producing a display like the one in Figure 8-4.

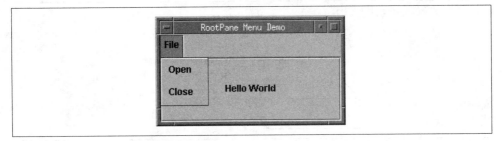

Figure 8-4. JRootPane with a JMenuBar

As with RootExample.java, we can get at these pieces using the root component:

```
    // Snippet from RootExample2.java
    JRootPane root = getRootPane();

    // Create a menu bar.
    JMenuBar bar = new JMenuBar();
    JMenu menu = new JMenu("File");
    bar.add(menu);
    menu.add("Open");
    menu.add("Close");
    root.setJMenuBar(bar);

    // Add a button to the content pane.
    root.getContentPane().add(new JButton("Hello World"));
```

In this case, the getRootPane() and setJMenuBar() calls could have been replaced with a single setJMenuBar(bar) call. Note that the menu bar property on the Swing containers is called JMenuBar.

The previous two root pane examples were intended to give you an understanding of how the JRootPane really works. Typically, however, your code does not work with

JRootPane directly. We'll get a better understanding of why when we get to the discussion of RootPaneContainer. For now, here's a version of the last example that shows how you'd really write that code:

```java
// RootExample3.java
//
import javax.swing.*;
import java.awt.*;

public class RootExample3 extends JFrame {
    public RootExample3() {
        super("RootPane Menu Demo");
        setSize(220,100);
        setDefaultCloseOperation(EXIT_ON_CLOSE);

        // Create a menu bar.
        JMenuBar bar = new JMenuBar();
        JMenu menu = new JMenu("File");
        bar.add(menu);
        menu.add("Open");
        menu.add("Close");
        setJMenuBar(bar);

        // Add a button to the content pane.
        getContentPane().add(new JButton("Hello World"));
    }

    public static void main(String[] args) {
        RootExample3 re3 = new RootExample3();
        re3.setVisible(true);
    }
}
```

The Glass Pane

JRootPane may seem a bit confusing at first glance. The important thing to remember is that in most cases, all you need to worry about is adding your component to the content pane and possibly setting a menu bar. As we noted earlier, the menu bar and content pane are part of the layered pane, which we'll look at in detail in the next section. In this section, we'll explain the other component contained by JRootPane: the "glass pane."

The glass pane is a component that is laid out to fill the entire pane. By default, it is an instance of JPanel, but it can be replaced with any Component. JRootPane's implementation of the addImpl() method ensures that the glass pane is the first component in the container, meaning that it will be painted last. In other words, the glass pane allows you to place components "above" any other components in the pane. Because of this, it generally makes sense for the glass pane to be nonopaque; otherwise, it will cover everything in the layered pane. It's important to remember that when the layout of the JRootPane is performed, the placement of the contents of the glass pane will have no effect on the placement of the contents of the layered pane (and its content pane). Both sets of components are placed within the same component space, overlapping each other as necessary. It's also important to realize that the components in the various panes are all equal when it comes to receiving input: mouse events are sent to any component in the JRootPane, whatever part of the pane it happens to be in.

This last note brings us a common use of the glass pane: blocking mouse events from the other components. As a rule, mouse events are sent to the "top" component if components are positioned on top of each other. If the top component has registered mouse listeners, the events are not sent to the covered components. We'll create a new JPanel to use as the glass pane. The panel will listen for all mouse events (and do nothing with them). Once the Start button is clicked, the glass pane is made visible—and none of the buttons in the main application work. The main application is not technically disabled, but the mouse events are going only to the glass pane and its components. After a few seconds, the glass pane will be hidden, allowing the underlying components to be used again. Figure 8-5 shows the application with the glass pane activated.

Figure 8-5. JRootPane with an active glass pane (which contains the progress bar)

This demo simulates situations in which your application starts an action that takes a long time to complete, and you don't want the user clicking on everything in sight if he gets impatient. Database queries and network resource lookups are great examples of tasks that can require a lot of time. You can adapt the glass pane for any similar scenario in your own programs. You should also remember that it is a regular JPanel component. As you can see in Figure 8-5, we show a Please wait... message and a progress bar to keep the user informed about what's going on. You could add other components, or even a Cancel button that the user can press to halt the operation if he gets tired of waiting.

Here's the code for this example. Of course, this one is more fun to run.

```
// GlassExample.java
//
import javax.swing.*;
import java.awt.*;
import java.awt.event.*;

// Show how a glass pane can be used to block mouse events.
public class GlassExample extends JFrame {
  JPanel glass = new JPanel(new GridLayout(0, 1));
  JProgressBar waiter = new JProgressBar(0, 100);
  Timer timer;

  public GlassExample( ) {
    super("GlassPane Demo");
    setSize(500, 300);
    setDefaultCloseOperation(EXIT_ON_CLOSE);

    // Set up the glass pane with a little message and a progress bar.
    JPanel controlPane = new JPanel(new GridLayout(2,1));
    controlPane.setOpaque(false);
    controlPane.add(new JLabel("Please wait..."));
    controlPane.add(waiter);
    glass.setOpaque(false);
    glass.add(new JLabel( )); // Padding...
    glass.add(new JLabel( ));
    glass.add(controlPane);
    glass.add(new JLabel( ));
    glass.add(new JLabel( ));
    glass.addMouseListener(new MouseAdapter( ) {});
    glass.addMouseMotionListener(new MouseMotionAdapter( ) {});
    setGlassPane(glass);

    // Now set up a few buttons and images for the main application.
    JPanel mainPane = new JPanel( );
    mainPane.setBackground(Color.white);
    JButton redB = new JButton("Red");
    JButton blueB = new JButton("Blue");
    JButton greenB = new JButton("Green");
    mainPane.add(redB);
    mainPane.add(greenB);
    mainPane.add(blueB);
    mainPane.add(new JLabel(new ImageIcon("oreilly.gif")));

    // Attach the pop-up debugger to the main app buttons so you
    // see the effect of making a glass pane visible.
    PopupDebugger pd = new PopupDebugger(this);
    redB.addActionListener(pd);
    greenB.addActionListener(pd);
    blueB.addActionListener(pd);

    // And last but not least, our button to launch the glass pane
    JButton startB = new JButton("Start the big operation!");
    startB.addActionListener(new ActionListener( ) {
        public void actionPerformed(java.awt.event.ActionEvent A) {
```

```
          glass.setVisible(true);
          startTimer( );
        }
      });

  Container contentPane = getContentPane( );
  contentPane.add(mainPane, BorderLayout.CENTER);
  contentPane.add(startB, BorderLayout.SOUTH);
}

// A quick method to start up a 10-second timer and update the progress bar
public void startTimer( ) {
  if (timer == null) {
    timer = new Timer(1000, new ActionListener( ) {
        int progress = 0;
        public void actionPerformed(ActionEvent A) {
          progress += 10;
          waiter.setValue(progress);

          // Once we hit 100%, remove the glass pane and reset the progress bar
          // stuff.
          if (progress >= 100) {
            progress = 0;
            timer.stop( );
            glass.setVisible(false);
            waiter.setValue(0);
          }
        }
      });
  }
  if (timer.isRunning( )) {
    timer.stop( );
  }
  timer.start( );
}

// A graphical debugger that pops up whenever a button is pressed
public class PopupDebugger implements ActionListener {
  private JFrame parent;
  public PopupDebugger(JFrame f) {
    parent = f;
  }
  public void actionPerformed(ActionEvent ae) {
    JOptionPane.showMessageDialog(parent, ae.getActionCommand( ));
  }
}

public static void main(String[] args) {
  GlassExample ge = new GlassExample( );
  ge.setVisible(true);
}
}
```

Note that the lines:

```
glass.addMouseListener(new MouseAdapter( ) {});
glass.addMouseMotionListener(new MouseMotionAdapter( ) {});
```

block mouse events from reaching the hidden components (remember, the glass pane fills the entire frame) because the events are sent to the first component (starting at the top) with registered listeners. Any time a mouse event method is called, it will do nothing since we just extended the empty-implementation adapter classes. However, forgetting these lines allows the events to pass through to our application.

Avoiding Unnecessary Layers

The following code fragment shows a common mistake:

```
JPanel panel = new JPanel( );
panel.add(someStuff);
JFrame f = new JFrame( );
f.getContentPane( ).add(panel);
```

There's nothing fundamentally wrong with this code. It will work just fine. However, there's an extra layer that's just not necessary. Recall from the beginning of this section that the content pane is initialized to an instance of JPanel. There's nothing special about that panel, and you should feel free to use it. A better implementation of the code fragment would be:

```
JFrame f = new JFrame( );
Container panel = f.getContentPane( ); // Cast to JPanel if you want to.
panel.add(someStuff);
```

It's also important to keep in mind that the content pane can be any arbitrary container—it doesn't have to be a JPanel. If you want to fill the content pane with a scrollable region, or perhaps with a tabbed pane, you can replace the content pane with a JScrollPane or JTabbedPane. For example:

```
JScrollPane scroll = new JScrollPane(new JTextPane( ));
JFrame f = new JFrame( );
f.setContentPane(scroll); // Not f.getContentPane( ).add(scroll);
```

A reasonable rule of thumb is that if you are only going to add a single component to the content pane and you want it to fill the entire pane, don't add to the content pane—replace it. Of course, replacing the content pane does leave you in charge of the background color and opacity as well. Sometimes the defaults for these properties are not what you want, so you should be aware you may need to tweak the pane before final production.

Properties

Table 8-2 shows the properties and default values defined by JRootPane. The background property is set to the default "control" (component) color defined in the UIManager.

Table 8-2. JRootPane properties

Property	Data type	get	is	set	Default value
accessibleContext°	AccessibleContext	•			JRootPaneAccessibleJRoot-Pane()
background°	Color	•		•	UIManager.getColor("control")
contentPane	Container	•		•	JPanel()
defaultButton[b]	JButton	•		•	null
doubleBuffered	boolean	•		•	true
glassPane	Component	•		•	JPanel()
JMenuBar*	JMenuBar	•		•	null
layeredPane	JLayeredPane	•		•	JLayeredPane()
layout°	LayoutManager	•		•	RootLayout()
optimizedDrawingEnabled	boolean		•		false
validateRoot°	boolean		•		true
windowDecorationStyle[1.4]	int	•		•	JRootPane.NONE

[1.4]since 1.4, [b]bound, °overridden

*This property replaces the deprecated menuBar property.

See also properties from the JComponent class (Table 3-6).

The contentPane is initially set to a JPanel with a BorderLayout, while glassPane is set to a nonopaque, invisible JPanel with a default (FlowLayout) layout manager. A new instance of JLayeredPane is the default value for layeredPane, and by default the JMenuBar property is set to null. The contentPane is contained by the layered pane's FRAME_CONTENT_LAYER (see "The JLayeredPane Class" for further explanation).

Note that the set() methods for the JMenuBar and contentPane properties take care of placing these components within the JLayeredPane, so you typically don't have to worry about the layered pane at all.

The inherited doubleBuffered property (see "Double Buffering" in Chapter 3) is true by default, and you'll usually leave it that way unless you do some fancy background painting. The layout property defaults to a new instance of the protected inner class RootLayout. Since the glass pane and the content pane occupy the same bounds, no optimization is needed, so optimizedDrawingEnabled returns false.

The defaultButton property was introduced in Chapter 5. This property allows a JButton to be specified as the default for the container. The default button is pressed if the user presses Enter (or some other UI-defined key) while the pane has focus (unless some other focused component, like a JTextField, handles the key). This is a very convenient feature when presenting a user with information to be viewed and acknowledged because it keeps the user from having to use the mouse.

Introduced in SDK 1.4, the windowDecorationStyle property allows you to set the border and window controls shown from the root pane. Classes like JOptionPane and JFileChooser set this property for you. If you start with a generic JWindow or JDialog though, you can now control the look of the window. The decoration style options are shown in Table 8-3.

Table 8-3. JRootPane constants

Constant	Type	Description
COLOR_CHOOSER_DIALOG	int	Color chooser decoration type
ERROR_DIALOG	int	Error dialog decoration type
FILE_CHOOSER_DIALOG	int	File chooser decoration type
INFORMATION_DIALOG	int	Error dialog decoration type
NONE	int	Type indicating no decorations
PLAIN_DIALOG	int	Plain dialog decoration type
QUESTION_DIALOG	int	Question dialog decoration type
WARNING_DIALOG	int	Warning dialog decoration type

Revalidate

The remaining property listed in Table 8-2 is the validateRoot property. JRootPane overrides isValidateRoot() to return true. This causes the container to be validated (meaning that its contents will be redisplayed) as a result of any call to revalidate() on one of its children or their descendants. This simplifies the process of dealing with components that change dynamically.

In older versions (prior to 1.2), if the font size of a component changed (for example), you needed to call invalidate() on the component and then validate() on its container to ensure that the component would be resized appropriately. With revalidate(), only one call is necessary. Furthermore, the way revalidate() is implemented allows multiple revalidate() calls to be handled at once, much like multiple repaint() calls are handled at the same time by the AWT.

Here's a simple example using revalidate():

```
// RevalidateExample.java
//
import javax.swing.*;
import java.awt.*;
import java.awt.event.*;

public class RevalidateExample extends JFrame {

  public RevalidateExample() {
    super("Revalidation Demo");
    setSize(300,150);
    setDefaultCloseOperation(EXIT_ON_CLOSE);
```

```
    // Create a single button.
    Font font = new Font("Dialog", Font.PLAIN, 10);
    final JButton b = new JButton("Add");
    b.setFont(font);

    Container c = getContentPane();
    c.setLayout(new FlowLayout());
    c.add(b);

    // Increase the size of the button's font each time it's clicked.
    b.addActionListener(new ActionListener() {
      int size = 10;

      public void actionPerformed(ActionEvent ev) {
        b.setFont(new Font("Dialog", Font.PLAIN, ++size));
        b.revalidate();   // Invalidates the button and validates its root pane
      }
    });
  }

  public static void main(String[] args) {
    RevalidateExample re = new RevalidateExample();
    re.setVisible(true);
  }
}
```

In this example, we create a single button and add it to the content pane of a JFrame (which uses a JRootPane). Each time the button is clicked, we increase the size of the button's font. As a result, the button needs to be resized to accommodate the larger label. To make this happen, we simply call revalidate( ) on the button. Note that the button could have been nested inside any number of other containers below the root pane, and this would still work properly. As long as there is an ancestor of the revalidated component that returns true to isValidateRoot( ), the container is validated. It would require a very specific effort on your part (maybe because you want complete control over component painting) to ignore a call for revalidation. You would have to be sure to unset the validateRoot property (by subclassing) on all of your component's parents.

Constructor

Only one constructor is available for the JRootPane class:

public JRootPane( )

Create a new pane with the default property values specified in Table 8-2.

The RootPaneContainer Interface

As we've said, the top-level Swing containers all use the JRootPane class as their single child component. In order to make it easier to work with these containers, Swing provides a common interface that each of them implement. This interface,

---

RootPaneContainer, defines methods for accessing the common properties available in JRootPane, as well as for the root pane itself. This is what allows for the shortcuts we described in the previous section.

The classes that implement this interface typically delegate the methods to their contained JRootPane. For example, getContentPane( ) would be implemented like this:

```
public Container getContentPane( ) {
    return getRootPane( ).getContentPane( );
}
```

Properties

This interface is made up entirely of accessors for the JRootPane and its properties, shown in Table 8-4. Notice that the root pane's JMenuBar is not available in this interface. This is because certain containers (JWindow, specifically) don't typically contain menus. This is not to say that you couldn't use one if you really wanted to (accessing it from the JRootPane), but access to the menu bar is not directly supported by the interface.

Table 8-4. RootPaneContainer properties

Property	Data type	get	is	set	Default value
contentPane	Container	•		•	
glassPane	Component	•		•	
layeredPane	JLayeredPane	•		•	
rootPane	JRootPane	•			

The JLayeredPane Class

We have already seen some of the panes (the glass and content panes, for example) accessible through the JRootPane class. Though it doesn't make much use of it directly, JRootPane introduces a class called JLayeredPane. JLayeredPane is a container that manages its components via layers so that components in the upper layers are painted on top of components in the lower layers. This gives you something that was difficult to get with AWT: complete control over which components are painted on top and which are hidden.

The easiest way to understand how this works is to look at a very simple example.

```
// SimpleLayers.java
//
import javax.swing.*;
import java.awt.Color;

public class SimpleLayers extends JFrame {
    public SimpleLayers( ) {
        super("LayeredPane Demonstration");
```

```
      setSize(200, 150);
      setDefaultCloseOperation(EXIT_ON_CLOSE);

      JLayeredPane lp = getLayeredPane( );

      // Create three buttons.
      JButton top = new JButton( );
      top.setBackground(Color.white);
      top.setBounds(20, 20, 50, 50);
      JButton middle = new JButton( );
      middle.setBackground(Color.gray);
      middle.setBounds(40, 40, 50, 50);
      JButton bottom = new JButton( );
      bottom.setBackground(Color.black);
      bottom.setBounds(60, 60, 50, 50);

      // Place the buttons in different layers.
      lp.add(middle, new Integer(2));
      lp.add(top, new Integer(3));
      lp.add(bottom, new Integer(1));
   }

   public static void main(String[] args) {
      SimpleLayers sl = new SimpleLayers( );
      sl.setVisible(true);
   }
}
```

In this example, we add three colored buttons to a JLayeredPane. The top button is
placed in layer 3, the middle in layer 2, and the bottom in layer 1. Recall that the
Component.add( ) method takes an Object as a second parameter, so we must create
Integer objects to identify the layers, rather than just passing in ints. When we run
this example, we see (in Figure 8-6) that the white (if your L&F allows custom button colors) button (the one with the highest layer, 3) is drawn above the gray button
(in layer 2), which is drawn above the black button (layer 1). The order in which the
buttons were added has no significance.

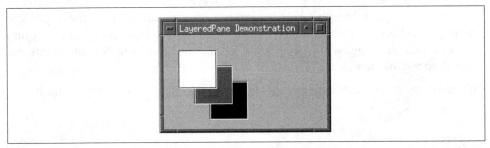

Figure 8-6. JLayeredFrame example with three buttons, each in their own layer

The actual values used for the layers are not important, only their relative ordering.
We could just as easily have used 10, 20, and 30 as the layer values.

Properties

JLayeredPane defines default values for the properties listed in Table 8-5. The layout property is set to null by default. This works fine when the pane's layers are containers themselves, each managing the layout of a particular layer, or when only a single component is added to each layer. If multiple components are added to a single layer, however, they will be laid out with no layout manager. This is why the RootLayout class described earlier explicitly lays out the components it adds to a single layer of its layered pane.

Table 8-5. JLayeredPane properties

Property	Data type	get	is	set	Default value
accessibleContext°	AccessibleContext	•			AccessibleJLayeredPane( )
layout°	LayoutManager	•		•	null
optimizedDrawingEnabled°	boolean	•			true

°overridden

See also properties from the JComponent class (Table 3-6).

The optimizedDrawingEnabled property is defined in JComponent and allows a component's children to be drawn more efficiently if they can be guaranteed not to overlap. In JComponent, this property is always true. In JLayeredPane, it is true only if the components in the pane do not overlap.

Constants

JLayeredPane defines several constants. The six shown in Figure 8-7 (and listed in Table 8-6) are Integer objects, used to define specific layers available to users of the class.

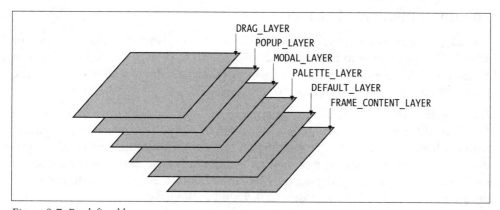

Figure 8-7. Predefined layers

Table 8-6. JLayeredPane constants

Constant	Type	Description
DEFAULT_LAYER	Integer	Used for most components (0)
DRAG_LAYER	Integer	Used when dragging objects on the screen to ensure that they appear on top of everything else as they are being dragged (400)
FRAME_CONTENT_LAYER	Integer	Used only for the content pane and menu bar (−30,000)
LAYER_PROPERTY	String	The name of the layer client property
MODAL_LAYER	Integer	Used to display modal pop-up windows above other components (200)
PALETTE_LAYER	Integer	Used to display floating toolbars or palettes (100)
POPUP_LAYER	Integer	Used to ensure that pop ups (including tooltips) are displayed above the components that generate them (300)

Remember, any number can be used as a layer number; these are provided as useful defaults. However, it's generally not a good idea to mix your own values with these constants, since there's no guarantee they won't change (this would be very unlikely, but it's definitely poor coding practice to assume the exact values of symbolic constants). Instead, you should choose to use either these constants or define your own layer values.

LAYER_PROPERTY is used as a client property name on any JComponents added to the pane. The client property value is an Integer representing the component's layer. (The constant is itself just a String.)

Constructor

public JLayeredPane()
   This constructor creates a new pane with a null layout manager.

Adding Components to Layers

The add() methods described below (implemented in java.awt.Container) are not actually reimplemented in this class, but it's important to understand how they can be used with JLayeredPane. In order to gain this understanding, we'll first explain the use of the term *position* with respect to this class.

A component's position in a layer determines the order in which it will be drawn. This is no different from a component's position in a simple container. Components with the lowest position numbers are drawn last (on top). Components with a position of −1 are added with the next highest position number, so they will drawn first (on bottom). This is best understood by looking at a quick example. Assume we have three components in a layer at positions 0, 1, and 2. We have:

   A B C

Now, if we add D to position 1, it shoves B and C down:

 A D B C

Adding E to position −1 sticks E at the end (currently position 4) and yields:

 A D B C E

Adding F to position 5 gives us:

 A D B C E F

F occupies the lowest screen position, and A occupies the highest. If we paint these components, they will be painted in the following order:

 F E C B D A

That is, F will be drawn first (on bottom) and A will be drawn last.

When working with multiple layers, nothing changes. The only difference is that all components in a given layer are painted before any components in the next layer, regardless of their positions within a layer. Note that the ordering of layers places the components in the *highest* numbered layer on top, while the ordering of positions places the component with the *lowest* numbered position on top. So, if we have:

 Layer 1: A B (A is at position 0; B is at position 1)
 Layer 2: C D
 Layer 3: E F

The components (shown with "layer,position" subscripts) will be painted in this order:

 $B_{1,1}$ $A_{1,0}$ $D_{2,1}$ $C_{2,0}$ $F_{3,1}$ $E_{3,0}$

The component (E) with the highest layer (3) and lowest position (0) is painted last (on top), as shown in Figure 8-1.

Here's how the various versions of Component.add( ) work with JLayeredPane. Rather than supply things like NORTH as a constraint on where to add things, we pass an Integer representing the layer we want to use. Again, these add( ) methods are *not* reimplemented in JLayeredPane; they're covered here only for the purpose of explaining how they work in this context. Each version of add( ) is explained in terms of how it will call addImpl( ), a protected method that *is* implemented in this class and is also described below.

public Component add(Component comp)
   Results in a call to addImpl(comp, null, -1).

public Component add(Component comp, int index)
   Results in a call to addImpl(comp, null, index).

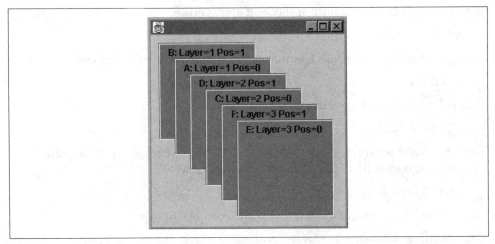

Figure 8-8. Paint order of layered components

public void add(Component comp, Object constraints)
> Results in a call to addImpl(comp, constraints, -1). The constraints argument should be an integer specifying which layer to add comp to.

public void add(Component comp, Object constraints, int index)
> Results in a call to addImpl(comp, constraints, index). The input object should be an integer specifying the layer to add the component to.

public Component add(String name, Component comp)
> Should not be used with JLayeredPane. If it is, it results in a call to addImpl(comp, name, -1). Since name is not an integer, it is ignored.

protected void addImpl(Component comp, Object constraints, int index)
> This implementation of addImpl checks to see if the given constraint object is an integer, and if so, uses it as the component's layer. If the constraint object is null (or anything other than an integer), the component's layer is set by calling getLayer( ) (described later in this chapter).

Layer management methods

JLayeredPane makes it easy to manipulate layers and the components within them by providing the following methods:

public int getComponentCountInLayer(int layer)
> Return the number of components currently in the specified layer.

public Component[] getComponentsInLayer(int layer)
> Return an array containing the Components currently in the specified layer.

public int getIndexOf(Component c)
> Return the absolute index of the given component. This ignores the pane's layers completely. The component with the highest index is the first component

painted, meaning that it appears under all other components (which are painted in decreasing order). Since this method ignores the abstractions, it can be useful in conjunction with methods such as remove( ) (mentioned below).

public int getLayer(Component c)

Return the layer in which the given component has been placed. If the given component is a JComponent, the layer is determined by getting its LAYER_PROPERTY. If it is not a JComponent, it is looked up in an internal hashtable used for mapping non-JComponents to layers. In either case, if the layer cannot be determined as described, the DEFAULT_LAYER is returned.

public int getPosition(Component c)

Return a component's position within its layer.

public int highestLayer( )

Return the highest numbered layer in which a child is contained. If there are no children, 0 is returned.

public int lowestLayer( )

Return the lowest numbered layer in which a child is contained. If there are no children, 0 is returned.

public void moveToBack(Component c)

Move the specified component to the "back" of its layer.

public void moveToFront(Component c)

Move the specified component to the "front" of its layer (position 0).

public void remove(int index)

Remove the specified component (the index is an absolute index, not layer-based) from the pane.

public void setLayer(Component c, int layer)
public void setLayer(Component c, int layer, int position)

Set the layer and position (which defaults to -1 in the first case) for the given component and repaint the component. Note that these methods do not add the component to the pane; add( ) must still be called. Alternatively, a single call to add(c, new Integer(layer)) or add(c, new Integer(layer), position) could be made. If the given component is a JComponent, its layer is stored by setting the LAYER_PROPERTY on the component itself. If not, the component's layer is stored in an internal hash table that maps from non-JComponents to layers.

public void setPosition(Component c, int position)

Set a component's position within its layer (determined by calling getLayer(c)).

Static methods

public static int getLayer(JComponent c)

Use the LAYER_PROPERTY to get the layer for a given Swing component. Normally, the getLayer( ) instance method should be used.

public static JLayeredPane getLayeredPaneAbove(Component c)

> Search the component hierarchy from the given component upward, returning the first JLayeredPane it finds. This allows you to find the layered pane in which a component has been placed. If none is found, it returns null.

public static void putLayer(JComponent c, int layer)

> Set a component's layer by assigning a value to its LAYER_PROPERTY. It does not cause a repaint as the setLayer( ) instance method does. Normally, setLayer( ) should be used.

Basic RootPaneContainers

For the rest of this chapter, we'll look at some basic containers (JFrame, JWindow, and JApplet) that implement RootPaneContainer and use JRootPane. First, we'll take a quick look at a simple interface called WindowConstants.

The WindowConstants Interface

WindowConstants is a simple interface containing only constants. It is implemented by JFrame, JDialog, and JInternalFrame.

Constants

The constants defined in WindowConstants specify possible behaviors in response to a window being closed. These values are shown in Table 8-7.

Table 8-7. JWindowConstants constants

Constant	Type	Description
DISPOSE_ON_CLOSE	int	Disposes window when closed
DO_NOTHING_ON_CLOSE	int	Does nothing when closed
EXIT_ON_CLOSE[1.4],[*]	int	Exits the virtual machine when closed
HIDE_ON_CLOSE	int	Hides window when closed

[1.4]since 1.4

[*]This constant was added in 1.4, although a matching constant was defined in the 1.3 JFrame class.

In the next section, we'll look at a strategy for exiting the application in response to a frame being closed.

The JFrame Class

The most common Swing container for Java applications is the JFrame class. Like java.awt.Frame, JFrame provides a top-level window with a title, border, and other platform-specific adornments (e.g., minimize, maximize, and close buttons). Because it uses a JRootPane as its only child, working with a JFrame is slightly different than working with an AWT Frame. An empty JFrame is shown in Figure 8-9.

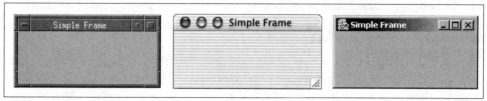

Figure 8-9. Empty JFrame instances on Unix, Mac, and Windows platforms

The primary difference is that calls to add( ) must be replaced with calls to getContentPane( ).add( ). In fact, the addImpl( ) method is implemented so that a call made directly to add( ) throws an Error. (The error message tells you not to call add( ) directly.)

Properties

JFrame defines the properties shown in Table 8-8. The accessibleContext property is as expected. ContentPane, glassPane, layeredPane, and JMenuBar are really properties of JRootPane (described earlier in the chapter). JFrame provides direct access to these panes, as required by the RootPaneContainer interface.

Table 8-8. JFrame properties

Property	Data type	get	is	set	Default value
accessibleContext[o]	AccessibleContext	•			JFrame.Accessible-JFrame( )
background[o]	Color	•		•	UIManager.getColor ("control")
contentPane[o]	Container	•		•	From rootPane
defaultCloseOperation	int	•		•	HIDE_ON_CLOSE
glassPane[o]	Component	•		•	From rootPane
JMenuBar[o]	JMenuBar	•		•	From rootPane
layeredPane[o]	JLayeredPane	•		•	From rootPane
layout[o]	LayoutManager	•		•	BorderLayout( )
rootPane[o,*]	JRootPane	•		•	JRootPane( )
rootPaneCheckingEnabled[p]	boolean		•	•	true
title[o]	String	•		•	""

[o]overridden, [p]protected

*The setRootPane( ) method is protected.

See also the java.awt.Frame class.

The defaultCloseOperation is set to HIDE_ON_CLOSE, a value taken from WindowConstants. This indicates that closing a JFrame window results in a call to setVisible(false).

The layout property is listed here because JFrame overrides setLayout( ) to throw an Error if an attempt is made to change the layout manager, rather than set the layout manager of the frame's content pane.

The rootPane property is set to a new instance of JRootPane when the frame is created and cannot be changed (via public methods). The rootPaneCheckingEnabled property determines whether you get those error messages when trying to add components directly to the root pane.

The accessors for the title property are inherited from Frame. This property can also be set in the JFrame constructor.

Constructors

All constructors can now (since 1.4) potentially throw HeadlessException if the graphics environment is operating in a "headless" mode, meaning that there is no display, keyboard, or mouse. This would be true, for example, in a servlet environment that used Swing to generate graphics to be sent to a web browser as downloaded image files.

The versions that specify a GraphicsConfiguration (introduced in 1.3 for JFrame) allow you to select the display device on which the dialog should appear if your application is running in a multi-screen environment.

public JFrame( )
public JFrame(GraphicsConfiguration gc)
>Create a new unnamed, invisible frame. Nothing appears in the title bar of the frame.

public JFrame(String title)
public JFrame(GraphicsConfiguration gc, String title)
>Create an invisible frame with the specified title.

Protected Methods

JFrame has a few protected methods that you should know about. If you extend JFrame, you can override them to alter the default behavior. In particular, if you don't want the frame responding to windowClosing( ) events at all, you can provide an empty implementation of the processWindowEvent( ) method. This will leave you with the responsibility of closing the frame programmatically. The next section has an example of extending processWindowEvent( ) to confirm that the user really wants to close the frame.

protected void frameInit( )

Called by the constructor to enable key and window events, set the root pane, and set the background color. The last thing this method does is set the `rootPaneCheckingEnabled` field to true.

protected void processWindowEvent(WindowEvent e)

Allow the superclass implementation to process the event. The superclass then handles window-closing events based on the current default close operation for the frame. For `HIDE_ON_CLOSE`, the frame is made invisible; for `DISPOSE_ON_CLOSE`, the frame is made invisible and disposed of; and for `DO_NOTHING_ON_CLOSE`, predictably, nothing is done.

Exiting Frames

In many applications, closing the main application frame should cause the program to exit (shutting down the virtual machine). The default implementation, however, is only to hide the frame when it is closed, leaving the virtual machine running with no visible frame. We'll briefly look at two simple ways to get the program to exit when the frame is closed.

The simplest thing to do is to set the close operation to exit:

```
// FrameClose1.java
//
import javax.swing.JFrame;

public class FrameClose1 {
  public static void main(String[] args) {
    JFrame mainFrame = new JFrame( );

    // Exit app when frame is closed.
    mainFrame.setDefaultCloseOperation(JFrame.EXIT_ON_CLOSE);
    mainFrame.setSize(320, 240);
    mainFrame.setVisible(true);
  }
}
```

Another alternative that works with SDKs prior to 1.3 is to add a `WindowListener` to the frame, calling `System.exit( )` in the `windowClosing( )` method. Here's a simple example:

```
// FrameClose2.java
//
import javax.swing.JFrame;
import java.awt.event.*;

public class FrameClose2 {
  public static void main(String[] args) {
    JFrame mainFrame = new JFrame( );
```

```
    // Exit app when frame is closed.
    mainFrame.addWindowListener(new WindowAdapter() {
      public void windowClosing(WindowEvent ev) {
        System.exit(0);
      }
    });

    mainFrame.setSize(320, 240);
    mainFrame.setVisible(true);
  }
}
```

If you get tired of writing this same block of code in every frame that needs to close
properly, you might want to use an extension of JFrame that supports this feature.
Here's one possible implementation of such a class:

```
// ExitFrame.java
//
import javax.swing.JFrame;
import java.awt.event.WindowEvent;

// A very simple extension of JFrame that defaults to EXIT_ON_CLOSE for
// its close operation. Relies on the 1.3 or higher SDK.
public class ExitFrame extends JFrame {

  public ExitFrame() {
    super();
    setDefaultCloseOperation(EXIT_ON_CLOSE);
  }

  public ExitFrame(String title) {
    super(title);
    setDefaultCloseOperation(EXIT_ON_CLOSE);
  }
}
```

You can use this class just like you'd use a JFrame. If you don't want the program to
exit when the user closes the frame, just change the default close action to one of the
values defined in WindowConstants.

A more common strategy is to display a dialog box asking something like, "Are you
sure?" when the user tries to close the frame. JOptionPane (which we'll discuss in
detail in Chapter 10) makes this very easy to do. All you need to do is reimplement
your processWindowEvent( ) method like this:

```
protected void processWindowEvent(WindowEvent e) {
  if (e.getID() == WindowEvent.WINDOW_CLOSING) {
    int exit = JOptionPane.showConfirmDialog(this, "Are you sure?");
    if (exit == JOptionPane.YES_OPTION) {
      System.exit(0);
    }
  }
  // If you don't want listeners processing the WINDOW_CLOSING events, you could put
  // this next call in an else block for the if (e.getID( )...) statement. That way,
```

```
    // only the other types of Window events (iconification, activation, etc.) would be
    // sent out.
    super.processWindowEvent(e);
}
```

The JWindow Class

JWindow is an extension of java.awt.Window that uses a JRootPane as its single component. Other than this core distinction, JWindow does not change anything defined by
the Window class.

In AWT, one common reason for using the Window class was to create a pop-up
menu. Since Swing explicitly provides a JPopupMenu class (see Chapter 14), there is no
need to extend JWindow for this purpose. The only time you'll use JWindow is if you
have something that needs to be displayed in its own window without the adornments added by JFrame. Remember, this means that the window can only be moved
or closed programmatically (or via the user's platform-specific window manager controls, if available).

One possible use for JWindow would be to display a splash screen when an application is starting up. Many programs display screens like this, containing copyright
information, resource loading status, etc. Here's such a program:

```
// SplashScreen.java
//
import java.awt.*;
import javax.swing.*;

public class SplashScreen extends JWindow {
  private int duration;
  public SplashScreen(int d) {
    duration = d;
  }

  // A simple little method to show a title screen in the center of the screen for
  // the amount of time given in the constructor
  public void showSplash( ) {
    JPanel content = (JPanel)getContentPane( );
    content.setBackground(Color.white);

    // Set the window's bounds, centering the window.
    int width = 450;
    int height =115;
    Dimension screen = Toolkit.getDefaultToolkit( ).getScreenSize( );
    int x = (screen.width-width)/2;
    int y = (screen.height-height)/2;
    setBounds(x,y,width,height);

    // Build the splash screen.
    JLabel label = new JLabel(new ImageIcon("oreilly.gif"));
```

```
    JLabel copyrt = new JLabel
       ("Copyright 2002, O'Reilly & Associates", JLabel.CENTER);
    copyrt.setFont(new Font("Sans-Serif", Font.BOLD, 12));
    content.add(label, BorderLayout.CENTER);
    content.add(copyrt, BorderLayout.SOUTH);
    Color oraRed = new Color(156, 20, 20,  255);
    content.setBorder(BorderFactory.createLineBorder(oraRed, 10));

    // Display it.
    setVisible(true);

    // Wait a little while, maybe while loading resources.
    try { Thread.sleep(duration); } catch (Exception e) {}

    setVisible(false);
  }

  public void showSplashAndExit() {
    showSplash();
    System.exit(0);
  }

  public static void main(String[] args) {
    // Throw a nice little title page up on the screen first.
    SplashScreen splash = new SplashScreen(10000);
    // Normally, we'd call splash.showSplash() and get on with the program.
    // But, since this is only a test...
    splash.showSplashAndExit();
  }
}
```

All this program does is create a JWindow containing a pair of labels and display it in the center of the screen. In a real application, the title screen might be displayed while various system resources are being loaded (consider using a ProgressMonitor in this case). When run, this example displays a simple window in the center of the screen, as shown in Figure 8-10.

Figure 8-10. JWindow used as a splash screen

Properties

JWindow defines the properties shown in Table 8-9. The contentPane, glassPane, and layeredPane are really properties of JRootPane (described earlier in the chapter).

Direct access is provided for convenience. Unlike JFrame (and JApplet, described below), JWindow does not provide direct access to the root pane's menu bar. This is just an indication of JWindow's intended usage. If you have some compelling reason to display a menu bar on a JWindow, you can always access it through the root pane or just add it as a component.

Table 8-9. JWindow properties

Property	Data type	get	is	set	Default value
accessibleContext[o]	AccessibleContext	•			JWindow.AccessibleJWindow()
contentPane[o]	Container	•		•	From rootPane
glassPane[o]	Component	•		•	From rootPane
layeredPane[o]	JLayeredPane	•		•	From rootPane
layout[o]	LayoutManager	•		•	BorderLayout()
rootPane[o, *]	JRootPane	•		•	JRootPane()
rootPaneCheckingEnabled[p]	boolean		•	•	true

[o]overridden, [p]protected

*The setRootPane() method is protected.

See also the java.awt.Window class.

The layout property is listed here because JWindow overrides setLayout() to throw an Error if an attempt is made to change the layout manager, rather than set the layout manager of the window's content pane.

The rootPane property is set to a new instance of JRootPane when the frame is created and cannot be changed using public methods.

Constructors

public JWindow()
> Create a new, invisible window associated with no particular owner. This uses a package-private method in SwingUtilities to make a "fake" frame that serves as the owner. This makes this window a top-level window with no focus dependencies.

public JWindow(JFrame frame)
public JWindow(Window window)
> Create a new, invisible window associated with the given frame or window. A window created with a valid (i.e., non-null) association is focusable only when the associated frame or window is visible on the screen.

public JWindow(GraphicsConfiguration gc)
public JWindow(Window window, GraphicsConfiguration gc)

Create a new, invisible window (possibly associated with the given window) using the given graphics configuration. The GraphicsConfiguration object lets you create windows on things such as virtual screens.

The JApplet Class

JApplet is a simple extension of java.applet.Applet to use when creating Swing programs designed to be used in a web browser (or *appletviewer*). As a direct subclass of Applet, JApplet is used in much the same way, with the init( ), start( ), and stop( ) methods still playing critical roles. The primary thing JApplet provides that Applet does not is the use of a JRootPane as its single display component. The properties and methods described below should look a lot like those described in the previous sections on JFrame and JWindow. Figure 8-11 shows a JApplet running in *appletviewer*.

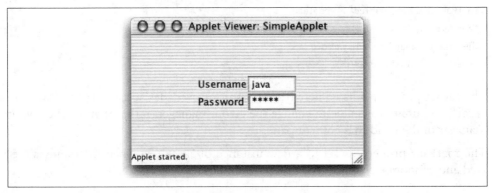

Figure 8-11. A JApplet running in the SDK appletviewer

Here's the code for this simple applet:

```
// SimpleApplet.java
//
import javax.swing.*;
import javax.swing.border.*;
import java.awt.*;

public class SimpleApplet extends JApplet {
  public void init( ) {
    JPanel p = new JPanel( );
    p.setLayout(new GridLayout(2, 2, 2, 2));
    p.add(new JLabel("Username"));
    p.add(new JTextField( ));
    p.add(new JLabel("Password"));
```

```
      p.add(new JPasswordField( ));
      Container content = getContentPane( );
      content.setLayout(new GridBagLayout( )); // Used to center the panel
      content.add(p);
   }
}
```

Using JApplet in browsers is a bit trickier. You should have a browser that supports at least the 1.2 release of the JRE. You typically end up using the Java Plug-in. The Plug-in allows you to specify which version of the JRE you want to use. The applet code itself doesn't change, but your HTML page is quite a bit different. For example, here's the simple HTML page with the <applet> tag to use with the *appletviewer*:

```
<HTML>
<HEAD><TITLE>JApplet Demo Page</TITLE></HEAD>
<BODY BGCOLOR="#FFFFFF">
<H1>JApplet Demo Page</H1>
If you see the login applet in this window, your plug-in has
been successfully installed and configured. <b>Congratulations!</b>
<hr>
<applet code=SimpleApplet width=300 height=200>
  <param name="bogus" value="just testing">
</applet>
<hr>
</BODY>
</HTML>
```

Pretty straightforward. Now here's the converted code that should replace the <applet> tag from the example above. We used the SDK's *HtmlConverter* application to produce this page that brings up the applet from Figure 8-11 in a browser with the Java Plug-in:

```
<!--"CONVERTED_APPLET"-->
<!-- HTML CONVERTER -->
<OBJECT
    classid="clsid:8AD9C840-044E-11D1-B3E9-00805F499D93"
    WIDTH = 300 HEIGHT = 200
    codebase="http://java.sun.com/products/plugin/autodl/jinstall-1_3-win.
cab#Version=1,3,0,0">
    <PARAM NAME = CODE VALUE = SimpleApplet >

    <PARAM NAME="type" VALUE="application/x-java-applet;version=1.3">
    <PARAM NAME="scriptable" VALUE="false">
    <PARAM NAME = "bogus" VALUE ="just testing">

<COMMENT>
<EMBED
        type="application/x-java-applet;version=1.3"
        CODE = SimpleApplet
        WIDTH = 300
        HEIGHT = 200
        bogus = "just testing"
    scriptable=false
```

```
            pluginspage="http://java.sun.com/products/plugin/index.html#download">
            <NOEMBED>

            </NOEMBED>
      </EMBED>
      </COMMENT>
</OBJECT>
<!--"END_CONVERTED_APPLET"-->
```

Not an obvious conversion, but fortunately, you can always use the converter tool to help you out. (You may want to run the converter from the 1.3 release of the SDK. This will allow you to support "1.3 and higher" if you want maximum compatibility for old versions of the Plug-in.) If you get deep into producing Swing applets, you should check out the full details on the Java Plug-in at *http://java.sun.com/products/plugin/index.html*.

One happy note to end this discussion: more and more browsers are supporting the Java Plug-in with a "use this plug in as the default for applets" type of option. With this in place, you don't need the converted HTML at all. The regular <applet> tags run just swell.

Hiding the Warning Message

Older versions of the popular browsers do not allow applets to access the system event queue. As a result, a warning message is printed to the Java console, indicating that the applet attempted to access the system event queue and failed. If you find this warning sufficiently annoying, Swing provides a workaround that allows you to suppress it. (You don't have to worry about this if you use the Java Plug-in; see the previous section for more details.) Just implement a constructor for your applet with the following code:

```
    getRootPane().putClientProperty("defeatSystemEventQueueCheck", Boolean.TRUE);
```

In AWT, applets rarely (if ever) had constructors. With Swing, a constructor (which must have no arguments) is a good place to set client properties like this one.

Threading Issues

Since JApplets are typically used within an existing Java virtual machine (from the web browser), you need to be careful about Swing threading issues. A good rule of thumb is that any adding or manipulation of components should be done in the init() method. If you choose to interact with Swing components in the start() method, you should be sure to execute the code in the event dispatch thread using the SwingUtilities.invokeLater() or SwingUtilities.invokeAndWait() methods.

```
    // SimpleApplet2.java
    //
    import javax.swing.*;
    import java.awt.*;
```

```
public class SimpleApplet2 extends JApplet {
  public SimpleApplet2() {
    // Suppress warning message on older versions if needed:
    //   getRootPane().putClientProperty("defeatSystemEventQueueCheck",
    //   Boolean.TRUE);
  }

  public void start() {
    SwingUtilities.invokeLater(new Runnable() {
      public void run() { // Run in the event thread.
        JPanel p = new JPanel();
        p.setLayout(new GridLayout(2, 2, 2, 2));
        p.add(new JLabel("Username"));
        p.add(new JTextField());
        p.add(new JLabel("Password"));
        p.add(new JPasswordField());
        Container content = getContentPane();
        content.setLayout(new GridBagLayout()); // Used to center the panel
        content.add(p);
        validate();
      }
    });
  }
}
```

Of course, in this example, we could just move this code to init( ) and safely do away with invokeLater( ). But if you start working with things like dynamic tables or trees in your applet, this approach is ideal. For more information on threading issues in Swing, see Chapter 1 for an introduction and Chapter 28 for more details.

Properties

JApplet defines the properties and default values shown in Table 8-10. The contentPane, glassPane, layeredPane, and JMenuBar properties are really properties of JRootPane (described earlier in the chapter). Direct access is provided to them for convenience.

Table 8-10. JApplet properties

Property	Data type	get	is	set	Default value
accessibleContext[o]	AccessibleContext	•			JApplet.AccessibleJApplet( )
contentPane[o]	Container	•		•	From rootPane
glassPane[o]	Component	•		•	From rootPane
layeredPane[o]	JLayeredPane	•		•	From rootPane
layout[o]	LayoutManager	•		•	BorderLayout( )

[o]overridden, [p]protected

*The setRootPane( ) method is protected.

See also the java.applet.Applet class.

Table 8-10. JApplet properties (continued)

Property	Data type	get	is	set	Default value
JMenuBar[o]	JMenuBar	•		•	From rootPane
rootPane[o],*	JRootPane	•		•	JRootPane( )
rootPaneCheckingEnabled[p]	boolean		•	•	true

[o]overridden, [p]protected

*The setRootPane( ) method is protected.

See also the java.applet.Applet class.

The layout property is listed here because JApplet overrides setLayout( ) to throw an Error if an attempt is made to change the layout manager, rather than set the layout manager of the applet's content pane.

The rootPane property is set when the applet is created. It cannot be changed via public methods.

Constructor

public JApplet()

Create a new applet and ensure that the timerQueue is running. This is how browsers (and *appletviewer*) create new applets. If you supply a constructor with an applet, perhaps to disable event queue checking, remember that browsers expect an applet constructor to have no arguments. The constructor sets the applet's foreground color to black and its background color to white.

User Interface Method

public void update(Graphics g)

Override Container.update( ) to do nothing but call paint( ). This is consistent with the implementation of update( ) provided by JComponent (and the implementation used by JFrame).

In this chapter:
- Simulating a Desktop
- The JInternalFrame Class
- The JDesktopPane Class
- The DesktopManager Interface
- Building a Desktop

CHAPTER 9

Internal Frames

Simulating a Desktop

Some GUI applications keep their entire interface in a single root window, which looks like a desktop environment and contains internal "windows" and icons, elements you'd find on the actual desktop. This style of interface was first used in early versions of the Windows operating system because, at that time, the operating system didn't support multiple, overlapping real windows for each application, so there was no alternative.

While there are still a few special circumstances in which this kind of interface is actually desirable (for example, if you're creating an emulation of another computer or a virtual environment and want to keep that world clearly distinct in its own window), most applications would be better off using real windows on the actual desktop.

Applications that stick to a virtual desktop interface out of habit do their users a disservice in a number of ways. Because their internal frames (simulated windows) are restricted to exist within the application's root window, the user has to compromise between making that window very large so there is room to position the application's windows in a convenient way, and keeping it small so that the windows of other applications can be seen and accessed conveniently. It's usually impossible to come up with a happy medium. The user is also prevented from overlapping windows of this application with windows of any other application, even if this would provide a better workflow.

Most of the perceived advantages of using a simulated desktop environment in a typical application can be achieved in a better way by thoughtful use of application palettes and the positioning of separate windows. If (despite all these caveats) it turns out that you *do* need to create and manage your own desktop in a window, Swing can accommodate you.

In this chapter, we'll look at a collection of classes Swing provides to allow you to create this type of application in Java. At the end of the chapter, we'll provide a large sample program that shows how to implement a variety of useful features.

Overview

Before looking at each of the classes involved in the Swing desktop/internal frame model, we'll take a moment for an overview of how they all work together. Figure 9-1 shows the relationships between the classes we'll be covering in this chapter.

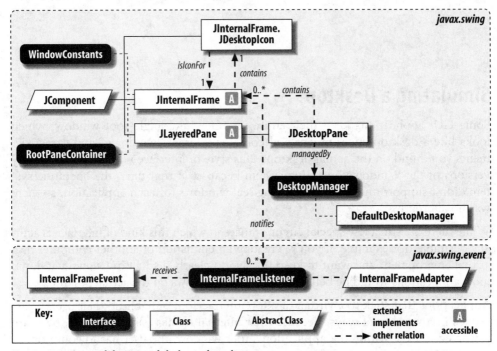

Figure 9-1. Internal frame and desktop class diagram

A JInternalFrame is a container that is similar to a JFrame. The key difference is that internal frames can exist only within some other Java container. JInternalFrame implements the following three interfaces: Accessible, WindowConstants, and RootPaneContainer.

Each internal frame keeps a reference to an instance of the static inner class called JDesktopIcon. Like real frames, JInternalFrames can be iconified. JDesktopIcon is the class responsible for taking the place of the frame when it is iconified.

Though not required, JInternalFrames are typically used inside of a JDesktopPane. JDesktopPane is an extension of JLayeredPane that adds direct support for managing a collection of JInternalFrames in layers. JDesktopPane uses an object called a DesktopManager to control how different behavior, like iconification or maximization, is carried out. A default implementation of this interface, DefaultDesktopManager, is provided. We'll see how all of this functionality is broken down as we cover the various classes and interfaces involved.

One more thing to notice about Figure 9-1 is that JInternalFrame supports a type of listener called InternalFrameListener. This interface contains methods like those defined by the AWT WindowListener class, with slightly different names, using InternalFrameEvents rather than WindowEvents as input.

The JInternalFrame Class

JInternalFrame provides the ability to create lightweight frames that exist inside other components. An internal frame is managed entirely within some other Java container, just like any other component, giving the program complete control over iconification, maximization, resizing, etc. Despite looking like "real" windows, the underlying windowing system knows nothing of the existence of internal frames.[*] Figure 9-2 shows what internal frames look like in various L&Fs.

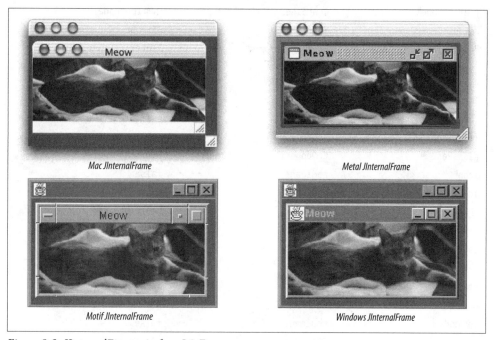

Figure 9-2. JInternalFrames in four L&Fs

---

[*] Note that JInternalFrame extends JComponent, not JFrame or Frame, so this statement should seem logical.

There's quite a lot to discuss about JInternalFrames, but most of their power comes when they are used inside a JDesktopPane. This section provides a quick overview of the properties, constructors, and methods available in JInternalFrame, and a more detailed discussion of using internal frames follows.

Properties

JInternalFrame defines the properties and default values shown in Table 9-1. The background and foreground properties are delegated to the frame's content pane.

Table 9-1. JInternalFrame properties

Property	Data type	get	is	set	Default value
accessibleContext[o]	AccessibleContext	•			JInternalFrame.AccessibleJInternalFrame()
closable	boolean		•	•	false
closed[b,c]	boolean		•	•	false
contentPane[b,o]	Container	•		•	From rootPane
defaultCloseOperation	int	•		•	DISPOSE_ON_CLOSE[1.3]
desktopIcon	JInternalFrame.JDesktopIcon	•		•	JInternalFrame.JDesktopIcon()
desktopPane	JDesktopPane	•			null
focusCycleRoot[1.4,o]	boolean		•	•	true (can't be changed)
focusCycleRootAncestor[1.4,o]	Container				null (will never change)
frameIcon[b]	Icon	•		•	null
glassPane[b,o]	Component	•		•	From rootPane()
icon[b,c]	boolean		•	•	false
iconifiable	boolean		•	•	false
JMenuBar[b,o]	JMenuBar	•		•	From rootPane()
layer[1.3]	int	•		•	0 (set available since 1.3)
layeredPane[b,o]	JLayeredPane	•		•	From rootPane()
maximizable	boolean		•	•	false
maximum[b,c]	boolean		•	•	false
normalBounds[1.3]	Rectangle	•		•	Non-maximized size
resizable	boolean		•	•	false
rootPane[b,o]	JRootPane	•			JRootPane()
selected[b,c]	boolean		•	•	false
title[b]	String	•		•	""

[1.3]since 1.3, [1.4]since 1.4, [b]bound, [c]constrained, [o]overridden

See also properties from the JComponent class (Table 3-6).

Table 9-1. JInternalFrame properties (continued)

Property	Data type	get	is	set	Default value
UI[b]	InternalFrameUI	•		•	From L&F
UIClassID[o]	String	•			"InternalFrameUI"
warningString	String	•			null

[1.3]since 1.3, [1.4]since 1.4, [b]bound, [c]constrained, [o]overridden

See also properties from the JComponent class (Table 3-6).

Three pairs of properties indicate whether something can be done to a frame and whether that thing is currently done to the frame. They are: closable/closed, iconifiable/icon, and maximizable/maximum. Note that closed, icon, and maximum are constrained properties.

The contentPane, glassPane, layeredPane, and JMenuBar properties come from the RootPaneContainer interface and are taken directly from the frame's JRootPane. The rootPane property is set to a new JRootPane when the frame is constructed.

The value of the defaultCloseOperation property defaults to WindowConstants. DISPOSE_ON_CLOSE. This means that when the user clicks the frame's close widget, the frame is hidden, and its dispose( ) method is called. (Prior to SDK 1.3, the default was HIDE_ON_CLOSE.)

The closed property is one of four constrained properties in this class, which means that attempts to set them could be vetoed. Code that sets these properties must be wrapped in try/catch blocks to handle the potential for a PropertyVetoException. As of this writing, these remain the only constrained properties you'll encounter in the standard Swing classes.

The desktopIcon reflects how the frame is displayed when iconified. A JDesktopIcon (which leaves the rendering to the L&F) is created for the frame when it is instantiated. The desktopPane property provides a convenient way to access the JDesktopPane containing the frame, if there is one.

focusCycleRoot and focusCycleRootAncestor relate to the improved focus traversal mechanism introduced in SDK 1.4 and described in "Focus and Focus Cycle Methods" in Chapter 3. For internal frames the focusCycleRoot property is always true, and focusCycleRootAncestor is always null because an internal frame is always the root of a focus cycle.

frameIcon is the icon painted inside the frame's titlebar (usually on the far left). By default, there is no icon. However, the Basic L&F checks to see if a frameIcon has been set and, if not, paints the "java cup" icon. This explains why an icon appears in the Windows L&F frame shown in Figure 9-2, but not in the others (which provide their own paint( ) implementations, rather than using the one provided by the Basic L&F).*

The `layer` property controls the frame's current layer, if it has been placed in a JLayeredPane. Since SDK 1.3, it has been possible to change a frame's layer by setting this property. The `normalBounds` property reflects (or changes) the size that the frame occupies when it's not maximized. If the frame is not maximized when `getNormalBounds` is called, it returns the same value as `getBounds`.

The `resizable` property indicates whether the frame can be resized by dragging its edges or corners, and `selected` indicates whether the frame has been selected (this typically determines the color of the titlebar). `selected` is a constrained property. `title` contains the string for the titlebar.

The `UI` property holds the current L&F implementation for the frame, and `UIClassID` reflects the class ID for internal frames.

Finally, the `warningString` property, which is always `null`, is used to specify the string that should appear in contexts where the frame might be insecure. This is the technique used by `java.awt.Window` to display a string like "Warning: Applet Window" when a Java window is displayed from an applet. Since `JInternalFrame`s are always fully enclosed by some other top-level container, this property is always `null`.

Events

`JInternalFrame` fires an `InternalFrameEvent` (discussed later in this chapter) whenever the frame's state changes.

The following standard methods are provided for working with events:

```
public void addInternalFrameListener(InternalFrameListener l)
public void removeInternalFrameListener(InternalFrameListener l)
public InternalFrameListener[] getInternalFrameListeners( ) (since 1.4)
```

Like all the other Swing classes, `JInternalFrame` fires `PropertyChangeEvents` when the value of any bound property is changed. `JInternalFrame` is unique in that it is the only Swing class that uses vetoable changes for some properties (`closed`, `icon`, `maximum`, and `selected`).

Constants

Table 9-2 shows the constants defined in this class. They are all strings and contain the names of the bound properties.

---

* The `BasicLookAndFeel` is an abstract base class that all the Swing L&Fs extend. For more information, see Chapter 26.

Table 9-2. JInternalFrame constants

Constant	Property
CONTENT_PANE_PROPERTY	Indicates that the content pane has changed
FRAME_ICON_PROPERTY	Indicates that the frame's icon has changed
GLASS_PANE_PROPERTY	Indicates that the glass pane has changed
IS_CLOSED_PROPERTY	Indicates that the frame has been opened or closed
IS_ICON_PROPERTY	Indicates that the frame as been iconified or deiconified
IS_MAXIMUM_PROPERTY	Indicates that the frame has been maximized or minimized
IS_SELECTED_PROPERTY	Indicates that the frame has been selected or deselected
LAYERED_PANE_PROPERTY	Indicates that the layered pane has changed
MENU_BAR_PROPERTY	Indicates that the menu bar has changed
ROOT_PANE_PROPERTY	Indicates that the root pane has changed
TITLE_PROPERTY	Indicates that the frame's title has changed

Constructors

JInternalFrame provides constructors that allow several of its boolean properties to be set at creation time. By default, resizable, closable, maximizable, and iconifiable are all set to false.

public JInternalFrame()
public JInternalFrame(String title)
   Create a new frame with all four properties set to false.

public JInternalFrame(String title, boolean resizable)
public JInternalFrame(String title, boolean resizable, boolean closable)
public JInternalFrame(String title, boolean resizable, boolean closable, boolean maximizable)
public JInternalFrame(String title, boolean resizable, boolean closable, boolean maximizable, boolean iconifiable)
   Allow one to four of the frame's boolean properties to be set at creation time.

JLayeredPane Methods

These methods are applicable only if the frame is contained by a JLayeredPane (otherwise, they do nothing).

public void moveToBack()
public void toBack()
   Call the containing layered pane's moveToBack() method, causing the frame to be the first (bottom) component painted in its layer. toBack() just calls moveToBack(), and the presence of both stems from historical inconsistency in the API.

public void moveToFront( )
public void toFront( )
>Call the containing layered pane's `moveToFront( )` method, causing the frame to be the last (top) component painted in its layer. These methods are equivalent.

Miscellaneous Public Methods

public void dispose( )
>Make the frame invisible, unselected, and closed.

public void doDefaultCloseAction( )
>Cause the frame to act exactly as if the Close button had been clicked. Available since 1.3.

public Component getFocusOwner( )
>If the frame is active, return the child that has focus (otherwise, return `null`). Available since 1.3.

public Component getMostRecentFocusOwner( )
>If the frame is active, this method returns the same value as `getFocusOwner`. Otherwise, it returns the value that `getFocusOwner` would return if the frame were active. Available since 1.4.

public void pack( )
>Like `Frame`'s `pack( )` method, this method causes the frame to be resized according to the preferred size of its components.

public void reshape(int x, int y, int width, int height)
>Call its superclass implementation and then force a repaint of the frame, so that decorations such as the title bar are painted.

public void restoreSubcomponentFocus( )
>Request that the frame restore focus to the most recent focus owner. Called by the UI when the frame is reactivated (e.g., by clicking on the title bar). Available since 1.3.

public void show( )
>Make the frame visible and select it, bringing it to the front of its layer.

public void updateUI( )
>Called to indicate that the L&F for the frame has changed.

Use of the Glass Pane

`JInternalFrame` is the only Swing class that uses the glass pane (see "The Glass Pane" in Chapter 8 for a general discussion). To be precise, `JInternalFrame` itself doesn't do anything special with the glass pane, but the default UI implementation (`BasicInternalFrameUI`) does. This class toggles the visibility of an internal frame's glass pane each time the state of the frame's selected property changes. When the frame is selected, the glass pane is made invisible, allowing components inside the frame to be accessed with the mouse. But when the frame is not selected, the glass pane is made visible. This means that the first time you click anywhere within an unselected internal frame, the mouse click does not get through to the component within the frame that you clicked on, but is instead intercepted by the glass pane, causing the frame to be selected (and causing the glass pane to be removed).

The Metal Look-and-Feel JInternalFrame.isPalette Client Property

If you plan to use the Metal L&F in your application, you can take advantage of a special custom property supported by MetalInternalFrameUI. This client property allows you to define an internal frame as a palette. This effectively amounts to removing the thick border from the frame. This is a technique commonly used in word-processing or graphics-editing programs to provide small windows that contain a set of convenient edit buttons. If you couple the use of this client property with the use of the desktop's PALETTE_LAYER (discussed later), you have a nice borderless frame that floats above your other internal frames. Here's an example of how you'd use this property:

```
JInternalFrame palette = new JInternalFrame( ); // Use any constructor.
palette.putClientProperty("JInternalFrame.isPalette", Boolean.TRUE);
palette.setBounds(0, 0, 50, 150);
JDesktopPane desk = new JDesktopPane( );
desk.add(palette, JDesktopPane.PALETTE_LAYER);
```

Other L&Fs quietly ignore this property. (If you'd like a framework in which to try out this code, there is a full-blown example program for working with internal frames at the end of this chapter that you can use as a starting point.)

The JInternalFrame.JDesktopIcon Class

JDesktopIcon is a static inner class of JInternalFrame that provides an iconified view of a frame. JInternalFrame instantiates a JDesktopIcon when the frame is created. The class extends JComponent and, like other Swing components, leaves all details of its visual appearance to its UI delegate.

Note that this class has no relation at all to the Swing Icon interface.

 You should not work with the JDesktopIcon class directly—the Javadoc for this inner class indicates that it will go away in a future Swing release.

The InternalFrameEvent Class

As we described earlier in the chapter, JInternalFrames fire InternalFrameEvents when the state of the frame changes. These are standard AWTEvent subclasses, providing a number of constants to define the type of change that was made to the frame. Since SDK 1.3, it also provides a getInternalFrame method to retrieve the associated frame.

Constants

Table 9-3 shows constants defined as possible values for the event ID.

Table 9-3. InternalFrameEvent constants

Constant	Type	Description
INTERNAL_FRAME_ACTIVATED	int	The frame has been activated, typically causing the title bar to change to a special color and the frame to gain focus.
INTERNAL_FRAME_CLOSED	int	The frame has been closed (sent anytime the frame is closed).
INTERNAL_FRAME_CLOSING	int	The frame is about to be closed (sent when the user clicks the closebox on the frame).
INTERNAL_FRAME_DEACTIVATED	int	The frame has been deactivated, typically causing the title bar to change to a default color and the frame to lose focus.
INTERNAL_FRAME_DEICONIFIED	int	The frame has been restored from an icon.
INTERNAL_FRAME_ICONIFIED	int	The frame has been iconified.
INTERNAL_FRAME_OPENED	int	The frame has been opened.
INTERNAL_FRAME_FIRST	int	The first integer value used to represent the above event IDs.
INTERNAL_FRAME_LAST	int	The last integer value used to represent the above event IDs.

The InternalFrameListener Interface

JInternalFrame fires InternalFrameEvents to registered InternalFrameListeners. This interface defines the following set of methods (which have a one-to-one correspondence to the methods in the java.awt.event.WindowListener interface).

Methods

All of these methods, except for internalFrameClosing( ), are called by the JInternalFrame when its properties are changed:

public abstract void internalFrameActivated(InternalFrameEvent e)
> The frame has been activated, typically meaning that it gains focus and is brought to the front.

public abstract void internalFrameClosed(InternalFrameEvent e)
> The frame has been closed.

public abstract void internalFrameClosing(InternalFrameEvent e)
   The frame is closing. This is called by the L&F when the close button is clicked.

public abstract void internalFrameDeactivated(InternalFrameEvent e)
   The frame has been deactivated.

public abstract void internalFrameDeiconified(InternalFrameEvent e)
   The frame has been restored from an icon.

public abstract void internalFrameIconified(InternalFrameEvent e)
   The frame has been reduced to an icon.

public abstract void internalFrameOpened(InternalFrameEvent e)
   A previously closed frame has been opened.

The InternalFrameAdapter Class

This class follows the standard AWT 1.1 listener/adapter pattern by providing empty implementations of the seven methods defined in the `InternalFrameListener` interface. If you are interested only in certain types of events, you can create a subclass of this adapter that implements only the methods you care about.

Methods

The following methods have empty implementations in this class:

```
public void internalFrameActivated(InternalFrameEvent e)
public void internalFrameClosed(InternalFrameEvent e)
public void internalFrameClosing(InternalFrameEvent e)
public void internalFrameDeactivated(InternalFrameEvent e)
public void internalFrameDeiconified(InternalFrameEvent e)
public void internalFrameIconified(InternalFrameEvent e)
public void internalFrameOpened(InternalFrameEvent e)
```

The JDesktopPane Class

JDesktopPane is an extension of `JLayeredPane`, which uses a `DesktopManager` to control the placement and movement of frames. Figure 9-3 shows what `JDesktopPane` looks like in several L&Fs. Like its superclass, `JLayeredPane` has a `null` layout manager. Components added to it must be placed at absolute locations with absolute sizes because it is intended to house `JInternalFrames`, which rely on the user to determine their placement.

Another reason for using `JDesktopPane` is to allow pop-up dialog boxes to be displayed using `JInternalFrames`. This is discussed in detail in the next chapter.

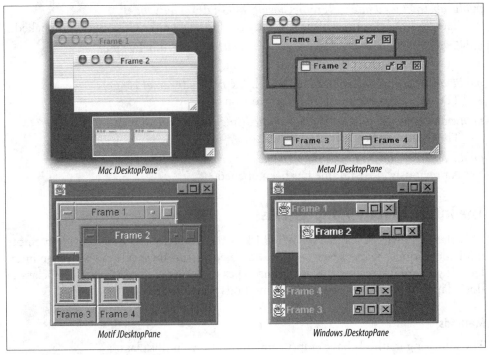

Mac JDesktopPane

Metal JDesktopPane

Motif JDesktopPane

Windows JDesktopPane

Figure 9-3. JDesktopPanes in four L&Fs

Properties

Table 9-4 shows the properties defined by JDesktopPane. The allFrames property provides access to all JInternalFrames contained by the desktop. The desktopManager property holds the DesktopManager object supplied by the pane's L&F. (We'll cover the responsibilities of the DesktopManager in the next section.) The opaque property defaults to true for JDesktopPanes, and isOpaque( ) is overridden so that it always returns true. UI contains the DesktopPaneUI implementation, and UIClassID contains the class ID for JDesktopPane.

Table 9-4. JDesktopPane properties

Property	Data type	get	is	set	Default value
accessibleContext[o]	AccessibleContext	•			JDesktopPane.AccessibleJDesktopPane( )
allFrames	JInternalFrame[]	•			Empty array
desktopManager	DesktopManager	•		•	From L&F
dragMode[1.3]	int	•		•	LIVE_DRAG_MODE

[1.3]since 1.3, [o]overridden

See also properties from the JLayeredPane class (Table 8-5).

Table 9-4. JDesktopPane properties (continued)

Property	Data type	get	is	set	Default value
opaque[o]	boolean		•	•	true
selectedFrame[1.3]	JInternalFrame	•		•	Depends on current state
UI	DesktopPaneUI	•		•	From L&F
UIClassID[o]	String	•			"DesktopPaneUI"

[1.3]since 1.3, [o]overridden

See also properties from the JLayeredPane class (Table 8-5).

Constructor

public JDesktopPane( )
> Create a new desktop and call updateUI( ), resulting in the L&F implementation installing a DesktopManager.

Methods

public JInternalFrame[] getAllFramesInLayer(int layer)
> Return all frames that have been added to the specified layer. This includes frames that have been iconified.

public void updateUI( )
> Called to indicate that the L&F for the desktop should be set.

The DesktopManager Interface

This interface is responsible for much of the management of internal frames contained by JDesktopPanes. It allows an L&F to define exactly how it wants to manage things such as frame activation, movement, and iconification. Most of the methods in InternalFrameUI implementations should delegate to a DesktopManager object. As described earlier, DesktopManagers are contained by JDesktopPane objects and are intended to be set by the L&F. You can also create your own variations on the supplied implementations to provide custom behavior, as shown in the example that concludes this chapter.

Methods

The majority of the methods in this interface act on a given JInternalFrame. However, those methods that could be applied to other types of components do not restrict the parameter unnecessarily (they accept any JComponent), despite the fact that they are typically used only with JInternalFrames. If you implement your own DesktopManager or other L&F classes, you may find a need for this flexibility.

public abstract void activateFrame(JInternalFrame f)
> Called to indicate that the specified frame should become active (is gaining focus).

public abstract void beginDraggingFrame(JComponent f)
> Called to indicate that the specified frame is now being dragged. The given component is normally a JInternalFrame.

public abstract void beginResizingFrame(JComponent f, int direction)
> Called to indicate that the specified frame will be resized. The direction comes from SwingConstants and must be NORTH, SOUTH, EAST, WEST, NORTH_EAST, NORTH_WEST, SOUTH_EAST, or SOUTH_WEST, representing the edge or corner being dragged (although this value is currently ignored by all provided implementations). The given component is normally a JInternalFrame. When resizing is complete, endResizingFrame( ) is called.

public abstract void closeFrame(JInternalFrame f)
> Called to indicate that the specified frame should be closed.

public abstract void deactivateFrame(JInternalFrame f)
> Called to indicate that the specified frame is no longer active (has lost focus).

public abstract void deiconifyFrame(JInternalFrame f)
> Called to indicate that the specified frame should no longer be iconified.

public abstract void dragFrame(JComponent f, int newX, int newY)
> Called to indicate that the specified frame should be moved from its current location to the newly specified coordinates. The given component is normally a JInternalFrame.

public abstract void endDraggingFrame(JComponent f)
> Called to indicate that the specified frame is no longer being dragged. The given component is normally a JInternalFrame.

public abstract void endResizingFrame(JComponent f)
> Called to indicate that the specified frame is no longer being resized. The given component is normally a JInternalFrame.

public abstract void iconifyFrame(JInternalFrame f)
> Called to indicate that the specified frame should be iconified.

public abstract void maximizeFrame(JInternalFrame f)
> Called to indicate that the specified frame should be maximized.

public abstract void minimizeFrame(JInternalFrame f)
> Called to indicate that the specified frame should be minimized. Note that this is not the same as iconifying the frame. Typically, calling this method causes the frame to return to its size and position before it was maximized.

public abstract void openFrame(JInternalFrame f)
> Called to add a frame and display it at a reasonable location. This is not often called because frames are normally added directly to their parent.

public abstract void resizeFrame(JComponent f, int newX, int newY, int newWidth,
   int newHeight)

> Called to indicate that the specified frame has been resized. Note that resizing is still in progress (many calls to this method may be made while the frame is being resized) after this method completes. The given component is normally a `JInternalFrame`.

public abstract void setBoundsForFrame(JComponent f, int newX, int newY,
   int newWidth, int newHeight)

> Called to set a new size and location for a frame. The given component will normally be a `JInternalFrame`.

The DefaultDesktopManager Class

`DefaultDesktopManager` is a default implementation of the `DesktopManager` interface. It serves as the base class for the Windows and Motif L&Fs, while the Metal L&F uses it without modification. In this section, we'll give a brief explanation of how each of the methods in the interface is implemented by this class.

Methods

public void activateFrame(JInternalFrame f)

> Call `setSelected(false)` on all other `JInternalFrames` contained by the specified frame's parent that are in the same layer as the given frame. It then moves the given frame to the front of its layer and selects it.

public void closeFrame(JInternalFrame f)

> Remove the given frame from its parent. It also removes the frame's icon (if displayed). It sets the frame's previous bounds to `null`.

public void deiconifyFrame(JInternalFrame f)

> Remove the given frame's icon from its parent and add the frame itself in its place. This method then tries to select the given frame if it can receive focus.

public void dragFrame(JComponent f, int newX, int newY)

> Call `setBoundsForFrame()` with the given location and current dimensions.

public void iconifyFrame(JInternalFrame f)

> Remove the given frame from its parent and add the frame's desktop icon. Before adding the icon, it checks to see if it has ever been iconified. If not, it calls `getBoundsForIconOf()` to set the icon's bounds. This is done only once for a given frame, ensuring that each time a frame is iconified, it returns to the same location on the desktop.

public void maximizeFrame(JInternalFrame f)

> Maximize the given frame so that it fills its parent. This method also saves the frame's previous bounds for use in `minimizeFrame()`. Once the frame has been

maximized, it is also selected. This method can be called on an iconified frame, causing it to be deiconified and maximized.

public void minimizeFrame(JInternalFrame f)
Set the frame's bounds to its previous bounds. If there are no previous bounds (previous bounds are set by calling `maximizeFrame( )`), the frame is not resized.

public void openFrame(JInternalFrame f)
Get the desktop icon for the given frame. If the icon's parent is non-null, the icon is removed from the parent, and the frame is added. If its parent is null, this method does nothing.

public void resizeFrame(JComponent f, int newX, int newY, int newWidth,
  int newHeight)
Call `setBoundsForFrame( )` with the given location and dimensions.

public void setBoundsForFrame(JComponent f, int newX, int newY, int newWidth,
  int newHeight)
Move and resize the given frame (using `setBounds( )`) and validate the frame if the size was actually changed.

public void beginDraggingFrame(JComponent f)
public void beginResizingFrame(JComponent f, int direction)
public void endDraggingFrame(JComponent f)
public void endResizingFrame(JComponent f)
Provide support for faster dragging if the desktop's `dragMode` requires it.

public void deactivateFrame(JInternalFrame f)
If the frame was selected, deselect it.

Protected methods

This default implementation provides several convenience methods, which it uses in the methods described above. The methods relate to desktop icon management and the management of a frame's previous size (when maximized). If you subclass `DefaultDesktopManager`, these methods will probably be of use to you.

The frame's previous bounds and an indication of whether it has ever been iconified are stored in client properties on the frame itself.* The property names used are `previousBounds` (which holds a `Rectangle`) and `wasIconOnce` (which holds a `Boolean`).

protected Rectangle getBoundsForIconOf(JInternalFrame f)
Get the bounds for the given frame's icon. The width and height are taken directly from the size of the icon. The icon is placed in the lower-left corner of the desktop. If an icon has already been placed in this corner, the icon is placed directly to the right, continuing until an unclaimed position along the bottom of

---

* See "Client Properties" in Chapter 3 for an explanation of JComponent's client property feature.

the frame is found. If there is no space along the bottom, a new row of icons is started directly above the first row. Once a frame has been iconified, its icon's location is set, and the icon always returns to the same spot (unless it is moved by the user).

protected Rectangle getPreviousBounds(JInternalFrame f)
Return the frame's previous bounds (set when the frame is maximized). These bounds are retrieved from the frame's `previousBounds` client property.

protected void removeIconFor(JInternalFrame f)
Remove the given frame's icon from its parent and repaint the region under the icon.

protected void setPreviousBounds(JInternalFrame f, Rectangle r)
Save the previous bounds of a frame. This is done by saving the frame's previous bounds in the frame itself, using the client property, `previousBounds`. This is generally called by `maximizeFrame( )`, with the data being used in a subsequent `minimizeFrame( )` call.

protected void setWasIcon(JInternalFrame f, Boolean value)
Called by `iconifyFrame( )` to indicate whether the frame has, at some time, been iconified. This is done by saving the boolean `value` in the frame itself, using the client property `wasIconOnce`. This is used to determine whether the icon's bounds have been defined.

protected boolean wasIcon(JInternalFrame f)
Determine whether a frame has ever been iconified (if it has, bounds are already defined for the icon). This is done by returning the `wasIconOnce` client property on the frame.

Building a Desktop

In this section, we'll pull together some of the things we've discussed in the previous section to create an application using `JDesktopPane`, `JInternalFrame`, and a custom `DesktopManager`. The example will show:

- The effect of adding frames to different layers of the desktop
- How to display a background image ("wallpaper") on the desktop
- How to keep frames from being moved outside of the desktop
- How to deiconify, move, and resize internal frames by frame "tiling"
- How to take advantage of `JInternalFrame`'s constrained properties by requiring that there be at least one noniconified frame on the desktop

Figure 9-4 shows what the application looks like when it's running. Here, we see the desktop with three frames, plus a fourth that has been iconified. The frames titled "Lo" are in a lower layer than the "Up" frames. No matter which frame is active or how the frames are arranged, the "Up" frame always appears on top of the others.

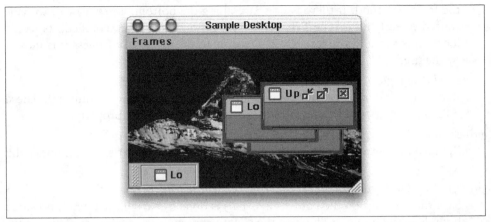

Figure 9-4. SampleDesktop layered frames and background image

Frames in the same layer can be brought to the front of that layer by clicking on the frame. This display also shows the use of a background image (what good is a desktop if you can't put your favorite image on the background, right?). This image is added to a very low layer (the lowest possible Java int, actually) to ensure that it is always painted behind anything else in the desktop. Figure 9-5 shows the same display after the frames have been "tiled."

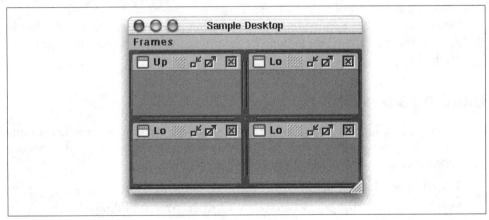

Figure 9-5. SampleDesktop with tiled frames

Now, let's take a look at some of the code used to create this example. There are three primary classes:

SampleDesktop

> This is the main class, which we chose to create as a JFrame that uses a JDesktopPane as its content pane. SampleDesktop has two inner classes. AddFrameAction is an Action used to add frames to the desktop. Recall from Chapter 3 that actions are a

nice way to encapsulate functionality that you might want to invoke from multiple locations. The other inner class, IconPolice, is responsible for ensuring that if there is only a single frame on the desktop, it cannot be iconified.

SampleDesktopMgr
An extension of DefaultDesktopManager that keeps frames from being moved outside the bounds of the desktop.

TileAction
A generic action class that can be used to tile all frames on a given desktop.

Let's take a look at these classes piece by piece. The complete source listing is provided at the end of the chapter.

Setting Things Up

The first thing to look at is the SampleDesktop constructor:

```
public SampleDesktop(String title) {
    super(title);
    setDefaultCloseOperation(EXIT_ON_CLOSE);

    // Create a desktop and set it as the content pane. Don't set the layered
    // pane, since it needs to hold the menu bar too.
    desk = new JDesktopPane();
    setContentPane(desk);

    // Install our custom desktop manager.
    desk.setDesktopManager(new SampleDesktopMgr());
    createMenuBar();
    loadBackgroundImage();
}
```

We set the frame's content pane to our new JDesktopPane. Since we won't be adding anything else to the body of the frame, this is a good idea. We could also have called getContentPane().add(desk), but, as we discussed in Chapter 8, this just introduces an unnecessary extra level (the content pane would then be a JPanel holding only our JDesktopPane). The more important thing to avoid is calling setLayeredPane(desk). Remember, the layered pane is responsible for rendering the menu bar too. If you did this, the menu bar would still be drawn at the top of the frame, but your desktop would be filling the same space, allowing frames to be placed over the menu.

The createMenuBar() method called here just adds a few options to the frame's menu bar. It uses instances of AddFrameAction for adding new frames (at "Up" and "Lo" levels), and it uses an instance of TileAction to support frame tiling. See the complete code listing at the end of this section for more details on this method.

The loadBackgroundImage() method looks like this:

```
protected void loadBackgroundImage() {
    ImageIcon icon = new ImageIcon("images/matterhorn.gif");
```

```
    JLabel l = new JLabel(icon);
    l.setBounds(0, 0, icon.getIconWidth( ), icon.getIconHeight( ));

    desk.add(l, new Integer(Integer.MIN_VALUE));
}
```

This method just creates a large JLabel containing an image and adds this label to the lowest possible layer of the desktop. This ensures that nothing is ever painted behind the background. In this example, we don't make any effort to resize or tile the background image, but it certainly could be done.

Adding Frames to the Desktop

The AddFrameAction class is an Action we've added to the menu bar. When fired, AddFrameAction instantiates a JInternalFrame and adds it to the specified layer of the desktop. Here's the code for the actionPerformed( ) method of this class:

```
public void actionPerformed(ActionEvent ev) {
  JInternalFrame f = new JInternalFrame(name, true, true, true, true);
  f.addVetoableChangeListener(iconPolice);
  f.setBounds(0, 0, 120, 60);
  desk.add(f, layer);
  f.setVisible(true);  // Needed since 1.3
}
```

The important things to notice here are that we set the bounds, not just the size, of the new frame, and we explicitly make it visible. We get the name of the frame from the name of the action being handled. If you don't specify a location (we've specified [0,0], the upper-left corner) for the frame, it won't appear on the desktop when you add it. Remember, there's no layout manager controlling the location of the components in a JDesktopPane. Also, starting with SDK 1.3, internal frames start out invisible until you explicitly make them visible, just like regular frames.

Veto Power

In the previous code block, we added a VetoableChangeListener to each new frame we created. This listener is an instance of another inner class called IconPolice. The purpose of this class is to ensure that the last frame on the desktop cannot be iconified. This may not be the most useful thing in the world to do, but it shows how to use JInternalFrame's constrained properties. Here's the code for this class:

```
class IconPolice implements VetoableChangeListener {
  public void vetoableChange(PropertyChangeEvent ev)
    throws PropertyVetoException {
    String name = ev.getPropertyName( );
    if (name.equals(JInternalFrame.IS_ICON_PROPERTY)
        && (ev.getNewValue( ) == Boolean.TRUE)) {
      JInternalFrame[] frames = desk.getAllFrames( );
      int count = frames.length;
      int nonicons = 0; // How many are not icons?
```

```
      for (int i = 0; i < count; i++) {
        if (!frames[i].isIcon()) {
          nonicons++;
        }
      }
      if (nonicons <= 1) {
        throw new PropertyVetoException("Invalid Iconification!", ev);
      }
    }
  }
}
```

If you haven't used constrained properties before, this code may look a little strange. The idea behind constrained properties is that before a property is changed, all registered listeners are given the opportunity to "veto" the change. This is done by throwing a PropertyVetoException from the vetoableChange( ) method, as we've done here.

Bounding the frames

The next class to look at is our custom desktop manager called SampleDesktopMgr. This class is an extension of DefaultDesktopManager, which overrides the default implementation of dragFrame( ). This is the method called any time the frame is moved. The new implementation simply checks the new location of the frame to see if the requested change of bounds will result in part of the frame moving outside of the desktop. If so, it adjusts the coordinates so that the frame is only moved to the edge of the desktop. The code for this method is included at the end of the chapter.

This class is included only as a useful example of the type of thing you might want to do with a desktop manager. If you don't mind frames being moved off the desktop, you can always just use DefaultDesktopManager (the default).

Moving Things Around

The last class in this example is called TileAction. Its job is to resize all of the frames and lay them out in a grid on a desktop. There are a few interesting things that take place in the actionPerformed( ) method of this class. First, we get all of the frames on the desktop and determine where each frame should be placed and how big it should be based on the size of the desktop and the total number of frames. For the details of how this is calculated, see the full code listing at the end of the chapter.

Next, we iterate over all of the frames on the desktop, deiconifying any iconified frames and then setting the size and location of each frame. Here's the block of code that does this work:

```
for (int i = 0; i < rows; i++) {
  for (int j = 0; j < cols && ((i * cols) + j < count); j++) {
    JInternalFrame f = allframes[(i * cols) + j];
```

```
          if (!f.isClosed() && f.isIcon()) {
            try {
              f.setIcon(false);
            }
            catch (PropertyVetoException ex) {}
          }
          desk.getDesktopManager().resizeFrame(f, x, y, w, h);
          x += w;
        }
        y += h;       // Start the next row.
        x = 0;
      }
```

We call setIcon() on the frame rather than calling deiconifyFrame() on the DesktopManager. We do this because deiconifyFrame() does not actually change the state of the icon property in the frame, which can result in unexpected behavior down the road. Figure 9-6 shows the sequence of calls (only certain significant calls are identified) made when we call setIcon(false).

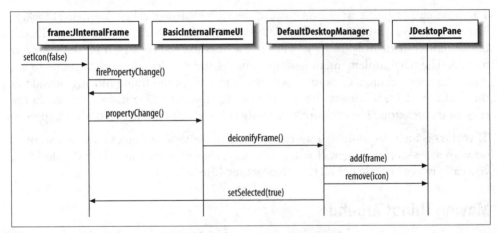

Figure 9-6. setIcon() sequence diagram

Note that the UI delegate is registered as a listener for property change events. When it hears that a frame is being deiconified, it calls deiconifyFrame() on the desktop manager. This object then adds the frame to its container (the desktop pane in this case), removes the icon, and selects the newly added frame.

Once the frame is deiconified, we relocate and resize it by calling the resizeFrame() method on the desktop manager:

```
    desk.getDesktopManager().resizeFrame(f, x, y, w, h);
```

We call this method (instead of just calling setBounds() on the frame) because it validates the frame after setting its bounds.

Source Code

Here's the complete source code (three files) for this example:

```java
// SampleDesktop.java
//
import javax.swing.*;
import java.awt.event.*;
import java.awt.*;
import java.util.*;
import java.beans.*;

// An example that shows how to do a few interesting things using JInternalFrames,
// JDesktopPane, and DesktopManager
public class SampleDesktop extends JFrame {

  private JDesktopPane desk;
  private IconPolice iconPolice = new IconPolice( );

  public SampleDesktop(String title) {
    super(title);
    setDefaultCloseOperation(EXIT_ON_CLOSE);

    // Create a desktop and set it as the content pane. Don't set the layered
    // pane, since it needs to hold the menu bar too.
    desk = new JDesktopPane( );
    setContentPane(desk);

    // Install our custom desktop manager.
    desk.setDesktopManager(new SampleDesktopMgr( ));

    createMenuBar( );
    loadBackgroundImage( );
  }

  // Create a menu bar to show off a few things.
  protected void createMenuBar( ) {
    JMenuBar mb = new JMenuBar( );
    JMenu menu = new JMenu("Frames");

    menu.add(new AddFrameAction(true));  // Add "upper" frame.
    menu.add(new AddFrameAction(false)); // Add "lower" frame.
    menu.add(new TileAction(desk));      // Add tiling capability.

    setJMenuBar(mb);
    mb.add(menu);
  }

  // Here, we load a background image for our desktop.
  protected void loadBackgroundImage( ) {
    ImageIcon icon = new ImageIcon("images/matterhorn.gif");
    JLabel l = new JLabel(icon);
    l.setBounds(0,0,icon.getIconWidth( ),icon.getIconHeight( ));
```

```java
      // Place the image in the lowest possible layer so nothing can ever be painted
      // under it.
      desk.add(l, new Integer(Integer.MIN_VALUE));
   }

   // This class adds a new JInternalFrame when requested.
   class AddFrameAction extends AbstractAction {
      public AddFrameAction(boolean upper) {
         super(upper ? "Add Upper Frame" : "Add Lower Frame");
         if (upper) {
            this.layer = new Integer(2);
            this.name = "Up";
         }
         else {
            this.layer = new Integer(1);
            this.name = "Lo";
         }
      }

      public void actionPerformed(ActionEvent ev) {
         JInternalFrame f = new JInternalFrame(name, true, true, true, true);
         f.addVetoableChangeListener(iconPolice);

         f.setBounds(0, 0, 120, 60);
         desk.add(f, layer);
         f.setVisible(true);  // Needed since 1.3
      }

      private Integer layer;
      private String name;
   }

   // A simple vetoable change listener that insists that there is always at least one
   // noniconified frame (just as an example of the vetoable properties)
   class IconPolice implements VetoableChangeListener {
      public void vetoableChange(PropertyChangeEvent ev)
         throws PropertyVetoException
      {
         String name = ev.getPropertyName();
         if (name.equals(JInternalFrame.IS_ICON_PROPERTY)
               && (ev.getNewValue() == Boolean.TRUE)) {
            JInternalFrame[] frames = desk.getAllFrames();
            int count = frames.length;
            int nonicons = 0; // How many are not icons?
            for (int i = 0; i < count; i++) {
               if (!frames[i].isIcon()) {
                  nonicons++;
               }
            }
            if (nonicons <= 1) {
               throw new PropertyVetoException("Invalid Iconification!", ev);
            }
         }
      }
   }
}
```

```java
  // A simple test program
  public static void main(String[] args) {
    SampleDesktop td = new SampleDesktop("Sample Desktop");

    td.setSize(300, 220);
    td.setVisible(true);
  }
}


// SampleDesktopMgr.java
//
import javax.swing.*;
import java.awt.event.*;
import java.awt.*;
import java.util.*;
import java.beans.*;

// A DesktopManager that keeps its frames inside the desktop
public class SampleDesktopMgr extends DefaultDesktopManager {

  // This is called whenever a frame is moved. This implementation keeps the frame
  // from leaving the desktop.
  public void dragFrame(JComponent f, int x, int y) {
    if (f instanceof JInternalFrame) {  // Deal only with internal frames.
      JInternalFrame frame = (JInternalFrame)f;
      JDesktopPane desk = frame.getDesktopPane();
      Dimension d = desk.getSize();

      // Nothing all that fancy below, just figuring out how to adjust
      // to keep the frame on the desktop
      if (x < 0) {                // Too far left?
        x = 0;                    // Flush against the left side.
      }
      else {
        if (x + frame.getWidth() > d.width) {    // Too far right?
          x = d.width - frame.getWidth();        // Flush against right side.
        }
      }
      if (y < 0) {               // Too high?
        y=0;                     // Flush against the top.
      }
      else {
        if (y + frame.getHeight() > d.height) {   // Too low?
          y = d.height - frame.getHeight();       // Flush against the bottom.
        }
      }
    }

    // Pass along the (possibly cropped) values to the normal drag handler.
    super.dragFrame(f, x, y);
  }
}
```

```
// TileAction.java
//
import javax.swing.*;
import java.awt.event.*;
import java.awt.*;
import java.beans.*;

// An action that tiles all internal frames when requested
public class TileAction extends AbstractAction {
  private JDesktopPane desk; // The desktop to work with

  public TileAction(JDesktopPane desk) {
    super("Tile Frames");
    this.desk = desk;
  }

  public void actionPerformed(ActionEvent ev) {

    // How many frames do we have?
    JInternalFrame[] allframes = desk.getAllFrames( );
    int count = allframes.length;
    if (count == 0) return;

    // Determine the necessary grid size.
    int sqrt = (int)Math.sqrt(count);
    int rows = sqrt;
    int cols = sqrt;
    if (rows * cols < count) {
      cols++;
      if (rows * cols < count) {
        rows++;
      }
    }

    // Define some initial values for size and location.
    Dimension size = desk.getSize( );

    int w = size.width / cols;
    int h = size.height / rows;
    int x = 0;
    int y = 0;

    // Iterate over the frames, deiconifying any iconified frames and then
    // relocating and resizing each.
    for (int i = 0; i < rows; i++) {
      for (int j = 0; j < cols && ((i * cols) + j < count); j++) {
        JInternalFrame f = allframes[(i * cols) + j];

        if (!f.isClosed( ) && f.isIcon( )) {
          try {
            f.setIcon(false);
          }
```

```
            catch (PropertyVetoException ignored) {}
        }

        desk.getDesktopManager().resizeFrame(f, x, y, w, h);
        x += w;
    }
    y += h; // Start the next row.
    x = 0;
    }
  }
}
```

Swing Dialogs

In most applications, information occasionally needs to be displayed for a brief period of time, often just long enough for the user to read it and click OK or perhaps enter a value, such as a password. Swing provides the JOptionPane class to make creating such simple dialog boxes extremely easy—in many cases requiring just one line of code.

Applications may also serve more complex dialog needs, such as providing a property editor in which a set of related values can be modified, with an appropriate interface. Swing's JDialog class supports such general-purpose dialogs. JDialogs can also be non-modal,* which means the user does not need to close the dialog before interacting with other application windows. When possible, implementing such an interface yields a more pleasant and productive user experience.

Even though JOptionPane makes it very easy (for the programmer) to pop up a dialog, bear in mind that this will disrupt the flow of activity for users and force them to deal with the dialog before they can proceed with their underlying task. While this is sometimes unavoidable or even appropriate, it is usually worth trying to find less disruptive alternatives (direct manipulation, a non-modal floating notification, or some other non-modal approach). This may require more work on the part of the developer but will result in a better application. And if the application is widely adopted, the benefits are multiplied across the entire user base.

The JDialog Class

JDialog is the Swing version of its superclass, java.awt.Dialog. It provides the same key features described in Chapter 8† in the discussion of JWindow, JFrame, and

---

* A modal dialog forces the user to interact only with that dialog until it is dismissed.

† Certain parts of this chapter assume that you have read at least part of Chapter 8.

JApplet: it uses a JRootPane as its container, and it provides default window-closing behavior. Since JDialog extends java.awt.Dialog, it has a heavyweight peer and is managed by the native windowing system. Figure 10-1 shows how JDialog fits into the class hierarchy.

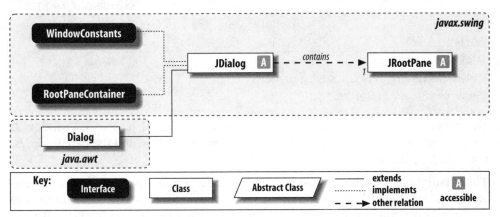

Figure 10-1. JDialog class diagram

Properties

JDialog defines the properties and default values listed in Table 10-1. The content-Pane, glassPane, JMenuBar, and layeredPane properties are taken from rootPane, which is set to a new JRootPane by the constructor.

Table 10-1. JDialog properties

Property	Data type	get	is	set	Default value
accessibleContext[o]	AccessibleContext	•			JDialog.AccessibleJDialog( )
contentPane[o]	Container	•		•	From rootPane
defaultCloseOperation	int	•		•	HIDE_ON_CLOSE
defaultLookAndFeelDecorated[s, 1.4]	boolean		•	•	Depends on L&F, often false
glassPane[o]	Component	•		•	From rootPane
JMenuBar[o]	JMenuBar	•		•	null
layeredPane[o]	JLayeredPane	•		•	From rootPane
layout[o]	LayoutManager	•		•	BorderLayout
modal*	boolean		•	•	false

[1.4]since 1.4, [o]overridden, [s]static

*Inherited from Dialog; can be set in JDialog constructors.

See also the java.awt.Dialog class.

Table 10-1. JDialog properties (continued)

Property	Data type	get	is	set	Default value
parent*	Container		•		SwingUtilities.get-SharedOwnerFrame( )
rootPane	JRootPane	•			JRootPane
title*	String	•		•	""

1.4since 1.4, ºoverridden, sstatic

*Inherited from Dialog; can be set in JDialog constructors.

See also the java.awt.Dialog class.

The defaultCloseOperation specifies how the dialog should react if its window is closed. The valid values come from the WindowConstants class, and the default operation is to hide the dialog.

The defaultLookAndFeelDecorated property provides a hint about whether newly created JDialogs should have their window decorations (such as title bars, controls to manipulate or close the window, and the like) drawn by the current L&F. This is only a hint; setting it to true has no effect if the L&F is unable to provide decorations or the window manager is unable to create undecorated windows.

The layout property is listed here because JDialog overrides setLayout( ) to throw an Error if an attempt is made to change the layout manager, rather than set the layout manager of the dialog's content pane.

The parent and title properties are inherited from Component and Dialog, respectively. Both are listed here because they can be set in the JDialog constructors.

The modal property is listed in this table because the JDialog constructors allow this property (inherited from Dialog) to be set. If a dialog is modal, no other window can be active while the dialog is displayed. As noted previously, such a restriction on the user's actions should be avoided if it's possible to design a better approach.

Constructors

There are many constructors to choose from, but they are all variations of the two fully specified constructors listed here, omitting one or more parameters from the end. The difference between the two families of constructors is whether the owner of the JDialog is a Frame or a Dialog. Note that it is valid to supply no owner by passing null as the first argument to any of the constructors or by using the zero argument constructor. The primary role of the owner is to dispose of any windows (including dialogs) that it owns when the owner itself is disposed.

public JDialog()
> Create a new dialog without a specified parent frame. An invisible owner frame is obtained from `SwingUtilities.getSharedOwnerFrame( )`.

public JDialog(Dialog owner, String title, boolean modal, GraphicsConfiguration gc)
> Create a dialog with the given owner dialog, title, modal setting, and `Graphics-Configuration`.

public JDialog(Frame owner, String title, boolean modal, GraphicsConfiguration gc)
> Create a dialog with the given owner frame, title, modal setting, and `Graphics-Configuration`.

All constructors can now (since 1.4) potentially throw `HeadlessException` if the graphics environment is operating in a "headless" mode, meaning that there is no display, keyboard, or mouse. This would be true, for example, in a servlet environment that used Swing to generate graphics to be sent to a web browser as downloaded image files.

The versions that specify a `GraphicsConfiguration` (also introduced in 1.4) allow you to select the display device on which the dialog should appear if your application is running in a multi-screen environment.

Public Methods

public void setLocationRelativeTo(Component c)
> Set the dialog's location based on the location of the given component. The dialog is centered within (if the component is larger than the dialog) or over (if the dialog is larger) the input component. If specified component is not currently displayed, this method centers the dialog on the screen. Note that this method has no effect on the dialog's parent, even if the input component is a different `Frame`.

public void update(Graphics g)
> This implementation of `update( )` just calls `paint( )`.

The JOptionPane Class

`JOptionPane` is a utility class used to create complex `JDialog`s and `JInternalFrame`s (the latter of which is used for lightweight dialogs). Figure 10-2 shows where `JOptionPane` fits into the class hierarchy; Figure 10-3 shows `JOptionPane` in four L&Fs. It provides a range of convenient ways to create common pop-up modal dialog boxes, which significantly reduces the amount of code you are required to write, at the expense of forcing the user to drop whatever she's doing and react to the pop up.

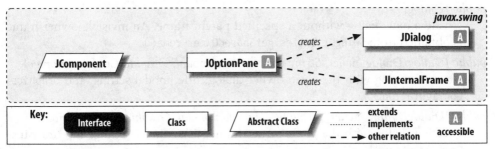

Figure 10-2. JOptionPane class diagram

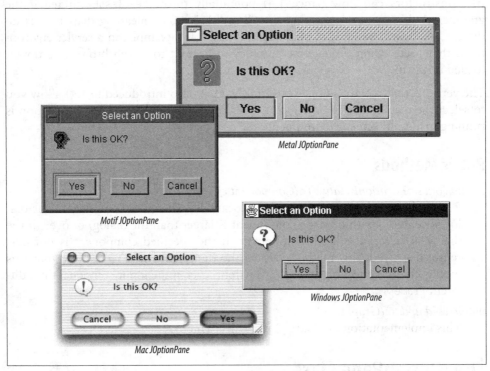

Figure 10-3. JOptionPanes (showing internal confirm dialogs) in four L&Fs

For example, to create a very simple dialog window with the text "Click OK after you read this" and an OK button without JOptionPane, you'd have to write something like this:

```
public void showSimpleDialog(JFrame f) {
final JDialog d = new JDialog(f, "Click OK", true);
d.setSize(200, 150);
JLabel l = new JLabel("Click OK after you read this", JLabel.CENTER);
d.getContentPane().setLayout(new BorderLayout());
d.getContentPane().add(l, BorderLayout.CENTER);
JButton b = new JButton("OK");
```

```
    b.addActionListener(new ActionListener( ) {
      public void actionPerformed(ActionEvent ev) {
        d.setVisible(false);
        d.dispose( );
      }
    });
    JPanel p = new JPanel( );       // Flow layout will center button.
    p.add(b);
    d.getContentPane( ).add(p, BorderLayout.SOUTH);
    d.setLocationRelativeTo(f);
    d.setVisible(true);
  }
```

That's quite a lot of work for such a conceptually simple task. Using JOptionPane, this method can be replaced with:

```
JOptionPane.showMessageDialog(f, "Click OK after you read this",
  "Click OK", JOptionPane.INFORMATION_MESSAGE);
```

Figure 10-4 shows the dialogs created by these two examples.

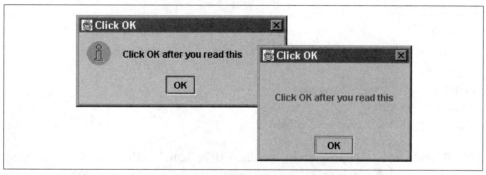

Figure 10-4. JDialogs created with (left) and without (right) JOptionPane

Properties

JOptionPane defines the properties listed in Table 10-2. The maxCharactersPerLine property specifies the maximum number of characters the L&F should display on a single line. By default there is no limit. To change this value, you must subclass JOptionPane.[*]

---

[*] If you subclass JOptionPane for this purpose, you'll need to construct instances of your subclasses rather than using the static methods (which will just construct JOptionPane objects, ignoring your subclass).

Table 10-2. *JOptionPane properties*

Property	Data type	get	is	set	Default value
accessibleContext°	AccessibleContext	•			JOptionPane. AccessibleJOptionPane()
icon[b]	Icon	•		•	null
initialSelectionValue[b]	Object	•		•	null
initialValue[b]	Object	•		•	null
inputValue[b]	Object	•		•	null
maxCharactersPerLineCount	int	•			Integer.MAX_VALUE
message[b]	Object	•		•	"JOptionPane Message"
messageType[b]	int	•		•	PLAIN_MESSAGE
options[b]	Object[]	•		•	null
optionType[b]	int	•		•	DEFAULT_OPTION
rootFrame[s]	Frame	•		•	From L&F
selectionValues[b]	Object[]	•		•	null
UI	JOptionPaneUI	•		•	From L&F
UIClassID°	String	•			"OptionPaneUI"
value[b]	Object	•		•	null
wantsInput[b]	boolean	•		•	false

[b]bound, °overridden, [s]static

See also properties from the JComponent class (Table 3-6).

The UI and UIClassID properties are defined as usual. value specifies the value selected by the user and is set by the L&F when the user closes the dialog.

rootFrame is a static "property" that controls the default root Frame to be used when calling static "show" methods that don't take a Frame parameter.

wantsInput indicates whether the pane is expecting input (beyond just clicking a JButton) from the user.

The other properties (as well as more on value and wantsInput) are discussed in detail throughout the chapter.

JOptionPane Structure

The dialogs created by JOptionPane are made up of four basic elements, some of which may be null. These elements are shown in Figure 10-5. (The input appearing in the frame's title bar is not part of the JOptionPane itself but can be set using the static dialog-creation methods.)

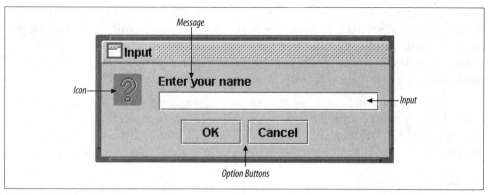

Figure 10-5. JOptionPane structure

The elements are:

An icon

> The icon usually provides some visual indication of the type of message being displayed. The icons used for four Swing L&Fs are shown in Figure 10-7.

A message area

> The message area usually contains a simple textual message. However, it can actually be any arbitrary Object. We'll discuss how different types of objects are displayed later in this chapter.

A data input area

> This area allows the user to enter a value or make a selection in response to the message. Typically, this is a JTextField, JComboBox, or JList, but this is entirely up to the L&F.

A set of option buttons

> For example, OK and Cancel.

Using JOptionPane

There are basically two ways to use JOptionPane. The simplest, demonstrated by the example at the beginning of this section, is to invoke one of the many static methods of the class. These methods all result in a JDialog or JInternalFrame being displayed immediately for the user. The methods return when the user clicks one of the buttons in the dialog.

The other way to use JOptionPane is to instantiate it using one of the many constructors and then call createDialog() or createInternalFrame(). These methods give you access to the JDialog or JInternalFrame and allow you to control when and where they are displayed. In most cases, the static methods will do everything you need. As with JDialog constructors, the static methods can (since 1.4) potentially throw a HeadlessException if the graphics environment is operating in a "headless" mode, meaning that there is no display, keyboard, or mouse.

It's worth noting that JOptionPane extends JComponent. When you instantiate JOptionPane, you actually have a perfectly usable component, laid out with the structure we described earlier. If you wanted to, you could display the component directly, but it typically makes sense to use it only in a dialog or internal frame.

All of the methods in JOptionPane that result in the creation of a JDialog create modal dialogs, but the methods that display JInternalFrames do not enforce modality. When the internal frame dialog is displayed, the other windows in your application can still receive focus. Typically, you will create modal dialogs. The situations in which you might use internal frames are discussed in the preceding chapter. See "Using internal frame dialogs with JDesktopPane" later in this chapter for more information about working with dialogs as internal frames.

Events

JOptionPane fires a PropertyChangeEvent any time one of the bound properties listed in Table 10-6 changes value. This is the mechanism used to communicate changes from the JOptionPane to the JOptionPaneUI, as well to the anonymous inner class listeners JOptionPane creates to close the dialog when the value or inputValue property is set by the L&F.

Constants

Tables 10-3 through 10-6 list the many constants defined in this class. They fall into four general categories:

Message types
    Used to specify what type of message is being displayed

Option types
    Used to specify what options the user should be given

Options
    Used to specify which option the user selected

Properties
    Contains the string names of the pane's bound properties

Table 10-3. JOptionPane constants for specifying the desired message type

Constant	Type	Description
ERROR_MESSAGE	int	Used for error messages
INFORMATION_MESSAGE	int	Used for informational messages
PLAIN_MESSAGE	int	Used for arbitrary messages
QUESTION_MESSAGE	int	Used for question dialogs
WARNING_MESSAGE	int	Used for warning messages

Table 10-4. JOptionPane constants for specifying the user's options

Constant	Type	Description[a]
DEFAULT_OPTION	int	OK button
OK_CANCEL_OPTION	int	OK and Cancel buttons
YES_NO_CANCEL_OPTION	int	Yes, No, and Cancel buttons
YES_NO_OPTION	int	Yes and No buttons

[a] The actual button labels are determined by the L&F. Currently, Swing L&Fs use the strings shown here. In future releases, these strings will be internationalized.

Table 10-5. JOptionPane selected option (and other "value") constants

Constant	Type	Description
CANCEL_OPTION	int	Cancel button pressed
CLOSED_OPTION	int	No button pressed, e.g., when the window is closed
NO_OPTION	int	No button pressed
OK_OPTION	int	OK button pressed
YES_OPTION	int	Yes button pressed
UNINITIALIZED_VALUE	Object	Value indicating that no value has been set for the pane

Table 10-6. JOptionPane bound property name constants

Constant	Type	Description
ICON_PROPERTY	String	Displayed icon
INITIAL_SELECTION_VALUE_PROPERTY	String	Initially selected value
INITIAL_VALUE_PROPERTY	String	Initially focused button
INPUT_VALUE_PROPERTY	String	Value entered by the user
MESSAGE_PROPERTY	String	Message displayed to the user
MESSAGE_TYPE_PROPERTY	String	Type of message displayed
OPTION_TYPE_PROPERTY	String	Type of options provided
OPTIONS_PROPERTY	String	List of nondefault options provided
SELECTION_VALUES_PROPERTY	String	Selection values available to user
VALUE_PROPERTY	String	Option selected by user
WANTS_INPUT_PROPERTY	String	Whether pane requires input

Four Dialog Types

JOptionPane provides static methods for creating four types of dialogs (see Table 10-7 and the examples that follow).[*] Each of these types can be automatically enclosed in either a JDialog or a JInternalFrame. The four types are:

Input Dialog
> Provides some way (typically a JTextField, JComboBox, or JList) for the user to enter data. Always includes two buttons: OK and Cancel.

Confirm Dialog
> Asks a user to confirm some information. Includes buttons such as Yes, No, OK, and Cancel.

Message Dialog
> Displays information to the user. Includes a single OK button.

Option Dialog
> Displays arbitrary data to the user. May contain any set of buttons for the user to choose from.

The first three types are somewhat restrictive, making it easy to create the most common types of dialogs. Option Dialog is more flexible, giving you complete control. Also, keep in mind that you can use the constructors to instantiate JOptionPane objects directly. These objects will then be Option Dialogs, again allowing you complete control.

Constructors

public JOptionPane( )
public JOptionPane(Object message)
public JOptionPane(Object message, int messageType)
public JOptionPane(Object message, int messageType, int optionType)
public JOptionPane(Object message, int messageType, int optionType, Icon icon)
public JOptionPane(Object message, int messageType, int optionType, Icon icon, Object[] options)
public JOptionPane(Object message, int messageType, int optionType, Icon icon, Object[] options, Object initialValue)
> These constructors allow JOptionPanes to be created and held over time (unlike the static methods listed below, which create panes that are used only once).

---

[*] Note that these dialog types are not different Java classes. They simply represent common types of dialog boxes used in applications.

Static Dialog Display Methods

There are more static "show" methods (used to create and display JDialog and JInternalFrame objects that contain JOptionPanes) than can be listed here; chances are good that there is a variant that does what you want with the parameters you have available. The authoritative list is in the JOptionPane Javadoc, and a summary is presented in Table 10-7.

Dialog Creation Method Parameters

Table 10-7 summarizes the parameter types, names, and default values for JOptionPane's constructors and static dialog creation methods. The parameters are listed (top to bottom) in the order they occur in the methods. Parameters that do not apply to a given column are left blank. In the rest of this section, we'll explain how each of these parameters affects the dialog's display. After that, we'll show some examples of dialogs and internal frames created using specific JOptionPane methods and constructors.

Component parentComponent

> For JDialogs, this is the dialog's parent. The dialog is centered on this component when it is displayed. For JInternalFrames, this parameter is used to find a container for the frame. If parentComponent is a JDesktopPane, the internal frame is added to its MODAL_LAYER. Otherwise, an attempt is made to see if parentComponent is contained (possibly recursively) by a JDesktopPane.* If so, the frame is added to the containing desktop's MODAL_LAYER.

> If neither of these apply, the parentComponent's parent (if it has no parent, a RuntimeException is thrown) is used as the container, and the frame is added with BorderLayout.CENTER constraints.

> This last option, while supported, rarely gives you what you're looking for. Since the dialog is added with BorderLayout constraints, your parentComponent's parent should be using a BorderLayout, or you may have various problems (e.g., GridBagLayout throws an exception if you add a component with constraints, other than a GridBagConstraints object). Even if you have a container with a BorderLayout, remember that the dialog fills the entire center of the container causing it to be resized as necessary, possibly to an unusable size. All of this leads to a simple rule: to make your life easier, create only internal dialogs within JDesktopPanes. See the example at the end of the chapter to see how to do this when you're not already using a JDesktopPane in your interface.

---

* getDesktopPaneForComponent searches a parent component chain for a JDesktopPane. It is static and public, so you are free to use it yourself. It takes a single Component as its parameter.

Table 10-7. *JOptionPane constructor/dialog creation method parameters, defaults, and return types*

Parameter type	Parameter name	JOptionPane constructors	InputDialog	ConfirmDialog	MessageDialog	Option-Dialog
Component	parentComponent		null[a]	Required[a]	Required[a]	Required[a]
Object	message	"JOptionPane Message"	Required	Required	Required	Required
String	title		"Input"	"Select an Option"	"Message"	Required
int	optionType	PLAIN_MESSAGE[b]		YES_NO_CANCEL_OPTION		Required
int	messageType	DEFAULT_OPTION[b]	QUESTION_MESSAGE	QUESTION_MESSAGE	INFORMATION_MESSAGE	Required
Icon	icon	null	null	null	null	Required
Object[]	selectionValues		null			
Object	initialSelectionValue		null			
Object[]	options	null				Required
Object	initialValue	null				Required
Return type			String/Object	int	void	int

[a] If null, a default Frame is used. This Frame is returned by the static getRootFrame method and can be set using the static setRootFrame method.
[b] The order of the optionType and messageType parameters for the constructors is reversed; messageType must come first.

parentComponent is allowed to be null, in which case a default Frame is used. This Frame is returned by the static method getRootFrame, and the default can be changed by calling the static method setRootFrame.

Object message

This is the message that will be displayed in the dialog. Typically, it is a simple String object. However, the methods allow this to be any arbitrary object. It's up to the L&F to determine how to handle other objects. Typically (for the Swing L&Fs), if the message is a Component, it is displayed as is. If it is an Icon, it is wrapped in a JLabel and displayed. If message is an Object[], the elements of the array are recursively expanded (applying these same rules) and added to form a vertical column. Any other types passed in are added as strings by calling the object's toString( ) method.

Note that the flexibility of this parameter allows you to use any arbitrary component (including containers with many other components inside) as the "message" for the dialog. Figure 10-6 shows an internal dialog that was created by passing in a custom calendar component as the message parameter.

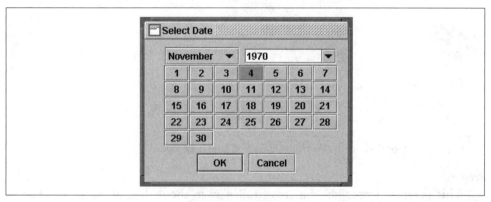

Figure 10-6. Custom component in a JOptionPane internal dialog

String title

This parameter contains the string that appears on the dialog's title bar. Note that this parameter does not apply to the JOptionPane constructors since JOptionPane itself does not have a title bar.

int optionType

This parameter determines which options the user is given for dismissing the dialog. This parameter applies only to Confirm Dialogs, Option Dialogs, and JOptionPane constructors. As a rule, Input Dialogs have an OK button and a Cancel button. Message Dialogs have only an OK button. For the other types of dialogs, this parameter may be one of these values: DEFAULT_OPTION, YES_NO_OPTION, YES_NO_CANCEL_OPTION, or OK_CANCEL_OPTION. Again, it's up to the L&F to determine how to interpret these, but you can confidently assume that YES_NO_OPTION provides a Yes and a No button, and so on. The DEFAULT_OPTION value provides a single OK button.

If you want a different set of buttons, you need to use an Option Dialog, which allows you to specify any arbitrary set of buttons via the options parameter.

int messageType

This parameter indicates the type of dialog to create. The possible values are: WARNING_MESSAGE, QUESTION_MESSAGE, INFO_MESSAGE, ERROR_MESSAGE, and PLAIN_ MESSAGE. It's up to the L&F to determine how to interpret these options. Usu-ally, the value of the parameter determines the icon displayed in the dialog. Figure 10-7 shows the icons used by several L&Fs (note that in some cases there isn't a distinct icon for each messageType). This default icon can be overridden by passing in a non-null value for the icon parameter. There is no icon associated with PLAIN_MESSAGE.

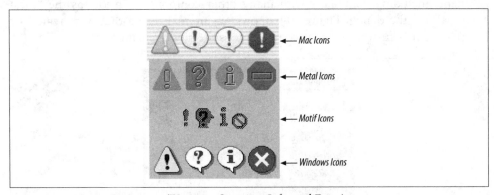

Figure 10-7. JOptionPane icons (Warning, Question, Info, and Error)

Icon icon

This parameter specifies the Icon to display in the dialog, allowing you to fur-ther customize the display. If it is set to null, the icon is determined based on the messageType. To have no icon displayed, pass PLAIN_MESSAGE as the messageType.

Object[] selectionValues

This parameter is used only in Input dialogs. It allows you to specify a set of selections for the user to choose from. As you might expect, it's up to the L&F to determine how to supply these options to the user. It's common for a JComboBox to be used when there are only a few values and to have it replaced by a scroll-ing JList (with a selection mode of MULTIPLE_INTERVAL_SELECTION) when there are many. In either case, the array of objects is passed directly to the list or combo box for interpretation. (See the documentation of these components for details on how different object types are interpreted.) If the selectionValues parameter is null, a JTextField is used for data entry.

`Object initialSelectionValue`

> This parameter also applies only to Input Dialogs. It allows you to specify which of the options supplied in `selectionValues` should be initially selected.

`Object[] options`

> This parameter applies only to `JOptionPane` constructors and Option Dialogs. It allows you to specify the set of option buttons the user will see. Using `null` here indicates that the `optionType` should be used to determine the set of buttons displayed. Useful parameter types for this parameter are `String` and `Icon`. These are used to construct `JButton` objects. `Components` passed in via this parameter are added as is.* Any other input objects are used to create `JButtons` with a label generated by calling `toString( )` on the object.

`Object initialValue`

> This parameter (also available only for constructors and Option Dialogs) allows you to specify a default option from the list supplied by the `options` parameter. Note that this works only if the `options` parameter is non-null. This value determines which button has initial focus. In addition, if the initial value is a `JButton`, it becomes the default button on the root pane that contains it (if there is one). For example, specifying `{"Register", "Not yet"}` as the `options` and `Register` as the `initialValue` causes the `Register` button to have initial focus and be the default button.

Simple Examples

The following are a few examples that show some of things you can do with `JOptionPane` static methods and constructors.

Here's an input dialog with more than 20 selection values. This results in the creation of a `JList` (Figure 10-8):

```
JOptionPane.showInputDialog(null, "Please choose a name", "Example 1",
    JOptionPane.QUESTION_MESSAGE, null, new Object[] {
    "Amanda", "Colin", "Don", "Fred", "Gordon", "Janet", "Jay", "Joe",
    "Judie", "Kerstin", "Lotus", "Maciek", "Mark", "Mike", "Mulhern",
    "Oliver", "Peter", "Quaxo", "Rita", "Sandro", "Tim", "Will"}, "Joe");
```

Here's another input dialog. This time, we don't provide any selection values, so we get a `JTextField`. The default value we supply is entered in the field when it comes up (Figure 10-9).

```
JOptionPane.showInputDialog(null, "Please enter your name", "Example 2",
    JOptionPane.QUESTION_MESSAGE, null, null, "Shannon");
```

---

* This is not as useful as it sounds, as no event listeners are added for the components. It would be nice if a future release at least supported passing `JButtons` by having the L&F add an action listener for them, like the one it adds to `JButtons` it creates.

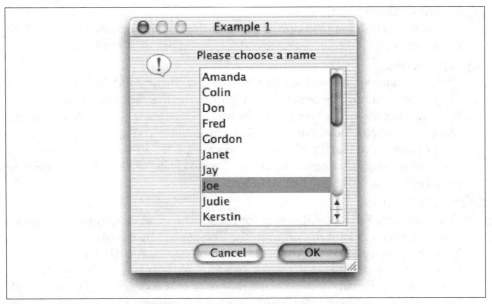

Figure 10-8. Input dialog (JList)

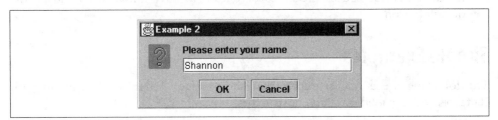

Figure 10-9. Input dialog (JTextField)

Next, we'll try a message dialog with a custom icon (Figure 10-10):

```
JOptionPane.showMessageDialog(null, "Have a nice day.", "Example 3",
    JOptionPane.INFORMATION_MESSAGE, new ImageIcon("images/smile.gif"));
```

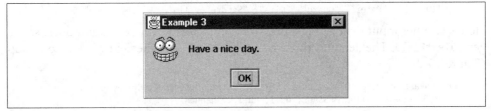

Figure 10-10. Message dialog with a custom Icon

Here's a very simple confirm dialog (Figure 10-11):

```
JOptionPane.showConfirmDialog(null, "Are you sure?", "Example 4",
    JOptionPane.YES_NO_CANCEL_OPTION);
```

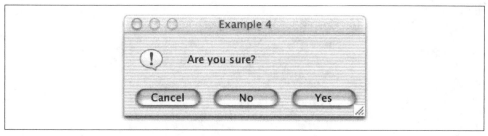

Figure 10-11. Confirm dialog

Next, we'll get a little fancy and create an internal frame dialog with custom option buttons (Figure 10-12):

```
JOptionPane.showInternalOptionDialog(desk, "Please select a color",
    "Example 5", JOptionPane.DEFAULT_OPTION, JOptionPane.QUESTION_MESSAGE,
    null, new Object[] {"Red", "Green", "Blue"}, "Blue");
```

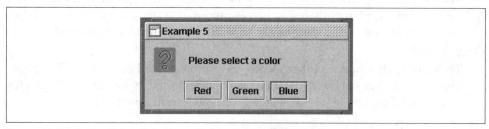

Figure 10-12. Internal frame dialog with custom buttons

Finally, let's use a JOptionPane constructor and place the new pane inside a regular Swing container. This is a strange thing to do, but it's perfectly valid (Figure 10-13).

```
JFrame f = new JFrame( );
Container c = f.getContentPane( );
c.setLayout(new BorderLayout( ));
JOptionPane op = new JOptionPane("Stop!", JOptionPane.WARNING_MESSAGE);
JPanel p = new JPanel(new FlowLayout( ));
p.add(op);
c.add(p);
c.add(new JLabel("Example 6", JLabel.CENTER), BorderLayout.NORTH);
f.setVisible(true);
```

Getting the Results

Now that we've seen how to create all sorts of useful dialog boxes, it's time to take a look at how to retrieve information about the user's interaction with the dialog. Table 10-7 showed the return types of the various methods. Here's a quick summary of what the returned values mean.

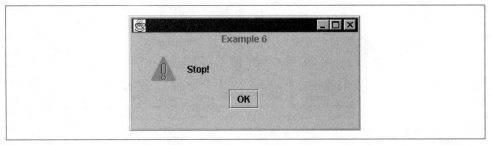

Figure 10-13. A JOptionPane inside a Swing container

Input Dialogs

> The versions that do not take an array of selection values return a String. This is the data entered by the user. The methods that do take an array of selection values return an Object reflecting the selected option. It's up to the L&F to determine the component used for presenting the options. Typically, a JComboBox is used if there are fewer than 20 choices, and a JList is used if there are 20 or more.* In any case, if the user presses the Cancel button, null is returned.

Confirm Dialogs

> These methods return an int reflecting the button pressed by the user. The possible values are: YES_OPTION, NO_OPTION, CANCEL_OPTION, and OK_OPTION. CLOSED_OPTION is returned if the user closes the window without selecting anything.

Message Dialogs

> These methods have void return types because they do not request a user response.

Option Dialogs

> If no options are specified, this method returns one of the constant values YES_OPTION, NO_OPTION, CANCEL_OPTION, and OK_OPTION. If options are explicitly defined, the return value gives the index to the array of options that matches the button selected by the user. CLOSED_OPTION is returned if the user closes the window without selecting anything.

Getting a value from a JOptionPane you've instantiated directly is also very simple. The value is obtained by calling the pane's getValue() method. This method returns an Integer value using the same rules as those described for option dialogs with two small variations. Instead of returning an Integer containing CLOSED_OPTION, getValue() returns null if the dialog is closed. Also, if you call getValue() before the user has made a selection (or before displaying the dialog at all, for that matter), it will return UNINITIALIZED_VALUE. To get the value of user input (from a JTextField, JComboBox, or JList), call getInputValue(). This will return the entered String or the selected Object

---

* Prior to SDK 1.4, the JList allowed the user to highlight multiple selections even though only the first could be detected. This has been fixed to allow only a single selection to be highlighted.

(which may also be a String). Note that, just as with the static "show" methods, there's no way to find out about multiple selections the user may have made when there are more than 20 choices.

The following example contains code to retrieve results from JOptionPanes.

A Comparison: Constructors Versus Static Methods

We've talked quite a bit about the two fundamental ways to create dialogs using JOptionPane: instantiate a JOptionPane and ask it to put itself into a JDialog or JInternalFrame, which you then display, or create and display the dialog in a single step by invoking one of the many static "show" methods.

The basic trade-off is this: using the static methods is a bit easier, but using a constructor allows you to hold onto and reuse the JOptionPane instance, a tempting feature if the pane is fairly complex and you expect to display it frequently (if you use the static methods, the option pane is recreated each time you call). The significance of this difference depends largely on the complexity of the pane. Because of lingering issues that make reusing JOptionPane problematic, it's still best to avoid this feature (see the note in the discussion following this example program for details).

The following example shows the differences between using JOptionPane's static methods and its constructors. It allows both internal and noninternal dialogs to be created, showing how each is done.

```
// OptPaneComparison.java
//
import javax.swing.*;
import java.awt.event.*;
import java.awt.*;
import java.beans.*;

public class OptPaneComparison extends JFrame {

  public static void main(String[] args) {
    JFrame f = new OptPaneComparison("Enter your name");
    f.setVisible(true);
  }

  public OptPaneComparison(final String message) {
    setDefaultCloseOperation(EXIT_ON_CLOSE);

    final int msgType = JOptionPane.QUESTION_MESSAGE;
    final int optType = JOptionPane.OK_CANCEL_OPTION;
    final String title = message;

    setSize(350, 200);
```

```
// Create a desktop for internal frames.
final JDesktopPane desk = new JDesktopPane( );
setContentPane(desk);

// Add a simple menu bar.
JMenuBar mb = new JMenuBar( );
setJMenuBar(mb);

JMenu menu = new JMenu("Dialog");
JMenu imenu = new JMenu("Internal");
mb.add(menu);
mb.add(imenu);
final JMenuItem construct = new JMenuItem("Constructor");
final JMenuItem stat = new JMenuItem("Static Method");
final JMenuItem iconstruct = new JMenuItem("Constructor");
final JMenuItem istat = new JMenuItem("Static Method");
menu.add(construct);
menu.add(stat);
imenu.add(iconstruct);
imenu.add(istat);

// Create our JOptionPane. We're asking for input, so we call setWantsInput.
// Note that we cannot specify this via constructor parameters.
optPane = new JOptionPane(message, msgType, optType);
optPane.setWantsInput(true);

// Add a listener for each menu item that will display the appropriate
// dialog/internal frame.
construct.addActionListener(new ActionListener( ) {
  public void actionPerformed(ActionEvent ev) {

    // Create and display the dialog.
    JDialog d = optPane.createDialog(desk, title);
    d.setVisible(true);

    respond(getOptionPaneValue( ));
  }
});

stat.addActionListener(new ActionListener( ) {
  public void actionPerformed(ActionEvent ev) {
    String s = JOptionPane.showInputDialog
      (desk, message, title, msgType);
    respond(s);
  }
});

iconstruct.addActionListener(new ActionListener( ) {
  public void actionPerformed(ActionEvent ev) {

    // Create and display the dialog.
    JInternalFrame f = optPane.createInternalFrame(desk, title);
    f.setVisible(true);
```

```
      // Listen for the frame to close before getting the value from it.
      f.addPropertyChangeListener(new PropertyChangeListener() {
        public void propertyChange(PropertyChangeEvent ev) {
          if ((ev.getPropertyName( ).equals(JInternalFrame.IS_CLOSED_PROPERTY))
          && (ev.getNewValue( ) == Boolean.TRUE)) {
            respond(getOptionPaneValue( ));
          }
        }
      });
    }
  });

  istat.addActionListener(new ActionListener() {
    public void actionPerformed(ActionEvent ev) {
      String s = JOptionPane.showInternalInputDialog
        (desk, message, title, msgType);
      respond(s);
    }
  });
}

// This method gets the selected value from the option pane and resets the
// value to null so we can use it again.
protected String getOptionPaneValue( ) {

  // Get the result . . .
  Object o = optPane.getInputValue( );
  String s = "<Unknown>";
  if (o != null)
    s = (String)o;

  Object val = optPane.getValue( ); // which button?

  // Check for Cancel button or closed option.
  if (val != null) {
    if (val instanceof Integer) {
      int intVal = ((Integer)val).intValue( );
      if((intVal == JOptionPane.CANCEL_OPTION) ||
        (intVal == JOptionPane.CLOSED_OPTION))
        s = "<Cancel>";
    }
  }

  // A little trick to clean the text field. It is updated only if the initial
  // value is changed. To do this, we'll set it to a dummy value ("X")
  // and then clear it.
  optPane.setValue("");
  optPane.setInitialValue("X");
  optPane.setInitialValue("");

  return s;
}
```

```
    protected void respond(String s) {
      if (s == null)
        System.out.println("Never mind.");
      else
        System.out.println("You entered: " + s);
    }

    protected JOptionPane optPane;
  }
```

The user interface for this example (Figure 10-14) is simple. We provide two menus: one to create standard dialogs and one to create internal frame dialogs. Each menu allows us to create a dialog using the JOptionPane we're holding (created via a constructor) or create a new dialog with a static method call.

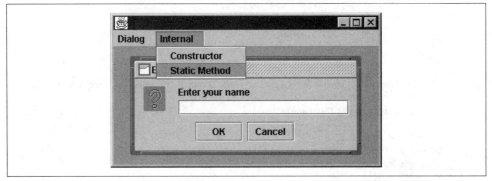

Figure 10-14. OptPaneComparison display

There are a few details here worth pointing out. First, notice that we called setWantsInput(true) on our JOptionPane object. This is how we create a pane that looks like those created by the showInputDialog( ) methods. Without this call, there would not be a text field in our dialog.

The next point of interest is the way we handle the JInternalFrame we get from the JOptionPane. Since this is just an ordinary internal frame, we don't have any simple way to block while we wait for input. Instead, we add a property change listener to the frame, which will wait for the frame to be closed. Alternatively, we could have added a property change listener to the JOptionPane and listened for the INPUT_VALUE_PROPERTY.

One last thing to point out is the little trick at the end of our getOptionPaneValue( ) method. We want to clear the value from the text field so that it won't show up there the next time we use the same option pane. Since we have no way of getting to the text field directly, and no way of explicitly clearing the value,* we resort to making two changes to the initial value of the field. The reason we have to make two calls is

---

* The setValue( ) call with an empty string might seem promising, but it isn't enough.

that the text field is cleared only when the `initialValue` property *changes*. If we just set it to an empty string every time, that wouldn't be considered a change, so the field wouldn't be updated.

In this example, we held onto the `JOptionPane` object. You might be tempted to hold onto the `JDialog` you get from the pane instead. This is generally not a good idea. The `JOptionPane` "disposes" of the dialog when it closes, meaning that, among other things, its peer is destroyed. It's easier to reuse the `JOptionPane`. Similar difficulties arise if you try to reuse the `JInternalFrame` created by the `JOptionPane`. Reusing the `JOptionPane` seems like a safer strategy, but there are still problems.

 Reusing a `JOptionPane` is not recommended. Read this section for details.

If you experiment with the program carefully, you'll discover some lingering and subtle problems with any attempt to reuse a single `JOptionPane` for multiple interactions with the user—for example, use the `Constructor` method in the `Dialog` menu, enter a name, and then click on OK. Then try the same method again, enter some text (or not, it doesn't make a difference), and close the window manually instead of clicking on either of the buttons. The program will report that you entered the same name as when you last clicked on OK, and there's no way to get it to forget this! You can even show the dialog multiple times and click on Cancel. If you then show it and close the window again, you'll see that the program still believes you entered the name you last said "OK" to.

This problem, on top of the fact that we needed to resort to trickery to get an empty initial value displayed at all, suggests that any savings in efficiency we might gain by reusing a `JOptionPane` are more than offset by the fact that, at least as it is currently implemented, this is not a safe or well-supported thing to do.

If you want to see even more disturbing behavior, remove the line in the "little trick" that reads `optPane.setValue("")`. The program seems at first to work the same way, but if you use the Constructor option in the Internal menu and try to enter the same name more than once, the OK button fails to work, leaving the internal frame open. Trying to cancel that method twice in a row fails in the same way.

Nonstatic Methods

Most of the methods defined in `JOptionPane` are static (or accessors for the pane's properties). Here are the only other nonstatic methods in the class:

public JDialog createDialog(Component parentComponent, String title)
> Create a new `JDialog` containing this `JOptionPane`. The dialog's parent is the specified component, and the input string is used as the window's title. The dialog is

centered on the input parent component. This method is used by all of the static "show dialog" methods, and it is also the method to use when you construct a `JOptionPane` directly and want to use it in a dialog.

public JInternalFrame createInternalFrame(Component parentComponent, String title)
Create a new `JInternalFrame` containing this `JOptionPane`. The frame's parent is the specified component, and the input string is used as the frame's title. The parent component is used to search (up the parent chain) for an enclosing `JDesktopPane`. (See the detailed discussion of the `parentComponent` parameter earlier in this chapter.) This method is used by all of the static "show internal frame" methods; it is the method to use when you construct a `JOptionPane` directly and want to use it in an internal frame.

public void selectInitialValue()
Select the initial value, causing the default button to receive focus. If you are going to use a `JOptionPane` to display a dialog multiple times, you should call this method before making the dialog visible.

public void updateUI()
Called to indicate that the L&F has changed.

Miscellaneous Static Methods

In addition to all of the static methods defined for showing dialogs (of which we saw some examples earlier), several other static methods are also defined:

public static Frame getFrameForComponent(Component parentComponent)
Search the parent hierarchy of the given `Component` until it finds a `Frame`, which it returns. If it encounters a `null` parent (or if the input component is `null`), it returns the result of a call to `getRootFrame()`.

public static JDesktopPane getDesktopPaneForComponent(Component parentComponent)
Search the parent hierarchy of the given `Component` until it finds a `JDesktopPane`, which it returns. If it encounters a `null` parent (or if the input component is `null`), it returns `null`.

public static void setRootFrame(Frame newRootFrame)
Set a default `Frame` to be used when an attempt is made to create a dialog and a parent `Frame` cannot be found.

public static Frame getRootFrame()
Return the value set by `setRootFrame()`. The value is initially determined by the L&F.

Using Internal Frame Dialogs with JDesktopPane

In order to get the best results when using internal frame dialogs created by JOptionPane, the dialogs need to be placed in a JDesktopPane. However, this may not be convenient if your application does not use a JDesktopPane. In this section, we'll show how you can easily adapt your application to use a JDesktopPane so that you can use internal frame dialogs.

Recall that JDesktopPane has a null layout manager, leaving the management of the location of its contents up to the DesktopManager and the user. This makes JDesktopPane a poor choice when you just need a container in which to build your main application. As a result, if you want to have an internal frame dialog displayed in a "normal" container, you need a solution that gives you the features of both JDesktopPane and a more layout-friendly container.

This is actually a pretty straightforward goal to achieve. You need to create a JDesktopPane and add your application container to it so that it fills an entire layer of the desktop. When there are no internal frames displayed, this looks the same as if you were displaying the application container alone. The benefit is that when you need to add an internal frame dialog, you have a desktop to add it to.

Here's a simple example that shows how this works. It also shows how you can make sure your container fills the desktop, even if the desktop changes size (since there's no layout manager, this won't happen automatically).

```
// DialogDesktop.java
//
import javax.swing.*;
import java.awt.event.*;
import java.awt.*;

// A frame that can easily support internal frame dialogs
public class DialogDesktop extends JFrame {

  public DialogDesktop(String title) {
    super(title);
    setDefaultCloseOperation(EXIT_ON_CLOSE);

    final JDesktopPane desk = new JDesktopPane( );
    setContentPane(desk);

    // Create our "real" application container; use any layout manager we want.
    final JPanel p = new JPanel(new GridBagLayout( ));
```

```
      // Listen for desktop resize events so we can resize p. This will ensure that
      // our container always fills the entire desktop.
      desk.addComponentListener(new ComponentAdapter( ) {
        public void componentResized(ComponentEvent ev) {
          Dimension deskSize = desk.getSize( );
          p.setBounds(0, 0, deskSize.width, deskSize.height);
          p.validate( );
        }
      });

      // Add our application panel to the desktop. Any layer below the MODAL_LAYER
      // (where the dialogs will appear) is fine. We'll just use the default in
      // this example.
      desk.add(p);

      // Fill out our app with a few buttons that create dialogs.
      JButton input = new JButton("Input");
      JButton confirm = new JButton("Confirm");
      JButton message = new JButton("Message");
      p.add(input);
      p.add(confirm);
      p.add(message);

      input.addActionListener(new ActionListener( ) {
        public void actionPerformed(ActionEvent ev) {
          JOptionPane.showInternalInputDialog(desk, "Enter Name");
        }
      });

      confirm.addActionListener(new ActionListener( ) {
        public void actionPerformed(ActionEvent ev) {
          JOptionPane.showInternalConfirmDialog(desk, "Is this OK?");
        }
      });

      message.addActionListener(new ActionListener( ) {
        public void actionPerformed(ActionEvent ev) {
          JOptionPane.showInternalMessageDialog(desk, "The End");
        }
      });
    }

    // A simple test program
    public static void main(String[] args) {
      DialogDesktop td = new DialogDesktop("Desktop");
      td.setSize(350, 250);
      td.setVisible(true);
    }
  }
```

Most of this class is just a sample program proving that the strategy works. The key ideas come early on in the code. The first important thing is the creation of a JDesktopPane, which we set as the frame's content pane. We then add the "real" application container to the desktop. The last important detail is the little ComponentListener we add to the desktop pane to ensure that our main application container is resized when the size of the desktop changes. Figure 10-15 shows what the simple test program looks like after expanding it slightly, with two of the internal dialogs open.

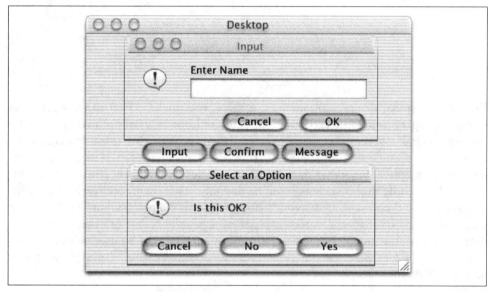

Figure 10-15. DialogDesktop display

Specialty Panes and Layout Managers

With all the spiffy Swing components out there, you might expect to see a few new layout managers to help place them, and you wouldn't be disappointed. The Swing package includes several layout managers. However, most of these managers are designed for specific containers—JScrollPane has its own ScrollPaneLayout manager, for example. The Swing package also includes several new convenience containers that handle things such as scrolling and tabs. (We'll take a close look at these containers and their associated layout managers in this chapter.) Figure 11-1 shows a class diagram of Swing's specialty panes and their layout managers. The OverlayLayout and SpringLayout general layout managers can be used with any containers. We tackle them separately at the end of this chapter. (SpringLayout was added in SDK 1.4.)

The JSplitPane Class

The JSplitPane component allows you to place two (and only two) components side by side in a single pane. You can separate the pane horizontally or vertically, and the user can adjust this separator graphically at runtime. You have probably seen such a split pane approach in things like a file chooser or a news reader. The top or left side holds the list of directories or news subject lines while the bottom (or right side) contains the files or body of the currently selected directory or article. To get started, Figure 11-2 shows a simple split pane example that shows two text areas with a horizontal split. You can adjust the width of the split by grabbing the divider and sliding it left or right.

Even with the code required to make the text areas behave (more on that in Chapter 19), the following example is still fairly simple. If you are looking to get up and running with a quick split pane, this is the way to go.

```
// SimpleSplitPane.java
// A quick test of the JSplitPane class
//
```

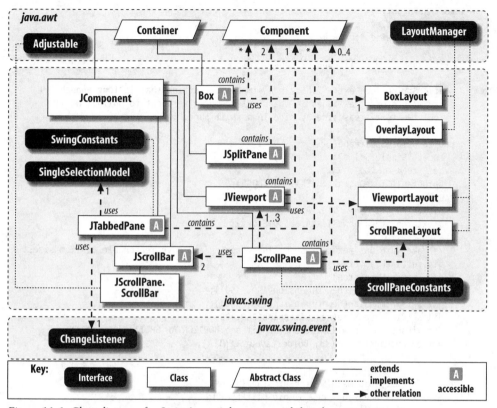

Figure 11-1. Class diagram for Swing's specialty panes and their layout managers

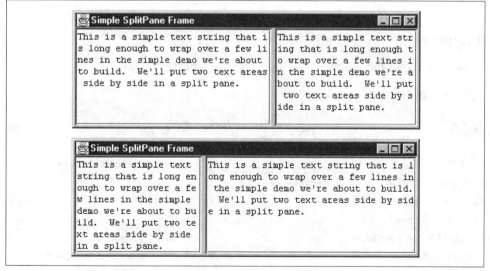

Figure 11-2. Simple JSplitPane with two text areas

```
import java.awt.*;
import java.awt.event.*;
import javax.swing.*;

public class SimpleSplitPane extends JFrame {

    static String sometext = "This is a simple text string that is long enough " +
        "to wrap over a few lines in the simple demo we're about to build.  We'll " +
        "put two text areas side by side in a split pane.";

    public SimpleSplitPane( ) {
        super("Simple SplitPane Frame");
        setSize(450, 200);
        setDefaultCloseOperation(EXIT_ON_CLOSE);

        JTextArea jt1 = new JTextArea(sometext);
        JTextArea jt2 = new JTextArea(sometext);

        // Make sure our text boxes do line wrapping and have reasonable minimum sizes.
        jt1.setLineWrap(true);
        jt2.setLineWrap(true);
        jt1.setMinimumSize(new Dimension(150, 150));
        jt2.setMinimumSize(new Dimension(150, 150));
        jt1.setPreferredSize(new Dimension(250, 200));
        JSplitPane sp = new JSplitPane(JSplitPane.HORIZONTAL_SPLIT, jt1, jt2);
        getContentPane( ).add(sp, BorderLayout.CENTER);
    }

    public static void main(String args[]) {
        SimpleSplitPane ssb = new SimpleSplitPane( );
        ssb.setVisible(true);
    }
}
```

Properties

Table 11-1 shows the properties contained in the JSplitPane class.

Table 11-1. JSplitPane properties

Property	Data type	get	is	set	Default value
accessibleContext[o]	AccessibleContext	•			JSplitPane. AccessibleJSplitPane( )
bottomComponent	Component	•		•	null
continuousLayout[b]	boolean		•	•	false
dividerLocation[b,*]	int	•		•	-1

[1.3]since 1.3, [b]bound, [o]overridden

*These properties return -1 only if no UI is defined for this component. Normally, the UI is queried for its current value.

See also properties from the JComponent class (Table 3-6).

Table 11-1. JSplitPane properties (continued)

Property	Data type	get	is	set	Default value
dividerSize[b]	int	•		•	5
lastDividerLocation	int	•		•	0
leftComponent	Component	•		•	null
maximumDividerLocation*	int	•			-1
minimumDividerLocation*	int	•			-1
oneTouchExpandable[b]	boolean		•	•	false
orientation[b]	int	•		•	HORIZONTAL_SPLIT
resizeWeight[b, 1.3]	double	•		•	0.0
rightComponent	Component	•		•	null
topComponent	Component	•		•	null
UI[b]	SplitPaneUI	•			From L&F
UIClassID[o]	String	•			"SplitPaneUI"

[1.3]since 1.3, [b]bound, [o]overridden

*These properties return -1 only if no UI is defined for this component. Normally, the UI is queried for its current value.

See also properties from the JComponent class (Table 3-6).

The properties of JSplitPane primarily relate to the divider. You can get and set its size, location, and orientation, and its minimum and maximum bounds. Of particular interest is the oneTouchExpandable property. If this value is set to true, the UI should provide a component that can quickly collapse or expand the divider. For your programming convenience, four component properties are available. Note that the component properties bottomComponent and rightComponent refer to the same object, as do topComponent and leftComponent. This way, you can refer to your components in a fashion that's consistent with the orientation of your split pane. The resizeWeight property affects how new space is allocated if the split pane itself is resized. The default of 0.0 distributes all of the size change to the bottom-right component; 1.0 goes entirely to the top-left component. If the continuousLayout property is true, both sides of the pane are updated as often as possible while the user moves the divider. Otherwise, the components are resized and redrawn only after the divider location is set. Continuous layout can be a performance problem and is often just awkward. The lastDividerLocation property saves the previous location of the divider and can be used to undo a change in the divider's position.

Constants

Several constants are defined for use with the JSplitPane class (see Table 11-2). Some of these constants name the various properties in a split pane while others provide constraints for where to place a component or where to place the split.

Table 11-2. JSplitPane constants

Constant	Type	Description
BOTTOM	String	Add a component to the bottom of a vertically split pane.
CONTINUOUS_LAYOUT_PROPERTY	String	Used in property change events to specify that the continuousLayout property has been changed.
DIVIDER	String	Add a component as the divider for the pane.
DIVIDER_LOCATION_PROPERTY[1.3]	String	Used in property change events to specify that the dividerLocation property has changed.
DIVIDER_SIZE_PROPERTY	String	Used in property change events to specify that the dividerSize property has changed.
HORIZONTAL_SPLIT	int	One of the valid values for the orientation property of a JSplitPane object. This type of split creates a vertical divider, resulting in a set of left/right components.
LAST_DIVIDER_LOCATION_PROPERTY	String	Used in property change events to specify that the lastDividerLocation property has changed.
LEFT	String	Add a component to the left of a horizontally split pane.
ONE_TOUCH_EXPANDABLE_PROPERTY	String	Used in property change events to specify that the oneTouchExpandable property has changed.
ORIENTATION_PROPERTY	String	Used in property change events to specify that the orientation property has changed.
RESIZE_WEIGHT_PROPERTY[1.3]	String	Used in property change events to specify that the resizeWeight property has changed.
RIGHT	String	Add a component to the right of a horizontally split pane.
TOP	String	Add a component to the top of a vertically split pane.
VERTICAL_SPLIT	int	One of the valid values for the orientation property of a JSplitPane object. This type of split creates a horizontal divider, resulting in a set of top/bottom components.

[1.3]since 1.3

Constructors

public JSplitPane( )

This constructor is a "demo" constructor. It sets up a horizontal split with a left button and right button (both JButton components) already defined and added.

public JSplitPane(int orientation)

public JSplitPane(int orientation, boolean continuousLayout)

These constructors allow you to pick your initial split (horizontal or vertical) using the constants HORIZONTAL_SPLIT and VERTICAL_SPLIT. No components are added to either pane. If you give a true value as the continuousLayout argument to the second constructor, both panes are repainted continuously as the user moves the divider. (This property is false by default—you just see a line showing the proposed divider location while you move the divider.)

public JSplitPane(int orientation, Component leftOrTop, Component bottomOrRight)
public JSplitPane(int orientation, boolean continuousLayout, Component leftOrTop,
  Component bottomOrRight)

> These constructors allow you to pick your orientation and the initial components for each pane. Depending on the orientation you choose, the first component is placed in the left or top pane, and the second component fills the other pane. If you give a true value as the continuousLayout argument to the second constructor, both panes are repainted continuously as the user moves the divider.

Control Methods

public void remove(Component comp)
public void remove(int index)
public void removeAll( )

> Remove components from the split pane. Typically, you use the first of these methods to remove one component at a time.

public void resetToPreferredSizes( )

> Reset the sizes of the components to their preferred sizes. The preferred size of a component is determined by the UI manager for the split pane. The preferred size of a split pane is the sum of the preferred sizes of its children (including the divider).

public void setDividerLocation(double position)

> This convenience method does the pixel calculating for you so that you can specify a position for the divider. The position you give is the fraction of the whole pane given to the left of the pane (for a horizontal split) or the top of the pane (for a vertical split). For example, with a horizontal split, a value of 0.75 assigns 75% of the pane to the component on the left. The position must be a value between 0 and 1. If it isn't, you get an IllegalArgumentException.

Minimum and Preferred Sizes

When setting up your split panes, watch out for the minimum and preferred sizes of the two components. If you look back at the code for Figure 11-2, you can see we forcibly set the minimum sizes of the two text areas. The boundaries observed by the divider in a split pane are dictated by the minimum sizes of the two components. Some components, such as JTextArea, define their minimum size as the size they are initially shown with. That often works fine, but in the case of the split pane, it means that you cannot adjust the division between the two text areas (as both are already at their minimum sizes). The same is true for containers such as panels or the JScrollPane we discuss in the next section.

You should also set the *preferred* size of the first component if you want the split pane to come up correctly the first time. In the previous example, if you remove the line that sets the preferred size of jt1, then jt1 comes up with room for one row of text, and jt2 takes everything else. Of course, you could also set the dividerLocation property before making the split pane visible. (Note that if you are using an older version of the JDK—such as 1.2.2—you have to set the preferred size.)

The JScrollPane Class

The JScrollPane class offers a more flexible version of the ScrollPane class found in the AWT package. Beyond the automatic scrollbars, you can put in horizontal and vertical headers as well as active components in the corners of your pane. (Figure 11-6 shows the exact areas available in a JScrollPane, which is managed by the ScrollPaneLayout class.)

Many Swing components use JScrollPane to handle their scrolling. The JList component, for example, does not handle scrolling on its own. Instead, it concentrates on presenting the list and making selection easy, assuming you'll put it inside a JScrollPane if you need scrolling. Figure 11-3 shows a simple JScrollPane in action with a JList object.

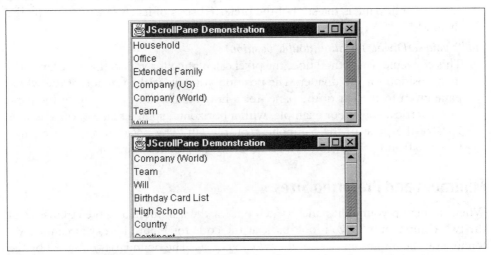

Figure 11-3. JScrollPane showing two portions of a list that is too long for one screen

This particular example does not take advantage of the row or column headers. The scrollpane adds the scrollbars automatically, but only "as needed." If we were to resize the window to make it much larger, the scrollbars would become inactive. Here's the code that builds this pane:

```
// ScrollList.java
// A simple JScrollPane
//
```

```
import javax.swing.*;
import java.awt.*;

public class ScrollList extends JFrame {

  JScrollPane scrollpane;

  public ScrollList() {
    super("JScrollPane Demonstration");
    setSize(300, 200);
    setDefaultCloseOperation(EXIT_ON_CLOSE);

    String categories[] = { "Household", "Office", "Extended Family",
                            "Company (US)", "Company (World)", "Team",
                            "Will", "Birthday Card List", "High School",
                            "Country", "Continent", "Planet" };
    JList list = new JList(categories);
    scrollpane = new JScrollPane(list);

    getContentPane( ).add(scrollpane, BorderLayout.CENTER);
  }

  public static void main(String args[]) {
    ScrollList sl = new ScrollList( );
    sl.setVisible(true);
  }
}
```

A similar technique can be used with many of the Swing components, including JPanel, JTree, JTable, and JTextArea. Chapter 15 discusses the JTable class and its particular use of JScrollPane.

While you will certainly use JScrollPane with many of the Swing components, you can also build your own components and drop them into a scrollable area. You may bundle up a piece of your user interface into one panel and make that panel scrollable.

Here's a short example that takes the items from our previous list and turns them into a basic census form. As you can see in Figure 11-4, the form itself is a panel with a size of 600×400 pixels. We display it inside a JScrollPane and make the application 300×200.

The only change from our first program is that we now have to build the census panel from scratch. We build a JPanel containing various labels and radio buttons, and slap it into a JScrollPane. The only logic involved is figuring out whether we're adding a label or a button, and getting the buttons into appropriate ButtonGroups (one group per row).

```
// ScrollDemo.java
// A simple JScrollPane demonstration
//
import javax.swing.*;
```

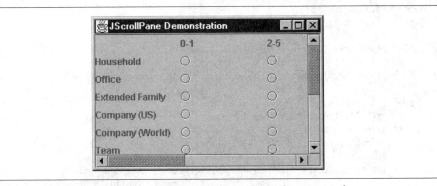

Figure 11-4. A JScrollPane with a component larger than the application window

```java
import java.awt.*;
import java.awt.event.*;

public class ScrollDemo extends JFrame {

  JScrollPane scrollpane;

  public ScrollDemo() {
    super("JScrollPane Demonstration");
    setSize(300, 200);
    setDefaultCloseOperation(EXIT_ON_CLOSE);
    init();
    setVisible(true);
  }

  public void init() {
    JRadioButton form[][] = new JRadioButton[12][5];
    String counts[] = { "", "0-1", "2-5", "6-10", "11-100", "101+" };
    String categories[] = { "Household", "Office", "Extended Family",
                            "Company (US)", "Company (World)", "Team",
                            "Will", "Birthday Card List", "High School",
                            "Country", "Continent", "Planet" };
    JPanel p = new JPanel();
    p.setSize(600, 400);
    p.setLayout(new GridLayout(13, 6, 10, 0));
    for (int row = 0; row < 13; row++) {
      ButtonGroup bg = new ButtonGroup();
      for (int col = 0; col < 6; col++) {
        if (row == 0) {
          p.add(new JLabel(counts[col]));
        }
        else {
          if (col == 0) {
            p.add(new JLabel(categories[row - 1]));
          }
          else {
            form[row - 1][col - 1] = new JRadioButton();
            bg.add(form[row -1][col - 1]);
```

```
                    p.add(form[row -1][col - 1]);
                }
            }
        }
    }
    scrollpane = new JScrollPane(p);
    getContentPane( ).add(scrollpane, BorderLayout.CENTER);
}

public static void main(String args[]) {
    new ScrollDemo( );
}
}
```

Properties

Table 11-3 shows how the JScrollPane properties grant you access to the five main components (not the corners) and the scrollbar policies. The valid values for horizontalScrollBarPolicy and verticalScrollBarPolicy are defined in the ScrollPaneConstants interface (see Table 11-8). The validateRoot property is always true to ensure that revalidation calls to any of the pane's descendants cause the scrollpane and all of its descendants to be validated, and that revalidation doesn't go any further than the JScrollPane, which would be redundant. The wheelScrollingEnabled property, added in SDK 1.4, allows you to enable or disable support for mice with a middle-wheel button.

Table 11-3. JScrollPane properties

Property	Data type	get	is	set	Default value
accessibleContext[o]	AccessibleContext	•			JScrollPane.AccessibleJScrollPane( )
columnHeader[b]	JViewport	•			null
columnHeaderView	Component			•	
componentOrientation[b, o]	int	•		•	ComponentOrientation.UNKNOWN
horizontalScrollBar[b]	JScrollBar	•			null
horizontalScrollBarPolicy[b]	int	•		•	HORIZONTAL_SCROLLBAR_AS_NEEDED
layout[b, o]	LayoutManager	•		•	new ScrollPaneLayout( )
opaque	boolean		•		false
rowHeader[b]	JViewport	•			null
rowHeaderView	Component			•	
UI	ScrollPane-UI	•		•	From L&F

[1.4]since 1.4, [b]bound, [o]overridden

See also properties from the JComponent class (Table 3-6).

Table 11-3. JScrollPane properties (continued)

Property	Data type	get	is	set	Default value
UIClassID[o]	String				"ScrollPaneUI"
validateRoot	boolean	•			true
verticalScrollbar[b]	JScrollBar	•			null
verticalScrollBarPolicy[b]	int	•		•	VERTICAL_SCROLLBAR_AS_NEEDED
viewport[b]	JViewport	•			null
viewportBorder[b]	Border	•		•	null
viewportBorderBounds	Rectangle	•			
viewportView	Component			•	
wheelScrollingEnabled[b, 1.4]	boolean	•		•	true

[1.4]since 1.4, [b]bound, [o]overridden

See also properties from the JComponent class (Table 3-6).

Given that you already have a viewport set up for the row and column headers, or the main viewport itself, you can use the columnHeaderView, rowHeaderView, and viewportView properties to modify the contents of these viewports. Note that the set accessors for these properties don't create new viewport objects; they simply set the view to display the given component.

Constructors

public JScrollPane( )
public JScrollPane(Component view)
public JScrollPane(Component view, int verticalScrollBarPolicy,
* int horizontalScrollBarPolicy)*
public JScrollPane(int verticalScrollBarPolicy, int horizontalScrollBarPolicy)

Create new scrollpanes. You can start off by specifying the view (i.e., the component to scroll), the scrollbar policies, or both. Just make sure you get the scrollbar policies in the right order! Of course, any of these pieces can be specified or changed after the scrollpane has been created. See the setViewportView( ) method later in this chapter.

Pane Component Methods

public JScrollBar createHorizontalScrollBar( )
public JScrollBar createVerticalScrollBar( )

Used by the UI for the scrollpane to create the scrollbars you see. You can override these methods if you want to use a specific subclass of the JScrollBar class.

public JViewport createViewport()
> Create the JViewport object that contains the main view you see. You can override this to use your own subclass of JViewport.

public Component getCorner(String whichCorner)
public void setCorner(String whichCorner, Component corner)
> Get or set the component in the corner of a scrollpane. The whichCorner argument can be any one of the corner strings from the ScrollPaneConstants class (see Table 11-4). You can add any component you like to the corners.

Headers and Corners

Neither of the previous examples took advantage of the additional features provided by JScrollPane over the AWT ScrollPane class. You can add headers to your scrolling panes and even put active components in the corners. Figure 11-5 shows an expanded example of our census program with headers and an "Information" button in the upper-left corner.

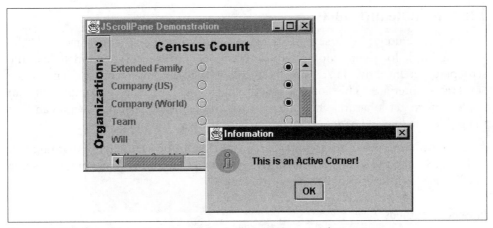

Figure 11-5. A JScrollPane with a button in the upper-left corner that opens a pop up

The code to add to the init( ) method for our demo is straightforward:

```
// Add in some JViewports for the column and row headers.
JViewport jv1 = new JViewport();
jv1.setView(new JLabel(new ImageIcon("columnlabel.gif")));
scrollpane.setColumnHeader(jv1);
JViewport jv2 = new JViewport();
jv2.setView(new JLabel(new ImageIcon("rowlabel.gif")));
scrollpane.setRowHeader(jv2);

// And throw in an information button
JButton jb1 = new JButton(new ImageIcon("question.gif"));
jb1.addActionListener(new ActionListener() {
  public void actionPerformed(ActionEvent ae) {
```

```
            JOptionPane.showMessageDialog(null,
                "This is an Active Corner!", "Information",
                JOptionPane.INFORMATION_MESSAGE);
        }
    } );
    scrollpane.setCorner(ScrollPaneConstants.UPPER_LEFT_CORNER, jb1);
```

We use a JLabel inside a JViewport for each header. The viewport in the headers allows the JScrollPane to synchronize header scrolling with the main viewport. We'll look at the JViewport class in more detail later in this chapter.

When you set up corner components, remember that if your scrollbars are on an as-needed basis, your corners could disappear. In our example, if we moved the information button to the upper-right corner and then made the window tall enough to contain the entire census form, the vertical scrollbar would disappear, and so would the Information button. You can alleviate this problem by setting the appropriate scrollbar policy to "always." That way, your corners stick around even when the scrollbars are not active.

The Scrollable Interface

You may have noticed that several Swing components rely on JScrollPane to do the scrolling work for them. Most of those components, like JList, seem to use the scrollpane intelligently. That's not by accident. These components implement the Scrollable interface. This interface defines five methods that a component can implement to get a natural effect out of the scrollpane. By "natural" we mean that things like the line and page increments behave the way you would expect.

A component does not need to implement Scrollable to be scrollable. Anything you add to a JScrollPane scrolls properly. The Scrollable interface merely provides some intelligence to make scrolling more convenient.

Increment methods

public int getScrollableBlockIncrement(Rectangle visibleRect, int orientation,
  int direction)
public int getScrollableUnitIncrement(Rectangle visibleRect, int orientation,
  int direction)

These methods should be used to return the appropriate increment amount required to display the next logical row or column of the component, depending on the value of orientation. orientation can be either SwingConstants.HORIZONTAL or SwingConstants.VERTICAL. The unit increment specifies (in pixels) how to display the next logical row or column; the block increment (also pixels) specifies how to "page" horizontally or vertically. The current position of the component is determined by visibleRect. The direction argument has a positive (> 0) value for moving down or right and a negative value (< 0) for moving up or left.

Viewport dimension methods

The other methods of the interface dictate the relation between the visible area of the scrollable component and the viewport it is displayed in:

public Dimension getPreferredScrollableViewportSize( )
> This method should return the preferred size of the viewport containing the component. This value may or may not be the same as the value returned by getPreferredSize( ) for the component. If you recall JList, you'll realize that the preferred size of the component itself is a dimension big enough to display all of the items in the list. The preferred size for the viewport, however, would only be big enough to display some particular number of rows in the list.

public boolean getScrollableTracksViewportHeight( )
public boolean getScrollableTracksViewportWidth( )
> These methods can be used to effectively disable horizontal or vertical scrolling in a scrollpane. If you return true for either of these methods, you force the component's height (or width) to match that of its containing viewport. An example might be a text area component that supports word wrapping. Since the text will wrap regardless of the width of the component, you could have getScrollableTracksViewportWidth( ) return true. As the scrollpane is resized, the vertical scrollbar still moves up and down through the text, but the horizontal scrollbar is not used. Returning false, then, indicates that the component's height (or width) is determined irrespective of the viewport's dimensions. A scrollpane might then display a scrollbar to allow the user to view the entire component.

The JScrollPane.ScrollBar class

protected class JScrollPane.ScrollBar extends JScrollBar implements UIResource
> By default, the scrollbars used in a JScrollPane are instances of this class. These scrollbars are a bit smarter than regular scrollbars. They check with the view to see if it implements the Scrollable interface. If it does (and if you did not explicitly set the unit and block increments), then these scrollbars ask the view to provide what it thinks are the appropriate values.

The ScrollPaneLayout Class

The JScrollPane class is actually just a panel with a hard-working layout manager and some convenient access methods for the manager. While you probably will not use this class on its own, the ScrollPaneLayout class is the manager that provides layout control for the nine areas of a JScrollPane object:

- Viewport
- Row header
- Column header

- Vertical scrollbar
- Horizontal scrollbar
- Four corners (upper left, upper right, lower left, and lower right)

These nine components are laid out as shown in Figure 11-6.

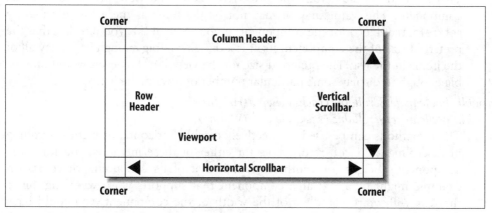

Figure 11-6. The layout areas managed by ScrollPaneLayout

The column headers and scrollbars behave like the four compass positions (North, South, East, and West) of a BorderLayout-managed panel. The vertical components are as wide as they need to be and as tall as the viewport. The horizontal components are as tall as they need to be and as wide as the viewport. The difference from the BorderLayout-managed panels is that the ScrollPaneLayout panels have four corners. Each corner can be a regular component (or blank). The corners appear based on the visibility of the headers and scrollbars. For example, if both of the scrollbars are visible, the lower-right corner component would be available. The valid values for these positions are defined in the ScrollPaneConstants interface (see Table 11-4).

Table 11-4. ScrollPaneLayout constant values

Location string from ScrollPaneConstants	Component location
VIEWPORT	Main viewing area, typically a JViewport component
COLUMN_HEADER	The column header (a row), typically a JViewport component
ROW_HEADER	The row header (a column), typically a JViewport component
HORIZONTAL_SCROLLBAR	The horizontal scrollbar for the viewport; must be a JScrollBar component
VERTICAL_SCROLLBAR	The vertical scrollbar for the viewport; must be a JScrollBar component
LOWER_LEFT_CORNER	The southwest corner, typically empty
LOWER_RIGHT_CORNER	The southeast corner, typically empty
UPPER_LEFT_CORNER	The northwest corner, typically empty
UPPER_RIGHT_CORNER	The northeast corner, typically empty

The `ScrollPaneLayout` class also contains several methods for manipulating the scrollbars associated with the viewport (via `JScrollPane`'s properties; see Table 11-1). Both the horizontal and vertical scrollbars have policies that determine when (and if) they show up. You can set and retrieve the scrollbar policies using these methods with constants defined in the `ScrollPaneConstants` interface listed in Table 11-5.

Table 11-5. ScrollPaneLayout policy constants from ScrollPaneConstants

ScrollPaneConstants constant	Type	Effect on Scrollbar component
HORIZONTAL_SCROLLBAR_ALWAYS	int	Always keeps a horizontal scrollbar around, even if the viewport extent area is wide enough to display the entire component
HORIZONTAL_SCROLLBAR_AS_NEEDED	int	Shows a horizontal scrollbar whenever the extent area is smaller than the full component
HORIZONTAL_SCROLLBAR_NEVER	int	Never shows a horizontal scrollbar, even if the component is wider than the viewport extent area
VERTICAL_SCROLLBAR_ALWAYS	int	Always keeps a vertical scrollbar around, even if the viewport extent area is tall enough to display the entire component
VERTICAL_SCROLLBAR_AS_NEEDED	int	Shows a vertical scrollbar whenever the extent area is smaller than the full component
VERTICAL_SCROLLBAR_NEVER	int	Never shows a vertical scrollbar, even if the component is taller than the viewport extent area
HORIZONTAL_SCROLLBAR_POLICY	String	The name of the horizontal scrollbar policy property for use with property change events
VERTICAL_SCROLLBAR_POLICY	String	The name of the vertical scrollbar policy property for use with property change events

Properties

This layout manager treats the various components as properties, with the usual property access methods. However, since `ScrollPaneLayout` is really just a layout manager, you don't set the components, you add them to the `JScrollPane`. Table 11-6 shows the components managed by a `ScrollPaneLayout`.

Table 11-6. ScrollPaneLayout properties

Property	Data type	get	is	set	Default value
columnHeader	JViewport	•			null
corner	Component	•			null
horizontalScrollBar	JScrollBar	•			null
rowHeader	JViewport	•			null
verticalScrollbar	JScrollBar	•			null
viewport	JViewport	•			null

The columnHeader, rowHeader, and viewport components are all of type JViewport. (We will look at that class in the next section, but basically, it provides easy access for placing a viewable rectangle over a component.) If the entire component fits in the rectangle, you can see all of the component. If not, the parts outside the rectangle are cropped. The corner property is indexed using constant values from Table 11-4.

As with other layout managers, you rarely add or remove components directly through the manager; that task is handled by the container. As you saw earlier, the JScrollPane class contains the methods necessary to add or replace any of these nine components. It also contains methods to retrieve these components, but the retrieval methods are provided through the layout manager, too, for convenience.

public Rectangle getViewportBorderBounds(JScrollPane sp)
  Return the bounding rectangle for sp's viewport border.

public void syncWithScrollPane(JScrollPane sp)
  This method can be used with your own customized scrollpane layout manager to synchronize the components associated with the scrollpane sp and this manager. That way, any components already added to sp are appropriately recognized by your layout manager.

JViewport

You use the JViewport class to create a view of a potentially large component in a potentially small place. We say "potentially" because the view can encompass the entire component or just a piece of it. In the JScrollPane class, a viewport is used to show a piece of the main component, and the scrollbars provide the user with control over which piece they see. JViewport accomplishes this using the normal clipping techniques, but it guarantees that an appropriately sized view of the component is displayed. The JScrollPane class also uses JViewport objects for the row and column headers.

Most of the time, you'll leave JViewport alone and use one of the other panes, like JScrollPane, to display your components. However, nothing prevents you from using JViewport objects, and you can certainly subclass this to create some interesting tools, such as an image magnifier pane. In such a pane, you'd still have to write the magnifying code—JViewport would just make it easy to see pieces of a magnified image. (The discussion of the new SpringLayout manager later in this chapter does show an example of using a JViewport on its own.)

Properties

The JViewport class has the properties shown in Table 11-7. The useful properties of JViewport deal with the view component. The view property lets you get or set the component this viewport is viewing. viewSize and viewPosition control the size and position of the area that's displayed. viewSize is normally equal to the size of the viewport, unless the component is smaller than the viewport. In that case, viewSize equals the component's size, and all of it is displayed. viewPosition is relative to the top-left corner of the component being displayed. If the backingStoreEnabled property is true, this JViewport object double-buffers the display of its contents. The isOptimizedDrawingEnabled( ) call always returns false to force the viewport's paint( ) method to be called, rather than allowing repaint calls to notify the viewport's children individually.

Table 11-7. JViewport properties

Property	Data type	get	is	set	Default value
accessibleContext	AccessibleContext	•			JViewport. AccessibleJViewport( )
backingStoreEnabled	boolean		•	•	false
changeListeners[1.4]	ChangeListener[]	•			Empty array
extentSize	Dimension	•		•	Size of the component
insets*	Insets	•			Insets(0, 0, 0, 0)
optimizedDrawingEnabled[o]	boolean		•		false
scrollMode[1.3]	int	•		•	BLIT_SCROLL_MODE
view	Component	•		•	null
viewPosition	Point	•		•	Point(0, 0)
viewRect	Rectangle	•			Rect(getViewPosition( ), getExtentSize( ))
viewSize	Dimension	•		•	Dimension(0, 0)

[1.3]since 1.3, [1.4]since 1.4, [o]overridden

*These get methods override JComponent and are final.

See also "The ViewportLayout Class" later in the chapter and properties of the JComponent class (Table 3-6).

The scrollMode property can also affect repaint performance. The constants for valid scrolling modes are shown in Table 11-8.

Table 11-8. JViewport scrolling-mode constants

JViewport constant	Type	Effect on Scrollbar component
BLIT_SCROLL_MODE[1.3]	int	The default scrolling mode; the fastest for most applications.
BACKINGSTORE_SCROLL_MODE[1.3]	int	Uses an off-screen graphics context to do its scrolling. As the Javadoc notes, this can be advantageous, but requires a good deal more RAM.
SIMPLE_SCROLL_MODE[1.3]	int	Swing 1.0 and 1.1 scrolling behavior. You will almost always want one of the other modes.

[1.3]since 1.3

Events

The JViewport class fires a ChangeEvent whenever the view size, view position, or extent size changes.

public void addChangeListener(ChangeListener l)
public void removeChangeListener(ChangeListener l)
> Add or remove a change listener for the viewport's ChangeEvents.

Constructor

public JViewport()
> Create an empty JViewport object. You can put something in the viewport using the setView( ) method.

Useful methods

public void repaint(long delay, int x, int y, int width, int height)
> Override the usual repaint( ) call to make sure that only one repaint( ) is performed. This method translates the repaint rectangle to the parent's coordinate system and tells the parent to repaint( ). Presumably, if the rectangle doesn't need to be repainted, nothing happens, although the parent could have its own overridden repaint( ) method.

public void scrollRectToVisible(Rectangle rect)
> Try to make the area represented by rect visible in the viewport.

public void setBounds(int x, int y, int width, int height)
> Override the resize method in JComponent to make sure the backing store for this image is correct if the width or height changes from the current dimensions.

public Dimension toViewCoordinates(Dimension size)
public Point toViewCoordinates(Point p)
> Translate the incoming Dimension or Point objects into corresponding objects relative to the current view. If your viewport supported logical coordinates, these methods would need to be overridden.

The ViewportLayout Class

As with the ScrollPaneLayout class, this class is meant to be used with a JViewport object, not for general use. That is to say, rather than attach this layout manager to your container, you should simply use a JViewport for your container. (Recall that you can place any component—such as a JPanel—within the viewport area.)

ViewportLayout is a straightforward implementation of the AWT LayoutManager interface and keeps the view in a useful position during resizing.

The JTabbedPane Class

The tabbed pane is now a fixture in applications for option displays, system configuration displays, and other multiscreen UIs. In the AWT, you have access to the CardLayout layout manager, which can be used to simulate the multiscreen behavior, but it contains nothing to graphically activate screen switching—you must write that yourself. Figure 11-7 shows that with the JTabbedPane, you can create your own tabbed pane, with tab activation components, very quickly.

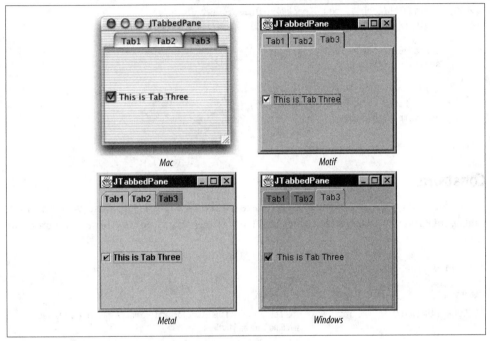

Figure 11-7. A simple tabbed pane with three tabs in several L&Fs

Here's the code that generated this simple application. We use the tabbed pane as our real container and create new tabs using the addTab( ) method. Note that each tab can contain exactly one component. As with a CardLayout-managed container, you quite often add a container as the one component on the tab. That way, you can then add as many other components to the container as necessary.

```
// SimpleTab.java
// A quick test of the JTabbedPane component
//
import java.awt.*;
import java.util.*;
import java.awt.event.*;
import javax.swing.*;
```

```
public class SimpleTab extends JFrame {

    JTabbedPane jtp;

    public SimpleTab( ) {
      super("JTabbedPane");
      setSize(200, 200);
      Container contents = getContentPane( );
      jtp = new JTabbedPane( );
      jtp.addTab("Tab1", new JLabel("This is Tab One"));
      jtp.addTab("Tab2", new JButton("This is Tab Two"));
      jtp.addTab("Tab3", new JCheckBox("This is Tab Three"));
      contents.add(jtp);

      setDefaultCloseOperation(EXIT_ON_CLOSE);
      setVisible(true);
    }

    public static void main(String args[]) {
      new SimpleTab( );
    }
}
```

Constants

Two constants, shown in Table 11-9, were added in SDK 1.4 for use with the new tabLayoutPolicy property. See Figure 11-8 for an example of these constants in action.

Table 11-9. JTabbedPane constants

Constant	Type	Description
SCROLL_TAB_LAYOUT[1.4]	int	This policy restricts tabs to one row and provides a spinner to access tabs by scrolling back and forth.
WRAP_TAB_LAYOUT[1.4]	int	This policy stacks tabs into multiple rows if they will not fit cleanly on one row. This is the default behavior prior to the 1.4 release.

[1.4]since 1.4

Properties

The JTabbedPane class has the properties listed in Table 11-10. For a tabbed pane, the properties are much simpler than for the scrollpane. You have access to the selection model (see Chapter 14 for a discussion of SingleSelectionModel and DefaultSingleSelectionModel), the currently selected tab—available by component (selectedComponent) or index (selectedIndex), and the total number of tabs for this panel. The tabRunCount property tells you how many rows (or runs) the pane is using currently to display all of the tabCount tabs. You can also control the location of the tabs using the tabPlacement property, which can be any of the TOP, BOTTOM, LEFT, or RIGHT constants defined in SwingConstants.

Table 11-10. JTabbedPane properties

Property	Data type	get	is	set	Default value
accessibleContext[b, o]	AccessibleContext	•			JTabbedPane. AccessibleJTabbedPane( )
backgroundAt[i]	Color	•		•	L&F-dependent
boundsAt[i]	Rectangle	•			
changeListeners[1.4]	ChangeListener[]	•			Empty array
componentAt[i]	Component	•		•	
disabledIconAt[i]	Icon	•		•	
displayed-MnemonicAt[b, i, 1.4]	int	•		•	-1
enabledAt[i]	boolean		•	•	
foregroundAt[i]	Color	•		•	L&F-dependent
iconAt[i]	Icon	•		•	
mnemonicAt[b, i, 1.4]	int	•		•	0 (no mnemonic)
model[b]	SingleSelectionModel	•		•	DefaultSingleSelectionModel( )
selectedComponent	Component	•		•	null
selectedIndex	int	•		•	-1
tabCount	int	•			0
tabLayoutPolicy[b, 1.4]	int	•		•	WRAP_TAB_LAYOUT
tabPlacement[b]	int	•		•	SwingConstants.TOP
tabRunCount	int	•			0
titleAt[b,i]	String	•		•	
toolTipTextAt[i, 1.3]	String	•		•	
UI	TabbedPaneUI	•		•	null
UIClassID[o]	String				"TabbedPaneUI"

[1.3]since 1.3, [1.4]since 1.4, [b]bound, [i]indexed, [o]overridden

See also properties from the JComponent class (Table 3-6).

The tabLayoutPolicy, added in SDK 1.4, allows you choose how to handle large numbers of tabs on a pane. Figure 11-8 shows an example of the two possibilities for this policy. (You'll find the source code for this example in the *TooManyTabs.java* file for this chapter.) Also new with 1.4, mnemonicAt and displayedMnemonicAt add support for mnemonics to the tabs. The mnemonicAt property sets the actual mnemonic for the tab. The displayedMnemonicAt property provides a hint to the L&F as to which character should be decorated in the tab. (For example, X is the mnemonic, but you want the *second* X underlined.) Note that not all L&Fs support this feature.

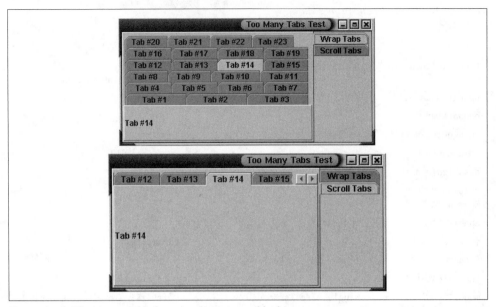

Figure 11-8. The two possible layout policies in a tabbed pane

Events

In addition to the property change events generated for the model and tabPlacement properties, JTabbedPane also generates change events whenever the tab selection changes. On its own, a JTabbedPane listens to the change events coming from the tabs to keep the user interface in sync with the selected tab. Of course, you can add your own listener to the pane. SingleSelectionModel uses the ChangeEvent class to report a new tab selection.

public void addChangeListener(ChangeListener l)
public void removeChangeListener(ChangeListener l)
    Add or remove a listener for change events from this tabbed pane.

protected ChangeListener createChangeListener()
    Create a listener that can route change events from the selection model for the pane to the fireStateChanged( ) method. The protected inner class JTabbedPane. ModelListener is used to accomplish the redirection.

Constructors

public JTabbedPane()
    Create an empty tabbed pane to which you can add new tabs with one of the tab methods listed below. The tabs are placed along the top of the pane.

public JTabbedPane(int tabPlacement)
> Create an empty tabbed pane to which you can add new tabs with one of the tab methods listed below. The tabs are placed according to `tabPlacement`—which can be one of TOP, BOTTOM, LEFT, or RIGHT—from the `SwingConstants` interface.

public JTabbedPane(int tabPlacement, int tabLayoutPolicy)
> In 1.4 or later, create an empty tabbed pane to which you can add new tabs with one of the tab methods listed below. The tabs are placed according to `tabPlacement`—which can be one of TOP, BOTTOM, LEFT, or RIGHT—from the `SwingConstants` interface. If there are too many tabs to fit on one row, they will wrap or scroll according to the `tabLayoutPolicy`.

Tab Methods

Once you have a tabbed pane set up, you can add, remove, and modify tabs at any time.

public void addTab(String title, Component comp)
public void addTab(String title, Icon tabIcon, Component comp)
public void addTab(String title, Icon tabIcon, Component comp, String tip)
> These methods allow you to add (append, really) a tab to the pane. You must specify the tab's component (`comp`) and `title`. If the component is `null`, the tab still appears, but it does not behave appropriately. When you select a tab with a `null` component, the previously selected tab's component remains visible. The title may be `null`. Optionally, you can also specify an icon (`tabIcon`) and a tooltip (`tip`) for the tab. As with the title, `null` values for these arguments do not cause any problems. Each of these methods builds up an appropriate call to `insertTab( )`.

public int indexAtLocation(int x, int y)
> Added in SDK 1.4, this method returns the index of the tab that contains the given coordinates (or -1 if no tab contains them).

public void insertTab(String title, Icon tabIcon, Component comp, String tip, int index)
> This method does all of the work of getting tabs into place on the pane. You specify the tab's title, icon, tooltip (all of which can be `null`), component, and the index to insert the component. If you supply an index larger than the tab count, an `ArrayIndexOutOfBoundsException` is thrown.

public Component add(Component component)
public Component add(String title, Component component)
public Component add(Component component, int index)
public void add(Component component, Object constraints)
public void add(Component component, Object constraints, int index)
> These methods are alternatives for adding tabs to a tabbed pane, in case you don't want to use `addTab( )` or `insertTab( )`. They are more in keeping with the standard `add( )` method for containers. If you supply an `index`, the tab is inserted

at that index. If you supply constraints, it should be either a String or an Icon object for use in the tab. (If the constraints object isn't a String or an Icon, it is ignored.) If you do not supply a title or constraint to label the tab, the tabbed pane uses component.getName( ).

public void remove(Component component)
Remove the tab with a match to component. If a match cannot be found, nothing happens.

public void removeAll( )
Remove all tabs from the tabbed pane.

public void removeTabAt(int index)
This method allows you to remove a given tab. As with insertTab( ), an inappropriate index value causes an ArrayIndexOutOfBoundsException.

public int indexOfComponent(Component comp)
public int indexOfTab(String title)
public int indexOfTab(Icon icon)
These methods allow you to look up a tab at runtime. If you use the second or third methods, the first tab with a matching title or icon is returned.

Miscellaneous Methods

Tabbed panes also support the notion of tooltips and do most of the work for you. However, you do need to set the tooltip text when you add the tab; no "setToolTipText( )" method exists.

public String getToolTipText(MouseEvent event)
This method overrides the getToolTipText( ) call from JComponent to return the tooltip appropriate for the tab your mouse cursor is on.

Figure 11-9 shows our first tabbed pane with tooltips active.

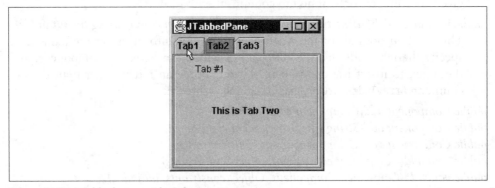

Figure 11-9. A tabbed pane with tooltips active

Here are the modifications to the code needed to make this work. We just add a null icon and the tooltip text (the last arguments) to the addTab( ) methods:

```
jtp = new JTabbedPane( );
jtp.addTab("Tab1", null, new JLabel("This is Tab One"), "Tab #1");
jtp.addTab("Tab2", null, new JButton("This is Tab Two"), "Tab #2");
jtp.addTab("Tab3", null, new JCheckBox("This is Tab Three"), "Tab #3");
contents.add(jtp);
```

You should also check out the example for the BoxLayout class later in this chapter. It contains a tabbed pane interface. One tab dynamically controls the enabledAt property for each of the other tabs.

Layout Managers

Beyond these specialty panes with their dedicated layout managers, the Swing package also includes some general layout managers you can use with your own code. You can use the new BoxLayout to make things like toolbars and OverlayLayout to make things like layered labels.

The BoxLayout class is a manager that gives you one row or column to put everything in. It's great for toolbars and button ribbons. It also comes with its very own convenience container called Box. The Box class is a lightweight container that requires a BoxLayout manager. While you can certainly use the BoxLayout class to control your own panel, frame, or other container, the Box class provides several shortcuts for dealing with components in a boxed layout. You'll often find that using a Box is easier than creating a panel or frame that you control with a BoxLayout manager.

The Box Class

Let's start with a look at the convenience container that puts the BoxLayout manager to use. The Box class is a lightweight container object whose primary purpose is to let you add components to a horizontal or vertical box without having to think about getting the constraints right. (As of SDK 1.4, Box extends JComponent.) You use the normal Container.add( ) method to place components in the box. Components are placed left to right (or top to bottom) in the order you add them.

Properties

Table 11-11 shows the properties of the Box class. You are not allowed to change a box's layout manager, so the setLayout accessor always throws an AWTError.

Table 11-11. Box properties

Property	Data type	get	is	set	Default value
accessibleContext[o]	AccessibleContext	•			box.AccessibleBox
layout[o]	layoutManager	•		•	BoxLayout

[o]overridden

See also properties from the JComponent class (Table 3-6).

Constructor

public Box(int alignment)

Create a container with a BoxLayout manager using the specified alignment. The possible values for the alignment are BoxLayout.X_AXIS (a horizontal box) and BoxLayout.Y_AXIS (a vertical box). (Refer to Figure 11-13 for an example of vertical and horizontal boxes.) Usually, you use the createVerticalBox( ) or createHorizontalBox( ) methods to make new boxes.

Creation method

Two convenience routines exist for creating boxes. You can create your own using the constructor, but these are sometimes easier.

public static Box createHorizontalBox( )
public static Box createVerticalBox( )

These methods create new Box components with the appropriate alignment.

Spacing and resizing methods

The Box class provides several static helper components for spacing and resizing controls. You can add these components as you would add any other component to the box.

public static Component createGlue( )
public static Component createHorizontalGlue( )
public static Component createVerticalGlue( )

These methods create "glue" components that you can place between two fixed-size components. Glue might be a misnomer; it doesn't cause the components to stay in one place. Rather, glue acts like a gooey filler: it lets a component shift when the parent container is resized and takes up the slack. The idea is that glue is malleable and stretchable compared to a strut or rigid area. Rather than forcing the components to change their sizes to consume new space, you can put glue components anywhere you want blank space. It's important to remember, however, that glue components really are components. When resizing a box, all of the components—the glue and the buttons in our examples—will have their sizes adjusted, up to their minimum or maximum limits.

The horizontal and vertical glue components stretch along the appropriate axis, while the generic glue component can stretch in both directions, if necessary. Figure 11-10 shows how a resize affects buttons in a Box. Without glue, the buttons grow as the contour is resized. With glue, the buttons still change, but they don't change as much; the glue takes up much of the extra space.

Here's the code to add glue to both sides of the buttons:

```
// HBoxWithGlue.java
// A quick test of the box layout manager using the Box utility class
//
```

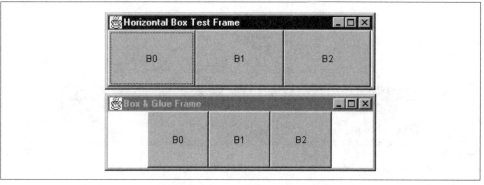

Figure 11-10. A Box container after being resized without (top) and with (bottom) glue components

```java
import java.awt.*;
import java.awt.event.*;
import javax.swing.*;

public class HBoxWithGlue extends JFrame {

  public HBoxWithGlue() {
    super("Box & Glue Frame");
    setSize(350, 100);
    Box box = Box.createHorizontalBox();
    setContentPane(box);
    box.add(Box.createHorizontalGlue());
    for (int i = 0; i < 3; i++) {
      Button b = new Button("B" + i);
      box.add(b);
    }
    box.add(Box.createHorizontalGlue());
    setDefaultCloseOperation(EXIT_ON_CLOSE);
    setVisible(true);
  }

  public static void main(String args[]) {
    HBoxWithGlue bt = new HBoxWithGlue();
  }
}
```

public static Component createRigidArea(Dimension d)
public static Component createHorizontalStrut(int width)
public static Component createVerticalStrut(int width)

These methods create rigid spaces. You can use these methods to force gaps between components. This is useful if you are trying to create groups of components in a toolbar. The rigid area creates an invisible component that has a fixed width and height. The horizontal strut has a fixed width and a variable height. The vertical strut has a fixed height and a variable width. Figure 11-11 has some examples of strut components before and after a resize.

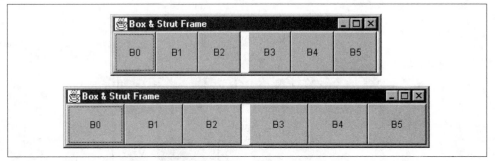

Figure 11-11. Strut components being resized inside a Box container

Here's the code for the strut example:

```
// HBoxWithStrut.java
//
import java.awt.*;
import java.awt.event.*;
import javax.swing.*;

public class HBoxWithStrut extends JFrame {

  public HBoxWithStrut() {
    super("Box & Strut Frame");
    setSize(370, 80);
    Box box = Box.createHorizontalBox();
    setContentPane(box);
    for (int i = 0; i < 3; i++) {
      Button b = new Button("B" + i);
      box.add(b);
    }

    // Add a spacer between the first three buttons and the last three buttons.
    box.add(Box.createHorizontalStrut(10));
    for (int i = 3; i < 6; i++) {
      Button b = new Button("B" + i);
      box.add(b);
    }
    setDefaultCloseOperation(EXIT_ON_CLOSE);
    setVisible(true);
  }

  public static void main(String args[]) {
    HBoxWithStrut bt = new HBoxWithStrut();
  }
}
```

The Box.Filler Class

The struts and glue components used in the various create methods above use a public inner class called Filler. The Filler inner class extends Component and provides mechanisms to specify fixed or variable widths and heights. It has no visual presence, but as you saw in the above examples, it can play a role in the layout process for a container.

While this class is public and can be used directly, the static convenience methods found in the Box class are probably easier to use.

Properties

Table 11-12 shows the properties found in the Filler class. The size properties all store their values in protected fields inherited from Component. Glue components are created by putting zeros in the minimum and preferred sizes, and Short.MAX_VALUE in the maximum sizes. Strut (and rigid area) components are created by putting exactly the same value in each of the three size categories.

Table 11-12. Box.Filler properties

Property	Data type	get	is	set	Default value
accessibleContext	AccessibleContext	•			Box.Filler.AccessibleBoxFiller()
maximumSize°	Dimension	•			Set by constructor
minimumSize°	Dimension	•			Set by constructor
preferredSize°	Dimension	•			Set by constructor

°overridden

See also the java.awt.Component class.

Constructor

public Filler(Dimension min, Dimension pref, Dimension max)
> Create a new Filler object with the given minimum, preferred, and maximum sizes.

Shape method

The Filler class has only one other method beyond those required to support accessibility:

public void changeShape(Dimension min, Dimension pref, Dimension max)
> Set the Filler object's minimum, preferred, and maximum sizes.

The BoxLayout Class

If you want only the layout manager for your own container, this is the class you need. The BoxLayout class implements the LayoutManager2 interface from the java.awt package. This class and its predecessor, LayoutManager, are discussed in detail in John Zukowski's *Java AWT Reference* (O'Reilly), which provides an excellent background on layout managers in general. Although it is no longer in print, you can download a copy in PDF format from this book's web site, *http://www.oreilly.com/ catalog/jswing2/*.

Figure 11-12 shows an example of a simple form that allows individual rows to be as tall as they need to be. Notice that we pad the top and bottom rows with glue, which keeps the form vertically centered on the tab.

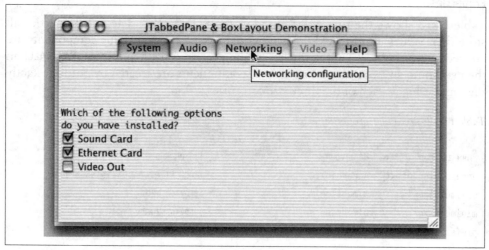

Figure 11-12. A BoxLayout attached to a normal JPanel (and active JTabbedPane tooltips)

Here's the code for this example:

```
// SysConfig.java
// A demonstration of the JTabbedPane class for displaying and manipulating
// configuration information. The BoxLayout class is used to lay out the first tab
// quickly.
//
import java.awt.*;
import java.awt.event.*;
import javax.swing.*;
import javax.swing.event.*;

public class SysConfig extends JFrame {
  JTabbedPane config = new JTabbedPane( );

  public SysConfig( ) {
    super("JTabbedPane & BoxLayout Demonstration");
    setSize(500,300);
    setDefaultCloseOperation(EXIT_ON_CLOSE);

    JPanel configPane = new JPanel( );
    configPane.setLayout(new BoxLayout(configPane, BoxLayout.Y_AXIS));
    JTextArea question = new JTextArea("Which of the following options\n" +
                                 "do you have installed?");
    // Now configure the text area to show up properly inside the box. This is part
    // of the "high art" of Swing.
```

```
        question.setEditable(false);
        question.setMaximumSize(new Dimension(300,50));
        question.setAlignmentX(0.0f);
        question.setBackground(configPane.getBackground( ));

        JCheckBox audioCB = new JCheckBox("Sound Card", true);
        JCheckBox nicCB = new JCheckBox("Ethernet Card", true);
        JCheckBox tvCB = new JCheckBox("Video Out", false);

        configPane.add(Box.createVerticalGlue( ));
        configPane.add(question);
        configPane.add(audioCB);
        configPane.add(nicCB);
        configPane.add(tvCB);
        configPane.add(Box.createVerticalGlue( ));

        JLabel audioPane = new JLabel("Audio stuff");
        JLabel nicPane = new JLabel("Networking stuff");
        JLabel tvPane = new JLabel("Video stuff");
        JLabel helpPane = new JLabel("Help information");

        audioCB.addItemListener(new TabManager(audioPane));
        nicCB.addItemListener(new TabManager(nicPane));
        tvCB.addItemListener(new TabManager(tvPane));

        config.addTab("System", null, configPane, "Choose Installed Options");
        config.addTab("Audio", null, audioPane, "Audio system configuration");
        config.addTab("Networking", null, nicPane, "Networking configuration");
        config.addTab("Video", null, tvPane, "Video system configuration");
        config.addTab("Help", null, helpPane, "How Do I...");

        getContentPane( ).add(config, BorderLayout.CENTER);
    }

    class TabManager implements ItemListener {
        Component tab;
        public TabManager(Component tabToManage) {
            tab = tabToManage;
        }

        public void itemStateChanged(ItemEvent ie) {
            int index = config.indexOfComponent(tab);
            if (index != -1) {
                config.setEnabledAt(index, ie.getStateChange( ) == ItemEvent.SELECTED);
            }
            SysConfig.this.repaint( );
        }
    }

    public static void main(String args[]) {
        SysConfig sc = new SysConfig( );
        sc.setVisible(true);
    }
}
```

Constants

The BoxLayout class contains the two constants listed in Table 11-13.

Table 11-13. BoxLayout constants

Constant	Type	Description
X_AXIS	int	Used with the constructor to create a manager that lays out components along a horizontal axis. This constant can also be used with the constructor for the Box class.
Y_AXIS	int	Used with the constructor to create a manager that lays out components along a vertical axis. This constant can also be used with the constructor for the Box class.

Constructor

public BoxLayout(Container target, int axis)

The only constructor for this layout manager; it takes as input the container to manage and how the components should be laid out: left to right (X_AXIS) or top to bottom (Y_AXIS). Figure 11-13 shows an example of a horizontal panel (A) and a vertical panel (B). To prove this BoxLayout is just a layout manager, we'll use regular AWT panels and buttons.

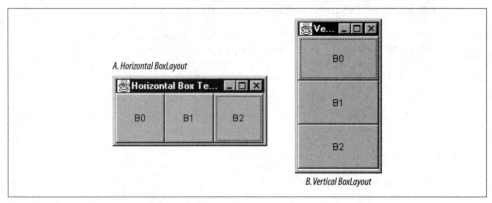

Figure 11-13. Horizontal and vertical BoxLayout-managed panels

Here's a look at the code to generate the horizontal box. (You need to change the axis you use in the constructor to get the vertical box. That example is online as *VBox.java*.)

```
// HBox.java
// A quick test of the BoxLayout manager using the Box utility class
//
import java.awt.*;
import java.awt.event.*;
import javax.swing.*;

public class HBox extends JFrame {
```

```
    public HBox( ) {
      super("Horizontal Box Test Frame");
      setSize(200, 100);
      Panel box = new Panel( );

      // Use BoxLayout.Y_AXIS if you want a vertical box.
      box.setLayout(new BoxLayout(box, BoxLayout.X_AXIS));
      setContentPane(box);
      for (int i = 0; i < 3; i++) {
        Button b = new Button("B" + i);
        box.add(b);
      }
      setDefaultCloseOperation(EXIT_ON_CLOSE);
      setVisible(true);
    }

    public static void main(String args[]) {
      HBox bt = new HBox( );
    }
  }
```

Well, maybe that's not really exciting since you can do the same thing with a well-constructed grid-layout manager. But the BoxLayout class does allow for components to be different sizes, unlike the GridLayout class. Recall from Figure 11-13 that we had a two-line text area as well as several checkbox components. The text area is somewhat taller than the checkboxes, but that doesn't bother the BoxLayout manager. Figure 11-14 shows the same application with altered background for the components. You can see the actual size of each component with respect to the layout manager.

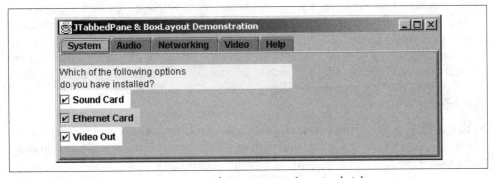

Figure 11-14. The BoxLayout manager with components of varying heights

Box alignments

One other thing to note about the BoxLayout class is the off-axis alignment of the components, dictated by the alignmentX and alignmentY properties of the Component class. For example, in a vertical box, the alignmentX property of the first component is used to determine the horizontal position of a component relative to the other components. Likewise, the alignmentY property dictates the vertical alignment of components in a horizontal BoxLayout.

The default alignments for the various components can throw things off. In the code example for Figure 11-13, we set the alignmentX property of the JTextArea to 0.0 to keep everything left-aligned. Without that manual adjustment, the text area tries to center itself on the screen. The checkboxes that follow then line up with their left edges on the same imaginary line as the center of the text area. Sometimes that's exactly what you want, but sometimes it isn't. Just be aware that some components occasionally need tweaking.

The OverlayLayout Class

Another layout manager in the Swing package is the OverlayLayout class. This layout manager is more of a facilitating manager for some of the Swing components, such as JMenuItem and AbstractButton. The purpose of this layout manager is to place components on top of each other based on some alignment points. This allows things like buttons and menu items to manage icons and text in the same visual area. Recall that a "center" alignment for a button with both an icon and a text label places the text directly over the icon. OverlayLayout understands how to arrange components that overlap.

The alignment points are values between 0.0 and 1.0 for both the horizontal and vertical axes. (For the horizontal axis, 0.0 is the left side of the component, 1.0 is the right side. The vertical axis runs from 0.0 at the top to 1.0 at the bottom.) You assign a horizontal and vertical pair of points to each component in the container. OverlayLayout then arranges the components so that their alignment points all occupy the same spot. To accomplish the previous icon and text example, you would set the alignments for the icon to 0.5 horizontal and 0.5 vertical. You would do the same for the text. However, if you wanted the text to show up underneath the icon but still centered horizontally, you would set the icon's alignments to 0.5 horizontal and 1.0 vertical. The text would use 0.5 horizontal and 0.0 vertical. Figure 11-15 illustrates these two scenarios.

As noted for BoxLayout, the OverlayLayout class implements the LayoutManager2 interface from the java.awt package. Again, you can find out more about layout managers in *Java AWT Reference* by John Zukowski (O'Reilly).

Constructor

One constructor does exist for creating an OverlayLayout manager:

public OverlayLayout(Container target)
    Create a layout manager for managing the components in a given container. Note that calling this constructor does not install the resulting layout manager for target. You still need to call setLayout( ). For example:

```
JPanel p1 = new JPanel( );
OverlayLayout overlay = new OverlayLayout(p1);
p1.setLayout(overlay);
```

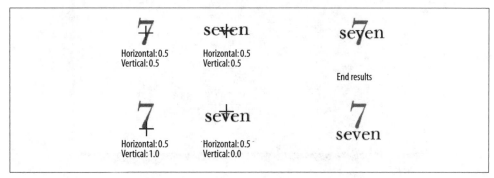

Figure 11-15. Arranging with OverlayLayout (crosshairs represent alignment points)

An OverlayLayout Example

Rather than contrive an example using the `OverlayLayout` manager, Figure 11-16 shows a simple program that lets you play with three buttons inside a panel, with an `OverlayLayout` manager running. You can type in the X- and Y-alignment values between 0.0 and 1.0 into text fields along the bottom. The text fields are organized as X and Y alignments for each of the three buttons (B1, B2, and B3 respectively). Click the Update button. The buttons in the floating panel rearrange themselves according to the values you enter. The gridlines show the bounds of the panel and its center. Try changing several of the values; this will give you an idea of how this layout manager might be used.

In Figure 11-16, you can see we placed B2 above and to the right of B1. We gave B3 centered alignment (0.5) for both axes. You can see how its center corresponds to the origin created by the polar opposite constraints of the other buttons—not the center of the container.

Admittedly, you probably won't be lining up buttons using this layout manager, but imagine controlling a multiline, multiicon label. This layout manager could prove useful in such situations.

Here's the code that produced this example. As with many of the examples, this one is more fun if you compile and run the program itself.

```
// OverlayTest.java
//
import java.awt.*;
import java.awt.event.*;
import javax.swing.*;

public class OverlayTest extends JFrame {
```

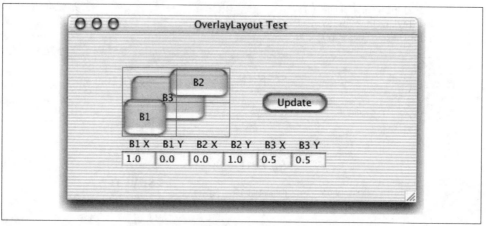

Figure 11-16. A demonstration of the OverlayLayout manager on three components

```
public OverlayTest( ) {
    super("OverlayLayout Test");
    setSize(500, 300);
    setDefaultCloseOperation(EXIT_ON_CLOSE);

    final Container c = getContentPane( );
    c.setLayout(new GridBagLayout( ));

    final JPanel p1 = new GridPanel( );
    final OverlayLayout overlay = new OverlayLayout(p1);
    p1.setLayout(overlay);

    final JButton jb1 = new JButton("B1");
    final JButton jb2 = new JButton("B2");
    final JButton jb3 = new JButton("B3");

    Dimension b1 = new Dimension(60, 50);
    Dimension b2 = new Dimension(80, 40);
    Dimension b3 = new Dimension(100, 60);

    jb1.setMinimumSize(b1);
    jb1.setMaximumSize(b1);
    jb1.setPreferredSize(b1);
    jb2.setMinimumSize(b2);
    jb2.setMaximumSize(b2);
    jb2.setPreferredSize(b2);
    jb3.setMinimumSize(b3);
    jb3.setMaximumSize(b3);
    jb3.setPreferredSize(b3);

    SimpleReporter reporter = new SimpleReporter( );
    jb1.addActionListener(reporter);
    jb2.addActionListener(reporter);
    jb3.addActionListener(reporter);
```

```
        p1.add(jb1);
        p1.add(jb2);
        p1.add(jb3);

        JPanel p2 = new JPanel();
        p2.setLayout(new GridLayout(2,6));
        p2.add(new JLabel("B1 X", JLabel.CENTER));
        p2.add(new JLabel("B1 Y", JLabel.CENTER));
        p2.add(new JLabel("B2 X", JLabel.CENTER));
        p2.add(new JLabel("B2 Y", JLabel.CENTER));
        p2.add(new JLabel("B3 X", JLabel.CENTER));
        p2.add(new JLabel("B3 Y", JLabel.CENTER));
        p2.add(new JLabel(""));

        final JTextField x1 = new JTextField("0.0", 4); // B1 x alignment
        final JTextField y1 = new JTextField("0.0", 4); // B1 y alignment
        final JTextField x2 = new JTextField("0.0", 4);
        final JTextField y2 = new JTextField("0.0", 4);
        final JTextField x3 = new JTextField("0.0", 4);
        final JTextField y3 = new JTextField("0.0", 4);

        p2.add(x1);
        p2.add(y1);
        p2.add(x2);
        p2.add(y2);
        p2.add(x3);
        p2.add(y3);


        GridBagConstraints constraints = new GridBagConstraints();
        c.add(p1, constraints);

        constraints.gridx = 1;
        JButton updateButton = new JButton("Update");
        updateButton.addActionListener(new ActionListener() {
            public void actionPerformed(ActionEvent ae) {
                jb1.setAlignmentX(Float.valueOf(x1.getText().trim()).floatValue());
                jb1.setAlignmentY(Float.valueOf(y1.getText().trim()).floatValue());
                jb2.setAlignmentX(Float.valueOf(x2.getText().trim()).floatValue());
                jb2.setAlignmentY(Float.valueOf(y2.getText().trim()).floatValue());
                jb3.setAlignmentX(Float.valueOf(x3.getText().trim()).floatValue());
                jb3.setAlignmentY(Float.valueOf(y3.getText().trim()).floatValue());

                p1.revalidate();
            }
        });
        c.add(updateButton, constraints);

        constraints.gridx = 0;
        constraints.gridy = 1;
        constraints.gridwidth = 2;
        c.add(p2, constraints);
    }
```

```
        public static void main(String args[]) {
            OverlayTest ot = new OverlayTest();
            ot.setVisible(true);
        }

        public class SimpleReporter implements ActionListener {
            public void actionPerformed(ActionEvent ae) {
                System.out.println(ae.getActionCommand());
            }
        }

        public class GridPanel extends JPanel {
            public void paint(Graphics g) {
                super.paint(g);
                int w = getSize().width;
                int h = getSize().height;

                g.setColor(Color.red);
                g.drawRect(0,0,w-1,h-1);
                g.drawLine(w/2,0,w/2,h);
                g.drawLine(0,h/2,w,h/2);
            }
        }
    }
```

When the user clicks Update, we receive an ActionEvent. The listener for this event does all the real work. We then query all the text fields, convert their contents into numbers, and set the alignment values. To make the new alignments take effect, we invalidate the layout and tell our panel to redo its layout.

The SizeRequirements Class

Laying out all of these components for the different layout managers involves a lot of calculations that can be quite similar. The layout manager needs to end up with a list of (x,y) coordinates for each component as well as a list of widths and heights. The SizeRequirements class provides several convenience methods for doing exactly these kinds of calculations.

Layout managers generally need two types of calculations: aligned and tiled. You can see both of these kinds of calculations in action with the FlowLayout manager. If you place two buttons and a list on a panel managed by FlowLayout, you get the components laid out left to right, each vertically centered relative to the others. The left-to-right x coordinates and widths for each component are an example of tiled requirements. The y coordinates and heights are an example of aligned requirements. You can perform both types of calculations with the static methods of this class. One thing to remember when using SizeRequirements, however, is that it calculates only one axis at a time—you can't make one call to get both the (x, y) and (width, height) lists. It's not really a big hassle though; just make one call for the x and width values and another for the y and height values.

Fields

public float alignment
> This field represents the actual alignment used for the component. A "center" alignment would be 0.5. A "left" alignment (when calculating widths) would be 0.0.

public int maximum
> This field represents the maximum size allowed for this component. If you are calculating widths, this should be the same as getMaximumSize( ).width for the component. For heights, this should be the same as getMaximumSize( ).height.

public int minimum
> This field represents the minimum size required for this component. If you are calculating widths, this should be the same as getMinimumSize( ).width for the component. For heights, this should be the same as getMinimumSize( ).height.

public int preferred
> This field represents the preferred size for this component. If you are calculating widths, this should be the same as getPreferredSize( ).width for the component. For heights, this should be the same as getPreferredSize( ).height.

Constructors

public SizeRequirements( )
> This constructor creates a SizeRequirements object with centered alignment and all sizes set to 0.

public SizeRequirements(int min, int pref, int max, float a)
> This constructor creates a SizeRequirements object with the given alignment a, minimum size min, preferred size pref, and maximum size max.

Methods

public static int[] adjustSizes(int delta, SizeRequirements[] children)
> Return an array of new preferred sizes for children based on delta. delta should be a change in the allocated space. The children are shortened or lengthened to accommodate the new allocation.

public static void calculateAlignedPositions(int allocated, SizeRequirements total, SizeRequirements[] children, int[] offsets, int[] spans)
public static void calculateTiledPositions(int allocated, SizeRequirements total, SizeRequirements[] children, int[] offsets, int[] spans)
> These methods calculate the offsets (x or y coordinates) and spans (widths or heights) for components that are to be laid out in an aligned or tiled manner, respectively. For example, if you were laying out a single row of buttons, you could use this method to calculate the x coordinate for the upper-left corner and the width of the button. The allocated parameter dictates how much space is allocated while total determines the overall SizeRequirements for the

children. (This value can be null or can be easily retrieved by calling getAlignedSizeRequirements( ) or getTiledSizeRequirements( ), respectively.)

public static SizeRequirements
  getAlignedSizeRequirements(SizeRequirements[] children)
    This method calculates the space required for a group of children (themselves described by a SizeRequirements object in the array) that should be aligned according to their individual alignments. The resulting SizeRequirements object has an alignment of 0.5. If children has zero elements, a default SizeRequirements object is returned.

public static SizeRequirements getTiledSizeRequirements(SizeRequirements[] children)
    This method calculates the space required for a group of children (themselves described by a SizeRequirements object in the array) that should be placed end to end, or tiled. The resulting SizeRequirements object has an alignment of 0.5. If children has zero elements, a default SizeRequirements object is returned.

The SpringLayout Class

With SDK 1.4, a new—but not really new—layout manager was added. The SpringLayout manager uses the notion of springs and struts to keep everything in place. A version of SpringLayout existed in the early alpha and betas of the Swing package, but it was not included because the Swing team felt it still needed too much work. While it still needs a bit of work, it has come a long way. Its inclusion in SDK 1.4 is a testament to that progress. The class diagram for SpringLayout and its helpers is shown in Figure 11-17.

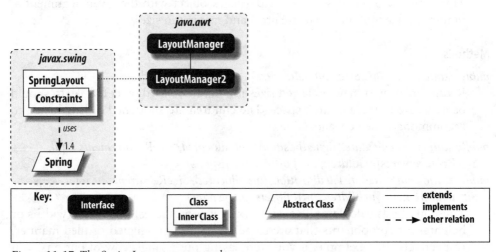

Figure 11-17. The SpringLayout manager classes

Before you dive too deeply into this layout manager, you should know that its purpose in life is to aid GUI builders and other code-generating tools. It can certainly be hand-coded—and we have the examples to prove it—but you'll often leave this layout manager to the aforementioned tools. (If you want a flexible replacement for the GridBagLayout, you might want to take a look at the RelativeLayout manager written by our own Jim Elliott. The complete package with docs, tutorial, and source code can be found on this book's web site, *http://www.oreilly.com/catalog/jswing2/*.)

Springs and Struts

Now that you're here for the long haul, let's look at the core of the SpringLayout manager's approach to component layout: spring and struts. A *spring* is effectively a triplet representing a range of values. It contains its minimum, preferred, and maximum lengths. A *strut* is a spring with all the spring removed—its minimum, preferred, and maximum lengths are identical. With SpringLayout at the helm, you use springs and struts to specify the bounds (x, y, width, height) of all your components. (You can mimic the null layout manager by using only struts.)

The not-so-obvious big win in this layout manager is that springs can be anchored between the edges of components and will maintain their relationship even when the container is resized. This makes it possible to create layouts that would be difficult in other managers. While you could probably use a grand GridBagLayout to do the trick, SpringLayout should provide better performance once it's all fixed up and finalized.

Figure 11-18 shows a simple application that uses SpringLayout. We position directional buttons over a large picture for navigation. Notice how the North button stays horizontally centered and anchored to the top edge of the application after we resize the frame. The other buttons behave similarly. Just to reiterate, you could certainly accomplish this with nested containers or a properly constructed GridBagLayout; the SpringLayout should simply prove to be the most maintainable over the long haul. We'll look at the source code for this example after we examine the API in more detail.

Constants

The SpringLayout class thinks of components in terms of their edges. Several constants have been defined for the edges, as shown in Table 11-14.

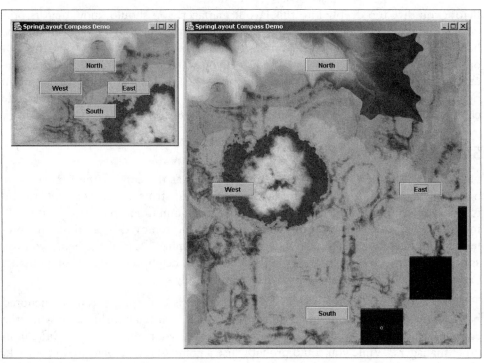

Figure 11-18. A SpringLayout-managed container at two different sizes

Table 11-14. SpringLayout constants

Constant	Type	Description
NORTH	String	The top edge of the component. Corresponds to the y value of the component's bounding box.
SOUTH	String	The bottom edge of the component. Corresponds to the y value of the bounding box plus the height of the component.
WEST	String	The left edge of the component. Corresponds to the x value of the component's bounding box.
EAST	String	The right edge of the component. Corresponds to the x value of the bounding box plus the width of the component.

Constructor

The only constructor for SpringLayout is the default constructor. Similar to the way one uses GridBagLayout and CardLayout, you'll want to keep a reference to your SpringLayout manager handy.

public SpringLayout()

Create a new SpringLayout manager.

Constraint Methods

As with other layout managers, a majority of the methods in SpringLayout are devoted to meeting the contract of the LayoutManager and LayoutManager2 interfaces. The methods that make this manager interesting, however, are the methods dealing with components' constraints.

public SpringLayout.Constraints getConstraints(Component c)
> This method returns the entire set of constraints (the springs on all four edges) for the given component. We discuss the Constraints inner class in the next section.

public Spring getConstraint(String edgeName, Component c)
> This method returns a particular spring for the specified edge (edgeName) of the given component (c).

public void putConstraint(String e1, Component c1, int pad, String e2, Component c2)
public void putConstraint(String e1, Component c1, Spring s, String e2, Component c2)
> These methods place a constraint (spring) between two edges. The first method is just a convenience method that uses pad to create a strut. e1 and c1 are associated with the dependent component while e2 and c2 refer to the anchor.

No method exists for setting all of the constraints at one time, but you can use the object returned by the getConstraints( ) method to manipulate all of the edges on a component.

Here's the source code for the example application shown in Figure 11-18. Notice the three primary means of positioning components in a SpringLayout. We add the North and South buttons to the container with prebuilt constraints. The East and West buttons are positioned by retrieving their existing constraints and setting up the bounding box for the component. For example, the North and East buttons are set up like this:

```
// Add North button.
c.add(nb, new SpringLayout.Constraints(northX, offsetS, widthS, heightS));

// Add East button.
c.add(eb);
sl.getConstraints(eb).setX(eastX);
sl.getConstraints(eb).setY(eastY);
sl.getConstraints(eb).setWidth(widthS);
sl.getConstraints(eb).setHeight(heightS);
```

As an example of the third mechanism for positioning components, the viewport for the graphics image is laid out using several putConstraint( ) calls:

```
c.add(viewport);
// The order here is important. You need to have a valid width and height
// in place before binding the (x,y) location.
sl.putConstraint(SpringLayout.SOUTH, viewport, Spring.minus(borderS),
                SpringLayout.SOUTH, c);
```

```
      sl.putConstraint(SpringLayout.EAST, viewport, Spring.minus(borderS),
                   SpringLayout.EAST, c);
      sl.putConstraint(SpringLayout.NORTH, viewport, topBorder, SpringLayout.NORTH, c);
      sl.putConstraint(SpringLayout.WEST, viewport, leftBorder, SpringLayout.WEST, c);
```

You might notice some funky springs in this example. We'll explain the centering spring and the sum( ) and minus( ) methods in the section on the Spring class itself.

```
// CompassButtons.java
//
import javax.swing.*;
import java.awt.*;

public class CompassButtons extends JFrame {

    JButton nb = new JButton("North");
    JButton sb = new JButton("South");
    JButton eb = new JButton("East");
    JButton wb = new JButton("West");
    JViewport viewport = new JViewport( );

    public CompassButtons( ) {
        super("SpringLayout Compass Demo");
        setSize(500,300);
        setDefaultCloseOperation(EXIT_ON_CLOSE);

        SpringLayout sl = new SpringLayout( );
        Container c = getContentPane( );
        c.setLayout(sl);

        int offset = 50;   // Gap between buttons and outside edge
        int w      = 80;   // Width of buttons
        int h      = 26;   // Height of buttons
        int border =  3;   // Border around viewport

        Spring offsetS      = Spring.constant(offset);
        Spring borderS      = Spring.constant(border);
        Spring widthS       = Spring.constant(w);
        Spring halfWidthS   = FractionSpring.half(widthS);
        Spring heightS      = Spring.constant(h);
        Spring halfHeightS  = FractionSpring.half(heightS);
        Spring leftEdgeS    = sl.getConstraint(SpringLayout.WEST, c);
        Spring topEdgeS     = sl.getConstraint(SpringLayout.NORTH, c);
        Spring rightEdgeS   = sl.getConstraint(SpringLayout.EAST, c);
        Spring bottomEdgeS  = sl.getConstraint(SpringLayout.SOUTH, c);
        Spring xCenterS     = FractionSpring.half(rightEdgeS);
        Spring yCenterS     = FractionSpring.half(bottomEdgeS);
        Spring leftBorder   = Spring.sum(leftEdgeS, borderS);
        Spring topBorder    = Spring.sum(topEdgeS, borderS);

        Spring northX = Spring.sum(xCenterS, Spring.minus(halfWidthS));
        Spring southY = Spring.sum(bottomEdgeS, Spring.minus(Spring.sum(heightS,
                                                                offsetS)));
        Spring eastX = Spring.sum(rightEdgeS, Spring.minus(Spring.sum(widthS, offsetS)));
        Spring eastY = Spring.sum(yCenterS, Spring.minus(halfHeightS));
```

```
        c.add(nb, new SpringLayout.Constraints(northX, offsetS, widthS, heightS));
        c.add(sb, new SpringLayout.Constraints(northX, southY, widthS, heightS));

        c.add(wb);
        sl.getConstraints(wb).setX(offsetS);
        sl.getConstraints(wb).setY(eastY);
        sl.getConstraints(wb).setWidth(widthS);
        sl.getConstraints(wb).setHeight(heightS);

        c.add(eb);
        sl.getConstraints(eb).setX(eastX);
        sl.getConstraints(eb).setY(eastY);
        sl.getConstraints(eb).setWidth(widthS);
        sl.getConstraints(eb).setHeight(heightS);

        c.add(viewport); // This sets a bounds of (0,0,pref_width,pref_height)
        // The order here is important. You need to have a valid width and height
        // in place before binding the (x,y) location.
        sl.putConstraint(SpringLayout.SOUTH, viewport, Spring.minus(borderS),
                    SpringLayout.SOUTH, c);
        sl.putConstraint(SpringLayout.EAST, viewport, Spring.minus(borderS),
                    SpringLayout.EAST, c);
        sl.putConstraint(SpringLayout.NORTH, viewport, topBorder,
                    SpringLayout.NORTH, c);
        sl.putConstraint(SpringLayout.WEST, viewport, leftBorder,
                    SpringLayout.WEST, c);

        ImageIcon icon = new ImageIcon(getClass().getResource("terrain.gif"));
        viewport.setView(new JLabel(icon));

        // Hook up the buttons. See the CompassScroller class (online) for details
        // on controlling the viewport.
        nb.setActionCommand(CompassScroller.NORTH);
        sb.setActionCommand(CompassScroller.SOUTH);
        wb.setActionCommand(CompassScroller.WEST);
        eb.setActionCommand(CompassScroller.EAST);
        CompassScroller scroller = new CompassScroller(viewport);
        nb.addActionListener(scroller);
        sb.addActionListener(scroller);
        eb.addActionListener(scroller);
        wb.addActionListener(scroller);

        setVisible(true);
    }

    public static void main(String args[]) {
        new CompassButtons();
    }
}
```

The SpringLayout.Constraints Inner Class

SpringLayout.Constraints embodies the spring constraints placed on a single component in a SpringLayout-managed container. It holds the bounding box for a component, but it uses Spring references rather than ints for the x, y, width, and height properties.

Properties

The Constraints inner class consists entirely of the properties shown in Table 11-15. With the exception of the constraint property, these properties mimic the Rectangle class often used to describe the bounds of components. The constraint property is indexed by edge name (a String). See Table 11-14 for a list of valid edge names and their respective relationships to the x, y, width, and height properties.

Table 11-15. SpringLayout.Constraints properties

Property	Data type	get	is	set	Default value
constraint[i]	Spring	•		•	null
height	Spring	•		•	null
width	Spring	•		•	null
x	Spring	•		•	null
y	Spring	•		•	null

[i]indexed (by String values; see Table 11-14)

Constructors

There are several constructors for building a Constraints object. You might want to do this if you intend to build the constraints before adding the component to its container. (You can use the Container.add(Component, Object) method to accomplish this.)

public SpringLayout.Constraints( )
public SpringLayout.Constraints(Spring x, Spring y)
public SpringLayout.Constraints(Spring x, Spring y, Spring width, Spring height)
> These constructors all build Constraints objects. Any unspecified property is left as a null value. The first constructor creates a completely empty Constraints object while the second leaves the width and height properties null.

The Spring Class

So what are these Spring objects we keep seeing everywhere? Recall that they are essentially a collection of three values: a minimum, a maximum, and a preferred value. You can use a spring to describe the height property of a text area, for example. Its minimum is 25 pixels; its maximum is the height of the screen, say 1024, and its preferred height is 8 rows, or 200. By the same token, you can create a strut by specifying a spring with identical values for all three properties. For example, a text field might have 25 for its minimum, maximum, and preferred height.

Beyond the basic expandability of a spring, you can do some fun things with them. Springs can be manipulated using mathematical concepts (and achieve a semantically correct result). For example, you can add two springs together. The new spring consists of the sum of the minimums, the sum of the preferred values, and the sum of the preferred maximums. You can also negate a spring and effectively multiply each of its values by −1. Summing with a negated spring, then, becomes a difference operation.

Now here's where things get really interesting. When you sum two springs, the result is not calculated immediately. The resulting spring stores a reference to the two operand springs. When needed, the summed spring queries its subsprings, which has the practical upshot of making springs dynamic. If you change one spring in a sum, the sum changes too. This turns out to be very useful in layout managers. Attach a spring to the bottom of the container, and it stretches whenever the container stretches.

Consider the y property for the South button in the application shown in Figure 11-18. We can use subtraction to keep the button 50 pixels above the bottom of the frame, even after the frame has been resized:

```
Spring offset = Spring.sum(buttonHeight, Spring.constant(50));
Spring southY = Spring.sum(bottom, Spring.minus(offset));
```

Figure 11-19 shows the details of each spring behind this button. (You can refer back to the code for the syntax when creating all the springs you see in the diagram.)

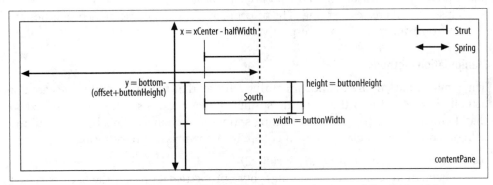

Figure 11-19. Constructing the x, y, width, and height springs (and struts) for the South button

Constant

Only one constant is defined for the Spring class, as shown in Table 11-16.

Table 11-16. Spring constant

Constant	Type	Description
UNSET	int	An indicator that this property has not yet been calculated. (Its internal value is Integer.MIN_VALUE.) Can be used as a notification to recalculate any cached values.

Properties

The properties for Spring shown in Table 11-17 are fairly straightforward. In addition to the minimum, maximum, and preferred properties, you can read and write the current value of the spring. Notice that the minimum, maximum and preferred properties are read-only. You can extend Spring if you need a more dynamic spring.

Table 11-17. Spring properties

Property	Data type	get	is	set	Default value
maximum	int	•			UNSET
minimum	int	•			UNSET
preferred	int	•			UNSET
value	int	•		•	UNSET

Creating springs

The default constructor for Spring is protected. It's (obviously) meant for subclasses. To create a spring, use the factory-style constant( ) methods:

public static Spring constant(int pref)
> This method creates a strut. The minimum, preferred, and maximum properties are all set to pref.

public static Spring constant(int min, int pref, int max)
> This method creates a spring. The minimum, preferred, and maximum properties are set from min, pref and max, respectively.

Manipulation methods

Three manipulations are defined for springs. Recall that the calculated values are not actually hardcoded into the resulting springs. References to s1 and s2 are stored so that if either spring changes, the resulting springs also change. (This is done with the help of a private inner class extension of Spring known as a "proxy spring.")

public static Spring max(Spring s1, Spring s2)
> This method returns a new spring whose properties represent the Math.max( ) of the respective properties of s1 and s2. In other words, the minimum property of the new spring is the max of s1.getMinimum( ) and s2.getMinimum( ).

public static Spring minus(Spring s)
> This method returns a new spring whose properties represent the negative of the respective properties of s1. In other words, the minimum property of the new spring is -s1.getMinimum( ).

public static Spring sum(Spring s1, Spring s2)
> This method returns a new spring whose properties represent the sum of the respective properties of s1 and s2. In other words, the minimum property of the new spring is equal to s1.getMinimum( ) + s2.getMinimum( ).

Other operations

As mentioned earlier, you can combine the manipulation methods to create other operations. In particular, Spring.sum(s1, Spring.minus(s2)) returns the difference of the respective properties in s1 and s2. The Math.min( ) function can be mimicked using Spring.minus(Spring.max(Spring.minus(s1), Spring.minus(s2))). Try it on paper—it really works!

Arranging Components

The combination of Spring math operations and constraints can make certain layouts easy to create (and easy to manipulate). We say "easy" in the "if you're designing a GUI builder" sense, of course. Figure 11-20 shows four buttons laid out in a vertical row with various Spring constraints holding them in place.

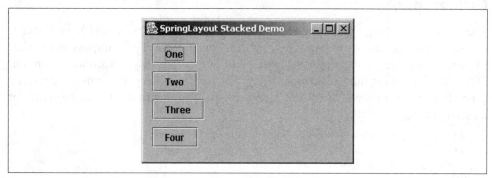

Figure 11-20. Vertically stacked buttons in a SpringLayout

To show off more of the Spring constraint combinations, we varied the layout code for these buttons:

```
// We'll leave all buttons at their preferred widths and heights. b1 is placed at
// (10,10).
c.add(b1);
sl.getConstraints(b1).setX(offsetS);
sl.getConstraints(b1).setY(offsetS);

// b2 is placed at (10, offset + b1.height + offset).
c.add(b2);
sl.getConstraints(b2).setX(offsetS);
sl.getConstraints(b2).setY(Spring.sum(Spring.sum(offsetS,
                    sl.getConstraints(b1).getHeight( )), offsetS));

// b3 is placed at (10, b2.south + offset).
c.add(b3);
sl.getConstraints(b3).setX(offsetS);
sl.getConstraints(b3).setY(Spring.sum(offsetS,
                    sl.getConstraint(SpringLayout.SOUTH, b2)));
```

```
// b4 is placed at (b3.west, b3.south + offset).
c.add(b4);
sl.putConstraint(SpringLayout.WEST, b4, 0, SpringLayout.WEST, b3);
sl.putConstraint(SpringLayout.NORTH, b4, offsetS, SpringLayout.SOUTH, b3);
```

You can use any one of the techniques shown on all the buttons, if you are so inclined. That said, there are a few consequences to the constraints we created in this example. For example, look at the y constraint of b2. It is simply the sum of two offsets and the height of b1. It is not dependent on the bottom edge of b1. It doesn't care where b1 is placed. The y constraints of b3 and b4, however, are dependent. If b2 moves down, so does b3—and if b3 moves down, so does b4.

One other fun constraint in this example is the left edge of b4. We tied it to the left edge of b3. If you change the x constraint of b3, b4 follows.

Custom Springs

There are some things that cannot be duplicated using sum( ), minus( ), and max( ). For those things, you can simply extend the Spring class. The compass navigation example in Figure 11-18 keeps the North and South buttons horizontally centered. (The East and West buttons are vertically centered.) To keep the buttons centered even after the user resizes the frame, we need a new Spring that returns the center of a parent spring:

```
// FractionSpring.java
//
import javax.swing.Spring;

public class FractionSpring extends Spring {

  protected Spring parent;
  protected double fraction;

  public FractionSpring(Spring p, double f) {
    if (p == null) {
      throw new NullPointerException("Parent spring cannot be null");
    }
    parent = p;
    fraction = f;
  }

  public int getValue( ) {
    return (int)Math.round(parent.getValue( ) * fraction);
  }

  public int getPreferredValue( ) {
    return (int)Math.round(parent.getPreferredValue( ) * fraction);
  }
  public int getMinimumValue( ) {
    return (int)Math.round(parent.getMinimumValue( ) * fraction);
  }
```

```
public int getMaximumValue( ) {
  return (int)Math.round(parent.getMaximumValue( ) * fraction);
}

public void setValue(int val) {
  // Uncomment this next line to watch when our spring is resized:
  // System.err.println("Value to setValue: " + val);
  if (val == UNSET) {
    return;
  }
  throw new UnsupportedOperationException("Cannot set value on a derived spring");
}

public static FractionSpring half(Spring s) {
  return new FractionSpring(s, 0.5);
}
}
```

If you look a bit closer, this class can actually handle any multiplier value. The factory method half( ) produces the spring we need most often, but you can use the public constructor to supply an alternative. You could certainly write other factory methods for common values you find useful. Maybe a goldenMean( ) method is in your future?

One method that you should pay attention to is setValue( ). In several derived springs (like our FractionSpring), the setValue( ) call does not make sense. Normally, we throw an UnsupportedOperationException to indicate that this required method from our abstract parent does not really apply. However, the special value UNSET can be used to help in a particular scenario: value caching. If the current value of the spring comes from an expensive operation, you can cache that value. If your spring is bound to another spring, such as the border of your container, changing the size of the container causes a chain of UNSET values to be passed to dependent springs. You could watch for UNSET and recalculate your spring values only when you receive it. (Try uncommenting the println( ) in our setValue( ) method and rerun the example. You should see four UNSET calls each time you resize the frame—one for each button.)

While it may take a few tries to wrap your brain around SpringLayout and Spring math, you can accomplish some complex layouts with one container and a single, efficient layout manager.

Other Panes

Chapter 10 showed you the basic "panes" such as JOptionPane. With the containers and layout managers shown in this chapter, you can create just about any pane you like. However, there are some very common application panes that we have not yet discussed. Chapter 12 describes some of the other panes available, including a file chooser and a color chooser.

CHAPTER 12
Chooser Dialogs

> **In this chapter:**
> - The JFileChooser Class
> - The File Chooser Package
> - The Color Chooser
> - The JColorChooser Class
> - Developing a Custom Chooser Panel
> - Developing a Custom Preview Panel
> - Developing a Custom Dialog

Just about every application you write these days needs to have a mechanism for opening and saving files. In the AWT, you can use the FileDialog class, but this is a heavyweight dialog that lacks the flexibility of the Swing components we've seen so far. The JFileChooser is Swing's answer to the FileDialog. The Swing package also contains a helper dialog for choosing colors (a common task during application configuration). We'll look at both of these dialogs in this chapter.

To get things started, Figure 12-1 shows the class hierarchy of the pieces we'll be looking at in this chapter.

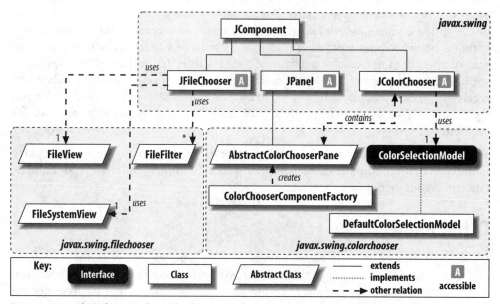

Figure 12-1. Class diagram for JFileChooser and JColorChooser

The JFileChooser Class

Since it plays such an integral role in just about every commercial application, let's look at the file chooser first. The JFileChooser class bundles a directory pane and typical selection buttons into a handy interface. Figure 12-2 shows the dialog window you get when you select the Save option of a simple application. As you might expect, other L&Fs can also be applied to this chooser.

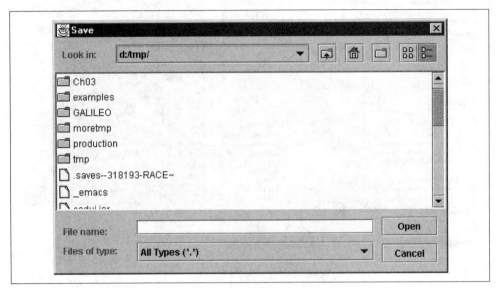

Figure 12-2. The JFileChooser save dialog (Metal L&F)

Figure 12-3 shows sample file choosers for open and save dialogs in the Windows, Motif, and Mac OS X L&Fs.

The application itself reports only which file (or files, if you use the Open option) you chose to open or save. Our application has a Pick Directory button that restricts the chooser to directories. The event handlers for each button do most of the interesting work. In each case, we create a new JFileChooser object, make any changes to the default properties that we need for the particular action, and then show the dialog. As you will see from the constants discussed later, the int returned from the showDialog( ) method indicates whether the user accepted a file selection or canceled the dialog. If we have a successful selection, our example application puts the name of the file into a display label.

Here's the code that generated the application. For this quick test, we create each file chooser dialog as we need it. You do not have to do this. You can save a reference to these dialogs and reuse them, just as you would other pop ups.

```
// SimpleFileChooser.java
// A simple file chooser to see what it takes to make one of these work
//
```

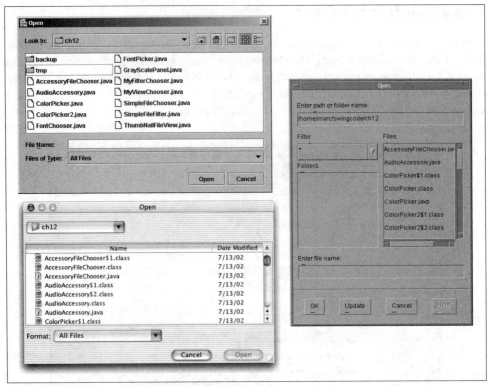

Figure 12-3. JFileChooser in the Metal, Motif, and Mac L&Fs

```java
import java.awt.*;
import java.awt.event.*;
import java.io.*;
import javax.swing.*;

public class SimpleFileChooser extends JFrame {

    public SimpleFileChooser() {
      super("File Chooser Test Frame");
      setSize(350, 200);
      setDefaultCloseOperation(EXIT_ON_CLOSE);

      Container c = getContentPane();
      c.setLayout(new FlowLayout());

      JButton openButton = new JButton("Open");
      JButton saveButton = new JButton("Save");
      JButton dirButton = new JButton("Pick Dir");
      final JLabel statusbar =
                  new JLabel("Output of your selection will go here");

      // Create a file chooser that opens up as an Open dialog.
      openButton.addActionListener(new ActionListener() {
```

```java
      public void actionPerformed(ActionEvent ae) {
        JFileChooser chooser = new JFileChooser( );
        chooser.setMultiSelectionEnabled(true);
        int option = chooser.showOpenDialog(SimpleFileChooser.this);
        if (option == JFileChooser.APPROVE_OPTION) {
          File[] sf = chooser.getSelectedFiles( );
          String filelist = "nothing";
          if (sf.length > 0) filelist = sf[0].getName( );
          for (int i = 1; i < sf.length; i++) {
            filelist += ", " + sf[i].getName( );
          }
          statusbar.setText("You chose " + filelist);
        }
        else {
          statusbar.setText("You canceled.");
        }
      }
    });

    // Create a file chooser that opens up as a Save dialog.
    saveButton.addActionListener(new ActionListener( ) {
      public void actionPerformed(ActionEvent ae) {
        JFileChooser chooser = new JFileChooser( );
        int option = chooser.showSaveDialog(SimpleFileChooser.this);
        if (option == JFileChooser.APPROVE_OPTION) {
          statusbar.setText("You saved " + ((chooser.getSelectedFile( )!=null)?
                       chooser.getSelectedFile( ).getName( ):"nothing"));
        }
        else {
          statusbar.setText("You canceled.");
        }
      }
    });

    // Create a file chooser that allows you to pick a directory
    // rather than a file.
    dirButton.addActionListener(new ActionListener( ) {
      public void actionPerformed(ActionEvent ae) {
        JFileChooser chooser = new JFileChooser( );
        chooser.setFileSelectionMode(JFileChooser.DIRECTORIES_ONLY);
        int option = chooser.showOpenDialog(SimpleFileChooser.this);
        if (option == JFileChooser.APPROVE_OPTION) {
          statusbar.setText("You opened " + ((chooser.getSelectedFile( )!=null)?
                       chooser.getSelectedFile( ).getName( ):"nothing"));
        }
        else {
          statusbar.setText("You canceled.");
        }
      }
    });

    c.add(openButton);
    c.add(saveButton);
    c.add(dirButton);
```

```
      c.add(statusbar);
    }

    public static void main(String args[]) {
      SimpleFileChooser sfc = new SimpleFileChooser();
      sfc.setVisible(true);
    }
  }
```

Properties

The JFileChooser class uses the properties shown in Table 12-1 for configuring most of the dialog's functionality.

Table 12-1. FileChooser properties

Property	Data type	get	is	set	Default value
acceptAllFileFilter	FileFilter	•			From L&F
acceptAllFileFilterUsed[b, 1.3]	boolean		•	•	true
accessibleContext	AccessibleContext	•			FileChooser. accessibleJFileChooser( )
accessory[b]	JComponent	•		•	null
actionListeners[1.4]	ActionListener[]	•			Empty array
approveButtonMnemonic[b, #]	int	•		•	0 (no mnemonic)
approveButtonText[b]	String	•		•	null
approveButtonToolTipText[b]	String	•		•	null
choosableFileFilters[b, *]	FileFilter[]	•			{getAcceptAllFileFilter( )}
controlButtonsAreShown[b, 1.3]	boolean	•		•	true
currentDirectory[b]	File	•		•	User's home directory
dialogTitle	String	•		•	null
dialogType[b]	int	•		•	OPEN_DIALOG
directorySelectionEnabled*	boolean		•		false
dragEnabled[1.4]	boolean	•		•	false
fileFilter[b]	FileFilter	•		•	AcceptAllFileFilter( )
fileHidingEnabled[b]	boolean		•	•	true
fileSelectionEnabled+	boolean		•		true

[1.3]since 1.3, [1.4]since 1.4, [b]bound, [o]overridden

[#]This property also has a set method that accepts a char argument.

[*]File filters are set using separate add, remove, and reset methods, which are discussed later.

[+]These properties are based on the fileSelectionMode property.

[$]Exists but is not implemented in 1.2, is partially implemented in 1.3, and is fully implemented in 1.4.

See also properties from the JComponent class (Table 3-6).

Table 12-1. FileChooser properties (continued)

Property	Data type	get	is	set	Default value
fileSelectionMode[b]	int	•		•	FILES_ONLY
fileSystemView[b]	FileSystemView	•		•	FileSystemView.getFileSystemView( )
fileView[b]	FileView	•		•	null
multiSelectionEnabled[b, $]	boolean		•	•	false
selectedFile[b]	File	•		•	null
selectedFiles[b]	File[]	•		•	Empty array
UI[b]	SplitPaneUI	•		•	From L&F
UIClassID[o]	String	•			"FileChooserUI"

[1.3]since 1.3, [1.4]since 1.4, [b]bound, [o]overridden

#This property also has a set method that accepts a char argument.

*File filters are set using separate add, remove, and reset methods, which are discussed later.

+These properties are based on the fileSelectionMode property.

$Exists but is not implemented in 1.2, is partially implemented in 1.3, and is fully implemented in 1.4.

See also properties from the JComponent class (Table 3-6).

The acceptAllFileFilter property provides access to the most common filter which, not surprisingly, accepts all files. You can set a more restrictive filter through the fileFilter property, or get a list of all the filters this dialog knows about with the choosableFileFilters property. The filters can also be affected by the fileHidingEnabled property, which, if true, does not display hidden files (such as files starting with "." on Unix systems). You can determine whether the dialog looks for files, directories, or both during the selection using the directorySelectionEnabled and fileSelectionEnabled convenience properties. The fileSelectionMode property is the real determining factor. You can use this property to select files, directories, or both with some of the constants presented later. Regardless of whether directories are selectable, double-clicking a directory opens that directory and makes it the new currentDirectory for the chooser. The number of files that can be selected (one or many) is determined by the multiSelectionEnabled property, which was fully implemented in the 1.4 release. (It was not implemented at all in 1.2. In 1.3, it can select multiple files, but the text field indicating which files are currently selected is not updated after the first file.) The selectedFile property contains the lead selection while the selectedFiles property holds several filenames, if multiple selections are allowed.

The remaining properties dictate the visual appearance of the dialog. You can create save, open, and custom dialogs with the dialogType property and some of the constants discussed later. The icons and descriptions used for files and folders are managed with the fileView and fileSystemView properties. (The data types supporting these properties are discussed in more detail in the next section.) You can customize the text in the dialog by setting the `dialogTitle` property for the pop up's title, the `approveButtonText` property for the OK button, and the `approveButtonToolTipText` property for the button's tooltip text. The `approveButtonMnemonic` property is a virtual key value (one of the `VK_` constants from `KeyEvent`) representing the letter you want underscored in the Approve button. Note that in setting this property, you can alternatively pass a `char` value to the set method.

File Chooser Accessories

The accessory property provides developers with an interesting hook into the dialog. You can create a custom component and attach it to the dialog. A typical example of such an accessory is an image viewer that shows you a thumbnail of any image file you have selected in the file selection window. Figure 12-4 shows a similar component that allows you to play music (*.au, .wav, .aiff*) files.

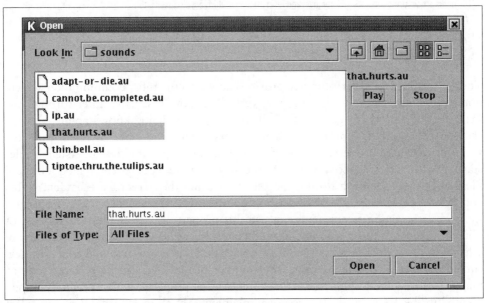

Figure 12-4. A file chooser with an audio accessory that can play a selected .au file

Here's the code for the accessory. To react to the user selecting a new file, your accessory needs to implement the `PropertyChangeListener` interface. (We attach it as a listener in the main application following this code.) Notice how we check the property change being reported in the `propertyChange()` method, so that we react only to new file selections. If it is a file selection event, we grab the new filename from the `PropertyChangeEvent` object. The `propertyChange()` method is the heart of the program. You should use this method to update your accessory as the user moves around the filesystem. We also use the `setCurrentClip()` method to keep the accessory's GUI in sync with the selected file. This keeps the Play and Stop buttons inactive for non-audio files so that users don't try to play a text file.

```java
// AudioAccessory.java
// A simple accessory for JFileChooser that lets you play music clips
//
import javax.swing.*;
import java.awt.*;
import java.net.*;
import java.beans.*;
import java.io.*;
import java.applet.*;
import java.awt.event.*;

public class AudioAccessory extends JPanel implements PropertyChangeListener,
ActionListener {

  AudioClip currentClip;
  String currentName="";
  JLabel fileLabel;
  JButton playButton, stopButton;

  public AudioAccessory( ) {
    // Set up the accessory. The file chooser will give us a reasonable size.
    setLayout(new BorderLayout( ));
    add(fileLabel = new JLabel("Clip Name"), BorderLayout.NORTH);
    JPanel p = new JPanel( );
    playButton = new JButton("Play");
    stopButton = new JButton("Stop");
    playButton.setEnabled(false);
    stopButton.setEnabled(false);
    p.add(playButton);
    p.add(stopButton);
    add(p, BorderLayout.CENTER);

    playButton.addActionListener(new ActionListener( ) {
      public void actionPerformed(ActionEvent e) {
        if (currentClip != null) {
          currentClip.stop( );
          currentClip.play( );
        }
      }
    });
    stopButton.addActionListener(new ActionListener( ) {
      public void actionPerformed(ActionEvent e) {
        if (currentClip != null) {
          currentClip.stop( );
        }
      }
    });
  }

  public void propertyChange(PropertyChangeEvent e) {
    String pname = e.getPropertyName( );
```

```
    if (JFileChooser.SELECTED_FILE_CHANGED_PROPERTY.equals(pname)) {
      // The user selected a file in the chooser.
      File f = (File)e.getNewValue();

      // Be reasonably sure it's an audio file.
      if ((f != null) &&
          (f.getName().toLowerCase().endsWith(".au") ||
           f.getName().toLowerCase().endsWith(".wav") ||
           f.getName().toLowerCase().endsWith(".aif") ||
           f.getName().toLowerCase().endsWith(".aiff"))
        ) {
        setCurrentClip(f);
      }
      else {
        setCurrentClip(null);
      }
    }
  }

  public void setCurrentClip(File f) {
    if (currentClip != null) { currentClip.stop(); }
    // Make sure we have a real file; otherwise, disable the buttons.
    if ((f == null) || (f.getName() == null)) {
      fileLabel.setText("no audio selected");
      playButton.setEnabled(false);
      stopButton.setEnabled(false);
      return;
    }

    // It seems that the audio file is real, so load it and enable the buttons.
    String name = f.getName();
    if (name.equals(currentName)) {
      // Same clip they just loaded; make sure the player is enabled
      fileLabel.setText(name);
      playButton.setEnabled(true);
      stopButton.setEnabled(true);
      return;
    }
    currentName = name;
    try {
      URL u = new URL("file:///" + f.getAbsolutePath());
      currentClip = Applet.newAudioClip(u);
    }
    catch (Exception e) {
      e.printStackTrace();
      currentClip = null;
      fileLabel.setText("Error loading clip.");
    }
    fileLabel.setText(name);
    playButton.setEnabled(true);
    stopButton.setEnabled(true);
  }
```

```
    public void actionPerformed(ActionEvent ae) {
      // Be a little cavalier here. We're assuming the dialog was just
      // approved or canceled, so we should stop any playing clip.
      if (currentClip != null) { currentClip.stop( ); }
    }
  }
```

Here's the application code that inserts the accessory into the chooser. The only real change we make is to the Open button's actionPerformed( ) method. Before we make the chooser visible, we use setAccessory( ) to get our audio accessory in place. We then attach the accessory as a property change listener to the chooser. This step ensures that the accessory is notified as the user selects new files.

```
// AccessoryFileChooser.java
//
import java.awt.*;
import java.awt.event.*;
import java.io.*;
import javax.swing.*;

public class AccessoryFileChooser extends JFrame {
  JFileChooser chooser = null;
  JLabel statusbar;

  public AccessoryFileChooser( ) {
    super("Accessory Test Frame");
    setSize(350, 200);
    setDefaultCloseOperation(EXIT_ON_CLOSE);
    Container c = getContentPane( );
    c.setLayout(new FlowLayout( ));

    JButton accButton = new JButton("Accessory");
    statusbar = new JLabel("Output of your selection will go here");
    chooser = new JFileChooser( );
    AudioAccessory aa = new AudioAccessory( );
    chooser.setAccessory(aa);
    chooser.addPropertyChangeListener(aa);  // To receive selection changes
    chooser.addActionListener(aa);     // To receive Approve/Cancel button events

    accButton.addActionListener(new ActionListener( ) {
      public void actionPerformed(ActionEvent ae) {
        int option = chooser.showOpenDialog(AccessoryFileChooser.this);
        if (option == JFileChooser.APPROVE_OPTION) {
          statusbar.setText("You chose " +
            ((chooser.getSelectedFile( )!=null)?
             chooser.getSelectedFile( ).getName( ):"nothing"));
        }
        else {
          statusbar.setText("You canceled.");
        }
      }
    });
    c.add(accButton);
```

```
      c.add(statusbar);
    }

    public static void main(String args[]) {
      AccessoryFileChooser afc = new AccessoryFileChooser();
      afc.setVisible(true);
    }
  }
```

Events

In addition to the property change events generated by most other Swing components, the JFileChooser also generates action events when the user clicks on the OK or Cancel buttons. The event is fired after the dialog is hidden.

public void addActionListener(ActionListener l)
public void removeActionListener(ActionListener l)
> If you want to listen directly to the OK or Cancel button events, you can add an ActionListener to the dialog. The accessory example listens to such events to stop playing any active audio clip.

public void approveSelection()
public void cancelSelection()
> You can programmatically fire an approval or a cancelation using these methods, simulating clicking on the OK or Cancel buttons. This can be useful if your accessory provides its own way of saying yes or no to the current selection. Both methods use the fireActionPerformed() method to send out the events. The APPROVE_SELECTION and CANCEL_SELECTION constants (listed later) are used for the appropriate command string.

protected void fireActionPerformed(String command)
> This protected method fires off a newly generated ActionEvent with the given command as the actionCommand of the event.

Constants

The JFileChooser class has several constants. These constants can be broken into two categories:

- The constants used for property change events, shown in Table 12-2
- The constants used as various property values, shown in Table 12-3

Table 12-2. FileChooser property names (for property change events)

Constant	Type	Description
ACCEPT_ALL_FILE_FILTER_USED_CHANGED_PROPERTY	String	The name used for the acceptAllFileFilterUsed property
ACCESSORY_CHANGED_PROPERTY	String	The name used for the accessory property

Constant	Type	Description
APPROVE_BUTTON_MNEMONIC_CHANGED_PROPERTY	String	The name used for the approveButtonMnemonic property
APPROVE_BUTTON_TEXT_CHANGED_PROPERTY	String	The name used for the approveButtonText property
APPROVE_BUTTON_TOOL_TIP_TEXT_CHANGED_PROPERTY	String	The name used for the approveButtonToolTipText property
CHOOSABLE_FILE_FILTER_CHANGED_PROPERTY	String	The name used for the choosableFileFilters property
CONTROL_BUTTONS_ARE_SHOWN_CHANGED_PROPERTY	String	The name used for the controlButtonsAreShown property
DIALOG_TITLE_CHANGED_PROPERTY	String	The name used for the dialogTitle property
DIALOG_TYPE_CHANGED_PROPERTY	String	The name used for the dialogType property
DIRECTORY_CHANGED_PROPERTY	String	The name used for the currentDirectory property
FILE_FILTER_CHANGED_PROPERTY	String	The name used for the fileFilter property
FILE_HIDING_CHANGED_PROPERTY	String	The name used for the fileHiding-Enabled property
FILE_SELECTION_MODE_CHANGED_PROPERTY	String	The name used for the fileSelectionMode property
FILE_SYSTEM_VIEW_CHANGED_PROPERTY	String	The name used for the fileSystemView property
FILE_VIEW_CHANGED_PROPERTY	String	The name used for the fileView property
MULTI_SELECTION_ENABLED_CHANGED_PROPERTY	String	The name used for the multiSelectionEnabled property
SELECTED_FILE_CHANGED_PROPERTY	String	The name used for the selectedFile property
SELECTED_FILES_CHANGED_PROPERTY	String	The name used for the selectedFiles property

The constants in Table 12-3 provide values for many of the properties in the JFile-Chooser class.

Table 12-3. FileChooser dialog constants

Constant	Type	Description
APPROVE_OPTION	int	The return value from the showDialog( ) methods, indicating that the user selected the approve option
APPROVE_SELECTION	String	The string to be used for the actionCommand property of the ActionEvent generated when the user approves the current selection

Table 12-3. FileChooser dialog constants (continued)

Constant	Type	Description
CANCEL_OPTION	int	The return value from the showDialog( ) methods, indicating that the user selected the cancel option
CANCEL_SELECTION	String	The string to be used for the actionCommand property of the ActionEvent generated when the user cancels the current selection
CUSTOM_DIALOG	String	A valid option for the dialogType property, indicating that this dialog supports a user-defined operation
DIRECTORIES_ONLY	int	A valid option for the fileSelectionMode property, indicating that only directories can be selected
ERROR_OPTION	int	The return value from the showDialog( ) methods, indicating that an error occurred
FILES_AND_DIRECTORIES	int	A valid option for the fileSelectionMode property, indicating that both files and directories can be selected
FILES_ONLY	int	A valid option for the fileSelectionMode property, indicating that only files can be selected
OPEN_DIALOG	int	A valid option for the dialogType property, indicating that this dialog is selecting files to be opened
SAVE_DIALOG	int	A valid option for the dialogType property, indicating that this dialog is selecting a file to be saved

Constructors

public JFileChooser( )

> Create a file chooser starting at the user's home directory. File choosers do not make a distinction between open and save at creation time. That aspect of a chooser is dictated by the dialogType property, which can be set at any time.

public JFileChooser(File currentDirectory)
public JFileChooser(String currentDirectoryPath)

> These constructors create new choosers starting at the specified directory.

public JFileChooser(FileSystemView fsv)
public JFileChooser(File currentDirectory, FileSystemView fsv)
public JFileChooser(String currentDirectoryPath, FileSystemView fsv)

> These constructors are similar to their above counterparts, but you can now specify the particular filesystem view you want to use. While the default filesystem views are not very interesting, this would be the easiest way to instantiate a file chooser using any custom view you might build from scratch. FileSystemView is discussed in more detail later in this chapter.

FileFilter Methods

The choosableFileFilters property does not have a proper "set" method, but you can modify the set of available filters using these methods:

public void addChoosableFileFilter(FileFilter filter)
public void removeChoosableFileFilter(FileFilter filter)
> Add or remove filters. The `FileFilter` class is discussed in detail later in this chapter.

public void resetChoosableFileFilters()
> Reset the list of choosable file filters to contain only the original "accept all" filter.

File and Directory Methods

The file methods check files to find the appropriate names, descriptions, and icons to display in the chooser according to the active `FileView` and `FileFilter` objects. If you open a `JFileChooser` and switch to the detail view of the files, you'll see many of these methods in action.

public boolean accept(File f)
> Return `true` if file f should be displayed.

public void changeToParentDirectory()
> Programmatically move the current directory up one level. At the root level, this method has no effect.

public void ensureFileIsVisible(File f)
> Ensure file f is visible in the chooser, which may mean changing the scroll location of the file list.

public String getDescription(File f)
> Return a description of file f. A common description is simply the file's name.

public Icon getIcon(File f)
> Return an icon to display in the chooser for file f. The icon could change depending on the type of file.

public String getName(File f)
> Return the name of file f. The chooser relies on the active `FileView` object to decide a file's name. The `FileView` object could alter the file's name for display—for example, to create an ISO 9660–compliant name.

public String getTypeDescription(File f)
> Return a brief description of the type of file f. The detail view of a directory might use this information.

public boolean isTraversable(File f)
> Return `true` if the file is a folder and can be opened.

public void rescanCurrentDirectory()
> Reload the current directory if its contents have changed.

Dialog Methods

protected JDialog createDialog(Component parent) throws HeadlessException

> This method allows you to easily create a dialog from subclasses that override JFileChooser's behavior. (For example, you can create a subclass that always produces choosers with a particular set of file filters.)

public int showDialog(Component parent, String approveButtonText)

> Make the dialog visible. If parent is not an instance of Frame, then the containing Frame object for parent is located and used. This method returns ACCEPT_OPTION if the user accepts a file, CANCEL_OPTION if the user cancels, or ERROR_OPTION if the user closes the dialog. Use this version of showDialog( ) to create a custom dialog with text you specify for the OK button (as opposed to one of the other show methods).

public int showOpenDialog(Component parent)
public int showSaveDialog(Component parent)

> You can use these methods to display chooser dialogs that have Open or Save on the Approve button. The dialogs are shown relative to the parent component.

The File Chooser Package

Under javax.swing, you'll find a package of helper classes for the JFileChooser. The javax.swing.filechooser package contains several classes for displaying and filtering files.

The FileFilter Class

The FileFilter class can be used to create filters for JFileChooser dialogs. The class contains only two abstract methods. It's important to note that extensions are not the only way to judge a file's fitness for a particular filter. The Mac filesystem, for example, can understand the creator of a file regardless of the file's name. On Unix systems, you might write a filter to display only files that are readable by the current user.

Constructor

public FileFilter( )

> The FileFilter class receives this default constructor at compile time; it is not defined in the class itself.

Filter methods

public abstract boolean accept(File f)

Return `true` if file `f` matches this filter. Note that you must explicitly accept directories (`f.isDirectory()` `==` `true`) if you want to allow the user to navigate into any subfolders.

public abstract String getDescription()

Return a short description to appear in the filters pulldown on the chooser. An example would be "Java Source Code" for any *.java* files.

Figure 12-5 shows a file chooser with custom filters for multimedia file types.

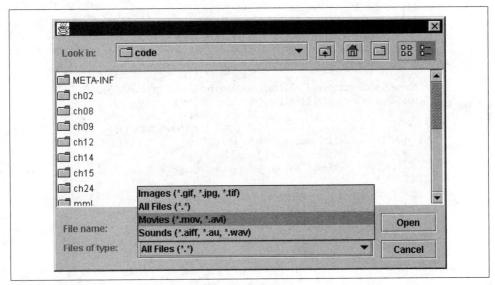

Figure 12-5. A custom set of filters for use with JFileChooser

Here's the code for the application. Before we make this chooser visible, we create and insert the three new filters for our media types. Other than that, it's pretty much the same code as our previous applications. The Swing demos included in the SDK provide access to a similar extension-based file filter class. However, we use this example anyway, as it illustrates the inner workings of a filter that should seem familiar to most programmers.

```
// MyFilterChooser.java
// Just a simple example to see what it takes to make one of these filters work
//
import java.awt.*;
import java.awt.event.*;
import java.io.*;
import javax.swing.*;
```

```
public class MyFilterChooser extends JFrame {
  public MyFilterChooser( ) {
    super("Filter Test Frame");
    setSize(350, 200);
    setDefaultCloseOperation(EXIT_ON_CLOSE);

    Container c = getContentPane( );
    c.setLayout(new FlowLayout( ));

    JButton openButton = new JButton("Open");
    final JLabel statusbar = new JLabel("Output of your selection will go here");

    openButton.addActionListener(new ActionListener( ) {
      public void actionPerformed(ActionEvent ae) {
        String[] pics = new String[] {"gif", "jpg", "tif"};
        String[] audios = new String[] {"au", "aiff", "wav"};
        JFileChooser chooser = new JFileChooser( );
        chooser.addChoosableFileFilter(new SimpleFileFilter(pics,
                                       "Images (*.gif, *.jpg, *.tif)"));
        chooser.addChoosableFileFilter(new SimpleFileFilter(".MOV"));
        chooser.addChoosableFileFilter(new SimpleFileFilter(audios,
                                       "Sounds (*.aiff, *.au, *.wav)"));
        int option = chooser.showOpenDialog(MyFilterChooser.this);
        if (option == JFileChooser.APPROVE_OPTION) {
          if (chooser.getSelectedFile( )!=null)
            statusbar.setText("You chose " + chooser.getSelectedFile( ).getName( ));
        }
        else {
          statusbar.setText("You canceled.");
        }
      }
    });

    c.add(openButton);
    c.add(statusbar);
    setVisible(true);
  }

  public static void main(String args[]) {
    MyFilterChooser mfc = new MyFilterChooser( );
  }
}
```

Here's the implementation of the filter class. You pass in an extension (or list of extensions) and a description of the extension(s) to the constructor. If you don't supply a description, the constructor builds a simple one for you based on the extensions you passed in. The only real work this class does happens in the accept( ) method, where we look to see if the file presented matches one of the supplied extensions.

```
// SimpleFileFilter.java
// A straightforward, extension-based example of a file filter. This should be
// replaced by a "first class" Swing class in a later release of Swing.
//
```

```
import javax.swing.filechooser.*;
import java.io.File;

public class SimpleFileFilter extends FileFilter {

  String[] extensions;
  String description;

  public SimpleFileFilter(String ext) {
    this (new String[] {ext}, null);
  }

  public SimpleFileFilter(String[] exts, String descr) {
    // Clone and lowercase the extensions
    extensions = new String[exts.length];
    for (int i = exts.length - 1; i >= 0; i--) {
      extensions[i] = exts[i].toLowerCase( );
    }
    // Make sure we have a valid (if simplistic) description.
    description = (descr == null ? exts[0] + " files" : descr);
  }

  public boolean accept(File f) {
    // We always allow directories, regardless of their extensions.
    if (f.isDirectory( )) { return true; }

    // It's a regular file, so check the extension.
    String name = f.getName( ).toLowerCase( );
    for (int i = extensions.length - 1; i >= 0; i--) {
      if (name.endsWith(extensions[i])) {
        return true;
      }
    }
    return false;
  }

  public String getDescription( ) { return description; }
}
```

The FileView Class

Another abstract helper class in the javax.swing.filechooser package is the FileView class. This class is implemented by the various L&Fs to supply icons and descriptions for the basic file and folder entries in the filesystem. While each L&F has a default implementation of this class, you can write your own and attach it to a file chooser to supply custom icons and descriptions for interesting types of files.

Constructor

public FileView()
    The FileView class has only this default constructor.

Methods

All of the methods for the FileView class are abstract and take one File as an argument. You fill in these methods to present a clean, consistent view of all files throughout the file chooser. Most custom views end up making decisions based on file information, such as the file's name or extension, before returning a result from these methods.

public abstract String getName(File f)
> Return the name of file f. While it's quite easy to return f.getName( ), you might want to return an all-uppercase version or a cross-platform, CD-ROM–compliant (ISO 9660) name, etc.

public abstract String getDescription(File f)
> Return a description of the file. The description could be a short abstract of the file's contents. Your file chooser might not necessarily display this information.

public abstract String getTypeDescription(File f)
> Return a description of the type of the file, such as "Directory" or "Bitmap Image."

public abstract Icon getIcon(File f)
> Return an icon appropriate for file f. This could be a folder icon, a file icon, or some specific icon based on other file information, such as its extension.

public abstract boolean isTraversable(File f)
> Answer questions about whether a directory can be opened. For example, Unix and Windows NT/2000 can prevent users from accessing directories for which they don't have permission. You could check permissions and return false if the user is not allowed to open a given folder. Rather than get an error when trying to open the folder, the user doesn't get the chance to try.

Figure 12-6 is an example of a custom FileView that (slowly!) displays tiny representations of any *.gif* or *.jpg* files in the directory instead of the generic icons. Since it loads the real image and scales it, rather than storing some separate set of real icons, you shouldn't try this on your collection of 5,000 JPEG clip-art images. It's great for small directories, though. This example also relies on the MetalIconFactory, so it does not run (properly) under other L&Fs. To avoid this problem, we force the use of the Metal L&F in the main( ) method by setting the swing.defaultlaf system property.

Following is the code for this particular file view. Look at the getIcon( ) method. That's where we decide which icon to return for a particular file. In this implementation, we list all directories as traversable and return a rather generic type description for our files. Notice that in the getName( ) method we check for an empty string. On Windows platforms, this empty string corresponds to one of the drive letters. The "name" of the file is empty, but the path contains the appropriate information, so we return that. If you're curious about the MetalIconFactory that we use to get the file and folder icons, check out Chapter 26.

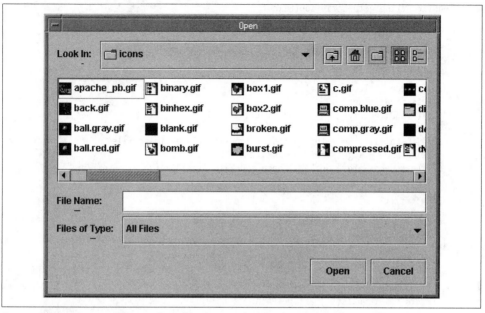

Figure 12-6. A custom file view for a file chooser that displays icons of image files

You might notice that we store a Component object (rather than JComponent) as our image observer. The reason for this is twofold. First, that's one class the createImage() method is defined in. Second, one obvious choice for the observer is the frame containing the application, which is frequently a JFrame, and JFrame does not descend from JComponent.

```java
// ThumbNailFileView.java
// A simple implementation of the FileView class that provides a 16 x 16 image of
// each GIF or JPG file for its icon. This could be SLOW for large images, as we
// simply load the real image and then scale it.
//
import java.io.File;
import java.awt.*;
import javax.swing.*;
import javax.swing.filechooser.*;
import javax.swing.plaf.metal.MetalIconFactory;

public class ThumbNailFileView extends FileView {

  private Icon fileIcon = MetalIconFactory.getTreeLeafIcon();
  private Icon folderIcon = MetalIconFactory.getTreeFolderIcon();
  private Component observer;

  public ThumbNailFileView(Component c) {
    // We need a component to create our icon's image.
    observer = c;
  }
```

```java
  public String getDescription(File f) {
    // We won't store individual descriptions, so just return the
    // type description.
    return getTypeDescription(f);
  }

  public Icon getIcon(File f) {
    // Is it a folder?
    if (f.isDirectory()) { return folderIcon; }

    // It's a file, so return a custom icon if it's an image file.
    String name = f.getName().toLowerCase();
    if (name.endsWith(".jpg") || name.endsWith(".gif")) {
      return new Icon16(f.getAbsolutePath());
    }

    // Return the generic file icon if it's not.
    return fileIcon;
  }

  public String getName(File f) {
    String name = f.getName();
    return name.equals("") ? f.getPath() : name;
  }

  public String getTypeDescription(File f) {
    String name = f.getName().toLowerCase();
    if (f.isDirectory()) { return "Folder"; }
    if (name.endsWith(".jpg")) { return "JPEG Image"; }
    if (name.endsWith(".gif")) { return "GIF Image"; }
    return "Generic File";
  }

  public Boolean isTraversable(File f) {
    // We'll mark all directories as traversable.
    return f.isDirectory() ? Boolean.TRUE : Boolean.FALSE;
  }

  public class Icon16 extends ImageIcon {
    public Icon16(String f) {
      super(f);
      Image i = observer.createImage(16, 16);
      i.getGraphics().drawImage(getImage(), 0, 0, 16, 16, observer);
      setImage(i);
    }

    public int getIconHeight() { return 16; }
    public int getIconWidth() { return 16; }

    public void paintIcon(Component c, Graphics g, int x, int y) {
      g.drawImage(getImage(), x, y, c);
    }
  }
}
```

Here's the application that uses this file view implementation. The only real change from the previous applications is in the properties we set for the chooser and our forced use of the Metal L&F.

```java
// MyViewChooser.java
// A simple example to see what it takes to make one of these FileViews work
//
import java.awt.*;
import java.awt.event.*;
import java.io.*;
import javax.swing.*;

public class MyViewChooser extends JFrame {
  JFrame parent;
  public MyViewChooser() {
    super("File View Test Frame");
    setSize(350, 200);
    setDefaultCloseOperation(EXIT_ON_CLOSE);
    parent = this;

    Container c = getContentPane();
    c.setLayout(new FlowLayout());

    JButton openButton = new JButton("Open");
    final JLabel statusbar = new JLabel("Output of your selection will go here");

    openButton.addActionListener(new ActionListener() {
      public void actionPerformed(ActionEvent ae) {
        JFileChooser chooser = new JFileChooser();

        // Set up our own file view for the chooser.
        chooser.setFileView(new ThumbNailFileView(MyViewChooser.this));

        int option = chooser.showOpenDialog(parent);
        if (option == JFileChooser.APPROVE_OPTION) {
          statusbar.setText("You chose " + chooser.getSelectedFile().getName());
        }
        else {
          statusbar.setText("You cancelled.");
        }
      }
    });

    c.add(openButton);
    c.add(statusbar);
  }

  public static void main(String args[]) {
    System.setProperty("swing.defaultlaf",
                       "javax.swing.plaf.metal.MetalLookAndFeel");
    MyViewChooser vc = new MyViewChooser();
    vc.setVisible(true);
  }
}
```

The FileSystemView Class

Another detail missing from the normal FileChooser dialog is a system-independent way of asking for a look at the entire filesystem. On Windows machines, for example, there are several "root" directories—one for each floppy drive, hard drive, CD drive, etc. On Unix systems (which includes Mac OS X), there is only one root directory, named "/". The abstract FileSystemView class is meant to be a source for system-independent views that map nicely to the real filesystem underneath your application. Currently, both Unix and Win32 systems have real implementations, and others are planned for release. (MacOS X relies on a Unix view of things.) Systems that do not have a full implementation use a generic filesystem view, similar to what is available through the standard java.io.File class.

Class instantiation method

public static FileSystemView getFileSystemView()
> The default implementation checks the file separator character to decide which filesystem view to return. A / returns a Unix view, \ returns a Win32 view, and everything else gets the generic view.

File and folder methods

If you do plan to build your own filesystem view, the following methods are the key pieces to look at:

public abstract File createNewFolder(File containingDir) throws IOException
> Create a new folder with some default name appropriate to the filesystem.

public File[] getFiles(File dir, boolean useFileHiding)
> Return a list of all of the files in dir. If useFileHiding is true, each file in dir is checked with isHiddenFile() before being added to the list.

public File[] getRoots()
> Return a list of "root" directories. On Unix or Mac OS X systems, this is the / directory. On Windows machines, this is a list of the active drive letters. In OS X, secondary partitions (including mounted removable media) are listed in the /Volumes directory. Users are accustomed to thinking of these as separate entities, so you might want to add your own code to include them as separate "roots."

public boolean isHiddenFile(File f)
> Return true if file f is a hidden file. What makes a file a hidden file differs from system to system.

public boolean isRoot(File f)
> Return true if file f maps to a root directory.

The Color Chooser

As the name indicates, the JColorChooser component is designed to allow users to pick a color. If your application supports customized environments (like the foreground, background, and highlight colors for text), this control might come in handy. You can pick a color from a palette and then look at that color in a preview panel that shows you how your color looks with black and white. The dialog also has an RGB mode that allows you to pick the exact amounts of red, blue, and green using sliders. The standard color chooser window looks like Figure 12-7.

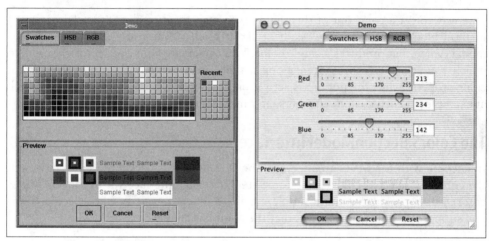

Figure 12-7. The default JColorChooser dialog in Swatches (left) and RGB (right) modes

The JColorChooser class provides a static method for getting this pop up going quickly. Here's the code that produced the screens in Figure 12-7:

```java
// ColorPicker.java
// A quick test of the JColorChooser dialog
//
import java.awt.*;
import java.awt.event.*;
import javax.swing.*;

public class ColorPicker extends JFrame {

  public ColorPicker() {
    super("JColorChooser Test Frame");
    setSize(200, 100);
    final Container contentPane = getContentPane();
    final JButton go = new JButton("Show JColorChooser");
    go.addActionListener(new ActionListener() {
      public void actionPerformed(ActionEvent e) {
        Color c;
        c = JColorChooser.showDialog(((Component)e.getSource()).getParent(),
                 "Demo", Color.blue);
```

```
        contentPane.setBackground(c);
      }
    });
    contentPane.add(go, BorderLayout.SOUTH);
    setDefaultCloseOperation(EXIT_ON_CLOSE);
  }

  public static void main(String args[]) {
    ColorPicker cp = new ColorPicker();
    cp.setVisible(true);
  }
}
```

One way to get a color out of this dialog is to wait for it to close (the showDialog( ) method blocks) and store the result of showDialog( ). But you are not limited to a modal dialog that produces a single color. You can create your own color choosers to which you attach a ChangeListener object that can detect any change in the current color property while the pop up is active, or even after it has been closed. We'll look at examples of such custom choosers later in this chapter.

The ColorSelectionModel Interface

In keeping with the MVC architecture, the JColorChooser uses a model to represent the currently selected color. The ColorSelectionModel interface (in the javax.swing. colorchooser package) is quite simple, having only one property (the selected color) and support for notifying listeners that the color has changed.

Property

The ColorSelectionModel class supports one property, shown in Table 12-4. The selectedColor property lets you access the color currently stored in the model.

Table 12-4. ColorSelectionModel property

Property	Data type	get	is	set	Description
selectedColor	Color	•		•	

Events

To indicate that the selected color has changed, implementations of ColorSelection-Model should fire a ChangeEvent whenever the selectedColor property changes.

Following the standard naming conventions, the following methods are required for managing ChangeEvent listeners:

public void addChangeListener(ChangeListener l)
public void removeChangeListener(ChangeListener l)

> As you might expect, these methods allow you to add and remove listener objects interested in receiving event notifications.

The DefaultColorSelectionModel Class

The `DefaultColorSelectionModel` class (in `javax.swing.colorchooser`) provides a straightforward implementation of the `ColorSelectionModel` interface. This is the selection model used by default in the `JColorChooser` class.

Properties

Table 12-5 shows the default value `DefaultColorSelectionModel` provides for the property inherited from `ColorSelectionModel`.

Table 12-5. DefaultColorSelectionModel properties

Property	Data type	get	is	set	Default value
changeListeners[1.4]	ChangeListener[]	•			Empty array
selectedColor[o]	Color	•		•	Color.white

[1.4]since 1.4, [o]overridden

Events

Because `DefaultColorChooserModel` implements `ColorChooserModel`, it fires a Change-Event whenever the `selectedColor` property changes.

In addition to the `addChangeListener()` and `removeChangeListener()` methods required by `ColorChooserModel`, the following method is provided to aid in dispatching change events:

protected fireStateChanged()
> You can use this method to fire a `ChangeEvent` whenever the color in the model is updated.

Constructors

public DefaultColorSelectionModel()
public DefaultColorSelectionModel(Color color)
> These constructors create new `DefaultColorSelectionModel` objects. If you call the first constructor with no color, `Color.white` is used.

The JColorChooser Class

The `JColorChooser` class allows you to create a standard dialog with a color palette from which users can select a color.

Properties

In addition to the typical UI properties of Swing components, the color chooser has the properties listed in Table 12-6. The `chooserPanels` property contains an array of all the chooser panels currently associated with this color chooser. You can get and set the entire array at once or, more commonly, you can add and remove chooser panels using some of the methods described later. The color property contains the currently selected color in the chooser. (This property is just a convenient access point for the selectedColor property of the selectionModel.) The previewPanel property contains the JComponent subclass that previews your color choice. (You can see an example of the default preview panel in Figure 12-7.) The selectionModel property dictates which selection model the chooser uses. The dragEnabled property allows you to drag colors from the chooser to another part of your application, but no transferHandler (inherited from JPanel) is in place to support this feature yet. You would need to supply a handler to make this property meaningful.

Table 12-6. JColorChooser properties

Property	Data type	get	is	set	Default value
accessibleContext	AccessibleContext	•			JColorChooser.AccessibleJColorChooser( )
chooserPanels[b]	AbstractColorChooserPanel[]	•		•	null
color	Color	•		•	Color.white
dragEnabled[1.4]	boolean	•		•	false
previewPanel[b]	JComponent	•		•	null
selectionModel[b]	ColorSelectionModel	•		•	DefaultColorSelectionModel
UI[b]	ColorChooserUI	•		•	From L&F
UIClassID[o]	String	•			"ColorChooserUI"

[1.4]since 1.4, [b]bound, [o]overridden

See also properties from the JComponent class (Table 3-6).

Events (Inherited from JComponent)

On its own, JColorChooser supports only PropertyChangeEvents, like all other Swing components. Using the static createDialog( ) method described below, you can attach your own ChangeListener to the color selection model for your chooser and react to changes in color anywhere in your program. You can even create a standalone chooser and add it to the container of your choice.

Constants

The JColorChooser class defines several constants for the property names used when firing PropertyChangeEvents, as shown in Table 12-7.

Table 12-7. JColorChooser property names for property change events

Constant	Type	Description
CHOOSER_PANELS_PROPERTY	String	The name of the chooserPanels property
PREVIEW_PANEL_PROPERTY	String	The name of the previewPanel property
SELECTION_MODEL_PROPERTY	String	The name of the selectionModel property

Constructors

public JColorChooser( )
public JColorChooser(Color initialColor)
public JColorChooser(ColorSelectionModel model)
> These constructors create new JColorChooser panes. The first two versions use a DefaultColorSelectionModel. In the first two versions, where you do not specify an initial color, Color.white is used. In the last version, the color is extracted from the model.

Dialog Methods

public static JDialog createDialog(Component c, String title, boolean modal,
  JColorChooser chooserPane, ActionListener okListener,
  ActionListener cancelListener)
> Create a (possibly modal) dialog window, with chooserPane as its main component. With this convenience method, you can add your own action listeners for the OK and Cancel buttons.

public static Color showDialog(Component c, String title, Color initialColor)
> Create a modal dialog that waits for the user to press either the OK or Cancel button. If the user clicks on OK, the current color in the chooser is returned; otherwise, null is returned. No errors or exceptions are raised if the user cancels.

Chooser Methods

public void addChooserPanel(AbstractColorChooserPanel panel)
> Add a new tab to the color chooser and place panel on that tab. An example using a custom chooser panel appears later in this chapter.

public AbstractColorChooserPanel removeChooserPanel(AbstractColorChooserPanel
  panel)
> Remove a panel from the chooser. If panel is found on one of the tabs, it is removed and returned. If the panel is not found, null is returned.

public void setColor(int c)
public void setColor(int r, int g, int b)
> You can use these methods as alternate ways of setting the color. They both affect the color property of JColorChooser. The first method expects a single

RGB color (where the 1-byte alpha channel is ignored). The second method takes red, green, and blue values ranging from 0 to 255.

The AbstractColorChooserPanel Class

If you don't find the two chooser panels sufficient for your needs, you can write your own chooser panel and add it to the chooser along with the others. If you decide to do that, the AbstractColorChooserPanel (in the javax.swing.colorchooser package) is your starting point. This class has several properties you can fill in and a few abstract methods you must supply. Both of the panels in Figure 12-7 are based on this class. Later, we'll take a look at writing our own custom chooser panel.

Properties

The AbstractColorChooserPanel supports the properties shown in Table 12-8. The smallDisplayIcon and displayName properties should return values used in the tabs of the JColorChooser's tabbed pane. They can be null, but you should have at least one return a valid object, so that your tab contains some form of identification. The colorSelectionModel property accesses the colorSelectionModel of the enclosing chooser. The mnemonic and displayedMnemonicIndex properties are hints to the L&F to provide keyboard shortcuts to access this panel. The defaults simply mean that no mnemonic is available—the panel must be activated via the mouse or Tab/arrow key navigation.

Table 12-8. AbstractColorChooserPanel properties

Property	Data type	get	is	set	Default value
colorSelectionModel	ColorSelectionModel	•			DefaultColorSelection-Model( )
displayedMnemonicIndex[1.4]	int	•			-1
displayName*	String	•			
largeDisplayIcon*	Icon	•			
mnemonic[1.4]	int	•			0 (no mnemonic)
smallDisplayIcon*	Icon	•			

[1.4]since 1.4

*The get call is abstract and must be supplied by the programmer, so no default value is available.

See also properties from the JPanel class (Table 8-1).

Protected helper method

protected Color getColorFromModel( )
> This protected method retrieves the current color from the ColorSelectionModel attached to this chooser panel.

Chooser panel methods

You'll need to override and use the following methods when developing your own panels. (You can see an example of a custom panel in the next section.)

protected abstract void buildChooser()
> Called to build your chooser panel when the color chooser is ready for it. It should be called only once.

public void installChooserPanel(JColorChooser enclosingChooser)
> This method is called when you add your chooser panel to the color chooser's tabbed pane. It registers this panel as a listener for change events coming from the chooser's `ColorSelectionModel`. You don't normally need to override this method, but if you do, be sure to call the corresponding method from the superclass.

public void uninstallChooserPanel(JColorChooser enclosingChooser)
> Called when the panel is removed from the chooser's tabbed pane. As you might expect, the panel is unregistered from the selection model. And, as with `installChooserPanel()`, call the corresponding method from the superclass if you plan to override this. (You aren't required to call the superclass, but if you don't, you need to be sure that your `install()` and `uninstall()` methods cooperate.)

public abstract void updateChooser()
> This method should update your chooser panel to reflect the current color in the `ColorSelectionModel`. It is called automatically when the panel is added to the chooser, so you do not have to figure out the current color in the constructor or `buildChooser()` method.

The ColorChooserComponentFactory Class

The `ColorChooserComponentFactory` class provides a few small methods for creating components common to a color chooser panel. The default chooser panels you see in `JColorChooser` come from this class, but you are certainly not restricted to using these components.

Methods

public static AbstractColorChooserPanel[] getDefaultChooserPanels()
> Return an array containing instances of the package-private `DefaultRGBChooser-Panel`, `DefaultSwatchChooserPanel`, and `DefaultHSBChooserPanel` classes. These are the panels attached to the RGB, HSB, and Swatches tabs in Figure 12-7.

public static JComponent getPreviewPanel()
> Return an instance of the package-private `DefaultPreviewPanel` class. This is the preview panel used in the screenshots in Figure 12-7.

Developing a Custom Chooser Panel

If you look at the JColorChooser component, you'll realize that it is really just a tabbed pane with a color previewer below it. You can have as many chooser panels in it as you like. Let's take a brief look at a panel that can be added to a color chooser. We'll create a simple panel for selecting a shade of gray with one slider rather than pushing each slider for red, green, and blue to the same value. Figure 12-8 shows the resulting panel; its source code is presented here.

```java
// GrayScalePanel.java
// A simple implementation of the AbstractColorChooserPanel class. This class
// provides a slider and a text field for picking out a shade of gray.
//
import java.awt.*;
import java.awt.event.*;
import javax.swing.*;
import javax.swing.event.*;
import javax.swing.colorchooser.*;

public class GrayScalePanel extends AbstractColorChooserPanel
                            implements ChangeListener, ActionListener {

  JSlider scale;
  JTextField percentField;

  // Set up our list of grays. We'll assume we have all 256 possible shades,
  // and we'll do it when the class is loaded.
  static Color[] grays = new Color[256];
  static {
    for (int i=0; i<256; i++) { grays[i] = new Color(i, i, i); }
  }

  public GrayScalePanel() {
    setLayout(new GridLayout(0, 1));

    // Create the slider and attach us as a listener.
    scale = new JSlider(JSlider.HORIZONTAL, 0, 255, 128);
    scale.addChangeListener(this);

    // Set up our display for the chooser.
    add(new JLabel("Pick your shade of gray:", JLabel.CENTER));
    JPanel jp = new JPanel();
    jp.add(new JLabel("Black"));
    jp.add(scale);
    jp.add(new JLabel("White"));
    add(jp);

    JPanel jp2 = new JPanel();
    percentField = new JTextField(3);
    percentField.setHorizontalAlignment(SwingConstants.RIGHT);
    percentField.addActionListener(this);
    jp2.add(percentField);
```

```
      jp2.add(new JLabel("%"));
      add(jp2);
   }

   // We did this work in the constructor, so we can skip it here.
   protected void buildChooser() { }

   // Make sure the slider is in sync with the other panels.
   public void updateChooser() {
      Color c = getColorSelectionModel().getSelectedColor();
      scale.setValue(toGray(c));
   }

   protected int toGray(Color c) {
      int r = c.getRed();
      int g = c.getGreen();
      int b = c.getBlue();
      // Grab the luminance the same way GIMP does.
      return (int)Math.round(0.3 * r + 0.59 * g + 0.11 * b );
   }

   // Pick a name for our tab in the chooser.
   public String getDisplayName() { return "Gray Scale"; }

   // No need for an icon
   public Icon getSmallDisplayIcon() { return null; }
   public Icon getLargeDisplayIcon() { return null; }
   // Finally, update the selection model as our slider changes.
   public void stateChanged(ChangeEvent ce) {
      getColorSelectionModel().setSelectedColor(grays[scale.getValue()]);
      percentField.setText("" + (100-(int)Math.round(scale.getValue() / 2.55)));
   }

   public void actionPerformed(ActionEvent ae) {
      int val = 100 - Integer.parseInt(ae.getActionCommand());
      getColorSelectionModel().setSelectedColor(grays[(int)(val * 2.55)]);
   }
 }
```

Here's the application that produced the new chooser. The only real change is that
we manually build the list of chooser panels for our chooser in the ColorPicker2
constructor:

```
// ColorPicker2.java
// A quick test of the JColorChooser dialog
//
import java.awt.*;
import java.awt.event.*;
import javax.swing.*;
import javax.swing.colorchooser.*;

public class ColorPicker2 extends JFrame {
```

Figure 12-8. A custom chooser panel added directly to a JColorChooser object

```java
JFrame parent;
Color c;

public ColorPicker2( ) {
  super("JColorChooser Test Frame");
  setSize(200, 100);
  parent=this;
  final JButton go = new JButton("Show JColorChoser");
  final Container contentPane = getContentPane( );
  go.addActionListener(new ActionListener( ) {
    final JColorChooser chooser = new JColorChooser( );
    boolean first = true;
    public void actionPerformed(ActionEvent e) {
      if (first) {
        first = false;
        GrayScalePanel gsp = new GrayScalePanel( );
        chooser.addChooserPanel(gsp);
      }
      JDialog dialog = JColorChooser.createDialog(parent, "Demo 2", true,
                   chooser, new ActionListener( ) {
                         public void actionPerformed(ActionEvent e) {
                           c = chooser.getColor( );
                         }}, null);
      dialog.setVisible(true);
      contentPane.setBackground(c);
```

```
      }
   });
   contentPane.add(go);
   setDefaultCloseOperation(EXIT_ON_CLOSE);
}

public static void main(String args[]) {
   ColorPicker2 cp2 = new ColorPicker2();
   cp2.setVisible(true);
}
}
```

Developing a Custom Preview Panel

In addition to creating custom color chooser panels, you can create your own pre-view panel. You can use any JComponent—just set the previewPanel property. As you update the color in the chooser, the foreground property of the preview panel changes. You can extend a container like JPanel and override the setForeground( ) method to gain more control over what parts of the pane are updated. Figure 12-9 shows a simple custom preview pane. We add two labels: one to show the fore-ground color (this label says, "This is a custom preview pane") and one to show the background color.

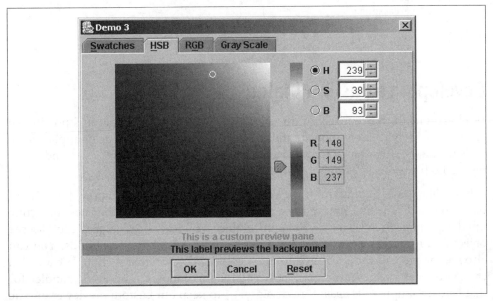

Figure 12-9. A custom preview panel added in a JColorChooser object

Remember that some L&Fs don't allow you to set the foreground or background colors of some components. If you're on a Mac OS X system, for example, you can run ColorPicker3 this way:

```
% java -Dswing.defaultlaf=javax.swing.plaf.metal.MetalLookAndFeel ColorPicker3
```

This custom pane is added to our ColorPicker3 chooser by setting the previewPanel property after we create the chooser object:

```
chooser.setPreviewPanel(new CustomPane());
```

Here's the code for the CustomPane class. We build it as an inner class.

```
public class CustomPane extends JPanel {
  JLabel j1 = new JLabel("This is a custom preview pane", JLabel.CENTER);
  JLabel j2 = new JLabel("This label previews the background", JLabel.CENTER);
  public CustomPane() {
    super(new GridLayout(0,1));
    j2.setOpaque(true);  // Otherwise, the background color won't show up
    add(j1);
    add(j2);
  }

  public void setForeground(Color c) {
    super.setForeground(c);
    if (j1 != null) {
      j1.setForeground(c);
      j2.setBackground(c);
    }
  }
}
```

Developing a Custom Dialog

While you might rely entirely on the standard color chooser dialog, it is possible to create a color chooser component and use it inside your own dialogs or applications. Let's take a look at a fancy font chooser that lets you pick the face, style, and color. Figure 12-10 shows an example of such a dialog.

It looks like a lot is going on in the code that built this dialog window, but it's not really that bad. The first part of the code is devoted to the tedious business of setting up the graphical-interface pieces. Notice that we create a regular JColorChooser object and never call either the showDialog() or createDialog() methods. You can also see the piece of code required to catch color updates in that section. We attach a ChangeListener to the ColorSelectionModel for the chooser. The event handler for that listener simply calls updatePreviewColor() to keep our custom previewer in sync with the color shown in the chooser.

You'll notice that we're storing our font information in a SimpleAttributeSet object. This object is used with the JTextPane class (and you can find out more about it in

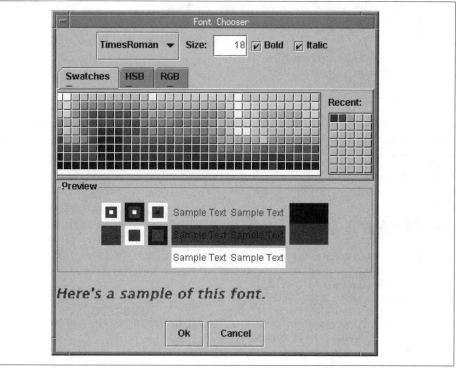

Figure 12-10. A custom dialog window, with a JColorChooser as one piece of it

Chapter 22). For right now, just know that it has some convenient methods for storing text attributes, such as the font name, bold/italic, and size.

Here's the startup code:

```
// FontChooser.java
// A font chooser that allows users to pick a font by name, size, style, and color.
// The color selection is provided by a JColorChooser pane. This dialog builds an
// AttributeSet suitable for use with JTextPane.
//
import javax.swing.*;
import javax.swing.event.*;
import javax.swing.colorchooser.*;
import javax.swing.text.*;
import java.awt.*;
import java.awt.event.*;

public class FontChooser extends JDialog implements ActionListener {

    JColorChooser colorChooser;
    JComboBox fontName;
    JCheckBox fontBold, fontItalic;
    JTextField fontSize;
    JLabel previewLabel;
```

```
SimpleAttributeSet attributes;
Font newFont;
Color newColor;

public FontChooser(Frame parent) {
  super(parent, "Font Chooser", true);
  setSize(450, 450);
  attributes = new SimpleAttributeSet();

  // Make sure that if the user cancels, the window does the right thing.
  addWindowListener(new WindowAdapter() {
    public void windowClosing(WindowEvent e) {
      closeAndCancel();
    }
  });

  // Start the long process of setting up our interface.
  Container c = getContentPane();

  JPanel fontPanel = new JPanel();
  fontName = new JComboBox(new String[] {"TimesRoman", "Helvetica", "Courier"});
  fontName.setSelectedIndex(1);
  fontName.addActionListener(this);
  fontSize = new JTextField("12", 4);
  fontSize.setHorizontalAlignment(SwingConstants.RIGHT);
  fontSize.addActionListener(this);
  fontBold = new JCheckBox("Bold");
  fontBold.setSelected(true);
  fontBold.addActionListener(this);
  fontItalic = new JCheckBox("Italic");
  fontItalic.addActionListener(this);

  fontPanel.add(fontName);
  fontPanel.add(new JLabel(" Size: "));
  fontPanel.add(fontSize);
  fontPanel.add(fontBold);
  fontPanel.add(fontItalic);

  c.add(fontPanel, BorderLayout.NORTH);

  // Set up the color chooser panel and attach a change listener so that color
  // updates are reflected in our preview label.
  colorChooser = new JColorChooser(Color.black);
  colorChooser.getSelectionModel().addChangeListener(new ChangeListener() {
    public void stateChanged(ChangeEvent e) {
      updatePreviewColor();
    }
  });
  c.add(colorChooser, BorderLayout.CENTER);

  JPanel previewPanel = new JPanel(new BorderLayout());
  previewLabel = new JLabel("Here's a sample of this font.");
  previewLabel.setForeground(colorChooser.getColor());
  previewPanel.add(previewLabel, BorderLayout.CENTER);
```

```
    // Add in the OK and Cancel buttons for our dialog box.
    JButton okButton = new JButton("Ok");
    okButton.addActionListener(new ActionListener( ) {
      public void actionPerformed(ActionEvent ae) {
        closeAndSave( );
      }
    });
    JButton cancelButton = new JButton("Cancel");
    cancelButton.addActionListener(new ActionListener( ) {
      public void actionPerformed(ActionEvent ae) {
        closeAndCancel( );
      }
    });

    JPanel controlPanel = new JPanel( );
    controlPanel.add(okButton);
    controlPanel.add(cancelButton);
    previewPanel.add(controlPanel, BorderLayout.SOUTH);

    // Give the preview label room to grow.
    previewPanel.setMinimumSize(new Dimension(100, 100));
    previewPanel.setPreferredSize(new Dimension(100, 100));

    c.add(previewPanel, BorderLayout.SOUTH);
  }
```

Let's pause and take a look at the next section of code. The actionPerformed( )
method monitors our font choices from the buttons and text field at the top of our
dialog. As font attributes change, we keep the AttributeSet object updated and
update our display label. (The listener for the color part of our dialog was attached
directly to the color chooser in the above code.) The updatePreviewFont( ) and
updatePreviewColor( ) methods allow us to change the font and color of the preview
label separately. That's a bit more efficient, especially when the user is picking a
color with an RGB slider.

```
    // Something in the font changed, so figure out what and make a
    // new font for the preview label.
    public void actionPerformed(ActionEvent ae) {
      // Check the name of the font.
      if (!StyleConstants.getFontFamily(attributes)
                      .equals(fontName.getSelectedItem( ))) {
        StyleConstants.setFontFamily(attributes, (String)fontName.getSelectedItem( ));
      }
      // Check the font size (no error checking yet).
      if (StyleConstants.getFontSize(attributes) !=
                              Integer.parseInt(fontSize.getText( ))) {
        StyleConstants.setFontSize(attributes, Integer.parseInt(fontSize.getText( )));
      }
      // Check to see if the font should be bold.
      if (StyleConstants.isBold(attributes) != fontBold.isSelected( )) {
        StyleConstants.setBold(attributes, fontBold.isSelected( ));
      }
```

```
  // Check to see if the font should be italic.
  if (StyleConstants.isItalic(attributes) != fontItalic.isSelected()) {
    StyleConstants.setItalic(attributes, fontItalic.isSelected());
  }
  // And update our preview label
  updatePreviewFont();
}

// Get the appropriate font from our attributes object and update
// the preview label.
protected void updatePreviewFont() {
  String name = StyleConstants.getFontFamily(attributes);
  boolean bold = StyleConstants.isBold(attributes);
  boolean ital = StyleConstants.isItalic(attributes);
  int size = StyleConstants.getFontSize(attributes);

  // Bold and italic don't work properly in beta 4.
  Font f = new Font(name, (bold ? Font.BOLD : 0) + (ital ? Font.ITALIC : 0), size);
  previewLabel.setFont(f);
}

// Get the appropriate color from our chooser and update previewLabel.
protected void updatePreviewColor() {
  previewLabel.setForeground(colorChooser.getColor());
  // Manually force the label to repaint.
  previewLabel.repaint();
}
```

The last segment of code helps us with the shutdown stage for our dialog. The getNewFont( ) and getNewColor( ) methods allow us to retrieve the selected font and color once the dialog is closed. We can also get the complete attribute set using getAttributes( ). The closeAndSave( ) method stores the font and color information from our preview label into newFont and newColor while closeAndCancel( ) puts null into both fields. After showing this dialog, the application using it should check the value of newFont or newColor to determine whether the user accepted a font choice.

```
public Font getNewFont() { return newFont; }
public Color getNewColor() { return newColor; }
public AttributeSet getAttributes() { return attributes; }

public void closeAndSave() {
  // Save font and color information.
  newFont = previewLabel.getFont();
  newColor = previewLabel.getForeground();

  // Close the window.
  setVisible(false);
}

public void closeAndCancel() {
  // Erase any font information and then close the window.
  newFont = null;
```

```
      newColor = null;
      setVisible(false);
    }
  }
```

Here's the application that puts this dialog to use. It's similar to our first color picker. A single button in the application causes the font chooser dialog to be displayed, and whatever font the user picks through the dialog becomes the font for the button. As with that first program, the main work is done here in the actionPerformed( ) method of the button's event handler. Notice how the application checks the new font choice to see if it is null.

```
// FontPicker.java
// A quick test of the FontChooser dialog
//
import java.awt.*;
import java.awt.event.*;
import javax.swing.*;
import javax.swing.colorchooser.*;

public class FontPicker extends JFrame {

  Color c;

  public FontPicker( ) {
    super("JColorChooser Test Frame");
    setSize(200,100);
    final JButton go = new JButton("Show FontChooser");
    go.addActionListener(new ActionListener( ) {
      final FontChooser chooser = new FontChooser(FontPicker.this);
      boolean first = true;
      public void actionPerformed(ActionEvent e) {
        chooser.setVisible(true);
        // If we got a real font choice, then update our go button.
        if (chooser.getNewFont( ) != null) {
          go.setFont(chooser.getNewFont( ));
          go.setForeground(chooser.getNewColor( ));
        }
      }
    });
    getContentPane( ).add(go);
    setDefaultCloseOperation(EXIT_ON_CLOSE);
  }

  public static void main(String args[]) {
    FontPicker fp = new FontPicker( );
    fp.setVisible(true);
  }
}
```

As you develop more commercial applications, you may end up writing some of your own choosers. (A DateChooser would be a good start!) Following the API style for the file and color choosers described in this chapter will make it easier to write your own chooser.

Borders

Swing provides eight unique styles of borders and allows you to combine them to form more elaborate versions. This chapter introduces you to the Swing borders and shows you how to work with and configure them. At the end of the chapter, we show you how to create a border of your own.

Introducing Borders

Figure 13-1 shows the standard borders that Swing provides. There are eight border styles: bevel, soft bevel, empty, etched, line, matte, titled, and compound. The MatteBorder gives you two borders in one: the border area can be filled with either a solid color or an icon. (This figure shows only the icon; you can see a better example of both in Figure 13-11.)

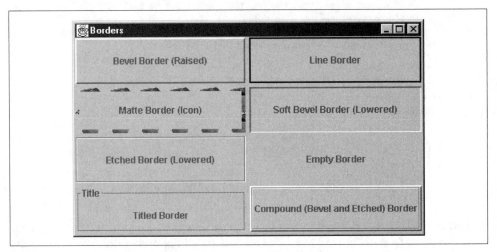

Figure 13-1. Borders in Swing

You can place a border around any Swing component that extends JComponent. The JComponent class contains a border property that is inherited by all Swing components. (Top-level components that don't inherit from JComponent, like JFrame and JDialog, can't have borders.) By default, the border property is null (no border), but you can access and modify it. Once you've set a component's border, the component paints itself using that border from that point on, and the insets of the border replace the component's default insets.

Here's how to set a component's border:

```
JLabel label = new JLabel("A Border");
mylabel.setBorder(new BevelBorder(BevelBorder.LOWERED));
```

Borders are grouped into a separate package within the Swing hierarchy, javax. swing.border. Figure 13-2 shows the classes within this package. The borders included with Swing directly or indirectly extend the AbstractBorder class, which in turn implements the fundamental Border interface and provides a number of helpful housekeeping methods that any implementation can use. (This is an example of the useful *skeletal implementation* pattern for working with interfaces described in Joshua Bloch's outstanding *Effective Java Programming Language Guide* [Addison-Wesley].) You'll almost certainly want to use the same technique if you develop your own border.

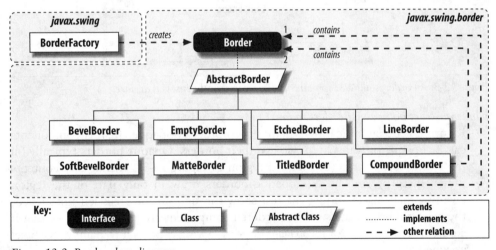

Figure 13-2. Border class diagram

Borders can be combined to form more elaborate compound borders. The lower-right corner of Figure 13-1 shows an example of a compound border. We combined an etched border (on the inside) with a raised bevel border (on the outside). Swing allows you to mix any number of border styles into a single border object. This gives Swing borders a useful compositional feature not often found in other graphical toolkits.

The Border Interface

The Border interface contains three methods.

Methods

public abstract void paintBorder(Component c, Graphics g, int x, int y, int width, int height)

> Draw the border. The border is drawn onto the graphics context g with the location and dimensions provided. paintBorder( ) must calculate exactly what area it can paint by checking the border's insets.

public abstract Insets getBorderInsets(Component c)

> Return an Insets object that reports the minimum amount of space the border needs to paint itself around the given component. Borders must never paint outside this insets region (shown shaded in Figure 13-3). When the border property is set, it replaces the native insets of the component with those of the border.

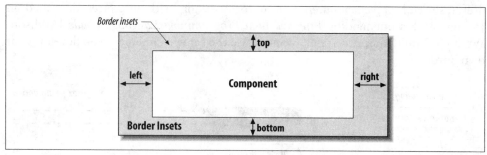

Figure 13-3. A border is allowed to paint itself only within the insets it declares

public abstract boolean isBorderOpaque( )

> Return a boolean indicating whether the border is opaque. Just as components can be opaque or transparent, so can their borders. Opaque borders typically fill the entire border area (the shaded region in Figure 13-3), erasing any contents drawn there previously. Nonopaque borders draw in only part of the region given by their insets and let the rest show through. In the areas left untouched, the background graphics of the bordered component are preserved. Note that if a border returns true for its opaque property, Swing expects it to paint every pixel assigned to it.

Painting Borders Correctly

The golden rule of creating borders is: "Never paint in the component's region." Here's a border that violates this rule:

```
public class WrongBorder extends AbstractBorder {
    public WrongBorder( ) {}
```

```
public void paintBorder(Component c, Graphics g, int x, int y,
                        int width, int height) {
    g.setColor(Color.black);
    g.fillRect(x, y, width, height);        // Bad
}
public boolean isBorderOpaque() { return true;}
public Insets getBorderInsets(Component c) {
    return new Insets(20, 20, 20, 20);
}
}
```

Look carefully at the paintBorder( ) method. The last four parameters passed in to the method can be used to calculate the total screen area of the component—*including* the border insets. We decided to paint our border by creating a single filled rectangle that fills the entire component space. While drawing the border, however, we painted over the underlying component and violated the golden rule.

The correct approach is to obtain the insets of the border region and draw rectangles only in that space, as shown:

```
public void paintBorder(Component c, Graphics g, int x, int y,
                        int width, int height) {
    Insets insets = getBorderInsets(c);
    g.setColor(Color.black);

    //  Draw rectangles around the component, but do not draw
    //  in the component area itself.
    g.fillRect(x, y, width, insets.top);
    g.fillRect(x, y, insets.left, height);
    g.fillRect(x+width-insets.right, y, insets.right, height);
    g.fillRect(x, y+height-insets.bottom, width, insets.bottom);
}
```

The AbstractBorder Class

AbstractBorder is the superclass that all Swing borders extend. Although not mandatory, borders of your own design can also extend AbstractBorder. You will probably want to do this in order to take advantage of the utility methods it contains. AbstractBorder provides default implementations of the three methods of the Border interface. If you subclass AbstractBorder to create your own border, you should override at least the paintBorder( ) and getBorderInsets( ) methods. AbstractBorder also provides methods to calculate the area of the component being bordered and to simplify determining the orientation of a component (important for internationalization).

Property

AbstractBorder has the property shown in Table 13-1. The default implementation of the borderOpaque property returns false. If you create a border that is opaque, you should override it and return true.

Table 13-1. AbstractBorder property

Property	Data type	get	is	set	Default value
borderOpaque°	boolean		•		false

°overridden

Constructor

public AbstractBorder()
   The only constructor; it takes no arguments.

Methods

public void paintBorder(Component c, Graphics g, int x, int y, int width, int height)
   This empty method is required by the `Border` interface; it should be overridden by a subclass to perform the actual rendering of the border.

public Insets getBorderInsets(Component c)
public Insets getBorderInsets(Component c, Insets i)
   Return an `Insets` object with 0 for each inset. Subclasses should override both of these methods to report the true area required by their border. The second version of this method modifies and returns the supplied `Insets` object, `i` (this allows you to reuse the same object for efficiency).

public Rectangle getInteriorRectangle(Component c, int x, int y, int width, int height)
   This nonstatic method calls the static version, using a reference to the component's current border.

public static Rectangle getInteriorRectangle(Border b, int x, int y, int width, int height)
   This static method calculates the area representing a component being bordered by the supplied border. It returns the result as a `Rectangle` object. This method is useful for pinpointing the area of the inner component in which borders shouldn't draw (or as a component author, where to draw).

Now that we're done with the preliminaries, let's look at the borders that Swing provides.

Swing Borders

The following sections discuss Swing's built-in border classes in detail.

The BevelBorder and SoftBevelBorder Classes

A *bevel* is another name for a slanted edge. The `BevelBorder` class can be used to simulate a raised or lowered edge with a slant surrounding the component, similar to the appearance of a button. The default bevel edge is two pixels wide on all sides. Figure 13-4 shows two bevel borders, the first raised and the second lowered.

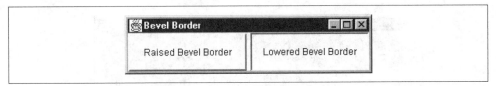

Figure 13-4. Raised and lowered bevel borders

Notice how the border creates the illusion of three dimensions. The bevel border simulates a light source above and to the left of the object (this light source location must be consistent for all 3D components in order to be effective). The border is then drawn with four colors: an outer and inner *highlight* color and an outer and inner *shadow* color. The highlight colors represent the two surfaces of the bevel facing toward the light while the shadow colors represent the surfaces facing away from the light. Figure 13-5 shows how a bevel border uses the highlight and shadow colors.

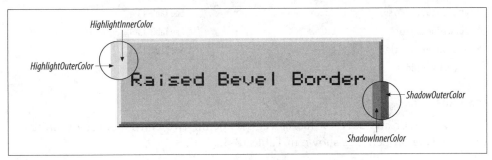

Figure 13-5. The four colors of a bevel border

When the bevel is raised, the top and left sides of the border are highlighted, and the bottom and right sides of the border are shadowed. This presents the appearance of the surface protruding above the background. When the bevel is lowered, the highlighted and shadowed surfaces are reversed, and the border appears to sink into the background. A bevel border is two pixels wide on all sides. The *inner* color represents the inner pixels for the border; the *outer* color represents the outer pixels.

The beveled border in Swing has a subclass, `SoftBevelBorder`, that can be used to simulate a subtle raised or lowered edge around a component. In fact, the only difference from the regular `BevelBorder` is that the soft beveled edge is slightly thinner on two of its four sides and provides for small rounded corners. Figure 13-6 shows a pair of soft bevel borders; if your eyes are really good, you may be able to tell the difference between these and the plain bevel borders.

Properties

Table 13-2 shows the properties of `BevelBorder` and `SoftBevelBorder`. The `bevelType` property shows whether the border appears raised or lowered. The `borderOpaque` property is `true` by default for a bevel border and `false` for a soft bevel border.

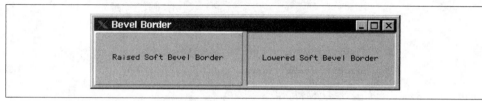

Figure 13-6. Soft bevel borders in Swing

Table 13-2. BevelBorder and SoftBevelBorder properties

Property	Data type	get	is	set	Default value
bevelType	int	•			BevelBorder.RAISED
borderOpaque[o]	boolean			•	See text
highlightInnerColor[1.3]	Color	•			See Table 13-4
highlightOuterColor[1.3]	Color	•			See Table 13-4
shadowInnerColor[1.3]	Color	•			See Table 13-4
shadowOuterColor[1.3]	Color	•			See Table 13-4

[1.3]since 1.3, [o]overridden

Constants

The BevelBorder and SoftBevelBorder classes define two constants used to initialize the bevelType property, as shown in Table 13-3.

Table 13-3. BevelBorder and SoftBevelBorder constants

Constant	Data type	Definition
RAISED	int	Raised bevel border
LOWERED	int	Lowered bevel border

Default colors

If colors are not specified in the constructor, they are derived from the component using the border, as shown in Table 13-4. In this table, background refers to the component's background color.

Table 13-4. Default colors for bevel borders

Property	Color
highlightOuterColor	background.brighter().brighter()
highlightInnerColor	background.brighter()
shadowOuterColor	background.darker().darker()
shadowInnerColor	background.darker()

Constructors

public BevelBorder(int bevelType)
public BevelBorder(int bevelType, Color highlight, Color shadow)
public BevelBorder(int bevelType, Color highlightOuter, Color highlightInner,
  Color shadowOuter, Color shadowInner)
> These constructors can be used to set the initial property values of the BevelBorder. The constructor is the only way the colors of the bevel border can be set; there are no mutator methods for the color variables.

public SoftBevelBorder(int bevelType)
public SoftBevelBorder(int bevelType, Color highlight, Color shadow)
public SoftBevelBorder(int bevelType, Color highlightOuter, Color highlightInner,
  Color shadowOuter, Color shadowInner)
> These constructors can be used to set the initial property values of the SoftBevelBorder. The definitions are identical to BevelBorder constructors.

In the constructors with two Color arguments, the given colors set the highlightInner and shadowOuter properties. highlightOuter is set to highlight.darker( ), and shadowInner is set to shadow.brighter( ).

Methods

public Insets getBorderInsets(Component c)
public Insets getBorderInsets(Component c, Insets i)
> Return an Insets object specifying an inset of two pixels on each side for BevelBorder and three pixels on each side for SoftBevelBorder. The second version of this method modifies and returns the supplied Insets object, i, allowing a single instance to be reused for efficiency.

public Color getHighlightInnerColor(Component c)
public Color getHighlightOuterColor(Component c)
public Color getShadowInnerColor(Component c)
public Color getShadowOuterColor(Component c)
> Retrieve various colors that would be used to draw the border if attached to an arbitrary component; the colors are used as shown in Figure 13-5.

public void paintBorder(Component c, Graphics g, int x, int y, int width, int height)
> Draw the beveled border within the graphics context of the component.

Changing borders on the fly

Here is a short program that creates four labels. Each label draws a bevel border around itself when the mouse pointer enters the component's region and erases it when the mouse leaves the region. This kind of "rollover" effect has become a popular feature in some applications' toolbars. Modifying the program to use soft bevel borders would be trivial.

```java
//  BevelExample.java
//
import java.awt.*;
import java.awt.event.*;
import javax.swing.*;
import javax.swing.border.*;

public class BevelExample extends JPanel {

    BevelBorder bevel;
    EmptyBorder empty;
    JLabel label[] = new JLabel[4];

    public BevelExample() {
        super(true);
        setLayout(new GridLayout(1, 4));

        bevel = new BevelBorder(BevelBorder.RAISED);
        empty = new EmptyBorder(5, 5, 5, 5);

        label[0] = new JLabel("Home");
        label[1] = new JLabel("Back");
        label[2] = new JLabel("Forward");
        label[3] = new JLabel("Stop");

        for (int i = 0; i < label.length; i++) {
            label[i].setHorizontalAlignment(JLabel.CENTER);
            label[i].addMouseListener(new RolloverListener());
            label[i].setBorder(empty);
            add(label[i]);
        }
    }

    public static void main(String s[]) {
        JFrame frame = new JFrame("Bevel Border");
        frame.setDefaultCloseOperation(JFrame.EXIT_ON_CLOSE);
        frame.setSize(400, 100);
        frame.setContentPane(new BevelExample());
        frame.setVisible(true);
    }

    // Inner class to respond to mouse events for the "rollover" effect
    class RolloverListener extends MouseAdapter {
        public void mouseEntered(MouseEvent e) {
            ((JLabel)e.getComponent()).setBorder(bevel);
            repaint();
        }

        public void mouseExited(MouseEvent e) {
            ((JLabel)e.getComponent()).setBorder(empty);
            repaint();
        }
```

```
                public void mouseClicked(MouseEvent e) {
                    String text = ((JLabel)e.getComponent()).getText();
                    System.out.println("You clicked " + text + "!");
                }
            }
        }
```

Figure 13-7 shows the results of our example.

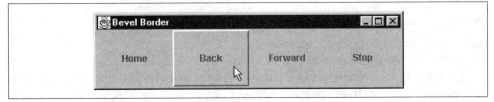

Figure 13-7. Working with bevel borders

The Empty Border Class

The EmptyBorder class is used to place empty space around a component. The size of the space on each side is defined by the border's insets, which are set in the constructor. Figure 13-8 shows an empty border with 20 pixels on all sides surrounding a JLabel. (Note that we used two other borders to denote the boundaries of the EmptyBorder.)

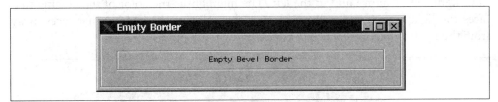

Figure 13-8. An empty border with two etched borders surrounding it

Properties

Table 13-5 shows the properties of the EmptyBorder class.

Table 13-5. EmptyBorder properties

Property	Data type	get	is	set	Default value
borderInsets[1.3]	Insets	•			None (set in constructor)
borderOpaque[o]	boolean			•	false

[1.3]since 1.3, [o]overridden

Constructors

public EmptyBorder(int top, int left, int bottom, int right)
public EmptyBorder(Insets insets)
  Create an empty border with the given insets.

public void paintBorder(Component c, Graphics g, int x, int y, int width, int height)
  Since this is an empty border, this method does nothing.

Method

public Insets getBorderInsets(Component c)
public Insets getBorderInsets(Component c, Insets i)
  Return the insets that would be used with the specified component. The first
  version of this method returns an Insets object with the insets specified in the
  constructor (this is the same as the borderInsets property). The second version
  of the method modifies and returns the supplied Insets object i for efficiency,
  reducing the number of throwaway objects created.

The EtchedBorder Class

An etched border is a single etching that surrounds the target component. The etching consists of adjacent lines of two colors, a highlight and a shadow, and can be
raised or lowered. Like bevel borders, etched borders render themselves by simulating a light source above and to the left. The highlight is the color of the etching that
faces the light source while the shadow is the color of the etching that faces away
from the light source. An etched border is shown in Figure 13-9.

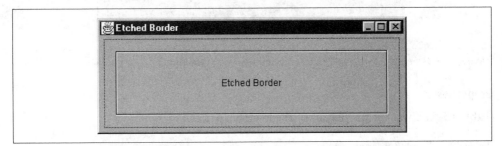

Figure 13-9. A lowered etched border in Swing

An etched border is very similar to a bevel border. By carefully manipulating the colors, you can create an EtchedBorder from a BevelBorder.

Properties

The properties for the EtchedBorder class are shown in Table 13-6. The borderOpaque
property always returns true, indicating that this border paints over all of its allocated pixels. The etchType tells whether the etch appears raised or lowered. Finally,

the highlightColor and shadowColor properties indicate the two colors used to simulate the etching. If no values are given, brighter and darker variations of the background color of the component are used for highlightColor and shadowColor, respectively.

Table 13-6. EtchedBorder properties

Property	Data type	get	is	set	Default value
borderOpaque[o]	boolean		•		true
etchType	int	•			EtchedBorder.LOWERED
highlightColor[1.3]	Color	•			null
shadowColor[1.3]	Color	•			null

[1.3]since 1.3, [o]overridden

Constants

EtchedBorder contains two constants used to initialize the etchType property, as shown in Table 13-7.

Table 13-7. EtchedBorder constants

Constant	Data type	Definition
RAISED	int	A raised border
LOWERED	int	A lowered border

Constructors

public EtchedBorder( )

Create a simple lowered etched border. The colors of the border's highlight and shadow default to the brighter( ) and darker( ) shades of the background color of any bordered component.

public EtchedBorder(Color highlight, Color shadow)

Create a lowered etched border using the specified highlight and shadow colors for the etching. There are no mutators ("set" methods) for the color fields; they can be set only during construction.

public EtchedBorder(int etchType)

Create a simple etched border of the etch type passed in. The colors of the border's highlight and shadow default to the brighter( ) and darker( ) shades of the background color of any bordered component.

public EtchedBorder(int etchType, Color highlight, Color shadow)

Create an etched border of the type passed in using the specified highlight and shadow colors for the etching. Note that there are no mutators for any of the properties; they can be set only during construction.

Miscellaneous

public Insets getBorderInsets(Component c)
public Insets getBorderInsets(Comonent c, Insets i)
> Return an Insets object specifying an inset of 2 on each side. The second version of this method modifies and returns the given Insets object, i.

public Color getHighlightColor(Component c)
public Color getShadowColor(Component c)
> Retrieve the colors that would be used to draw the shadowed and highlighted parts of the border on the specified component.

public void paintBorder(Component c, Graphics g, int x, int y, int width, int height)
> Cause the border to paint itself with the graphics context of the component.

The LineBorder Class

The LineBorder class creates a border consisting of a line of arbitrary thickness around the component. Unlike the beveled or etched borders, the line is a single color and is not shaded. Since SDK 1.3, you can specify that the border use (very subtly) rounded corners. Figure 13-10 shows two different line borders, each with a different thicknesses.

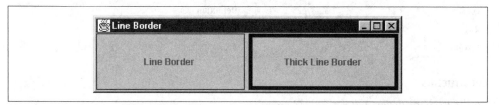

Figure 13-10. Line borders in Swing

Properties

The properties for the LineBorder object are shown in Table 13-8. The borderOpaque property always returns true, indicating that this border paints over all of its allocated pixels. The others describe the way it will be drawn; all are read-only and can be set only during construction.

Table 13-8. LineBorder properties

Property	Data type	get	is	set	Default value
borderOpaque[o]	boolean		•		true
lineColor	Color	•			From constructor

[o]overridden

Table 13-8. LineBorder properties (continued)

Property	Data type	get	is	set	Default value
roundedCorners	boolean		•		false
thickness	int		•		1

ºoverridden

Constructors

public LineBorder(Color color)
public LineBorder(Color color, int thickness)
public LineBorder(Color color, int thickness, boolean roundedCorners)
    Create a lined border with a specific color and an optional thickness and (since SDK 1.3) possibly rounded corners. The thickness defaults to 1, and the corners to nonrounded.

Methods

public Insets getBorderInsets(Component c)
public Insets getBorderInsets(Component c, Insets i)
    Return an Insets object; the inset on each side is equal to the thickness of the line, as specified in the constructor. The second version of this method modifies and returns the given Insets object, i.

public void paintBorder(Component c, Graphics g, int x, int y, int width, int height)
    Cause the border to paint itself with the graphics context of the component.

Miscellaneous

The LineBorder class contains two shortcut methods allowing you to reuse objects for certain commonly used kinds of borders. These methods reduce garbage collection by returning the same object each time they are called. (The ability to safely and easily support this kind of shared object reuse is one of the major advantages of writing immutable classes like LineBorder.)

public static Border createBlackLineBorder()
    Return the equivalent of LineBorder(Color.black, 1).

public static Border createGrayLineBorder()
    Return the equivalent of LineBorder(Color.gray, 1).

The MatteBorder Class

In art and photography, a *mat* is often used to offset a picture from its frame. In Swing, matte[*] borders perform the same function, separating a component from everything else. A matte border in Swing can be either a solid color or a repeated image icon. The color or icon fills the entire space reserved by the border's insets.

With a MatteBorder, you have the choice of constructing the object with either a Color or an Icon. If you choose a color, the color flood-fills the entire space reserved for the border. If you use an icon, the icon tiles or wallpapers itself throughout the entire area of the MatteBorder. Figure 13-11 shows both kinds of MatteBorder.

Figure 13-11. Various matte borders in Swing

Properties

MatteBorder extends the EmptyBorder class. The borderOpaque property can be either true or false, depending on how the border is used. If the MatteBorder is drawn exclusively with a solid color, then the border is opaque, and the property has a value of true. If the border is used with an image, the image may contain transparency, and the property has a value of false. (See Table 13-9.)

Table 13-9. MatteBorder properties

Property	Data type	get	is	set	Default value
borderInsets[1.3]	Insets	•			None (set in constructor)
borderOpaque[o]	boolean			•	None (depends on kind; see text)

[1.3]since 1.3, [o]overridden

 Be careful if you use an image icon with a MatteBorder without explicitly setting the insets. The resulting border insets are the width and height of the icon used, which (depending on how much space the layout manager gives) could paint over part of your component.

---

[*] This is Sun's misspelling, not ours, perhaps by association with the matte paintings in motion picture special effects.

Constructors

public MatteBorder(Icon tileIcon)
> Create a matte border by calculating the insets from the icon passed in. The border's top and bottom height matches the height of the icon, while the border's left and right width matches the width of the icon.

public MatteBorder(Insets borderInsets, Color matteColor)
public MatteBorder(int top, int left, int bottom, int right, Color matteColor)
> Create a matte border with the specified insets using the solid color specified by matteColor.

public MatteBorder(Insets borderInsets, Icon tileIcon)
public MatteBorder(int top, int left, int bottom, int right, Icon tileIcon)
> Create a matte border with the specified insets. Instead of using a flood-filled color, however, the specified icon is wallpapered throughout the border's space.

Methods

public Insets getBorderInsets(Component c)
public Insets getBorderInsets(Component c, Insets i)
> Retrieve information about the component's insets (the component isn't used; the value returned is the same as that obtained through the borderInsets property). The insets depend on how the border was constructed. If the insets were specified explicitly in the constructor, those insets are returned. If the border uses an icon and insets weren't specified explicitly, the width of the icon is used as the inset on the left and right sides, and the height of the icon is used on the top and bottom. The second version of this method modifies and returns the given Insets object, i, to reduce the number of garbage objects created.

public void paintBorder(Component c, Graphics g, int x, int y, int width, int height)
> Cause the border to paint itself with the graphics context of the component.

Two kinds of matte borders

Here is a program that displays the two types of matte borders from Figure 13-11.

```
// MatteExample.java
//
import java.awt.*;
import javax.swing.*;
import javax.swing.border.*;

public class MatteExample extends JPanel {

    public MatteExample( ) {
        super(true);
        this.setLayout(new GridLayout(1, 2, 5, 5));

        JLabel label1 = new JLabel("Matte Border");
        JLabel label2 = new JLabel("Matte Border (Icon)");
```

```
        label1.setHorizontalAlignment(JLabel.CENTER);
        label2.setHorizontalAlignment(JLabel.CENTER);

        Icon icon = new ImageIcon("plant.gif");
        MatteBorder matte = new MatteBorder(35, 35, 35, 35, Color.blue);
        MatteBorder matteicon = new MatteBorder(35, 35, 35, 35, icon);
        label1.setBorder(matte);
        label2.setBorder(matteicon);

        add(label1);
        add(label2);
    }

    public static void main(String s[]) {
        JFrame frame = new JFrame("Matte Borders");
        frame.setDefaultCloseOperation(JFrame.EXIT_ON_CLOSE);
        frame.setSize(500, 200);
        frame.setContentPane(new MatteExample( ));
        frame.setVisible(true);
    }
}
```

The TitledBorder Class

The TitledBorder class takes an arbitrary border and adds a descriptive string to it. This title string can be placed in one of six different positions around the component and can be set to appear above, below, or overlaid on the border. In addition, you can specify the font and color of the title string. Figure 13-12 enumerates all of the explicit title positions and justifications available.

 Since SDK 1.3, there are also two logical positions, LEADING and TRAILING, which position the title relative to the direction in which text flows under the current locale. For better internationalization support, use LEADING and TRAILING rather than the explicit LEFT or RIGHT positions.

You can use any style of border in conjunction with a TitledBorder by setting the TitledBorder's own border property. For example, the borders in Figure 13-12 are used in conjunction with a BevelBorder. The default border style, however, is an EtchedBorder. A titled, etched border (with the title at the top leading corner) has a strong tradition of being used in many applications to group a set of related user-interface elements visually inside of a larger window.

Properties

The properties for the TitledBorder class are given in Table 13-10. The border property contains the border that is being titled. It can be any border that implements the Border interface. The read-only borderOpaque property always returns false; the titled

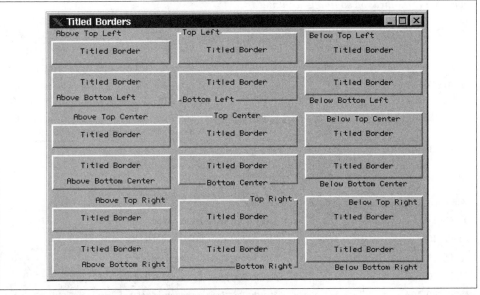

Figure 13-12. Title positions and justifications

border does not color all of its pixels. The title property holds the string that is displayed with this border. titleColor is the string's color, titleFont represents its font, size, and style. titleJustification and titlePosition tell where the title appears in relation to the component and the border. See Tables 13-11 and 13-12 for their values.

Table 13-10. TitledBorder properties

Property	Data type	get	is	set	Default value
border	Border	•		•	From L&F
borderOpaque°	boolean		•		false
title	String	•		•	""
titleColor	Color	•		•	From L&F
titleFont	Font	•		•	From L&F
titleJustification	int	•		•	LEADING[1.3]
titlePosition	int	•		•	TOP

[1.3]since 1.3, °overridden

Table 13-11. Justification constants

Property	Data type	Default value
DEFAULT_JUSTIFICATION	int	Use the default justification, which is LEADING.
LEFT	int	Place the title string on the left side of the border.

[1.3]since 1.3

Table 13-11. *Justification constants (continued)*

Property	Data type	Default value
CENTER	int	Place the title string in the center of the border.
RIGHT	int	Place the title string on the right side of the border
LEADING[1.3]	int	Locale-sensitive positioning to the left for text that is oriented left-to-right, to the right if right-to-left.
TRAILING[1.3]	int	Locale-sensitive to the right for text that is oriented left-to-right, to the left if right-to-left.

[1.3]since 1.3

Table 13-12. *Position constants*

Constant	Data type	Definition
DEFAULT_POSITION	int	Place the text in the default position, TOP.
ABOVE_TOP	int	Place the text above the top line of the border.
TOP	int	Place the text on the top line of the border.
BELOW_TOP	int	Place the text below the top line of the border.
ABOVE_BOTTOM	int	Place the text above the bottom line of the border.
BOTTOM	int	Place the text on the bottom line of the border.
BELOW_BOTTOM	int	Place the text below the bottom line of the border.

Constructors

public TitledBorder(String title)
public TitledBorder(Border border)
public TitledBorder(Border border, String title)
public TitledBorder(Border border, String title, int titleJustification, int titlePosition)
public TitledBorder(Border border, String title, int titleJustification, int titlePosition, Font titleFont)
public TitledBorder(Border border, String title, int titleJustification, int titlePosition, Font titleFont, Color titleColor)

Create a `TitledBorder` instance with the specified properties. Any border that implements the `Border` interface can be used for the border property. The justification and position constants are enumerated in Tables 13-11 and 13-12. Default values for omitted properties are shown in Table 13-10.

Miscellaneous

public Insets getBorderInsets(Component c)
public Insets getBorderInsets(Component c, Insets i)

Return an Insets object that describes the insets being used by the titled border; the insets depend on both the underlying border and the font and position of the border's title. The second version of this method tries to reduce garbage creation by modifying and returning the given Insets object, i, but it can't perform this optimization if the underlying border doesn't extend AbstractBorder (and thus may lack a corresponding method).

public void paintBorder(Component c, Graphics g, int x, int y, int width, int height)
Cause the border to paint itself with the graphics context of the component.

public Dimension getMinimumSize(Component c)
Return the minimum size of this border, including the border and text.

Using a titled border

Here is a short program that creates the image displayed in Figure 13-13:

```java
// TitledExample.java
//
import java.awt.*;
import javax.swing.*;
import javax.swing.border.*;

public class TitledExample extends JPanel {

    public TitledExample( ) {
        super(true);

        this.setLayout(new GridLayout(1, 1, 5, 5));

        JLabel label = new JLabel("Titled Border");
        label.setHorizontalAlignment(JLabel.CENTER);

        TitledBorder titled = new TitledBorder("Title");
        label.setBorder(titled);

        add(label);
    }

    public static void main(String s[]) {
        JFrame frame = new JFrame("Borders");
        frame.setDefaultCloseOperation(JFrame.EXIT_ON_CLOSE);
        frame.setSize(200, 100);
        frame.setContentPane(new TitledExample( ));
        frame.setVisible(true);
    }
}
```

Figure 13-13. A simple title border

The CompoundBorder Class

You can combine two borders to create more elaborate displays with the CompoundBorder class. The insets of both borders are added together to form the insets of the resulting compound border object. The component renders the outside border first, followed by the inside border. You can compound borders recursively so that any number of borders can be embedded inside of a CompoundBorder object:

```
CompoundBorder comp = new CompoundBorder(new CompoundBorder(new EtchedBorder( ),
                                   new EmptyBorder(10, 10, 10, 10)),
                 new MatteBorder(20, 20, 20, 20, Color.red));
```

The preceding code yields the border in Figure 13-14.

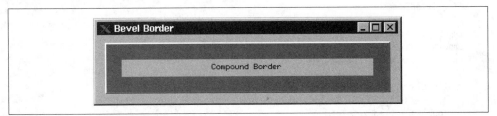

Figure 13-14. A compound border

Properties

Table 13-13 lists the properties of the CompoundBorder class. The insideBorder and outsideBorder properties hold the borders that are combined. If both of the borders in the compound border are opaque, the borderOpaque property is true. Otherwise, the property is false.

Table 13-13. CompoundBorder properties

Property	Data type	get	is	set	Default value
borderOpaque[o]	boolean		•		See text
insideBorder	Border	•			null
outsideBorder	Border	•			null

[o]overridden

Constructors

public CompoundBorder( )
> Initialize an empty compound border with no outside or inside border. Because there are no mutators ("set" methods) for any border property, you will probably never invoke this constructor.

public CompoundBorder(Border outsideBorder, Border insideBorder)
> Create a compound border object with the specified inside and outside borders.

Miscellaneous

public Insets getBorderInsets(Component c)
public Insets getBorderInsets(Component c, Insets i)
> Return an Insets object describing the insets used by the compound border; the inset on each side is the sum of the insets of the borders being combined in this compound border. The second version of this method modifies and returns the given Insets object, i, to help reduce the number of temporary garbage objects created.

public void paintBorder(Component c, Graphics g, int x, int y, int width, int height)
> Cause the border to paint itself with the graphics context of the component.

The BorderFactory Class

The BorderFactory class (which is in the javax.swing package) allows you to call various static methods to create borders. Instead of declaring new instances for each border, the factory class attempts to reuse previously defined (cached) borders, thus saving memory. It's a good idea to get in the habit of using this factory if you create a lot of borders in your application. Currently, only a few borders are actually cached. But in future releases, additional border caching may be added to this class. The fact that most border classes are *immutable* (i.e., they contain no mutator methods that would allow them to be changed) is an excellent design choice that enables this kind of instance sharing safely and easily even in a multithreaded environment like Java.

Methods

public static Border createBevelBorder(int bevelType)
> Create a BevelBorder of the specified type (either raised or lowered). This method returns a cached border rather than creating a new one.

public static Border createBevelBorder(int bevelType, Color highlight, Color shadow)
> Create a BevelBorder of the specified type (either raised or lowered), with the appropriate highlight and shadow colors.

public static Border createBevelBorder(int bevelType, Color highlightOuter,
Color highlightInner, Color shadowOuter, Color shadowInner)
> Create a BevelBorder of the specified type (either raised or lowered), with the appropriate highlight and shadow colors.

public static Border createEmptyBorder()
> Create an EmptyBorder. This method returns a cached border rather than creating a new one.

public static Border createEmptyBorder(int top, int left, int bottom, int right)
> Create an EmptyBorder with the specified size.

public static Border createEtchedBorder( )
> Create a default `EtchedBorder`. This method returns a cached border rather than creating a new one.

public static Border createEtchedBorder(Color highlight, Color shadow)
> Create an `EtchedBorder` with the appropriate highlight and shadow colors.

public static Border createEtchedBorder(int bevelType)
> Since SDK 1.3, this method allows you to create nonlowered etched borders. Returns a cached border rather than creating a new one each time.

public static Border createEtchedBorder(int bevelType, Color highlight, Color shadow)
> Since SDK 1.3, this method allows you to create nonlowered etched borders using particular colors.

public static Border createLineBorder(Color color)
> Create a `LineBorder` with the specified color.

public static Border createLineBorder(Color color, int thickness)
> Create a `LineBorder` with the specified color and thickness.

public static Border createLoweredBevelBorder( )
> Create a lowered `BevelBorder`. This method returns a cached border rather than creating a new one.

public static Border createRaisedBevelBorder( )
> Create a raised `BevelBorder`. This method returns a cached border rather than creating a new one.

public static CompoundBorder createCompoundBorder( )
> Create an empty `CompoundBorder`.

public static CompoundBorder createCompoundBorder(Border outsideBorder, Border insideBorder)
> Create a `CompoundBorder` by combining the two borders passed in.

public static MatteBorder createMatteBorder(int top, int left, int bottom, int right, Color color)
> Create a `MatteBorder` with the specified size and color.

public static MatteBorder createMatteBorder(int top, int left, int bottom, int right, Icon titleIcon)
> Create a `MatteBorder` with the specified size, tile-filling it with instances of the specified icon `titleIcon`.

public static TitledBorder createTitledBorder(Border border)
> Create a `TitledBorder` from border.

public static TitledBorder createTitledBorder(Border border, String title)
> Create a `TitledBorder` from border. The border's title is the `title` string passed in, positioned at the upper left of the border.

public static TitledBorder createTitledBorder(Border border, String title,
  int titleJustification, int titlePosition)

> Create a `TitledBorder` from the `Border` passed in. The border's title, justification, and position are also passed in.

public static TitledBorder createTitledBorder(Border border, String title,
  int titleJustification, int titlePosition, Font titleFont)

> Create a `TitledBorder` from the `Border` passed in. The border's title, justification, position, and font are all passed in.

public static TitledBorder createTitledBorder(Border border, String title,
  int titleJustification, int titlePosition, Font titleFont, Color titleColor)

> Create a `TitledBorder` from the `Border` passed in. The border's title is the `title` string passed in. The justification, position, font, and color of the border are also dictated by the variables passed in.

public static TitledBorder createTitledBorder(String title)

> Create a `TitledBorder` with the given title.

Creating Your Own Border

Creating your own border is simple when you extend the `AbstractBorder` class. You need to define three things: how to draw the border, whether it is opaque, and what its insets are. To accomplish this, you must implement `paintBorder()`, both `isBorderOpaque()` methods, and `getBorderInsets()`. The hard part of coming up with your own border is doing something creative with the `Graphics` primitives in the `paintBorder()` method. A reminder: make sure that you paint only in the insets region that you define for yourself. Otherwise, you could be painting over the component you intend to border.

Let's take a look at a simple border:

```
// CurvedBorder.java
//
import java.awt.*;
import javax.swing.border.*;

public class CurvedBorder extends AbstractBorder
{
    private Color wallColor = Color.gray;
    private int sinkLevel = 10;

    public CurvedBorder() { }
    public CurvedBorder(int sinkLevel) { this.sinkLevel = sinkLevel; }
    public CurvedBorder(Color wall) { this.wallColor = wall; }
    public CurvedBorder(int sinkLevel, Color wall)     {
```

```
            this.sinkLevel = sinkLevel;
            this.wallColor = wall;
    }

    public void paintBorder(Component c, Graphics g, int x, int y, int w, int h)
    {
        g.setColor(getWallColor());

        // Paint a tall wall around the component.
        for (int i = 0; i < sinkLevel; i++) {
            g.drawRoundRect(x+i, y+i, w-i-1, h-i-1, sinkLevel-i, sinkLevel);
            g.drawRoundRect(x+i, y+i, w-i-1, h-i-1, sinkLevel, sinkLevel-i);
            g.drawRoundRect(x+i, y, w-i-1, h-1, sinkLevel-i, sinkLevel);
            g.drawRoundRect(x, y+i, w-1, h-i-1, sinkLevel, sinkLevel-i);
        }
    }

    public Insets getBorderInsets(Component c) {
        return new Insets(sinkLevel, sinkLevel, sinkLevel, sinkLevel);
    }
    public Insets getBorderInsets(Component c, Insets i) {
        i.left = i.right = i.bottom = i.top = sinkLevel;
        return i;
    }
    public boolean isBorderOpaque() { return true; }
    public int getSinkLevel() { return sinkLevel; }
    public Color getWallColor() { return wallColor; }
}
```

This border draws round rectangles in succession around the component. The rectangles are offset from each other so that it appears that the component is depressed into the surface. The sinkLevel property defines how "deep" the depression should appear. Note that we define the border insets to match the sinkLevel property. We draw four round rectangles on each pass, instead of just one—this ensures that each pixel is filled between rectangles, which won't be the case if we use just one. (If you want to see what we mean, try commenting out some of the drawRoundRect() calls.) Finally, the wallColor property specifies the border's color.

Here is an excerpt from the source that you can use to surround a slider with this border. Figure 13-15 shows the result.

```
JSlider mySlider = new JSlider();
mySlider.setMajorTickSpacing(20);
mySlider.setMinorTickSpacing(10);
mySlider.setPaintTicks(true);
mySlider.setPaintLabels(true);

CurvedBorder border = new CurvedBorder(10, Color.darkGray);
mySlider.setBorder(border);
```

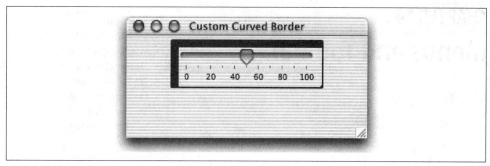

Figure 13-15. A custom curved border

## CHAPTER 14

Menus and Toolbars

This chapter discusses Swing menus and toolbars. Menus are the richer and more flexible of the two, so they encompass most of the chapter. They tend to be the first thing users explore in learning a new application, so it's fitting that Swing provides a great deal of freedom in laying out menu components.

Toolbars allow you to group buttons, combo boxes, and other elements together in repositionable panels; these tools can assist the user in performing many common tasks. You can add any component to a Swing toolbar, even non-Swing components. In addition, Swing allows the toolbar to be dragged from the frame and positioned inside a child window for convenience.

Introducing Swing Menus

Swing menu components are subclasses of JComponent. Consequently, they have all the benefits of a Swing component, and you can treat them as such with respect to layout managers and containers.

Here are some notable features of the Swing menu system:

- Icons can augment or replace menu items.
- Menu items can be radio buttons.
- Keyboard accelerators can be assigned to menu items; these appear next to the menu item text.
- Most standard Swing components can be used as menu items.

Swing provides familiar menu separators, checkbox menu items, pop-up menus, and submenus for use in your applications. In addition, Swing menus support keyboard accelerators and "underline" style (mnemonic) shortcuts, and you can attach menu bars to the top of Swing frames with a single function that adjusts the frame insets accordingly. On the Macintosh, your application can be configured so that this method places the menu bar at the top of the screen, where users expect to find it. Figure 14-1 defines the various elements that make up the menu system in Swing.

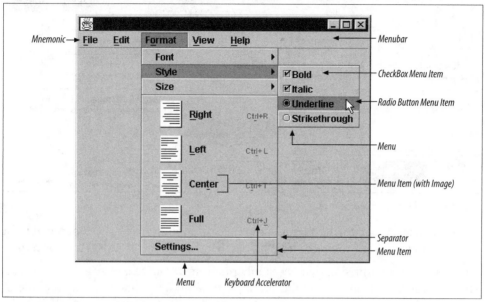

Figure 14-1. The elements of the Swing menu system

Note that not all platforms support underline-style mnemonics. Notably, on the Macintosh (which has never provided this sort of user interface) mnemonics do not appear at all in the system menu bar, and though they are visible in the actual menus, they do not work in either place. If your application uses mnemonics, you should consider grouping the code to set them up into a separate method that is invoked only when running on a platform that supports them.

All platforms do support accelerators (shortcuts) but have different conventions about the key used to invoke them. You can take advantage of the Toolkit method getMenuShortcutKeyMask to always use the right key.

Menu Hierarchy

The class diagram for Swing menus is shown in Figure 14-2.

You might be surprised to find AbstractButton in the hierarchy, but menus and menu items have many features in common with Swing buttons. For example, menu items can be highlighted (when the mouse pointer passes over them), they can be clicked to indicate that the user has made a choice, they can be disabled and grayed like buttons, and they can be assigned action commands to assist with event handling. JCheckBoxMenuItem and JRadioButtonMenuItem can even be toggled between two

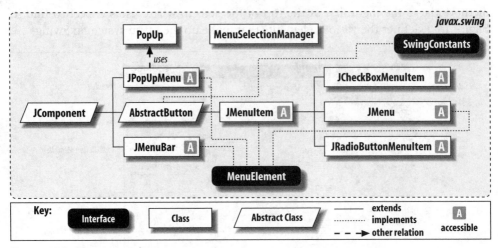

Figure 14-2. Swing menu diagram

selection states. Since Swing menu components share much of the functionality of Swing buttons, it is appropriate and efficient that they inherit from `AbstractButton`.

It may also seem surprising that `JMenu` inherits from `JMenuItem`, instead of vice-versa. This is because each `JMenu` contains an implicit menu item that serves as the title of the menu. You'll often hear this part of the menu called the *title button*. When the user presses or drags the mouse cursor over the title button, the corresponding menu appears. Note, however, that menus do not have to be anchored to a menu bar. You can embed them in other menus, where they act as submenus. This means that the title button must be able to act as a menu item, which would not be possible if the hierarchy was reversed. We discuss this behavior in more detail when we cover the `JMenu` class later in this chapter.

Almost all of the menu classes implement the `MenuElement` interface. The `MenuElement` interface outlines standardized methods that dictate how each Swing menu component behaves when it encounters user input, such as keyboard or mouse events. Swing menu classes typically process these mouse and keyboard events and pass notifications to the component delegates, which handle any necessary redrawing of the component. These methods work in tandem with the `MenuSelectionManager` class. While you rarely need to implement the `MenuElement` interface, it helps to know how it works. We show how to implement this interface later in the chapter.

Getting Your Feet Wet

Okay, it's time to jump in. Here is a flashy program that introduces much of the basic Swing menu functionality:

```
// IntroExample.java
//
```

```java
import java.awt.*;
import java.awt.event.*;
import javax.swing.*;

public class IntroExample extends JMenuBar {

    String[] fileItems = new String[] { "New", "Open", "Save", "Exit" };
    String[] editItems = new String[] { "Undo", "Cut", "Copy", "Paste" };
    char[] fileShortcuts = { 'N','O','S','X' };
    char[] editShortcuts = { 'Z','X','C','V' };

    public IntroExample( ) {

        JMenu fileMenu = new JMenu("File");
        JMenu editMenu = new JMenu("Edit");
        JMenu otherMenu = new JMenu("Other");
        JMenu subMenu = new JMenu("SubMenu");
        JMenu subMenu2 = new JMenu("SubMenu2");

        // Assemble the File menus with mnemonics.
        ActionListener printListener = new ActionListener( ) {
                public void actionPerformed(ActionEvent event) {
                    System.out.println("Menu item [" + event.getActionCommand( ) +
                                        "] was pressed.");
                }
            };
        for (int i=0; i < fileItems.length; i++) {
            JMenuItem item = new JMenuItem(fileItems[i], fileShortcuts[i]);
            item.addActionListener(printListener);
            fileMenu.add(item);
        }

        // Assemble the File menus with keyboard accelerators.
        for (int i=0; i < editItems.length; i++) {
            JMenuItem item = new JMenuItem(editItems[i]);
            item.setAccelerator(KeyStroke.getKeyStroke(editShortcuts[i],
                Toolkit.getDefaultToolkit( ).getMenuShortcutKeyMask( ), false));
            item.addActionListener(printListener);
            editMenu.add(item);
        }

        // Insert a separator in the Edit menu in Position 1 after "Undo".
        editMenu.insertSeparator(1);

        // Assemble the submenus of the Other menu.
        JMenuItem item;
        subMenu2.add(item = new JMenuItem("Extra 2"));
        item.addActionListener(printListener);
        subMenu.add(item = new JMenuItem("Extra 1"));
        item.addActionListener(printListener);
        subMenu.add(subMenu2);

        // Assemble the Other menu itself.
        otherMenu.add(subMenu);
```

```
otherMenu.add(item = new JCheckBoxMenuItem("Check Me"));
item.addActionListener(printListener);
otherMenu.addSeparator( );
ButtonGroup buttonGroup = new ButtonGroup( );
otherMenu.add(item = new JRadioButtonMenuItem("Radio 1"));
item.addActionListener(printListener);
buttonGroup.add(item);
otherMenu.add(item = new JRadioButtonMenuItem("Radio 2"));
item.addActionListener(printListener);
buttonGroup.add(item);
otherMenu.addSeparator( );
otherMenu.add(item = new JMenuItem("Potted Plant",
                     new ImageIcon("image.gif")));
item.addActionListener(printListener);

// Finally, add all the menus to the menu bar.
add(fileMenu);
add(editMenu);
add(otherMenu);
  }

  public static void main(String s[]) {
    JFrame frame = new JFrame("Simple Menu Example");
    frame.setDefaultCloseOperation(JFrame.EXIT_ON_CLOSE);
    frame.setJMenuBar(new IntroExample( ));
    frame.pack( );
    frame.setVisible(true);
  }
}
```

This example creates a menu bar with three simple menus, attaching mnemonics to
the menu items of the File menu and keyboard accelerators to the menu items of the
Edit menu. Figure 14-3 shows a mosaic of the different menus that the program produces. It also shows how the Edit menu looks on two different platforms, with the
proper accelerator key (Control or Command) used on each.

In the third menu, we've enhanced the last item with a GIF image of a potted plant.
In addition, the first menu item in the Other menu is actually a submenu that pops
out to a second submenu, underscoring the recursive nature of menus. If you select
any of the menus, you are rewarded with a simple text output that tells you what you
clicked:

```
Menu item [New] was pressed.
Menu item [Radio 1] was pressed.
```

Don't worry if you do not understand all the classes and methods at this point. We
will examine each menu component in detail shortly.

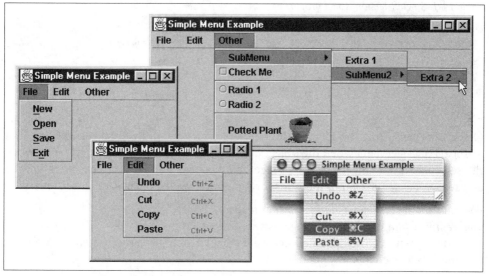

Figure 14-3. A sample of Swing menu effects

Menu Bar Selection Models

In all GUI environments, menu components allow only one selection to be made at a time. Swing is no exception. Swing provides a data model that menu bars and menus can use to emulate this behavior: the SingleSelectionModel.

The SingleSelectionModel Interface

Objects implementing the SingleSelectionModel interface do exactly what its name suggests: they maintain an array of possible selections and allow one element in the array to be chosen at a time. The model holds the index of the selected element. If a new element is chosen, the model resets the index representing the chosen element and fires a ChangeEvent to each of the registered listeners.

Properties

Objects implementing the SingleSelectionModel interface contain the properties shown in Table 14-1. The selected property is a boolean that tells if there is a selection. The selectedIndex property is an integer index that represents the currently selected item.

Table 14-1. SingleSelectionModel properties

Property	Data type	get	is	set	Default value
selected	boolean			•	
selectedIndex	int	•		•	

Events

Objects implementing the SingleSelectionModel interface must fire a ChangeEvent (not a PropertyChangeEvent) when the object modifies its selectedIndex property, i.e., when the selection has changed. The interface contains the standard addChangeListener() and removeChangeListener() methods for maintaining a list of ChangeEvent listeners.

void addChangeListener(ChangeListener listener)
void removeChangeListener(ChangeListener listener)
> Add or remove the specified ChangeListener from the list of listeners receiving this model's change events.

Method

The SingleSelectionModel interface contains one other method:

public void clearSelection()
> Clear the selection value, forcing the selected property to return false.

The DefaultSingleSelectionModel Class

Swing provides a simple default implementation of the SingleSelectionModel interface in the DefaultSingleSelectionModel class.

Properties

DefaultSingleSelectionModel contains just the properties required by the SingleSelectionModel interface, as shown in Table 14-2. The selectedIndex property is an integer index that represents the currently selected item. The default value of -1 indicates that there is no selection. The selected property is a boolean that returns true if the selectedIndex is anything other than -1, and false otherwise.

Table 14-2. DefaultSingleSelectionModel properties

Property	Data type	get	is	set	Default value
selected	boolean			•	false
selectedIndex	int	•		•	-1

Events and methods

The DefaultSingleSelectionModel object provides all the events and methods specified by the SingleSelectionModel interface discussed earlier.

The JMenuBar Class

Swing's JMenuBar class supersedes the AWT MenuBar class. This class creates a horizontal menu bar component with zero or more menus attached to it. JMenuBar uses the DefaultSingleSelectionModel as its data model because the user can raise, or *activate*, only one of its menus at a given time. Once the mouse pointer leaves that menu, the class removes the menu from the screen (or *cancels* it, in Swing lingo), and all menus again become eligible to be raised. Figure 14-4 shows the class hierarchy for the JMenuBar component.

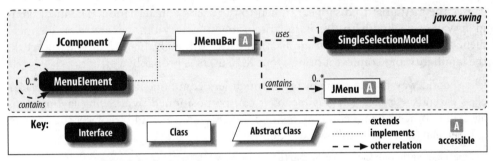

Figure 14-4. JMenuBar class diagram

You can add JMenu objects to the menu bar with the add( ) method of the JMenuBar class. JMenuBar then assigns an integer index based on the order in which the menus were added. The menu bar displays the menus from left to right on the bar according to their assigned index. In theory, there is one exception: the help menu. You are supposed to be allowed to mark one menu as the help menu; the location of the help menu is up to the L&F. In practice, trying to do this results in JMenuBar throwing an Error.

Menu Bar Placement

You can attach menu bars to Swing frames or applets in one of two ways. First, you can use the setJMenuBar( ) method of JFrame, JDialog, JApplet, or JInternalFrame:

```
JFrame frame = new JFrame("Menu");
JMenuBar menuBar = new JMenuBar();

// Attach the menu bar to the frame.
frame.setJMenuBar(menuBar);
```

The setJMenuBar( ) method is analogous to the setMenuBar( ) method of java.awt.Frame. Like its predecessor, setJMenuBar( ) allows the L&F to determine the location of the menu (typically, it anchors the menu bar to the top of a frame, adjusting the frame's internal Insets accordingly). Both JApplet and JDialog contain a setJMenuBar( ) method—this means that you can add menu bars to both applets and dialogs. Either way, be sure not to confuse the setJMenuBar( ) method with the older setMenuBar( ) method of AWT when working with Swing menus, or the compiler complains bitterly.

If your application is running on a Macintosh, the Mac L&F can be configured to place menu bars at the top of the screen, where Mac users expect to find them. Setting the system property com.apple.macos.useScreenMenuBar to true activates this behavior. It's disabled by default because most Java programs do not expect this behavior, and they must be coded properly to deal with it. Notably, the Aqua Human Interface Guidelines require that the menu bar is always visible. If your application has any frames that lack menu bars, whenever one of these gains focus, it causes the menu bar to disappear, much to the user's consternation. The most common way of dealing with this is to write a menu factory that generates an identical menu bar for each frame your application uses. Although this is a little extra work, the familiarity and comfort it brings your Mac users is probably worth it.

The second way to add a menu bar is much less common. Recall that the JMenuBar class extends JComponent. This means it can be positioned by a Swing layout manager like other Swing components. For example, we could replace the call to setJMenuBar( ) with the following code:

```
menuBar.setBorder(new BevelBorder(BevelBorder.RAISED));
frame.getContentPane( ).add(menuBar, BorderLayout.SOUTH);
```

This places the menu bar at the bottom of the frame, as shown in Figure 14-5. (Note that we set a beveled border around the menu bar to help outline its location.) It would even be possible to add two or three menu bars in different locations. Swing does not require a single menu bar to be anchored to the top of a frame. Because they extend JComponent, multiple menu bars can be positioned anywhere inside a container.

 You have to add at least one named menu to a menu bar for it to gain any thickness. Otherwise, it appears as a thin line—similar to a separator.

Of course, you'd never actually want to do this without a very compelling reason. It robs the L&F of its opportunity to place the menu bar in the appropriate location. Moving something as fundamental as a menu bar is almost certain to cause confusion and usability challenges for your users; having multiple menu bars would be baffling.

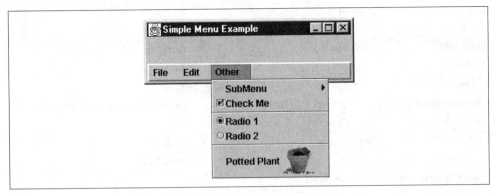

Figure 14-5. JMenuBar positioned as a Swing component

Properties

The properties of the JMenuBar class are shown in Table 14-3. menu is an indexed property that references each JMenu attached to the menu bar. The read-only menuCount property maintains a count of these attached menus. Remember that the single selection model allows only one menu to be activated at a time. If any menu is currently activated, the selected property returns true; otherwise, the property returns false. The componentAtIndex property accesses the menu associated with the given index. It is similar to the indexed menu property, except the contents are cast to a Component. If there is no component associated with that index, the getComponentAtIndex( ) accessor returns null. The component property returns a reference to this (i.e., the menu bar itself); subElements returns an array consisting of the menus on the menu bar.

Table 14-3. JMenuBar properties

Property	Data type	get	is	set	Default value
accessibleContext[o]	AccessibleContext	•			JMenuBar.AccessibleJMenuBar( )
borderPainted[b]	boolean		•	•	true
component	Component	•			this
componentAtIndex[i]	Component	•			true
helpMenu[u]	JMenu	•		•	Throws an Error
layout[o]	LayoutManager	•		•	BoxLayout(X_AXIS)
margin[b]	Insets	•		•	null
menuCount	int	•			0

[b]bound, [i]indexed, [o]overridden, [u]unimplemented

See also properties from the JComponent class (Table 3-6).

Table 14-3. JMenuBar properties (continued)

Property	Data type	get	is	set	Default value
menu[i]	JMenu	•			null
selected	boolean		•		false
selectionModel[b]	SingleSelectionModel	•		•	DefaultSingleSelectionModel()
subElements	MenuElement[]	•			
UI[b]	MenuBarUI	•		•	From L&F
UIClassID[o]	String	•			"MenuBarUI"

[b]bound, [i]indexed, [o]overridden, [u]unimplemented

See also properties from the JComponent class (Table 3-6).

The margin property controls the amount of space between the menu bar's border and its menus while the borderPainted property can be used to suppress the painting of the menu bar's border even if the border property has a non-null value. Setting borderPainted to false prevents the normal painting of the border. For more information about Swing borders, see Chapter 13.

The helpMenu property is supposed to allow you to designate one JMenu as the help menu (which has a special location in some operating systems), but this property has never been implemented, and using it throws an Error even in SDK 1.4. You can take advantage of the fact that the menu bar uses a BoxLayout to insert "glue" to position your (ordinary) help menu at the right edge when appropriate, but this shifts the burden of knowing when to do that (based on the current L&F) to your code, which is unfortunate.

Constructor

public JMenuBar( )

Create and initialize an empty JMenuBar object.

Menu

public JMenu add(JMenu menu)

You can use this method to attach a JMenu to the menu bar set. Because of the BoxLayout of JMenuBar, menus are displayed on the menu bar from left to right in the order that you add( ) them. The method returns a reference to the JMenu that was passed in, allowing you to string together calls—for example, menubar.add(menu).add(menuitem).

Miscellaneous

public int getComponentIndex(Component c)
> Return the index associated with the component reference passed in. If there is no match to the component, the method returns a -1. The only type of component it makes sense to pass in is JMenu.

public void setSelected(Component c)
> Force the menu bar (and its associated model) to select a particular menu, which fires a ChangeEvent in the menu bar's single selection model. This method, for example, is called when a mnemonic key for a particular menu is pressed. Note that this is different than the boolean selected property listed in Table 14-3.

public void updateUI( )
> Force the UIManager to refresh the L&F of the component, based on the current UI delegate.

JMenuBar also implements the methods specified by the MenuElement interface, which is covered later in this chapter.

The JMenuItem Class

Before discussing menus, we should introduce the JMenuItem class. Figure 14-6 shows the class diagram for the JMenuItem component.

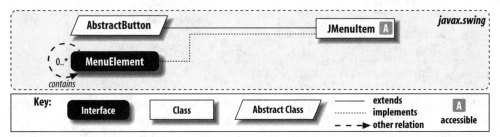

Figure 14-6. JMenuItem class diagram

A JMenuItem serves as a wrapper for strings and images to be used as elements in a menu. The JMenuItem class is essentially a specialized button and extends the AbstractButton class. Its behavior, however, is somewhat different from standalone buttons. When the mouse pointer is dragged over a menu item, Swing considers the menu item to be *selected*. If the user releases the mouse button while over the menu item, it is considered to be chosen and should perform its action.

There is an unfortunate conflict in terminology here. Swing considers a menu item selected when the mouse moves over it, as updated by the MenuSelectionManager and classes that implement the `MenuElement` interface. On the other hand, Swing considers a button selected when it remains in one of two persistent states, such as a checkbox button remaining in the checked state until clicked again. So when a menu item is selected, its button model is really *armed*. Conversely, when a menu item is deselected, its button model is disarmed. Finally, when the user releases the mouse button over the menu item, the button is considered to be clicked, and the `AbstractButton`'s `doClick( )` method is invoked.

Menu Item Shortcuts

Menu items can take both keyboard accelerators and (on some platforms) mnemonics. Mnemonics are an artifact of buttons; they appear as a single underline below the character that represents the shortcut. Keyboard accelerators, on the other hand, are inherited from `JComponent`. With menu items, they have the unique side effect of appearing in the menu item. (Their exact appearance and location is up to the L&F.) Figure 14-7 shows both mnemonics and keyboard accelerators.

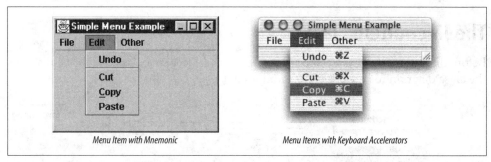

Figure 14-7. Mnemonics and keyboard accelerators

Keyboard accelerators and mnemonics perform the same function: users can abbreviate common GUI actions with keystrokes. However, a mnemonic can be activated only when the button (or menu item) it represents is visible on the screen. Menu item keyboard accelerators can be invoked any time the application has the focus— whether the menu item is visible or not. Also, as noted, accelerators work on all platforms and all L&Fs while mnemonics are less universal. Menus may be assigned both at once.

Let's look at programming both cases. Keyboard accelerators typically use a variety of keystrokes: function keys, command keys, or an alphanumeric key in combination with one or more modifiers (e.g., Shift, Ctrl, or Alt). All of these key combinations can be represented by the `javax.swing.KeyStroke` class, but only some of them are appropriate for the platform and L&F in use. Hence, you can assign a keyboard accelerator to a menu item by setting its accelerator property with a KeyStroke object configured using the default toolkit's menuShortcutKeyMask property, as follows:

```
JMenuItem m = new JMenuItem("Copy");
m.setAccelerator(KeyStroke.getKeyStroke('C',
    Toolkit.getDefaultToolkit().getMenuShortcutKeyMask(), false));
```

Under Metal, this sets the accelerator to Ctrl-C, which is the letter C typed in combination with the Ctrl key. The accelerator appears at the right side of the menu item (though again, the position is up to the L&F). The KeyStroke class is covered in more detail in Chapter 27.

The second, less universal, way to set a shortcut is through the mnemonic property of the AbstractButton superclass:

```
JMenuItem mi = new JMenuItem("Copy");
mi.setMnemonic('C');
```

The mnemonic property underlines the character you pass into the setMnemonic( ) method. Note that mnemonic characters cannot take modifiers; they are simple letters. Be sure to use a letter that exists in the menu item's label. Otherwise, nothing is underlined, and the user will not know how to activate the keyboard shortcut. Also be sure to set up mnemonics only if you're running on a platform and L&F that support them.

As of SDK 1.4, you can use the displayedMnemonicIndex property to cope with menu items containing multiple copies of the character you're using as a mnemonic, if it makes more sense for a later instance to be underlined (for example, the common Save As menu item in which the uppercase "A" should get the underline). To achieve this, once you set up the mnemonic, call setDisplayedMnemonicIndex with a value of 5.

Images

In Swing, menu items can contain (or consist entirely of) icons. This can be a visual aid if the icon can convey the intended meaning more clearly. You can pass an Icon object to the constructor of the JMenuItem class as follows:

```
JMenu menu = new JMenu("Justify");

// The first two menu items contain text and an image. The third
// uses only the image.
menu.add(new JMenuItem("Center", new ImageIcon("center.gif")));
menu.add(new JMenuItem("Right", new ImageIcon("right.gif")));
menu.add(new JMenuItem(new ImageIcon("left.gif")));
```

By default, the text is placed to the left of the image. This is shown on the left in Figure 14-8. As you can see, this often misaligns the images to the right of the text, especially if there is a menu item consisting only of an image. If the menu item images are all the same width, you can improve the appearance of your menus by altering the text's position using the setHorizontalTextAlignment( ) method:

```
JMenu menu = new JMenu("Justify");

// The first two menu items contain text and an image. The third
// uses only the image. The text is now set to the right.
JMenuItem item1= new JMenuItem("Center", new ImageIcon("center.gif")));
item1.setHorizontalTextAlignment(SwingConstants.RIGHT);
JMenuItem item2= new JMenuItem("Right", new ImageIcon("right.gif")));
item2.setHorizontalTextAlignment(SwingConstants.RIGHT);

// Now add the menu items to the menu.
menu.add(item1);
menu.add(item2);
menu.add(new JMenuItem(new ImageIcon("left.gif")));
```

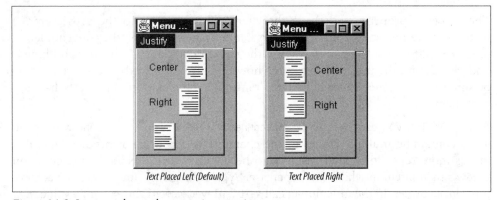

Figure 14-8. Image and text placement in menu items

This positions the text on the other side of the images, as shown on the right of Figure 14-8. You can trace the setHorizontalTextAlignment( ) method up the class hierarchy to the AbstractButton class. As we mentioned before, the JMenuItem class is a button object with respect to its text and image. AbstractButton contains a setVerticalTextAlignment( ) method as well, so if the accompanying image is taller than the menu item text, you can use this method to set the text's vertical position as well. (See the AbstractButton class in Chapter 5 and the OverlayLayout class in Chapter 11 for more information about alignment with menu items and buttons.) The image is placed to the left of the text if you construct a menu item from an Action object (more on this later in the chapter).

Java supports image transparency, so if you require some parts of an image to be transparent, you can specify a "transparent" color in the GIF file (many paint programs allow you to do this), or you can create a specialized color filter that seeks out specific pixel colors and changes their opacity before passing the resulting Image onto the menus. The former is much easier.

Event Handling

There are a number of ways to process events from menu items. Because menu items inherit ActionEvent functionality from AbstractButton, one approach is to assign an action command to each menu item (this is often done automatically with named components) and attach all of the menu items to the same ActionListener. Then, in the actionPerformed( ) method of the listener, use the event's getActionCommand( ) method to obtain the action command of the menu item generating the event. This tells the listener which menu item has been clicked, allowing it to react accordingly. This is the approach used in *IntroExample.java* earlier in this chapter and *PopupMenuExample.java*, which is discussed later.

Alternatively, you can register a separate ActionListener class with each menu item, which takes the guesswork out of determining the menu item selected. However, Swing allows you to go a step further. The most object-oriented approach is to create a specialized Action class that corresponds to each of the tasks a user might request of your application. This lets you bundle the code for each program action together with the action's name, icon, keystrokes, and other attributes in one place. You can then use this Action to create the menu item, which automatically sets the item's text, image, accelerator, and so on.

This technique is particularly powerful if you want to be able to invoke the same action in multiple ways (such as from a toolbar as well as a menu). You can use the same Action instance to create the menu item and toolbar button, and they'll both have appropriate labels and appearances. If the application needs to disable the action because it's not currently appropriate, calling setEnabled on the Action instance automatically updates all user interface elements associated with the action (thus dimming both your menu item and toolbar button). Similarly, changing other attributes of the action, such as its name or icon, automatically updates any associated user-interface components.

Although prior to SDK 1.3 it wasn't possible to construct a JMenuItem from an Action directly, adding the Action to a JMenu or JPopupMenu had the same effect: the menu would create and configure an appropriate JMenuItem for you.

Properties

The properties for the JMenuItem class are shown in Table 14-4. Most of the properties shown are superclass properties reconfigured to ensure that the menu item's "button" acts like a menu item should. The borderPainted property is always false;

menu items never take a border. The focusPainted property is also false to ensure that a focus rectangle is never drawn around the menu item. horizontalTextPosition and horizontalAlignment are both initialized to JButton.LEFT. This places the text to the left of the image icon and places the text and image icon on the left side of the menu item. (See the previous example for information on how to reconfigure this.)

Table 14-4. JMenuItem properties

Property	Data type	get	is	set	Default value
acceleratorb	KeyStroke	•		•	null
accessibleContexto	Accessible Context	•			JMenuItem. AccessibleJMenuItem( )
armedb, o	boolean		•	•	false
borderPaintedo	boolean		•	•	false
componento	Component	•			
enabledo	boolean		•	•	true
focusPaintedo	boolean		•	•	false
horizontalAlignmento	int	•		•	JButton.LEFT
horizontalTextPositiono	int	•		•	JButton.LEFT
menuDragMouseListeners1.4	MenuDragMouseListener[]	•			
menuKeyListeners1.4	MenuKeyListener[]	•			
modelo	ButtonModel	•		•	DefaultButtonModel( )
subElementso	MenuElement[]	•			
UIb	MenuItemUI			•	From L&F
UIClassIDo	String	•			"MenuItemUI"

1.4since 1.4, bbound, ooverridden

See also properties from the AbstractButton class (Table 5-5).

The accelerator property sets the keyboard accelerator for the menu item; the accelerator is typically drawn to the right of the menu item string. The armed property simply maps a boolean down to the armed state of the component model, ButtonModel. You can use this to programmatically select the menu item, if needed. The enabled property is a boolean that indicates whether the user can select the menu item. If the menu item is disabled, JMenuItem automatically grays the text and associated image. As discussed earlier, the most powerful way to control the enabled state of a menu item is to associate it with an Action object so that it automatically tracks the action's enabled state. The subElements property provides an array of submenus contained in this menu item.

Constructors

JMenuItem( )
JMenuItem(Action action)
JMenuItem(Icon icon)
JMenuItem(String string)
JMenuItem(String string, Icon icon)
JMenuItem(String string, int mnemonic)

Create a menu item with the appropriate icon or string. You also have the option to specify a mnemonic if you initialize with a string. Since Version 1.3, you can use the properties of an Action to directly configure the properties of the JMenuItem.

Events

JMenuItems send many different kinds of events. Perhaps the most important are ActionEvents, which are fired when an item is selected. ChangeEvents are fired when button properties change. Methods for adding and removing listeners for these events are inherited from AbstractButton.

JMenuItem also uses special events for reporting mouse motions and key presses on top of the menu item. These are the MenuDragMouseEvent and MenuKeyEvent. Here are the methods for registering listeners for these events:

addMenuDragMouseListener (MenuDragMouseListener 1)
removeMenuDragMouseListener (MenuDragMouseListener 1)

These methods add or remove a specific MenuDragMouseListener interested in being notified when there is a MenuDragMouseEvent.

addMenuKeyListener (MenuKeyListener 1)
removeMenuKeyListener (MenuKeyListener 1)

These methods add or remove a specific MenuKeyListener interested in being notified when there is a MenuKeyEvent.

The following methods provide support for firing these events, though you will probably never need to call them:

public void processMenuDragMouseEvent (MenuDragMouseEvent e)

Fire a specific MenuDragMouseEvent notification based on the type of MouseEvent that was observed. If the MouseEvent listed was MOUSE_ENTERED, for example, the menu invokes the fireMenuDragMouseEntered( ) method.

public void processMenuKeyEvent (MenuKeyEvent e)

Fire a specific MenuKeyEvent notification based on the type of MenuKeyEvent that was observed. If the MenuKeyEvent listed was KEY_RELEASED, for example, the menu invokes the fireMenuKeyReleased( ) method.

Method

public void updateUI( )

Force the current UI manager to reset the current delegate for the component, thus updating the component's L&F.

Menu Element Interface

public void menuSelectionChanged(boolean isIncluded)
public MenuElement[] getSubElements( )
public Component getComponent( )
public void processMouseEvent(MouseEvent event, MenuElement path[],
    MenuSelectionManager manager)
public void processKeyEvent(KeyEvent event, MenuElement path[],
    MenuSelectionManager manager)

Implement the MenuElement interface, discussed later in this chapter.

The MenuDragMouseEvent Class

Swing generates a series of events while the mouse is dragging across an open menu. One event, MenuDragMouseEvent, describes the drag in relation to a particular menu item. You can listen for these events by adding an object that implements MenuDragMouseListener to the addMenuDragMouseListener( ) method of JMenuItem. The object implementing MenuDragMouseListener will have four separate methods that can be invoked in response to a mouse drag inside a menu; each one indicates exactly what happened with the drag. Table 14-5 shows the properties of the MenuDragMouseEvent.

Properties

Table 14-5. MenuDragMouseEvent properties

Property	Data type	get	is	set	Default value
clickCount[o]	int	•			
id[o]	int	•		•	
manager	MenuSelectionManager	•			
modifiers[o]	Object	•		•	
path	MenuElement[]	•			
popupTrigger[o]	boolean		•		
source	Object	•			
when[o]	long	•			

[o]overridden

See also java.awt.event.MouseEvent.

Table 14-5. MenuDragMouseEvent properties (continued)

Property	Data type	get	is	set	Default value
x°	int			•	
y°	int		•	•	

°overridden

See also `java.awt.event.MouseEvent`.

There are no defaults for the event; all properties are set in the constructor. The `source` property indicates the object that sent the event. The `id` property describes the type of event that was fired. The `when` property gives the event a timestamp. The `modifiers` property allows you to test various masks to see which mouse button is being pressed, as well as the Alt, Ctrl, Shift, and Meta keys. The `x` and `y` properties give the current location of the mouse pointer relative to the component in question. The `clickCount` property describes how many times a mouse button has been clicked prior to this drag. The `popupTrigger` property indicates whether this mouse event should cause a popup menu to appear. The `path` property gives an ordered array of `MenuElement` objects, describing the path to this specific menu. Finally, the `manager` property contains a reference to the current `MenuSelectionManager` for this menu system.

Constructor

public MenuDragMouseEvent(Component source, int id, long when, int modifiers,
  int x, int y, int clickCount, boolean popupTrigger, MenuElement[] path,
  MenuSelectionManager manager)
    Initialize each of the properties described in Table 14-5 with the specified values.

The MenuDragMouseListener Interface

The `MenuDragMouseListener` interface, which is the conduit for receiving the `MenuDragMouseEvent` objects, contains four methods. One method is called when the mouse is dragged inside the menu item, the second when the mouse is released inside the menu item. Finally, the last two are called when the mouse is dragged into a menu item, or dragged out of a menu item.

Methods

public abstract void menuDragMouseDragged(PopupMenuEvent e)
    Called when the mouse is dragged inside of a menu item.

public abstract void menuDragMouseReleased(PopupMenuEvent e)
    Called when the mouse has been released inside of a menu item.

public abstract void menuDragMouseEntered(PopupMenuEvent e)
    Called when the mouse is being dragged, and has entered a menu item.

public abstract void menuDragMouseExited(PopupMenuEvent e)
    Called when the mouse is being dragged, and has exited a menu item.

The MenuKeyEvent Class

Swing also generates an event when a specific menu item receives a key event. Note that the key event does not have to be directed at the specific menu (i.e., an accelerator or mnemonic). Instead, the menu item responds to any key events generated while the menu pop up containing it is showing on the screen. You can listen for these events by adding an object that implements MenuKeyListener to the addMenuKeyListener() method of JMenuItem. The object implementing MenuKeyListener will have three separate methods that can be invoked in response to a menu key event.

Table 14-6 shows the properties of MenuKeyEvent. There are no defaults for the event; all properties are set in the constructor. The source property indicates the object that sent the event. The id property describes the type of event that was fired. The when property gives the event a timestamp. The modifiers property allows you to test various masks to see which mouse button is being pressed, as well as the Alt, Ctrl, Shift, and Meta keys. The keyCode and keyChar properties describe the key that was actually pressed. The path property gives an ordered array of MenuElement objects, describing the path to this specific menu. Finally, the manager property contains a reference to the current MenuSelectionManager.

Table 14-6. MenuKeyEvent properties

Property	Data Type	get	is	set	Default Value
id[o]	int	•		•	
keyChar[o]	char	•		•	
keyCode[o]	int	•			
manager	MenuSelectionManager	•			
modifiers[o]	Object	•		•	
path	MenuElement[]	•			
source	Object	•			
when[o]	long	•			

[o]overridden

See also java.awt.event.keyEvent.

Constructor

public MenuDragMouseEvent(Component source, int id, long when, int keyCode, char keyChar, MenuElement[] path, MenuSelectionManager manager)
    This constructor takes each of the properties described in Table 14-6.

The MenuKeyListener Interface

The MenuKeyListener interface, which is the conduit for receiving the MenuKeyEvent objects, contains three methods. One method is called when a key is typed (i.e., pressed and released) while the second is called after a key is pressed. This third is called after a key is released. Note that if a key is pressed and held down for a few seconds, Swing emulates the traditional key behavior: it considers the key both "typed" and "pressed" again.

Methods

public abstract void menuKeyTyped(MenuKeyEvent e)
  Called when a key intended for this menu element is both pressed and released.

public abstract void menuKeyPressed(MenuKeyEvent e)
  Called when a key intended for this menu element is pressed.

public abstract void menuKeyReleased(MenuKeyEvent e)
  Called when a key intended for this menu element is released.

Menu items cannot exist by themselves; they must be embedded in menus. Swing implements two closely related styles of menus: anchored menus and pop-up menus. Swing uses the JMenu and JPopupMenu classes to implement these menus.

The JPopupMenu Class

Pop-up menus are an increasingly popular user-interface feature. These menus are not attached to a menu bar; instead, they are free-floating menus that associate themselves with an underlying component. This component is called the *invoker*. Linked to specific interface elements, pop-up menus are nicely context-sensitive. They are brought into existence by a platform-dependent pop-up trigger event that occurs while the mouse is over the invoking component. In AWT and Swing, this trigger is typically a mouse event. Once raised, the user can interact with the menu normally. Figure 14-9 is an example of a pop-up menu in Swing.

You can add or insert JMenuItem, Component, or Action objects to the pop-up menu with the add( ) and insert( ) methods. The JPopupMenu class assigns an integer index to each menu item and orders them based on the layout manager of the pop-up menu. In addition, you can add separators to the menu by using the addSeparator( ) method; these separators also count as an index. Figure 14-10 shows the class diagram for the JPopupMenu component. Starting with SDK 1.4, pop-up menus use the Popup class to actually draw themselves. This class is also used for other briefly displayed interface elements like tooltips.

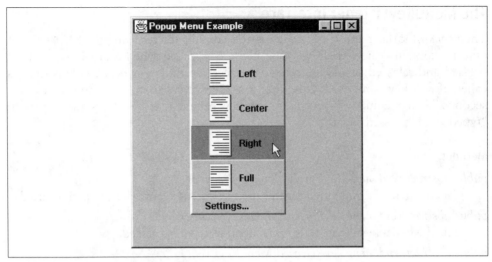

Figure 14-9. A pop-up menu in Swing

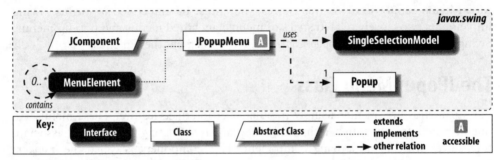

Figure 14-10. JPopupMenu class diagram

Displaying the Pop-up Menu

Pop-up menus are usually raised by invoking the show( ) method in response to a platform-specific pop-up trigger. The show( ) method sets the location and invoker properties of the menu before making it visible. Pop ups are automatically canceled by a variety of events, including clicking a menu item; resizing an invoking component; or moving, minimizing, maximizing, or closing the parent window. (You won't need to worry about canceling pop-up menus.) You raise the pop-up menu at the right time by checking all your MouseEvents to see if they're the pop-up trigger. A word to the wise: if a MouseEvent is the pop-up trigger, be sure not to pass it on to your superclass, or Swing could cancel the pop-up menu immediately after raising it! Also, be sure to check both pressed and released events because some platforms use one or the other. The easiest way to do that is to check *all* mouse events. Here's a processMouseEvent( ) method that raises a pop-up menu upon receiving the appropriate trigger:

```
public void processMouseEvent(MouseEvent e) {
    if (e.isPopupTrigger( )) {
        popup.show(this, e.getX( ), e.getY( ));
    }
    else {
        super.processMouseEvent(e);
    }
}
```

Note the use of isPopupTrigger( ) in java.awt.event.MouseEvent to check whether the mouse event is a trigger in a platform-independent way. Since SDK 1.3, JPopupMenu has an equivalent method you can use in the same way.

When the mouse moves outside the component, Swing no longer sends pop-up trigger events to that component, and its pop-up menu cannot be raised. This gives you the opportunity to define different pop-up menus for different underlying components, adding context sensitivity to your interface.

Properties

The properties of the JPopupMenu class are shown in Table 14-7. Pop-up menus have many properties. The visible property tells whether the pop-up menu is currently showing on the screen; you can use the setVisible( ) method to show or hide the pop up, but if it is a free-floating pop up, it is much easier to use the show( ) method. The location property provides the coordinates on the screen where the pop-up menu is or has been raised. The read-only margin property gives the amount of space between the pop-up window border and an imaginary rectangle surrounding the individual menu items.

Table 14-7. JPopupMenu properties

Property	Data type	get	is	set	Default value
accessibleContext[o]	AccessibleContext	•			JPopupMenu. accessibleJPopupMenu( )
borderPainted	boolean		•	•	true
component	Component	•			
componentAtIndex[i]	Component	•			
invoker	Component	•		•	
label[b]	String	•		•	""
layout[o]	LayoutManager	•		•	GridBagLayout( )

[1.4]since 1.4, [b]bound, [i]indexed, [o]overridden

See also properties from the JMenuItem class (Table 14-4).

Table 14-7. JPopupMenu properties (continued)

Property	Data type	get	is	set	Default value
lightWeightPopupEnabled	boolean		•	•	getDefaultLightWeightPop-upEnabled( )
location[o]	Point			•	
margin	Insets	•			
popupMenuListeners[1.4]	PopupMenuListener[]	•			
popupSize	Dimension			•	
selectionModel	SingleSelectionModel	•			DefaultSingleSelectionMo-del( )
subElements	MenuElement[]	•			
UI[b]	PopupMenuUI	•		•	BasicPopupMenuUI( )
UIClassID[o]	String	•			"PopupMenuUI"
visible[b, o]	boolean		•	•	false

[1.4]since 1.4, [b]bound, [i]indexed, [o]overridden

See also properties from the JMenuItem class (Table 14-4).

The invoker property is a reference to the component that is responsible for hosting the pop-up menu. The borderPainted property indicates whether the pop-up menu should paint its border. The label property gives each pop-up menu a specific label; the individual L&F is free to use or ignore this property as it sees fit. Note that label is a String and not a JLabel. componentAtIndex is an indexed property that returns the component at the specified index.

The lightWeightPopupEnabled property allows the programmer to enable or disable the potential use of lightweight components to represent the pop-up menu. If the property is set to true, Swing uses a lightweight component when the pop-up is inside the top-level component's drawing space, and a heavyweight when the pop-up extends beyond its space. If your interface uses any heavyweight components, they interfere with lightweight pop ups, so you should turn off this feature. You can set the default value of this property for all pop-up menus using the static setDefaultLightWeightPopupEnabled( ) method.

Events

JPopupMenu objects fire a PopupMenuEvent under two conditions: when the menu becomes visible or invisible, or is canceled without a menu item selection. The class contains the standard addPopupMenuListener( ) and removePopupMenuListener( ) methods for maintaining a list of PopupMenuEvent subscribers.

public void addPopupMenuListener(PopupMenuListener l)
public void removePopupMenuListener(PopupMenuListener l)
    Add or remove a PopupMenuListener from the object's event queue.

The ability to be notified right before the pop-up menu becomes visible gives you the opportunity to tweak the state and contents of the menu based on the current state of your application, which can make your interface even more helpful and context-sensitive.

Note that when the pop-up menu is canceled, it also becomes invisible, so two events are potentially triggered. The cancelation event itself seems to be fired rarely in current implementations, though. If you need to know when the menu goes away, use the popupMenuWillBecomeInvisible handler.

Constructors

public JPopupMenu( )
public JPopupMenu(String title)
> Create an empty pop-up menu. The second constructor accepts a String as the title of the pop-up menu.

Menu Items

public JMenuItem add(JMenuItem menuItem)
public Component add(Component c)
public JMenuItem add(Action a)
> Add various elements to the pop-up menus. Objects extending either JMenuItem or JComponent can be added, but the latter functions best if it implements the MenuElement interface. If you specify an Action, its many properties are used to derive an appropriate JMenuItem, and its text is placed to the right of any image icon. The item retains its association with the action so that updates to the action (changes in name, icon, enabled state, etc.) are reflected by the item. The resulting JMenuItem is then returned, which you can use to alter its formatting.

public JMenuItem insert(Action a, int index)
public Component insert(Component component, int index)
> Insert a specific menu item at a particular index. You can pass in a JComponent or an Action to these methods. If you use a JComponent, it's best if it implements the MenuElement interface. If you specify an Action, its various properties are used to derive an appropriate JMenuItem, and its text is placed to the right of any image icon. As usual, the item retains its association with the action. The resulting JMenuItem is then returned, which you can use to alter its formatting. All menu item indices that were previously at or after the specified position are incremented.

public void addSeparator( )
> Add a separator to the pop-up menu. Typically, a separator consists of a single horizontal line drawn across the pop-up menu. Note that, like menu items, the separator counts as an index in the menu. The separator used is an instance of an inner class, not the regular JSeparator; it is always horizontal.

Display

public void show(Component invoker, int x, int y)
> Paint the pop-up menu at the requested coordinates. The method takes a reference to the invoking component. It is functionally equivalent to the following calls: setInvoker( ), setLocation( ), and setVisible( ).

public void setPopupSize(int width, int height)
> An alternate way to establish a preferred size for the pop up. (The other way is the popupSize property, which takes a Dimension.)

Miscellaneous

public int getComponentIndex(Component c)
> Return the index associated with the component reference c. If there is no match to the component passed in, the method returns -1.

public static boolean getDefaultLightWeightEnabled
> Return the default value for the lightWeightPopupEnabled property.

public boolean isPopupTrigger(MouseEvent e)
> Since SDK 1.3, an alternate way to check whether a given mouse event should trigger a pop-up menu in the current L&F.

public static void setDefaultLightWeightPopupEnabled(boolean aFlag)
> Set the default value of the lightWeightPopupEnabled property, which controls whether a lightweight or heavyweight component is used for the pop up.

public void setSelected(Component c)
> Force the pop-up menu's model to select a particular menu item. This forces a property change event in the pop-up menu's single selection model.

public void updateUI( )
> Force the default user interface manager to update itself, thus resetting the delegate to display a new PopupMenuUI.

Menu Element Interface

public void menuSelectionChanged(boolean isIncluded)
public MenuElement[] getSubElements( )
public Component getComponent( )
public void processMouseEvent(MouseEvent event, MenuElement path[],
  MenuSelectionManager manager)
public void processKeyEvent(KeyEvent event, MenuElement path[],
  MenuSelectionManager manager)
> Implement the MenuElement interface, which is covered later in this chapter.

Using Pop-up Menus

Here is a program that demonstrates the use of the JPopupMenu class. The example is similar to the one that generated Figure 14-9, except that the pop up communicates events from the pop-up menu and from each of its menu items.

```java
// PopupMenuExample.java
//
import java.awt.*;
import java.awt.event.*;

import javax.swing.*;
import javax.swing.border.*;
import javax.swing.event.*;

public class PopupMenuExample extends JPanel {

    public JPopupMenu popup;

    public PopupMenuExample() {
        popup = new JPopupMenu();
        ActionListener menuListener = new ActionListener() {
            public void actionPerformed(ActionEvent event) {
                System.out.println("Popup menu item [" +
                                event.getActionCommand() + "] was pressed.");
            }
        };
        JMenuItem item;
        popup.add(item = new JMenuItem("Left", new ImageIcon("left.gif")));
        item.setHorizontalTextPosition(JMenuItem.RIGHT);
        item.addActionListener(menuListener);
        popup.add(item = new JMenuItem("Center", new ImageIcon("center.gif")));
        item.setHorizontalTextPosition(JMenuItem.RIGHT);
        item.addActionListener(menuListener);
        popup.add(item = new JMenuItem("Right", new ImageIcon("right.gif")));
        item.setHorizontalTextPosition(JMenuItem.RIGHT);
        item.addActionListener(menuListener);
        popup.add(item = new JMenuItem("Full", new ImageIcon("full.gif")));
        item.setHorizontalTextPosition(JMenuItem.RIGHT);
        item.addActionListener(menuListener);
        popup.addSeparator();
        popup.add(item = new JMenuItem("Settings . . ."));
        item.addActionListener(menuListener);

        popup.setLabel("Justification");
        popup.setBorder(new BevelBorder(BevelBorder.RAISED));
        popup.addPopupMenuListener(new PopupPrintListener());

        addMouseListener(new MousePopupListener());
    }

    // An inner class to check whether mouse events are the pop-up trigger
    class MousePopupListener extends MouseAdapter {
```

```
        public void mousePressed(MouseEvent e) { checkPopup(e); }
        public void mouseClicked(MouseEvent e) { checkPopup(e); }
        public void mouseReleased(MouseEvent e) { checkPopup(e); }

        private void checkPopup(MouseEvent e) {
            if (e.isPopupTrigger()) {
                popup.show(PopupMenuExample.this, e.getX(), e.getY());
            }
        }
    }

    // An inner class to show when pop-up events occur
    class PopupPrintListener implements PopupMenuListener {
        public void popupMenuWillBecomeVisible(PopupMenuEvent e) {
            System.out.println("Popup menu will be visible!");
        }
        public void popupMenuWillBecomeInvisible(PopupMenuEvent e) {
            System.out.println("Popup menu will be invisible!");
        }
        public void popupMenuCanceled(PopupMenuEvent e) {
            System.out.println("Popup menu is hidden!");
        }
    }

    public static void main(String s[]) {
        JFrame frame = new JFrame("Popup Menu Example");
        frame.setDefaultCloseOperation(JFrame.EXIT_ON_CLOSE);
        frame.setContentPane(new PopupMenuExample());
        frame.setSize(300, 300);
        frame.setVisible(true);
    }
}
```

The interesting parts of this program are the methods of MousePopupListener. These call a private method, checkPopup(), to see if we've received an event that should raise the pop-up menu. If we get a valid trigger event, we show the pop up at the mouse location. This is an alternative to the approach of overriding processMouseEvent() that was demonstrated in "Displaying the Pop-up Menu."

The PopupMenuEvent Class

This is a simple event that tells listeners that the target pop-up menu is about to become visible or invisible, or that it has been canceled. Note that it doesn't tell which one has occurred. The object implementing PopupMenuListener will define three separate methods that can be called by a pop-up menu; each one indicates exactly what happened with the target pop-up menu object.

Constructor

public PopupMenuEvent(Object source)
    The constructor takes a reference to the object that fired the event.

The PopupMenuListener Interface

The `PopupMenuListener` interface, which is the conduit for receiving the `PopupMenuEvent` objects, contains three methods. One method is called when the pop up is canceled, and the other two indicate that the pop up is about to show or hide itself. This interface must be implemented by any listener object that wishes to be notified of changes to the pop-up menu.

Methods

public abstract void popupMenuCanceled(PopupMenuEvent e)
> Called when the target pop-up menu is canceled or removed from the screen. (This seems to be called rarely in practice.)

public abstract void popupMenuWillBecomeInvisible(PopupMenuEvent e)
> Called when the pop-up menu is about to be removed from the screen.

public abstract void popupMenuWillBecomeVisible(PopupMenuEvent e)
> Called when the pop-up menu is about show itself on the screen. This is an excellent opportunity to update the contents of the menu (or their enabled states) based on current application conditions.

The JMenu Class

The `JMenu` class represents the anchored menus attached to a `JMenuBar` or another `JMenu`. Menus directly attached to a menu bar are called *top-level* menus. Submenus, on the other hand, are not attached to a menu bar but to a menu item that serves as its title. This menu item title is typically marked by a right arrow, indicating that its menu appears alongside the menu item if the user selects it. See Figure 14-11.

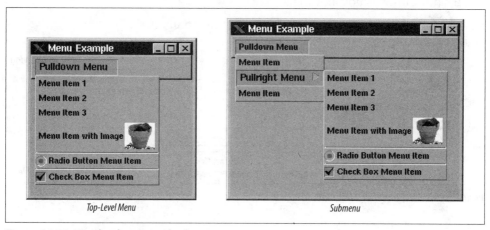

Figure 14-11. Top-level menu and submenu

JMenu is a curious class. It contains a MenuUI delegate, but it uses a ButtonModel for its data model. To see why this is the case, it helps to visualize a menu as two components: a menu item and a pop-up menu. The menu item serves as the title. When it is pressed, it signals the pop-up menu to show itself either below or directly to the right of the menu item. JMenu actually extends the JMenuItem class, which makes it possible to implement the title portion of the menu. This, in effect, makes it a specialized button. On some platforms you can use the mnemonic property of the JMenuItem superclass to define a shortcut for the menu's title and, consequently, the menu. In addition, you can use the enabled property of JMenuItem to disable the menu if desired.

As with pop-up menus, you can add or insert JMenuItem, Component, or Action objects in the pop-up portion of the menu by calling the add( ) and insert( ) methods. You can also add a simple string to the menu; JMenu creates the corresponding JMenuItem object for you internally. The JMenu class assigns an integer index to each menu item and orders them based on the layout manager used for the menu. You can also add separators to the menu by using the addSeparator( ) method.

 You cannot use keyboard accelerators with JMenu objects (top-level or submenu), because accelerators trigger actual program actions, not simply the display of a menu from which actions can be chosen. On some platforms you can use the setMnemonic( ) method to set a shortcut to bring up the menu, but the only universal, reliable approach is to assign keyboard accelerators to the non-submenu JMenuItems that trigger program actions.

You can programmatically cause the submenu to pop up on the screen by setting the popupMenuVisible property to true. Be aware that the pop up does not appear if the menu's title button is not showing.

Figure 14-12 shows the class diagram for the JMenu component.

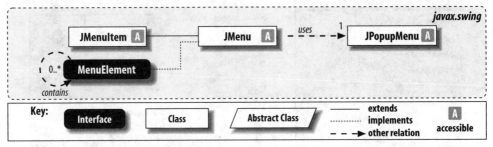

Figure 14-12. JMenu class diagram

Properties

The JMenu properties are listed in Table 14-8. JMenu uses a JPopupMenu to represent its list of menu items. If you wish to access that underlying menu, you can do so using the popupMenu property. The popupMenuVisible property tracks whether the menu's pop-up portion is currently visible. As noted, setting this to true when the title button is visible causes the pop up to appear. JMenu also contains a selected property, which indicates if the user has selected the title button of the menu. Both properties should mirror each other.

Table 14-8. JMenu properties

Property	Data type	get	is	set	Default value
accessibleContext[o]	AccessibleContext	•			JMenu.accessibleJMenu( )
component	Component	•			
componentOrientation[1.4, o]	ComponentOrientation	•		•	From L&F
delay	int	•		•	0
itemCount	int	•			0
item[i]	JMenuItem	•			null
layout[o]	LayoutManager	•		•	OverlayLayout( )
menuComponentCount	int	•			0
menuComponent[i]	Component	•			null
menuComponents	Component[ ]	•			
menuListeners[1.4]	MenuListener[ ]	•			
model[o]	ButtonModel	•		•	DefaultButtonModel( )
popupMenu	JPopupMenu	•			
popupMenuVisible	boolean		•	•	false
selected	boolean		•	•	false
subElements	MenuElement[ ]	•			
tearOff[u]	boolean		•		Throws an Error
topLevelMenu	boolean		•		
UI[b]	MenuUI			•	From L&F
UIClassID	String	•			"MenuUI"

[1.4]since 1.4, [b]bound, [i]indexed, [o]overridden, [u]unimplemented

See also properties from the JMenuItem class (Table 14-4).

The topLevelMenu property has the value true if this JMenu is directly attached to a menu bar and is not a submenu. item is an indexed property that allows access to each of the JMenuItem objects in the menu, while itemCount maintains a count of all of the JMenuItem objects that are present. The delay property specifies the amount of time, in milliseconds, that the underlying menu waits to appear or disappear after receiving the corresponding event. The delay must be set to a positive integer, or setDelay( ) throws an IllegalArgumentException.

The menuComponent property is a more generalized version of the item property; it returns the component at the given index as a Component rather than as a JMenuItem. In addition, the menuComponentCount property retains a count of the menu items, separators, and other components currently in the menu. The menuComponents property lets you access each of the items in the menu, returned as an array of Component objects.

The componentOrientation property is used to accommodate non-Western languages in which text does not flow left to right. JMenu overrides this property in order to properly pass changes on to the JPopupMenu delegate it uses.

 The tearOff property is not yet implemented and is reserved for (increasingly dubious) future use in Swing. Trying to use it throws an Error (rather than something more appropriate like an UnsupportedOperationException). Since an Error is supposed to indicate a catastrophic failure of the virtual machine, using this property will almost certainly crash your application.

Constructor

public JMenu( )
public JMenu(Action a)
public JMenu(String s)
public JMenu(String s, boolean b)
> Initialize a default JMenu. You have the option of specifying a string for the JMenu to display—as well as a boolean for the tearOff property (which is ignored)—or binding it to an Action.

Menu Items

public JMenuItem add(JMenuItem menuItem)
public Component add(Component c)
public void add(String s)
public JMenuItem add(Action a)
> Add various elements to the menus. Objects from both JMenuItem and JComponent can be added, but the latter functions best if it implements the MenuElement interface. If you specify a String as the parameter, a menu item with the appropriate label is created. If you specify an Action, its text and icon properties are used to derive an appropriate JMenuItem, and its text is placed to the right of the icon. It retains its association with the action and is updated to reflect

changes to its properties. The resulting JMenuItem is returned, which you can use to alter its formatting.

public void addSeparator( )

Add a separator to the menu. Typically, a separator consists of a single horizontal line drawn across the menu.

public void insert(String s, int index)
public JMenuItem insert(JMenuItem mi, int index)
public JMenuItem insert(Action a, int index)

Insert a specific menu item at a particular index. The index must be positive, or the method throws an IllegalArgumentException. You can pass in a JMenuItem, a String, or an Action to these methods. If you specify a String as the parameter, a menu item with the appropriate label is created. If you specify an Action, its text and icon properties are used to derive an appropriate JMenuItem, and its text is placed to the right of the icon. As usual, the menu retains its association with the action. The resulting JMenuItem is returned, which you can use to alter its formatting. All menu items that were previously at or after the specified position are increased by one.

public void insertSeparator(int index)

Insert a horizontal separator at the position specified by the integer index. The index must be positive, or the method throws an IllegalArgumentException. All menu items' indices that were previously at or after the specified position are increased by one.

public void remove(JMenuItem item)
public void remove(int index)

Remove the menu item that matches the JMenuItem passed in or that currently occupies the specified integer index. If there are no matches (or if the position does not exist), no changes are made to the menu. If the function is successful, all menu items' indices following the removed menu item are reduced by one.

public void removeAll( )

Remove all of the items from the menu.

Miscellaneous

public void updateUI( )

Force the default user interface manager to update itself, thus resetting the delegate to display a new MenuUI.

public void setMenuLocation(int x, int y)

Set a custom location at which the menu appears when shown.

public boolean isMenuComponent(Component c)
> Determine whether the component c is present anywhere in the menu. This method searches all submenus as well.

public String paramString( )
> Return a `String` specifying the current state of the menu properties (intended for debugging purposes).

Event

`JMenu` objects fire a `MenuEvent` when the user has selected or deselected the menu's title button. The `JMenu` object contains the standard `addChangeListener( )` and `removeChangeListener( )` methods for maintaining a list of `MenuEvent` subscribers.

public void addMenuListener(MenuListener listener)
public void removeMenuListener(MenuListener listener)
> Add or remove a `MenuListener` from the list of listeners receiving this menu's events.

MenuElement Interface

public void menuSelectionChanged(boolean isIncluded)
public MenuElement[] getSubElements( )
public Component getComponent( )
public void processKeyEvent(KeyEvent event, MenuElement path[],
*   MenuSelectionManager manager)*
> Implement the `MenuElement` interface, which is covered later in this chapter.

Working with Menus

Here is a program that demonstrates the use of the `JMenu` class. In this program, we use Swing's `Action` class to process the menu events. (We'll also use actions for toolbars later in this chapter.)

```
//  MenuExample.java
//
import java.awt.*;
import java.awt.event.*;
import javax.swing.*;
import javax.swing.border.*;

public class MenuExample extends JPanel {

    public JTextPane pane;
    public JMenuBar menuBar;

    public MenuExample( ) {
        menuBar = new JMenuBar( );
```

```
        JMenu formatMenu = new JMenu("Justify");
        formatMenu.setMnemonic('J');

        MenuAction leftJustifyAction = new MenuAction("Left",
                                new ImageIcon("left.gif"));
        MenuAction rightJustifyAction = new MenuAction("Right",
                                 new ImageIcon("right.gif"));
        MenuAction centerJustifyAction = new MenuAction("Center",
                                  new ImageIcon("center.gif"));
        MenuAction fullJustifyAction = new MenuAction("Full",
                                new ImageIcon("full.gif"));

        JMenuItem item;
        item = formatMenu.add(leftJustifyAction);
        item.setMnemonic('L');
        item = formatMenu.add(rightJustifyAction);
        item.setMnemonic('R');
        item = formatMenu.add(centerJustifyAction);
        item.setMnemonic('C');
        item = formatMenu.add(fullJustifyAction);
        item.setMnemonic('F');

        menuBar.add(formatMenu);
        menuBar.setBorder(new BevelBorder(BevelBorder.RAISED));

    }

    class MenuAction extends AbstractAction {

        public MenuAction(String text, Icon icon) {
            super(text,icon);
        }

        public void actionPerformed(ActionEvent e) {
            try { pane.getStyledDocument().insertString(0 ,
                "Action ["+e.getActionCommand()+"] performed!\n", null);
            } catch (Exception ex) { ex.printStackTrace(); }
        }
    }

    public static void main(String s[]) {

        MenuExample example = new MenuExample();
        example.pane = new JTextPane();
        example.pane.setPreferredSize(new Dimension(250, 250));
        example.pane.setBorder(new BevelBorder(BevelBorder.LOWERED));

        JFrame frame = new JFrame("Menu Example");
        frame.setDefaultCloseOperation(JFrame.EXIT_ON_CLOSE);
        frame.setJMenuBar(example.menuBar);
        frame.getContentPane().add(example.pane, BorderLayout.CENTER);
        frame.pack();
        frame.setVisible(true);
    }
}
```

Our Actions are all instances of the inner class MenuActions. As we add each Action to the menu, it creates an appropriate JMenuItem (with the image left-justified) and returns it to us. This allows us to manipulate the resulting menu item in any way we want; in this case, we add a mnemonic for each item. You can run this program on various platforms to see if they support mnemonics. You shouldn't rely on mnemonics as a key part of your user interface in a program intended for multiple platforms (in fact, you should avoid setting them at all unless you are sure the platform supports them).

The resulting program produces a menu bar with a single menu, as shown in Figure 14-13. The menu contains four menu items and is similar in appearance to the pop-up example. When the user clicks any menu item, Swing generates an ActionEvent to be processed by the actionPerformed( ) method of our MenuAction class. As in the previous examples, this results in the name of the menu item being printed. For variety, we have added a simple JTextPane to display the results of our menu choice, instead of using the system output. See Chapters 19 and 22 for more information on JTextPane.

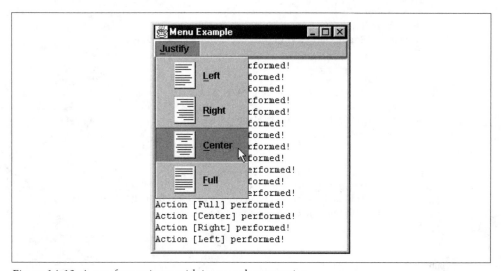

Figure 14-13. A set of menu items with icons and mnemonics

The MenuEvent Class

This is a simple event that tells listeners that the target menu has been raised, selected, or canceled. Note that it doesn't tell which one has occurred. The listener defines three separate methods that can be called to deliver the menu event; each one tells exactly what happened.

Constructor

public MenuEvent(Object source)
> The constructor takes a reference to the object that fires the event.

The MenuListener Interface

The MenuListener interface, which is the conduit for receiving MenuEvents, specifies three methods. One method is called when the menu is canceled; the other two are called when the title button of the menu is selected or deselected. This interface must be implemented by any listener object that needs to be notified of changes to the menu object.

Methods

public abstract void menuCanceled(MenuEvent e)
> This method is called when the menu is canceled or removed from the screen.

public abstract void menuDeselected(MenuEvent e)
> This method is called when the target menu's title button is deselected.

public abstract void menuSelected(MenuEvent e)
> This method is called when the target menu's title button is selected.

Selectable Menu Items

So far, we've covered traditional menu items that produce a simple, text-oriented label associated with an action. But that's not the only type of item to which users are accustomed. Swing provides for two selectable menu items: the checkbox menu item and the radio button menu item.

The JCheckBoxMenuItem Class

Checkbox menu items are represented by the JCheckBoxMenuItem class. As you might have guessed, this object behaves similarly to the JCheckBox object. By clicking on a checkbox menu item, you can toggle a UI-defined checkmark that generally appears to the left of the menu item's label. There is no mutual exclusion between adjoining JCheckBoxMenuItem objects—the user can check any item without affecting the state of the others. Figure 14-14 shows the class diagram for the JCheckBoxMenuItem component.

Properties

Table 14-9 shows the properties of the JCheckBoxMenuItem class. JCheckBoxMenuItem inherits the JMenuItem model (ButtonModel) and its accessors. The JCheckBoxMenuItem class also contains two additional component properties. The state property has the value true if the menu item is currently in the checked state, and false if it is not. The

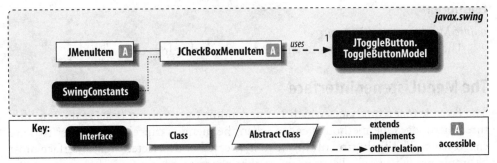

Figure 14-14. JCheckBoxMenuItem class diagram

`selectedObjects` property contains an `Object` array of size one, consisting of the text of the menu item if it is currently in the checked state. If it is not, `getSelectedObjects()` returns `null`. The `getSelectedObjects()` method exists for compatibility with AWT's `ItemSelectable` interface.

Table 14-9. JCheckBoxMenuItem properties

Property	Data type	get	is	set	Default value
accessibleContext[o]	AccessibleContext	•			JCheckBoxMenuItem. AccessibleJCheckBoxMenuItem()
selectedObjects[o]	Object[]	•			
state	boolean	•		•	false
UI[b]	CheckBoxMenuItemUI	•		•	From L&F
UIClassID[o]	String	•			"CheckBoxMenuItem"

[b]bound, [o]overridden

See also properties from the `JMenuItem` class (Table 14-4).

Constructors

public JCheckBoxMenuItem()
public JCheckBoxMenuItem(Action action)
public JCheckBoxMenuItem(Icon icon)
public JCheckBoxMenuItem(String text)
public JCheckBoxMenuItem(String text, Icon icon)
public JCheckBoxMenuItem(String text, boolean checked)
public JCheckBoxMenuItem(String text, Icon icon, boolean checked)

These constructors initialize the `JCheckBoxMenuItem` with a specified action (since Version 1.3), icon, or string. The additional boolean value initializes the `state` property, specifying whether the menu item is initially checked.

Miscellaneous

public void updateUI()

Force the current UI manager to reset and repaint the delegate for the component, thus updating the component's L&F.

Using Checkbox Menu Items

Here's a program using the JCheckBoxMenuItem class. It is similar to the JMenu example, except that each menu item now has a checkmark next to it. We've done nothing to make the items mutually exclusive; that comes next. We have, however, reworked the code to use more-portable keyboard accelerators rather than mnemonics. Note that we used M (middle) as the accelerator for the Center option because C is generally reserved for Copy. Figure 14-15 shows the result.

```java
// CheckBoxMenuItemExample.java
//
import java.awt.*;
import java.awt.event.*;
import javax.swing.*;
import javax.swing.border.*;

public class CheckBoxMenuItemExample extends JPanel {
    public JTextPane pane;
    public JMenuBar menuBar;
    public JToolBar toolBar;

    public CheckBoxMenuItemExample() {
        menuBar = new JMenuBar();
        JMenu justifyMenu = new JMenu("Justify");
        ActionListener actionPrinter = new ActionListener() {
            public void actionPerformed(ActionEvent e) {
                try { pane.getStyledDocument().insertString(0 ,
                    "Action ["+e.getActionCommand()+"] performed!\n", null);
                } catch (Exception ex) { ex.printStackTrace(); }
            }
        };
        JCheckBoxMenuItem leftJustify = new
            JCheckBoxMenuItem("Left", new ImageIcon("left.gif"));
        leftJustify.setHorizontalTextPosition(JMenuItem.RIGHT);
        leftJustify.setAccelerator(KeyStroke.getKeyStroke('L',
                Toolkit.getDefaultToolkit().getMenuShortcutKeyMask()));
        leftJustify.addActionListener(actionPrinter);
        JCheckBoxMenuItem rightJustify = new
            JCheckBoxMenuItem("Right", new ImageIcon("right.gif"));
        rightJustify.setHorizontalTextPosition(JMenuItem.RIGHT);
        rightJustify.setAccelerator(KeyStroke.getKeyStroke('R',
                Toolkit.getDefaultToolkit().getMenuShortcutKeyMask()));
        rightJustify.addActionListener(actionPrinter);
```

```
JCheckBoxMenuItem centerJustify = new
        JCheckBoxMenuItem("Center", new ImageIcon("center.gif"));
centerJustify.setHorizontalTextPosition(JMenuItem.RIGHT);
centerJustify.setAccelerator(KeyStroke.getKeyStroke('M',
                Toolkit.getDefaultToolkit().getMenuShortcutKeyMask()));
centerJustify.addActionListener(actionPrinter);
JCheckBoxMenuItem fullJustify = new
        JCheckBoxMenuItem("Full", new ImageIcon("full.gif"));
fullJustify.setHorizontalTextPosition(JMenuItem.RIGHT);
fullJustify.setAccelerator(KeyStroke.getKeyStroke('F',
                Toolkit.getDefaultToolkit().getMenuShortcutKeyMask()));
fullJustify.addActionListener(actionPrinter);

justifyMenu.add(leftJustify);
justifyMenu.add(rightJustify);
justifyMenu.add(centerJustify);
justifyMenu.add(fullJustify);

menuBar.add(justifyMenu);
menuBar.setBorder(new BevelBorder(BevelBorder.RAISED));

    }

    public static void main(String s[]) {
        CheckBoxMenuItemExample example = new CheckBoxMenuItemExample();
        example.pane = new JTextPane();
        example.pane.setPreferredSize(new Dimension(250, 250));
        example.pane.setBorder(new BevelBorder(BevelBorder.LOWERED));

        JFrame frame = new JFrame("Menu Example");
        frame.setDefaultCloseOperation(JFrame.EXIT_ON_CLOSE);
        frame.setJMenuBar(example.menuBar);
        frame.getContentPane().add(example.pane, BorderLayout.CENTER);
        frame.pack();
        frame.setVisible(true);
    }
}
```

The JRadioButtonMenuItem Class

Swing implements radio button menu items with the JRadioButtonMenuItem class. As you might expect, it shares the characteristics of the JRadioButton class and is intended to represent a group of mutually exclusive choices. Some L&Fs indicate this exclusivity visually by showing circular "buttons" to the left of the selectable choices.

Even though L&Fs visually distinguish between checkbox and radio button items, the distinction can be subtle and unfamiliar to users, so it's a good idea to use separators (see "The JSeparator Class" later in this chapter) as well as other visual cues that suggest the logical grouping of mutually exclusive items within the menu.

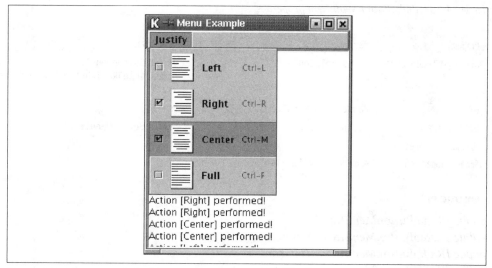

Figure 14-15. A series of checkbox menu items

Although you might expect otherwise, radio button menu items don't enforce mutual exclusion by themselves. Instead, you need to use a ButtonGroup object to limit the user to a single selection. Figure 14-16 shows the class diagram for the JRadioButtonMenuItem component.

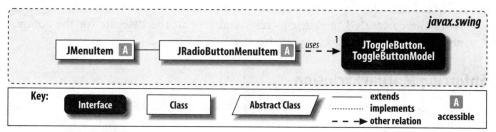

Figure 14-16. Radio button menu item class diagram

Properties

Table 14-10 shows the properties of the JRadioButtonMenuItem class. Unlike JCheckBoxMenuItem, there is no state property that indicates the current selection state of the menu item. Instead, you typically use this class in conjunction with a ButtonGroup, which contains a getSelected( ) method for extracting the correct object.

Table 14-10. JRadioButtonMenuItem properties

Property	Data type	get	is	set	Default value
accessibleContext[o]	AccessibleContext	•			JRadioButtonMenuItem. AccessibleJRadioButtonMenu-Item( )
UI[b]	RadioButtonMenuItemUI	•		•	From L&F
UIClassID[o]	String	•			"RadioButtonMenuItem"

[b]bound, [o]overridden

See also properties from the JMenuItem class (Table 14-4).

Constructor

public JRadioButtonMenuItem( )
public JRadioButtonMenuItem(Action action)
public JRadioButtonMenuItem(Icon icon)
public JRadioButtonMenuItem(String text)
public JRadioButtonMenuItem(String text, Icon icon)
> Initialize the JRadioButtonMenuItem with the specified action (since Version 1.3), icon, or string.

Miscellaneous

public void updateUI( )
> Force the current UI manager to reset and repaint the delegate for the component, thus updating the component's L&F.

Enforcing Mutual Exclusion

The following program shows how to implement the mutually exclusive nature of radio button menu items:

```
//  RadioButtonMenuItemExample.java
//
import java.awt.*;
import java.awt.event.*;
import javax.swing.*;
import javax.swing.border.*;

public class RadioButtonMenuItemExample extends JPanel {

    public JTextPane pane;
    public JMenuBar menuBar;
    public JToolBar toolBar;

    public RadioButtonMenuItemExample( ) {
        menuBar = new JMenuBar( );
        JMenu justifyMenu = new JMenu("Justify");
```

```java
        ActionListener actionPrinter = new ActionListener( ) {
            public void actionPerformed(ActionEvent e) {
                try { pane.getStyledDocument( ).insertString(0 ,
                    "Action ["+e.getActionCommand( )+"] performed!\n", null);
                } catch (Exception ex) { ex.printStackTrace( ); }
            }
        };
        JRadioButtonMenuItem leftJustify = new
                JRadioButtonMenuItem("Left", new ImageIcon("left.gif"));
        leftJustify.setHorizontalTextPosition(JMenuItem.RIGHT);
        leftJustify.setAccelerator(KeyStroke.getKeyStroke('L',
                    Toolkit.getDefaultToolkit( ).getMenuShortcutKeyMask( )));
        leftJustify.addActionListener(actionPrinter);
        JRadioButtonMenuItem rightJustify = new
                JRadioButtonMenuItem("Right", new ImageIcon("right.gif"));
        rightJustify.setHorizontalTextPosition(JMenuItem.RIGHT);
        rightJustify.setAccelerator(KeyStroke.getKeyStroke('R',
                    Toolkit.getDefaultToolkit( ).getMenuShortcutKeyMask( )));
        rightJustify.addActionListener(actionPrinter);
        JRadioButtonMenuItem centerJustify = new
                JRadioButtonMenuItem("Center", new ImageIcon("center.gif"));
        centerJustify.setHorizontalTextPosition(JMenuItem.RIGHT);
        centerJustify.setAccelerator(KeyStroke.getKeyStroke('M',
                    Toolkit.getDefaultToolkit( ).getMenuShortcutKeyMask( )));
        centerJustify.addActionListener(actionPrinter);
        JRadioButtonMenuItem fullJustify = new
                JRadioButtonMenuItem("Full", new ImageIcon("full.gif"));
        fullJustify.setHorizontalTextPosition(JMenuItem.RIGHT);
        fullJustify.setAccelerator(KeyStroke.getKeyStroke('F',
                    Toolkit.getDefaultToolkit( ).getMenuShortcutKeyMask( )));
        fullJustify.addActionListener(actionPrinter);

        ButtonGroup group = new ButtonGroup( );
        group.add(leftJustify);
        group.add(rightJustify);
        group.add(centerJustify);
        group.add(fullJustify);

        justifyMenu.add(leftJustify);
        justifyMenu.add(rightJustify);
        justifyMenu.add(centerJustify);
        justifyMenu.add(fullJustify);

        menuBar.add(justifyMenu);
        menuBar.setBorder(new BevelBorder(BevelBorder.RAISED));
    }

    public static void main(String s[]) {

        RadioButtonMenuItemExample example = new
                                    RadioButtonMenuItemExample( );
        example.pane = new JTextPane( );
        example.pane.setPreferredSize(new Dimension(250, 250));
        example.pane.setBorder(new BevelBorder(BevelBorder.LOWERED));
```

```
        JFrame frame = new JFrame("Menu Example");
        frame.setDefaultCloseOperation(JFrame.EXIT_ON_CLOSE);
        frame.setJMenuBar(example.menuBar);
        frame.getContentPane( ).add(example.pane, BorderLayout.CENTER);
        frame.pack( );
        frame.setVisible(true);
    }
}
```

Figure 14-17 shows the result. We use a `ButtonGroup` object to make our `JRadioButtonMenuItems` mutually exclusive. Selecting any of the menu items deselects the others. Since text justification is mutually exclusive, this example shows how you would implement a real justification menu.

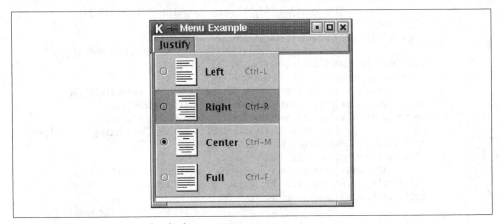

Figure 14-17. An example of radio button menu items

The JSeparator Class

You may have noticed that both `JMenu` and `JPopupMenu` contain `addSeparator( )` methods to add separators to menus. In doing so, each class instantiates a `JSeparator` object and positions it in the menu. However, `JSeparator` exists as a component unto itself outside of menus, and, because it extends `JComponent`, it can be positioned inside a container like any other Swing component. `JSeparator` is a simple component that provides separation between logical groups of menu items. In some L&Fs it shows up as a horizontal line drawn across its entire width; in others, it is invisible and just adds a little extra space between elements. It has no model, only a delegate.

Properties

Table 14-11 shows the properties of `JSeparator`.

Table 14-11. JSeparator properties

Property	Data type	get	is	set	Default value
accessibleContext[o]	AccessibleContext	•			JSeparator.accessibleJSeparator( )
orientation	int	•		•	SwingConstants.HORIZONTAL
UI[b]	SeparatorUI	•		•	From L&F
UIClassID[o]	String	•			"SeparatorUI"

[b]bound, [o]overridden

See also properties from the JComponent class (Table 3-6).

Constructor

JSeparator( )
JSeparator(int orientation)

Create a separator. By default, this separator is horizontal; if you specify an orientation, it should be either SwingConstants.HORIZONTAL or SwingConstants.VERTICAL.

Miscellaneous

public void updateUI( )

Force the current UI manager to reset and repaint the delegate for the component, thus updating the component's L&F.

Using a Separator Outside of a Menu

We've already seen how a separator can be used in menus to highlight the grouping of menu items. However, separators are components in themselves and can be used for a variety of tasks. Here is a program that adds a separator between a series of buttons:

```
// SeparatorExample.java
//
import java.awt.*;
import java.awt.event.*;
import javax.swing.*;
import javax.swing.border.*;

public class SeparatorExample extends JPanel {

    public SeparatorExample( ) {
        super(true);

        setLayout(new BoxLayout(this, BoxLayout.Y_AXIS));
        Box box1 = new Box(BoxLayout.X_AXIS);
        Box box2 = new Box(BoxLayout.X_AXIS);
        Box box3 = new Box(BoxLayout.X_AXIS);

        box1.add(new JButton("Press Me"));
        box1.add(new JButton("No Me!"));
```

```
        box1.add(new JButton("Ignore Them!"));
        box2.add(new JSeparator());
        box3.add(new JButton("I'm the Button!"));
        box3.add(new JButton("It's me!"));
        box3.add(new JButton("Go Away!"));

        add(box1);
        add(box2);
        add(box3);
    }

    public static void main(String s[]) {

        SeparatorExample example = new SeparatorExample();

        JFrame frame = new JFrame("Separator Example");
        frame.setDefaultCloseOperation(JFrame.EXIT_ON_CLOSE);
        frame.setContentPane(example);
        frame.pack();
        frame.setVisible(true);
    }
}
```

This code yields the interface shown in Figure 14-18. Note that on platforms where separators are invisible, they are difficult or impossible to notice when used in this unorthodox way. (Even in this example, in which the separator has a visual representation, it's pretty hard to see!)

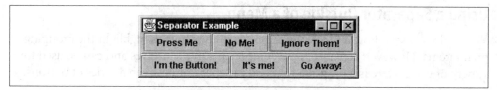

Figure 14-18. A standalone separator between two groups of buttons

The MenuElement Interface

As we saw in the previous examples, one nice feature of Swing menus is that we are not constrained to using text for menu items. However, the possibilities don't have to stop with icons, either. In fact, with a little work you can create or extend any Java component to serve as a menu item. There is one catch: your new menu item must implement the MenuElement interface. Swing declares five methods in the MenuElement interface; these methods are called by Swing's internal MenuSelectionManager when various actions take place.

Why is this necessary? Let's look at the traditional menu item, such as the Paste item in the Edit menu. When the user raises the Edit menu, and the mouse passes over the Paste menu item, the menu item typically highlights itself, usually by changing color. This tells the user that releasing (or clicking, depending on the L&F) the mouse button chooses the Paste option. When the mouse leaves the menu item, it returns to its normal color. However, what if we wanted to make the text bold instead of highlighting it? What if we wanted to substitute another icon image in the menu item when the mouse passed over it? By calling the methods of this interface, menus allow menu items to define their own unique behavior.

Methods

public void processMouseEvent(MouseEvent event,MenuElement path[],
  MenuSelectionManager manager)

> This method handles events triggered by the mouse. In addition to the MouseEvent, the current path of selected menu elements is provided, as well as a reference to the current menu selection manager. You can take whatever action you feel is necessary with this method.

public void processKeyEvent(KeyEvent event, MenuElement path[],
  MenuSelectionManager manager)

> This method handles events triggered by keystrokes. In addition to the KeyEvent, the current path of selected menu elements is provided as well as a reference to the current menu selection manager. You can take whatever action you feel is necessary in this method.

public void menuSelectionChanged(boolean isIncluded)

> Called when the menu element is added or removed from the current target menu.

public MenuElement[] getSubElements()

> Return an array of subelements for the target MenuElement. This is needed in the event that a particular menu element has a submenu.

public Component getComponent()

> Return a reference to the component responsible for painting the menu item.

Making Arbitrary Components into Menu Elements

It is relatively easy to convert any Swing component into a menu element and drop it in a menu. Here is a program that places a JSlider inside a pop-up menu and uses it as a hidden control for an underlying component.

```
//  MenuElementExample.java
//
import java.awt.*;
import java.awt.event.*;

import javax.swing.*;
import javax.swing.border.*;
import javax.swing.event.*;

public class MenuElementExample extends JPanel {
```

```java
public JPopupMenu popup;
SliderMenuItem slider;
int theValue = 0;

public MenuElementExample( ) {

    popup = new JPopupMenu( );
    slider = new SliderMenuItem( );

    popup.add(slider);
    popup.add(new JSeparator( ));

    JMenuItem ticks = new JCheckBoxMenuItem("Slider Tick Marks");
    ticks.addActionListener(new ActionListener( ) {
        public void actionPerformed(ActionEvent event) {
            slider.setPaintTicks(!slider.getPaintTicks( ));
        }
    });
    JMenuItem labels = new JCheckBoxMenuItem("Slider Labels");
    labels.addActionListener(new ActionListener( ) {
        public void actionPerformed(ActionEvent event) {
            slider.setPaintLabels(!slider.getPaintLabels( ));
        }
    });
    popup.add(ticks);
    popup.add(labels);
    popup.addPopupMenuListener(new PopupPrintListener( ));

    addMouseListener(new MousePopupListener( ));
}

// Inner class to check whether mouse events are the pop-up trigger
class MousePopupListener extends MouseAdapter {
    public void mousePressed(MouseEvent e) { checkPopup(e); }
    public void mouseClicked(MouseEvent e) { checkPopup(e); }
    public void mouseReleased(MouseEvent e) { checkPopup(e); }

    private void checkPopup(MouseEvent e) {
        if (e.isPopupTrigger( )) {
            popup.show(MenuElementExample.this, e.getX( ), e.getY( ));
        }
    }
}

// Inner class to print information in response to pop-up events
class PopupPrintListener implements PopupMenuListener {
    public void popupMenuWillBecomeVisible(PopupMenuEvent e) { }

    public void popupMenuWillBecomeInvisible(PopupMenuEvent e) {
        theValue = slider.getValue( );
        System.out.println("The value is now " + theValue);
    }
```

```
            public void popupMenuCanceled(PopupMenuEvent e) {
                System.out.println("Popup menu is hidden!");
            }
        }

        public static void main(String s[]) {
            JFrame frame = new JFrame("Menu Element Example");
            frame.setDefaultCloseOperation(JFrame.EXIT_ON_CLOSE);
            frame.setContentPane(new MenuElementExample());
            frame.setSize(300, 300);
            frame.setVisible(true);
        }

        // Inner class that defines our special slider menu item
        class SliderMenuItem extends JSlider implements MenuElement {

            public SliderMenuItem() {
                setBorder(new CompoundBorder(new TitledBorder("Control"),
                                new EmptyBorder(10, 10, 10, 10)));

                setMajorTickSpacing(20);
                setMinorTickSpacing(10);
            }

            public void processMouseEvent(MouseEvent e, MenuElement path[],
                                    MenuSelectionManager manager) {}

            public void processKeyEvent(KeyEvent e, MenuElement path[],
                                    MenuSelectionManager manager) {}

            public void menuSelectionChanged(boolean isIncluded) {}

            public MenuElement[] getSubElements() {return new MenuElement[0];}

            public Component getComponent() {return this;}
        }
    }
```

As with our previous pop-up example, PopupMenuExample, we implement MouseListener and check incoming mouse events to see whether to show the pop up. The inner class SliderMenuItem implements the MenuElement interface, and is the focus of our example. In this case, it's fairly easy. Our menu slider never has subelements, doesn't have a concept of a selection, and doesn't need to do anything special with mouse or key events.

The interface resulting from our example is shown in Figure 14-19. We provide a JSlider object, a separator, and two JCheckBoxMenuItem objects, which control the state of the slider. The slider is also surrounded by a titled border. When the user adjusts the slider and dismisses the pop up, we print the current value of the slider to the standard output. With a little bit of imagination, you can do just about anything with a pop-up menu. Of course, if it's something unexpected, you should carefully consider whether it is likely to confuse or confound your users.

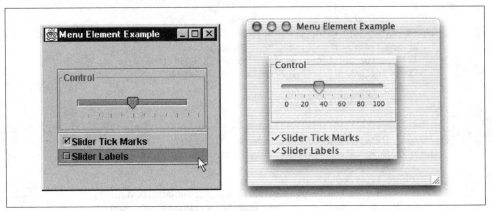

Figure 14-19. A JSlider masquerading as a pop-up menu element in two L&Fs

Toolbars

Toolbars are another approach to providing access to commonly used application features. They are more likely than menus to use graphical representations of commands. Because they remain on-screen at all times (unlike menus, which drop down only when activated) they can provide a useful "dashboard" for indicating the current state of the application. On the other hand, they take up more room than menu bars, so it's good to let the user decide whether they should be visible at all.

Toolbars have the ability to "tear" themselves from their location within a frame and embed their components in a moveable standalone window. This gives the user the freedom to drag the toolbar anywhere on the screen. In addition, toolbars can "dock" in locations where the layout manager can support them.

The JToolBar Class

Like the menu bar, the JToolBar class is a container for various components. You can add any component to the toolbar, including buttons, combo boxes, and even additional menus. Like menus, the toolbar is easiest to work with when paired with Action objects.

When a component is added to the toolbar, it is assigned an integer index that determines its display order from left to right. While there is no restriction on the type of component that can be added, the toolbar generally looks best if it uses components that are the same vertical height. Note that toolbars have a default border installed by the L&F. If you don't like the default, you can override the border with one of your own using the setBorder( ) method. Alternatively, you can deactivate the drawing of the border by setting the borderPainted property to false.

JToolBar has its own separator that inserts a blank space on the toolbar; you can use the addSeparator( ) method to access this separator. Separators are useful if you want to add space between groups of related toolbar components. The separator for toolbars is actually an inner class. Be sure not to confuse this separator with the JSeparator class.

Figure 14-20 shows the class diagram for the JToolBar component.

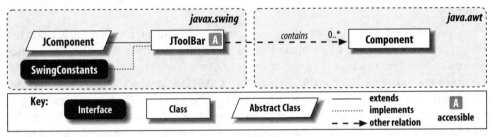

Figure 14-20. JToolBar class diagram

Floating toolbars

Although toolbars can be easily positioned in Swing containers, they do not have to stay there. Instead, you can "float" the toolbar by holding the mouse button down while the cursor is over an empty section of the toolbar (that is, not over any of its components) and dragging. This places the toolbar in a moveable child window; you can position it anywhere in the viewing area. Toolbars can then reattach themselves to specific locations, or *hotspots*, within the frame. Letting go of the toolbar while dragging it over a hotspot anchors the toolbar back into the container. Figure 14-21 is an example of a floating toolbar.

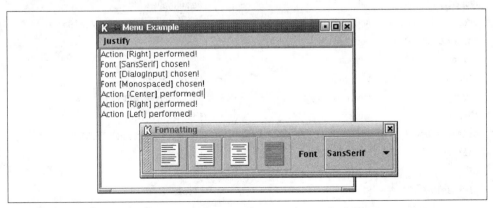

Figure 14-21. A floating toolbar

It is best to place a toolbar in a container that supports the BorderLayout. If you intend to make the toolbar floatable, place it along either the north, south, east, or west side of the container, and leave the remaining sides open. This allows the toolbar to define anchor spots when it is being dragged and ensures that the resulting layout is not ambiguous.

If you want to disable floating, you can reset the floatable property to false:

```
JToolBar toolBar = new JToolBar();
toolBar.setFloatable(false);
```

Properties

The properties of the JToolBar class are shown in Table 14-12. The borderPainted property defines whether the toolbar should paint its border. The JToolBar constructor resets the layout manager of the component to a BoxLayout along the x axis (this becomes a y-axis BoxLayout if the orientation is VERTICAL), which it uses to place any child components. The margin property defines the insets that appear between the toolbar's edges and its components. The floatable property defines whether the toolbar can be separated from the container and "floated" in a standalone window. You can use the indexed componentAtIndex property to access any of the components on the toolbar. The orientation property determines whether the toolbar is horizontal or vertical. Its value must be either HORIZONTAL or VERTICAL (constants defined in SwingConstants). Attempting to set orientation to some other value throws an IllegalArgumentException. Finally, starting with SDK 1.4, rollover can be set to cause the toolbar's button borders to be drawn only when the mouse is hovering over them, a style of interface popularized by dynamic web sites. Not all L&Fs honor a true value for rollover.

Table 14-12. JToolBar properties

Property	Data type	get	is	set	Default value
accessibleContext	AccessibleContext	•			JToolBar.AccessibleJToolBar()
borderPainted[b]	boolean		•	•	true
componentAtIndex[i]	Component	•			
floatable[b]	boolean		•	•	true
layout[o]	LayoutManager	•		•	BoxLayout(X_AXIS)
margin[b]	Insets	•		•	Insets(0,0,0,0)
orientation[b]	int	•		•	SwingConstants.HORIZONTAL
rollover[1.4, b]	boolean		•	•	false
UI[b]	ToolBarUI	•		•	From L&F
UIClassID[o]	String	•			"ToolBarUI"

[1.4]since 1.4, [b]bound, [i]indexed, [o]overridden

See also properties from the JComponent class (Table 3-6).

Event

JToolbar generates a `PropertyChangeEvent` when any of its bound properties are changed.

Constructor

public JToolBar( )
public JToolBar(int orientation)
public JToolBar(String name)
public JToolBar(String name, int orientation)

Create a `JToolBar`, optionally supplying a name that appears as a title when the toolbar is floating (the ability to assign a name started with SDK 1.3). The orientation is horizontal by default; if you specify an orientation, it must be `SwingConstants.HORIZONTAL` or `SwingConstants.VERTICAL`.

Adding actions

public JButton add(Action a)

Add an `Action` to the toolbar. The method creates a simple `JButton` with the text of the action placed below its image.[*] It then returns the `JButton`, allowing you to reset any of the button's attributes. (As you'd expect, the method for adding a component to a toolbar is inherited from `Container`.)

Miscellaneous

public void updateUI( )

Force the current `UIManager` to repaint the UI delegate for the component, updating the component's L&F.

public int getComponentIndex(Component c)

Return the integer index of the component c, or -1 if it's not found. Note that any separators in the toolbar take up index positions.

public void addSeparator( )
public void addSeparator(Dimension size)

Add a separator to the toolbar. Be sure not to confuse the toolbar separator with `JSeparator`, which is a separate Swing component. The toolbar separator created by this method is simply a blank area of space used to provide spacing between groups of toolbar components. The size is normally up to the toolbar, though you can specify the separator's size explicitly if you wish.

---

[*] In SDK 1.3, Sun discouraged the use of this method without actually deprecating it. People have pointed out that there is no adequate replacement, and this has been acknowledged. So use it, but keep your eye out for news.

Creating a Toolbar

The following example adds a toolbar to the JMenu example and provides a glimpse of the true power of using Action objects for building a user interface.

To add some interesting complexity, we also allow the user to choose a font from a combo box, showing that you can use other kinds of components in a toolbar. Note that we add the combo box and a JLabel for it as separate components and that the combo box uses its own actionPerformed( ) method.

```java
// ToolBarExample.java
//
import java.awt.*;
import java.awt.event.*;
import javax.swing.*;
import javax.swing.border.*;
import javax.swing.event.*;

public class ToolBarExample extends JPanel {

    public JTextPane pane;
    public JMenuBar menuBar;
    public JToolBar toolBar;
    String fonts[] = {"Serif","SansSerif","Monospaced","Dialog","DialogInput"};

    public ToolBarExample( ) {
        menuBar = new JMenuBar( );

        // Create a set of actions to use in both the menu and toolbar.
        DemoAction leftJustifyAction = new DemoAction("Left",
            new ImageIcon("left.gif"), "Left justify text", 'L');
        DemoAction rightJustifyAction = new DemoAction("Right",
            new ImageIcon("right.gif"), "Right justify text", 'R');
        DemoAction centerJustifyAction = new DemoAction("Center",
            new ImageIcon("center.gif"), "Center justify text", 'M');
        DemoAction fullJustifyAction = new DemoAction("Full",
            new ImageIcon("full.gif"), "Full justify text", 'F');

        JMenu formatMenu = new JMenu("Justify");
        formatMenu.add(leftJustifyAction);
        formatMenu.add(rightJustifyAction);
        formatMenu.add(centerJustifyAction);
        formatMenu.add(fullJustifyAction);
        menuBar.add(formatMenu);

        toolBar = new JToolBar("Formatting");
        toolBar.add(leftJustifyAction);
        toolBar.add(rightJustifyAction);
        toolBar.add(centerJustifyAction);
        toolBar.add(fullJustifyAction);

        toolBar.addSeparator( );
        JLabel label = new JLabel("Font");
        toolBar.add(label);
```

```
        toolBar.addSeparator( );
        JComboBox combo = new JComboBox(fonts);
        combo.addActionListener(new ActionListener( ) {
            public void actionPerformed(ActionEvent e) {
                try { pane.getStyledDocument( ).insertString(0,
                    "Font [" + ((JComboBox)e.getSource( )).getSelectedItem( ) +
                    "] chosen!\n", null);
                } catch (Exception ex) { ex.printStackTrace( ); }
            }
        });
        toolBar.add(combo);

        // Disable one of the Actions.
        fullJustifyAction.setEnabled(false);
    }

    public static void main(String s[]) {

        ToolBarExample example = new ToolBarExample( );
        example.pane = new JTextPane( );
        example.pane.setPreferredSize(new Dimension(250, 250));
        example.pane.setBorder(new BevelBorder(BevelBorder.LOWERED));
        example.toolBar.setMaximumSize(example.toolBar.getSize( ));

        JFrame frame = new JFrame("Menu Example");
        frame.setDefaultCloseOperation(JFrame.EXIT_ON_CLOSE);
        frame.setJMenuBar(example.menuBar);
        frame.getContentPane( ).add(example.toolBar, BorderLayout.NORTH);
        frame.getContentPane( ).add(example.pane, BorderLayout.CENTER);
        frame.pack( );
        frame.setVisible(true);
    }

    class DemoAction extends AbstractAction {

        public DemoAction(String text, Icon icon, String description,
                          char accelerator) {
            super(text, icon);
            putValue(ACCELERATOR_KEY, KeyStroke.getKeyStroke(accelerator,
                    Toolkit.getDefaultToolkit( ).getMenuShortcutKeyMask( )));
            putValue(SHORT_DESCRIPTION, description);
        }

        public void actionPerformed(ActionEvent e) {
            try { pane.getStyledDocument( ).insertString(0,
                    "Action [" + getValue(NAME) + "] performed!\n", null);
            } catch (Exception ex) { ex.printStackTrace( ); }
        }
    }
}
```

Note the efficiency we've achieved: by creating a single set of Actions to represent our justification modes, we can create a corresponding menu entry or toolbar button in a single line of code. Each has the appropriate label and/or icon, accelerator key (for menus), and tooltip. Try holding your mouse over the buttons to see the tooltip. Also notice that by disabling the Full justify action we automatically disabled both the corresponding menu item and toolbar button. When an action is disabled, all the associated components are notified of the property change. In our program, both the menu item and the toolbar button for full justification are grayed, as shown in Figure 14-22.

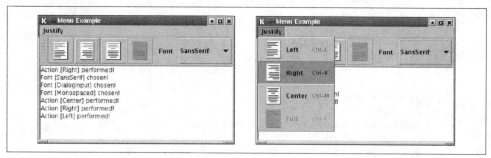

Figure 14-22. Disabling actions automatically grays the toolbar and menu representations

To see the toolbar float, click on the textured area at the left edge and drag it outside the window. You can also drag it to any edge of the frame to anchor it at that position.

A JToolBar is a regular Swing component, so you can use more than one in an application. If you do so, and you wish to make the toolbars floatable, it is best to place each toolbar in a concentric BorderLayout container, leaving the other three sides unpopulated. This ensures that the toolbars maintain their respective positions if they are both dragged to a new side.

CHAPTER 15

Tables

Tables represent one of the most common formats for viewing data. Database records are easy to sort and choose from a table. Statistics on disk usage can be displayed for several computers or several time periods all at once. Stock market quotes can be tracked. And where would sales presentations be without tables? Well, the JTable class in the Swing package now gives you access to a single component that can handle all of the preceding examples and more.

Without getting fancy, you can think of tables as an obvious expression of two-dimensional data. In fact, the JTable class has a constructor that takes an Object[][] argument and displays the contents of that two-dimensional array as a table with rows and columns. For example, Figure 15-1 shows how a table of string objects falls out very quickly.

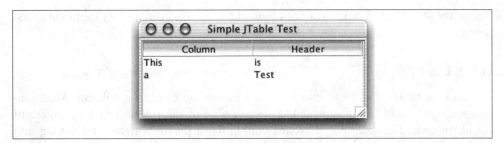

Figure 15-1. A simple JTable with a two-dimensional array of strings for data

This program was generated with very little code. All we did was set up a JTable object with a String[][] argument for the table data and a String[] argument for the table's headers. Rather than adding the table itself directly to our window, we enclose it in a scrollpane:

```
// SimpleTable.java
// A test of the JTable class using default table models and a convenience
// constructor
//
```

```
import java.awt.*;
import javax.swing.*;

public class SimpleTable extends JFrame {

    public SimpleTable() {
        super("Simple JTable Test");
        setSize(300, 200);
        setDefaultCloseOperation(EXIT_ON_CLOSE);

        JTable jt = new JTable(new String[][] { {"This", "is"}, {"a", "Test"} },
                               new String[] {"Column", "Header"});
        JScrollPane jsp = new JScrollPane(jt);
        getContentPane().add(jsp, BorderLayout.CENTER);
    }

    public static void main(String args[]) {
        SimpleTable st = new SimpleTable();
        st.setVisible(true);
    }
}
```

As you can see, we rely entirely on the data models built for us and simply pass in our data (a String[][] object) and our column headers (a String[] object). JTable takes care of the rest. With the default models, you can select multiple rows, edit individual cells, and listen for selection events. But of course, you are not restricted to the default models, and you can produce some pretty interesting effects if you decide to roll your own.

The JTable Class

Before we get ahead of ourselves, let's look at the JTable class and its supporting cast members.

Table Columns

With Swing tables, the basic unit is not an individual cell but a column. Most columns in real-world tables represent a certain type of information that is consistent for all records. For example, a record containing a person's name is a String and might be the first column of the table. For every other record (row), the first cell is always a String. The columns do not need to all have the same data type. The same record could hold not only a person's name, but whether or not they owned a computer. That column would hold Boolean values, not String values. The models supporting JTable reflect this view of the world. There is a TableModel that handles the contents of each cell in the table. You will also find a TableColumnModel that tracks the state of the columns in the table (how many columns, the total width, whether or not you can select columns, etc.).

The ability to store different types of data also affects how the table draws the data. The table column that maps to the "owns a computer" field could use a JCheckBox object for the cells of this column while using regular JLabel objects for the cells of other columns. But again, each column has one data type and one class responsible for drawing it.

Now, as the JTable class evolves, you may find alternate ways to think about tables without relying so heavily on columns. You'll want to keep an eye on the API in future releases of the Swing package. Figure 15-2 shows how the classes of the JTable package fit together.

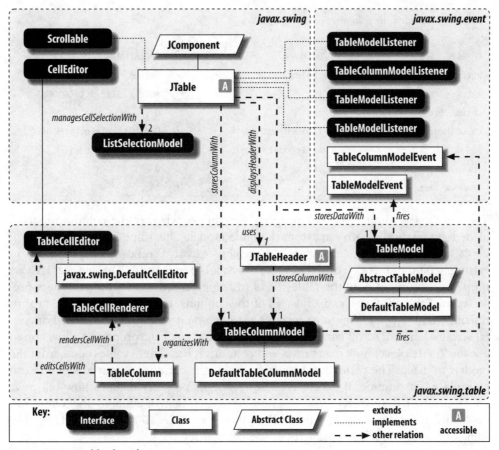

Figure 15-2. JTable class diagram

Well, we made it this far without officially discussing the JTable class itself. Dynamic data and database queries are handled entirely by the table model underneath the display. So what can you do with a JTable object? The JTable class gives you control over the appearance and behavior of the table. You can control the spacing of columns, their resizability, their colors, and so on. The JTable object is the source of row selections. Through delegation, you can add and remove rows and columns directly with the JTable object.

Properties

The appearance of a JTable is manipulated almost entirely through its properties. To make things a bit more manageable, we'll break the properties up into three smaller tables: one for row, column, and cell properties; one for selection properties; and one for visual properties. Table 15-1 covers the row, column, and cell properties.

Table 15-1. JTable row, column, and cell properties

Property	Data type	get	is	set	Default value
autoCreateColumnsFromModel	boolean	•		•	false
autoResizeMode	int	•		•	AUTO_RESIZE_ALL_COLUMNS
columnCount	int	•			0
columnModel	TableColumnModel	•		•	DefaultTableColumnModel()
model	TableModel	•		•	DefaultTableModel()
rowCount	int	•			0
rowHeight	int	•		•	16

The autoCreateColumnsFromModel property determines whether the column model is loaded automatically with data from the table model. This value is set to true if you don't supply a non-null ColumnModel to the constructor. (You can always replace an existing column model with the setColumnModel() method.) The autoResizeMode property determines how the table reacts to being resized. Using the constants presented in Table 15-4, you can adjust all of the columns, only the last column, or shut resizing off altogether. You must turn off autoresizing if you want to use the horizontal scrollbar in your scroll pane. The columnCount and rowCount properties allow you to ask the JTable object how many rows and columns it has. These values come from the models in place. The columnModel property holds the current column model and can be replaced at runtime, if necessary. The rowHeight property dictates how tall rows are, in pixels. This property must be a number greater than or equal to one. Other values cause the setRowHeight() method to throw an IllegalArgumentException. The value of rowHeight includes the vertical intercell spacing.

Table 15-2 lists the selection-related properties of the JTable class. The selectionModel property holds the ListSelectionModel object that handles row selections, and the selectionMode property applies to that model. (You can control the column selections with the selectionModel property of the TableColumnModel for your table.) The cellSelectionEnabled, columnSelectionAllowed, and rowSelectionAllowed properties determine whether you can select cells, columns, or rows. If cells are selectable, only cells can be selected, regardless of the row and column properties. With cell selection turned on and row and column selection turned off, you can still select a range of cells. With an active selection on your table, the selectedColumn, selectedColumnCount, selectedColumns, selectedRow, selectedRowCount, and selectedRows give you access to the various parts of that selection. The selectedRow and selectedColumn properties store the anchor selection (i.e., the first selection) from their respective selection models.

Table 15-2. JTable selection properties

Property	Data type	get	is	set	Default value
cellSelectionEnabled	boolean	•		•	false
columnSelectionAllowed	boolean	•		•	false
rowSelectionAllowed	boolean	•		•	true
selectedColumn	int	•			-1
selectedColumnCount	int	•			0
selectedColumns	int[]	•			int[0]
selectedRow	int	•			-1
selectedRowCount	int	•			0
selectedRows	int[]	•			int[0]
selectionMode	int			•	MULTIPLE_INTERVAL_SELECTION
selectionModel	ListSelectionModel	•		•	DefaultListSelectionModel

Table 15-3 covers the remaining properties of the JTable class. The cellEditor property determines the cell editor currently in use. When you start editing, the JTable class looks up your column and asks it for an editor. If the column has one, that editor is used; otherwise, a default editor for the column's class type is used. If no cell is currently being edited, this property is null. If you want your table to support automatic drag initiation, set the dragEnabled property to true. The gridColor, selectionBackground, and selectionForeground properties determine the color used for the grid lines and selection text. The intercellSpacing property determines the horizontal and vertical spacing around each cell in the table. The preferredScrollableViewportSize property determines the preferred size of the scrollpane for the table. The scrollableTracksViewportHeight and scrollableTracksViewportWidth properties are always false, which indicates that making the viewport around the table should not resize the table to fit the viewport (assuming you have placed the table in a scrollpane). You can control which lines show up on the table with showGrid, showHorizontalLines, and showVerticalLines. Use setShowGrid( ) as a convenient way to turn both horizontal and vertical lines on or off at the same time. The tableHeader property is used to store a JTableHeader object for your table. This header can be used in a JScrollPane as the column header for your table. (No row header counterpart is provided, but you can see an example of creating one in the next chapter.) The `rowMargin` property determines the amount of empty space between rows. This is really just a more convenient way of getting at the height information in the `intercellSpacing` property.

Table 15-3. JTable visual and editing properties

Property	Data type	get	is	set	Default value
accessibleContext[o]	AccessibleContext	•			JTable. AccessibleJTable
cellEditor	TableCellEditor	•		•	null
dragEnabled[1.4]	boolean	•		•	false
gridColor	Color	•		•	From L&F
intercellSpacing	Dimension	•		•	Dimension(1, 1)
preferredScrollableViewportSize[o]	Dimension	•		•	Dimension(450, 400)
rowMargin	int	•		•	1
scrollableTracksViewportHeight[o]	boolean	•			false
scrollableTracksViewportWidth[o]	boolean	•			false
selectionBackground[b]	Color	•		•	From L&F
selectionForeground[b]	Color	•		•	From L&F
showGrid	boolean			•	true
showHorizontalLines	boolean	•		•	true
showVerticalLines	boolean	•		•	true
tableHeader	JTableHeader	•		•	JTableHeader(column-Model)
UI[b]	TableUI	•		•	From L&F
UIClassID[o]	String	•			"TableUI"

[b]bound, [o]overridden, [1.4]since 1.4

See also properties from the `JComponent` class (Table 3-6).

Examples

To see some of the more interesting properties in action, the following example sets up a simple (contrived) data set. We shut off autoresizing so that horizontal scrolling works properly. We also set the selection mode so that any range of cells can be selected. (We'll look at responding to selection events in the next section.)

Here's the source code that built the table in Figure 15-3:

```
// TableFeature.java
// A test of the JTable class using default table models and a convenience
// constructor
//
import java.awt.*;
import javax.swing.*;
```

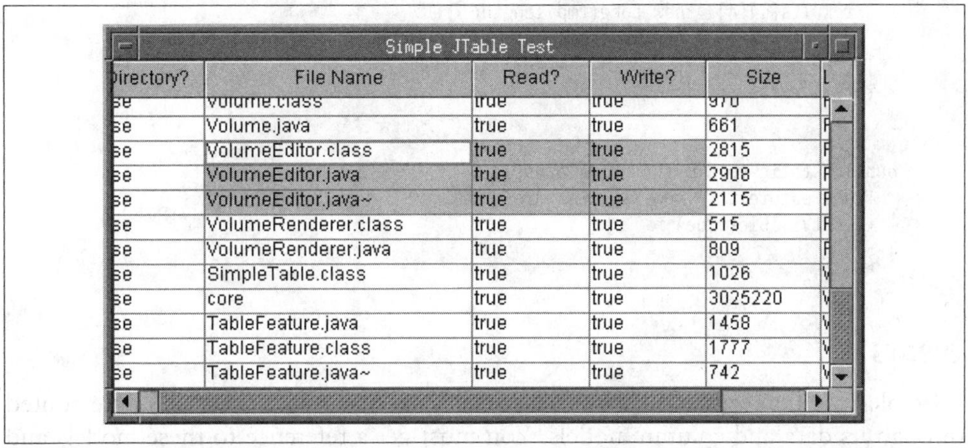

Figure 15-3. A simple JTable in a JScrollPane with a range of cells selected

```java
import java.util.Date;
import java.io.File;

public class TableFeature extends JFrame {

  String titles[] = new String[] {
    "Directory?", "File Name", "Read?", "Write?", "Size", "Last Modified"
  };

  public TableFeature( ) {
    super("Simple JTable Test");
    setSize(300, 200);
    setDefaultCloseOperation(EXIT_ON_CLOSE);

    File pwd = new File(".");
    Object[][] stats = getFileStats(pwd);

    JTable jt = new JTable(stats, titles);
    jt.setAutoResizeMode(JTable.AUTO_RESIZE_OFF);
    jt.setColumnSelectionAllowed(true);

    JScrollPane jsp = new JScrollPane(jt);
    getContentPane( ).add(jsp, BorderLayout.CENTER);
  }

  public Object[][] getFileStats(File dir) {
    String files[] = dir.list( );
    Object[][] results = new Object[files.length][titles.length];

    for (int i=0; i < files.length; i++) {
      File tmp = new File(files[i]);
      results[i][0] = new Boolean(tmp.isDirectory( ));
      results[i][1] = tmp.getName( );
      results[i][2] = new Boolean(tmp.canRead( ));
      results[i][3] = new Boolean(tmp.canWrite( ));
```

```
      results[i][4] = new Long(tmp.length());
      results[i][5] = new Date(tmp.lastModified());
    }
    return results;
  }

  public static void main(String args[]) {
    TableFeature tf = new TableFeature();
    tf.setVisible(true);
  }
}
```

Events

All table-specific events you would expect to see from the JTable class are routed
through its data and column models. You must get a reference to these models and
attach listeners to the models directly, with code like this example, which uses our
custom EEL utility discussed in Chapter 3:

```
TableModel myModel = new MyTableModel();  // Some valid TableModel class
JTable table = new JTable(myModel);
EEL eel = EEL.getInstance();
eel.addGui();
// Listen for added/removed/updated rows.
myModel.addTableModelListener(eel);
TableColumnModel columnModel = table.getColumnModel();
// Listen for added/removed/moved columns.
columnModel.addTableColumnModelListener(eel);
// Listen for row selections.
myTable.getSelectionModel().addListSelectionListener(eel);
// Listen for column selections.
columnModel.getSelectionModel.addListSelectionListener(eel);
```

You can see a more detailed example using the selection listeners later in this chapter. Examples using model listeners appear in Chapter 16.

Constants

Table 15-4 shows the constants defined in JTable. These constants specify how columns behave when you resize the entire table or adjust a single column; they are
used for the autoResizeMode property.

Table 15-4. JTable constants

Constant	Data type	Description
AUTO_RESIZE_ALL_COLUMNS	int	When a table is resized, all columns are resized proportionately.
AUTO_RESIZE_LAST_COLUMN	int	When a table is resized, resize the last column only.

Table 15-4. JTable constants (continued)

Constant	Data type	Description
AUTO_RESIZE_NEXT_COLUMN	int	When a column is resized, resize the next column too. For example, if you make column N bigger, column N+1 shrinks.
AUTO_RESIZE_OFF	int	When a table is resized, do not resize the columns at all.
AUTO_RESIZE_SUBSEQUENT_COLUMNS	int	When a column is resized, resize all subsequent columns proportionally to preserve the overall width of the table.

Constructors

public JTable( )

Create a new JTable object using a DefaultTableModel, a DefaultTableColumnModel, and a DefaultListSelectionModel for its models.

public JTable(TableModel dm)
public JTable(TableModel dm, TableColumnModel cm)
public JTable(TableModel dm, TableColumnModel cm, ListSelectionModel sm)

These constructors allow you to specify the exact table model, table column model, and (row) list selection model you want to use. If you want to specify only the column or list selection model, you can pass null as an argument for the other models, and the appropriate default model is created and used.

public JTable(int numRows, int numColumns)

This constructor builds a default table model with the specified number of rows and columns. Default table column and list selection models are also used.

public JTable(Vector data, Vector columnNames)
public JTable(Object data[][], Object columnNames[])

Populate tables by filling the custom table model with data and naming the columns with columnNames. In the case of the first constructor, it is assumed that the data vector is a vector containing other vectors, one for each row of data. The data argument can contain any type of object. The table does its best to render the objects in the array appropriately, using labels generated by calling toString( ) on the objects if necessary. While the columnNames argument can also contain an array of any type of object, a String[] is the most common. The default table header renderer uses column names (or the toString( ) result of nonstring objects) to label columns.

The table models used by these constructors are not instances of DefaultTableModel. If you retrieve the table model, you can interact with it only through the TableModel interface.

Other Interesting Methods

Here are a few other methods to remember. These methods allow you to control tables programmatically. If you have other buttons or keyboard shortcuts for things like selecting matching records, these methods come in handy.

public void addColumnSelectionInterval(int index0, int index1)
public void addRowSelectionInterval(int index0, int index1)

> Programmatically extend the column and row selections on the table. Discontiguous selections must be added as separate contiguous intervals. The value of index0 does not have to be less than or equal to index1, but an IllegalArgumentException results if either index is outside the range of valid columns.

public void clearSelection()

> This method removes all selection intervals (both rows and columns) currently active in the table.

public int columnAtPoint(Point p)

> Given an (x,y) coordinate p relative to the upper-left corner of this JTable component, return the column that contains that point. (This method returns -1 if p is not contained by any of the table's columns.) Along with the rowAtPoint() method, you can take advantage of this method to track where the mouse is in the table.

public boolean editCellAt(int row, int col, EventObject event)

> Open the cell at (row, col) for editing. Fancy editors can alter their behavior or appearance based on the initiating action passed as event. If you do not require a specific event, you can create a simple MouseEvent of type MOUSE_CLICKED with a click count of 2.

public void moveColumn(int column, int targetColumn)

> This method relocates the column at index column to become the column at index targetColumn. This comes in handy if you have layout wizards that allow users to organize the columns separate from the table itself.

public void removeColumn(TableColumn column)

> This method allows you to completely delete a column.

public void removeColumnSelectionInterval(int index0, int index1)
public void removeRowSelectionInterval(int index0, int index1)

> Subtract a selection interval (columns or rows, respectively) from the active selection. This action is not the same as clearing the selection. If the current selection has more items than you remove, the remaining items stay selected.

public int rowAtPoint(Point p)

> Given an (x,y) coordinate p relative to the upper-left corner of this JTable component, return the row that contains that point. (This method returns -1 if p is not contained by any of the table's rows.) Along with the columnAtPoint()

method, you can take advantage of this method to track where the mouse is in the table.

public void selectAll( )

Select all cells (or all rows and all columns, if you prefer) in the table. This method is the opposite of the clearSelection( ) method. Whether this selection is reported as rows, columns, or cells depends on how the columnSelectionAllowed and rowSelectionAllowed properties are set.

The TableColumn Class

The TableColumn class is the starting point for building your columns. It supplies access to all the basic components of an individual column. This class should not be confused with the TableColumnModel interface. That model, discussed in the next section, dictates the form of a collection of table columns, which then makes up a full table.

Properties

The TableColumn class has the properties listed in Table 15-5.

Table 15-5. TableColumn properties

Property	Data type	get	is	set	Default value
cellEditor	TableCellEditor	•		•	null
cellRenderer[b]	TableCellRenderer	•		•	null
headerRenderer[b]	TableCellRenderer	•		•	null
headerValue[b]	Object	•		•	null
identifier	Object	•		•	null
maxWidth	int	•		•	Integer.MAX_VALUE
minWidth	int	•		•	15
modelIndex	int	•		•	0
propertyChangeListeners[1.4]	PropertyChangeListener[]	•			Empty array
resizable	boolean	•		•	true
width[b]	int	•		•	75

[b]bound, [1.4]since 1.4

The cellEditor, cellRenderer, and headerRenderer properties determine which components are used to draw (and possibly edit) cell values. The default value of null for these properties indicates that a default renderer or editor should be built and used. The headerValue property is accessible to the headerRenderer for drawing an appropriate header. The identifier property is used to identify a column uniquely. If an identifier is not specified, the getIdentifier( ) method returns the current headerValue. The minWidth and maxWidth properties determine the minimum and maximum width in pixels for the column. By setting these properties to the same value, you can create a fixed-width column. The current width of the column is stored in the width property. The modelIndex determines the index value used when rendering or editing the column to get the appropriate data values. It is normally set in the constructor and does not need to be modified after that. Relocating the column onscreen has no effect on the model index. The resizable property affects only the user's ability to manually resize columns—you can programmatically resize a column at any time.

Constants

Four of the properties have descriptive constants that are used with property change events. These constants are listed in Table 15-6.

Table 15-6. TableColumn constants

Constant	Type	Description
CELL_RENDERER_PROPERTY	String	The property name of the cellRenderer property
COLUMN_WIDTH_PROPERTY	String	The property name of the columnWidth property
HEADER_RENDERER_PROPERTY	String	The property name of the headerRenderer property
HEADER_VALUE_PROPERTY	String	The property name of the headerValue property

Event

The only event generated by the TableColumn class is a property change event that is generated when any of the column's bound properties (cellRenderer, headerRenderer, headerValue, and width) are changed.

public void addPropertyChangeListener(PropertyChangeListener l)
public void removePropertyChangeListener(PropertyChangeListener l)
> Add or remove a property change listener interested in receiving events from this column.

Constructors

The following constructors exist for building TableColumn objects:

public TableColumn( )
> Create an empty column with the default property values.

public TableColumn(int modelIndex)
> Create an empty column with the specified modelIndex.

public TableColumn(int modelIndex, int width)
> Create an empty column with the specified `modelIndex` and `width` in pixels. The `minWidth` and `maxWidth` properties keep their default values.

public TableColumn(int modelIndex, int width, TableCellRenderer cellRenderer, Table-CellEditor cellEditor)
> Create an empty column with the specified `modelIndex`, `width` in pixels, `cellRenderer`, and `cellEditor`. The renderer or editor arguments can be `null`, in which case the appropriate default is used.

Another useful method

While the get/set methods for the properties constitute a majority of the `TableColumn` class, the following method does provide a bit of functionality:

public void sizeWidthToFit( )
> Force the width of the column to match that of its header, even if it means modifying the `minWidth` or `maxWidth` properties.

The TableColumnModel Interface

A single column is not a very interesting table—an interesting list, maybe, but not a table. To handle real tables (even ones with only one column), we need a model for storing several columns as a collection. The `TableColumnModel` interface provides that functionality in the Swing package. As you may have noticed from Figure 15-2, the `JTable` class has a column model in addition to a table model. While the table model provides the specific values for the cells in a column, the column model provides information such as the column margins and whether or not column selections are allowed.

The `TableColumnModel` interface manages column selections and column spacing. For managing selections, you have access to the usual selection properties, such as the number of selected columns and the selection model in place. For dealing with column spacing, you can control the column margins and view the total column width.

Properties

`TableColumnModel` has the properties listed in Table 15-7. The `columnCount` property returns the number of columns supported by this model. While this might seem like redundant information, given that the table model (discussed later in this chapter) knows how many columns it supports, the next chapter examines some column models that do not use all of the columns available in the table model. The `columnMargin` property dictates how much space should be left between columns. That spacing is included when calculating the value of the `totalColumnWidth`. You can turn column selection on or off with the `columnSelectionAllowed` property. If column selections are allowed, you can then use the `selectionModel`, `selectedColumns`, and selectedColumnCount properties to work with the selections. As with other selections, you can use the selectionModel to programmatically affect the selected columns if needed.

Table 15-7. TableColumnModel properties

Property	Data type	get	is	set	Default value
column[i]	TableColumn	•			
columns	Enumeration	•			
columnCount	int	•			
columnMargin	int	•		•	
columnSelectionAllowed	boolean	•		•	
selectedColumnCount	int	•			
selectedColumns	int[]	•			
selectionModel	ListSelectionModel	•		•	
totalColumnWidth	int	•			

[i]indexed

The column and columns properties let you access the table's columns themselves. The index used as an argument to getColumn( ) refers to the column's index in the column model, which doesn't necessarily match the index of the column in the table model, or the order in which columns appear on the screen.

Event

Any class implementing the TableColumnModel interface has to support the ColumnModelEvent, which is generated when a column's view size, position, or extent size changes. The interface defines the standard addColumnModelListener( ) and removeColumnModelListener( ) methods, but the implementing class is responsible for the code that fires the events when columns are added, removed, or moved.

public void addColumnModelListener(TableColumnModelListener l)
public void removeColumnModelListener(TableColumnModelListener l)
   Add or remove a listener interested in changes to this column model.

Column methods

The TableColumnModel interface defines several methods for working with the columns in the model:

public void addColumn(TableColumn column)
   Append column to the current column model.

public int getColumnIndex(Object identifier)
public int getColumnIndexAtX(int xPixel)

> Return the column model (screen) index of a column, either with a header matching `identifier` or at the specified `xPixel` location on the screen.

public void moveColumn(int index, int newIndex)

> Move the column at `index` to `newIndex`. Other columns should be shifted as needed to accommodate the moved column. This visually relocates the column on the screen only. The table model does not change.

public void removeColumn(TableColumn column)

> Delete column from the column model. Columns following the removed column are shifted one index to fill the gap.

The DefaultTableColumnModel Class

The `DefaultTableColumnModel` class implements the `TableColumnModel` interface and serves as the column model if you do not specify a model in the `JTable` constructor. It also works as a good starting point for creating your own column models. You inherit everything you need; just override the methods you want to change.

Properties

The `DefaultTableColumnModel` class inherits all of its properties from the `TableColumnModel` interface and supplies the default values shown in Table 15-8.

Table 15-8. DefaultTableColumnModel properties

Property	Data type	get	is	set	Default value
column[i,o]	TableColumn	•			
columns[o]	Enumeration	•			
columnCount[o]	int	•			0
columnMargin[o]	int	•		•	1
columnSelectionAllowed[o]	boolean	•		•	false
selectedColumnCount[o]	int	•			0
selectedColumns[o]	int[]	•			null
selectionModel[o]	ListSelectionModel	•		•	DefaultListSelectionModel()
totalColumnWidth[o]	int	•			0

[i]indexed, [o]overridden

Events

The DefaultTableColumnModel supports the ColumnModelEvent events that are dictated by the TableColumnModel interface, but it includes several convenience methods beyond simply attaching listeners:

protected void fireColumnAdded(TableColumnModelEvent e)
protected void fireColumnMarginChanged( )
protected void fireColumnMoved(TableColumnModelEvent e)
protected void fireColumnRemoved(TableColumnModelEvent e)
protected void fireColumnSelectionChanged(ListSelectionEvent e)

> These helper methods are used to fire events when columns are added, resized, relocated, removed, or selected. They also allow you to fire column-based events to create your own column model by extending this class.

public void addColumnModelListener(TableColumnModelListener x)
public void removeColumnModelListener(TableColumnModelListener x)

> Add or remove a listener for TableColumnModelEvents fired by this model.

protected void propertyChange(PropertyChangeEvent e)
protected void valueChanged(ListSelectionEvent e)

> The DefaultTableColumnModel listens to some of these events to keep the visual state of the table in sync. The COLUMN_WIDTH_PROPERTY change events (from one of the added TableColumn objects) cause the width cache for the table to be recalculated. The valueChanged( ) method listens for new column selections and fires a column selection changed event.

Constructor

public DefaultTableColumnModel( )

> Set up a new DefaultTableColumnModel with the default values for properties listed in Table 15-8.

Other useful methods

public void addColumn(TableColumnColumn)
public int getColumnIndex(Object identifier)
public int getColumnIndexAtX(int xPixel)
public void moveColumn(int index, int newindex)
public void removeColumn(TableColumn column)

> These methods provide straightforward implementation of the abstract methods required by the TableColumnModel interface.

The TableColumnModelEvent Class

Many of the events fired by the DefaultTableColumnModel class use this event class to encode the columns that were affected. Notice that these events describe something happening to a contiguous group of columns, unlike the selection events. There is no direct support for things like removing a discontiguous selection of columns. You must generate a different event for each contiguous range of columns that needs to be removed.

Event methods

public int getFromIndex()
public int getToIndex()

Use these methods to find the affected columns. If only a single column is affected, these methods return the same value.

The TableColumnModelListener Interface

If you want to listen to any of the column model events, you must implement the `TableColumnModelListener` interface and register as a listener for these events. Not surprisingly, the event-firing methods from the `DefaultTableColumnModel` class reflect the types of events this interface defines:

public void columnAdded(TableColumnModelEvent e)
public void columnMarginChanged(ChangeEvent e)
public void columnMoved(TableColumnModelEvent e)
public void columnRemoved(TableColumnModelEvent e)
public void columnSelectionChanged(ListSelectionEvent e)

Use these methods to react to changes in the column model. While you cannot add a `ListSelectionListener` directly to the column model if you care only about column selections, you can retrieve the selection model (using `getSelectionModel()`) and attach a listener to that object.

Implementing a Column Model

Here's a custom column model that keeps all of its columns in alphabetical order as they are added:

```
// SortingColumnModel.java
// A simple extension of the DefaultTableColumnModel class that sorts
// incoming columns
//
import javax.swing.table.*;

public class SortingColumnModel extends DefaultTableColumnModel {

  public void addColumn(TableColumn tc) {
    super.addColumn(tc);
    int newIndex = sortedIndexOf(tc);
```

```
        if (newIndex != tc.getModelIndex()) {
          moveColumn(tc.getModelIndex(), newIndex);
        }
      }

  protected int sortedIndexOf(TableColumn tc) {
    // Just do a linear search for now.
    int stop = getColumnCount();
    String name = tc.getHeaderValue().toString();

    for (int i = 0; i < stop; i++) {
      if (name.compareTo(getColumn(i).getHeaderValue().toString()) <= 0) {
        return i;
      }
    }
    return stop;
  }
}
```

Implementing the model is simple. We override addColumn() to add the column to the superclass and then move it into the appropriate position. You can use this column model with any data model. The next section goes into much more detail on the table model used to store the real data, so for this simple example, we'll use the DefaultTableModel class to hold the data. Once we have our table model and our column model, we can build a JTable with them. Then, any columns we add are listed in alphabetical order (by the header), regardless of the order in which they were added. The result looks like Figure 15-4.

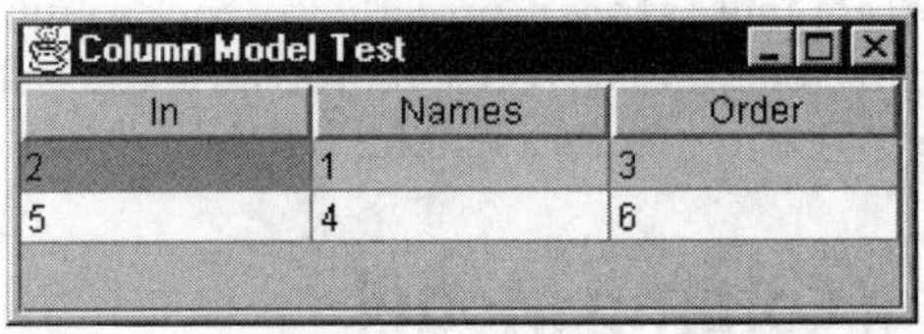

Figure 15-4. A sorting column model; the columns are sorted by name as they are added

Here's the code that puts the table and column models together:

```
// ColumnExample.java
// A test of the JTable class using default table models and a convenience
// constructor
import java.awt.*;
import javax.swing.*;
import javax.swing.table.*;

public class ColumnExample extends JFrame {

  public ColumnExample() {
    super("Abstract Model JTable Test");
    setSize(300, 200);
    setDefaultCloseOperation(EXIT_ON_CLOSE);
```

```
            DefaultTableModel dtm = new DefaultTableModel(new String[][] {
                               {"1", "2", "3"}, {"4", "5", "6"} },
                               new String[] {"Names", "In", "Order"});
            SortingColumnModel scm = new SortingColumnModel( );
            JTable jt = new JTable(dtm, scm);
            jt.createDefaultColumnsFromModel( );

            JScrollPane jsp = new JScrollPane(jt);
            getContentPane( ).add(jsp, BorderLayout.CENTER);
        }

        public static void main(String args[]) {
            ColumnExample ce = new ColumnExample( );
            ce.setVisible(true);
        }
    }
```

There's no trick here. All we do is create our sorting column model and use it when we create the JTable. You can find other examples of custom column models in the next chapter.

Table Data

We've seen the TableColumnModel, which stores a lot of information about the structure of a table but doesn't contain the actual data. The data that's displayed in a JTable is stored in a TableModel. The TableModel interface describes the minimum requirements for a model that supplies the information necessary to display and edit a table's cells and to show column headers. The AbstractTableModel fills out most of the TableModel interface, but leaves the methods for retrieving the actual data undefined. The DefaultTableModel extends AbstractTableModel and provides an implementation for storing data as a vector of vectors. We'll look at both the abstract and default table models in more detail later in this chapter.

The TableModel Interface

All of the table models start with this interface. A table model must be able to give out information on the number of rows and columns in the table and have access to the values of the cells of the table. The TableModel interface also has methods that can be used to encode information about the columns of the table (such as a localized name or class type) separate from the column model.

Properties

The TableModel interface supports the properties shown in Table 15-9. The columnCount is the number of columns in the data model. This does not have to match the number of columns reported by the column model. Likewise, `rowCount` is the number of rows in the data model. `columnName` and `columnClass` are indexed properties that let you retrieve the name of the column and the class of objects in the column. The name used in the table model is distinct from anything used in the `TableColumn` class. For both properties, remember that the index refers to the table model, regardless of where the column appears on the screen.

Table 15-9. TableModel properties

Property	Data type	get	is	set	Default value
columnCount	int	•			
rowCount	int	•			

Events

As you may have come to expect from other models in the Swing package, the `TableModel` has its own event type, `TableModelEvent`, generated whenever the table changes. A full discussion of the `TableModelEvent` class and the `TableModelListener` appears later in this chapter.

public void addTableModelListener(TableModelListener l)
public void removeTableModelListener(TableModelListener l)
> Add or remove listeners interested in receiving table model events.

Cell methods

These methods let you obtain and change the values of individual cells:

public Object getValueAt(int rowIndex, int columnIndex)
> Return the value of the cell at (`rowIndex`, `columnIndex`). Base types (`int`, `float`, etc.) are wrapped in an appropriate `Object`.

public boolean isCellEditable(int rowIndex, int columnIndex)
> Return true if the cell at (`rowIndex`, `columnIndex`) can be edited.

public void setValueAt(Object aValue, int rowIndex, int columnIndex)
> Set the value of the cell at (`rowIndex`, `columnIndex`) to aValue. As with the getValueAt( ) method, you may need to wrap primitive data types in an `Object` (like `Integer`) before using them to set the value of a cell.

The AbstractTableModel Class

This class implements many of the methods of the `TableModel` interface, leaving the really important ones to you. If you want to build your own table model, this is the place to start. (In fact, the documentation shipped with the Swing package even recommends starting here, rather than with the `DefaultTableModel` presented in the next section.) The three unimplemented methods from `TableModel` are:

```
public abstract int getColumnCount( )
public abstract int getRowCount( )
public abstract Object getValueAt(int row, int col)
```

With these methods, you can build your own table model better suited to the kinds of data you want to display. You can extend this model to support databases and even dynamic data.

Other properties available through the `AbstractTableModel` are shown in Table 15-10.

Table 15-10. AbstractTableModel properties

Property	Data type	get	is	set	Default value
cellEditable[ii,o]	boolean		•		false
columnClass[i]	Class	•			Object.class
columnCount[o]	int	•			Abstract
columnName[i]	String	•			"A" for column 1, "B" for column 2, etc. " " for an invalid index.
rowCount[o]	int	•			Abstract
valueAt[ii, o]	Object	•		•	Getter is abstract. Setter is empty implementation (creating a read-only table by default).

[i]indexed, [ii]double indexed (by row and column), [o]overridden

As a starting point, let's look at recreating the file list table with our own data model. For fun, we'll throw in support for the column headers and column types as well. (This is not one of the requirements of a minimal table model, but it makes the table look more professional.) Here's the source code for the model:

```
// FileModel.java
// A custom table model to display information on a directory of files
//
import javax.swing.table.*;
import java.util.Date;
import java.io.File;

public class FileModel extends AbstractTableModel {

  String titles[] = new String[] {
    "Directory?", "File Name", "Read?", "Write?", "Size", "Last Modified"
  };

  Class types[] = new Class[] {
    Boolean.class, String.class, Boolean.class, Boolean.class,
    Number.class, Date.class
  };
```

```
  Object data[][];

  public FileModel() { this("."); }

  public FileModel(String dir) {
    File pwd = new File(dir);
    setFileStats(pwd);
  }

  // Implement the methods of the TableModel interface we're interested
  // in. Only getRowCount(), getColumnCount(), and getValueAt() are
  // required. The other methods tailor the look of the table.
  public int getRowCount() { return data.length; }
  public int getColumnCount() { return titles.length; }
  public String getColumnName(int c) { return titles[c]; }
  public Class getColumnClass(int c) { return types[c]; }
  public Object getValueAt(int r, int c) { return data[r][c]; }

  // Our own method for setting/changing the current directory
  // being displayed. This method fills the data set with file info
  // from the given directory. It also fires an update event, so this
  // method could also be called after the table is on display.
  public void setFileStats(File dir) {
    String files[] = dir.list();
    data = new Object[files.length][titles.length];

    for (int i=0; i < files.length; i++) {
      File tmp = new File(files[i]);
      data[i][0] = new Boolean(tmp.isDirectory());
      data[i][1] = tmp.getName();
      data[i][2] = new Boolean(tmp.canRead());
      data[i][3] = new Boolean(tmp.canWrite());
      data[i][4] = new Long(tmp.length());
      data[i][5] = new Date(tmp.lastModified());
    }

    // Just in case anyone's listening
    fireTableDataChanged();
  }
}
```

And here's the source for the simple application that creates and displays the JTable.
Notice how simple it is to make the JTable with a custom model:

```
// FileTable.java
// A test frame for the custom table model
import java.awt.*;
import javax.swing.*;
import java.util.Date;
import java.io.File;

public class FileTable extends JFrame {
```

```
public FileTable( ) {
  super("Custom TableModel Test");
  setSize(300, 200);
  setDefaultCloseOperation(EXIT_ON_CLOSE);

  FileModel fm = new FileModel( );
  JTable jt = new JTable(fm);
  jt.setAutoResizeMode(JTable.AUTO_RESIZE_OFF);
  jt.setColumnSelectionAllowed(true);

  JScrollPane jsp = new JScrollPane(jt);
  getContentPane( ).add(jsp, BorderLayout.CENTER);
}

public static void main(String args[]) {
  FileTable ft = new FileTable( );
  ft.setVisible(true);
}
}
```

Instead of supplying the data and headers in the JTable constructor, we built them into our own table model, and then created the JTable with our own model. That also gave us control over the column types. Figure 15-5 shows the results of our custom model.

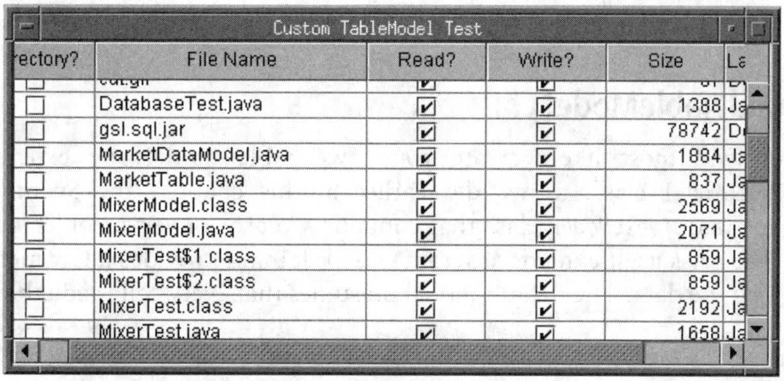

Figure 15-5. A JTable built with a custom TableModel class

Events

public void addTableModelListener(TableModelListener l)
public void removeTableModelListener(TableModelListener l)

Add or remove listeners for table model events coming from this model. The listeners are used in the various event-firing methods, which are presented next.

public void fireTableDataChanged()
public void fireTableStructureChanged()
public void fireTableRowsInserted(int first, int last)
public void fireTableRowsUpdated(int first, int last)
public void fireTableRowsDeleted(int first, int last)
public void fireTableCellUpdated(int row, int col)

These methods call `fireTableChanged()` after constructing an appropriate `TableModelEvent` object. `fireTableDataChanged()` indicates that all of the cells in the table might have changed, but the columns of the table are still intact. On the other hand, the `fireTableStructureChanged()` method indicates that the actual columns present in the model may have changed (in name, type, or even number) as well.

public void fireTableChanged(TableModelEvent e)

Reports event e to any registered listeners. Programmers usually start with one of the preceding `fireTable...()` methods.

Another useful method

The `AbstractTableModel` class has one other useful method:

public int findColumn(String columnName)

An easy mechanism for looking up columns by their associated names. This is a linear search, so large tables may need to override this.

The DefaultTableModel Class

While you will most likely create your own table models by extending the `AbstractTableModel` class, as we did earlier in this chapter, the Swing package includes a `DefaultTableModel` class that contains a `Vector` of `Vector` objects to house the data. The class itself extends `AbstractTableModel` and provides a few methods for manipulating the data. The default model presumes that every cell is editable.

Properties

The `DefaultTableModel` class provides default values to the properties inherited from the `TableModel` interface. These values are shown in Table 15-11.

Table 15-11. DefaultTableModel properties

Property	Data type	get	is	set	Default value
cellEditable[ii, o]	boolean			•	true
cellSelected[ii]	boolean		•		false
columnClass[i, o]	Class	•			Object.class

[i]indexed, [ii]double indexed (by row and column), [o]overridden

Table 15-11. DefaultTableModel properties (continued)

Property	Data type	get	is	set	Default value
columnCount[o]	int	•			0
columnName[i, o]	String	•			"A" for column 1, "B" for column 2, etc. "" for an invalid index.
columnSelected[i]	boolean		•		false
rowCount[o]	int	•			0
rowSelected[i]	boolean		•		false
valueAt[ii, o]	Object	•		•	Data-dependent

[i]indexed, [ii]double indexed (by row and column), [o]overridden

Events

The DefaultTableModel class does not support any new event types, but since it does contain real data, it provides the following helper methods to generate events:

public void newDataAvailable(TableModelEvent e)
public void newRowsAdded(TableModelEvent e)
public void rowsRemoved(TableModelEvent e)

Fire the appropriate table model events. If e is null, the model assumes that all the associated data has changed and creates an appropriate event.

Constructors

public DefaultTableModel()

Build a DefaultTableModel with zero rows and zero columns.

public DefaultTableModel(int numRows, int numColumns)

Build a DefaultTableModel with the specified number of rows and columns.

public DefaultTableModel(Vector columnNames, int numRows)
public DefaultTableModel(Object[] columnNames, int numRows)

Build a DefaultTableModel with the specified number of rows. The number of columns matches the number of elements in the columnNames vector (or array), which also supplies the names for the columns in the column header.

public DefaultTableModel(Vector data, Vector columnNames)
public DefaultTableModel(Object[] [] data, Object[] columnNames)

Build a DefaultTableModel with the number of rows determined by the data object and the number of columns determined by the columnNames object. The data vector columns are padded or truncated to match the number of columns dictated by the columnNames vector.

The Object arrays are converted to vectors (or vectors of vectors in the case of Object[][]).

Other useful methods

With the DefaultTableModel class, you can get and set the data directly. These methods work in addition to the usual getValueAt( ) and setValueAt( ) methods for individual cells.

public Vector getDataVector( )

> Return the row vector, which itself contains vectors representing the collection of cells (one for each column) for each row.

public void setDataVector(Object[][] newData, Object[] columnIDs)
public void setDataVector(Vector newData, Vector columnIDs)

> Set the new data (as a vector of vectors) for the model. The columnIDs field can be null, or it can contain the names of columns that are returned by getColumnName( ). (Although you can create column IDs that are not of type String, the getColumnName( ) method converts them to strings using the toString( ) method.) The first column ID is mapped to the first column in newData, the second column ID to the second column, and so on.

public void addColumn(Object columnID)
public void addColumn(Object columnID, Object[] columnData)
public void addColumn(Object columnID, Vector columnData)

> Add a new column to the model. The first version inserts null values into the rows currently in the table. Both the second and third versions insert values into the current rows up to their size or the number of rows, and null values after that if more rows exist. (If, for example, you had 20 rows but supplied a vector of 18 objects, the last 2 rows would receive null values.) The columnID field must not be null.

public void addRow(Object[] rowData)
public void addRow(Vector rowData)

> Append new rows to the table. Like the padding that occurs with adding columns, the row's data is truncated or extended as necessary to match the current number of columns in the table.

public void insertRow(int row, Object[] rowData)
public void insertRow(int row, Vector rowData)

> Insert a new row at row in the table. As with the addRow( ) methods, the size of the rowData vector is adjusted to match the number of columns in the table.

public void moveRow(int startIndex, int endIndex, int toIndex)

> Move a range of rows (from startIndex to endIndex inclusive) to a new location (toIndex). The other rows are shifted accordingly.

public void removeRow(int index)

> Delete the row at index from the table.

public void setColumnIdentifiers(Object[] columnIDs)
public void setColumnIdentifiers(Vector columnIDs)

> Set the identifiers for the columns in the table to `columnIDs`. The number of identifiers passed in dictates the number of columns in the table.

public void setNumRows(int newSize)

> Change the number of rows in the current table. If `newSize` is less than the current table size, the extra rows are truncated. If `newSize` is larger than the current table size, extra rows (new `Vector(getColumnCount())` objects) are added to pad the table to `newSize` rows.

The TableModelEvent Class

Several methods of the `AbstractTableModel` class help you fire events to report changes in your data model. All of the methods build an appropriate `TableModelEvent` object and send it to any registered listeners through the `fireTableChanged()` method.

Properties

The `TableModelEvent` class encompasses the properties listed in Table 15-12.

Table 15-12. TableModelEvent properties

Property	Data type	get	is	set	Default value
column	int	•			
firstRow	int	•			
lastRow	int	•			
type	int	•			

The `column` property shows the column affected by this event, which could be a specific column or `ALL_COLUMNS`. Likewise, `firstRow` and `lastRow` identify the first and last row in a range of rows affected by this event; either property may be a specific column or `HEADER_ROW`. `lastRow` is always greater than or equal to `firstRow`. Finally, `type` indicates which type of event occurred; its value is one of the constants `INSERT`, `UPDATE`, or `DELETE`.

Constants

The properties and constructors can use several constants, defined in the `TableModelEvent` class and shown in Table 15-13.

Table 15-13. *TableModelEvent constants*

Constant	Data Type	Description
ALL_COLUMNS	int	Indicates that the event is not localized on one column.
DELETE	int	One of the values that can be returned by the getType( ) call; indicates that rows have been deleted from the model.
HEADER_ROW	int	This constant can be used in place of a normal first row value to indicate that the metadata (such as column names) of the table has changed.
INSERT	int	One of the values that can be returned by the getType( ) call; indicates that rows have been inserted into the model.
UPDATE	int	One of the values that can be returned by the getType( ) call; indicates that data in some of the rows has changed. The number of rows and columns has not changed.

The TableModelListener Interface

As you saw in previous examples, the JTable class listens to model events to keep the view of the table consistent with the model. If you want to monitor changes in a table yourself, implement this interface. Only one method exists for event notification, and you register the listener with the model itself, not with the JTable.

public void tableChanged(TableModelEvent e)
> Called for any table model events your model generates. You can use getType( ) to distinguish events of different types.

Dynamic Table Data

Since we've already seen some simple examples of table models at work in a JTable object, let's look at some more interesting ones.

You can take advantage of the convenience methods that generate TableModelEvent objects to create a table model that responds to dynamic data. A classic example of dynamic table data is stock market quotes. Of course, you have to pay for the quote feed, but if you've done that, you can use a JTable to show off your portfolio.

Just to try out dynamic data, we'll simulate a stock market where Swing components are the traded commodities. The heart of this simulator is MYOSM, which sets up a thread to play with the values of the components so that we have changing data to look at. The example contains two different constructors. One constructor for MYOSM simply starts the updater thread. This is the version our final application uses since the JTable we build is showing off the stock quotes; the other constructor creates its own JFrame that monitors and displays the changes. If you run MYOSM as an application, that's the version you'll see.

Here's the code for our stock market. (The Stock class is available online, but isn't particularly interesting, so we didn't list it.)

```
//MYOSM.java
// Make Your Own Stock Market: a simple stock market simulator that contains a
// few stocks and their current prices (and deltas). It randomly adjusts the
// prices on stocks to give a dynamic feel to the data.
//
import javax.swing.*;
import java.awt.*;
import java.util.*;

public class MYOSM extends JFrame implements Runnable {

  Stock[] market = {
    new Stock("JTree", 14.57),
    new Stock("JTable", 17.44),
    new Stock("JList", 16.44),
    new Stock("JButton", 7.21),
    new Stock("JComponent", 27.40)
  };
  boolean monitor;
  Random rg = new Random( );
  Thread runner;

  public MYOSM( ) {
    // Not meant to be shown as a real frame
    super("Thread only version...");
    runner = new Thread(this);
    runner.start( );
  }

  // This version creates a real frame so that you can see how the typical stocks
  // are updated. It's not meant to be used with other programs, but rather as a
  // debugging tool to make sure the market runs smoothly.
  public MYOSM(boolean monitorOn) {
    super("Stock Market Monitor");
    setSize(400, 100);
    setDefaultCloseOperation(EXIT_ON_CLOSE);
    monitor = monitorOn;

    getContentPane( ).add(new JLabel("Trading is active.  " +
        "Close this window to close the market."),
        BorderLayout.CENTER);
    runner = new Thread(this);
    runner.start( );
  }

  // Here's the heart of our stock market. In an infinite loop, just pick a
  // random stock and update its price. To make the program interesting, we'll
  // update a price every second.
  public void run( ) {
    while(true) {
      int whichStock = Math.abs(rg.nextInt( )) % market.length;
      double delta = rg.nextDouble( ) - 0.4;
      market[whichStock].update(delta);
      if (monitor) {
```

```
        market[whichStock].print( );
      }
      try {
        Thread.sleep(1000);
      }
      catch(InterruptedException ie) {
      }
    }
  }

  public Stock getQuote(int index) {
    return market[index];
  }

  // This method returns the list of all the symbols in the market table.
  public String[] getSymbols( ) {
    String[] symbols = new String[market.length];
    for (int i = 0; i < market.length; i++) {
      symbols[i] = market[i].symbol;
    }
    return symbols;
  }

  public static void main(String args[]) {
    MYOSM myMarket = new MYOSM(args.length > 0);
    myMarket.setVisible(true);
  }
}
```

With this stock market class producing dynamic data, you need a model that can listen for that data. Use a polling method to extract new data at intervals. If your data source generated events, you could also create a table model that listened for the events and updated your table immediately after receiving a change event. (If updating your table is costly, polling might make more sense.)

Here's the table model that works in conjunction with the dynamic data source. Notice that we implement Runnable so that we can start a thread to control the polling frequency. Apart from that, the data model handles the same tasks as the previous data models. We return the appropriate column names and values for individual cells.

```
// MarketDataModel.java
//
import javax.swing.table.*;
import javax.swing.*;

public class MarketDataModel extends AbstractTableModel
implements Runnable {

  Thread runner;
  MYOSM market;
  int delay;
```

```
public MarketDataModel(int initialDelay) {
  market = new MYOSM( );
  delay = initialDelay * 1000;
  Thread runner = new Thread(this);
  runner.start( );
}

Stock[] stocks = new Stock[0];
int[] stockIndices = new int[0];
String[] headers = {"Symbol", "Price", "Change", "Last updated"};

public int getRowCount( ) { return stocks.length; }
public int getColumnCount( ) { return headers.length; }

public String getColumnName(int c) { return headers[c]; }

public Object getValueAt(int r, int c) {
  switch(c) {
  case 0:
    return stocks[r].symbol;
  case 1:
    return new Double(stocks[r].price);
  case 2:
    return new Double(stocks[r].delta);
  case 3:
    return stocks[r].lastUpdate;
  }
  throw new IllegalArgumentException("Bad cell (" + r + ", " + c +")");
}

public void setDelay(int seconds) { delay = seconds * 1000; }
public void setStocks(int[] indices) {
  stockIndices = indices;
  updateStocks( );
  fireTableDataChanged( );
}

public void updateStocks( ) {
  stocks = new Stock[stockIndices.length];
  for (int i = 0; i < stocks.length; i++) {
    stocks[i] = market.getQuote(stockIndices[i]);
  }
}

public void run( ) {
  while(true) {
    // Blind update...we could check for real deltas if necessary
    updateStocks( );

    // We know there are no new columns, so don't fire a data change; fire only a
    // row update. This keeps the table from flashing
    fireTableRowsUpdated(0, stocks.length - 1);
```

```
        try { Thread.sleep(delay); }
        catch(InterruptedException ie) {}
      }
    }
  }
```

Most of the code is fairly simple. getValueAt( ) merely looks up the appropriate value from the table's data, taking into account the column requested so it can return an appropriate type of object. The one trick is that our model doesn't necessarily track all the stocks simulated by MYOSM. The model provides a setStocks( ) method that lets you select the stocks that interest you and populates the model's data accordingly. setStocks( ) fires a TableModelEvent indicating that the table's data has changed; in particular, rows (but not columns) may have been added or deleted. The model's run( ) method fires a similar event with each update, indicating that the data in the rows has been updated. With this model in place, we can create a table using the same simple code, but this time, we update the table every five seconds. Figure 15-6 shows the results.

Symbol	Price	Change	Last updated
JTree	15.869534361302238	-0.21524222439481...	Mon Apr 13 12:06...
JTable	19.961719137676603	0.5279226639231799	Mon Apr 13 12:06...
JList	18.078289384149496	0.20606051830177...	Mon Apr 13 12:06...

Figure 15-6. A table model that generates dynamic (and precise!) data

Just to be complete, here's the code for this application that displays our market simulator. Notice that only the model passed to the JTable constructor really changed from the previous table application.

```java
// MarketTable.java
// A test of the JTable class using default table models and a convenience
// constructor
//
import java.awt.*;
import javax.swing.*;

public class MarketTable extends JFrame {

  public MarketTable( ) {
    super("Dynamic Data Test");
    setSize(300, 200);
    setDefaultCloseOperation(EXIT_ON_CLOSE);

    // Set up our table model with a 5-second polling delay.
    MarketDataModel mdm = new MarketDataModel(5);

    // Pick which stocks we want to watch...
    mdm.setStocks(new int[] { 0, 1, 2 });
```

```
    // ...and pop up the table.
    JTable jt = new JTable(mdm);
    JScrollPane jsp = new JScrollPane(jt);
    getContentPane( ).add(jsp, BorderLayout.CENTER);
  }

  public static void main(String args[]) {
    MarketTable mt = new MarketTable( );
    mt.setVisible(true);
  }
}
```

Database Data

Another popular source of information for table displays is database records. You can create a table model that connects to a database and produces rows and columns based on the results of queries you send. Figure 15-7 shows a simple application that passes any query you type to the database. The table displays the results from your query. The column headings (and even the number of columns) are taken directly from the database and depend entirely on the query and the database contents.

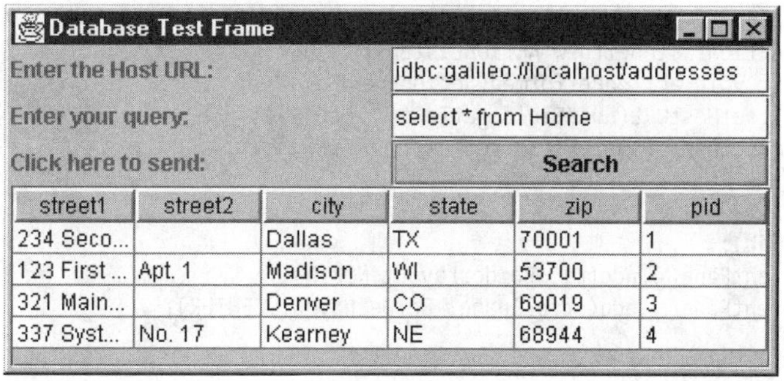

Figure 15-7. A database query result table example

In this example, each new search causes a fireTableChanged( ), since the query may have new columns. If we could count on the columns remaining the same, we could use the fireTableRowsUpdated( ) method, like we did with the dynamic data example.

Here is the code to build this application. Most of the work is setting up the labels and text fields that serve as our graphical interface, but take a look at the anonymous event handler for the Search button. This is where we pass the database URL and query to our model. We'll use the URL and query as the starting point for discussing the model code below.

```
// DatabaseTest.java
//
import java.awt.*;
import java.awt.event.*;
```

```
import javax.swing.*;
import javax.swing.table.*;

public class DatabaseTest extends JFrame {

    JTextField hostField;
    JTextField queryField;
    QueryTableModel qtm;

    public DatabaseTest() {
        super("Database Test Frame");
        setDefaultCloseOperation(EXIT_ON_CLOSE);
        setSize(350, 200);

        qtm = new QueryTableModel();
        JTable table = new JTable(qtm);
        JScrollPane scrollpane = new JScrollPane(table);
        JPanel p1 = new JPanel();
        p1.setLayout(new GridLayout(3, 2));
        p1.add(new JLabel("Enter the Host URL: "));
        p1.add(hostField = new JTextField());
        p1.add(new JLabel("Enter your query: "));
        p1.add(queryField = new JTextField());
        p1.add(new JLabel("Click here to send: "));

        JButton jb = new JButton("Search");
        jb.addActionListener(new ActionListener() {
          public void actionPerformed(ActionEvent e) {
            qtm.setHostURL(hostField.getText().trim());
            qtm.setQuery(queryField.getText().trim());
          }
        } );
        p1.add(jb);
        getContentPane().add(p1, BorderLayout.NORTH);
        getContentPane().add(scrollpane, BorderLayout.CENTER);
    }

    public static void main(String args[]) {
        DatabaseTest tt = new DatabaseTest();
        tt.setVisible(true);
    }
}
```

Following is the code for the query model. Rather than hold a vector of vectors, we'll store a vector of String[] objects to facilitate retrieving the values. This query table contains all of the code required to connect to a database server using a JDBC driver. The server and driver we are using were both written by Brian Cole and are available along with the rest of the code in this chapter at *http://www.oreilly.com/catalog/ jswing2*.

We have code similar to all of our previous examples for the basic methods from the AbstractTableModel class, which we extend. But we have to add support for a changing host and query. If the host stays the same from the last query that was run, we can continue to use the same connection. If not, we close the old connection and build a new one. When we set the query, however, we have to send it to the database server, and then update the table once we get the response. Notice that this example fires a full table-changed event at the end of the setQuery( ) call. With our open-ended query form, chances are we'll get back some very different results from query to query, so we don't bother trying to send only modification events. If you're unfamiliar with SQL or the JDBC code throughout this class, check out *Database Programming with JDBC and Java* by George Reese (O'Reilly).

```java
// QueryTableModel.java
// A basic implementation of the TableModel interface that fills out a Vector of
// String[] structure from a query's result set
//
import java.sql.*;
import java.io.*;
import java.util.Vector;
import javax.swing.*;
import javax.swing.table.*;

public class QueryTableModel extends AbstractTableModel {
  Vector cache;  // Will hold String[] objects
  int colCount;
  String[] headers;
  Connection db;
  Statement statement;
  String currentURL;

  public QueryTableModel() {
    cache = new Vector();
    new gsl.sql.driv.Driver();
  }

  public String getColumnName(int i) { return headers[i]; }
  public int getColumnCount() { return colCount; }
  public int getRowCount() { return cache.size();}

  public Object getValueAt(int row, int col) {
    return ((String[])cache.elementAt(row))[col];
  }

  public void setHostURL(String url) {
    if (url.equals(currentURL)) {
      // Same database; we can leave the current connection open
      return;
    }
    // Oops...new connection required
    closeDB();
    initDB(url);
    currentURL = url;
  }
```

```java
    // All the real work happens here; in a real application, we'd probably perform the
    // query in a separate thread.
    public void setQuery(String q) {
      cache = new Vector();
      try {
        // Execute the query and store the result set and its metadata.
        ResultSet rs = statement.executeQuery(q);
        ResultSetMetaData meta = rs.getMetaData();
        colCount = meta.getColumnCount();

        // Now we must rebuild the headers array with the new column names.
        headers = new String[colCount];
        for (int h=1; h <= colCount; h++) {
          headers[h-1] = meta.getColumnName(h);
        }

        // Now we must file the cache with the records from our query. This would not
        // be practical if we were expecting a few million records in response to our
        // query, but we aren't, so we can do this.
        while (rs.next()) {
          String[] record = new String[colCount];
          for (int i=0; i < colCount; i++) {
            record[i] = rs.getString(i + 1);
          }
          cache.addElement(record);
        }
        fireTableChanged(null); // Notify everyone that we have a new table.
      }
      catch(Exception e) {
        cache = new Vector();   // Blank it out and keep going.
        e.printStackTrace();
      }
    }

    public void initDB(String url) {
      try {
        db = DriverManager.getConnection(url);
        statement = db.createStatement();
      }
      catch(Exception e) {
        System.out.println("Could not initialize the database.");
        e.printStackTrace();
      }
    }

    public void closeDB() {
      try {
        if (statement != null) { statement.close(); }
        if (db != null) {        db.close(); }
      }
      catch(Exception e) {
```

```
            System.out.println("Could not close the current connection.");
            e.printStackTrace();
        }
    }
}
```

This model does not support database updates using any of the entries you see in the table. You could certainly support that feature if you needed to. The Swing package has a more complete result-set model called the JDBCAdapter in the table examples directory if you want another example of database and JTable communication.

Yet More Useful Methods

public void setDefaultRenderer(Class columnClass, TableCellRenderer renderer)
> Add a new renderer for a particular type of data, given by the columnClass.

public void addColumnSelectionInterval(int index0, int index1)
public void addRowSelectionInterval(int index0, int index1)
> Programmatically add an interval of rows or columns to the current selection. The appropriate selectionAllowed property must be set to true for this to work.

public void clearSelection()
> Clear any selection that might exist on the table. Nothing happens if no selection exists.

public void removeColumnSelectionInterval(int index0, int index1)
public void removeRowSelectionInterval(int index0, int index1)
> Remove row or column intervals from the current selection.

public void selectAll()
> Select the entire table.

public void setColumnSelectionInterval(int index0, int index1)
public void setRowSelectionInterval(int index0, int index1)
> Set the selection on the table to the given column or row interval.

public void moveColumn(int column, int targetColumn)
> Move the column at the index given by column to the new targetColumn index by delegating the request to the column model. Other columns are shifted as needed to make room for (and close the gap left by) the relocated column.

The JTableHeader Class

The JTableHeader class is an extension of JComponent and serves as the header component for tables. It not only dictates the basic color and font used for the header, but also the resizability and relocatability of the columns in the table. If you have an appropriate renderer for the header, you can also enable tooltips for the header. An example of custom renderers appears in Chapter 16.

Properties

The JTableHeader class has the properties listed in Table 15-14.

Table 15-14. JTableHeader properties

Property	Data type	get	is	set	Default value
accessibleContext[o]	AccessibleContext	•			JTableHeader. AccessibleJTableHeader()
columnModel	TableColumnModel	•		•	DefaultColumnModel()
draggedColumn	TableColumn	•		•	null
draggedDistance	int	•		•	0
opaque[o]	boolean		•	•	true
reorderingAllowed	boolean	•		•	true
resizingAllowed	boolean	•		•	true
resizingColumn	TableColumn	•		•	null
table	JTable	•		•	null
UI[b]	TableHeaderUI	•		•	From L&F
UIClassID[o]	String	•			"TableHeaderUI"
updateTableInRealTime	boolean	•		•	true

[b]bound, [o]overridden

See also properties from the JComponent class (Table 3-6).

The columnModel property is the TableColumnModel in place for the header. This is normally set through the constructor during the JTable initializeLocalVars() call. The draggedColumn and resizingColumn properties return the TableColumn object that the user has moved or resized. You can control whether the user is allowed to move or resize columns using the reorderingAllowed and resizingAllowed properties. The updateTableInRealTime property dictates whether the column being moved or resized is visually updated during the move or after. If this property is false, only the column headers move until the action is complete, and then the table is updated. The table property represents the companion table for the header.

Selecting Table Entries

All this, and all we can do is render and edit data in a table. "What about selecting data?" you ask. Yes, we can do that, too. And, as you might expect, the ListSelectionModel (discussed in Chapter 7) drives us through these selections. Unlike most of the other components, however, the two-dimensional JTable has two selection models, one for rows and one for columns.

Figure 15-8 shows an application that allows you to turn on and off the various selections allowed on a table (cell, row, and column). As you select different rows and columns, two status labels show you the indices of the selected items.

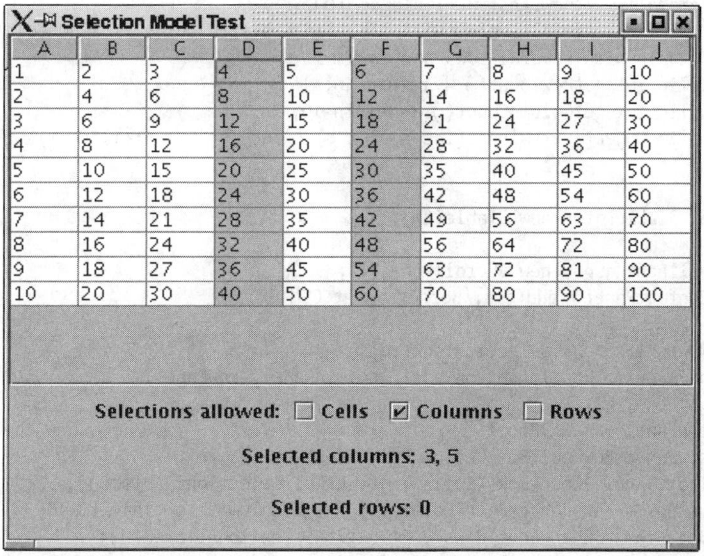

Figure 15-8. A table that lets you select rows, columns, or cells

Let's look at the code for this example. Most of the work is getting the interface you see running. Once that's done, we attach our two reporting labels as listeners to the row selection and column selection models. The interesting part of the code is the ListSelectionListener, written as an inner class. This class tracks any ListSelectionModel and updates a label with the currently selected indices every time it changes. (Those indices are retrieved using the getSelectedIndices() method we wrote ourselves.) Since we rely on only the list selection model, we can use the same event handler for both the row and the column selections.

```
// SelectionExample.java
// A simple multiplication table with the ability to play with row and column
// selections. You can alter the cell, column, and row selection properties
// of the table at runtime.
//
import java.awt.*;
import java.awt.event.*;
import javax.swing.*;
import javax.swing.event.*;
import javax.swing.table.*;

public class SelectionExample extends JFrame {
```

```
public SelectionExample( ) {
  super("Selection Model Test");
  setSize(450, 350);
  setDefaultCloseOperation(EXIT_ON_CLOSE);

  TableModel tm = new AbstractTableModel( ) {
    // We'll create a simple multiplication table to serve as a noneditable
    // table with several rows and columns.
    public int getRowCount( ) { return 10; }
    public int getColumnCount( ) { return 10; }
    public Object getValueAt(int r, int c) { return "" + (r+1)*(c+1); }
  };

  final JTable jt = new JTable(tm);

  JScrollPane jsp = new JScrollPane(jt);
  getContentPane( ).add(jsp, BorderLayout.CENTER);

  // Now set up our selection controls.
  JPanel controlPanel, buttonPanel, columnPanel, rowPanel;

  buttonPanel = new JPanel( );
  final JCheckBox cellBox, columnBox, rowBox;
  cellBox = new JCheckBox("Cells", jt.getCellSelectionEnabled( ));
  columnBox = new JCheckBox("Columns", jt.getColumnSelectionAllowed( ));
  rowBox = new JCheckBox("Rows", jt.getRowSelectionAllowed( ));
  cellBox.addActionListener(new ActionListener( ) {
    public void actionPerformed(ActionEvent ae) {
      jt.setCellSelectionEnabled(cellBox.isSelected( ));
      columnBox.setSelected(jt.getColumnSelectionAllowed( ));
      rowBox.setSelected(jt.getRowSelectionAllowed( ));
    }
  } );

  columnBox.addActionListener(new ActionListener( ) {
    public void actionPerformed(ActionEvent ae) {
      jt.setColumnSelectionAllowed(columnBox.isSelected( ));
      cellBox.setSelected(jt.getCellSelectionEnabled( ));
    }
  } );

  rowBox.addActionListener(new ActionListener( ) {
    public void actionPerformed(ActionEvent ae) {
      jt.setRowSelectionAllowed(rowBox.isSelected( ));
      cellBox.setSelected(jt.getCellSelectionEnabled( ));
    }
  } );

  buttonPanel.add(new JLabel("Selections allowed:"));
  buttonPanel.add(cellBox);
  buttonPanel.add(columnBox);
  buttonPanel.add(rowBox);
```

```
      columnPanel = new JPanel();
      ListSelectionModel csm = jt.getColumnModel().getSelectionModel();
      JLabel columnCounter = new JLabel("(Selected Column Indices Go Here)");
      csm.addListSelectionListener(new SelectionDebugger(columnCounter, csm));
      columnPanel.add(new JLabel("Selected columns:"));
      columnPanel.add(columnCounter);

      rowPanel = new JPanel();
      ListSelectionModel rsm = jt.getSelectionModel();
      JLabel rowCounter = new JLabel("(Selected Row Indices Go Here)");
      rsm.addListSelectionListener(new SelectionDebugger(rowCounter, rsm));
      rowPanel.add(new JLabel("Selected rows:"));
      rowPanel.add(rowCounter);

      controlPanel = new JPanel(new GridLayout(0, 1));
      controlPanel.add(buttonPanel);
      controlPanel.add(columnPanel);
      controlPanel.add(rowPanel);

      getContentPane().add(controlPanel, BorderLayout.SOUTH);
  }

  public static void main(String args[]) {
    SelectionExample se = new SelectionExample();
    se.setVisible(true);
  }

  public class SelectionDebugger implements ListSelectionListener {
    JLabel debugger;
    ListSelectionModel model;

    public SelectionDebugger(JLabel target, ListSelectionModel lsm) {
      debugger = target;
      model = lsm;
    }
    public void valueChanged(ListSelectionEvent lse) {
      if (!lse.getValueIsAdjusting()) {
        // Skip all the intermediate events.
        StringBuffer buf = new StringBuffer();
        int[] selection = getSelectedIndices(model.getMinSelectionIndex(),
                                    model.getMaxSelectionIndex());
        if (selection.length == 0) {
          buf.append("none");
        }
        else {
          for (int i = 0; i < selection.length -1; i++) {
            buf.append(selection[i]);
            buf.append(", ");
          }
          buf.append(selection[selection.length - 1]);
        }
        debugger.setText(buf.toString());
      }
    }
  }
```

```
// This method returns an array of selected indices. It's guaranteed to
// return a non-null value.
protected int[] getSelectedIndices(int start, int stop) {
  if ((start == -1) || (stop == -1)) {
    // No selection, so return an empty array
    return new int[0];
  }

  int guesses[] = new int[stop - start + 1];
  int index = 0;
  // Manually walk through these.
  for (int i = start; i <= stop; i++) {
    if (model.isSelectedIndex(i)) {
      guesses[index++] = i;
    }
  }

  // Pare down the guess array to the real thing.
  int realthing[] = new int[index];
  System.arraycopy(guesses, 0, realthing, 0, index);
  return realthing;
    }
  }
}
```

It is definitely worth pointing out that for this specific application we could have retrieved the array of selected row indices from the JTable object and the array of selected column indices from the table's column model. Those classes have methods similar to our getSelectedIndices( ) method. However, that would have required two separate handlers. But quite honestly, outside this example, two separate handlers might be easier to write and maintain.

Rendering Cells

You can build your own renderers for the cells in your table. By default, you get renderers for Boolean types (JCheckBox for display and editing), ImageIcon types, Number types (right-justified JTextField), and Object types (JTextField). However, you can specify a particular renderer for a class type or for a particular column, or even for a particular cell.

The TableCellRenderer Interface

This interface provides access to a rendering component without defining what the component does. This works because a renderer functions by rubber-stamping a component's image in a given location. The only method this interface defines initializes and returns just such a component:

public abstract Component getTableCellRendererComponent(JTable table, Object value, boolean isSelected, boolean hasFocus, int row, int column)

This model takes a value, which can also be retrieved by getting the cell at row, column of table, and returns a component capable of drawing the value in a table cell (or anywhere, really). The resulting drawing can be affected by the selection state of the object and whether it currently has the keyboard focus.

The DefaultTableCellRenderer Class

The javax.swing.table package includes a default renderer that produces a JLabel to display text for each cell in the table. The JTable class uses this renderer to display Numbers, Icons, and Objects. JTable creates a new default renderer and then aligns it correctly and attaches an appropriate icon, depending on the type of data. Object objects are converted to strings using toString( ) and are shown as regular labels. Number objects are shown right-aligned, and Icons are shown using centered labels. Boolean values do not use DefaultTableCellRenderer; instead, they use a private renderer class that extends JCheckBox. Go back and take a look at Figure 15-5 for an example of how this renderer works on different types of data.

Properties

The DefaultTableCellRenderer modifies three properties of the JLabel class, as shown in Table 15-15. The color values are used as the "unselected" foreground and background colors for text. You might recall that the selected foreground and background colors are governed by the JTable class. If you set either of these properties to null, the foreground and background colors from JTable are used.

Table 15-15. DefaultTableCellRenderer properties

Property	Data type	get	is	set	Default value
background	Color	•		•	null
foreground	Color	•		•	null
opaque	boolean		•	•	true

See also properties from the JLabel class (Table 4-1).

Of course, we can also build our own renderer based on DefaultTableCellRenderer. Here's an example renderer we can use with our FileModel from Figure 15-5. This renderer puts an exclamation point icon in front of any file size greater than some threshold value (passed to the constructor of our renderer).

```
// BigRenderer.java
// A renderer for numbers that shows an icon in front of big numbers
//
```

```
import java.awt.*;
import javax.swing.*;
import javax.swing.table.*;

public class BigRenderer extends DefaultTableCellRenderer {
  double threshold;
  Icon bang = new ImageIcon("bang.gif");

  public BigRenderer(double t) {
    threshold = t;
    setHorizontalAlignment(JLabel.RIGHT);
    setHorizontalTextPosition(SwingConstants.RIGHT);
  }

  public Component getTableCellRendererComponent(JTable table,
    Object value, boolean isSelected, boolean hasFocus, int row, int col)
  {
    // Be a little paranoid about where the user tries to use this renderer.
    if (value instanceof Number) {
      if (((Number)value).doubleValue() > threshold) {
        setIcon(bang);
      }
      else {
        setIcon(null);
      }
    }
    else {
      setIcon(null);
    }
    return super.getTableCellRendererComponent(table, value, isSelected,
                    hasFocus, row, col);
  }
}
```

To attach this renderer to our table, we add a few lines of code to the `FileTable` class:

```
JTable jt = new JTable(fm);
// ...
jt.setDefaultRenderer(Number.class, new BigRenderer(1000));
```

Figure 15-9 shows the results of this renderer in action with the new `FileTable2` class.

The CellRendererPane Class

This utility class was built to keep renderers from propagating repaint() and validate() calls to the components using renderer components such as JTree and JList. If you played around with creating your own renderers for any of the Swing components that use them, you'll recall that you did not use this class yourself. This pane is often wrapped around the renderer, and its various paintComponent() methods are used to do the actual drawing. You do not normally need to worry about this class.

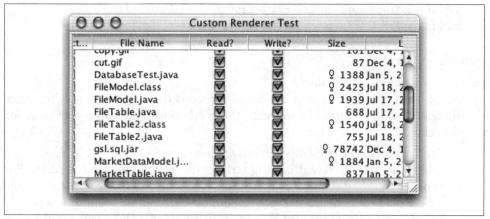

Figure 15-9. A custom renderer (note the icons) applied to a file information table

Editing Cells

In addition to custom renderers, you can also create custom editors for your table cells. (Actually, the basic stuff in this section also applies to the JTree class.) You have several options ranging from straightforward to completely homegrown.

The CellEditor Interface

This interface governs the basic functionality required of an editor. It has methods for retrieving a new value and determining when to start and stop editing. The basic process for editing is:

- The user clicks the required number of times on the cell (varies from editor to editor).
- The component (usually JTree or JTable) replaces the cell with its editor.
- The user types or chooses a new value.
- The user ends the editing session (e.g., pressing Enter in a text field).
- The editor fires a change event to interested listeners (usually the tree or table containing the cell), stating that editing is finished.
- The component reads the new value and replaces the editor with the cell's renderer.

Events

The CellEditor interface requires methods for adding and removing cell editor listeners, which are objects interested in finding out whether editing is finished or canceled. The CellEditorListener class is discussed later in the chapter.

```
public abstract void addCellEditorListener(CellEditorListener l)
public abstract void removeCellEditorListener(CellEditorListener l)
```

Methods

public Object getCellEditorValue()

Access the only property of a cell editor, which is the cell's current value. After successful editing, a table or tree calls this method to retrieve the new value for the cell.

public abstract boolean isCellEditable(EventObject anEvent)

Should return true if anEvent is a valid trigger for starting this kind of editor. For example, if you want the user to double-click on a field to invoke the editor, this method would test whether anEvent is a double-click mouse event. If it was only a single-click, you could return false. If it was a double-click, you could return true.

public abstract boolean shouldSelectCell(EventObject anEvent)

This method should return true if the cell to be edited should also be selected. While you usually want to select the cell, there are some situations in which not selecting the cell is preferable. For example, you might be implementing a table that lets the user edit cells that are part of an ongoing selection. Since you want the selection to remain in place, you would implement this method to return false. The cell can still be edited.

public abstract boolean stopCellEditing()
public abstract void cancelCellEditing()

You should use these methods to tell the editor to stop editing the cell. The stopCellEditing() method indicates that editing is over and that the new value supplied should replace the old value of the cell. The cancelCellEditing() method indicates that editing is over and that the new value the user entered (if any) should be ignored. The stopCellEditing() method can return a false value if the editor is unable to stop editing. (This might occur if your editor validates input and currently contains an invalid entry.) As an example, you can use these to programmatically stop or cancel editing before starting to edit another cell or upon losing focus.

The TableCellEditor Interface

To begin any custom cell editor devoted to tables, we need to start with the TableCellEditor interface. This interface defines one method that returns our editor:

public Component getTableCellEditorComponent(JTable table, Object value, boolean isSelected, int row, int column)

Return a component capable of editing a value. This method should initialize the editor (to reflect the value and isSelected arguments) and may also affect the table. You could dull the color of the rest of the row or table while editing one cell, for example.

The DefaultCellEditor class (discussed below) provides a good implementation of this interface. Unless you're doing something exotic, you should be able to base your cell editors on the DefaultCellEditor class. (In Chapter 16, we do have a slightly exotic example that uses a JSlider and a pop-up window to create an editor in .)

The CellEditorListener Interface

The CellEditorListener interface defines how an object can listen for events generated by a cell editor. Cell editors generate a ChangeEvent when editing is canceled or stopped (a better term might be "finished"). Typically, the object "hosting" the editor (for example, a JTree allowing the user to enter a new filename) would register as a listener. When the event occurs, the JTree reads the cell's new value from the editor, tears down the editor, and repaints the cell with its new value.

public void editingStopped(ChangeEvent e)
> Indicate that successful editing has been completed. You can get the new value of the cell from the editor component, which is contained in the source property of the change event.

public void editingCanceled(ChangeEvent e)
> Indicate editing has been canceled. You should ignore any partially edited value that might be present in the editor.

The DefaultCellEditor Class

Swing provides a default editor with a fair amount of flexibility. The DefaultCellEditor class implements the CellEditor interface and provides constructors that let you use a text field, checkbox, or combo box for entering the new value.

Properties

The DefaultCellEditor class contains the properties listed in Table 15-16. The cellEditorValue property contains the value of the cell editor. This value can be used or ignored when editing stops, depending on whether editing is stopped or canceled. The clickCountToStart property determines how many clicks it takes to begin editing a cell. For checkboxes and combo boxes, this value is 1; for text fields, the default value of this property is 2, meaning that the user has to double-click to start editing. The component property contains the actual component that the cell editor returns when getTableCellEditorComponent( ) or getTreeCellEditorComponent( ) is called.

Table 15-16. DefaultCellEditor properties

Property	Data type	get	is	set	Default value
cellEditorValue[o]	Object	•			null
clickCountToStart	int	•		•	Determined by constructor
component	Component	•			Determined by constructor

[o]overridden

Events

As dictated by the CellEditor interface, the DefaultCellEditor class implements the add and remove methods for cell editor listeners. It also provides these convenience methods for generating those events:

protected void fireEditingStopped( )
protected void fireEditingCanceled( )
> Both of these methods notify registered listeners that editing has stopped. The cell editor is listed as the source of these events.

Constructors

You can create your own cell editor using any of the following constructors. You can also preconfigure any of the components you pass in. For example, you might pass in a right-justified text field or a checkbox with custom icons.

public DefaultCellEditor(JTextField x)
public DefaultCellEditor(JCheckBox x)
public DefaultCellEditor(JComboBox x)
> These constructors create editors with the most common components: a JCheckBox for boolean values, a JComboBox for a list of well-defined choices, and a JTextField for any value that can be represented as a String.

Tree and table editor methods

Most of the methods in DefaultCellEditor are implementations of the CellEditor methods. The only other methods in the DefaultCellEditor class that are new are the methods required to implement the TableCellEditor and TreeCellEditor interfaces.

public Component getTreeCellEditorComponent(JTree tree, Object value,
*   boolean isSelected, boolean expanded, boolean leaf, int row)*
> Return a valid tree cell editor (discussed in more detail in Chapter 17).

public Component getTableCellEditorComponent(JTable table, Object value, boolean
*   isSelected, int row, int column)*
> Return a valid table cell editor (discussed earlier).

Figure 15-10 shows an example of a JTable outfitted with a DefaultCellEditor made out of a combo box.

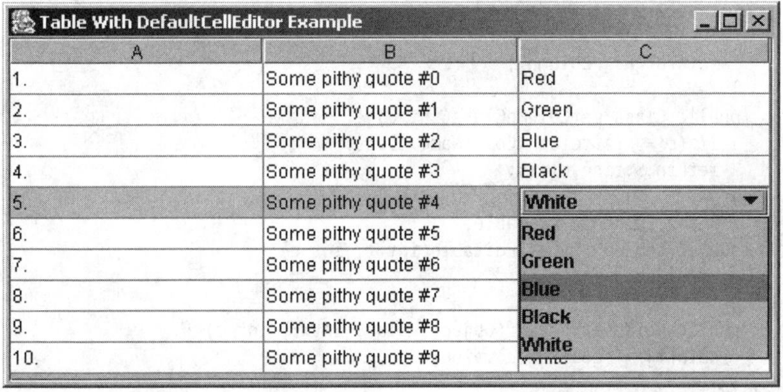

Figure 15-10. A JTable with a pop-up cell editor built from the DefaultCellEditor class

The data in the table is entirely contrived, but look at how simple it was to set up the combo box editor. In our data model we say that one column has a particular type (a simple inner class called ColorName in our case). Then we register a new DefaultCellEditor as the default editor for that type. Here's the complete source code:

```java
// ColorTable.java
//
import javax.swing.table.*;
import java.awt.*;
import java.awt.event.*;
import javax.swing.*;

public class ColorTable extends JFrame {
  ColorName colors[] = {
    new ColorName("Red"), new ColorName("Green"), new ColorName("Blue"),
    new ColorName("Black"), new ColorName("White")
  };

  public ColorTable() {
    super("Table With DefaultCellEditor Example");
    setSize(500,300);
    setDefaultCloseOperation(EXIT_ON_CLOSE);

    JTable table = new JTable(new AbstractTableModel() {
        ColorName data[] = {
          colors[0], colors[1], colors[2], colors[3], colors[4],
          colors[0], colors[1], colors[2], colors[3], colors[4]
        };
        public int getColumnCount() { return 3; }
        public int getRowCount() { return 10;  }
```

```
        public Object getValueAt(int r, int c) {
          switch (c) {
          case 0:  return (r + 1) + ".";
          case 1:  return "Some pithy quote #" + r;
          case 2:  return data[r];
          }
          return "Bad Column";
        }
        public Class getColumnClass(int c) {
          if (c == 2) return ColorName.class;
          return String.class;
        }
        // Make Column 2 editable.
        public boolean isCellEditable(int r, int c) {
          return c == 2;
        }
        public void setValueAt(Object value, int r, int c) {
          data[r] = (ColorName)value;
        }
      });

    table.setDefaultEditor(ColorName.class,
                    new DefaultCellEditor(new JComboBox(colors)));
    table.setDefaultRenderer(ColorName.class, new DefaultTableCellRenderer());
    table.setRowHeight(20);
    getContentPane().add(new JScrollPane(table));
  }

  public static void main(String args[]) {
    ColorTable ex = new ColorTable();
    ex.setVisible(true);
  }

  public class ColorName {
    String cname;
    public ColorName(String name) { cname = name; }
    public String toString() { return cname; }
  }
}
```

Next Steps

There are many other things you can do with JTable and its various supporting models. While we don't have time or space to present all of them, we will take a look at a few more interesting examples of JTable features in Chapter 16.

CHAPTER 16

Advanced Table Examples

In this chapter, we're going to take a different approach. Tables are extremely flexible, useful gadgets. Here, we're going to show you how to put tables to work in more advanced situations. Most of these examples require working on the TableModel itself or the TableColumnModel. But once you know what you're doing, subclassing these models is fairly easy and gives you a lot of flexibility.

We will look at four examples:

- A scrollable table with row headers. Remember that a JTable understands column headers but doesn't have any concept of a row header. Also, remember that a JScrollPane understands both column and row headers. In this example, we'll show you how to add row headers to a JTable and make them work properly within a JScrollPane.

- A table that has an extremely large number of rows. Scrolling stops working well when you have more than a few hundred rows. We'll build a table with 10,000 rows, let you page up and down to select a range of 100 rows within the table, and then scroll back and forth within that more limited range.

- A table with a custom editor and renderer for working with cells that contain something other than just text. We'll represent a numeric value with a slider. The user can also move the slider to edit the value.

- A TableChart component that builds pie charts based on the TableModel class used by JTable. In this example, the JTable is almost superfluous, although it provides a convenient way to edit the data in the pie chart. The real point is that the TableModel is a powerful abstraction that can be put to use even when there's no table around.

A Table with Row Headers

As we promised, this is a table with headers for both rows and columns. The JTable handles the column headers itself; we need to add machinery for the rows. Figure 16-1 shows the resulting table. It shows column labels, plus two data columns from a larger table. Scrolling works the way you would expect. When you scroll vertically, the row headers scroll with the data. You can scroll horizontally to see other data columns, but the row headers remain on the screen.

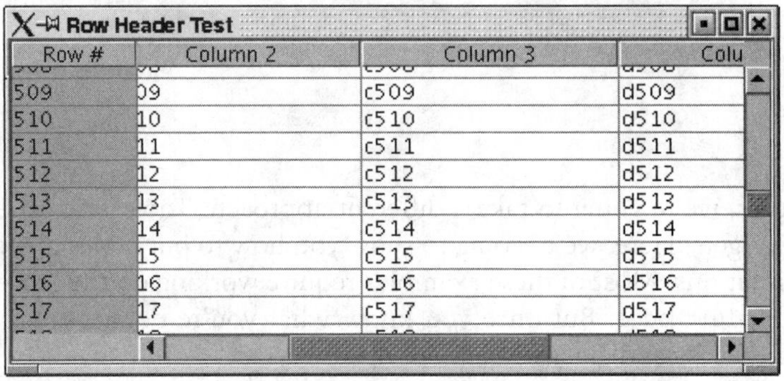

Figure 16-1. A table with both row and column headers

The trick is that we really have two closely coordinated tables: one for the row headers (a table with only one column) and one for the data columns. There is a single TableModel, but separate TableColumnModels for the two parts of the larger table. In the figure, the gray column on the left is the row header; it's really column 0 of the data model.

To understand what's going on, it helps to remember how a Swing table models data. The TableModel itself keeps track of all the data for the table, i.e., the values that fill in the cells. There's no reason why we can't have two tables that share the same table model—that's one of the advantages of the model-view-controller architecture. Likewise, there's no reason why we can't have data in the table model that isn't displayed; the table model can keep track of a logical table that is much larger than the table we actually put on the screen. This is particularly important in the last example, but it's also important here. The table that implements the row headers uses the first column of the data model and ignores everything else; the table that displays the data ignores the first column.

The TableColumnModel keeps track of the columns and is called whenever we add, delete, or move a column. One way to implement tables that use or ignore parts of our data is to build table column models that do what we want, which is add only a particular column (or group of columns) to the table. That's the approach we've chosen. Once we have our models, it is relatively simple to create two JTables that use the same `TableModel`, but different `TableColumnModels`. Each table displays only the columns that its column model allows. When we put the tables next to each other, one serves as the row header, and the other displays the body. Depending on the data you put in your tables, you could probably automate many of these steps. Here is the code for our not-so-simple table:

```java
// RowHeaderTable.java
//
import java.awt.*;
import java.awt.event.*;
import javax.swing.*;
import javax.swing.table.*;

public class RowHeaderTable extends JFrame {

  public RowHeaderTable( ) {
    super("Row Header Test");
    setSize(300, 200);
    setDefaultCloseOperation(EXIT_ON_CLOSE);


    TableModel tm = new AbstractTableModel( ) {
      String data[] = {"", "a", "b", "c", "d", "e"};
      String headers[] = {"Row #", "Column 1", "Column 2", "Column 3",
                          "Column 4", "Column 5"};
      public int getColumnCount( ) { return data.length; }
      public int getRowCount( ) { return 1000; }
      public String getColumnName(int col) { return headers[col]; }

      // Synthesize some entries using the data values and the row number.
      public Object getValueAt(int row, int col) {
        return data[col] + row;
      }
    };

    // Create a column model for the main table. This model ignores the first
    // column added and sets a minimum width of 150 pixels for all others.
    TableColumnModel cm = new DefaultTableColumnModel( ) {
      boolean first = true;
      public void addColumn(TableColumn tc) {
        // Drop the first column, which will be the row header.
        if (first) { first = false; return; }
        tc.setMinWidth(150);  // Just for looks, really...
        super.addColumn(tc);
      }
    };

    // Create a column model that will serve as our row header table. This model
    // picks a maximum width and stores only the first column.
    TableColumnModel rowHeaderModel = new DefaultTableColumnModel( ) {
      boolean first = true;
      public void addColumn(TableColumn tc) {
        if (first) {
```

```
        tc.setMaxWidth(tc.getPreferredWidth( ));
        super.addColumn(tc);
        first = false;
      }
      // Drop the rest of the columns; this is the header column only.
    }
  };

  JTable jt = new JTable(tm, cm);

  // Set up the header column and hook it up to everything.
  JTable headerColumn = new JTable(tm, rowHeaderModel);
  jt.createDefaultColumnsFromModel( );
  headerColumn.createDefaultColumnsFromModel( );

  // Make sure that selections between the main table and the header stay in sync
  // (by sharing the same model).
  jt.setSelectionModel(headerColumn.getSelectionModel( ));

  // Make the header column look pretty.
  //    headerColumn.setBorder(BorderFactory.createEtchedBorder( ));
  headerColumn.setBackground(Color.lightGray);
  headerColumn.setColumnSelectionAllowed(false);
  headerColumn.setCellSelectionEnabled(false);

  // Put it in a viewport that we can control.
  JViewport jv = new JViewport( );
  jv.setView(headerColumn);
  jv.setPreferredSize(headerColumn.getMaximumSize( ));

  // Without shutting off autoResizeMode, our tables won't scroll correctly
  // (horizontally, anyway).
  jt.setAutoResizeMode(JTable.AUTO_RESIZE_OFF);

  // We have to manually attach the row headers, but after that, the scroll
  // pane keeps them in sync.
  JScrollPane jsp = new JScrollPane(jt);
  jsp.setRowHeader(jv);
  jsp.setCorner(ScrollPaneConstants.UPPER_LEFT_CORNER,
                headerColumn.getTableHeader( ));
  getContentPane( ).add(jsp, BorderLayout.CENTER);
}

public static void main(String args[]) {
  RowHeaderTable rht = new RowHeaderTable( );
  rht.setVisible(true);
}
}
```

The various models we use—our subclasses of `AbstractTableModel` and `DefaultTableColumnModel`—are anonymous inner classes. The new table model doesn't do anything really interesting; it just keeps track of the raw data. There's an

---

array of column headers; the data itself is computed in the getValueAt( ) method. Of course, in a real example, you'd have some way of looking up real data.

Our TableColumnModels are where the magic happens. The addColumn( ) method, which they override, is called whenever a column is added to a table. The first of our two models, cm, keeps track of the body of the table. The first time it is called, it returns without doing anything—effectively ignoring the first column in the table, which is the column of row headers. (It does set the local variable first to false, indicating that it already processed the headers.) For subsequent columns, addColumn( ) behaves the way you would expect: it sets a minimum column width, then calls the method in the superclass to insert the column in the table.

The other table column model, rowHeaderModel, overrides addColumn( ) to do the opposite: it inserts the first column (the row header) into the table and ignores all the other columns. Notice that we manually set the maximum width of the header column. Without this action, the header column would try to be as wide as the main table—leaving no room for the main table to display itself. This value could be passed in to the constructor of a regular inner class, or you could calculate an appropriate width. These classes make the assumption that column 0 (the row headers) is added to the table first and never added again. As long as the table isn't editable, that assumption is valid. If the table were editable, we would have to add some logic to make sure we always know which column we're working on.

The rest of the code is almost self-explanatory. We create two JTable objects: jt (for the body) and headerColumn (for the row headers). We start by telling our tables to build their columns because we specified our own column models. Our tables use the same TableModel and the appropriate TableColumnModel. To make sure that row selection for the two tables is always in sync, we give them both the same SelectionModel. We give headerColumn a different color and disable column and cell selection. The only thing left is to arrange the display. We create a separate JViewport to display the row headers and put the header column in it. Then we disable autoresize mode for the main table; this is necessary to make the scrollbars work properly. (Things get confusing if a table inside a scrollpane tries to resize itself.) Finally, we create a JScrollPane from jt. To get the row headers into the scrollpane, we add the viewport (which already contains headerColumn) to the JScrollPane by calling setRowHeader( ). Then we just slap the JScrollPane, which now contains both tables, into our JFrame's content pane, and we're done.

Large Tables with Paging

Working conveniently with very large tables can be a pain. Scrolling up and down is fine as long as the table is only a few hundred lines long, but when it gets larger, a tiny movement in the scrollbar can change your position by a few thousand rows. One way to solve this is by combining paging with scrolling. We'll create a table with

10,000 rows (large enough to make scrolling through the entire table a hassle) and add buttons to page up and down 100 rows at a time. Within any group of 100 rows, you can use the scrollbar as usual to move around. Figure 16-2 shows the result.

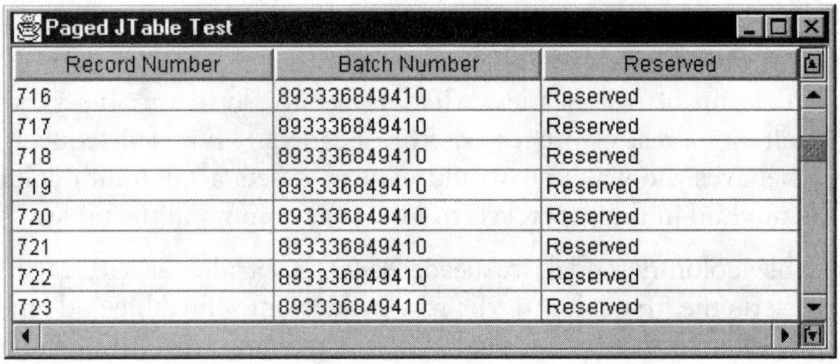

Figure 16-2. A paging (and scrolling) table

In this example, we're using a simple trick. There are really two tables to worry about: a logical table that contains all 10,000 rows, which might represent records that were read from a database, and the physical table that's instantiated as a JTable object and displayed on the screen. To do this trick, we implement a new table model, PagingModel, which is a subclass of AbstractTableModel. This table model keeps track of the data for the entire logical table: all 10,000 rows. However, when a JTable asks it for data to display, it pretends it knows only about the 100 rows that should be on the screen at this time. It's actually quite simple. (And we don't even need to worry about any column models; the default column model is adequate.)

Here's the PagingModel code used to track the 10,000 records:

```
// PagingModel.java
// A larger table model that performs "paging" of its data. This model reports a
// small number of rows (e.g., 100 or so) as a "page" of data. You can switch pages
// to view all of the rows as needed using the pageDown( ) and pageUp( ) methods.
// Presumably, access to the other pages of data is dictated by other GUI elements
// such as up/down buttons, or maybe a text field that allows you to enter the page
// number you want to display.
//
import javax.swing.table.*;
import javax.swing.*;
import java.awt.event.*;
import java.awt.*;

public class PagingModel extends AbstractTableModel {

  protected int pageSize;
  protected int pageOffset;
  protected Record[] data;
```

```java
public PagingModel() {
  this(10000, 100);
}

public PagingModel(int numRows, int size) {
  data = new Record[numRows];
  pageSize = size;

  // Fill our table with random data (from the Record() constructor).
  for (int i=0; i < data.length; i++) {
    data[i] = new Record();
  }
}

// Return values appropriate for the visible table part.
public int getRowCount() { return Math.min(pageSize, data.length); }
public int getColumnCount() { return Record.getColumnCount(); }

// Work only on the visible part of the table.
public Object getValueAt(int row, int col) {
  int realRow = row + (pageOffset * pageSize);
  return data[realRow].getValueAt(col);
}

public String getColumnName(int col) {
  return Record.getColumnName(col);
}

// Use this method to figure out which page you are on.
public int getPageOffset() { return pageOffset; }

public int getPageCount() {
  return (int)Math.ceil((double)data.length / pageSize);
}

// Use this method if you want to know how big the real table is. You could also
// write "getRealValueAt()" if needed.
public int getRealRowCount() {
  return data.length;
}

public int getPageSize() { return pageSize; }
public void setPageSize(int s) {
  if (s == pageSize) { return; }
  int oldPageSize = pageSize;
  pageSize = s;
  pageOffset=(oldPageSize * pageOffset) / pageSize;
  fireTableDataChanged();
}

// Update the page offset and fire a data changed event (all rows).
public void pageDown() {
  if (pageOffset < getPageCount() - 1) {
```

```
      pageOffset++;
      fireTableDataChanged( );
    }
  }

  // Update the page offset and fire a data changed (all rows).
  public void pageUp( ) {
    if (pageOffset > 0) {
      pageOffset--;
      fireTableDataChanged( );
    }
  }

  // We provide our own version of a scrollpane that includes
  // the Page Up and Page Down buttons by default.
  public static JScrollPane createPagingScrollPaneForTable(JTable jt) {
    JScrollPane jsp = new JScrollPane(jt);
    TableModel tmodel = jt.getModel( );

    // Don't choke if this is called on a regular table...
    if (! (tmodel instanceof PagingModel)) {
      return jsp;
    }

    // Go ahead and build the real scrollpane.
    final PagingModel model = (PagingModel)tmodel;
    final JButton upButton = new JButton(new ArrowIcon(ArrowIcon.UP));
    upButton.setEnabled(false);  // Starts off at 0, so can't go up
    final JButton downButton = new JButton(new ArrowIcon(ArrowIcon.DOWN));
    if (model.getPageCount( ) <= 1) {
      downButton.setEnabled(false);  // One page...can't scroll down
    }

    upButton.addActionListener(new ActionListener( ) {
      public void actionPerformed(ActionEvent ae) {
        model.pageUp( );

        // If we hit the top of the data, disable the Page Up button.
        if (model.getPageOffset( ) == 0) {
          upButton.setEnabled(false);
        }
        downButton.setEnabled(true);
      }
    } );

    downButton.addActionListener(new ActionListener( ) {
      public void actionPerformed(ActionEvent ae) {
        model.pageDown( );

        // If we hit the bottom of the data, disable the Page Down button.
        if (model.getPageOffset( ) == (model.getPageCount( ) - 1)) {
          downButton.setEnabled(false);
```

```
        }
        upButton.setEnabled(true);
      }
    } );

    // Turn on the scrollbars; otherwise, we won't get our corners.
    jsp.setVerticalScrollBarPolicy
        (ScrollPaneConstants.VERTICAL_SCROLLBAR_ALWAYS);
    jsp.setHorizontalScrollBarPolicy
        (ScrollPaneConstants.HORIZONTAL_SCROLLBAR_ALWAYS);

    // Add in the corners (page up/down).
    jsp.setCorner(ScrollPaneConstants.UPPER_RIGHT_CORNER, upButton);
    jsp.setCorner(ScrollPaneConstants.LOWER_RIGHT_CORNER, downButton);

    return jsp;
  }
}
```

The PagingModel constructor fills an array with all our data. (The Record object does something simple to generate meaningless data; in real life, we could be getting data from a database, J2EE call, XML-RPC, or any number of live sources.) Most of the methods in the PagingModel are fairly self-explanatory. The interesting ones have something to do with the table's rows. getRowCount( ) isn't computationally complex, but is typical of what we'll see: if the table is too big for one page, it returns pageSize, which is the number of rows we want to display. getValueAt( ) is only slightly more complex: it translates the desired row from the physical table into the actual row within the much larger logical table and returns the appropriate data. (We don't need to do anything to the column, but we would if we were making a table that paged in two directions.) We've added some convenience methods— getPageOffset( ), getPageCount( ), and getRealRowCount( )—to provide information about the table's actual size and the portion we're looking at.

The pageDown( ) and pageUp( ) methods are a bit more interesting. These are called when the user clicks on either of the paging buttons displayed with the table. When the user pages, these methods increment or decrement the model's pageOffset variable, which records the current offset into the table. This effectively means that the data in the physical table (the table we display) has changed, although nothing has changed in the logical table at all. Because the physical table has changed, we call fireTableDataChanged( ), which fires a TableModelEvent that tells the JTable to reload all the data. When it's created, the JTable registers itself as a listener for table model events.

Our table doesn't let you change the page increment, but that would be a useful feature, so we provide a setPageSize( ) method. This method is interesting because, again, changing the page size does nothing to the logical table, but it effectively adds or deletes rows from the physical JTable on the screen.

The last important task that our table model has to perform is to build a JScrollPane that knows how to work properly with our table. This is implemented in the createPagingScrollPaneForTable( ) method. This method starts by getting a JScrollPane and then modifying it to work appropriately. The modifications are really quite simple. We create a pair of buttons to control the paging (the icons for the buttons are implemented by the rather simple ArrowIcon class, which we haven't shown); we wire the buttons to the pageUp( ) and pageDown( ) methods of our table model; and we include some logic to disable buttons when we reach the top or bottom of the table. Finally, we turn on the scrollpane's scrollbars and add the buttons in the upper- and lower-right corners. Remember that if the scrollbars aren't enabled, there won't be any place to put the buttons.

Our table is currently static: it displays but cannot update data. How would you implement table updates? We'll leave this as a thought experiment. There's some simple bookkeeping that you'd have to do, but the most interesting part would be implementing setValueAt( ) in the PagingModel class. Like getValueAt( ), it would have to translate between logical rows in the data and physical rows in the JTable. It would have to call fireTableDataChanged( ) to generate a table model event and cause the JTable to update the display. But you would also need a way to set the value of the cells that are not visible. For real applications, you might consider writing your own getRealValueAt( ) and setRealValueAt( ) that do not map incoming row values.

Here's the very simple Record class; it just provides column names and generates meaningless data, one record (row) at a time:

```
// Record.java
// A simple data structure for use with the PagingModel demo
//
public class Record {
  static String[] headers = { "Record Number", "Batch Number", "Reserved" };
  static int counter;
  String[] data;

  public Record() {
    data = new String[] { "" + (counter++), "" + System.currentTimeMillis(),
            "Reserved" };
  }

  public String getValueAt(int i) { return data[i]; }

  public static String getColumnName(int i) { return headers[i]; }
  public static int getColumnCount() { return headers.length; }
}
```

Here's the application that brings up the JTable using our paging model:

```
// PagingTester.java
//
import java.awt.*;
import java.awt.event.*;
```

```
import javax.swing.*;
import javax.swing.table.*;

public class PagingTester extends JFrame {

  public PagingTester( ) {
    super("Paged JTable Test");
    setSize(300, 200);
    setDefaultCloseOperation(EXIT_ON_CLOSE);

    PagingModel pm = new PagingModel( );
    JTable jt = new JTable(pm);

    // Use our own custom scrollpane.
    JScrollPane jsp = PagingModel.createPagingScrollPaneForTable(jt);
    getContentPane( ).add(jsp, BorderLayout.CENTER);
  }

  public static void main(String args[]) {
    PagingTester pt = new PagingTester( );
    pt.setVisible(true);
  }
}
```

We just create an instance of our PagingModel to hold the data and construct a JTable with that model. Then we get a paging scrollpane from the JTable and add that scrollpane to the content pane of a JFrame.

A Table with Custom Editing and Rendering

Recall from the previous chapter that you can build your own editors and renderers for the cells in your table. One easy customization is altering the properties of the DefaultTableCellRenderer, which is an extension of JLabel. You can use icons, colors, text alignment, borders, and anything that can change the look of a label.

You don't have to rely on JLabel, though. Developers come across all types of data. Some of that data is best represented as text—some isn't. For data that requires (or at least enjoys the support of) alternate representations, your renderer can extend any component. To be more precise, it can extend Component, so your options are boundless. We look at one of those options next.

A Custom Renderer

Figure 16-3 shows a table containing audio tracks in a mixer format, using the default renderer. We have some track information, such as the track name, its start and stop times, and two volumes (left and right channels, both using integer values from 0 to 100) to control.

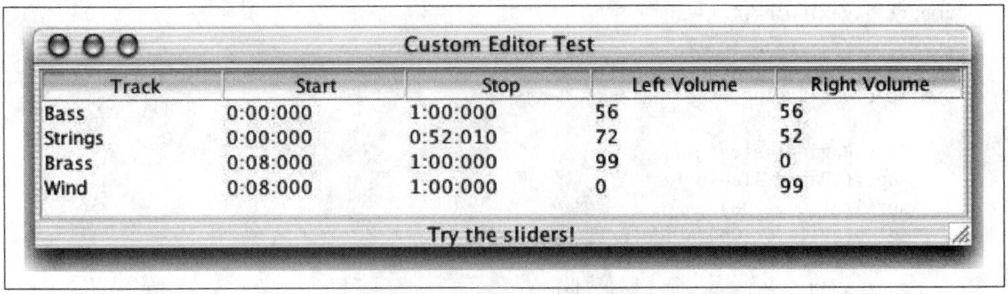

Figure 16-3. A standard table with cells drawn by the DefaultTableCellRenderer

We'd really like to show our volume entries as sliders. The sliders give us a better indication of the relative volumes. Figure 16-4 shows the application with a custom renderer for the volumes.

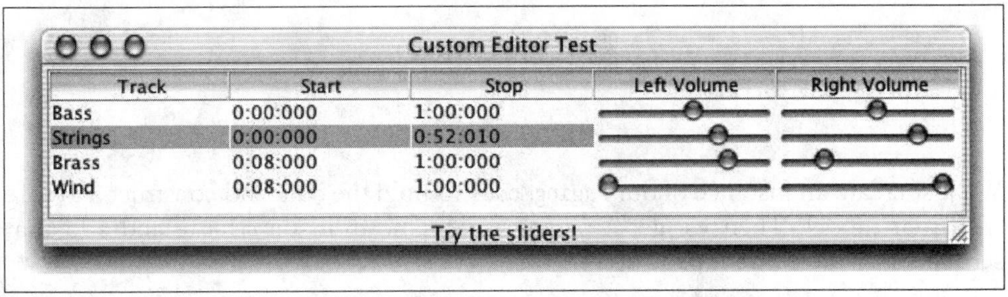

Figure 16-4. A standard table with the volume cells drawn by VolumeRenderer

The code for this example involves two new pieces and a table model for our audio columns. First, we must create a new renderer by implementing the `TableCellRenderer` interface ourselves. Then, in the application code, we attach our new renderer to our volume columns. The model code looks similar to the models we have built before. The only real difference is that we now have two columns using a custom `Volume` class. The following `Volume` class encodes an integer. The interesting thing about this class is the `setVolume()` method, which can parse a `String`, `Number`, or other `Volume` object.

```
// Volume.java
// A simple data structure for track volumes on a mixer
//
public class Volume {
  private int volume;

  public Volume(int v) { setVolume(v); }
  public Volume() { this(50); }

  public void setVolume(int v) { volume = (v < 0 ? 0 : v > 100 ? 100 : v); }
  public void setVolume(Object v) {
    if (v instanceof String) {
      setVolume(Integer.parseInt((String)v));
    }
```

```
    else if (v instanceof Number) {
      setVolume(((Number)v).intValue( ));
    }
    else if (v instanceof Volume) {
      setVolume(((Volume)v).getVolume( ));
    }
  }

  public int getVolume( ) { return volume; }

  public String toString( ) { return String.valueOf(volume); }
}
```

Here's the model code. We store a simple `Object[][]` structure for our data, a separate array for the column headers, and another array for the column class types. We make every cell editable by always returning true for the `isCellEditable( )` method. The `setValue( )` method checks to see if we're setting one of the volumes, and if so, we don't simply place the new object into the array. Rather, we set the volume value for the current object in the data array. Then, if someone builds an editor that returns a `String` or a `Number` rather than a `Volume` object, we still keep our `Volume` object intact.

```
// MixerModel.java
// An audio mixer table data model. This model contains the following columns:
//   Track name (String)
//   Track start time (String)
//   Track stop time (String)
//   Left channel volume (Volume, 0 . . 100)
//   Right channel volume (Volume, 0 . . 100)
//
import javax.swing.table.*;

public class MixerModel extends AbstractTableModel {

  String headers[] = {"Track", "Start", "Stop", "Left Volume", "Right Volume"};
  Class columnClasses[] = {String.class, String.class, String.class,
                           Volume.class, Volume.class};
  Object  data[][] = {
    {"Bass", "0:00:000", "1:00:000", new Volume(56), new Volume(56)},
    {"Strings", "0:00:000", "0:52:010", new Volume(72), new Volume(52)},
    {"Brass", "0:08:000", "1:00:000", new Volume(99), new Volume(0)},
    {"Wind", "0:08:000", "1:00:000", new Volume(0), new Volume(99)},
  };

  public int getRowCount( ) { return data.length; }
  public int getColumnCount( ) { return headers.length; }
  public Class getColumnClass(int c) { return columnClasses[c]; }
  public String getColumnName(int c) { return headers[c]; }
  public boolean isCellEditable(int r, int c) { return true; }
  public Object getValueAt(int r, int c) { return data[r][c]; }

  // Do something extra here so that if we get a String object back (from a text
  // field editor), we can still store that as a valid Volume object. If it's just a
  // string, then stick it directly into our data array.
```

```
    public void setValueAt(Object value, int r, int c) {
      if (c >= 3) { ((Volume)data[r][c]).setVolume(value);}
      else {data[r][c] = value;}
    }

    // A quick debugging utility to dump the contents of our data structure
    public void dump() {
      for (int i = 0; i < data.length; i++) {
        System.out.print("|");
        for (int j = 0; j < data[0].length; j++) {
          System.out.print(data[i][j] + "|");
        }
        System.out.println();
      }
    }
  }
}
```

Here's the application that displays the window and table. Notice how we attach a specific renderer to the Volume class type without specifying which columns contain that data type, using the setDefaultRenderer( ) method. The table uses the results of the TableModel's getColumnClass( ) call to determine the class of a given column and then uses getDefaultRenderer( ) to get an appropriate renderer for that class.

```
// MixerTest.java
//
import java.awt.*;
import javax.swing.*;

public class MixerTest extends JFrame {

  public MixerTest() {
    super("Customer Editor Test");
    setSize(600,160);
    setDefaultCloseOperation(EXIT_ON_CLOSE);

    MixerModel test = new MixerModel();
    test.dump();
    JTable jt = new JTable(test);
    jt.setDefaultRenderer(Volume.class, new VolumeRenderer());
    JScrollPane jsp = new JScrollPane(jt);
    getContentPane().add(jsp, BorderLayout.CENTER);
  }

  public static void main(String args[]) {
    MixerTest mt = new MixerTest();
    mt.setVisible(true);
  }
}
```

Now we build our renderer. As you saw with the DefaultTableCellRenderer class, to create a new renderer, we often just extend the component that does the rendering. Then we initialize the component with the getTableCellRendererComponent( ) method and return a reference to that component. That is exactly what we do with this rather simple VolumeRenderer class. We extend the JSlider class and, in the getTableCell-RendererComponent() method, set the position of the slider's knob and return the slider. This doesn't allow us to edit volume values, but at least we get a better visual representation.

```java
// VolumeRenderer.java
// A slider renderer for volume values in a table
//
import java.awt.Component;
import javax.swing.*;
import javax.swing.table.*;

public class VolumeRenderer extends JSlider implements TableCellRenderer {

  public VolumeRenderer() {
    super(SwingConstants.HORIZONTAL);
    // Set a starting size. Some 1.2/1.3 systems need this.
    setSize(115,15);
  }

  public Component getTableCellRendererComponent(JTable table, Object value,
                                                 boolean isSelected,
                                                 boolean hasFocus,
                                                 int row,int column) {
    if (value == null) {
      return this;
    }
    if (value instanceof Volume) {
      setValue(((Volume)value).getVolume());
    }
    else {
      setValue(0);
    }
    return this;
  }
}
```

A Custom Editor

Of course, the next obvious question is how to make the sliders usable for editing volume values. To do that, we write our own VolumeEditor class that implements the TableCellEditor interface.

The following code implements a TableCellEditor for Volume objects from scratch. The fireEditingCanceled() method shows how to cancel an editing session, and fireEditingStopped() shows how to end a session and update the table. In both cases, it's a matter of firing a ChangeEvent identifying the editor for the appropriate listeners. When editing is canceled, you must restore the cell's original value.

To help with this new editor, we provide a pop-up window inner class that has two buttons: an "OK" button (which displays a green checkmark) and a "cancel" button (a red "x"). This pop up extends the JWindow class and gives us room to grow if we need to. (The JSlider class can take advantage of the Enter key to accept a new value, and the Escape key can be used to cancel. If we need anything else, our pop-up helper is the right way to go.) As a bonus, the pop up clearly indicates which volume is actively being edited, as you can see in Figure 16-5.

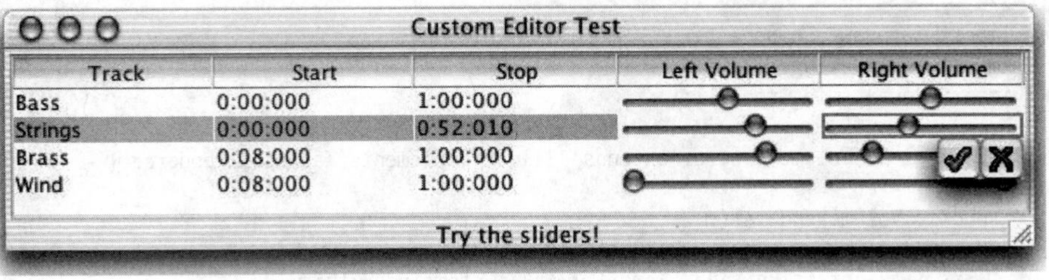

Figure 16-5. Our custom volume editor in action with the pop-up accept and cancel buttons

Here's the source code for this editor. Pay special attention to the code we use to connect the pop-up helper to the editor (so we can properly stop or cancel editing when the user clicks a button).

```java
// VolumeEditor.java
// A slider editor for volume values in a table
//
import java.awt.*;
import java.awt.event.*;
import java.util.*;
import javax.swing.*;
import javax.swing.table.*;
import javax.swing.event.*;

public class VolumeEditor extends JSlider implements TableCellEditor {

  public OkCancel helper = new OkCancel();
  protected transient Vector listeners;
  protected transient int originalValue;
  protected transient boolean editing;

  public VolumeEditor() {
    super(SwingConstants.HORIZONTAL);
    listeners = new Vector();
  }

  // Inner class for the OK/cancel pop-up window that displays below the active
  // scrollbar. Its position will have to be determined by the editor when
  // getTableCellEditorComponent() is called.
  public class OkCancel extends JWindow {
    private JButton okB = new JButton(new ImageIcon("accept.gif"));
    private JButton cancelB = new JButton(new ImageIcon("decline.gif"));
    private int w = 50;
    private int h = 24;
```

```java
  public OkCancel() {
    setSize(w,h);
    setBackground(Color.yellow);
    JPanel p = new JPanel(new GridLayout(0,2));
    // p.setBorder(BorderFactory.createLineBorder(Color.gray));
    // okB.setBorder(null);
    // cancelB.setBorder(null);
    p.add(okB);
    p.add(cancelB);
    setContentPane(p);

    okB.addActionListener(new ActionListener() {
      public void actionPerformed(ActionEvent ae) {
        stopCellEditing();
      }
    });

    cancelB.addActionListener(new ActionListener() {
      public void actionPerformed(ActionEvent ae) {
        cancelCellEditing();
      }
    });
  }
}

public Component getTableCellEditorComponent(JTable table, Object value,
                                            boolean isSelected,
                                            int row, int column) {
  if (value == null) {
    return this;
  }
  if (value instanceof Volume) {
    setValue(((Volume)value).getVolume());
  }
  else {
    setValue(0);
  }
  table.setRowSelectionInterval(row, row);
  table.setColumnSelectionInterval(column, column);
  originalValue = getValue();
  editing = true;
  Point p = table.getLocationOnScreen();
  Rectangle r = table.getCellRect(row, column, true);
  helper.setLocation(r.x + p.x + getWidth() - 50, r.y + p.y + getHeight());
  helper.setVisible(true);
  return this;
}

// CellEditor methods
public void cancelCellEditing() {
  fireEditingCanceled();
  editing = false;
  helper.setVisible(false);
}
```

```
public Object getCellEditorValue( ) {return new Integer(getValue( ));}

public boolean isCellEditable(EventObject eo) {return true;}

public boolean shouldSelectCell(EventObject eo) {
  return true;
}

public boolean stopCellEditing( ) {
  fireEditingStopped( );
  editing = false;
  helper.setVisible(false);
  return true;
}

public void addCellEditorListener(CellEditorListener cel) {
  listeners.addElement(cel);
}

public void removeCellEditorListener(CellEditorListener cel) {
  listeners.removeElement(cel);
}

protected void fireEditingCanceled( ) {
  setValue(originalValue);
  ChangeEvent ce = new ChangeEvent(this);
  for (int i = listeners.size( ) - 1; i >= 0; i--) {
    ((CellEditorListener)listeners.elementAt(i)).editingCanceled(ce);
  }
}

protected void fireEditingStopped( ) {
  ChangeEvent ce = new ChangeEvent(this);
  for (int i = listeners.size( ) - 1; i >= 0; i--) {
    ((CellEditorListener)listeners.elementAt(i)).editingStopped(ce);
  }
}
}
```

You can make this the active editor for volume objects by using the setDefaultEditor( )
method:

```
JTable table = new JTable(new MixerModel( ));
table.setDefaultEditor(Volume.class, new VolumeEditor( ));
```

Once it's in place, you can use the sliders to edit the volumes. Because we always
return true when asked isCellEditable( ), the sliders are always active. If you want,
you can make them a muted color until the user double-clicks on one and then make
that slider active. When the user stops editing by selecting another entry, the active
slider should return to its muted color. The DefaultCellEditor does a lot of the work
for you.

Charting Data with a TableModel

Our last example shows that the table machinery isn't just for building tables; you can use it to build other kinds of components (like the pie chart in Figure 16-6). If you think about it, there's no essential difference between a pie chart, a bar chart, and many other kinds of data displays; they are all different ways of rendering data that's logically kept in a table. When that's the case, it is easy to use a `TableModel` to manage the data and build your own component for the display.

With AWT, building a new component was straightforward: you simply created a subclass of `Component`. With Swing, it's a little more complex because of the distinction between the component itself and the user-interface implementation. But it's not terribly hard, particularly if you don't want to brave the waters of the Pluggable L&F. In this case, there's no good reason to make pie charts that look different on different platforms, so we'll opt for simplicity. We'll call our new component a `TableChart`; it extends `JComponent`. Its big responsibility is keeping the data for the component updated; to this end, it listens for `TableModelEvents` from the `TableModel` to determine when changes have been made.

To do the actual drawing, `TableChart` relies on a delegate, `PieChartPainter`. To keep things flexible, `PieChartPainter` is a subclass of `ChartPainter`, which gives us the option of building other kinds of chart painters (bar chart painters, etc.) in the future. `ChartPainter` extends `ComponentUI`, which is the base class for user interface delegates. Here's where the model-view-controller architecture comes into play. The table model contains the actual data, `TableChart` is a controller that tells a delegate what and when to paint, and `PieChartPainter` is the view that paints a particular kind of representation on the screen.

Just to prove that the same `TableModel` can be used with any kind of display, we also display an old-fashioned `JTable` using the same data—which turns out to be convenient because we can use the `JTable`'s built-in editing capabilities to modify the data. If you change any field (including the name), the pie chart immediately changes to reflect the new data.

The `TableChart` class is particularly interesting because it shows the "other side" of table model event processing. In the `PagingModel` of the earlier example, we had to generate events as the data changed. Here, you see how those events might be handled. The `TableChart` has to register itself as a `TableModelListener` and respond to events so that it can redraw itself when you edit the table. The `TableChart` also implements one (perhaps unsightly) shortcut: it presents the data by summing and averaging along the columns. It would have been more work (but not much more) to present the data in any particular column, letting the user choose the column to be displayed. (See Figure 16-6.)

Here's the application that produces both the pie chart and the table. It includes the `TableModel` as an anonymous inner class. This inner class is very simple, much simpler

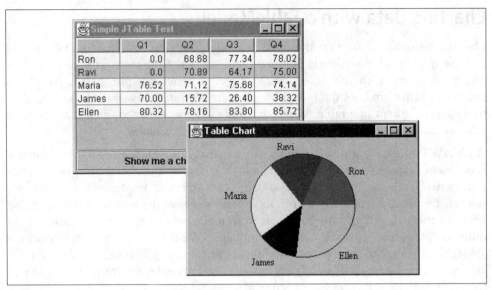

Figure 16-6. A chart component using a TableModel

than the models we used earlier in this chapter; it provides an array for storing the data, methods to get and set the data, and methods to provide other information about the table. Notice that we provided an isCellEditable() method that always returns true (the default method always returns false). Because we're allowing the user to edit the table, we must also override setValueAt(); our implementation updates the data array and calls fireTableRowsUpdated() to notify any listeners that data has changed and they need to redraw. The rest of ChartTester just sets up the display; we display the pie chart as a pop up.

```java
// ChartTester.java
//
import java.awt.*;
import java.awt.event.*;
import javax.swing.*;
import javax.swing.table.*;

public class ChartTester extends JFrame {

  public ChartTester() {
    super("Simple JTable Test");
    setSize(300, 200);
    setDefaultCloseOperation(EXIT_ON_CLOSE);

    TableModel tm = new AbstractTableModel() {
      String data[][] = {
        {"Ron", "0.00", "68.68", "77.34", "78.02"},
        {"Ravi", "0.00", "70.89", "64.17", "75.00"},
        {"Maria", "76.52", "71.12", "75.68", "74.14"},
```

```
            {"James", "70.00", "15.72", "26.40", "38.32"},
            {"Ellen", "80.32", "78.16", "83.80", "85.72"}
        };
        String headers[] = { "", "Q1", "Q2", "Q3", "Q4" };
        public int getColumnCount() { return headers.length; }
        public int getRowCount() { return data.length; }
        public String getColumnName(int col) { return headers[col]; }
        public Class getColumnClass(int col) {
            return (col == 0) ? String.class : Number.class;
        }

        public boolean isCellEditable(int row, int col) { return true; }
        public Object getValueAt(int row, int col) { return data[row][col]; }
        public void setValueAt(Object value, int row, int col) {
            data[row][col] = (String)value;
            fireTableRowsUpdated(row,row);
        }
    };

    JTable jt = new JTable(tm);
    JScrollPane jsp = new JScrollPane(jt);
    getContentPane().add(jsp, BorderLayout.CENTER);

    final TableChartPopup tcp = new TableChartPopup(tm);
    JButton button = new JButton("Show me a chart of this table");
    button.addActionListener(new ActionListener() {
        public void actionPerformed(ActionEvent ae) {
            tcp.setVisible(true);
        }
    } );
    getContentPane().add(button, BorderLayout.SOUTH);
}

public static void main(String args[]) {
    ChartTester ct = new ChartTester();
    ct.setVisible(true);
}
}
```

The TableChart object is actually made of three pieces. The TableChart class extends JComponent, which provides all the machinery for getting a new component on the screen. It implements TableModelListener because it has to register and respond to TableModelEvents.

```
// TableChart.java
// A chart-generating class that uses the TableModel interface to get
// its data
//
import java.awt.*;
import java.awt.event.*;
import javax.swing.*;
import javax.swing.event.*;
import javax.swing.table.*;
```

```java
public class TableChart extends JComponent implements TableModelListener {

  protected TableModel model;
  protected ChartPainter cp;
  protected double[] percentages;  // Pie slices
  protected String[] labels;       // Labels for slices
  protected String[] tips;         // Tooltips for slices

  protected java.text.NumberFormat formatter =
              java.text.NumberFormat.getPercentInstance( );

  public TableChart(TableModel tm) {
    setUI(cp = new PieChartPainter( ));
    setModel(tm);
  }

  public void setTextFont(Font f) { cp.setTextFont(f); }
  public Font getTextFont( ) { return cp.getTextFont( ); }

  public void setTextColor(Color c) { cp.setTextColor(c); }
  public Color getTextColor( ) { return cp.getTextColor( ); }

  public void setColor(Color[] clist) { cp.setColor(clist); }
  public Color[] getColor( ) { return cp.getColor( ); }

  public void setColor(int index, Color c) { cp.setColor(index, c); }
  public Color getColor(int index) { return cp.getColor(index); }

  public String getToolTipText(MouseEvent me) {
    if (tips != null) {
      int whichTip = cp.indexOfEntryAt(me);
      if (whichTip != -1) {
        return tips[whichTip];
      }
    }
    return null;
  }

  public void tableChanged(TableModelEvent tme) {
    // Rebuild the arrays only if the structure changed.
    updateLocalValues(tme.getType( ) != TableModelEvent.UPDATE);
  }

  public void setModel(TableModel tm) {
    // Get listener code correct.
    if (tm != model) {
      if (model != null) {
        model.removeTableModelListener(this);
      }
      model = tm;
      model.addTableModelListener(this);
      updateLocalValues(true);
    }
  }
```

```
public TableModel getModel( ) { return model; }

// Run through the model and count every cell (except the very first column,
// which we assume is the slice label column).
protected void calculatePercentages( ) {
  double runningTotal = 0.0;
  for (int i = model.getRowCount( ) - 1; i >= 0; i--) {
    percentages[i] = 0.0;
    for (int j = model.getColumnCount( ) - 1; j >=0; j--) {

      // First, try the cell as a Number object.
      Object val = model.getValueAt(i,j);
      if (val instanceof Number) {
        percentages[i] += ((Number)val).doubleValue( );
      }
      else if (val instanceof String) {
        // Oops, it wasn't numeric, so try it as a string.
        try {
          percentages[i]+=Double.valueOf(val.toString( )).doubleValue( );
        }
        catch(Exception e) {
          // Not a numeric string. Give up.
        }
      }
    }
    runningTotal += percentages[i];
  }

  // Make each entry a percentage of the total.
  for (int i = model.getRowCount( ) - 1; i >= 0; i--) {
    percentages[i] /= runningTotal;
  }
}

// This method just takes the percentages and formats them as tooltips.
protected void createLabelsAndTips( ) {
  for (int i = model.getRowCount( ) - 1; i >= 0; i--) {
    labels[i] = (String)model.getValueAt(i, 0);
    tips[i] = formatter.format(percentages[i]);
  }
}

// Call this method to update the chart. We try to be more efficient here by
// allocating new storage arrays only if the new table has a different number of
// rows.
protected void updateLocalValues(boolean freshStart) {
  if (freshStart) {
    int count = model.getRowCount( );
    if ((tips == null) || (count != tips.length)) {
      percentages = new double[count];
      labels = new String[count];
      tips = new String[count];
    }
  }
}
```

```
        calculatePercentages();
        createLabelsAndTips();

        // Now that everything's up-to-date, reset the chart painter with the new
        // values.
        cp.setValues(percentages);
        cp.setLabels(labels);

        // Finally, repaint the chart.
        repaint();
    }
}
```

The constructor for TableChart sets the user interface for this class to be the PieChartPainter (which we discuss shortly). It also saves the TableModel for the component by calling our setModel() method; providing a separate setModel() (rather than saving the model in the constructor) lets us change the model at a later time—a nice feature for a real component, though we don't take advantage of it in this example. We also override getToolTipText(), which is called with a MouseEvent as an argument. This method calls the ChartPainter's indexOfEntryAt() method to figure out which of the model's entries corresponds to the current mouse position, looks up the appropriate tooltip, and returns it.

tableChanged() listens for TableModelEvents. It delegates the call to another method, updateLocalValues(), with an argument of true if the table's structure has changed (e.g., rows added or deleted), and false if only the values have changed. The rest of TableChart updates the data when the change occurs. The focal point of this work is updateLocalValues(); calculatePercentages() and createLabelsAndTips() are helper methods that keep the work modular. If updateLocalValues() is called with its argument set to true, it finds out the new number of rows for the table and creates new arrays to hold the component's view of the data. It calculates percentages, retrieves labels, makes up tooltips, and calls the ChartPainter (the user interface object) to give it the new information. It ends by calling repaint() to redraw the screen with updated data.

ChartPainter is the actual user-interface class. It is abstract; we subclass it to implement specific kinds of charts. It extends the ComponentUI class, which makes it sound rather complex, but it isn't. We've made one simplifying assumption: the chart looks the same in any L&F. (The component in which the chart is embedded changes its appearance, but that's another issue—and one we don't have to worry about.) All our ComponentUI has to do is implement paint(), which we leave abstract, forcing the subclass to implement it. Our other abstract method, indexOfEntryAt(), is required by TableChart.

```
// ChartPainter.java
// A simple, chart-drawing UI base class. This class tracks the basic fonts and
// colors for various types of charts, including pie and bar. The paint() method is
// abstract and must be implemented by subclasses for each type.
//
```

```
import java.awt.*;
import java.awt.event.*;
import javax.swing.*;
import javax.swing.plaf.*;

public abstract class ChartPainter extends ComponentUI {

    protected Font textFont = new Font("Serif", Font.PLAIN, 12);
    protected Color textColor = Color.black;
    protected Color colors[] = new Color[] {
        Color.red, Color.blue, Color.yellow, Color.black, Color.green,
        Color.white, Color.gray, Color.cyan, Color.magenta, Color.darkGray
    };
    protected double values[] = new double[0];
    protected String labels[] = new String[0];

    public void setTextFont(Font f) { textFont = f; }
    public Font getTextFont() { return textFont; }

    public void setColor(Color[] clist) { colors = clist; }
    public Color[] getColor() { return colors; }

    public void setColor(int index, Color c) { colors[index] = c; }
    public Color getColor(int index) { return colors[index]; }

    public void setTextColor(Color c) { textColor = c; }
    public Color getTextColor() { return textColor; }

    public void setLabels(String[] l) { labels = l; }
    public void setValues(double[] v) { values = v; }

    public abstract int indexOfEntryAt(MouseEvent me);
    public abstract void paint(Graphics g, JComponent c);
}
```

There's not much mystery here. Except for the two abstract methods, these methods just maintain various simple properties of ChartPainter: the colors used for painting, the font, and the labels and values for the chart.

The real work takes place in the PieChartPainter class, which implements the indexOfEntryAt( ) and paint( ) methods. The indexOfEntryAt( ) method allows our TableChart class to figure out which tooltip to show. The paint( ) method allows us to draw a pie chart of our data.

```
// PieChartPainter.java
// A pie chart implementation of the ChartPainter class
//
import java.awt.*;
import java.awt.event.*;
import javax.swing.*;
import javax.swing.plaf.*;

public class PieChartPainter extends ChartPainter {
```

```java
protected static PieChartPainter chartUI = new PieChartPainter();
protected int originX, originY;
protected int radius;

private static double piby2 = Math.PI / 2.0;
private static double twopi = Math.PI * 2.0;
private static double d2r   = Math.PI / 180.0; // Degrees to radians
private static int xGap = 5;
private static int inset = 40;

public int indexOfEntryAt(MouseEvent me) {
  int x = me.getX() - originX;
  int y = originY - me.getY();  // Upside-down coordinate system

  // Is (x,y) in the circle?
  if (Math.sqrt(x*x + y*y) > radius) { return -1; }

  double percent = Math.atan2(Math.abs(y), Math.abs(x));
  if (x >= 0) {
    if (y <= 0) { // (IV)
      percent = (piby2 - percent) + 3 * piby2; // (IV)
    }
  }
  else {
    if (y >= 0) { // (II)
      percent = Math.PI - percent;
    }
    else { // (III)
      percent = Math.PI + percent;
    }
  }
  percent /= twopi;
  double t = 0.0;
  if (values != null) {
    for (int i = 0; i < values.length; i++) {
      if (t + values[i] > percent) {
        return i;
      }
      t += values[i];
    }
  }
  return -1;
}

public void paint(Graphics g, JComponent c) {
  Dimension size = c.getSize();
  originX = size.width / 2;
  originY = size.height / 2;
  int diameter = (originX < originY ? size.width - inset
                                    : size.height - inset);
  radius = (diameter / 2) + 1;
  int cornerX = (originX - (diameter / 2));
  int cornerY = (originY - (diameter / 2));
```

```
      int startAngle = 0;
      int arcAngle = 0;
      for (int i = 0; i < values.length; i++) {
        arcAngle = (int)(i < values.length - 1 ?
                            Math.round(values[i] * 360) :
                            360 - startAngle);
        g.setColor(colors[i % colors.length]);
        g.fillArc(cornerX, cornerY, diameter, diameter,
                   startAngle, arcAngle);
        drawLabel(g, labels[i], startAngle + (arcAngle / 2));
        startAngle += arcAngle;
      }
      g.setColor(Color.black);
      g.drawOval(cornerX, cornerY, diameter, diameter);  // Cap the circle.
    }

    public void drawLabel(Graphics g, String text, double angle) {
      g.setFont(textFont);
      g.setColor(textColor);
      double radians = angle * d2r;
      int x = (int) ((radius + xGap) * Math.cos(radians));
      int y = (int) ((radius + xGap) * Math.sin(radians));
      if (x < 0) {
        x -= SwingUtilities.computeStringWidth(g.getFontMetrics(), text);
      }
      if (y < 0) {
        y -= g.getFontMetrics().getHeight();
      }
      g.drawString(text, x + originX, originY - y);
    }

    public static ComponentUI createUI(JComponent c) {
      return chartUI;
    }
  }
}
```

There's nothing really complex here; it's just a lot of trigonometry and a little bit of simple AWT drawing. paint( ) is called with a graphics context and a JComponent as arguments; the JComponent allows you to figure out the size of the area we have to work with.

Here's the code for the pop up containing the chart:

```
// TableChartPopup.java
//
import java.awt.*;
import java.awt.event.*;
import javax.swing.*;
import javax.swing.table.*;

public class TableChartPopup extends JFrame {

  public TableChartPopup(TableModel tm) {
    super("Table Chart");
```

```
      setSize(300,200);
      TableChart tc = new TableChart(tm);
      getContentPane( ).add(tc, BorderLayout.CENTER);
    // Use the following line to turn on tooltips:
    ToolTipManager.sharedInstance( ).registerComponent(tc);
      }
   }
```

As you can see, the TableChart component can be used on its own without a JTable. We just need a model to base it on. You could expand this example to chart only selected rows or columns, but we'll leave that as an exercise that you can do on your own.

CHAPTER 17

Trees

One crucial component that found its way into the Swing set is the tree. Tree components help you visualize hierarchical information and make traversal and manipulation of that information much more manageable. A tree consists of *nodes,* which can contain either a user-defined object along with references to other nodes, or a user-defined object only. (Nodes with no references to other nodes are commonly called *leaves*.) In modern windowing environments, the directory list is an excellent example of a tree. The top of the component is the root directory or drive, and under that is a list of subdirectories. If the subdirectories contain further subdirectories, you can look at those as well. The actual files found in any directory in this component are the leaves of the tree.

Any data with parent-child relationships can be displayed as a tree. Another common example is an organizational chart. In such a chart, every management position is a node, with child nodes representing the employees under the manager. The organizational chart's leaves are the employees who are not in management positions, and its root is the president or CEO. Of course, real organizations don't always adhere to a strict tree structure. In a tree, each node has exactly one parent node, with the exception of the root node, which cannot have a parent (so trees are not cyclic). This means—in the world of trees—that two managers cannot manage the same employee.

In short, whenever you have a clearly defined hierarchy, you can express that hierarchy as a tree. Swing implements trees with the JTree class and its related models. With trees, as with tables, it's particularly important to understand the models. The JTree itself merely coordinates the tree's display.

A Simple Tree

Before we look at the models supporting the JTree class, let's look at a very simple example of a tree built with some of the various L&Fs (Figure 17-1). The `javax.swing.DefaultMutableTreeNode` class serves as our node class. You don't have to worry about specifically making a node a leaf. If the node has no references to other nodes by the time you display it, it's a leaf.

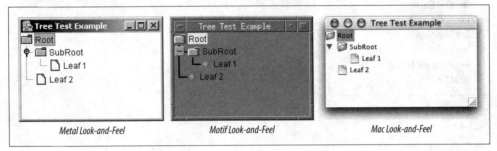

Figure 17-1. A simple JTree in the Metal, Motif, and Mac L&Fs

This example works by building up a series of unconnected nodes (using the `DefaultMutableTreeNode` class) and then connecting them. As long as we stick to the default classes provided with the tree package, we can build a regular model out of our nodes quite quickly. In this example, we build the model based on an empty root node, and then populate the tree by attaching the other nodes to the root or to each other. You can also build the tree first, and then create the model from the root node. Both methods have the same result. With a valid tree model in place, we can make a real JTree object and display it.

```
// TestTree.java
// A simple test to see how we can build a tree and populate it
//
import java.awt.*;
import java.awt.event.*;
import javax.swing.*;
import javax.swing.tree.*;

public class TestTree extends JFrame {

  JTree tree;
  DefaultTreeModel treeModel;

  public TestTree( ) {
    super("Tree Test Example");
    setSize(400, 300);
    setDefaultCloseOperation(EXIT_ON_CLOSE);
  }

  public void init( ) {
    // Build up a bunch of TreeNodes. We use DefaultMutableTreeNode because the
    // DefaultTreeModel can use it to build a complete tree.
    DefaultMutableTreeNode root = new DefaultMutableTreeNode("Root");
    DefaultMutableTreeNode subroot = new DefaultMutableTreeNode("SubRoot");
    DefaultMutableTreeNode leaf1 = new DefaultMutableTreeNode("Leaf 1");
    DefaultMutableTreeNode leaf2 = new DefaultMutableTreeNode("Leaf 2");
```

```
    // Build our tree model starting at the root node, and then make a JTree out
    // of it.
    treeModel = new DefaultTreeModel(root);
    tree = new JTree(treeModel);

    // Build the tree up from the nodes we created.
    treeModel.insertNodeInto(subroot, root, 0);
    // Or, more succinctly:
    subroot.add(leaf1);
    root.add(leaf2);

    // Display it.
    getContentPane( ).add(tree, BorderLayout.CENTER);
  }

  public static void main(String args[]) {
    TestTree tt = new TestTree( );
    tt.init( );
    tt.setVisible(true);
  }
}
```

As you can see, the action happens in the init( ) method. We create several nodes using the DefaultMutableTreeNode class. The DefaultTreeModel class provides us with a basis for working with the tree, and we add our nodes to that model. All the trees in this chapter follow the same basic steps—gathering nodes, creating a tree, and populating the tree—though again, not necessarily in that order. We also look at other things you can do with trees, including how to catch selection events and how to change the presentation of the nodes and leaves.

And just to prove that it's not hard to listen to selections from a tree, Figure 17-2 shows an expanded example that displays the most recently selected item in a JLabel at the bottom of the application.

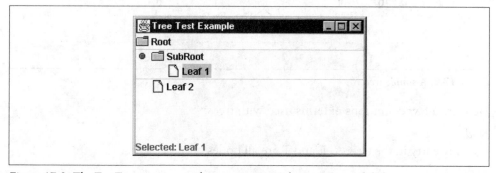

Figure 17-2. The TestTree program with an active TreeSelectionListener label

To make this work, we add a listener directly to the JTree object. The listener responds much like a ListSelectionListener, but is slightly modified to handle the specifics of tree selections. (For example, selection intervals may have to cross over an expanded node, and all the nodes under the expanded entry must also be selected.) Even though we allow multiple entries to be selected, we show only the lead entry of the selection to keep output simple. Here's the chunk of code we need to add to the init( ) method in the TestTree class:

```
// Create and add our message label for the selection output.
final JLabel messageLabel = new JLabel("Nothing selected.");
add(messageLabel, BorderLayout.SOUTH);

// Add our selection listener and have it report to
// our messageLabel.
tree.addTreeSelectionListener(new TreeSelectionListener( ) {
  public void valueChanged(TreeSelectionEvent tse) {
    TreePath tp = tse.getNewLeadSelectionPath( );
    messageLabel.setText("Selected: " + tp.getLastPathComponent( ));
  }
});
```

Of course, you should be sure to import javax.swing.event.* to access the TreeSelectionListener and TreeSelectionEvent classes.

Tree Terminology

Let's look at a simple tree made up of the letters A–Z, shown in Figure 17-3.

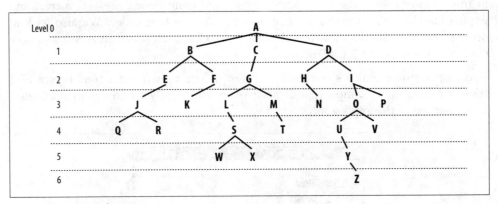

Figure 17-3. A simple tree

Here are a few definitions of terms used with trees:

Node
> Any entry in the tree. A, J, and T are all nodes.

Root
> The top-level entry of the tree. A root cannot have a parent, and a tree can have only one root. The root in this example is A.

Child
> Any of the nodes attached below a given node. M is a child of G.

Parent

The node attached above a given node. Any typical node has only one parent, and the root of the tree is the only node with no parent. G is the parent of M, and C is the parent of G.

Sibling

Any child of a node's parent. A node is also its own sibling. B's siblings are B, C, and D.

Descendant

Any child, or child of a child, or child of a child of a child, etc. A node is also its own descendant. L, S, W, and X are the descendants of L.

Ancestor

Any parent, or parent's parent, or parent's parent's parent, etc. A node is also its own ancestor. A, D, I, and P are the ancestors of P.

Level

The distance (measured in number of ancestors) from a node to the root node. The biggest level is also called the height or depth of a tree. A's level is 0, while T's level is 4.

Path

A list of nodes leading from one node to another. Typically, a path is from the root to another node.

Row

In a graphical representation of a tree, the mapping of a path to a corresponding row number on the screen. A would always be row 0, while other nodes might map to different rows, depending on which nodes are expanded and which are collapsed. If you think of taking a snapshot of a JTree and converting it to a JList, the row of the entry in the tree would correspond to the index of the entry in the list.

Collapsed

In a visual representation of a tree, a node is "collapsed" if you cannot see any of its children. In our example, none of the nodes are collapsed.

Expanded

In a visual representation of a tree, a node is "expanded" if you can see its children. In our example, all the nodes are expanded. (While you can expand or collapse a leaf, it has no effect, as leaves have no children by definition.)

Visible

A visible node is one that can be seen without expanding any of its parents. In a visual representation of a tree, a node might be offscreen (in a scrollpane, for example) but still be considered visible.

As a quick overview, Figure 17-4 details how the various tree classes work together to display a tree. We'll look at each of these classes in detail. JTrees use TreeCellRenderers to graphically display a tree represented by a TreeModel. TreeModels encode a tree using TreeNodes that contain an Object (your data for that node) and possibly references to other TreeNodes. Once displayed, the nodes of the tree can be selected according to the rules of a TreeSelectionModel. If supported, you can edit any one of the nodes in the tree using a TreeCellEditor.

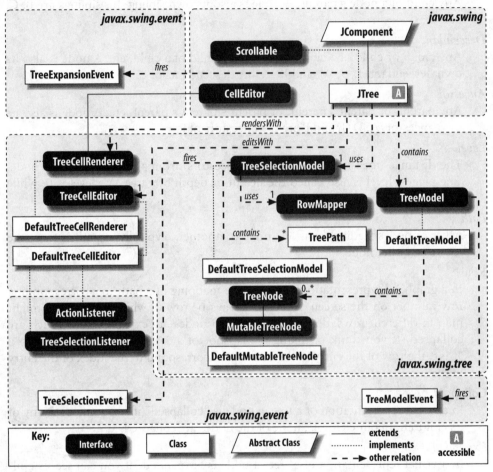

Figure 17-4. JTree class diagram

Tree Models

Looking at Figure 17-4 you can get an overview of where all the tree pieces come from. As with many of the Swing components you've seen already, the models supporting the data for trees play a crucial role in making the component run. Two interfaces are particularly important: TreeModel, which describes how to work with tree data, and TreeSelectionModel, which describes how to select nodes.

The TreeModel Interface

To get started, you need a tree model. The TreeModel interface is the starting point for your model. You don't have to start from scratch; there is a default implementation (DefaultTreeModel) that you can subclass or just look at for ideas. (We'll look at this class later in the chapter.)

Property

The TreeModel has one root property, listed in Table 17-1. This read-only property designates the root of a tree: by definition, the node that has no parent. All other nodes in your tree are descendants of this node.

Table 17-1. TreeModel property

Property	Data type	get	is	set	Default value
root	Object	•			

Events

The tree model uses the TreeModelEvent class defined in the javax.swing.event package. A TreeModelEvent indicates that the tree changed: one or more nodes were added, modified, or deleted. You will find a more detailed discussion in "Tree Events," later in this chapter.

public void addTreeModelListener(TreeModelListener l)
public void removeTreeModelListener(TreeModelListener l)
   Add or remove listeners interested in receiving tree model events.

Miscellaneous methods

Several miscellaneous methods are defined in this model for querying the tree and its structure. Although the actual data structures are defined by the classes that implement the model, the model works as if every node maintains an array of its children, which in turn can be identified by an index into the array.

public Object getChild(Object parent, int index)
   Given a parent object, return the child node at the given index. In many cases, if you specify an invalid index or try to get a child from a leaf, you should receive an ArrayIndexOutOfBoundsException. Of course, this is user-definable. It would also be possible to create a model that simply returned a null or default child.

public int getChildCount(Object parent)
   Given a parent node, return the number of children this node has. Leaves return a value of 0.

public int getIndexOfChild(Object parent, Object child)
> Given a parent node and an object, return the index of the child in the parent's children array. If the child object is not a child of this parent, it returns -1.

public boolean isLeaf(Object node)
> Check to see if the given node is a leaf. By definition, a leaf has no children. This method does not distinguish between a "real" leaf (a node that should never have a child) and nodes that simply do not have a child at the time you query them. If you need to distinguish between these types of nodes, look at the allowsChildren property of the TreeNode class.

public void valueForPathChanged(TreePath path, Object newValue)
> Notify the tree of a change to the user-defined object contained in the node path points to.

The DefaultTreeModel Class

The DefaultTreeModel class puts together a basic tree model using TreeNode objects. (We'll look at TreeNode in the next section.) This DefaultTreeModel is the basis for the first example we built. It implements the TreeModel interface and adds a few new methods. If you're in a mood to create your own tree, this is a great place to start. Each node's data is really just an Object reference, pointing to just about anything you could want to represent. (Base types, of course, must be wrapped up in objects.) You can usually get away with building on a DefaultTreeModel, unless you need to impose a specific structure, such as limiting the number of children a node can have. Normally, the children of a node are just kept in a vector, so no limits exist.

One other note about tree models: if you plan to allow multiple threads to access your model, you need to find a synchronization point. A conservative approach to thread safety dictates that you lock on the root node of the tree. Less conservative approaches require a bit of searching to make sure that you are not locking on a descendant of a node that is already locked. (If you did, it's possible the other thread would delete one of your ancestors, and thus delete you.)

Properties

The DefaultTreeModel class contains the properties listed in Table 17-2. It provides a root property (inherited from TreeModel) and a boolean property (asksAllowsChildren) to determine whether the tree model asks a node if it can accept children before inserting them. This property allows you to write nodes that can reject the addition of a child at runtime.

Table 17-2. DefaultTreeModel properties

Property	Data type	get	is	set	Default value
asksAllowsChildren*	boolean			•	false
root°	Object	•		•	null
treeModelListeners[1.4]	TreeModelListener[]	•			null

[1.4]since 1.4, °overridden

*The read method for the asksAllowsChildren property is asksAllowsChildren( ).

Events

The DefaultTreeModel fires a TreeModelEvent whenever the tree is changed. It implements the standard methods for registering listeners, plus a number of convenience methods for firing different versions of the TreeModelEvent.

public void addTreeModelListener(TreeModelListener l)
public void removeTreeModelListener(TreeModelListener l)
  Add or remove listeners interested in receiving tree model events.

protected void fireTreeNodesChanged(Object source, Object path[], int childIndices[], Object children[])
protected void fireTreeNodesInserted(Object source, Object path[], int childIndices[], Object children[])
protected void fireTreeNodesRemoved(Object source, Object path[], int childIndices[], Object children[])
protected void fireTreeStructureChanged(Object source, Object path[], int childIndices[], Object children[])
  Send a TreeModelEvent to the appropriate method of all registered TreeModelListeners. The main difference between fireTreeNodesChanged( ) and fireTreeStructureChanged( ) is that the latter represents a significant change to the overall structure of the tree, while the former is typically used for minor changes, such as notifying listeners that the user data stored in a particular set of nodes has changed, or that the visual representation of those nodes has changed. These methods should be called from one of the public node change methods below. All these methods assume an ascending order for the child indices.

public void nodeChanged(TreeNode node)
  Use this method any time you update a node to notify the model that the representation of this node may have changed. This is used most often to indicate that the user data in a node was edited.

public void nodesChanged(TreeNode node, int childIndices[])
  Similar to nodeChanged( ). Use this method any time you update the children of a node and need to notify the model that the representation of those children may have changed.

public void nodesWereInserted(TreeNode node, int childIndices[])

>This method indicates that you have added children to a node. The indices of the children you added must be sorted in ascending order.

public void nodesWereRemoved(TreeNode node, int childIndices[])

>This method indicates that you have removed children from a node. The indices of the children you removed must be sorted in ascending order.

public void nodeStructureChanged(TreeNode node)

>If you have completely rearranged the children (and possibly grandchildren and great grandchildren, etc.) of the node, call this method. It in turn calls the `fireTreeStructureChanged( )` method.

public void valueForPathChanged(TreePath path, Object newValue)

>Use this method to set the value of the user-defined object stored in this node. This method calls `nodesChanged( )` for you. If you have subclassed `DefaultTreeModel` to create your own tree model, and that model uses specific user-defined objects in its nodes, override this method to make sure that the appropriate type of object is put into the node. For example, if your tree nodes store base types, manually extract the base value out of the wrapper object passed to this method.

Constructors

public DefaultTreeModel(TreeNode root)
public DefaultTreeModel(TreeNode root, boolean asksAllowsChildren)

>Create a new tree model implemented with `TreeNode` objects for the nodes. These constructors set up the given node as the root of the tree. If you specify true for the `asksAllowsChildren` argument of the second constructor, the model checks the node to see if it allows children before deciding whether the node is a leaf.

Miscellaneous methods

The `DefaultTreeModel` contains several methods to help you query and update the contents of your tree. These methods should help you add and remove nodes, as well as update the tree whenever you make other changes (such as changing user data).

public TreeNode[] getPathToRoot(TreeNode node)
protected TreeNode[] getPathToRoot(TreeNode node, int depth)

>Return an array of `TreeNode` objects from the root down to the specified node. (The protected version uses depth as a marker to aid in its recursive discovery of the path. Normally, you use the public method.)

public void insertNodeInto(MutableTreeNode child, MutableTreeNode parent,
  int index)

>Attach the child node to the parent node at the given index. If the index is larger than the child count (meaning more than just "the next possible index"), an `ArrayIndexOutOfBoundsException` is thrown.

public void reload()

public void reload(TreeNode node)

> Refresh the tree, presumably after it is modified in some fashion. The first method reloads the tree from the root down while the second call starts with the specified node. These methods are very useful when you are dynamically modifying the tree. For example, deleting a node does not immediately update JTree's display; call reload( ) on the parent of the deleted node to refresh the tree.

public void removeNodeFromParent(MutableTreeNode node)

> Remove a node from its parent. The node is not destroyed but is placed in an array for use with nodesWereRemoved( ), which generates the appropriate model event for you.

Working with Tree Models

The TestTree example earlier in the chapter shows the DefaultTreeModel in action. However, if you want to build a more tailored tree, you can extend DefaultTreeModel and control things like the addition and removal of nodes. (Of course, if you want to build a tree model out of something other than TreeNode objects, you need to build your own class and implement the TreeModel interface. You could even have the model generate the tree dynamically.)

As an example, we build a model that sorts incoming children using DefaultMutableTreeNode for the nodes. This type of model works for mailbox managers and other places where the user can create folders and subfolders any old time. (Trees that support Drag and Drop insertions would definitely benefit.) Figure 17-5 shows an example tree that uses the SortTreeModel to load a hierarchy of files and folders. This particular example supplies a case-insensitive comparator so that the filenames don't arrange themselves in that annoying uppercase-before-lowercase thing.

We extend DefaultTreeModel and provide a new method for adding children to the model that does not require an index. We then calculate the proper (comparator-determined) index and insert the node using the super.insertNodeInto( ) call.

Here is the SortTreeModel class:

```
// SortTreeModel.java
// This class is similar to the DefaultTreeModel, but it keeps
// a node's children in alphabetical order.
import javax.swing.tree.*;
import java.util.Comparator;

public class SortTreeModel extends DefaultTreeModel {
  private Comparator comparator;

  public SortTreeModel(TreeNode node, Comparator c) {
    super(node);
    comparator = c;
  }
```

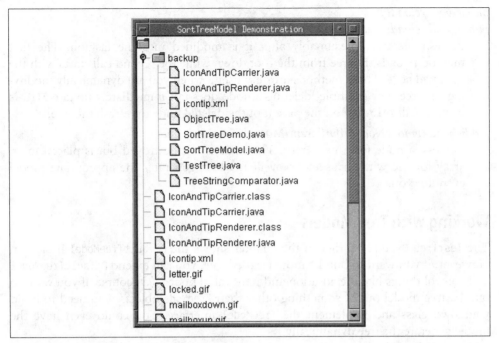

Figure 17-5. A case-insensitive sorting tree

```java
public SortTreeModel(TreeNode node, boolean asksAllowsChildren, Comparator c) {
  super(node, asksAllowsChildren);
  comparator = c;
}

public void insertNodeInto(MutableTreeNode child, MutableTreeNode parent) {
  int index = findIndexFor(child, parent);
  super.insertNodeInto(child, parent, index);
}

public void insertNodeInto(MutableTreeNode child, MutableTreeNode par, int i) {
  // The index is useless in this model, so just ignore it.
  insertNodeInto(child, par);
}

// Perform a recursive binary search on the children to find the right
// insertion point for the next node.
private int findIndexFor(MutableTreeNode child, MutableTreeNode parent) {
  int cc = parent.getChildCount();
  if (cc == 0) {
    return 0;
  }
  if (cc == 1) {
    return comparator.compare(child, parent.getChildAt(0)) <= 0 ? 0 : 1;
  }
  return findIndexFor(child, parent, 0, cc - 1);  // First and last index
}
```

```
    private int findIndexFor(MutableTreeNode child, MutableTreeNode parent,
                             int i1, int i2) {
      if (i1 == i2) {
        return comparator.compare(child, parent.getChildAt(i1)) <= 0 ? i1 : i1 + 1;
      }
      int half = (i1 + i2) / 2;
      if (comparator.compare(child, parent.getChildAt(half)) <= 0) {
        return findIndexFor(child, parent, i1, half);
      }
      return findIndexFor(child, parent, half + 1, i2);
    }
  }
```

If you want to see a model built from scratch, check out the algebraic expression tree model (*ExpressionTreeModel.java*) from our online examples. It stores expressions, as a computer language parser might view and evaluate such things. The ExprTree1 class starts the demonstration.

The JTree Class

Now that you've seen all the tree models and some of the default implementations, let's look at the visual representation we can give them. The JTree class can build up trees out of several different objects, including a TreeModel. JTree extends directly from JComponent and represents the visual side of any valid tree structure.

As another example of hierarchical data, let's look at a tree that displays XML documents. (We'll leave the details of XML to Brett McLaughlin and his excellent *Java and XML* book. Of course, as our own Bob Eckstein also wrote the *XML Pocket Reference*, we'll include a shameless plug for that, too.) Here's an entirely contrived XML document that contains several layers of data:

```
<?xml version="1.0"?>
<simple>
 <level1 attr="value" a2="v2">
   This is arbitrary data...
   <emptytag1 />
   <et2 a1="v1"/>
   <level2 more="attributes">
     <input type="text" name="test"/>
   </level2>
 </level1>

 <!-- one more level to test...--><test/>
 <one>
  <two>
   <three>
    <four/>
    <five/><fiveA/>
   </three>
   <six/>
   <seven>
```

```
    <eight/>
    </seven>
  </two>
  <nine/>
</one>
<multi><line>test</line></multi>
</simple>
```

Figure 17-6 shows the representation of this document in a JTree.

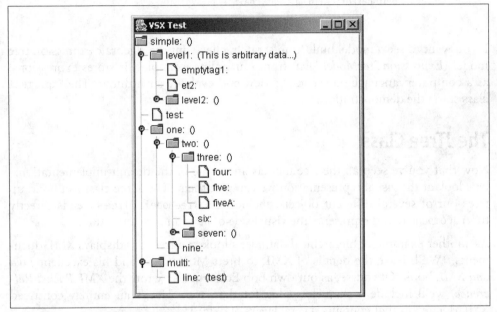

Figure 17-6. A JTree built by parsing an XML document

In this example, we treat XML tags with children as nodes and tags without children as leaves. Any tag with actual data (not counting the attributes—more on those later) shows that data in its label. We create a simple inner class to store the tags as they are generated by the XML parser. The other inner class, XMLTreeHandler, fills in the tree model based on the parser's events.

Here's the source code for *VSX.java*, our Very Simple XML example:

```java
// VSX.java
import javax.swing.*;
import javax.swing.tree.*;
import java.util.*;
import java.io.*;
import org.xml.sax.*;
import org.xml.sax.helpers.*;
import javax.xml.parsers.*;

public class VSX {
```

```java
public TreeModel parse(String filename) {
  SAXParserFactory factory = SAXParserFactory.newInstance();
  XMLTreeHandler handler = new XMLTreeHandler();
  try {
    // Parse the input.
    SAXParser saxParser = factory.newSAXParser();
    saxParser.parse( new File(filename), handler);
  }
  catch (Exception e) {
    System.err.println("File Read Error: " + e);
    e.printStackTrace();
    return new DefaultTreeModel(new DefaultMutableTreeNode("error"));
  }
  return new DefaultTreeModel(handler.getRoot());
}

public static class XMLTreeHandler extends DefaultHandler {
  private DefaultMutableTreeNode root, currentNode;
  public DefaultMutableTreeNode getRoot() {
    return root;
  }

  // SAX parser handler methods
  public void startElement(String namespaceURI, String lName, String qName,
                           Attributes attrs) throws SAXException {
    String eName = lName; // Element name
    if ("".equals(eName)) eName = qName;
    Tag t = new Tag(eName, attrs);
    DefaultMutableTreeNode newNode = new DefaultMutableTreeNode(t);
    if (currentNode == null) {
      root = newNode;
    }
    else {
      // Must not be the root node
      currentNode.add(newNode);
    }
    currentNode = newNode;
  }

  public void endElement(String namespaceURI, String sName, String qName)
  throws SAXException {
    currentNode = (DefaultMutableTreeNode)currentNode.getParent();
  }

  public void characters(char buf[], int offset, int len) throws SAXException {
    String s = new String(buf, offset, len).trim();
    ((Tag)currentNode.getUserObject()).addData(s);
  }
}

public static class Tag {
  private String name;
  private String data;
  private Attributes attr;
```

```java
    public Tag(String n, Attributes a) { name = n; attr = a; }

    public String getName() { return name; }
    public Attributes getAttributes() { return attr; }
    public void setData(String d) { data = d; }
    public String getData() { return data; }

    public void addData(String d) {
      if (data == null) {
        setData(d);
      }
      else {
        data += d;
      }
    }

    public String getAttributesAsString() {
      StringBuffer buf = new StringBuffer(256);
      for (int i = 0; i < attr.getLength(); i++) {
        buf.append(attr.getQName(i));
        buf.append("=\"");
        buf.append(attr.getValue(i));
        buf.append("\"");
      }
      return buf.toString();
    }

    public String toString() {
      String a = getAttributesAsString();
      return name + ": " + a + (data == null ? "" :" (" + data + ")");
    }
  }

  public static void main(String args[]) {
    if (args.length != 1) {
      System.err.println("Usage is: java VSX testfile.xml");
      System.exit(1);
    }
    JFrame frame = new JFrame("VSX Test");
    VSX parser = new VSX();
    JTree tree = new JTree(parser.parse(args[0]));
    frame.getContentPane().add(new JScrollPane(tree));
    frame.setDefaultCloseOperation(JFrame.EXIT_ON_CLOSE);
    frame.setSize(300,400);
    frame.setVisible(true);
  }
}
```

The parse() method does most of the work in this example. The events from the SAXParser are used to determine the structure of the tree. Once the document is parsed, that model is used to build the JTree object that we display inside a JScrollPane.

Properties

The JTree class contains properties (shown in Table 17-3) for manually displaying and editing tree cells if you need this control. The editable property specifies whether cells can be edited (i.e., modified by users). The toggleClickCount property allows you to specify how many clicks are required to start editing a tree node. The cellEditor, cellRenderer, and invokesStopCellEditing properties affect the components used to display and manipulate trees. Setting invokesStopCellEditing to true forces changes to a cell to be saved if editing is interrupted.

Table 17-3. JTree properties

Property	Data type	get	is	set	Default value
accessibleContext[o]	AccessibleContext	•			JTree. AccessibleJTree( )
anchorSelectionPath[1.3]	TreePath	•		•	null
cellEditor[b]	TreeCellEditor	•		•	null
cellRenderer[b]	TreeCellRenderer	•		•	null
collapsed[1.4,i,o,*]	boolean		•		
dragEnabled[1.4]	boolean	•		•	false
editable[b,o]	boolean		•	•	false
editing	boolean		•		false
editingPath	TreePath	•			null
expanded[1.4,i,o,*]	boolean		•		
expandsSelectedPaths	boolean	•		•	true
fixedRowHeight	boolean		•		true
invokesStopCellEditing[b]	boolean	•		•	false
largeModel[b]	boolean	•		•	false
lastSelectedPathComponent	Object	•			null
leadSelectionPath	TreePath	•		•	null
leadSelectionRow	int	•			-1
maxSelectionRow	int	•			From selection model
minSelectionRow	int	•			From selection model
model[b]	TreeModel	•		•	null
opaque[b,o]	boolean		•	•	true
preferredScrollableViewportSize	Dimension	•			From L&F

[1.3]since 1.3, [1.4]since 1.4, [b]bound, [i]indexed, [o]overridden

*Indexed by int and TreePath.

+A value of −1 indicates variable row heights.

See also properties of the JComponent class (Table 3-6).

Table 17-3. JTree properties (continued)

Property	Data type	get	is	set	Default value
rootVisible[b]	boolean		•	•	true
rowCount	int	•			
rowHeight[b, +]	int	•		•	16
rowSelected[i]	boolean	•			
scrollableTracksViewportHeight	boolean	•			false
scrollableTracksViewportWidth	boolean	•			false
scrollsOnExpand[b]	boolean	•		•	true
selectionEmpty	boolean		•		From selection model
selectionModel[b]	TreeSelectionModel	•		•	DefaultTreeSelectionModel()
selectionPath	TreePath	•		•	From selection model
selectionPaths	TreePath[]	•		•	From selection model
selectionRows	int[]	•		•	From selection model
showsRootHandles[b]	boolean	•		•	false
toggleClickCount[1.3]	int	•		•	2
treeExpansionListeners[1.4]	TreeExpansionListener[]	•			Empty array
treeSelectionListeners[1.4]	TreeSelectionListener[]	•			Empty array
treeWillExpandListeners[1.4]	TreeWillExpandListener[]	•			Empty array
UI[b, o]	TreeUI	•		•	From L&F
UIClassID[o]	String	•			"TreeUI"
visibleRowCount[b]	int	•		•	20

[1.3]since 1.3, [1.4]since 1.4, [b]bound, [i]indexed, [o]overridden

*Indexed by int and TreePath.

+A value of −1 indicates variable row heights.

See also properties of the JComponent class (Table 3-6).

The display of the tree itself inside a scrollpane is managed by the preferredScrollableViewportSize, scrollableTracksViewportHeight, and scrollableTracksViewportWidth properties. The preferred viewport size specifies the desired size of the viewport showing the tree. Both of the tracking properties are false to indicate that changing the size of the viewport containing the tree does not affect the calculated width or height of the tree. They can be overridden for specialized behavior. For example, if you placed your tree in a JScrollPane, and the width of that pane were suddenly changed so that a given node might not be visible without scrolling, you could turn on tooltips for the long node and supply a string that contained the entire path for that node. The tooltip pop up would show the whole path without scrolling, regardless of the viewport size.

Several properties give you access to the state of selections for a tree. Properties such as anchorSelectionPath, leadSelectionPath, leadSelectionRow, minSelectionRow, and maxSelectionRow indicate the location of various selected entries. An anchor path is the first entry the user clicked (which may or may not be the same as the min/max selections). You can determine whether a programmatic selection change visually expands the children of a node with the expandsSelectedPaths property. The lastSelectedPath property tracks the most recently selected path.

If you need more control over selections, you can use the selectionModel property. You can modify the current model or even install your own custom model. Most of the time, however, you can just use JTree properties like selectionEmpty, selectionPath, selectionPaths, and selectionRows to let you know exactly which (if any) nodes in the tree are selected.

The JTree class also provides properties that allow you to control the tree's appearance regardless of the display and editing mechanisms used. Many aspects of the tree's appearance are based on the concept of a "row," which is a single item currently displayed in the tree. You can control the row height and root display style with the rowHeight, fixedRowHeight, rootVisible, and showsRootHandles properties. fixedRowHeight specifies that all rows must have the same height; if it is false, row heights may vary. rootVisible is true if the tree's root is displayed; if it is false, the root is omitted. Its initial value depends on which constructor you call. If scrollsOnExpand is true, expanding any node automatically scrolls the tree so that as many of the node's children as possible are visible. showsRootHandles determines whether the one-touch expand/collapse control (or "handle") appears for the root node.

Another interesting property of trees is largeModel. Some UI managers pay attention to this property and alter their behavior if it is set to true, presumably to increase the efficiency of updates and model events. The size of the tree that merits using this property depends largely on your application, but if you're wondering if your tree could benefit from a large model, try turning the property on and playing with your tree to see if you notice a performance gain.

Several indexed properties give you a quick view of the state of the tree. The rowSelected property tells you whether a particular row is selected. The expanded and collapsed properties tell you whether a row is, well, expanded or collapsed.

SDK 1.4 introduced access to the event listeners attached to the tree through the treeExpansionListeners, treeSelectionListeners, and treeWillExpandListeners properties.

Many methods of the JTree class should be considered accessors for properties we haven't listed in Table 17-3. This omission is intentional (though not undebated).

We felt it would be clearer if these methods were discussed with similar methods that don't fit the "property" patterns.

Events

The JTree class adds support for the expansion and selection events shown in Table 17-4. We will look at these events in greater detail (with examples) in "Tree Events" later in this chapter.

Table 17-4. JTree events

Event	Description
TreeExpansionEvent	A tree node has been (or will be) expanded or collapsed.
TreeSelectionEvent	A row (path) has been selected or, if more than one row can be selected, a row has been added or removed from the current selection.

The TreeEvents class in the code for this chapter reports all the events generated by the JTree object. These events are supported by the following methods:

public void addTreeExpansionListener(TreeExpansionListener l)
public void removeTreeExpansionListener(TreeExpansionListener l)
  Add or remove listeners interested in receiving tree expansion events.

public void addTreeWillExpandListener (TreeWillExpandListener tel)
public void removeTreeWillExpandListener (TreeWillExpandListener tel)
  Add or remove listeners interested in receiving "tree will expand" events. Note that no "TreeWillExpandEvent" class exists. The methods of the TreeWillExpandListener interface (discussed later in this chapter) use TreeExpansionEvent objects.

public void addTreeSelectionListener(TreeSelectionListener l)
public void removeTreeSelectionListener(TreeSelectionListener l)
  Add or remove listeners interested in receiving tree selection events.

public void fireTreeCollapsed(TreePath collapsedPath)
public void fireTreeExpanded(TreePath expandedPath)
  Notify any registered TreeExpansionListener objects that a path has collapsed or expanded. The collapsedPath and expandedPath arguments are used to construct a new TreeExpansionEvent with this JTree as the source.

public void fireTreeWillExpand(TreePath path) throws ExpandVetoException
public void fireTreeWillCollapse(TreePath path) throws ExpandVetoException
  Notify registered listeners that a tree node is about to expand or collapse. The path argument constructs a new TreeExpansionEvent object sent to the listeners. The ExpandVetoException class is discussed later in the "Tree Events" section of this chapter.

protected void fireValueChanged(TreeSelectionEvent selectionEvent)

Notify registered TreeSelectionListener objects that a selection event has occurred. Whenever a listener registers with this JTree, an event redirector is set up to grab the selection events coming from the tree selection model and pass them to the listener with this JTree as the source. You do not need to worry about the selection model to attach a listener. You attach the listener to the JTree itself, and the redirector does the work.

JTree also generates property change events whenever any of its bound properties are modified.

Constants

The constants provided with the JTree class are used for reporting the names of bound properties in property change events and are listed in Table 17-5.

Table 17-5. JTree string constants for property change events

ANCHOR_SELECTION_PATH_PROPERTY[1.3]	ROOT_VISIBLE_PROPERTY
CELL_EDITOR_PROPERTY	ROW_HEIGHT_PROPERTY
CELL_RENDERER_PROPERTY	SCROLLS_ON_EXPAND_PROPERTY
EDITABLE_PROPERTY	SELECTION_MODEL_PROPERTY
EXPANDS_SELECTED_PATHS_PROPERTY[1.3]	SHOWS_ROOT_HANDLES_PROPERTY
INVOKES_STOP_CELL_EDITING_PROPERTY	TOGGLE_CLICK_COUNT_PROPERTY[1.3]
LARGE_MODEL_PROPERTY	TREE_MODEL_PROPERTY
LEAD_SELECTION_PATH_PROPERTY[1.3]	VISIBLE_ROW_COUNT_PROPERTY

[1.3]since 1.3

Constructors

public JTree()

Create a tree using a DefaultTreeModel object as its base. You should probably use one of the other constructors to get an interesting tree. The default tree is populated with some meaningless sample content.

public JTree(TreeNode root)
public JTree(TreeNode root, boolean asksAllowsChildren)

Build new trees using the node root as the root of the tree. These constructors also use the DefaultTreeModel as their model.

public JTree(TreeModel model)

Build a tree using the model provided. The model argument contains the root of the tree.

public JTree(Object value[])
public JTree(Vector value)
public JTree(Hashtable value)

Build a DefaultTreeModel object and use the inner class `JTree.DynamicUtilTreeNode` to populate the tree using the value argument as children. If any element in value is itself an `Object[]`, a `Vector`, or a `Hashtable`, a node is built for that element, and its contents become children of the node. This recursive process continues until all elements and their contents are explored.

The last constructor is great for simple data structures that you want to display as a tree. Figure 17-7 shows the tree that results when you display a hashtable.

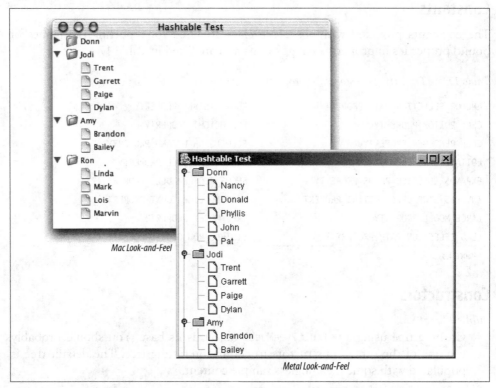

Figure 17-7. JTrees built from a hashtable and a DefaultTreeModel in Mac and Metal L&Fs

Even though this tree is larger than the tree in Figure 17-1, it takes less code to set it up:

```
// ObjectTree.java
//
import java.awt.*;
import java.awt.event.*;
import javax.swing.*;
```

```
import javax.swing.tree.*;
import java.util.*;

public class ObjectTree extends JFrame {

  JTree tree;
  String[][] sampleData = {
    {"Amy"}, {"Brandon", "Bailey"},
    {"Jodi"}, {"Trent", "Garrett", "Paige", "Dylan"},
    {"Donn"}, {"Nancy", "Donald", "Phyllis", "John", "Pat"},
    {"Ron"}, {"Linda", "Mark", "Lois", "Marvin"}
  };

  public ObjectTree( ) {
    super("Hashtable Test");
    setSize(400, 300);
    setDefaultCloseOperation(EXIT_ON_CLOSE);
  }

  public void init( ) {
    Hashtable h = new Hashtable( );
    // Build up the hashtable using every other entry in the String[][] as a key,
    // followed by a String[] "value."
    for (int i = 0; i < sampleData.length; i+=2) {
      h.put(sampleData[i][0], sampleData[i + 1]);
    }
    tree = new JTree(h);
    getContentPane( ).add(tree, BorderLayout.CENTER);
  }

  public static void main(String args[]) {
    ObjectTree tt = new ObjectTree( );
    tt.init( );
    tt.setVisible(true);
  }
}
```

Selection Methods

One of the primary functions the JTree class provides is programmer access to the selection status of the tree. (Most of these functions work with a selection model discussed in "Tree Selections.") We'll say more about this later, but selections may be based on either rows or paths. A row is a displayed element in a tree; you refer to a row by its index. A path is a list of nodes from the root to the selected node.

addSelectionInterval(int row1, int row2)

Add the paths between row1 and row2 to the current selection. It uses getPathBetweenRows( ) to collect the list of paths to add.

public void addSelectionPath(TreePath path)
public void addSelectionPaths(TreePath paths[])
public void addSelectionRow(int row)
public void addSelectionRows(int rows[])

> Add to the current selection on the tree. If you supply an array of paths or integers, each of the paths or rows indicated is selected. If any path or row is not currently visible, it is made visible.

public void clearSelection()

> Clear the current selection completely.

public boolean isPathSelected(TreePath path)

> Return true if the given path is in the current selection. It is the TreePath equivalent of the get method for the rowSelected property.

public void removeSelectionInterval(int row1, int row2)

> Remove the paths between row1 and row2 from the current selection. It uses getPathBetweenRows( ) to collect the list of paths to deselect.

public void removeSelectionPath(TreePath path)
public void removeSelectionPaths(TreePath paths[])
public void removeSelectionRow(int row)
public void removeSelectionRows(int rows[])

> Remove pieces of the current selection dictated by the rows or paths provided as arguments. If a specified path or row is not in the current selection, it is ignored, and any remaining rows or paths are deselected.

public void setSelectionInterval(int row1, int row2)

> Set the current selection to represent the paths between row1 and row2. It uses getPathBetweenRows( ) to collect the list of paths to select.

public void setSelectionPath(TreePath path)
public void setSelectionPaths(TreePath paths[])
public void setSelectionRow(int row)
public void setSelectionRows(int rows[])

> Set the current selection on the tree. If you supply an array of paths or integers, each of the indicated paths or rows is selected. If any path or row is not currently visible, it is made visible.

Expansion Methods

For any entry in your tree, you can check to see if it is currently expanded or collapsed. A node is considered expanded if the nodes in its path are also expanded. (This applies to leaves as well.) You can also programmatically control the collapsing and expanding of parts of your tree. All of the following methods accept either a TreePath or a row (int) argument.

public void collapsePath(TreePath path)
public void collapseRow(int row)
> Collapse the given path or row if needed. (In the case of the path argument, the last component of the path is collapsed.) Once collapsed, it tries to make the path visible as well.

public void expandPath(TreePath path)
public void expandRow(int row)
> Expand the given path or row if needed. Once expanded, it tries to make the path visible as well.

public boolean isCollapsed(int row)
public boolean isCollapsed(TreePath path)
> Return true if any node in the given path or row is not currently expanded. If every node is expanded, these methods return false.

public boolean isExpanded(int row)
public boolean isExpanded(TreePath path)
> Return true if the given path or row is currently fully expanded. If any nodes in the path are not expanded, these methods return false.

public boolean hasBeenExpanded(TreePath path)
> Return true if the path has ever been expanded.

Path and Row Methods

public TreePath getClosestPathForLocation(int x, int y)
public int getClosestRowForLocation(int x, int y)
> Return the path or row closest to a given location (x,y) in the component, relative to its upper-left corner. These methods return null only if nothing is visible. If you need to be sure that the point (x,y) is actually inside the bounds for the path or row returned, you need to check that yourself. The getPathForLocation( ) and getRowForLocation( ) methods do a basic check and return null if the point falls outside the closest row, if this is all you need.

public Rectangle getPathBounds(TreePath path)
> Return the Rectangle object that encompasses the specified path, if that path is not currently visible. The scrollPathToVisible( ) method calls this to show a particular path on the screen. If the path is already visible, this method returns null.

public TreePath getPathForLocation(int x, int y)
> A more restricted version of getClosestPathForLocation( ). If x or y ends up outside the bounds of the path returned by the closest path call, this method returns null.

public TreePath getPathForRow(int row)
> Return the path associated with the specified row. If row is an invalid value (less than zero or greater than the number of rows in the current tree) or is not currently visible, this method returns null.

public Rectangle getRowBounds(int row)
> This method functions like getPathBounds( ) for the given row.

public int getRowForLocation(int x, int y)
> A more restricted version of getClosestRowForLocation( ). If x or y is outside the bounds of the row returned by the closest row call, this method returns -1.

public int getRowForPath(TreePath path)
> Return the row number for the last component in path. If any part of path is not visible, or if path is null, this method returns -1.

public boolean isVisible(TreePath path)
> Return true if the given path is currently visible. Recall that a visible path is any path you can see in the tree without expanding a parent node—not necessarily one that is onscreen at the moment.

public void makeVisible(TreePath path)
> Make path visible if it is not already visible.

public void scrollPathToVisible(TreePath path)
public void scrollRowToVisible(int row)
> If the tree is in a scrollpane, scroll the given path or row to make it appear in the pane. A path is expanded up to its last component, if need be, to make it visible. (By definition, rows are always visible.) The tree must be in a scrollable environment (like a JScrollPane or JViewport) for this to work.

Editing Methods

public void cancelEditing( )
> Cancel editing of a tree cell. If no cell is being edited, this method has no effect.

public TreeNode getEditingPath( )
> Return the path to the element in the tree currently being edited. If the tree is not being edited, this method returns null.

public boolean isEditing( )
> Return true if the current selection is being edited.

public boolean isPathEditable(TreePath path)
> Return the value of the editable property for a given path. If it returns true, the path can be edited. The UI manager calls this method before editing a node so that a subclass of JTree can override it and say yes or no based on some appropriate criteria. (For example, you could allow editing of leaves but not editing of folders.)

public void startEditingAtPath(TreePath path)

    Try to start editing the last element in path. This might fail if the cell editor will not edit that element.

public boolean stopEditing()

    Stop the tree from being edited. If the tree is not being edited, this method has no effect. It returns true if the tree was being edited and the cell editor stopped successfully. It returns false otherwise—for example, if the tree was not being edited or the editor could not be stopped.

JTree Inner Classes

protected class JTree.AccessibleJTree

    This class represents the accessible implementation for JTree.

public static class JTree.DynamicUtilTreeNode

    Various constructors of the JTree class use this inner class to build tree nodes out of arrays, vectors, and hashtables.

protected static class JTree.EmptySelectionModel

    As its name implies, this inner class provides an implementation of the TreeSelectionModel interface (by extending DefaultTreeSelectionModel) that does not allow any selections.

protected class JTree.TreeModelHandler

    Manage the expandedState cache by listening to expansion and modification events coming from the model.

protected class JTree.TreeSelectionRedirector

    This class contains methods for redirecting the source of events. Typically, this is done when the tree model generates an event, but the JTree object associated with that model needs to be listed as the source of the event.

Tree Nodes and Paths

You probably noticed that the DefaultTreeModel class depends on TreeNode and TreePath objects. In a tree, a TreeNode represents an individual piece of data stored at a particular point in a tree, and a path represents a collection of these pieces that are directly related to each other (in an ancestor/descendant relationship). Let's look at the classes that make up the typical nodes and paths.

The TreeNode Interface

A TreeNode is the basic unit of a tree. This interface defines the minimum properties and access routines a typical tree model expects to see in its nodes.

Properties

The TreeNode interface contains the properties listed in Table 17-6. The TreeNode properties are straightforward and deal with the structure of the node. The parent property holds a valid value for every node in a tree, except the root. The childAt property lets you access a particular child in the tree. The childCount property contains the number of children associated with this node, if it allows children. If the node does not allow children, it is probably a leaf, but it is also possible to have a mutable tree node that has no children, or does not allow children, and yet is not a leaf. (An empty directory with no write permissions would be an example of such a node.)

Table 17-6. TreeNode properties

Property	Data type	get	is	set	Default value
allowsChildren	boolean	•			
childAt[i]	TreeNode	•			
childCount	int	•			
leaf	boolean		•		
parent	TreeNode	•			

[i]indexed

Notice that the children are not properties of a TreeNode. This is not to say that a TreeNode does not have children, but rather the accessor methods do not fit the "property" definition.

Child access methods

public int getIndex(TreeNode node)
public Enumeration children( )

> Access the children associated with a particular node. You can pick the child by node via getIndex( ); you can also use the childAt property accessor, getChildAt( ), to pick a child by index number. If you want all the nodes under a parent, the children( ) method returns an enumeration of those nodes.

The MutableTreeNode Interface

The MutableTreeNode interface extends the TreeNode interface to include basic manipulation methods for the children and the user data. If you set about defining your own nodes, this is a good place to start.

Properties

The MutableTreeNode class contains the properties listed in Table 17-7. MutableTreeNode adds write access to the parent property from the TreeNode interface and gives you access to user data. You should note, however, that setParent() expects a MutableTreeNode while getParent() simply returns a TreeNode. The userObject property contains the data that makes a TreeNode interesting. You can use this property to store any arbitrary object. All other properties are inherited without change.

Table 17-7. MutableTreeNode properties

Property	Data type	get	is	set	Default value
parent[o]	MutableTreeNode	•		•	
userObject	Object			•	

[o]overridden

See also properties of the TreeNode interface (Table 17-6).

Mutation methods

The mutation methods of MutableTreeNode allow you to access and modify the node's children as well as its parent:

public void insert(MutableTreeNode child, int index)

Insert a child into the children array maintained by the node. The position of the new child is given by index. If you want to append a child, the index should be the node's getChildCount( ) + 1.

public void remove(int index)
public void remove(MutableTreeNode node)

Remove a child from the node; the child may be specified by its index or by the child node itself.

public void removeFromParent( )

Remove the node from its parent. This assumes that the parent is also a mutable node and allows the removal of children.

The DefaultMutableTreeNode Class

DefaultMutableTreeNode inherits many of its properties from the MutableTreeNode and TreeNode interfaces. It supplies the default values shown in Table 17-8. The properties that are not inherited describe relationships of various nodes and paths in a tree. We felt it would be easiest to explain these properties as methods. The properties are listed in Table 17-8 for completeness, but you should read the section on structure methods for details on their uses.

Table 17-8. DefaultMutableTreeNode properties

Property	Data type	get	is	set	Default value
allowsChildren°	boolean	•		•	false
childAt^i,o	TreeNode	•			
childCount°	int	•			0
depth	int	•			0
firstChild	TreeNode	•			null
firstLeaf	DefaultMutableTreeNode	•			null
lastChild	TreeNode	•			null
lastLeaf	DefaultMutableTreeNode	•			null
leaf°	boolean		•		true
leafCount	int	•			0
level	int	•			0
nextLeaf	DefaultMutableTreeNode	•			null
nextNode	DefaultMutableTreeNode	•			null
nextSibling	DefaultMutableTreeNode	•			null
parent°	MutableTreeNode*	•		•	null
path	TreeNode[]	•			Array with this node as the sole element
previousLeaf	DefaultMutableTreeNode	•			null
previousNode	DefaultMutableTreeNode	•			null
previousSibling	DefaultMutableTreeNode	•			null
root	TreeNode	•			null
root	boolean		•		false
siblingCount	int	•			0
userObject°	Object	•		•	null
userObjectPath	Object[]	•		•	null

^i indexed, ° overridden

*The get method for the parent property returns a TreeNode object.

See also properties of the MutableTreeNode class (Table 17-7).

Constant

The DefaultMutableTreeNode class contains one constant, as shown in Table 17-9.

Table 17-9. DefaultMutableTreeNode constant

Constant	Type	Description
EMPTY_ENUMERATION	Enumeration	The enumeration methods listed later in this chapter return this constant if the enumeration you ask for is empty.

Constructors

public DefaultMutableTreeNode( )
public DefaultMutableTreeNode(Object userObject)
public DefaultMutableTreeNode(Object userObject, boolean allowsChildren)

Build new tree nodes that carry an optional userObject. You can also specify whether this child should be allowed to contain children. If you set allowsChildren to false, an IllegalStateException is thrown any time you try to insert or add a child to this node. By default, the user object is null, and children are allowed.

Structure methods

The structure methods listed here provide easy ways to modify and query the structure of a tree. You can check the relation of a given node to any other node and even retrieve specific relatives (children, parent, siblings) of a node. Many of these methods could be considered accessors for various properties; we thought it would be easier to discuss and contrast their behavior if we listed them as methods. In our discussion, we'll refer frequently to the tree made out of letters in Figure 17-3. Figure 17-8 shows a JTree built with the same structure using DefaultMutableTreeNode nodes and the DefaultTreeModel.

public void add(MutableTreeNode child)

Remove the node child from its current position (if any) and append it to the end of the child array for this node. It throws IllegalStateException if this node does not allow children and throws IllegalArgumentException if child is null.

public TreeNode getChildAfter(TreeNode child)

Retrieve the next child for this node after the specified child. If child is the last node in the child array, it returns null. If child does not exist at this node, an IllegalArgumentException is thrown. (For node A, the child after B is C, and the child after C is D.)

public TreeNode getChildBefore(TreeNode child)

Retrieve the previous child for this node after the specified child. If child is the first node in the child array, it returns null. If child does not exist at this node, an IllegalArgumentException is thrown. (For node A, the child before node B is null, and the child before node C is B.)

public int getDepth( )

Return the depth of the tree starting from this node. This is an expensive operation because you must traverse the entire tree starting at this node to get the correct answer. (For node A, the depth is 6; for node G, the depth is 3.)

public TreeNode getFirstChild( )

Retrieve the first child in the child array of this node. If this node does not have any children, it throws a NoSuchElementException. (For node I, the first child is O.)

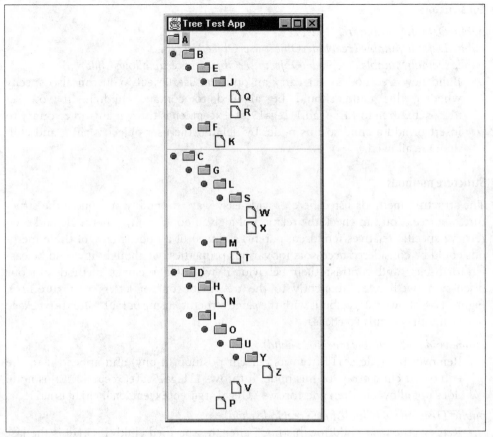

Figure 17-8. The JTree representation of the tree in Figure 17-3

public DefaultMutableTreeNode getFirstLeaf( )

Get the first leaf that is a descendant of this node. If this node has no children, it is itself a leaf, so it returns this. (For node B, the first leaf is Q; for node W, the first leaf is W.)

public int getIndex(TreeNode child)

Return the index of child in the node's child array. It returns –1 if child does not exist at this node. (For node S, the index of W is 0. For node S again, the index of T is –1.)

public TreeNode getLastChild( )

Retrieve the last child in the child array of this node. If this node does not have any children, it throws a NoSuchElementException. (For node I, the last child is P.)

public DefaultMutableTreeNode getLastLeaf( )

Get the last leaf that is a descendant of this node. If this node has no children, it is itself a leaf, so it returns this. (For node B, the last leaf is K; for node D, the last leaf is P.)

public int getLeafCount( )

Return the number of leaves that are descendants of this node. If this node has no children, it is itself a leaf, so it returns 1. If a node has children, however, it is not a leaf, so it does not count itself. (For both nodes C and G, the leaf count is 3.)

public int getLevel( )

Return the current level of this node with relation to the root of the tree (i.e., its distance from the root). If this node is the root, its level is 0. (For node A, the level is 0; for node M, the level is 3.)

public DefaultMutableTreeNode getNextLeaf( )

Return the next node in the parent's tree that is a leaf. If this is the last node in its parent's tree, it returns null. It does not matter whether this node is a leaf or not. (For node H, the next leaf is Z.)

public DefaultMutableTreeNode getNextNode( )

Return the next node in the tree, where "next" is defined in terms of a preorder traversal of the tree. If this node is the last in a preorder traversal, it returns null. See the preorderEnumeration( ) method later in this chapter for a more detailed discussion of preorder traversals. (For node E, the next node is J; for node T, the next node is D.)

public DefaultMutableTreeNode getNextSibling( )

Return the next child in this parent's child array. If this node is the last (or only) child, it returns null. (For node Q, the next sibling is R; for node D, the next sibling is null.)

public TreeNode[] getPath( )

Return the path from the root to this node as an array of TreeNode objects. (The path for node R is A B E J R.)

public DefaultMutableTreeNode getPreviousLeaf( )

Return the previous node in the parent's tree that is a leaf. If this is the first node in the parent's tree, it returns null. It does not matter whether this node is a leaf or not. (For node H, the previous leaf is null; for node T, the previous leaf is X.)

public DefaultMutableTreeNode getPreviousNode( )

Return the previous node in the tree, where "previous" is defined in terms of a preorder traversal of the tree. If this node is the first in a preorder traversal, it returns null. See the preorderEnumeration( ) method later in the chapter for a more detailed discussion of preorder traversals. (For node E, the previous node is B; for node C, the previous node is K.)

public DefaultMutableTreeNode getPreviousSibling( )

Return the previous child in this parent's child array. If this node is the first (or only) child, it returns null. (For node Q, the previous sibling is null; for node D, the previous sibling is C.)

public TreeNode getRoot( )

Retrieve the root of the tree this node belongs to. Any given tree has exactly one root, where a root is defined as the node with a `null` parent. (For any node in the example tree, including A, the root is A.)

public TreeNode getSharedAncestor(DefaultMutableTreeNode node2)

Find the closest shared ancestor for this node and the given node2. If node2 is a descendant of this node, this node is the common ancestor (and vice versa). The "worst" case for two nodes in the same tree would be to have the root as the only shared ancestor. If node2 is not in this node's tree, it returns `null`. (For nodes J and K, the shared ancestor is B; for nodes J and V, the shared ancestor is A.)

public int getSiblingCount( )

Return the number of siblings for this node. Since a node is its own sibling, this method returns the child count for this node's parent. (For node Q, the sibling count is 2; for node K, the sibling count is 1.)

public Object[] getUserObjectPath( )

Return all user objects along the path from the root to this node. It may contain `null`s if some nodes along the path have no user object. Recall that a user object is any arbitrary piece of data you wish to store with a node. In a filesystem tree that stores file and folder names as user objects, for example, this method returns an array of String objects where each string represents a directory in the path, and the last string represents the selected file.

public void insert(MutableTreeNode node, int index)

Insert a new node as a child to this node at the given index. If index is larger than `getChildCount( ) + 1`, it generates an `ArrayIndexOutOfBoundsException`. If node is null or is an ancestor of this node, it generates an `IllegalArgumentException`. If this node doesn't accept children (`allowsChildren` is false), it generates an `IllegalStateException`.

public boolean isLeaf( )

Return `true` if this node has no children. This method does not check the `allowsChildren` property. (Node B returns `false`; node R returns `true`.)

public boolean isNodeAncestor(TreeNode node2)

Return true if node2 is an ancestor of this node. (E, B, and A are all ancestors of node E.)

public boolean isNodeChild(TreeNode node2)

Return true if node2 is in this node's child array. (For node G, L returns `true` while S returns `false`.)

public boolean isNodeDescendant(DefaultMutableTreeNode node2)

Return true if node2 is a descendant of this node. (For node G, both L and S return true, but C and H return `false`.)

public boolean isNodeRelated(DefaultMutableTreeNode node2)

Return true if node2 is in the same tree as this node. (Any two nodes listed in our example are part of the same tree, so they all return true.)

public boolean isNodeSibling(TreeNode node2)

Return true if node2 is a sibling of this node. (For node Q, R is a sibling, but S is not.)

public boolean isRoot()

Return true if this node is the root of its tree. "Rootness" is determined by having a null parent. (A is the root of the tree.)

public void remove(int index)
public void remove(MutableTreeNode node)

Remove a child from this node. In the first version, if an invalid index number is given, you receive an ArrayIndexOutOfBoundsException. In the second version, if the node given does not exist as a child, you receive an IllegalArgumentException. The child is given a null parent after removal.

public void removeAllChildren()

Remove all the children attached to this node. It does nothing if no children exist.

public void removeFromParent()

Remove this node from its parent. This works like a call to getParent(). remove(this) by creating a new tree rooted at this node.

Enumeration methods

If you want to look at all the nodes in a tree, you should use one of the following enumeration methods to get that list of nodes. The enumeration does not build a copy of the tree, but it does keep track of where you are in the tree, and when you call the nextElement() method, you get the correct next element according to the traversal you picked. The code to traverse (or search) a tree looks something like this:

```
Enumeration e = root.breadthFirstEnumeration();
while (e.hasMoreElements()) {
    DefaultMutableTreeNode node = (DefaultMutableTreeNode)e.nextElement();
    System.out.print(node.getUserObject() + " ");
    // Or do something else more interesting with the node
}
System.out.println();
```

public Enumeration breadthFirstEnumeration()

A breadth-first traversal starts looking at the root node, then goes to its children, in ascending index order. After each child is looked at, the traversal moves on to the children of the root's first child and so on. The tree in Figure 17-3 produces the following breadth-first output:

A B C D E F G H I J K L M N O P Q R S T U V W X Y Z

A breadth-first traversal works if you are searching a very large tree for some item, and you expected to find the item near the top of the tree.

public Enumeration depthFirstEnumeration()
public Enumeration postorderEnumeration()

Depth-first (sometimes called *postorder*) traversals start with the root, go to its first child, go to that node's first child, and so on. The first node it actually "looks" at is the first leaf it hits. Then it backs up one level and goes to other children of that first leaf's parent. In our example, the depth-first traversal produces this output:

Q R J E K F B W X S L T M G C N H Z Y U V O P I D A

A depth-first traversal is useful if you expect to find the leaves of a tree interesting and want to start working with them quickly. For example, in a filesystem, a depth-first enumeration would get you to a file object right away.

public Enumeration preorderEnumeration()

Preorder traversals start at the root, look at it, then move on to the first child, look at it, then move on to its first child, look at it, and so on. The preorder output of the example looks like this:

A B E J Q R F K C G L S W X M T D H N I O U Y Z V P

A preorder traversal is useful for dumping out a tree that represents some parsed data. In the filesystem example, such a traversal would be useful if you need information about each node as you traverse before you look at any of its children. A breadth-first search would give you all of the top-level directories first, which is not what we want. A depth-first search would not let us look at a directory until we had already seen its children—also not what we want.

public Enumeration children()
public Enumeration pathFromAncestorEnumeration(TreeNode ancestor)

These last two enumerations do not give you the entire tree, but rather an interesting piece of it. The children() call is inherited from TreeNode and gives an enumeration of the immediate children of this node. The pathFromAncestorEnumeration() gives you a list of all the nodes from the root down to this node. (The children of A are B, C, and D. The path from the ancestor for node N is A D H N.)

public Enumeration getExpandedDescendants(TreePath parent)

Return an enumeration of all currently expanded nodes that are descendants of parent. If parent is null or is not expanded itself, null is returned.

The TreePath Class

If you look at a collection of these node objects from one node to one of its descendants, you have a path. The TreePath class is straightforward, but it does have some convenience methods for comparing and dealing with paths. A TreePath is a read-only object. If you want to change the structure of the path, you need to interact with the model, not the path. (These paths serve as a "view" of a tree branch but are not part of an existing tree.)

Properties

The TreePath class has five simple properties. The values of these properties, shown in Table 17-10, are set by the constructor, and after that are read-only.

Table 17-10. TreePath properties

Property	Data type	get	is	set	Default value
lastPathComponent	Object	•			
parentPath	TreePath	•			
path	Object[]	•			
pathComponent[i]	Object	•			
pathCount	int	•			

[i]indexed

The path property is the array of tree nodes from the root to another node. Since the path is an Object array and not a TreeNode array, you can still use a TreePath to describe a path in a tree with custom nodes, such as our expression tree. The parentPath is a TreePath leading up to (and including) the parent of this node. pathCount is the number of nodes in the path property. lastPathComponent lets you access the last node on the path, and the indexed property, pathComponent, lets you retrieve any node.

Constructors

public TreePath(Object singlePath)
public TreePath(Object[] path)

Build a TreePath object out of one or several Objects. If you want a path represented by just one node, you can use the first version of the constructor. Typically, paths consist of several nodes from the root down to some interesting node, in which case you'd use the second version. A TreePath should reflect all the nodes from the root down, but there is no check involved if you tried to create a "partial" path from an ancestor node that was not necessarily the root. However, other classes dealing with TreePath objects expect the first entry in the path to be the root of the tree.

protected TreePath()

This constructor is provided for subclasses that may choose to use other arguments to initialize a path.

protected TreePath(TreePath parent, Object lastElement)
protected TreePath(Object[] path, int length)

> These constructors create new TreePath objects by returning the path with a length of the root to lastElement or of length nodes long, respectively. If you want to create a TreePath by lengthening a given path, see the pathByAddingChild( ) method below.

Miscellaneous methods

public boolean isDescendant(TreePath path)

> Return true if path is a descendant of this path. The given path is considered a descendant of this path if path contains all the nodes found in this path. This differs from equals( ) in that path could be longer than this path and still be a descendant. If this path is null, it returns false.

public TreePath pathByAddingChild(Object child)

> Return a new TreePath object created by appending child to this path. The child argument cannot be null.

Tree Selections

After the tree is built and looks the way you want it to, you need to start working with selections so it does something useful. The JTree class introduced many of the selection manipulation methods already, but let's take a closer look at the model for selecting paths in a tree and the DefaultSelectionModel provided in the javax.swing. tree package. If you're comfortable with selection models, you probably won't find anything surprising here and may want to skip to "Rendering and Editing."

Selections are based on rows or paths. It's important to realize the distinction between a "row" and a "path" for trees. A path contains the list of nodes from the root of the tree to another node. Paths exist regardless of whether or not you plan to display the tree.

Rows, however, are completely dependent on the graphical display of a tree. The easiest way to think about a row is to think of the tree as a JList object. Each item in the list is a row on the tree. That row corresponds to some particular path. As you expand and collapse folders, the number of rows associated with the tree changes. It's the RowMapper object's job to relate a row number to the correct path.

Depending on your application, you may find rows or paths more efficient. If your program deals mostly with the user object data, paths are a good choice. If you're working with the graphical interface (automatically expanding folders and the like), rows may be more useful.

The RowMapper Interface

Tree selections make extensive use of the RowMapper interface. (In the absence of a RowMapper, you simply cannot retrieve information on rows in the tree from classes like TreeSelectionModel. TreePath information is still available, and the tree, its model, and the selection model will all continue to work just fine.) It is a simple interface with one method:

public int[] getRowsForPaths(TreePath paths[])

> The UI for your tree should implement this to return a list of row indices matching the supplied paths. If any of the paths are null or not visible, -1 should be placed in the return int array. While this may seem like an obvious task, you must account for the expanded or collapsed state of the nodes in the tree; remember that there's no such thing as a collapsed row. This is one reason why the JTree class cannot simply use a ListSelectionModel.

The TreeSelectionModel Interface

Now for the heart of selections. The TreeSelectionModel interface determines what a tree selection can look like.

Properties

TreeSelectionModel contains the properties listed in Table 17-11. The selection model properties deal primarily with the current selection on the tree. The notion of a "lead" selection stems from the fact that a selection can happen as a process, not only as a single event. The lead selection is the most recently added cell in the selection. It might be the only path selected, but it might also be the most recent selection out of several in a range or discontiguous group of selections. If the selection contains more than one path, the getSelectionPath( ) method returns the first selection in the path, which may or may not be the same thing as getLeadSelectionPath( ). It's also good to remember that, if it has children, selecting a "folder" node in a tree does not imply selecting all the nodes underneath it.

Having said that, the rest of the properties are fairly self-explanatory. minSelectionRow and maxSelectionRow let you get the smallest and largest selected row numbers. rowMapper holds a utility that manages the mapping between paths and row numbers. selectionPaths and selectionRows let you access the rows or paths currently selected. selectionCount tells you the number of rows selected.

Table 17-11. TreeSelectionModel properties

Property	Data type	get	is	set	Default value
leadSelectionPath	TreePath	•			
leadSelectionRow	int	•			

Table 17-11. TreeSelectionModel properties (continued)

Property	Data type	get	is	set	Default value
maxSelectionRow	int	•			
minSelectionRow	int	•			
rowMapper	RowMapper	•		•	
rowSelected	boolean		•		
selectionCount	int	•			
selectionMode	int	•		•	
selectionPath	TreePath	•		•	
selectionPaths	TreePath[]	•		•	
selectionRows	int[]	•			
selectionEmpty	boolean		•		

Constants

The value of the selectionMode property must be one of the constants listed in Table 17-12 and defined in the TreeSelectionModel interface.

Table 17-12. TreeSelectionModel constants

Constant	Type	Description
SINGLE_TREE_SELECTION	int	Allows only one path in the tree to be selected at any one time. Choosing a new path deselects the previous choice.
CONTIGUOUS_TREE_SELECTION	int	Allows several paths to be selected; they must be in a continuous block. The block ranges from the minSelectionRow to the maxSelectionRow.
DISCONTIGUOUS_TREE_SELECTION	int	Allows several paths to be selected; they can be any set of nodes, contiguous or otherwise.

Events

The TreeSelectionModel requires classes that implement the model to implement methods for registering listeners for property change events and tree selection events. TreeSelectionEvent is discussed in greater detail in "Tree Events" later in this chapter.

public void addPropertyChangeListener(PropertyChangeListener l)
public void removePropertyChangeListener(PropertyChangeListener l)

Add or remove listeners interested in receiving property change events.

public void addTreeSelectionListener(TreeSelectionListener l)
public void removeTreeSelectionListener(TreeSelectionListener l)

Add or remove listeners interested in receiving tree selection events. These methods differ from the JTree methods for adding or removing listeners, in that the event source sent to these listeners is the selection model, whereas the event source sent to the JTree selection listeners is the tree itself.

Selection methods

Many of these methods will look familiar if you read through the section on the JTree class. A tree passes along many of the selection calls to the selection model that supports it so that you can deal primarily with the tree itself.

public void addSelectionPath(TreePath path)
public void addSelectionPaths(TreePath paths[])
> Augment the current selection with the supplied path or paths.

public void clearSelection()
> Clear the current selection, leaving the selection empty. If nothing is selected before calling clearSelection( ), this method should have no effect.

public boolean isPathSelected(TreePath path)
public boolean isRowSelected(int row)
> Return true if the path or row specified is in the current selection.

public void removeSelectionPath(TreePath path)
public void removeSelectionPaths(TreePath paths[]))
> Remove the listed path or paths from the current selection. Any selected paths not specified remain selected.

public void resetRowSelection()
> Update the set of currently selected rows. This would be done if the row mapper changes, for example.

The DefaultTreeSelectionModel Class

Swing provides a default implementation of the tree selection model that supports all three modes of selection. You can see this model in use in the example earlier in this chapter.

Properties

The DefaultTreeSelectionModel inherits its properties from the TreeSelectionModel interface and supplies the default values listed in Table 17-13.

Table 17-13. DefaultTreeSelectionModel properties

Property	Data type	get	is	set	Default value
leadSelectionPath[o]	TreePath	•			null
leadSelectionRow[o]	int	•			-1

[1.4]since 1.4, [b]bound, [o]overridden

Table 17-13. DefaultTreeSelectionModel properties (continued)

Property	Data type	get	is	set	Default value
maxSelectionRow[o]	int	•			-1
minSelectionRow[o]	int	•			-1
propertyChangeListeners[1.4]	PropertyChangeListener[]	•			Empty array
rowMapper[o]	RowMapper	•		•	null
rowSelected[o]	boolean		•		false
selectionCount[o]	int	•			0
selectionMode[b,o]	int	•		•	DISCONTIGUOUS_TREE_SELECTION
selectionPath[o]	TreePath	•		•	null
selectionPaths[o]	TreePath[]	•		•	null
selectionRows[o]	int[]	•			null
selectionEmpty[o]	boolean		•		true
treeSelectionListeners[1.4]	TreeSelectionListener[]	•			Empty array

[1.4]since 1.4, [b]bound, [o]overridden

Events

The DefaultTreeSelectionModel supports the same property change and tree selection events as the TreeSelectionModel interface:

public void addPropertyChangeListener(PropertyChangeListener l)
public void removePropertyChangeListener(PropertyChangeListener l)
> Add or remove listeners interested in receiving property change events.

public void addTreeSelectionListener(TreeSelectionListener l)
public void removeTreeSelectionListener(TreeSelectionListener l)
> Add or remove listeners interested in receiving tree selection events. These events come from the DefaultTreeSelectionModel rather than JTree itself.

protected void fireValueChanged(TreeSelectionEvent event)
> Notify all registered TreeSelectionListener objects associated with this selection that the selection has changed.

Constant

The DefaultTreeSelectionModel contains one constant, as shown in Table 17-14.

Table 17-14. DefaultTreeSelectionModel constant

Constant	Type	Description
SELECTION_MODE_PROPERTY	String	The name of the selection mode property used in property change events

Constructor

public DefaultTreeSelectionModel( )

Create an instance of the default selection model with all properties initialized to the default values listed in Table 17-13.

Tree Events

Trees generate three types of events worth mentioning. Apart from the obvious selection events (TreeSelectionEvent, TreeSelectionListener), you can receive expansion events (TreeExpansionEvent, TreeExpansionListener, TreeWillExpandListener) from the graphical side, and you can catch structural changes to the model itself (TreeModelEvent, TreeModelListener).

Figure 17-9 shows a simple program that uses the Every Event Listener (EEL) class (described in Chapter 3) to display all events that come from selecting, expanding, and editing a tree. (We use a tree built by the default JTree constructor.) For editing, you can change the text of a node or add and remove nodes so that you can monitor model events.

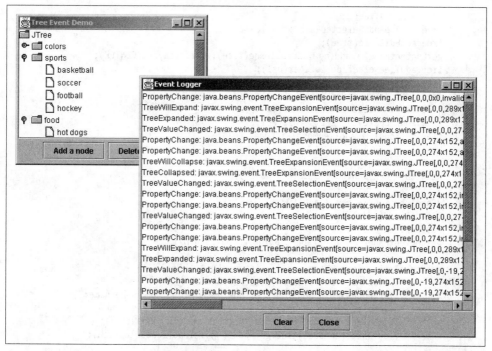

Figure 17-9. The JTree events as reported by our EEL utility

Here's the source code required to hook up all the various events:

```java
// TreeEvents.java
//
import java.awt.*;
import java.awt.event.*;
import javax.swing.*;
import javax.swing.event.*;
import javax.swing.tree.*;

public class TreeEvents extends JFrame implements TreeSelectionListener {

    JButton addB, deleteB;
    JTree tree;
    DefaultMutableTreeNode leadSelection;

    public TreeEvents() {
        super("Tree Event Demo");
        setSize(300,200);
        setDefaultCloseOperation(EXIT_ON_CLOSE);

        EEL eel = EEL.getInstance();
        eel.addGui();

        tree = new JTree();
        tree.setExpandsSelectedPaths(true);
        tree.setEditable(true);
        getContentPane().add(new JScrollPane(tree), BorderLayout.CENTER);
        tree.addTreeSelectionListener(eel);
        tree.addTreeSelectionListener(this);
        tree.addTreeExpansionListener(eel);
        tree.addTreeWillExpandListener(eel);
        tree.addPropertyChangeListener(eel);
        tree.getModel().addTreeModelListener(eel);

        addB = new JButton("Add a node");
        deleteB = new JButton("Delete a node");

        JPanel buttonP = new JPanel();
        buttonP.add(addB);
        buttonP.add(deleteB);
        getContentPane().add(buttonP, BorderLayout.SOUTH);

        addB.addActionListener(new ActionListener() {
            public void actionPerformed(ActionEvent ae) {
                String nodeName = JOptionPane.showInputDialog("New node name:");
                if (leadSelection != null) {
                    leadSelection.add(new DefaultMutableTreeNode(nodeName));
                    ((DefaultTreeModel)tree.getModel()).reload(leadSelection);
                }
                else {
                    JOptionPane.showMessageDialog(TreeEvents.this, "No Parent...");
                }
            }
        });
```

```
            deleteB.addActionListener(new ActionListener( ) {
                public void actionPerformed(ActionEvent ae) {
                    if (leadSelection != null) {
                        DefaultMutableTreeNode parent =
                            (DefaultMutableTreeNode) leadSelection.getParent( );
                        if (parent == null) {
                            JOptionPane.showMessageDialog(TreeEvents.this, "Can't delete root");
                        }
                        else {
                            parent.remove(leadSelection);
                            leadSelection = null;
                            ((DefaultTreeModel)tree.getModel( )).reload(parent);
                        }
                    }
                    else {
                        JOptionPane.showMessageDialog(TreeEvents.this, "No Selection...");
                    }
                }
            });
        eel.showDialog( );
    }

    public void valueChanged(TreeSelectionEvent e) {
        TreePath leadPath = e.getNewLeadSelectionPath( );
        if (leadPath != null) {
            leadSelection = (DefaultMutableTreeNode)leadPath.getLastPathComponent( );
        }
    }

    public static void main(String args[]) {
        TreeEvents te = new TreeEvents( );
        te.setVisible(true);
    }
}
```

The TreeModelEvent Class

The TreeModelEvent class encapsulates model changes by specifying the path that has changed as well as information on the children of that path.

Properties

The TreeModelEvent has several properties as shown in Table 17-15. If the event contains information about the affected children of a node, you can retrieve the indices and the children themselves with the childIndices and children properties, respectively. The path and treePath properties provide access to the main node of the event. Whether you look at that node through a TreePath object or through an Object array depends on your program; both methods lead to the same node.

Table 17-15. TreeModelEvent properties

Property	Data type	get	is	set	Default value
childIndices	int[]	•			
children	Object[]	•			
path	Object[]	•			
treePath	TreePath	•			

Constructors

public TreeModelEvent(Object source, Object path[], int childIndices[],
  Object children[])
public TreeModelEvent(Object source, TreePath path, int childIndices[],
  Object children[])
    Allow you to build an event that encompasses the children of a modified node.
    This type of event is useful if the references to the node's children have changed,
    or if the number of children has changed.

public TreeModelEvent(Object source, Object path[])
public TreeModelEvent(Object source TreePath path)
    If the modified node is the only interesting node for this event (if its value
    changed, but nothing happened to its children, for example), you can use these
    constructors.

The TreeModelListener Interface

The TreeModelListener interface requires that listeners implement the following
methods:

public void treeNodesChanged(TreeModelEvent e)
public void treeNodesInserted(TreeModelEvent e)
public void treeNodesRemoved(TreeModelEvent e)
    Indicate that nodes were changed, inserted, or removed, respectively.

public void treeStructureChanged(TreeModelEvent e)
    Indicate that the tree structure has changed significantly (such as several sub-
    trees being deleted) and may require more analysis than can be performed on the
    nodes and children retrievable through the event object e.

We can use this class of events to monitor the state of the tree. For example, consider a tree that represents a filesystem. Any time we change the tree, we want to
update the supporting filesystem. Listening for model changes would be the precise
clue we need to perform the required updates.

The TreeSelectionEvent Class

Selection events occur whenever a user (or program, for that matter) changes the selection on a tree. For example, if you went through a directory tree and manually selected 12 discontiguous files, that would generate 12 selection events, each building on the last. If you were to pick 12 contiguous files by selecting the first file and using a modifier to pick the last, that would generate only two selection events. (Both of these examples assume that nothing was originally selected.) As with list selections, *unselecting* something also counts as a selection event. In many cases where more than one file can be selected, you shouldn't listen for selection events directly, but rather provide an OK button or some other means for the user to finalize the current selection.

Properties

The properties for TreeSelectionEvent are shown in Table 17-16. Not surprisingly, they are similar to the selection properties available for the JTree class.

Table 17-16. TreeSelectionEvent properties

Property	Data type	get	is	set	Default value
addedPath	boolean		•		Set by constructor
newLeadSelectionPath	TreePath	•			Set by constructor
oldLeadSelectionPath	TreePath	•			Set by constructor
path	TreePath	•			Set by constructor
paths	TreePath[]	•			Set by constructor

Constructors

public TreeSelectionEvent(Object source, TreePath path, boolean isNew,
  TreePath oldLeadSelectionPath, TreePath newLeadSelectionPath)
  Build a TreeSelectionEvent centered on one path. The isNew argument determines whether the selection is an addition to (true) or a removal from (false) the current selection.

public TreeSelectionEvent(Object source, TreePath paths[], boolean areNew[],
  TreePath oldLeadSelectionPath, TreePath newLeadSelectionPath)
  Build a selection event that starts off with multiple selections in place. This would be useful in a filesystem tree for selecting things that matched a filter, like all the *.java* files.

Methods

public Object cloneWithSource(Object newSource)

 This clever method allows you to clone an event and modify the source component that ostensibly generated the event. This is great for a component that delegates some or all of its visual presence to a tree. You can use this method in an event adapter to pass on the event to some other listener, with the new component listed as the source.

public boolean isAddedPath(int index)
public boolean isAddedPath(TreePath path)

 Check an arbitrary specified path or index to see if it was added to the current selection. This can be useful if you are interested in the status of a single path but the event was generated with an array of new paths.

The TreeSelectionListener Interface

The TreeSelectionListener interface carries only one method:

public void valueChanged(TreeSelectionEvent e)

 Called whenever the selection on a tree changes. The DefaultTreeModel uses this method even for selections caused programmatically.

The TreeExpansionEvent Class

Normally, the tree UI expands and collapses elements of a tree for you. However, if you want to listen for and react to these events, you can do so. The TreeExpansionEvent class covers both expanding and collapsing a tree node.

Property

The sole property for TreeExpansionEvent is shown in Table 17-17.

Table 17-17. TreeExpansionEvent property

Property	Data type	get	is	set	Default value
path	TreePath	•			Set by constructor

Constructor

public TreeExpansionEvent(Object source, TreePath path)

 The source for this constructor is most often the tree itself, but it's certainly possible to imagine a GUI trigger as the source for a collapse or expand call.

The TreeExpansionListener Interface

To catch expansion or collapse events yourself, you can implement the TreeExpansionListener interface, which provides the following two methods:

public void treeExpanded(TreeExpansionEvent e)
public void treeCollapsed(TreeExpansionEvent e)
  Called when a path is collapsed or expanded.

Pending Expansion Events

JDK 1.2 introduced two classes that help you listen and react to expansion events before they occur. The TreeWillExpandListener interface allows you to register interest in pending expansion events. Implementations of this interface throw an ExpandVetoException if they decide that the expansion or collapse should not be allowed.

The TreeWillExpandListener interface

This interface gives you access to the expansion events (both expanding and collapsing) before the event takes place in the tree itself. The only reason you would want to hear about such an event rather than listening for the real expansion event is if you want to do something with the tree before it changes. The interface provides the following two methods:

public void treeWillExpand(TreeExpansionEvent event) throws ExpandVetoException
public void treeWillCollapse(TreeExpansionEvent event) throws ExpandVetoException
  Implement these methods to react to pending expansion events.

The ExpandVetoException class

The most common reason for listening to pending expansion events is that you may want to stop them from occurring. If the user does not have permission to expand a folder in a filesystem, for example, you could have a listener check each expand event. If you find a case where an expansion or collapse should not occur, your listener can throw an ExpandVetoException. Each of the listener methods mentioned above can throw this exception. The JTree setExpandedState( ) method catches these exceptions, and, if one is thrown, the node is left alone, and the fireTreeExpanded( ) or fireTreeCollapsed( ) method is never called. ExpandVetoException's constructors are:

public ExpandVetoException(TreeExpansionEvent event)
public ExpandVetoException(TreeExpansionEvent event, String message)
  Similar to other exception classes, these constructors build new exceptions with the proposed expansion event and an optional message.

Rendering and Editing

As with the table cells covered in previous chapters, you can create your own tree cell renderers and editors. The default renderers and editors usually do the trick, but you're probably reading this because they don't do the trick for you, so forge onward! If you went through building your own renderers and editors for tables, you'll find this material quite familiar. The tree uses renderers and editors in much the same way that tables do. In fact, you might recall that the `DefaultCellEditor` class can return both table and tree cell editors.

Rendering Nodes

Why would you want to render a node? Good question. One reason is that you want to modify the L&F of a tree without writing a whole UI package for trees. If you had some special way of presenting the "selected" look, for example, you could write your own tree renderer and still use the default L&F for your other components. You might want to render something other than a string with an icon for the nodes of your tree. Or, as we mentioned above, you might want tooltips that vary based on the particular node you rest your cursor on. "Because I can" is also a good reason.

But I just want to change the icons!

Before we tackle creating our own renderers, we should point out that the Metal L&F lets you modify the set of icons used by a tree for the leaves and folders. To change the icons, use the `UIManager` class and the L&F icons for trees. You can also use the client property `JTree.lineStyle` to affect the type of lines drawn from folders to leaves. Chapter 26 has much more detail on L&Fs, but this short example should get you started for the tree-specific properties.

Call the `putClientProperty()` method on your instance of the tree to set its line style. Your choices of styles are:

Horizontal
: Thin horizontal lines drawn above each top-level entry in the tree (the default)

Angled
: The Windows-style, right-angle lines from a folder to each of its leaves

None
: No lines at all

Call the `UIManager.put()` method to modify the icons used by all trees. The icons you can replace are:

Tree.openIcon
: Used for opened folders

Tree.closedIcon
: Used for closed folders

`Tree.leafIcon`
> Used for leaves

`Tree.expandedIcon`
> Used for the one-touch expander when its node is expanded

`Tree.collapsedIcon`
> Used for the one-touch expander when its node is collapsed

Thus, if t is a JTree, and icon is some kind of Icon, the code:

```
t.putClientProperty ("JTree.lineStyle", "Angled");
UIManager.put ("Tree.openIcon", icon);
```

sets the tree's line style to Angled and sets the icon for opened folders to icon.

Figure 17-10 shows a tree with custom icons and angled lines connecting the nodes. (This is also a sample of a JTree used for some hierarchical data other than a filesystem. Here, we have a Virtual Reality Markup Language [VRML] world builder with the containers representing composite scenes and the leaves representing atomic objects in the world.)

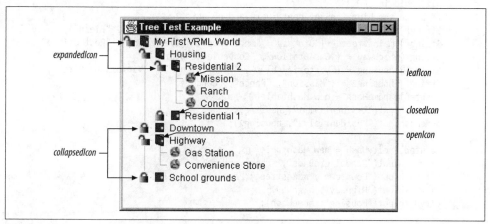

Figure 17-10. A sample JTree with custom icons and line style

Here's the code that installed these customizations. The customizations happen in two places. The various icons used throughout the tree are installed in our constructor and apply to any tree instance we create. The lineStyle property is something we associated with the particular instance of JTree in our init( ) method. Again, this property affects only the Metal L&F.

```
// TestTree3.java
// A simple test to see how we can build a tree and customize its icons
//
import java.awt.*;
import java.util.*;
import java.awt.event.*;
import javax.swing.*;
```

```
import javax.swing.plaf.*;
import javax.swing.tree.*;

public class TestTree3 extends JFrame {

  JTree tree;
  DefaultTreeModel treeModel;

  public TestTree3( ) {
    super("Tree Test Example");
    setSize(200, 150);
    setDefaultCloseOperation(EXIT_ON_CLOSE);

    // Add our own customized tree icons.
    UIManager.put("Tree.leafIcon", new ImageIcon("world.gif"));
    UIManager.put("Tree.openIcon", new ImageIcon("door.open.gif"));
    UIManager.put("Tree.closedIcon", new ImageIcon("door.closed.gif"));
    UIManager.put("Tree.expandedIcon", new ImageIcon("unlocked.gif"));
    UIManager.put("Tree.collapsedIcon", new ImageIcon("locked.gif"));
  }

  public void init( ) {
    // Build the hierarchy of containers and objects.
    String[] schoolyard = {"School", "Playground", "Parking Lot", "Field"};
    String[] mainstreet = {"Grocery", "Shoe Shop", "Five & Dime", "Post Office"};
    String[] highway = {"Gas Station", "Convenience Store"};
    String[] housing = {"Victorian_blue", "Faux Colonial", "Victorian_white"};
    String[] housing2 = {"Mission", "Ranch", "Condo"};
    Hashtable homeHash = new Hashtable( );
    homeHash.put("Residential 1", housing);
    homeHash.put("Residential 2", housing2);

    Hashtable cityHash = new Hashtable( );
    cityHash.put("School grounds", schoolyard);
    cityHash.put("Downtown", mainstreet);
    cityHash.put("Highway", highway);
    cityHash.put("Housing", homeHash);

    Hashtable worldHash = new Hashtable( );
    worldHash.put("My First VRML World", cityHash);

    // Build our tree out of our big hashtable.
    tree = new JTree(worldHash);

    // Pick an angled line style.
    tree.putClientProperty("JTree.lineStyle", "Angled");
    getContentPane( ).add(tree, BorderLayout.CENTER);
  }

  public static void main(String args[]) {
    TestTree3 tt = new TestTree3( );
    tt.init( );
    tt.setVisible(true);
  }
}
```

The DefaultTreeCellRenderer Class

[JDK 1.2 introduced another alternative to the L&F setup for trees. In addition to setting up icons and line styles as we do in the previous example, you can use the DefaultTreeCellRenderer class and its properties to customize tree display. DefaultTreeCellRenderer is an extension of the JLabel class that implements the TreeCellRenderer interface (discussed later) and is devoted to tailoring your tree's display.

Properties

Table 17-18 shows the properties associated with this new class:

Table 17-18. DefaultTreeCellRenderer properties

Property	Data type	get	is	set	Default value
background[o],*	Color	•		•	From L&F
backgroundNonSelectionColor	Color	•		•	From L&F
backgroundSelectionColor	Color	•		•	From L&F
borderSelectionColor	Color	•		•	From L&F
closedIcon	Icon	•		•	From L&F
defaultClosedIcon	Icon	•			From L&F
defaultLeafIcon	Icon	•			From L&F
defaultOpenIcon	Icon	•			From L&F
font[o],*	Font	•		•	From L&F
leafIcon	Icon	•		•	From L&F
openIcon	Icon	•		•	From L&F
preferredSize[o],+	Dimension	•		•	From L&F
textNonSelectionColor	Color	•		•	From L&F
textSelectionColor	Color	•		•	From L&F

[o]overridden

*This property has an overridden set( ) method that does not allow UIResource objects (such as ColorUIResource and FontUIResource) as its argument.

+This property overrides the get( ) method to increase the width of the preferred size by three pixels.

The various properties let you configure the icons for leaves, open folders, and closed folders. You can also control the colors used for the text and selected elements.

Constructor

The DefaultTreeCellRenderer class has only one constructor:

public DefaultTreeCellRenderer()
　　　Return a new instance of the class.

The default renderer can be very handy for changing the L&F of one tree as opposed to every tree. Figure 17-11 shows an example of such a tree in a split pane. The top tree is a normal tree. The tree on the bottom was built with the same data, but it alters the icons of its renderer.

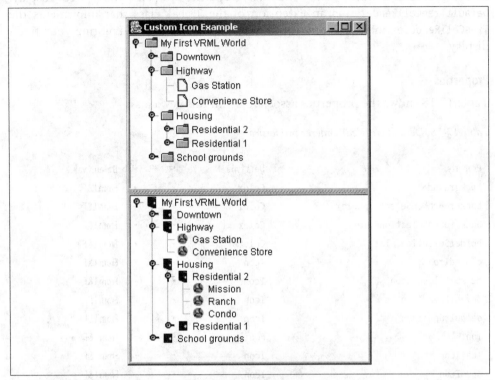

Figure 17-11. Sample JTrees; the second tree uses custom icons

Here's the code that produced the trees and custom icons for the second tree:

```
// Build our tree out of our big hashtable.
tree1 = new JTree(worldHash);
tree2 = new JTree(worldHash);
DefaultTreeCellRenderer renderer = (DefaultTreeCellRenderer)tree2.getCellRenderer( );
renderer.setClosedIcon(new ImageIcon("door.closed.gif"));
renderer.setOpenIcon(new ImageIcon("door.open.gif"));
renderer.setLeafIcon(new ImageIcon("world.gif"));
```

Custom Renderers

What if we wanted more tailored icons or node-specific tooltips or even HTML text for the nodes? Such features would require writing our own renderer. Our XML tree uses the default folder and leaf icons, which are more appropriate for files and filesystems. We can write a custom renderer that uses icons specified by the XML tags if they're available. (It uses the default icons if not.) Figure 17-12 shows such a renderer in action.

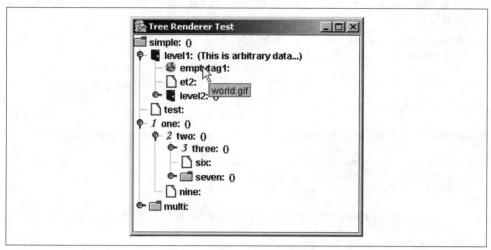

Figure 17-12. XML JTree tree with a custom interface and tooltips

The TreeCellRenderer Interface

With the TreeCellRenderer interface and your favorite Component subclass, you can render a tree cell any way you like, regardless of the L&F in place. While you can return any component as a renderer, because of the problems with mixing heavy-weight and lightweight components, you'll probably want to return a subclass of JComponent. If you want multiple components to do your rendering (or your editing, for that matter), extending Container is a good place to start. This interface defines one method:

public Component getTreeCellRendererComponent(JTree tree, Object value,
   boolean selected, boolean expanded, boolean leaf, int row, boolean hasFocus)
     This method takes as arguments all the information relevant to rendering a tree node. You are free to ignore any argument that doesn't interest you, or you can go directly to the tree node, value. You can then create and return a component that draws your node correctly.

A simple way to build your first renderer is to extend the JLabel class. You'll probably want to keep some other state information around as well. The following is the code that built the above renderer. When the program renders a cell or displays a cell's tooltip (by calling getTreeCellRendererComponent( )), we set the current color for the foreground and background according to the selected status of our object. We could also query our object for other bits of information, if needed.

We implement the IconAndTipCarrier interface to let our renderer know it should use a custom icon and text for the tooltips. IconAndTipCarrier was written for this example and has only two methods: getIcon( ) and getToolTipText( ). To get the more interesting tooltips working, we override the getToolTipText( ) method to return a different string for each node or leaf. In our case, we show the filename of the icon being used.

```java
// IconAndTipRenderer.java
// A renderer for our XML cells
//
import java.awt.*;
import javax.swing.*;
import javax.swing.tree.*;

public class IconAndTipRenderer extends JLabel implements TreeCellRenderer {

  Color backColor = new Color(0xFF, 0xCC, 0xFF);
  Icon openIcon, closedIcon, leafIcon;
  String tipText = "";

  public IconAndTipRenderer(Icon open, Icon closed, Icon leaf) {
    openIcon = open;
    closedIcon = closed;
    leafIcon = leaf;
    setBackground(backColor);
    setForeground(Color.black);
  }

  public Component getTreeCellRendererComponent(JTree tree, Object value,
                                                boolean selected,
                                                boolean expanded, boolean leaf,
                                                int row, boolean hasFocus) {
    setText(value.toString( ));
    if (selected) {
      setOpaque(true);
    }
    else {
      setOpaque(false);
    }

    // Try to find an IconAndTipCarrier version of the current node.
    IconAndTipCarrier itc = null;
    if (value instanceof DefaultMutableTreeNode) {
      Object uo = ((DefaultMutableTreeNode)value).getUserObject( );
      if (uo instanceof IconAndTipCarrier) {
        itc = (IconAndTipCarrier)uo;
      }
    }
    else if (value instanceof IconAndTipCarrier) {
      itc = (IconAndTipCarrier)value;
    }
    if ((itc != null) && (itc.getIcon( ) != null)) {
      // Great! Use itc's values to customize this label.
      setIcon(itc.getIcon( ));
      tipText = itc.getToolTipText( );
```

```
            }
          else {
            // Hmmm, nothing available, so rely on the defaults.
            tipText = " ";
            if (expanded) {
              setIcon(openIcon);
            }
            else if (leaf) {
              setIcon(leafIcon);
            }
            else {
              setIcon(closedIcon);
            }
          }
          return this;
        }

        // Override the default to send back different strings for folders and leaves.
        public String getToolTipText( ) {
          return tipText;
        }
      }
```

Here are the lines in *VSX2.java* that create the new renderer and tell our tree to use it instead of the default renderer:

```
// Steal the default icons from a default renderer.
DefaultTreeCellRenderer rend1 = new DefaultTreeCellRenderer( );
IconAndTipRenderer rend2 = new IconAndTipRenderer(
  rend1.getOpenIcon( ),
  rend1.getClosedIcon( ),
  rend1.getLeafIcon( ));
tree.setCellRenderer(rend2);
```

If you want the tooltips to be active, you have to register the tree with the ToolTipManager (see Chapter 27 for details) like so:

```
ToolTipManager.sharedInstance( ).registerComponent(tree);
```

Editing Nodes

One of the other things you may want to do with a tree node is edit it. Each L&F shipped with Swing implements basic text field editors for tree nodes, but it is possible to use other components to edit nodes. In fact, since editors are just subclasses of Component, you can even build your own editor.

For example, we can create an expression editor (see Figure 17-13) that picks one of two possible components. If you want to edit an operator, you get a JComboBox with the four supported operators in the list. If you want to edit an integer, you get a JTextField.

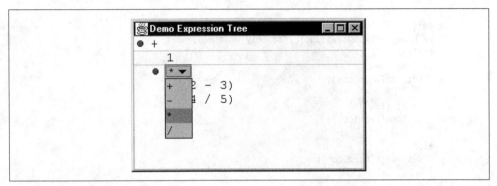

Figure 17-13. Expression tree with a custom editor for the operator nodes

The TreeCellEditor Interface

Like the TreeCellRenderer interface, the TreeCellEditor interface has one method:

public Component getTreeCellEditorComponent(JTree tree, Object value,
  boolean selected, boolean expanded, boolean leaf, int row)
    Configure the editor just before it pops up on the screen. In our example, we use
    this method to select the current operator in the combo box or to set the current
    text value for the text field.

In addition to this method, you also need to keep track of things like whether you
can even edit this tree node. Most of that information comes from the CellEditor
interface (which TreeCellEditor extends).

The DefaultTreeCellEditor Class

JDK 1.2 introduced another useful component to the tree package: the
DefaultTreeCellEditor class. This class can be used to supply an editor for your tree
cells that lets icons associated with the cells remain on the screen during editing.
(This was a problem in previous releases.) You can use a default text field to edit
cells or wrap your own custom editor in this class to use the start-up and rendering
features. The DefaultTreeCellEditor class starts editing a cell after a triple-click of
the mouse or after a "click-pause-click wait for 1,200 milliseconds" sequence.

Properties

Table 17-19 lists the DefaultTreeCellEditor properties.

Table 17-19. DefaultTreeCellEditor properties

Property	Data type	get	is	set	Default value
borderSelectionColor	Color	•		•	From L&F
cellEditorValue⁰	Object	•			
font⁰	Font	•		•	From L&F
tree*	JTree			•	From constructor

⁰overridden

*This property has a protected set( ) method.

The font and borderSelectionColor properties determine the visible qualities of the editor. The cellEditorValue property comes from the CellEditor interface discussed in detail in Chapter 27. (It contains the current value stored in the editor.) The tree property is the JTree whose cell is being edited.

Events

As dictated by the CellEditor interface, the DefaultTreeCellEditor class generates ChangeEvent objects for cell editor events. The usual add and remove methods are present:

public void addCellEditorListener( )
public void removeCellEditorListener( )
> Register and unregister listeners interested in finding out the editor has a new value for the cell. One such listener is the tree currently being edited.

Constructors

Two constructors allow you to build your own version of the "default" editor:

public DefaultTreeCellEditor(JTree tree, DefaultTreeCellRenderer renderer)
> Call the next constructor with the supplied tree and renderer arguments and pass null for the editor.

public DefaultTreeCellEditor(JTree tree, DefaultTreeCellRenderer renderer,
TreeCellEditor editor)
> Build a default editor with the given tree and renderer used. If you supply null for the editor, a DefaultCellEditor with a text field is created for you. (You can read more about the DefaultCellEditor class in Chapter 27.) This constructor gives you an editor that displays the proper icon from renderer while the user is editing the cell. For simple editors, this provides a smooth transition into editing a cell. For more complex editors, the icon can get in the way.

CellEditor and TreeCellEditor methods

The `DefaultTreeCellEditor` class implements the `TreeCellEditor` interface (and by extension, the `CellEditor` interface). The methods from these interfaces are present in the class. The methods for `CellEditor` are usually delegated to the `realEditor` component. Chapter 27 has more details on the `CellEditor` interface.

One of the most common tasks a cell editor encounters is validating the input provided by the user. The default editor has no skill in this area, but if we build our own editors, we can add as much functionality as we need.

Two ways of validating input come to mind. An easy way is to restrict the input to a range of choices. The `JComboBox` class is an excellent candidate for this type of work. We can supply a list of valid values, and the user picks something from the list. Another way of handling input is testing the value before you accept it. If the user supplies an invalid entry, just leave the editor open. If she supplies a valid entry, accept it and close the editor. We'll build both types of editors in the example below.

For the tree itself, we need one class that we can designate as our editor. That class, in turn, delegates its editing capabilities to one of the two editors mentioned above. This delegating class does not have to be a component itself since the actual editor the tree uses comes from the `getTreeCellEditorComponent()` call, which returns the real editing component. In our case, it returns an `EmailEditor` or an `EditorComboBox`, depending on whether we're editing a node or a leaf. However, `EmailTreeCellEditor` does have to implement the `TreeCellEditor` interface; as you can see from the code, after the real editors are set up, it delegates the other methods to the current editor:

```java
// EmailTreeCellEditor.java
//
import javax.swing.*;
import javax.swing.event.*;
import java.awt.*;
import java.awt.event.*;
import java.util.*;
import javax.swing.tree.*;

public class EmailTreeCellEditor implements TreeCellEditor {

    EditorComboBox nodeEditor;
    EmailEditor leafEditor;
    CellEditor currentEditor;

    static String[] emailTypes = { "Home", "Work", "Pager", "Spam" };

    public EmailTreeCellEditor() {

        EmailEditor tf = new EmailEditor();
        EditorComboBox cb = new EditorComboBox(emailTypes);

        nodeEditor = cb;
        leafEditor = tf;
    }
```

```
    public Component getTreeCellEditorComponent(JTree tree, Object value,
                                                boolean isSelected,
                                                boolean expanded,
                                                boolean leaf, int row) {
        if (leaf) {
            currentEditor = leafEditor;
            leafEditor.setText(value.toString());
        }
        else {
            currentEditor = nodeEditor;
            nodeEditor.setSelectedItem(
                ((DefaultMutableTreeNode)value).getUserObject());
        }
        return (Component)currentEditor;
    }

    public Object getCellEditorValue() {
        return currentEditor.getCellEditorValue();
    }

    // All cells are editable in this example.
    public boolean isCellEditable(EventObject event) {
        return true;
    }

    public boolean shouldSelectCell(EventObject event) {
        return currentEditor.shouldSelectCell(event);
    }

    public boolean stopCellEditing() {
        return currentEditor.stopCellEditing();
    }

    public void cancelCellEditing() {
        currentEditor.cancelCellEditing();
    }

    public void addCellEditorListener(CellEditorListener l) {
        nodeEditor.addCellEditorListener(l);
        leafEditor.addCellEditorListener(l);
    }

    public void removeCellEditorListener(CellEditorListener l) {
        nodeEditor.removeCellEditorListener(l);
        leafEditor.removeCellEditorListener(l);
    }
}
```

Next, we need to set up our first custom editor. For nodes, we want a combo box that gives us some address categories as choices. The EditorComboBox class is really a bit more flexible than that. It accepts any array of objects as an argument to its constructor and returns a JComboBox editor containing that list as its choices.

This class also implements the CellEditor interface so that it can perform the duties required of an editor. As you saw in the above code, the EmailTreeCellEditor delegates most of its responsibilities here. In setting up the constructor, we attach an action listener that stops the editing process when the user chooses one of the items in the list. The JTree object using this editor registers as a CellEditorListener when you begin editing a node. It then waits for the ChangeEvent that we distribute in the fireEditingStopped( ) method before removing the editor component from the screen. Using the isCellEditable( ) method, we'll start editing if the user right-clicks on our node.

```java
// EditorComboBox.java
// A CellEditor JComboBox subclass for use with Trees (and possibly tables)
//
import javax.swing.*;
import javax.swing.event.*;
import java.awt.event.*;
import java.awt.*;
import java.util.*;

public class EditorComboBox extends JComboBox implements CellEditor {

  String value;
  Vector listeners = new Vector( );

  // Mimic all the constructors people expect with ComboBoxes.
  public EditorComboBox(Object[] list) {
    super(list);
    setEditable(false);
    value = list[0].toString( );

    // Listen to our own action events so that we know when to stop editing.
    addActionListener(new ActionListener( ) {
      public void actionPerformed(ActionEvent ae) {
        if (stopCellEditing( )) {
          fireEditingStopped( );
        }
      }
    });
  }

  // Implement the CellEditor methods.
  public void cancelCellEditing( ) { }

  // Stop editing only if the user entered a valid value.
  public boolean stopCellEditing( ) {
    try {
      value = (String)getSelectedItem( );
      if (value == null) { value = (String)getItemAt(0); }
      return true;
    }
    catch (Exception e) {
```

```
    // Something went wrong.
    return false;
  }
}

public Object getCellEditorValue() {
  return value;
}

// Start editing when the right mouse button is clicked.
public boolean isCellEditable(EventObject eo) {
  if ((eo == null) ||
      ((eo instanceof MouseEvent) && (((MouseEvent)eo).isMetaDown()))) {
    return true;
  }
  return false;
}

public boolean shouldSelectCell(EventObject eo) { return true; }

// Add support for listeners.
public void addCellEditorListener(CellEditorListener cel) {
  listeners.addElement(cel);
}

public void removeCellEditorListener(CellEditorListener cel) {
  listeners.removeElement(cel);
}

protected void fireEditingStopped() {
  if (listeners.size() > 0) {
    ChangeEvent ce = new ChangeEvent(this);
    for (int i = listeners.size() - 1; i >= 0; i--) {
      ((CellEditorListener)listeners.elementAt(i)).editingStopped(ce);
    }
  }
}
  }
}
```

The next step is to build our editor delegate for the leaves. We'll use the same approach, but this time, we will make sure that the user enters a valid value. We do this in the stopCellEditing() method. If the value in the text field does not look like an email address (i.e., does not have an "@" in it somewhere), we return false and do *not* fire the ChangeEvent. (See Chapter 20 for a more proactive approach to restricting the text field input.) This leaves the text field on the screen. Until the user types a valid email address into the text field, pressing Enter has no effect, and the editor remains visible.

```
// EmailEditor.java
//
import javax.swing.*;
import javax.swing.event.*;
import java.awt.event.*;
```

```
import java.awt.*;
import java.util.*;

public class EmailEditor extends JTextField implements CellEditor {
  String value = "";
  Vector listeners = new Vector( );

  // Mimic all the constructors people expect with text fields.
  public EmailEditor( ) { this("", 5); }
  public EmailEditor(String s) { this(s, 5); }
  public EmailEditor(int w) { this("", w); }
  public EmailEditor(String s, int w) {
    super(s, w);
    // Listen to our own action events so that we know when to stop editing.
    addActionListener(new ActionListener( ) {
      public void actionPerformed(ActionEvent ae) {
        if (stopCellEditing( )) { fireEditingStopped( ); }
      }
    });
  }

  // Implement the CellEditor methods.
  public void cancelCellEditing( ) { setText(""); }

  // Stop editing only if the user entered a valid value.
  public boolean stopCellEditing( ) {
    try {
      String tmp = getText( );
      int at = tmp.indexOf("@");
      if (at != -1) {
        value = tmp;
        return true;
      }
      return false;
    }
    catch (Exception e) {
      // Something went wrong (most likely we don't have a valid integer).
      return false;
    }
  }

  public Object getCellEditorValue( ) { return value; }

  // Start editing when the right mouse button is clicked.
  public boolean isCellEditable(EventObject eo) {
    if ((eo == null) ||
        ((eo instanceof MouseEvent) &&
         (((MouseEvent)eo).isMetaDown( )))) {
      return true;
    }
    return false;
  }

  public boolean shouldSelectCell(EventObject eo) { return true; }
```

```
    // Add support for listeners.
    public void addCellEditorListener(CellEditorListener cel) {
      listeners.addElement(cel);
    }

    public void removeCellEditorListener(CellEditorListener cel) {
      listeners.removeElement(cel);
    }

    protected void fireEditingStopped( ) {
      if (listeners.size( ) > 0) {
        ChangeEvent ce = new ChangeEvent(this);
        for (int i = listeners.size( ) - 1; i >= 0; i--) {
          ((CellEditorListener)listeners.elementAt(i)).editingStopped(ce);
        }
      }
    }
  }
}
```

And of course, as the last step, we must register this new delegating editor with our
JTree object in the init( ) method of the EmailTree class:

```
tree.setCellEditor(new EmailTreeCellEditor( ));
tree.setEditable(true);
```

If you recall from the constructor descriptions for DefaultTreeCellEditor, you can
also use that class to keep the icon associated with a node on the screen while you
are editing. To accomplish this, you could use the following code:

```
DefaultTreeCellRenderer renderer = (DefaultTreeCellRenderer)tree.getCellRenderer( );
EmailTreeCellEditor emailEditor = new EmailTreeCellEditor( );
DefaultTreeCellEditor editor = new DefaultTreeCellEditor(
    tree, renderer, emailEditor);
tree.setCellEditor(editor);
```

Look-and-Feel Helper Classes

JDK 1.2 added three other classes to the tree package that help the L&F code do its
job:

AbstractLayoutCache
> The abstract base class for calculating layout information for an L&F. This
> includes dealing with icons and row height information. The details of these cal-
> culations are left to subclasses.

FixedHeightLayoutCache (extends AbstractLayoutCache)
> This class assumes a fixed height for all tree cells and does not accept heights
> less than or equal to 0.

VariableHeightLayoutCache (extends AbstractLayoutCache)
> This class allows variable heights for cells, checking with the cell renderer if a
> specified height is less than or equal to 0.

The documentation for these classes notes that they will become "more open" with future releases of the JDK. (As of the 1.4 release, that same note still exists. Ah, well.) Fortunately, the JTree class itself is not concerned with these classes—there are no methods for setting or modifying the layout cache. The L&F classes, however, do use these classes, and developers building their own L&Fs may want to look closer.

What Next?

With this control over the look of a tree and its contents, you can create some impressive interfaces for a wide variety of data and your own network management software that lets you browse domains and subdomains and computers and users. Any hierarchy of information you can think of can be shown graphically.

It is worth pointing out, however, that you are not restricted to graphical applications with these models. You can use DefaultTreeModel to store regular, hierarchical data, even if you have no intention of displaying the data on a screen. The model is flexible and provides a good starting point if you don't have any tree data structures of your own lying around.

CHAPTER 18
Undo

In many applications (word processors, spreadsheets, and board games, to name a few), the user is given the opportunity to undo changes made to the state of the application. In a word processor you can undo deletions. In a chess game, you're often allowed to take back undesirable moves (typically after realizing your queen has just been banished from the board). Without support, providing these undo capabilities can be a lot of work for the programmer, especially if you want to provide a powerful undo system that keeps a history of undoable operations and allows them to be undone and redone indefinitely.

Thankfully, Swing provides a collection of classes and interfaces that support this advanced undo functionality. Within the Swing packages, only the classes in the `javax.swing.text` package currently use these facilities, but you are free to use undo in any component you create or extend. You can even use it for undoing things that may not be directly associated with a UI component (like a chess move). It's important to realize that the undo facility is not tied in any way to the Swing components themselves. One could easily argue that the package might be more logically called "java.util.undo." None of the classes or interfaces in the `javax.swing.undo` package use any other Swing object.

In this chapter, we'll look at everything Swing provides to support undo, but we won't get into the details of how the text components use this facility (Chapter 22 does the honors in that department).

The Swing Undo Facility

The `javax.swing.undo` package contains two interfaces and seven classes (two of which are exception classes). These, along with a listener interface and event class from the `javax.swing.event` package, comprise the undo facility shown in Figure 18-1.

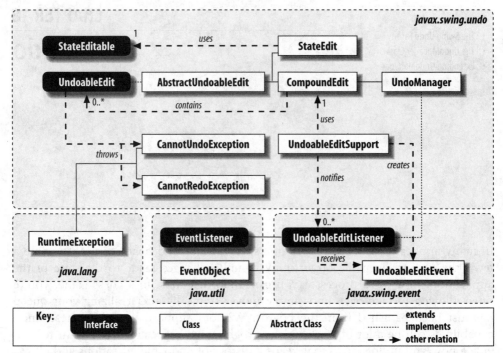

Figure 18-1. The Swing undo facility

Here is a brief overview of each class:

UndoableEdit

> The base interface for just about everything else in the undo package. It serves as an abstraction for anything in an application that can be undone.

AbstractUndoableEdit

> The default implementation of UndoableEdit provides a starting point for building new UndoableEdit classes. It provides a simple set of rules for determining whether undo and redo requests are allowable (based on whether the edit has already been undone, redone, or killed). Despite its name, it is not an abstract class. This is really just a technicality since the default implementation is not at all useful as it is, so you'd never want to instantiate one.

CompoundEdit

> This extension of AbstractUndoableEdit allows multiple edits to be grouped together into a single edit. Those familiar with the classic *Design Patterns* by Erich Gamma et al. (Addison-Wesley) will recognize this construct as a basic implementation of the Composite pattern.

UndoableEditEvent

> This event class can be used to notify listeners that an undoable edit has been made.

UndoableEditListener

    The listener interface to which UndoableEditEvents are sent. It contains a single method called undoableEditHappened( ).

UndoManager

    An extension of CompoundEdit that can manage a list of edits to be undone or redone in sequence. UndoManager implements UndoableEditListener, so it can be added to many components that generate UndoableEditEvents, allowing it to manage edits from multiple sources in a single undo list.

StateEdit

    An extension of AbstractUndoableEdit that can be used for edits that are undone or redone by changing a set of property values representing the state of the application (or some aspect of it) before and after the edit.

StateEditable

    This interface must be implemented by objects wishing to use StateEdit. The StateEdit constructor accepts a StateEditable and calls its two methods, storeState( ) and restoreState( ), to manage the editable's state.

UndoableEditSupport

    This class provides support facilities for classes that need to support undo. It simplifies the processes of managing listeners, firing events, and grouping multiple edits.

CannotUndoException *and* CannotRedoException

    These exception classes extend RuntimeException and are thrown when an undo or redo attempt is made while the edit is not in the correct state (e.g., calling redo( ) on an edit that has not yet been undone).

Now that we have a basic understanding of what we have to work with, let's look at the details of each of these interfaces and classes.

The UndoableEdit Interface

The UndoableEdit interface defines a set of operations that can be performed on any object that needs to provide undo and redo functionality. Typically, classes that implement this interface are fairly small. Instances of these classes represent single, undoable changes ("edits") made to the state of the application or some component of the application.

UndoableEdits can be thought of as being in one of three states, as shown in the state diagram in Figure 18-2. Since UndoableEdit is just an interface, it can't really enforce this state model. However, this is the intended state model, and the AbstractUndoableEdit class described in the next section does enforce it. Alternate implementations of this interface should not deviate from this model.

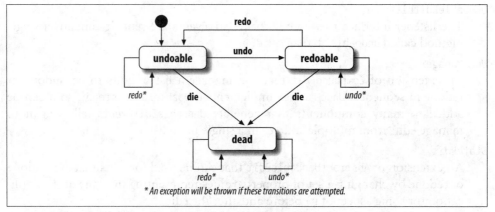

Figure 18-2. UndoableEdit state chart

When initially created, the edit represents some change that has just been done and is now *undoable*.* Once the edit is undone, it becomes *redoable*. Having been undone, it may be redone, causing it to become *undoable* again. This sequence can be repeated indefinitely. If, for whatever reason, an edit can no longer be used, it can be "killed," taking it to the *dead* state. Once killed, the edit can no longer be undone or redone. Dead is dead.

 The die( ) method provides a mechanism for edits to explicitly release any resources they may be holding, rather than waiting until the edits are garbage-collected.

Properties

Table 18-1 shows the properties defined by UndoableEdit.

Table 18-1. UndoableEdit properties

Property	Data type	get	is	set	Default value
presentationName	String	•			
redoPresentationName	String	•			
significant	boolean	•			
undoPresentationName	String	•			

UndoableEdits are typically displayed to a user, allowing the user to decide to undo or redo some action that was performed. In support of this, UndoableEdit provides three

---

* Throughout this chapter, we'll use *italics* when we refer to the "state" of an edit. These states do not usually map directly to any field or method provided by the undo classes; they simply provide an easy way to talk about the state of an edit.

properties that name an edit: presentationName, undoPresentationName, and redoPresentationName. These properties might have values such as delete, undo delete, and redo delete, respectively. The last two names are typically just variations on the first.

The significant property may be used to distinguish edits of different levels of importance. An insignificant edit, for example, might not be displayed to the user, instead being performed as a side effect of some other edit.

To understand the idea of an insignificant edit, think of a computer chess game. The process of making a move might consist of clicking on a piece, causing the square the piece is sitting on to change color, then clicking on the destination square, completing the move. You might implement the game's undo capability by having an edit responsible for changing the color of the square of the selected piece and another edit representing the move itself. The first edit is not the type of edit you'd want to display to the user. Instead, you'd track this as an insignificant edit.

Edit-merging methods

UndoableEdit provides two methods for merging the changes described by two edits into a single edit. Implementations of these methods are under no obligation to support this merging feature. Such implementations simply return false, indicating that no merging of the edits was done.

The addEdit() and replaceEdit() methods are similar. addEdit() asks the edit it is invoked upon to absorb an input edit, and replaceEdit() asks the edit if it would like to replace the input edit. The idea is that addEdit() is called on an existing edit, passing in a new one, while replaceEdit() is called on a new edit, passing in an existing one.

Absorbing edits can be useful in a variety of scenarios. One use of this feature might be to group together a series of "delete-character" edits created as a user holds down the Delete or Backspace key. By merging these into a single edit, the user would be able to undo the series of deletions with a single undo operation, rather than having to undo each individual character.

For another example, consider our chess game again. If a user clicked on three different pieces before deciding which one to move, each subsequent piece selection edit would probably want to replace the previous one so that the temporary selections don't become part of the *undoable* history.

public abstract boolean addEdit(UndoableEdit anEdit)
> This method asks the edit to absorb anEdit. If the edit is able to do so, it returns true. If not, it returns false. If anEdit is absorbed, it is no longer undoable or redoable by itself (i.e., canUndo() and canRedo() should return false, and undo() and redo() should throw exceptions). If anEdit is no longer needed, die() should be called on it.

public abstract boolean replaceEdit(UndoableEdit anEdit)

> This method asks this edit to replace anEdit. If the edit is able to do so, it returns true. If not, it returns false. If anEdit is replaced, it should no longer be undoable or redoable by itself (i.e., canUndo( ) and canRedo( ) should return false, and undo( ) and redo( ) should throw exceptions). If anEdit is no longer needed, die( ) should be called on it.

For more information on these methods, see the discussion of CompoundEdit.

Other methods

public abstract boolean canRedo()

> This method returns true if the edit currently can be redone, implying that a subsequent redo( ) call should not throw a CannotRedoException.

public abstract boolean canUndo()

> This method returns true if the edit currently can be undone, implying that a subsequent undo( ) call should not throw a CannotUndoException.

public abstract void die()

> This method is called to indicate that the edit can no longer be undone or redone. Any state being held by the edit can be released, and subsequent calls to undo( ) or redo( ) should throw exceptions.

public abstract void redo() throws CannotRedoException

> This method is called to redo an edit that has previously been undone. If the edit cannot be redone (perhaps because it has not been undone yet), a CannotRedoException should be thrown.

public abstract void undo() throws CannotUndoException

> Called to undo an edit. If the edit cannot be undone (perhaps because it has already been undone), a CannotUndoException should be thrown.

The AbstractUndoableEdit Class

This implementation of UndoableEdit provides useful default behavior for the methods defined in the interface. It enforces the state model described in the previous section using two internal boolean properties, *alive* and *done*. A new AbstractUndoableEdit is both *alive* and *done*. A call to die( ) makes it no longer *alive*. A call to undo( ) makes it no longer *done*, while redo( ) makes it *done* again. In order for an edit to be undone, it must be both *alive* and *done*. To be redone, it must be *alive* but not *done*.

Subclasses of AbstractUndoableEdit should take advantage of this fundamental state support by calling super.undo( ) and super.redo( ) in the first line of their undo( ) and redo( ) methods, respectively. This frees the subclass from having to worry about enforcing the edit's state model.

Properties

Table 18-2 shows the default values `AbstractUndoableEdit` specifies for the properties defined in `UndoableEdit`.

Table 18-2. AbstractUndoableEdit properties

Property	Data type	get	is	set	Default value
presentationName°	String	•			""
redoPresentationName°	String	•			"Redo"*
significant°	boolean		•		true
undoPresentationName°	String	•			"Undo"*

°overridden

*As of SDK 1.3.1, these values are UI resources retrieved from the `UIManager` class.

The `presentationName` property is empty by default. `RedoPresentationName` and `undoPresentationName` are formed by appending `presentationName` to `RedoName` and `UndoName` (protected constants, see below), respectively. By default, all `AbstractUndoableEdits` are significant.

There is no way to change the values of these properties once the object is created. Concrete edit classes need to provide some way (possibly just returning a constant value from the property accessor) to define the presentation name.

Constants

Table 18-3 shows the two protected constants that `AbstractUndoableEdit` defines. These constants are used by default when forming the `redoPresentationName` and `undoPresentationName` properties. In the 1.2.x and 1.3.0 releases, their values were hardcoded English strings. Starting with 1.3.1, these values are retrieved using the `UIManager.getString()` method with the keys `"AbstractUndoableEdit.redoText"` and `"AbstractUndoableEdit.undoText"`, respectively.

Table 18-3. AbstractUndoableEdit constants

Constant	Type	Description
RedoName^d	String	`String ("Redo")` prepended to the presentation name to form the undo presentation name
UndoName^d	String	`String ("Undo")` prepended to the presentation name to form the undo presentation name

^ddeprecated as of 1.3.1

Constructor

public AbstractUndoableEdit()

Create a new edit. The edit is initially *alive* and *done*.

UndoableEdit methods

The following methods provide a simple default implementation of the UndoableEdit interface:

public boolean addEdit(UndoableEdit anEdit)
> Always return false. Merging edits is not directly supported by this class.

public boolean canRedo()
> Return true if the edit is *alive* (die( ) has not been called) and not *done* (it has been undone).

public boolean canUndo()
> Return true if the edit is *alive* (die( ) has not been called) and *done* (it has not already been undone, or it has been undone and redone).

public void die( )
> Set a flag indicating that the edit is no longer *alive*.

public void redo( ) throws CannotRedoException
> Call canRedo( ) and throw an exception if it returns false. Otherwise, it sets a flag to indicate that the edit is *done*.

public boolean replaceEdit(UndoableEdit anEdit)
> Always return false. Merging of edits is not directly supported by this class.

public void undo( ) throws CannotUndoException
> Call canUndo( ) and throw an exception if it returns false. Otherwise, it sets a flag to indicate that the edit is no longer *done*.

Creating a toggle edit

In this example, we'll create a simple extension of AbstractUndoableEdit called UndoableToggleEdit.* This edit provides the ability to undo clicking on a JToggleButton (or one of its subclasses, JRadioButton or JCheckBox). A program using this new edit creates a new UndoableToggleEdit each time the toggle button is clicked. If undo( ) is called on the edit, it changes the state of the button back to its previous state. A redo( ) call sets the button back to the state it was in when it was passed into the UndoableToggleEdit constructor. Here's the source code for this new edit class:

```
// UndoableToggleEdit.java
//
import javax.swing.*;
import javax.swing.undo.*;

// An UndoableEdit used to undo the clicking of a JToggleButton
public class UndoableToggleEdit extends AbstractUndoableEdit {
```

---

* We'll use this class throughout the examples in this chapter, so it's probably a good idea to make sure you understand its purpose.

```
      private JToggleButton button;
      private boolean selected;

      // Create a new edit for a JToggleButton that has just been toggled.
      public UndoableToggleEdit(JToggleButton button) {
         this.button = button;
         selected = button.isSelected();
      }

      // Return a reasonable name for this edit.
      public String getPresentationName() {
         return "Toggle " + button.getText() + " " +
         (selected ? "on" : "off");
      }

      // Redo by setting the button state as it was initially.
      public void redo() throws CannotRedoException {
         super.redo();
         button.setSelected(selected);
      }

      // Undo by setting the button state to the opposite value.
      public void undo() throws CannotUndoException {
         super.undo();
         button.setSelected(!selected);
      }
   }
}
```

We inherit most of our behavior from AbstractUndoableEdit. The most important thing to learn from this class is that the edit keeps track of enough information to undo or redo an operation. In our case, this is done by holding a reference to the toggle button the edit applies to, as well as by keeping a boolean to hold the value of the toggle. For more complex undo capabilities, your edit classes probably need more information than this.

Another important thing to notice is that both undo() and redo() call their super implementations to ensure that the edit is in the appropriate state.

Next, let's look at a small application that shows how we might use this new edit class. In this (admittedly worthless) application, we create three toggle buttons that we place in the center of a frame. Below these toggle buttons, we add two JButtons— one for undo and one for redo. Each time one of the toggle buttons is pressed (see the actionPerformed() method in the SimpleListener inner class), we create a new UndoableToggleEdit (discarding any previous edit). At this time, we also update the labels on our undo and redo buttons using the names defined by the new edit.

If the undo button is clicked, we call undo() on the edit, which changes the state of the last toggle button we clicked. Clicking the redo button switches it back again by calling redo() on the edit.

When we initially create the edit or when we perform an undo or redo (note the finally blocks in the two anonymous listener classes), we enable or disable the undo and redo buttons based on the edit's response to canUndo( ) and canRedo( ).

For now, we can only undo the most recent edit. Later in the chapter, we'll present a similar example that supports multiple undo operations. Here's the source code for this sample application:

```
// UndoableToggleApp.java
//
import javax.swing.*;
import javax.swing.event.*;
import javax.swing.undo.*;
import java.awt.*;
import java.awt.event.*;

// A sample app showing the use of UndoableToggleEdit
public class UndoableToggleApp extends JFrame {

  private UndoableEdit edit;
  private JButton undoButton;
  private JButton redoButton;

  // Create the main frame and everything in it.
  public UndoableToggleApp( ) {

    // Create some toggle buttons (and subclasses).
    JToggleButton tog = new JToggleButton("ToggleButton");
    JCheckBox cb = new JCheckBox("CheckBox");
    JRadioButton radio = new JRadioButton("RadioButton");

    // Add our listener to each toggle button.
    SimpleListener sl = new SimpleListener( );
    tog.addActionListener(sl);
    cb.addActionListener(sl);
    radio.addActionListener(sl);

    // Lay out the buttons.
    Box buttonBox = new Box(BoxLayout.Y_AXIS);
    buttonBox.add(tog);
    buttonBox.add(cb);
    buttonBox.add(radio);

    // Create undo and redo buttons (initially disabled).
    undoButton = new JButton("Undo");
    redoButton = new JButton("Redo");
    undoButton.setEnabled(false);
    redoButton.setEnabled(false);

    // Add a listener to the undo button. It attempts to call undo( ) on the
    // current edit, then enables/disables the undo/redo buttons as appropriate.
    undoButton.addActionListener(new ActionListener( ) {
      public void actionPerformed(ActionEvent ev) {
        try {
```

```
        edit.undo( );
      } catch (CannotUndoException ex) { ex.printStackTrace( ); }
      finally {
        undoButton.setEnabled(edit.canUndo( ));
        redoButton.setEnabled(edit.canRedo( ));
      }
    }
  });

  // Add a redo listener, which is just like the undo listener,
  // but for redo this time.
  redoButton.addActionListener(new ActionListener( ) {
    public void actionPerformed(ActionEvent ev) {
      try {
        edit.redo( );
      } catch (CannotRedoException ex) { ex.printStackTrace( ); }
      finally {
        undoButton.setEnabled(edit.canUndo( ));
        redoButton.setEnabled(edit.canRedo( ));
      }
    }
  });

  // Lay out the undo/redo buttons.
  Box undoRedoBox = new Box(BoxLayout.X_AXIS);
  undoRedoBox.add(Box.createGlue( ));
  undoRedoBox.add(undoButton);
  undoRedoBox.add(Box.createHorizontalStrut(2));
  undoRedoBox.add(redoButton);
  undoRedoBox.add(Box.createGlue( ));

  // Lay out the main frame
  Container content = getContentPane( );
  content.setLayout(new BorderLayout( ));
  content.add(buttonBox, BorderLayout.CENTER);
  content.add(undoRedoBox, BorderLayout.SOUTH);
  setSize(400, 150);
}

public class SimpleListener implements ActionListener {
  // When a toggle button is clicked, we create a new UndoableToggleEdit (which
  // replaces any previous edit). We then get the edit's undo/redo names and set
  // the undo/redo button labels. Finally, we enable/disable these buttons by
  // asking the edit what we are allowed to do.
  public void actionPerformed(ActionEvent ev) {
    JToggleButton tb = (JToggleButton)ev.getSource( );
    edit = new UndoableToggleEdit(tb);
    undoButton.setText(edit.getUndoPresentationName( ));
    redoButton.setText(edit.getRedoPresentationName( ));
    undoButton.getParent( ).validate( );
    undoButton.setEnabled(edit.canUndo( ));
    redoButton.setEnabled(edit.canRedo( ));
  }
}
```

```
    // Main program just creates the frame and displays it
    public static void main(String[] args) {
      JFrame f = new UndoableToggleApp();
      f.setDefaultCloseOperation(JFrame.EXIT_ON_CLOSE);
      f.setVisible(true);
    }
}
```

Figure 18-3 shows what this application looks like after we've played with it for a while. We just got through toggling the radio button and then clicking on the undo button.

Figure 18-3. Sample UndoableToggleApp display

The CompoundEdit Class

CompoundEdit is a subclass of AbstractUndoableEdit that supports the aggregation of multiple edits into a single composite edit. After a CompoundEdit is created, UndoableEdits can be added by calling addEdit( ). Once all edits have been added, a new method, end( ), must be called on the CompoundEdit to indicate that the creation of the edit is complete (after this point, addEdit( ) just returns false). Only after end( ) has been called can the edit be undone. CompoundEdit implements undo( ) and redo( ) by calling the appropriate method on each of the edits added to it, allowing all of them to be executed at once.

Figure 18-4 shows a state chart very similar to the one we saw for UndoableEdit. The key difference is that a CompoundEdit is initially *inProgress* and does not allow either undo( ) or redo( ). The end( ) method must be called after adding the edits to the CompoundEdit to enable undo.

Properties

CompoundEdit defines the properties shown in Table 18-4. inProgress is the only new property here. It indicates whether edits may be added to the CompoundEdit. Initially true, this property is set to false when end( ) is called. It never changes back to true after that.

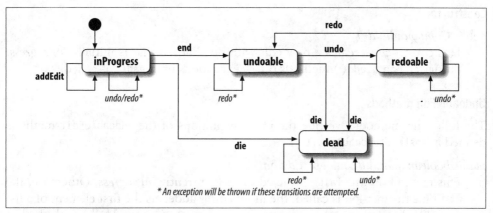

Figure 18-4. CompoundEdit state chart

Table 18-4. CompoundEdit properties

Property	Data type	get	is	set	Default value
inProgress	boolean			•	true
presentationName°	String	•			""
redoPresentationName°	String	•			"Redo"
significant°	boolean		•		false
undoPresentationName°	String	•			"Undo"

°overridden

See also properties from the AbstractUndoableEdit class (Table 18-2).

The values of presentationName, redoPresentationName, and undoPresentationName are initially the same as the values defined in AbstractUndoableEdit. However, once edits are added, these values are set to the values of the corresponding properties of the last edit added.

The significant property is initially false. Once edits are added, this value is determined by checking the significance of the child edits. If any of them are set to true, the CompoundEdit is considered to be significant.

Protected field

protected Vector edits
> This is where the CompoundEdit stores its edits. New edits are added to the end of the vector.

Constructor

public CompoundEdit( )

> This constructor creates a new edit with no children that is initially *inProgress*.
> The undo( ) and redo( ) methods throw exceptions until end( ) is called.

UndoableEdit methods

The following methods override the implementations of the `UndoableEdit` methods
defined in `AbstractUndoableEdit`:

public boolean addEdit(UndoableEdit anEdit)

> This method returns `false` if the edit is not currently *inProgress*. Otherwise, the
> first time the method is called, the input edit is added as the first element of a list
> of child edits. Subsequent calls are given the opportunity to merge with the last
> edit in the list. This is done by calling `addEdit(anEdit)` on the last edit in the list.
> If this returns `false` (indicating that the last edit did not absorb the new edit),
> `anEdit.replaceEdit(lastEdit)` is called to see if the new edit can replace the last
> edit. If this returns `true` (indicating that the new edit can replace the last edit),
> the last edit is removed from the list, and the new edit is added in its place. If
> not, the last edit is left in the list, and the new edit is added to the end of the list.
>
> Figure 18-5 shows a sequence diagram for this method. In this example, the last
> edit does not absorb the new edit, but the new edit does replace the previous last
> edit. We show the last two operations in italics to indicate that these are not
> actual method calls on the compound edit.

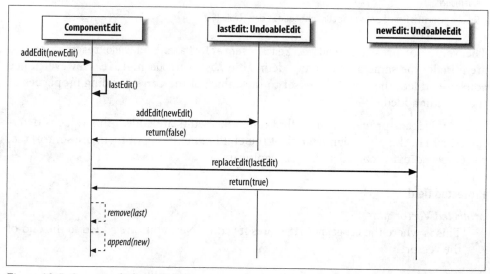

Figure 18-5. CompoundEdit.addEdit( ) sequence diagram

public boolean canRedo( )

> Return true if the edit is not *inProgress* and super.canRedo( ) returns true.

public boolean canUndo( )

> Return true if the edit is not *inProgress* and super.canUndo( ) returns true.

public void die( )

> Call die( ) on each of the child edits in reverse order. It then calls super.die( ).

public void redo( ) throws CannotRedoException

> Call super.redo( ) to make sure redo is allowed. It then calls redo( ) on each of its children in the order they were added.

public void undo( ) throws CannotUndoException

> Call super.undo( ) to make sure undo is allowed. It then calls undo( ) on each of its children in the reverse of the order they were added.

Other methods

public void end( )

> Indicate that no more edits will be added. After this method is called, the edit is no longer *inProgress*.

protected UndoableEdit lastEdit( )

> Return the last edit added, or null if no edits have been added yet.

Using Compound Edits

The following example is a modification of the UndoableToggleApp from the previous section. This version uses CompoundEdit to allow multiple button toggles to be undone at once. Each time one of the toggle buttons is clicked, a new UndoableToggleEdit is created and added to a CompoundEdit. Once you've toggled as many buttons as you want, you can click the end button, which causes end( ) to be called on the CompoundEdit and enables the undo button. Clicking on this button causes undo( ) to be called on the CompoundEdit, which in turn calls undo( ) on each of the UndoableToggleEdits that were added to it. Clicking on one of the toggle buttons again causes the CompoundEdit to be replaced with a new one, to which new edits will be added until the end button is pressed again.

Here's the source code for this example. Much of it is unchanged from the UndoableToggleApp example, so we've highlighted the significant changes.

```
// UndoableToggleApp2.java
//
import javax.swing.*;
import javax.swing.event.*;
import javax.swing.undo.*;
import java.awt.*;
import java.awt.event.*;
```

```
// A sample app showing the use of UndoableToggleEdit and CompoundEdit
public class UndoableToggleApp2 extends JFrame {

    private CompoundEdit edit;
    private JButton undoButton;
    private JButton redoButton;
    private JButton endButton;

    // Create the main frame and everything in it.
    public UndoableToggleApp2( ) {

        // Create some toggle buttons (and subclasses).
        JToggleButton tog = new JToggleButton("ToggleButton");
        JCheckBox cb = new JCheckBox("CompoundEdit ExampleCheckBox");
        JRadioButton radio = new JRadioButton("RadioButton");

        // Add our listener to each toggle button.
        SimpleListener sl = new SimpleListener( );
        tog.addActionListener(sl);
        cb.addActionListener(sl);
        radio.addActionListener(sl);

        // Lay out the buttons.
        Box buttonBox = new Box(BoxLayout.Y_AXIS);
        buttonBox.add(tog);
        buttonBox.add(cb);
        buttonBox.add(radio);

        // Create undo and redo buttons (initially disabled).
        undoButton = new JButton("Undo");
        redoButton = new JButton("Redo");
        endButton = new JButton("End");
        undoButton.setEnabled(false);
        redoButton.setEnabled(false);
        endButton.setEnabled(false);

        // Add a listener to the undo button. It attempts to call undo( ) on the
        // current edit, then enables/disables the undo/redo buttons as appropriate.
        undoButton.addActionListener(new ActionListener( ) {
            public void actionPerformed(ActionEvent ev) {
                try {
                    edit.undo( );
                } catch (CannotUndoException ex) { ex.printStackTrace( ); }
                finally {
                    undoButton.setEnabled(edit.canUndo( ));
                    redoButton.setEnabled(edit.canRedo( ));
                }
            }
        });

        // Add a redo listener, which is just like the undo listener, but for redo this
        // time.
        redoButton.addActionListener(new ActionListener( ) {
            public void actionPerformed(ActionEvent ev) {
```

```
        try {
          edit.redo( );
        } catch (CannotRedoException ex) { ex.printStackTrace( ); }
        finally {
          undoButton.setEnabled(edit.canUndo( ));
          redoButton.setEnabled(edit.canRedo( ));
        }
      }
    });

    // Add an end listener. This listener will call end( ) on the CompoundEdit and
    // update the undo/redo buttons.
    endButton.addActionListener(new ActionListener( ) {
      public void actionPerformed(ActionEvent ev) {
        edit.end( );
        endButton.setEnabled(false);
        undoButton.setEnabled(edit.canUndo( ));
        redoButton.setEnabled(edit.canRedo( ));
      }
    });

    // Lay out the undo/redo/end buttons.
    Box undoRedoEndBox = new Box(BoxLayout.X_AXIS);
    undoRedoEndBox.add(Box.createGlue( ));
    undoRedoEndBox.add(undoButton);
    undoRedoEndBox.add(Box.createHorizontalStrut(2));
    undoRedoEndBox.add(redoButton);
    undoRedoEndBox.add(Box.createHorizontalStrut(2));
    undoRedoEndBox.add(endButton);
    undoRedoEndBox.add(Box.createGlue( ));

    // Lay out the main frame.
    Container content = getContentPane( );
    content.setLayout(new BorderLayout( ));
    content.add(buttonBox, BorderLayout.CENTER);
    content.add(undoRedoEndBox, BorderLayout.SOUTH);
    setSize(400, 150);
  }

  public class SimpleListener implements ActionListener {
    public void actionPerformed(ActionEvent ev) {
      if (edit == null || edit.isInProgress( ) == false)
        edit = new CompoundEdit( );

      JToggleButton tb = (JToggleButton)ev.getSource( );
      UndoableEdit togEdit = new UndoableToggleEdit(tb);
      edit.addEdit(togEdit);
      endButton.setEnabled(true);
      undoButton.setEnabled(edit.canUndo( ));
      redoButton.setEnabled(edit.canRedo( ));
    }
  }
}
```

```
    // Main program just creates the frame and displays it.
    public static void main(String[] args) {
      JFrame f = new UndoableToggleApp2();
      f.setDefaultCloseOperation(JFrame.EXIT_ON_CLOSE);
      f.setVisible(true);
    }
  }
```

The UndoableEditEvent Class

UndoableEditEvent is an event class (it extends java.util.EventObject) defined in the javax.swing.event package. It is used by components that support undo to notify interested listeners (implementing UndoableEditListener) that an UndoableEdit has been performed.

A little later in the chapter, we'll see an example that uses the UndoableEditEvent class and the UndoableEditListener interface.

Property

UndoableEditEvent defines the property shown in Table 18-5. The edit property contains the UndoableEdit that was generated, causing this event to be fired.

Table 18-5. UndoableEditEvent property

Property	Data type	get	is	set	Default value
edit	UndoableEdit	•			

See also the java.util.EventObject class.

Constructor

public UndoableEditEvent(Object source, UndoableEdit edit)
> Create a new event with the specified event source and UndoableEdit.

The UndoableEditListener Interface

Classes that generate UndoableEditEvents fire these events to UndoableEditListeners. This is a simple interface (like UndoableEditEvent, it can be found in the javax.swing. event package), defining a single method:

public abstract void undoableEditHappened(UndoableEditEvent e)
> Called when an undoable operation is performed on an object that supports undo. The event e can be used to obtain the new UndoableEdit.

The UndoManager Class

UndoManager is an extension of CompoundEdit that can track a history of edits, allowing them to be undone or redone one at time. Additionally, it implements UndoableEditListener by calling addEdit( ) each time an UndoableEditEvent is fired. This allows a single UndoManager to be added as a listener to many components that support undo, providing a single place to track all edits and populate an undo menu for the entire application.

It may seem a bit strange that UndoManager extends CompoundEdit. We'll explain why shortly, but first it's important to understand the primary ways in which UndoManager acts differently than CompoundEdit. For starters, when you add an edit to an UndoManager, it is placed in a list of edits available for undo. When you call undo( ), only the first (significant) edit is undone. This is different from the behavior of CompoundEdit, in which a call to undo( ) results in a call to undo( ) on all of the added edits.

Another major difference between UndoManager and its superclass is the semantics of the inProgress property. In CompoundEdit, we could add new edits only when we were *inProgress*, and only after calling end( ) could undo( ) or redo( ) be called. In contrast, UndoManager allows undo( ) and redo( ) to be called while it is *inProgress*. Furthermore, when end( ) is called, it stops supporting sequential undo/redo behavior and starts acting like CompoundEdit (undo( ) and redo( ) call their superclass implementations when the UndoManager is not *inProgress*).

For the strong-hearted,[*] Figure 18-6 shows a state chart for the UndoManager class.[†] For several reasons, this chart is considerably more complicated than the ones in the previous sections. First, as mentioned earlier, UndoManager has the curious behavior that once end( ) is called, it begins to act (for the most part) like a CompoundEdit. This is why we have the transition from the *inProgress* state to a new superstate (*notInProgress*, for lack of a better name), the contents of which look just like the CompoundEdit state chart (see Figure 18-4).

This state chart is also complicated because, within the *inProgress* state, whether we are *undoable*, *redoable*, or both (*undoableOrRedoable*) depends on whether all of the edits have been undone or redone. For example, if there are two edits in the UndoManager and we've undone one, we are *undoableOrRedoable*. We can undo the remaining edit, or redo the one we've undone. If we choose to undo the remaining edit, we go from *undoableOrRedoable* to *redoable* since there are no more edits to undo. However, if there were still more undoable edits, we'd have stayed in the

---

[*] All others might want to skip ahead to the description of Figure 18-7.

[†] This chart assumes that all edits are significant. For details on why this is important, see the descriptions of the editToBeUndone( ) and editToBeRedone( ) methods later in this section.

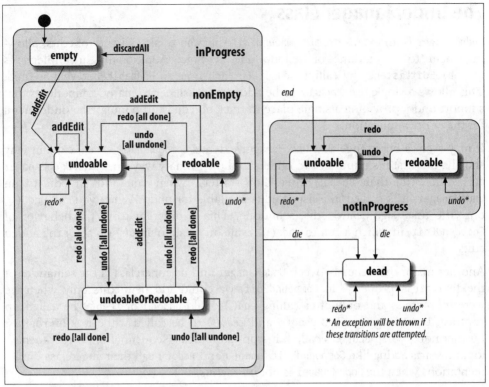

Figure 18-6. UndoManager state chart

undoableOrRedoable state. Or, if we'd chosen to redo the undone edit, there would be no more redoable edits, so we'd go from *undoableOrRedoable* to *undoable*.

Another factor that contributes to the complexity is that any time we add a new edit, we are no longer able to redo past undos because the new edit takes the place of the last undone edit, and all pending redoable edits are dropped. Therefore, any time we add an edit, we go to the *undoable* state.

A Codeless Example

Figure 18-7 attempts to simplify the explanation of UndoManager state transitions by showing how the UndoManager handles additions, undos, and redos for a sample scenario. This example shows that the most typical use of UndoManager is straightforward, despite all its complexity. We add three edits to the UndoManager and then undo each of them. We then redo the first edit. At this point, we could redo the second edit or undo the first edit again. In the example, we instead add a new edit. Adding an edit causes any edits that appear later in the list (those edits that originated latest) to be lost. In this example, that causes our initial second and third edits to be dropped from the manager before the new edit is added. Finally, we undo this new edit.

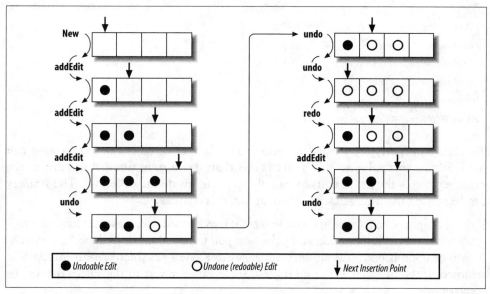

Figure 18-7. UndoManager example

Transformer?

Probably the most nonintuitive things about the design of UndoManager are its extension from CompoundEdit and the fact that after its end( ) method is called, an UndoManager is essentially transformed into a CompoundEdit. The idea is to use an UndoManager in a temporary capacity during a specific editing task and then later be able to treat all of the edits given to the UndoManager as a single CompoundEdit.

As an example, consider a spreadsheet application. The process of editing the formula for a single cell can be managed by an UndoManager, allowing small changes to be undone and redone. Once the formula has been committed, the UndoManager's end( ) method can be called, and the manager begins to act like a CompoundEdit. This edit can then be handed off to a primary undo manager, allowing the entire formula change to be undone as a single edit.

Properties

UndoManager defines the properties shown in Table 18-6.

Table 18-6. UndoManager properties

Property	Data type	get	is	set	Default value
limit	int	•		•	100
redoPresentationName°	String	•			"Redo"
undoOrRedoPresentationName	String	•			"Undo"
undoPresentationName°	String	•			"Undo"

°overridden

See also properties from the CompoundEdit class (Table 18-4).

The limit property represents the maximum number of edits the UndoManager can hold. Setting this value so that limit is less than the current number of edits in the manager causes the list of edits to be reduced to fit inside the new limit. The strategy for decreasing the list size is described later in this chapter.

If the manager is *inProgress*, the redoPresentationName and undoPresentationName properties are set to the values returned by the next edit to be redone or undone, respectively. If redo or undo is not possible, AbstractUndoEdit.Redo or AbstractUndoableEdit.Undo is returned. If the manager is not *inProgress*, these values revert to the values defined by CompoundEdit.

A new property, undoOrRedoPresentationName, is defined in this class. This property is used only when limit is set to 1. It returns the value of undoPresentationName if the single edit was not undone, or the value of redoPresentationName if it was.

Constructor

public UndoManager()
  Create a new manager containing no edits, with a limit of 100.

UndoableEditListener Method

This method is defined in the UndoableEditListener interface implemented by UndoManager:

public void undoableEditHappened(UndoableEditEvent e)
  Call addEdit( ), passing in the UndoableEdit stored in the input event.

UndoableEdit Methods

UndoManager overrides the following UndoableEdit methods:

public synchronized boolean addEdit(UndoableEdit anEdit)
  If the manager is *inProgress*, this method adds anEdit at the current insertion point. Any undone edits are removed from the manager, and die( ) is called on

each of them in reverse order (the last edit added is killed first). If the manager is not *inProgress*, this method returns `false`.

public synchronized boolean canRedo( )

> If the `UndoManager` is *inProgress*, this method uses `editToBeRedone( )` (described later) to find the next significant redoable edit. If an edit is found, and it returns `true` when `canRedo( )` is called on it, this method returns `true`. If the manager is not *inProgress*, `super.canRedo( )` is called, making the manager act like a `CompoundEdit`.

public synchronized boolean canUndo( )

> If the `UndoManager` is *inProgress*, this method uses `editToBeUndone( )` to find the next significant undoable edit. If an edit is found and returns `true` when `canUndo( )` is called on it, this method returns `true`. If the manager is not *inProgress*, `super.canUndo( )` is called, making the manager act like a `CompoundEdit`.

public synchronized void redo( ) throws CannotRedoException

> If the `UndoManager` is *inProgress*, this method uses `editToBeRedone( )` to find the next significant redoable edit (the most recently undone edit). If an edit is found, `redoTo( )` is called to redo all edits up to the next significant one. If no edit is found, an exception is thrown. If the manager is not *inProgress*, `super.redo( )` is called, making the manager act like a `CompoundEdit`.

public synchronized void undo( ) throws CannotUndoException

> If the `UndoManager` is *inProgress*, this method uses `editToBeUndone( )` to find the next significant undoable edit. If an edit is found, `undoTo( )` is called to undo all edits up to the next significant one. If no edit is found, an exception is thrown. If the manager is not *inProgress*, `super.undo( )` is called, making the manager act like a `CompoundEdit`.

 Calling `undo( )` and then calling `redo( )` does not necessarily put you right back where you started. Any insignificant edits undone by the `undo( )` call are not redone by a subsequent `redo( )` call.

Public Methods

The following methods are introduced in the `UndoManager` class:

public synchronized void discardAllEdits( )

> Remove all edits from the `UndoManager`, calling `die( )` on them in the order they were added.

public synchronized boolean canUndoOrRedo( )

> This method is intended to be used when the manager is limited to holding a single edit (`limit == 1`). If the edit has been undone, it returns the result of a call to `canRedo( )`; otherwise, it returns the result of a call to `canUndo( )`.

public synchronized void undoOrRedo() throws CannotRedoException, CannotUndoException

> This method is intended to be used when the manager is limited to holding a single edit (`limit == 1`). If the edit has been undone, it calls `redo()`; otherwise, it calls `undo()`.

Protected Methods

These methods are used internally by the `UndoManager` to manage its list of edits. They provide support for ignoring insignificant edits and removing edits that are no longer accessible.

protected UndoableEdit editToBeRedone()

> Return the next edit to be redone. This is simply the last significant edit that was undone. Any insignificant edits are skipped. If there are no significant redoable edits available, this method returns `null`.

protected UndoableEdit editToBeUndone()

> Return the next edit to be undone. This is the last significant edit that was either redone or added. Any insignificant edits are skipped. If there are no significant undoable edits available, this method returns `null`.

protected void trimEdits(int from, int to)

> Remove the specified range of edits from the manager (if `from` is greater than `to`, it does nothing). The `die()` method is called on each removed edit in reverse order (`to` down to `from`). If the insertion point was within the trimmed range, it is reset to the value of `from`.

protected void trimForLimit()

> Reduce the number of edits to fit within the set `limit` for this manager. If the number of edits is not greater than `limit`, it does nothing. Otherwise, it removes edits from either end of the list (or both), trying to end up with equal numbers of undoable and redoable edits (or as close as possible). For example, if there are 10 edits, half of which had been undone, and `limit` is reduced to 6, the first 2 undone edits (those that were undone first) and the first 2 edits added (those that would be undone last) are removed. This leaves six edits (the new `limit`), three of which have been undone.

protected void redoTo(UndoableEdit edit) throws CannotRedoException

> Start with the last undone edit and call `redo()` on each edit in the list, stopping after calling `redo()` on the input edit. An `ArrayIndexOutOfBoundsException` will be thrown if the input edit is not found before reaching the end of the edit list.

protected void undoTo(UndoableEdit edit) throws CannotUndoException

> Start with the last redone or added edit and call `undo()` on each edit in the list, stopping after calling `undo()` on the input edit. An `ArrayIndexOutOfBoundsException`

will be thrown if the input edit is not found before reaching the beginning of the edit list.

Using an Undo Manager

In the previous examples, we created UndoableEdits in our main program each time we were notified of an action that we wanted to allow the user to undo. A more desirable strategy is to make the component that generated the action responsible for creating the UndoableEdit and firing an UndoableEditEvent, passing us the edit. Using an UndoManager, we can then easily provide the user with the ability to undo and redo as many changes as necessary.

For this example to work, we need to provide a component that generates UndoableEdits and allows UndoableEditListeners to be added and removed. In keeping with the examples provided so far in this chapter, we'll do this by creating an extension of JToggleButton that fires an UndoableEditEvent each time its state is toggled. This event will contain an UndoableToggleEdit (the class introduced in the "Creating a toggle edit" section) that can be used to undo the toggle. To keep the example as simple as possible, we'll allow only a single listener to be added to the button. In a real application, you should maintain a list of interested listeners instead.* Here's the code for this event-generating button class:

```
// UndoableJToggleButton.java
//
import java.awt.event.*;
import javax.swing.*;
import javax.swing.event.*;
import javax.swing.undo.*;

// Sample undoable toggle button class. Supports only a single listener to
// simplify the code.
public class UndoableJToggleButton extends JToggleButton {
  private UndoableEditListener listener;

  // For this example, we'll just provide one constructor.
  public UndoableJToggleButton(String txt) {
    super(txt);
  }

  // Set the UndoableEditListener.
  public void addUndoableEditListener(UndoableEditListener l) {
    listener = l; // Should ideally throw an exception if listener != null
  }

  // Remove the UndoableEditListener.
  public void removeUndoableEditListener(UndoableEditListener l) {
```

* Later in the chapter, we'll introduce UndoableEditSupport, a class that simplifies this process.

```
        listener = null;
    }

    // We override this method to call the super implementation first (to fire the
    // action event) and then fire a new UndoableEditEvent to our listener.
    protected void fireActionPerformed(ActionEvent ev) {

        // Fire the ActionEvent as usual.
        super.fireActionPerformed(ev);

        if (listener != null) {
            listener.undoableEditHappened(new UndoableEditEvent(this,
                new UndoableToggleEdit(this)));
        }
    }
  }
}
```

As you can see, all we've done here is override `fireActionPerformed()` so that each
time an `ActionEvent` is fired (indicating that the button was toggled), we also create
and fire a new `UndoableEditEvent`. Of course, the strategy for generating edits varies
considerably based on the type of class you're making undoable.

Now let's look at a program that uses an `UndoManager` to allow the undo of multiple
toggle button edits. In this example, we'll create three `UndoableJToggleButtons` and
provide undo and redo buttons that allow the user to undo and redo up to 100 (the
default limit) button toggles.

This example doesn't take advantage of the fact that `UndoManager` implements
`UndoableEditListener` by adding the manager as a listener to our undoable buttons.
We want to do more than track the edit when it is generated; we also want to update
the user interface so that the user knows that the undo and redo options are available. To support this, we instead add our own `UndoableEditListener` inner class, calling `addEdit()` on the `UndoManager` each time an event is fired and then updating our
undo and redo buttons appropriately.

 Lack of listener support has been identified by the Swing team as an
important hole in the current `UndoManager`. Look for more support in
this area in a future release. At the end of the chapter, we show how
you can extend the current `UndoManager` to give it better listener
support.

Here's the source code, again similar in structure to the previous examples:

```
// UndoableToggleApp3.java
//
import javax.swing.*;
import javax.swing.event.*;
import javax.swing.undo.*;
import java.awt.*;
import java.awt.event.*;
```

```java
// A sample app showing the use of UndoManager
public class UndoableToggleApp3 extends JFrame {

    private UndoManager manager = new UndoManager();
    private JButton undoButton;
    private JButton redoButton;

    // Create the main frame and everything in it.
    public UndoableToggleApp3() {

        // Create some toggle buttons.
        UndoableJToggleButton tog1 = new UndoableJToggleButton("One");
        UndoableJToggleButton tog2 = new UndoableJToggleButton("Two");
        UndoableJToggleButton tog3 = new UndoableJToggleButton("Three");

        // Add our listener to each toggle button.
        SimpleUEListener sl = new SimpleUEListener();
        tog1.addUndoableEditListener(sl);
        tog2.addUndoableEditListener(sl);
        tog3.addUndoableEditListener(sl);

        // Lay out the buttons.
        Box buttonBox = new Box(BoxLayout.Y_AXIS);
        buttonBox.add(tog1);
        buttonBox.add(tog2);
        buttonBox.add(tog3);

        // Create undo and redo buttons (initially disabled).
        undoButton = new JButton("Undo");
        redoButton = new JButton("Redo");
        undoButton.setEnabled(false);
        redoButton.setEnabled(false);

        // Add a listener to the undo button. It attempts to call undo() on the
        // UndoManager, then enables/disables the undo/redo buttons as appropriate.
        undoButton.addActionListener(new ActionListener() {
            public void actionPerformed(ActionEvent ev) {
                try {
                    manager.undo();
                } catch (CannotUndoException ex) { ex.printStackTrace(); }
                finally {
                    updateButtons();
                }
            }
        });

        // Add a redo listener, which is just like the undo listener.
        redoButton.addActionListener(new ActionListener() {
            public void actionPerformed(ActionEvent ev) {
                try {
                    manager.redo();
                } catch (CannotRedoException ex) { ex.printStackTrace(); }
                finally {
                    updateButtons();
```

```
          }
        }
      });

      // Lay out the undo/redo buttons.
      Box undoRedoBox = new Box(BoxLayout.X_AXIS);
      undoRedoBox.add(Box.createGlue( ));
      undoRedoBox.add(undoButton);
      undoRedoBox.add(Box.createHorizontalStrut(2));
      undoRedoBox.add(redoButton);
      undoRedoBox.add(Box.createGlue( ));

      // Lay out the main frame.
      getContentPane( ).setLayout(new BorderLayout( ));
      getContentPane( ).add(buttonBox, BorderLayout.CENTER);
      getContentPane( ).add(undoRedoBox, BorderLayout.SOUTH);
      setSize(400, 150);
  }

  public class SimpleUEListener implements UndoableEditListener {
    // When an UndoableEditEvent is generated (each time one of the buttons is
    // pressed), we add it to the UndoManager and then get the manager's undo/redo
    // names and set the undo/redo button labels. Finally, we enable/disable these
    // buttons by asking the manager what we are allowed to do.
    public void undoableEditHappened(UndoableEditEvent ev) {
      manager.addEdit(ev.getEdit( ));
      updateButtons( );
    }
  }

  // Method to set the text and state of the undo/redo buttons
  protected void updateButtons( ) {
    undoButton.setText(manager.getUndoPresentationName( ));
    redoButton.setText(manager.getRedoPresentationName( ));
    undoButton.getParent( ).validate( );
    undoButton.setEnabled(manager.canUndo( ));
    redoButton.setEnabled(manager.canRedo( ));
  }

  // Main program just creates the frame and displays it
  public static void main(String[] args) {
    JFrame f = new UndoableToggleApp3( );
    f.setDefaultCloseOperation(JFrame.EXIT_ON_CLOSE);
    f.setVisible(true);
  }
}
```

Figure 18-8 shows the application running. Before taking this screenshot, we toggled each of the buttons in order and then undid the third toggle. Notice that we can now retoggle button Three or undo the previous toggle (button Two).

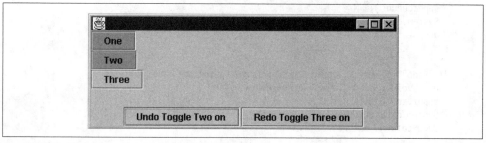

Figure 18-8. Undoing and redoing toggle buttons

Understanding the UndoManager

There are a lot of subtle details about `UndoManager` that may be hard to understand without seeing them in action. In this section, we'll try to provide a concrete example of how all these little things work. To do so, let's create a very simple `UndoableEdit` implementation that is not associated with any component. It will help us see what the `UndoManager` is doing in certain situations. All this class does is output various bits of useful information when its methods are called:

```
// SampleUndoableEdit.java
//
import javax.swing.undo.*;
import java.util.*;

public class SampleUndoableEdit extends AbstractUndoableEdit {

  private boolean isSignificant;
  private boolean isReplacer;
  private int number;
  private boolean allowAdds;
  private Vector addedEdits;
  private UndoableEdit replaced;

  // Create a new edit with an identifying number. The boolean arguments define
  // the edit's behavior.
  public SampleUndoableEdit(int number, boolean allowAdds,
                            boolean isSignificant,
                            boolean isReplacer) {
    this.number = number;
    this.allowAdds = allowAdds;
    if (allowAdds)
      addedEdits = new Vector();
    this.isSignificant = isSignificant;
    this.isReplacer = isReplacer;
  }

  // "Undo" the edit by printing a message to the screen.
  public void undo() throws CannotUndoException {
```

```
    super.undo();
    System.out.print("Undo " + number);
    dumpState();
}

// "Redo" the edit by printing a message to the screen.
public void redo() throws CannotRedoException {
    super.redo();
    System.out.print("Redo " + number);
    dumpState();
}

// If allowAdds is true, we store the input edit. If not, just return false.
public boolean addEdit(UndoableEdit anEdit) {
    if (allowAdds) {
        addedEdits.addElement(anEdit);
        return true;
    }
    else
        return false;
}

// If isReplacer is true, we store the edit we are replacing.
public boolean replaceEdit(UndoableEdit anEdit) {
    if (isReplacer) {
        replaced = anEdit;
        return true;
    }
    else
        return false;
}

// Significance is based on constructor parameter.
public boolean isSignificant() {
    return isSignificant;
}

// Just return our identifier.
public String toString() {
    return "<" + number + ">";
}

// Debug output.
public void dumpState() {
    if (allowAdds && addedEdits.size() > 0) {
        Enumeration e = addedEdits.elements();
        System.out.print(" (absorbed: ");
        while (e.hasMoreElements()) {
            System.out.print(e.nextElement());
        }
        System.out.print(")");
    }
```

```
      if (isReplacer && replaced != null) {
        System.out.print(" (replaced: " + replaced + ")");
      }
      System.out.println( );
    }
  }
```

In our main program, we'll add instances of this new edit class to an UndoManager to show how different features work. We won't step through this program line by line. The comments in the code and in the output serve as an explanation of the different UndoManager features (and quirks) being shown:

```java
// UndoManagerDetails.java
//
import javax.swing.undo.*;

// An example that shows lots of little UndoManager details
public class UndoManagerDetails {
  public static void main(String[] args) {
    UndoManager mgr = new UndoManager( );

    // Show how insignificant edits are skipped over.
    //
    //                                # adds? sig? replace?
    mgr.addEdit(new SampleUndoableEdit(1, false, true, false));
    mgr.addEdit(new SampleUndoableEdit(2, false, true, false));
    mgr.addEdit(new SampleUndoableEdit(3, false, false, false));
    mgr.addEdit(new SampleUndoableEdit(4, false, false, false));

    System.out.println("-------------------------");
    System.out.println("Insignificant edit example");
    System.out.println("-------------------------");
    mgr.undo( );
    mgr.redo( );
    System.out.println(mgr.canRedo( )); // No more sig. edits

    // Show how edits that call add/replace are used.
    //
    //                                # adds? sig? replace?
    mgr.addEdit(new SampleUndoableEdit(5, true,  true, false));
    mgr.addEdit(new SampleUndoableEdit(6, false, true, false));
    System.out.println("--------------------------------");
    System.out.println("Absorbed (by addEdit) edit example");
    System.out.println("--------------------------------");
    mgr.undo( );
    mgr.discardAllEdits( );

    //                                # adds? sig? replace?
    mgr.addEdit(new SampleUndoableEdit(1, false, true, false));
    mgr.addEdit(new SampleUndoableEdit(2, false, true, true));
    System.out.println("-----------------------------------");
    System.out.println("Absorbed (by replaceEdit) edit example");
    System.out.println("-----------------------------------");
```

```
mgr.undo( );
System.out.println(mgr.canUndo( ));

// Show how changing limit works.
mgr.discardAllEdits( );

//                                  # adds? sig? replace?
mgr.addEdit(new SampleUndoableEdit(1, false, true, false));
mgr.addEdit(new SampleUndoableEdit(2, false, true, false));
mgr.addEdit(new SampleUndoableEdit(3, false, true, false));
mgr.addEdit(new SampleUndoableEdit(4, false, true, false));
mgr.addEdit(new SampleUndoableEdit(5, false, true, false));
mgr.addEdit(new SampleUndoableEdit(6, false, true, false));
System.out.println("----------------------");
System.out.println("Changing limit example");
System.out.println("----------------------");
mgr.undo( );
mgr.undo( );
mgr.undo( );          // Now 3 undoable, 3 redoable
mgr.setLimit(4); // Now 2 undoable, 2 redoable!
while (mgr.canUndo( ))
  mgr.undo( );
while (mgr.canRedo( ))
  mgr.redo( );

// undoOrRedo example
mgr.discardAllEdits( );
mgr.setLimit(1);

//                                  # adds? sig? replace?
mgr.addEdit(new SampleUndoableEdit(1, false, true, false));
System.out.println("------------------");
System.out.println("undoOrRedo example");
System.out.println("------------------");
System.out.println(mgr.getUndoOrRedoPresentationName( ));
mgr.undoOrRedo( );
System.out.println(mgr.getUndoOrRedoPresentationName( ));
mgr.undoOrRedo( );

// Show how UndoManager becomes a CompositeEdit.
mgr.discardAllEdits( );
mgr.setLimit(100);

//                                  # adds? sig? replace?
mgr.addEdit(new SampleUndoableEdit(1, false, true, false));
mgr.addEdit(new SampleUndoableEdit(2, false, true, false));
mgr.addEdit(new SampleUndoableEdit(3, false, true, false));
System.out.println("------------------------------");
System.out.println("Transform to composite example");
System.out.println("------------------------------");
mgr.end( );
mgr.undo( );
mgr.redo( );
```

```
        // Show that adds are no longer allowed. Note that addEdit( ) returns true in
        // pre-JDK 1.2 Swing releases. This is fixed in JDK 1.2.
        System.out.println(mgr.addEdit(
          new SampleUndoableEdit(4, false, true, false)));
        mgr.undo( ); // Note that edit 4 is not there.
      }
    }
```

Here's the output generated by this program. We've added some comments to the output in *constant width italic*.

```
--------------------------
Insignificant edit example
--------------------------
Undo 4 // Three undos from a single mgr.undo( ) call
Undo 3
Undo 2
Redo 2 // But mgr.redo( ) only redoes the significant one!
false  // ...and there are no more redos
--------------------------------
Absorbed (by addEdit) edit example
--------------------------------
Undo 5 (absorbed: <6>) // Edit 6 was absorbed by edit 5 and undone.
-------------------------------------
Absorbed (by replaceEdit) edit example
-------------------------------------
Undo 2 (replaced: <1>) // Edit 1 was replaced by edit 2 and undone.
false // No more edits to undo
---------------------
Changing limit example
---------------------
Undo 6 // We perform three undos...
Undo 5
Undo 4 // ...and then set the limit to 4, which trims from both ends.
Undo 3 // Only two undos left...
Undo 2
Redo 2 // and then four redos are available.
Redo 3
Redo 4
Redo 5
-----------------
undoOrRedo example
-----------------
Undo    // undoOrRedoPresentationName is "Undo" here...
Undo 1 // ...then we do an undoOrRedo( )...
Redo    // ...and it's now "Redo".
Redo 1
-----------------------------
Transform to composite example
-----------------------------
Undo 3 // Because we called end( ), undo( ) undoes all the edits...
Undo 2
Undo 1
```

```
Redo 1 // ...and redo() redoes them all.
Redo 2
Redo 3
true   // addEdit() claims the edit was added (returns false in JDK 1.2),
Undo 3 // but edit 4 never got added because end() had been called.
Undo 2
Undo 1
```

All the details in this example can be a little overwhelming, but don't let this keep you from using UndoManager. For most applications, the basic features of UndoManager (shown in the first example in this section) give you everything you need to provide your users with powerful undo capabilities.

At the end of this chapter, we'll show how you might extend UndoManager to add functionality. We'll create an undo manager that gives us access to the edits it contains and notifies us any time an edit is added.

The StateEditable Interface

So far in this chapter, we've seen that the responsibility for undoing or redoing an edit lies in the UndoableEdit object itself. The Swing undo package provides another mechanism for handling undo and redo, which is based on the idea of letting an "outside object" define its state before and after a series of changes are made to it. Once these *pre* and *post* states of the object are defined, a StateEdit toggles back and forth between these states, undoing and redoing the changes. The outside object is responsible for defining the object's significant state and must implement the StateEditable interface, which defines the methods listed below.

Methods

StateEditable defines two simple methods:

public void storeState(Hashtable state)
> Called to ask the object to store its current state by inserting attributes and values as key/value pairs into the given Hashtable.

public void restoreState(Hashtable state)
> Called to tell the object to restore its state, based on the key/value pairs found in the given Hashtable.

The StateEdit Class

StateEdit is an extension of AbstractUndoableEdit that is used to toggle between two arbitrary states. These states are defined by a StateEditable associated with the StateEdit. When the edit is created, it gets the current (*pre*) state from the StateEditable. Later, when end() is called on the edit (presumably after some changes have been made to the state of the StateEditable), it again gets the current (*post*) state from the StateEditable. After this point, undo() and redo() calls result in the state of the StateEditable being toggled back and forth between the *pre* and *post* states. Figure 18-9 shows a typical sequence of method calls between an application object (some object in the system that is managing edits), a StateEdit, its StateEditable, and the two Hashtables used to store the state of the StateEditable.

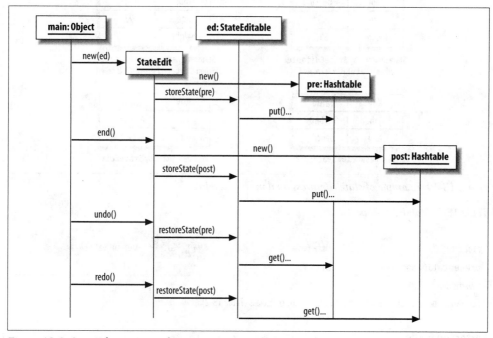

Figure 18-9. StateEdit sequence diagram

State optimization

It's important to understand that StateEdit optimizes its representation of the states returned by the StateEditable. This is done by removing all duplicate key/value pairs from the *pre* and *post* Hashtables, keeping only those values that have changed. This is important to understand because it means the StateEditable cannot assume that all keys and values stored by its storeState( ) method are in the table that is passed into restoreState( ).

Figure 18-10 shows an example of how this works. The top two tables show the complete state as returned by the StateEditable. The bottom two tables show the tables as they appear after StateEdit.end( ) has compressed them to remove duplicate data. This is how the tables would look when passed to StateEditable.restoreState( ).

Property

Table 18-7 shows the default property value defined by StateEdit. The presentationName property defaults to null if not specified in the StateEdit constructor. All other properties are defined by the superclass.

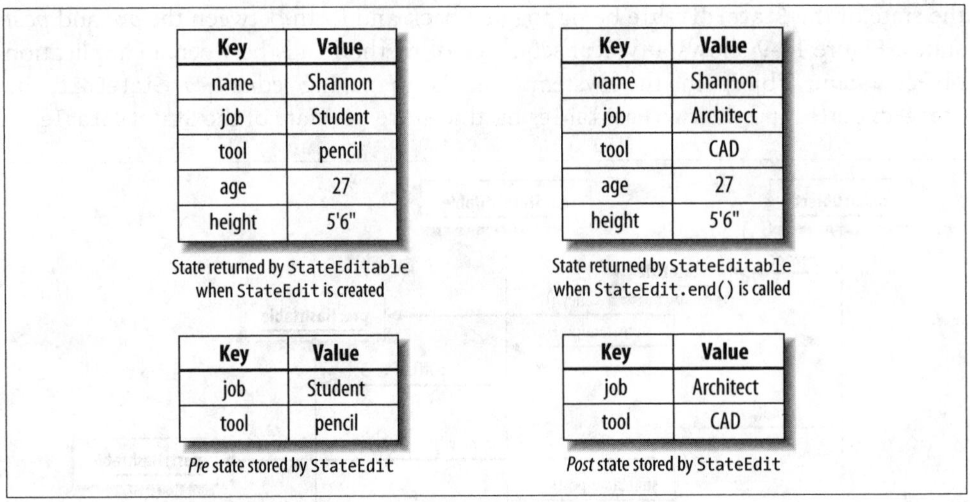

Key	Value
name	Shannon
job	Student
tool	pencil
age	27
height	5'6"

State returned by StateEditable
when StateEdit is created

Key	Value
name	Shannon
job	Architect
tool	CAD
age	27
height	5'6"

State returned by StateEditable
when StateEdit.end() is called

Key	Value
job	Student
tool	pencil

Pre state stored by StateEdit

Key	Value
job	Architect
tool	CAD

Post state stored by StateEdit

Figure 18-10. Example of state compression done by StateEdit

Table 18-7. StateEdit property

Property	Data type	get	is	set	Default value
presentationName°	String			•	null

°overridden

See also properties from the AbstractUndoableEdit class (Table 18-2).

Protected fields

The following fields are available to subclasses of StateEdit:

protected StateEditable object
> The StateEditable associated with this edit.

protected Hashtable preState
protected Hashtable postState
> The Hashtables used to store the state information.

protected String undoRedoName
> The presentation name used for this edit.

Constructors

public StateEdit(StateEditable anObject)
> Create a new edit that saves and restores its state using the given StateEditable. StateEdit calls init( ) to set up the initial state.

public StateEdit(StateEditable anObject, String name)
> Create a new edit that saves and restores its state using the given StateEditable. It uses the given name as its presentationName and calls init( ) to set up the initial state.

UndoableEdit methods

The following methods override the `AbstractUndoableEdit` implementations of methods in the `UndoableEdit` interface. These methods should be called only after end( ), but they don't enforce this restriction and thus may produce confusing results.* In practice, you should ensure that end( ) is called before allowing undo( ) or redo( ) to be called on the edit.

public void redo( )†

Call `super.redo( )` to ensure that the edit can be redone and then call `restoreState( )` on the edit's `StateEditable`, passing in the `Hashtable` that was populated when end( ) was called on the edit.

public void undo( )‡

Call `super.undo( )` to ensure that the edit can be undone and then call `restoreState( )` on the edit's `StateEditable`, passing in the `Hashtable` that was populated when the edit was constructed.

New public method

The following new method is defined in this class.

public void end( )

Called to indicate that the state of the `StateEditable` has changed. The `storeState( )` method is called on the `StateEditable` to determine its *post* state. This method then uses `removeRedundantState( )` to compress the *pre* and *post* state `Hashtables`. Note that the `StateEdit` is not fully ready to handle undo( ) and redo( ) requests until this method has been called.

Protected methods

protected void init (StateEditable anObject, String name)

Called by the constructors to set the initial state of the edit. It stores the input `StateEditable` and edit name (used for the `presentationName` property) and creates a new `Hashtable`, which it passes to the input `StateEditable`'s `storeState( )` method. This new `Hashtable` now holds the edit's *pre* state.

---

* Calling undo( ) basically works. The problem is that a subsequent call to canRedo( ) would then return true. However, if you then called redo( ), the Hashtable passed to restoreState( ) would be null since it is not created until end( ) is called. Future Swing releases will probably throw exceptions in these abnormal cases.

† CannotRedoException is not listed in the throws clause of this method as it was in the superclass version. This is valid only because this exception extends RuntimeException. Since super.redo( ) is called, this method *will* throw a CannotRedoException if the edit has already been undone.

‡ CannotUndoException is not listed in the throws clause of this method as it was in the superclass version. This is valid only because this exception extends RuntimeException. Since super.undo( ) is called, this method *will* throw a CannotUndoException if the edit has already been undone.

protected void removeRedundantState( )

This method is called by end( ) to remove any duplicate key/value pairs from the *pre* and *post* Hashtables. Only entries that have the same key and value are removed from the tables. Comparisons are done using the equals( ) method. See Figure 18-10 for an illustration of how this method is used.

StateEdit example

Here's one last version of our toggle button application. In this example, we'll use a StateEdit to store the state of all three toggle buttons. The user can determine when we start and stop the creation of the edit (buttons are provided for these functions). The main application frame serves as the StateEditable, and its storeState( ) method stores the selected property of each of its buttons in the input Hashtable. The boldface code shows the differences between this example and UndoableToggleApp2:

```java
// UndoableToggleApp4.java
//
import javax.swing.*;
import javax.swing.event.*;
import javax.swing.undo.*;
import java.awt.*;
import java.awt.event.*;
import java.util.Hashtable;

// A sample app showing the use of StateEdit(able)
public class UndoableToggleApp4 extends JFrame implements StateEditable {

    private JToggleButton tog;
    private JCheckBox cb;
    private JRadioButton radio;

    private JButton undoButton;
    private JButton redoButton;
    private JButton startButton;
    private JButton endButton;

    private StateEdit edit;

    // Create the main frame and everything in it.
    public UndoableToggleApp4( ) {

        // Create some toggle buttons (and subclasses).
        tog = new JToggleButton("ToggleButton");
        cb = new JCheckBox("CheckBox");
        radio = new JRadioButton("RadioButton");

        // Add our listener to the buttons.
        SimpleListener sl = new SimpleListener( );
        tog.addActionListener(sl);
        cb.addActionListener(sl);
        radio.addActionListener(sl);
```

```
// Lay out the buttons.
Box buttonBox = new Box(BoxLayout.Y_AXIS);
buttonBox.add(tog);
buttonBox.add(cb);
buttonBox.add(radio);

// Create undo, redo, start, and end buttons.
startButton = new JButton("Start");
endButton = new JButton("End");
undoButton = new JButton("Undo");
redoButton = new JButton("Redo");
startButton.setEnabled(true);
endButton.setEnabled(false);
undoButton.setEnabled(false);
redoButton.setEnabled(false);

// Add a listener to the start button. It creates a new StateEdit,
// passing in this frame as the StateEditable.
startButton.addActionListener(new ActionListener() {
  public void actionPerformed(ActionEvent ev) {
    edit = new StateEdit(UndoableToggleApp4.this);
    startButton.setEnabled(false);
    endButton.setEnabled(true);
    // undoButton.setEnabled(edit.canUndo());
    //
    // NOTE: We really don't want to be able to undo until end() is pressed,
    // but StateEdit does not enforce this for us!
    undoButton.setEnabled(false);
    redoButton.setEnabled(edit.canRedo());
  }
});

// Add a listener to the end button. It will call end() on the StateEdit.
endButton.addActionListener(new ActionListener() {
  public void actionPerformed(ActionEvent ev) {
    edit.end();
    startButton.setEnabled(true);
    endButton.setEnabled(false);
    undoButton.setEnabled(edit.canUndo());
    redoButton.setEnabled(edit.canRedo());
  }
});

// Add a listener to the undo button. It attempts to call undo() on the
// current edit, then enables/disables the undo/redo buttons as appropriate.
undoButton.addActionListener(new ActionListener() {
  public void actionPerformed(ActionEvent ev) {
    try {
      edit.undo();
    } catch (CannotUndoException ex) { ex.printStackTrace(); }
```

```
      finally {
        undoButton.setEnabled(edit.canUndo( ));
        redoButton.setEnabled(edit.canRedo( ));
      }
    }
  }
});

  // Add a redo listener, which is just like the undo listener.
  redoButton.addActionListener(new ActionListener( ) {
    public void actionPerformed(ActionEvent ev) {
      try {
        edit.redo( );
      } catch (CannotRedoException ex) { ex.printStackTrace( ); }
      finally {
        undoButton.setEnabled(edit.canUndo( ));
        redoButton.setEnabled(edit.canRedo( ));
      }
    }
  });

  // Lay out the state/end and undo/redo buttons.
  Box undoRedoBox = new Box(BoxLayout.X_AXIS);
  undoRedoBox.add(Box.createGlue( ));
  undoRedoBox.add(startButton);
  undoRedoBox.add(Box.createHorizontalStrut(2));
  undoRedoBox.add(endButton);
  undoRedoBox.add(Box.createHorizontalStrut(2));
  undoRedoBox.add(undoButton);
  undoRedoBox.add(Box.createHorizontalStrut(2));
  undoRedoBox.add(redoButton);
  undoRedoBox.add(Box.createGlue( ));

  // Lay out the main frame.
  Container content = getContentPane( );
  content.setLayout(new BorderLayout( ));
  content.add(buttonBox, BorderLayout.CENTER);
  content.add(undoRedoBox, BorderLayout.SOUTH);
  setSize(400, 150);
}

public class SimpleListener implements ActionListener {
  // When any toggle button is clicked, we turn off the undo and redo buttons,
  // reflecting the fact that we can only undo/redo the last set of state changes
  // as long as no additional changes have been made.
  public void actionPerformed(ActionEvent ev) {
    undoButton.setEnabled(false);
    redoButton.setEnabled(false);
  }
}

// Save the state of the app by storing the current state of the three buttons.
// We'll use the buttons themselves as keys and their selected state as values.
public void storeState(Hashtable ht) {
  ht.put(tog, new Boolean(tog.isSelected( )));
```

```
      ht.put(cb, new Boolean(cb.isSelected()));
      ht.put(radio, new Boolean(radio.isSelected()));
  }

  // Restore state based on the values we saved when storeState() was called. Note
  // that StateEdit discards any state info that did not change from between the
  // start state and the end state, so we can't assume that the state for all three
  // buttons is in the Hashtable.
  public void restoreState(Hashtable ht) {
    Boolean b1 = (Boolean)ht.get(tog);
    if (b1 != null)
      tog.setSelected(b1.booleanValue());
    Boolean b2 = (Boolean)ht.get(cb);
    if (b2 != null)
      cb.setSelected(b2.booleanValue());
    Boolean b3 = (Boolean)ht.get(radio);
    if (b3 != null)
      radio.setSelected(b3.booleanValue());
  }

  // Main program just creates the frame and displays it
  public static void main(String[] args) {
    JFrame f = new UndoableToggleApp4();
    f.setDefaultCloseOperation(JFrame.EXIT_ON_CLOSE);
    f.setVisible(true);
  }
}
```

Note that we could have used whatever keys and values we needed to store the current state in the storeState() method. We simplified this example by using the button itself as the key and a Boolean to hold the value. There are no restrictions on the keys and values you choose, as long as they are Objects, and the storeState() and restoreState() methods are implemented to use the same keys.

The UndoableEditSupport Class

UndoableEditSupport is a simple utility class for classes that need to support undo.[*] It provides methods for adding and removing UndoableEditListeners, as well as a postEdit() method used to send an UndoableEditEvent to the added listeners. Additionally, it allows multiple edits to be added to it and fired as a single CompoundEdit.

Properties

UndoableEditSupport defines the properties shown in Table 18-8. updateLevel reflects the current level of nesting of beginUpdate() calls. (See "Nested edit support" later in

---

[*] Presently, none of the Swing classes that support undo actually use this class. Instead, they manage their edits and listeners themselves.

this section for more information on this property.) As with other event-generating classes in Swing, a convenience property to retrieve currently registered listeners—undoableEditListeners in this case—was added in SDK 1.4.

Table 18-8. UndoableEditSupport properties

Property	Data type	get	is	set	Default value
undoableEditListeners[1.4]	UndoableEditListener[]	•			Empty array
updateLevel	int	•			0

[1.4]since 1.4

Protected fields

The following fields are available to subclasses of UndoableEditSupport:

protected CompoundEdit compoundEdit
This is the edit used to group together multiple edits that are added between beginUpdate( ) and endUpdate( ) calls. See "Nested edit support" later in this section.

protected Vector listeners
This is where the list of listeners is stored.

protected Object realSource
Hold the event source used for all events fired by this object. If the source is set when the UndoableEditSupport is created, that object is sent as the source of all events. Otherwise, the UndoableEditSupport itself becomes the source.

protected int updateLevel
This is where the updateLevel property is stored.

Constructors

public UndoableEditSupport( )
Create a new support object, which uses itself as the source object for any events it fires.

public UndoableEditSupport(Object r)
Create a new support object, which uses the given object as the source for any events it fires.

UndoableEditEvent/listener support methods

The following methods allow an undo-capable object to use an UndoableEditSupport object to manage event listeners:

public synchronized void addUndoableEditListener(UndoableEditListener l)
Add the given listener to a list of listeners to be notified of new UndoableEdits.

public synchronized void removeUndoableEditListener(UndoableEditListener l)

> Remove the specified listener.

public synchronized void postEdit(UndoableEdit e)

> If updateLevel is 0, this method uses _postEdit( ) to send an UndoableEditEvent to all added listeners. If updateLevel is not 0, this method adds the input edit to a CompoundEdit to be fired later. See the beginUpdate( ) and endUpdate( ) methods for more details on the use of CompoundEdit.

protected void _postEdit(UndoableEdit e)

> This protected method is used by postEdit( ) and endUpdate( ). It creates a new UndoableEditEvent containing the input edit and sends it to all registered listeners by calling undoableEditHappened( ) on each.

Nested edit support

The following methods allow the UndoableEditSupport class to consolidate multiple edits into a single CompoundEdit, to be fired after a series of edits have been added. To use these methods, the object using the support object first calls beginUpdate( ). Each subsequent postEdit( ) call causes the input edit to be added to a single CompoundEdit. When endUpdate( ) is called, an UndoableEditEvent containing the CompoundEdit is fired.

If multiple beginUpdate( ) calls are made, the support object keeps track of the level of nesting using the updateLevel property. Only when the number of endUpdate( ) calls matches the number of beginUpdate( ) calls is the CompoundEdit finally fired. Regardless of how many times beginUpdate( ) is called, only a single CompoundEdit is created.

public synchronized void beginUpdate()

> This method indicates that subsequent postEdit( ) calls should result in the input edit being added to a CompoundEdit. It increments updateLevel and, if the updateLevel is 0, creates a new CompoundEdit.

public synchronized void endUpdate()

> Decrement updateLevel. If updateLevel is 0, it calls end( ) on the CompoundEdit and then calls _postEdit( ) to deliver the edit to the support object's listeners.

protected CompoundEdit createCompoundEdit()

> Return a new CompoundEdit. A subclass could override this method to return a different CompoundEdit implementation if desired.

Figure 18-11 shows how to use beginUpdate( ) and endUpdate( ). We add a total of four edits to the support object. Notice that the first endUpdate( ) call does nothing but decrement the current level. The next endUpdate( ), which brings the level to 0, causes the composite edit containing the four added edits to be fired.

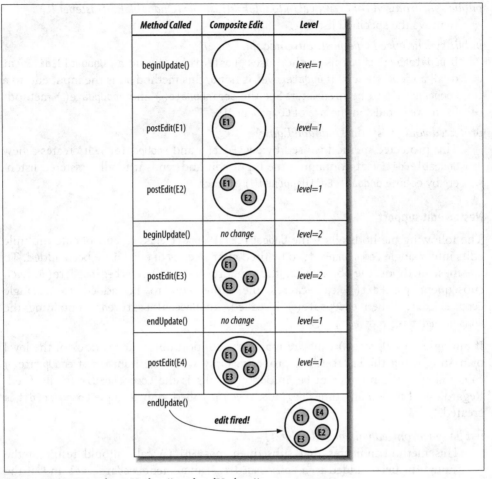

Method Called	Composite Edit	Level
beginUpdate()		level=1
postEdit(E1)		level=1
postEdit(E2)		level=1
beginUpdate()	*no change*	level=2
postEdit(E3)		level=2
endUpdate()	*no change*	level=1
postEdit(E4)		level=1
endUpdate()	*edit fired!*	

Figure 18-11. Using beginUpdate() and endUpdate()

Using Undoable Edit Support

Earlier in this chapter, we created a simple undoable toggle button class. To keep that example simple, we allowed only a single listener to be added to the button. In this example (just a new implementation of the same class), we'll show how easily we can use UndoableEditSupport to allow multiple listeners to be added and notified. Differences from our earlier implementation are bolded.

```
// UndoableJToggleButton2.java
//
import java.awt.event.*;
import javax.swing.*;
import javax.swing.event.*;
import javax.swing.undo.*;
```

```
// Sample undoable toggle button class using UndoableEditSupport
public class UndoableJToggleButton2 extends JToggleButton {

    private UndoableEditSupport support;

    // For this example, we'll provide just one constructor.
    public UndoableJToggleButton2(String txt) {
        super(txt);
        support = new UndoableEditSupport(this);
    }

    // Add an UndoableEditListener using our support object.
    public void addUndoableEditListener(UndoableEditListener l) {
        support.addUndoableEditListener(l);
    }

    // Remove an UndoableEditListener using our support object.
    public void removeUndoableEditListener(UndoableEditListener l) {
        support.addUndoableEditListener(l);
    }

    // Override this method to call the super implementation first (to fire the
    // action event) and then fire a new UndoableEditEvent to our listeners using
    // our support object.
    protected void fireActionPerformed(ActionEvent ev) {

        // Fire the ActionEvent as usual.
        super.fireActionPerformed(ev);

        support.postEdit(new UndoableToggleEdit(this));
    }
}
```

The CannotRedoException Class

This class is an extension of RuntimeException thrown when an attempt is made to redo an UndoableEdit that cannot be redone (typically because it has not yet been undone or because it has been "killed").

There are no properties, constructors (other than the implicit default), or methods defined in this class.

The CannotUndoException Class

This class is an extension of RuntimeException thrown when an attempt is made to undo an UndoableEdit that cannot be undone (typically because it has already been undone, or because it has been "killed").

There are no properties, constructors (other than the implicit default), or methods defined in this class.

Extending UndoManager

Now that we've looked at all of the classes and interfaces in the undo framework, we'll look at a few ideas for extending the functionality it provides.

In this example, we'll extend UndoManager to add a few extra features. The first thing we'll add is the ability to get a list of the edits stored in the manager. This is a simple task of returning the contents of the edits vector inherited from CompoundEdit. We also provide access to an array of significant undoable edits and an array of significant redoable edits. These might be useful in a game like chess, in which we want to provide a list of past moves.

The next major feature we add is support for listeners. At this writing, the current UndoManager does not have any way of notifying you when it receives edits. As we saw in an earlier example, this means that you have to listen to each edit-generating component if you want to update the user interface to reflect new undoable or redoable edits as they occur. In our manager, we simply add the ability to add and remove undoable edit listeners to the undo manager itself. Each time an edit is added, the undo manager fires an UndoableEditEvent to any registered listeners. This way, we can just add the undo manager as a listener to each edit-generating component and then add a single listener to the undo manager to update the UI.

The methods of our new undo manager can be divided into two groups, each supporting one of the two features we're adding. We'll split the source code listing along these lines so we can talk about each set of methods independently. Here's the first half:

```java
// ExtendedUndoManager.java
//
import javax.swing.event.*;
import javax.swing.undo.*;
import java.util.Enumeration;
import java.util.Vector;

// An extension of UndoManager that provides two additional features:
// (1) The ability to add and remove listeners
// (2) The ability to gain more extensive access to the edits being managed
public class ExtendedUndoManager extends UndoManager
  implements UndoableEditListener {

  private ExtendedUndoableEditSupport support =
    new ExtendedUndoableEditSupport();

  private Object source; // The source of the last edit

  // Return the complete list of edits in an array.
  public synchronized UndoableEdit[] getEdits() {
    UndoableEdit[] array = new UndoableEdit[edits.size()];
    edits.copyInto(array);
    return array;
```

```
    }

    // Return all currently significant undoable edits. The first edit is the next one
    // to be undone.
    public synchronized UndoableEdit[] getUndoableEdits() {
      int size = edits.size();
      Vector v = new Vector(size);
      for (int i=size-1;i>=0;i--) {
        UndoableEdit u = (UndoableEdit)edits.elementAt(i);
        if (u.canUndo() && u.isSignificant())
          v.addElement(u);
      }
      UndoableEdit[] array = new UndoableEdit[v.size()];
      v.copyInto(array);
      return array;
    }

    // Return all currently significant redoable edits. The first edit is the next one
    // to be redone.
    public synchronized UndoableEdit[] getRedoableEdits() {
      int size = edits.size();
      Vector v = new Vector(size);
      for (int i=0; i<size; i++) {
        UndoableEdit u = (UndoableEdit)edits.elementAt(i);
        if (u.canRedo() && u.isSignificant())
          v.addElement(u);
      }
      UndoableEdit[] array = new UndoableEdit[v.size()];
      v.copyInto(array);
      return array;
    }
```

The first method here is simple. All we do is copy the edits from the edits vector into an array and return it. The other two methods are nearly identical. They are a little more complicated than they ideally should be because we don't have access to the current insertion point into the edits vector (which would split the list right between the undoable and redoable edits). Instead, we just iterate over the elements, building up a list of significant undoable or redoable edits.

Here are the methods we added to support listeners:

```
    // UndoableEditListener Method Support (ExtendedUndoManager.java, part 2)
    //

    // Add an edit and notify our listeners.
    public synchronized boolean addEdit(UndoableEdit anEdit) {
      boolean b = super.addEdit(anEdit);
      if (b)
        support.postEdit(anEdit); // If the edit was added, notify listeners.
      return b;
    }

    // When an edit is sent to us, call addEdit() to notify any of our listeners.
    public synchronized void undoableEditHappened(UndoableEditEvent ev) {
```

```
        UndoableEdit ue = ev.getEdit();
        source = ev.getSource();
        addEdit(ue);
    }

    // Add a listener to be notified each time an edit is added to this manager.
    // This makes it easy to update undo/redo menus as edits are added.
    public synchronized void addUndoableEditListener(UndoableEditListener l) {
        support.addUndoableEditListener(l);
    }

    // Remove a listener from this manager.
    public synchronized void removeUndoableEditListener(UndoableEditListener l) {
        support.removeUndoableEditListener(l);
    }

    // A simple extension of UndoableEditSupport that lets us specify the event
    // source each time we post an edit
    class ExtendedUndoableEditSupport extends UndoableEditSupport {

        // Post an edit to added listeners.
        public synchronized void postEdit(UndoableEdit ue) {
            realSource = source; // From our enclosing manager object
            super.postEdit(ue);
        }
    }
}
```

The first method here is a customized implementation of addEdit( ). For the most part, we leave this method to the superclass. The only thing we've added is a call to UndoableEditSupport.postEdit( ). Any time an edit is added to the undo manager, we notify its listeners. The idea is that a single listener, probably responsible for updating an Undo menu, is added to the undo manager.

The next method is the undoableEditHappened( ) method from the UndoableEditListener interface. This is the method called each time any edit-generating component in the application fires an UndoableEdit. In this method, we first store the source of the event (we'll see how we use this shortly) and then call addEdit( ).

The next two methods simply use UndoableEditSupport to manage interested listeners.

Finally, we define a small inner class called ExtendedUndoableEditSupport. This is an extension of UndoableEditSupport that we use to set the correct event source each time the ExtendedUndoManager fires an UndoableEditEvent. Rather than declaring the undo manager as the source of the event, we use the real source of the event that was passed to the undo manager's undoableEditHappened( ) method. Note that realSource, which is a protected field in UndoableEditSupport, becomes the source object in the fired UndoableEditEvent.

CHAPTER 19

Text 101

Swing provides an extensive collection of classes for working with text in user interfaces. In fact, because there's so much provided for working with text, Swing's creators placed most of it into its own package: javax.swing.text. This package's dozens of interfaces and classes (plus the six concrete component classes in javax.swing) provide a rich set of text-based models and components complex enough to allow endless customization yet simple to use in the common case.

In this chapter we'll look at JTextComponent, the base class for all of the text components shown in Figure 19-1, and then discuss JTextField, JPasswordField, and JTextArea. Then we'll introduce what's going on behind the scenes. We save the more complex model, event, and view classes for later, but we occasionally refer to things you may want to investigate further in the next four chapters.

JFormattedTextField is an extension of JTextField with formatting and object-parsing abilities. We'll devote Chapter 20 to JFormattedTextField and its related classes.

Swing text components allow you to customize certain aspects of the L&F without much work. This includes the creation of custom carets (cursors), custom highlighting, and custom key bindings to associate Actions with special key combinations. These features are covered in Chapter 21.

We describe JTextPane in Chapter 22 and discuss styles, the Document model and Views. Style features include structured text supporting multiple fonts and colors, and even embedded Icons and Components.

Finally, we turn to JEditorPane in Chapter 23 and see how all of this is tied together by something called an EditorKit. EditorKits allow you to define which view objects should be used, which special actions your editor will support, and how your documents can be input and output via streams. You can even register EditorKits for specific content types to enable JEditorPanes to handle those content types automatically.

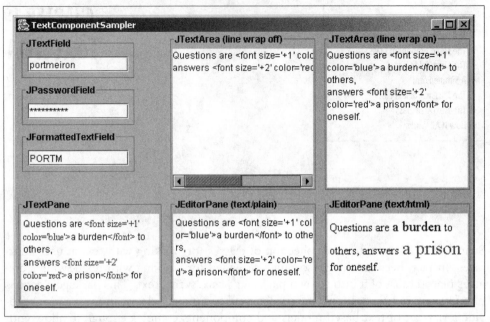

Figure 19-1. A sample of Swing text components

The Swing Text Components

Despite all the complexity and power Swing's text components provide, it's still pretty simple to do most things. Figure 19-1 shows each of the six Swing text components, plus an extra JTextArea (to show a different wrapping style) and an extra JEditorPane (to show a different EditorKit).

```
// TextComponentSampler.java
//
import javax.swing.*;
import javax.swing.text.*;
import javax.swing.border.*;
import java.awt.*;

public class TextComponentSampler extends JFrame {

  public static String word = "portmeiron";
  public static String markup =
    "Questions are <font size='+1' color='blue'>a burden</font> to others,\n" +
    "answers <font size='+2' color='red'>a prison</font> for oneself.";

  public TextComponentSampler() {
    super("TextComponentSampler");

    JTextField tf = new JTextField(word, 12);
    JPasswordField pf = new JPasswordField(word, 12);
```

```
MaskFormatter formatter = null;
try { formatter = new MaskFormatter("UUUUU");
    } catch (java.text.ParseException ex) { }
JFormattedTextField ftf = new JFormattedTextField(formatter);
ftf.setColumns(12);
ftf.setValue(word);

JTextArea ta1 = new JTextArea(markup);
JScrollPane scroll1 = new JScrollPane(ta1);

JTextArea ta2 = new JTextArea(markup);
ta2.setLineWrap(true);
ta2.setWrapStyleWord(true);
JScrollPane scroll2 = new JScrollPane(ta2);

JTextPane tp = new JTextPane( );
tp.setText(markup);
// Create an AttributeSet with which to change color and font.
SimpleAttributeSet attrs = new SimpleAttributeSet( );
StyleConstants.setForeground(attrs, Color.blue);
StyleConstants.setFontFamily(attrs, "Serif");
// Apply the AttributeSet to a few blocks of text.
StyledDocument sdoc = tp.getStyledDocument( );
sdoc.setCharacterAttributes(14, 29, attrs, false);
sdoc.setCharacterAttributes(51, 7, attrs, false);
sdoc.setCharacterAttributes(78, 28, attrs, false);
sdoc.setCharacterAttributes(114, 7, attrs, false);
JScrollPane scroll3 = new JScrollPane(tp);

JEditorPane ep1 = new JEditorPane("text/plain", markup);
JScrollPane scroll4 = new JScrollPane(ep1);

JEditorPane ep2 = new JEditorPane("text/html", markup);
JScrollPane scroll5 = new JScrollPane(ep2);

// Done creating text components; now lay them out and make them pretty.
JPanel panel_tf = new JPanel( );
JPanel panel_pf = new JPanel( );
JPanel panel_ftf = new JPanel( );
panel_tf.add(tf);
panel_pf.add(pf);
panel_ftf.add(ftf);

panel_tf.setBorder(new TitledBorder("JTextField"));
panel_pf.setBorder(new TitledBorder("JPasswordField"));
panel_ftf.setBorder(new TitledBorder("JFormattedTextField"));
scroll1.setBorder(new TitledBorder("JTextArea (line wrap off)"));
scroll2.setBorder(new TitledBorder("JTextArea (line wrap on)"));
scroll3.setBorder(new TitledBorder("JTextPane"));
scroll4.setBorder(new TitledBorder("JEditorPane (text/plain)"));
scroll5.setBorder(new TitledBorder("JEditorPane (text/html)"));

JPanel pan = new JPanel(new FlowLayout(FlowLayout.LEFT));
pan.add(panel_tf);
```

```
        pan.add(panel_pf);
        pan.add(panel_ftf);

        Container contentPane = getContentPane( );
        contentPane.setLayout(new GridLayout(2, 3, 8, 8));

        contentPane.add(pan);
        contentPane.add(scroll1);
        contentPane.add(scroll2);
        contentPane.add(scroll3);
        contentPane.add(scroll4);
        contentPane.add(scroll5);
    }

    public static void main(String args[]) {
        JFrame frame = new TextComponentSampler( );
        frame.setDefaultCloseOperation(JFrame.EXIT_ON_CLOSE);
        frame.setSize(600, 450);
        frame.setVisible(true);
    }
}
```

Unlike java.awt.TextArea, the multiline Swing text components lack built-in scroll-bars. If you want scrollbars—and you almost always do—you must create your own JScrollPane. Fortunately, this is easy to do. Just replace add(myTextComp) with add(new JScrollPane(myTextComp)). In most L&Fs, scrollbars do not appear unless they are needed.

The JTextComponent Class

The six concrete Swing text component classes have quite a bit in common. Conse-quently, they share a common base class, JTextComponent. Figure 19-2 shows the class hierarchy for the Swing text components. As you can see, the concrete text compo-nents are in the javax.swing package with the rest of the Swing component classes, but JTextComponent and all its supporting classes can be found in javax.swing.text.

JTextComponent is an abstract class that serves as the base class for all text-based Swing components. It defines a large number of properties and methods that apply to its subclasses. In this introductory chapter, we'll pass quickly over many of these properties, as they require an understanding of the underlying model and view aspects of the text framework.

Properties

JTextComponent defines the properties and default values shown in Table 19-1. document is a reference to the Document model for the component, where the component's con-tent data is stored. (We'll discuss the details of the Document interface in Chapter 22.) The UI property for all text components is a subclass of javax.swing.plaf.TextUI.

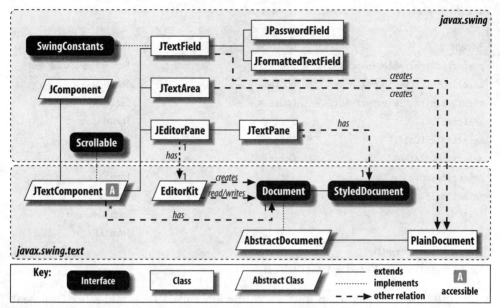

Figure 19-2. The Swing text components

Table 19-1. JTextComponent properties

Property	Data type	get	is	set	Default value
accessibleContext[o]	AccessibleContext	•			AccessibleJTextComponent
actions	Action[]	•			From the UI's EditorKit
caret[b]	Caret	•		•	null
caretColor[b]	Color	•		•	null
caretPosition	int	•		•	From caret
disabledTextColor[b]	Color	•		•	null
document[b]	Document	•		•	null
dragEnabled[1.4]	boolean	•		•	false
editable[b]	boolean	•	•	•	true
focusAccelerator[b]	char	•		•	'\0'
highlighter[b]	Highlighter	•		•	null
keymap[b]	Keymap	•		•	null
layout[o]	LayoutManager	•		•	null
margin[b]	Insets	•		•	From UI
navigationFilter[1.4]	NavigationFilter	•		•	null

[1.4]since 1.4, [b]bound, [o]overridden

See also properties from the JComponent class (Table 3-6).

Table 19-1. JTextComponent properties (continued)

Property	Data type	get	is	set	Default value
preferredScrollableViewportSize[o]	Dimension	•			Preferred size of component
scrollableTracksViewportHeight[o]	boolean	•			See below
scrollableTracksViewportWidth[o]	boolean	•			See below
selectedText	String	•			From document
selectedTextColor[b]	Color	•		•	null
selectionColor[b]	Color	•		•	null
selectionEnd	int	•		•	From caret
selectionStart	int	•		•	From caret
text	String	•		•	From document
UI[b]	TextUI	•		•	From L&F

[1.4]since 1.4, [b]bound, [o]overridden

See also properties from the JComponent class (Table 3-6).

accessibleContext refers to an instance of the inner class AccessibleJTextComponent that implements the AccessibleText interface, which is described in Chapter 25.

The actions property specifies a list of Actions (such as page-up, change-font, or paste-from-clipboard) that are available to the component. The actual list is created by the component's EditorKit, which we'll cover in detail in Chapter 23. This read-only property exists for the convenience of the text component and those who sub-class it, and the presence or absence of an Action on the list does not mean that Action is or is not installed in the component's active Keymap or InputMap.

caret represents the location at which data is inserted into the document (in other words, the cursor position; Swing uses the term caret instead of cursor). highlighter is an object responsible for drawing highlighted text. keymap allows you to specify, for example, the keystrokes that cause text to be cut (e.g., Ctrl-X) or pasted (e.g, Command-V). We'll discuss all three of these in Chapter 21.

caretColor, disabledTextColor, selectionColor, and selectedTextColor simply spec-ify the color used to render the caret, disabled text, selection background, and selected text, respectively.[*]

The dragEnabled property, new in SDK 1.4, should be set to true to enable auto-matic drag handling (if the L&F supports it). Because automatic drag could possibly change the way text-selection gestures are interpreted, the default value for this prop-erty is false. Note that the accessor method is named getDragEnabled( ), not isDragEnabled( ), as convention would dictate.

---

[*] The regular text color is stored in the inherited foreground property.

The editable property indicates whether the document can be edited. If this property is set to false, characters typed into the component are not inserted—the component is used only for displaying.

The focusAccelerator property specifies the key that can be used to give focus to the text component. The default value (\0) indicates that no focus accelerator has been set.

The inherited layout property defaults to null because the layout of text components is handled by the View hierarchy (more on this later). The margin property specifies the distance between the component's text and its border (using an instance of java.awt.Insets).

navigationFilter (if not null) is used by the caret to restrict cursor movement.

The selectedText and text properties are managed by the component's Document while selectionStart, selectionEnd, and caretPosition delegate to the caret.

The preferredScrollableViewportSize property (from the Scrollable interface) simply delegates to getPreferredSize(). The values of the other two properties from the Scrollable interface, scrollableTracksViewportHeight and scrollableTracksViewport-Width, are determined by the size of the JViewport containing the component. If the viewport is larger than the preferred size of the component, these properties are true. Otherwise (or if the component's parent is not a JViewport), they are false.

Events

JTextComponent fires a CaretEvent any time the state of the component's Caret changes. So any time the cursor position changes, an event is fired. The only exception is that while a selection is being made (the mouse is being dragged), events are not fired as the cursor moves, only when the mouse is released and the selection has been created.

The following standard methods are provided for working with caret events. (Note that the getCaretListeners() method was introduced in SDK 1.4.)

```
public void addCaretListener(CaretListener listener)
public void removeCaretListener(CaretListener listener)
public CaretListener[] getCaretListeners()
```

The CaretEvent class and CaretListener interface are described in detail in Chapter 21.

In addition to firing CaretEvents, JTextComponents naturally fire property change events when the values of bound properties are changed.

Constants

Table 19-2 defines the JTextComponent constants. There are no constants defined for any bound properties other than focusAccelerator, but there is nothing special about FOCUS_ACCELERATOR_KEY, and its solitary existence as a constant is most likely evidence of an oversight with respect to the other bound properties.

Table 19-2. JTextComponent constants

Constant	Type	Description
DEFAULT_KEYMAP	String	The name of the default keymap used by all text components. This string can be used as a parameter to the static getKeymap( ) method.
FOCUS_ACCELERATOR_KEY	String	The bound property name for the focus accelerator, used when firing property change events.

Constructor

public JTextComponent( )

Create a new editable component and update the UI (causing many of the null properties listed in Table 19-1 to be set).

Clipboard Methods

These methods allow you to move data to and from the system clipboard:

public void copy( )

Copy the currently selected range in the component's model to the system clipboard. No change is made to the document itself.

public void cut( )

Copy the currently selected range in the component's model to the system clipboard. The selected range (if any) is removed from the document.

public void paste( )

Copy the contents of the system clipboard into the document. If there is an active selection, it is replaced by the pasted contents. If there is no selection, the contents are inserted in front of the current insert position (caret).

Selection Methods

These methods are concerned with selecting (highlighting) text:

public void moveCaretPosition(int pos)

Form a selection by moving the caret to the specified position. The selection begins at the location specified when setCaretPosition( ) was last called. It throws an IllegalArgumentException if pos is not between 0 and getText( ).length( ).

public void replaceSelection(String content)

Replace the currently selected area with content. If there is no current selection, the input text is inserted at the current caret position.

public void select(int selectionStart, int selectionEnd)

Select an area of the document bounded by the input offsets. This method is implemented by calling setCaretPosition( ) and moveCaretPosition( ), but it does not throw an exception even if selectionStart or selectionEnd is out of bounds. According to the documentation for JTextComponent, setCaretPosition( ) and moveCaretPosition( ) should be called directly instead of calling select( ), which is provided only for backward compatibility.

public void selectAll( )

Select all the text in the component.

View Methods

These methods provide mappings between model and view coordinate systems (e.g., pixel (53,71) of the view might correspond to character 42 of the document). They also provide information necessary for scrolling the text component.

public int getScrollableUnitIncrement(Rectangle visibleRect, int orientation,
  int direction)

public int getScrollableBlockIncrement(Rectangle visibleRect, int orientation,
  int direction)

Return the "unit" and "block" scroll increments (in pixels) desired by the component. The default implementation returns 10% and 100% of the size of the visible area, respectively. Subclasses are expected to compute a scroll increment that exposes some logical portion of the display, such as a row or column of data. The input Rectangle defines the size of the current view area. The orientation must be either SwingConstants.VERTICAL or SwingConstants.HORIZONTAL. The direction indicates which direction to scroll. Negative values indicate a scroll up or left; positive values indicate down or right. For more information on scrolling, see "The Scrollable Interface" in Chapter 11.

public Rectangle modelToView(int pos) throws BadLocationException

Convert the input position to an area in the view coordinate system. pos is an offset into the content of the text component.

public int viewToModel(Point pt)

Return the offset of the character found at the location described by pt.

Working with Keymaps

The Swing text components allow you to map keystrokes to specified actions. This capability existed before the more flexible and universal InputMap and ActionMap mechanisms emerged. (These are discussed in "Keyboard Events" in Chapter 3.) The Keymap-based methods are still available for backward compatibility and were reimplemented using the new framework. The following methods are defined in the JTextComponent base class and are discussed in more detail in Chapter 21:

public static Keymap addKeymap(String name, Keymap parent)
> Create a new Keymap with the specified parent. If the input map name is not null, the new Keymap is added to an internal table using the map name.

public static Keymap getKeymap(String name)
> Return the Keymap associated with the given name.

public static Keymap removeKeymap(String name)
> Remove (and return) the Keymap specified by the input map name.

public static void loadKeymap(Keymap map, JTextComponent.KeyBinding[] bindings, Action[] actions)
> This static utility method can be used to insert Action bindings into a Keymap.

Other Methods

public String getText(int offset, int len) throws BadLocationException
> Return a portion of the text starting at the input offset (the distance, in characters, from the beginning of the document) containing the requested number of characters.

public void write(Writer out) throws IOException
> Write the contents of the document to the given Writer. The default implementation stores the document as plain text, but subclasses may produce alternate data formats, such as HTML.

public void read(Reader in, Object desc) throws IOException
> Set the contents of the component from a Reader. The default implementation reads plain text, but subclasses may handle more complex formats, such as HTML. The second parameter is intended to describe the stream and may be null. If it's not, it is added as a property of the document; HTML documents and the JEditorKit use URLs as descriptions to help resolve relative hyperlinks.

public void updateUI( )
> This method is called to indicate that the L&F has changed.

The JTextField Class

JTextField allows the user to enter a single line of text, scrolling the text if its size exceeds the physical size of the field. A JTextField fires an ActionEvent to any registered ActionListeners (including the Action set via the setAction() method, if any) when the user presses the Enter key.

JTextFields (and all JTextComponents) are automatically installed with a number of behaviors appropriate to the L&F, so cut/copy/paste, special cursor movement keys, and text-selection gestures should work without any extra intervention on your part.

The following program presents a JTextField for the user to edit (shown in Figure 19-3). The JTextField is initially right-justified, but the justification changes each time the Enter key is pressed.

```java
// JTextFieldExample.java
//
import javax.swing.*;
import java.awt.event.*;

public class JTextFieldExample {

  public static void main(String[] args) {

    final JTextField tf = new JTextField("press <enter>", 20);
    tf.setHorizontalAlignment(JTextField.RIGHT);

    tf.addActionListener(new ActionListener() {
        public void actionPerformed(ActionEvent e) {
          int old = tf.getHorizontalAlignment();
          if (old == JTextField.LEFT) tf.setHorizontalAlignment(JTextField.RIGHT);
          if (old == JTextField.RIGHT) tf.setHorizontalAlignment(JTextField.CENTER);
          if (old == JTextField.CENTER) tf.setHorizontalAlignment(JTextField.LEFT);
        }
      });

    JFrame frame = new JFrame("JTextFieldExample");
    frame.setDefaultCloseOperation(JFrame.EXIT_ON_CLOSE);
    frame.getContentPane().setLayout(new java.awt.FlowLayout());
    frame.getContentPane().add(tf);
    frame.setSize(275, 75);
    frame.setVisible(true);
    tf.requestFocus();
  }
}
```

Properties

Table 19-3 shows the properties defined by JTextField. The document property defaults to a new instance of PlainDocument, and the UIClassID is TextFieldUI.

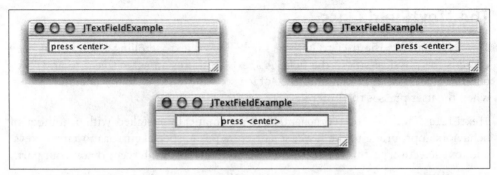

Figure 19-3. JTextFields shown with different alignments

Table 19-3. JTextField properties

Property	Data type	get	is	set	Default value
accessibleContext[o]	AccessibleContext	•			AccessibleJTextField
action[1.3]	Action	•		•	null
actionCommand	String			•	null
actions[o]	Action[]	•			From superclass plus NotifyAction
columns	int	•		•	0
document[b, o]	Document	•		•	PlainDocument()
font[b, o]	Font	•		•	From superclass
horizontalAlignment[b]	int	•		•	LEADING
horizontalVisibility	BoundedRangeModel	•			DefaultBoundedRangeModel
preferredSize[b, o]	Dimension	•		•	Width based on columns and font
scrollOffset	int	•		•	From horizontal visibility
UIClassID[o]	String	•			"TextFieldUI"
validateRoot[o]	boolean		•		true

[1.3]since 1.3, [b]bound, [o]overridden

See also properties from the JTextComponent class (Table 19-1).

The value of the accessibleContext property is an AccessibleJTextField, which extends JTextComponent.AccessibleJTextComponent.

The actionCommand string is used in ActionEvents fired by the text field. If a non-null value has not been explicitly set, the current contents of the field are used as the ActionEvent's action command.

action keeps track of an Action associated with this field. The field keeps its enabled and toolTipText properties synchronized with the Action. Also, the Action receives any ActionEvents fired by the field.

The actions property appears here because JTextField adds NotifyAction to the array of utility actions inherited from its superclass. NotifyAction is used to indicate that the contents of the field have been "accepted" by the user, typically by pressing Enter.

The columns property specifies the displayed width of the field, which is unrelated to the length of the field's content (which is generally unbounded). If the value of columns is 0, the width returned by getPreferredSize( ) (unless set explicitly with setPreferredSize( )) is just long enough to display the field's content text and changes when the user adds or deletes characters, which means the displayed field dynamically resizes when it is revalidated under FlowLayout or any other layout manager that respects getPreferredSize( ).* If columns is not 0, the width returned by getPreferredSize( ) defaults to columns times the pixel width of the lowercase character m in the field's font. (Unfortunately, it doesn't quite work as it should. The width returned represents the width of the entire component, including the rectangle drawn around the text, so it is often not quite wide enough for the designated number of m characters to fit without scrolling.) The font property is listed in the table because setFont( ) is overridden to update the preferredSize calculation (if necessary) and revalidate the component (so the new font is drawn).

horizontalAlignment indicates where text appears in the field. Valid values are LEFT, CENTER, RIGHT, LEADING, and TRAILING (defined in SwingConstants). LEADING has the same effect as LEFT (and TRAILING as RIGHT) unless the field is in an environment where text reads from right to left.

horizontalVisibility is a BoundedRangeModel (see Chapter 6) that defines the portion of the text displayed if the text is too long for the field. Its minimum is 0, and its maximum is equal to the size of the text field or the total length of the text, whichever is bigger (in pixels). Its extent is the width of the text field (in pixels), and its value is the offset from the beginning of the text currently showing at the left edge of the field. shiftOffset simply provides direct access to horizontalVisibility's value property.

When validateRoot is true, calling revalidate( ) on the JTextField does not revalidate its parent. isValidateRoot( ) is true unless JTextField is contained within a JViewPort.

Events

JTextField objects fire ActionEvents any time the Enter key is pressed, indicating that the user is finished with the field.

---

* This is actually up to the UI delegate, but existing L&Fs behave as described.

The JTextField class contains the following standard methods for working with ActionEvents:

```
public void addActionListener(ActionListener l)
public void removeActionListener(ActionListener l)
public ActionListener[] getActionListeners()
```

Additionally, the following method is provided:

public void postActionEvent()
Fire an ActionEvent to all registered listeners.

In addition to firing ActionEvents, a JTextField fires a PropertyChangeEvent whenever the horizontalAlignment or action properties are updated.

Constant

JTextField defines the constant shown in Table 19-4.

Table 19-4. JTextField constant

Constant	Type	Description
notifyAction	String	The name of the action used to send notification that the field's contents have been accepted

This action name is used by TextFieldUI implementations to map a keystroke (typically Enter) to the Action provided by JTextField, which notifies listeners that something has been entered in the field.

Constructors

public JTextField()
Create a new text field with no content. The columns property defaults to 0.

public JTextField(String text)
Create a new text field with the given text. The columns property defaults to 0.

public JTextField(int columns)
Create a new text field with the specified number of columns.

public JTextField(String text, int columns)
Create a new text field with the specified number of columns, displaying the given text.

public JTextField(Document doc, String text, int columns)
Create a new text field that uses the specified document model (covered in detail in Chapter 22) and number of columns. If the string is null, the Document's text is displayed. Otherwise, the string replaces the Document's content and is displayed.

Methods

Almost all the public methods are property accessors or event management methods that have already been covered. The only exception is listed below:

public void scrollRectToVisible(Rectangle r)

> Adjust the field's visibility based on the x value of the Rectangle parameter. The other three values of the rectangle (y, width, height) are ignored. It ensures that the specified x-coordinate in pixels (not characters), relative to the leftmost text position, is visible. If the specified x-coordinate is already visible, no scrolling occurs.

A Simple Form

One of the most common user-interface constructs is the basic form. Typically, forms are made up of labels and fields, with the label describing the text to be entered in the field. Here's a primitive TextForm class that shows the use of mnemonics, tooltips, and basic accessibility support. Note that we call setLabelFor( ) to associate each label with a text field. This association allows the mnemonics to set the focus and, together with setToolTipText( ), supports accessibility (see Chapter 25).

```java
// TextForm.java
//
import javax.swing.*;
import java.awt.event.*;
import java.awt.*;

// A simple label/field form panel
public class TextForm extends JPanel {

    private JTextField[] fields;

    // Create a form with the specified labels, tooltips, and sizes.
    public TextForm(String[] labels, char[] mnemonics, int[] widths, String[] tips) {
        super(new BorderLayout( ));
        JPanel labelPanel = new JPanel(new GridLayout(labels.length, 1));
        JPanel fieldPanel = new JPanel(new GridLayout(labels.length, 1));
        add(labelPanel, BorderLayout.WEST);
        add(fieldPanel, BorderLayout.CENTER);
        fields = new JTextField[labels.length];

        for (int i=0; i < labels.length; i+=1) {
            fields[i] = new JTextField( );
            if (i < tips.length) fields[i].setToolTipText(tips[i]);
            if (i < widths.length) fields[i].setColumns(widths[i]);

            JLabel lab = new JLabel(labels[i], JLabel.RIGHT);
            lab.setLabelFor(fields[i]);
            if (i < mnemonics.length) lab.setDisplayedMnemonic(mnemonics[i]);
```

```
      labelPanel.add(lab);
      JPanel p = new JPanel(new FlowLayout(FlowLayout.LEFT));
      p.add(fields[i]);
      fieldPanel.add(p);
    }
  }

  public String getText(int i) {
    return( fields[i].getText() );
  }

  public static void main(String[] args) {
    String[] labels = { "First Name", "Middle Initial", "Last Name", "Age" };
    char[] mnemonics = { 'F', 'M', 'L', 'A' };
    int[] widths = { 15, 1, 15, 3 };
    String[] descs = { "First Name", "Middle Initial", "Last Name", "Age" };

    final TextForm form = new TextForm(labels, mnemonics, widths, descs);

    JButton submit = new JButton("Submit Form");

    submit.addActionListener(new ActionListener() {
        public void actionPerformed(ActionEvent e) {
          System.out.println(form.getText(0) + " " + form.getText(1) + ". " +
                             form.getText(2) + ", age " + form.getText(3));
        }
      });

    JFrame f = new JFrame("Text Form Example");
    f.setDefaultCloseOperation(JFrame.EXIT_ON_CLOSE);
    f.getContentPane().add(form, BorderLayout.NORTH);
    JPanel p = new JPanel();
    p.add(submit);
    f.getContentPane().add(p, BorderLayout.SOUTH);
    f.pack();
    f.setVisible(true);
  }
}
```

We've included a simple main( ) method here to show how this form class might be used. Clearly, much could be done to make this simple class more flexible and powerful. That aside, Figure 19-4 shows what we get.

Understanding JTextField Sizing

Depending on how you construct your JTextField, and how it is laid out in its container, you may be a bit surprised by its size when it appears on the screen. Here are three things to watch out for:

Height stretching

JTextField's getPreferredSize( ) method returns a reasonable height—the height of the field's font plus enough for the border—but layout managers such

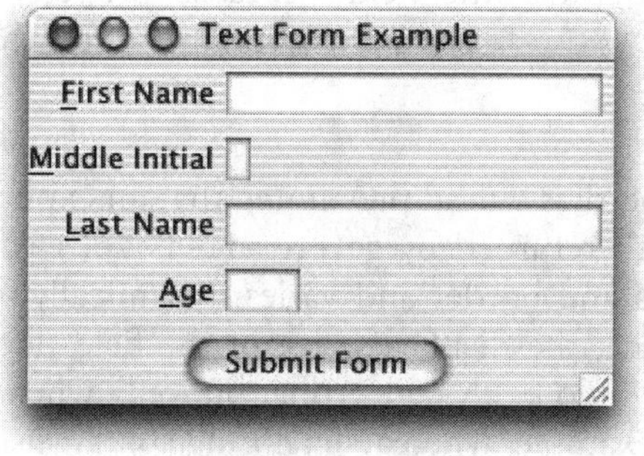

Figure 19-4. A simple text form

as BorderLayout (west, center, and east positions) and GridLayout ignore this and stretch the field vertically. The field handles vertical stretching by centering its single line of text within its too-tall editing area. A little stretching may look OK, but it doesn't take much to distort the field. To prevent stretching, place the JTextField inside a JPanel (which defaults to FlowLayout), then add the JPanel to the container.

Note that the north and south positions of BorderLayout do respect the height returned by getPreferredSize( ). The width is ignored instead. The field is stretched to cover the entire width of the container.

Skimpy columns

Specifying the number of columns your JTextField should have, by either creating it with one of the constructors that takes a columns parameter or by explicitly calling setColumns( ), may not actually produce a field capable of displaying that many columns without scrolling. This is especially true for narrow fields (less than four columns) and fields with constant-width fonts.

This tight squeeze happens because of the sizing of the component using the lowercase character m of the field's font, as described earlier. getPreferredSize( ) returns a width that is the number of columns times the pixel width of m. Because the field's border occupies some of this space, the field can be too small for its contents. This isn't a problem for wide fields with proportional fonts because most of the characters the user enters are narrower than an m, so there is enough slack to cover the field's border. Otherwise, you may have to implement a workaround.

A simple and effective workaround for this problem is to specify one more column than you actually need. Another workaround is to do something like this:

```
// A hack to make a JTextField really two columns wide
JTextField tf = new JTextField("mm");
tf.setPreferredSize( tf.getPreferredSize( ) );
tf.setText(""); // Empty the field.
```

This works only because the field's `columns` property defaults to 0. (When `columns` is nonzero, `setPreferredSize()` does not affect the width, though it does affect the height.)

Dynamic width

If the `columns` property is 0 (and presuming that an explicit `preferredSize` hasn't been set), the width returned by `getPreferredSize()` is just enough to display the field's contents and border and varies dynamically when the user edits the contents. In practice, the displayed size of the field does not change on every keystroke, which would be disconcerting, but only when the field is revalidated. This happens, for example, when an enclosing container is resized.

Still, you probably don't want your fields to change size at all. There are several ways to make sure they don't. You can use a layout manager that ignores the width returned by `getPreferredSize()`, such as `GridLayout` or `BorderLayout` (north and south positions). You can specify a nonzero value for `columns` in the constructor (or via `setColumns()`). Alternately, you can specify an explicit width (and height) with `setPreferredSize()`.

Restricting input

One of the most common extensions of a text field is a field that enforces some type of restriction on the text that may be entered into it (uppercase only, numbers only, no more than 10 characters, and so on). With a `java.awt.TextField`, such restrictions can be enforced by filtering key events. In earlier versions of Swing, this was done by creating a restricted document model. As of SDK 1.4, Swing provides a `JFormattedTextField` (described in Chapter 20) for this purpose.

The JPasswordField Class

A `JPasswordField` is a text field in which an echo character (* by default) is displayed in place of the characters typed by the user. This feature is generally used when entering passwords to avoid showing the password on the screen. Except for the quirky display, `JPasswordField` behaves like an ordinary `JTextField`, though some steps have been taken to enhance the password field's security.

One reason that `JPasswordField` is a separate class from `JTextField` in Swing (which is not the case in the analogous AWT classes) is so the L&F can treat them differently by specifying different UI delegates. The UI delegate is responsible for hiding the input characters in a `JPasswordField`.

Properties

Table 19-5 shows the properties defined by `JPasswordField`. `JPasswordField` has its own unique `UIClassID` value. The value for `accessibleContext` property is

---

AccessibleJPasswordField, an inner class that extends the JTextField. AccessibleJTextField class. The echoChar property specifies the character to be displayed in the field each time a key is pressed. This character is used to hide the actual input characters, though the L&F may choose to ignore it and hide the input characters some other way.

Table 19-5. JPasswordField properties

Property	Data type	get	is	set	Default value
accessibleContext⁰	AccessibleContext	•			AccessibleJPasswordField
echoChar	char	•		•	'*'
password	char[]	•			
text⁰	string	•		•	
UIClassID⁰	String	•			"PasswordFieldUI"

⁰overridden

See also properties from the JTextComponent class (Table 19-1).

In the interest of security, the getText( ) accessor methods have been deprecated in the JPasswordField field. To get the entered password, it is recommended that the getPassword( ) method be used instead. getPassword( ) returns a mutable char[] array, not an immutable String, so that you can clobber the password with '\0' characters when you are done with it.

Constructors

public JPasswordField( )
> Create a new password text field with zero columns.

public JPasswordField(String text)
> Create a new field containing the text (displayed using the echo character).

public JPasswordField(int columns)
> Create a new password field with the requested number of columns.

public JPasswordField(String text, int columns)
> Create a new password field with the specified number of columns, containing the supplied text (displayed using the echo character).

public JPasswordField(Document doc, String text, int columns)
> This constructor (called by all the others) creates a new password field that uses the specified document model and number of columns. If text is null, the Document's current text is "displayed" with the echo character. Otherwise, text replaces the Document's content and is "displayed." This constructor sets the echo character as an asterisk (*).

Data Protection Methods

public void cut( )
public void copy( )

These methods are overridden to disable cut and copy behavior in password fields. They simply call the L&F's `provideErrorFeedback( )` method, which typically emits a beep. If these methods were not overridden, it would be possible for hidden passwords to be copied from password fields and pasted into nonhidden fields.

public string getText(int offs, int len) throws BadLocationException

Defined in this class only for the purpose of being marked as deprecated. The `getPassword( )` method should be used instead.

Miscellaneous Methods

public boolean echoCharIsSet( )

Indicate whether an echo character has been set. Note that a default echo character (*) is defined, so this method always returns true unless the echo character is explicitly set to '\0'.

The JTextArea Class

The `JTextArea` class displays multiple lines of text in a single font and style. Its default behavior is not to wrap lines of text, but line-wrapping can be enabled on word or character boundaries. Figure 19-5 shows a `JTextArea`.

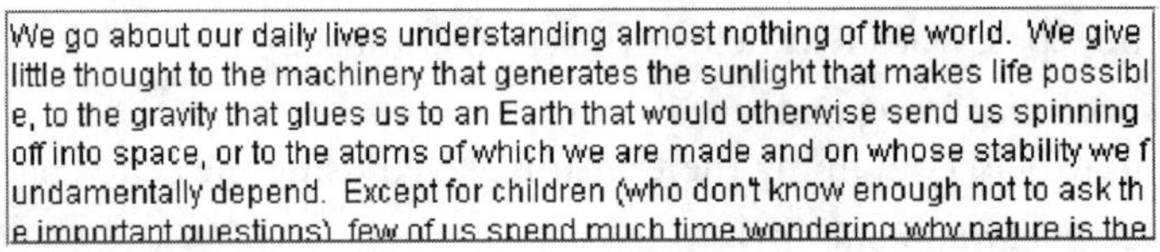

Figure 19-5. JTextArea

Like all Swing `JTextComponents` (but unlike `java.awt.TextArea`), `JTextArea` lacks integrated scrollbars. Fortunately, it is easy to embed a `JTextArea` inside a `JScrollPane` for seamless scrolling. (`JTextArea` implements the `Scrollable` interface, so `JScrollPane` can be intelligent about scrolling it.)

`JTextArea` handles newlines in a cross-platform way. Line separators in text files can be newline (\n), carriage return (\r), or carriage return newline (\r\n), depending on the platform. Swing's text components remember which line separator was originally used, but always use a newline character to represent one in memory. So always use \n when working with the content of a text component. When writing the content back to disk (or to whatever destination you give the write( ) method), the text component translates newlines back to the remembered type. If there is no remembered type (because the content was created from scratch), newlines are translated to the value of the line.separator system property.

Properties

JTextArea defines properties shown in Table 19-6. AccessibleJTextArea is an inner class that extends JTextComponent.AccessibleJTextComponent.

Table 19-6. JTextArea properties

Property	Data type	get	is	set	Default value
accessibleContext[o]	AccessibleContext	•			AccessibleJTextArea
columns	int	•		•	0
font[b, o]	Font	•		•	From superclass
lineCount	int	•			From document
lineWrap[b]	boolean	•		•	false
preferredScrollableViewportSize[o]	Dimension	•			See comments below
preferredSize[b, o]	Dimension	•		•	See comments below
rows	int	•		•	0
scrollableTracksViewportWidth[o]	boolean	•			See comments below
tabSize[b]	int	•		•	8
UIClassID[o]	String	•			"TextAreaUI"
wrapStyleWord[b]	boolean	•		•	false

[b]bound, [o]overridden

See also properties from the javax.swing.text.JTextComponent class (Table 19-1).

The rows and columns properties specify the number of rows and columns to be displayed by the component. If they are nonzero, they determine the value of preferredScrollableViewportSize and the minimum dimensions for preferredSize, based on the size of font. For variable-width fonts, the width of each column is based on the width of the lowercase character m. The font property is listed here because setFont( ) has been overridden to revalidate the component, allowing it to resize based on the size of the new font.

By default, the preferredSize property makes the JTextArea just big enough to display all of the component's text, but not smaller in either dimension than the values defined in the rows and columns properties. The size of the text area changes dynamically as text is inserted or deleted. This is just what you want if you're using a

JScrollPane, but it can be surprising under FlowLayout.* (The JTextArea resizes immediately on each keystroke without waiting for an external revalidation.)

lineCount provides access to the number of lines in the component's document. This has nothing to do with how much of the content is currently visible. What constitutes a "line" is document-dependent but is typically a sequence of characters that ends with a newline.

The lineWrap property indicates whether a line of text should wrap if it is too long for the allocated width of the component. If lineWrap is false, the ends of long lines are completely hidden from the user unless you're using a JScrollPane. The scrollableTracksViewportWidth property is true when line wrap is on, false otherwise.

The wrapStyleWord property determines where line wrapping occurs. If true, the component attempts to wrap only at word boundaries (see Figure 19-6). The default is false. (This property is ignored unless lineWrap is set to true.)

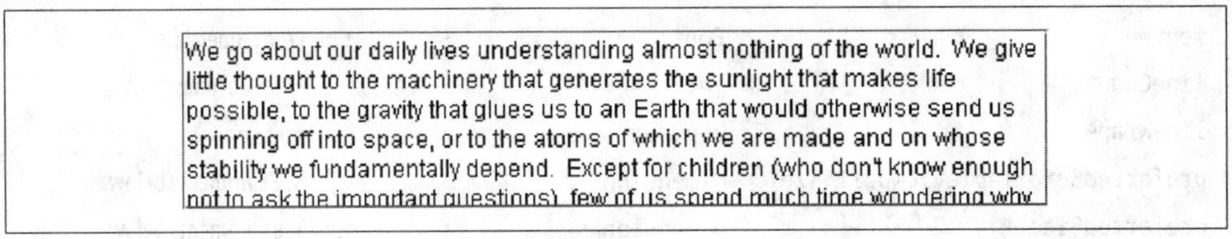

We go about our daily lives understanding almost nothing of the world. We give little thought to the machinery that generates the sunlight that makes life possible, to the gravity that glues us to an Earth that would otherwise send us spinning off into space, or to the atoms of which we are made and on whose stability we fundamentally depend. Except for children (who don't know enough not to ask the important questions) few of us spend much time wondering why

Figure 19-6. JTextArea with lineWrap and wrapStyleWord set to true

The tabSize property specifies the number of columns that a tab character should expand to.

Events

JTextArea does not fire any new event types. It inherits event behavior from JTextComponent and fires property change events when the lineWrap, wrapStyleWord, or tabSize properties are changed.

Constructors

public JTextArea()
    Create a default text area.

public JTextArea(int rows, int columns)
    Create a text area with the specified number of rows and columns.

public JTextArea(String text)
    Create a text area displaying the specified text.

---

* Or under any other layout manager that respects getPreferredSize( ).

public JTextArea(String text, int rows, int columns)
> Create a text area with the specified number of rows and columns displaying the given text.

public JTextArea(Document doc)
> Create a text area that uses the specified Document.

public JTextArea(Document doc, String text, int rows, int columns)
> Create a text area with the specified number of rows and columns that uses the specified Document. If text is null, the Document's current text is displayed. Otherwise, text replaces the Document's content and is displayed. All the other constructors invoke this one.

Text Manipulation Methods

The following convenience methods make it easy to modify the contents of the text area's document model:

public void append(String str)
> Append the given text to the end of the document.

public void insert(String str, int pos)
> Insert the specified text at the given position (offset from the beginning of the document). To insert text at the beginning of the document, use a position of 0.

public void replaceRange(String str, int start, int end)
> Replace a section of the document beginning with the character at the start position and ending with the character at the end position with the given string. The string may be null, in which case a deletion is performed.

Line Transformation Methods

These methods can be used to find the character offset of a given line (see the distinction between line and row in the "Properties" section) and vice-versa. Note that the first line of the document is line 0, the first character of the document is at offset 0, and that newlines count as characters in the document.

public int getLineStartOffset(int line) throws BadLocationException
> Return the character offset (from the beginning of the document) that marks the beginning of the specified line number.

public int getLineEndOffset(int line) throws BadLocationException
> Return the character offset (from the beginning of the document) that marks the end of the specified line number. This is actually the offset of the *first character* of the *next* line.

public int getLineOfOffset(int offset) throws BadLocationException
> Return the line number that contains the given character offset (from the beginning of the document).

The following example shows how these three methods work:

```
// OffsetTest.java
//
import javax.swing.*;
import javax.swing.text.*;

public class OffsetTest {
    public static void main(String[] args) {
        JTextArea ta = new JTextArea();
        ta.setLineWrap(true);
        ta.setWrapStyleWord(true);
        JScrollPane scroll = new JScrollPane(ta);

        // Add three lines of text to the JTextArea.
        ta.append("The first line.\n");
        ta.append("Line Two!\n");
        ta.append("This is the 3rd line of this document.");

        // Print some results.
        try {
            for (int n=0; n < ta.getLineCount(); n+=1)
                System.out.println("line " + n + " starts at " +
                    ta.getLineStartOffset(n) + ", ends at " + ta.getLineEndOffset(n));
            System.out.println();

            int n = 0;
            while (true) {
                System.out.print("offset " + n + " is on ");
                System.out.println("line " + ta.getLineOfOffset(n));
                n += 13;
            }
        } catch (BadLocationException ex) { System.out.println(ex); }

        // Layout
        JFrame f = new JFrame();
        f.setDefaultCloseOperation(JFrame.EXIT_ON_CLOSE);
        f.getContentPane().add(scroll, java.awt.BorderLayout.CENTER);
        f.setSize(150, 150);
        f.setVisible(true);
    }
}
```

When run, this little program produces the following output, along with the frame shown in Figure 19-7. Remember that newlines count as characters in the document.

```
line 0 starts at 0, ends at 16
line 1 starts at 16, ends at 26
line 2 starts at 26, ends at 65

offset 0 is on line 0
offset 13 is on line 0
offset 26 is on line 2
offset 39 is on line 2
```

```
offset 52 is on line 2
offset 65 is on javax.swing.text.BadLocationException: Can't translate offset to line
```

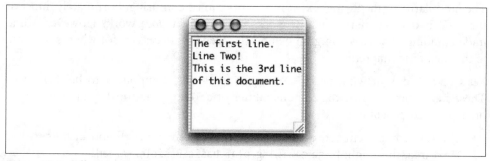

Figure 19-7. OffsetTest frame

Notice that getLineEndOffset( ) returns an index of the character *after* the last character in the specified line. getLineOfOffset(65) throws a BadLocationException even though 65 is returned as the ending offset for line 2.

Understanding JTextArea Layout

Here are tips for laying out your JTextAreas:

Use a JScrollPane
Almost every JTextArea in a real-world application should be embedded in a JScrollPane. The exception might be a JTextArea set to be read-only via setEditable(false), in which it would be impossible for the user to enter text that is pushed past the JTextArea's allocated area. But even then, some of its content might be invisible to the user if the L&F installs a font larger than you expect. It's usually safe to use a JScrollPane because in most L&Fs, scrollbars don't show up unless they are needed. Installing a JScrollPane is as easy as replacing add(myTextArea) with add(new JScrollPane(myTextArea)) in your code. (JScrollPanes are described in Chapter 11.)

Give it size
The default size of a JTextArea is small, allowing only a handful of characters to be displayed. Typing some text into a small JTextArea causes scrollbars to appear, leaving even less space to display text. Or, if it's not in a JScrollPane, the JTextArea grows larger bit by bit as the user types. Neither of these is likely to be what you want, so be sure that your JTextArea is laid out with adequate size. There are three ways to do this. You can use a layout manager that ignores the preferredSize, such as GridLayout or (probably most popular) the center position of BorderLayout. You can specify nonzero values for rows and columns in the constructor (or by using setRows( ) and setColumns( )). Finally, you can specify an explicit size with setPreferredSize( ).

How It All Works

The modularity of the Swing text components can be confusing. Fortunately, most of the time it doesn't matter *how* it works as long as it *does* work. However, some understanding of what's going on behind the scenes is necessary for what is to come in the next four chapters.

Let's take a look at what needs to happen for a text component to be displayed. These behaviors describe the responsibilities of a JTextArea, but they are similar for other JTextComponents:

- The text component retrieves its UI delegate from the L&F and installs it. For JTextArea, this might be javax.swing.plaf.basic.BasicTextAreaUI.

- The UI delegate may set properties such as font, foreground, and selection color. The UI delegate may also set the caret, highlighter, InputMaps and ActionMap. The maps allow text components to respond to L&F-specific keyboard commands for actions such as cut/copy/paste, select-all, caret-to-end-of-line, page-down, and so on.

- The UI delegate also instantiates an EditorKit. For JTextArea this might be javax.swing.text.DefaultEditorKit. Most of the Actions in the text component's array come from the EditorKit.

- If the text component's constructor didn't receive a Document, it creates one. JTextArea creates its Document (a PlainDocument) directly, but other text components delegate this to the EditorKit.

- The Document is responsible for storing the component's text content. It does this by breaking it into a hierarchy of one or more Elements. Each Element can hold part of the Document's content and some style information. JTextArea creates one Element for each line of text and ignores style information. Other text components can be more sophisticated.

- The text component registers itself as a listener for events it needs to track. This includes registering as a DocumentListener so it can update itself in response to any changes that occur in its Document.

- The text component may delegate or partially delegate preferredSize, minimumSize, and maximumSize to the UI delegate. JTextArea does this, but if its rows and columns properties are nonzero, it enforces a minimum on preferredSize.

- The UI delegate is responsible for painting the component, but it uses the EditorKit to paint the text content. The EditorKit does this by way of a ViewFactory. The ViewFactory creates a hierarchy of one or more View objects from the hierarchy of Element objects. The View hierarchy is then painted to the screen. A one-to-one correspondence from Element to View is typical but not required of the ViewFactory.

In this chapter, we've shown how easy it is to do simple things with the Swing text framework. However, if you want to do more than we've demonstrated in this chapter, Swing has a lot to offer. In the next four chapters, we'll examine the rest of the Swing text package, building many interesting and powerful sample programs as we go.

Formatted Text Fields

Swing provides extended functionality for text fields through the JFormattedTextField class introduced in SDK 1.4. A JFormattedTextField can display its value in a friendly (and locale-specific) way, enforce restrictions on its value, be used to edit non-String objects, and permit its value (or part of its value) to be incremented or decremented with the keyboard.

Figure 20-1 shows several JFormattedTextFields, but for the full effect you may wish to run the SimpleFTF program and play with it a bit. Most of the fields show locale-specific formatting. The Integer field puts delimiters between millions and thousands and between thousands and units. It changes its appearance (by dropping the delimiters) temporarily when it gains focus. An invalid value either adjusts to the closest valid value or reverts to the most recent valid value when a field loses focus, depending on the field. (For example, try changing the date to February 34.) Also, be sure to notice how elements of the Date field can be incremented and decremented with the up arrow and down arrow keys. (The L&F specifies keys for incrementing and decrementing, but existing L&Fs use the up arrow and down arrow. In addition, the Enter and Escape keys usually commit and cancel an edit, respectively.)

You might also notice some nonintuitive behavior. Attempting to edit the first Float field drops all but the first digit after the decimal point, and text input in the URL field defaults to *overwrite* mode (not the expected *insert* mode). As a workaround for the former, see the second Float field in SimpleFTF. For the latter, see the DefaultFormatter and its setOverwriteMode property later in this chapter.

Here's the code for SimpleFTF:

```
// SimpleFTF.java
//
import javax.swing.*;

public class SimpleFTF extends JPanel {
```

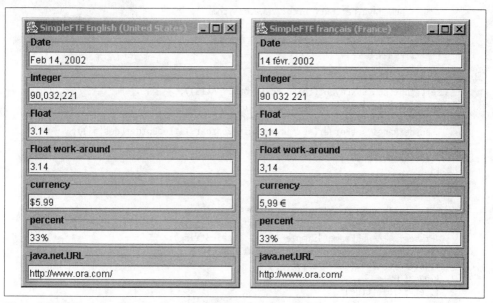

Figure 20-1. JFormattedTextFields in two different locales

```java
public SimpleFTF( ) {
    JFormattedTextField ftf[] = new JFormattedTextField[7];
    String des[] = new String[ftf.length]; // Description of each field

    des[0] = "Date";
    ftf[0] = new JFormattedTextField(new java.util.Date( ));

    des[1] = "Integer";
    ftf[1] = new JFormattedTextField(new Integer(90032221));

    des[2] = "Float";
    ftf[2] = new JFormattedTextField(new Float(3.14));

    des[3] = "Float work-around"; // Manually specify a NumberFormat.
    ftf[3] = new JFormattedTextField(java.text.NumberFormat.getInstance( ));
    ftf[3].setValue(new Float(3.14));

    des[4] = "currency";
    ftf[4] = new JFormattedTextField(java.text.NumberFormat.getCurrencyInstance( ));
    ftf[4].setValue(new Float(5.99));

    des[5] = "percent";
    ftf[5] = new JFormattedTextField(java.text.NumberFormat.getPercentInstance( ));
    ftf[5].setValue(new Float(0.33));

    des[6] = "java.net.URL"; // Works via 1-arg String constructor and toString( )
    java.net.URL u = null;
    try {
```

```
      u = new java.net.URL("http://www.ora.com/");
    } catch (java.net.MalformedURLException ignored) { }
    ftf[6] = new JFormattedTextField(u);
    ftf[6].setColumns(24);

    // Add each ftf[] to a BoxLayout.
    setLayout(new BoxLayout(this, BoxLayout.Y_AXIS));
    for (int j=0; j < ftf.length; j+=1) {
      JPanel borderPanel = new JPanel(new java.awt.BorderLayout( ));
      borderPanel.setBorder(new javax.swing.border.TitledBorder(des[j]));
      borderPanel.add(ftf[j], java.awt.BorderLayout.CENTER);
      add(borderPanel);
    }
  }

  public static void main(String argv[]) {
    String localeString = java.util.Locale.getDefault( ).getDisplayName( );
    JFrame f = new JFrame("SimpleFTF " + localeString);
    f.setDefaultCloseOperation(JFrame.EXIT_ON_CLOSE);
    f.setContentPane(new SimpleFTF( ));
    f.pack( );
    f.setVisible(true);
  }
}
```

Figure 20-2 shows the classes associated with JFormattedTextField. We'll describe each Swing class in turn.

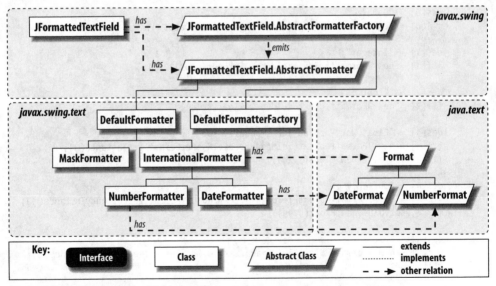

Figure 20-2. JFormattedTextField class diagram

The JFormattedTextField Class

`JFormattedTextField` extends `JTextField` primarily by having a value property in addition to its content (accessed by the text property). The user may manipulate the field's content, but its value doesn't (necessarily) change until the user *commits* the edit. If the user cancels the edit, the content reverts back to the most recent valid value.

The field's value may be of any `Object` type, but it is displayed and edited as a `String`. The field uses its formatter to translate between `Object` and `String` representations.

`JFormattedTextField` works by maintaining an `AbstractFormatterFactory` (defined as a public abstract inner class). Whenever the field receives focus, it obtains an `AbstractFormatter` (another public abstract inner class) from the factory to oversee editing until it loses focus. It also queries the factory for a formatter at other times, such as when it loses focus or when `setValue()` is called.

The factory does not generally create new objects (as other factory classes typically do), but usually just hands out an appropriate existing formatter instance for the field to use. The factory is used to permit different formatters to be used for viewing versus editing, not to support a variety of different types. `JFormattedTextField` does support a variety of types, but its constructor creates a custom factory for the type passed in. So if you create a new `JFormattedTextField(new java.util.Date())`, every formatter it gets from its factory is for dates,[*] and it rejects user input that looks like a `java.net.URL` or some other class.[†]

Properties

Table 20-1 shows the properties defined by `JFormattedTextField`. It has its own unique `UIClassID` value but does not override the inherited `accessibleContext`. The document property is listed in the table only because `JFormattedTextField` overrides `setDocument()` to register itself as a listener for the new document and remove itself as a listener for the previous one.

---

[*] Unless you replace the factory, of course, using `setFormatterFactory()`.

[†] Subclasses of `java.lang.Number` are an exception of sorts. By default, `JFormattedTextField` creates the same factory for any subclass of `java.lang.Number`. So, for example, a simple formatted text field created with a `java.lang.Integer` accepts floating-point values. See "Handling Numerics" later in this chapter.

Table 20-1. JFormattedTextField properties

Property	Data type	get	is	set	Default value
actions[o]	Action[]	•			From superclass plus CommitAction, CancelAction
document[b,o]	Document	•		•	PlainDocument
editValid	boolean		•		true
focusLostBehavior	int	•		•	COMMIT_OR_REVERT
formatter[b]	JFormattedTextField. AbstractFormatter	•			null
formatterFactory[b]	JFormattedTextField. AbstractFormatterFactory	•		•	null
UIClassID[o]	String	•			"FormattedTextFieldUI"
value[b]	Object	•		•	null

[b]bound, [o]overridden

See also properties from the JTextField class (Table 19-3).

The actions property appears here because JFormattedTextField adds CommitAction and CancelAction to the array of utility actions inherited from the superclass. CommitAction extends JTextField's NotifyAction to call commitEdit() (to set the current edit as the value) before firing. CancelAction resets value, canceling the current edit (if any).

editValid is false if the current edit does not meet the field's formatting requirements, and true otherwise. This property is managed by the field's formatter. If the formatter permits the field to be in a temporary invalid state, it needs to update the value of this property appropriately.

formatter is the AbstractFormatter installed to oversee editing and is obtained from the formatterFactory. (Note that this is technically the case even if you instantiated the JFormattedTextField with the constructor that takes an AbstractFormatter. The constructor simply creates an unsophisticated formatterFactory that always returns the formatter you passed in. Whenever the field receives or loses focus, it queries the factory for an AbstractFormatter and receives your formatter.) The formatter is used to convert between the value (which may be any Object type) and its String representation displayed in the field.

The formatterFactory is responsible for supplying the field with a formatter whenever it asks for one. All of JFormattedTextField's constructors, except for the default constructor, use their arguments to create the formatterFactory. The default constructor leaves a null value for formatterFactory, but a factory is created the first time setValue() is called with a non-null argument.

value is the most recent valid content of the field, which may not be the current content of the field if an edit is in progress. Because of this, it is usually wise to call the field's commitEdit( ) method before calling getValue( ).*

The focusLostBehavior property specifies how the field behaves when it loses focus. The legal values are COMMIT_OR_REVERT, REVERT, COMMIT, and PERSIST. These are described in Table 20-2. (Some formatters "push" values when an edit is in progress and ignore the value of this property.) This property doesn't help you if you want an invalid field to refuse to lose focus, but you can do that with an InputVerifier like this:

```
myFTF.setInputVerifier(new InputVerifier( ) {
  public boolean verify(JComponent input) {
    if (!(input instanceof JFormattedTextField))
      return true; // Give up focus.
    return ((JFormattedTextField)input).isEditValid( );
} });
```

See "The InputVerifier Class" at the end of this chapter for details.

Events

JFormattedTextField does not fire any new event types. It inherits event behavior from JTextField and fires property change events when the values of the value, formatter, or formatterFactory properties are changed.

Constants

Table 20-2 defines the JFormattedTextField constants. These are the legal values of the focusLostBehavior property.

Table 20-2. JFormattedTextField constants

Constant	Type	Description
COMMIT	int	When the field loses focus, commitEdit( ) is called. If commitEdit( ) throws a ParseException, the field retains its invalid content.
COMMIT_OR_REVERT	int	When the field loses focus, commitEdit( ) is called. If commitEdit( ) throws a ParseException, the field reverts to its most recent valid content.
REVERT	int	When the field loses focus, it reverts to its most recent valid content.
PERSIST	int	Nothing happens when the field loses focus. (It retains its current content.)

---

* Especially if the focusLostBehavior property is set to PERSIST. In the other cases it is likely that the field lost focus (causing its value to be committed or reverted) when the user clicked on the button or other GUI element that resulted in this call to getValue( ). Calling commitEdit( ) is easy enough that it makes sense to do it unless you're sure it isn't required.

Constructors

public JFormattedTextField()
> Create a new formatted text field with no formatter factory.

public JFormattedTextField(Object value)
> Create a new formatted text field with the specified initial value. A formatter factory is automatically created based on the type of value. This constructor can handle java.util.Date, subclasses of java.lang.Number, or any class with a constructor that takes a single String argument.* Use one of the other constructors to support other types.

public JFormattedTextField(java.text.Format format)
> Create a new formatted text field. A simple formatter factory is automatically created based on format.

public JFormattedTextField(JFormattedTextField.AbstractFormatter formatter)
> Create a new formatted text field and set formatterFactory to the result of calling new DefaultFormatterFactory(formatter).

public JFormattedTextField(JFormattedTextField.AbstractFormatterFactory factory)
> Create a new formatted text field with the specified formatter factory.

public JFormattedTextField(JFormattedTextField.AbstractFormatterFactory factory,
Object value)
> Create a new formatted text field with the specified initial value, then set formatterFactory to the specified factory.

Public Method

public void commitEdit() throws java.text.ParseException
> Attempt to set the current content of the field as the value. It uses the field's formatter to convert from String to Object type.

Handling Numerics

To a certain extent, JFormattedTextField treats the types Float, Double, Integer, Long, Short, and Byte (all subclasses of java.lang.Number) as interchangeable. This can sometimes be surprising. For example, with this field:

```
JFormattedTextField ftf = new JFormattedTextField(new Integer(4));
```

you might expect to be able to retrieve the value like this:

```
int val = ((Integer)ftf.getValue()).intValue(); // Incorrect
```

---

* This works only if the constructor can accept strings generated by the toString() method.

This code is likely to throw a ClassCastException because ftf.getValue() might return one of the other numeric types if the user has edited the field.* A safer way to retrieve the value is:

```
int val = ((Number)ftf.getValue()).intValue(); // Correct
```

Casting to Number like this always works because the methods floatValue(), doubleValue(), integerValue(), longValue(), shortValue(), and byteValue() are all defined in the java.lang.Number class.

If for some reason you want to force getValue() to return a specific numeric type, this can be done by instantiating a NumberFormat, calling its setValueClass() method, and passing the NumberFormat into the JFormattedTextField constructor.

The JFormattedTextField.AbstractFormatter Class

AbstractFormatter is an abstract inner class of JFormattedTextField that defines the basic API for formatters. Usually, there is no reason to extend AbstractFormatter directly since DefaultFormatter (discussed in the next section) provides a more complete starting point.

Public methods

public abstract Object stringToValue(String text) throws java.text.ParseException
public abstract String valueToString(Object value) throws java.text.ParseException
These two methods are the heart of the formatter API. They are used by the field to convert between the field's value (which may be any Object type) and the String representation displayed in the field. If conversion is impossible, a java.text.ParseException is thrown. In particular, the stringToValue() method throws a ParseException if its argument is not valid. Returning without throwing a ParseException indicates that the input was deemed valid.

public void install(JFormattedTextField ftf)
Immediately after a JFormattedTextField obtains a formatter from its formatterFactory, it calls this method so the formatter can initialize itself for a new field. AbstractFormatter's implementation of this method stores ftf for later use (by the getFormattedTextField() method, for example) and sets the text content of the field. It also installs any values returned by getActions(), getDocumentFilter(), and getNavigationFilter() on ftf. (AbstractFormatter returns null in all three of those methods but is prepared for subclasses not to.) Subclasses may override this method if they wish to add listeners to the field or its Document or to modify the field's selection or caret position.

---

* By default, it tends to return either a Long or a Double, but it's not so simple even when knowing that. A field showing 5.008 may return a Double value, but if the user shortens it to 5.00 with the Backspace key, it may now return a Long value (despite the presence of the decimal point).

public void uninstall()
> JFormattedTextField calls this method on its formatter just before it obtains a new formatter from its formatterFactory to undo anything done in the install() method. Subclasses that override install() may need to override uninstall() also.

Protected methods

protected JFormattedTextField getFormattedTextField()
> Return the JFormattedTextField on which this formatter is installed.

protected Action[] getActions()
> AbstractFormatter's implementation returns null. Subclasses may override this method to add one or more Actions to the field's ActionMap. An Action is invoked only if its name matches something in the field's InputMap. Formatters may be especially interested in "increment", "decrement", and "reset-field-edit", which most L&Fs assign to the up arrow, down arrow, and Escape keys, respectively. See Appendix B for a complete list.

protected DocumentFilter getDocumentFilter()
> AbstractFormatter's implementation returns null. Subclasses may override this method to set a DocumentFilter on the field. (See "The DocumentFilter Class" in Chapter 22.)

protected NavigationFilter getNavigationFilter()
> AbstractFormatter's implementation returns null. Subclasses may override this method to set a NavigationFilter on the field. (See "The NavigationFilter Class" in Chapter 22.)

protected void invalidEdit()
> Call this method to provide error feedback (for example, when the user attempts to enter an invalid character into the field). AbstractFormatter's implementation simply calls the field's invalidEdit() method.

protected void setEditValid(boolean valid)
> This utility method simply passes its argument to the field's setEditValid() method. The formatter is responsible for keeping the field's editValid property up to date.

protected Object clone() throws CloneNotSupportedException
> Because JFormattedTextFields cannot share a formatter, the clone is in an unattached state and may be installed on some other JFormattedTextField.

The DefaultFormatter Class

DefaultFormatter is a concrete implementation of AbstractFormatter that provides enough functionality for many purposes. It can be used for classes with a constructor that takes a single String. To support other classes, you may have to override

---

DefaultFormatter's stringToValue( ) method and its valueToString( ) method if the class's toString( ) method is not adequate.

DefaultFormatter maintains the field's editValid property, checking to see if the current edit is valid after every user keystroke and calling setEditValid( ) as appropriate.

Properties

Table 20-3 shows the properties defined by DefaultFormatter.

Table 20-3. DefaultFormatter properties

Property	Data type	get	is	set	Default value
allowsInvalid	boolean	•		•	true
commitsOnValidEdit	boolean	•		•	false
overwriteMode	boolean	•		•	true
valueClass	Class	•		•	null

The allowsInvalid property controls whether the field's content may be temporarily invalid during an edit. Consider an integer field with a current value of 25 that the user wants to change to 19. The user may decide to do this by pressing the Backspace key twice, then the 1 key and the 9 key. After the first backspace, the content of the field is 2. After the second backspace, the content of the field is the empty string, but if allowsInvalid were false, this would not be allowed (since the empty string is not a valid integer), and the field would refuse to allow the 2 to be deleted. Setting this property to false can be effective in certain cases but should be done only after careful consideration.

commitsOnValidEdit controls how often a field's value is set during an edit. If this property is true, then the field attempts to commit its content after every keystroke. The default value is false, which means the field does not commit until something special happens, such as when the field loses focus or the user presses the Enter key. Consider again the situation from the previous paragraph. After the first backspace, the field shows 2. If commitsOnValidEdit is false, nothing is committed, and the field's value remains 25. If the user later cancels the edit (using the Escape key, for example), the content of the field reverts to 25. If commitsOnValidEdit is true, the 2 is committed immediately, and the field's value becomes 2.

When the overwriteMode property is true, characters entered by the user (and even pastes from the clipboard) replace characters in the field. When it is false (insert mode), new characters are inserted without deleting any of the existing characters. The default value is true, which is often not what you want. Subclasses of DefaultFormatter often call setOverwriteMode(false) in their constructors.

The valueClass property determines the type of object that the stringToValue( ) method attempts to return. It is usually fine for this property to remain null, in which case stringToValue( ) attempts to return an object of the same type* as getFormattedTextField.getValue( ). (If you override the stringToValue( ) method, the valueClass property is ignored unless you handle it manually or invoke super. stringToValue( ).)

Constructor

public DefaultFormatter( )
> Create a new DefaultFormatter with default property values.

Public Methods

public abstract Object stringToValue(String text) throws java.text.ParseException
> This method uses reflection to attempt to instantiate an object using a constructor that takes a single String argument. The object instantiated is of the type specified by the formatter's valueClass property or, if null, of the same type as the field's current value. If that class doesn't have a public String constructor, or if the constructor throws an exception, this method throws a ParseException. Subclasses frequently override this behavior.

public abstract String valueToString(Object value) throws java.text.ParseException
> This method simply returns value.toString( ). Subclasses may override this behavior.

public void install(JFormattedTextField ftf)
> This method is overridden to move the caret to the beginning of the field. Except for that, it delegates to the superclass.

Example

Here, we extend DefaultFormatter to create a formatter that can edit combinations such as those used by combination locks. The String representation of a combination is something like 15-45-22 or 35-30-11-19. The Object representation is an int[ ] array.† We override stringToValue( ) and valueToString( ) to convert between these representations, and we override getActions( ) so that the number under the caret can be incremented or decremented from the keyboard. We also provide a sample

---

* Numerics (Float, Double, Integer, Long, Short, and Byte) are an exception. This might be a good reason to call setValueClass( ). See "Handling Numerics," earlier in this chapter.

† We could have chosen any object type, including java.util.Vector or a custom Combination class, instead of int[ ].

main( ) method that shows how CombinationFormatter could be used. (See Figure 20-3.)

```java
// CombinationFormatter.java
//
import javax.swing.*;
import javax.swing.text.*;

public class CombinationFormatter extends DefaultFormatter {

  public CombinationFormatter( ) {
    setOverwriteMode(false);
  }

  public Object stringToValue(String string) throws java.text.ParseException {
    // Input: string of form "15-45-22" (any number of hyphen-delimited numbers)
    // Output: int array
    String s[] = string.split("-");
    int a[] = new int[s.length];
    for (int j=0; j<a.length; j+=1)
      try {
        a[j] = Integer.parseInt(s[j]);
      } catch (NumberFormatException nfe) {
        throw new java.text.ParseException(s[j] + " is not an int", 0);
      }
    return a;
  }

  public String valueToString(Object value) throws java.text.ParseException {
    // Input: int array
    // Output: string of numerals separated by hyphens
    if (value == null) return null;
    if (! (value instanceof int[]))
      throw new java.text.ParseException("expected int[]", 0);
    int a[] = (int[])value;
    StringBuffer sb = new StringBuffer( );
    for (int j=0; j < a.length; j+=1) {
      if (j > 0) sb.append('-');
      sb.append(a[j]);
    }
    return sb.toString( );
  }

  protected Action[] getActions( ) {
    Action[] actions = { new CombinationIncrementer("increment", 1),
                         new CombinationIncrementer("decrement", -1) };
    return actions;
  }

  // Begin inner class -----------------------------------------

  public class CombinationIncrementer extends AbstractAction {
    protected int delta;
```

```
      public CombinationIncrementer(String name, int delta) { // Constructor
        super(name); // 'name' must match something in the component's InputMap or else
                     // this Action is not invoked automatically. Valid names include
                     // "reset-field-edit", "increment", "decrement", and "unselect"
                     // (see Appendix B).
        this.delta = delta;
      }

      public void actionPerformed(java.awt.event.ActionEvent ae) {
        JFormattedTextField ftf = getFormattedTextField(); // From AbstractFormatter
        if (ftf == null) return;
        String text = ftf.getText();
        if (text == null) return;
        int pos = ftf.getCaretPosition();

        int hyphenCount = 0;
        for (int j=0; j < pos; j+=1) // How many hyphens precede the caret?
          if (text.charAt(j) == '-') hyphenCount += 1;
        try {
          int a[] = (int[])stringToValue(text);
          a[hyphenCount] += delta; // Change the number at caret position.
          if (a[hyphenCount] < 0) a[hyphenCount] = 0;
          String newText = valueToString(a);
          ftf.setText(newText); // Does not retain caret position
          if ((text.charAt(pos) == '-') && (newText.length() < text.length()) )
            pos -= 1; // Don't let caret move past - when 10 changes to 9.
          ftf.setCaretPosition(pos);
        } catch (Exception e) { return; }
      }
    }
  }
  // End inner class ----------------------------------------

  public static void main(String argv[]) {
    // A demo main() method to show how CombinationFormatter could be used
    int comb1[] = { 35, 11, 19 };
    int comb2[] = { 10, 20, 30 };

    final JFormattedTextField field1 =
      new JFormattedTextField(new CombinationFormatter());
    field1.setValue(comb1);

    final JFormattedTextField field2 =
      new JFormattedTextField(new CombinationFormatter());
    field2.setValue(comb2);

    JPanel pan = new JPanel();
    pan.add(new JLabel("Change the combination from"));
    pan.add(field1);
    pan.add(new JLabel("to"));
    pan.add(field2);
```

```
      JButton b = new JButton("Submit");
     b.addActionListener(new java.awt.event.ActionListener( ) {
       public void actionPerformed(java.awt.event.ActionEvent ae) {
         try {
           field1.commitEdit( ); // Make sure current edit (if any) is committed.
           field2.commitEdit( );
         } catch (java.text.ParseException pe) { }
         int oldc[] = (int[])field1.getValue( );
         int newc[] = (int[])field2.getValue( );
         //
         // Code to validate oldc[] and change to newc[] goes here.
         //
       }
     });
     pan.add(b);

     JFrame f = new JFrame("CombinationFormatter Demo");
     f.setDefaultCloseOperation(JFrame.EXIT_ON_CLOSE);
     f.setContentPane(pan);
     f.setSize(360, 100);
     f.setVisible(true);
   }
 }
```

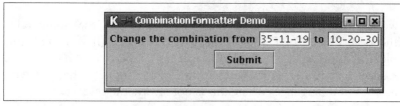

Figure 20-3. JFormattedTextFields using CombinationFormatters

Some combination locks require each combination to have exactly three numbers and require each number to be no higher than 59. CombinationFormatter doesn't enforce either of these restrictions, but it wouldn't be hard to incorporate them.

The MaskFormatter Class

MaskFormatter is a subclass of DefaultFormatter that formats strings by matching them against a mask. The mask is a string of literals and nonliterals. The nonliterals (listed and described in Table 20-4) are wildcards that match a family of characters. Literals match only themselves. A single quote preceding a nonliteral (or another single quote) turns it into a literal. So, for example, the mask "ABa'A#''Hb" consists of the nonliteral A, the literal B, the literal a, the literal A, the nonliteral #, the literal ', the nonliteral H, and the literal b. The string "1BaA1'1b" matches this mask.

Table 20-4. Mask nonliterals (case-sensitive)

char	Matches	Notes
*	Any character	
A	Any alphanumeric character	Tested by `Character.isLetterOrDigit()`
?	Any alphabetic character	Tested by `Character.isLetter()`
U	Uppercase alphabetic	Like ? but lowercase is mapped to uppercase
L	Lowercase alphabetic	Like ? but uppercase is mapped to lowercase
#	Any numeric character	Tested by `Character.isDigit()`
H	Any hexadecimal numeric	Like # but includes abcdefABCDEF
'		Precedes any character in this table to create a literal

The `JFormattedTextField` in Figure 19-1 (and the code that follows it) uses a simple `MaskFormatter` with mask "UUUUU".

A `MaskFormatter` installed on a `JFormattedTextField` controls the caret so that by default it skips over literals and lands on nonliterals, which is nice. It can also be configured (by setting the `valueContainsLiteralCharacters` property to `false`) to have `getValue()` skip the literals, so the above string would be returned as "111" instead of "1BaA1'1b".

`MaskFormatter` works with Unicode characters, so, for example, the nonliteral # matches any Unicode `DECIMAL_DIGIT_NUMBER`, not just ASCII 0-9. (If you think this might be a problem, take a look at the `validCharacters` property.) In general, one character in the mask matches exactly one character of the input string, but with Unicode there may be a few languages where this is not always the case.

If you're trying to do something more complicated than `MaskFormatter` allows, such as specifying a more granular group of characters or permitting strings to vary in length, see "Formatting with Regular Expressions," later in this chapter.

Properties

Table 20-5 shows the properties defined by `MaskFormatter`.

Table 20-5. MaskFormatter properties

Property	Data type	get	is	set	Default value
allowsInvalid[o]	boolean	•		•	false
invalidCharacters	String	•		•	null
mask	String	•		•	null

[o]overridden

See also properties from the `DefaultFormatter` class (Table 20-3).

Table 20-5. MaskFormatter properties (continued)

Property	Data type	get	is	set	Default value
placeholder	char		•	•	' ' (space)
placeholderCharacter	String		•	•	null
validCharacters	String		•	•	null
valueContainsLiteralCharacters	boolean		•	•	true

°overridden

See also properties from the DefaultFormatter class (Table 20-3).

The allowsInvalid property is listed here because MaskFormatter overrides it to default to false (which is usually what you want with MaskFormatter) and uses it to control an additional aspect of its behavior. If allowsInvalid is false, the field's caret skips over literals and lands on nonliterals.

The mask property described earlier is key to MaskFormatter. It can be set in the constructor or through the setMask( ) method, both of which are declared to throw a ParseException if the mask is invalid. This is an annoyance because the only way to make an invalid mask is to escape a literal (or to put a single ' at the end), and even then no exception actually gets thrown (at least not in Version 1.4.1).

The placeholder and placeholderCharacter properties determine what happens if the string is shorter than the mask. Let's say the mask has length 6, but the input string is only 4 characters long. If the 5th slot of the mask is a literal, then that literal is copied into the 5th slot of the string. If not, the 5th slot of the placeholder string is consulted. If placeholder is not null and has a length of at least 5, and if this is the formatter's initial attempt at formatting (not a subsequent attempt), then the 5th slot of the placeholder string is copied. Otherwise, the value of placeholderCharacter is copied. (If the input string is longer than the mask, excess characters are ignored.)

validCharacters and invalidCharacters place restrictions on which characters can match nonliterals in the mask. The type of these properties is String, but think of them as (case-sensitive) sets of characters. If validCharacters is not null, then any character matching a nonliteral must appear in the validCharacters string. Excluding a character from the validCharacters string prevents it from matching anything. If invalidCharacters is not null, then any character appearing in the invalidCharacters string is also illegal, even if it also appears in the validCharacters string.

If the valueContainsLiteralCharacters property is set to false, then the stringToValue( ) method (and hence the field's getValue( ) method) strips the literals out of the string it returns. For example, if the mask is 20## and the field holds 2013, getValue( ) returns 2013 if valueContainsLiteralCharacters is true, but 13 if valueContainsLiteralCharacters is false.

Constructors

public MaskFormatter( )
> Create a new MaskFormatter with no mask.

public MaskFormatter(String mask) throws java.text.ParseException
> Create a new MaskFormatter with the specified mask.

Public Methods

public abstract Object stringToValue(String text) throws java.text.ParseException
> This method is overridden to strip out any mask literals from text (but only if valueContainsLiteralCharacters is false) before delegating to the superclass. The valueClass property is honored. (See DefaultFormatter's stringToValue( ) method.)

public abstract String valueToString(Object value) throws java.text.ParseException
> This method returns value.toString( ), appending placeholder or literal mask characters if necessary.

The InternationalFormatter Class

InternationalFormatter is a subclass of DefaultFormatter that delegates most of its work to an object of type java.text.Format (which is always a subclass since java.text.Format itself is abstract). Many of these subclasses provide internationalization support through awareness of locales, hence the name InternationalFormatter.

InternationalFormatter is rarely used directly. It is a repository for the common functionality of its two subclasses, DateFormatter and NumberFormatter.

Properties

Table 20-6 shows the properties defined by InternationalFormatter.

Table 20-6. InternationalFormatter properties

Property	Data type	get	is	set	Default value
format	java.text.Format	•		•	null
minimum	Comparable	•		•	null
maximum	Comparable	•		•	null
overwriteMode[o]	boolean	•		•	false

[o]overridden

See also properties from the DefaultFormatter class (Table 20-3).

The format property is key to InternationalFormatter and is used by the valueToString( ) and stringToValue( ) methods to translate between the field's Object and String representations. It can be set in the constructor or via the setFormat( ) method.

The minimum and maximum properties can constrain the value of the field. If minimum is not null, value may not be less than minimum. If maximum is not null, value may not be greater than maximum. These may be of any type that implements the Comparable interface. (Provided it hasn't already been set, calling setMinimum( ) or setMaximum( ) also sets the formatter's valueClass property.)

InternationalFormatter overrides the overwriteMode property, setting it to false.

Constructors

public InternationalFormatter( )
> Create a new InternationalFormatter with no Format.

public InternationalFormatter(java.text.Format format)
> Create a new InternationalFormatter with the specified Format.

Public Methods

public Object stringToValue(String text) throws java.text.ParseException
> This method is overridden to throw a ParseException if the value is less than minimum (if minimum is not null) or more than maximum (if maximum is not null). Otherwise, it delegates to getFormat( ).parseObject(text), allowing any ParseException to propagate. The valueClass property is honored.

public String valueToString(Object value) throws java.text.ParseException
> This method delegates to getFormat( ).format(value).

public Format.Field[] getFields(int offset)
> Return the Format.Field constants that correspond to the given offset of the field's text, or an empty array if there is no text. This can be used to determine the subfield at that offset (for example, DAY_OF_WEEK in a DateFormat).

The DateFormatter Class

DateFormatter is a subclass of InternationalFormatter that uses an object of type java.text.DateFormat as its format. JFormattedTextField instantiates a DateFormatter for itself if you pass a java.util.Date or a java.text.DateFormat into its constructor. With a java.util.Date, the format is localized to the default locale. This is usually what you want, but if you want your program to use the same date format no matter where in the world it is run, construct your JFormattedTextField with a specific java. text.DateFormat.

Most of the `DateFormatter` implementation is concerned with providing support to increment and decrement subfields of any date from the keyboard. It does a nice job with this. If you haven't done so yet, you might want run the `SimpleFTF` program and play with the date field.

Properties

`DateFormatter` does not define any properties beyond those it inherits (see Table 20-6). The `minimum` and `maximum` properties can be handy if you want the field to be restricted to a specific range of dates.

Constructors

public DateFormatter()
> Create a new `DateFormatter` and call `java.text.DateFormat.getDateInstance()` to set the `format` to the formatting style of the current locale.

public DateFormatter(java.text.DateFormat format)
> Create a new `DateFormatter` with the specified `format`.

The NumberFormatter Class

`NumberFormatter` is a subclass of `InternationalFormatter` that uses an object of type `java.text.NumberFormat` as its format. `JFormattedTextField` instantiates a `NumberFormatter` for itself if you pass a subclass of `Number` or a `java.text.NumberFormat` into its constructor. With a subclass of `Number`, the format is localized to the current locale. Again, this is usually what you want, but if you want your program to use the same number format no matter where in the world it is run, construct your `JFormattedTextField` with a specific `java.text.NumberFormat`.

Properties

`NumberFormatter` does not define any properties beyond those it inherits (see Table 20-6). The `minimum` and `maximum` properties can be handy if you want the field to be restricted to a specific range.

Constructors

public NumberFormatter()
> Create a new `NumberFormatter` and call `java.text.NumberFormat.getNumberInstance()` to set the `format`, which is a general-purpose format for the current locale.

public NumberFormatter(java.text.NumberFormat format)
> Create a new `NumberFormatter` with the specified `format`.

Public Method

public Object stringToValue(String text) throws java.text.ParseException
NumberFormatter does not technically override this method, but (through private methods) does alter how it works slightly. This method should succeed if valueClass has been set to Integer, Long, Short, Byte, Float, or Double, even though those classes don't have constructors that take a single String argument.

The JFormattedTextField.AbstractFormatterFactory Class

AbstractFormatterFactory is an abstract inner class of JFormattedTextField that defines the basic API (a single method) for formatter factories. There is usually no reason to extend AbstractFormatterFactory directly. Instantiate a DefaultFormatterFactory instead.

Each JFormattedTextField has its own factory. See the description of formatter factories in "The JFormattedTextField Class" earlier in this chapter.

Public method

public abstract JFormattedTextField.AbstractFormatter
  getFormatter(JFormattedTextField tf)
This method returns a formatter for tf to use. Simple factories return the same formatter instance (not even a clone) each time. Sophisticated factories might examine tf and return different formatters depending on whether it has focus, whether it is enabled, etc.

The DefaultFormatterFactory Class

DefaultFormatterFactory is Swing's only concrete implementation of AbstractFormatterFactory. It holds one or more formatters and decides which one to give to the field depending on whether the field has focus and whether the field's value is null.

Properties

Table 20-7 shows the formatter properties defined by DefaultFormatterFactory.

Table 20-7. DefaultFormatterFactory properties

Property	Data type	get	is	set	Default value
defaultFormatter	JFormattedTextField.AbstractFormatter	•		•	null
displayFormatter	JFormattedTextField.AbstractFormatter	•		•	null
editFormatter	JFormattedTextField.AbstractFormatter	•		•	null
nullFormatter	JFormattedTextField.AbstractFormatter	•		•	null

`defaultFormatter` is used if one of the other formatter properties is `null`. It is common for `defaultFormatter` to be the only non-null formatter property, in which case the field uses the `defaultFormatter` exclusively.

`displayFormatter` is intended for use when the field does not have focus. It may be `null`, in which case `defaultFormatter` is used instead.

`editFormatter` is intended for use when the field has focus. It may be `null`, in which case `defaultFormatter` is used instead.

`nullFormatter` is intended for use when the field's content is `null`. It may be `null`, in which case `displayFormatter` or `editFormatter` (depending on whether the field has focus) is used instead. (If `displayFormatter`/`editFormatter` is also `null`, `defaultFormatter` is used.)

Constructors

public DefaultFormatterFactory()
> Create a new `DefaultFormatterFactory` with no formatters.

public DefaultFormatterFactory(
  JFormattedTextField.AbstractFormatter defaultFormatter)
public DefaultFormatterFactory(
  JFormattedTextField.AbstractFormatter defaultFormatter, JFormattedTextField.
  AbstractFormatter displayFormatter)
public DefaultFormatterFactory(
  JFormattedTextField.AbstractFormatter defaultFormatter, JFormattedTextField.
  AbstractFormatter displayFormatter, JFormattedTextField.
  AbstractFormatter editFormatter)
public DefaultFormatterFactory(
  JFormattedTextField.AbstractFormatter defaultFormatter, JFormattedTextField.
  AbstractFormatter displayFormatter, JFormattedTextField.
  AbstractFormatter editFormatter, JFormattedTextField.
  AbstractFormatter nullFormatter)
> Create a new `DefaultFormatterFactory` with the specified `defaultFormatter`, `displayFormatter`, `editFormatter`, and `nullFormatter`. Versions that lack one or more of the parameters act as though `null` were passed for the missing parameter.

Public Method

public JFormattedTextField.AbstractFormatter getFormatter(JFormattedTextField tf)
> If `tf.getValue()` is `null` and `nullFormatter` is not, this method returns `nullFormatter`. If `tf` has focus and `editFormatter` is not `null`, this method returns `editFormatter`. If `tf` does not have focus and `displayFormatter` is not `null`, this method returns `displayFormatter`. Otherwise, this method returns `defaultFormatter`.

Example

This program demonstrates two simple ways to use DefaultFormatterFactory. The first creates a factory that provides different formatters depending on whether the field has focus. The second changes a field's format "midstream" by completely replacing its factory. Figure 20-4 shows what the example looks like. Try tabbing between the fields and watch how the format of the top field changes (as the bottom's does when you click on the change format button).

```java
// FactoryDemo.java
//
import javax.swing.*;
import javax.swing.text.*;
import java.awt.*;
import java.awt.event.*;
import javax.swing.border.TitledBorder;
import java.text.ParseException;

public class FactoryDemo {

  public static JPanel demo1( ){
    // Demo 1: Field with different formats with and without focus

    JPanel pan = new JPanel(new BorderLayout( ));
    pan.setBorder(new TitledBorder("Demo 1: format toggles with focus"));

    MaskFormatter withFocus = null, withoutFocus = null;
    try { withFocus = new MaskFormatter("LLLL");
        withoutFocus = new MaskFormatter("UUUU");
        } catch (ParseException pe) { }

    DefaultFormatterFactory factory =
        new DefaultFormatterFactory(withoutFocus, null, withFocus);

    JFormattedTextField field = new JFormattedTextField(factory);
    field.setValue("Four");
    pan.add(field, BorderLayout.CENTER);

    return pan;
  }

  public static JPanel demo2( ){
    // Demo 2: Change the format of a field when the user presses a button. We can't
    // call field.setFormatter( ) because it's a protected method. (It wouldn't work
    // anyway. The old factory would replace our new formatter with an "old" one next
    // time the field gains or loses focus.) Instead, send a new factory to
    // field.setFormatterFactory( ).

    JPanel pan = new JPanel(new BorderLayout( ));
    pan.setBorder(new TitledBorder("Demo 2: change format midstream"));
```

```
      MaskFormatter lowercase = null;
      try { lowercase = new MaskFormatter("LLLL");
          } catch (ParseException pe) { }
      final JFormattedTextField field = new JFormattedTextField(lowercase);
      field.setValue("Fore");
      pan.add(field, BorderLayout.CENTER);

      final JButton change = new JButton("change format");
      JPanel changePanel = new JPanel( );
      changePanel.add(change);
      pan.add(changePanel, BorderLayout.SOUTH);

      change.addActionListener(new ActionListener( ) {
        public void actionPerformed(ActionEvent ae) {
          try {
            field.commitEdit( ); // Commit current edit (if any).
            MaskFormatter uppercase = new MaskFormatter("UUUU");
            DefaultFormatterFactory factory = new DefaultFormatterFactory(uppercase);
            field.setFormatterFactory(factory);
            change.setEnabled(false);
          } catch (ParseException pe) { }
        }
      });

      return pan;
    }

    public static void main(String argv[]) {
      JFrame f = new JFrame("FactoryDemo");
      f.setDefaultCloseOperation(JFrame.EXIT_ON_CLOSE);
      f.getContentPane( ).add(demo1( ), BorderLayout.NORTH);
      f.getContentPane( ).add(demo2( ), BorderLayout.SOUTH);
      f.setSize(240, 160);
      f.setVisible(true);
    }
  }
}
```

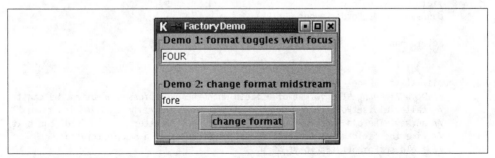

Figure 20-4. Formatter factory variations

Formatting with Regular Expressions

If you are a fan of regular expressions, you might be wondering whether Swing provides any direct support for using regular expressions with JFormattedTextFields. The answer is no. There is no direct support, but it's easy to write your own formatter for regular expressions.

```java
// RegexPatternFormatter.java -- formatter for regular expressions
//
import javax.swing.*;
import javax.swing.text.*;

public class RegexPatternFormatter extends DefaultFormatter {

  protected java.util.regex.Matcher matcher;

  public RegexPatternFormatter(java.util.regex.Pattern regex) {
    setOverwriteMode(false);
    matcher = regex.matcher(""); // Create a Matcher for the regular expression.
  }

  public Object stringToValue(String string) throws java.text.ParseException {
    if (string == null) return null;
    matcher.reset(string); // Set 'string' as the matcher's input.

    if (! matcher.matches()) // Does 'string' match the regular expression?
      throw new java.text.ParseException("does not match regex", 0);

    // If we get this far, then it did match.
    return super.stringToValue(string); // Honors the valueClass property
  }


  public static void main(String argv[]) {
    // A demo main() method to show how RegexPatternFormatter could be used

    JLabel lab1 = new JLabel("even length strings:");
    java.util.regex.Pattern evenLength = java.util.regex.Pattern.compile("(..)*");
    JFormattedTextField ftf1 =
        new JFormattedTextField(new RegexPatternFormatter(evenLength));

    JLabel lab2 = new JLabel("no vowels:");
    java.util.regex.Pattern noVowels = java.util.regex.Pattern.compile("[^aeiou]*",
        java.util.regex.Pattern.CASE_INSENSITIVE);
    RegexPatternFormatter noVowelFormatter = new RegexPatternFormatter(noVowels);
    noVowelFormatter.setAllowsInvalid(false); // Don't allow user to type vowels.
    JFormattedTextField ftf2 = new JFormattedTextField(noVowelFormatter);

    JFrame f = new JFrame("RegexPatternFormatter Demo");
    f.setDefaultCloseOperation(JFrame.EXIT_ON_CLOSE);
    JPanel pan1 = new JPanel(new java.awt.BorderLayout());
    pan1.add(lab1, java.awt.BorderLayout.WEST);
    pan1.add(ftf1, java.awt.BorderLayout.CENTER);
```

```
        lab1.setLabelFor(ftf1);
        f.getContentPane().add(pan1, java.awt.BorderLayout.NORTH);
        JPanel pan2 = new JPanel(new java.awt.BorderLayout());
        pan2.add(lab2, java.awt.BorderLayout.WEST);
        pan2.add(ftf2, java.awt.BorderLayout.CENTER);
        lab2.setLabelFor(ftf2);
        f.getContentPane().add(pan2, java.awt.BorderLayout.SOUTH);
        f.setSize(300, 80);
        f.setVisible(true);
    }
}
```

Figure 20-5 shows what this example looks like when it runs. Notice that the top field enforces its format only when you tab away from it; if it has an odd-length value at that point, it reverts to the previous value. The bottom field validates as you type; the example shows what happens if you try to type in the entire alphabet.

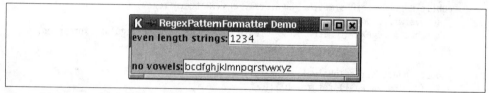

Figure 20-5. Formatting with regular expressions

Now you know everything there is to know about JFormattedTextFields, but before we close let's explore one more class: InputVerifier. InputVerifiers are often convenient to use with JFormattedTextFields, which is why we cover them here, but InputVerifiers can be attached to any JComponent, not just to JFormattedTextFields.

The InputVerifier Class

InputVerifier is an abstract class introduced in SDK 1.3. Subclasses of InputVerifier can be attached to JComponents to control whether they are willing to give up focus. Typically, this is done to force the user to put a component in a "valid" state before allowing the user to transfer focus to another component.

A brief example of using an InputVerifier with a JFormattedTextField appeared earlier in this chapter. (See the focusLostBehavior property of the JFormattedTextField class.)

Public Methods

public abstract boolean verify(JComponent input)

Return true if the component should give up focus, or false to keep focus. You should implement this method to examine the component and make the determination, but you should not produce any side effects on the component.

public boolean shouldYieldFocus(JComponent input)

This method is called when the user attempts to transfer focus from the given component elsewhere. Return true if the component should give up focus, or false to keep focus. This method is permitted to produce side effects. InputVerifier's implementation simply defers to the verify() method, but implementing classes may override either. Typically, subclasses provide only a verify() method unless they intend to produce side effects.

CHAPTER 21

Carets, Highlighters, and Keymaps

In this chapter:
• Carets
• Highlighters
• Keymaps

Like some of the other Swing components (JTree, for example), the text components allow you to do a certain amount of customization without having to implement your own L&F. Certain aspects of these components' behavior and appearance can be modified directly through properties of JTextSCComponent. This chapter explains how to modify three such components: carets, highlighters, and keymaps.

With the more flexible text components (JEditorPane and anything that extends it, including JTextPane), you can control the View objects created to render each Element of the Document model. In this chapter, we'll concentrate on the classes and interfaces related to modifying text components without dealing with View objects. Chapter 23 discusses custom View classes.

JTextComponent has three UI-related properties that you can access and modify directly. These properties are defined by the following interfaces:

Caret
> Keeps track of where the insertion point is located and defines how it is displayed. This includes its size and shape, its blink rate (if any), etc. (Don't confuse this with java.awt.Cursor, which tracks the mouse, not the insertion point.)

Highlighter
> Keeps track of which text should be highlighted and how that text is visually marked. Typically, this is done by painting a solid rectangle "behind" the text, but this is up to the implementation of this interface.

Keymap
> Defines a hierarchy of Actions to be performed when certain keys are pressed. For example, pressing Ctrl-C may copy some text, or Command-V may paste at the current caret location. This is considered an L&F feature because different native L&Fs have different default keymaps.

As you might expect, Swing provides default implementations of these interfaces. Figure 21-1 shows these classes and interfaces and the relationships between them. Note that each Caret and Highlighter is associated with a single JTextComponent (set by its install( ) method) while Keymap has no direct relation to any JTextComponent, and therefore can be used by multiple components.

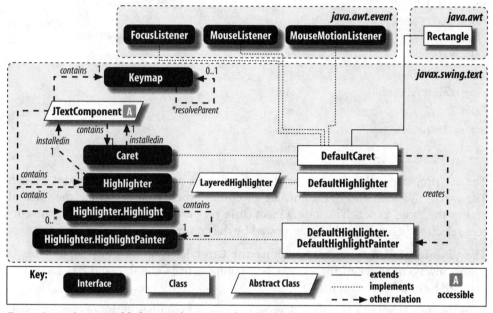

Figure 21-1. Caret, Highlighter, and Keymap class diagram

In the next few sections, we'll take a closer look at these interfaces as well as the default implementations for Caret and Highlighter. The default implementation of Keymap is an inner class of JTextComponent, which we can't subclass directly. When we get to that discussion, we'll see why we typically won't need to.

Carets

Carets represent the location where new text is inserted.

The Caret Interface

The Caret interface provides a number of useful features for dealing with text insertion and selection.

Properties

The Caret interface defines the properties shown in Table 21-1. The blinkRate property specifies the number of milliseconds between Caret blinks. A value of 0 indicates that the Caret shouldn't blink at all.

Table 21-1. Caret properties

Property	Data type	get	is	set	default Value
blinkRate	int	•		•	
dot	int	•		•	
magicCaretPosition	Point	•		•	
mark	int	•			
selectionVisible	boolean		•	•	
visible	boolean		•	•	

The dot property is the current Caret position as an offset into the Document model. The mark is the other end of the current selection. If there is no selection, the value of mark is the same as dot. The selectionVisible property designates whether the current selection (if any) should be decorated by the component's Highlighter.

The visible property indicates whether the Caret itself should be visible. This is almost always true when the Caret's text component is editable and has focus but may not be in other situations.

magicCaretPosition is a Point used when moving among lines with uneven end positions to ensure that the up and down arrow keys produce the desired effect. For example, consider the following text:

```
Line 1 is long
Line 2
Line 3 is long
```

If the caret was initially positioned before the o in long in line 3, you'd expect the up arrow key to move the caret to the end of line 2. A second up arrow press should move the caret just before the o in long on the first line. This is where the "magic" comes in. The first time the up arrow is pressed, magicCaretPosition is set to the old caret location so that this position's x-coordinate can be used if the up arrow is pressed again. You will probably never need to do anything with this property since the DefaultEditorKit manages it.

Events

Whenever the Caret's position changes, a ChangeEvent should be fired to any interested ChangeListeners. Caret defines the following standard methods for managing event listeners:

```
public abstract void addChangeListener(ChangeListener l)
public abstract void removeChangeListener(ChangeListener l)
```

Methods

In addition to the accessors for the properties listed earlier, the Caret interface defines the following four methods:

public void install(JTextComponent c)
> Signal that the Caret is responsible for the given component. In addition to giving the Caret access to the component, it also provides access to the Document model (to which the Caret can listen so it can update the caret location when text is added or removed).

public void deinstall(JTextComponent c)
> Signal that the Caret is no longer responsible for the given component. The Caret should no longer be used once this method has been called.

public void moveDot(int dot)
> Called when a selection is being made. It should update the Caret to the specified position and update the JTextComponent's Highlighter to reflect the new selection range.

public void paint(Graphics g)
> Render the Caret using the given Graphics object.

The DefaultCaret Class

The DefaultCaret class provides a basic implementation of the Caret interface that renders itself as a thin vertical line. This class extends Rectangle; implements the FocusListener, MouseListener, and MouseMotionListener interfaces; and reacts to events sent to these listeners when they are fired by its installed JTextComponent.

As we'll see, extending DefaultCaret is a great way to create your own Caret without having to worry about most of the complicated details.

Properties

DefaultCaret does not add any properties to the Caret interface except the ones it inherits from java.awt.Rectangle. Table 21-2 shows the default values it supplies.

Table 21-2. DefaultCaret properties

Property	Data type	get	is	set	Default value
blinkRate	int	•		•	0
dot	int	•		•	0
magicCaretPosition	Point	•		•	null
mark	int	•			0
selectionVisible	boolean		•	•	false
visible	boolean		•	•	false

See also the properties of java.awt.Rectangle (not in this book).

Events

A ChangeEvent is fired to registered listeners whenever the caret's position changes. The following standard methods are provided for working with ChangeEvents. (Note that the getChangeListeners( ) method did not exist prior to SDK 1.4, and getListeners( ) did not exist prior to SDK 1.3.)

```
protected void fireStateChanged( )
public void addChangeListener(ChangeListener l)
public void removeChangeListener(ChangeListener l)
public ChangeListener[] getChangeListeners( )
public EventListener[] getListeners(Class listenerType)
```

Constructor

public DefaultCaret( )
 Create a nonblinking DefaultCaret.

Caret methods

DefaultCaret provides the following implementations of the methods defined by the Caret interface:

public void install(JTextComponent c)
 Set the caret's component property and register a FocusListener, MouseListener, MouseMotionListener, and PropertyChangeListener for the component as well as a DocumentListener for the component's Document. For the first three it registers itself, either directly or indirectly. For the other two it registers an instance of UpdateHandler, an inner class.

public void deinstall(JTextComponent c)
 Remove all the listeners registered by the install( ) method, set the component property to null, and (if the blink rate has been set) stop the Timer that controls the blinking (see Chapter 27).

---

public void moveDot(int dot)
> Move the Caret to the specified position and update the component's Highlighter so it can highlight the area over which the cursor has been dragged.

public void paint(Graphics g)
> Convert the current caret position (dot) to view coordinates, then render the caret by drawing a thin vertical line. Subclasses that override this method must also override the damage( ) method (or else g's clipping area may be off, which can prevent the caret from being drawn).

FocusListener methods

These methods are implemented from the FocusListener interface:

public void focusGained(FocusEvent e)
> Called when the caret's component gains focus. If the component is enabled and editable, the caret becomes visible.

public void focusLost(FocusEvent e)
> Called when the caret's component loses focus. A permanent loss of focus (in which e.isTemporary( ) returns false) causes the caret to become invisible.

Mouse methods

These methods are implemented from the MouseListener and MouseMotionListener interfaces. They define how DefaultCaret behaves in response to mouse gestures.

public void mouseClicked(MouseEvent e)
> Update the position of the caret. A double-click selects a word; a triple-click selects a line.

public void mouseDragged(MouseEvent e)
> Call moveCaret( ) (described later).

public void mousePressed(MouseEvent e)
> Call positionCaret( ) (described later) and request focus for the caret's component if it is enabled.

public void mouseEntered(MouseEvent e)
public void mouseExited(MouseEvent e)
public void mouseMoved(MouseEvent e)
public void mouseReleased(MouseEvent e)
> These methods do nothing in this implementation.

Protected methods

In addition to implementing all of the methods defined in the Caret interface, DefaultCaret adds several useful methods of its own:

protected void adjustVisibility(Rectangle nloc)

Called whenever the caret's position changes. This implementation calls the component's `scrollRectToVisible()` method (from the proper thread using `SwingUtilities.invokeLater()` if necessary) to ensure that the caret is visible. Subclasses may choose to change this policy.

protected void damage(Rectangle r)

This is an important method in the implementation of `DefaultCaret`. It is responsible for asking the caret's component to partially repaint itself, which causes the caret to be actually drawn. It is also responsible for setting values to the caret's x, y, width, and height fields (inherited from `java.awt.Rectangle`) so that other parts of `DefaultCaret`'s implementation know where (in screen coordinates) the caret is located. This information is used, for example, to erase the previous location of the caret when the caret moves. Also, it sometimes determines the clipping area of the `Graphics` object passed into `paint()`. The next section explains in detail how this works.

protected final JTextComponent getComponent()

Provide access to the caret's component. The `install()` method (which is called when the `Caret` is added to the component) stores the component for future use, making it available here.

protected Highlighter.HighlightPainter getSelectionPainter()

Return an object capable of making highlight decorations, which can be passed to the `addHighlight()` method of the component's `Highlighter` when a new selection is made. This implementation returns an instance of `DefaultHighlightPainter` (an inner class of `DefaultHighlighter`) with a value of `null` for its color property. This and other classes related to `Highlighter` are covered later in this chapter.

protected void moveCaret(MouseEvent e)

Called when the mouse is dragged (by `mouseDragged()`) or Shift-clicked (indirectly by `mousePressed()`), which usually updates the current selection.

protected void positionCaret(MouseEvent e)

Called when the mouse is clicked (indirectly by `mousePressed()`). It moves the dot without making a selection. It also clears the `magicCaretPosition` property.

protected final void repaint()

This method simply calls getComponent().repaint(x, y, width, height), which eventually causes the paint() method to be called. The caret's x, y, width, and height fields should have been set properly by the damage() method. Unlike most Swing methods, repaint() is thread-safe.

Custom Carets

Let's take a crack at creating our own Caret. The typical way to create a custom caret is to extend DefaultCaret and override paint() and damage(). That's what we'll do for CornerCaret, a simple five-pixel-by-five-pixel, L-shaped caret, but we'll also add a

constructor to make it blink by default. To use this new caret, simply call
setCaret(new CornerCaret()) on any Swing text component. (The main() method is
provided for demonstration purposes only. CornerCaret would be complete without
it.)

```java
// CornerCaret.java
//
import javax.swing.*;
import javax.swing.text.*;
import java.awt.*;

public class CornerCaret extends DefaultCaret {

  public CornerCaret() {
    setBlinkRate(500); // Half a second
  }

  protected synchronized void damage(Rectangle r) {
    if (r == null) return;
    // Give values to x,y,width,height (inherited from java.awt.Rectangle).
    x = r.x;
    y = r.y + (r.height * 4 / 5 - 3);
    width = 5;
    height = 5;
    repaint(); // Calls getComponent().repaint(x, y, width, height)
  }

  public void paint(Graphics g) {
    JTextComponent comp = getComponent();
    if (comp == null) return;

    int dot = getDot();
    Rectangle r = null;
    try {
      r = comp.modelToView(dot);
    } catch (BadLocationException e) { return; }
    if (r == null) return;

    int dist = r.height * 4 / 5 - 3; // Will be distance from r.y to top

    if ( (x != r.x) || (y != r.y + dist) ) {
      // paint() has been called directly, without a previous call to
      // damage(), so do some cleanup. (This happens, for example, when the
      // text component is resized.)
      repaint(); // Erase previous location of caret.
      x = r.x; // Set new values for x,y,width,height.
      y = r.y + dist;
      width = 5;
      height = 5;
    }

    if ( isVisible() ) {
      g.setColor(comp.getCaretColor());
```

```
            g.drawLine(r.x, r.y + dist, r.x, r.y + dist + 4);   // Five vertical pixels
            g.drawLine(r.x, r.y + dist + 4, r.x + 4, r.y + dist + 4); // Five horiz px
        }
    }

    public static void main(String args[]) {
        JFrame frame = new JFrame("CornerCaret demo");
        frame.setDefaultCloseOperation(JFrame.EXIT_ON_CLOSE);
        JTextArea area = new JTextArea(8, 32);
        area.setCaret(new CornerCaret());
        area.setText("This is the story\nof the hare who\nlost his spectacles.");
        frame.getContentPane().add(new JScrollPane(area), BorderLayout.CENTER);
        frame.pack();
        frame.setVisible(true);
    }
}
```

There are several things worth mentioning here.

First, damage() gets a Rectangle directly as a parameter, but paint() has to obtain one manually via getComponent().modelToView() (or getComponent().getUI().modelToView()). Despite this, the fields of the rectangles are the same. The x and y fields are the coordinates of the cursor, though y is at the top of the text, not the baseline. The value of height depends on the font, but the value of width is meaningless (probably 0).

The paint() method should check whether the cursor is visible before drawing anything and is expected to honor the value of the component's caretColor property. Because the caret is drawn "over" (after) the component's content, large cursors must take care not to obscure the text underneath. (One way to handle this is to draw in XOR [eXclusive OR] mode.) See Figure 21-2.

The damage() method is responsible for setting the value of the caret's x, y, width, and height fields (inherited from Rectangle) to cover anything that is drawn by paint(). If not, only part (or possibly none) of the caret actually appears after paint() is called, or caret fragments may be left behind when the caret moves. Finally, damage() calls the caret's repaint() method, which eventually causes the paint() method to be called.

FancyCaret is more complicated than CornerCaret because it is rendered using the width of the character it is on. It also draws the caret in XOR mode, which allows the text to show through the caret.

When a pixel is drawn in XOR mode, its new color does not necessarily become the drawing color. Instead, its new color becomes a mix of its previous color and the drawing color. If the previous color is the same as the drawing color, the new color is the XOR color. If the previous color is the same as the XOR color, the new color is the drawing color. If the previous color is a third color, the new color is some undefined (but reasonable) other color. FancyCaret takes advantage of this by setting the

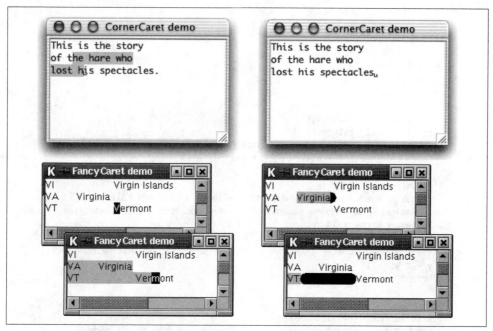

Figure 21-2. Demonstrations of the CornerCaret and FancyCaret

drawing color to the caret color and the XOR color to the component's background color. Here's the code:

```java
// FancyCaret.java
//
import javax.swing.*;
import javax.swing.text.*;
import java.awt.*;

public class FancyCaret extends DefaultCaret {

  protected synchronized void damage(Rectangle r) {
    if (r == null) return;

    // Give values to x,y,width,height (inherited from java.awt.Rectangle).
    x = r.x;
    y = r.y;
    height = r.height;
    // A value for width was probably set by paint(), which we leave alone. But the
    // first call to damage() precedes the first call to paint(), so in this case we
    // must be prepared to set a valid width or else paint() receives a bogus clip
    // area, and caret is not drawn properly.
    if (width <= 0) width = getComponent().getWidth();

    repaint(); // Calls getComponent().repaint(x, y, width, height)
  }
```

```java
public void paint(Graphics g) {
  JTextComponent comp = getComponent();
  if (comp == null) return;

  int dot = getDot();
  Rectangle r = null;
  char dotChar;
  try {
    r = comp.modelToView(dot);
    if (r == null) return;
    dotChar = comp.getText(dot, 1).charAt(0);
  } catch (BadLocationException e) { return; }

  if ( (x != r.x) || (y != r.y) ) {
    // paint() has been called directly, without a previous call to
    // damage(), so do some cleanup. (This happens, for example, when the
    // text component is resized.)
    repaint(); // Erase previous location of caret.
    x = r.x;   // Update dimensions (width is set later in this method).
    y = r.y;
    height = r.height;
  }

  g.setColor(comp.getCaretColor());
  g.setXORMode(comp.getBackground()); // Do this to draw in XOR mode.

  if (dotChar == '\n') {
    int diam = r.height;
    if (isVisible())
      g.fillArc(r.x-diam/2, r.y, diam, diam, 270, 180); // Half-circle
    width = diam / 2 + 2;
    return;
  }

  if (dotChar == '\t') try {
    Rectangle nextr = comp.modelToView(dot+1);
    if ((r.y == nextr.y) && (r.x < nextr.x)) {
      width = nextr.x - r.x;
      if (isVisible()) g.fillRoundRect(r.x, r.y, width, r.height, 12, 12);
      return;
    }
    else dotChar = ' ';
  } catch (BadLocationException e) { dotChar = ' '; }

  width = g.getFontMetrics().charWidth(dotChar);
  if (isVisible()) g.fillRect(r.x, r.y, width, r.height);
}

public static void main(String args[]) {
  JFrame frame = new JFrame("FancyCaret demo");
  frame.setDefaultCloseOperation(JFrame.EXIT_ON_CLOSE);
  JTextArea area = new JTextArea(8, 32);
  area.setCaret(new FancyCaret());
  area.setText("VI\tVirgin Islands \nVA      Virginia\nVT\tVermont");
```

```
        frame.getContentPane( ).add(new JScrollPane(area), BorderLayout.CENTER);
        frame.pack( );
        frame.setVisible(true);
    }
}
```

The paint( ) method uses g.getFontMetrics( ).charWidth( ) to determine how wide to render the caret,* but this complicates things. The damage( ) method can't call charWidth( ) because it doesn't have access to a Graphics object, so it relies on paint( ) to set the width field. At first glance, it seems that this shouldn't work because paint( ) is called after damage( ), not before. But in practice, paint( ) is called twice when the caret moves: once before damage( ) (this one doesn't actually draw anything because its clip area is not set correctly) and once after (this one does draw the caret).

FontMetrics.charWidth( ) returns 0 for tabs and newlines, so they need special handling. FancyCaret shows off by drawing a half-circle for a newline and a rounded rectangle for a tab. This could be considered overkill, but it is important that something with positive width is drawn or else the caret disappears when the user moves it onto a tab or newline, which can be disorienting.

The CaretListener Interface

If you want to keep track of the position of a Caret in a JTextComponent, you don't actually need to interact directly with the component's Caret. Instead, you can simply add a CaretListener to the component.

Method

The CaretListener interface contains one method:

public void caretUpdate(CaretEvent e)
    Called any time the caret's position changes.

The CaretEvent Class

As you'd expect, there's a CaretEvent class to go along with the CaretListener we just introduced. This is actually an abstract class. The only concrete subclass is a package-private inner class within JTextComponent.

Properties

CaretEvent defines the properties shown in Table 21-3. dot indicates the current caret location while mark shows the end of the selection, if there is one (otherwise, it is the same as dot).

---

* FancyCaret is too simplistic for the more complex Swing text components (JTextPane and JEditorPane) that support multiple fonts. For these we would need to determine from the Document model the particular Font in use at the dot location and call g.getFontMetrics(theParticularFont).

Table 21-3. *CaretEvent properties*

Property	Data type	get	is	set	Default value
dot	int	•			Abstract
mark	int	•			Abstract

Constructor

public CaretEvent(Object source)
> Create a new event. Subclasses must manage the dot and mark properties themselves. Since caret positions change frequently, it's best to create a single CaretEvent object and reuse it each time the caret position changes.

Highlighters

Highlighters determine how text is marked to make it stand out. The order in which we discuss the highlighter interfaces may seem counterintuitive. The basic Highlighter interface is so straightforward that you'll rarely need to work with it directly, so we will describe it later. At this point, we discuss the interface you're most likely to use first: the Highlighter.HighlightPainter interface.

The Highlighter.HighlightPainter Interface

This is an inner interface of the Highlighter interface. If you want to change the way that highlights are drawn in your text component, this is the interface you'd implement.

Implementations of Highlighter.HighlightPainter are returned by Caret implementations and passed to Highlighter implementations (described later in this section; there are a lot of interfaces working together), which use them to decorate the area "behind" a selection. The only concrete implementation that's provided in Swing is DefaultHighlighter.DefaultHighlightPainter, which paints highlights as a solid background rectangle of a specified color.

This interface consists of a single paint( ) method. Unlike the paint( ) method of Caret, this method is called before the text itself is rendered, so there's no need to worry about obscuring text or XOR mode.

Method

public void paint(Graphics g, int p0, int p1, Shape bounds, JTextComponent c)
> Render a highlighter behind the text of the specified component. The p0 and p1 parameters specify offsets into the document model defining the range to be highlighted. The bounds parameter defines the bounds of the specified component.

A Custom HighlightPainter

Here's a sample implementation of the Highlighter.HighlightPainter interface that paints highlights as thick underlines instead of as the usual solid rectangle. To use this highlight painter, we need to set a Caret that returns an instance of our highlight painter in its getSelectionPainter() method. The main() method in this example (provided for demonstration purposes only since the highlight painter would be complete without it) shows one way of doing this.

```java
// LineHighlightPainter.java
// An implementation of HighlightPainter that underlines text with a thick line
import javax.swing.*;
import javax.swing.text.*;
import java.awt.*;

public class LineHighlightPainter implements Highlighter.HighlightPainter {

  // Paint a thick line under one line of text, from r extending rightward to x2.
  private void paintLine(Graphics g, Rectangle r, int x2) {
    int ytop = r.y + r.height - 3;
    g.fillRect(r.x, ytop, x2 - r.x, 3);
  }

  // Paint thick lines under a block of text.
  public void paint(Graphics g, int p0, int p1, Shape bounds, JTextComponent c) {

    Rectangle r0 = null, r1 = null, rbounds = bounds.getBounds();
    int xmax = rbounds.x + rbounds.width; // x-coordinate of right edge
    try {  // Convert positions to pixel coordinates.
      r0 = c.modelToView(p0);
      r1 = c.modelToView(p1);
    } catch (BadLocationException ex) { return; }
    if ((r0 == null) || (r1 == null)) return;

    g.setColor( c.getSelectionColor() );

    // Special case if p0 and p1 are on the same line
    if (r0.y == r1.y) {
      paintLine(g, r0, r1.x);
      return;
    }

    // First line, from p1 to end-of-line
    paintLine(g, r0, xmax);

    // All the full lines in between, if any (assumes that all lines have
    // the same height--not a good assumption with JEditorPane/JTextPane)
    r0.y += r0.height;    // Move r0 to next line.
    r0.x = rbounds.x;     // Move r0 to left edge.
    while (r0.y < r1.y) {
      paintLine(g, r0, xmax);
      r0.y += r0.height; // Move r0 to next line.
    }
```

```
  // Last line, from beginning-of-line to p1
  paintLine(g, r0, r1.x);
}

public static void main(String args[]) {

  // Extend DefaultCaret as an anonymous inner class.
  Caret lineHighlightPainterCaret = new DefaultCaret() {
    private Highlighter.HighlightPainter lhp = new LineHighlightPainter();
    // Override getSelectionPainter to return the LineHighlightPainter.
    protected Highlighter.HighlightPainter getSelectionPainter() {
      return lhp;
    }
  };

  JFrame frame = new JFrame("LineHighlightPainter demo");
  frame.setDefaultCloseOperation(JFrame.EXIT_ON_CLOSE);
  JTextArea area = new JTextArea(9, 45);
  area.setCaret(lineHighlightPainterCaret);
  area.setLineWrap(true);
  area.setWrapStyleWord(true);
  area.setText("This is the story\nof the hare who\nlost his spectacles.");
  frame.getContentPane().add(new JScrollPane(area), BorderLayout.CENTER);
  frame.pack();
  frame.setVisible(true);
}
}
```

All we've done here is override the paint( ) method to paint thin (three-pixel) rectangles under each line of text in the highlighted region. For this example, we've assumed that each line of text has the same height. This is fine for JTextField and JTextArea, but if you want to customize the highlighting of more complex text components, you need to take the different fonts into account. Figure 21-3 shows the LineHighlightPainter in action.

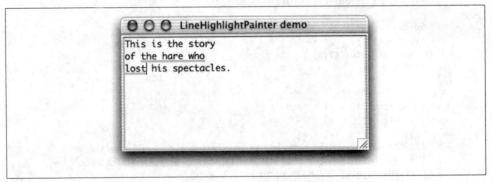

Figure 21-3. The LineHighlightPainter

The Highlighter.Highlight Interface

The second inner interface of `Highlighter` is the `Highlighter.Highlight` interface. It is used by `Highlighter` to represent a single range of text to be decorated. The only implementation is a package-private inner class of `DefaultHighlighter`.

Properties

Table 21-4 shows the properties defined by the `Highlighter.Highlight` interface. The `startOffset` and `endOffset` properties reflect the range of a given highlighted area as offsets into the document model. The other property, `painter`, is responsible for rendering the `Highlight`. The only methods in this interface are the accessors for the three properties.

Table 21-4. Highlighter.Highlight properties

Property	Data type	get	is	set	Default value
endOffset	int	•			
painter	Highlighter.HighlightPainter	•			
startOffset	int	•			

The Highlighter Interface

The `Highlighter` interface is responsible for marking background areas of a text component to "highlight" selected portions of the text. `Highlighter`s can be used not only to highlight the current text selection but also for other purposes. For example, you could choose to highlight all the misspelled words in the document.

`Highlighter` defines two inner interfaces (described above) to manage its highlights. `Highlighter.Highlight` keeps track of a single highlighted area while `Highlighter.HighlightPainter` is responsible for painting a highlighted area. Refer to Figure 21-1 to see how the various classes and interfaces are related.

Property

Table 21-5 shows the property defined by the `Highlighter` interface. The single property, `highlights`, is an array of individual areas to be highlighted.

Table 21-5. Highlighter property

Property	Data type	get	is	set	Default value
highlights	Highlighter.Highlight[]	•			

Methods

public Object addHighlight(int p0, int p1, Highlighter.HighlightPainter p)
  throws BadLocationException
  Add a new highlight covering the specified range (from document offset p0 to offset p1) using the specified `Highlighter.HighlightPainter` (see above) to perform the rendering. If you don't want to create your own `HighlightPainter`, you may pass in `DefaultHighlighter.DefaultPainter` (a public static field that `DefaultHighlighter` provides for this purpose). The return value is a "tag" object that can be passed to `changeHighlight( )` and `removeHighlight( )`. (Implementations of this interface should document the specific type of the object this method returns.)

public void changeHighlight(Object tag, int p0, int p1) throws BadLocationException
  Take an existing highlight (tag) and change it to refer to a different portion of the document. The tag should be either an object returned by `addHighlight( )` or one of the elements returned by `getHighlights( )`.

public void install(JTextComponent c)
  Called when a UI is installed on a text component. This provides access to the component, its UI delegate, and its `Document` model.

public void deinstall(JTextComponent c)
  Called when the UI is removed from a text component. Any references stored in the `install( )` method should be dropped here, and any listeners unregistered.

public void paint(Graphics g)
  Render all the highlights.

public void removeAllHighlights( )
  Remove all of the `Highlighter`'s highlights.

public void removeHighlight(Object tag)
  Remove a single highlight. The tag should be either an object returned by `addHighlight( )` or one of the elements returned by `getHighlights( )`.

Adding Multiple Highlights

Here's an example of a program that adds multiple highlights, one for each vowel. The results of running it are shown in Figure 21-4.

```java
// MultiHighlight.java
//
import javax.swing.*;
import javax.swing.text.*;
import java.awt.event.*;
import java.awt.BorderLayout;

public class MultiHighlight implements ActionListener {
```

```
private JTextComponent comp;
private String charsToHighlight;

public MultiHighlight(JTextComponent c, String chars) {
  comp = c;
  charsToHighlight = chars;
}

public void actionPerformed(ActionEvent e) {
  // Highlight all characters that appear in charsToHighlight.
  Highlighter h = comp.getHighlighter();
  h.removeAllHighlights();
  String text = comp.getText();

  for (int j=0; j < text.length(); j+=1) {
    char ch = text.charAt(j);
    if (charsToHighlight.indexOf(ch) >= 0) try {
      h.addHighlight(j, j+1, DefaultHighlighter.DefaultPainter);
    } catch (BadLocationException ble) { }
  }
}

public static void main(String args[]) {
  JFrame frame = new JFrame("MultiHighlight");
  frame.setDefaultCloseOperation(JFrame.EXIT_ON_CLOSE);
  JTextArea area = new JTextArea(5, 20);
  area.setText("This is the story\nof the hare who\nlost his spectacles.");
  frame.getContentPane().add(new JScrollPane(area), BorderLayout.CENTER);

  JButton b = new JButton("Highlight All Vowels");
  b.addActionListener(new MultiHighlight(area, "aeiouAEIOU"));
  frame.getContentPane().add(b, BorderLayout.SOUTH);
  frame.pack();
  frame.setVisible(true);
}
}
```

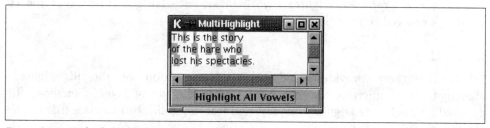

Figure 21-4. Multiple highlights

The LayeredHighlighter Class

LayeredHighlighter is an abstract class that implements the Highlighter interface. It doesn't provide an implementation for any of the Highlighter methods (for that, see

DefaultHighlighter in the next section) but declares one abstract method used by View objects.

Method

public abstract void paintLayeredHighlights(Graphics g, int p0, int p1,
    Shape viewBounds, JTextComponent editor, View view)
    Leaf views call this method to render any layered highlights that have overlapping offsets.

The DefaultHighlighter Class

The DefaultHighlighter class provides a useful implementation of the Highlighter interface. (It extends LayeredHighlighter.)

Properties

DefaultHighlighter adds one new property to the one it inherits. Table 21-6 shows its two properties.

Table 21-6. DefaultHighlighter properties

Property	Data type	get	is	set	Default value
highlights°	Highlighter.Highlight[]	•			Empty array
drawsLayeredHighlights	boolean	•		•	true

°overridden
See also the properties of Highlighter (Table 21-5).

The drawsLayeredHighlights property changes the behavior of the addHighlight() method. If the Highlighter.HighlightPainter object passed into addHighlight() is an instance of LayeredHighlighter.LayerPainter, DefaultHighlighter takes special advantage of it only if the value of this property is true.

Static field

DefaultHighlighter provides a default implementation of the Highlighter.HighlightPainter interface that can be passed to the addHighlight() method. (Its declared type is LayeredHighlighter.LayerPainter, a public abstract class that implements HighlightPainter.)

public static final LayeredHighlighter.LayerPainter DefaultPainter
    This highlighter renders a solid-color rectangular highlight. It uses the color specified by the component's selectionColor property.

Constructor

public DefaultHighlighter()
> Create a new DefaultHighlighter.

Methods

The following methods implement the `Highlighter` interface:

public Object addHighlight(int p0, int p1, Highlighter.HighlightPainter p)
throws BadLocationException
> Add a new highlight using the `createPosition()` method on the component's `Document` to track the specified beginning and end, even as changes are made to it. It returns an instance of a package-private inner class implementing `Highlighter.Highlight`.

public void changeHighlight(Object tag, int p0, int p1) throws BadLocationException
> Clean up the area previously highlighted by the given highlight and reset it. `tag` should be a `Highlight` returned from either `addHighlight()` or `getHighlights()`.

public void deinstall(JTextComponent c)
> Called when the UI is removed from a text component. It drops the reference to the component supplied by `install()`.

public void install(JTextComponent c)
> Called when a UI is installed on a text component. It clears any existing highlights and stores the given component for use in other methods.

public void paint(Graphics g)
> Call `paint()` on the `HighlightPainter` defined for each `Highlight`.

public void removeAllHighlights()
> Remove all of the `Highlighter`'s highlights and clean up the areas they covered.

public void removeHighlight(Object tag)
> Remove the given highlight and clean up the area it covered. `tag` should be a `Highlight` returned from either `addHighlight()` or `getHighlights()`.

There's also one method that's not part of the `Highlighter` interface:

public void paintLayeredHighlights(Graphics g, int p0, int p1, Shape viewBounds,
JTextComponent editor, View view)
> Render any layered highlights that have overlapping offsets.

The DefaultHighlighter.DefaultHighlightPainter Class

An instance of this inner class is returned by `DefaultCaret`'s `getSelectionPainter()` method. It paints highlights as a solid background rectangle of a specified color.

You might want to instantiate one of these if you want to set your own color for a highlight. If you want to use the color specified by the component's `selectionColor` property, you can avoid a redundant object creation by using the instance made available to you through DefaultHighlighter's DefaultPainter field.

Property

This inner class defines the property shown in Table 21-7. The color property defines the color used to draw highlights. It can be set only in the constructor.

Table 21-7. DefaultHighlighter.DefaultHighlightPainter property

Property	Data type	get	is	set	Default value
color	Color			•	From constructor

Constructor

public DefaultHighlightPainter(Color c)
> Create a new painter that uses the specified color. If the color is null, the highlights are drawn with the component's selectionColor.

Methods

public void paint(Graphics g, int offs0, int offs1, Shape bounds, JTextComponent c)
> Determine the pixel locations of the given endpoints and draw a rectangle to highlight the specified region. If the two offsets are on different lines, three rectangles are drawn: one from the start point to the end of that line, another that highlights any full lines that follow, and a third from the start of the next line up to the last offset.

public void paintLayer(Graphics g, int offs0, int offs1, Shape bounds,
JTextComponent c, View view)
> Render just the part of the highlight that corresponds to the specified view.

Keymaps

A Keymap contains mappings from KeyStrokes* to Actions and provides a variety of methods for accessing and updating these mappings.

The Keymap Interface

One last interface you can use to customize your application without implementing your own L&F is Keymap.

---

* KeyStroke is discussed in more detail in Chapter 27. Basically, it's just a representation of a key being typed, containing both the key code and any key modifiers (Ctrl, Alt, etc.).

Normally, an L&F defines a set of meaningful keystrokes. For example, Windows users expect Ctrl-C to copy text and Ctrl-V to paste while the Mac uses the Command key instead. Ctrl-Insert and Shift-Insert perform the same tasks for Motif users. These key sequences work as expected in Swing text components because of the Keymap installed by the L&F. This interface lets you change or augment this behavior.

The Keymap interface has been available to Swing text components since the beginning. SDK 1.3 introduced the more flexible and universal keyboard event system based on InputMaps and ActionMaps (described in Chapter 3). The techniques illustrated in this section remain useful: Keymap support was reimplemented using the new mechanism for backward compatibility. This approach is still quite convenient if all you need is to add a couple of keyboard commands to a text component. Also be sure to learn how to use InputMap and ActionMap directly—they give you more capabilities, in many more situations.

Properties

The Keymap interface defines the properties shown in Table 21-8. The boundAction and boundKeyStrokes properties contain the Actions and KeyStrokes (both part of the javax.swing package) local to the Keymap.

Table 21-8. Keymap properties

Property	Data type	get	is	set	Default value
boundActions	Action[]	•			
boundKeyStrokes	KeyStroke[]	•			
defaultAction	Action	•		•	
name	String	•			
resolveParent	Keymap	•		•	

The defaultAction property represents the action to be used when there is no action defined for a key. It is typically set to an instance of the DefaultKeyTypedAction inner class from the DefaultEditorKit. However, if you want to catch all keystrokes (perhaps to implement an editor like *vi* that inserts text only when it is in insert mode), you could define your own default action. defaultAction may be null, but the getDefaultAction( ) method should consult the resolveParent before returning null.

name is an arbitrary name given to the map. It may be null, but then the keymap will not be found by JTextComponent methods that refer to keymaps by name.

Finally, the resolveParent is another Keymap used to resolve any keys that are not defined locally in the map, thus creating a linear hierarchy of Keymaps. If an appropriate Action is not defined locally, the parent keymap is consulted (unless the parent is null).

Methods

Several methods defined in the Keymap interface allow mappings from KeyStrokes to Actions to be added, removed, and queried:

public abstract void addActionForKeyStroke(KeyStroke key, Action a)
> Add the Action to be performed for the given KeyStroke.

public abstract Action getAction(KeyStroke key)
> Determine the action for the given keystroke. If the action is not found in the Keymap, the resolveParent (if any) should be consulted before returning null. (The defaultAction should *not* be consulted. If the caller wishes to fall back on the keymap's defaultAction, it must call the getDefaultAction( ) method manually.)

public abstract KeyStroke[] getKeyStrokesForAction(Action a)
> Return all KeyStrokes that map to the specified Action. This includes KeyStrokes maintained by the resolveParent, unless mapped elsewhere locally.

public abstract boolean isLocallyDefined(KeyStroke key)
> Signal whether the specified KeyStroke is defined in the Keymap. The resolveParent should *not* be checked.

public abstract void removeBindings()
> Remove all KeyStroke to Action bindings from the Keymap. (Should not affect the resolveParent.)

public abstract void removeKeyStrokeBinding(KeyStroke keys)
> Remove the binding for the specified KeyStroke. (Should not affect the resolveParent.)

Keymap Implementation

Unlike Caret and Highlighter, the Keymap interface does not have a public default implementation. The JTextComponent class defines DefaultKeymap as a package-private inner class. This implementation uses a Hashtable to map from KeyStrokes to Actions. (So each KeyStroke maps to no more than one Action.)

There are a few ways to change the Keymap used by your text components. One option is to call getKeymap( ) on the component and add any new actions directly to that map. Doing this may change the mappings for all JTextComponents in the application if the L&F is sharing a single Keymap for every component (which is what the Swing L&Fs do). This is not a big problem if the actions you add work with all types of text components, but it is probably not the best approach.

A better approach is to define a new Keymap that uses the default Keymap (installed by the L&F) as its parent. The new Keymap contains only the mappings you define and passes any other keystrokes up to the default map. As the next example shows, this is done by calling JTextComponent.addKeymap( ). This method takes the name of your new map and the parent map to be used and returns a new Keymap for you to add mappings to. Since this is a static method, once you've made this call and added to the new map, you can use the new map for any other JTextComponents by calling:

```
myComponent.setKeymap(JTextComponent.getKeymap("MyKeymapName"))
```

Adding Keyboard Actions

Here's a quick example showing how easy it is to add keyboard functionality to Swing text components. In this example, we'll enable Ctrl-W to select a word, Ctrl-L to select a line, and Ctrl-U to convert words to uppercase.* JTextArea provides Actions for select-word and select-line via the getActions( ) method, but we create our own upcase-word Action as an inner class. All we have to do is create a Keymap containing the mappings we want, and we'll be able to make selections or upcase words with a simple key press. Here's the code to do this:

```java
// KeymapExample.java
//
import javax.swing.*;
import javax.swing.text.*;
import java.util.Hashtable;
import java.awt.event.*;
import java.awt.BorderLayout;

// A simple example showing how to add Actions for KeyStrokes
public class KeymapExample {
  public static void main(String[] args) {

    // Start with a simple JTextArea, get its Keymap to use as our parent,
    // and create a new map called "KeymapExampleMap".
    JTextArea area = new JTextArea(6, 32);
    Keymap parent = area.getKeymap();
    Keymap newmap = JTextComponent.addKeymap("KeymapExampleMap", parent);

    // Add Ctrl-U: change current word to uppercase (our own action).
    KeyStroke u = KeyStroke.getKeyStroke(KeyEvent.VK_U, InputEvent.CTRL_MASK);
    Action actionU = new UpWord(); // An inner class (defined below)
    newmap.addActionForKeyStroke(u, actionU);

    // Get all the actions JTextArea provides for us.
    Action actionList[] = area.getActions();
    // Put them in a Hashtable so that we can retreive them by Action.NAME.
    Hashtable lookup = new Hashtable();
    for (int j=0; j < actionList.length; j+=1)
      lookup.put(actionList[j].getValue(Action.NAME), actionList[j]);

    // Add Ctrl-L: select current line (action provided for us).
    KeyStroke L = KeyStroke.getKeyStroke(KeyEvent.VK_L, InputEvent.CTRL_MASK);
```

---

* Of course, a robust implementation would want to be sensitive to the modifier key that's commonly used in the current L&F rather than blindly using Ctrl.

```
    Action actionL = (Action)lookup.get(DefaultEditorKit.selectLineAction);
    newmap.addActionForKeyStroke(L, actionL);

    // Add Ctrl-W: select current word (action provided for us).
    KeyStroke W = KeyStroke.getKeyStroke(KeyEvent.VK_W, InputEvent.CTRL_MASK);
    Action actionW = (Action)lookup.get(DefaultEditorKit.selectWordAction);
    newmap.addActionForKeyStroke(W, actionW);

    // Set the JTextArea's Keymap to be our new map.
    area.setKeymap(newmap);

    // Show the TextPane.
    JFrame f = new JFrame("KeymapExample");
    f.setDefaultCloseOperation(JFrame.EXIT_ON_CLOSE);
    f.getContentPane().add(new JScrollPane(area), BorderLayout.CENTER);
    area.setText("This is the story\nof the hare who\nlost his spectacles.");
    f.pack();
    f.setVisible(true);
  }

  // Begin inner class.
  public static class UpWord extends TextAction {
    public UpWord() {
      super("uppercase-word-action");
    }

    public void actionPerformed(ActionEvent e) {
      // Change current word (or selected words) to uppercase.
      JTextComponent comp = getTextComponent(e);
      if (comp == null) return;
      Document doc = comp.getDocument();
      int start = comp.getSelectionStart();
      int end = comp.getSelectionEnd();
      try {
        int left = javax.swing.text.Utilities.getWordStart(comp, start);
        int right = javax.swing.text.Utilities.getWordEnd(comp, end);
        String word = doc.getText(left, right-left);
        doc.remove(left, right-left);
        doc.insertString(left, word.toUpperCase(), null);
        comp.setSelectionStart(start); // Restore previous position/selection.
        comp.setSelectionEnd(end);
      } catch (BadLocationException ble) { return; }
    }
  } // End inner class.
}
```

 If you're sure your code won't need to be compatible with SDKs prior to 1.4, you should consider adding code to check whether the document extends AbstractDocument and, if it does, use its replace() method rather than separate calls to delete() and insert(). This makes the Action work better with any JFormattedTextFields or DocumentFilters that accept the final text but not the intermediate state.

Don't worry about understanding everything about the actions we added here. (Text actions are covered in detail in Chapter 23.) The important things to understand are the following basic steps:

1. Get the current map (the default set by the L&F).

2. Create a new map with the old map as its parent by calling the static addKeymap( ) method in JTextComponent.

3. Get the desired KeyStrokes using the KeyStroke.getKeyStroke( ) method, along with a few constants defined in the java.awt.event package. The java.awt.event.KeyEvent class defines constant values for many common keys while java.awt.event.InputEvent defines masks for Shift, Ctrl, Alt, and Meta.

4. Add the KeyStroke/Action pair to the new Keymap.

5. Set the new map as the map for our JTextComponent.

Styled Text Panes

In this chapter we'll discuss Swing's most powerful text component, JTextPane, as well as the Document model and the many classes and interfaces that go along with it. All text components use the Document interface to interact with their models. JTextPane uses the StyledDocument interface, an extension of the Document interface with style-manipulation methods.

This is a long chapter because there are so many classes and interfaces used by Document and its ilk. You may have no immediate need to learn about some of these classes, especially those in the latter half of the chapter. Don't feel that you must read the chapter straight through.

The JTextPane Class

JTextPane is a multiline text component that can display text with multiple fonts, colors, and even embedded images. It supports named hierarchical text styles and has other features that can help implement a word processor or a similar application.

Technically, JTextPane is a subclass of JEditorPane, but it usually makes more sense to think of JTextPane as a text component in its own right. JEditorPane uses "editor kits" to handle text in various formats (such as HTML or RTF) in a modular way. Use a JEditorPane when you want to view or edit text in one of these formats. Use a JTextPane when you want to handle the text yourself. We'll cover JEditorPane and editor kits (including JTextPane's editor kit, StyledEditorKit) in Chapter 23.

Properties

JTextPane defines the properties shown in Table 22-1. document and styledDocument are both names for the same property. The model returned by getDocument() always implements StyledDocument (which is an interface that extends Document). Attempting to call setDocument() with a Document that is not a StyledDocument throws an

`IllegalArgumentException`. (The `Document` and `StyledDocument` interfaces are described in detail later in this chapter.)

Table 22-1. JTextPane properties

Property	Data type	get	is	set	Default value
characterAttributes	AttributeSet	•			
document[o]	Document	•		•	Value of styledDocument
editorKit[b,o]	EditorKit	•		•	StyledEditorKit
inputAttributes	MutableAttributeSet	•			
logicalStyle	Style	•		•	
paragraphAttributes	AttributeSet	•			
styledDocument	StyledDocument	•		•	DefaultStyledDocument
UIClassID[o]	String	•			"TextPaneUI"

[b]bound, [o]overridden

See also properties from the JTextComponent class (Table 19-1) and the JEditorPane class (Table 23-1). (Not shown are the contentType, page, and accessibleContext properties, inherited from JEditorPane.)

The `inputAttributes`, `characterAttributes`, `paragraphAttributes`, and `logicalStyle` properties are not properties of the JTextPane itself, but of the text under the caret. The types of these properties are related: the `Style` interface extends the `MutableAttributeSet` interface, which extends the `AttributeSet` interface. (We'll tackle these interfaces in "AttributeSets and Styles" later in this chapter.) The values of these properties are stored by the pane's `styledDocument`* and typically change as the position of the caret moves. Because of this (and also because the `setCharacterAttributes( )` and `setParagraphAttributes( )` methods require an extra boolean parameter, which makes them invalid as JavaBeans property mutators), we elaborate on these methods later in this chapter in "Attribute and Style Methods."

The `editorKit` property is inherited from JEditorPane, but there is little or no reason to deal with it directly. The `editorKit` defaults to an instance of `StyledEditorKit`. Attempting to set an editor kit that is not a `StyledEditorKit` (or a subclass) throws an `IllegalArgumentException`.

Constructors

public JTextPane( )
Create an empty text pane.

---

* Actually, inputAttributes is maintained by the pane's editorKit, which is a CaretListener of the Document. This read-only property is used by JTextPane when text is inserted. The newly inserted text will have the same attributes as the text immediately preceding it.

public JTextPane(StyledDocument doc)
> Create a text pane displaying the specified document.

Attribute and Style Methods

These methods manipulate the character attributes, paragraph attributes, and logical styles of the pane's document. *Character attributes* include font and text color. *Paragraph attributes* can also include paragraph indentation and spacing. *Styles* are groups of attributes that can be reused throughout the document. *Named styles* are styles that have been assigned a name. The document keeps track of these styles so you can look them up and reuse or modify them later. Changing the attributes of a style changes all text that is tagged with that style.

You can apply *logical styles* to whole paragraphs. Logical styles define a baseline set of attributes that can be overridden by local paragraph or character attributes. (See the discussion in "The StyledDocument Interface" later in this chapter for more details.) When setting the logical style for a paragraph, you can use a named style to facilitate reuse. We do this in the example editor later in the chapter, presenting a menu of the named styles.

Rather than operating on one attribute at a time, the attribute and style methods operate on collections of attributes held in objects implementing AttributeSet, MutableAttributeSet, or Style.

The accessor methods may return null if there is no content at the caret position or if there are no attributes to return. The mutator methods are thread-safe, so (unlike most Swing methods) they can be called safely by threads other than the event-dispatching thread.

public AttributeSet getCharacterAttributes()
> Return the character attributes that apply to the text at the caret position. Only the current caret position is used; any selected text is ignored.

public MutableAttributeSet getInputAttributes()
> This method delegates to the pane's editorKit (by calling its method of the same name). The effect is identical to calling getCharacterAttributes(), except the result is mutable. One way to change how inserted text appears in the pane is to manipulate the MutableAttributeSet returned by this method, but it is often easier to call setCharacterAttributes() instead.

public void setCharacterAttributes(AttributeSet attr, boolean replace)
> Apply the specified attributes to the selected characters. Even if there is no selection, the attributes apply (by updating inputAttributes) to any new text inserted at the current caret location. If you want the new set of attributes to completely replace the existing set (instead of augmenting it), use true for the replace argument.

public AttributeSet getParagraphAttributes()
Return the paragraph attributes for the text at the caret position. Only the current caret position is used; any selected text is ignored.

public void setParagraphAttributes(AttributeSet attr, boolean replace)
Apply the supplied attributes to any selected (or partially selected) paragraphs. If there is no selection, the attributes are applied to the paragraph at the current caret position. If you want the new set of attributes to completely replace the existing set (instead of augmenting it), use true for the replace argument.

public Style getLogicalStyle()
Return the Style that applies to the paragraph containing the caret. Any selected text is ignored.

public void setLogicalStyle(Style s)
Set the Style for the paragraph containing the caret. Any selected text is ignored.

Insertion/Replacement Methods

In addition to displaying text, JTextPane can display Icons and arbitrary Components. This flexibility makes it possible to display documents with embedded images or interactive documents such as HTML forms.

There are three insertion methods: one inserts text, one inserts an Icon, and one inserts a Component. Despite their dissimilar names, all three work the same way. The new insertion replaces the current selection or, if there is no selection, appears at the current caret position. (If you want to insert at a position other than the caret position, you can do so by manipulating the pane's document directly.) If you want to insert without replacing the current selection, you need to "deselect" before calling one of these methods. Here's one way to do this:

```
pane.getCaret().setDot(pane.getCaretPosition());
```

These methods are thread-safe, so (unlike most Swing methods) they can be called safely by threads other than the event-dispatching thread.

public void replaceSelection(String content)
Insert the specified text into the document, replacing anything currently selected. If content is null, it deletes the current selection. Any new text uses the attributes specified by the inputAttributes property.

public void insertIcon(Icon c)
Insert an Icon into the document, replacing anything currently selected.

public void insertComponent(Component c)

Insert a Component into the document,[*] replacing the current selection. The component is laid out relative to the text baseline, according to its alignmentY property (see Table 3-6). If c is a JComponent, calling c.setAlignmentY(0.8) places 80% of the component above the baseline.

Here's a short example showing how these methods work. We create a JTextPane with three buttons that insert a text string, button, and icon. Figure 22-1 shows it after it's been played with a bit.

```java
// PaneInsertionMethods.java
//
import javax.swing.*;
import java.awt.BorderLayout;
import java.awt.event.*;

// Show how icons, components, and text can be added to a JTextPane.
public class PaneInsertionMethods {

    public static void main(String[] args) {

        final JTextPane pane = new JTextPane();

        // Button to insert some text
        JButton textButton = new JButton("Insert Text");
        textButton.addActionListener(new ActionListener() {
            public void actionPerformed(ActionEvent event) {
                pane.replaceSelection("text");
            }
        });

        // Button to insert an icon
        final ImageIcon icon = new ImageIcon("bluepaw.gif");
        JButton iconButton = new JButton(icon);
        iconButton.addActionListener(new ActionListener() {
            public void actionPerformed(ActionEvent event) {
                pane.insertIcon(icon);
            }
        });

        // Button to insert a button
        JButton buttonButton = new JButton("Insert Button");
        buttonButton.addActionListener(new ActionListener() {
            public void actionPerformed(ActionEvent event) {
                pane.insertComponent(new JButton("Click Me"));
            }
        });
```

[*] Note that while it is usually fine for multiple JTextPanes to share the same Document, it can be a problem if you plan to use this method because it is forbidden to add a Component to more than one Container.

```
    // Layout
    JPanel buttons = new JPanel( );
    buttons.add(textButton);
    buttons.add(iconButton);
    buttons.add(buttonButton);

    JFrame frame = new JFrame( );
    frame.setDefaultCloseOperation(JFrame.EXIT_ON_CLOSE);
    frame.getContentPane( ).add(pane, BorderLayout.CENTER);
    frame.getContentPane( ).add(buttons, BorderLayout.SOUTH);
    frame.setSize(360,180);
    frame.setVisible(true);
  }
}
```

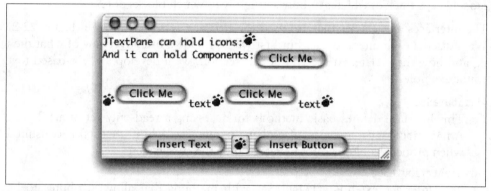

Figure 22-1. JTextPane containing JButtons and ImageIcons

Named Style Methods

JTextPane provides three methods for dealing with named styles, but it doesn't manage the styles itself, delegating this to its document instead. See the similarly named methods in the StyledDocument interface, the DefaultStyledDocument class, and the StyleContext class (later in this chapter) for more details on named styles.

public Style getStyle(String name)
> Return a named Style previously added to this document.

public void removeStyle(String name)
> Remove a named Style from this document. (It may also be removed from other StyledDocuments that share the same set of Styles.)

public Style addStyle(String name, Style parent)
> Create and return a new, empty Style and add it to the document's style hierarchy. The name of the new style is name, which may be null if you want to create

an unnamed style.* The parent parameter (if not null) is the Style used to resolve attributes not found in the new Style.

This method is poorly named. It doesn't "add" anything to its Style argument, but rather creates a new Style with the supplied name and parent.

AttributeSets and Styles

AttributeSet and its relatives are used to hold collections of attributes that can be used by styled text components (including JTextPane). For example, an AttributeSet might comprise an attribute for font size, an attribute for foreground color, and an attribute for indentation. Each attribute is simply a key/value pair. The Document model keeps track of which attribute sets apply to which blocks of text.

The interfaces and classes that are used for attribute sets are shown in Figure 22-2. We'll discuss each one in detail, but first we'll provide a brief overview of what they do and how they relate. At the end of this section, we'll develop a Style-based text editor example.

AttributeSet

>   This interface defines basic methods for accessing a read-only set of attributes. An AttributeSet may have a "resolving parent," which (if it exists) is consulted when property lookups can't be resolved by the current set.

MutableAttributeSet

>   This interface extends AttributeSet with methods that allow attributes to be added, given new values, or deleted from the set.

Style

>   This interface extends MutableAttributeSet to add two things: an optional name for the style and support for adding and removing ChangeEventListeners.

SimpleAttributeSet

>   A basic implementation of the MutableAttributeSet interface.

StyleConstants

>   This class defines the standard attribute keys used by Swing's text components. It also defines some static utility methods for getting and setting attribute values from attribute sets.

StyleContext

>   This utility class provides two services: it can create new AttributeSets in a space-efficient manner, and it manages a shared pool of named Style and Font information.

* Unnamed styles can be used but can't be accessed by the getStyle( ) and removeStyle( ) methods.

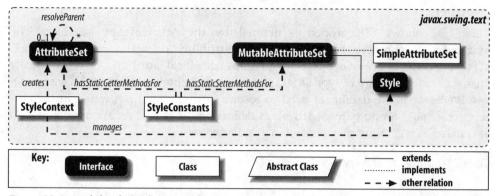

Figure 22-2. High-level AttributeSet class diagram

Since Swing does not provide a top-level public implementation of the Style interface, when you need a Style, you must request it from a StyleContext.* If you need a MutableAttributeSet, you can instantiate a SimpleAttributeSet using one of its constructors. If you want an AttributeSet, you can ask the default StyleContext for one or you can instantiate a SimpleAttributeSet.

The AttributeSet Interface

AttributeSet is an interface for a read-only collection of an arbitrary set of key/value pairs. The attribute value can be any arbitrary Object. The attribute key can also be any arbitrary object, but in practice it is almost always one of the constants defined in the StyleConstants class. StyleConstants defines standard attribute keys for font names and styles, foreground and background colors, indentation, and so on. These keys follow the Type-Safe Enumeration pattern, a clean way for Java programs to define typed constants for use in methods and interfaces.

AttributeSets can be structured in a hierarchy, so it's easy (and common) to say "this AttributeSet is just like that AttributeSet except it has a new foreground color and turns on italics." This hierarchy is maintained through the resolveParent property.

An AttributeSet's resolving parent (if not null) is another AttributeSet. The relationship between an AttributeSet and its resolving parent is much like the inheritance relationship between a Java class and its superclass: attributes not found in the local AttributeSet are searched for in its resolving parent, just as method implementations not found in a class are searched for in its superclass. This can go on indefinitely until the attribute is found or a set with no parent is reached.

---

* Which StyleContext do you use? The static StyleContext.getDefaultStyleContext( ) method returns the system's default StyleContext, but it is probably better to ask your JTextPane, which has style methods that delegate (eventually) to its StyleContext. For an example, see "A Stylized Editor" later in this chapter.

Properties

Table 22-2 shows the properties defined by the `AttributeSet` interface. The `attributeCount` property is the number of attributes defined locally by the set. `attributeNames` is an `Enumeration` containing the local attribute keys (not really "names," since keys are of type `Object`, and probably obtained from `StyleConstants`). `resolveParent` is the parent set used to resolve attribute keys not found in the current set, or null for no parent. Attributes defined in the parent set are not counted in `attributeCount`, nor are they present in `attributeNames`.

Table 22-2. AttributeSet properties

Property	Data type	get	is	set	Default value
attributeCount	int	•			
attributeNames	Enumeration	•			
resolveParent	AttributeSet	•			

Constants

`AttributeSet` defines the constants shown in Table 22-3.

Table 22-3. AttributeSet constants

Constant	Data type	Description
NameAttribute	Object	An implementation that chooses to store its name as an attribute pair should use this as the attribute key.
ResolveAttribute	Object	An implementation that chooses to store its `resolveParent` as an attribute pair should use this constant as the attribute key.

Methods

public Object getAttribute(Object key)

Search for an attribute whose key matches the one supplied. If the attribute is not found locally, the set's resolving parent is searched (if it exists). This process continues up the hierarchy until the attribute is found. If the value cannot be found, null is returned.

Note that `StyleConstants` provides static utility methods that are often more convenient to use than this method. `StyleConstants.getFontSize(mySet)` can replace this more complex code:

```
((Integer)mySet.getAttribute(StyleConstants.FontSize)).intValue( )
```

These methods differ, however, if `mySet` (including its resolving ancestors) does not have an attribute for font size. In this case, `StyleConstants.getFontSize( )` returns a default value (12) while `mySet.getAttribute( )` returns null (which causes a `NullPointerException` if you blindly attempt to call its `intValue( )` method).

public boolean containsAttribute(Object key, Object value)
> Return `true` if this set (or its resolving ancestors) contains the attribute key and its value matches (in the sense of `equals( )`) value.

public boolean containsAttributes(AttributeSet attrs)
> Return `true` if this set (or its resolving ancestors) contains values for all of the attributes in the given `AttributeSet`, and all of these values match. Note that this comparison does not include attributes contributed by any parent attribute sets. This distinction is not spelled out in the `AttributeSet` documentation but is true of standard implementations.

public boolean isDefined(Object key)
> Return `true` if the given attribute key is defined locally in this set. The resolving ancestors are not searched.

public AttributeSet copyAttributes()
> Create and return a clone of this `AttributeSet`.

public boolean isEqual(AttributeSet attrs)
> Return `true` if this set and the given set are equivalent. What this means exactly is left up to the implementation, and Swing's implementations can be a bit sloppy with respect to the resolving parents. For example, two `SimpleAttributeSets` are considered equivalent if all the attributes defined locally in the one on which you invoke the method have matches anywhere in the resolving hierarchy of the other, and both sets have the same number of locally defined attributes at the top level. In this case it is possible for an attribute defined locally in the second set, even at the top level, to fail to match anything in its comrade's resolving hierarchy, so this kind of "equivalence" is not symmetric. (Though such an example is possible, it would be convoluted because, due to how `SimpleAttributeSet` is implemented, both sets would have to have the same resolving parent.)

Inner interfaces

`AttributeSet` contains four inner interfaces. Each of these is entirely empty and serves only to mark attribute keys as belonging to a particular category. There is no requirement that attribute keys implement these interfaces, but most of the keys that Swing uses do.

```
public interface CharacterAttribute
public interface ColorAttribute
public interface FontAttribute
public interface ParagraphAttribute
```

The MutableAttributeSet Interface

`MutableAttributeSet` is an extension of the `AttributeSet` interface that provides methods for modifying (as opposed to just examining) the attributes in a set.

Property

`MutableAttributeSet` does not define any properties beyond those it inherits from `AttributeSet` but does extend the `resolveParent` read/write property by providing the `setResolveParent( )` mutator method. (See Table 22-4.)

Table 22-4. MutableAttributeSet property

Property	Data type	get	is	set	Default value
resolveParent°	AttributeSet	•		•	

°overridden

See also properties from the `AttributeSet` interface (Table 22-2).

Methods

public void addAttribute(Object key, Object value)

> Add an attribute to this set with the given key and value. If an attribute with the same key exists locally in this set, the new value replaces it. Be wary of using a mutable object (such as a `StringBuffer`) as an attribute value because `MutableAttributeSet` presumes that the attribute value `Object` does not change while it is part of the set. (Instead of altering the attribute value `Object` itself, use this method to replace it with a different `Object`.)

> Note that `StyleConstants` provides static utility methods that are often more convenient to use than this method. For example, `StyleConstants.setFontSize(mySet,14)` can replace this more complex code:

```
mySet.addAttribute(StyleConstants.FontSize, new Integer(14));
```

public void addAttributes(AttributeSet attrs)

> Add all the attributes present in the supplied `AttributeSet` to this set. Swing's implementations ignore the resolving parent of attrs and add only the locally defined attributes.

public void removeAttribute(Object key)

> Remove the attribute with the specified key from this set. This method has no effect if there is no matching local key.

public void removeAttributes(AttributeSet attrs)

> Remove the attributes that match those in the supplied `attrs` (in both key and value). If you want attributes removed even if the values don't match, call `removeAttributes(attrs.getAttributeNames( ))` instead.

public void removeAttributes(Enumeration names)

> Remove all attributes with keys that match those found in `names`.

The Style Interface

Style is a simple extension of MutableAttributeSet that allows a set of attributes to be given a name. This allows the Style to be easily referenced (e.g., by JTextPane's getStyle( ) method, which takes a name String as an argument and returns the requested Style). Style names are often used to populate a menu in the user interface, allowing the user to select a named Style for a block of text.

In addition, Style provides support for registering change listeners that will be notified whenever the attributes that define a Style are modified.

Property

Table 22-5 shows the property defined by the Style interface. The only property added by Style is the name property. It is permissible for a Style to be unnamed, in which case getName( ) returns null.

Table 22-5. Style property

Property	Data type	get	is	set	Default value
name	String			•	

See also properties from the MutableAttributeSet interface (Table 22-4).

Constants

Style does not define any constants beyond those it inherits from AttributeSet; one of these is NameAttribute. We mention it here because an implementation that chooses to store its name as an attribute pair should use NameAttribute as the attribute key.

Events

When a change is made to the attributes that make up a Style, listeners registered for change events are notified. The Style interface includes the following standard methods for registering change listeners:

```
public void addChangeListener(ChangeListener l)
public void removeChangeListener(ChangeListener l)
```

The SimpleAttributeSet Class

Swing provides a basic implementation of the MutableAttributeSet interface that uses a Hashtable to maintain its attributes. This is Swing's only top-level public class implementing AttributeSet or MutableAttributeSet.

Properties

Table 22-6 shows the default property values defined by `SimpleAttributeSet`. A newly created `SimpleAttributeSet` contains an empty `Hashtable`. The `resolveParent` (when set) is stored in the table just like the other attributes are, using the constant `ResolveAttribute`* as the key. This means that the `attributeCount` property includes this attribute, and `attributeNames` includes this object. The `empty` property is `false` if the set has any local attributes, even if the set's only local attribute is its `resolveParent`.

Table 22-6. SimpleAttributeSet properties

Property	Data type	get	is	set	Default value
attributeCount[o]	int	•			0
attributeNames[o]	Enumeration	•			**Empty** Enumeration
empty	boolean		•		true
resolveParent[o]	AttributeSet	•		•	null

[o]overridden

Constant

In addition to those it inherits from the `AttributeSet` interface, `SimpleAttributeSet` defines the constant shown in Table 22-7.

Table 22-7. SimpleAttributeSet constant

Constant	Data type	Description
EMPTY	AttributeSet	An empty, immutable AttributeSet

Constructors

public SimpleAttributeSet()
> Create a new set containing no attributes.

public SimpleAttributeSet(AttributeSet source)
> Create a set containing the attributes and values from the given set. It does not use source as a resolving parent; it just copies its local attributes. (But note that this could very well set the resolveParent to be the same as source's resolveParent.)

---

* SimpleAttributeSet inherits this constant from the AttributeSet interface, but StyleConstants also defines this constant. AttributeSet.ResolveAttribute, SimpleAttributeSet.ResolveAttribute, and StyleConstants. ResolveAttribute are three names for the same constant.

Add/remove methods

public void addAttribute(Object key, Object value)

> Add an attribute to this set with the given key and value. If an attribute with the specified key already exists locally in this set, the supplied value replaces it. (The use of a `Hashtable` as the attribute storage mechanism prohibits an attribute from having a value of null. `Hashtable.put( )` would throw a `NullPointerException`.)
>
> Note that `StyleConstants` provides more convenient static utility methods. `StyleConstants.setFontSize(mySet,14)` can replace `mySet.addAttribute(Style-Constants.FontSize, new Integer(14))`, for example.

public void addAttributes(AttributeSet attrs)

> Add all of the attributes defined locally in the supplied `AttributeSet` to this set.

public void removeAttribute(Object key)

> Remove the attribute with the specified key from this set. It is removed only from the local set, not from any resolving ancestors. This method has no effect if there is no matching local key.

public void removeAttributes(AttributeSet attrs)

> Remove all of the local attributes that match (in both key and value) a local attribute in attrs. If you want attributes removed even if the values don't match, call `removeAttributes(attrs.getAttributeNames( ))` instead.

public void removeAttributes(Enumeration names)

> Remove all local attributes with keys that match those found in names.

Query methods

public Object getAttribute(Object key)

> Search for an attribute whose key matches the given key. If the attribute is not found locally, the set's resolving ancestors (if any) are searched. If the value cannot be found, null is returned.
>
> Note that `StyleConstants` provides more convenient static utility methods. `StyleConstants.getFontSize(mySet)` can be used instead of this more complex code:
>
> > `((Integer)mySet.getAttribute(StyleConstants.FontSize)).intValue( )`
>
> These methods differ, however, if mySet (including its resolving ancestors) does not have an attribute for font size. In this case `StyleConstants.getFontSize( )` returns a default value (12), while `mySet.getAttribute( )` returns null (which throws a `NullPointerException` if you attempt to call its `intValue( )` method).

public boolean containsAttribute(Object key, Object value)

> Return true if this set (or its resolving ancestors) contains the attribute key and its value matches (in the sense of equals( )) value.

public boolean containsAttributes(AttributeSet attrs)

> Return true if this set (or its resolving ancestors) contains values for all of the local attributes in the given `AttributeSet`, and all of these values match.

public boolean isDefined(Object key)

> Return true if the given attribute key is defined locally in this set. Resolving ancestors are not searched.

public boolean isEqual(AttributeSet attr)

> Return true only if the given set has the same contents (attribute keys and values, including the pseudoattribute for the resolving parent) as the current set. The precise behavior of this method is it returns true if the given set has the same number of local attributes as this set and if `containsAttributes(attr)` returns true. This is only an approximation of actual equivalence.

public AttributeSet copyAttributes()

> Create and return a copy of this set. Except for the declared return type, this method is identical to the `clone( )` method.

The StyleConstants Class

This class defines a collection of well-known attribute keys. You are free to use attributes of any `Object` type as the keys in the attribute sets you create, but the attribute keys defined here are the ones that `JTextPane` expects to see and knows how to handle. (Barring customization on your part, other attributes are typically ignored.)

`StyleConstants` also provides static utility methods for getting and setting these well-known attributes. These are handy for three reasons:

- They free you from having to use attribute keys directly.
- They take care of wrapping and unwrapping base types into their `Object` counterparts. (boolean to `java.lang.Boolean`, int to `Integer`, etc.)
- The get methods return default values (instead of `null`) when they are unable to find an appropriate attribute pair.*

Consider the code needed to retrieve the font size from one attribute set and to set the font size of another set to be two points larger. Without these static utility methods, the code looks something like this:

```
Object sizeObj = origSet.getAttribute(StyleConstants.FontSize);
int size = (sizeObj == null) ? 12 : ((Integer)sizeObj).intValue( );
otherSet.addAttribute(StyleConstants.FontSize, new Integer(size+2));
```

---

* Therefore, if you want to be able to detect the absence of an attribute, don't use `StyleConstants`'s static methods. Instead, call the `AttributeSet`'s `getAttribute( )` method directly. You should also be aware that the default values that `StyleConstants` provides are not universal. For example, without a `Background` attribute, `StyleConstants.getBackground( )` returns `Color.black`, but `JTextFrame` uses the color specified by its `Background` property (inherited from `Component`/`JComponent`).

With them, the code can be as simple as:

```
int size = StyleConstants.getFontSize(origSet);
StyleConstants.setFontSize(otherSet, size+2);
```

Attribute key constants and utility methods

Usually, we cover a class's constants and methods separately, but we make an exception for StyleConstants. The following tables show the constants defined by StyleConstants, grouped by how they are used. Each row contains an attribute key constant, the object type used by the key's values, the utility methods that get or set values using that key, and the default value returned by the get method when it is unable to find a value using the key.

Character attribute keys. Table 22-8 shows the constants and utility methods for character attributes.

Table 22-8. StyleConstants: character attribute values

Constant	Value type	Public static methods[a]	Default
Background	Color	Color getBackground(aset) void setBackground(maset, Color bg)	Color.black
BidiLevel	Integer	int getBidiLevel(aset) void setBidiLevel(maset, int bidi)	0
Bold	Boolean	boolean isBold(aset) void setBold(maset, boolean b)	false
ComponentAttribute	Component	Component getComponent(aset) void setComponent(maset, Component c)[b]	null
FontFamily	String	String getFontFamily(aset) void setFontFamily(maset, String fam)	"Mono-spaced"
FontSize	Integer	int getFontSize(aset) void setFontSize(maset, int s)	12
Foreground	Color	Color getForeground(aset) void setForeground(maset, Color fg)	Color.black
IconAttribute	Icon	Icon getIcon(aset) void setIcon(maset, Icon i)[c]	null
Italic	Boolean	boolean isItalic(aset) void setItalic(maset, boolean b)	false
Strikethrough	Boolean	boolean isStrikethrough(aset) void setStrikethrough(maset, boolean b)	false
Subscript	Boolean	boolean isSubscript(aset) void setSubscript(maset, boolean b)	false

Table 22-8. StyleConstants: character attribute values (continued)

Constant	Value type	Public static methods[a]	Default
Superscript	Boolean	boolean isSuperscript(aset) void setSuperscript(maset, boolean b)	false
Underline	Boolean	boolean isUnderline(aset) void setUnderline(maset, boolean b)	false

[a] The first argument's type declaration is omitted for brevity. The type of aset in the get methods is AttributeSet. The type of maset in the set methods is MutableAttributeSet. If a get method is unable to find the appropriate attribute in the set, it returns the value listed in the Default column.

[b] The setComponent( ) method actually sets two attributes. It sets ComponentAttribute as expected, but it also sets AbstractDocument.ElementNameAttribute to ComponentElementName. Though attribute sets usually specify the style in which text should be displayed, these attributes specify that a Component should *replace* the text.

[c] The setIcon( ) method actually sets two attributes. It sets IconAttribute as expected, but it also sets AbstractDocument. ElementNameAttribute to IconElementName. Though attribute sets usually specify the style in which text should be displayed, these attributes designate that an Icon should *replace* the text.

The FontSize, FontFamily, Bold, and Italic attributes together determine the character's font. A method in the StyleContext class may save you the trouble of retrieving these attribute values separately: getFont(AttributeSet attr) examines the values of these four properties (plus Subscript and Superscript, which can alter the actual size of the font) and returns an appropriate java.awt.Font object.

The Foreground and Background attributes determine the color in which the characters are painted. The Subscript and Superscript attributes alter the font size and placement. The Strikethrough and Underline attributes determine whether the character is decorated with lines below or through it, respectively.

The BidiLevel attribute is the character's bidirectional level as defined by the Unicode bidi algorithm. This is used to determine whether the character is a left-to-right character or a right-to-left character.

ComponentAttribute and IconAttribute are used to specify a Component or an Icon that might be displayed instead of the character, but this replacement does not happen unless AbstractDocument.ComponentNameAttribute is set as well. The setComponent( ) and setIcon( ) methods therefore set this attribute in addition to ComponentAttribute or IconAttribute. (There is no special significance to the "Attribute" suffix of these constants.)

Paragraph attribute keys. Table 22-9 shows the constants and utility methods for paragraph attributes.

Table 22-9. StyleConstants: paragraph attribute values

Constant	Value type	Public static methods[a]	Default
Alignment	Integer	int getAlignment(aset) void setAlignment(maset, int a)	ALIGN_LEFT[b]
FirstLineIndent	Float	float getFirstLineIndent(aset) void setFirstLineIndent(maset, float i)	0
LeftIndent	Float	float getLeftIndent(aset) void setLeftIndent(maset, float i)	0
LineSpacing	Float	float getLineSpacing(aset) void setLineSpacing(maset, float i)	0
Orientation	Not used		
RightIndent	Float	float getRightIndent(aset) void setRighIndent(maset, float i)	0
SpaceAbove	Float	float getSpaceAbove(aset) void setSpaceAbove(maset, float i)	0
SpaceBelow	Float	float getSpaceBelow(aset) void setSpaceBelow(maset, float i)	0
TabSet	TabSet[c]	TabSet getTabSet(aset) void setTabSet(maset, TabSet tabs)	null

[a] The first argument's type declaration is omitted for brevity. The type of aset in the get methods is AttributeSet. The type of maset in the set methods is MutableAttributeSet. If a get method is unable to find the appropriate attribute in the set, it returns the value in the Default column.

[b] See Table 22-11 for the values that can be assigned to this attribute.

[c] The TabSet class is described later in this chapter.

The Alignment attribute determines how the paragraph is justified. Table 22-11 lists values for left-, right-, center-, and full-justification. (Don't confuse Alignment with Orientation; StyleConstants mysteriously defines an attribute key for Orientation even though it is not used by Swing.)

The LeftIndent, RightIndent, SpaceAbove, and SpaceBelow attributes specify an amount of extra space (in points) on the left, right, top, and bottom of the paragraph, respectively. The LineSpacing attribute determines how much extra vertical space (in points) appears between consecutive lines of the paragraph.

The FirstLineIndent attribute determines how far (in points) to indent the first line of the paragraph with respect to the remaining lines. It may have a negative value to create a hanging indent.

The TabSet attribute is a collection of TabStops that determine the placement of text with embedded tab (\t) characters. A TabSet supports any number of left, right, centering, or decimal-aligned TabStops. We discuss the TabSet and TabStop classes later in this chapter.

Other attribute keys. Table 22-10 shows some keys for attributes that aren't used directly to specify the styling text. These attributes are for the convenience of classes that implement the `AttributeSet/Style` interfaces for storing extra information. `StyleConstants` does not provide any utility methods for these attributes.

Table 22-10. StyleConstants: other attribute values

Constant	Value type	Notes
ComposedTextAttribute	java.text.AttributedString	
ModelAttribute	Object	Used for HTML form elements
NameAttribute	String	Another name for AttributeSet. NameAttribute
ResolveAttribute	AttributeSet	Another name for AttributeSet. ResolveAttribute

`NameAttribute` and `ResolveAttribute` have the same values as the like-named constants defined by the `AttributeSet` interface. An implementation of `AttributeSet` (and its subinterfaces) that chooses to store its `ResolveParent` or its name (remember that the `Style` interface defines a name property) as an attribute pair should use these constants as the attribute keys. This is exactly how `SimpleAttributeSet` is implemented.

`ComposedTextAttribute` is an attribute key that is coupled with a value of type `java.text.AttributedString`, which is a class that has its own way of storing styled text. If a renderer encounters this attribute, it delegates drawing to the static `Utilities.drawComposedText( )` method.

`ModelAttribute` is used by `HTMLEditorKit` and `JEditorPane` to attach a component model (`ListModel`, `ComboBoxModel`, etc.) to an HTML form element.

Attribute value constants

`StyleConstants` also defines a few constants used as attribute values (not attribute keys). These are shown in Table 22-11.

Table 22-11. StyleConstants: attribute values not used as keys

Constant	Type	Associated attribute key
ALIGN_CENTER	int	Alignment
ALIGN_JUSTIFIED	int	Alignment
ALIGN_LEFT	int	Alignment
ALIGN_RIGHT	int	Alignment
ComponentElementName	String	AbstractDocument.ElementNameAttribute
IconElementName	String	AbstractDocument.ElementNameAttribute

The values of the `Alignment` paragraph attribute determine how any extra space is allocated to a line of text. The default is `ALIGN_LEFT`, which puts all the extra space on the right side, pushing the line of text against the left margin. `ALIGN_RIGHT` puts the extra space on the left, pushing the line of text to the right. `ALIGN_CENTER` puts equal space on the left and right, centering the text on the line. And finally, `ALIGN_JUSTIFIED` spreads out the extra space within the line of text, making the line flush with both the left and right margins.

`ComponentElementName` and `IconElementName` are character attribute values intended to be paired with `AbstractDocument.ElementNameAttribute` (a constant not provided by `StyleConstants`) as the attribute key. If the value of this attribute is `ComponentElementName`, the renderer attempts to display the value (a `Component`) of the `ComponentAttribute` attribute instead of the text. If the value of this attribute is `IconElementName`, the renderer attempts to display the value (an `Icon`) of the `IconAttribute` attribute instead of the text. In essence, this character attribute allows a `Component` or `Icon` to take the place of text (usually a single space) in the `Document` model. This attribute is set automatically by the `setComponent( )` and `setIcon( )` methods.

StyleConstants inner classes

`StyleConstants` has four public static inner classes that correspond to the four inner interfaces defined by `AttributeSet`. These are shown in Table 22-12.

Table 22-12. The public static inner classes of StyleConstants

Inner class name	Implements	Contains which attribute keys?
`CharacterConstants`	`AttributeSet.CharacterAttribute`	Listed in Table 22-8
`ColorConstants`	`AttributeSet.ColorAttribute,` `AttributeSet.CharacterAttribute`	`Foreground, Background`
`FontConstants`	`AttributeSet.FontAttribute,` `AttributeSet.CharacterAttribute`	`FontFamily, FontSize, Bold,` `Italic`[a]
`ParagraphConstants`	`AttributeSet.ParagraphAttribute`	Listed in Table 22-9

[a] Note that the names inside the inner class are `Family`, `Size`, `Bold`, and `Italic`.

You don't need to worry about these inner classes because all of the constant keys they define are also defined in the outer class. However, they can be used with the `instanceof` operator to identify the category of an attribute. For example:

```
if (someAttr instanceof AttributeSet.ParagraphAttribute)
    doSomething( );
// Or the equivalent:
if (someAttr instanceof StyleConstants.ParagraphAttribute) ...
```

The StyleContext Class

A `StyleContext` is, in essence, a class that caches style-related objects. This can be important because styled documents tend to have many blocks of text with the same attributes, and we'd like each of these blocks to share a single `AttributeSet` object rather than have its own (but identical) `AttributeSet`.

Consider the common case in which you want to extend JTextPane to make it easy to append text in different colors. A naïve way to do this would be:

```
public class ColorPane extends JTextPane {
  public void append(Color c, String s) { // Naive implementation
    // Bad: instiantiates a new AttributeSet object on each call
    SimpleAttributeSet aset = new SimpleAttributeSet();
    StyleConstants.setForeground(aset, c);

    int len = getText().length();
    setCaretPosition(len); // Place caret at the end (with no selection).
    setCharacterAttributes(aset, false);
    replaceSelection(s); // There is no selection, so insert at caret.
  }
}
```

This does work, but it's not good code because it instantiates a `SimpleAttributeSet` object on every call. Suppose we want to display the numbers 1 through 400 in different colors (the primes in red, the perfect squares in blue, and the rest in black) in a ColorPane:

```
ColorPane pane = new ColorPane();
for (int n=1; n <= 400; n+=1) {
  if (isPrime(n)) {
    pane.append(Color.red, String.valueOf(n));
  } else if (isPerfectSquare(n)) {
    pane.append(Color.blue, String.valueOf(n));
  } else {
    pane.append(Color.black, String.valueOf(n));
  }
}
```

This causes 400 `SimpleAttributeSet` objects to be instantiated, even though we're using only 3 colors. Object creation is not hugely expensive, but creating 397 objects we don't really need does chew up some processing time. More than that, the pane's Document might keep references to all 400 AttributeSets, preventing the garbage collector from reclaiming them until the Document itself is reclaimed.

This is where the StyleContext comes in. Instead of creating an AttributeSet ourselves, we simply ask the StyleContext for one. It creates a new object for us if it must, but first it sees if the AttributeSet we're looking for resides in its cache. If so, it gives us the cached AttributeSet so we can reuse it.

StyleContext isn't hard to use. Fixing ColorPane to use it[*] is only a two-line change:

```
public class ColorPane extends JTextPane {
  public void append(Color c, String s) { // Better implementation--uses StyleContext
```

---

[*] Another worthy change is to replace len = getText().length() with len = getDocument().getLength(). This is because getText() has to perform a moderate amount of work to convert the pane's content into String form, and this work is wasted if we're interested only in its length. There's no reason not to make this change except that we don't introduce the Document interface until later in this chapter.

```
        StyleContext sc = StyleContext.getDefaultStyleContext();
        AttributeSet aset = sc.addAttribute(SimpleAttributeSet.EMPTY,
                                    StyleConstants.Foreground, c);

        int len = getText().length();
        setCaretPosition(len);  // Place caret at the end (with no selection).
        setCharacterAttributes(aset, false);
        replaceSelection(s); // There is no selection, so insert at caret.
    }
}
```

With this change, the first time we ask for a blue attribute set (for number 1), StyleContext instantiates one for us and adds it to its cache. The next time we ask for a blue attribute set (for number 4), it returns the cached set. No new object is instantiated. The same goes for the red and black sets, so only three AttributeSets are instantiated during the processing of 400 (or even 4,000) numbers.

StyleContext caches three kinds of style-related objects: AttributeSets, Fonts, and named Styles. For AttributeSets and Fonts, it makes sense to use the "default" StyleContext, as we did in the code for ColorPane. The static getDefaultStyleContext() method returns a StyleContext that is intended to be shared, and it makes sense to share as much as possible.

For Styles, though, sharing demands some caution because of the possibility for name-clashes. For example, two documents may define a style named "headline" in completely different ways. Because of this, a Document that supports named styles (including a DefaultStyledDocument, which JTextPane usually uses) creates its own StyleContext instead of using the default.[*] So when dealing with named styles, it is safer to use the style methods provided by your text component (which delegates to its Document) or by your Document (which delegates to its StyleContext) instead of the default StyleContext.

It's worth mentioning a few things about StyleContext's font handling. First, there is a handy getFont() method that "retrieves" an actual java.awt.Font from an AttributeSet, even though AttributeSets store font information as separate attributes for font family, font size, bold, etc. Second, StyleContext does cache Font objects but doesn't cache FontMetrics objects, even though it has a getFontMetrics() method.

Properties

Table 22-13 shows the properties defined by the StyleContext class. The styleNames property provides access to the names of all Styles created by this StyleContext. The

---

[*] Each Swing text component has a Document, and every Document uses a StyleContext. For efficiency, the plainer Documents all use the default StyleContext. Although DefaultStyledDocument doesn't normally share styles in this way, it has constructors that allow you to specify which StyleContext it should use. So if you want named Styles to be shared, it is possible to pass the default StyleContext (or any other StyleContext) into the constructor.

StyleContext starts out with one Style, which takes its name from the DEFAULT_STYLE constant and doesn't have any attributes. The emptySet property simply gives you SimpleAttributeSet.EMPTY, which is an immutable, empty AttributeSet that doesn't have any attributes. The changeListeners() property gives you an array containing the StyleContext's registered change listeners.

Table 22-13. StyleContext properties

Property	Data type	get	is	set	Default value
changeListeners[1.4]	ChangeListener[]	•			Empty array
emptySet	AttributeSet	•			SimpleAttributeSet.EMPTY
styleNames	Enumeration (each element is a String)	•			An Enumeration containing only the String constant DEFAULT_STYLE

[1.4]since 1.4

Events

A ChangeEvent is fired whenever a new Style is created by, or an existing Style is removed from, the StyleContext.* The following two methods are provided for managing ChangeListeners:

```
public void addChangeListener(ChangeListener l)
public void removeChangeListener(ChangeListener l)
```

Constant

The StyleContext class defines the constant shown in Table 22-14.

Table 22-14. StyleContext constant

Name	Data type	Description
DEFAULT_STYLE	String	The name of the default (initially empty) style

Constructor

public StyleContext()
> Instantiate a StyleContext that contains only a default style with no attributes. Invoke the constructor when you want to create a brand new StyleContext instead of sharing an existing one, such as the one returned by getDefaultStyleContext().

Static default accessor method

public static final StyleContext getDefaultStyleContext()
> Return a StyleContext that is intended to be shared.

---

* When attributes are added, changed, or removed from a Style, the Style itself notifies all listeners that registered with that Style. StyleContext fires a ChangeEvent only when an entire Style is added or removed.

AttributeContext methods

These methods (along with the accessor for the emptySet property) implement the AbstractDocument.AttributeContext interface. This interface exists so that Documents can expose their font-caching methods.* StyleContext is the only class in Swing that implements this interface.

public synchronized AttributeSet addAttribute(AttributeSet old, Object key,
 Object value)

This method returns an AttributeSet similar to old except that it has the specified value as the value for an attribute with the specified key. It tries to return a set in its cache. If it has to, it instantiates a new AttributeSet, adds it to the cache, and returns it. The value passed in for old may be an empty set, such as SimpleAttributeSet.EMPTY, or the set returned by getEmptySet().

This method is poorly named. It doesn't "add" anything to its AttributeSet argument, but it might create a slightly different AttributeSet and add it to the cache.

public synchronized AttributeSet addAttributes(AttributeSet old, AttributeSet attr)

This method is the same as AddAttribute() except that it finds or creates a set whose contents include the results of adding *all* the attributes defined in attr to old, not just a single new attribute.

public synchronized AttributeSet removeAttribute(AttributeSet old, Object key)

This method returns an AttributeSet similar to old except that it lacks an attribute with the specified key. It tries to return a set in its cache. If it has to, it instantiates a new AttributeSet, adds it to the cache, and returns it.

This method is poorly named. It doesn't "delete" anything from its AttributeSet argument, but it might create a smaller AttributeSet and add it to the cache.

public synchronized AttributeSet removeAttributes(AttributeSet old, AttributeSet attrs)

This method is the same as RemoveAttribute() except that it finds or builds a set that includes only those attributes in old that have no matching value in attr. If you want attributes removed even if the values don't match, call removeAttributes(old.getAttributeNames()) instead.

public synchronized AttributeSet removeAttributes(AttributeSet old,
 Enumeration names)

This method is the same as RemoveAttribute() except that it returns the result of removing all attributes with keys that match those found in names.

public synchronized void reclaim(AttributeSet a)

Signal that the AttributeSet is no longer used, and the StyleContext is free to remove it from its cache. This method was more important before the advent of weak references with SDK 1.2.

---

* They don't have to expose their named-style methods because the interfaces that support styles provide their own style methods. See "The StyledDocument Interface" for more details.

Font and color accessor methods

public Font getFont(String family, int style, int size)

This method returns a `java.awt.Font` with the requested font family, style, and size. It tries to return a `Font` in the cache. If it has to, it instantiates a new `Font`, adds it to the cache, and returns it. (The style parameter should be a bitwise "or" of `Font.PLAIN`, `Font.BOLD`, and `Font.ITALIC`.)

public Font getFont(AttributeSet attr)

Look up the font attributes defined in `attr` (`FontFamily`, `FontSize`, `Bold`, `Italic`, `Subscript`, and `Superscript`) and return an appropriate `java.awt.Font`. Caching behavior is similar to the three-argument `getFont()` method.

public FontMetrics getFontMetrics(Font f)

Equivalent to `Toolkit.getDefaultToolkit.getFontMetrics(f)`. No caching is performed for `FontMetrics` objects, but subclasses may override this behavior.

public Color getForeground(AttributeSet attr)
public Color getBackground(AttributeSet attr)

Equivalent to `StyleConstants.getForeground(attr)` and `StyleConstants.getBackground(attr)`. No caching is performed for `Color` objects, but subclasses may override this.

Style management methods

public Style addStyle(String name, Style parent)

Create a new, empty `Style`, add it to the cache, and return it. The name of the new style is `name`, which may be `null` to create an unnamed style.* The `parent` parameter (if not `null`) indicates that the existing `Style` used to resolve attributes is not found in the new `Style`.

This method is poorly named. It doesn't "add" anything to its `Style` argument, but it creates a new `Style` with the given name and resolving parent.

public Style getStyle(String name)

Return the cached `Style` with the given `name` or `null` if it isn't found.

public void removeStyle(String name)

Signal that the named `Style` is no longer used, and the `StyleContext` is free to remove it from its cache.

Serialization methods

The following static methods define a mechanism for reading and writing an `AttributeSet` to a stream. They are written so that the constant attribute keys defined in `StyleConstants` are recognized when the stream is read, allowing references to the existing singleton objects to be used instead of creating new instances. For example,

---

* Unnamed styles are not cached nor can they be accessed by the `getStyle()` method.

---

when StyleConstants.Bold is encountered while a serialized AttributeSet is read, the AttributeSet uses the shared StyleConstants.Bold instance instead of creating its own instance of the key. This is critical because it allows the keys to be compared with the highly efficient reference equality (the == operator) rather than with a much more expensive equals( ) method.

public static void registerStaticAttributeKey(Object key)
Register an attribute key as a well-known key. When an attribute with the given key is written to a stream, a special marker is used so that it can be recognized when it is read back in. All attribute keys defined in StyleConstants are registered using this method. If you define additional attribute keys that you want to ensure will exist as singletons (nonreplicated objects), you should register them using this method. Such keys must not be Serializable, as this is how writeAttributeSet( ) determines if it needs to save the keys in a special format.

public static Object getStaticAttributeKey(Object key)
Return the special marker that can be used to represent key in serialization.

public static Object getStaticAttribute(Object skey)
Given skey, the special marker used in serialization, return the original key.

public static void writeAttributeSet(ObjectOutputStream out, AttributeSet a)
  throws IOException
Write the contents of the given set to the specified stream. Any non-Serializable keys are looked up in the set of keys registered by calls to the registerStaticAttributeKey( ) method. All attribute values must be Serializable.

public static void readAttributeSet(ObjectInputStream in, MutableAttributeSet a)
  throws ClassNotFoundException, IOException
Read a set of attributes from the given stream, adding them to the input set. When an attribute key that matches a key registered by a call to registerStaticAttributeKey( ) is read, the registered singleton key is returned.

public void readAttributes(ObjectInputStream in, MutableAttributeSet a)
  throws ClassNotFoundException, IOException
public void writeAttributes(ObjectOutputStream out, AttributeSet a)
  throws IOException
These methods simply call the static readAttributeSet( ) and writeAttributeSet( ) methods.

A Stylized Editor

Though we have yet to cover the Document model, we've learned enough to implement a substantial example that shows how to create Styles and apply them to paragraphs in a document. This mini word processor has the following features:

- The user can define Styles using a simple dialog box that allows attributes such as font size, line spacing, bold, and italics to be specified.

- The user can set the Style for the paragraph at the cursor position.
- The user can modify a Style and see the changes reflected in all paragraphs using the modified Style.

This last item demonstrates why the Style interface includes methods for registering ChangeListeners. We'll have to write the code that modifies the Style, but when a Style changes, JTextPane redraws the affected text automatically.

The example consists of two classes: StyleFrame and StyleBox. StyleFrame is the main application frame. It contains a JTextPane for editing text and a JMenuBar that allows the user to create and modify Styles, and set the Style for the paragraph at the current cursor position. StyleBox is a simple dialog containing various JTextFields, JComboBoxes, and JCheckBoxes that allow the user to define several paragraph attributes.

We'll look at StyleBox first to get an idea of what the program can do. Figure 22-3 shows two sample StyleBoxes. The first shows the "default" Style that we get from the document when it's created. The second shows a specification for a "Title" Style that uses a large, bold font and places extra space above and below the text.

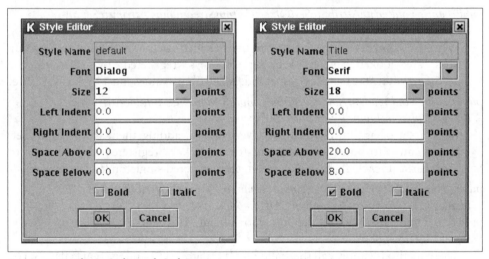

Figure 22-3. Editing Styles with StyleBox

Here's the code for this class. There's a lot of code related to the creation and layout of all the data entry components. Feel free to ignore these details and concentrate on the fillStyle() and loadFromStyle() methods. These show how to set attributes on a Style object and how to retrieve attributes from an already populated Style (which we do when the user wants to modify a Style).

```
// StyleBox.java
//
import javax.swing.*;
```

```java
import javax.swing.text.*;
import java.awt.*;

public class StyleBox extends JPanel {
    // Control panel that can be used to edit a style's paragraph attributes

    private static final String[] fonts = {"Monospaced", "Serif", "SansSerif"};
    private static final String[] sizes = {"8", "10", "12", "18", "24", "36"};

    private JTextField nameField;
    private JComboBox fontCombo, sizeCombo;
    private JTextField leftField, rightField, aboveField, belowField;
    private JCheckBox boldCheck, italicCheck;

    public StyleBox() {
        // Create the fields and lay them out.
        super(new BorderLayout(4, 4));
        JPanel labelPanel = new JPanel(new GridLayout(8, 1, 0, 2));
        JPanel valuePanel = new JPanel(new GridLayout(8, 1, 0, 2));
        add(labelPanel, BorderLayout.WEST);
        add(valuePanel, BorderLayout.CENTER);
        JLabel lab;
        JPanel sidePanel;

        lab = new JLabel("Style Name", SwingConstants.RIGHT);
        labelPanel.add(lab);
        nameField = new JTextField();
        lab.setLabelFor(nameField);
        valuePanel.add(nameField);

        lab = new JLabel("Font", SwingConstants.RIGHT);
        labelPanel.add(lab);
        fontCombo = new JComboBox(fonts);
        fontCombo.setEditable(true); // User may enter custom value
        lab.setLabelFor(fontCombo);
        valuePanel.add(fontCombo);

        lab = new JLabel("Size", SwingConstants.RIGHT);
        labelPanel.add(lab);
        sizeCombo = new JComboBox(sizes);
        sizeCombo.setEditable(true); // User may enter custom value
        lab.setLabelFor(sizeCombo);
        sidePanel = new JPanel(new BorderLayout(4, 0));
        sidePanel.add(sizeCombo, BorderLayout.CENTER);
        sidePanel.add(new JLabel("points"), BorderLayout.EAST);
        valuePanel.add(sidePanel);

        lab = new JLabel("Left Indent", SwingConstants.RIGHT);
        labelPanel.add(lab);
        leftField = new JTextField();
        lab.setLabelFor(leftField);
        sidePanel = new JPanel(new BorderLayout(4, 0));
        sidePanel.add(leftField, BorderLayout.CENTER);
```

```
    sidePanel.add(new JLabel("points"), BorderLayout.EAST);
    valuePanel.add(sidePanel);

    lab = new JLabel("Right Indent", SwingConstants.RIGHT);
    labelPanel.add(lab);
    rightField = new JTextField( );
    lab.setLabelFor(rightField);
    sidePanel = new JPanel(new BorderLayout(4, 0));
    sidePanel.add(rightField, BorderLayout.CENTER);
    sidePanel.add(new JLabel("points"), BorderLayout.EAST);
    valuePanel.add(sidePanel);

    lab = new JLabel("Space Above", SwingConstants.RIGHT);
    labelPanel.add(lab);
    aboveField = new JTextField( );
    lab.setLabelFor(aboveField);
    sidePanel = new JPanel(new BorderLayout(4, 0));
    sidePanel.add(aboveField, BorderLayout.CENTER);
    sidePanel.add(new JLabel("points"), BorderLayout.EAST);
    valuePanel.add(sidePanel);

    lab = new JLabel("Space Below", SwingConstants.RIGHT);
    labelPanel.add(lab);
    belowField = new JTextField( );
    lab.setLabelFor(belowField);
    sidePanel = new JPanel(new BorderLayout(4, 0));
    sidePanel.add(belowField, BorderLayout.CENTER);
    sidePanel.add(new JLabel("points"), BorderLayout.EAST);
    valuePanel.add(sidePanel);

    boldCheck = new JCheckBox("Bold");
    italicCheck = new JCheckBox("Italic");
    sidePanel = new JPanel(new GridLayout(1, 2));
    sidePanel.add(boldCheck);
    sidePanel.add(italicCheck);
    valuePanel.add(sidePanel);

    clear( ); // Sets initial values, etc.
  }

  public void clear( ) {
    // Reset all fields (also set nameField to be editable).
    nameField.setText("");
    nameField.setEditable(true);
    fontCombo.setSelectedIndex(0);
    sizeCombo.setSelectedIndex(2);
    leftField.setText("0.0");
    rightField.setText("0.0");
    aboveField.setText("0.0");
    belowField.setText("0.0");
    boldCheck.setSelected(false);
    italicCheck.setSelected(false);
  }
```

```
public String getStyleName( ) {
  // Return the name of the style.
  String name = nameField.getText( );
  if (name.length( ) > 0)
    return name;
  else
    return null;
}

public void fillStyle(Style style) {
  // Mutate 'style' with the values entered in the fields (no value checking --
  // could throw NumberFormatException).
  String font = (String)fontCombo.getSelectedItem( );
  StyleConstants.setFontFamily(style, font);

  String size = (String)sizeCombo.getSelectedItem( );
  StyleConstants.setFontSize(style, Integer.parseInt(size));

  String left = leftField.getText( );
  StyleConstants.setLeftIndent(style, Float.valueOf(left).floatValue( ));

  String right = rightField.getText( );
  StyleConstants.setRightIndent(style, Float.valueOf(right).floatValue( ));

  String above = aboveField.getText( );
  StyleConstants.setSpaceAbove(style, Float.valueOf(above).floatValue( ));

  String below = belowField.getText( );
  StyleConstants.setSpaceBelow(style, Float.valueOf(below).floatValue( ));

  boolean bold = boldCheck.isSelected( );
  StyleConstants.setBold(style, bold);

  boolean italic = italicCheck.isSelected( );
  StyleConstants.setItalic(style, italic);
}

// Load the form from an existing Style.
public void loadFromStyle(Style style) {
  nameField.setText(style.getName( ));
  nameField.setEditable(false); // Don't allow name change.

  String fam = StyleConstants.getFontFamily(style);
  fontCombo.setSelectedItem(fam);

  int size = StyleConstants.getFontSize(style);
  sizeCombo.setSelectedItem(Integer.toString(size));

  float left = StyleConstants.getLeftIndent(style);
  leftField.setText(Float.toString(left));

  float right = StyleConstants.getRightIndent(style);
  rightField.setText(Float.toString(right));
```

```
        float above = StyleConstants.getSpaceAbove(style);
        aboveField.setText(Float.toString(above));

        float below = StyleConstants.getSpaceBelow(style);
        belowField.setText(Float.toString(below));

        boolean bold = StyleConstants.isBold(style);
        boldCheck.setSelected(bold);

        boolean italic = StyleConstants.isItalic(style);
        italicCheck.setSelected(italic);
    }
}
```

One class ties this whole example together. StyleFrame is a JFrame that provides a
JTextPane for editing text and a JMenuBar for working with Styles and exiting the
application. The Style menu (see Figure 22-4) contains two submenus (Set Logical
Style and Modify Style) and one menu item (Create New Style). The submenus each
contain a list of the Styles that have been created (plus default, the Style we get for
free).

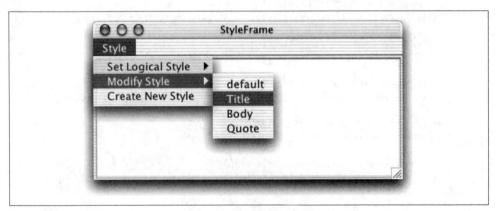

Figure 22-4. StyleFrame example menus

The menu options function as follows:

Set Logical Style
> When a Style is selected from this menu, the setLogicalStyle( ) method is
> called on the frame's JTextPane, which assigns the Style to the entire paragraph
> in which the caret is positioned.[*]

Modify Style
> When a Style is selected from this submenu, the StyleBox is displayed and pop-
> ulated with the existing definition of the selected Style. Once changes are made

---

[*] We could add code to assign the Style to multiple highlighted paragraphs, but first we need to learn more
about the Document model.

and the dialog is closed, the existing Style is "refilled" by the StyleBox. This causes the Style to fire a property change event, which alerts its listeners to redraw all paragraphs that use the modified Style.

Create New Style

When this item is selected, a dialog box is displayed showing an empty StyleBox to define a new Style. When the dialog is closed, a new Style is created by calling addStyle( ) on the JTextPane. We then ask the StyleBox to fill the new Style with the entered data. Finally, the new Style is added to the Set Logical Style and Modify Style menus.

Here's the code for this class:

```java
// StyleFrame.java
//
import javax.swing.*;
import javax.swing.text.*;
import java.awt.*;
import java.awt.event.*;

public class StyleFrame extends JFrame implements ActionListener {
    // A JTextPane with a menu for Style manipulation

    protected StyleBox styleBox;
    protected JTextPane textPane;
    protected JMenuBar menuBar;
    protected JMenu applyStyleMenu, modifyStyleMenu;
    protected JMenuItem createItem;

    public StyleFrame( ) {
        super("StyleFrame");

        styleBox = new StyleBox( );
        textPane = new JTextPane( );
        getContentPane( ).add(new JScrollPane(textPane), BorderLayout.CENTER);

        // Set up menu.
        menuBar = new JMenuBar( );
        JMenu styleMenu = new JMenu("Style");
        menuBar.add(styleMenu);
        setJMenuBar(menuBar);

        applyStyleMenu = new JMenu("Set Logical Style");
        applyStyleMenu.setToolTipText(
            "set the Logical Style for the paragraph at caret location");
        styleMenu.add(applyStyleMenu);

        modifyStyleMenu = new JMenu("Modify Style");
        modifyStyleMenu.setToolTipText(
            "redefine a named Style (will affect paragraphs using that style)");
        styleMenu.add(modifyStyleMenu);
```

```java
        createItem = new JMenuItem("Create New Style");
        createItem.setToolTipText(
            "define a new Style (which can then be applied to paragraphs)");
        createItem.addActionListener(this);
        styleMenu.add(createItem);

        // Add the default style to applyStyleMenu and modifyStyleMenu.
        createMenuItems(StyleContext.DEFAULT_STYLE);
    }

    protected void createMenuItems(String styleName) {
        // Add 'styleName' to applyStyleMenu and modifyStyleMenu.
        JMenuItem applyItem = new JMenuItem(styleName);
        applyItem.addActionListener(this);
        applyStyleMenu.add(applyItem);

        JMenuItem modifyItem = new JMenuItem(styleName);
        modifyItem.addActionListener(this);
        modifyStyleMenu.add(modifyItem);
    }

    public void actionPerformed(ActionEvent e) {
        // Determine which menuItem was invoked and process it.
        JMenuItem source = (JMenuItem)e.getSource();

        if ( applyStyleMenu.isMenuComponent(source) ) {
            // Apply an existing style to the paragraph at the caret position.
            String styleName = source.getActionCommand();
            Style style = textPane.getStyle(styleName);
            textPane.setLogicalStyle(style);
        }

        if ( source == createItem ) {
            // Define a new Style and add it to the menus.
            styleBox.clear();
            int response = JOptionPane.showConfirmDialog(this, styleBox,
                "Style Editor", JOptionPane.OK_CANCEL_OPTION,
                JOptionPane.PLAIN_MESSAGE);
            if (response == JOptionPane.OK_OPTION &&
                styleBox.getStyleName() != null) {
                String styleName = styleBox.getStyleName();
                Style style = textPane.addStyle(styleName, null);
                styleBox.fillStyle(style);
                createMenuItems(styleName); // Add new Style to the menus.
            }
        }

        if ( modifyStyleMenu.isMenuComponent(source) ) {
            // Redefine a Style (automatically redraws paragraphs using Style).
            String styleName = source.getActionCommand();
            Style style = textPane.getStyle(styleName);
            styleBox.loadFromStyle(style);
```

```
        int response = JOptionPane.showConfirmDialog(this, styleBox,
            "Style Editor", JOptionPane.OK_CANCEL_OPTION,
            JOptionPane.PLAIN_MESSAGE);
        if (response == JOptionPane.OK_OPTION) styleBox.fillStyle(style);
    }
}

    public static void main(String[] args) {
        JFrame frame = new StyleFrame();
        frame.setDefaultCloseOperation(JFrame.EXIT_ON_CLOSE);
        frame.setSize(400, 300);
        frame.setVisible(true);
    }
}
```

Well, folks, that's it! With these two classes (fewer than 300 lines of code), we've created the beginnings of a potentially powerful Style-based text editor. Figure 22-5 shows several different Styles similar to the ones used in this book.

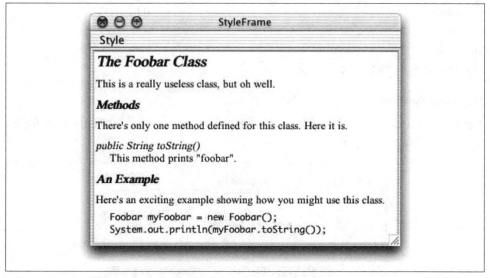

Figure 22-5. StyleFrame example

With a little extra effort, we could add code to StyleFrame to support character styles (which could be applied to individual words within a paragraph) or to StyleBox to support derived styles (use the resolveParent to allow the user to say things like "this style is just like that style except for the foreground color").

The TabStop Class

We came across TabSet and TabStop back in our discussion of the SwingConstants class, but now let's take a closer look. TabStop, as you might guess, is used to describe a tab position. This information is used by the text View classes to correctly handle the display of tabs encountered in the Document model.

Properties

The TabStop class defines the properties listed in Table 22-15. The alignment property specifies how the text following a tab should be positioned relative to the tab. The legal values for this property are shown in Table 22-16. The leader property describes what should be displayed leading up to the tab. Legal values for this property are shown in Table 22-17, but this property is ignored by the rest of Swing,* so setting its value has no effect. The position property specifies the location of the tab (in pixels from the margin).

Table 22-15. TabStop properties

Property	Data type	get	is	set	Default value
alignment	int		•		ALIGN_LEFT
leader[a]	int		•		LEAD_NONE
position	float		•		From constructor

[a] Swing ignores the value of this property.

Alignment constants

Table 22-16 lists the valid values for the alignment property. (See Figure 22-6 for an example of how they look.)

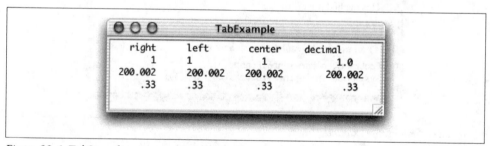

Figure 22-6. TabStop alignment

Table 22-16. TabStop alignment constants

Constant	Data type	Description
ALIGN_BAR	int	Text after the tab starts at the tab position (the same behavior as ALIGN_LEFT).
ALIGN_CENTER	int	Text after the tab is centered over the tab's position.

---

* Actually, there is one obscure corner of Swing that does respect the leader property: the code that knows how to write an RTF file to disk. Except for that, it is completely ignored (at least as of SDK 1.4.1).

Table 22-16. TabStop alignment constants (continued)

Constant	Data type	Description
ALIGN_DECIMAL	int	Text after the tab is aligned so that the first decimal point is located at the tab position. (If there is no decimal point, it behaves like ALIGN_RIGHT.)
ALIGN_LEFT	int	Text after the tab starts at the tab's position.
ALIGN_RIGHT	int	Text after the tab ends at the tab's position.

Leader constants

Table 22-17 lists values for the leader property and describes what they would do if this feature were implemented.

Table 22-17. TabStop leader constants

Constant	Description
LEAD_DOTS	Precede tab with a series of dots.
LEAD_EQUALS	Precede tab with a series of equal signs.
LEAD_HYPHENS	Precede tab with a series of hyphens.
LEAD_NONE	Precede tab with blank space.
LEAD_THICKLINE	Precede tab with a thick line.
LEAD_UNDERLINE	Precede tab with a thin line.

Constructors

public TabStop(float pos)
> Create a TabStop with the specified position, an alignment of ALIGN_LEFT, and a leader of LEAD_NONE.

public TabStop(float pos, int align, int leader)
> Create a TabStop with the specified position, alignment, and leader. (Again, the leader value is ignored by Swing.)

The TabSet Class

It is often useful to define a series of TabStops that should be applied to a given block of text. TabSet allows you to do this and defines a few convenient methods for looking up the TabStops contained in the set. TabSets are immutable—once the TabStops are defined (in the constructor), they cannot be added or removed.

This class bundles a collection of TabStops so that they can be applied to a block of text using an AttributeSet. Note that even if you only want to set one TabStop, you still have to wrap it in a TabSet to use it.

Properties

The TabSet class defines the properties shown in Table 22-18. The indexed tab property is used to access a given TabStop while the tabCount property holds the number of TabStops defined in the set.

Table 22-18. TabSet properties

Property	Data type	get	is	set	Default value
tab[i]	TabStop	•			From constructor
tabCount	int	•			From constructor

[i]indexed

Constructor

public TabSet(TabStop tabs[])
  Create a set containing the supplied array of TabStops.

Methods

public TabStop getTabAfter(float location)
  Return the first TabStop past the given location or null if there are none.

public int getTabIndex(TabStop tab)
  Return the index of the given TabStop or -1 if it isn't found.

public int getTabIndexAfter(float location)
  Return the index of the first TabStop past the given location or -1 if there are none.

Example

Here's a quick example of using a TabSet in a JTextPane (Figure 22-6). It's as simple as it looks. The only thing to watch out for is to call setParagraphAttributes( ), not setCharacterAttributes( ), since tabs don't apply at the character level.

```
// TabExample.java
//
import javax.swing.*;
import javax.swing.text.*;

// Demonstrate a TabSet in a JTextPane.
public class TabExample {

  public static void main(String[] args) {

    JTextPane pane = new JTextPane( );
    TabStop[] tabs = new TabStop[4];
```

```
    tabs[0] = new TabStop( 60, TabStop.ALIGN_RIGHT,   TabStop.LEAD_NONE);
    tabs[1] = new TabStop(100, TabStop.ALIGN_LEFT,    TabStop.LEAD_NONE);
    tabs[2] = new TabStop(200, TabStop.ALIGN_CENTER,  TabStop.LEAD_NONE);
    tabs[3] = new TabStop(300, TabStop.ALIGN_DECIMAL, TabStop.LEAD_NONE);
    TabSet tabset = new TabSet(tabs);

    StyleContext sc = StyleContext.getDefaultStyleContext( );
    AttributeSet aset =
      sc.addAttribute(SimpleAttributeSet.EMPTY, StyleConstants.TabSet, tabset);
    pane.setParagraphAttributes(aset, false);
    pane.setText("\tright\tleft\tcenter\tdecimal\n"
                +"\t1\t1\t1\t1.0\n"
                +"\t200.002\t200.002\t200.002\t200.002\n"
                +"\t.33\t.33\t.33\t.33\n");

    JFrame frame = new JFrame("TabExample");
    frame.setContentPane(new JScrollPane(pane));
    frame.setDefaultCloseOperation(JFrame.EXIT_ON_CLOSE);
    frame.setSize(360, 120);
    frame.setVisible(true);
  }
}
```

The Document Model

The Document is the M part of the MVC (Model-View-Controller) architecture for all
of Swing's text components. It is responsible for the text content of the component
as well as relevant style information for text components that support styled text.
The Document model must be simple enough to be used by JTextField, but powerful
and flexible enough to be used by JTextPane and JEditorPane. Swing accomplishes
this by providing the classes and interfaces shown in Figure 22-7.

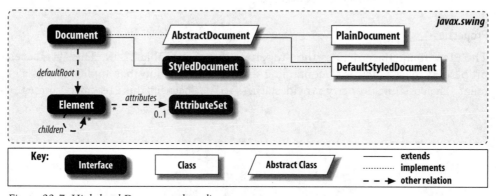

Figure 22-7. High-level Document class diagram

Basically, a Document partitions its content into small pieces called Elements. Each Element is small enough that its style information can be represented by a single AttributeSet. The Elements are organized into a tree structure* with a single root.

Swing provides the Document interface, which doesn't support styled text, and the StyledDocument interface, which does. But note that there is no StyledElement interface. Swing provides a single Element interface that does support style. The simpler document types (such as PlainDocument, which JTextField and JTextArea use by default) use Elements but don't assign any style information to them.

The Element Interface

The Element interface is used to describe a portion of a document. But note that an Element does not actually *contain* a portion of the document; it just defines a way of structuring a portion. It maintains a start offset and end offset into the actual text content, which is stored elsewhere by the Document.

Each Element may have style information, stored in an AttributeSet, that applies to the entire Element. Figure 22-8 gives an example of how a Document that supports styled text must change a single Element representing a phrase in italics into a subtree of Elements when a word in the middle is changed from italic to bold.

The branch Element may have an AttributeSet of its own, though how this is interpreted is up to the implementing class. The point is probably moot because the classes in Swing that implement Element also implement MutableAttributeSet, with the resolveParent (unless explicitly set otherwise) defaulting to the parent Element. Even if the resolveParent is explicitly set, the Element's getAttribute( ) method is overridden to consult its parent in the Element tree if it doesn't find a value through its resolveParent.

Properties

The Element interface defines the properties shown in Table 22-19. The attributes property is the AttributeSet containing the style information that applies to this element. The document property provides access to the Document this Element describes.

---

* The term Element applies to the interior nodes of the tree as well as to the leaf nodes. So it is more accurate to say that the Document partitions its content into small pieces called LeafElements. The interior nodes are called BranchElements, and each may have an arbitrary number of child Elements.

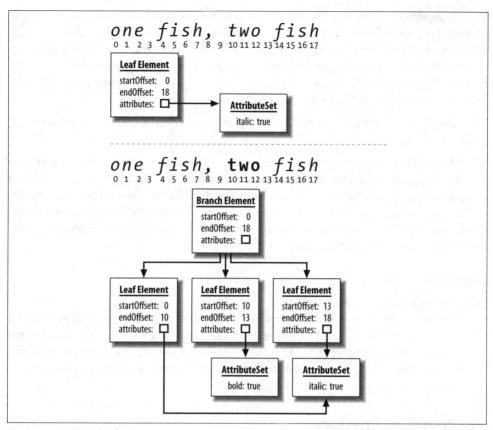

Figure 22-8. Sample Element structure

Table 22-19. Element properties

Property	Data type	get	.is	set	Default value
attributes	AttributeSet	•			
document	Document	•			
element[i]	Element	•			
elementCount	int	•			
endOffset	int	•			
leaf	boolean		•		
name	String	•			
parentElement	Element	•			
startOffset	int	•			

[i]indexed

The `elementCount` property specifies the number of children (possibly zero) the `Element` has, and `element` is an indexed property for accessing those children. The children are always kept in order, so you are assured that `getElement(0)` affects offsets in the document that appear before those affected by `getElement(1)`. If this `Element` has no children, the `leaf` property is `true`. The `parentElement` property is the `Element` that contains this `Element`, or `null` if this `Element` is a root.

The `name` property is a brief name for the `Element` and is often one of the values listed in Table 22-23.

The `startOffset` and `endOffset` properties are offsets into the document text that specify the portion of the document the `Element` covers. Expect these values to change as text is inserted in or deleted from the document. These offsets are relative to the beginning of the document, not relative to the `parentElement`'s `startOffset`. (Note that `endOffset` actually points to the position after the last character of the `Element`, as depicted in Figure 22-8.)

Element lookup method

public int getElementIndex(int offset)
> Return the index of the child element closest to the given offset (relative to the beginning of the `Document`). The return value can be used as the index for the `element` property to retrieve the child `Element` itself. If the element that you invoke this method on is a leaf element (and therefore has no children), it returns `-1`.

The Document Interface

The `Document` interface is the foundation of the document model used by all Swing text components. It defines methods for manipulating the text content, methods for registering event listeners, and methods for accessing the `Element` tree.

Actually, `Document` supports the existence of multiple `Element` trees, though typically there is only one. The idea is to support multiple ways of structuring the same document content. For example, a play could have one `Element` tree organized by act/scene/line and another organized by page/paragraph/sentence. Both trees cover the entire text of the play, just in different ways. (It would be a mistake to have one tree cover Act I and another tree cover Act II. If that's what you want, use two separate `Documents`.)

Properties

Table 22-20 shows the properties defined by the `Document` interface. They are fairly straightforward. The `defaultRootElement` property is the root of this `Document`'s `Element` tree, or if this `Document` has more than one tree, the root of the "default" tree. The `rootElements` property is an array of all the tree roots, including `defaultRootElement`.

Table 22-20. Document properties

Property	Data Type	get	is	set	Default value
defaultRootElement	Element	•			
endPosition	Position	•			
length	int	•			
rootElements	Element[]	•			
startPosition	Position	•			

The length property is the total number of "characters" in the Document. This contains all the actual characters in the document, including tabs and newlines* embedded Components and Icons (which count as one "character" each).

The startPosition and endPosition properties are offsets to the beginning and end (actually, one position past the last character) of the current document text. The type of these properties is Position, which keeps track of a particular location in a Document as text is inserted or deleted over time. We cover Position later in this chapter.

Events

Implementations of the Document interface fire DocumentEvents to indicate changes to the Document's contents. Document types that support undo also fire UndoableEditEvents. UndoableEditEvent and UndoableEditListener are covered in Chapter 18. DocumentEvent and DocumentListener are discussed later in this chapter.

Document defines the following standard methods for managing event listeners:

```
public void addDocumentListener(DocumentListener listener)
public void removeDocumentListener(DocumentListener listener)
public void addUndoableEditListener(UndoableEditListener listener)
public void removeUndoableEditListener(UndoableEditListener listener)
```

Constants

Document defines the two constants shown in Table 22-21, which are intended to be used as keys when calling the getProperty( ) and putProperty( ) methods.

Table 22-21. Document constants

Constant	Type	Description
StreamDescriptionProperty	String	The key used to store a description of the stream the Document was created from, if it was initialized from a stream and anything is known about the stream
TitleProperty	String	The key used to store the Document's name, if it has one

---

* Recall that newlines are always stored in memory as \n, regardless of how the current platform writes them in a file, so they always count as one character.

Text manipulation methods

These methods manipulate the contents of the Document. They all throw a BadLocationException if you attempt to reference a document offset that does not exist (for example, if you try to insert text at offset 200 of a 100-character Document). BadLocationException (defined later in this chapter) is used throughout the text package to signal this condition.

public String getText(int offset, int length) throws BadLocationException
> Retrieve length characters of text starting at the specified offset into the Document.

public void getText(int offset, int length, Segment txt) throws BadLocationException
> Equivalent to getText(offset, length), except for efficiency, the text is not returned as a String. Instead, the requested text is placed into the supplied Segment object. (We discuss the Segment class later in this chapter.)

public void insertString(int offset, String str, AttributeSet a)
> *throws BadLocationException*
> Insert the specified string (with the specified style attributes) at the specified offset into the Document and update its Element tree(s) to reflect the change. The AttributeSet may be null.

public void remove(int offset, int len) throws BadLocationException
> Delete length characters of text starting at the specified offset into the Document and update its Element tree(s) to reflect the change. Some versions of Swing spuriously call this method with a length of zero, so implementations should be prepared to handle this case.

Other methods

public Position createPosition(int offset) throws BadLocationException
> Return a Position object used to track the content of the Document at the specified offset as text is inserted or deleted over time.

public Object getProperty(Object key)
public void putProperty(Object key, Object value)
> Retrieve and set (respectively) arbitrary properties associated with the document. These properties can be used to store such things as the document's title, author, etc.

public void render(Runnable r)
> Execute the given Runnable, guaranteeing that the content of the model is not changed while the Runnable is running. The Runnable itself must not alter the model. This method allows the Document to be painted without concerns about its contents changing during the painting process. It is called by the TextUI's paint( ) method.

The AbstractDocument Class

Much of the implementation of the Document interface is provided by the AbstractDocument class. One significant feature provided by this default implementation is a basic locking mechanism. Unlike most methods in Swing, certain methods in the classes that make up the document model are thread-safe. AbstractDocument is specifically designed so that it may be used by multiple threads. It also defines several important inner classes/interfaces:

Content

>An inner interface that defines the API for storing and accessing the text content of the Document. Implementations of this interface may or may not support undoable edits.

AttributeContext

>An inner interface that defines an API for AttributeSet caching. See "Attribute-Context methods" earlier in this chapter.

LeafElement

>An inner class that provides a concrete implementation of the Element interface. This class is tailored for Elements that directly represent content and have no children.

BranchElement

>An inner class that provides a concrete implementation of the Element interface. This class is tailored for interior Elements with one or more child Elements.

AbstractElement

>An abstract inner class that is the superclass of both LeafElement and BranchElement. It implements the MutableAttributeSet interface in addition to Element.* The resolveParent of the AttributeSet defaults to the parent Element in the Element tree unless explicitly set otherwise. Even if set otherwise, the AttributeSet getValue( ) method consults the parent Element in the Element tree if it doesn't find a value through the resolveParent.

>This means that the attributes of the Element apply to its children in the Element tree, but attributes of the child Elements override parent values.

DefaultDocumentEvent *and* ElementEdit

>These inner classes descend from AbstractUndoableEdit and are used for event notification.

Properties

AbstractDocument defines the properties shown in Table 22-22. The important ones are defined by the Document interface. The documentProperties property (a

---

* AbstractDocument.AbstractElement also implements the TreeNode interface. See Chapter 17.

java.util.Dictionary) allows direct access to the storage mechanism used in support of the getProperty( ) and putProperty( ) methods defined by Document. documentListeners and undoableEditListeners provide access to any registered listeners on the Document (as does the getListeners( ) method).

Table 22-22. AbstractDocument properties

Property	Data type	get	is	set	Default value
asynchronousLoadPriority	int	•		•	-1
bidiRootElement	Element	•			
defaultRootElement[o]	Element	•			Abstract
documentFilter[1.4]	DocumentFilter	•		•	null
documentListeners[1.4]	DocumentListener[]	•			null
documentProperties	Dictionary	•		•	null
endPosition[o]	Position	•			
length[o]	int	•			0
rootElements[o]	Element[]	•			{ defaultRootElement, bidiRootElement }
startPosition[o]	Position	•			
undoableEditListeners[1.4]	UndoableEditListener[]	•			null

[1.4]since 1.4, [o]overridden

The documentFilter property (if not null) is an object that oversees and can influence any insertions, replacements, or deletions within the documentFilter's text content. We cover the DocumentFilter class later in this chapter.

In addition to the expected defaultRootElement, AbstractDocument defines a bidiRootElement property, which is useful only if you're interested in the bidirectional level (as defined by the Unicode bidi algorithm) in mixed left-to-right and right-to-left text.

The asynchronousLoadPriority property is not used outside of HTMLEditorKit. A value less than zero indicates that the Document should not be loaded asynchronously.

Events

AbstractDocument fires DocumentEvents and UndoableEditEvents when changes are made to the document. It implements the following standard methods for managing event listeners:

```
public void addDocumentListener(DocumentListener listener)
public void removeDocumentListener(DocumentListener listener)
```

```
public DocumentListener[] getDocumentListeners( ) (since 1.4)
public void addUndoableEditListener(UndoableEditListener listener)
public void removeUndoableEditListener(UndoableEditListener listener)
public UndoableEditListener[] getUndoableEditListeners( ) (since 1.4)
public EventListener[] getListeners(Class listenerType) (since 1.3)
protected void fireChangedUpdate(DocumentEvent e)
protected void fireInsertUpdate(DocumentEvent e)
protected void fireRemoveUpdate(DocumentEvent e)
protected void fireUndoableEditUpdate(UndoableEditEvent e)
```

Constants

`AbstractDocument` defines an attribute key constant and four attribute value constants for that key. These public constants are shown in Table 22-23.

Table 22-23. AbstractDocument constants

Constant	Data type	Description
BidiElementName	String	name value typically used by bidi `Elements`
ContentElementName	String	name value typically used by `LeafElements`
ElementNameAttribute	String	Attribute key used to store element names
ParagraphElementName	String	name value often used by `BranchElements`
SectionElementName	String	Possible name value for "higher" `BranchElements`

Also see Table 22-11 for two additional values for the `ElementNameAttribute` key.

Constructors

Since `AbstractDocument` is an abstract class, its constructors are called only by subclasses. The constructors require arguments that are implementations of inner interfaces defined by `AbstractDocument`. Fortunately, Swing provides implementations for us.

protected AbstractDocument(AbstractDocument.Content data, AbstractDocument. AttributeContext context)

The data argument is responsible for actually holding the text content of the Document and should be an object of type GapContent.[*] Because the caret is allowed to be placed immediately after the last character of the Document, AbstractDocument expects a single newline character (which it calls the "implied break") to be already present in this object when it is passed to its constructor. (The GapContent and StringContent insert this character automatically in their

---

[*] Swing provides another implementation of the `AbstractDocument.Content` interface called `StringContent`, but it is inefficient compared to GapContent. The GapContent and StringContent classes are covered later in this chapter.

constructors.) The context argument caches AttributeSets (for efficiency) and should be an object of type StyleContext.

protected AbstractDocument(AbstractDocument.Content data)
> Equivalent to calling the two-argument version of the constructor, passing StyleContext.getDefaultStyleContext( ) as the second argument.

Locking methods

AbstractDocument implements a basic locking mechanism that ensures that, at any given time, there is either a single writer of the document or zero or more readers. That is, if no one is writing to the document, anyone is allowed to read it or write to it. Once someone begins writing, no one is able to read until the writer has finished.

Certain methods that technically "read" the document (such as getText( )) do not actually obtain a read lock to do so. The only method that obtains a read lock is the render( ) method, meaning that you are not guaranteed document stability when other access methods are implemented.

This locking scheme is supported by the following methods. If you decide to use the existing document types, you don't have to understand all the details; the locks are exploited automatically. But if you decide to implement your own document type, it is important to understand how this works. Any code that modifies the text content, the Element tree, or the Document properties should be framed like this:

```
try {
  writeLock( );
  // Code that messes with the Document goes here.
} finally { writeUnlock( ); }
```

protected final void writeLock()
> Block until able to obtain the write lock. If the write lock is held by another thread, or if there are any readers, this method waits until it is notified that the state of the locks has changed before making an attempt to obtain the lock. Once the lock has been obtained, this method returns, and no other read or write locks can be obtained until the lock is released.

protected final void writeUnlock()
> Release the write lock, allowing waiting readers or writers to obtain locks.

protected final Thread getCurrentWriter()
> Return the thread currently holding the write lock or null if there is none.

public final void readLock()
> Block until able to obtain a read lock. If another thread holds the write lock, this method waits until it is notified that the lock has been released before trying to obtain the lock again. Multiple threads may hold read locks simultaneously.

public final void readUnlock()

> Called to indicate that the current thread is no longer reading the document. If this was the only reader, writing may begin (threads waiting for the lock are notified).

public void render(Runnable r)

> Called to render the Document visually. It obtains a read lock, ensuring that no changes are made to the Document during the rendering process. It then calls the input Runnable's run()* method. This method *must not* attempt to modify the Document since deadlock occurs if it tries to obtain a write lock. When the run() method completes (either naturally or by throwing an exception), the read lock is released. Note that there is nothing in this method directly related to rendering the Document. It could technically be used to execute any arbitrary code while holding a read lock.

Text manipulation methods

These methods read and write the underlying Document content. The methods that modify the content must obtain a write lock before proceeding.

public String getText(int offset, int length) throws BadLocationException

> Retrieve length characters of text starting at the specified offset into the Document. (This method does not obtain a read lock while accessing the Document's content.)

public void getText(int offset, int length, Segment txt) throws BadLocationException

> Equivalent to getText(offset, length), except for efficiency, the text is not returned as a String. Instead, the requested text is placed into the supplied Segment object. (Segment is discussed in depth later in this chapter.)

public void insertString(int offset, String str, AttributeSet attrs)
  throws BadLocationException

> Insert the specified string (with the specified style attributes) at the specified offset into the Document. This method blocks until it can obtain the Document's write lock. After performing the insertion, it fires a DocumentEvent and (if this is an undoable edit) an UndoableEditEvent().

public void remove(int offset, int len) throws BadLocationException

> Delete length characters of text starting at the specified offset into the Document. Like insertString(), this method blocks until it can obtain a write lock. After the removal, it fires a DocumentEvent and (if this is an undoable edit) an UndoableEditEvent().

public void replace(int offset, int length, int offset, String text, AttributeSet attrs)
  throws BadLocationException

> Equivalent to calling remove(offset, length) followed by insertString(offset, text, attrs). This is for the benefit of classes (particularly DocumentFilter and

---

* It calls this method directly from the current Thread. No new Thread is created.

JFormattedTextField) that prefer to see a replacement as a single edit instead of as a separate deletion and insertion. Subclasses may or may not actually implement this as a single atomic edit. (This method was introduced in SDK 1.4.)

Other public methods

public Position createPosition(int offs) throws BadLocationException
Return a Position object used to track the content of the Document at the specified offset even as text is inserted or deleted over time.

public abstract Element getParagraphElement(int pos)
Return the Element representing the paragraph that contains the specified Document offset. It is up to the subclass to decide exactly what "paragraph" means.

public Object getProperty(Object key)
public void putProperty(Object key, Object value)
Retrieve and set (respectively) properties associated with the document. The properties are stored in the documentProperties Dictionary.

The PlainDocument Class

PlainDocument is a concrete subclass of AbstractDocument used for simple documents that do not need to manage complex formatting styles. The JTextField and JTextArea classes use PlainDocument as their default model. It's worth noting that PlainDocument provides more power than these components typically need. As a subclass of AbstractDocument, it supports AttributeSets, allowing the document to contain different fonts, colors, font styles, etc. These attributes are ignored when rendering the simple text components that use this document type.

The Elements that make up a PlainDocument correspond to distinct lines of text that end with a newline (\n). Each line of text maps to a single LeafElement. All of these LeafElements are contained by a single BranchElement (the Document's root Element). PlainDocument always keeps its Element tree structured as two levels like this, but subclasses are free to implement other schemes.

Properties

PlainDocument does not define any properties beyond those of AbstractDocument (see Table 22-22), though of course it provides implementations for abstract methods, such as getDefaultRootElement( ). PlainDocument does support setting its tab stop size, but clients must do this using putProperty(TabSizeAttribute, new Integer(size)) rather than with a set method. The default tab stop size is 8.

Constants

PlainDocument defines the constants shown in Table 22-24.

Table 22-24. PlainDocument constants

Constant	Data type	Description
lineLimitAttribute	String	Attribute key used to store the maximum length of a line, if any
tabSizeAttribute	String	Attribute key used to store the size of tab stops

The attribute values paired with these keys should be of type Integer. Swing never uses lineLimitAttribute, but PlainView does respect tabSizeAttribute when it draws text with tabs.

Constructors

public PlainDocument( )
> Call the constructor below, passing in a new instance of GapContent.

public PlainDocument(AbstractDocument.Content content)
> Create a new document using the specified Content. It adds a document property reflecting a default tab size of 8 and creates a default root Element. This constructor was protected prior to SDK 1.4.

Public methods

The only new methods defined in this class are the following:

public Element getParagraphElement(int pos)
> Because PlainDocument has an Element for each line of text, this method returns the Element for the line containing the specified offset into the Document.

public void insertString(int offset, String str, AttributeSet a)
throws BadLocationException
> Because JTextField and its subclasses have only a single line of text, PlainDocument overrides this method to change newlines into spaces when it determines that it is appropriate to do so. Otherwise, the behavior is the same as it is in the superclass.

Restriction example

Figure 19-1 shows a JFormattedTextField that restricts the length of its content. It is possible to achieve the same effect by using a custom Document model. Before the advent of JFormattedTextField and DocumentFilter in SDK 1.4, this was the only good way to restrict a field's content. In any case, it demonstrates how easy it can be to subclass PlainDocument.

Here's the code for our custom Document model that restricts the length of its content. One complication is that the replace( ) method was added to AbstractDocument in SDK 1.4. We need to override replace( ), or else the user could exceed our length limit by selecting all and pasting in a bunch of text. But since our implementation calls super.replace( ), it won't even compile on versions prior to 1.4. There are ways around this (e.g., reflection), but it's not worth it for this simple example. With Version 1.4 and later, it's easier to use a JFormattedTextField anyway.

```
// MaxLengthDocument.java
//
import javax.swing.*;
import javax.swing.text.*;

// An extension of PlainDocument that restricts the length of its content
public class MaxLengthDocument extends PlainDocument {

  private int max;

  // Create a Document with a specified max length.
  public MaxLengthDocument(int maxLength) {
    max = maxLength;
  }

  // Don't allow an insertion to exceed the max length.
  public void insertString(int offset, String str, AttributeSet a)
            throws BadLocationException {
    if (getLength() + str.length() > max)
        java.awt.Toolkit.getDefaultToolkit().beep();
    else super.insertString(offset, str, a);
  }

  // We'd need to override replace() as well if running under SDK 1.4.

  // A sample main() method that demonstrates using MaxLengthDocument with a
  // JTextField. Note that new JFormattedTextField(new MaskFormatter("*****")) would
  // be easier.
  public static void main(String[] args) {

    Document doc = new MaxLengthDocument(5); // Set maximum length to 5.
    JTextField field = new JTextField(doc, "", 8);

    JPanel flowPanel = new JPanel();
    flowPanel.add(field);
    JFrame frame = new JFrame("MaxLengthDocument demo");
    frame.setContentPane(flowPanel);
    frame.setDefaultCloseOperation(JFrame.EXIT_ON_CLOSE);
    frame.setSize(160, 80);
    frame.setVisible(true);
  }
}
```

The StyledDocument Interface

StyledDocument is an extension of the Document interface that can associate different styles with different parts of its text content. StyledDocument has methods that can assign new style attributes to blocks of text. It also supports named Styles.

This interface defines the notions of "character attributes," "paragraph attributes," and "logical styles." This isn't so much a distinction of the attribute itself as it is a description of where it applies. For example, a green foreground color could be set as a character attribute, a paragraph attribute, or an attribute of a logical style. (Some attributes, such as indentation, affect only the paragraph level.) Character attributes apply to LeafElements; paragraph attributes apply to BranchElements. Logical styles also apply to BranchElements but can be overridden by local attributes. These local overrides can be either paragraph or character attributes.

The implementing class decides exactly how it structures its Element tree, and therefore what "paragraph" means.

Properties

StyledDocument does not define any properties beyond those it inherits from Document (see Table 22-20). Note that although logicalStyle, characterElement, and paragraphElement appear (by mechanical interpretation of the JavaBeans specification) to be indexed properties of StyledDocument, the "index" associated with them is a character offset into the document, not a simple array index. We omit these "properties" here and discuss the methods and those related to them in the descriptions that follow.

Style application methods

The superinterface's insertString( ) method takes an AttributeSet, but if you want to change the style attributes of text already in the Document, you need to use the methods defined here:

public void setCharacterAttributes(int offset, int length, AttributeSet s, boolean replace)
> This method applies the given attributes to the specified portion of the Document. If you want the new set of attributes to completely replace the existing set (instead of augmenting it), use true for the replace argument.

public void setParagraphAttributes(int offset, int length, AttributeSet s,
boolean replace)
> This method applies the given attributes to the paragraphs contained (or partially contained) by the specified range. If you want the new set of attributes to completely replace the existing set (instead of augmenting it), use true for the replace argument.

public void setLogicalStyle(int offset, Style s)
> This method applies the supplied Style to the paragraph that contains the specified document offset. The new Style replaces any previous logical Style.

Query methods

These methods are used to retrieve style information at a particular document offset:

public Element getCharacterElement(int offset)
> Return the `LeafElement` that contains the specified document offset. If you're interested only in the character attributes, call `getAttributes( )` on the element that is returned.

public Element getParagraphElement(int offset)
> Return the `BranchElement` representing the paragraph that contains the specified document offset. If you're interested only in the paragraph attributes, call `getAttributes( )` on the element that is returned.

public Style getLogicalStyle(int offset)
> Return the logical `Style` in effect for the paragraph that contains the given document offset, if there is one.

StyleContext delegation methods

The `StyledDocument` interface defines several methods that exactly match methods provided by the `StyleContext` class. Though implementing classes could theoretically do something different, in practice they just delegate to an instance of `StyleContext`. (See "The StyleContext Class" earlier in this chapter for a description of these methods.)

```
public Style getStyle(String nm)
public Style addStyle(String nm, Style parent)
public void removeStyle(String nm)
public Color getForeground(AttributeSet attr)
public Color getBackground(AttributeSet attr)
public Font getFont(AttributeSet attr)
```

The DefaultStyledDocument Class

`DefaultStyledDocument` is the implementation of `StyledDocument` that `JTextPane` uses by default. It inherits much of its functionality from `AbstractDocument` but adds methods for style handling. `DefaultStyledDocument` structures its `Element` tree as shown in Figure 22-9. This, together with Figure 22-8, gives a good idea of how `DefaultStyledDocument` works.

This default root has a child for each paragraph (delimited by the newline character, \n) in the `Document`. Each of these is a `BranchElement` with one or more `LeafElement` children. The number of `LeafElements` depends on the character attributes of the paragraph. Within a paragraph, any block of text with differing character attributes requires its own `LeafElement`. If the entire paragraph has the same set of character attributes, the corresponding `BranchElement` has only a single child.

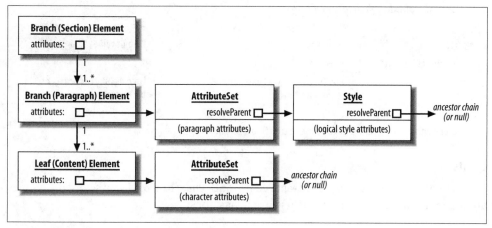

Figure 22-9. DefaultStyledDocument element tree structure

Character attributes are stored in the AttributeSets attached to the LeafElements. Paragraph attributes are stored in the AttributeSets attached to the BranchElements (excluding the root). Logical Styles are stored as the resolving parents of the AttributeSets that hold the paragraph attributes (recall that the Style interface extends AttributeSet). The AttributeSets that hold the character attributes and the logical Style attributes may have resolving parents, but the AttributeSets that hold the paragraph attributes may not (unless there is no logical Style assigned to that paragraph).

Figure 22-9 doesn't show a resolveParent link between the AttributeSet for character attributes and the AttributeSet for paragraph attributes, and in practice there doesn't need to be one. All the Element objects that DefaultStyledDocument creates are subclasses of AbstractDocument.AbstractElement—which knows how to climb the Element tree when looking for attribute values. Keep this in mind if you plan to subclass DefaultStyledDocument to create your own Document types.

DefaultStyledDocument sometimes refers to the root as the "section" Element, the middle tier as the "paragraph" Elements, and the leaf tier as the "content" Elements. DefaultStyledDocument always keeps its Element tree structured in three levels like this, but subclasses are free to implement other schemes.

Properties

DefaultStyledDocument defines the properties shown in Table 22-25. The default-RootElement is the same as the one described earlier. The styleNames property is an Enumeration with the names of all the named Styles available to this Document.

Table 22-25. DefaultStyledDocument properties

Property	Data type	get	is	set	Default value
defaultRootElement⁰	Element	•			
styleNames	Enumeration (the type of each element is String)	•			From the StyleContext set in the constructor

⁰overridden

See also properties from the AbstractDocument class (Table 22-22).

Events

DefaultStyledDocument fires DocumentEvents and UndoableEditEvents when changes are made to the document, just as its superclass does.

Constant

DefaultStyledDocument defines the constant shown in Table 22-26.

Table 22-26. DefaultStyledDocument constant

Name	Data type	Description
BUFFER_SIZE_DEFAULT	int	Default size for the GapContent object created by two of DefaultStyledDocument's constructors (value is 4096)

Constructors

public DefaultStyledDocument( )
> Instantiate a DefaultStyledDocument with a new GapContent and a new (unshared) StyleContext object. If you want to use the default StyleContext to share styles, call a version that lets you pass StyleContext.getDefaultStyleContext( ) instead.

public DefaultStyledDocument(StyleContext context)
> Instantiate a DefaultStyledDocument with a new GapContent and the supplied StyleContext.

public DefaultStyledDocument(AbstractDocument.Content content,
  StyleContext context)
> Instantiate a DefaultStyledDocument with the supplied Content model and StyleContext. The context argument is responsible for actually holding the text content of the Document and should be an object of type GapContent.* Because the caret is allowed to be placed immediately after the last character of the Document, DefaultStyledDocument expects a newline character (which it calls the "implied

---

* Swing provides another implementation of the AbstractDocument.Content interface called StringContent, but it is inefficient compared to GapContent. The GapContent and StringContent classes are covered later in this chapter.

break") to be already present in this object when it is passed to its constructor. (The GapContent and StringContent insert this character automatically in their constructors.)

Content style methods

The insertString( ), replace( ), remove( ), and getText( ) methods inherited from AbstractDocument query and alter the document's text content. The following methods query and alter the style attributes assigned to the text content:

public Element getCharacterElement(int offset)
> Return the LeafElement that contains the specified document offset. If you're interested only in the character attributes, call getAttributes( ) on the result.

public void setCharacterAttributes(int offset, int length, AttributeSet s, boolean replace)
> This method obtains a write lock, applies the supplied attributes to the specified portion of the Document, and fires events to notify listeners of the change. If you want the new set of attributes to completely replace the existing set (instead of augmenting it), use true for the replace argument. Setting character attributes often causes new Elements to be added to the Element tree. (See Figure 22-8 for an illustration of this.)

public Element getParagraphElement(int offset)
> Return the BranchElement representing the paragraph that contains the specified document offset (the one on the middle level of the Element tree, not the root). Call getAttributes( ) on the result if you're interested only in the paragraph attributes.

public void setParagraphAttributes(int offset, int length, AttributeSet s,
* boolean replace)*
> This method obtains a write lock, applies the given attributes to the paragraphs contained (or partially contained) by the specified range, and fires events to notify listeners of the change. If you want the new set of attributes to completely replace the existing set (instead of augmenting it), use true for the replace argument. Unlike setCharacterAttributes( ), this method does not change the structure of the Element tree.

public Style getLogicalStyle(int offset)
> Return the logical Style assigned to the paragraph that contains the specified document offset. This is done by finding the AttributeSet for this offset's paragraph attributes and returning its resolving parent. (If casting the resolveParent to Style fails, it returns null.)

public void setLogicalStyle(int offset, Style s)
> This method obtains a write lock, sets the style for the paragraph containing the specified offset, and fires events to notify listeners of the change. This is done by finding the AttributeSet for this offset's paragraph attributes and setting its resolving parent to the given Style. The new Style replaces any previous logical

Style (or any previous resolveParent of the paragraph attributes). Note that attributes of the logical Style may be overridden by existing paragraph attributes, so they may have no effect.

StyleContext delegation methods

The DefaultStyledDocument has several methods that delegate to the StyleContext established by its constructors. (See "The StyleContext Class" for a full description of these methods.)

public Style getStyle(String nm)
public Style addStyle(String nm, Style parent)
public void removeStyle(String nm)

These methods retrieve, create, and delete named Styles available to the Document.

public Color getForeground(AttributeSet attr)
public Color getBackground(AttributeSet attr)
public Font getFont(AttributeSet attr)

These methods are discussed in "The StyleContext Class."

StyledDocument example

Here's a quick example that manipulates a pane's StyledDocument to draw parentheses, brackets, and braces in different colors. It sets each half of a matching pair to the same color and sets mismatches to red. The interesting work happens in the run( ) method. To keep things simple, it doesn't try to ignore quoted parentheses or those in comments.

```
// ParenMatcher.java
//
import javax.swing.*;
import javax.swing.text.*;
import java.awt.event.*;
import java.awt.Color;
import java.awt.BorderLayout;

// A simple paren matcher
public class ParenMatcher extends JTextPane implements Runnable {

  public static Color[] matchColor = { Color.blue, Color.magenta, Color.green };
  public static Color badColor = Color.red;

  private AttributeSet[] matchAttrSet;
  private AttributeSet badAttrSet;

  public ParenMatcher( ) {
    // Create an array of AttributeSets from the array of Colors.
    StyleContext sc = StyleContext.getDefaultStyleContext( );
    badAttrSet = sc.addAttribute(SimpleAttributeSet.EMPTY,
                    StyleConstants.Foreground, badColor);
```

```
      matchAttrSet = new AttributeSet[matchColor.length];
      for (int j=0; j < matchColor.length; j+=1)
        matchAttrSet[j] = sc.addAttribute(SimpleAttributeSet.EMPTY,
                                   StyleConstants.Foreground, matchColor[j]);
    }

    // Match and color the parens/brackets/braces.
    public void run() {
      StyledDocument doc = getStyledDocument();
      String text = "";
      int len = doc.getLength();
      try {
        text = doc.getText(0, len);
      } catch (BadLocationException ble) { }
      java.util.Stack stack = new java.util.Stack();
      for (int j=0; j < text.length(); j+=1) {
        char ch = text.charAt(j);
        if (ch == '(' || ch == '[' || ch == '{') {
          int depth = stack.size();
          stack.push(""+ch+j); // Push a String containing the char and the offset.
          AttributeSet aset = matchAttrSet[depth % matchAttrSet.length];
          doc.setCharacterAttributes(j, 1, aset, false);
        }
        if (ch == ')' || ch == ']' || ch == '}') {
          String peek = stack.empty() ? "." : (String)stack.peek();
          if (matches(peek.charAt(0), ch)) { // Does it match?
            stack.pop();
            int depth = stack.size();
            AttributeSet aset = matchAttrSet[depth % matchAttrSet.length];
            doc.setCharacterAttributes(j, 1, aset, false);
          }
          else { // Mismatch
            doc.setCharacterAttributes(j, 1, badAttrSet, false);
          }
        }
      }

      while (! stack.empty()) { // Anything left in the stack is a mismatch.
        String pop = (String)stack.pop();
        int offset = Integer.parseInt(pop.substring(1));
        doc.setCharacterAttributes(offset, 1, badAttrSet, false);
      }
    }

    // Unset the foreground color (if any) whenever the user enters text
    // (if not for this, text entered after a paren would catch the paren's color).
    public void replaceSelection(String content) {
      getInputAttributes().removeAttribute(StyleConstants.Foreground);
      super.replaceSelection(content);
    }

    // Return true if 'left' and 'right' are matching parens/brackets/braces.
    public static boolean matches(char left, char right) {
      if (left == '(') return (right == ')');
```

```
      if (left == '[') return (right == ']');
      if (left == '{') return (right == '}');
      return false;
    }

    public static void main(String[] args) {
      JFrame frame = new JFrame("ParenMatcher");

      final ParenMatcher matcher = new ParenMatcher();
      matcher.setText("int fact(int n) {\n"
                    +"  if (n <= 1) return 1;\n"
                    +"  return(n * fact(n-1));\n"
                    +"}\n");
      frame.getContentPane().add(new JScrollPane(matcher), BorderLayout.CENTER);

      JButton matchButton = new JButton("match parens");
      matchButton.addActionListener(new ActionListener() {
        public void actionPerformed(ActionEvent ae) { matcher.run(); }
      });
      frame.getContentPane().add(matchButton, BorderLayout.SOUTH);

      frame.setDefaultCloseOperation(JFrame.EXIT_ON_CLOSE);
      frame.setSize(200, 150);
      frame.setVisible(true);
    }
}
```

Document Events

When changes are made to a Document, observers of the Document are notified by the
event types DocumentEvent and UndoableEditEvent, defined in the javax.swing.event
package. UndoableEditEvent and its associated listener interface are discussed in
Chapter 18. In this section, we'll look at DocumentEvent and its relatives.

The DocumentListener Interface

Document uses this interface to notify its registered listeners of changes. It calls one of
three methods depending on the category of change and passes a DocumentEvent to
specify the details.

Methods

public void changedUpdate(DocumentEvent e)

Signal that an attribute or set of attributes has changed for some of the
Document's content. The DocumentEvent specifies exactly which part of the
Document is affected.

public void insertUpdate(DocumentEvent e)

> Signal that text has been inserted into the Document. The DocumentEvent specifies which part of the Document's content is new.

public void removeUpdate(DocumentEvent e)

> Signal that text has been removed from the Document. The DocumentEvent specifies where the text was located in the Document before it was deleted.

Suppose we want the parentheses matcher we wrote in the last section to update its colors "live" instead of waiting for the user to click on a button. All we have to do is register with the pane's Document as a DocumentListener. Whenever we're notified that text has been inserted or deleted, we recolor the parentheses. It's that easy.

We do have to be careful not to call run( ) directly from insertUpdate( ) or removeUpdate( ). This results in an IllegalStateException when our code attempts to obtain the Document's write lock. The solution is to avoid coloring the parentheses until the Document is finished with its event dispatching, which is easily done with SwingUtilities.invokeLater( ).

```
// LiveParenMatcher.java
//
import javax.swing.*;
import javax.swing.text.*;
import javax.swing.event.*;

// Like ParenMatcher but continuously colors as the user edits the document
public class LiveParenMatcher extends ParenMatcher implements DocumentListener {

  public LiveParenMatcher( ) {
    super( );
    getDocument( ).addDocumentListener(this);
  }

  public void changedUpdate(DocumentEvent de) {
    // No insertion or deletion, so do nothing
  }

  public void insertUpdate(DocumentEvent de) {
    SwingUtilities.invokeLater(this); // Will call run( )
  }

  public void removeUpdate(DocumentEvent de) {
    SwingUtilities.invokeLater(this); // Will call run( )
  }

  public static void main(String[] args) {
    JFrame frame = new JFrame("LiveParenMatcher");
    frame.setContentPane(new JScrollPane(new LiveParenMatcher( )));
    frame.setDefaultCloseOperation(JFrame.EXIT_ON_CLOSE);
    frame.setSize(300, 200);
    frame.setVisible(true);
  }
}
```

If an insertion is made that doesn't contain any parentheses, brackets, or braces, it is wasteful to recolor the text because the colors don't change. A more sophisticated program would recognize this and not attempt to recolor. We'll add this feature to our LiveParenMatcher example in the next section.

The DocumentEvent Interface

A DocumentEvent is fired when a change is made to a Document. It contains information about the portion of the Document that was modified along with information about the details of the change.

Unlike most events, DocumentEvent is an interface rather than a class. This is so an undo-capable class (such as AbstractDocument) can create an event implementation that extends a class from the undo package and implements DocumentEvent. We'll see the details of how this works over the next few pages.

Properties

Table 22-27 shows the properties defined by the DocumentEvent interface. The document property is the Document object that fired this event. The offset and length properties specify where the change took place (the affected characters) relative to the beginning of the document. The type property indicates the kind of change that occurred. It is one of three constants from the Document.EventType inner class (described next): INSERT, REMOVE, CHANGE.

Table 22-27. DocumentEvent properties

Property	Data type	get	is	set	Default value
document	Document	•			
length	int	•			
offset	int	•			
type	DocumentEvent.EventType	•			

Element tree details

public DocumentEvent.ElementChange getChange(Element elem)
> Use this method to discover what changes were made to the structure of the Document's Element tree. It returns an ElementChange object (described later in this chapter) that stores the child Elements that were added and/or deleted from the parent Element you passed in as an argument. If no child Elements were added or deleted, this method returns null, even if large changes were made to some of the child Elements.

Here's how we can change our insertUpdate( ) method to query the DocumentEvent and recolor the parentheses only when appropriate:

```
public void insertUpdate(DocumentEvent de) {
   Document doc = de.getDocument( );
   int offset = de.getOffset( );
   int length = de.getLength( );
   String inserted = "";
   try {
     inserted = doc.getText(offset, length);
   } catch (BadLocationException ble) { }

   for (int j=0; j < inserted.length( ); j+=1) {
     char ch = inserted.charAt(j);
     if (ch == '(' || ch == '[' || ch == '{' ||
         ch == ')' || ch == ']' || ch == '}'  ) {
       SwingUtilities.invokeLater(this); // Will call run( )
       return; // No need to check further
     }
   }
}
```

Note that this wouldn't work for removeUpdate( ). The values returned by getOffset( ) and getLength( ) refer to the content of the Document before the deletion occurred.

The DocumentEvent.EventType Class

This inner class is simply a type-safe enumeration used to define different types of DocumentEvents. It has no public constructors, so the only instances of the class are the three constants listed in Table 22-28.

Table 22-28. DocumentEvent.EventType constants

Constant	Type	Description
CHANGE	DocumentEvent.EventType	Attributes have changed.
INSERT	DocumentEvent.EventType	Content has been inserted.
REMOVE	DocumentEvent.EventType	Content has been removed.

The DocumentEvent.ElementChange Interface

This inner interface of DocumentEvent describes a set of Element changes made to a single parent Element. The changes may include adding new children, deleting existing children, or both (a replacement). An ElementChange is generated only when entire Elements are added or removed from a parent element. For example, merely deleting content from a child does not generate an ElementChange unless you remove the entire child Element.

Properties

Table 22-29 shows the properties defined by the DocumentEvent.ElementChange interface. The childrenAdded and childrenRemoved properties indicate the set of child Elements that was added to or removed from the Element represented by the element property. The array contents are in the order the Elements appear (or used to appear) within their parent Element. The index property indicates where the children were added or removed (an index into the Element's child list, not a document offset). If childrenAdded is empty, the index indicates the location of the first element removed; otherwise, it indicates the location of the first added element.

Table 22-29. DocumentEvent.ElementChange properties

Property	Data type	get	is	set	Default value
childrenAdded	Element[]	•			
childrenRemoved	Element[]	•			
element	Element	•			
index	int	•			

DocumentEvent.ElementChange is used in a small debugging example in the next section.

The ElementIterator Class

This utility class performs a depth-first traversal of an Element tree. It is similar to Enumeration in concept, but there are differences. In particular, ElementIterator has separate methods for retrieving the first and subsequent Elements.

Constructors

public ElementIterator(Document document)
    Create an iterator that begins at the given Document's default root element.

public ElementIterator(Element root)
    Create an iterator that begins at the specified root Element.

Methods

public Element first()
    Reset the iterator to the first Element and return it.

public Element next()
    Move the iterator to the next Element and return it. If there are no more Elements, return null.

public Element current()
    Return the current Element in the iterator.

public int depth()

Return the depth of the current Element. The depth of the iterator's root is 1, the depth of the root's children is 2, and so on.

public Element previous()

Return the previous Element. It does not change the state of the iterator, so calling next(); previous(); next(); previous(); moves the iterator forward by two Elements.

public Object clone()

Return a copy of the iterator. The clone is positioned at the same point as the original iterator.

In this debugging example, we use an ElementIterator to search for non-null ElementChange objects:

```
public void removeUpdate(DocumentEvent de) {
    // Print some debugging information.
    ElementIterator iter = new ElementIterator(de.getDocument());

    for (Element elem = iter.first(); elem != null; elem = iter.next()) {
        DocumentEvent.ElementChange change = de.getChange(elem);
        if (change != null) { // null means there was no change in elem
            System.out.println("Element "+elem.getName() + " (depth " +
                iter.depth()+") changed its children: " +
                change.getChildrenRemoved().length+" children removed, " +
                change.getChildrenAdded().length+" children added.\n");
        }
    }
}
```

The Segment Class

We saw the Segment class back in the Document interface's getText() method. It is essentially a char array that allows fast access to a segment of text. The motivation is entirely speed. To this end, it breaks some fundamental rules of object-oriented programming by exposing its data as public fields. If a data source already has the requested text in a char array, it can just replace the Segment's array with its own (so you will be sharing it) and set the index fields appropriately.

Think of using Segment as you would String. Strings are immutable once the constructor is done with them, and you should treat Segments this way too, at least most of the time. When accessing a Segment, use the retrieval methods instead of accessing the array directly.

Properties

Table 22-30 shows the properties defined by Segment. The beginIndex and endIndex properties define the portion of the char array that contains meaningful data. The index property represents the current position in the array and is manipulated by the retrieval methods. The `partialReturn` property allows you to trade convenience for speed. If you set this property to `true`, you get only as much text as can be managed without copying, which may be less than you asked for. (You can always ask for the rest later.)

Table 22-30. Segment properties

Property	Data type	get	is	set	Default value
beginIndex	int	•			
endIndex	int	•			
index	int	•		•	
partialReturn[1.4]	boolean		•	•	false

[1.4]since 1.4

Constant

Segment defines the constant shown in Table 22-31.

Table 22-31. DefaultStyledDocument constant

Constant	Data type	Description
DONE	char	Char value returned when index is out of bounds (same value as `java.text.CharacterIterator.DONE`)

Fields

public char array[]
    The array of characters used to store the data. It should not be modified.

public int offset
    The offset into the array that represents the beginning of the meaningful text.

public int count
    The number of characters that comprise the meaningful text.

Constructors

public Segment()
    Create a Segment with no data.

public Segment(char array[], int offset, int count)
    Create a Segment that references an existing array. The `offset` and `count` delimit the portion of the array that contains meaningful text.

Methods

public char current( )

Return the char at the location specified by the index property.

public char next( )

Increment the index property and return the char at the new location. (If positioned at endIndex, this method returns DONE instead.)

public char previous( )

Decrement the index property and return the char at the new location. (If positioned at beginIndex, this method returns DONE instead.)

public char first( )

Set index to the value of the beginIndex property and return the char at the new location.

public char last( )

Set index to the value of the endIndex property and return the char at the new location.

public String toString( )

Return the Segment as a String of length count.

public Object clone( )

Create a shallow copy of the Segment. (That is, the char array is shared.)

We can now reimplement our insertUpdate( ) method to use a Segment when it queries the Document for the inserted text. It's pretty straightforward.

```
public void insertUpdate(DocumentEvent de) {
    Document doc = de.getDocument( );
    int offset = de.getOffset( );
    int length = de.getLength( );
    Segment seg = new Segment( );
    try {
        doc.getText(offset, length, seg); // Text placed in Segment
    } catch (BadLocationException ble) { }

    // Iterate through the Segment.
    for (char ch = seg.first( ); ch != seg.DONE; ch = seg.next( ))
        if (ch == '(' || ch == '[' || ch == '{' ||
            ch == ')' || ch == ']' || ch == '}'  ) {
            SwingUtilities.invokeLater(this); // Will call run( )
            return; // No need to check further
        }
}
```

The AbstractDocument.Content Interface

We briefly mentioned this interface earlier, but let's take a closer look. The five methods of this interface define the API that AbstractDocument uses to actually store its text content. Many methods in AbstractDocument simply delegate to its Content model. (We discuss Swing's two implementations of this interface, StringContent and GapContent, next.)

Methods

public int length( )
    Return the current length of the content.

public String getString(int where, int len) throws BadLocationException
    Return a String containing the specified range of text.

public void getChars(int where, int len, Segment txt) throws BadLocationException
    Place the specified range of text in the supplied Segment object. This is often faster than calling getString( ).

public UndoableEdit insertString(int where, String str) throws BadLocationException
    Insert the specified string at the requested offset in the content. If the Content model supports undo, an UndoableEdit object is returned; otherwise, this method returns null.

public UndoableEdit remove(int where, int len) throws BadLocationException
    Remove the specified range of characters from the document content. If the Content model supports undo, an UndoableEdit object is returned; otherwise, this method returns null.

public Position createPosition(int offset) throws BadLocationException
    Create a Position that tracks the content at the specified offset as text is inserted or deleted over time.

The StringContent Class

The StringContent class is an implementation of the AbstractDocument.Content interface that maintains its content in consecutive cells of a character array. This is very inefficient because part of the array must be copied every time a character is inserted or deleted (except at the very end). This was the default Content model for all text components in the early days of Swing, before GapContent was perfected.

StringContent does support undoable edits, so the insertString( ) and remove( ) methods always return non-null UndoableEdit objects. It expands its character array (by doubling) when it gets too small and keeps its Position objects in a Vector that it updates when necessary.

Constructors

public StringContent( )
    Create an array with a default initial size (10) containing a single newline character.

public StringContent(int initialLength)
    Create an array with the specified initial size containing a single newline character.

The GapContent Class

The GapContent class is an implementation of the AbstractDocument.Content interface and is the default Content model. Its inspiration was the venerable Emacs text editor, which employs a similar storage scheme for its buffers.

GapContent takes advantage of the fact that text is typically inserted sequentially. In other words, if the user inserts a character at position 10 in the document, chances are good that the next insertion is at position 11. With StringContent, each insertion results in an array copy to make room for the new text. In contrast, GapContent keeps a "gap" in its character array, located at the current insertion point. When text is entered, the gap gets smaller, but no characters need to be copied in the array (except the newly entered ones). When the insertion point moves one slot left or right, only a single character has to be copied to maintain the gap at the insertion point.

Like StringContent, GapContent expands its array when necessary and supports undoable edits. The insertString( ) and remove( ) methods always return non-null UndoableEdit objects. GapContent keeps its Position objects sorted so it can easily find the marks that need to be updated when the gap is shifted.

Constructors

public GapContent( )
> Create a content object with a default initial array size (10) containing a single newline character.

public GapContent(int initialLength)
> Create a content object with the specified initial array size containing a single newline character.

AbstractDocument.Content methods

The following methods implement the AbstractDocument.Content interface:

public Position createPosition(int offset) throws BadLocationException
> Create a Position at the specific document offset. This implementation manages a sorted array of positions to make it easy to find the marks that need to be updated when the gap is shifted.

public void getChars(int where, int len, Segment chars) throws BadLocationException
> Populate the given Segment with the requested text (len characters, starting at where). If the requested text falls entirely on one side of the gap, the Segment refers to the internal array. If not, the result depends on the value of the Segment's partialReturn property. If partialReturn is false (the default), a new array that contains the specified range with no gap is created for the Segment. If it is true, the Segment refers to the internal array, but only the characters below the

gap are available through the Segment. (Examine the Segment's count field to see how many characters are available.)

public String getString(int where, int len) throws BadLocationException
Return the requested portion of the content in String form.

public UndoableEdit insertString(int where, String str) throws BadLocationException
Insert the specified text at the given location. The gap and Positions are adjusted as necessary. This method returns an UndoableEdit that can be used to restore the content to its previous state.

public int length()
Return the length of the content. The gap does not count in this value.

public UndoableEdit remove(int where, int nitems) throws BadLocationException
Remove the specified range of characters from the content. The gap and Positions are updated as necessary. This method returns an UndoableEdit that can be used to restore the content to its previous state.

Undo Event Example

We learned about Swing's undo classes in Chapter 18, but let's see an undo example with text components. All we have to do is register with the Document as an UndoableEditListener, and we'll automatically receive UndoableEditEvents.

In this example, we subclass the StyleFrame program in "A Stylized Editor" to add menu items and buttons for undo/redo. We create a pair of Action objects as inner classes that are in charge of enabling/disabling the menu items and button. We also register the Actions as UndoableEditListeners so they can update themselves. We do this through calls to textPane.getDocument().addUndoableEditListener().

So when you type characters, the menu item and the button say Undo addition. When you delete characters, they say Undo deletion. And when you change the logical style of a paragraph, they say Undo style change. It just works. (See Figure 22-10.)

```
// UndoStyleFrame.java
//
import javax.swing.*;
import javax.swing.undo.*;
import javax.swing.event.*;
import java.awt.event.*;

// Add undo support to the StyleFrame example (keep just the most recent edit to keep
// things simple).
public class UndoStyleFrame extends StyleFrame {

  protected UndoAct undoAction = new UndoAct(); // An Action for undo
  protected RedoAct redoAction = new RedoAct(); // An Action for redo

  public UndoStyleFrame() {
    super();
    setTitle("UndoStyleFrame");
```

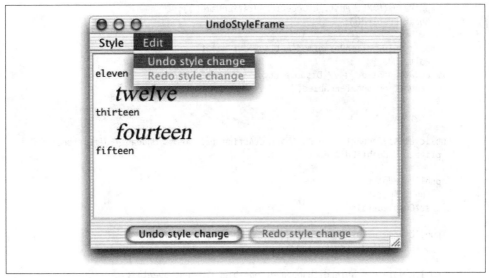

Figure 22-10. Undo in a JTextFrame

```
      // Register the Actions as undo listeners (we inherited textPane).
      textPane.getDocument( ).addUndoableEditListener(undoAction);
      textPane.getDocument( ).addUndoableEditListener(redoAction);

      // Create menu for undo/redo.
      JMenu editMenu = new JMenu("Edit");
      editMenu.add(new JMenuItem(undoAction));
      editMenu.add(new JMenuItem(redoAction));
      menuBar.add(editMenu); // we inherited menuBar from superclass

      // Create buttons for undo/redo.
      JPanel buttonPanel = new JPanel( );
      buttonPanel.add(new JButton(undoAction));
      buttonPanel.add(new JButton(redoAction));
      getContentPane( ).add(buttonPanel, java.awt.BorderLayout.SOUTH);
   }

   // Begin inner classes ------------

   public class UndoAct extends AbstractAction implements UndoableEditListener {
      private UndoableEdit edit;

      public UndoAct( ) {
         super("Undo");
         setEnabled(false);
      }
      public void updateEnabled( ) {
         setEnabled(edit.canUndo( ));
      }
      public void undoableEditHappened(UndoableEditEvent event) {
         edit = event.getEdit( );
```

```
      putValue(NAME, edit.getUndoPresentationName());
      updateEnabled();
    }
    public void actionPerformed(ActionEvent ae) {
      edit.undo();
      updateEnabled(); // Disable undo.
      redoAction.updateEnabled(); // Enable redo.
    }
  }

  public class RedoAct extends AbstractAction implements UndoableEditListener {
    private UndoableEdit edit;

    public RedoAct() {
      super("Redo");
      setEnabled(false);
    }
    public void updateEnabled() {
      setEnabled(edit.canRedo());
    }
    public void undoableEditHappened(UndoableEditEvent event) {
      edit = event.getEdit();
      putValue(NAME, edit.getRedoPresentationName());
      updateEnabled();
    }
    public void actionPerformed(ActionEvent ae) {
      edit.redo();
      updateEnabled(); // Disable redo.
      undoAction.updateEnabled(); // Enable undo.
    }
  }

  // End inner classes ------------

  public static void main(String[] args) {
    JFrame frame = new UndoStyleFrame();
    frame.setDefaultCloseOperation(JFrame.EXIT_ON_CLOSE);
    frame.setSize(400, 300);
    frame.setVisible(true);
  }
}
```

The BadLocationException Class

This exception is thrown by many of the text classes to indicate that an attempt has been made to access an invalid Document offset.

Constructor

public BadLocationException(String message, int offset)
  Create a new exception as a result of an attempt to access the specified offset.

Method

public int offsetRequested()
> Return the offending offset that caused the exception to be thrown.

The Position Interface

Position is an interface used to represent a location in a Document. Positions are intended to have more lasting value than simple Document offsets. For example, if you set a Position at the beginning of a sentence and then insert text before the sentence, the Position is still located at the beginning of the sentence, even though its offset has changed.

Property

Table 22-32 shows the property defined by the Position interface. The offset property indicates the Position's current offset from the start of the Document. The only method in this interface is the accessor for this property, getOffset().

Table 22-32. Position property

Property	Data type	get	is	set	Default value
offset	int	•			

The Position.Bias Class

This is a very simple static inner class used to define a type-safe enumeration. The values of the enumeration indicate a position's bias toward the character before or after a location. The idea is that there is slightly more detail in saying "the user clicked nearest offset 14 from the left" versus "the user clicked nearest offset 14." Bias can also be useful with bidirectional text.

Though a fair number of Swing's text methods take an argument of type Position. Bias, support for it is spotty. Most of those methods ignore the Bias argument.

Constants

As a type-safe enumeration, Position.Bias has no public constructors, so the only instances of the class are the two constants listed in Table 22-33.

Table 22-33. Position.Bias constants

Constant	Data type	Description
Backward	Position.Bias	A bias toward the previous character in the model
Forward	Position.Bias	A bias toward the next character in the model

Views

In our discussion of how Swing represents styled text, we haven't mentioned how it is actually drawn on the screen. That's where the View classes come in. They form most of the V part of the MVC architecture for text components and are responsible for rendering the text.

The way this works is a tree of View objects is created from the Document's Element tree. (Examples of this are shown in Figure 22-11.) For DefaultStyledDocuments in a JTextPane, the View tree is modeled closely on the structure of the Element tree, with almost a one-to-one mapping from Elements to Views. A PlainDocument in a JTextArea is handled more simply, with a single View object that paints the entire Element tree.

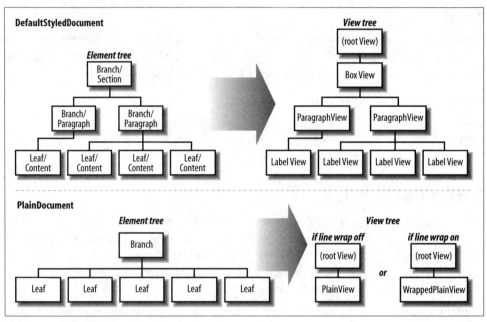

Figure 22-11. View trees created from Element trees

Notice that the View trees have a root View above what could be considered the "natural" root. This was done to ease the implementation of the other View classes, which can now all assume that they have a non-null parent in the View tree. So that each child doesn't have to register as a DocumentListener, the root View also takes care of dispatching DocumentEvents to its children. The actual type of the root View is a package-private inner class. (You are free to create a View tree with any root you like, so this does not always need to be the case. The implementations of the TextUI.getRootView( ) method that Swing provides do return a package-private View class.)

Creation of the View tree is often handled by the text component's TextUI, but if its EditorKit returns a non-null value from its getViewFactory( ) method, this task is delegated to the factory. This gives the more complex text components (such as JEditorPane, discussed in Chapter 23) a powerful tool for customizing their appearance.

The ViewFactory Interface

Implementations of the ViewFactory interface determine the kind of View object that needs to be created for each Element passed in to the factory. We'll see more of the ViewFactory interface in the next chapter.

Method

public View create(Element elem)
     Return a View for the given Element.

The View Class

This abstract class is the base class for a score of View types (see Figure 22-12) and provides basic functionality for drawing part of a Document's content. Before we cover the properties and methods of View, we should note a few potentially confusing details.

Float coordinates

The View classes follow the lead of the 2D API and use float values to specify x and y coordinates. It is usually safe to convert these to ints if you prefer.

Shape versus Rectangle

Many View methods take arguments of type java.awt.Shape. The Shape interface is implemented by many classes that represent geometric shapes, including java.awt. Rectangle. Theoretically, a View class can take advantage of nonrectangular rendering areas, but the existing View classes treat Shape objects as Rectangles. You can convert a Shape into a Rectangle (int coordinates) by calling someShape.getBounds( ), or you can convert a Shape into a Rectangle2D (float coordinates) by calling someShape. getBounds2D( ).

Span and allocation

The term *span* refers to a distance (typically a float) in a particular direction while *allocation* refers to the area (a Shape) in which a View is drawn. These terms are used frequently in the View source code and documentation, so we'll use them too.

Axis

An *axis* value should be either X_AXIS or Y_AXIS (int constants). View has several indexed properties that expect the index to be one of these two values. (The exception is the view property. getView(n) requests the *n*th child of the View.)

Bias

Many View methods have a parameter of type Position.Bias (see the previous discussion). There are only two values for an object of this type: Bias.Forward and Bias.Backward. The idea is that the addition of a Bias refines a Document offset somewhat. Without a Bias, if a user clicks to an offset of 5, then you know the click was either on the right half of the 4th character or on the left half of the 5th. The Bias parameter distinguishes between the two cases.

That said, Swing's handling of Position.Bias is spotty. Many method implementations simply ignore the Bias parameter, and many callers blindly pass in Bias.Forward. Should you decide to do the same, you would be in good company.

Properties

The View class defines the properties shown in Table 22-34.

Table 22-34. View properties

Property	Data type	get	is	set	Default value
alignment[i]	float	•			0.5
attributes	AttributeSet	•			From element
container	Container	•			From parent
document	Document	•			From element
element	Element	•			From constructor
endOffset	int	•			From element
graphics[1.3]	Graphics	•			
maximumSpan[i]	float	•			(resizeWeight<=0 ? preferredSpan : Integer.MAX_VALUE)
minimumSpan[i]	float	•			(resizeWeight<=0 ? preferredSpan : 0)
parent	View	•		•	null
preferredSpan[i]	float	•			Abstract
resizeWeight[i]	int	•			0
startOffset	int	•			From element
view[i]	View	•			null
viewCount	int	•			0

[i]indexed, [1.3]since 1.3

Table 22-34. View properties (continued)

Property	Data type	get	is	set	Default value
viewFactory	ViewFactory	•			From parent
visible	boolean		•		true

ⁱindexed, 1.3since 1.3

The properties are defined as follows:

attributes

> This property defines the AttributeSet used by the View to render an Element. By default, the Element's attributes are used. However, View objects should access the attributes through the getAttributes( ) accessor to allow View-specific attributes to be added to the Element's attributes or to allow the attributes to be converted in some way by the View subclasses.

container

> This property is the Container ultimately responsible for this View. This View uses the container's coordinate system as its own, without performing any translation for child Views. We refer to this coordinate system as *view coordinates*.

element

> This property is the Element this View is responsible for rendering. The document, startOffset, and endOffset properties are taken directly from the element property.

viewCount

> This property defines the number of children this View has, and the indexed view property gives access to specific children. Typically, only subclasses of CompositeView (plus root Views) have any children.

viewFactory

> This property is the factory that was used to create this View and can be used to create child View objects.

graphics

> This property is a java.awt.Graphics object that can be used to determine font characteristics. (The paint( ) method is passed a Graphics object for drawing, so it doesn't need to use this one.)

visible

> This property reflects whether the View should be drawn on the screen..

alignment

> This property specifies the desired alignment for the View for each axis. 0 indicates origin alignment, 1 indicates alignment to the full span away from the origin, and 0.5 (the default) indicates centered alignment.

The other four properties help determine the minimum, maximum, and preferred size of the component using the View. preferredSpan reflects the View's preferred size along a particular axis. resizeWeight is used to determine the minimum and maximum size of the View. A value of 0 (or less) indicates that the view should not be resized. The minimumSpan and maximumSpan of a View with a resizeWeight of 0 are equal to the preferredSpan. Otherwise (if resizeWeight > 0), the minimumSpan is considered to be 0 while the maximumSpan is Integer.MAX_VALUE.

Constructor

public View(Element elem)
> Instantiate a View for the given Element. Since the View class is abstract, this is called only from the subclass constructors.

Constants

View defines the constants shown in Table 22-35. The first four are used in the getBreakWeight( ) method, which is described later. The other two apply to the three properties that are indexed based on an axis.

Table 22-35. View constants

Name	Data type	Description
BadBreakWeight	int	The View should not be broken into fragments for formatting purposes.
ExcellentBreakWeight	int	The View supports splitting, and this is a very good place to break.
ForcedBreakWeight	int	The View supports splitting, and it must be broken here to be displayed properly.
GoodBreakWeight	int	The View supports splitting, but there is probably a better break location.
X_AXIS	int	Used to specify the x-axis (another name for SwingConstants. HORIZONTAL).
Y_AXIS	int	Used to specify the y-axis (another name for SwingConstants. VERTICAL).

Abstract methods

These three key methods must be implemented by all concrete subclasses of View:

public abstract void paint(Graphics g, Shape allocation)
> Lay out and paint the View within the bounds of the given Shape with the given Graphics. The allocation may be different than the last time the View was painted, so the View must be prepared to reorganize its layout appropriately. For efficiency, there is usually no clipping region set on the Graphics object. It's the View's responsibility to stay within the allocation (or explicitly call g.setClip(allocation)). Also, you can't be sure that the Graphics object has any other settings (foreground color, background color, etc.).

public abstract Shape modelToView(int offset, Shape allocation, Position.Bias b)
> *throws BadLocationException*
> Convert from a Document offset to view coordinates. The return value should be a small Rectangle (or another Shape) that designates the region in which the

character at that offset is drawn. Be prepared for the Position.Bias argument to be null, in which case it should be treated as Position.Bias.Forward.

public abstract int viewToModel(float x, float y, Shape allocation, Position. Bias biasReturn[])
Convert from view coordinates to a Document offset. The return value should be the Document offset closest to point (x, y). You should set the value of biasReturn[0] to Bias.Forward or Bias.Backward to indicate whether the given point is closer to the next character or the previous one. (If you're less scrupulous and always set it to Bias.Forward, you won't be alone, but set it correctly if you can.)

In the method descriptions that follow, we describe the functions of the methods for a generic subclass of View. These functions are not what the methods usually do in the View class itself. The View class does provide implementations, but they are often empty or minimal (i.e., they always return null or always return this).

Translation methods

These methods (with the addition of two of the above abstract methods) translate between Document offsets and view coordinates. Views use the same coordinate system as the text component in which they are drawn.

public Shape modelToView(int p0, Position.Bias b0,int p1, Position.Bias b1, Shape allocation) throws BadLocationException
Like the abstract modelToView( ) method, but returns a Shape that binds a range of characters instead of a single character. (p0 and p1 are Document offsets.)

public int getNextVisualPositionFrom(int offset, PositionBias bias, Shape a, int direction, Position.Bias[] biasReturn) throws BadLocationException
This method determines where the caret goes when the user presses one of the arrow keys. The direction parameter is one of SwingConstants.NORTH, SOUTH, EAST, or WEST. The input and output are both Document offsets, so handling EAST and WEST is easy. NORTH and SOUTH might need to be converted into view coordinates and then reconverted. The View class has a good implementation that tries to respect magicCaretPosition (if any) and calls Utilities.getPostionAbove( ) and getPositionBelow( ) for NORTH and SOUTH. You should set the value of biasReturn[0] to Bias.Forward or Bias.Backward as appropriate.

public int getViewIndex(int offset, Shape allocation) throws BadLocationException
Return the index of the child View that corresponds to the given Document offset, or -1 if no such child exists. This method was introduced in SDK 1.3.

public int getViewIndex(float x, float y, Shape allocation)
  throws BadLocationException
    Return the index of the child View that corresponds to the given point, or -1 if no such child exists. This method was introduced in SDK 1.4.

public String getToolTipText(float x, float y, Shape allocation)
    Return the tooltip for the given point, or null if there is none. This method was introduced in SDK 1.4 to support the display of ALT text from HTML IMG tags in JEditorPane.

Break methods

public View breakView(int axis, int offset, float pos, float length)
    Return a new View for painting part of this View's content. The new View should start at the given offset into the Document, which can be anywhere in the range defined by the View's startOffset and endOffset properties. Ideally, the new View should have a span of length along the given axis. The pos argument designates the starting position (along the same axis) for the new View's allocation. Most Views ignore this argument except for things such as calculating the positions of tab stops. Views that support breaking typically implement this by calling the createFragment() method after determining an offset for the far side of the break. Views that don't support breaking return themselves unbroken (via return this).

    Suppose we're trying to draw lines of text that are 400 pixels wide and we've already drawn 280 pixels worth of text on the current line. We could call breakView(X_AXIS, offset, 280, 120) in an attempt to fill out the line. The View returned may or may not have the horizontal span we asked for.

public int getBreakWeight(int axis, float pos, float length)
    Return a "score" indicating how appropriate it would be to break this View into a piece with the given length along the given axis (from the start of the View, i.e., from the Document offset designated by its startOffset property). The return value should be one of the constants from Table 22-35. The pos argument designates the starting position (along the same axis) of the View's allocation. Most Views ignore this argument except for things such as calculating the positions of tab stops.

public View createFragment(int p0, int p1)
    Return a new View for painting part of this View's content. The new View should cover the Document from offset p0 to offset p1, which are in the range defined by the View's startOffset and endOffset properties. Views that don't support breaking return themselves unbroken (via return this).

Tree management methods

These methods (introduced in SDK 1.3) allow the structure of the View tree to be modified. In Views that don't support children, these methods do nothing.

public void insert(int index, View v)
 Insert a child View at the given index.

public void append(View v)
 Add a child View to the end; equivalent to insert(getViewCount( ), v).

public void remove(int index)
 Remove the child View at the given index.

public void removeAll( )
 Remove all of this View's children.

public void replace(int index, int length, View[] views)
 Replace some child Views (starting at index) with some other Views. The length argument may be 0, resulting in a pure insertion. The views array may be null, resulting in a pure deletion.

Layout methods

The way that Views are laid out is based on how Components are laid out, except that each axis is handled separately. Both View and Component have preferredSize, minimumSize, and maximumSize properties. View's setSize( ) method resembles a combination of Component's doLayout( ) and setSize( ) methods. View's preferenceChanged( ) method is analogous to invalidate( ) in Component.

public void setSize(float width, float height)
 Set the size of the View and lay out any children. This method may be called with the same arguments as the previous call to ensure that the layout is up-to-date.

public void preferenceChanged(View child, boolean width, boolean height)
 A child View calls this method to indicate to its parent that its preferredSpan has changed, identifying itself and the axis (one or both) of the change. Any cached size information for the child should be discarded, and preferenceChanged( ) should be called on this View's parent (grandparent of the child). A preferenceChanged( ) on the root View triggers a revalidate( ) on the text component.

public Shape getChildAllocation(int index, Shape a)
 The parameters are the Shape that is the allocation for this View (the parent) and a child index, and the Shape returned is the allocation for the child. (The child's allocation should be entirely inside the parent's.) This is an important method because many of the View methods require an allocation argument. So you need the value returned by this method to call them.

Update methods

If every View object registers as a DocumentListener, there is a flurry of redundant activity each time the document changes. To ameliorate this, only the root View registers itself and uses these methods to forward DocumentEvents down the tree. A child View is notified only if the event applies to that child.

public void changedUpdate(DocumentEvent e, Shape a, ViewFactory f)
public void insertUpdate(DocumentEvent e, Shape a, ViewFactory f)
public void removeUpdate(DocumentEvent e, Shape a, ViewFactory f)
> These methods have the same names and purposes as those defined in the DocumentListener interface, but have extra arguments to pass the View its current allocation and a ViewFactory that can be used to rebuild its children if necessary.

The View Classes

Swing provides an almost overwhelming number of View classes. Figure 22-12 shows them and the relationships between them. (Note that the View types used by JTextArea and JTextPane are depicted in Figure 22-11.)

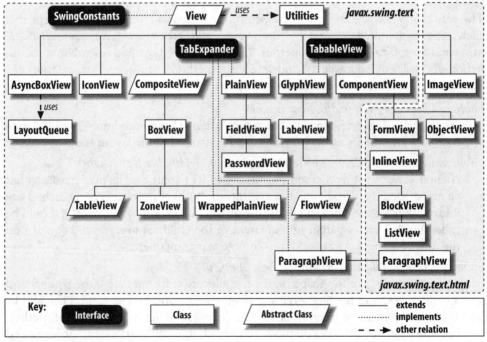

Figure 22-12. View class diagram

It's not worth discussing every `View` class in detail, but here's a brief description of each:

PlainView

Displays one or more nonwrapped lines of text in a single font and color.

FieldView

A subclass of `PlainView` used by `JTextField`. It knows how to perform alignment on a single line of text.

PasswordView

A subclass of `FieldView` used by `JPasswordField`.

GlyphView

Displays a block of styled text, but all in the same style (such as the text represented by a leaf in the `Element` tree). This `View` supports breaking, so the text may wrap across several lines.

LabelView

A subclass of `GlyphView` that doesn't behave any differently except that it caches character attributes to speed up painting. (It has nothing to do with `JLabel`.)

ComponentView

Knows how to display embedded `Components`.

IconView

Knows how to display embedded `Icons`.

CompositeView

An abstract class customized to handle children. There is no requirement that all `Views` that use child `Views` must extend this class, but they do in practice.

BoxView

A subclass of `CompositeView` that tiles its child `Views` along an axis (as when paragraphs are tiled down a page, for example).

WrappedPlainView

A subclass of `BoxView` that displays one or more paragraphs of text in a single font and color. Each paragraph is managed by a child `View` (an instance of a package-private inner class) and is wrapped if necessary.

FlowView

An abstract subclass of `BoxView` that defines a "flow strategy" for laying out children amid constraints.

ParagraphView

An subclass of `FlowView` that knows how to display an indented paragraph of text that may have a mix of styles.

ZoneView

A subclass of `BoxView` that attempts to be memory-efficient by deferring the creation of child `Views` until they are needed. This can be useful for displaying (parts of) very large `Element` trees, but this class is unused in Swing.

AsyncBoxView

Behaves like BoxView but performs layout on a low-priority thread in an attempt to free up the GUI thread for other things. The thread and pending layout tasks are managed by the LayoutQueue class.

TableView

An abstract class in which each child View represents a row, and each grandchild View represents a cell.

In addition to these, there are several View classes in the javax.swing.text.html package that are used by JEditorPane to display HTML. These are listed in Table 22-36. (JEditorPane is the topic of the next chapter.)

Table 22-36. View classes in the javax.swing.text.html package

View class	Used for
BlockView	`<blockquote>`, `<pre>`, `<center>`, `<div>`, `<li>`, `<dl>`, `<dd>`, parent View for others
FormView	`<input>`, `<select>`, `<textarea>` (HTML forms)
ImageView	`<img>`
InlineView	Inline text
ListView	`<ul>`, `<ol>`, `<dir>`, `<menu>`
ObjectView	Component specified in `<object>` tag
ParagraphView	`<p>` (including implied `<p>` tags), `<dt>`, `<h1>`, `<h2>`, `<h3>`, `<h4>`, `<h5>`, `<h6>`

As of SDK 1.4, ObjectView supports an interesting feature. If you include a tag like this:

```
<object classid='javax.swing.JButton'>
    <param name='text' value='push me'>
    <param name='toolTipText' value='go ahead and push me...'>
</object>
```

in your HTML, ObjectView instantiates the Object and (if it is a Component, including JComponent) renders it with the rest of the HTML. This works for any Object type, but (at least for now) the `<param>` tag works only for properties of type String.

The TabExpander Interface

TabExpander is a simple interface implemented by View classes that know how to expand tabs.

Method

public abstract float nextTabStop(float x, int tabOffset)

Return the next tab stop position after the specified position. Values are expressed in points. For example, a View with tab stops every 80 points, starting at 0, would return 240.0 for an input of 227.0. The second parameter is the

---

Document offset of the tab, which can be used to look up the kind of tab when multiple tab types are supported.

The TabableView Interface

This interface is implemented by View classes that need to take tab settings into account when calculating their preferredSpan. In general, a View instance that implements this interface functions correctly with respect to tabs only if its parent View implements the TabExpander interface.

Methods

public abstract float getTabbedSpan(float x, TabExpander e)
> Return a value indicating the span of the View, starting at the specified point and using the supplied TabExpander to expand tabs.

public abstract float getPartialSpan(int p0, int p1)
> Return a value indicating the span needed to cover the range delimited by the specified document offsets. Implementations may assume that there are no tabs in the given range.

The Utilities Class

This class defines a number of static methods used by the text package. Some of these methods are key to the View classes. Many of the method signatures clash with the rest of the Swing text API. For example, parameters in the view coordinate system are declared to be ints, not floats.

Public static methods

public static final int getWordStart(JTextComponent c, int offset)
> *throws BadLocationException*
public static final int getWordEnd(JTextComponent c, int offset)
> *throws BadLocationException*
> Return the Document offset at the beginning (or one position past the end) of the word at the specified Document offset.

public static final int getPreviousWord(JTextComponent c, int offset)
> *throws BadLocationException*
public static final int getNextWord(JTextComponent c, int offset)
> *throws BadLocationException*
> Return the Document offset at the beginning of the word that precedes or follows the specified offset.

public static final int getRowStart(JTextComponent c, int offset)
  throws BadLocationException
public static final int getRowEnd(JTextComponent c, int offset)
  throws BadLocationException
> Return the `Document` offset corresponding to the start or end of the row containing the specified offset.

public static final int getPositionAbove(JTextComponent c, int offset, int x)
  throws BadLocationException
public static int getPositionBelow(JTextComponent c, int offset, int x)
  throws BadLocationException
> Return the document position closest to the given x view coordinate in the row above or below the row containing the specified `offset`.

public static final Element getParagraphElement(JTextComponent c, int offset)
> Return the paragraph `Element` corresponding to the specified `Document` offset. If the component's model is a `StyledDocument`, it delegates to the model's `getParagraphElement( )` method. Otherwise, the `Document`'s `defaultRootElement` is queried for the child containing the given offset.

public static final int getBreakLocation(Segment s, FontMetrics metrics, int x0, int x,
  TabExpander e, int startOffset)
> Try to find a suitable line-break location by looking for whitespace in the supplied `Segment`. `x0` and `x` (both in view coordinates) are the start and intended end of the span. The return value is a `Document` offset. The `TabExpander` may be `null`, but then tabs are counted as spaces.

public static final int drawTabbedText(Segment s, int x, int y, Graphics g,
  TabExpander e, int startOffset)
> Draw the `Segment`'s text, starting at `startOffset`, to the supplied `Graphics` at the specified point (x, y) in view coordinates. The `TabExpander` may be `null`, but then tabs are counted as spaces. The return value is the x-coordinate at the end of the drawn text.

public static final int getTabbedTextWidth(Segment s, FontMetrics metrics, int x,
  TabExpander e, int startOffset)
> Return the width (in view coordinates) of the `Segment`'s text, starting at `startOffset`, with tabs expanded. The x argument is the starting position of the text in view coordinates. The `TabExpander` may be `null`, but then tabs are counted as spaces.

public static final int getTabbedTextOffset(Segment s, FontMetrics metrics, int x0,
  int x, TabExpander e, int startOffset)
> Return the offset into the given `Segment` corresponding to the view coordinate x. The `x0` coordinate specifies the `View` location of the start of the text. The `TabExpander` may be `null`, but then tabs are counted as spaces.

public static final int getTabbedTextOffset(Segment s, FontMetrics metrics, int x0,
   int x, TabExpander e, int startOffset, boolean round)
   This is the same as the previous method if round is true. If round is false, when x
   falls between two characters, it returns the offset of the left one even if the right
   one is closer.

The DocumentFilter Class

DocumentFilter is a class that oversees calls to insertString( ), remove( ), and
replace( ) on any subclass of AbstractDocument. It can allow the edit to occur, substitute another edit, or block it entirely. Because all of Swing's Document classes inherit
from AbstractDocument, this means you can attach a DocumentFilter to pretty much
any Swing text component. The Document interface does not define a
setDocumentFilter( ) method though, so you have to cast the object returned by the
getDocument( ) method to AbstractDocument before you can set the DocumentFilter.
DocumentFilter was introduced in SDK 1.4.

Here's how DocumentFilter works. AbstractDocument's insertString( ), remove( ),
and replace( ) methods check for the existence of a DocumentFilter. If there is one,
they forward the call to the like-named method of the DocumentFilter object. But the
DocumentFilter methods are passed an extra parameter called the FilterBypass. The
FilterBypass object has its own insertString( ), remove( ), and replace( ) methods,
and these actually change the Document's content.

It's important that DocumentFilter methods call FilterBypass methods because an
endless calling loop occurs if the Document methods are called. The delegation to the
DocumentFilter is "bypassed" in FilterBypass. FilterBypass also provides a
getDocument( ) method so the DocumentFilter can examine the contents of the
Document before deciding whether to allow an edit.

Constructor

public DocumentFilter( )
   Instantiate a DocumentFilter that allows all edits to occur.

Methods

DocumentFilter's methods allow all edits to occur by default, so you override only the
ones you want to be more restrictive.

```
public void insertString(DocumentFilter.FilterBypass fb, int offset,
   String text, AttributeSet attr) throws BadLocationException
public void remove(DocumentFilter.FilterBypass fb, int offset, int length)
   throws BadLocationException
public void replace(DocumentFilter.FilterBypass fb, int offset,
   int length, String text, AttributeSet attr) throws BadLocationException
```

DocumentFilter.FilterBypass methods

```
public Document getDocument( )
public void insertString(int offset, String text, AttributeSet attr)
  throws BadLocationException
public void remove(int offset, int length) throws BadLocationException
public void replace(int offset, int length, String text,
    AttributeSet attr) throws BadLocationException
```

Here's a simple example of a DocumentFilter that doesn't allow lowercase letters in the Document. All it does is convert the input String to uppercase before delegating to the FilterBypass.

```java
// UpcaseFilter.java
// A simple DocumentFilter that maps lowercase letters to uppercase
import javax.swing.*;
import javax.swing.text.*;

public class UpcaseFilter extends DocumentFilter {

  public void insertString(DocumentFilter.FilterBypass fb, int offset,
                 String text, AttributeSet attr) throws BadLocationException
  {
    fb.insertString(offset, text.toUpperCase( ), attr);
  }

  // No need to override remove( ); inherited version allows all removals.

  public void replace(DocumentFilter.FilterBypass fb, int offset, int length,
                 String text, AttributeSet attr) throws BadLocationException
  {
    fb.replace(offset, length, text.toUpperCase( ), attr);
  }

  public static void main(String[] args) {
    DocumentFilter dfilter = new UpcaseFilter( );

    JTextArea jta = new JTextArea( );
    JTextField jtf = new JTextField( );
    ((AbstractDocument)jta.getDocument( )).setDocumentFilter(dfilter);
    ((AbstractDocument)jtf.getDocument( )).setDocumentFilter(dfilter);

    JFrame frame = new JFrame("UpcaseFilter");
    frame.getContentPane( ).add(jta, java.awt.BorderLayout.CENTER);
    frame.getContentPane( ).add(jtf, java.awt.BorderLayout.SOUTH);
    frame.setDefaultCloseOperation(JFrame.EXIT_ON_CLOSE);
    frame.setSize(200, 120);
    frame.setVisible(true);
  }
}
```

Note that even though the text area and the text field each have their own Document, they share the same DocumentFilter instance. Unless your DocumentFilter needs to store state information, you can instantiate one DocumentFilter and attach it to as many AbstractDocuments as you like.

The NavigationFilter Class

The NavigationFilter class is similar to the DocumentFilter class except that it oversees caret positioning instead of edits to the Document. Like DocumentFilter, NavigationFilter was introduced in SDK 1.4. Unlike DocumentFilter, you can easily install a NavigationFilter on any Swing text component without having to perform a cast. Just pass your NavigationFilter into the component's setNavigationFilter() method, and the component's Caret will filter all movement through it. NavigationFilters can also be specified by subclasses of AbstractFormatter (see Chapter 20).

Two of NavigationFilter's methods work just like DocumentFilter's methods. The Caret's moveDot() and setDot() methods check for the existence of a NavigationFilter. If there is one, they forward the call to the like-named method of the NavigationFilter object. But the NavigationFilter methods are passed an extra parameter called the FilterBypass. The FilterBypass object has its own moveDot() and setDot() methods, and these actually change the position of the Caret. FilterBypass also provides access to the Caret via its getCaret() method.

A third method, getNextVisualPositionFrom(), is called by the default caret movement Actions[*] when they are acting on a component that has a NavigationFilter. Thus, a NavigationFilter can completely control how the caret reacts to the arrow keys. (If no NavigationFilter exists, the default caret movement Actions call the like-named method of the appropriate View object instead. See "The View Class" earlier in this chapter.) There is no FilterBypass involved with this method.

Constructor

public NavigationFilter()
   Instantiate a NavigationFilter that reproduces the default caret movement behavior.

Methods

NavigationFilter's methods reproduce the default caret movement behavior, so you override only the ones you want to behave differently.

---

[*] These Actions are defined in DefaultEditorKit (see Chapter 23) and are bound by the existing L&Fs to the arrow keys (to move the caret) and Shift-arrow keys (to extend the current selection).

public void setDot(NavigationFilter.FilterBypass fb, int dot, Position.Bias bias)
public void moveDot(NavigationFilter.FilterBypass fb, int dot, Position.Bias bias)

> The bias parameter is not present in the corresponding methods in the Caret interface. Except for forwarding it to the FilterBypass methods when necessary, you can ignore it.

public int getNextVisualPositionFrom(JTextComponent comp, int pos, Position.
Bias bias, int direction, Position.Bias[] biasRet) throws BadLocationException

> See the like-named method in "The View Class" for a description of this method. The default implementation delegates (by way of the component's TextUI) to the appropriate View object. If you override this method, you can call super. getNextVisualPositionFrom(comp, pos, bias, biasRet) to determine where the caret would go if there is no NavigationFilter. Note that the caret is not guaranteed to actually appear at the offset returned by this method because the NavigationFilter's moveDot( ) and setDot( ) methods may not allow it.

NavigationFilter.FilterBypass methods

```
public Caret getCaret( )
public void setDot(int dot, Position.Bias bias)
public void moveDot(int dot, Position.Bias bias)
```

This was a long chapter, but now you know all about Swing's handling of styled text. You have only one more chapter to go, and then the Swing text components will no longer hold any mysteries for you. In the next chapter we cover the last of the Swing text components: the flexible and powerful JEditorPane.

Editor Panes and Editor Kits

Over the last four chapters we've covered just about all the classes and interfaces that make up the Swing text framework. In this chapter, we'll look at a class that ties everything together: `EditorKit`. An `EditorKit` pulls together the document model, document view, document editing actions, and document I/O strategy, serving as a central reference point for a given document type.

In addition to looking at `EditorKit` and its subclasses, this chapter introduces the `TextAction` class (an abstract extension of `AbstractAction`) and the many useful concrete action classes available as inner classes of the `EditorKit` subclasses. These actions include basic functions such as copying and pasting text as well as style-oriented tasks such as changing font characteristics.

Throughout the chapter, we build simple but powerful editors for working with increasingly complex content types, moving from plain text to styled text to HTML. Finally, we discuss the process for creating your own editor kit.

The JEditorPane Class

`JEditorPane` is an extension of `JTextComponent` capable of displaying various types of content, such as HTML and RTF. It is not intended to be used as a full-featured web browser, but it can be used to view simple HTML and is ideal for integrating online help into Java applications.

`JEditorPane`s work closely with `EditorKit` objects. An `EditorKit` plugs into the editor pane to customize it for a particular content type. Without an `EditorKit` telling it how to work, a `JEditorPane` can't function. We discuss `EditorKit` in the next section.

Figure 23-1 shows the `JEditorPane` in action, displaying a portion of the Javadoc for the `JEditorPane` class. Here's the code:

```
// HTMLExample.java
//
```

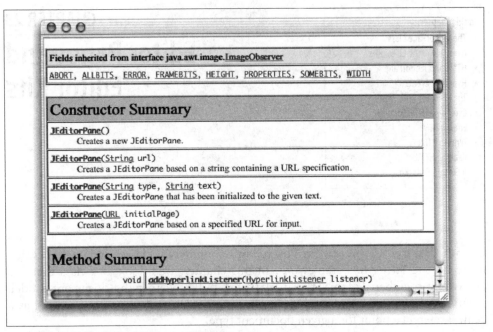

Figure 23-1. JEditorPane showing an HTML page

```java
import javax.swing.*;
import javax.swing.event.*;
import java.io.*;

public class HTMLExample {
  public static void main(String[] args) {
    JEditorPane pane = null;
    try {
      pane = new JEditorPane(args[0]);
    }
    catch (IOException ex) {
      ex.printStackTrace(System.err);
      System.exit(1);
    }
    pane.setEditable(false);

    // Add a hyperlink listener.
    final JEditorPane finalPane = pane;
    pane.addHyperlinkListener(new HyperlinkListener( ) {
      public void hyperlinkUpdate(HyperlinkEvent ev) {
        try {
          if (ev.getEventType( ) == HyperlinkEvent.EventType.ACTIVATED)
            finalPane.setPage(ev.getURL( ));
        } catch (IOException ex) { ex.printStackTrace(System.err); }
      }
    });
```

```
        JFrame frame = new JFrame();
        frame.setDefaultCloseOperation(JFrame.EXIT_ON_CLOSE);
        frame.setContentPane(new JScrollPane(pane));
        frame.setSize(350,400);
        frame.setVisible(true);
    }
}
```

We've created a minimal HTML browser.* In a real application, you'd want to do things like change the cursor while new pages are being loaded and handle exceptions more elegantly. The anonymous inner class in this example shows a quick way to enable hyperlinks when viewing text in a JEditorPane. We'll look at the classes and methods used here in the next few sections.

Properties

Table 23-1 shows the properties defined by JEditorPane. The accessibleContext property depends on the type of EditorKit in use. If an HTMLEditorKit is installed, a special AccessibleJEditorPaneHTML object is used. Otherwise, its superclass, AccessibleJEditorPane, is used. AccessibleJEditorPane extends the JTextComponent. AccessibleJTextComponent class.

Table 23-1. JEditorPane properties

Property	Data type	get	is	set	Default value
accessibleContext[o]	AccessibleContext	•			AccessibleJEditorPane or AccessibleJEditorPaneHTML
contentType	String	•		•	From editorKit
editorKit[b]	EditorKit	•		•	null
focusTraversalPolicy[1.4, o]	FocusTraversalPolicy		•		true
page	URL	•		•	null
scrollableTracks-ViewportWidth[o]	boolean	•			true
UIClassID[o]	String	•			"EditorPaneUI"

[1.4]since 1.4, [b]bound, [o]overridden

See also properties from the JTextComponent class (Table 19-1).

The contentType property reflects the type of content displayed by the editor. This value is taken from the installed EditorKit and typically has values such as "text/plain", "text/html", and "text/rtf". The editorKit supplies everything needed to work with a particular content type.

---

* This simple browser will not handle all HTML pages. Swing is still being enhanced to provide better HTML support. However, significant progress has been made since earlier releases.

A custom FocusTraversalPolicy property is installed so the Tab key does not move focus to the next component.* The page property specifies the URL of the current page being displayed. The scrollableTracksViewportWidth property is true for this class.

Events

JEditorPanes fire a special type of event called a HyperlinkEvent, which is typically fired when the user clicks on a hyperlink; the program normally responds by loading a new page. To support this event type, a corresponding event class and listener interface are available in the javax.swing.event package. These are described briefly at the end of this section.

As you'd expect, the following methods are provided for working with these events:

```
public synchronized void addHyperlinkListener(HyperlinkListener listener)
public synchronized void removeHyperlinkListener(HyperlinkListener
    listener)
public synchronized HyperlinkListener[] getHyperlinkListeners()
public void fireHyperlinkUpdate(HyperlinkEvent e)
```

JEditorPane objects also fire PropertyChangeEvents when the editorKit property is changed. getHyperlinkListeners() was introduced in SDK 1.4. While not restricted to HTML documents by any means, HTML is a natural and familiar environment for hyperlinks (so we have chosen to detail them in "HTML and JEditorPane" later in this chapter).

Constructors

The following constructors are provided. Note that the last two may throw an IOException if they are unable to load the specified URL (including if the server returns an HTTP error).

public JEditorPane()
    Create an empty pane.

public JEditorPane(String url) throws IOException
public JEditorPane(URL initialPage) throws IOException
    Create a pane displaying the specified URL. contentType and editorKit are set based on the content type of the URLConnection created from the given URL. Because these constructors attempt to open a URL, they may throw an IOException if the URL cannot be found.

* In previous versions this was implemented using the (now deprecated) managingFocus property.

EditorKit Methods

The following methods are available for managing EditorKits. You won't need to use any of these methods unless you're defining your own EditorKits for working with various content types.

public EditorKit getEditorKitForContentType(String type)
Return an EditorKit for the given content type. An attempt is made to create the appropriate EditorKit if one has not already been set (via a call to setEditorKitForContentType( )). If the appropriate EditorKit cannot be created, a DefaultEditorKit is returned.

public void setEditorKitForContentType(String type, EditorKit k)
Explicitly set the EditorKit to be used for a given content type.

public static EditorKit createEditorKitForContentType(String type)
Attempt to create a new EditorKit instance for the given content type. In order for this method to return a non-null object, the content type must be associated with an editor kit class name via registerEditorKitForContentType( ).

public static void registerEditorKitForContentType(String type, String classname)
Called to associate a content type with an editor kit class name. It is called four times in the JEditorPane initializer block. These calls define the mappings shown in Table 23-2.

Table 23-2. Default content type mappings

Content type	Class
application/rtf	javax.swing.text.rtf.RTFEditorKit
text/html	javax.swing.text.html.HTMLEditorKit
text/plain	javax.swing.JEditorPane.PlainEditorKit (a package-private subclass of DefaultEditorKit)
text/rtf	javax.swing.text.rtf.RTFEditorKit

public static String getEditorKitClassNameForContentType(String type)
Return the class name associated with the specified content type (introduced in SDK 1.3).

Miscellaneous Methods

public void setPage(String url) throws IOException
A convenience method used to set the current page, given a URL string. An IOException is thrown if the given URL cannot be loaded.

public void scrollToReference(String reference)
Used by setPage( ) to scroll the display to the specified reference within the current document. This method provides support for URLs containing named

anchors, like events.html#february. Note that this method works only with HTML documents. It was protected prior to SDK 1.4 but is now available to everyone.

Overview of the Editor Kits

The following sections provide an overview of the various editor kits. With minor variations, this information applies to all editor kits.

The EditorKit Class

The EditorKit class is the abstract base class for all editor kits. It has a number of methods that define the model (e.g., createDefaultDocument( )), the view (e.g., getViewFactory( )), the capabilities (getActions( )), and the I/O strategy (read( ) and write( )) for a given type of document content. Figure 23-2 shows the EditorKit class and the many classes and interfaces it interacts with.

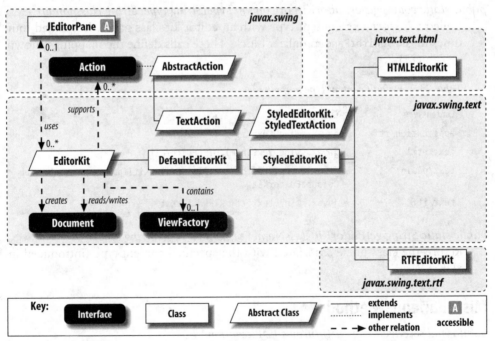

Figure 23-2. EditorKit class diagram

This figure shows several important things about the EditorKit class. First, each EditorKit instance is typically associated with a single JEditorPane (though in some cases, it doesn't care). The EditorKit defines how to create a default Document as well as how to read and write the Document to a stream. In addition, each EditorKit may define a `ViewFactory` responsible for creating `View` objects for each `Element` in the Document. Finally, the diagram shows that an `EditorKit` may define a set of `Actions` that it supports.

The other classes shown in the diagram are the subclasses of `EditorKit` and `AbstractAction`. We'll look at each of these classes, as well as some inner classes not shown on the diagram, throughout this chapter.

Properties

`EditorKit` defines the properties shown in Table 23-3. The actions property defines the set of actions that can be used on a text component, which uses a model and a view produced by this `EditorKit`. `contentType` indicates the MIME type of the data that this kit supports. The `viewFactory` property is the `ViewFactory` object used to create `View` objects for the `Elements` of the document type produced by the kit. The accessors for all three of these properties are abstract.

Table 23-3. EditorKit properties

Property	Data type	get	is	set	Default value
actions	Action[]	•			Abstract
contentType	String	•			Abstract
viewFactory	ViewFactory	•			Abstract

Abstract methods

The following methods must be defined by implementations of this class:

public abstract Object clone()
> Return a copy of the editor kit. `EditorKit` implements `Cloneable` so that new instances can be created quickly.

public abstract Caret createCaret()
> Create a new `Caret` to be used with the `JEditorPane`. However, this method is currently not called anywhere within Swing—Carets are initially installed via the `createCaret()` method in `BasicTextUI` and can be changed via a call to `setCaret()` on any `JTextComponent`.

public abstract Document createDefaultDocument()
> Called by the `BasicTextUI` when installing a UI for a component and by `JTextComponent` before loading a new document from a stream. It should return a new `Document` object of the appropriate type for the kit. Figure 23-3 shows how this method is called when a new `JEditorPane` is created without specifying a document.

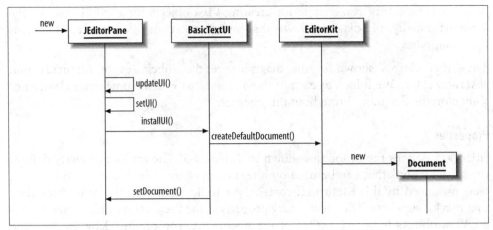

Figure 23-3. Default document creation using EditorKit

public abstract void read(InputStream in, Document doc, int pos)
    throws IOException, BadLocationException
public abstract void read(Reader in, Document doc, int pos)
    throws IOException, BadLocationException
> Populate the given Document, based on data read from the stream or reader. The data read is inserted at the specified document position (use 0 if this is a new, empty document).

public abstract void write(OutputStream out, Document doc, int pos, int len)
    throws IOException, BadLocationException
public abstract void write(Writer out, Document doc, int pos, int len)
    throws IOException, BadLocationException
> Write the specified portion of the document to the specified stream. To write the entire document, call write(aWriter, aDoc, 0, aDoc.getLength( )).

These read( ) and write( ) methods support any arbitrary text format. For simple text, the data read and written is plain text; more advanced editor kits might be able to read attribute and style information or well-defined markup languages like HTML or XML.

Other methods

These methods are not abstract, but the default implementations do nothing:

public void install(JEditorPane c)
> Called once the content type for the JEditorPane has been determined. It associates the kit with the editor pane. Subclasses that need to query or listen to the editor pane for any reason should take advantage of this method.

public void deinstall(JEditorPane c)
> Called when the JEditorPane changes its editor kit. For example, subclasses may take advantage of this method to remove listeners from the pane.

The TextAction Class

Way back in Chapter 3, we introduced the `Action` interface and the `AbstractAction` default implementation. To quickly review, `Actions` are a way to encapsulate some common piece of functionality, along with an associated name, icon, and other attributes. `Action` extends the `ActionListener` interface, so any `Action` can be added as a listener to components that fire `Action` events.

When working with any word processor or basic editor, you perform "actions" all the time. The simplest example occurs every time you type a character. Some action is performed to add that character to the document and the display. More interesting examples include making a segment of text bold, copying a selection of text, or changing the current font.

Swing provides support for many of these common activities through classes that extend the `TextAction` abstract class. The specific actions available are defined as inner classes of the `EditorKit` subclasses. We'll cover each of these in the sections that follow. In this section, we'll briefly cover the `TextAction` class itself, so you understand what all these new actions have in common. Appendix B lists all the actions provided by Swing's standard components.

Note that if you want to define your own `Action` implementations that manipulate text components, they don't have to extend `TextAction`. In most cases you'll want to because its `getTextComponent()` method makes it convenient to create a single instance that can work with multiple text components.

Constructor

public TextAction(String name)
> Pass the action name up to its superclass, where it is assigned to the `Action.NAME` property. Recall from the discussion of `Action` that this property is typically the primary key used to identify actions.

Static method

public static final Action[] augmentList(Action[] list1, Action[] list2)
> Add the actions in the second list to those in the first list. Any action names in both lists are mapped to the `Action` specified in the second list. This method can be used by an `EditorKit` that adds new actions to the actions supported by its superclass.

Protected methods

protected final JTextComponent getFocusedComponent( )
> Return JTextComponent.getFocusedComponent( ).

protected final JTextComponent getTextComponent(ActionEvent e)
> Determine the currently active text component, allowing actions to be shared by multiple text components. If the given event has a JTextComponent as its target, that component is returned. If not, the result of getFocusedComponent( ) is returned.

The DefaultEditorKit Class

DefaultEditorKit, a subclass of EditorKit, provides a great deal of default behavior applicable to most document types. As we'll see, the most interesting features available in this class are provided by the actions it supports through its numerous inner classes.

When used directly, DefaultEditorKit supports only plain-text data. Its actions deal with tasks such as copying and pasting data, and its I/O methods read and write only plain text. However, the important thing about this class is that it can be extended to add more features, and the actions it defines are still useful. We'll see extensions of DefaultEditorKit in the sections that follow.

Properties

DefaultEditorKit defines values for the properties shown in Table 23-4. Each action is an instance of an inner class capable of performing a given task. The contentType for editors using DefaultEditorKit is "text/plain", indicating that styled text is not supported. The viewFactory property is set to null, indicating that users of this class must provide ViewFactory support via the TextUI.

Table 23-4. DefaultEditorKit properties

Property	Data type	get	is	set	Default value
actions⁰	Action[]	•			Array of 53* TextAction objects
contentType⁰	String	•			"text/plain"
viewFactory⁰	ViewFactory	•			null

⁰overridden

*As of 1.4; there were 47 when Swing was first released.

See also properties from the EditorKit class (Table 23-3).

Constants

DefaultEditorKit defines 52[*] action names (Strings, shown in Table 23-5) as constant values, though their names aren't all-caps as you'd expect given the Java naming conventions. All but six of these names are public; six are declared with default (package) access and are thus intended for internal use. Behind each action name is an inner class (some classes are used by multiple actions) that extends TextAction to carry out the action. Several of these action classes are public, so we describe them in more detail after this section. However, even with the nonpublic classes, you can get to an instance of the action using these constants, along with the actions property. The following example shows a common strategy for doing this. We store all the actions in a local Hashtable so that we can access them by name. In this example, we then retrieve the "cut" action from the table using the DefaultEditorKit.cutAction constant:

```
Hashtable actionHash = new Hashtable( );
Action[] actions = edKit.getActions( );
for (int i=0; i<actions.length; i++) {
  String name = (String)actions[i].getValue(Action.NAME);
  actionHash.put(name, actions[i]);
}
Action cut = (Action)actionHash.get(DefaultEditorKit.cutAction);
```

Table 23-5. DefaultEditorKit action name constants

Constant	Description
backwardAction	Move the caret back one position.
beepAction	Create a beep (Toolkit.beep( )).
beginAction	Move the caret to the beginning of the document.
beginLineAction	Move the caret to the beginning of the current line.
beginParagraphAction	Move the caret to the beginning of the current paragraph.
beginWordAction	Move the caret to the beginning of the current word.
copyAction	Copy the selected region and place it on the system clipboard.
cutAction	Cut the selected region and place it on the system clipboard.
defaultKeyTypedAction	Insert the pressed key (default when there is no special key mapping for a pressed key).
deleteNextCharAction	Delete the character following the caret position.
deletePrevCharAction	Delete the character before the caret position.
downAction	Move the caret down one position.

[n]Not public (declared with default package access).

---

[*] The keen observer will notice that the properties table indicated that there were 53 actions available. One action is not defined as a constant but is still available under the name dump-model. This action just calls dump( ) on the document of the currently focused JTextComponent (assuming it's an AbstractDocument), causing the model structure to be printed to System.err.

Table 23-5. DefaultEditorKit action name constants (continued)

Constant	Description
endAction	Move the caret to the end of the document.
endLineAction	Move the caret to the end of the current line.
endParagraphAction	Move the caret to the end of the current paragraph.
endWordAction	Move the caret to the end of the current word.
forwardAction	Move the caret forward one position.
insertBreakAction	Insert a line or paragraph break (\n) into the document; if there is a current selection, it is removed first.
insertContentAction	Insert content into the document; if there is a current selection, it is removed first.
insertTabAction	Insert a tab character into the document; if there is a current selection, it is removed first.
nextWordAction	Move the caret to the beginning of the next word.
pageDownAction	Page the document down.
pageUpAction	Page the document up.
pasteAction	Paste the contents of the system clipboard at the caret position; if there is a current selection, it is replaced by the pasted content.
previousWordAction	Move the caret to the beginning of the previous word.
readOnlyAction	Set the editor to read-only mode; results in a call to setEditable(false) on the JTextComponent.
selectAllAction	Highlight the entire document.
selectionBackwardAction	Adjust the current selection by moving the caret back one position.
selectionBeginAction	Adjust the current selection by moving the caret back to the beginning of the document.
selectionBeginLineAction	Adjust the current selection by moving the caret back to the beginning of the current line.
selectionBeginParagraphAction	Adjust the current selection by moving the caret back to the beginning of the current paragraph.
selectionBeginWordAction	Adjust the current selection by moving the caret back to the beginning of the current word.
selectionDownAction	Adjust the current selection by moving the caret down one row.
selectionEndAction	Adjust the current selection by moving the caret to the end of the document.
selectionEndLineAction	Adjust the current selection by moving the caret to the end of the current line.
selectionEndParagraphAction	Adjust the current selection by moving the caret to the end of the current paragraph.
selectionEndWordAction	Adjust the current selection by moving the caret to the end of the current word.
selectionForwardAction	Adjust the current selection by moving the caret forward one position.

nNot public (declared with default package access).

Table 23-5. DefaultEditorKit action name constants (continued)

Constant	Description
selectionNextWordAction	Adjust the current selection by moving the caret to the beginning of the next word.
selectionPageDownAction[n]	Page the document down, moving the selection.
selectionPageLeftAction[n]	Page the document left, moving the selection.
selectionPageRightAction[n]	Page the document right, moving the selection.
selectionPageUpAction[n]	Page the document up, moving the selection.
selectionPreviousWordAction	Adjust the current selection by moving the caret to the beginning of the previous word.
selectionUpAction	Adjust the current selection by moving the caret down one row.
selectLineAction	Select the current line.
selectParagraphAction	Select the current paragraph.
selectWordAction	Select the current word.
toggleComponentOrientationAction[n]	Switches the component's orientation (between left-to-right and right-to-left).
unselectAction[n]	Eliminate any selection without affecting its content.
upAction	Move the caret up one position.
writableAction	Set the editor to writable mode; results in a call to setEditable(true) on the JTextComponent.

[n]Not public (declared with default package access).

It would have been nice if EditorKit had been enhanced to take advantage of ActionMap to spare us this sort of effort. Perhaps someday…

Using actions

Let's look at a simple example that shows how these actions can be used. This program creates a JTextArea and adds all the available actions to a menu (the list is pretty long, so we split it into two submenus). As we discussed in Chapter 14, we can add these Action objects directly to the menu. The default action names appear as menu selections.

Since JTextArea gets its actions from the DefaultEditorKit, you'll see each of the actions listed in Table 23-5 when you run this program. By blindly adding all the actions, we avoid interacting with the editor kit directly in this program. At the end of this section, we'll look at a much more useful example that uses DefaultEditorKit directly.

```
// TextActionExample.java
//
import javax.swing.*;
import javax.swing.text.*;
```

```
// Simple TextAction example
public class TextActionExample {
  public static void main(String[] args) {

    // Create a text area.
    JTextArea ta = new JTextArea( );
    ta.setLineWrap(true);

    // Add all actions to the menu (split into two menus to make it more usable).
    Action[] actions = ta.getActions( );
    JMenuBar menubar = new JMenuBar( );
    JMenu actionmenu = new JMenu("Actions");
    menubar.add(actionmenu);

    JMenu firstHalf = new JMenu("1st Half");
    JMenu secondHalf = new JMenu("2nd Half");
    actionmenu.add(firstHalf);
    actionmenu.add(secondHalf);

    int mid = actions.length/2;
    for (int i=0; i<mid; i++) {
      firstHalf.add(actions[i]);
    }
    for (int i=mid; i<actions.length; i++) {
      secondHalf.add(actions[i]);
    }

    // Show it.
    JFrame f = new JFrame( );
    f.setDefaultCloseOperation(JFrame.EXIT_ON_CLOSE);
    f.getContentPane( ).add(ta);
    f.setJMenuBar(menubar);
    f.setSize(300, 200);
    f.setVisible(true);
  }
}
```

That's all there is to it! All we did was call getActions( ) on the JTextArea (which ultimately retrieved the actions from a DefaultEditorKit) and added each action to the menu. Of course, most of these actions would never be provided as menu options, and for those that would, you'd want to change the label (the default labels are all lowercase, and the words are hyphen-separated, as in cut-to-clipboard). The example at the end of the section is a bit more realistic.

Constructor

public DefaultEditorKit()
    This default constructor defines no behavior.

Methods

The following methods provide default implementations for all the abstract methods defined in EditorKit:

public Object clone( )
>   Return a new DefaultEditorKit.

public Caret createCaret( )
>   Return null. See EditorKit.createCaret( ).

public Document createDefaultDocument( )
>   Create a new PlainDocument instance and return it.

public void read(InputStream in, Document doc, int pos)
>   *throws IOException, BadLocationException*
public void read(Reader in, Document doc, int pos)
>   *throws IOException, BadLocationException*
>   Read plain text from the supplied Reader (in), adding the text at the specified position. The version that takes an InputStream simply wraps the stream in an InputStreamReader and calls the other version.

public void write(OutputStream out, Document doc, int pos, int len)
>   *throws IOException, BadLocationException*
public void write(Writer out, Document doc, int pos, int len)
>   *throws IOException, BadLocationException*
>   Write len plain text characters to the supplied Writer (out), starting at position pos. The version that takes an OutputStream simply wraps the stream in an OutputStreamWriter and calls the other version.

Useful Actions

In the next few sections, we'll give a brief overview of some key actions defined as public static inner classes of DefaultEditorKit. The first of these is the default action used to insert text into the active JTextComponent. The constructors aren't described individually, as they simply set up the proper name for each action. We'll simply describe the actionPerformed method that implements the purpose of each action. In each case, the method has the standard signature, public void actionPerformed(ActionEvent e).

DefaultEditorKit.DefaultKeyTypedAction
>   Insert the actionCommand value from the ActionEvent into the active JTextComponent using replaceSelection( ). If the first character has a value less than 0x20, this does nothing. This action adds ordinary (noncommand) keystrokes to the document's content.

DefaultEditorKit.BeepAction
>   Call Toolkit.getDefaultToolkit( ).beep( ) to produce an audible alert.

`DefaultEditorKit.CopyAction`

Call copy( ) on the active JTextComponent, if it can be determined.

`DefaultEditorKit.CutAction`

Call cut( ) on the active JTextComponent, if it can be determined.

`DefaultEditorKit.InsertBreakAction`

Replace the active JTextComponent's current selection with a newline character (\n). If there is no selection, a newline is inserted.

`DefaultEditorKit.InsertContentAction`

Insert the actionCommand value from the event into the active JTextComponent, using replaceSelection( ). If the action command is null, a beep is sounded.

`DefaultEditorKit.InsertTabAction`

Replace the active JTextComponent's current selection with a tab character (\t). If there is no selection, a tab is inserted.

`DefaultEditorKit.PasteAction`

Call paste( ) on the active JTextComponent.

A Simple Text Editor

In the next example, we'll show how to provide some of the things you'd expect from a basic editor. Our first editor supports the following features:

- Cut, copy, and paste via toolbar buttons, menu selection, and default key shortcuts
- Select-all capability via menu selection
- Quick keyboard navigation using `nextWordAction`, `previousWordAction`, `selectionNextWordAction`, and `selectionPreviousWordAction`
- Saving and loading documents

When we run it, our simple editor looks something like Figure 23-4.[*]

Here's the source code for SimpleEditor. It's designed to be easily extensible, allowing us to add features of the more advanced editor kits. This class serves as the base class for the other examples in this chapter.

```
// SimpleEditor.java
//
import javax.swing.*;
import javax.swing.text.*;
import java.awt.*;
import java.io.*;
import java.awt.event.*;
import java.util.Hashtable;
```

---

[*] Text in this and subsequent figures is from "Computing Machinery and Intelligence" by A.M. Turing (*Mind*, 1950).

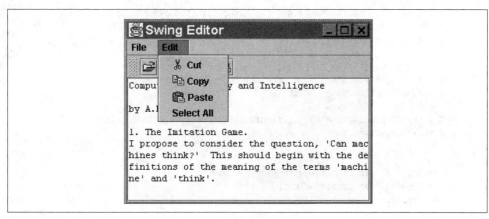

Figure 23-4. SimpleEditor

```java
// An example showing several DefaultEditorKit features. This class is designed
// to be easily extended for additional functionality.

public class SimpleEditor extends JFrame {

  public static void main(String[] args) {
    SimpleEditor editor = new SimpleEditor();
    editor.setDefaultCloseOperation(JFrame.EXIT_ON_CLOSE);
    editor.setVisible(true);
  }

  // Create an editor.
  public SimpleEditor() {
    super("Swing Editor");
    textComp = createTextComponent();
    makeActionsPretty();

    Container content = getContentPane();
    content.add(textComp, BorderLayout.CENTER);
    content.add(createToolBar(), BorderLayout.NORTH);
    setJMenuBar(createMenuBar());
    setSize(320, 240);
  }

  // Create the JTextComponent subclass.
  protected JTextComponent createTextComponent() {
    JTextArea ta = new JTextArea();
    ta.setLineWrap(true);
    return ta;
  }

  // Add icons and friendly names to actions we care about.
  protected void makeActionsPretty() {
    Action a;
    a = textComp.getActionMap().get(DefaultEditorKit.cutAction);
    a.putValue(Action.SMALL_ICON, new ImageIcon("icons/cut.gif"));
    a.putValue(Action.NAME, "Cut");
```

```
        a = textComp.getActionMap( ).get(DefaultEditorKit.copyAction);
        a.putValue(Action.SMALL_ICON, new ImageIcon("icons/copy.gif"));
        a.putValue(Action.NAME, "Copy");

        a = textComp.getActionMap( ).get(DefaultEditorKit.pasteAction);
        a.putValue(Action.SMALL_ICON, new ImageIcon("icons/paste.gif"));
        a.putValue(Action.NAME, "Paste");

        a = textComp.getActionMap( ).get(DefaultEditorKit.selectAllAction);
        a.putValue(Action.NAME, "Select All");
    }

    // Create a simple JToolBar with some buttons.
    protected JToolBar createToolBar( ) {
        JToolBar bar = new JToolBar( );

        // Add simple actions for opening and saving.
        bar.add(getOpenAction( )).setText("");
        bar.add(getSaveAction( )).setText("");
        bar.addSeparator( );

        // Add Cut/Copy/Paste buttons.
        bar.add(textComp.getActionMap( ).get(DefaultEditorKit.cutAction)).setText("");
        bar.add(textComp.getActionMap( ).get(DefaultEditorKit.copyAction)).setText("");
        bar.add(textComp.getActionMap( ).get(DefaultEditorKit.pasteAction)).setText("");
        return bar;
    }

    // Create a JMenuBar with file and edit menus.
    protected JMenuBar createMenuBar( ) {
        JMenuBar menubar = new JMenuBar( );
        JMenu file = new JMenu("File");
        JMenu edit = new JMenu("Edit");
        menubar.add(file);
        menubar.add(edit);

        file.add(getOpenAction( ));
        file.add(getSaveAction( ));
        file.add(new ExitAction( ));
        edit.add(textComp.getActionMap( ).get(DefaultEditorKit.cutAction));
        edit.add(textComp.getActionMap( ).get(DefaultEditorKit.copyAction));
        edit.add(textComp.getActionMap( ).get(DefaultEditorKit.pasteAction));
        edit.add(textComp.getActionMap( ).get(DefaultEditorKit.selectAllAction));
        return menubar;
    }

    // Subclass can override to use a different open action.
    protected Action getOpenAction( ) { return openAction; }

    // Subclass can override to use a different save action.
    protected Action getSaveAction( ) { return saveAction; }

    protected JTextComponent getTextComponent( ) { return textComp; }
```

```
private Action openAction = new OpenAction( );
private Action saveAction = new SaveAction( );

private JTextComponent textComp;
private Hashtable actionHash = new Hashtable( );

// ********** ACTION INNER CLASSES ********** //

// A very simple exit action
public class ExitAction extends AbstractAction {
  public ExitAction( ) { super("Exit"); }
  public void actionPerformed(ActionEvent ev) { System.exit(0); }
}

// An action that opens an existing file
class OpenAction extends AbstractAction {
  public OpenAction( ) {
    super("Open", new ImageIcon("icons/open.gif"));
  }

  // Query user for a filename and attempt to open and read the file into the
  // text component.
  public void actionPerformed(ActionEvent ev) {
    JFileChooser chooser = new JFileChooser( );
    if (chooser.showOpenDialog(SimpleEditor.this) !=
        JFileChooser.APPROVE_OPTION)
      return;
    File file = chooser.getSelectedFile( );
    if (file == null)
      return;

    FileReader reader = null;
    try {
      reader = new FileReader(file);
      textComp.read(reader, null);
    }
    catch (IOException ex) {
      JOptionPane.showMessageDialog(SimpleEditor.this,
      "File Not Found", "ERROR", JOptionPane.ERROR_MESSAGE);
    }
    finally {
      if (reader != null) {
        try {
          reader.close( );
        } catch (IOException x) {}
      }
    }
  }
}

// An action that saves the document to a file
class SaveAction extends AbstractAction {
```

```
public SaveAction( ) {
  super("Save", new ImageIcon("icons/save.gif"));
}

// Query user for a filename and attempt to open and write the text component's
// content to the file.
public void actionPerformed(ActionEvent ev) {
  JFileChooser chooser = new JFileChooser( );
  if (chooser.showSaveDialog(SimpleEditor.this) !=
      JFileChooser.APPROVE_OPTION)
    return;
  File file = chooser.getSelectedFile( );
  if (file == null)
    return;

  FileWriter writer = null;
  try {
    writer = new FileWriter(file);
    textComp.write(writer);
  }
  catch (IOException ex) {
    JOptionPane.showMessageDialog(SimpleEditor.this,
    "File Not Saved", "ERROR", JOptionPane.ERROR_MESSAGE);
  }
  finally {
    if (writer != null) {
      try {
        writer.close( );
      } catch (IOException x) {}
    }
  }
}
}
}
```

Let's look at a few of the methods from this example. The first interesting method is
called makeActionsPretty( ). This method adds icons to the actions we're going to
display and changes the text for these actions. This way, our user interface displays
nice names like Cut instead of cut-to-clipboard. It uses the ActionMap associated with
the text component to look up the standard actions, as described in Chapter 3.

In createToolBar( ), we get instances of two inner classes, OpenAction and
SaveAction, and add them to our JToolBar. We get these actions by calling
getOpenAction( ) and getSaveAction( ) to allow subclasses to provide different implementations of these actions. We then get the cut, copy, and paste actions. We've
chosen not to display the text for the actions in the toolbar, so we call setText("")
on the JButton returned by each add( ) call. For more details on Swing's handy
JToolBar class, see Chapter 14.

The createMenuBar( ) method is similar to createToolBar( ). We add two additional actions here: exit and select-all. In this method, we don't strip the text from the menu items, allowing both the icon and text to be displayed.

Finally, we define action classes for exiting the application, and for opening and saving files. These last two actions call the JTextComponent's read( ) and write( ) methods, which take advantage of the editor kit's read( ) and write( ) methods. For more details on another handy Swing class we've used here, JFileChooser, see Chapter 12.

If you compare this example to the version from our first edition,* you'll see some good evidence of the maturation of Swing over the last few years. We've been able to remove an entire page of code because of features that Swing now gives us for free. ActionMaps eliminated the need for our own code to organize and look up the text components' Actions. We also had a method that added entries to the component's KeyMap for moving around by word and extending the selection using the keyboard. We made no effort to do this in an L&F-appropriate way. Luckily, the new InputMap associated with JTextArea provides all these capabilities for us, and it is L&F-sensitive. In the Windows, Metal, and Motif L&Fs, you can move the caret a word at a time by holding down Ctrl while pressing an arrow key; in the Mac L&F, the Command key serves this purpose. In all L&Fs, holding down Shift during cursor movement extends the selection in that direction.

The StyledEditorKit Class

StyledEditorKit extends DefaultEditorKit to provide additional features for styled text. It is the kit used by the JTextPane class. Like DefaultEditorKit, this class defines a number of new TextActions. In this class, all of these action classes are public. We'll look at each of them at the end of this section.

Properties

StyledEditorKit defines the properties and default values shown in Table 23-6. The actions property is the set of actions defined for DefaultEditorKit, augmented with actions for setting text alignment and font family, size, and style attributes. The exact actions provided are shown in Table 23-7. In this table, the first column is the inner class name, the next column is the action name (Action.NAME), and the last column lists parameter values passed to the specific action class constructor. Additional actions can be created by instantiating the desired action class and passing different values to the constructor.

---

* You can download the first edition's examples at *http://www.oreilly.com/catalog/jswing*. You'll find *Simple-Editor.java* in in the *ch24* directory.

Table 23-6. StyledEditorKit properties

Property	Data type	get	is	set	Default value
actions[o]	Action[]			•	DefaultEditorKit's actions and 18 more
characterAttributeRun	Element	•			null
inputAttributes	MutableAttributeSet	•			
viewFactory[o]	ViewFactory	•			StyledViewFactory( )

[o]overridden

See also properties from the DefaultEditorKit class (Table 23-4).

Table 23-7. StyledEditorKit default actions

Action name	Action class	Constructor argument
center-justify	AlignmentAction	StyleConstants.ALIGN_CENTER
font-bold	BoldAction	
font-family-Monospaced	FontFamilyAction	"Monospaced"
font-family-SansSerif	FontFamilyAction	"SansSerif"
font-family-Serif	FontFamilyAction	"Serif"
font-italic	ItalicAction	
font-size-8	FontSizeAction	8
font-size-10	FontSizeAction	10
font-size-12	FontSizeAction	12
font-size-14	FontSizeAction	14
font-size-16	FontSizeAction	16
font-size-18	FontSizeAction	18
font-size-24	FontSizeAction	24
font-size-36	FontSizeAction	36
font-size-48	FontSizeAction	48
font-underline	UnderlineAction	
insert-break	StyledInsertBreakAction	
left-justify	AlignmentAction	StyleConstants.ALIGN_LEFT
right-justify	AlignmentAction	StyleConstants.ALIGN_RIGHT

The characterAttributeRun property indicates the Element in which the caret is currently located. This is updated whenever the kit's JEditorPane fires a CaretEvent. Similarly, the inputAttributes property provides access to the attribute set in use at the current caret position. This property is used by the JTextPane class whenever content is added to the document.

The viewFactory defined by StyledEditorKit is an inner class capable of creating View objects for different types of Elements. The View objects created by this factory depend on the name property of the Element passed to the create( ) method, as shown in Table 23-8.

Table 23-8. StyledEditorKit.StyledViewFactory view creation policy

Element name	View class created
AbstractDocument.ContentElementName	LabelView
AbstractDocument.ParagraphElementName	ParagraphView
AbstractDocument.SectionElementName	BoxView
AbstractDocument.ComponentElementName	ComponentView
AbstractDocument.IconElementName	IconView
Other	LabelView

Constructor

public StyledEditorKit( )
> This default constructor provides no behavior.

EditorKit methods

These methods override those defined in DefaultEditorKit or EditorKit:

public Object clone( )
> Return a new StyledEditorKit that is a copy of this editor kit.

public Document createDefaultDocument( )
> Return a new instance of DefaultStyledDocument.

public void install(JEditorPane c)
> Called when the kit is associated with a JEditorPane. It adds itself (actually, an instance of a nonpublic inner class) as a CaretListener of the given pane.

public void deinstall(JEditorPane c)
> Called to indicate that the given pane is no longer using this kit. It removes the caret listener added by install( ).

The StyledEditorKit.StyledTextAction Class

As discussed earlier, StyledEditor defines several public inner classes to perform actions related to styled text. This public abstract class extends TextAction and serves as the base class for all the other action inner classes.

Constructor

public StyledTextAction(String nm)
> Pass the action name up to the superclass.

Protected methods

These protected methods are available to any subclass of StyledTextAction. None of them does anything really new, they just save you a few steps for certain common tasks. If you define your own styled text actions, some of these methods will come in handy.

protected final JEditorPane getEditor(ActionEvent e)
> Provide convenient access to the JEditorPane with which the given event is associated. If neither the event source nor the currently focused component is a JEditorPane, this method throws an IllegalArgumentException.

protected final StyledDocument getStyledDocument(JEditorPane e)
> This convenience method gets the current document from the given pane and returns it as a StyledDocument. If the document is not an instance of StyledDocument (or a subclass), this method throws an IllegalArgumentException.

protected final StyledEditorKit getStyledEditorKit(JEditorPane e)
> This convenience method gets the current editor kit from the given pane and returns it as a StyledEditorKit. If it is not an instance of StyledEditorKit (or a subclass), this method throws an IllegalArgumentException.

protected final void setCharacterAttributes(JEditorPane editor, AttributeSet attr, boolean replace)
> Set the character attributes for the currently selected text, if there is a selection, or the current input attributes. The replace parameter indicates whether the given attributes should replace the existing ones or be added.

protected final void setParagraphAttributes(JEditorPane editor, AttributeSet attr, boolean replace)
> Call setParagraphAttributes( ) for the currently selected range of the given editor pane.

The following seven classes are public, static extensions of the StyledTextAction abstract class. Instances of these classes are provided as default actions for the StyledEditorKit, but you can create additional instances if the exact action you want is not provided as a default. Each class contains only a constructor and its actionPerformed( ) method, so we'll detail only the interesting methods as we did for DefaultEditorKit's actions.

Unless otherwise noted, each of these classes uses the setCharacterAttributes( ) method, defined in StyledTextAction, to update the attributes for the current selection, if there is one, or the attributes for text to be inserted.

The StyledEditorKit.FontFamilyAction class

public FontFamilyAction(String name, String family)
> Create an action with the supplied name to establish the specified font family (SansSerif, Serif, or the like).

public void actionPerformed(ActionEvent e)
> By default, set the current font family to the value established by the constructor. However, if the target of the event matches the current JEditorPane, and the event's actionCommand property is not null, the action command is used as the new font family instead.

The StyledEditorKit.FontSizeAction class

public FontSizeAction(String name, int size)
> Create an action with the specified name and font size.

public void actionPerformed(ActionEvent e)
> By default, set the current font size to the value established by the constructor. However, if the target of the given event matches the current JEditorPane, and the event's actionCommand property is not null, the action command (converted from a String to an int) is used as the new font size instead.

The StyledEditorKit.ForegroundAction class

public ForegroundAction(String name, Color fg)
> Create an action with the specified name and color.

public void actionPerformed(ActionEvent e)
> By default, set the current foreground color to the value established by the constructor. However, if the target of the given event matches the current JEditorPane, and the event's actionCommand property is not null, the action command is used as the new color instead.

> The task of converting the actionCommand string to a Color is handled by the Color.decode( ) method. Typically, colors are written as hexadecimal numbers in which the first eight bits represent red, the next eight represent green, and the last eight represent blue. For example, 0xFF0000 is red, 0x000000 is black, and 0xFF00FF is magenta. All Color.decode( ) does is convert such a string to the corresponding Color.

The StyledEditorKit.AlignmentAction class

public AlignmentAction(String name, int alignment)
> Create an action with the given name and alignment value. The value must be one of the alignment constants defined in SwingConstants: ALIGN_LEFT, ALIGN_CENTER, ALIGN_RIGHT, or ALIGN_JUSTIFIED.

public void actionPerformed(ActionEvent e)

By default, set the current alignment to the value established by the constructor. However, if the target of the given event matches the current JEditorPane, and the event's actionCommand property is not null, the numeric value of the action command (the String is parsed as an int) is used as the new alignment instead.

Note that unlike the other action classes discussed here, this one uses setParagraphAttributes( ) rather than setCharacterAttributes( ) since alignment is a paragraph property.

The StyledEditorKit.BoldAction class

public void actionPerformed(ActionEvent e)

Check the current attribute set to see if the bold attribute is turned on and toggle this value for the current selection or specified attributes.

The StyledEditorKit.ItalicAction class

public void actionPerformed(ActionEvent e)

Check the current input attribute set to see if the italic attribute is turned on and toggle this value for the current selection or input attributes.

The StyledEditorKit.UnderlineAction class

public void actionPerformed(ActionEvent e)

Check the current attribute set to see if the underline attribute is turned on and toggle this value for the current selection or given attributes.

A Better Editor

Earlier in this chapter, we created a class called SimpleEditor that used some of the actions provided by DefaultEditorKit. Now we'll extend that class to create StyleEditor, which uses many of the new actions we've just introduced. When run, StyledEditor looks like Figure 23-5.

There's not a lot in this class that's new. We override several of the methods defined in SimpleEditor to add actions to the toolbar and menu. These include actions for changing the font's style, size, and family. We also take advantage of the text component's InputMap to add new key mappings that change the font style since these aren't built into Swing the way SimpleEditor's actions were. We use the default AWT toolkit's getMenuShortcutKeymask( ) method to accomplish this in an L&F-appropriate manner. Under most L&Fs, the keys Ctrl-B, Ctrl-I, and Ctrl-U toggle bold, italics and underlining while in the Mac L&F, Command-B, Command-I, and Command-U are used instead.

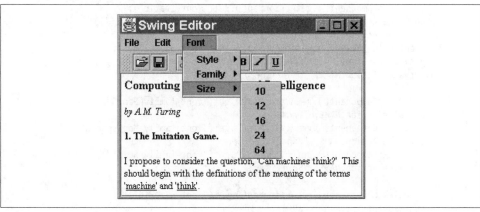

Figure 23-5. StyledEditor: a text editor that supports user-defined styles

Here's the code for our new and improved editor:

```
// StyledEditor.java
//
import javax.swing.*;
import javax.swing.text.*;
import java.awt.event.*;
import java.awt.Toolkit;

// An extension of SimpleEditor that adds styled-text features
public class StyledEditor extends SimpleEditor{

  public static void main(String[] args) {
    StyledEditor editor = new StyledEditor();
    editor.setVisible(true);
    editor.setDefaultCloseOperation(JFrame.EXIT_ON_CLOSE);
  }

  // Create a styed editor.
  public StyledEditor() {
    updateInputMap();  // Install our style-related keystrokes
  }

  // Override to create a JTextPane.
  protected JTextComponent createTextComponent() {
    return new JTextPane();
  }

  // Add icons and friendly names for font actions.
  protected void makeActionsPretty() {
    super.makeActionsPretty();

    Action a;
    a = getTextComponent().getActionMap().get("font-bold");
    a.putValue(Action.SMALL_ICON, new ImageIcon("icons/bold.gif"));
    a.putValue(Action.NAME, "Bold");
```

```
    a = getTextComponent( ).getActionMap( ).get("font-italic");
    a.putValue(Action.SMALL_ICON, new ImageIcon("icons/italic.gif"));
    a.putValue(Action.NAME, "Italic");
    a = getTextComponent( ).getActionMap( ).get("font-underline");
    a.putValue(Action.SMALL_ICON, new ImageIcon("icons/underline.gif"));
    a.putValue(Action.NAME, "Underline");

    a = getTextComponent( ).getActionMap( ).get("font-family-SansSerif");
    a.putValue(Action.NAME, "SansSerif");
    a = getTextComponent( ).getActionMap( ).get("font-family-Monospaced");
    a.putValue(Action.NAME, "Monospaced");
    a = getTextComponent( ).getActionMap( ).get("font-family-Serif");
    a.putValue(Action.NAME, "Serif");

    a = getTextComponent( ).getActionMap( ).get("font-size-10");
    a.putValue(Action.NAME, "10");
    a = getTextComponent( ).getActionMap( ).get("font-size-12");
    a.putValue(Action.NAME, "12");
    a = getTextComponent( ).getActionMap( ).get("font-size-16");
    a.putValue(Action.NAME, "16");
    a = getTextComponent( ).getActionMap( ).get("font-size-24");
    a.putValue(Action.NAME, "24");
  }

  // Add key mappings for font style features.
  protected void updateInputMap( ) {
    // Extend the input map used by our text component.
    InputMap map = getTextComponent( ).getInputMap( );
    int mask = Toolkit.getDefaultToolkit( ).getMenuShortcutKeyMask( );
    KeyStroke bold = KeyStroke.getKeyStroke(KeyEvent.VK_B, mask, false);
    KeyStroke italic = KeyStroke.getKeyStroke(KeyEvent.VK_I, mask, false);
    KeyStroke under = KeyStroke.getKeyStroke(KeyEvent.VK_U, mask, false);
    map.put(bold, "font-bold");
    map.put(italic, "font-italic");
    map.put(under, "font-underline");
  }

  // Add font actions to the toolbar.
  protected JToolBar createToolBar( ) {
    JToolBar bar = super.createToolBar( );
    bar.addSeparator( );

    bar.add(getTextComponent( ).getActionMap( ).get("font-bold")).setText("");
    bar.add(getTextComponent( ).getActionMap( ).get("font-italic")).setText("");
    bar.add(getTextComponent( ).getActionMap( ).get("font-underline")).setText("");

    return bar;
  }

  // Add font actions to the menu.
  protected JMenuBar createMenuBar( ) {
    JMenuBar menubar = super.createMenuBar( );
    JMenu font = new JMenu("Font");
    menubar.add(font);
```

```
        JMenu style = new JMenu("Style");
        JMenu family = new JMenu("Family");
        JMenu size = new JMenu("Size");
        font.add(style);
        font.add(family);
        font.add(size);

        style.add(getTextComponent().getActionMap().get("font-bold"));
        style.add(getTextComponent().getActionMap().get("font-underline"));
        style.add(getTextComponent().getActionMap().get("font-italic"));

        family.add(getTextComponent().getActionMap().get("font-family-SansSerif"));
        family.add(getTextComponent().getActionMap().get("font-family-Monospaced"));
        family.add(getTextComponent().getActionMap().get("font-family-Serif"));

        size.add(getTextComponent().getActionMap().get("font-size-10"));
        size.add(getTextComponent().getActionMap().get("font-size-12"));
        size.add(getTextComponent().getActionMap().get("font-size-16"));
        size.add(getTextComponent().getActionMap().get("font-size-24"));

        // Don't forget that we can define new actions too!
        size.add(new StyledEditorKit.FontSizeAction("64", 64));

        return menubar;
    }
}
```

The last thing we do is create a new action using one of the StyledEditorKit inner classes, to remind ourselves that we're not restricted to those actions defined as defaults by the kit. We're free to create new instances as needed.

Saving styled documents

One feature that's missing from our StyledEditor is the ability to read and write styled text. Unfortunately, StyledEditorKit does not override the read() and write() methods, so any documents saved from our StyledEditor are saved as plain text. To fix this problem, we'd ideally want to create a new editor kit that saved all the Style and Element information associated with the Document.

For now, we'll provide an alternative solution by extending our editor once again and adding the ability to serialize the Document object to a file and then read it back in.* Note that we'll actually serialize all the attribute and style information that is part

---

* It's worth mentioning two drawbacks to this strategy. First, serialization saves the state of the entire Document object. This is less efficient than designing your own representation for saving a document—though these days, when one common word processor routinely produces large files for relatively small documents, this disadvantage might not be significant. More important, serialization from one version of Java is not likely to be compatible with another. So you could save a document with this editor running under 1.3, upgrade to 1.4, and find that you can't read any documents you saved. Java is moving to a more durable XML- and JavaBeans-based file format, but DefaultStyledDocument doesn't yet expose enough of its contents to work this way.

of the document. We can't do the same sort of thing in an editor kit subclass because the editor kit's read( ) methods are set up to read the contents of a file into an *existing* document. Serializing the entire document and then reading it back would not fit this model, since the process of reading a serialized object creates a new document.

Here's the source for an editor that allows styled documents to be saved and opened without losing their text attributes. All we've done is provided new implementations of the getSaveAction( ) and getOpenAction( ) methods and defined the new actions returned by these methods.

```java
// IOStyledEditor.java
//
import javax.swing.*;
import javax.swing.text.*;
import java.awt.event.*;
import java.io.*;

// An extension of StyledEditor that adds document serialization
public class IOStyledEditor extends StyledEditor {

  public static void main(String[] args) {
    IOStyledEditor te = new IOStyledEditor( );
    te.setDefaultCloseOperation(JFrame.EXIT_ON_CLOSE);
    te.setVisible(true);
  }

  // Provide a new open action.
  protected Action getOpenAction( ) {
    if (inAction == null)
      inAction = new InAction( );
    return inAction;
  }

  // Provide a new save action.
  protected Action getSaveAction( ) {
    if (outAction == null)
      outAction = new OutAction( );
    return outAction;
  }

  private Action inAction;
  private Action outAction;

  // An action that saves the document as a serialized object
  class OutAction extends AbstractAction {
    public OutAction( ) {
      super("Serialize Out", new ImageIcon("icons/save.gif"));
    }

    public void actionPerformed(ActionEvent ev) {
      JFileChooser chooser = new JFileChooser( );
      if (chooser.showSaveDialog(IOStyledEditor.this) !=
          JFileChooser.APPROVE_OPTION)
```

```
        return;
      File file = chooser.getSelectedFile();
      if (file == null)
        return;

      FileOutputStream writer = null;
      try {
        Document doc = getTextComponent().getDocument();
        writer = new FileOutputStream(file);
        ObjectOutputStream oos = new ObjectOutputStream(writer);
        oos.writeObject(doc);  // Write the document.
      }
      catch (IOException ex) {
        JOptionPane.showMessageDialog(IOStyledEditor.this,
        "File Not Saved", "ERROR", JOptionPane.ERROR_MESSAGE);
      }
      finally {
        if (writer != null) {
          try {
            writer.close();
          } catch (IOException x) {}
        }
      }
    }
  }

// An action that reads the document as a serialized object
class InAction extends AbstractAction {
  public InAction() {
    super("Serialize In", new ImageIcon("icons/open.gif"));
  }
  public void actionPerformed(ActionEvent ev) {
    JFileChooser chooser = new JFileChooser();
    if (chooser.showOpenDialog(IOStyledEditor.this) !=
        JFileChooser.APPROVE_OPTION)
      return;
    File file = chooser.getSelectedFile();
    if (file == null)
      return;
    FileInputStream reader = null;
    try {
      reader = new FileInputStream(file);
      ObjectInputStream ois = new ObjectInputStream(reader);
      Object o = ois.readObject();  // Read the document.
      getTextComponent().setDocument((Document)o);
    }
    catch (IOException ex) {
      JOptionPane.showMessageDialog(IOStyledEditor.this,
      "File Input Error", "ERROR", JOptionPane.ERROR_MESSAGE);
    }
    catch (ClassNotFoundException ex) {
      JOptionPane.showMessageDialog(IOStyledEditor.this,
      "Class Not Found", "ERROR", JOptionPane.ERROR_MESSAGE);
    }
```

```
        finally {
          if (reader != null) {
            try {
              reader.close( );
            } catch (IOException x) {}
          }
        }
      }
    }
  }
```

As you can see from the code, all we've done is take advantage of the fact that the Swing document classes are serializable. This allows us to write the Document model out to a file and read it back in without losing any of the information contained in the model. If something goes wrong while reading or writing the file, an appropriate warning dialog pops up using the JOptionPane class from Chapter 10.

HTML and JEditorPane

As we discussed in Chapter 19, Swing provides (somewhat spotty) support for working with the Web's most common markup language, HTML. Fortunately, as Swing matures, the HTML support in the JEditorPane class improves.

The support for reading, writing, and displaying HTML through the JEditorPane class is provided by the HTMLEditorKit and associated classes. This class is an extension of the generic DefaultEditorKit class and is devoted (not surprisingly) to HTML files. You might recall from the previous discussion of EditorKit that there are three basic parts of an editor kit: its parser, its file writer, and its association with a ViewFactory. While we have looked briefly at these pieces before, here we focus on their implementation in HTMLEditorKit.

Along the way, we'll see how to extend some of these pieces to do custom work in the context of an HTML document. We decided that a detailed discussion of the classes that extend the editor kit would not be interesting to a majority of our readers, so we concentrate on the more immediately useful classes. However, if you want to see the details and play with the internals of the HTMLEditorKit, we have two entire chapters devoted to this topic on the book's web site (*http://www.oreilly.com/catalog/ jswing2*). Throughout this discussion, we'll point you to that material if you want more detail than we've provided here.

Much of the information in those chapters describes how you can extend HTML with custom tags. Adding custom tags to HTML is not really a good idea in most cases. You are better off using XML, which is by definition extensible, for that purpose. A great book to start with is *Java and XML* by Brett McLaughlin—from O'Reilly, of course.

If you're just looking for basic HTML editing and rendering, you'll be in good shape after reading the rest of this chapter. If you need to support custom tags or write your own ViewFactory, grab the online chapters.

A Quick Browser Example

Before we get down to business on the API, here's an example of the HTMLEditorKit's power. In a very small amount of code, we can create a web browser. This mini-browser contains nothing more than two labels, a text field, and a JEditorPane controlled by the HTMLEditorKit. The browser is similar to the very first example in this chapter, but we've added the ability to enter URLs, and we show the destination URL in the status bar whenever you mouse over a hyperlink. (We also added support for hyperlinks inside HTML frames.)

We'll cover all the parts in more detail, but if you can't wait to get started with your own browser, pay special attention to the *SimpleLinkListener.java* file. That's where most of the real work in this example occurs.* If all you need to do is display HTML text in your application, this is the example to look at (or perhaps the even simpler one at the start of the chapter).

Here's the code for this mini-browser. The first file, *MiniBrowser.java*, sets up the basic Swing components you can see in Figure 23-6, namely a text field for entering new URLs, a JEditorPane for displaying the current page, and a label at the bottom of the frame to function as the status bar. (The status bar reflects the "go to" URL when you place your mouse cursor over a hyperlink.) The second file, *SimpleLinkListener.java*, handles the hyperlink events.

```
// MiniBrowser.java
//
import javax.swing.*;
import javax.swing.text.*;
import java.awt.event.*;
import java.awt.*;
import java.io.File;

public class MiniBrowser extends JFrame {

  private JEditorPane jep;

  public MiniBrowser(String startingUrl) {
    // First, just get a screen up and visible, with an appropriate handler in place
    // for the kill window command.
```

---

* The original version of this browser appeared in Marc's article, "Patch the Swing HTMLEditorKit," *Java-World,* January 1999 (*http://www.javaworld.com/javaworld/jw-01-1999/jw-01-swing.html*). Our derivative code is used with permission. Thanks also to Mats Forslöf (at Marcwell, in Sweden) for his improvements to the original version. Feel free to check out the article, but be aware that the patch mentioned fixes a pre-1.3 bug.

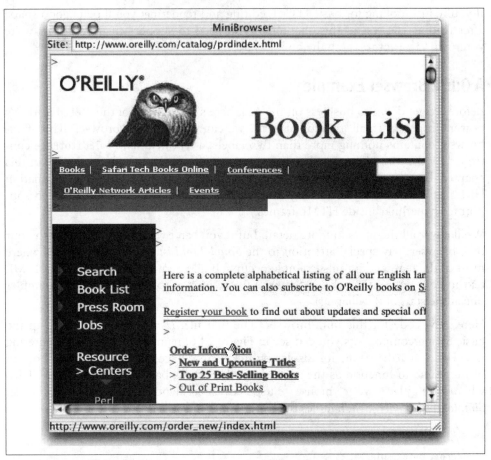

Figure 23-6. MiniBrowser on a Mac OS X system displaying www.oreilly.com

```
super("MiniBrowser");
setSize(400,300);
setDefaultCloseOperation(EXIT_ON_CLOSE);

// Now set up our basic screen components, the editor pane, the text field for
// URLs, and the label for status and link information.
JPanel urlPanel = new JPanel();
urlPanel.setLayout(new BorderLayout());
JTextField urlField = new JTextField(startingUrl);
urlPanel.add(new JLabel("Site: "), BorderLayout.WEST);
urlPanel.add(urlField, BorderLayout.CENTER);
final JLabel statusBar = new JLabel(" ");

// Here's the editor pane configuration. It's important to make the
// "setEditable(false)" call; otherwise, our hyperlinks won't work. (If the text
// is editable, then clicking on a hyperlink simply means that you want to change
// the text, not follow the link.)
jep = new JEditorPane();
jep.setEditable(false);
```

```
      try {
        jep.setPage(startingUrl);
      }
      catch(Exception e) {
        statusBar.setText("Could not open starting page.  Using a blank.");
      }
      JScrollPane jsp = new JScrollPane(jep);

      // Get the GUI components onto our content pane.
      getContentPane( ).add(jsp, BorderLayout.CENTER);
      getContentPane( ).add(urlPanel, BorderLayout.NORTH);
      getContentPane( ).add(statusBar, BorderLayout.SOUTH);

      // Last but not least, hook up our event handlers.
      urlField.addActionListener(new ActionListener( ) {
        public void actionPerformed(ActionEvent ae) {
          try {
            jep.setPage(ae.getActionCommand( ));
          }
          catch(Exception e) {
            statusBar.setText("Error: " + e.getMessage( ));
          }
        }
      });
      jep.addHyperlinkListener(new SimpleLinkListener(jep, urlField, statusBar));
  }

  public static void main(String args[]) {
    String url = "";
    if (args.length == 1) {
      url = args[0];
      if (!(url.startsWith("http:") || url.startsWith("file:"))) {
        // If it's not a fully qualified URL, assume it's a file.
        if (url.startsWith("/")) {
          // Absolute path, so just prepend "file:"
          url = "file:" + url;
        }
        else {
          try {
            // Assume it's relative to the starting point.
            File f = new File(url);
            url = f.toURL( ).toString( );
          }
          catch (Exception e) {
            url = "http://www.oreilly.com/";
          }
        }
      }
    }
    else {
      url = "http://www.oreilly.com/";
    }
    new MiniBrowser(url).setVisible(true);
  }
}
```

Here's *SimpleLinkListener.java*. Notice that the "entered" and "exited" event handlers do not bother with the mouse cursor. As of SDK 1.3, the mouse cursor is automatically updated as you enter and exit hyperlinks. All we do is update the status bar. Don't worry too much about the hyperlink handling; we'll tackle that topic in the next section. We hope that you have seen enough event-handling code in Java to find this class familiar without reading the details yet.

```java
// SimpleLinkListener.java
// A hyperlink listener for use with JEditorPane. This listener changes the cursor
// over hyperlinks based on enter/exit events and also loads a new page when a valid
// hyperlink is clicked.
import java.awt.*;
import java.awt.event.*;
import java.io.*;
import java.util.*;
import javax.swing.*;
import javax.swing.event.*;
import javax.swing.text.*;
import javax.swing.text.html.*;

public class SimpleLinkListener implements HyperlinkListener {

  private JEditorPane pane;        // The pane we're using to display HTML

  private JTextField  urlField;    // An optional text field for showing the current
                                   // URL being displayed

  private JLabel statusBar;        // An optional label for showing where a link would
                                   // take you

  public SimpleLinkListener(JEditorPane jep, JTextField jtf, JLabel jl) {
    pane = jep;
    urlField = jtf;
    statusBar = jl;
  }

  public SimpleLinkListener(JEditorPane jep) {
    this(jep, null, null);
  }

  public void hyperlinkUpdate(HyperlinkEvent he) {
    HyperlinkEvent.EventType type = he.getEventType();
    if (type == HyperlinkEvent.EventType.ENTERED) {
      // Enter event. Fill in the status bar.
      if (statusBar != null) {
        statusBar.setText(he.getURL().toString());
      }
    }
    else if (type == HyperlinkEvent.EventType.EXITED) {
      // Exit event. Clear the status bar.
      if (statusBar != null) {
        statusBar.setText(" "); // Must be a space or it disappears
      }
```

```
    }
    else if (type == HyperlinkEvent.EventType.ACTIVATED) {
      // Jump event. Get the URL and, if it's not null, switch to that page in the
      // main editor pane and update the "site url" label.
      if (he instanceof HTMLFrameHyperlinkEvent) {
        // Ahh, frame event; handle this separately.
        HTMLFrameHyperlinkEvent  evt = (HTMLFrameHyperlinkEvent)he;
        HTMLDocument doc = (HTMLDocument)pane.getDocument();
        doc.processHTMLFrameHyperlinkEvent(evt);
      } else {
        try {
          pane.setPage(he.getURL());
          if (urlField != null) {
            urlField.setText(he.getURL().toString());
          }
        }
        catch (FileNotFoundException fnfe) {
          pane.setText("Could not open file: <tt>" + he.getURL() +
                      "</tt>.<hr>");
        }
        catch (Exception e) {
          e.printStackTrace();
        }
      }
    }
  }
}
```

Hyperlink Events

JEditorPanes fire a type of event called a HyperlinkEvent. Typically, this event is fired when the user clicks on a hyperlink in the currently displayed document; the program normally responds by loading a new page. To support this event type, a related event class and listener interface are available in the javax.swing.event package.

The HyperlinkListener Interface

The HyperlinkListener interface (found in javax.swing.event) defines a single method, used to respond to hyperlink activations:

public abstract void hyperlinkUpdate(HyperlinkEvent e)

> Called to indicate that a hyperlink request has been made. Typical implementations of this method obtain the new URL from the event and call setPage() on the associated JEditorPane. See the JEditorPane example earlier in the chapter to learn how this method can be used.

The HyperlinkEvent Class

The HyperlinkEvent class (found in javax.swing.event) describes a hyperlink request.

Properties

HyperlinkEvent defines the properties shown in Table 23-9. The URL property contains a java.net.URL object that can be used to retrieve URL content represented by the event. The description property allows a description of the link (typically, the text of the hyperlink) to be supplied. This can be useful when the URL property is null, such as when the hyperlink can't be parsed well enough to create a URL object. The eventType property defines the type of event that has occurred.

Table 23-9. HyperlinkEvent properties

Property	Data type	get	is	set	Default value
description	String	•			null
eventType	HyperlinkEvent.EventType	•			From constructor
sourceElement[1.4]	Element	•			null
URL	java.net.URL	•			From constructor

[1.4]since 1.4

See also the java.util.EventObject class (not covered in this book).

Constructors

public HyperlinkEvent(Object source, HyperlinkEvent.EventType type, URL u)
public HyperlinkEvent(Object source, HyperlinkEvent.EventType type, URL u,
  String desc)
public HyperlinkEvent(Object source, HyperlinkEvent.EventType type, URL u,
  String desc, Element sourceElement)
    Create a new event with the specified properties. The u argument represents the destination of the link. The value of the type parameter is taken from the constant values defined in the HyperlinkEvent.EventType class: ENTERED, EXITED, and ACTIVATED. The desc parameter is optional. The sourceElement argument is also optional (and can be null). It represents the originating anchor Element from the HTML Document.

Inner classes

public static final class EventType
    This simple inner class is a type-safe enumeration that defines three constants of type HyperlinkEvent.EventType. These constants are ENTERED, EXITED, and, ACTIVATED. As the cursor enters and exits a hyperlinked area of the document,

ENTERED and EXITED events are fired. The ACTIVATED constant indicates that a hyperlink has been activated (clicked) by the user.

Prior to the 1.3 release of the SDK, ENTERED and EXITED events were not fired. The aforementioned January 1999 *JavaWorld* article discusses a workaround for the 1.2 and 1.1 releases.

The HTMLFrameHyperlinkEvent Class

Another event that can arrive at your doorstep in the hyperlinkUpdate( ) method is the HTMLFrameHyperlinkEvent class from the javax.swing.text.html package. (We know, we know. Why isn't it part of the event package? Well, it is quite specific to HTML content whereas the concept of a hyperlink is supposed to be more generic.) This event is similar in content and purpose to the regular HyperlinkEvent and indeed extends that class. It carries information relating to HTML frames—specifically, the target frame for the hyperlink. target is the one new property this class adds, as shown in Table 23-10

Table 23-10. HTMLFrameHyperlinkEvent property

Property	Data type	get	is	set	Default value
target	String	•			null

See also the javax.swing.HyperlinkEvent class (Table 23-9).

If you look back at the code for the SimpleLinkListener class, you can see where we look for this type of event. ENTERED and EXITED hyperlink events are treated the same—we just update our status bar. However, if the user activates a link, we need to see where its destination lies. If the link is an instance of HTMLFrameHyperlinkEvent, we have to treat it differently. Fortunately, we don't have to do much work. The HTMLDocument class knows how to handle these events, so we just pass it to our document.

We should note a few things about frame-related hyperlink events. They are not well-supported in SDK 1.2. They do exist there, but are probably best left out of the picture. Even in the 1.4 release, these events are not handled as gracefully as you might hope. For example, the _blank target does not open a new window in the current implementation of JEditorPane. To support such a target, you would need to monitor the target property of any incoming ACTIVATED HTMLFrameHyperlinkEvent object and launch your own new window if necessary.

The HTMLEditorKit Class

The API for the HTMLEditorKit is more or less what you might expect from an editor kit if you made it through Chapters 19–22 on Swing text components. We'll take a brief look at the API and then go through examples of how to work with this editor kit.

Inner Classes

As you can see in Figure 23-7, HTMLEditorKit defines several inner classes. These inner classes are integral to the display and editing of HTML content. While we don't want to spend too much time on the details of these classes, you should know about them. We list them here as a quick reference.

public static class HTMLEditorKit.HTMLFactory
   The view factory implementation for HTML.

public static class HTMLEditorKit.HTMLTextAction
   An Action for inserting HTML into an existing document.

public static class HTMLEditorKit.InsertHTMLTextAction
   An extension of HTMLTextAction that allows you to insert arbitrary HTML content. This one is quite handy. For example, we can create an action for a toolbar or menu that inserts a copyright:

```
private final static String COPY_HTML =
    "<p>&copy; 2002, O'Reilly &amp; Associates</p>";
Action a = new HTMLEditorKit.InsertHTMLTextAction("InsertCopyright",
    COPY_HTML, HTML.Tag.BODY, HTML.Tag.P);
a.putValue(Action.SMALL_ICON, new ImageIcon("icons/cpyrght.gif"));
a.putValue(Action.NAME, "Copyright Text");
```

   The action can be added to a toolbar or menu, just like the others in the StyledEditor example. We end up with a one-touch button that adds our copyright information to the page.

public static class HTMLEditorKit.LinkController
   The event listener that translates mouse events into the (often) more desirable HyperlinkEvents.

public static class HTMLEditorKit.Parser
   A parser to read an input stream of HTML.

public static class HTMLEditorKit.ParserCallback
   An implementation of a callback for use while loading an HTML document.

Properties

Apart from some of the obvious properties you might expect from an editor kit—the content type and parser, for example—several other display properties for HTML documents are present in the HTMLEditorKit class. These properties are shown in Table 23-11.

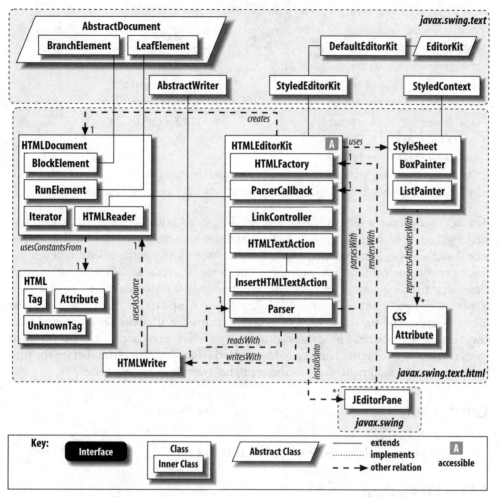

Figure 23-7. *HTMLEditorKit class diagram*

Table 23-11. *HTMLEditorKit properties*

Property	Data type	get	is	set	Default value
actionsº	Action[]	•			Standard text actions plus HTML-specific actions*
contentTypeº	String	•			"text/html"
defaultCursor[1.3]	Cursor	•		•	System default cursor
inputAttributes	MutableAttributeSet	•			Defined by default.css†

[1.3]since 1.3, ºoverridden

*See Appendix B for a list of these actions.

†This file is in the *javax/swing/text/html* directory and is most often pulled from the *rt.jar* file.

See also properties from the EditorKit class (Table 23-3) and the StyledEditorKit class (Table 23-6).

Table 23-11. HTMLEditorKit properties (continued)

Property	Data type	get	is	set	Default value
linkCursor[1.3]	Cursor	•		•	System "hand" cursor
parser	HTMLEditorKit.Parser	•			ParserDelegate( )
styleSheet	StyleSheet	•		•	Defined by default.css[†]
viewFactory[o]	ViewFactory	•			HTMLFactory( )

[1.3]since 1.3, [o]overridden

*See Appendix B for a list of these actions.

†This file is in the *javax/swing/text/html* directory and is most often pulled from the *rt.jar* file.

See also properties from the EditorKit class (Table 23-3) and the StyledEditorKit class (Table 23-6).

The actions property lists available text actions. In addition to standard actions like making text bold or italic, the HTML additions let you insert images, horizontal rules, and anchors (among other things). The editor kit stores the MIME type for the document in the contentType property. The defaultCursor and linkCursor properties dictate the cursor to be displayed over normal text (defaultCursor) and over hyperlinks (linkCursor). As of SDK 1.3, the visual update of the cursor happens automatically. The inputAttributes property returns the attribute set associated with the current stylesheet. The parser property provides easy access to the installed parser that reads content. The styleSheet and viewFactory properties dictate the presentation of the document. Both of these can be overridden in subclasses.

Constructor

public HTMLEditorKit( )
> Construct a simple instance of the HTMLEditorKit class.

Editor Kit Methods

If you intend to create your own subclass of the HTMLEditorKit, these methods will come in handy. Overriding them allows you to control exactly which steps from the parent class are performed.

public void install(JEditorPane c)
> Called when the editor kit is associated with an editor pane. This is where the default link controller is attached to the editor pane so that hyperlink activity is reported to any HyperlinkListener objects correctly.

public void deinstall(JEditorPane c)
> Called to remove an editor kit from an editor pane if, for example, a new, non-HTML document is loaded into the pane.

HTML Document Methods

These methods allow you to create, modify, and save HTML documents program-matically. Again, if you want to simply *display* HTML text in a JEditorPane, none of these are necessary.

public Document createDefaultDocument()
> Create a blank document that you can use to build an HTML page from scratch. HTML can be inserted using the insertHTML() method.

public void insertHTML(HTMLDocument doc, int offset, String html, int popDepth,
> *int pushDepth, HTML.Tag insertTag) throws BadLocationException, IOException*
>> Insert HTML into an existing document. You can insert images, formatted text, or even hyperlinks. The doc is the document where the html will be inserted. popDepth and pushDepth indicate how many closing and opening tags, respec-tively, are required to insert the html. For just a simple insert, both can be 0. The insertTag parameter dictates the tag associated with the HTML in the docu-ment hierarchy—obviously closely associated with the html you supply. Insert-ing content beyond the end or before the beginning of the document throws a BadLocationException.

public void read(Reader in, Document doc, int pos)
> *throws IOException, BadLocationException*
>> Manually read HTML text into an existing document starting at pos. The Reader supplied (in) should not have a parser attached to it, as the parser from the edi-tor kit is used.

public void write(Writer out, Document doc, int pos, int len)
> *throws IOException, BadLocationException*
>> Save some or all of a document as HTML. To save the entire document, pos should start at 0 and len should be doc.length(). Examples of the read() and write() methods appear in "Editing HTML" later in this chapter.

Extending HTMLEditorKit

As a quick example of how we might extend this class to add some functionality of our own, let's look at an editor kit that spits out debugging information as we load documents. This allows us to see the steps involved in extending an editor kit, and it leaves us with a very useful tool for implementing other extensions (such as custom tags and attributes).

The first step, of course, is to create our extended editor kit. In this example, we cre-ate a debugging editor kit that spits out the styles loaded and the individual tags it passes by. Here's the code:

```
// DebugHTMLEditorKit.java
// A simple extension of the HTMLEditor kit that uses a verbose ViewFactory.
```

```
import javax.swing.*;
import javax.swing.text.*;
import javax.swing.text.html.*;
import javax.swing.event.*;
import java.awt.event.*;
import java.awt.*;
import java.io.Serializable;
import java.net.*;

public class DebugHTMLEditorKit extends HTMLEditorKit {
  public static HTML.Tag ORA = new HTML.UnknownTag("ora");
  public static AttributeSet currentAnchor;

  public void install(JEditorPane paneEditor) {
    super.install(paneEditor);
    StyleSheet ss = getStyleSheet();
    java.util.Enumeration e = ss.getStyleNames();
    while (e.hasMoreElements()) {
      System.out.println(e.nextElement());
    }
  }

  public ViewFactory getViewFactory() {
    return new VerboseViewFactory();
  }

  public static class VerboseViewFactory extends HTMLEditorKit.HTMLFactory
  {
    public View create(Element elem) {
      System.out.print("Element: " + elem.getName());
      Object o=elem.getAttributes().
        getAttribute(StyleConstants.NameAttribute);
      HTML.Tag kind = (HTML.Tag) o;
      System.out.println(" view as: " + o);
      dumpElementAttributes(elem);
      return super.create(elem);
    }

    private void dumpElementAttributes(Element elem) {
      AttributeSet attrs = elem.getAttributes();
      java.util.Enumeration names = attrs.getAttributeNames();
      while (names.hasMoreElements()) {
        Object key = names.nextElement();
        System.out.println("  " + key + " : " + attrs.getAttribute(key));
      }
      try {
        System.out.println("  " +
          elem.getDocument().getText(elem.getStartOffset(),
            elem.getEndOffset()));
      } catch (Exception e) { // We don't deal with null elements for now.
      }
    }
  }
}
```

Two methods extend `HTMLEditorKit`. First, we override the `install()` method to print our style information. Notice that we still call `super.install()`. Without that call, we would lose the hyperlink functionality. (Sometimes you want that—we'll see an example of modifying hyperlink behavior later in the chapter.)

Next, we override `getViewFactory()` to return an instance of our own factory (written as an inner class). In our case, we use the `create()` method as a springboard to dump debugging information for each document element that passes through. At the end, we return the standard view that `HTMLEditorKit` normally produces. It's in this method that you can send back any custom view factory you like. If you need to support a specific L&F that you can't get from a regular browser and stylesheets through HTML, a custom `ViewFactory` and `HTMLEditorKit` may be the ticket.

The HTMLDocument Class

While the editor kit is interesting in its own right, we can't do much beyond displaying web pages without looking at the `HTMLDocument` class. This class supports the basic structure of HTML pages. From this class you can view and manipulate the content of a given web page. Not coincidentally, this turns out to be handy for editing documents we plan to save as HTML.

Properties

The properties for `HTMLDocument` shown in Table 23-12 help define the appearance and behavior of the document.

Table 23-12. HTMLDocument properties

Property	Data type	get	is	set	Default value
base	URL	•		•	null
parser[1.3]	HTMLEditorKit.Parser	•		•	null*
preservesUnknownTags	boolean	•		•	true
styleSheet	StyleSheet	•			
tokenThreshold	int	•		•	Integer.MAX_VALUE

[1.3]since 1.3

*Set by `HTMLEdtiorKit.createDefaultDocument`

See also properties from the `DefaultStyledDocument` class (Table 22-25).

The base property reflects the base URL for relative hyperlink references. If you use the `setPage()` method of `JEditorPane`, this property is defined automatically from the HTML source. In other cases (such as manually reading an input stream), you may need to define this value yourself. The `tokenThreshold` property determines when page display begins. If you want some of your page to display as soon as possible, pick a relatively low value for this property. The default for `Integer.MAX_VALUE` is to wait for the entire document to load. The read-only `styleSheet` property gives you access to the stylesheet installed from the editor kit. You can change the initial stylesheet during the construction of this class, but you can also override individual styles defined in the current stylesheet at any time. The last property, `preservesUnknownTags`, determines whether non-HTML tags are kept in the document. If you turn off this feature, writing your document to an HTML file expunges unrecognized tags. (See the Javadoc for `HTML.Tag` for a list of recognized tags. The `HTML` class is covered next.)

Constructors

public HTMLDocument( )
public HTMLDocument(StyleSheet styles)
public HTMLDocument(AbstractDocument.Content c, StyleSheet styles)
> Create new `HTMLDocument` objects. The first constructor uses the default stylesheet from the `HTMLEditorKit`. Alternatively, you can supply your own stylesheet, or your own content model and stylesheet, respectively. The content model allows you to supply your own variation on HTML content, but we recommend sticking with the default model.

Public content methods

public void setParagraphAttributes(int offset, int length, AttributeSet s,
  boolean replace)
> Set the attribute(s) associated with the paragraph containing `offset`. If `replace` is `false`, `s` is merged with existing attributes. The `length` argument determines how many characters are affected by the new attributes. This is often the entire paragraph.

public void insertAfterEnd(Element elem, String htmlText)
  throws BadLocationException, IOException
public void insertAfterStart(Element elem, String htmlText)
  throws BadLocationException, IOException
public void insertBeforeEnd(Element elem, String htmlText)
  throws BadLocationException, IOException
public void insertBeforeStart(Element elem, String htmlText)
  throws BadLocationException, IOException
> Insert `htmlText` at the respective point (after the end, before the start, etc.) relative to `elem`. Note that `elem` cannot be a leaf for the `insertAfterStart( )` and `insertBeforeEnd( )` methods.

public void setInnerHTML(Element elem, String htmlText)
   throws BadLocationException, IOException
      Replace the children of `elem` with `htmlText`.

public void setOuterHTML(Element elem, String htmlText)
   throws BadLocationException, IOException
      Replace `elem` in its parent with `htmlText`.

The HTML Class

`HTMLEditorKit` and `HTMLDocument` are by far the most important classes in the `javax.swing.text.html` package. If you are working on custom editors or browsers, you will become quite familiar with these classes. Beyond these, though, are several important supporting classes, one of which is the `HTML` class, a small helper class that is still integral to the use of `HTMLEditorKit` and `HTMLDocument`.

Inner classes

The `HTML` class defines three inner classes. Tags and attributes each have their own subclasses of these inner classes. We won't go into detail about these inner classes here. You can find that information in the HTML Editor Kit chapters on the book's web site.

public static class HTML.Attribute
   Provide a template for creating a list of HTML attributes. Note that simply having an attribute in the list does not imply that it is supported by the `HTMLEditorKit`.

public static class HTML.Tag
   Provide a type for creating a list of HTML tags. Note that simply having a tag in the list does not imply that it is supported by the `HTMLEditorKit`. For example, the `<applet>` tag is defined but not supported when displaying HTML documents.

public static class HTML.UnknownTag
   This subclass of `HTML.Tag` allows the parser to produce valid entries for custom tags without modifying the parser. Any tag not recognized is created as an `UnknownTag` with a name corresponding to that used in the HTML document. For example, we could add `<ora>` tags to a document, and we would see them pass through the editor kit as `UnknownTag` objects. We have an example of using this class in the material on the web site, but if you are serious about custom tags, you should explore the XML tools available for Java, especially those included in SDK 1.4.

The StyleSheet Class

The last big piece of the HTML display puzzle is the StyleSheet class. This class defines the mechanisms for supporting cascading stylesheets. A stylesheet lists the formats available in a document along with the display characteristics of those formats. For example, it could dictate that all <p> paragraphs use 14-point Helvetica, all <h1> text use 28-point Helvetica, and all <h2> text use italicized 20-point Helvetica. This is, of course, an incomplete list, but you get the idea.

The Javadoc acknowledges that stylesheet support is incomplete in SDK 1.4. Each successive release of the swing.text.html package has included remarkable improvements. If you rely on this package for part of your application, you should make sure you have the latest possible version of Java. However, despite incomplete stylesheet support, you can still put it to use in your own applications. We look at an example of modifying the look of a standard HTML document through stylesheets at the end of this section.

Properties

The StyleSheet class defines a few properties, as shown in Table 23-13.

Table 23-13. StyleSheet properties

Property	Data Type	get	is	set	Default Value
base	URL	•		•	null
baseFontSize	int, String*			•	4
styleSheets	StyleSheet[]	•			null

*This property can be set as either an int or a String.

The baseFontSize property allows you to dictate the base font size for styles. The base size is used for normal <p> text, with larger fonts used for headers and smaller fonts used for sub- and superscripts. This font size is also the base for relative font sizes specified via <font> tags. The base property is the URL root for any relative URLs defined in the document. This property is normally set via the setPage( ) method of JEditorPane or the <base> header tag, but can be set manually if you are building a new document from scratch. You can use these two properties without creating a formal stylesheet. The styleSheets property returns an array of contained stylesheets. stylesheets can be arranged in a hierarchy to make construction and maintenance easier.

We have more detailed examples of altering HTML styles through the StyleSheet class in the chapter on the web site.

Editing HTML

Generally, editor kits serve as a collection point for everything you would need to read, write, edit, and display some type of content. The HTMLEditorKit in particular serves as just such a collection point for HTML content. In addition to the HTMLEditorKit class proper, several supporting classes aid in the process of reading HTML, displaying it in the framework of JEditorPane, and writing it to a stream. Specifically, we look at the javax.swing.text.html.parser package and the HTMLWriter class. The APIs for this section remain a bit opaque, but as we mentioned earlier, each new release of the SDK comes with increased support, functionality, and openness.

If you're not interested in the hows and wheres of reading and writing HTML, but still want to be able to edit HTML documents, go ahead and dive into this example. We extend the SimpleEditor from earlier in this chapter to support two things:

- More HTML actions, including horizontal rules, images, and hyperlinks
- A Save menu item to write the document as HTML

To get started, Figure 23-8 is a screenshot of our editor in action. The document you see was created from scratch using the editor.

Figure 23-8. The SimpleEditor extended to support HTML

Here's the HTML generated when you save the document:

```
<html>
  <head>

  </head>
  <body>
    <p>
      This is some simple text.
    </p>
    <hr>
```

```
    And <a href="http://www.ora.com">this is a link</a>.
    <p>
      Here's a picture:
      <img src="http://www.ora.com/animals/javasoap_red_firefish_flip.gif">

    </p>

  </body>
</html>
```

Not bad, eh? Not perfect, but certainly passable for prototypes and internal applications.

Let's look at the classes involved in this application, which is primarily the same as the StyledEditor. The primary change comes from the new actions we support. Rather than repeat the entire code for the editor (*HTMLEditor.java* in the source archive), we can concentrate on three specific actions: ImageAction, SaveAction, and TagAction.

Hyperlink Actions

The TagAction class supports the most interesting of the editor actions. You can create actions for any HTML tag that uses one (primary) attribute. In our simple editor, the only such tag of interest is the <a> tag, but this is still a popular tag. We create two separate instances of TagAction for the <a> tag: one for the href attribute version, and one for the name attribute. Here's the code for creating the actions:

```
a = new TagAction(HTML.Tag.A, "URL", HTML.Attribute.HREF);
a.putValue(Action.SMALL_ICON, new ImageIcon("icons/link.gif"));
a.putValue(Action.NAME, "Anchor Link");
a = new TagAction(HTML.Tag.A, "Name", HTML.Attribute.NAME);
a.putValue(Action.SMALL_ICON, new ImageIcon("icons/anchor.gif"));
a.putValue(Action.NAME, "Anchor Name");
```

These actions can then be stuffed back into the action hashtable we use for all the predefined text actions found in the StyledEditorKit.

The code for the TagAction class itself is fairly straightforward because we rely primarily on StyledEditorKit.StyledTextAction as a starting point:

```
public class TagAction extends StyledEditorKit.StyledTextAction {
  private HTML.Tag tag;
  private HTML.Attribute tagAttr;
  private String tagName;

  public TagAction(HTML.Tag t, String s, HTML.Attribute a) {
    super(s);
    tag = t;
    tagName = s;
    tagAttr = a;
  }
```

```
      public void actionPerformed(ActionEvent e) {
        JEditorPane editor = getEditor(e);
        if (editor != null) {
          String value = JOptionPane.showInputDialog(HTMLEditor.this,
            "Enter " + tagName +":");
          StyledEditorKit kit = getStyledEditorKit(editor);
          MutableAttributeSet attr = kit.getInputAttributes();
          boolean anchor = attr.isDefined(tag);
          if (anchor) {
            attr.removeAttribute(tag);
          }
          else {
            SimpleAttributeSet as = new SimpleAttributeSet();
            as.addAttribute(tagAttr, value);
            attr.addAttribute(tag, as);
          }
          setCharacterAttributes(editor, attr, false);
        }
      }
    }
```

This action starts by retrieving the editor (an instance of JEditorPane) associated with the event. The editor "associated with the event" is the editor pane with focus when the action occurred. There is no specific code required to attach an Action in a menu or toolbar to an editor. Once we have a valid editor, we use it to alter the selected text.

Anchor tags require at least one attribute, so we prompt the user for the proper information. With the attribute information in hand, we use the editor's StyledEditorKit to make a proper AttributeSet for our tag. We use that AttributeSet in turn to apply our tag to the text in the editor.

Inserting Images

The ImageAction class is similar to the TagAction class. We need to prompt the user for the image's source URL, but we don't link the image to any selected text. We simply insert it at the current cursor location. Here's the code for the ImageAction class:

```
public class ImageAction extends StyledEditorKit.StyledTextAction {
  public ImageAction() {
    super("InsertIMG");
  }

  public void actionPerformed(ActionEvent ae) {
    JEditorPane editor = getEditor(ae);
    HTMLEditorKit kit = (HTMLEditorKit)editor.getEditorKit();
    HTMLDocument doc = (HTMLDocument)editor.getDocument();
    String value = JOptionPane.showInputDialog(HTMLEditor.this, "Image file:");
    try {
      kit.insertHTML(doc, editor.getCaretPosition(),
        "<img src=\"" + value + "\">", 0, 0, HTML.Tag.IMG);
```

```
        }
        catch (Exception e) {
            JOptionPane.showMessageDialog(HTMLEditor.this,
            "Image Not Loaded", "ERROR", JOptionPane.ERROR_MESSAGE);
            e.printStackTrace();
        }
    }
}
```

Unlike the `TagAction` class, `ImageAction` requires the editor kit to be an `HTMLEditorKit` because `HTMLEditorKit` has a convenience routine to insert a chunk of HTML as plain text. No building of tags with attribute sets here. We just insert an `<img>` tag that refers to the user's chosen file, and we're done.

Saving as HTML

OK, so we can insert HTML into our editor. What we're really here for is reading and writing HTML. The power of the editor kits really starts to shine now. We don't have to write new `SaveAction` or `OpenAction` classes—the ones written for our `SimpleEditor` work just fine. `SimpleEditor` relies on the text component's `write()` method, which in turn queries the editor kit. The `HTMLEditorKit` supplies an instance of the `HTMLWriter` class to get the job done. This means that no extra code is required on our part, which is just the way we like it.

Writing HTML

The `write()` method from `JEditorPane` takes advantage of the writer installed as part of the `HTMLEditorKit`. In our previous example, that writer is the `HTMLWriter` class. Starting with a more generic styled document, you could also write HTML with `MinimalHTMLWriter`. The classes described in this section both extend from the `AbstractWriter` class. (See Figure 23-9.)

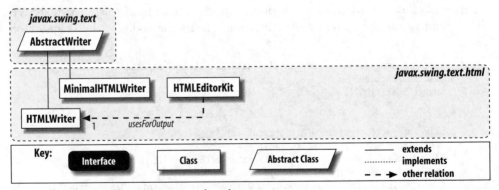

Figure 23-9. HTML document-writing class diagram

The AbstractWriter Class

In this chapter, we've talked about a variety of strategies for saving document content. As of SDK 1.2, a new class provides some assistance in creating a rendition of an in-memory document structure suitable for saving as human-readable text. It relies on the `ElementIterator` class. `AbstractWriter` supports indentation to clarify the document structure as well as maximum line length to keep the generated output easy to read.

`ElementIterator` is a simple iterator class (somewhat obviously) devoted to working with `Element` objects. It has the usual `next( )` and `previous( )` methods of any bidirectional iterator. Both return objects of type `Element`. Unlike the new iterators in the Collections API, there is no `hasNext( )` method. Instead, `next( )` or `previous( )` return `null` to signal the "end" of the stream. As with the constructors for `AbstractWriter`, an `ElementIterator` can be built on a `Document` or start from a particular `Element`. This class is covered in more depth in Chapter 22.

Properties

`AbstractWriter` defines the properties shown in Table 23-14.

Table 23-14. AbstractWriter properties

Property	Data type	get	is	set	Default value
canWrapLines[1.3, p]	boolean	•		•	true
currentLineLength[1.3, p]	int	•		•	
document[p]	Document	•			
elementIterator[p]	ElementIterator	•			
endOffset[1.3]	int	•			
indentLevel[1.3, p]	int	•			0
indentSpace[p]	int	•		•	2
lineEmpty[1.3, p]	boolean		•		
lineLength[1.3, p]	int	•		•	100
lineSeparator[1.3]	String	•		•	line.separator system property
startOffset[1.3]	int	•			
writer[1.3, p]	Writer	•			

[1.3]since 1.3, [p]protected

Several properties are read-only and simply help describe the state of the current writer. The document itself is available through the `document` property. The `elementIterator`, `endOffset`, `indentLevel`, `startOffset`, and `writer` properties all give you information about the writer (and a reference to the writer itself). If you are writing the entire document, `startOffset` is 0, and `endOffset` is the length of the document. The other read-only property, lineEmpty, can tell you if the current line the writer is working on is empty. The mutable properties help you configure how the output looks. The canWrapLines and lineLength let you dictate how long lines are "rendered" when written. If canWrapLines is true, and currentLineLength is greater than lineLength, the text is wrapped. How much space is used for each level of indentation is controlled by the indentSpace property. Likewise, the lineSeparator property dictates the line ending used during output.

Constant

Table 23-15 shows the single, protected constant defined by AbstractWriter.

Table 23-15. AbstractWriter constant

Constant	Data type	Description
NEWLINE	char	The newline character (\n)

Constructors

protected AbstractWriter(Writer w, Document doc)
protected AbstractWriter(Writer w, Document doc, int pos, int len)
> Create an object that assists in writing the specified Document or portion (starting at pos and running for len characters) of doc.

protected AbstractWriter(Writer w, Element root)
protected AbstractWriter(Writer w, Element root, int pos, int len)
> Create an object that assists in writing the elements below (and including) root. A portion of the elements (starting at pos and running for len characters) below root can also be specified.

Output-generating methods

The following methods write text to the Writer supplied in the constructor:

protected void indent() throws IOException
> Write a series of blank spaces according to the current indent level (see decrIndent() and incrIndent() later in this chapter).

protected void text(Element elem) throws BadLocationException, IOException
> Write the current text within the range of the given element (as returned by getText() which is discussed later in this chapter).

abstract protected void write() throws IOException, BadLocationException
> Must be implemented by subclasses to write the document. The intention is that subclasses call getElementIterator() and then iterate over the elements, using the other methods supplied by this class to produce the output.

protected void write(char ch) throws IOException

> Write the given character. If the maximum line length is reached, it also writes a NEWLINE character and calls indent( ).

protected void write(String str) throws IOException

> Write the given string. If the string is too long to fit on the current line, the method checks to see if it would fit on a new line. If so, the entire string is written on a new line. If not, the line is split between the current line and the next line.

protected void writeAttributes(AttributeSet attr) throws IOException

> Write a textual representation of the given set of attributes. Each attribute is written as "name=value".

Formatting methods

protected void incrIndent()

> Increment the indent level. The indent level is initially 0.

protected void decrIndent()

> Decrement the indent level.

The HTMLWriter Class

The HTMLWriter class is a fairly intricate example of extending AbstractWriter. HTMLWriter outputs HTMLDocument objects to a stream. The writer keeps all the tags (even ones it doesn't understand) intact and produces reasonably formatted HTML. Tags carry attributes exactly as you would expect. All attributes are enclosed in double quotes (<tag attribute="value">) to keep embedded spaces of attribute values intact and to conform to the HTML specification.

Constructors

Two constructors build a writer from a given HTMLDocument:

public HTMLWriter(Writer w, HTMLDocument doc)
public HTMLWriter(Writer w, HTMLDocument doc, int pos, int len)

> Both constructors require a Writer object (w) and an HTML document (doc) to write. The writer can be any valid writer, including a FileWriter or possibly an OutputStreamWriter chained on top of a Socket. The second version of the constructor creates a writer for a subset of doc specified by the starting offset pos and extending for len characters.

Writing method

Only one public writing method exists:

public void write( ) throws IOException, BadLocationException
> Write the document (or specified portion) to the given output stream. It loops through the element structure of the document and drives calls to the appropriate protected methods for the various elements it encounters. For example, if it encounters an HTML comment, it invokes the comment( ) method.

MinimalHTMLWriter

If you have a simple StyledDocument that was not initially an HTML document, you can still write it as HTML using the MinimalHTMLWriter. For example, we could add a "Save As" option to our StyledEditor class to output the document as HTML in addition to the usual method. Here's the code for the new Action:

```
class SaveAsHtmlAction extends AbstractAction {
    public SaveAsHtmlAction( ) {
        super("Save As...", null);
    }

    // Query user for a filename and attempt to open and write the text
    // component's content to the file.
    public void actionPerformed(ActionEvent ev) {
        JFileChooser chooser = new JFileChooser( );
        if (chooser.showSaveDialog(StyledEditor.this) !=
                JFileChooser.APPROVE_OPTION)
            return;
        File file = chooser.getSelectedFile( );
        if (file == null)
            return;
        FileWriter writer = null;
        try {
            writer = new FileWriter(file);
            MinimalHTMLWriter htmlWriter = new MinimalHTMLWriter(writer,
                (StyledDocument)textComp.getDocument( ));
            htmlWriter.write( );
        }
        catch (IOException ex) {
            JOptionPane.showMessageDialog(StyledEditor.this,
                "HTML File Not Saved", "ERROR", JOptionPane.ERROR_MESSAGE);
        }
        catch (BadLocationException ex) {
            JOptionPane.showMessageDialog(StyledEditor.this,
                "HTML File Corrupt", "ERROR", JOptionPane.ERROR_MESSAGE);
        }
        finally {
            if (writer != null) {
```

```
      try {
        writer.close();
      } catch (IOException x) {}
    }
  }
 }
}
```

You should see two substantive changes to the SaveAction class from the previous example. First, rather than let the textComp object (an instance of JEditorPane) write itself out, we create our MinimalHTMLWriter from a FileWriter object and the document from our textComp. The write() method of the htmlWriter() spits out an HTML version of our document. Unfortunately, you still have to be careful with this writer—it's not perfect yet. Figure 23-10 shows a screenshot of a simple document in our styled editor and the same document as HTML displayed inside a browser. Note that the HTML version is not quite perfect, as you can see from the fact that it displays differently in the browser than it does in our editor.

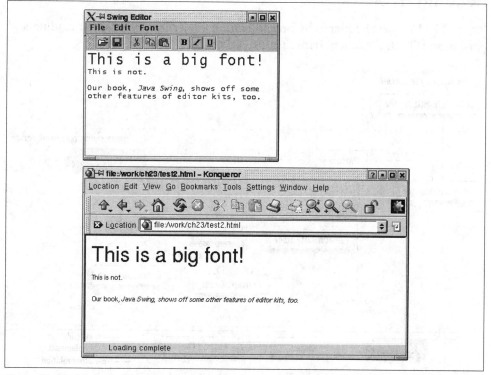

Figure 23-10. The StyledEditor document saved (not perfectly) as HTML and displayed in a browser

Constructors

`MinimalHTMLWriter` has two constructors:

public MinimalHTMLWriter(Writer w, StyledDocument doc)
public MinimalHTMLWriter(Writer w, StyledDocument doc, int pos, int len)
> Build writers for the given doc. The second version writes `len` characters of content starting from pos.

Public writing method

`MinimalHTMLWriter` has one public method for starting the writing process:

public void write( ) throws IOException, BadLocationException
> Write the document (or the specified part of the document) to the writer given in the constructor.

Reading HTML

Figure 23-11 shows the hierarchy breakdown for the classes involved in reading and parsing an HTML document with the `HTMLEditorKit`.

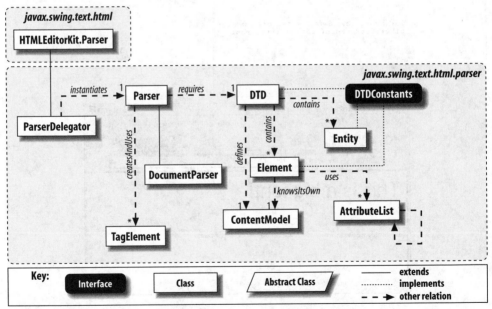

Figure 23-11. The class hierarchy for parsing HTML via HTMLEditorKit

Document Parsers

The first function involved in loading and displaying an HTML document is parsing it. The HTMLEditorKit class has hooks for returning a parser to do the job. The classes in the javax.swing.text.html.parser package implement a DTD-based* parser for this purpose.

But since we're here, let's look at the flow of an incoming HTML document. The editor kit instantiates a parser to read the document. ParserDelegator does what its name implies and delegates the actual parsing duties to another class—DocumentParser, in this case. ParserDelegator also handles loading the DTD used to create the real parser. Ostensibly, you could load your own DTD, but this whole process is rather tightly coupled to the HTML DTD supplied by the good folks at Sun. Once the parser is in place, you can send it a document and a ParserCallback instance and start parsing. As the parser finds tokens and data, it passes them off to the callback instance that does the real work of building the document.

You can display the document as it is built, or you can wait for the entire document to be loaded before displaying it. The tokenThreshold property from HTMLDocument determines exactly when the display work begins. See the discussion following Table 23-12 for more details on the token threshold.

A Custom EditorKit

Although Swing's HTML support is less than ideal, it is sufficient to handle inline help systems and aid in rapid prototyping. Each release of the SDK improves support and usability. It will continue to get better. In the meantime, if you're desperate for serious markup language support, you really should check out XML.

If you're interested in doing your own EditorKit work, look up the more detailed HTMLEditorKit chapters online. You should also check out the javax.swing.text.rtf package. It serves the same basic purpose as the HTML package but reads and writes RTF files. However, be aware that RTF seems to be even more plagued with "acceptable variants" than HTML. Make sure you test your output on an intended target system before rolling out your new commercial editor!

To round out this final section, we'll review the steps involved in creating your own editor kit. These steps include:

- Creating the EditorKit class
- Defining the Document type

---

* DTD stands for Document Type Definition. The editor kit uses its own compiled DTD based on HTML 3.2 rather than one of the public standard versions—another factor that complicates efforts to extend the tags supported.

- Defining new Actions
- Creating custom View classes
- Creating a ViewFactory
- Creating a "reader" and a "writer"
- Telling JEditorPane about your new kit

Create the EditorKit Class

First, create your EditorKit class. Depending on the type of documents you're going to support, you can subclass the abstract EditorKit base class or extend any of the existing kits we've covered in this chapter.

Much of the work in creating this class is covered in the steps that follow. In addition to those more complex issues, you should implement the following EditorKit methods:

public abstract Object clone()
> Strangely, the Swing implementations of this method just return a new instance of the editor kit subclass. It is probably a good idea to return a "true clone" here, although this method is not currently used within Swing.

public void install(JEditorPane c)
> Implement this method only if you want to access the JEditorPane using your editor kit. One possibility here is to add the kit as a listener of some type.

public void deinstall(JEditorPane c)
> Typically, you use this method only if you implement install() to add a listener of some sort. This method should remove the listener.

public abstract String getContentType()
> This method should be implemented to describe the type of content your kit handles. The Swing-provided editor kits return text/plain, text/html, and text/rtf. This method is important if you want JEditorPane to be able to use your editor kit automatically when it is asked to display URLs of the appropriate type. When determining which editor kit to use, JEditorPane uses the URLConnection object from the URL passed to its setPage() method to determine the content type of the URL.

Define the Document Type

Depending on the complexity of your editor kit, you may need to define a new Document class. The HTMLEditorKit does this, defining HTMLDocument as a subclass of DefaultStyledDocument.

Whether you use an existing document type or create your own, make sure createDefaultDocument( ) returns an instance of the type of document you want your kit to use.

Define New Actions

If you want your kit to assist in the creation of editors for your document type, you may want to define additional Action classes to perform certain activities. The three basic steps for creating any document editor are:

Define the new Action classes
> Create any new Action classes you want to provide. Review the discussion of the TextAction and StyledEditorKit.StyledTextAction classes; these may serve as useful base classes for any new Action classes you create.

Define default Action instances
> Define instances of your new Action classes (or existing Action classes) that you wish to provide as default actions for the kit. This is typically done by creating a static array. For example:

```
private static final Action[] defaultActions = {
    new MyNewAction(arg1, arg2),
    new MyOtherNewAction(arg1)
};
```

> Then, implement the getActions( ) method:

```
public Action[] getActions( ) {
    return TextAction.augmentList(super.getActions( ), this.defaultActions);
}
```

> This adds your new actions to the set of actions defined by your superclass.

Define constants for default actions
> In order for users to take advantage of your new default actions, you need to make the action names publicly available. The common pattern is to define a String constant for each action name. For example:

```
public static final String MY_NEW_ACTION = "my-new-action";
public static final String ANOTHER_NEW_ACTION = "another-new-action";
```

> The actual values of the String constants should match the Action.NAME properties defined for each of your default actions.

Create Custom View Classes

If you want your documents to be displayed in a special way, you may need to define your own view classes. It's a good idea to take a look at the available classes and see if they do what you need, or if they can be extended to provide the look you want. Also, be sure to take advantage of the static text painting methods provided by the javax.swing.text.Utilities class.

Note that you are not under any obligation to keep a one-to-one mapping from Elements to View objects. It's perfectly reasonable to define a single View that is responsible for a group of elements such as a table cell, row, or the entire table. The trade-off between many simple Views and fewer complex ones (right up to a single View that draws the entire document) is an architectural design choice that you'll make based on the normal considerations of performance, code complexity, and the like.

Create a ViewFactory Interface and View Classes

If you want to control the types of View objects created for the different types of Elements in your documents, implement a ViewFactory. This interface contains one method, create( ). A typical implementation of this interface looks something like this:

```
class MyFactory implements ViewFactory {
  public View create(Element e) {
    String name = e.getName( );
    if (name != null) {
      if (name.equals(AbstractDocument.ContentElementName)) {
        return new LabelView(e);
      }
      if (name.equals(SomeOtherElementName)) {
        return new SomeOtherView(e);
      }
    }
    return new LabelView(e); // A default
  }
}
```

The key thing is to ensure that the correct type of View is created for any Element types allowed in your documents. Note that you need to write this factory from scratch; there are no existing public factories (except for HTMLEditorKit.HTMLFactory) to subclass.

If you do implement your own ViewFactory, remember to implement the EditorKit. getViewFactory( ) method to return an instance of your factory class.

Create a "Reader" and a "Writer"

Potentially, the most time-consuming and challenging part of creating your own editor kit is defining and implementing a strategy for reading and writing documents in the correct format. For complex document types, it makes the most sense to implement this code in separate classes outside the editor kit.

However you choose to implement the parsing and saving operations (perhaps taking advantage of the AbstractWriter class), you need to provide implementations of the read( ) and write( ) methods (unless the implementations provided by the class

---

you're extending serve your purposes). Unless you have special requirements, you implement only the methods that work with the java.io Reader and Writer classes. If you're extending DefaultEditorKit, the other versions just call these.

Earlier in this chapter, we discussed the strategy of reading and writing styled documents using the built-in Java serialization mechanism. Depending on your needs, this may be a reasonable approach. Keep in mind that if you read in a serialized document, you'll have to copy all the attributes and content over to the document passed in to the read( ) method. While this may be a pain, it may be less trouble than defining your own document format and parser.

Tell JEditorPane About Your New Kit

If you want JEditorPane to use your editor kit when it encounters URLs of the appropriate MIME type, you need to register the kit with the JEditorPane class. This is done by calling either the static method registerEditorKitForContentType( ) or the nonstatic setEditorKitForContentType( ). The first method takes two strings: the content type your kit works with and the class name of your kit. You might call it like this:

```
JEditorPane.registerEditorKitForContentType("text/foo","mypackage.FooEdKit");
```

The other option takes the content type and an instance of the kit. For example:

```
JEditorPane ed = new JEditorPane( );
ed.setEditorKitForContentType("text/foo", new FooEditorKit( ));
```

If you go with the first version (which applies to all JEditorPane objects), keep in mind that JEditorPane won't know about your kit until this call is made, so you need to be sure to make the call before you expect your kit to be used.

This step is required only if you are using a standard MIME type that the java.net. URLConnection class knows about. This is the class JEditorPane uses to determine which editor kit to use when a new URL is specified. Of course, you can still register your editor kit even if you're not using a well-known MIME type, but you'll also need to call setContentType( ) on your JEditorPane since your document type won't be recognized automatically. The other option is to skip this step altogether and just call setEditorKit( ) on the JEditorPane.

At last, we've come to the close of this multi-chapter novella on the Swing text framework. If you've actually read it from beginning to end, congratulations! You now know everything there is to know about the powerful Swing text architecture. Well, OK, you may not know everything, but at least you know where to start looking.

No matter which road you took to reach this final paragraph, it's important not to let all the complexity scare you away from using the Swing text components. If you just need to do simple things, go back to Chapter 19 and revisit the examples provided there. If your requirements are more demanding, we hope the last four chapters have given you a better understanding of the framework.

Drag and Drop

Until the Java 2 platform hit the streets, Drag and Drop support (specifically, support for interacting with the native windowing system underneath the JVM) was lacking. The ability to let users drag a file from their file chooser into your application is almost a requirement of a modern, commercial user interface. The java.awt.dnd package gives you and your Java programs access to that support. You can now create applications that accept information dropped in from an outside source. You can also create Java programs that compile draggable information that you export to other applications. And, of course, you can add both the drop and drag capabilities to a single application to make its interface much richer and more intuitive.

"But wait!" you cry. "I recognize that package name. That's an AWT package!" You're right. Technically, Drag and Drop support is provided under the auspices of the AWT, not as a part of Swing. However, one driving force behind Swing is that it provides your application with a more mature, sophisticated user interface. Because Drag and Drop directly affects that maturity, we figured that you'd like to hear about it—even if it is not a part of Swing. And to try and hide that fact, we'll be using Swing components in all of the examples. However, we should note for completeness that Drag and Drop support can be added just as easily to good, old-fashioned AWT components—they just don't look as nice.

What Is Drag and Drop?

If you have ever used a graphical file system manager to move a file from one folder to another, you have used Drag and Drop (often abbreviated DnD). The term "drag and drop" refers to a GUI action in which the end user "picks up" an object such as a file or piece of text by moving the cursor over the object, clicking the mouse button, and, without releasing the button, "dragging" the object to a particular area of the screen and releasing the mouse button to "drop" the object. This process is meant to extend the desktop metaphor. Just like your real desktop, you can rearrange things by picking them up, moving them, and dropping them in a filing cabinet, a trash can, an in-box, a shoebox, or the floor.

Some programmers have added DnD functionality to individual components. For example, you might want to have a graphically rearrangeable JTree. Even without the DnD package, you can accomplish this with a clever bit of programming and a good deal of time. With the DnD package, however, not only do you not need the clever bit of programming, you are not limited to one component. You can drag information from one component to another in the same application, in two different Java applications (using separate JVMs), or even between your Java application and the native windowing system.

DnD and SDK 1.4

SDK 1.4 introduced several new features that make minimal DnD functionality easy to program for simple cases. On the drag side, many components now have a new boolean property called dragEnabled. If you set this property to true, you can "export" information by dragging it away from the component. Table 24-1 shows the Swing components that support the dragEnabled property and the format of the information they export.

Table 24-1 . Export capabilities of various Swing components

Component	Export data type(s)	Description
JColorChooser	application/x-java-jvm-local-objectref	Exports a reference to a java.awt.Color object. Imports a color TransferHandler property so you can accept such a drag.
JEditorPane	text/plain, other	If the content type for the editor is not plain text, the export contains both a plain-text version and an "other" version determined by the write( ) method of the editor pane.
JFileChooser	application/x-java-file-list	The files dragged out of a JFileChooser are set up in the same manner as those of a native file chooser. If you drop them on a Java drop site, the type is x-java-file-list.
JFormattedTextField	text/plain	Recall that the "format" in this text field refers to text validation, not visual formatting such as that found in HTML.
JList	text/plain text/html	Single items drag out as plain text. Multiple items generate a chunk of HTML representing an unordered list. Each item is one entry in the list.
JTable	text/plain text/html	Single cells drag out as plain text. Multiple cells generate a chunk of HTML representing a table bounding the cells.
JTextArea	text/plain	Any text dragged out is presented as plain text.

Component	Export data type(s)	Description
JTextField	text/plain	Any text dragged out is presented as plain text.
JTextPane	text/plain, other	If the content type for the text pane is not plain text, the export contains both a plain-text version and an "other" version determined by the write( ) method of the pane.
JTree	text/plain text/html	Single items drag out as plain text. Multiple items generate a chunk of HTML representing an unordered list. Each item is one entry in the list. The hierarchy of disparate tree nodes is not maintained (i.e., the exported HTML does not contain nested lists).

On the drop side, the text components all support basic drop functionality. Other components (JList, JTable, etc.) have a new property called transferHandler. If you set the transferHandler, you can easily accept dropped data of almost any type. Table 24-2 shows a list of the default import capabilities of several Swing components.

Table 24-2 . Import capabilities of several Swing components

Component	Import data type(s)	Description
JColorChooser	class=java.awt.Color	Any transfer with a representation class (or subclass) of Color is accepted.
JEditorPane	text/plain, other	Accepts incoming plain text as well as text with the same MIME type as the current document. (The read( ) method of the pane is used.)
JFormattedTextField	text/plain	Plain text is effectively typed into the field to maintain format validation.
JPasswordField	text/plain	Text can be inserted, but it is shown as stars or whatever the current echo character is set to display.
JTextArea	text/plain	Plain text is inserted at the current caret position.
JTextField	text/plain	Plain text is inserted at the current caret position.
JTextPane	text/plain, other	Accepts incoming plain text as well as text with the same MIME type as the current document. (The read( ) method of the pane is used.)

To get you going with the new "easy" stuff, let's start with an example. To show you the results of a drop, Figure 24-1 shows a screenshot of an all-encompassing transfer handler attached to a text area. You can drag all kinds of information: icons from your desktop, text from an editor, a chunk of cells from a spreadsheet, several items from a JTree in another window—just about anything. Drop your items in the text window, and it shows you the possible transfer flavors. If it knows how to handle any of the flavors (text, Java objects, etc.), it displays as much of the actual data as it can.

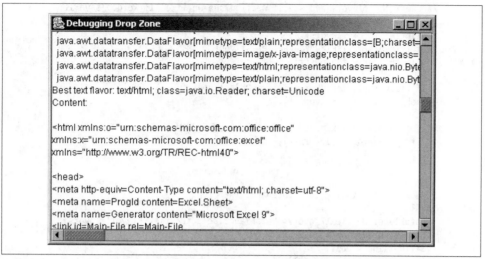

Figure 24-1. UberHandler demo with a drop from a Microsoft Excel® spreadsheet

The source code for this handler follows. The (simple) GUI application you see in Figure 24-1 is built in the main( ) method of this handler. You could certainly ignore this application and attach the handler to a more elegant debugger of your own devising.

```java
// UberHandler.java
import javax.swing.*;
import java.awt.event.*;
import java.awt.dnd.*;
import java.awt.datatransfer.*;
import java.io.*;

public class UberHandler extends TransferHandler {
  JTextArea output;

  public void TransferHandler( ) { }

  public boolean canImport(JComponent dest, DataFlavor[] flavors) {
    // You bet we can!
    return true;
  }

  public boolean importData(JComponent src, Transferable transferable) {
    // Here's the tricky part.
    println("Receiving data from " + src);
    println("Transferable object is: " + transferable);
    println("Valid data flavors: ");
    DataFlavor[] flavors = transferable.getTransferDataFlavors( );
    DataFlavor listFlavor = null;
    DataFlavor objectFlavor = null;
    DataFlavor readerFlavor = null;
    int lastFlavor = flavors.length - 1;
```

```
// Check the flavors and see if we find one we like. If we do, save it.
for (int f = 0; f <= lastFlavor; f++) {
  println("  " + flavors[f]);
  if (flavors[f].isFlavorJavaFileListType()) {
    listFlavor = flavors[f];
  }
  if (flavors[f].isFlavorSerializedObjectType()) {
    objectFlavor = flavors[f];
  }
  if (flavors[f].isRepresentationClassReader()) {
    readerFlavor = flavors[f];
  }
}

// Now try to display the content of the drop.
try {
  DataFlavor bestTextFlavor = DataFlavor.selectBestTextFlavor(flavors);
  BufferedReader br = null;
  String line = null;
  if (bestTextFlavor != null) {
    println("Best text flavor: " + bestTextFlavor.getMimeType());
    println("Content:");
    Reader r = bestTextFlavor.getReaderForText(transferable);
    br = new BufferedReader(r);
    line = br.readLine();
    while (line != null) {
      println(line);
      line = br.readLine();
    }
    br.close();
  }
  else if (listFlavor != null) {
    java.util.List list =
        (java.util.List)transferable.getTransferData(listFlavor);
    println(list);
  }
  else if (objectFlavor != null) {
    println("Data is a java object:\n" +
            transferable.getTransferData(objectFlavor));
  }
  else if (readerFlavor != null) {
    println("Data is an InputStream:");
    br = new BufferedReader((Reader)transferable.getTransferData(readerFlavor));
    line = br.readLine();
    while (line != null) {
      println(line);
    }
    br.close();
  }
  else {
    // Don't know this flavor type yet
    println("No text representation to show.");
  }
```

```
        println("\n\n");
    }
    catch (Exception e) {
      println("Caught exception decoding transfer:");
      println(e);
      return false;
    }
    return true;
}

public void exportDone(JComponent src, Transferable data, int action) {
    // Just let us know when it occurs.
    System.err.println("Export Done.");
}

public void setOutput(JTextArea jta) {
    output = jta;
}

protected void print(Object o) {
    print(o.toString());
}

protected void print(String s) {
    if (output != null) {
      output.append(s);
    }
    else {
      System.out.println(s);
    }
}

protected void println(Object o) {
    println(o.toString());
}

protected void println(String s) {
    if (output != null) {
      output.append(s);
      output.append("\n");
    }
    else {
      System.out.println(s);
    }
}

protected void println() {
    println("");
}

public static void main(String args[]) {
    JFrame frame = new JFrame("Debugging Drop Zone");
    frame.setSize(500,300);
    frame.setDefaultCloseOperation(JFrame.EXIT_ON_CLOSE);
```

```
        JTextArea jta = new JTextArea( );
        frame.getContentPane( ).add(new JScrollPane(jta));
        UberHandler uh = new UberHandler( );
        uh.setOutput(jta);
        jta.setTransferHandler(uh);

        frame.setVisible(true);
    }
}
```

Programming with DnD

So how do we add more complex DnD functionality to a component? On the surface, it's very easy. DnD uses the same technique as most other GUI features: events.
There are drag start events, drag source events, and drop events. To play with these
events, implement the corresponding listener interfaces. Sound familiar? For example, to respond to a dropped object, we create an event handler that implements the
DropTargetListener interface. What you do with the dropped object is the fun part.

Just to prove that this stuff really works, let's take a look at a simple example of the
drop listener (Figure 24-2). This application shows the names of any files you drag
from your native windowing system's file manager.

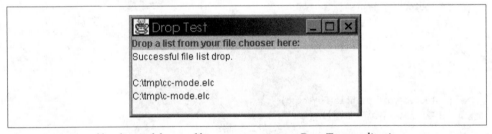

Figure 24-2. Two files dragged from a file manager onto our DropTest application

Admittedly, a screenshot does not do this test program justice. You really should
compile and run *DropTest.java* to get the full effect. But trust us, it does work! We'll
look at the source code for this example later in this section. With SDK 1.4, things
get significantly easier, but again, more of that to come. First let's look at an overview of what's involved.

You have three main areas to work with. A drop target accepts an incoming drag.
The process of accepting the dragged information generates a series of events that
you can respond to. The source of the dragged item might be your application,
another Java application, or a native windowing system application such as your file
manager. None of these matter to the drop target.

Your application can also be a source for draggable items. This functionality requires
the other two parts of DnD: a drag recognizer and a drag source. The drag recognizer is really just a glorified event adapter that listens for events that indicate if a

drag has begun. In the simplest cases, this is usually a `mouseDragged( )` event from the `MouseMotionListener` interface. (Later in this chapter, you will see how to make other events trigger a drag.) Once a drag is recognized, the drag source starts a drag and properly wraps the dragged information in an object that a drop target can recognize. Like the drop target, the information in a drag source is used inside your own application, another Java application, or a native application. Of course, all of these examples need to know what to do with the information once it arrives, but there are no *a priori* restrictions on where you drop your data.

While you definitely should familiarize yourself with the `DropTarget` and `DragSource` classes, the driving force behind the DnD package is events. There are events for each of the three major players: drop target events, recognizer events, and drag source events. Use recognizer events to start the whole process. Your response to target and source events dictates the behavior of your application. Let's look at a typical series of events in DnD scenarios (see Table 24-3).

Table 24-3. Common DnD event methods

Event on system	Gesture recognizer methods	Drag source methods	Drop target methods
Click and drag an item such as a file.	dragGestureRecognized( )		
Drag item into a possible drop area.		dragEnter( ) called first; dragOver( ) called continuously until exit	dragEnter( ) called first; dragOver( ) called continuously until exit
Drag item out of a possible drop area.		dragExit( )	dragExit( )
Drop the item on a target that accepts the drop.		dragExit( ) dragDropEnd( )*	dragExit( ) drop( )
Drop the item on a target that rejects the drop.		dragExit( ) dragDropEnd( )*	dragExit( ) drop( )
Drop the item on anything other than an active target.		dragExit( ) dragDropEnd( )*	

*You can determine the success status of a drop from the event passed to dragDropEnd( ).

Throughout the entire process, you can determine whether the user wants to copy or move the information based on keyboard modifiers such as the Control key. We'll describe the API for all of these events in the course of this chapter. Let's get started!

The Drop API

This example uses several of the classes found in the `java.awt.dnd` package. Here's how they fit together (see Figure 24-3). Remember that we're just looking at the drop side of DnD. We'll explore the drag side in the next section and autoscrolling at the end of this chapter.

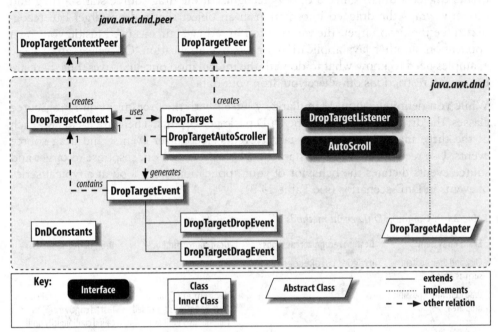

Figure 24-3. DnD class diagram for the drop side

The DropTarget Class

An obvious starting point for playing with this API is the DropTarget class. This class encapsulates the functionality you add to regular GUI components so that they can respond to drop events. You can make just about anything a drop target. Well, not *anything*, but any Component can be a drop target. Typically, you pick the component that responds to the drop—such as the text area in our example—but you can also pick a proxy component that simply helps produce all the right events while your event handler plays with the dropped data.

Note that just because the DropTarget class implements the DropTargetListener interface, this does not mean that the target is already handling drop events for you. The DropTarget class implementation of the interface supports the internal mechanisms for responding to events; it isn't used by us as programmers. We still have to create our own listener.

Properties

Table 24-4 lists five properties of the DropTarget class that govern the context of this target and its data transfer capabilities.

Table 24-4. DropTarget properties

Property	Data type	get	is	set	Default value
active	boolean		•	•	true
component	Component	•		•	null
defaultActions	int	•		•	ACTION_COPY_OR_MOVE
dropTargetContext	DropTargetContext	•			null
flavorMap	FlavorMap	•		•	SystemFlavorMap. getDefaultFlavorMap( )

The active property handles exactly what its name suggests: the active state of this target. If active is false, this target does not accept any dropped information. The component property references the component this target is using onscreen. Notice that you can set this property, too. You could have one DropTarget that uses a variety of components during different stages of your application. This is possible because dropTargetContext keeps a reference to the native peer supporting the drop target, and that native peer requires only that something onscreen can activate drop events.

The defaultActions and flavorMap properties determine the types of transfers (move, copy, link) and the types of data (filenames, strings, objects, etc.) you accept, respectively. The complete details of the FlavorMap class are beyond the scope of this chapter, but we'll look at the pertinent aspects later when we create our own data to drag. Fortunately, it is often simple to figure out what "flavor" a dropped object uses. If you know more about the incoming types of data than Java does, you can supply your own flavor map, but usually, the convenience methods supplied by the DataFlavor class are sufficient. You can easily find other Java classes, byte streams, and filename lists. For example, we'll be working with lists of files created by your windowing system's native file manager. You can use the isFlavorJavaFileListType( ) method to determine whether the user dropped valid filename data into your application. Many similar methods exist for the primary types of information that your Java application can handle.

Events

A DropTarget produces DropTargetEvent objects as the user enters, moves over, and exits the target, and eventually drops information on the target. Depending on the specific action—dragging actions such as entering and exiting versus dropping—a subclass of DropTargetEvent may be used. In either case, you implement the DropTargetListener interface to respond to these events.

public void addDropTargetListener(DropTargetListener l)
  throws TooManyListenersException
public void removeDropTargetListener(DropTargetListener l)
> These methods allow you to add or remove one listener at a time. Attempting to add more than one listener results in the `TooManyListenersException`.

The `DropTarget` class itself implements the `DropTargetListener` interface (discussed in detail later), so it defines the following methods:

public void dragEnter(DropTargetDragEvent dtde)
public void dragExit(DropTargetEvent dte)
public void dragOver(DropTargetDragEvent dtde)
public void drop(DropTargetDropEvent dtde)
public void dropActionChanged(DropTargetDragEvent dtde)
> These methods all trap drop events before the registered listener gets them. If the drop target is not active, these methods return without notifying the listener. Otherwise, the registered listener is notified, and the autoscroll mechanism is updated. (More on autoscrolling later in this chapter.)

Note that this trapping behavior prevents the drop target from being its own listener. You'll receive an `IllegalArgumentException` if you try to add the target as its own listener.

Constructors

Several constructors are available for creating `DropTarget` objects. Depending on how much of the default information you want (or how much information you need to supply at runtime after the `DropTarget` is instantiated), you can pick an appropriate constructor. You can create drop targets along with your components, or you can attach them at runtime. The latter might be useful if you have a dynamic interface because the visual component that accepts incoming drops can change.

public DropTarget()
> This constructor creates an "empty" drop target. It is currently an active target that supports copy or move operations. You still need to supply a component and a listener to make it useful.

public DropTarget(Component c, DropTargetListener dtl)
public DropTarget(Component c, int ops, DropTargetListener dtl)
public DropTarget(Component c, int ops, DropTargetListener dtl, boolean act)
public DropTarget(Component c, int ops, DropTargetListener dtl, boolean act,
  FlavorMap fm)
> These methods supply various parts of a typical target. The arguments include the component associated with the drop target (c), the listener responding to drop events (dtl), the drop operations supported (ops—copy and move are both supported by default; see Table 24-5 for the constant values to use for this argument),

whether the target is active (act, which is true by default), and a flavor map to use (fm, which is null by default).

Table 24-5. DnDConstants

Constant	Data type	Description
ACTION_COPY	int	Supports copying of dragged item(s).
ACTION_COPY_OR_MOVE	int	Supports copying or moving of dragged item(s).
ACTION_LINK ACTION_REFERENCE	int	Supports referencing dragged item(s). The definition of "reference" depends on your application and the native platform. (For example, you might use this operation to create a symbolic link or a shortcut to a file in a file browser application.) No direct mouse or keyboard action starts a link operation in the current implementation.
ACTION_MOVE	int	Supports moving dragged item(s).
ACTION_NONE	int	Does not support anything (i.e., ignore this action).

Typically, supplying the component, a listener, and the operations you want to support is sufficient to get started. If your drop target is active only in certain situations, starting out with a disabled target may be useful.

The DnDConstants Class

This quick little helper class defines the different types of actions (move, copy, and link) that are supported by the DnD framework. Notice that we say "DnD framework" and not just "DnD." The Java 2 API is ready for all of these actions, but your application or windowing system may not be. For example, while copy and move operations are universally understood, the link/reference operation is not. You might find that operation useful when dragging and dropping within a single application.

The DropTargetContext Class

As mentioned earlier, DropTargetContext supports a DropTarget with all the useful implementations. This class provides you with access to the DnD peer. Most of the methods update the native peer to keep the DnD state of your windowing system consistent.

For programmers, this class represents the primary location for interesting information when handling a drop or drag event. You can retrieve an instance of the context from any drop event and use it to provide user feedback. You can also use it to retrieve the drop target if you need it.

Properties

Reflecting the fact that this class serves primarily as peer support, many of its properties are protected (see Table 24-6).

Table 24-6. DropTargetContext properties

Property	Data type	get	is	set	Default value
component	Component	•			
currentDataFlavorsᴾ	DataFlavor[]	•			
currentDataFlavorsAsListᴾ	List	•			
dropTarget	DropTarget	•			
targetActionsᴾ	int	•		•	
transferableᴾ	Transferable	•			

ᴾprotected

The component and ropTarget properties are both publicly accessible and simply return references to the DropTarget object (and its Component) associated with this context. The currentDataFlavors and currentDataFlavorsAsList properties return the data flavors currently supported. This can be useful when updating a drag cursor. (For example, if the drop target cannot accept any of the current flavors, a "no drop" cursor can be displayed.) Which of these two properties you access depends entirely on your preference for using either an array of objects or a list. The targetActions property indicates the supported operations for the drop target. These actions can be any of the values from the DnDConstants class shown in Table 24-5. The transferable property is a bundled reference to the data being transferred by the DnD operation.

The protected TransferableProxy inner class wraps Transferable objects and, if possible, provides efficiencies when dealing with local objects (which were dragged and dropped in the same virtual machine). However, programmers' access to this class is restricted to subclasses of the DropTargetContext class.

In practice, you shouldn't worry about these classes since the event classes give you front-line access to most of the real action. But if you start low-level development on DnD support (for example, if you needed to remap the behavior of the native windowing system), you'll definitely need these classes.

The DropTargetListener Interface

If you want to respond to drop events, you need to implement the DropTargetListener interface and register with the DropTarget. You get only one listener per drop target. Unlike many other event handlers, which handle interfaces automatically, you must implement some of these interface methods yourself. Specifically, you need to accept or reject the operation generating the events. This acceptance or rejection keeps the visual clues—typically, the appearance of the mouse cursor—in sync with your application logic. We'll look at an example of this shortly.

Methods

The DropTargetListener methods break a drop event into five categories. These methods are similar to the MouseListener and MouseMotionListener methods. They describe the key moments in a drop process. Note that several variations of DropTargetEvent are used as arguments. These events are described in more detail in the next section.

public void dragEnter(DropTargetDragEvent dtde)
> Called when the user drags an item over an active drop target. If you implement this method, you should indicate at some point in the code whether you will accept a drop using either the acceptDrag( ) or rejectDrag( ) method of dtde.

public void dragExit(DropTargetEvent dte)
> Called when the user drags an item out of an active drop target.

public void dragOver(DropTargetDragEvent dtde)
> Called continuously while the user is over (inside the boundaries of) an active drop target. If you implement this method, at some point in the code you should indicate whether you will accept a drop using the acceptDrag( ) or rejectDrag( ) method of dtde.

public void drop(DropTargetDropEvent dtde)
> Called when the user drops a dragged item on an active drop target. All the hard work involved in accepting a drop starts here. As with the dragEnter( ) and dragOver( ) methods, you can initially accept or reject the drop, but eventually, you should terminate the drop process with a call to the dropComplete( ) method. Several examples of this method are presented throughout the rest of this chapter.

public void dropActionChanged(DropTargetDragEvent dtde)
> Called when the user changes the type of the drop. The most common change is from copy to move (or vice versa) by pressing (or releasing) a modifier key during the drag operation.

The DropTargetAdapter Class

As with other listeners in the java.awt.event package, the DropTargetListener interface comes with a companion adapter: DropTargetAdapter. This class was introduced in 1.4 and simply implements DropTargetListener, providing null bodies for each of the listener's methods.

The DropTargetEvent Class

The event-handling methods for a drop listener receive a DropTargetEvent. The DropTargetEvent class serves as the basis for the more specific events that are passed to the drop( ) and various drag methods. It provides access to the DropTargetContext through its only property, which is shown in Table 24-7.

Table 24-7. DropTargetEvent property

Property	Data type	get	is	set	Default value
dropTargetContext	DropTargetContext	•			From constructor

As its name implies, this property gives you access to the DropTargetContext associated with the target that generated the event. You can use the context to get at the GUI component associated with the event. (The getSource( ) method returns the DropTarget object, not the component.)

Depending on whether you pick up drag events or the final drop event, you get one of two DropTargetEvent subclasses: DropTargetDragEvent or DropTargetDropEvent. Both contain more or less the same information, but drop events give you the capacity to retrieve the transferred data.

The DropTargetDragEvent Class

As the user drags a piece of information over your drop target, several drag events are generated. You can monitor these events and use them to dynamically control the cursor or the drop target. You have probably seen a cursor change to a big "not here!" symbol over invalid drop targets.

Properties

The properties of a DropTargetDragEvent object should give you all the information you need to make such changes. These properties are listed in Table 24-8.

Table 24-8. DropTargetDragEvent properties

Property	Data type	get	is	set	Default value
currentDataFlavors	DataFlavor[]	•			
currentDataFlavorsAsList	List	•			
dropAction	int	•			
location	Point	•			
sourceActions	int	•			

The currentDataFlavors and currentDataFlavorsAsList properties give you access to the properties of the same name in the DropTargetContext class. The location property gives you the coordinates of the mouse pointer for this particular event. The dropAction property indicates which operation (move, copy, link) the user intends to perform while the sourceActions property indicates which operations the source of the data supports. If you find an incompatibility, you can reject the drag event using one of the drag methods described in the next section.

Drag methods

Once you have looked at the event, you can decide whether to accept it. The following methods facilitate announcing that decision. As you accept( ) or reject( ) the drag, the cursor should follow suit to give the user proper visual feedback.

public void acceptDrag(int dragOperation)
> This method indicates that you will accept the drag. The dragOperation argument dictates which operation is acceptable. If you want to accept both copy and move operations, you need to figure out which operation is currently underway and accept that operation. While you can syntactically accept an ACTION_COPY_OR_MOVE operation, you probably won't do the same thing for a copy as you would for a move. The example in the "Finishing Touches" section later in this chapter implements both copy and move logic.

public void rejectDrag( )
> This method indicates that you will not accept the drag.

Transfer data method

The DropTargetDragEvent also carries some information about the data wrapped up in the event.

public boolean isDataFlavorSupported(DataFlavor df)
> Similar to the currentDataFlavors property, this method gives you access to the method of the same name in the DropTargetContext. It returns true if df is a flavor that the drop target accepts.

The DropTargetDropEvent Class

This class is very similar to the DropTargetDragEvent class, but now that we have a real drop, we can gain access to the information that the user was dragging, not just the meta-information. We can also use the DropTargetDropEvent class to signal the original drag source of a successful (or failed) drop.

Properties

Similar to the drag version, the properties for DropTargetDropEvent shown in Table 24-9 give you access to just about everything that's useful.

Table 24-9. DropTargetDropEvent properties

Property	Data type	get	is	set	Default value
currentDataFlavors	DataFlavor[]	•			
currentDataFlavorsAsList	List	•			
dropAction	int	•			

Table 24-9. DropTargetDropEvent properties (continued)

Property	Data type	get	is	set	Default value
localTransfer	boolean		•		
location	Point	•			
sourceActions	int	•			
transferable	Transferable	•			

The currentDataFlavors, currentDataFlavorsAsList, dropAction, location, and sourceActions properties all mimic their respective counterparts in the DropTargetDragEvent class. There are also two new properties: localTransfer and transferable. The localTransfer property tells you whether the data being transferred came from the same virtual machine. You can use this information to process the transfer more efficiently. The transferable property is a Transferable object that represents the actual transferred data. Again, Transferable comes from the java.awt. datatransfer package, but we'll see some examples of extracting the data from a Transferable object in the code examples.

Drop methods

As with the drag events, you can accept or reject drops.

public void acceptDrop(int dropAction)
> This method accepts a drop of type dropAction. If you decide to accept the drop, call this method, process the drop, and then call the dropComplete( ) method.

public void rejectDrop( )
> This method rejects the drop.

public void dropComplete(boolean success)
> This method tells the source of the drag that the drop is complete. The success argument should be true if the drop is successful; otherwise, it should be false.

Transfer data method

As with the drag events, you can check for specific data flavor support.

public boolean isDataFlavorSupported(DataFlavor df)
> This method gives you access to the method of the same name in the DropTargetContext. It returns true if df is a flavor the drop target accepts.

Drop Example

Well, after all that, here's the source code from the file list drop application in Figure 24-2. This example simply generates status messages for most of the methods, but it does correctly process the drop event in the drop( ) method. Later examples put more of the listener methods to use.

```
/*
 * DropTest.java
 * A simple drop tester application
 */

import java.awt.*;
import java.awt.dnd.*;
import java.awt.datatransfer.*;
import java.awt.event.*;
import java.io.*;
import java.util.*;
import javax.swing.*;

public class DropTest extends JFrame {

  DropTarget dt;
  JTextArea ta;

  public DropTest() {
    super("Drop Test");
    setSize(300,300);
    setDefaultCloseOperation(EXIT_ON_CLOSE);

    // Make a quick label for instructions and create the
    // text area component.
    getContentPane( ).add(
    new JLabel("Drop a list from your file chooser here:"),
    BorderLayout.NORTH);
    ta = new JTextArea( );
    getContentPane( ).add(ta, BorderLayout.CENTER);

    // Set up our text area to recieve drops.
    // This class handles drop events.
    dt = new DropTarget(ta, new DebugDropListener( ));
    setVisible(true);
  }

  public class DebugDropListener implements DropTargetListener {
    // For now, we'll just report ancilliary events to the console,
    // including dragEnter, dragExit, dragOver, and dropActionChanged.
    public void dragEnter(DropTargetDragEvent dtde) {
      System.out.println("Drag Enter");
    }

    public void dragExit(DropTargetEvent dte) {
      System.out.println("Drag Exit");
    }

    public void dragOver(DropTargetDragEvent dtde) {
      System.out.println("Drag Over");
    }

    public void dropActionChanged(DropTargetDragEvent dtde) {
      System.out.println("Drop Action Changed");
    }
```

```
public void drop(DropTargetDropEvent dtde) {
    try {
      // Get the dropped object and try to figure out what it is.
      Transferable tr = dtde.getTransferable();
      DataFlavor[] flavors = tr.getTransferDataFlavors();
      for (int i = 0; i < flavors.length; i++) {
        System.out.println("Possible flavor: " + flavors[i].getMimeType());
        // Check for file lists specifically.
        if (flavors[i].isFlavorJavaFileListType()) {
          // Great! Accept copy drops.
          dtde.acceptDrop(DnDConstants.ACTION_COPY);
          ta.setText("Successful file list drop.\n\n");

          // Add the list of filenames to our text area.
          java.util.List list =
              (java.util.List)tr.getTransferData(flavors[i]);
          for (int j = 0; j < list.size(); j++) {
            ta.append(list.get(j) + "\n");
          }

          // If we made it this far, everything worked.
          dtde.dropComplete(true);
          return;
        }
      }
      // Hmm, the user must not have dropped a file list.
      System.out.println("Drop failed: " + dtde);
      dtde.rejectDrop();
    } catch (UnsupportedFlavorException e) {
      e.printStackTrace();
      dtde.rejectDrop();
    } catch (InvalidDnDOperationException e) {
      e.printStackTrace();
      dtde.rejectDrop();
    } catch (IOException e) {
      e.printStackTrace();
      dtde.rejectDrop();
    }
  }
}

public static void main(String args[]) {
  new DropTest();
}
}
```

The interesting code for this application is found in two methods: the constructor
and the drop() method. In the constructor, we build a simple application with a
label and a text area. Only one line is needed to create a drop target and associate it
with the text area:

```
dt = new DropTarget(ta, new DebugDropListener());
```

Now we have a drop target, and its associated component is the text area ta. The second argument is the `DropTargetListener` for the target. (We use an inner class to handle events in our example.)

The `drop( )` method deconstructs the dropped information. As mentioned before, this happens in a series of steps:

1. Check the MIME type of the transfer to make sure it's acceptable.
2. Accept the drop.
3. Retrieve the data from the `Transferable` object.
4. Mark the drop complete.

In our example, the first step is handled using a convenience method from the `DataFlavor` class. We look for a list of files specifically; if we find it, we proceed to the second step and call `acceptDrop( )`. Pulling the data out of the `Transferable` object is straightforward here, but we still must cast it as the appropriate type to do anything with it. (We'll see examples of other types of transferable data in the next section.) Finally, if nothing goes wrong, we mark the drop a success by calling `dropComplete(true)`. If we didn't find a file list, or if an error occurred while trying to retrieve the data, we call `rejectDrop( )`.

Transferable Contents

The DnD API uses the foundations laid by the system clipboard support in the `java.awt.datatransfer` package. We won't go into the gory details of data transfer here (we will see more of this package later), but we will expand our example to handle more than just a list of files:

```
public void drop(DropTargetDropEvent dtde) {
    try {
        // Get the dropped object and try to figure out what it is.
        Transferable tr = dtde.getTransferable( );
        DataFlavor[] flavors = tr.getTransferDataFlavors( );
        for (int i = 0; i < flavors.length; i++) {
            System.out.println("Possible flavor: " + flavors[i].getMimeType( ));
            // Check for file lists specifically.
            if (flavors[i].isFlavorJavaFileListType( )) {
                // Great! Accept copy drops...
                dtde.acceptDrop(DnDConstants.ACTION_COPY);
                ta.setText("Successful file list drop.\n\n");

                // Add the list of filenames to our text area.
                java.util.List list = (java.util.List)tr.getTransferData(flavors[i]);
                for (int j = 0; j < list.size( ); j++) {
                    ta.append(list.get(j) + "\n");
                }

                // If we made it this far, everything worked.
                dtde.dropComplete(true);
```

```
        return;
      }
      // Is it another Java object?
      else if (flavors[i].isFlavorSerializedObjectType()) {
        dtde.acceptDrop(DnDConstants.ACTION_COPY_OR_MOVE);
        ta.setText("Successful Object drop.\n\n");
        Object o = tr.getTransferData(flavors[i]);
        // Normally, we would try to cast o as something useful. For now, we just
        // want to print out a success message.
        ta.append("Object: " + o);
        dtde.dropComplete(true);
        return;
      }
      // How about an input stream?
      else if (flavors[i].isRepresentationClassInputStream()) {
        dtde.acceptDrop(DnDConstants.ACTION_COPY_OR_MOVE);
        ta.setText("Successful stream drop.\n\n");
        ta.read(new InputStreamReader((InputStream)tr.getTransferData(flavors[i])),
                "from a drop");
        dtde.dropComplete(true);
        return;
      }
    }
    System.out.println("Drop failed: " + dtde);
    dtde.rejectDrop();
  } catch (Exception e) {
    e.printStackTrace();
    dtde.rejectDrop();
  }
}
```

In this expanded drop( ) method, we check for two other common data transfer
types: a Java Object and an InputStream. If the type is a Java Object, we can simply
grab the transfer data directly using getTransferData( ). Presumably, your application knows which types of objects the user might be dragging in and can use
instanceof tests to determine what it received.

If the type is not an Object, we check to see if it can be represented by a stream. If so,
we open an InputStreamReader and grab the data. Text built outside of another Java
application can be transferred in this way.

The TransferHandler Class

If you are working with SDK 1.4 or later, recall that you can handle incoming drops
by simply setting the transferHandler property. A more complete example of this
class in action appears later in this chapter in the "Rearranging Trees" section, where
we show you how to create your own Transferable type.

Constants

Several constants are defined for the type of transfer you're performing. Those constants are shown in Table 24-10.

Table 24-10. TransferHandler constants

Constant	Data type	Description
COPY	int	Supports copying of dragged item(s)
COPY_OR_MOVE	int	Supports copying or moving dragged item(s)
MOVE	int	Supports moving dragged item(s)
NONE	int	Does not support anything (disables dragging)

Properties

The TransferHandler class comes with several read-only properties shown in Table 24-11. The copyAction, cutAction, and pasteAction properties all return Action objects that behave like their namesakes. For example, getCutAction( ) returns an action that calls the exportToClipboard( ) method with a MOVE type. The sourceActions property provides a way to track the operations supported by the source of the drag. As an example, your drag source may not support a delete operation (which is required for the move action), so you could report only the COPY type. The visualRepresentation property offers you the opportunity to display a custom icon during the drag (but support for this is not guaranteed).

Table 24-11. TransferHandler properties

Property	Data type	get	is	set	Default value
copyAction^s	Action	•			Package-private subclass of AbstractAction
cutAction^s	Action	•			Package-private subclass of AbstractAction
pasteAction^s	Action	•			Package-private subclass of AbstractAction
sourceActions	int	•			NONE if no property descriptor; COPY otherwise
visualRepresentation	Icon	•			null

^s static

Constructors

protected TransferHandler( )
> A convenience constructor for subclasses.

public TransferHandler(String property)
> This constructor sets up a handler based on the specified property. For example, the JColorChooser uses this type of handler for the color property. If you have JavaBeans, this is a simple way to drag and drop properties from one bean to another.

Methods

public void exportAsDrag(JComponent comp, InputEvent e, int action)
public void exportToClipboard(JComponent comp, Clipboard clip, int action)

These methods both start the export process. In the case of exportAsDrag( ), this means starting a drag event. In the case of exportToClipboard( ), this means using the specified clipboard (clip). The source of the event is given with comp, and the action (copy, link, or move) is also given.

protected void exportDone(JComponent source, Transferable data, int action)

This method is called at the completion of an export event. For drag events, this happens when the drop is completed (or rejected). For clipboards, it is called as soon as the clipboard contains the exported data (cut and copy actions do not wait for a corresponding paste action).

public boolean importData(JComponent comp, Transferable t)

This method does all the work on the import side. The source of the event (or target of the drop, if you prefer) is comp. The data is encapsulated in the Transferable object t. From t you can learn how to import the data or whether importing the data is necessary. You can then work with comp to accomplish the import. If the import succeeds, you should return true; return false otherwise.

public boolean canImport(JComponent comp, DataFlavor[] transferFlavors)

This straightforward method should return true if comp can import data via one of the flavors listed in transferFlavors. It should return false in all other cases.

protected Transferable createTransferable(JComponent c)

This is the workhorse for the export side. You should build (and return) a Transferable object based on the given component c. (If your handler is strictly for importing data, you can leave the default version of this method intact.)

The Drag Gesture API

Now that the drop side is working, how do we make the drag side go? First, we need a bit of background information. To successfully accomplish a drag in Java, we must first recognize what constitutes a drag gesture. A *drag gesture* is an action the user takes to indicate that she's starting a drag. Typically, this is a mouse drag event, but it is not hard to imagine other gestures that could be used. For example, a voice-activated system might listen for the words "pick up" or something similar.

The API for drag gestures is fairly simple. Four DnD classes and interfaces make up the core: DragGestureRecognizer, MouseDragGestureRecognizer, DragGestureListener, and DragGestureEvent, as shown in Figure 24-4.

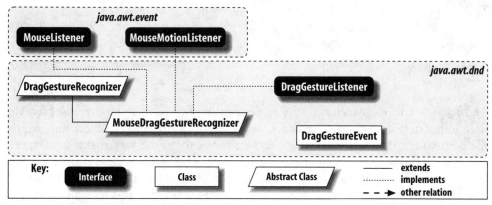

Figure 24-4. Drag recognition class diagram

The DragGestureRecognizer Class

At the heart of this API is the DragGestureRecognizer class. Basically, the recognizer is responsible for recognizing a sequence of events that says "start dragging." This can be quite different for different platforms, so the DragGestureRecognizer class is abstract and must be subclassed to create an appropriate implementation. (The MouseDragGestureRecognizer takes a few more steps to complete the class and makes assumptions about using a mouse as the trigger for drag events. You can use the tool-kit on your system to retrieve a concrete version.) This sounds more complex than it is. The idea is that you attach a drag gesture recognizer to a component with code similar to this:

```
JLabel jl = new JLabel("Drag Me!");
DragSource ds = new DragSource();
DragGestureRecognizer dgr = ds.createDefaultDragGestureRecognizer(
                    jl, DnDConstants.ACTION_COPY, this);
```

Now when you click on the jl label and start dragging, a drag gesture is recognized. The system then reports that recognition to your application through any registered DragGestureListener. An example is shown later in this section.

Properties

The DragGestureRecognizer uses the properties in Table 24-12 to hold information about a drag operation.

Table 24-12. DragGestureRecognizer properties

Property	Data type	get	is	set	Default value
component	Component	•		•	null
dragSource	DragSource	•			Passed through constructor

Table 24-12. DragGestureRecognizer properties (continued)

Property	Data type	get	is	set	Default value
sourceActions	int	•		•	ACTION_NONE
triggerEvent	InputEvent	•			null

The component property refers to the component registered as the source for possible drag initiations. The dragSource property represents a DragSource object that wraps the component that are generating drags in much the same way that a DropTarget object wraps components that are receiving drops. The sourceActions property is the set of acceptable drag operations (coming from DnDConstants) for the drag source. The triggerEvent returns the first in a list of events that led to this recognizer declaring that a drag started. If no drag is currently recognized, this property is null.

Events

As mentioned before, the DragGestureRecognizer reports its events to a DragGestureListener and sends a DragGestureEvent. The usual add and remove methods for the listener are available.

public void addDragGestureListener(DragGestureListener dgl)
  throws TooManyListenersException
public void removeDragGestureListener(DragGestureListener dgl)
> These methods supply the usual support for registering and unregistering listeners with the recognizer. Note that this is a unicast event; only one listener is allowed.

protected abstract void registerListeners( )
protected abstract void unregisterListeners( )
> These protected methods register (and unregister) the appropriate trigger event listeners with the component associated with this recognizer. For example, if a drag starts with the user dragging the mouse, these methods would register the recognizer with the component as a MouseMotionListener. The listeners that a subclass registers to receive depend entirely on the events that can trigger a drag.

protected void fireDragGestureRecognized(int dragAction, Point p)
> This method creates a DragGestureEvent and notifies the registered listener (if any) that a drag gesture has been recognized. The dragAction argument is one of the DnDConstants actions. The location of the mouse when the trigger event occurred is contained in p.

Fields

DragGestureRecognizer defines the following fields:

protected DragSource dragSource
protected Component component
protected int sourceActions
> These fields support the properties of the same names.

protected DragGestureListener dragGestureListener
> This field stores the active listener registered with the recognizer.

protected ArrayList events
> This field stores the list of events that triggered the recognition of a drag gesture. The `triggerEvent` property corresponds to the first element in this list. This field can be manipulated through the `appendEvent( )` and `resetRecognizer( )` methods.

Constructors

All of the constructors for `DragGestureRecognizer` are protected. Because the class is abstract, a subclass is needed to create an instance of `DragGestureRecognizer` anyway. In real programs, you would use the `DragSource.createDefaultDragGestureRecognizer( )` method or the `Toolkit.createDragGestureRecognizer( )` method to build a recognizer.

protected DragGestureRecognizer(DragSource ds)
protected DragGestureRecognizer(DragSource ds, Component c)
protected DragGestureRecognizer(DragSource ds, Component c, int sa)
protected DragGestureRecognizer(DragSource ds, Component c, int sa,
  DragGestureListener dgl)
> Create `DragGestureRecognizer` objects and use the supplied arguments to override the default property values for `dragSource`, `component`, and `sourceActions`, respectively. If supplied, `dgl` is used as the listener for any recognition events.

Trigger event list methods

Since it is possible a sequence of events (such as pressing the Tab key and then dragging the mouse) is responsible for causing a drag, the following methods help set up the list of trigger events correctly:

protected void appendEvent(InputEvent awtie)
> This method allows individual events to be stored in the recognizer. The list can be cleared using the `resetRecognizer( )` method.

public void resetRecognizer( )
> This method clears any events in the trigger event list. If a drag is currently in progress, it is effectively cancelled.

The MouseDragGestureRecognizer Class

For many applications, we use the mouse drag as the drag gesture. The `MouseDragGestureRecognizer` class implements the appropriate recognizer functions for us. Note that this class is still abstract. Individual platforms must subclass it and fill out the specifics of what constitutes a valid drag initiation. However, this class does make it much easier to create your own recognizer than to start from the DragGestureRecognizer class directly.

As you start playing with DnD functionality, you will probably rely on the prebuilt recognizers you can retrieve from the DragSource class.

Constructors

The MouseDragGestureRecognizer class contains the same set of constructors found in its parent class:

```
protected MouseDragGestureRecognizer(DragSource ds)
protected MouseDragGestureRecognizer(DragSource ds, Component c)
protected MouseDragGestureRecognizer(DragSource ds, Component c, int act)
protected MouseDragGestureRecognizer(DragSource ds, Component c, int act,
    DragGestureListener dgl)
```

Mouse methods

Because this class recognizes gestures started by mouse events, it implements both the MouseListener and MouseMotionListener interfaces. The following methods come from these interfaces:

public void mouseClicked(MouseEvent e)
public void mouseDragged(MouseEvent e)
public void mouseEntered(MouseEvent e)
public void mouseExited(MouseEvent e)
public void mouseMoved(MouseEvent e)
public void mousePressed(MouseEvent e)
public void mouseReleased(MouseEvent e)
   In the MouseDragGestureRecognizer class, these methods are all empty. Sub-classes must override the methods to provide appropriate functionality.

Listener methods

This class implements the two abstract methods inherited from DragGestureListener:

protected void registerListeners( )
protected void unregisterListeners( )
   These methods register and unregister this recognizer as a MouseListener and a MouseMotionListener with its component.

The Drag Gesture Events and Listeners

The DragGestureListener interface provides one method to indicate whether a drag gesture has been recognized:

```
public void dragGestureRecognized(DragGestureEvent dge)
```

The DragGestureEvent provides you with everything you need to know about the drag the user has initiated. If you like everything you see, you can start the drag process. If something is wrong (the wrong action, the wrong object to drag, the application is not in a draggable mode, etc.), you can ignore the gesture.

Properties

Most of the properties stored in a DragGestureEvent provide convenient access to similar properties in the DragGestureRecognizer that generated the event. These are listed in Table 24-13.

Table 24-13. DragGestureEvent properties

Property	Data type	get	is	set	Default value
component	Component	•			
dragAction	int	•			
dragOrigin	Point	•			
dragSource	DragSource	•			
sourceAsDragGestureRecognizer	DragGestureRecognizer	•			
triggerEvent	InputEvent	•			

The dragOrigin property corresponds to the location of the mouse when the gesture was recognized. The sourceAsDragGestureRecognizer property is merely a convenience property allowing you to access the source of the event as a DragGestureRecognizer rather than as an Object, which is what happens with the source property inherited from the EventObject class.

Event list methods

In discussing the DragGestureRecognizer fields, we noted that several events can be sequenced together to create a drag. The entire list of these events can be retrieved with these methods:

public Iterator iterator( )
> This method returns an iterator for the ArrayList storing the events. If you've worked with the Collections APIs, this method may be more to your liking.

public Object[] toArray( )
public Object[] toArray(Object[] array)
> These methods return the list of events in an Object array. The first method creates a new array, while the second fills the supplied array.

Drag initiation methods

We worry about DragGestureEvent objects because they have the mechanism for starting a drag operation. These methods are required to get a drag underway and usually appear in your dragGestureRecognized( ) method. Now you can package the data to be dragged and pick a cursor to indicate that a successful drag start has occurred. (You can pick one of the cursors predefined in the DragSource class. See Table 24-15 for a complete list.) This sounds worse than it is. Be sure to look at the example code to get an idea of the relatively small amount of programming required.

public void startDrag(Cursor dragCursor, Transferable transferable,
  DragSourceListener dsl) throws InvalidDnDOperationException
    This method starts a drag operation with the initial cursor defined by dragCursor. The data that will be transferred in the operation needs to be wrapped up in a Transferable object. The dsl argument should be the DragSourceListener associated with the drag source. Often, you can bundle the DragSourceListener and the DragGestureListener together in one class.

public void startDrag(Cursor dragCursor, Image dragImage, Point imageOffset,
  Transferable transferable, DragSourceListener dsl)
  throws InvalidDnDOperationException
    This method is similar to the first startDrag( ) with the exception of the dragImage and imageOffset arguments. If draggable images are supported on your platform (they may not be!), then you can supply an image and an offset to use during the drag operation. The offset represents the location of the mouse pointer relative to the upper-left corner of the image. You can find out if your platform supports drag images using the dragImageSupported property of the DragSource class, which is discussed in the next section.

A Simple Gesture

While they won't do us any good by themselves, we need to familiarize ourselves with these drag gestures before we can do anything with the DnD process. (This must be done in the 1.3 and 1.2 SDKs. In the 1.4 SDK, we need to do this only if we want more control over the drag process.) Here's a simple example of a JList object that will eventually contain draggable list items. Right now, we'll just make sure that we can recognize a drag gesture when it happens in our list object.

```
/*
 * GestureTest.java
 * A simple (?) test of the DragSource classes to
 * create a draggable object in a Java application
 */

import java.awt.*;
import java.awt.dnd.*;
import java.awt.datatransfer.*;
import java.awt.event.*;
import java.io.*;
import java.util.*;
import javax.swing.*;

public class GestureTest extends JFrame {
```

```
    DragSource ds;
    JList jl;
    String[] items = {"Java", "C", "C++", "Lisp", "Perl", "Python"};

    public GestureTest( ) {
      super("Gesture Test");
      setSize(200,150);
      setDefaultCloseOperation(EXIT_ON_CLOSE);

      // Create a JList object and add it to our application.
      jl = new JList(items);
      jl.setSelectionMode(ListSelectionModel.SINGLE_SELECTION);
      getContentPane( ).add(new JScrollPane(jl), BorderLayout.CENTER);

      // Now create a DragRecognizer with the DragSource class; you can
      // use a Toolkit if you prefer. Notice that we specify our JList
      // object when creating the recognizer, not when creating the drag
      // source.
      ds = new DragSource( );
      DragGestureRecognizer dgr = ds.createDefaultDragGestureRecognizer(
                            jl, DnDConstants.ACTION_COPY,
                            new DragGestureListener( ) {
          // Report the recognized drag event to the console.
          public void dragGestureRecognized(DragGestureEvent dge) {
            System.out.println("Drag Gesture Recognized!");
          }
        });

      setVisible(true);
    }

    public static void main(String args[]) {
      new GestureTest( );
    }
  }
}
```

The Drag API

Once you recognize a drag gesture, you can start an actual drag. The drag source
receives many of the same types of events as the drop target. Like a drop target, a
drag source has a native peer in the form of a DragSourceContext and receives events
as the user drags his object over the source and finally drops it on a drop target. As
shown in Figure 24-5, the class diagram for the Drag API is similar to that of the
Drop API.

The DragSource Class

The DragSource class, the flip side of DropTarget, provides support for creating draggable information. Recall from the beginning of this chapter that unlike the
DropTarget class, a regular GUI component is not used as a base. Rather, the base

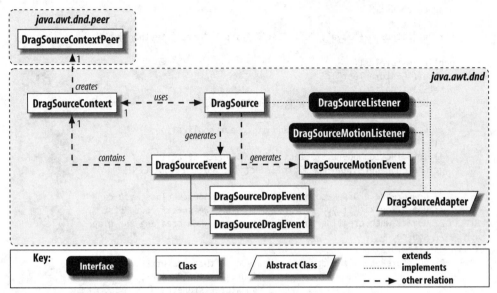

Figure 24-5. Class diagram of DnD's drag side

component for starting a drag is encapsulated in the DragGestureRecognizer. The recognizer can in turn start a drag for the DragSource. The DragSource class encompasses the context of the drag and provides a focal point for maintaining the visual state of the drag. For example, several predefined cursors that you can use during the drag operation are built into this class.

Properties

The DragSource class has only three properties, two of which are static and apply to the overall DnD system. These properties are shown in Table 24-14.

Table 24-14. DragSource properties

Property	Data type	get	is	set	Default value
defaultDragSource[s]	DragSource	•			
dragImageSupported[s]	boolean		•		
dragSourceListeners[1.4]	DragSourceListener[]	•			Empty array
dragSourceMotionListeners[1.4]	DragSourceMotionListener[]	•			Empty array
flavorMap	FlavorMap	•			

[s]static, [1.4]since 1.4

The defaultDragSource property provides a "platform" drag source that can be retrieved from any other class. Since you do not really associate a component with a drag source, you can rely entirely on this default source during your drags. (This is not required; you can build your own.) The flavorMap property stores the flavor map for the source to help translate between native names and MIME types. The dragImageSupported property indicates whether your system can drag an Image along with the cursor during a drag operation.

Constants

Several predefined cursors are at your disposal as constants in DragSource. These cursor constants can be used when starting a drag operation and are listed in Table 24-15. The sample images are merely representative of the types of cursors that appear. They may vary from system to system; with Java 2, you are certainly free to create your own.

Table 24-15. DragSource constants

Constant	Data type	Illustration
DefaultCopyDrop	Cursor	
DefaultCopyNoDrop	Cursor	
DefaultLinkDrop	Cursor	
DefaultLinkNoDrop	Cursor	
DefaultMoveDrop	Cursor	
DefaultMoveNoDrop	Cursor	

Events

DragSource generates two types of events and includes the appropriate add and remove methods. The listeners and drag events are described later in this section.

public void addDragSourceListener()
public void removeDragSourceListener()
    Manage listeners for source events such as reporting when a successful drop occurs on the drop side.

public void addDragSourceMotionListener()
public void removeDragSourceMotionListener()
    Manage listeners for source motion events. You might listen to motion events if you support any custom functionality based on the location of the mouse. (For example, if you still want to notice when a user passes into a particular part of the screen that is not a drop target.)

Constructor

DragSource has one public constructor:

public DragSource()
    This constructor creates a new DragSource.

Helper creation methods

The DragSource class has a few helper methods to create the other parts required for initiating a drag:

public DragGestureRecognizer createDefaultDragGestureRecognizer(Component c,
    int actions, DragGestureListener dgl)
public DragGestureRecognizer createDragGestureRecognizer(Class recognizerClass,
    Component c, int actions, DragGestureListener dgl)
    These methods can be used to create DragGestureRecognizer objects for your drag-capable component (c). Again, the actions argument comes from DnDConstants and dictates the types of actions (move, copy, link) that are acceptable. You can give a null listener for the dgl argument and attach one to the recognizer later. The second version of this method uses recognizerClass as a prototype for the recognizer. The recognizerClass argument should be a subclass of DragGestureRecognizer.

protected DragSourceContext createDragSourceContext(DragSourceContextPeer dscp,
    DragGestureEvent dgl, Cursor dragCursor, Image dragImage, Point imageOffset,
    Transferable t, DragSourceListener dsl)
    This protected method creates a new context object for the DragSource. As with other peer operations, this is not something you normally need to use. However, subclasses can override this to create context objects suited to a particular task, such as supplying a certain image to go with the drag operation.

Start methods

As you saw in the DragGestureEvent class, once a drag gesture has been recognized, you need to start the drag manually. You can use either the drag event versions, or if you need a bit more control, you can use any of the following methods as well:

public void startDrag(DragGestureEvent trigger, Cursor dragCursor,
    Transferable transferable, DragSourceListener dsl)
    throws InvalidDnDOperationException
    The simplest of the start methods, this requires only a trigger event (trigger), an initial cursor to display (dragCursor), the data to be transferred (transferable), and a source listener (which can be null). If the system is not in a state in which a drag initiation is allowed (typically because a peer DragSourceContext cannot be created), it throws the InvalidDnDOperationException.

public void startDrag(DragGestureEvent trigger, Cursor dragCursor,
   Transferable transferable, DragSourceListener dsl, FlavorMap flavorMap)
   throws InvalidDnDOperationException
      Similar to the previous method, this version allows you to specify your own fla-
      vor map.

public void startDrag(DragGestureEvent trigger, Cursor dragCursor,
   Image dragImage, Point dragOffset, Transferable transferable,
   DragSourceListener dsl) throws InvalidDnDOperationException
      If your system supports drag images, you can specify the image and the offset for
      the cursor location in that image. Remember that not all systems support drag
      images.

public void startDrag(DragGestureEvent trigger, Cursor dragCursor,
   Image dragImage, Point imageOffset, Transferable transferable,
   DragSourceListener dsl, FlavorMap flavorMap)
   throws InvalidDnDOperationException
      Similar to the other startDrag( ) methods, but you can specify both a drag image
      and a flavor map if you have them.

The DragSourceContext Class

As you may have gathered from the previous section, DragSource objects use a
DragSourceContext to handle the necessary native windowing code in much the same
way DropTarget objects do. You don't have to create an instance of this class on your
own, but you can access the context from the DragSource class if you need any of the
information provided by the context.

Properties

The properties for DragSourceContext are shown in Table 24-16. They are all read-only.

Table 24-16. DragSourceContext properties

Property	Data type	get	is	set	Default value
component	Component	•			
cursor	Cursor	•			
dragSource	DragSource	•			
sourceActions	int	•			
transferable	Transferable	•			
trigger	InputEvent	•			

These properties give you access to the "way things look" during a drag operation. With the exception of the cursor property, which can tell you which cursor is currently displayed, these properties are similar to those in the DragGestureEvent class.

Events

The DragSourceContext class is the source of DragSource events. By definition, the source of an event contains the appropriate add and remove methods for attaching listeners. While you can use these methods to attach (or detach) a listener, you typically pass in your listener when you call a startDrag() method. (The actual DragSourceEvent class is described in the next section.)

public void addDragSourceListener(DragSourceListener dsl)
  throws TooManyListenersException
public void removeDragSourceListener(DragSourceListener dsl)
  These methods add or remove a drag source listener for this context. Notice that this is a unicast event.

Protected constants

Table 24-17 defines four protected constants found in the DragSourceContext class.

Table 24-17. DragSourceContext constants

Constant	Data type	Description
CHANGED	int	The user action changed (usually between copy and move).
DEFAULT	int	Switches to the default cursor.
ENTER	int	The cursor entered a drop target.
OVER	int	The cursor is over a drop target.

These constants are used to identify cursor actions in the updateCurrentCursor() method, which is described later.

Constructors

You can create a DragSourceContext with its only constructor. However, you need a valid DragSourceContextPeer for your platform. Normally, you use the startDrag() methods, and a context is created for you.

```
    public DragSourceContext(DragSourceContextPeer dscp,
        DragGestureEvent trigger, Cursor dragCursor, Image dragImage,
        Point offset, Transferable t, DragSourceListener dsl)
```

Event methods

Like the DropTargetContext class, DragSourceContext implements the DragSourceListener interface itself.

---

public void dragEnter(DragSourceDragEvent dsde)
public void dragOver(DragSourceDragEvent dsde)
public void dragExit(DragSourceEvent dse)
public void dropActionChanged(DragSourceDragEvent dsde)
public void dragDropEnd(DragSourceDropEvent dsde)

> These methods come from the DragSourceListener interface. They trap incoming events and, if a valid listener exists, the events are passed on. The cursor is then updated for you automatically.

Miscellaneous methods

Two other methods round out the functionality of the DragSourceContext class:

public void transferablesFlavorsChanged( )

> This method can also be used to indicate that something has changed in the current drag process. If the data flavor for the Transferable object changes, this method can be called to notify the native peer of that change.

protected void updateCurrentCursor(int dropOp, int targetAct, int status)

> Each of the previous event methods use this method to update the cursor as the user moves around over potential drop targets and other parts of the application. The dropOp argument is the current action the user has undertaken. The targetAction argument lists the acceptable drop actions for the current target, and status indicates the type of update for the current cursor. This can be any of the values from Table 24-17.

The DragSourceListener Interface

If you care about events being sent to the drag source, you should implement the DragSourceListener interface. All drag events generated over the source object and the drop event (either an accepted drop over a valid drop target or a rejected drop) are sent here.

Event methods

The types of events presented here mimic the types we saw with the DropTargetListener interface:

public void dragEnter(DragSourceDragEvent dsde)

> This method handles events generated as the user enters a viable drop target.

public void dragOver(DragSourceDragEvent dsde)

> This method handles events that are generated continuously as the user moves around inside the bounds of a viable drop target.

public void dropActionChanged(DragSourceDragEvent dsde)

> If the user changes from copy to move or vice versa, this method receives that event.

public void dragExit(DragSourceEvent dse)
    This method handles the events generated when the user leaves the bounds of a viable target.

public void dragDropEnd(DragSourceDropEvent dsde)
    Not found in the `DropTargetListener` interface, this method is notified when a drop has completed on a drop target. Notification does not imply success; you need to check the dsde event for that. The events are discussed in the next section.

The DragSourceMotionListener Interface

If you care about events being sent while a drag is in motion, you should implement the `DragSourceMotionListener` interface. Introduced in 1.4, this interface allows you to listen in on the current position of a drag that is in progress. You might need this if you plan to respond to the location of the mouse cursor during a drag. While you probably won't use this interface, it is vital for any custom DnD support.

Event method

The event presented here is similar to the types found in the `MouseMotionListener` interface:

public void dragMouseMoved(DragSourceDragEvent dsde)
    This method handles events generated as the user moves the mouse after starting a drag.

The DragSourceAdapter Class

As with the `DropTargetAdapter` from the previous section, the drag source listeners have a companion adapter: `DragSourceAdapter`. This class was introduced in 1.4 and implements both `DragSourceListener` and `DragSourceMotionListener`. It provides null bodies for each of the listener's methods.

Drag Source Events

Not surprisingly, we have drag source events similar to the drop target events. The `DragSourceEvent` class serves as the base of the event hierarchy and gives you access to the source context through its sole property, shown in Table 24-18.

Table 24-18. DragSourceEvent property

Property	Data type	get	is	set	Default value
dragSourceContext	DragSourceContext	•			

Constructors

public DragSourceEvent(DragSourceContext dsc)
public DragSourceEvent(DragSourceContext dsc, int x, int y)

> If you have a valid `DragSourceContext`, you can build your own `DragSourceEvent` with this constructor. As of SDK 1.4, you can also specify (x,y) coordinates for the event.

The DragSourceDragEvent Class

The subclasses of `DragSourceEvent` distinguish between dragging events and drop events. `DragSourceDragEvent` is used in a majority of the events reported, with the exception of exit events and drop complete events.

Properties

The `DragSourceDragEvent` properties help you decide how the source of the drag should respond to various things the user does. Most of the properties deal with the types of actions the user can take and, of course, what the user is really doing. They are shown in Table 24-19.

Table 24-19. DragSourceDragEvent properties

Property	Data type	get	is	set	Default value
dropAction	int	•			
gestureModifiers	int	•			
targetActions	int	•			
userAction	int	•			

`dropAction` represents the effective drop action found by combining the user's currently selected drop action (`userAction`) and the actions acceptable to the target (`targetActions`). Differences in the `dropAction` and `userAction` can be used to provide helpful feedback to the user during the drag operation. The `gestureModifiers` property describes the state of any input modifiers, such as holding down the Control key.

The DragSourceDropEvent Class

While it's not required, your source might care about the success (or failure) of a drop. This class encapsulates the drop event and its status.

Properties

Table 24-20 shows the two properties available from a `DragSourceDropEvent`.

Table 24-20. DragSourceDropEvent properties

Property	Data type	get	is	set	Default value
dropAction	int	•			
dropSuccess	boolean	•			

The dropAction property contains the final drop action taken by the user. If the drop target accepts the drop, dropSuccess is true (false otherwise). You may recall the dropComplete( ) method from the DropTargetDropEvent class. The dropSuccess property reflects the value passed to that method.

Completing the Gesture

Now we can go back to our GestureTest program and finish the job. We'll complete the DragSource object and add some listener methods so that we can see the different events as they are reported to the DragSourceListener. You should pay attention to what we do in the dragGestureRecognized( ) method, which is where we manually start the drag operation. (See Figure 24-6.)

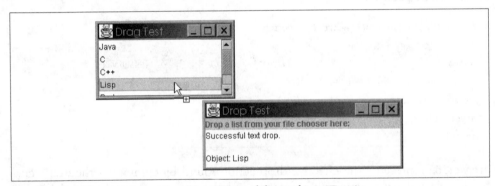

Figure 24-6. A drag operation started in a JList and dropped in a JTextArea

Here's the source for the complete DragTest application. (We used DropTest2 with the expanded drop( ) method for the receiving end.)

```
/*
 * DragTest.java
 * A simple (?) test of the DragSource classes to
 * create a draggable object in a Java application.
 */

import java.awt.*;
import java.awt.dnd.*;
import java.awt.datatransfer.*;
import java.awt.event.*;
import java.io.*;
import java.util.*;
import javax.swing.*;
```

```
public class DragTest extends JFrame implements DragSourceListener,
DragGestureListener {

  DragSource ds;
  JList jl;
  StringSelection transferable;
  String[] items = {"Java", "C", "C++", "Lisp", "Perl", "Python"};

  public DragTest( ) {
    super("Drag Test");
    setSize(200,150);
    setDefaultCloseOperation(EXIT_ON_CLOSE);

    // Set up our JList and DragRecognizer as before. This time, the difference is
    // that we use the recognized drag to start a real drag process.
    jl = new JList(items);
    jl.setSelectionMode(ListSelectionModel.SINGLE_SELECTION);
    getContentPane( ).add(new JScrollPane(jl), BorderLayout.CENTER);

    ds = new DragSource( );
    DragGestureRecognizer dgr = ds.createDefaultDragGestureRecognizer(
      jl, DnDConstants.ACTION_COPY, this);
    setVisible(true);
  }

  // In addition to reporting a successful gesture, create a piece of transferable
  // data using java.awt.datatransfer.StringSelection.
  public void dragGestureRecognized(DragGestureEvent dge) {
    System.out.println("Drag Gesture Recognized!");
    transferable = new StringSelection(jl.getSelectedValue( ).toString( ));
    ds.startDrag(dge, DragSource.DefaultCopyDrop, transferable, this);
  }

  public void dragEnter(DragSourceDragEvent dsde) {
    System.out.println("Drag Enter");
  }

  public void dragExit(DragSourceEvent dse) {
    System.out.println("Drag Exit");
  }

  public void dragOver(DragSourceDragEvent dsde) {
    System.out.println("Drag Over");
  }

  public void dragDropEnd(DragSourceDropEvent dsde) {
    System.out.print("Drag Drop End: ");
    if (dsde.getDropSuccess( )) {
      System.out.println("Succeeded");
    }
    else {
      System.out.println("Failed");
    }
  }
}
```

```
        public void dropActionChanged(DragSourceDragEvent dsde) {
          System.out.println("Drop Action Changed");
        }

        public static void main(String args[]) {
          new DragTest( );
        }
      }
```

With this version of the dragGestureRecognized( ) method, we create a real piece of
draggable information. In our particular case, we create a String object with the
StringSelection class. This object can be picked up by other Java applications as a
String or as a serialized Java object—admittedly, not the ideal transfer medium if
you are serious about dropping this text in a native application. Fortunately, the
StringSelection class also supports the "plain-text" flavor, which is more useful for
native applications.

While we won't waste the paper needed to present it here, you can see the 1.4 version of this example in the online code. (It's also somewhat boring because it just
works.) Check out *DragTest14.java* and *DropTest14.java*. Again, these examples
work so cleanly because they don't require any customization. We hope that you'll
be in the same position more often than not.

Rearranging Trees

The JTree class is a ripe candidate for the DnD system. Adding nodes to a tree, moving nodes from one tree to another, or even just rearranging the nodes within a single tree can all be accomplished quite easily with DnD gestures. Unfortunately, JTree
does not have any built-in support for these actions. The next few examples take a
look at extending JTree to include such features.

A TransferHandler Example

At the beginning of the chapter we mentioned that 1.4 made several parts of the DnD
API obsolete—at least for simple tasks. That point is worth reiterating. If you have a
simple drop target or a simple drag source that requires custom handling, you can
use the TransferHandler class and the transferHandler property of JComponent to do
most of your work.

One common feature of graphical trees is the ability to add nodes by dropping them
into an existing tree. While the TransferHandler approach cannot handle all of the
intricacies of adding and rearranging trees, it can make basic imports very straightforward.

Here's an example of a tree that can accept incoming lists of files from the native
windowing system. You can drag icons from your desktop or file manager and drop
them into the tree. They are appended to the root folder.

```
/*
 * FSTree.java
 * A sample component for dragging & dropping a collection of files
 * into a tree.
 */

import javax.swing.*;
import javax.swing.tree.*;
import java.awt.dnd.*;
import java.awt.datatransfer.*;
import java.util.List;
import java.util.Iterator;
import java.awt.Point;
import java.awt.Rectangle;
import java.awt.Insets;
import java.io.File;
import java.io.IOException;

public class FSTree extends JTree {

  public FSTree() { super(); init(); }
  public FSTree(TreeModel newModel) { super(newModel); init(); }
  public FSTree(TreeNode root) { super(root); init(); }
  public FSTree(TreeNode root, boolean asks) { super(root, asks); init();}

  private void init() {
    // We don't want to export anything from this tree, only import.
    setDragEnabled(false);
    setTransferHandler(new FSTransfer());
  }

  public class FSTransfer extends TransferHandler {
    public boolean importData(JComponent comp, Transferable t) {
      // Make sure we have the right starting points.
      if (!(comp instanceof FSTree)) {
        return false;
      }
      if (!t.isDataFlavorSupported(DataFlavor.javaFileListFlavor)) {
        return false;
      }

      // Grab the tree, its model, and the root node.
      FSTree tree = (FSTree)comp;
      DefaultTreeModel model = (DefaultTreeModel)tree.getModel();
      DefaultMutableTreeNode root = (DefaultMutableTreeNode)model.getRoot();
      try {
        List data = (List)t.getTransferData(DataFlavor.javaFileListFlavor);
        Iterator i = data.iterator();
        while (i.hasNext()) {
          File f = (File)i.next();
          root.add(new DefaultMutableTreeNode(f.getName()));
        }
        model.reload();
        return true;
```

```
      }
      catch (UnsupportedFlavorException ufe) {
        System.err.println("Ack! we should not be here.\nBad Flavor.");
      }
      catch (IOException ioe) {
        System.out.println("Something failed during import:\n" + ioe);
      }
      return false;
    }

    // We support only file lists on FSTrees.
    public boolean canImport(JComponent comp, DataFlavor[] transferFlavors) {
      if (comp instanceof FSTree) {
        for (int i = 0; i < transferFlavors.length; i++) {
          if (!transferFlavors[i].equals(DataFlavor.javaFileListFlavor)) {
            return false;
          }
        }
        return true;
      }
      return false;
    }
  }
}
```

As you can see, the majority of the work goes into overriding the two import methods from TransferHandler. The tree component is quite simple. We disable dragging and install our new DnD handler. The FSTransfer inner class iterates through the files dropped on the tree and appends them to the root folder. This example is more for show, so we just store the name of the file in the tree. A slightly more advanced FSTree would probably store the file itself.

While it's not exciting in static mode, after adding a few entries from the desktop of a Windows system, our new tree looks like Figure 24-7.

And here's the simple program that builds the instance of FSTree:

```
/*
 * FSTest.java
 * A quick test environment for the FSTree component.
 */

import javax.swing.*;
import javax.swing.tree.*;

public class FSTest extends JFrame {

  public FSTest() {
    super("FSTree Component Test");
    setSize(300,300);
    setDefaultCloseOperation(EXIT_ON_CLOSE);
```

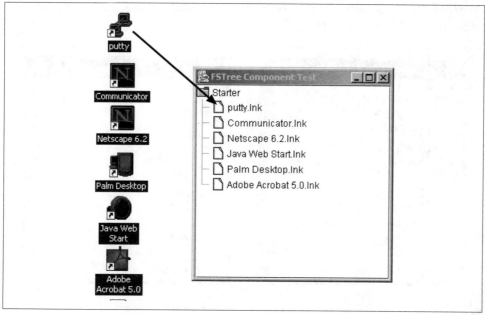

Figure 24-7. A drag operation resulting in a filled-out, drop-enabled JTree

```
    FSTree fst = new FSTree(new DefaultMutableTreeNode("Starter"));
    getContentPane().add(new JScrollPane(fst));
    setVisible(true);
  }

  public static void main(String args[]) {
    new FSTest();
  }
}
```

Of course, a slightly more advanced FSTree would allow you to add nodes to something other than the root folder. If you want to manage drops based on things such as the (x,y) coordinates where the drop occurred, the TransferHandler won't do the trick. You'll need to rely on the lower-level classes and events that we looked at in this chapter. The next section looks into that low-level control in more detail. If you use a 1.2 or 1.3 system, the process presented in the next section is the only way to go. But again, even if you have the TransferHandler mechanism from 1.4, it might not always be sufficient.

A Rearranging Example

We can apply all this lower-level DnD functionality to JTree objects to overcome a deficiency in the user interface. On its own, JTree has no facility for visually rearranging its leaves and branches. We can create appropriate DnD event handlers from scratch and our own transferable type to implement this functionality for any JTree we build. The code in this example works with SDK 1.2 and higher. Figure 24-8 shows the resulting tree.

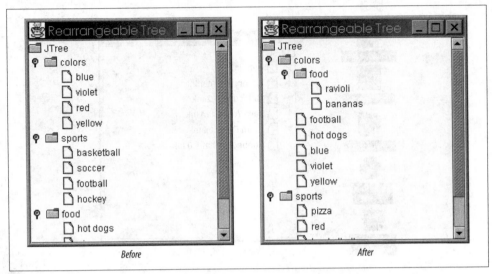

Figure 24-8. *An editable tree before and after items have been dragged and dropped*

"Before" and "after" screenshots still don't do this application justice. But notice that you can move entire folders as well as individual items. Any node can be dragged and dropped into any folder. You are, however, limited to dropping items into a folder. As with the other examples in this chapter, you must compile the code and play with the application to get the full effect. In the meantime, here's the source code for the Drag half of our example. Don't worry too much about the TransferableTreeNode class (we discuss this in greater detail in the next section). For now, just think of it as a DnD wrapper for a tree node.

```
/*
 * TreeDragSource.java
 * A more involved test of the DnD system to see if
 * we can create a self-contained, rearrangable JTree. This is
 * the Drop half.
 */

import java.awt.*;
import java.awt.dnd.*;
import java.awt.datatransfer.*;
import java.awt.event.*;
import java.io.*;
import java.util.*;
import javax.swing.*;
import javax.swing.tree.*;

public class TreeDragSource
implements DragSourceListener, DragGestureListener {
```

```
    DragSource source;
    DragGestureRecognizer recognizer;
    TransferableTreeNode transferable;
    DefaultMutableTreeNode oldNode;
    JTree sourceTree;

    public TreeDragSource(JTree tree, int actions) {
      sourceTree = tree;
      source = new DragSource();
      recognizer = source.createDefaultDragGestureRecognizer(
          sourceTree, actions, this);
    }

    // Drag gesture handler
    public void dragGestureRecognized(DragGestureEvent dge) {
      TreePath path = sourceTree.getSelectionPath();
      if ((path == null) || (path.getPathCount() <= 1)) {
        // We can't really move the root node (or an empty selection).
        return;
      }
      // Remember which node was dragged off so we can delete it to complete a move
      // operation.
      oldNode = (DefaultMutableTreeNode)path.getLastPathComponent();

      // Make a version of the node that we can use in the DnD system.
      transferable = new TransferableTreeNode(path);

      // And start the drag process. We start with a no-drop cursor, assuming that the
      // user won't want to drop the item right where she picked it up.
      source.startDrag(dge, DragSource.DefaultMoveNoDrop, transferable, this);

      // If you support dropping the node anywhere, you should probably start with a
      // valid move cursor:
      //      source.startDrag(dge, DragSource.DefaultMoveDrop, transferable, this);
    }

    // Drag event handlers
    public void dragEnter(DragSourceDragEvent dsde) { }
    public void dragExit(DragSourceEvent dse) { }
    public void dragOver(DragSourceDragEvent dsde) { }
    public void dropActionChanged(DragSourceDragEvent dsde) { }

    public void dragDropEnd(DragSourceDropEvent dsde) {
      if (dsde.getDropSuccess()) {
        // Remove the node only if the drop was successful.
        ((DefaultTreeModel)sourceTree.getModel())
            .removeNodeFromParent(oldNode);
      }
    }
  }
```

This allows us to recognize a drag and build a valid Transferable object to accompany the drag. The drop side needs to take the drop, figure out where it landed, and decide what to do with it. If the drop occurred over a folder and contained one of our special tree node objects, we accept the drop. If it was over a file or was not a tree node, we reject the drag. (And we finally get to put some of those weird JTree methods to use!)

```java
/*
 * TreeDropTarget.java
 * A more involved test of the DnD system to see if
 * we can create a self-contained, rearrangable JTree. This is
 * the Drop half.
 */

import java.awt.*;
import java.awt.dnd.*;
import java.awt.datatransfer.*;
import java.awt.event.*;
import java.io.*;
import java.util.*;
import javax.swing.*;
import javax.swing.tree.*;

public class TreeDropTarget implements DropTargetListener {

  DropTarget target;
  JTree targetTree;

  public TreeDropTarget(JTree tree) {
    targetTree = tree;
    target = new DropTarget(targetTree, this);
  }

  // Drop event handlers
  public void dragEnter(DropTargetDragEvent dtde) { }
  public void dragOver(DropTargetDragEvent dtde) { }
  public void dragExit(DropTargetEvent dte) { }
  public void dropActionChanged(DropTargetDragEvent dtde) { }

  public void drop(DropTargetDropEvent dtde) {
    // Figure out where the drop occurred (in relation to the target tree).
    Point pt = dtde.getLocation();
    TreePath parentpath = targetTree.getClosestPathForLocation(pt.x,pt.y);

    // For simplicity's sake, we'll assume that the tree uses the DefaultTreeModel
    // and DefaultMutableTreeNode classes.
    DefaultMutableTreeNode parent =
      (DefaultMutableTreeNode)parentpath.getLastPathComponent();

    // Now check to see if it was dropped on a folder. If not, reject it.
    if (parent.isLeaf()) {
      dtde.rejectDrop();
      return;
    }
```

```
    try {
      // Grab the data.
      Transferable tr = dtde.getTransferable( );
      DataFlavor[] flavors = tr.getTransferDataFlavors( );
      for (int i = 0; i < flavors.length; i++) {
        if (tr.isDataFlavorSupported(flavors[i])) {
          // It's a usable node, so pull it out of the transferable object and add it
          // to our tree.
          dtde.acceptDrop(DnDConstants.ACTION_MOVE);
          TreePath p = (TreePath)tr.getTransferData(flavors[i]);
          DefaultMutableTreeNode node =
            (DefaultMutableTreeNode)p.getLastPathComponent( );
          DefaultTreeModel model=(DefaultTreeModel)targetTree.getModel( );
          model.insertNodeInto(node, parent, 0);

          // Last but not least, mark the drop a success.
          dtde.dropComplete(true);
          return;
        }
      }
      dtde.rejectDrop( );
    } catch (Exception e) {
      e.printStackTrace( ); // Just for debugging, really
      dtde.rejectDrop( );
    }
  }
}
```

Putting it all together does not take much effort. If we want to create a single rearrangeable tree, we simply make it both a drag source and a drop target. With the separation of our DnD handlers, we can also enforce a "source-only" tree by attaching only the drag source half. Without the drop half, drops on the tree would simply be ignored.

```
/*
 * TreeDragTest.java
 * A more involved test of the DnD system to see if
 * we can create a self-contained, rearrangable JTree.  This is
 * the test framework that builds a tree and attaches both the
 * drag and the drop support.
 */

import java.awt.*;
import java.awt.dnd.*;
import java.awt.datatransfer.*;
import java.awt.event.*;
import java.io.*;
import java.util.*;
import javax.swing.*;
import javax.swing.tree.*;

public class TreeDragTest extends JFrame {
```

```
   TreeDragSource ds;
   TreeDropTarget dt;
   JTree tree;

   public TreeDragTest( ) {
     super("Rearrangeable Tree");
     setSize(300,200);
     setDefaultCloseOperation(EXIT_ON_CLOSE);

     // Create a quick JTree to use for demonstration purposes. The default
     // constructor for JTree creates just such a tree with a few categories such as
     // food and sports to play around with.
     tree = new JTree( );
     getContentPane( ).add(new JScrollPane(tree), BorderLayout.CENTER);

     ds = new TreeDragSource(tree, DnDConstants.ACTION_MOVE);
     dt = new TreeDropTarget(tree);
     setVisible(true);
   }

   public static void main(String args[]) {
     new TreeDragTest( );
   }
 }
```

Finishing Touches

With the DnD API, we can add a few more features to help us achieve the goal of user interface maturity. Since we can't drop our objects on other leaves, we really should keep the drag cursor consistent. If we're over a folder, we can accept the drag and show the "ok to drop here" cursor. If we're anywhere else, we'll reject the drag and show the "no drop" version. The current implementation of our handlers allows only nodes to be moved. We can include support for "copy or move" drags. (We can also keep our cursor in sync with the new support so users know whether they're copying or moving.) Once all this is working, we should also set up autoscrolling on our tree to give the user access to any off-screen parts of the tree.

Dynamic Cursors

If your application can use the new DnD support built into the 1.4 release, you shouldn't have to worry about cursor management. If you're using one of the older SDKs or building fancier custom support, read on.

The DnD package ships with some standard cursors for indicating "ok to drop" and "not ok to drop." These cursors are displayed automatically when you accept( ) or reject( ) an item as it is dragged over potential drop targets. Here's a look at the dragEnter( ) and dragOver( ) event handlers that check to see whether the mouse is over a folder in the tree. If it's not, we reject the drag. This rejection causes the cursor to update its appearance. (Note that with the new cursor features in Java 2, you can define your own cursors and use them here if you don't like the cursors supplied by your windowing system.)

```
private TreeNode getNodeForEvent(DropTargetDragEvent dtde) {
  // Use the same logic from the drop() method to see if the cursor is over a
  // folder in the target tree.
  Point p = dtde.getLocation();
  TreePath path = targetTree.getClosestPathForLocation(p.x, p.y);
  return (TreeNode)path.getLastPathComponent();
}

public void dragEnter(DropTargetDragEvent dtde) {
  dragOver(dtde);
}

public void dragOver(DropTargetDragEvent dtde) {
  TreeNode node = getNodeForEvent(dtde);
  if (node.isLeaf()) {
    dtde.rejectDrag();
  }
  else {
    // Start by supporting move operations.
    dtde.acceptDrag(DnDConstants.ACTION_MOVE);
  }
}
```

Changing the Drop Action

To support both move and copy operations, we need to make two modifications. Contrary to what you might infer from the names of the event-handling methods, we do not need to override the dropActionChanged( ) method. (You would override this method if you want to react to the change *during* the drag operation. We just want to react to the change when the data is finally dropped.) All we really need to do is make sure that our acceptDrag( ) methods handle both copy and move actions. Regrettably, you cannot accept the ACTION_MOVE_OR_COPY action to encompass both types of drops. You need to decide which type of drop occurred and accept that drop specifically. However, if you know you'll accept any drop the user can make, you can try the follwing trick. In *TreeDropTarget.java*, we had:

```
dtde.acceptDrag(DnDConstants.ACTION_MOVE);
```

We now have:

```
dtde.acceptDrag(dtde.getDropAction());
```

We just accept whatever the user's desired action is.

To complete the transaction properly, we need to make sure that during a copy operation we don't remove the original node. In *TreeDropSource.java*, we need a slightly smarter dragDropEnd( ) method:

```
public void dragDropEnd(DragSourceDropEvent dsde) {
    // To support move or copy, we have to check which occurred,
    // and remove the node only if it was a move operation.
    if (dsde.getDropSuccess() &&
        (dsde.getDropAction() == DnDConstants.ACTION_MOVE))
    {
      ((DefaultTreeModel)sourceTree.getModel())
            .removeNodeFromParent(oldNode);
    }
}
```

So now, if the user performs a copy rather than a move, we leave the source tree intact. Otherwise, we remove the node from the source tree just as we did before.

Autoscrolling

Often, a drop target is contained in a scrollable window. Word processors with text that can't fit on the screen and file managers with a large hierarchy of files and folders are common examples. If you want, you can create drop targets that set up an *autoscroll boundary*. This boundary allows a user in the middle of a drag operation to hold the mouse near an edge of your component, which causes the component scroll itself to show the previously hidden area.

Regretfully, this is not something that is implemented by default on components such as JTree and JTextArea. However, you can create autoscrolling versions of these classes by implementing the Autoscroll interface. (See Figure 24-9.)

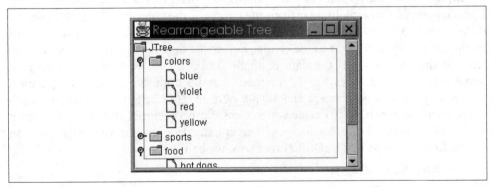

Figure 24-9. The editable tree with autoscroll boundaries drawn in

The Autoscroll Interface

For any component that can appear in a `JViewport` or `JScrollPane`, you can extend it and implement this interface. This allows `DropTarget` objects to monitor where your cursor is and initiate an autoscroll if necessary. Autoscrolling is handled by an auto-scroller, which is discussed in the next section.

Methods

The `Autoscroll` interface has only two methods:

public Insets getAutoscrollInsets( )
> This method returns an `Insets` object that describes the autoscroll activation areas of a target. Figure 24-9 shows a `JTree` with an outline of the insets drawn over the tree.

public void autoscroll(Point cursorLocn)
> This method is called by the autoscroller to force the component to reposition itself. Exactly where the component moves to (how fast, in which direction, etc.) is up to you. The `cursorLocn` argument gives you the location of the mouse cursor that prompted the scrolling request. You get full control over the scrolling. You can jump to a new location or use a loop to incrementally inch your way to the target.

We can add an inner class that extends `JTree` and implements this interface to achieve our autoscrolling, rearrangeable tree. Pay special attention to the `AutoscrollingJTree` class.

```
// AutoscrollTest.java
import java.awt.*;
import java.awt.dnd.*;
import java.awt.datatransfer.*;
import java.awt.event.*;
import java.io.*;
import java.util.*;
import javax.swing.*;
import javax.swing.tree.*;

public class AutoscrollTest extends JFrame {

    TreeDragSource ds;
    TreeDropTarget dt;
    JTree tree;

    public AutoscrollTest( ) {
        super("Rearrangeable Tree");
        setSize(300,200);
        setDefaultCloseOperation(EXIT_ON_CLOSE);

        // If you want autoscrolling, use this line:
        //    tree = new AutoScrollingJTree( );
```

```
       // Otherwise, use this line:
       //    tree = new JTree();
       getContentPane().add(new JScrollPane(tree), BorderLayout.CENTER);

       ds = new TreeDragSource(tree, DnDConstants.ACTION_COPY_OR_MOVE);
       dt = new TreeDropTarget(tree);
       setVisible(true);
   }

   public class AutoScrollingJTree extends JTree implements Autoscroll {
       private int margin = 12;

       public AutoScrollingJTree() { super(); }

       // You've been told to scroll because the mouse cursor is in your scroll zone.
       public void autoscroll(Point p) {
           // Figure out which row you're on.
           int realrow = getRowForLocation(p.x, p.y);
           Rectangle outer = getBounds();

           // Now decide if the row is at the top of the screen or at the bottom. Do this
           // so that the previous row (or the next row) is visible. If you're at the
           // absolute top or bottom, just return the first or last row, respectively.
           realrow = (p.y + outer.y <= margin ?
                       realrow < 1 ? 0 : realrow - 1 :
                       realrow < getRowCount() - 1 ? realrow + 1 : realrow);
           scrollRowToVisible(realrow);
       }

       // Calculate the insets for the *JTREE*, not the viewport the tree is in. This
       // makes it a bit messy.
       public Insets getAutoscrollInsets() {
           Rectangle outer = getBounds();
           Rectangle inner = getParent().getBounds();
           return new Insets(inner.y - outer.y + margin, inner.x - outer.x + margin,
               outer.height - inner.height - inner.y + outer.y + margin,
               outer.width - inner.width - inner.x + outer.x + margin);
       }

       // Use this method if you want to see the boundaries of the autoscroll active
       // region. Toss it out otherwise.
       public void paintComponent(Graphics g) {
           super.paintComponent(g);
           Rectangle outer = getBounds();
           Rectangle inner = getParent().getBounds();
           g.setColor(Color.red);
           g.drawRect(-outer.x + 12, -outer.y + 12, inner.width - 24, inner.height - 24);
       }
   }

   public static void main(String args[]) {
       new AutoscrollTest();
   }
}
```

In the autoscroll( ) method, we check to see if the cursor is near the top edge or the bottom edge. We use JTree's getRowForLocation( ) method to find the row closest to the cursor and then make the next (or previous) row visible. If you implemented this functionality for a component that did not have something like the scrollRowToVisible( ) method, you can grab the component's container and scroll it. (Most likely, the parent container is a JViewport, so you can code for this. Remember that even in a JScrollPane, the component is housed in a JViewport that is tied to the scrollbars.)

The getAutoscrollInsets( ) method looks a bit ugly since we need to supply insets that match the tree, not the viewport that contains the tree. As we expand the tree, it gets taller. As it gets taller, we need to make the bottom inset larger. Figure 24-10 illustrates the problem we're facing.

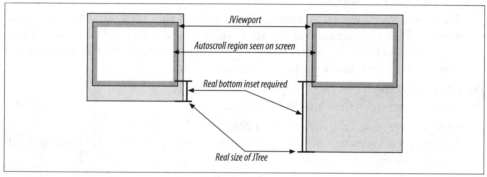

Figure 24-10. Real insets versus visible insets for a component in a JViewport

So, all the extra work in that method will take the varying size of the tree into account. Fortunately, this also works when the user resizes the application and changes the space allotted to the viewport. The performance of these calculations is surprisingly quick and should suffice for many applications. However, for performance fanatics, you can certainly modify this class to listen to component events on both the tree and the viewport. If either of these changes, you can reset the values of the insets, which do not change during the getAutoscrollInsets( ) method.

The DropTarget.DropTargetAutoScroller Class

As we mentioned earlier, there is a separate helper class involved in listening to the mouse cursor's position and causing a target to autoscroll when the cursor waits long enough in the active autoscroll region. The DropTarget class has an inner class called DropTargetAutoScroller devoted to this task. When you register a component with a drop target, the target checks to see if the component is an instance of Autoscroll. If so, it creates an autoscroller for you. You can, of course, subclass if you want different behavior from the autoscroller.

Constructor

The only constructor for the autoscroller is protected:

protected DropTarget.DropTargetAutoScroller(Component c, Point p)
> This creates an autoscroller for the component c and stores an initial value for the mouse location p. (This value is used to determine whether the mouse moved since the last time an autoscroll was performed.)

Methods

Three methods are present to start a scroll, stop a scroll, and update the mouse's location:

public void actionPerformed(ActionEvent e)
> The autoscroller works by timing the mouse. If this method sits in an active autoscroll region long enough, an autoscroll is started. To do this, it uses a Timer object that reports its ActionEvent to this class. This method then calls the autoscroll( ) method of your component.

protected void stop( )
> This method stops the autoscroller's timer.

protected void updateLocation(Point newLocn)
> This method keeps the autoscroller in sync with the mouse as it moves around, and restarts the timer if necessary.

CHAPTER 25

Programming with Accessibility

Accessibility is a Java feature that allows you to extend your programs by interfacing an application's components with *assistive technologies* that have special permission to use them. Assistive technologies are, in the narrowest sense, specialized tools that people can use to assist in interacting with your application; examples include voice-recognition and audio output. In a broader sense, however, assistive technologies can be robust application suites that can assist just about anybody with anything.

It helps to think of accessibility as a two-sided conversation. This conversation takes place between an assistive technology and the "accessibility-friendly" components of applications. Assistive technologies are quite powerful: Java grants them access to all the components in the virtual machine that they can interface with, as well as the ability to interface with the windowing event queue. The latter gives an assistive technology the ability to monitor graphical events. The former means that an assistive technology can directly interact with the GUI widgets of one or more applications quickly and easily, without disrupting the application beneath it.

In order for components to interface with assistive technologies, they must implement special "accessible" interfaces. (The Swing components already implement these interfaces.) There are six unique interfaces for exporting accessible functionality: one each for actions, component properties, selections, text properties, hyperlinks, and bounded-range values. For each type of accessibility exported, one or more objects inside that component can be directly manipulated through that interface. For example, the JTextField Swing component supports text accessibility. Therefore, a voice-recognition program can insert letters in the field by obtaining the text-accessible interface and copying out the words that the user has spoken.

As there are two sides to accessibility, there are also two programming packages to deal with: the Accessibility API and the Accessibility Utility API. The first API defines the interfaces and classes that the programmer must implement on the application side in order for the components to be accessibility-friendly. The Accessibility Utility

API, on the other hand, is a package of utilities that assistive technologies can incorporate into their own classes in order to "hook" into the JVM and interface with the application. Sun bundles the former with the Swing libraries. The latter is distributed independently, typically by the assistive technology vendor, similar to peripheral vendors providing drivers for their equipment.

Another way of creating an assistive interface in JDK 1.2 or higher is to take advantage of the MultiLookandFeel with one or more Swing components. For example, in addition to a graphical L&F, you might also redirect certain elements of the UI delegates to an audio output or a braille display. While a new L&F can technically be considered an assistive technology, this approach is better explained in Chapter 26.

IBM has developed a great site on developing accessible applications in Java. You can check out this resource at *http://www-3.ibm.com/able/accessjava.html*.

How Accessibility Works

Assistive technologies are a feature of Java. These technologies typically manifest themselves as a class archive, such as a JAR file, that resides separately on the user's local machine. As we mentioned earlier, however, Java offers assistive technologies a wide latitude of control over an application for two reasons:

- Java loads assistive technologies into the same virtual machine as the application (or applications) with which they intend to interface.
- Assistive technologies can use or even replace the virtual machine's sole windowing event queue (java.awt.EventQueue).

Let's take a look at an accessibility-enabled Java virtual machine (JVM). When a JVM is started, it searches a configuration file for a list of specialized classes (we'll provide specifics about this later in this chapter). If it finds them, it loads the classes into the same namespace as the application that it is about to execute. Thus, when the Java application starts, the assistive technologies start with it.

The second important step is replacing the GUI event queue with an appropriate queue for the assistive technology. Hence, the application, GUI event queue, and assistive technology work together to make accessibility possible. Figure 25-1 shows how an assistive technology interfaces with the JVM.

Evolving Accessibility Support

Before we get started, it's important to say that the accessibility features and even the approach to accessibility varies a bit depending on the version of Java you're using. The next few sections briefly describe the main differences you should be aware of; other differences are noted throughout the chapter.

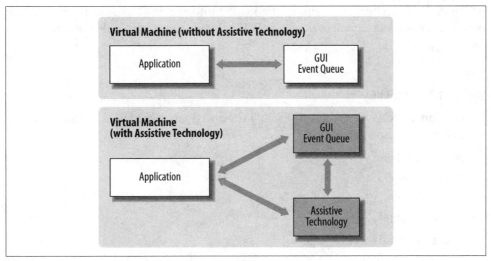

Figure 25-1. An assistive technology in the JVM

Version 1.1 accessibility

A 1.1 JVM searches the *awt.properties* configuration file for a list of specialized accessibility classes and, if they are there, loads them before starting up.

Here's a segment of the *awt.properties* file with the appropriate additions for JDK 1.1 accessibility highlighted in bold:

```
AWT.alt=Alt
AWT.meta=Meta

# Assistive technologies
AWT.assistive_technologies=SpeechRecognition
AWT.EventQueueClass=com.sun.java.accessibility.util.EventQueueMonitor

# Key names
AWT.enter=Enter
AWT.backSpace=Backspace
```

There are two important lines in the "Assistive technologies" section of this file. The line beginning `AWT.assistive_technologies=` refers to a class on the current `CLASSPATH` where Java can find an assistive technology. Each time the user starts the virtual machine, the assistive technology class is instantiated as well. The other line, `AWT.EventQueueClass=`, refers to an Accessibility Utility API class that aids accessibility by replacing the Java graphical event queue. (We will talk about this class later in the chapter.)

Version 1.2 accessibility

In 1.2 and beyond, the virtual machine loads a different file: *accessibility.properties* in the *jre/lib* directory. Whereas 1.1 required specifying the `AWTEventQueue` property explicitly, 1.2 and later handle this automatically. However, you still need to specify which assistive technologies should be loaded into the JVM at startup. Hence, the very brief *accessibility.properties* file for JDK 1.2 and later might look like this:

```
# Assistive technologies: only one line
assistive_technologies=SpeechRecognition
```

Version 1.3 accessibility

In addition to following the approach introduced in 1.2, SDK 1.3 added several classes and interfaces, including:

- AccessibleIcon
- AccessibleRelation
- AccessibleRelationSet
- AccessibleTable
- AccessibleTableModelChange

The other major change in 1.3 concerns the location of the low-level accessibility support code. In the 1.3 release, that code moved into the java.awt.Component and java.awt.Container classes, making it possible to use the same framework for light-weight AWT components.

As an interesting side note, Version 1.3 also added the java.awt.Robot class. While not specifically part of Swing or Accessibility, the Robot class allows for things such as screen captures and "mouse warping" (moving the mouse programmatically). If you intend to support assistive technologies such as screen magnification, this class is invaluable.

Version 1.4 accessibility

Improvements in accessibility support continue to evolve in subsequent Java versions; they build on the changes in 1.2 and 1.3 noted above. SDK 1.4 includes a few new classes and interfaces:

- AccessibleEditableText
- AccessibleExtendedComponent
- AccessibleExtendedTable
- AccessibleKeyBinding

Several other constants and properties were added, mostly to make it easier for developers to understand the assistive technologies in a given environment. For example, the javax.accessibility.assistive_technologies system property allows you to specify the assistive technologies to load at runtime. Two boolean properties, javax.accessibility. screen_reader_present and javax.accessibility.screen_magnifier_present, provide indications that particular technologies are installed and available on a system. While it is always a good idea to develop applications that are compatible with such technologies, developers who want to be extra careful on systems with these features can now do so.

One of the most welcome category of changes in the 1.4 release relates to navigation through and interactions with HTML pages. Support for <object> tags and keyboard link traversal are among the more notable additions.

The Accessibility Contract

In theory, accessibility defines a "contract" between an application and an assistive technology. The contract goes like this: in exchange for providing an alternate interface that allows users greater power to interact with my application, I will allow outside control of many or all of my components. With Swing, you do this by activating accessibility properties and interfaces inside your components. If you stick to the Swing components in your application, this is a trivial task—it's already done for you. However, if you're using AWT, it can be more difficult.

Let's take a look at the fine print:

- All accessibility-friendly components return a standardized accessible object on demand. This object has standardized methods that allow assistive technologies to query each component for its name, description, role (purpose), parent, children, and current state. In addition, the assistive technology can register to be notified in the event of a property change in the component. Finally, the assistive technology can access most component, text, selection, hypertext, action, or value properties in the component to be manipulated.

- The assistive technology can access and manipulate key information about the JVM, including a list of all the top-level windows, the location of the mouse, and the current focus. It also has the ability to inject events into the systemwide graphical event queue. In addition, with JDK 1.1 accessibility, assistive technologies can replace the windowing event queue with one of their own (this replacement is unnecessary with the Java 2 releases).

Note the last point. This allows the assistive technology to be able to "sniff" various GUI events at the system level and react accordingly. For example, if focus shifts from one application to another, a voice-recognition assistive technology can monitor that change to switch to a vocabulary appropriate for the new application.

How Do I Get It?

The exact procedure for implementing accessibility features depends on whether you are making a Swing application or an AWT application accessible.

Swing

If you are using Swing components in your application, then almost everything is taken care of for you. You need to do only two things to make your components accessibility-friendly: provide an accessible name and provide an accessible description for each component. In certain cases, these properties may be set for you automatically. If not, both are trivial additions, as shown below:

```
JTextField text = new JTextField( );
text.getAccessibleContext( ).setAccessibleName("Name");
text.getAccessibleContext( ).setAccessibleDescription("Enter A Name");
```

By having these two properties set in your components, any assistive technology that has been loaded into the JVM can successfully query the component to determine how it can best be used.

As we mentioned, these properties are often derived from other common attributes of the Swing components, such as labels and tooltips. The following has the same effect as the code we just showed:

```
JTextField text = new JTextField( );
JLabel label = new JLabel("Name");
label.setLabelFor(text);               // Sets text's accessibleName
text.setToolTipText("Enter a name");   // Sets text's accessibleDescription
```

AWT

SDK 1.3 added accessibility support to the Component and Container classes. While we heartily encourage you to write applications with Swing components, any applications that require AWT components can still be made accessible.

In general, if you are curious about the state of the accessibility package, check out *http://java.sun.com/products/jfc/accessibility.html*. From there you can link to all the latest additions and several good overviews of the goals (and the details) of javax.accessibility. (The accessibility tools have their own version numbers, so don't be alarmed if the latest version you see is a 1.3 release—that doesn't mean it won't work with the latest release of the Java 2 SDK.)

The Accessibility Package

Now let's discuss the issues an assistive technology encounters when hooking into an accessibility-friendly application.

The Path to Determining Accessibility

Almost all Swing objects support one or more forms of accessibility, which means that they implement the Accessible interface. However, for an assistive technology

---

to find out which types of accessibility an application supports, the technology needs to do some investigating. The typical course of action runs like this:

1. The assistive technology locates a desired component in the target application with the help of the Accessibility Utility APIs. Once found, it invokes the getAccessibleContext() method of the component object, which is the sole method of the Accessible interface. This method returns a customized AccessibleContext object, often an inner class of the component.

2. The assistive technology can then use the AccessibleContext object to retrieve the name, description, role, state, parent, and children components of the accessible component in question.

3. The assistive technology can register for any property change events in the component it's interested in.

4. The assistive technology can call upon several standardized methods to determine whether those types of accessibility are supported. All AccessibleContext objects have these interface methods. If any of these methods return null, then the component does not support the specific accessibility type.

5. If they are not null, the objects returned by each of the various methods can then be used to access the functionality on the component.

Different components implement different types of accessibility. For example, a tree might export accessibility action, selection, and component properties, while a button might simply export component properties. Components do not have to support all five steps. Hence, assistive technologies need to determine exactly which accessible functionality each component supports by querying that component for information.

The Accessible Interface

All components that need to export functionality to outside objects must implement the Accessible interface. This interface consists of only one method: getAccessible-Context(). Assistive technologies must always call this method first to retrieve an accessible-context object from the component. This object can then be used to query the component about its accessible capabilities.

Method

public abstract AccessibleContext getAccessibleContext()
  Return the AccessibleContext object of the current component, or null if the component does not support accessibility.

The AccessibleContext Class

The `AccessibleContext` class is the heart of accessibility. It bundles component information that any assistive technology can learn about. The class has three primary responsibilities. First, it allows access to the accessible properties of the host component: its name, role, description, and current state, as well as a parent object and a list of child objects, if applicable. Second, it provides the ability to register for any change events on those properties. Third, the `AccessibleContext` object is responsible for reporting the accessible functionality that the component exports. Technologies that obtain the `AccessibleContext` object of a component can then call upon the following methods to determine which types of accessible functionality can be used:

```
public AccessibleAction getAccessibleAction( )
public AccessibleComponent getAccessibleComponent( )
public AccessibleComponent getAccessibleEditableText( )   // 1.4
public AccessibleComponent getAccessibleIcon( )           // 1.3
public AccessibleSelection getAccessibleSelection( )
public AccessibleComponent getAccessibleTable( )          // 1.3
public AccessibleText getAccessibleText( )
public AccessibleValue getAccessibleValue( )
```

Each of these methods returns a special object that an assistive technology can use to modify properties or invoke functionality inside the component. In the event that a component does not support one or more types, the respective method returns `null`.

The `AccessibleContext` class contains several abstract methods. Hence, each component has its own subclass of `AccessibleContext` that is returned by the `getAccessibleContext( )` method of the `Accessible` interface.

Properties

Table 25-1 shows the properties of the `AccessibleContext` class. The most important are `accessibleName` and `accessibleDescription`. Both properties are usually set by the programmer of the host application. The `accessibleName` property gives a name to the component; some Swing components automatically set the accessible name as the text of the component. `accessibleDescription` gives a terse description of how the user should interact with the component.

Table 25-1. AccessibleContext properties

Property	Data type	get	is	set	Default value
accessibleAction	AccessibleAction	•			
accessibleChild[i]	Accessible	•			
accessibleChildrenCount[a]	int	•			
accessibleComponent	AccessibleComponent	•			
accessibleDescription[b]	String	•		•	

[1.3]since 1.3, [1.4]since 1.4, [a]abstract, [b]bound, [i]indexed

Table 25-1. AccessibleContext properties (continued)

Property	Data type	get	is	set	Default value
accessibleEditableText[1.4]	AccessibleEditableText				
accessibleIcon[1.3]	AccessibleIcon[]				
accessibleIndexInParent[a]	int	•			
accessibleName[b]	String	•		•	
accessibleParent	Accessible	•		•	
accessibleRelationSet	AccessibleRelationSet				
accessibleRole[a]	AccessibleRole	•			
accessibleSelection	AccessibleSelection	•			
accessibleStateSet[a]	AccessibleStateSet	•			
accessibleTable[1.3]	AccessibleTable	•			
accessibleText	AccessibleText	•			
accessibleValue	AccessibleValue	•			
locale[a]	Locale	•			

[1.3]since 1.3, [1.4]since 1.4, [a]abstract, [b]bound, [i]indexed

The read-only accessibleRole property defines the purpose of the component. Accessible role values are predefined constants, such as SCROLL_BAR or PUSHABLE_BUTTON; they essentially tell what the component is. The accessibleStateSet property reflects the current state of the accessible component. There are a host of states that a component can be in.

The accessibleAction, accessibleSelection, accessibleText, accessibleValue, and accessibleComponent properties refer to the individual types of accessibility supported by each component. Each property contains a read-only object, used exclusively for interfacing with the accessible area of the component. The get accessors for these methods return null if there's no accessible object of the requested type for this component. If you have looked at the Accessibility API, you might think there should be an accessibleHyperlink property, but no such property exists. To get an AccessibleHyperlink, use getAccessibleText() and check whether the result is an instance of AccessibleHypertext. Once you have an AccessibleHypertext object, call getLink() to get an AccessibleHyperlink.

The accessibleParent property places the component in its accessibility hierarchy. Note that the accessibility hierarchy may differ from the regular component hierarchy. For example, a CellRenderer object inside a Swing list component does not have the JList as its parent in the component hierarchy. However, it does have the JList as a parent in the accessibility hierarchy. That way, if an assistive technology wished to access the list itself, it is not cut off by limitations in the component hierarchy.

The accessibleChildrenCount, accessibleChild, and accessibleIndexInParent properties each give details about this component in the current accessibility hierarchy. accessibleChild is an indexed property that provides references to each of the component's accessible children, while accessibleChildrenCount is an integer that returns the number of accessible children present. If this component is the child of a parent component in the accessibility hierarchy, the accessibleIndexInParent property indicates which index the component currently holds.

Accessible names and descriptions

Assistive technologies use the accessibleName property to distinguish the component from others of the same type. With named components, such as those that extend AbstractButton, the accessible name is automatically extracted from its label. For all others, you should always set the accessibleName property when including the component in your application. With Swing components, you can set the accessibility name with the following code fragment:

```
mySwingComponent.getAccessibleContext.setAccessibleName("Execute");
```

An assistive technology attempts to reference a component by keying off of its name, so it's probably a good idea to stick with standardized names. In other words, if you create a JPopupMenu object containing various chemical elements, make sure to call it something reasonable like "Elements" and not "The Elements Popup Menu of Gerald's Application." The latter would be extremely difficult for assistive technologies to identify. A good rule of thumb is to keep the names short but unique.

You can set the accessibility description of each component with the following short segment of code:

```
myButton.getAccessibleContext( ).setAccessibleDescription(
   "Closes the dialog");
```

You can also set the description of a Swing component by giving it a tooltip string:

```
myButton.getAccessibleContext( ).setToolTipText("Closes the dialog");
```

Both approaches are equivalent. Assistive technologies can use the description property to learn more about the accessible component. The description is not as important as the name, but it frequently helps the user by providing instructions on how to work with a specific component.

Events

Objects extending the AccessibleContext class must fire a PropertyChangeEvent when one of its bound properties is modified. Assistive technologies listen for these events and modify their states or react in some fashion if such a change occurs.

public void addPropertyChangeListener(PropertyChangeListener listener)
public void removePropertyChangeListener(PropertyChangeListener listener)

Add or remove the specified `PropertyChangeListener` from the object's list of listeners.

public void firePropertyChange(String property, Object oldValue, Object newValue)

Fire a `PropertyChangeEvent` to all registered listeners indicating that the property has changed and provide both the old value and the new value of the property.

Constants

`AccessibleContext` uses the string constants listed in Table 25-2 to represent various properties when communicating change events.

Table 25-2. AccessibleContext constants

Constant	Description
ACCESSIBLE_ACTION_PROPERTY[1.3]	The supported set of actions has changed.
ACCESSIBLE_ACTIVE_DESCENDANT_PROPERTY	The active descendant of a component has changed.
ACCESSIBLE_CARET_PROPERTY	An `AccessibleText` component's caret property has changed.
ACCESSIBLE_CHILD_PROPERTY	The `accessibleChild` property has changed.
ACCESSIBLE_DESCRIPTION_PROPERTY	The `accessibleDescription` property has changed.
ACCESSIBLE_HYPERTEXT_OFFSET[1.4]	A hypertext element has received focus.
ACCESSIBLE_NAME_PROPERTY	The `accessibleName` property has changed.
ACCESSIBLE_SELECTION_PROPERTY	The `accessibleSelection` property has changed.
ACCESSIBLE_STATE_PROPERTY	The `accessibleStateSet` property has changed.
ACCESSIBLE_TABLE_CAPTION_CHANGED[1.3]	The table caption has changed.
ACCESSIBLE_TABLE_COLUMN_DESCRIPTION_CHANGED[1.3]	The column's description has changed.
ACCESSIBLE_TABLE_COLUMN_HEADER_CHANGED[1.3]	The column's header has changed.
ACCESSIBLE_TABLE_MODEL_CHANGED[1.3]	The table's model has changed.
ACCESSIBLE_TABLE_ROW_DESCRIPTION_CHANGED[1.3]	The row's description has changed.
ACCESSIBLE_TABLE_ROW_HEADER_CHANGED[1.3]	The row's header has changed.
ACCESSIBLE_TABLE_SUMMARY_CHANGED[1.3]	The table's summary has changed.
ACCESSIBLE_TEXT_PROPERTY	The `accessibleText` property has changed.
ACCESSIBLE_VALUE_PROPERTY	The `accessibleValue` property has changed.
ACCESSIBLE_VISIBLE_DATA_PROPERTY	The visual appearance of the component has changed.

[1.3]since 1.3, [1.4]since 1.4

Other Accessible Objects

Before going further, there are several simple objects in the accessibility package used by `AccessibleContext` that we should discuss in more detail.

The AccessibleState Class

Each accessible component can have one or more states associated with it. An assistive technology can query these states at any time to determine how best to deal with the component. The accessible states can only be retrieved, however, and not set. There are two classes that the `Accessible` package uses to handle states: `AccessibleState` and `AccessibleStateSet`.

The `AccessibleState` class contains an enumeration of static objects that define states that any accessible component can have. Note that a component can be in more than one state at any time. A list of the possible states that an accessible object can be in, along with a brief description of each, is shown in Table 25-3.

Table 25-3. AccessibleState constants

State	Meaning
ACTIVE	The window, dialog, or frame is the active one.
ARMED	The object, such as a button, has been pressed but not released, and the mouse cursor is still over the button.
BUSY	The object is busy processing and should not be interrupted.
CHECKED	The object is checked.
COLLAPSED	The object, such as a node in a tree, is collapsed.
EDITABLE	The object supports any form of editing.
ENABLED	The object is enabled.
EXPANDABLE	The object, such as a node in a tree, can report its children.
EXPANDED	The object, such as a node in a tree, is expanded.
FOCUSABLE	The object can accept the focus.
FOCUSED	The object has the focus.
HORIZONTAL	The object's orientation is horizontal.
ICONFIED	The object is iconified.
MODAL	The object is modal and must be closed before the user can switch to another window.
MULTI_LINE	The object is capable of using many lines of text.
MULTISELECTABLE	The object allows multiple children to be selected at the same time.
OPAQUE	The object is completely filled (i.e., paints every pixel) and thus does not allow transparency.
PRESSED	The object, such as a button, is being pressed but has not been released.
RESIZABLE	The object is resizable.
SELECTABLE	The object is capable of being selected from its parent.

Table 25-3. AccessibleState constants (continued)

State	Meaning
SELECTED	The object is selected.
SHOWING	The object and each of its ancestors are visible.
SINGLE_LINE	The object is capable of using only a single line of text.
TRANSIENT	The object is transient. In the context of accessibility, transient objects serve only to help other components perform some underlying duty, such as rendering to the screen. These objects do not generate change events that an assistive technology would be interested in, but are necessary to allow assistive technologies to query through the component hierarchy.
VERTICAL	The object's orientation is vertical.
VISIBLE	The object is visible.

Some of these states are specific to various objects. For example, a JButton cannot be COLLAPSED, and a JLabel cannot be EDITABLE. An assistive technology, however, should know which objects can have which states and how to act accordingly. Note that the individual states of AccessibleState are immutable objects. In order to work with a group (or set) of them, you will need the services of the AccessibleStateSet object.

Constructor

protected AccessibleState(String key)
> This protected constructor is called using any of the states listed above to instantiate an AccessibleState object. It is protected to allow each of the above constants to remain as a strongly typed, static enumeration of states. Follow this procedure if you subclass AccessibleState with your own states.

The AccessibleStateSet Class

Because an accessible component can have more than one accessible state at the same time, you must access each of the states through the use of an AccessibleStateSet object. This object is simply a repository (or set) of accessible states, as well as various methods that search and identify particular states. You can retrieve an AccessibleStateSet for each accessible component with the getAccessibleStateSet( ) accessor of the AccessibleContext object.

Constructors

AccessibleStateSet( )
> Create an empty state set.

AccessibleStateSet(AccessibleState[] states)
> Create a state set using the array of AccessibleState objects passed in to initialize itself.

Methods

The methods of `AccessibleStateSet` give you everything you need to manipulate the set:

public boolean add(AccessibleState state)
> Add a new `AccessibleState` to the set, returning `true` if successful. If the state is already present, it is not added, and the method returns `false`.

public void addAll(AccessibleState[] states)
> Add all the states specified in the array to the set, ignoring any that are already present.

public void clear()
> Clear all states from the state set.

public boolean contains(AccessibleState state)
> Return a `boolean` indicating whether the given `state` is included in the set.

public boolean remove(AccessibleState state)
> Remove a specific `AccessibleState` from the set, returning `true` if successful. If the state is not present in the set, the method returns `false`.

public AccessibleState[] toArray()
> Return all the states in the set as an array of `AccessibleState` objects.

The AccessibleRole Class

A common way to determine the purpose or function of an accessible component is to check its *accessibility role*. All accessibility roles are bundled inside the `AccessibleRole` class, which, like the `AccessibleState` class, consists only of static constants. An assistive technology can query these read-only roles from `AccessibleContext` to better determine which type of component it is dealing with. If a desired role does not exist in this class, you can always extend the `AccessibleRole` class into a subclass of your own and include the newly defined role there. Because they are all of type `AccessibleRole`, the static constants within this class can be used in conjunction with the `getAccessibleRole()` method of an `AccessibleContext` object.

Table 25-4 outlines each of the accessibility roles.

Table 25-4. AccessibleRole constants

Constant	Meaning
ALERT	Provides an alert to the user
AWT_COMPONENT	A generic AWT component
CANVAS[1.3]	An object that you can paint on and receive events from
CHECK_BOX	A dual-state button or checkbox
COLOR_CHOOSER	An object for selecting a color

[1.3]since 1.3, [1.4]since 1.4

Table 25-4. AccessibleRole constants (continued)

Constant	Meaning
COLUMN_HEADER	A header for a column of data
COMBO_BOX	A combo box component
DATE_EDITOR[1.4]	An editor that can manipulate Date and Time objects
DESKTOP_ICON	An internal frame that has been iconified
DESKTOP_PANE	A desktop pane that supports internal frames
DIALOG	A top-level dialog box
DIRECTORY_PANE	A specialty pane used to locate directories on a filesystem
FILE_CHOOSER	A specialty dialog box for choosing a file
FILLER	Any object that takes up space in a user interface
FONT_CHOOSER[1.4]	A component for picking fonts
FRAME	A top-level frame
GLASS_PANE	The glass pane of a frame or applet
GROUP_BOX[1.4]	Any bordered container
HYPERLINK[1.4]	A link in a hypertext document
ICON[1.3]	An icon (small graphic image)
INTERNAL_FRAME	An internal frame inside a desktop frame
LABEL	A string-based label
LAYERED_PANE	A layered-pane object
LIST	A list object
LIST_ITEM[1.3]	An element in a list
MENU	A standard menu that descends from a menu bar
MENU_BAR	A menu bar object
MENU_ITEM	A menu item inside a menu
OPTION_PANE	An object that displays a pop-up message
PAGE_TAB	An page tab object, typically a descendant of a page tab list
PAGE_TAB_LIST	A grouping of page tabs
PANEL	A panel object
PASSWORD_TEXT	A password text field that masks its entry text
POPUP_MENU	A pop-up menu
PROGRESS_BAR	A progress bar object
PUSH_BUTTON	A standard button
RADIO_BUTTON	A radio button
ROOT_PANE	The root pane of a frame
ROW_HEADER	A header for a row of data
SCROLL_BAR	A scrollbar

[1.3]since 1.3, [1.4]since 1.4

Table 25-4. AccessibleRole constants (continued)

Constant	Meaning
SCROLL_PANE	A scrollpane object
SEPARATOR	A lined separator used in conjunction with a layout manager
SLIDER	A slider object
SPIN_BOX[1.4]	A spinner component
SPLIT_PANE	A pane that is split into two adjustable halves
STATUS_BAR[1.4]	A label (or labels) used to show application status information
SWING_COMPONENT	A generic Swing component
TABLE	A table object
TEXT	A generic object that displays text
TOGGLE_BUTTON	A dual-state button that does not provide a separate state
TOOL_BAR	A toolbar object
TOOL_TIP	A tooltip object
TREE	A tree object
UNKNOWN	An unknown object
VIEWPORT	A viewport used in a scrollpane
WINDOW	A top-level window without a border or title

[1.3]since 1.3, [1.4]since 1.4

Constructor

protected AccessibleRole(String key)
> This is the only constructor for the AccessibleRole class. Note that the constructor is protected; there is no public constructor for this class. The constructor takes a single String that corresponds to the locale for each of the accessible roles. This locale determines how to translate each of the states and roles into a human-readable form.

Types of Accessibility

Accessible components can export several types of assistive functionalities—for example: actions, text properties, component properties, icon properties, selections, table properties, hypertext, and bounded-range value properties. Most of these functions are already present in the Swing components, so if you stick closely to Swing, you probably won't need to implement these interfaces in your components. In an effort to explain how one might implement these interfaces, we have provided a simple example showing how to add AccessibleAction support to an AWT-based component.

The AccessibleAction Interface

The `AccessibleAction` interface outlines the methods that an accessible object or component must have to export its actions. The idea is that an assistive technology can determine the correct action by obtaining the total number of actions that the component exports, then reviewing each of their descriptions to resolve the correct one. Once this has occurred, the `doAccessibleAction( )` method can be called with the correct index to invoke the required method.

Properties

The properties in Table 25-5 must be readable through the `AccessibleAction` interface. `accessibleActionCount` stores the number of accessible actions that the component implements. The indexed property `accessibleActionDescription` provides a string describing the action associated with the given index. The action with index 0 is the component's default action.

Table 25-5. AccessibleAction properties

Property	Data type	get	is	set	Default value
accessibleActionCount	int	•			
accessibleActionDescription[i]	Action	•			

[i]indexed

Method

public abstract boolean doAccessibleAction(int index)
   Invokes an action based on the given index. The method returns `false` if an action with that index does not exist. It returns `true` if successful.

The AccessibleComponent Interface

The `AccessibleComponent` interface should be supported by any component that is drawn to a graphical context on the screen. Assistive technologies can use this interface to change how the component is drawn. Almost all of the methods in this interface call equivalent methods in the `java.awt.Component` class, so you will find this accessibility type in almost every Swing component. Adding `AccessibleComponent` support to your own components is a trivial exercise.

Properties

The properties in Table 25-6 must be made available by classes that implement the `AccessibleComponent` interface. These properties should be fairly self-explanatory if you're familiar with the way `JComponents` work. The background and foreground properties let you manipulate the component's background and foreground colors. The cursor and font properties let you manipulate the component's cursor or font.

Table 25-6. AccessibleComponent properties

Property	Data type	get	is	set	Default value
background	Color	•		•	
bounds	Rectangle	•		•	
cursor	Cursor	•		•	
enabled	boolean		•	•	
focusTraversable	boolean		•		
font	Font	•		•	
foreground	Color	•		•	
location	Point	•		•	
locationOnScreen	Point	•			
showing	boolean		•		
size	Dimension	•		•	
visible	boolean		•	•	

The enabled, showing, and visible properties let you find out the component's status. A component that is enabled has AccessibleState.ENABLED as part of its accessibleStateSet property. Likewise, a component that is visible has AccessibleState.VISIBLE as part of its accessibleStateSet, and a component that is showing has AccessibleState.SHOWING as part of its accessibleStateSet. A visible component is showing only if all of its ancestors are also visible. Remember that it's possible for a component that's showing to be hidden by another component.

The location, locationOnScreen, bounds, and size properties let you find out about the real estate occupied by the component. location gives you access to the component's position in the parent container's coordinate system; locationOnScreen gives you access to the component's position in the screen's coordinate system. The bounds property is a Rectangle that describes the component's bounding box; the size property is a Dimension that gives you the component's width and height, including any insets or borders.

The focusTraversable property tells you whether this object can accept focus. If its value is true, the component also has AccessibleState.FOCUSABLE as part of its accessibleStateSet.

Events

Objects implementing the AccessibleComponent interface must be able to register listeners for focus events generated by the component.

public abstract void addFocusListener(FocusListener l)
public abstract void removeFocusListener(FocusListener l)
> Add or remove the specified FocusListener from the event listener list.

Methods

public abstract boolean contains(Point p)
> Return a boolean indicating whether the point passed in (in object coordinates) is within the bounding box of the component.

public abstract Accessible getAccessibleAt(Point p)
> Return a component that implements the Accessible interface under the point passed in, or null if one does not exist.

public abstract void requestFocus( )
> Make a request to grab the focus. Note that the method returns void; if it does not succeed, it will not notify the caller.

The AccessibleSelection Interface

AccessibleSelection is a simple interface that allows assistive technologies to query a component for information about its current selections. By selections, we mean choosing one or more items in a component, such as from a JList. The interface also contains methods that allow outside modification to the current set of selections.

The AccessibleSelection interface works by interfacing with two separate lists. The first is the standard *data list* of objects that have been added to the component, typically with an add( ) method. The second is the *selection list*; this list contains zero-based indexes into the former list. With Swing, the JList class is the most obvious candidate for implementing the AccessibleSelection interface. With this class, the interface simply monitors both the model and the selection model of the JList to complete its functionality.

Again, this is a case where the objects in the accessibility hierarchy differ from the traditional component hierarchy. Here, the accessible children of an AccessibleSelection component should be the objects returned by the getAccessibleSelection( ) method—in other words, the objects added to the selectable list. As you might guess, all the objects that can be selected must implement the Accessible interface.

Properties

The properties listed in Table 25-7 must be readable through the AccessibleSelection interface. The accessibleSelectionCount property tells you how many selections the user has made. accessibleSelection, which is indexed, lets you access a particular selection given by the index. accessibleChildSelected, which is also indexed, lets you find out whether a particular child of the component is on the selection list; in this case, the index refers to one of the component's children, and a true value indicates that the child specified by the index is on the selection list.

Table 25-7. AccessibleSelection properties

Property	Data type	get	is	set	Default value
accessibleSelectionCount	int	•			
accessibleSelection[i]	Accessible	•			
accessibleChildSelected[i]	boolean			•	

[i]indexed

Methods

public abstract void addAccessibleSelection(int index)
> Add the child referenced by index in the data list to the selection list. If the child is already present, it is not added again. If the selection list supports only one selection at a time, the child replaces the previous selection on the list.

public abstract void removeAccessibleSelection(int index)
> Remove the child referenced by index in the data list from the current selection list. If the child is not currently selected, this method has no effect.

public abstract void clearAccessibleSelection()
> Clear the selection list.

public abstract void selectAllAccessibleSelection()
> Add every child contained in the component to the selection list.

The AccessibleText Interface

The AccessibleText methods are used to export "editable" text to assistive technologies. By editable, we mean text that the user can normally click and change, as opposed to static text that you would see in labels or buttons. The AccessibleText interface provides several methods that allow you not only to change the text, but to obtain many of its attributes. The AccessibleText interface is generally used only with the Swing components because much of the required functionality is not available in AWT components.

Properties

The read-only properties in Table 25-8 must be made available by classes that implement the AccessibleText interface.

Table 25-8. AccessibleText properties

Property	Data type	get	is	set	Default value
caretPosition	int	•			
characterAttribute[i]	AttributeSet	•			
characterBounds[i]	Rectangle	•			
charCount	int	•			
selectedText	String	•			
selectionEnd	int	•			
selectionStart	int	•			

[i]indexed

Constants

The AccessibleText interface uses the constants listed in Table 25-9. The charCount property lets you retrieve the total number of characters in the text buffer. characterBounds lets you retrieve the Rectangle bounding the character at a given index. caretPosition gives you the index of the character directly to the right of the caret.

Table 25-9. AccessibleText constants

State	Meaning
CHARACTER	Retrieves the current character at or near the specified index
WORD	Retrieves the current word at or near the specified index
SENTENCE	Retrieves the current sentence at or near the specified index

Methods

public abstract String getAfterIndex(int part, int index)
> Return the current character, word, or sentence after the given index, depending on which AccessibleText constant is passed in.

public abstract String getAtIndex(int part, int index)
> Return the current character, word, or sentence from the given index, depending on which AccessibleText constant is passed in.

public abstract String getBeforeIndex(int part, int index)
> Return the current character, word, or sentence before the given index, depending on which AccessibleText constant is passed in.

public abstract int getIndexAtPoint(Point p)
> Take a Point in local coordinates and return an index to the text character that resides under the point. If there is no text under the given point, the method must return -1.

The AccessibleHypertext Interface

The AccessibleHypertext interface extends the AccessibleText interface to allow access to hypertext, such as you'd see in a web page. In order to determine whether a given component has any accessible hyperlinks in it, call the getAccessibleText( ) method of the component's AccessibleContext object and check to see if the object returned is an instance of the AccessibleHypertext interface. If it is, the resulting object is a special hypertext accessibility object that can be used to obtain not only the traditional accessible text information but also the number of hyperlinks in the page and AccessibleHyperlink objects for each link.

Properties

AccessibleHypertext defines the properties listed in Table 25-10. The linkCount property tells you the number of hyperlinks in the text. The indexed property linkIndex gives you the index of the hyperlink at the given character offset into the text. The link property itself, which is also indexed, lets you access the hyperlink specified by the index. For example, to find the hyperlink associated with character n, you could write:

```
AccessibleHyperlink h = getLink(getLinkIndex(n));
```

Table 25-10. AccessibleHypertext properties

Property	Data type	get	is	set	Default value
link[i]	AccessibleHyperlink	•			
linkCount	int	•			
linkIndex[i]	int	•			

[i]indexed

See also properties of the AccessibleText interface (Table 25-8).

The AccessibleHyperlink Class

The AccessibleHyperlink class is an abstract class that encapsulates an HTML hyperlink in a text document. Hyperlinks (and concrete extensions of the AccessibleHyperlink class) are found only inside the document models of a JEditorPane. The AccessibleHyperlink class implements the AccessibleAction interface, which normally provides support for any number of actions in accessible components. For the most part, AccessibleHyperlink objects have only one action associated with them, which results in loading the text pane with the HTML document or image associated with the link. AccessibleHyperlink objects are returned from the getLink( ) accessor of an AccessibleHypertext object.

Properties

The `AccessibleHyperlink` class defines the properties listed in Table 25-11. All of the properties are abstract. The `endIndex` and `startIndex` properties let you access the starting and ending offsets of this hyperlink in the document from which it came. The `valid` property is true if the document that this hyperlink points to is still valid (i.e., has not changed).

Table 25-11. AccessibleHyperlink properties

Property	Data type	get	is	set	Default value
accessibleActionAnchor[a,i]	Object	•			
accessibleActionCount[a]	int	•			
accessibleActionDescription[a,i]	String	•			
accessibleActionObject[a,i]	String	•			
endIndex[a]	int	•			
startIndex[a]	int	•			
valid[a]	boolean		•		

[a]abstract, [i]indexed

The remaining properties let you work with an `AccessibleAction` (or actions) associated with this hyperlink. `accessibleActionCount` lets you find out how many actions are associated with the hyperlink; this is usually one, but there can be more. If there are more, the first action is *not* considered the default. `accessibleActionDescription` lets you retrieve a `String` describing a particular action. `accessibleActionObject` lets you access an object representing the action itself. For example, given a hyperlink to the URL *http://www.oreilly.com/*, getAccessibleActionObject will return a Java URL pointing to *http://www.oreilly.com/*. Finally, `accessibleActionAnchor` gives you the object that is displayed on the screen to represent the link. For example, if the link is a clickable image, getAccessibleActionAnchor returns an `ImageIcon`; if the link is represented by text, this method returns a `String` containing the text.

Method

public abstract boolean doAccessibleAction(int index)
   This method performs the action specified by the given integer index.

The AccessibleValue Interface

The `AccessibleValue` interface is responsible for handling a bounded-range value property inside a component. For example, the current value of a slider would be considered an accessible value that a component can export to an assistive technology. This is a simple interface that contains only four methods. Note that the value's data type is the generic Number; it is up to the caller to ensure that the data type passed in is correct and that the value returned is cast to the correct object.

Methods

public abstract Number getCurrentAccessibleValue()
> Return the current value as a Number. If the value has not been initialized, this method returns null.

public abstract boolean setCurrentAccessibleValue(Number n)
> Attempt to set the current value to the number passed in. If the number passed in is not the correct type, or if it cannot be set, the method returns false. Otherwise, the method returns true.

public abstract Number getMinimumAccessibleValue()
> Return the current minimum value as a Number. The caller is responsible for casting the returned Number to the appropriate data type.

public abstract Number getMaximumAccessibleValue()
> Return the current maximum value as a Number. The caller is responsible for casting the returned Number to the appropriate data type.

Classes Added in SDK 1.3 and 1.4

The 1.3 and 1.4 SDKs both augmented the Accessibility package. Three interfaces in particular stand out: AccessibleIcon, AccessibleEditableText, and AccessibleTable.

The AccessibleIcon Interface

Added in the 1.3 release, the AccessibleIcon interface allows assistive technologies to get information about any icons on a component (such as a button or a label). Notice that the getAccessibleIcon( ) method from the AccessibleContext class returns an array of icons. While Swing labels and buttons do not support multiple icons, custom components can freely do so and still provide useful information to assistive technologies.

Properties

Table 25-12 lists the three descriptive properties for AccessibleIcon. accessibleIcon-Description is the most useful property and can be set through the accessible context as it is on other components.

Table 25-12. AccessibleIcon properties

Property	Data type	get	is	set	Default value
accessibleIconDescription	String	•		•	
accessibleIconHeight	int	•			
accessibleIconWidth	int	•			

The AccessibleEditableText Interface

While the AccessibleText interface has always been part of Swing, an editable representation for text did not exist. With the release of the 1.4 SDK, AccessibleEditableText fills that gap.

Property

As an extension of the AccessibleText interface, most of the properties for AccessibleEditableText are inherited. One writable property to alter the contents of the text component, textContents, was added. It is shown in Table 25-13.

Table 25-13. AccessibleEditableText property

Property	Data type	get	is	set	Default value
textContents	String			•	

Text manipulation methods

The remaining AccessibleEditableText methods allow assistive technologies to manipulate text in the editable component:

public void cut(int startIndex, int endIndex)
> This method cuts text in the component (between the given indices) and places it on the system clipboard.

public void delete(int startIndex, int endIndex)
> Similar to the cut( ) method, but the text is simply cleared—it is not sent to the clipboard.

public String getTextRange(int startIndex, int endIndex)
> This method returns the text between the given indices.

public void insertTextAtIndex(int index, String s)
> Insert the text in s at the point given by index. Similar to the paste( ) method below, but the string to insert is not retrieved from the clipboard.

public void paste(int startIndex)
> Insert the text on the clipboard at the point given by startIndex.

public void replaceText(int startIndex, int endIndex, String s)
> This method replaces the text between startIndex and endIndex with the text in s. Note that there is no variation for this method that takes the text directly from the clipboard.

public void selectText(int startIndex, int endIndex)
> This method can be used to programmatically select the text between the startIndex and endIndex.

public void setAttributes(int startIndex, int endIndex, AttributeSet as)
> This method can be used to programmatically alter the attributes of a range of text between startIndex and endIndex.

The AccessibleTable Interface

The 1.3 SDK also introduced an accessible interface for tables. This interface allows assistive technologies access to descriptive information on the table and its various parts (rows, columns, and cells).

Properties

The properties in Table 25-14 describe just about every part of a table you would expect to have access to. Some of the less obvious properties include accessibleAt, which returns the Accessible object at a given row and column. The accessibleCaption property is the table caption—which is not necessarily the same as the summary. The extent properties (accessibleColumnExtentAt and accessibleRowExtentAt) provide information on how many columns or rows, respectively, the Accessible object occupies. For example, an accessible spreadsheet might have an entry that occupies two or more "straddled" cells.

Table 25-14. AccessibleHyperlink properties

Property	Data type	get	is	set	Default value
accessibleAt[ii]	Accessible	•			
accessibleCaption	Accessible	•		•	
accessibleColumnCount	int	•			
accessibleColumnDescription[i]	Accessible	•		•	
accessibleColumnExtentAt[ii]	int	•			
accessibleColumnHeader	AccessibleTable	•		•	
accessibleColumnSelected[i]	boolean		•		
accessibleRowCount	int	•			
accessibleRowDescription[i]	Accessible	•		•	
accessibleRowExtentAt[ii]	int	•			

[i]indexed, [ii]double-indexed (row, column)

Table 25-14. AccessibleHyperlink properties (continued)

Property	Data type	get	.is	set	Default value
accessibleRowHeader	AccessibleTable	•		•	
accessibleRowSelected[i]	boolean		•		
accessibleSelected[ii]	boolean		•		
accessibleSummary	Accessible	•		•	
selectedAccessibleColumns	int[]	•			
selectedAccessibleRows	int[]	•			

[i]indexed, [ii]double-indexed (row, column)

Relations and Extended Information

Among the other accessibility pieces added in the 1.3 and 1.4 releases are the AccessibleRelation and AccessibleRelationSet classes. A new method in the AccessibleContext class gives you access to the relation set for an accessible component. A *relation set* is the collection of all relationships between this component and other components in the system. The AccessibleRelation class encodes these relationships. An AccessibleRelation can describe several relationships, including control (controller/controlled by), labeling (label for/labeled by), and membership.

Perhaps not surprisingly, the extended accessibility interfaces (AccessibleExtendedTable and AccessibleExtendedComponent) provide information above and beyond what's available through their parent interfaces, AccessibleTable and AccessibleComponent, respectively. The extended component interface describes information for onscreen components, including tooltip text, border text, and key bindings. The extended table information allows you to translate between row and column indices and a linear index of Accessible objects. For example, given a pair of row and column values, you can look up the Accessible object associated with that cell. Alternatively, you can take the index of a particular Accessible object and find out which row or column it is associated with.

The last big addition to the accessibility package is the AccessibleKeyBindings interface. This interface simply describes the key bindings (i.e., shortcuts and mnemonics) associated with a component. Again, this type of information is available in other formats from other places, but this interface gives assistive technologies a consistent view of the bindings as well as a consistent way of extracting the relevant parts.

Implementing AccessibleAction

Here is a short example that implements an AccessibleContext and the AccessibleAction interface for a simple AWT button:

```
// ActionExampleButton.java
//
```

```
import java.util.*;
import java.awt.*;
import java.awt.event.*;

import javax.swing.*;
import javax.accessibility.*;

public class ActionExampleButton extends Button
    implements ActionListener, Accessible {

    public ActionExampleButton() {
        super("Press this Button");
        addActionListener(this);
    }

    public AccessibleContext getAccessibleContext() {
        return (new ActionAccessibleContext());
    }

    public void actionPerformed(ActionEvent e) {
        System.out.println("The button was pressed!");
    }

    public void processActionEvent(ActionEvent e) {
        super.processActionEvent(e);
    }

    // This class contains the accessible context for the component. Many of the
    // abstract methods simply call the SwingUtilities class to get the job done;
    // this is advised if you can get away with it. Otherwise, see the source code
    // for SwingUtilities.
    class ActionAccessibleContext extends AccessibleContext {

        public ActionAccessibleContext() {
            super();
            setAccessibleName("Button");
            setAccessibleDescription("Press the Button");
        }

        public AccessibleRole getAccessibleRole() {
            // Fill in whatever role you want here.
            return (AccessibleRole.AWT_COMPONENT);
        }

        public AccessibleStateSet getAccessibleStateSet() {
            return SwingUtilities.getAccessibleStateSet(ActionExample.this);
        }

        public int getAccessibleIndexInParent() {
            return SwingUtilities.getAccessibleIndexInParent(ActionExample.this);
        }

        public int getAccessibleChildrenCount() {
            return SwingUtilities.getAccessibleChildrenCount(ActionExample.this);
        }
```

```
        public Accessible getAccessibleChild(int i) {
            return SwingUtilities.getAccessibleChild(ActionExample.this, i);
        }

        public Locale getLocale() {
            // Ask the component what its locale is.
            return ActionExample.this.getLocale();
        }

        public AccessibleAction getAccessibleAction() {
            return new AccessAction();
        }
    }

    // This class implements the AccessibleAction interface. Essentially, there
    // is only one action, which is the equivalent of clicking on the button.
    class AccessAction implements AccessibleAction {

        final int NUMBER_OF_ACTIONS = 1;
        final String DESCRIPTION = "Presses the button";

        public int getAccessibleActionCount() {
            return NUMBER_OF_ACTIONS;
        }

        public String getAccessibleActionDescription(int i) {
            if (i == 0)
                return (DESCRIPTION);
            else
                return null;
        }

        public boolean doAccessibleAction(int i) {
            if (i == 0) {
                // Simulate clicking on a button.
                ActionExample.this.processActionEvent(new ActionEvent(this,
                    ActionEvent.ACTION_PERFORMED,
                    ActionExample.this.getActionCommand()));
                return true;
            } else
                return false;
        }
    }

    public static void main(String s[]) {

        ActionExampleButton example = new ActionExampleButton();

        JFrame frame = new JFrame("AccessibleAction Example");
        frame.setDefaultCloseOperation(EXIT_ON_CLOSE);
        frame.getContentPane().add(example, BorderLayout.CENTER);
        frame.setSize(100, 100);
        frame.setVisible(true);
    }
}
```

The result is somewhat anticlimactic: the example creates a simple button on the screen, and nothing else. If you click on the button, the following output is displayed:

```
The button was pressed!
```

However, it is important to know that an assistive technology could incorporate itself into the virtual machine and find out the button's state and description and even cause the button to be clicked. In order to understand more about how this can occur, we need to talk about the accessibility utility classes.

The Accessibility Utility Classes

So far, we've seen how the Accessibility APIs help make Swing and AWT components easier to interface with assistive technologies. However, we haven't seen what's available on the other side of the contract. In reality, there are several classes that help assistive technologies interface with the JVM on startup, communicate with accessibility-friendly components, and capture and interpret various system events. These classes are called the *accessibility utility* classes. They are not part of Swing; instead, they exist as a separate package, com.sun.java.accessibility.util, which is distributed by Sun. (You can download this package from *http://java.sun.com/ products/jfc/*.) The utility classes are crucial to assistive technology developers who wish to create specialized solutions that can communicate with any accessibility-friendly application.

Specifically, the accessibility utility classes can provide assistive technologies with:

- A list of the top-level windows of all Java applications currently executing under that virtual machine
- Support for locating the window that has input focus
- Support for locating the current mouse position
- Registration for listening for when top-level windows appear and disappear
- The ability to register listeners for and insert events into the windowing event queue

For the purposes of this chapter, we will discuss only the central classes in the Accessibility Utilities API. We begin with the class that allows assistive technologies to bridge the gap in the application's component: EventQueueMonitor.

The EventQueueMonitor Class

The EventQueueMonitor class is, in effect, a gateway to the system event queue. This class provides the central functionality for any assistive technology to capture and interpret system events, monitor the mouse position, and locate components related to screen position. EventQueueMonitor is a subclass of the AWT EventQueue class. This allows it to masquerade as the system event queue for the current JVM. Recall that the system event queue has its own thread, inserting and removing windowing events as necessary. With the EventQueueMonitor class, an application can register listeners for and post events to the system event queue thread—a critical task for assistive technologies.

To do this in JDK 1.1,* the EventQueueMonitor must replace the traditional system event queue at startup. Currently, Java allows this to occur only if the following property is set in the *awt.properties* file:

```
AWT.EventQueueClass=com.sun.java.accessibility.util.EventQueueMonitor
```

The class listed must be relative to the current value of the CLASSPATH environment variable. If successfully located, Java instantiates this class (invoking its constructor) and uses it for the windowing event queue.

 Some ports of the Java 1.1.x virtual machine do not allow the replacement of the windowing event queue through the *awt.properties* file. While the Windows and Solaris versions of the JDK follow closely to the reference specification put out by Sun Microsystems for the virtual machine, others may not. If you experience problems with accessibility on your specific port of the JVM, contact the organization that created the port and request that they support this capability. Alternatively, use a newer JVM.

Upon startup, the EventQueueMonitor class also seeks out any assistive technologies by looking for the following entry in the *awt.properties* file:

```
#JDK 1.1
AWT.assistive_technologies=com.xxx.SpeechRecognition,com.xxx.Brailer
```

In JDK 1.2 and higher, you make a similar addition to *accessibility.properties*:

```
#JDK 1.2
assistive_technologies=com.xxx.SpeechRecognition,com.xxx.Brailer
```

Again, the comma-separated list of classes must be relative to the CLASSPATH. When these classes are found, the EventQueueMonitor class instantiates each of them in its own thread.

Note that the EventQueueMonitor class consists almost entirely of static methods. Because there can be only one system event queue per virtual machine, this allows assistive technologies to call upon its methods and access graphical events from any location. If you need to access the EventQueueMonitor object itself, you can always get at it through the Toolkit.getSystemEventQueue( ) method; however, this is rarely necessary.

---

* In JDK 1.2 and higher, the loading of the event queue monitor is not necessary.

Constructor

public EventQueueMonitor()

This default constructor is used to create a new instance of an `EventQueueMonitor`. The JVM invokes this at startup; it shouldn't be invoked by the user.

Initialization

In JDK 1.2 and higher, assistive technologies must not register for events before the GUI is ready. These methods allow you to find out when the GUI is ready. (They don't exist in the 1.1 version of accessibility.) As we show in the `AssistiveExample` class later in this chapter, assistive technologies typically call `isGUIInitialized()`; add themselves as a `GUIInitializedListener` if the GUI isn't initialized; and implement the `guiInitialized` method (required by the `GUIInitializedListener` interface), which is called when the GUI is ready. (Although this looks like a typical event registration pattern, no events are actually involved.)

public static void addGUIInitializedListener(GUIInitializedListener c)
public static void removeGUIInitializedListener(GUIInitializedListener c)

These methods add or remove a listener from the list of classes that are notified when the GUI subsystem of the JVM is ready to interface with assistive technologies. You should not attempt to register for any GUI events before this has occurred.

public static boolean isGUIInitialized()

Return a `boolean` indicating whether the GUI subsystem of the JVM is ready to interface with assistive technologies. You can check this in the constructor of your assistive technology class and, if it is `false`, register to be notified when it is safe to interface using the `addGUIInitializedListener()` method.

Methods

public static void addTopLevelWindowListener(TopLevelWindowListener l)

Register a listener method to be invoked if a top-level window is created in the current virtual machine.

public static Accessible getAccessibleAt(Point p)

Return the object implementing the `Accessible` interface that is directly below the point passed in, or `null` if such an object does not exist. If there is a component available that does not implement the `Accessible` interface, this method attempts to locate a translator object.

public static Point getCurrentMousePosition()

Return the current position of the mouse in screen coordinates.

public static Window[] getTopLevelWindows()

Return an array of each of the top-level windows in the current virtual machine.

public static Window getTopLevelWindowWithFocus()

Return a reference to the top-level window that has the focus.

protected static void maybeLoadAssistiveTechnologies()

This protected method performs the task of loading and instantiating any assistive technologies referenced in the *awt.properties* file in the current thread. If the current virtual machine is JDK 1.2 or greater, this method returns without loading any classes; with JDK 1.2, the Toolkit class has inherited this responsibility.

public void postEvent(AWTEvent theEvent)

Queue an AWTEvent to be dispatched in the system event queue.

public static void removeTopLevelWindowListener(TopLevelWindowListener l)

Remove a listener method from the top-level window event list.

protected static void queueWindowEvent(WindowEvent e)

This protected method queues a specific WindowEvent to be dispatched in the system event queue.

The AWTEventMonitor Class

The EventQueueMonitor works with two other classes to allow assistive technologies to monitor specific events. AWTEventMonitor is one of those classes. This class contains a series of protected listener arrays and allows applications to register listeners for any and all AWT events that pass through the event queue. This is done through static methods inside the class that can be called from anywhere.

Constructor

public AWTEventMonitor()

The default constructor. There is no need for the programmer to invoke it.

Methods

public static addActionListener(ActionListener l)
public static removeActionListener(ActionListener l)

Add or remove a listener for AWT ActionEvents to or from the monitor.

public static addAdjustmentListener(AdjustmentListener l)
public static removeAdjustmentListener(AdjustmentListener l)

Add or remove a listener for AWT AdjustmentEvents to or from the monitor.

public static addComponentListener(ComponentListener l)
public static removeComponentListener(ComponentListener l)

Add or remove a listener for AWT ComponentEvents to or from the monitor.

public static addContainerListener(ContainerListener l)
public static removeContainerListener(ContainerListener l)

Add or remove a listener for AWT ContainerEvents to or from the monitor.

public static addFocusListener(FocusListener l)
public static removeFocusListener(FocusListener l)
> Add or remove a listener for AWT FocusEvents to or from the monitor.

public static addItemListener(ItemListener l)
public static removeItemListener(ItemListener l)
> Add or remove a listener for AWT ItemEvents to or from the monitor.

public static addKeyListener(KeyListener l)
public static removeKeyListener(KeyListener l)
> Add or remove a listener for AWT KeyEvents to or from the monitor.

public static addMouseListener(MouseListener l)
public static removeMouseListener(MouseListener l)
> Add or remove a listener for AWT MouseEvents to or from the monitor.

public static addMouseMotionListener(MouseMotionListener l)
public static removeMouseMotionListener(MouseMotionListener l)
> Add or remove a listener for AWT MouseMotionEvents to or from the monitor.

public static addTextListener(TextListener l)
public static removeTextListener(TextListener l)
> Add or remove a listener for AWT TextEvents to or from the monitor.

public static addWindowListener(WindowListener l)
public static removeWindowListener(WindowListener l)
> Add or remove a listener for AWT WindowEvents to or from the monitor.

protected static getComponentWithFocus()
> Return the component that currently has the keyboard focus.

The SwingEventMonitor Class

The SwingEventMonitor extends the AWTEventMonitor class and provides event registration for all Swing events. This class contains a series of protected listener arrays and allows applications to register listeners for any and all AWT and Swing events that pass through the event queue. Note that SwingEventMonitor contains all the functionality of AWTEventMonitor; use this class to gain access to both types of windowing events.

Constructor

public SwingEventMonitor()
> The default constructor. There is no need for the programmer to invoke it.

Methods

public static addAncestorListener(AncestorListener l)
public static removeAncestorListener(AncestorListener l)
  Add or remove a listener for Swing AncestorEvents.

public static addCaretListener(CaretListener l)
public static removeCaretListener(CaretListener l)
  Add or remove a listener for Swing CaretEvents.

public static addCellEditorListener(CellEditorListener l)
public static removeCellEditorListener(CellEditorListener l)
  Add or remove a listener for Swing CellEditorEvents.

public static addChangeListener(ChangeListener l)
public static removeChangeListener(ChangeListener l)
  Add or remove a listener for Swing ChangeEvents.

public static addColumnModelListener(TableColumnModelListener l)
public static removeColumnModelListener(TableColumnModelListener l)
  Add or remove a listener for Swing TableColumnModelEvents.

public static addDocumentListener(DocumentListener l)
public static removeDocumentListener(DocumentListener l)
  Add or remove a listener for Swing DocumentEvents.

public static addListDataListener(ListDataListener l)
public static removeListDataListener(ListDataListener l)
  Add or remove a listener for Swing ListDataEvents.

public static addListSelectionListener(ListSelectionListener l)
public static removeListSelectionListener(ListSelectionListener l)
  Add or remove a listener for Swing ListSelectionEvents.

public static addMenuListener(MenuListener l)
public static removeMenuListener(MenuListener l)
  Add or remove a listener for Swing MenuEvents.

public static addPopupMenuListener(PopupMenuListener l)
public static removePopupMenuListener(PopupMenuListener l)
  Add or remove a listener for Swing PopupMenuEvents.

public static addPropertyChangeListener(PropertyChangeListener l)
public static removePropertyChangeListener(PropertyChangeListener l)
  Add or remove a listener for PropertyChangeEvents.

public static addTableModelListener(TableModelListener l)
public static removeTableModelListener(TableModelListener l)
  Add or remove a listener for Swing TableModelEvents.

public static addTreeExpansionListener(TreeExpansionListener l)
public static removeTreeExpansionListener(TreeExpansionListener l)
  Add or remove a listener for Swing TreeExpansionEvents.

public static addTreeModelListener(TreeModelListener l)
public static removeTreeModelListener(TreeModelListener l)
   Add or remove a listener for Swing `TreeModelEvents`.

public static addTreeSelectionListener(TreeSelectionListener l)
public static removeTreeSelectionListener(TreeSelectionListener l)
   Add or remove a listener for Swing `TreeSelectionEvents`.

public static addUndoableEditListener(UndoableEditListener l)
public static removeUndoableEditListener(UndoableEditListener l)
   Add or remove a listener for Swing `UndoableEditEvents`.

public static addVetoableChangeListener(VetoableChangeListener l)
public static removeVetoableChangeListener(VetoableChangeListener l)
   Add or remove a listener for `VetoableChangeEvents`.

The TopLevelWindowListener Interface

This is a simple listener that assistive technologies can implement and register with the `addTopLevelWindowListener( )` and `removeTopLevelWindowListener( )` methods of the `EventQueueMonitor` class if they want to receive notification when a top-level window is created or destroyed. The interface contains two methods.

Methods

public abstract void topLevelWindowCreated(Window w)
   Invoked when a top-level window has been created.

public abstract void topLevelWindowDestroyed(Window w)
   Invoked when a top-level window has been destroyed.

The GUIInitializedListener Interface

`GUIInitializedListener` is a simple interface added in the 1.2 Accessibility package. This interface contains a single method, `guiInitialized( )`, which is called via the `EventQueueMonitor` when the GUI subsystem of the JVM is ready to have assistive technologies interface with it (i.e., register event listeners for components).

Method

public void guiInitialized( )
   Invoked by the `EventQueueMonitor` when the GUI subsystem has completed initializing itself and is ready to interface with assistive technologies.

This interface is necessary because the GUI subsystem for JDK 1.2 and higher may not be ready to deal with outside technologies by the time the assistive technology is loaded into the virtual machine. Hence, you should always check in the constructor of your assistive technology class to see if the GUI is initialized (using the static method `EventQueueMonitor.isGUIInitialized( )`). If it isn't, register a class that implements this interface with the `EventQueueMonitor`.

When the GUI is ready, it invokes this method, and the assistive technology can complete its initialization. (See the example at the end of the chapter for the code to do this.)

Interfacing with Accessibility

The following code shows how to create a simple assistive technology that can monitor events on the system event queue and interface with accessible components. The example consists of one class, `AssistiveExample`. This class creates a small window containing two labels and five checkboxes, which are repeatedly updated when the mouse comes to rest over an accessible component for longer than half a second.

Note that while using 1.2 or higher accessibility, we have to check to see if the GUI is ready for us to start firing accessibility-related commands. We do this by checking the `EventQueueMonitor.isGUIInitialized( )` method. This method returns a `boolean` indicating whether the GUI will accept accessibility commands. If it does, then we're fine. If it doesn't, then we must register ourselves to be notified when the GUI becomes available. This uses the `GUIInitializedListener` interface, which we explained earlier.

To use the `AssistiveExample` class, simply create a new `AssistiveExample` object from an existing application. The constructor creates a frame and makes it visible. For an example, check the source of the `BigExample` class in the online code files for this chapter.

Finally, note that we have a single button in our assistive example that performs the first action reported by the accessible context. You can use the Tab key to bring this button into focus while pointing with the mouse, then press the space bar to fire the action.

```
//  AssistiveExample.java
//
import java.awt.*;
import java.awt.event.*;
import javax.swing.*;
import javax.swing.border.*;
import javax.accessibility.*;
import com.sun.java.accessibility.util.*;

public class AssistiveExample extends JPanel
    implements MouseMotionListener, ActionListener, GUIInitializedListener {

    Timer timer;
    static JFrame frame;
```

```
JLabel nameLabel = new JLabel( );
JLabel descriptionLabel = new JLabel( );
JLabel tableLabel = new JLabel( );

JCheckBox selectionCheckBox = new JCheckBox("Selection", false);
JCheckBox textCheckBox = new JCheckBox("Text", false);
JCheckBox valueCheckBox = new JCheckBox("Value", false);
JCheckBox componentCheckBox = new JCheckBox("Component", false);
JCheckBox actionCheckBox = new JCheckBox("Action", false);
JCheckBox hypertextCheckBox = new JCheckBox("Hypertext", false);
JCheckBox iconCheckBox = new JCheckBox("Icon", false);
JCheckBox tableCheckBox = new JCheckBox("Table", false);
JCheckBox editableTextCheckBox = new JCheckBox("EditableText", false);
JLabel classLabel = new JLabel( );
JLabel parentLabel = new JLabel( );
JLabel relationLabel = new JLabel( );
JButton performAction = new JButton("Perform Action");

public AssistiveExample( ) {
  frame = new JFrame("Assistive Example");
  // Insert the appropriate labels and checkboxes.
  setLayout(new GridLayout(0,1));   // Just make as many rows as we need.

  add(nameLabel);
  add(descriptionLabel);
  add(tableLabel);
  add(new JSeparator( ));
  add(actionCheckBox);
  add(componentCheckBox);
  add(editableTextCheckBox);
  add(hypertextCheckBox);
  add(iconCheckBox);
  add(selectionCheckBox);
  add(tableCheckBox);
  add(textCheckBox);
  add(valueCheckBox);
  add(classLabel);
  add(parentLabel);
  add(relationLabel);
  add(performAction);

  setBorder(new TitledBorder("Accessible Component"));

  performAction.addActionListener(this);

  frame.getContentPane( ).add(this, BorderLayout.CENTER);
  frame.setBounds(100,100,500,600);
  frame.setVisible(true);

  // Check to see if the GUI subsystem is initialized correctly. (This is needed in
  // JDK 1.2 and higher.) If it isn't ready, then we have to wait.
  if (EventQueueMonitor.isGUIInitialized( )) {
    createGUI( );
  } else {
```

```
      EventQueueMonitor.addGUIInitializedListener(this);
    }

    performAction.grabFocus();
  }

  public void guiInitialized() {
    createGUI();
  }

  public void createGUI() {
    // We want to track the mouse motions, so notify the Swing event monitor of this.
    SwingEventMonitor.addMouseMotionListener(this);

    // Start a Timer object to measure how long the mouse stays over a particular
    // area.
    timer = new Timer(500, this);
  }

  public void mouseMoved(MouseEvent e) {
    // If the mouse moves, restart the timer.
    timer.restart();
  }
  public void mouseDragged(MouseEvent e) {
    // If the mouse is dragged, restart the timer.
    timer.restart();
  }

  public void actionPerformed(ActionEvent e) {
    // Find the component currently under the mouse.
    Point currentPosition = EventQueueMonitor.getCurrentMousePosition();
    Accessible comp = EventQueueMonitor.getAccessibleAt(currentPosition);

    // If the user pressed the button, and the component has an accessible action,
    // then execute it.
    if (e.getActionCommand() == "Perform Action") {
      AccessibleContext context = comp.getAccessibleContext();
      AccessibleAction action = context.getAccessibleAction();

      if (action != null)
        action.doAccessibleAction(0);
      else
        System.out.println("No accessible action present!");
      return;
    }

    // Otherwise, the timer has fired. Stop it and update the window.
    timer.stop();
    updateWindow(comp);
  }

  private void updateWindow(Accessible component) {
    if (component == null) { return; }
```

```
    // Reset the checkboxes.
    actionCheckBox.setSelected(false);
    selectionCheckBox.setSelected(false);
    textCheckBox.setSelected(false);
    componentCheckBox.setSelected(false);
    valueCheckBox.setSelected(false);
    hypertextCheckBox.setSelected(false);
    iconCheckBox.setSelected(false);
    tableCheckBox.setSelected(false);
    editableTextCheckBox.setSelected(false);

    // Get the accessibile context of the component in question.
    AccessibleContext context = component.getAccessibleContext();
    AccessibleRelationSet ars = context.getAccessibleRelationSet();

    nameLabel.setText("Name: " + context.getAccessibleName());
    descriptionLabel.setText("Desc: " + context.getAccessibleDescription());
    relationLabel.setText("Relation: " + ars);

    // Check the context for each of the accessibility types.
    if (context.getAccessibleAction() != null)
      actionCheckBox.setSelected(true);
    if (context.getAccessibleSelection() != null)
      selectionCheckBox.setSelected(true);
    if (context.getAccessibleText() != null) {
      textCheckBox.setSelected(true);
      if (context.getAccessibleText() instanceof AccessibleHypertext)
        hypertextCheckBox.setSelected(true);
    }
    if (context.getAccessibleComponent() != null) {
      componentCheckBox.setSelected(true);
      classLabel.setText("Class: " + context.getAccessibleComponent());
      parentLabel.setText("Parent: " + context.getAccessibleParent());
    }
    if (context.getAccessibleValue() != null)
      valueCheckBox.setSelected(true);
    if (context.getAccessibleIcon() != null)
      iconCheckBox.setSelected(true);
    if ((context.getAccessibleTable() != null) ||
        (context.getAccessibleParent() instanceof JTable)) {
      tableCheckBox.setSelected(true);
      tableLabel.setText("Table Desc: " +
          context.getAccessibleParent().getAccessibleContext()
                .getAccessibleDescription());
    }
    else {
      tableLabel.setText("");
    }
    if (context.getAccessibleEditableText() != null)
      editableTextCheckBox.setSelected(true);
    repaint();
  }
}
```

Figure 25-2 shows the result. We've connected our assistive technology to a demo application called BigExample. (The only functioning component is the Exit menu item.) Because Swing components support accessibility, we didn't need to do much work beyond creating and adding the components to the application. Figure 25-3 shows our assistive technology attached to the accessible AWT button we developed earlier, proving that we can communicate with it.

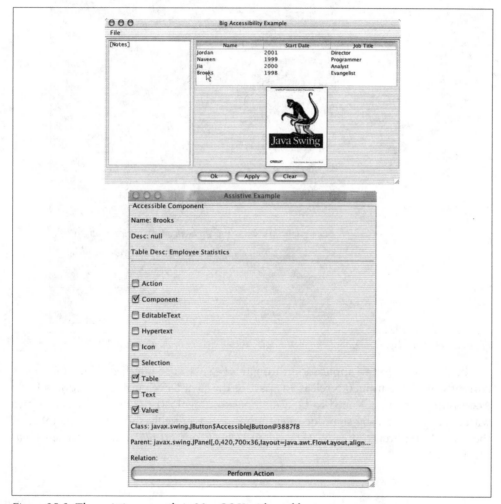

Figure 25-2. The assistive example in Mac OS X with a table

The Java Accessibility Helper

Developers serious about adding accessible support to their applications should consider taking advantage of the Java Accessibility Helper from Sun. This GUI tool allows developers to test applications from the assistive technology point of view. A test suite

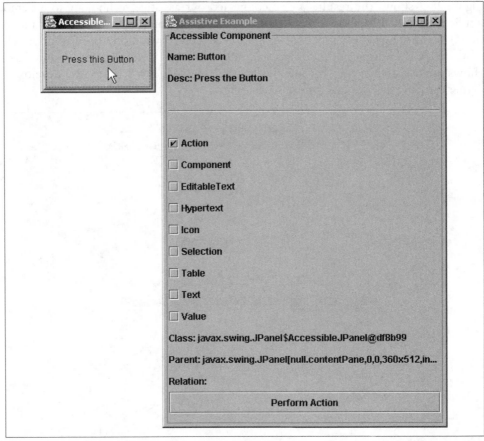

Figure 25-3. The assistive example on a Windows system with our customized AWT button

can be developed for an application through an easy-to-use interface. This free tool is currently available in its 0.6 release as part of the Java Developer Connection's Early Access program. You'll need to be a member to download the helper (which comes with some great step-by-step documentation), but you really should be a member of the JDC if you aren't already! (For details, check out *http://developer.java.sun.com/ developer/*.)

Look and Feel

In Chapter 1, we introduced the concept of Swing's Pluggable L&F (PLAF) architecture. In this chapter, we'll get into a variety of topics related to PLAF. The chapter includes:

- A discussion of the default L&F presented to users on different platforms, and the trade-offs involved in changing it for your application

- An overview of how the Swing component classes work together with the UI-delegate classes

- A detailed explanation of the various PLAF-related classes in the `javax.swing` package, as well as some of the important classes and interfaces from `javax.swing.plaf`

- An explanation of how PLAF fits into JFC's accessibility framework using `MultiLookAndFeel`.

- Detailed discussions of strategies for customizing the L&F of your applications using the following techniques:

  - Modification of specific component properties
  - Modification of resource defaults
  - Use of themes in the Metal L&F
  - Use of customized client properties in the Metal L&F
  - Replacement of specific UI delegates
  - Creation of a new L&F from scratch

This chapter contains a lot of technical detail. You can do a lot with Swing's PLAF architecture without understanding everything we cover here. If you're interested in customizing the L&F of your applications, but don't mind if there are a few things that don't quite make sense, you can skim the next few sections and jump right into "Look-and-Feel Customization." If you want to understand exactly how everything works, read on.

Mac OS X and the Default Look-and-Feel

On most platforms, unless the user or application has explicitly specified otherwise, Swing uses the Metal cross-platform L&F, and developers have likely become accustomed to this. With the advent of Mac OS X (which includes a tightly integrated Java environment that tracks Sun's latest releases), things change slightly. Mac users have strong expectations about the appearance and behavior of their applications, and Apple intends Java to be a first-class development environment on its OS. Because of this, the Mac L&F is the default under Mac OS X. This L&F allows Java applications to appear and behave like other Macintosh applications. This makes them more likely to be familiar to and adopted by Mac users.

As long as developers have made good use of Java's layout managers to account for differences in rendering between different machines, their applications translate to this new environment well. Unfortunately, not all applications have been designed in this way, and it is sometimes felt that the burden of testing under multiple different L&Fs is too difficult. Although you can use the mechanisms described later in this chapter to force your application to use a particular L&F (like the always available Metal), you should avoid taking this step lightly; it takes choices away from your users and definitely reduces the likelihood of the application's acceptance on highly consistent platforms like the Macintosh. If, despite this, you feel such a restriction is necessary, at least provide an easily found configuration option by which the users can choose to overrule you and use their preferred L&F at their own risk, so to speak.

If you do want to work with the Mac L&F, but lack a Mac on which you can test your application's layout, you can download the MacMetrics Metal theme from this book's web site: *http://www.oreilly.com/catalog/jswing2/*. This theme modifies Metal so that its components closely approximate the dimensions of the Mac L&F. It was graciously shared with us by Lee Ann Rucker who developed it while creating the Mac L&F itself. Figure 26-1 shows an example of how the theme alters a Metal interface. To use it, simply be sure *MacMetrics.jar* is in your application's classpath, and arrange for the following lines of code to be executed:

```
import javax.swing.plaf.metal.MetalLookAndFeel;
...
MetalLookAndFeel.setCurrentTheme(new MacMetricsTheme( ));
```

If you change the theme after any Swing components have already been created, you also need to call SwingUtilities.updateComponentTreeUI for each top-level container in your application, as discussed in "Changing the look-and-feel" later in this chapter.

Testing against the Metal, Motif, MacMetrics, and Windows L&Fs can provide some reassurance that your design is robust and cross-platform.

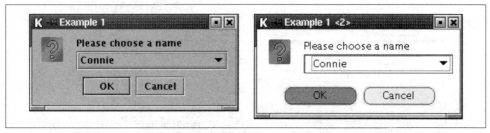

Figure 26-1. The defulat (left) and MacMetrics Metal themes on a Linux workstation

If you'd like your application to go even further in being a "good Mac citizen," we suggest you read Apple's technical note 2031, "Java Runtime Properties for Mac OS X," available at *http://developer.apple.com/technotes/tn/tn2031.html*. There, you'll learn how to enable Swing to use the global Macintosh menu bar (through a simple property setting that defaults to off because most Java applications haven't been designed to accommodate this style of interface). The document also discusses ways of taking advantage of hardware graphics acceleration and other Mac-specific features. There is an even more detailed discussion, including some very good advice, in Chapter 5 of *Early Adopter Mac OS X Java* (Wrox Press).

How Does It Work?

As you probably already know, each instance of a given Swing component uses a UI delegate to render the component using the style of the currently installed L&F. To really understand how things work, it helps to peek under the hood for a moment to see which methods are called at a few key points. The first point of interest is component creation time. When a new Swing component is instantiated, it must associate itself with a UI delegate object. Figure 26-2 shows the important steps in this process.*

In this figure, we show what happens when a new JTree component is created. The process is the same for any Swing component:

1. First, the constructor calls updateUI( ). Each Swing component class provides an updateUI( ) method that looks something like this:

   ```
   public void updateUI( ) {
       setUI((TreeUI)UIManager.getUI(this));
   }
   ```

2. The updateUI( ) method asks the UIManager class, described below, for an appropriate UI delegate object via its static getUI( ) method.

3. The UIManager consults an instance of UIDefaults (set up when the L&F was first installed) for the appropriate UI delegate.

---

* We do not show every method call. The illustration provides a high-level overview of the process.

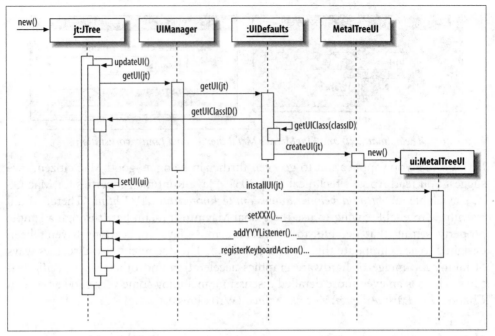

Figure 26-2. UI delegate installation

4. The `UIDefaults` object goes back to the component to get the UI class ID. In this `JTree` example, `"TreeUI"` is returned.

5. `UIDefaults` then looks up the `Class` object for the class ID. In this case, it finds the `MetalTreeUI` class.

6. The static method `createUI( )` is called (using reflection) on this UI delegate class. This static method is responsible for returning an instance of the UI delegate class. In some cases, a single instance is shared by all components. In other cases, a new instance is created each time. In this diagram, we show a new instance of `MetalTreeUI` being created and returned from `createUI( )`.

7. At last, the `JTree` has a UI delegate. The `updateUI( )` method now calls `setUI( )`.

8. If a UI delegate was already installed (in this example, we're creating a new component, so there is no delegate installed yet), `setUI( )` would call `uninstallUI( )` on the old delegate.

9. `setUI( )` now calls `installUI( )` on the new UI delegate, passing in the component.

10. The `installUI( )` methods for different components do different things. Often (as shown here), `installUI( )` is used to install listeners (allowing the UI delegate to keep track of changes made to the component), set defaults (e.g., fonts and colors), and add keyboard actions.

Now that the new component has been associated with its UI delegate, it can use the delegate for all L&F-related operations. The JComponent base class delegates the following methods to its UI:

- paintComponent( ) (called by paint( ); calls ui.update( ))
- getPreferredSize( )
- getMaximumSize( )
- getMinimumSize( )
- contains( )

 The three size accessors delegate to the UI only if a value has not been explicitly set on the component itself via a call to setPreferredSize( ), setMaximumSize( ), or setMinimumSize( ).

Now let's take a second look under the hood and see how the delegation of the painting process actually happens. The process in Figure 26-3 is pretty straightforward.

1. When the component is asked to update itself, it simply calls paint( ). Notice that this differs from java.awt.Component.update( ), which paints the component's background first. We'll see why this is important later in this chapter.

2. The JComponent.paint( ) method (after doing quite a few other things we won't get into here) calls paintComponent( ).

3. paintComponent( ) calls update( ) on the UI delegate.

4. Here (in ComponentUI.update( )), the background is painted only if the component is opaque. Then, the paint( ) method is called on the delegate.

5. The paint( ) method, implemented by the specific UI delegate classes, gets whatever information it needs from the component (which it receives as a parameter) and renders the component.

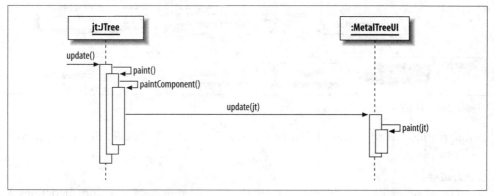

Figure 26-3. Swing painting delegation

We've left out a lot of details about the Swing painting mechanics in this example. If you want to know more about how this works, refer to the description of JComponent.paint( ) in Chapter 3. Our goal here is just to understand where the UI delegate fits in the painting process.

You should now have a basic understanding of how the Swing component classes work together with the UI delegates. In the next section, we'll explore the key classes and interfaces that make up the PLAF architecture.

Key Look-and-Feel Classes and Interfaces

In this section, we'll take an in-depth look at several key classes and interfaces that make up the Swing PLAF design. Figure 26-4 shows the relationships between the classes (and interfaces) we will examine in this section.

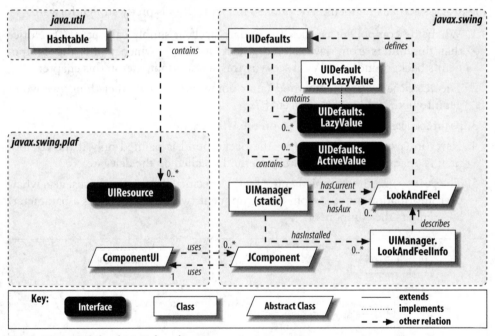

Figure 26-4. High-level L&F class diagram

Before we look at the details of each of these classes, we'll quickly describe the role each one plays:

LookAndFeel

>The abstract base class from which all the different L&Fs extend. It defines a number of static convenience methods, as well as some abstract methods required by every L&F.

UIDefaults

> An L&F is responsible for defining a set of default properties. UIDefaults is a Hashtable subclass that holds these properties. The properties include UIClassID to ComponentUI subclass mappings (e.g., "TreeUI" to MetalTreeUI) as well as lower-level defaults, such as colors and fonts.

UIDefaults.ActiveValue *and* UIDefaults.LazyValue

> These inner interfaces of UIDefaults enable some optimizations for resource values.

UIResource

> This is an empty interface (like Serializable or Cloneable) used to tag property values. It allows values defined by the L&F to be distinguished from values set by the user, as described in "The UIResource Interface" later in this chapter.

UIManager

> If you've ever changed the L&F of a Swing program at runtime, you're probably already familiar with this class. UIManager is responsible for tracking a global view of the L&Fs available in an application. It keeps track of the currently installed L&F and provides a mechanism to change the L&F. All of its methods are static, but it does provide a mechanism that allows multiple applets within a single virtual machine to use different L&Fs.

UIManager.LookAndFeelInfo

> This inner class is used to describe available L&Fs without actually having to load the L&F classes. UIManager uses this class to provide a list of available L&Fs.

ComponentUI

> This is the base class common to all UI delegates. It defines all of the methods related to painting and sizing that the different delegate subclasses must implement.

JComponent

> You're certainly familiar with this class by now—it's the base class for all of the Swing components. We include it in this diagram to show that at any time, each JComponent has a reference to a single ComponentUI. ComponentUI objects may, however, be shared by multiple components. JComponent was covered in gory detail back in Chapter 3.

The next several sections explore the details of each of these key players. After that, we'll be ready to look at a variety of ways that you can customize the L&F of your applications.

The LookAndFeel Class

The LookAndFeel class is the abstract base class from which all L&F implementations are derived. Extensions of this class are responsible for defining everything that's unique to a particular L&F. Figure 26-5 shows the inheritance hierarchy for the most common Swing L&F classes.

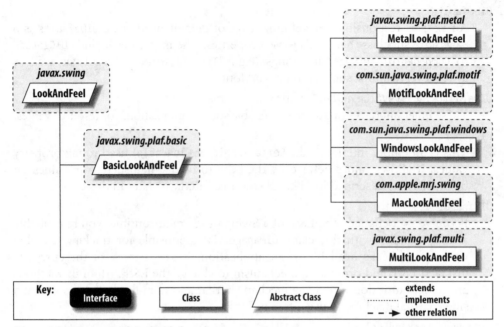

Figure 26-5. Swing LookAndFeel class diagram

Each L&F is defined in its own package.* This allows the numerous UI delegate classes and other support classes that make up the L&F to be conveniently grouped. The abstract BasicLookAndFeel class is the where the Swing L&F framework really lives. All of the abstractions for the various component UI classes are defined here. By extending the classes in the javax.swing.plaf.basic package, the other L&F packages (including ones you might create yourself) are relieved from having to worry about a lot of the details of the various component UI classes and can focus on rendering the components in a particular style.

Another special class in this diagram is the MultiLookAndFeel class, which allows you to use multiple L&Fs at the same time. This is used to provide accessibility support, perhaps by providing an L&F that speaks instead of drawing to the screen. Another possible use is automated UI testing. We'll get into the javax.swing.plaf.multi package later in the chapter.

Properties

The LookAndFeel class defines the properties shown in Table 26-1. As you can see, none of these properties have useful values defined in this base class (those listed as abstract have accessors that are abstract). The defaults property should be defined

---

* Note that the Windows and Motif L&Fs remain in the com.sun.java.swing.plaf package hierarchy.

by each L&F to contain the UI delegate class defaults, default system colors and fonts, etc. (We'll get into more detail on how `UIDefaults` is used later in the chapter.) The `description`, `ID`, and `name` properties just describe the L&F. Table 26-2 shows the values of these properties for the most common Swing L&Fs to give you an idea of how they are used.

Table 26-1. LookAndFeel properties

Property	Data type	get	is	set	Default value
defaults	UIDefaults	•			null
description	String	•			Abstract
ID	String	•			Abstract
name	String	•			Abstract
nativeLookAndFeel	boolean		•		Abstract
supportedLookAndFeel	boolean		•		Abstract
supportsWindowDecorations[1.4]	boolean	•			false

[1.4]since 1.4

Table 26-2. Property values for common Swing L&Fs

Look-and-feel	ID	Name	Description
MacLookAndFeel	Mac	MacOS	The MacOS L&F
MetalLookAndFeel	Metal	Metal	The Java L&F
MotifLookAndFeel	Motif	CDE/Motif	The CDE/Motif L&F
WindowsLookAndFeel	Windows	Windows	The Microsoft Windows L&F

The `nativeLookAndFeel` property indicates whether the L&F is designed to emulate the native L&F of the platform on which the application is currently running. For example, if you are running on a Windows machine, the `WindowsLookAndFeel` returns true if you invoke `isNativeLookAndFeel()`. Similarly, on a Solaris machine, the `MotifLookAndFeel` returns true while the `MacLookAndFeel` returns true on a Macintosh.

The `supportedLookAndFeel` property indicates whether the L&F is allowed to be used on the current platform. This was put in place primarily for legal reasons*—certain L&Fs may not be executed on platforms other than the native platform even if they're part of the standard Java distribution.

Finally, the `supportsWindowDecorations` property indicates whether the L&F can provide undecorated `RootPaneUI` instances. Such L&Fs support client-drawn window decorations (border, title bar, and controls for manipulating the window),

---

* Specifically, this was added to keep the `WindowsLookAndFeel` from being used on other platforms. The `MacLookAndFeel` is simply absent on non-Macintosh Java distributions.

allowing the L&F to take over the task of drawing these items from the underlying peer window.

Constructor

public LookAndFeel()
> The default constructor is available, so subclasses do not need to explicitly call one.

Methods

In addition to the accessors for the properties we listed earlier, the LookAndFeel base class defines the following public methods:

public void initialize()
> Perform any L&F-specific initialization needed, other than setting defaults. It is called by the UIManager just before invoking the getDefaults() method for the first time. The default implementation does nothing.

public void provideErrorFeedback(Component component)
> Invoked when the user tries to do something that's not allowed, such as pasting into an uneditable JTextField that has focus. The default implementation just beeps; subclasses can override this and provide additional feedback.

public String toString
> Return a string representation of the L&F, built from the description property and the L&F class name.

public void uninitialize()
> Used to perform cleanup before the L&F is replaced. This typically happens when a new L&F is chosen to replace the current one.

Static convenience methods

The following static methods are defined in this class. They are used by L&F subclasses to simplify common tasks.

public static Object getDesktopPropertyValue(String systemPropertyName,
*   Object fallbackValue)*
> Return the specified system desktop property by calling the default Toolkit's getDesktopProperty() method. If this method is null, fallbackValue is returned. Available since 1.4, this method provides convenient access to AWT's desktop property information. Desktop properties are platform-specific settings that track systemwide desktop themes that might be changed by the user during program execution. Because the properties vary by platform and may not exist at all on some platforms, few cross-platform programs use them.

public static void installBorder(JComponent c, String defaultBorderName)

Install a default border for the component if there is currently no border defined or if the current border is tagged as a UIResource. The border to install is retrieved from the UIManager using defaultBorderName as a key.

public static void installColors(JComponent c, String defaultBgName,
String defaultFgName)

Install default foreground and background colors for the component if they are not currently defined or if the current colors are tagged as UIResources. The colors to install are retrieved from the UIManager, using defaultBgName and defaultFgName as keys.

public static void installColorsAndFont(JComponent c, String defaultBgName,
String defaultFgName, String defaultFontName)

Call installColors( ) and install a default font using the same rules with respect to UIResources. A call to this method typically looks something like:

```
LookAndFeel.installColorsAndFont(theLabel, "Label.background",
    "Label.foreground", "Label.font");
```

public static Object makeIcon(Class baseClass, String gifFile)

Create a UIResource from the specified filename that can be entered into a defaults table. The filename should be relative to the directory containing the L&F classes so that it can be loaded by calling baseClass.getResourceAsStream( ). The returned object is a UIDefaults.LazyValue, meaning that the GIF is loaded only if it is needed.

public static void uninstallBorder(JComponent c)

Remove a default border from the component if the current border is tagged as a UIResource.

There are also a number of static methods for setting up key bindings that map KeyStrokes typed by the user to Actions that should be taken by components. The method makeKeyBindings has been available since Swing was introduced. A significantly improved keyboard-binding infrastructure was introduced with Version 1.3, which uses the InputMap and ActionMap classes to unify the two previous incompatible APIs. Three methods related to this new API were added to the LookAndFeel class: loadKeyBindings, makeComponentInputMap, and makeInputMap. The full details of the change in key-binding infrastructure (and the reasons behind it) are discussed in the *Swing Connection* article "Keyboard Bindings in Swing" at *http://java.sun.com/ products/jfc/tsc/special_report/kestrel/keybindings.html*.

In all of these methods, the specification of the keystrokes to associate with an action can either be KeyStroke objects or Strings describing a KeyStroke. In the latter case, an attempt is made to convert the string to a KeyStroke. This string may begin with any number of modifiers taken from the following list: shift, control, meta, alt, button1, button2, button3. The modifiers (if any) should be followed by the name of the key (the names defined in KeyEvent, without the VK_ at the beginning). For example, x would simply map to new `KeyStroke(0, KeyEvent.VK_X)` while Ctrl-Alt-Delete would map to:

```
new KeyStroke(InputEvent.CTRL_MASK|InputEvent.ALT_MASK, KeyEvent.VK_DELETE)
```

The UIDefaults Class

One of the key things that distinguishes an L&F is a set of default properties. These properties are stored in an extension of `java.util.Hashtable` called `UIDefaults`.

Any type of value that is important to an L&F can be stored in this table. The most common ones are fonts, colors, borders, icons, and, most importantly, UI-delegate class names. We'll get into the details of populating a `UIDefaults` object for a custom L&F in "Creation of a Custom Look-and-Feel" later in this chapter.

Starting with SDK 1.4, the `UIDefaults` class supports localized values for its defaults through new methods (and variants of existing methods) that add a `Locale` parameter.

Events

`UIDefaults` fires a `PropertyChangeEvent` any time a default is added to the table. If an individual property is added, the name of the property is the default's key. If a bulk addition is made, the property name is `"UIDefaults"`, and both the old and new property values reported are `null`.

The following event-related methods are defined:

public void addPropertyChangeListener(PropertyChangeListener listener)
public void removePropertyChangeListener(PropertyChangeListener listener)
    Define who receives notification when changes are made to the defaults.

public PropertyChangeListener[] getPropertyChangeListeners()
    Return an array, which may be empty, containing all the current (added and not yet removed) `PropertyChangeListeners` registered for `UIDefaults`. Available since SDK 1.4.

Constructors

UIDefaults()
    This is the default constructor; it creates an empty hashtable to hold the defaults for the L&F.

UIDefaults(Object[] keyValueList)
    This constructor accepts an array of objects and creates a defaults table initialized with the specified key/value pairs. The `keyValueList` array must be of even length, containing alternating keys and values. For example:

```
{ "textFont", new Font("Serif", Font.PLAIN, 12), "backgroundColor", Color.black }
```

Methods

If you are not creating your own L&F, you don't need to be concerned with the methods defined in UIDefaults. UIManager provides a set of static methods that perform the same functions on the UIDefaults object associated with the currently installed L&F:

public Object get(Object key)

> Like its Hashtable equivalent, this method returns the object associated with the given key. The method is overridden to provide special handling of two special types of values: ActiveValue and LazyValue. (These interfaces are described at the end of this section.) Values that are not of one of these special types are returned as is.

public Boolean getBoolean(Object key)
public Border getBorder(Object key)
public Color getColor(Object key)
public Dimension getDimension(Object key)
public Font getFont(Object key)
public Icon getIcon(Object key)
public Insets getInsets(Object key)
pulic int getInt(Object key)
public String getString(Object key)

> Provide type-safe access to certain types of properties. They return the object associated with the given key, attempting to cast it to the appropriate return type. If the cast is unsuccessful, the methods return null.

> As of SDK 1.4, all of the preceding get methods search the resource bundles associated with the UIDefaults using its default locale if the requested default is not present in the Hashtable. Each method also now has a variant with a second parameter of type Locale to allow lookup of a default for a specific locale.

public void setDefaultLocale(Locale l)
public Locale getDefaultLocale()

> These methods determine (or examine) the default Locale established for the UIDefaults, and thus affect the behavior of the single-parameter versions of the default-lookup methods. Available since Version 1.4.

public void addResourceBundle(String bundleName)
public void removeResourceBundle(String bundleName)

> Determine the list of resource bundles that are searched for localized values. When looking up the localized value for a default, the bundles are searched in the reverse order they were added (the most recent is searched first). Also since Version 1.4.

> Defaults stored in resource bundles don't support ActiveValue or LazyValue.

public ComponentUI getUI(JComponent target)

Return the UI-delegate object associated with the current L&F for the target component that was passed in. Locates the correct object by invoking the getUIClassID( ) method of the input component to obtain the correct name of the delegate, cross-referencing it against the class defaults table using the getUIClass( ) method, and invoking the UI delegate's static createUI( ) method to obtain an appropriate UI instance. If the method is unsuccessful, it invokes the getUIError( ) method.

public Class getUIClass(String uiClassID)
public Class getUIClass(String uiClassID, ClassLoader uiClassLoader)

These methods search the defaults table for the given class ID. The value from the table should be the class name of the appropriate UI delegate. After retrieving the class name, the name itself is used as a key into the table in an attempt to find the corresponding Class object. If the class is not already in the table, it is loaded by calling uiClassLoader.loadClass( ) or by calling Class.forName( ) if uiClassLoader is null. Once the class is found, it is added to the table (with its name as the key) so that subsequent calls to getUIClass( ) can get the class directly from the table. Note that the first version of this method calls the second with a null class loader.

public Object put(Object key, Object value)

Add the given key/value pair to the table. If the key already exists in the table, its value is replaced. If a new key is added, or if an existing key is assigned a new value, a PropertyChangeEvent is fired to all registered listeners. The property name sent with this event is the key. If the value is null, the key is removed from the table, and the PropertyChangeEvent is fired with a new value of null.

public void putDefaults(Object[] keyValueList)

Transfer all of the key/value pairs in the object array to the table, firing a single PropertyChangeEvent on completion. The property name in this event is "UIDefaults". (See the UIDefaults(Object[]) constructor for a description of the expected format of the input array.) Existing properties whose names are absent from the array are not affected by this method. If a null value is associated with a key in the array, the corresponding property is removed.

protected void getUIError(String msg)

Called if the getUI( ) method fails to successfully retrieve a UI delegate for its target component. By default, it just dumps a stack trace and continues. If you want to add specific functionality to handle errors, you can override this method in a subclass.

The UIDefaults.ActiveValue Interface

As we mentioned in the previous section, the UIDefaults.get( ) method handles two types of values differently. The first of these, ActiveValue, is used for properties that potentially need to be instantiated each time they are queried. Such properties typically include renderers and editors.

Method

The interface defines one method:

public abstract Object createValue(UIDefaults table)
Implementations of this method are expected to return a new instance of some class. When `UIDefaults.get( )` finds an `ActiveValue`, it invokes this method and returns the resulting object, rather than returning the `ActiveValue` itself.

Creating an ActiveValue

Implementations of this interface are typically very simple. For example:

```
Object myActiveValue  = new UIDefaults.ActiveValue( ) {
  public Object createValue(UIDefaults table) {
    return new MyThing( );
  }
};
```

The UIDefaults.LazyValue Interface

The other special type of value recognized by `UIDefaults.get( )` is the `LazyValue`. This interface allows properties to be lazily instantiated when they are asked for, avoiding the creation of values that may not be used. This is typically used for objects that take a long time to create, such as icons, or objects that are likely to be unused.

Method

The interface defines the following method:

public abstract Object createValue(UIDefaults table)
Implementations of this method are expected to return a new instance of some class. When `UIDefaults.get( )` finds a `LazyValue`, it invokes this method and replaces the value in the table with the resulting object. (See Figure 26-6.)

Creating a LazyValue

Prior to SDK 1.3, the typical code for a `LazyValue` was just like the code we presented for `ActiveValue`. The only difference was the intent. With `ActiveValue`, `createValue( )` is called every time a key is accessed. With `LazyValue`, `createValue( )` is called only once because the `LazyValue` object is replaced with the real value returned by `createValue( )`.

Unfortunately, performance benchmarking revealed that the savings of deferring the execution of the `createValue` methods was overwhelmed by the cost of class loading

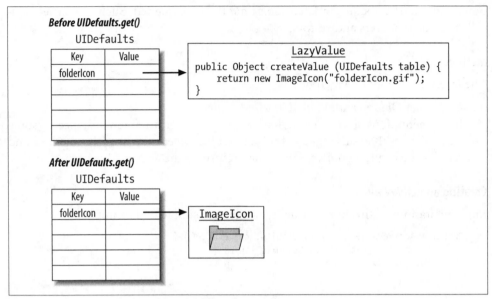

Figure 26-6. Conversion of a LazyValue

all the anonymous LazyValue implementations! To fix this, a new class was introduced. UIDefaults.ProxyLazyValue implements the LazyValue interface and uses reflection to create its proxied instance when asked to do so. Reflection allows the class-loading process to be deferred until the default is actually needed, thus finally achieving the performance gain that has always been the goal of the interface. When implementing your own L&F defaults, you should use the ProxyLazyValue class instead of creating new anonymous classes of the LazyValue interface.

Figure 26-7 shows how LazyValues and ActiveValues are handled differently by UIDefaults. Pay special attention to the differences in handling the second get( ) call.

The UIResource Interface

UIResource is an empty interface (similar in concept to java.io.Serializable or java.lang.Cloneable) used to tag L&F resource values that have been set by the L&F. The purpose of tagging these values is to allow Swing to distinguish between values set by the user and values set by the L&F. Consider the following scenario in which the L&F is changed during execution:

- User creates a JFoo component
- L&F installs a default foreground property with the value Color.blue
- User calls setForeground(Color.orange) on the new JFoo object
- User (or the application logic) changes the L&F
- New L&F installs its default foreground property with the value Color.red

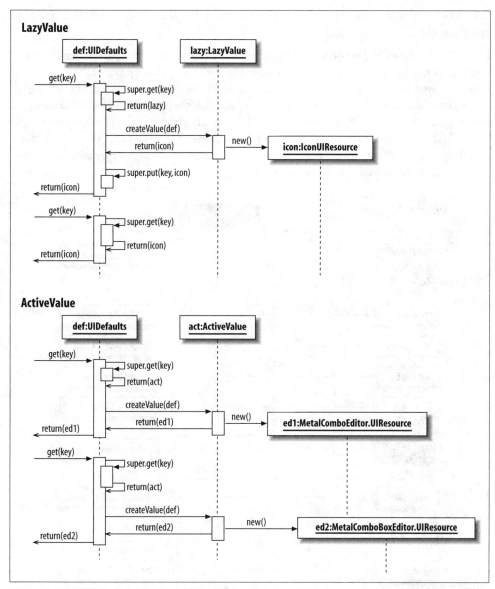

Figure 26-7. UIDefaults's handling of LazyValue and ActiveValue

Without the concept of UIResources, changing the L&F would cause all of the resource values (such as the foreground color in the above scenario) to be reset when the L&F is changed, since each L&F installs its defaults as part of its initialization process. Using UIResource to tag L&F-installed resource values allows Swing to make an instanceof UIResource check before installing the default values for new resources. If this operation returns false (indicating that the user changed the resource to something other than the default), the resource is not replaced by the new L&F. In our example, the foreground color would remain orange even after changing the L&F.

Figure 26-8 shows the various implementations of this interface, used when representing different types of resource values. The resource classes that extend existing classes (`ActionMapUIResource`, `ComponentInputMapUIResource`, `ColorUIResource`, `DimensionUIResource`, `FontUIResource`, `InputMapUIResource`, and `InsetsUIResource`) provide nothing more than constructors that simply pass their arguments up to the superclass. In the `BorderUIResource` and `IconUIResource` classes, a delegate object, which is the "real" resource, is held. Methods called on the resource object are just forwarded to the actual border or icon.[*]

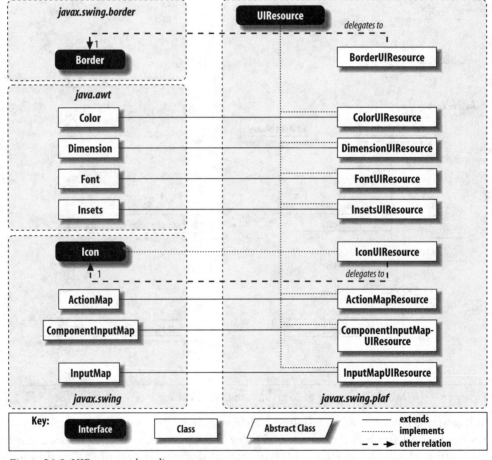

Figure 26-8. UIResource class diagram

---

[*] This delegation approach is necessary because `Border` and `Icon` are interfaces, not classes.

Static BorderUIResource methods

In addition to the delegation behavior described earlier, the `BorderUIResource` class defines four static methods used to access single instances of four common `Border` types tagged as `UIResources`. The methods are listed here for your convenience:

```
public static Border getEtchedBorderUIResource( )
public static Border getLoweredBevelBorderUIResource( )
public static Border getRaisedBevelBorderUIResource( )
public static Border getBlackLineBorderUIResource( )
```

This is similar to the role of the `BorderFactory` class, except that fewer borders are maintained, and they are specifically managed as `BorderUIResources`.

BorderUIResource inner classes

`BorderUIResource` defines static inner classes that subclass most[*] of the border classes defined in the `javax.swing.border` package. Each of these classes provides a set of constructors that map directly to the constructors provided by the real `Border` classes. See Chapter 13 for a list of these constructors.

```
public static class BevelBorderUIResource extends BevelBorder
    implements UIResource
public static class CompoundBorderUIResource extends CompoundBorder
    implements UIResource
public static class EmptyBorderUIResource extends EmptyBorder
    implements UIResource
public static class EtchedBorderUIResource extends EtchedBorderUI
    implements UIResource
public static class LineBorderUIResource extends LineBorder
    implements UIResource
public static class MatteBorderUIResource extends MatteBorder
    implements UIResource
public static class TitledBorderUIResource extends TitledBorder
    implements UIResource
```

The UIManager Class

`UIManager` provides a simple interface to a variety of information about the current L&F, as well as to any other available L&Fs. All of its methods are static, so you never need to instantiate a `UIManager`; you simply call its static methods. In this section, we'll look at a variety of ways that you can control the L&F of your applications using the `UIManager`.

---

[*] For whatever reason, there is no `SoftBevelBorderUIResource` defined.

The most common use of UIManager is to set the current L&F. If you don't want to use the L&F Swing selects by default, you simply call one of the setLookAndFeel() methods during initialization. For example:

```
public static void main(String[] args) {
  try {
   UIManager.setLookAndFeel(new com.sun.java.swing.plaf.motif.MotifLookAndFeel());
  } catch (UnsupportedLookAndFeelException e) {System.err.println("Bummer!");}
}
```

 As discussed in "Mac OS X and the Default Look-and-Feel" earlier in this chapter, think carefully before forcing a specific L&F on users of your application, and consider letting them overrule your choice.

LAFState

One issue that comes up whenever you have a static class is how to manage the fields of the class in a browser-based environment. It's important that one applet doesn't affect another by changing the value of some static field. In the case of the UIManager, it's important to ensure that the L&F used in one applet doesn't affect any other applets.

UIManager gets around this by storing much of the state in a private inner class called LAFState. Each application context has an associated LAFState, so there is no risk of an applet changing the L&F of another applet from some other source. This strategy is completely transparent to Swing developers.

UIManager look-and-feel concepts

The UIManager tracks a number of different L&F properties. These include:

Current L&F
> The most important L&F tracked by the UIManager is the L&F currently in use. The default value depends on the platform; it is usually the cross-platform L&F or (less often) the system L&F.

Cross-platform L&F
> This L&F is not modeled after a preexisting native L&F. By default, this is Swing's Metal L&F.

System L&F
> This L&F is designed to emulate the native L&F of the platform the application is currently running on. The value of this L&F (unsurprisingly) depends on the platform on which the program is running. The default implementation of UIManager checks the value of the os.name system property. If this contains the string Windows, the Windows L&F is used; the presence of Solaris or SunOS causes the Motif L&F to be used, and the string Mac results in an attempt to use the (nonexistent) com.sun.java.swing.plaf.mac.MacLookAndFeel. Any other platform

uses the cross-platform L&F. Of course, you shouldn't put too much stock in the default implementation; this is an obvious candidate for adjustment when porting Swing to a new platform. For example, in the shipping Mac OS X implementation, UIManager returns the correct string: com.apple.mrj.swing.MacLookAndFeel, as shown in Figure 26-5.

Installed L&Fs

This is the set of L&Fs currently available to the application, which depends on the platform.

Auxiliary L&Fs

This (possibly empty) set of L&Fs is used to provide accessibility support from a Swing application. They exist in conjunction with the current L&F to provide some sort of nongraphical representation of the display. A typical auxiliary L&F might be called AudioLookAndFeel. There are no auxiliary L&Fs by default.

The following example shows how you can verify the L&Fs defined by your system:

```java
// UIManagerDefaults.java
//
import javax.swing.*;

public class UIManagerDefaults {
  public static void main(String[] args) {
    System.out.println("Default look-and-feel:");
    System.out.println("  " + UIManager.getLookAndFeel().getName());

    UIManager.LookAndFeelInfo[] inst = UIManager.getInstalledLookAndFeels();
    System.out.println("Installed look-and-feels: ");
    for (int i=0;i<inst.length;i++) {
      System.out.println("   " + inst[i].getName());
    }

    LookAndFeel[] aux = UIManager.getAuxiliaryLookAndFeels();
    System.out.println("Auxiliary look-and-feels: ");
    if (aux != null) {
      for (int i=0;i<aux.length;i++) {
        System.out.println("   " + aux[i].getName());
      }
    }
    else {System.out.println("   <NONE>");}

    System.out.println("Cross-Platform:");
    System.out.println("  " + UIManager.getCrossPlatformLookAndFeelClassName());

    System.out.println("System:");
    System.out.println("  " + UIManager.getSystemLookAndFeelClassName());

    System.exit(0);
  }
}
```

Running this program on a Windows machine produces the following output:

```
Default look-and-feel:
   Metal Look and Feel
Installed look-and-feels:
   Metal
   CDE/Motif
   Windows
Auxiliary look-and-feels:
   <NONE>
Cross-Platform:
   javax.swing.plaf.metal.MetalLookAndFeel
System:
   com.sun.java.swing.plaf.windows.WindowsLookAndFeel
```

By contrast, running it on a Macintosh produces the following:*

```
Default look-and-feel:
   MacOS
Installed look-and-feels:
   Metal
   MacOS Adaptive
   CDE/Motif
   Windows
Auxiliary look-and-feels:
   <NONE>
Cross-Platform:
   javax.swing.plaf.metal.MetalLookAndFeel
System:
   com.apple.mrj.swing.MacLookAndFeel
```

Look-and-feel properties file

In the previous section, we examined the default values for various L&F properties. These defaults are hardcoded inside the UIManager version used by a given platform. Since all the useful methods in this class are static, there's no opportunity for you to change these defaults by extending UIManager. Instead, any changes to be made to these defaults must be made in the Swing properties file. During initialization, the UIManager looks for a file called *swing.properties* in the *lib* directory under the Java home directory defined by the java.home system property. (This is the mechanism Apple uses to make the Mac L&F the default on Mac OS X.)

Table 26-3 shows the various properties that you can define in this file, along with a description of their purpose. Default values for these properties vary, as described in the preceding section.

---

* Note in particular the different default L&F, as discussed at the beginning of this chapter.

Table 26-3. L&F options in Swing.properties

Property name	Purpose
swing.defaultlaf	Class name of the default L&F class
swing.auxiliarylaf	Comma-delimited list of auxiliary L&F class names
swing.plaf.multiplexinglaf	Class name of the multiplexing L&F class
swing.installedlafs	Comma-delimited list of installed L&F keys (used below)
swing.installedlaf.*.name	For each installed L&F, contains the L&F name indexed by the key used in swing.installedlafs
swing.installedlaf.*.class	For each installed L&F, contains the class name indexed by the key used in swing.installedlafs

The first three properties listed here must contain fully qualified class names. The swing.auxiliarylaf property may contain a comma-separated list of class names. The swing.installedlafs property should contain a comma-separated list of arbitrary L&F identifiers. Each identifier listed here must also have a name and class property defined for it.

Here's a hypothetical *swing.properties* file in which we explicitly set values for all of the possible properties:

```
swing.defaultlaf=com.sun.java.swing.plaf.motif.MotifLookAndFeel
swing.auxiliarylaf=audio.AudioLookAndFeel,braille.BrailleLookAndFeel
swing.plaf.multiplexinglaf=supermulti.SuperMultiLookAndFeel
swing.installedlafs=motif,metal,audio,braille
swing.installedlaf.motif.name=CDE/Motif
swing.installedlaf.motif.class=com.sun.java.swing.plaf.motif.MotifLookAndFeel
swing.installedlaf.metal.name=Metal
swing.installedlaf.metal.class=javax.swing.plaf.metal.MetalLookAndFeel
swing.installedlaf.audio.name=Audio
swing.installedlaf.audio.class=audio.AudioLookAndFeel
swing.installedlaf.braille.name=Braille
swing.installedlaf.braille.class=braille.BrailleLookAndFeel
```

These same property values may also be defined on the command line. For example, to start your Java application using the Motif L&F, all you have to do is enter this at the command line:

```
% java -Dswing.defaultlaf=com.sun.java.swing.plaf.motif.MotifLookAndFeel MyClass
```

Events

The UIManager class fires a PropertyChangeEvent any time the active L&F is changed. The property name in the event is lookAndFeel.

public static void addPropertyChangeListener(PropertyChangeListener listener)
public static void removePropertyChangeListener(PropertyChangeListener listener)
    Add or remove a PropertyChangeListener from the listener list.

UIDefaults convenience methods

UIManager defines a number of methods that simplify access to properties defined in the UIDefaults table of the currently installed L&F. These methods do nothing more than obtain the current UIDefaults object and call its corresponding method. It provides static versions of all the get methods listed in "The UIDefaults Class" earlier in this chapter, including the variants that specify a Locale.

Other static methods

public static void addAuxiliaryLookAndFeel(LookAndFeel laf)
> Add an auxiliary L&F. See "The MultiLookAndFeel" later in this chapter for more information.

public static LookAndFeel[] getAuxiliaryLookAndFeels()
> Return an array of objects representing the currently installed auxiliary L&Fs.

public static String getCrossPlatformLookAndFeelClassName()
> Return the name of the L&F class that is the default cross-platform L&F. This is hardcoded to return the Metal L&F class name.

public static UIDefaults getDefaults()
> Return the UIDefaults object associated with the current L&F, incorporating any defaults you have defined. See "Managing defaults" below for more information.

public static UIManager.LookAndFeelInfo[] getInstalledLookAndFeels()
> Return an array of UIManager.LookAndFeelInfo objects that identify the L&Fs currently installed on the system. This information is useful if you want to present the user with the names of the available L&Fs without going through the time-consuming process of actually instantiating all the L&F objects.

public static LookAndFeel getLookAndFeel()
> Retrieve the currently active L&F.

public static UIDefaults getLookAndFeelDefaults()
> Return the UIDefaults table defined for the current L&F, ignoring any defaults you have defined. See "Managing defaults" for more information.

public static String getSystemLookAndFeelClassName()
> Return the name of the L&F class native to the current platform.

public static ComponentUI getUI(JComponent target)
> Return the appropriate UI delegate for the component passed in. The delegate is instantiated from the current L&F.

public static void installLookAndFeel(String name, String className)
> Create a UIManager.LookAndFeelInfo entry from the two string parameters and add it to the installedLookAndFeels property.

public static void installLookAndFeel(UIManager.LookAndFeelInfo info)
> Add the given UIManager.LookAndFeelInfo object to the installedLookAndFeels property.

public static boolean removeAuxiliaryLookAndFeel(LookAndFeel laf)
> Remove an auxiliary L&F. Returns true if the L&F was found and removed.

public static void setInstalledLookAndFeels(UIManager.LookAndFeelInfo infos[])
> *throws SecurityException*
> Reset the list of currently installed L&Fs to those specified in the array infos.

Changing the look-and-feel

The following two methods change the L&F currently in use. If you call one of these methods before creating any Swing components (at the beginning of your main( ) or init( ) method, perhaps), you don't need to do anything else.

However, if you have already created any Swing components, you need to notify each of them that the L&F has changed so that they can get their new UI delegates. To do so, call the updateUI( ) method on every component in your application. Fortunately, Swing provides a method called SwingUtilities.updateComponentTree( ) that makes all of the updateUI() calls for you. All you have to do is pass in each of your top-level containers (typically JFrames, JWindows, and JApplets) one at a time. The SwingUtilities class, which is covered in detail in Chapter 27, takes care of updating the UI for each component contained in the component you pass in.

public static void setLookAndFeel(LookAndFeel newLookAndFeel)
> *throws UnsupportedLookAndFeelException*
> Reset the current L&F. If the given L&F is supported, the old L&F, if there is one, is uninitialized, and the new one is initialized. A property change event is fired to any registered listeners, indicating that the L&F for the system has been changed. This method also calls getDefaults( ) on the new L&F to set up the UI defaults.

public static void setLookAndFeel(String className) throws ClassNotFoundException,
> *InstantiationException, IllegalAccessException, UnsupportedLookAndFeelException*
> Set the current L&F, given the fully qualified name of a class that extends LookAndFeel. It attempts to turn the given class name into a LookAndFeel object and, if it is successful, passes this object to the other setLookAndFeel( ) method. Note the additional exceptions thrown by this method. These exceptions are actually thrown by the Class.forName( ) and Class.newInstance( ) methods, which are used to turn the given String into a LookAndFeel object.

Managing defaults

The UIManager tracks three levels of defaults, as shown in Figure 26-9.

As you know, each L&F defines a set of default values stored in a UIDefaults object. But this is only the beginning of the story. You are free to modify these default values in your application. If you do, the UIManager tracks these modifications in a separate UIDefaults object, which is hidden from you. When you ask for the current

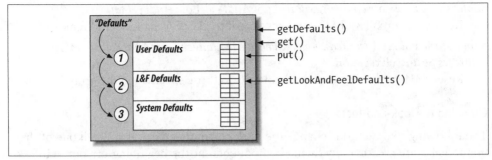

Figure 26-9. UIManager default management

defaults by calling getDefaults( ), or when you make a get( ) call to retrieve a specific key, you are actually accessing a sequence of UIDefaults objects. The values you have explicitly set have the highest priority, those set by the L&F are considered next, and those defined as system properties are considered only if there is no user- or L&F-defined property.[*]

Any defaults that your program explicitly sets remain defined, even if you change the L&F. If you want access to the defaults defined by the L&F, ignoring those you have overridden or added, you can call getLookAndFeelDefaults( ).

The UIManager.LookAndFeelInfo Class

This simple inner class is used to provide information about an L&F without having to load the L&F class itself. The UIManager provides a list of the available L&Fs by providing instances of these objects. The data stored in them can be used, for example, to populate a list of user-selectable L&Fs.

Properties

The properties listed in Table 26-4 make up the heart of this simple class. The name property contains a short name that describes the L&F, and the className property contains the fully qualified class name of the corresponding LookAndFeel implementation.

Table 26-4. UIManager.LookAndFeelInfo properties

Property	Data type	get	is	set	Default value
className	String	•			From constructor
name	String	•			From constructor

[*] Currently, UIManager defines only a single system default called "FocusManagerClassName". This is used by the FocusManager class to determine which FocusManager implementation to use. In the future, additional system defaults may be defined. Note that the new focus mechanism introduced in SDK 1.4 (and described in "Working with Focus" in Chapter 28) made this default obsolete by deprecating FocusManager. The value is still present, however.

Constructor

public LookAndFeelInfo(String name, String className)
Set the object's two properties.

Method

This is the only method other than the accessors for the two properties:

public String toString( )
Return a string built from the object's properties.

The ComponentUI Class

The abstract ComponentUI class, found in the com.sun.java.swing.plaf package, is the abstract class from which all UI delegates must inherit. It defines the core set of methods called by the JComponent base class, which all UI delegates must implement. Very few of the Swing components invoke component-specific methods on their UI objects, so the methods defined here form the core of the communication from the component classes to the UI classes.

In the Swing L&Fs, the individual delegate class names are typically formed by joining the L&F name, the component name (minus the J), and UI. For example, the Metal UI-delegate class for JSlider components is called MetalSliderUI. This naming convention is not enforced in any way, but it's a nice, simple standard that's well worth following.

Methods

Here are the methods defined in this abstract class. Note that they all take a JComponent. As we discussed in the chapter introduction, this means that the UI delegate does not need to keep a reference to the component and that the same delegate may be used for multiple components if desired.

public boolean contains(JComponent c, int x, int y)
Return a boolean indicating whether the specified component currently encompasses the specified point x, y. The default implementation simply delegates the call to the component by calling c.inside(x, y).

public int getAccessibleChildrenCount(JComponent c)
Return the number of accessible children in this object. This is delegated to the UI because a delegate might wish to represent different parts of itself as independently accessible components that don't map directly to Swing components. However, this default implementation just uses SwingUtilities.getAccessibleChildrenCount( ).

public Accessible getAccessibleChild(JComponent c, int i)
Return the accessible child at the specified index. The default implementation uses SwingUtilities.getAccessibleChild( ).

public Dimension getMaximumSize(JComponent c)

Return the maximum size for the given component. The default implementation returns `getPreferredSize( )`.

public Dimension getMinimumSize(JComponent c)

Should return the minimum size for the given component. The default implementation returns `getPreferredSize( )`.

public Dimension getPreferredSize(JComponent c)

Should return the preferred size for the given component. The default implementation returns `null`. If `JComponent` gets a `null` back from this method (or either of the two size methods listed previously), it defers the size query to its superclass (`Container`).

public void installUI(JComponent c)

Called just after the UI delegate is instantiated. The default implementation does nothing. Typically, this method adds listeners to the component, so the UI can update itself when the component changes state. It is also used to set various default values, such as fonts and colors.

public void paint(Graphics g, JComponent c)

Responsible for painting the component based on the component's current state. Since the implementation of this method is entirely component-specific, the default implementation does nothing. This method is called by the `update( )` method, which is described later. It is not called directly by `JComponent`.

public void uninstallUI(JComponent c)

Called as the current L&F is being removed. The default implementation does nothing. Subclasses typically use this method to release any resources they may have created and, most importantly, remove any listeners they added in `installUI( )`.

public void update(Graphics g, JComponent c)

Called by `JComponent.paintComponent( )`. If you're familiar with the old AWT update/paint mechanism, this method should also be familiar. The key difference is that this version of `update( )` fills the component's bounding rectangle with the background color only if the component is opaque. Whatever the opaqueness, this method finishes by calling `paint( )`.

Static method

public static ComponentUI createUI(JComponent c)

This static method, typically invoked by the `UIManager`, is used to obtain an instance of the component's UI delegate. This implementation actually throws an `Error`, since `createUI( )` should not be called on the abstract `ComponentUI` class, and subclasses are expected to define a valid implementation. Concrete subclasses of `ComponentUI` should return an instance (either a new one or a shared one) of their specific class.

The MultiLookAndFeel

Before we get into creating our own L&F, we'll take a quick detour to explore MultiLookAndFeel. This is the L&F that allows accessible interfaces to be incorporated into Swing applications. It can also be used to add sound effects, support for automated testing, and more.

By this point, you're probably at least aware of the concept of *accessibility* as it applies to JFC and Swing. If you read Chapter 25, you're aware of more than just the concept. The last piece of the accessibility puzzle is Swing's multiple L&F support.

The idea behind MultiLookAndFeel is to allow multiple L&Fs to be associated with each component in a program's GUI without the components having to do anything special to support them. By allowing multiple L&Fs, Swing makes it easy to augment a traditional L&F with auxiliary L&Fs, such as speech synthesizers or braille generators. Figure 26-10 gives a high-level view of how this might work.

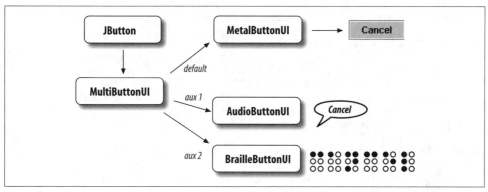

Figure 26-10. MultiLookAndFeel and Auxiliary L&F

In this diagram, we show a JButton in a multiplexing UI environment. The button's UI delegate is actually a MultiButtonUI, which is contained in the javax.swing.plaf.multi package. This is a special delegate that can support any number of additional ButtonUI objects. Here, we show the default UI delegate (MetalButtonUI) and two (hypothetical) auxiliary delegates, AudioButtonUI and BrailleButtonUI.

The MultiButtonUI (and all the other multiplexing delegates) keeps track of a vector of "real" UI objects. The first element in the vector is guaranteed to be the default, screen-based L&F. This default receives special treatment. When the JButton sends a query to its UI delegate, the MultiButtonUI forwards the query first to its default L&F, and then to each of the auxiliary L&Fs. If the method requires a return value, only the value returned from the default L&F is used; the others are ignored.

Creating an Auxilliary Look-and-Feel

Creating a fully implemented auxiliary L&F is beyond the scope of this book. However, we will throw something together to give you a feel for what it would take to build one.

In this example, we define an L&F called StdOutLookAndFeel. This simple-minded L&F prints messages to the screen to describe which component has the focus. To make the example reasonably concise, we show only the implementation of the UI delegate for JButtons, which does nothing more than print messages when a button gains or loses focus.

First, let's take a look at our StdOutLookAndFeel class:

```
// StdOutLookAndFeel.java
//
import javax.swing.*;
import javax.swing.plaf.*;

public class StdOutLookAndFeel extends LookAndFeel {

  // A few simple informational methods

  public String getName() { return "Standard Output"; }
  public String getID() { return "StdOut"; }
  public String getDescription() { return "The Standard Output Look and Feel"; }
  public boolean isNativeLookAndFeel() { return false; }
  public boolean isSupportedLookAndFeel() { return true; }

  // Our only default is the UI delegate for buttons.

  public UIDefaults getDefaults() {
    UIDefaults table = new UIDefaults();

    table.put("ButtonUI", "StdOutButtonUI");
    // In order to function, we'd also need lines here to define UI delegates
    // extending each of the following classes: CheckBoxUI, ComboBoxUI,
    // DesktopIconUI, FileChooserUI, InternalFrameUI, LabelUI,
    // PopupMenuSeparatorUI, ProgressBarUI, RadioButtonUI, ScrollBarUI,
    // ScrollPaneUI, SeparatorUI, SliderUI, SplitPaneUI, TabbedPaneUI,
    // TextFieldUI, ToggleButtonUI, ToolBarUI, ToolTipUI, TreeUI, and RootPaneUI.

    return table;
  }
}
```

As you can see, we've left out a lot of defaults that would be required for our L&F to be usable. In our case, we just map "ButtonUI" (the value of the UIClassID property for JButton) to our StdOutButtonUI class. Let's take a look at that class now:

```
// StdOutButtonUI.java
//
import java.awt.*;
```

```java
import java.awt.event.*;
import javax.accessibility.*;
import javax.swing.*;
import javax.swing.plaf.*;

public class StdOutButtonUI extends ButtonUI {

  // Use a single instance of this class for all buttons.
  private static StdOutButtonUI instance;

  private AccessListener listener = new AccessListener();

  // Return the single instance. If this is the first time, we create the
  // instance in this method too.
  public static ComponentUI createUI(JComponent c) {
    if (instance == null) {
      instance = new StdOutButtonUI();
    }
    return instance;
  }

  // Add a focus listener so we know when the buttons have focus.
  public void installUI(JComponent c) {
    JButton button = (JButton)c;
    button.addFocusListener(listener);
  }

  // Remove the focus listener.
  public void uninstallUI(JComponent c) {
    JButton button = (JButton)c;
    button.removeFocusListener(listener);
  }

  // Empty paint and update methods. An empty update() is critical!
  public void paint(Graphics g, JComponent c) {
  }

  public void update(Graphics g, JComponent c) {
  }

  public Insets getDefaultMargin(AbstractButton b) {
    return null; // Not called since we're auxiliary
  }

  // A focus listener. A real L&F would want to do a lot more.
  class AccessListener extends FocusAdapter {

    // We print some accessibility info when we get focus.
    public void focusGained(FocusEvent ev) {
      JButton b = (JButton)ev.getComponent();
      AccessibleContext access = b.getAccessibleContext();
      System.out.print("Focus gained by a ");
      System.out.print(access.getAccessibleRole().toDisplayString());
      System.out.print(" named ");
```

```
      System.out.println(access.getAccessibleName());
      System.out.print("Description: ");
      System.out.println(access.getAccessibleDescription());
    }

    // We print some accessibility info when we lose focus.
    public void focusLost(FocusEvent ev) {
      JButton b = (JButton)ev.getComponent();
      AccessibleContext access = b.getAccessibleContext();
      System.out.println("Focus leaving " + access.getAccessibleName());
    }
  }
}
```

The first method in this class is the static `createUI()` method, which is called to create an instance of our UI delegate. We chose to share an instance of `StdOutButtonUI` across all buttons, so we just return our single instance from this method. The next two methods, `installUI()` and `uninstallUI()`, are used to add and remove a `FocusListener` from the button. In a more realistic implementation, you'd likely be interested in listening for other types of events as well—this is where you'd register (and unregister) them.

Next, we define empty implementations of `paint()` and `update()`. Note the comment about the `update()` method. If we didn't override the default `update()` implementation, our auxiliary L&F, which should not affect the display in any way, would paint a solid rectangle in the location of opaque components.

We've also defined a small inner class called `AccessListener`. We've just made this class a `FocusListener` that displays a little information about the button any time it gains or loses focus. Note that we've taken advantage of Swing's support for accessibility by pulling information from the button's `AccessibleContext`.

Installing the MultiLookAndFeel

At this point, you may be wondering exactly how you use this new L&F. Obviously, we can't just call `UIManager.setLookAndFeel()` because we'd lose our graphical L&F that way. Luckily, Swing provides us with three other ways to install our auxiliary L&F. The first option is to explicitly tell the `UIManager` about the L&F. Placing the following line in our `main()` (or `init()` for an applet) method does the trick:

```
UIManager.addAuxiliaryLookAndFeel (new StdOutLookAndFeel () );
```

The second option is to use the Swing properties we discussed earlier in the chapter. If you want to make a global addition of the L&F, add the following to your *swing. properties* file:

```
swing.auxiliarylaf=StdOutLookAndFeel
```

The last option is very convenient if you're just playing around. All you have to do is tell the Java runtime about the L&F when you start it up, like this:

```
% java -Dswing.auxiliarylaf=StdOutLookAndFeel YourApp
```

Although this example is very sketchy, it should give you a sense of how to get started creating an auxiliary L&F and of the amount of work it takes.

Auditory Cues

SDK 1.4 introduced a framework for providing auditory cues in response to user interface actions without the complexity of adding an auxiliary L&F. Core support is provided by `BasicLookAndFeel` through an audio action map (see Table B-45 in Appendix B) that is available for use by subclasses.

It should be noted that, although the framework is in place, none of the standard L&Fs activate any sounds, at least as of SDK 1.4.1. Comments in the source code indicate that the activation has been temporarily disabled due to bugs in sound playback. So although this is an interesting area to watch, and you should feel free to experiment with customizations to activate various sounds, until Sun decides auditory cues are ready to be unleashed, it's probably best not to rely on them.

With that caveat, here's how the mechanism is set up. When `getAudioActionMap()` is called for the first time in `BasicLookAndFeel`, a series of initialization steps occur, with many opportunities for customization of the sort described in the next section:

1. The UI defaults are consulted to look up the list of sounds to be loaded, under the key `"auditoryCues.cueList"`. This is how Table B-45 gets its values.

2. For each cue, `createAudioAction()` is called to create the actual `Action` object that plays the sound. `BasicLookAndFeel` uses Java Sound to load and play named audio files, and the Metal L&F takes advantage of this mechanism, as shown in Table 26-5 (the files are in the `javax.swing.plaf.metal.sounds` package within the runtime JAR). The Windows L&F takes a different approach and maps the cues in the list to appropriate Windows desktop properties so they reflect the choices made in the user's native desktop themes. This mapping is shown in Table 26-6.

Table 26-5. Auditory cues mapped to sound files in MetalLookAndFeel

Auditory cue	File
CheckBoxMenuItem.commandSound	*MenuItemCommand.wav*
InternalFrame.closeSound	*FrameClose.wav*
InternalFrame.maximizeSound	*FrameMaximize.wav*
InternalFrame.minimizeSound	*FrameMinimize.wav*
InternalFrame.restoreDownSound	*FrameRestoreDown.wav*
InternalFrame.restoreUpSound	*FrameRestoreUp.wav*
MenuItem.commandSound	*MenuItemCommand.wav*
OptionPane.errorSound	*OptionPaneError.wav*
OptionPane.informationSound	*OptionPaneInformation.wav*

Table 26-5. *Auditory cues mapped to sound files in MetalLookAndFeel (continued)*

Auditory cue	File
OptionPane.questionSound	*OptionPaneQuestion.wav*
OptionPane.warningSound	*OptionPaneWarning.wav*
PopupMenu.popupSound	*PopupMenuPopup.wav*
RadioButtonMenuItem.commandSound	*MenuItemCommand.wav*

Table 26-6. *Auditory cues mapped to desktop properties in WindowsLookAndFeel*

Auditory cue	Desktop property
CheckBoxMenuItem.commandSound	win.sound.menuCommand
InternalFrame.closeSound	win.sound.close
InternalFrame.maximizeSound	win.sound.maximize
InternalFrame.minimizeSound	win.sound.minimize
InternalFrame.restoreDownSound	win.sound.restoreDown
InternalFrame.restoreUpSound	win.sound.restoreUp
MenuItem.commandSound	win.sound.menuCommand
OptionPane.errorSound	win.sound.hand
OptionPane.informationSound	win.sound.asterisk
OptionPane.questionSound	win.sound.question
OptionPane.warningSound	win.sound.exclamation
PopupMenu.popupSound	win.sound.menuPopup
RadioButtonMenuItem.commandSound	win.sound.menuCommand

3. Once the audio actions are created, BasicLookAndFeel associates each action with a sound file to be played when the action is performed. A protected method and inner AudioAction class provide support for this approach, and it's used by the Metal L&Fs, as shown in Table 26-5. Other L&Fs can override this and use different mechanisms to produce appropriate sounds; the Windows L&F does this to provide a link between the Java auditory cues and the sounds defined by the user's native desktop sound themes, which may change even while the Java application is running.

The UI delegates within the Basic L&F have been enhanced to trigger sounds at appropriate times. When one of these classes wishes to play a sound, it calls Basic-LookAndFeel.playSound( ), passing in the corresponding Action. The playSound( ) method doesn't always play the sound. It first checks to see if the action is present in the list contained in the UI defaults entry "AuditoryCues.playList". This list gives applications a chance to turn particular cues on and off, and it's here that the current implementation has blocked sounds from actually playing. If there were no sound bugs, the Metal L&F would include the sounds for the four kinds of OptionPane cues, and the Windows L&F would include all sound cues, in this list. At press time, the play list is always left empty. When `playSound( )` finds the action in the play list, it invokes the action's `actionPerformed( )` method to produce the sound.

There are a variety of ways to customize the sounds produced for the auditory cues. The discussion of the Windows L&F approach illustrates the most complex: you can create a custom L&F that overrides the mechanisms in `BasicLookAndFeel` that load and produce sounds. Without going nearly that far you can still achieve a great deal. By taking advantage of the UI defaults mechanism you can alter the sound used by default for a particular cue simply by setting up a link to your own audio file. For example:

```
UIManager.put("PopupMenu.popupSound", "myGreatBloop.au");
```

Finally, you can assign specific cues to a particular component by storing values in its own `ActionMap`. In this case you need to create the `Action` that plays the sound and assign it to the map. Suppose you have a `menuItem` that you want to play a special sound, which you encapsulated as `myMenuSoundAction`. Here's the code you'd use:

```
ActionMap menuMap = menuItem.getActionMap( );
menuMap.put("MenuItem.commandSound", myMenuSoundAction);
```

We hope this auditory cue mechanism will soon be reliable enough to be active in the shipping SDK so that we can all start taking advantage of it. In the meantime, this discussion of customization has been a good setup for the next topic.

Look-and-Feel Customization

In this section, we'll look at different ways that you can change the way components in your application appear. We'll start with the simplest approach—making property changes on a per-component basis—and work our way through several increasingly powerful (and complicated) strategies. In the last section, we'll show you how to build your own L&F from the ground up.

Modification of Component Properties

This is the most obvious way to change the look of a component, and it's certainly not new to Swing. At the very top of the Java component hierarchy, `java.awt.Component` defines a number of fundamental properties, including `foreground`, `background`, and `font`. If you want to change the way a specific component looks, you can always just change the value of these properties, or any of the others defined by the specific components you are using. As we said, this is nothing new to the Swing PLAF architecture, but we don't want to lose sight of the fact that you can still make many changes in this way.

Bear in mind that platform-specific L&F constraints on the rendering of certain components may prevent some property changes from being honored. For example, Mac buttons are always the same color.

Modification of the UI Defaults

Modifying component properties lets you customize individual components. But what if you want to make more global changes? What if you want to change things that aren't exposed as component properties?

This is where UIResources come into play. There are more than 300 different resources defined by the Swing L&Fs that you can tweak to change the way the components are displayed. These resources include icons, borders, colors, fonts, and more. (Appendix A shows a complete list of the properties defined by the Basic-LookAndFeel, the base class for all of the Swing-provided L&Fs.) Unfortunately, not all of the Swing L&Fs adhere strictly to these resource names. In the following example, several of the resource names we've used are specific to the Metal L&F.

Making global changes with defaults

In this example, we change the defaults for a variety of resources to give you an idea of the types of things you can affect. Specifically, we change the border used by buttons, the title font and icons used by internal frames, and the width used by scrollbars.

Because we're making these changes globally, any components that use these properties are affected by what we do.

```java
// ResourceModExample.java
//
import java.awt.*;
import java.awt.event.*;
import javax.swing.*;
import javax.swing.border.*;

public class ResourceModExample {
  public static void main(String[] args) {

    // A custom border for all buttons
    Border border = BorderFactory.createRaisedBevelBorder( );
    Border tripleBorder = new CompoundBorder(new CompoundBorder(
      border, border), border);

    UIManager.put("Button.border", tripleBorder);

    // Custom icons for internal frames
    UIManager.put("InternalFrame.closeIcon", new ImageIcon("close.gif"));
    UIManager.put("InternalFrame.iconizeIcon", new ImageIcon("iconify.gif"));
    UIManager.put("InternalFrame.maximizeIcon", new ImageIcon("maximize.gif"));
    UIManager.put("InternalFrame.altMaximizeIcon", new ImageIcon("altMax.gif"));

    // A custom internal frame title font
    UIManager.put("InternalFrame.titleFont", new Font("Serif", Font.ITALIC, 12));

    // Make scrollbars really wide.
```

```
        UIManager.put("ScrollBar.width", new Integer(30));

        // Throw together some components to show what we've done. Nothing below here is
        // L&F-specific.
        // **********************************
        JFrame f = new JFrame();
        f.setDefaultCloseOperation(JFrame.EXIT_ON_CLOSE);
        Container c = f.getContentPane();

        JDesktopPane desk = new JDesktopPane();
        c.add(desk, BorderLayout.CENTER);

        JButton cut = new JButton("Cut");
        JButton copy = new JButton("Copy");
        JButton paste = new JButton("Paste");

        JPanel p = new JPanel(new FlowLayout());
        p.add(cut);
        p.add(copy);
        p.add(paste);
        c.add(p, BorderLayout.SOUTH);

        JInternalFrame inf = new JInternalFrame("MyFrame", true, true, true, true);
        JLabel l = new JLabel(new ImageIcon("luggage.jpeg"));
        JScrollPane scroll = new JScrollPane(l);
        inf.setContentPane(scroll);
        inf.setBounds(10, 10, 350, 280);
        desk.add(inf);
        inf.setVisible(true);

        f.setSize(380, 360);
        f.setVisible(true);
    }
}
```

There's not really a lot to explain about the example. In the first part, we set a variety of resources, specifying our own border, icons, font, and scrollbar width. After that, we just threw together a few components to demonstrate the changes we made. We didn't have to do anything specific to our individual internal frame, scrollbar, or button objects—they used our new defaults automatically. This example produces the display shown in Figure 26-11. This example also illustrates the limitation brought up at the end of the previous section and shows that it applies to defaults in the same way it does to directly modifying component properties. Not every L&F honors all customizations that your code might request. Metal ignored the titleFont specification (as can be seen in the lefthand screenshot) while the Mac L&F used the requested font but enforced the Aqua Human Interface Guidelines with respect to the window control icons and scrollbar widths. Both L&Fs used the specified custom button borders.

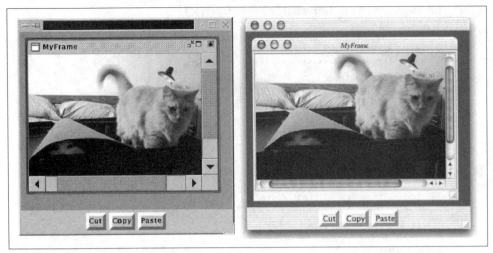

Figure 26-11. UI resource customization in the Metal (left) and Mac (right) L&Fs

Using Metal's Themes

The cross-platform Metal L&F defines a class called MetalTheme that allows you to customize the look of any application that uses Metal. This simple class encapsulates the colors and fonts used by the L&F. By creating your own theme, you can change the look of *every* component displayed by the Metal L&F.

Sound exciting? It gets better. What makes this feature especially nice is how easy it is to use. Here's an extension of the default theme (which uses three shades of blue for its primary colors) that replaces the familiar blue colors with shades of red:

```
// RedTheme.java
//
import javax.swing.plaf.*;
import javax.swing.plaf.metal.*;

public class RedTheme extends DefaultMetalTheme {
  public String getName() { return "Mars"; }

  private final ColorUIResource primary1 = new ColorUIResource(153, 102, 102);
  private final ColorUIResource primary2 = new ColorUIResource(204, 153, 153);
  private final ColorUIResource primary3 = new ColorUIResource(255, 204, 204);

  protected ColorUIResource getPrimary1() { return primary1; }
  protected ColorUIResource getPrimary2() { return primary2; }
  protected ColorUIResource getPrimary3() { return primary3; }
}
```

These last three methods are defined by MetalTheme to set the primary colors used by the Metal L&F. Everything Metal paints uses these colors (along with three shades of gray, plus black and white), so there's nothing more to do. To tell an application to use this new theme, we just need to add the following call to the beginning of the main( ) or init( ) method:

```
MetalLookAndFeel.setCurrentTheme(new RedTheme( ));
```

If you've already created any Swing components, you'll also need to call UIManager. setLookAndFeel(new MetalLookAndFeel( )) after you set the theme. Themes are queried only during the initialization phase, when all of the data from the theme is loaded into the UIDefaults. Of course, you'll also need to make sure your application is using the Metal L&F if that's not the platform default.

MetalTheme properties

The *RedTheme.java* example shows the most basic type of theme you can create; it doesn't scratch the surface of the flexibility Metal themes can provide. The MetalTheme abstract class actually defines all the properties shown in Table 26-7 (note that some of the accessors are abstract in MetalTheme). The default values for all of the colors are defined by the various base colors set by the theme, along with black and white. In some cases, the defaults are defined in terms of other properties from this table.

Table 26-7. MetalTheme properties

Property	Data type	get	is	set	Default value
acceleratorForeground	ColorUIResource	•			primary1
acceleratorSelectedForeground	ColorUIResource	•			black
control	ColorUIResource	•			secondary3
controlDarkShadow	ColorUIResource	•			secondary1
controlDisabled	ColorUIResource	•			secondary2
controlHighlight	ColorUIResource	•			white
controlInfo	ColorUIResource	•			black
controlShadow	ColorUIResource	•			secondary2
controlTextColor	ColorUIResource	•			controlInfo
controlTextFont	FontUIResource	•			Abstract
desktopColor	ColorUIResource	•			primary2
focusColor	ColorUIResource	•			primary2
highlightedTextColor	ColorUIResource	•			controlTextColor
inactiveControlTextColor	ColorUIResource	•			controlDisabled
inactiveSystemTextColor	ColorUIResource	•			secondary2
menuBackground	ColorUIResource	•			secondary3
menuDisabledForeground	ColorUIResource	•			secondary3
menuForeground	ColorUIResource	•			black
menuSelectedBackground	ColorUIResource	•			primary2

Table 26-7. MetalTheme properties (continued)

Property	Data type	get	is	set	Default value
menuSelectedForeground	ColorUIResource	•			black
menuTextFont	FontUIResource	•			Abstract
name	String	•			Abstract
primaryControl	ColorUIResource	•			primary3
primaryControlDarkShadow	ColorUIResource	•			primary1
primaryControlHighlight	ColorUIResource	•			white
primaryControlInfo	ColorUIResource	•			black
primaryControlShadow	ColorUIResource	•			primary2
separatorBackground	ColorUIResource	•			white
separatorForeground	ColorUIResource	•			primary1
subTextFont	FontUIResource	•			Abstract
systemTextColor	ColorUIResource	•			primary1
systemTextFont	FontUIResource	•			Abstract
textHighlightColor	ColorUIResource	•			primary3
userTextColor	ColorUIResource	•			black
userTextFont	FontUIResource	•			Abstract
windowBackground	ColorUIResource	•			white
windowTitleBackground	ColorUIResource	•			primary3
windowTitleFont	FontUIResource	•			Abstract
windowTitleForeground	ColorUIResource	•			black
windowTitleInactiveBackground	ColorUIResource	•			secondary3
windowTitleInactiveForeground	ColorUIResource	•			black

Abstract protected methods

As we saw in the previous table, `MetalTheme` defines six core colors (along with black and white) used to paint all Metal components. Subclasses of `MetalTheme` must implement the following six methods to define the core colors used by the theme:

```
protected abstract ColorUIResource getPrimary1( )
protected abstract ColorUIResource getPrimary2( )
protected abstract ColorUIResource getPrimary3( )
protected abstract ColorUIResource getSecondary1( )
protected abstract ColorUIResource getSecondary2( )
protected abstract ColorUIResource getSecondary3( )
```

Black and white

Some interesting (though arguably bizarre) effects could also be created by replacing the values of black and white. These `MetalTheme` methods return `Color.black` and `Color.white`, wrapped as `ColorUIResources`, by default:

```
protected ColorUIResource getBlack( )
protected ColorUIResource getWhite( )
```

Additional customization

`MetalTheme` defines one last method that allows you to use themes to change other aspects of the L&F:

public void addCustomEntriesToTable(UIDefaults table)
Called after the `MetalLookAndFeel` loads its default tables. The default implementation does nothing. Subclasses can take advantage of this hook to add any number of custom resource values to the defaults table. For example:

```
public void addCustomEntriesToTable(UIDefaults table) {
    table.put("Tree.openIcon", new ImageIcon("open.gif"));
    table.put("Tree.closedIcon", new ImageIcon("closed.gif"));
}
```

DefaultMetalTheme font properties

`DefaultMetalTheme` is a concrete extension of `MetalTheme`; its name property is `Steel`. It defines the defaults for the six abstract `Font` properties declared in `MetalTheme`. Table 26-8 shows the values of these fonts.

Table 26-8. DefaultMetalTheme fonts

Property	Font name	Font style	Font size
controlTextFont	Dialog	Font.BOLD	12
menuTextFont	Dialog	Font.BOLD	12
subTextFont	Dialog	Font.PLAIN	10
systemTextFont	Dialog	Font.PLAIN	12
userTextFont	Dialog	Font.PLAIN	12
windowTitleFont	Dialog	Font.BOLD	12

Protected DefaultMetalTheme base colors

We saw earlier that the `MetalTheme` class defines abstract accessor methods for six protected color resources. Table 26-9 shows the values defined for these colors by the `DefaultMetalTheme`.[*]

---

[*] `DefaultMetalTheme` also defines the package-private properties primary0, secondary0, and secondary4, but no current code seems to use them.

Table 26-9. Protected DefaultMetalTheme colors

Name	Color
primary1	(102, 102, 153)
primary2	(153, 153, 204)
primary3	(204, 204, 255)
secondary1	(102, 102, 102)
secondary2	(153, 153, 153)
secondary3	(204, 204, 204)

The primary colors all have equal parts red and green and a higher blue component. This is how you can tell that these values represent increasingly lighter shades of blue. Similarly, the secondary colors all have the same value for red, green, and blue, indicating that they represent increasingly lighter shades of gray.

As you can see, our simple RedTheme directly touched only three of the properties defined by MetalTheme. (Our previous discussion gave you everything there is to know about making even more drastic changes to the Metal L&F using themes.) All you have to decide is which of the font and color properties you want to change, and then override their respective accessor methods.

Remember, the team that designed the Metal L&F went through a good deal of trouble to make a clean, consistent L&F. As a rule, you're probably best off changing only the fonts and the primary and secondary colors (which define all the other colors). But if you want to, MetalTheme gives you the hooks to define all sorts of different color combinations.

Use of Metal's Client Properties

Another feature that's unique to the Metal L&F is the use of special client properties that allow a handful of components to be customized. To use these properties, you make a call that looks something like this:

```
myComponent.putClientProperty("JTree.lineStyle", "Angled");
```

Setting these client properties with any other L&F has no effect, unless it's a custom L&F that knows to look for these properties.

We've touched on most of these properties as they came up throughout the book, so we'll just briefly describe them here. Table 26-10 shows a breakdown of the various client properties used by Metal.*

---

* Note that JToolBar used to support an isRollover property, but this has been removed from the table.

Table 26-10. Metal L&F client properties

Component	Property	Data type	Default	Other values
JInternalFrame	isPalette	Boolean	false	true
JScrollBar	isFreeStanding	Boolean	true	false
JSlider	isFilled	Boolean	false	true
JTree	lineStyle	String	"Horizontal"	"Angled", "None"

To create the property key, just build a string from the component type and the property name—for example, JScrollBar.isFreeStanding.

JInternalFrame.isPalette

> Can be set to Boolean.TRUE to indicate that the border around the internal frame should not be painted.

JScrollBar.isFreeStanding

> Set to Boolean.FALSE by the Metal L&F for any scrollbars used by JScrollPanes. This setting just indicates that the scrollbar should be displayed flush against its borders. Normally, there is a small space around the scrollbar. Typically, you won't have reason to change this particular value.

JSlider.isFilled

> Can be set to Boolean.TRUE to cause the slider's "track" to be filled on one side to clearly differentiate the space on either side of the "thumb."

JTree.lineStyle

> This property can be set to Angled or None (or the default, Horizontal) to change the way the tree structure is drawn. By default, horizontal lines are drawn to separate branches of the tree. Setting this property to Angled causes short angled lines to be drawn between the nodes. As you might guess, setting it to None turns off both features.

Replacement of Individual UI Delegates

Say you're using an L&F that you're basically happy with, but there are a few components you wish had a slightly different appearance. If the changes you want to make can't be done by simply changing resource values, one option is to implement your own custom UI delegates for the components you want to change and then tell the UIManager to use your new classes instead of the L&F defaults.

Modifying a scrollbar

We'll show how this can be done with a very simple example. We've decided to toss aside the nice, clean consistent design of the Metal L&F by changing the way the thumb of the scrollbar is displayed. To keep the code as simple as possible, we're going to change the thumb from the Metal style with textured bumps to a simple solid black box.

We do not recommend making such random changes to existing L&Fs. In this particular example, we're breaking something the designers of the Metal L&F worked very hard to achieve—consistency. Keep in mind that this is an example that shows you *how* to do something. We'll leave it to you to have the good sense to know *when* to do it.

To do this, we need to create our own implementation of the `ScrollBarUI` class. Rather than starting from scratch, we'll extend `MetalScrollBarUI` and change only the methods we want to reimplement. In this case, we find that there's a method called `paintThumb()` that's responsible for rendering the thumb of the scrollbar. `paintThumb()` and `createUI()` are the only methods we're going to reimplement. Here's the source code for our new scrollbar UI delegate:

```java
// MyMetalScrollBarUI.java
//
import java.awt.*;
import javax.swing.*;
import javax.swing.plaf.*;
import javax.swing.plaf.metal.*;

// A simple extension of MetalScrollBarUI that draws the thumb as a solid
// black rectangle.
public class MyMetalScrollBarUI extends MetalScrollBarUI
{
  // Create our own scrollbar UI!
  public static ComponentUI createUI( JComponent c ) {
    return new MyMetalScrollBarUI();
  }

  // This method paints the scroll thumb. We've just taken the
  // MetalScrollBarUI code and stripped out all the
  // interesting painting code, replacing it with code that paints a
  // black box.
  protected void paintThumb(Graphics g, JComponent c, Rectangle thumbBounds)
  {
    if (!c.isEnabled()) { return; }

    g.translate( thumbBounds.x, thumbBounds.y );
    if ( scrollbar.getOrientation() == JScrollBar.VERTICAL ) {
      if ( !isFreeStanding ) {
        thumbBounds.width += 2;
      }
      g.setColor( Color.black );
      g.fillRect( 0, 0, thumbBounds.width - 2, thumbBounds.height - 1 );
      if ( !isFreeStanding ) {
        thumbBounds.width -= 2;
      }
    }
    else { // HORIZONTAL
      if ( !isFreeStanding ) {
        thumbBounds.height += 2;
      }
```

```
      g.setColor( Color.black );
      g.fillRect( 0, 0, thumbBounds.width - 1, thumbBounds.height - 2 );
      if ( !isFreeStanding ) {
        thumbBounds.height -= 2;
      }
    }
    g.translate( -thumbBounds.x, -thumbBounds.y );
  }
}
```

Pretty simple stuff. The first thing we did was define a new createUI( ) method.
Recall that this is the method JComponent calls when it is assigned a new UI delegate.
All we do is return a new instance of our modified scrollbar delegate.

The second method in our class is basically just a stripped-down version of
MetalScrollBarUI's paintThumb( ) method. In our implementation, we've removed all
the code that created a nice clean thumb, complete with shading and texture bumps,
replacing it with single calls to Graphics.fillRect( ).

Since we've extended MetalScrollBarUI, our new scrollbar delegate looks just like the
Metal scrollbar, except for the solid black thumb.

The only thing left to do is tell the UIManager to use our custom scrollbar delegate
instead of the L&F default. You can probably guess that this is simple. Here's what
we do:

```
UIManager.put("ScrollBarUI", "MyMetalScrollBarUI");
```

Once we make this call, any new scrollbars that are created use our custom UI delegate instead of the previously installed MetalScrollBarUI. Here's a little test program
to prove that this works:

```
// MetalModExample.java
//
import javax.swing.*;
import java.awt.*;
import java.io.*;

public class MetalModExample {
  public static void main(String[] args) {
    // Make sure we're using the Metal L&F, since the example needs it.
    try {
      UIManager.setLookAndFeel("javax.swing.plaf.metal.MetalLookAndFeel");
    }
    catch (Exception e) {
      System.err.println("Metal is not available on this platform?!");
      e.printStackTrace( );
      System.exit(1);
    }
    JComponent before = makeExamplePane( );

    // Replace the MetalScrollBarUI with our own!
    UIManager.put("ScrollBarUI", "MyMetalScrollBarUI");
```

```
        JComponent after = makeExamplePane();

        JFrame f = new JFrame();
        f.setDefaultCloseOperation(JFrame.EXIT_ON_CLOSE);

        Container c = f.getContentPane();
        c.setLayout(new GridLayout(2, 1, 0, 1));
        c.add(before);
        c.add(after);
        f.setSize(450, 400);
        f.setVisible(true);
    }

    // Create a scrollpane with a text area in it.
    public static JComponent makeExamplePane() {
        JTextArea text = new JTextArea();

        try {
            text.read(new FileReader("MetalModExample.java"), null);
        }
        catch (IOException ex) {}

        JScrollPane scroll = new JScrollPane(text);
        return scroll;
    }
}
```

We create two JScrollPanes, which use JScrollBars. The first one is created with the default scrollbar delegate. Then, we tell the UIManager to use our new UI delegate and create a second JScrollPane. Figure 26-12 shows the different scrollbars created by this example.

In this section, we've seen how easy it is to replace a single UI delegate. If you're creating a custom application, and you want to change specific components, this is a nice, easy way to make the changes. However, if you develop a set of custom delegates that you're particularly happy with, you might want to consider rolling them into your own custom L&F, so that you don't have to install each delegate in every program you write. The next section explores your options for creating a custom L&F.

Creation of a Custom Look-and-Feel

Everything we've covered in this chapter up to this point has been useful background information for the ultimate application customization strategy: creating your own L&F. As you might guess, this is not something you'll do in an afternoon, nor is it usually something you should consider doing at all. However, thanks to the L&F framework, it's not as difficult as you might think. In a few instances, it actually makes sense, such as when you're developing a game. You'll likely find that the most difficult part is coming up with a graphical design for each component.

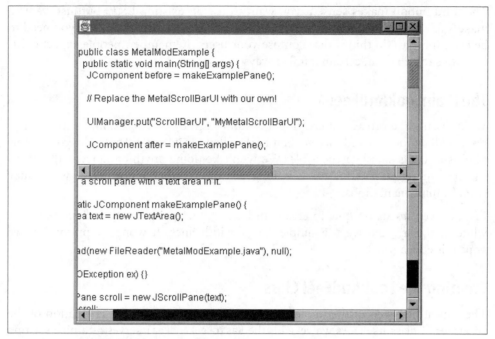

```
public class MetalModExample {
  public static void main(String[] args) {
    JComponent before = makeExamplePane();

    // Replace the MetalScrollBarUI with our own!

    UIManager.put("ScrollBarUI", "MyMetalScrollBarUI");

    JComponent after = makeExamplePane();
```

```
 a scroll pane with a text area in it.

atic JComponent makeExamplePane() {
ea text = new JTextArea();


ad(new FileReader("MetalModExample.java"), null);

DException ex) {}

Pane scroll = new JScrollPane(text);
```

Figure 26-12. Standard and customized Metal scrollbars

There are basically three different strategies for creating a new L&F:

- Start from scratch by extending LookAndFeel and extending each of the UI delegates defined in javax.swing.plaf.

- Extend the BasicLookAndFeel and each of the abstract UI delegates defined in javax.swing.plaf.basic.

- Extend an existing L&F, like MetalLookAndFeel, and change only selected components.

The first option gives you complete control over how everything works. It also requires a lot of effort. Unless you are implementing an L&F that is fundamentally different from the traditional desktop L&Fs, or you have some strong desire to implement your own L&F framework from scratch, we strongly recommend that you do not use this approach.

The next option is the most logical if you want to create a completely new L&F. This is the approach we'll focus on in this section. The BasicLookAndFeel has been designed as an abstract framework for creating new L&Fs. Each of the Swing L&Fs extends Basic. The beauty of using this approach is that the majority of the programming logic is handled by the framework—all you really have to worry about is how the different components should look.

The third option makes sense if you want to use an existing L&F, but just want to make a few tweaks to certain components. If you go with this approach, you need to be careful not to do things that confuse your users. Remember, people expect existing L&Fs to behave in certain familiar ways.

The PlainLookAndFeel

We'll discuss the process of creating a custom L&F by way of example. In this section, we'll define bits and pieces of an L&F called PlainLookAndFeel. The goal of this L&F is to be as simple as possible. We won't be doing anything fancy with colors, shading, or painting—this book is long enough without filling pages with fancy paint( ) implementations.

Instead, we'll focus on *how* to create an L&F. All of our painting is done in black, white, and gray, and we use simple, single-width lines. It won't be pretty, but we hope it is educational.

Creating the LookAndFeel Class

The logical first step in the implementation of a custom L&F is the creation of the LookAndFeel class itself. As we've said, the BasicLookAndFeel serves as a nice starting point. At a minimum, you'll need to implement the five abstract methods defined in the LookAndFeel base class (none of which is implemented in BasicLookAndFeel). Here's a look at the beginnings of our custom L&F class:

```
// PlainLookAndFeel.java
//
package plain;
import java.awt.*;
import javax.swing.*;
import javax.swing.border.*;
import javax.swing.plaf.*;
import javax.swing.plaf.basic.*;

public class PlainLookAndFeel extends BasicLookAndFeel {
  public String getDescription( ) { return "The Plain Look and Feel"; }
  public String getID( ) { return "Plain"; }
  public String getName( ) { return "Plain"; }
  public boolean isNativeLookAndFeel( ) { return false; }
  public boolean isSupportedLookAndFeel( ) { return true; }
  // ...
}
```

At this point, we have an L&F that actually compiles. Let's go a little further and make it useful. The next major step is to define the defaults for the L&F. This is similar to what we did earlier when we defined a few custom resources for an application. The difference is that now we are defining a complete set of resources for an entirely new L&F that can be used across many applications. The installation of defaults is handled by getDefaults( ), which has been broken down into three additional methods in BasicLookAndFeel.

BasicLookAndFeel.getDefaults( ) creates a UIDefaults table and calls the following three methods (in this order):

```
protected void initClassDefaults(UIDefaults table)
protected void initSystemColorDefaults(UIDefaults table)
protected void initComponentDefaults(UIDefaults table)
```

Let's look at these three steps in detail.

Defining class defaults

Defining class defaults is the process of enumerating the names of the classes your L&F uses for each of the UI delegates. One nice feature of the BasicLookAndFeel is that it defines concrete implementations of all of the UI-delegate classes. One big benefit is that you can test your new L&F as you're creating it, without having to specify every single delegate class. Instead, just define the ones you want to test and use the basic implementations for the others. Those that you define (since they're stored in a simple Hashtable) override any values previously defined by BasicLookAndFeel.

A typical implementation of this method looks something like this:

```
protected void initClassDefaults(UIDefaults table) {
    super.initClassDefaults(table); // Install the "basic" delegates.

    String plainPkg = "plain.";
    Object[] classes = {
        "ProgressBarUI", plainPkg + "PlainProgressBarUI",
            "SliderUI", plainPkg + "PlainSliderUI",
                "TreeUI", plainPkg + "PlainTreeUI",
        // ...
    };
    table.putDefaults(classes);
}
```

The first line calls the BasicLookAndFeel implementation, which installs each of the basic UI delegates. Next, we create a string containing the package name for our L&F classes. This is used in constructing the class names of each of our UI delegates. We then create an array of UIClassID to UI-delegate class name mappings. The items in this array should alternate between class IDs[*] and class names. Include such a mapping for each UI delegate your L&F implements.

---

[*] The UIClassID property for all Swing components can be formed by dropping the J from the class name and adding UI at the end. JButton's UIClassID is ButtonUI, JTree's is TreeUI, etc.

Defining look-and-feel colors

The next set of defaults typically defined are the color resources used by the L&F. You have a lot of flexibility in handling colors. As we saw earlier in the chapter, the Metal L&F defines all colors in terms of a color "theme," allowing the colors used by the L&F to be easily customized. This feature is specific to Metal, but you can implement a similar feature in your own L&F.

Colors are typically defined according to the colors specified in the `java.awt.` `SystemColor` class. These are the colors used by the `BasicLookAndFeel`, so if you are going to delegate any of the painting routines to Basic, it's important to define values for the system colors. Even if you are going to handle every bit of painting in your custom L&F, it's still a good idea, though it is not required, to use the familiar color names.

`BasicLookAndFeel` adds another protected method called `loadSystemColors()`. For non-native L&Fs, this simply maps an array of name/color value pairs into resource keys and `ColorUIResource` values. For example, a pair of entries in the array might be:

```
"control", "#FFFFFF"
```

This would result in a resource called `"control"` being added, with a value of the color white.

 The conversion from #FFFFFF to Color.white is done by the java.awt. Color.decode() method (which uses java.lang.Integer.decode()). This method takes a string representation of a color and converts it to a valid Color object. In this case, the # character indicates that we are specifying a hexadecimal (base-16) number. (You can also use the familiar 0x notation.) The first two characters (one byte) represent the red component of the color. The next two represent green, and the last two represent blue. In this example, all values are FF (255 decimal), which maps to the color white.

Using `loadSystemColors()` allows you to define the color values for your L&F by creating an array of key/value pairs, like the pair we just looked at. This array is then passed to `loadSystemColors()`, along with the `UIDefaults` table. Here's a sample implementation of `initSystemColorDefaults()`:

```
protected void initSystemColorDefaults(UIDefaults table) {
    String[] colors = {
                   "desktop", "#C0C0C0",
              "activeCaption", "#FFFFFF",
          "activeCaptionText", "#000000",
        "activeCaptionBorder", "#000000"
    // More of the same
    };
    loadSystemColors(table, colors, false);
}
```

Table 26-11 shows the 26 color keys used by `SystemColor` and `BasicLookAndFeel`.

Table 26-11. Standard system color properties

System color property	Description
desktop	Color of the desktop background
activeCaption	Color of the titlebar (captions) when the frame is active
activeCaptionText	Color of the titlebar text when the frame is active
activeCaptionBorder	Color of the titlebar border when the frame is active
inactiveCaption	Color of the titlebar (captions) when the frame is inactive
inactiveCaptionText	Color of the titlebar text when the frame is inactive
inactiveCaptionBorder	Color of the titlebar border when the frame is inactive
window	Color of the interior of the window
windowBorder	Color of the window border
windowText	Color of the window text
menu	Background color of menus
menuText	Color of the text in menu items
text	Background color of editable text
textText	Color of editable text
textHighlight	Background color of editable text when highlighted
textHighlightText	Color of editable text when highlighted
textInactiveText	Color of normally editable text that has been disabled
control	Standard color for controls such as buttons or scrollbar thumbs
controlText	Color for text inside controls
controlHighlight	Highlight color for controls
controlLtHighlight	Lighter highlight color for controls
controlShadow	Shadow color for controls
controlDkShadow	Darker shadow color for controls
scrollbar	Color to use for the background area of a scrollbar (where the thumb slides)
info	Background color for informational text
infoText	Color for informational text

Defining component defaults

The last method called by BasicLookAndFeel.getDefaults( ) is initComponentDefaults( ). This is where you define all of the colors, icons, borders, and other resources used by each of the individual component delegates. The BasicLookAndFeel implementation of this method defines over 300 different resource values for 40 delegate classes. We've cataloged these resources, along with the type of value expected for each, in Appendix A.

The good news is that you don't have to redefine all 300+ resource values in your custom L&F, though you certainly can. Many of the resources are colors and are defined in terms of the system colors we've already defined. For example, the Button.background resource defaults to the value defined for "control" while Button.foreground defaults to "controlText". As long as you've defined values for the system colors and you're happy with the system colors defined by the BasicLookAndFeel, you can get by with little or no changes to the component-level color resources. The amount of customization done in this method is really up to you. If you like the resource choices made by the BasicLookAndFeel, use them. If you want your own custom defaults, you can change them.

The Swing L&Fs follow a few useful steps that make the implementation of initComponentDefaults( ) easier to understand:

Define fonts

> Chances are there's a fixed set of fonts your L&F uses throughout its delegates. It's a good idea to define these up front so that you're not creating duplicate font resources throughout the method. Recall from earlier in the chapter that resources defined by the L&F should implement the UIResource interface, so we define our fonts as FontUIResource objects:

```
FontUIResource sansSerifPlain10 =
    new FontUIResource("SansSerif", Font.PLAIN, 10);
FontUIResource monospacedPlain10 =
    new FontUIResource("Monospaced", Font.PLAIN, 10);
```

Define colors

> If you plan to use colors not defined by the system colors, and you're not using a flexible color strategy like Metal's themes, remember to define them as ColorUIResources:

```
ColorUIResource green = new ColorUIResource(Color.green);
ColorUIResource veryLightGray = new ColorUIResource(240, 240, 240);
```

Define insets

> Several of the resource values are defined as java.awt.Insets. Again, it's convenient to define these values up front:

```
InsetsUIResource zeroInsets = new InsetsUIResource(0,0,0,0);
InsetsUIResource bigInsets = new InsetsUIResource(10,10,10,10);
```

Define borders

> If you're going to use the standard Swing borders for your components, recall that you can obtain singleton resource borders from the BorderUIResource class. For example:

```
Border etchedBorder = BorderUIResource.getEtchedBorderUIResource( );
Border blackLineBorder = BorderUIResource.getBlackLineBorderUIResource( );
```

This works great for defining simple borders. However, it's often useful to define dynamic borders that change based on the state of the component they are bordering. For example, when a button is pressed, it often draws its border differently than when it is in the default raised position. The Basic L&F provides a class called BasicBorders that includes inner classes for several common dynamic borders. We cover this class at the end of the chapter.

Define icons

Several components define a variety of Icon resources. There are two distinct types of icons you'll want to define: static and dynamic. Static icons are usually ImageIcons, loaded from small GIF files. They are used for things like tree nodes and JOptionPane dialogs. It's generally a good idea to define static icons using the UIDefaults.LazyValue interface (discussed earlier in the chapter) to avoid loading the images in applications that don't use the components they are associated with. The easiest strategy is just to use the LookAndFeel.makeIcon( ) method, which returns LazyValue instances,[*] to defer the loading of icons for your L&F classes. For example, to arrange the on-demand load of an image called *warning.gif* from the *icons* directory directly under the directory containing your L&F classes, you would use the following code:

```
Object warningIcon = LookAndFeel.makeIcon(getClass( ), "icons/warning.gif");
```

Table 26-12 summarizes the default icons loaded by BasicLookAndFeel. If you use the default resource values for these icons, be sure to supply an image for each of the icons (in the *icons* subdirectory). No default image files are defined.

Table 26-12. Image icons defined by BasicLookAndFeel

Resource name	Filename
FileChooser.detailsViewIcon	*DetailsView.gif*
FileChooser.homeFolderIcon	*HomeFolder.gif*
FileChooser.listViewIcon	*ListView.gif*
FileChooser.newFolderIcon	*NewFolder.gif*
FileChooser.upFolderIcon	*UpFolder.gif*
FileView.computerIcon	*Computer.gif*
FileView.directoryIcon	*Directory.gif*
FileView.fileIcon	*File.gif*
FileView.floppyDriveIcon	*FloppyDrive.gif*
FileView.hardDriveIcon	*HardDrive.gif*
InternalFrame.icon	*JavaCup.gif*
OptionPane.errorIcon	*Error.gif*
OptionPane.informationIcon	*Inform.gif*
OptionPane.questionIcon	*Question.gif*
OptionPane.warningIcon	*Warn.gif*
Tree.closedIcon	*TreeClosed.gif*
Tree.leafIcon	*TreeLeaf.gif*
Tree.openIcon	*TreeOpen.gif*

---

[*] You might wonder why this code wasn't changed to take advantage of the new UIDefaults.ProxyLazyValue class. It's likely the Swing authors realized this change would not provide much (if any) of a performance boost because every invocation of the makeIcon method shares the same anonymous implementation class.

It's more challenging to define icons that change based on the state of a component. The most obvious examples of dynamic icons are radio buttons and checkboxes. These icons paint themselves differently depending on whether they are selected and, typically, whether they are currently being pressed. We'll look at a strategy for implementing dynamic icons later in this chapter.

Define other resources

A variety of other resources, including Dimensions and Integer values, can also be defined as component resources. Remember, you can refer to Appendix A for a complete list.

Create defaults array

Now that you've defined all the common resources that might be shared by multiple components, it's time to put together an array of key/value pairs for the resources you want to define. This array is typically handled just like the others we've seen up to this point—entries in the array alternate between resource keys and values. Since there are potentially a very large number of resources being defined here, it's a good idea to group resources by component. Here's part of our PlainLookAndFeel defaults array definition:

```
Object[] defaults = {
  "Button.border", buttonBorder,
  "Button.margin", new InsetsUIResource(2, 2, 2, 2),
  "Button.font", sansSerifPlain10,

  "RadioButton.icon", radioButtonIcon,
  "RadioButton.pressed", table.get("controlLtHighlight"),
  "RadioButton.font", sansSerifPlain10,

  "CheckBox.icon", checkBoxIcon,
  "CheckBox.pressed", table.get("controlLtHighlight"),
  "CheckBox.font", sansSerifPlain10,

  "Slider.foreground", table.get("controlText")
};
```

Note that you aren't limited to the resources listed in Appendix A. In the code snippet, we added two custom resources called RadioButton.pressed and CheckBox.pressed that we use as background colors when the button is being pressed.

Remember two little details

We've covered almost everything you have to think about when implementing initComponentDefaults( ). There are two more important steps (one at the beginning and one at the end) to remember. The first thing you typically do is call super.initComponentDefaults( ). This loads all of the defaults defined by BasicLookAndFeel. If you don't do this, you are likely to have a runtime error when the BasicLookAndFeel tries to access some undefined resource. Of course, if you define all of the resources in your L&F, you don't have to make the super call. The last thing to do is load your defaults into the input UIDefaults table.

When it's complete, the `initComponentDefaults( )` method should look something like this:

```
protected void initComponentDefaults(UIDefaults table) {
  super.initComponentDefaults(table);

  // Define any common resources, lazy/active value resources, etc.

  Object[] defaults = {
    // Define all the defaults.
  };

  table.putDefaults(defaults);
}
```

Defining an Icon Factory

This is not a required step, but it can prove useful. The Swing L&Fs group the definitions of various dynamic icons into an icon factory class. This class serves as a holder of singleton instances of the various dynamic icons used by the L&F and contains the inner classes that actually define the icons.

Which icons, if any, you define in an icon factory is up to you. The Metal L&F uses its icon factory to draw all of its icons, except those used by JOptionPane. This allows Metal to change the color of its icons based on the current color theme, a task not easily achieved if the icons are loaded from GIF files.

For our purposes, we concentrate on defining dynamic icons. The PlainLookAndFeel uses GIFs for all of the static icons.

The easiest way to understand how to implement a dynamic icon is to look at a simple example. Here's a trimmed-down version of our PlainIconFactory class, showing how we implemented the radio button icon:

```
// PlainIconFactory.java
//
package plain;

import java.awt.*;
import javax.swing.*;
import javax.swing.plaf.*;
import java.io.Serializable;

public class PlainIconFactory {
  private static Icon radioButtonIcon;
  private static Icon checkBoxIcon; // Implemention trimmed from example

  // Provide access to the single RadioButtonIcon instance.
  public static Icon getRadioButtonIcon() {
    if (radioButtonIcon == null) {
      radioButtonIcon = new RadioButtonIcon( );
    }
```

```
      return radioButtonIcon;
   }

   // An icon for rendering the default radio button icon
   private static class RadioButtonIcon implements Icon, UIResource, Serializable
   {
      private static final int size = 15;

      public int getIconWidth() { return size; }
      public int getIconHeight() { return size; }

      public void paintIcon(Component c, Graphics g, int x, int y) {

         // Get the button and model containing the state we are supposed to show.
         AbstractButton b = (AbstractButton)c;
         ButtonModel model = b.getModel();

         // If the button is being pressed (and armed), change the BG color.
         // (NOTE: could also do something different if the button is disabled)

         if (model.isPressed() && model.isArmed()) {
           g.setColor(UIManager.getColor("RadioButton.pressed"));
           g.fillOval(x, y, size-1, size-1);
         }

         // Draw an outer circle.
         g.setColor(UIManager.getColor("RadioButton.foreground"));
         g.drawOval(x, y, size-1, size-1);

         // Fill a small circle inside if the button is selected.
         if (model.isSelected()) {
           g.fillOval(x+4, y+4, size-8, size-8);
         }
      }
   }
}
```

We provide a static getRadioButtonIcon( ) method that creates the icon the first time it's called. On subsequent calls, the single instance is returned immediately. We'll do the same thing for each dynamic icon we define. Next, we have the RadioButtonIcon inner class. Recall from Chapter 4 that there are three methods involved in implementing the Icon interface (the other interfaces, UIResource and Serializable, have no methods). Our implementations of getIconWidth( ) and getIconHeight( ) are simple; they just return a constant size.

The interesting code is in paintIcon( ). In this method, what we paint depends on the state of the button's model. In our implementation, we do two checks. First, we check to see if the button is being pressed. If so (and if the button is armed, meaning that the mouse pointer is still over the button), we paint a special background color. Then we paint a solid outer circle and perform a second check to see if the button is selected. If it is, we paint a solid circle inside the outer circle.

One thing to note here is that we chose to define a custom resource called RadioButton.pressed. Since there is no standard policy for showing that a button is pressed, we use this resource to define the background for our pressed button.

The really interesting thing about this new icon class is that for many L&Fs, defining this icon is all you need to do to for the delegate that uses it. In PlainLookAndFeel, we don't even define a PlainRadioButtonUI class at all. Instead, we just create a RadioButtonIcon and set it as the icon using the resource "RadioButton.icon". Figure 26-13 shows some RadioButtons using the PlainLookAndFeel. The first button is selected, the second is selected and is being held down, and the third is unselected.

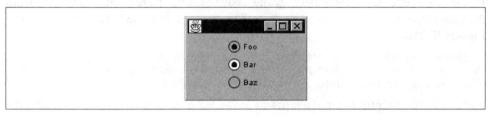

Figure 26-13. PlainIconFactory.RadioButtonIcon

Defining Custom Borders

Certain Swing components are typically rendered with some type of border around them. The javax.swing.border package defines a number of static borders that you can use. However, it's often desirable to create your own custom borders as part of your L&F. Also, certain borders (just like certain icons) should be painted differently depending on the state of the object they are being painted around.

The Swing L&Fs define custom borders in a class called *<L&F name>*Borders. Many of the inner classes defined in BasicBorders may be useful when defining your own L&F. These are the borders used by default by the BasicLookAndFeel. They include the following inner classes:

```
public static class ButtonBorder extends AbstractBorder
    implements UIResource
public static class FieldBorder extends AbstractBorder
    implements UIResource
public static class MarginBorder extends AbstractBorder
    implements UIResource
public static class MenuBarBorder extends AbstractBorder
    implements UIResource
public static class RadioButtonBorder extends ButtonBorder
public static class RolloverButtonBorder extends ButtonBorder
public static class SplitPaneBorder implements Border, UIResource
public static class ToggleButtonBorder extends ButtonBorder
```

It's probably not too important to understand the details of most of these inner classes. The important thing to know is that these are the borders installed for certain components by the `BasicLookAndFeel`.

One of these inner classes, `MarginBorder`, does deserve special mention. This class defines a border that has no appearance, but takes up space. It's used with components that define a margin property, specifically `AbstractButton`, `JToolBar`, and `JTextComponent`. When defining borders for these components, it's important to create a `CompoundBorder` that includes an instance of `BasicBorders.MarginBorder`. If you don't do this, your L&F ignores the component's margin property, a potentially confusing problem for developers using your L&F. Here's an example from `PlainLookAndFeel` in which we use a `MarginBorder` to define the border that we'll use for our `JButtons`:

```
Border marginBorder = new BasicBorders.MarginBorder();
Object buttonBorder = new BorderUIResource.CompoundBorderUIResource(
  new PlainBorders.ButtonBorder(), marginBorder);
```

Note that the `MarginBorder` constructor takes no arguments. It simply checks the component's margin property in its `paintBorder()` method. Using a `MarginBorder` with a component that has no margin property simply results in a border with insets of (0,0,0,0).

This example brings us back to the idea of creating a `PlainBorders` class that defines a set of borders for our L&F. Keep in mind that you don't have to do this. You're free to use the default borders provided by Basic, or even the simple borders defined by the `swing.border` package. Here's the `PlainBorders` class in which we define a single inner class for handling button borders:

```
// PlainBorders.java
//
package plain;

import java.awt.*;
import javax.swing.*;
import javax.swing.border.*;
import javax.swing.plaf.*;

public class PlainBorders {
  // An inner class for JButton borders
  public static class ButtonBorder extends AbstractBorder implements UIResource
  {
    private Border raised;  // Use this one by default.
    private Border lowered; // Use this one when pressed.

    // Create the border.
    public ButtonBorder() {
      raised = BorderFactory.createRaisedBevelBorder();
      lowered = BorderFactory.createLoweredBevelBorder();
    }
```

```
    // Define the insets (in terms of one of the others).
    public Insets getBorderInsets(Component c) {
      return raised.getBorderInsets(c);
    }

    // Paint the border according to the current state.
    public void paintBorder(Component c, Graphics g, int x, int y,
        int width, int height) {

      AbstractButton b = (AbstractButton)c;
      ButtonModel model = b.getModel();

      if (model.isPressed() && model.isArmed()) {
        lowered.paintBorder(c, g, x, y, width, height);
      }
      else {
        raised.paintBorder(c, g, x, y, width, height);
      }
    }
  }
}
```

For the sake of providing a very simple example, we've implemented our
ButtonBorder class using two other existing borders. Which of these borders is actually painted by our border is determined by the state of the button model.

The BasicGraphicsUtils Class

There's one more class from the Basic L&F worth knowing something about.
BasicGraphicsUtils defines a number of static utility methods that might be useful
when creating your own L&F.

Methods

public static void drawBezel(Graphics g, int x, int y, int w, int h, boolean isPressed,
  boolean isDefault, Color shadow, Color darkShadow, Color highlight)
public static void drawDashedRect(Graphics g, int x, int y, int width, int height)
public static void drawEtchedRect(Graphics g, int x, int y, int w, int h, Color control,
  Color shadow, Color darkShadow, Color highlight)
public static void drawGroove(Graphics g, int x, int y, int w, int h, Color shadow,
  Color highlight)
public static void drawLoweredBezel(Graphics g, int x, int y, int w, int h,
  Color shadow, Color darkShadow, Color highlight)
>   These methods can be used to draw various rectangles. The Basic L&F uses
>   these for many of its borders. Figure 26-14 shows several rectangles created by
>   these methods. The parameters shown in the four drawBezel() examples corre-
>   spond to isPressed and isDefault, respectively.

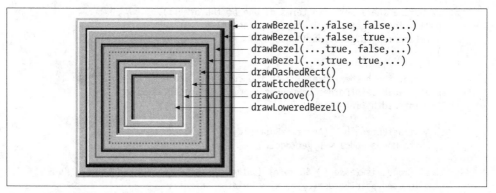

Figure 26-14. BasicGraphicsUtils

public static void drawString(Graphics g, String text, int underlinedChar, int x, int y)

Draw a String at the specified location. The first occurrence of underlinedChar is underlined. This is typically used to indicate mnemonics.

public static void drawStringUnderlineCharAt(Graphics g, String text,
  int underlinedIndex, int x, int y)

Draw a String at the specified location. The character whose index within the string is underlinedIndex is underlined. Introduced in Version 1.4, this method allows you to cope with situations in which your mnemonic's underline is more logical if it doesn't appear on the first instance of the corresponding character within the string.

public static Insets getEtchedInsets()
public static Insets getGrooveInsets()

Return the Insets used by the drawEtchedRect( ) and drawGroove( ) methods.

public static Dimension getPreferredButtonSize(AbstractButton b, int textIconGap)

Return the preferred size of a button based on its text, icon, insets, and the textIconGap parameter.

Creating the Individual UI Delegates

The key step in developing an L&F is creating a set of UI delegate classes for the various Swing components that can't be sufficiently customized just by setting resource values or defining custom borders and icons.

Unfortunately, a description of the methods involved in each individual UI delegate is beyond the scope of this book (we're starting to fear that no one will be able to lift it as it is!). Still, we don't want to leave you in the dark after coming so far, so we'll take a detailed look at a single example. For the rest of the chapter, we focus on the creation of the PlainSliderUI, but many of the steps along the way apply to other delegates as well.

Define a constructor

Constructors for UI delegates don't typically do much. The main thing to concern yourself with is whether you want to keep a reference to the component the delegate is rendering. Generally speaking, this is not necessary because the component is always passed as a parameter to methods on the delegate. However, if you're extending Basic, you do need to pay attention to the requirements of the Basic constructor. In the case of BasicSliderUI, we are required to pass a JSlider as an argument. Even though the current implementation of BasicSliderUI ignores it, to be safe, our constructor works the same way. Here's the beginning of our PlainSliderUI class:

```
// PlainSliderUI.java
//
package plain;
import java.awt.*;
import javax.swing.*;
import javax.swing.plaf.*;
import javax.swing.plaf.basic.*;

public class PlainSliderUI extends BasicSliderUI {
  // ...
  public PlainSliderUI(JSlider slider) {
    super(slider);
  }
  // ...
}
```

Define the factory method

The next important step is to define a createUI( ) factory method. This is how the delegate is created for a given component. Typically, all you need to do here is return a new instance of your UI delegate class. In some cases, it may be better to use a single instance of the UI delegate class for all components. In this case, createUI( ) always returns the same static object rather than creating a new one each time. If you go with this approach, make sure your delegate (including its superclass) doesn't hold any instance-specific component data.

In PlainSliderUI, our createUI( ) method just returns a new instance of PlainSliderUI:

```
public static ComponentUI createUI(JComponent c) {
  return new PlainSliderUI((JSlider)c);
}
```

Define installUI( ) and uninstallUI( ) (optional)

The installUI( ) and uninstall( ) methods give you an opportunity to initialize your UI delegate with information from the component it's rendering. Both methods take a single JComponent parameter, which can safely be cast to the appropriate type if needed.

If you're not extending the Basic L&F, you'll typically have quite a bit of work to do in the installUI( ) method. On the other hand, if you are taking advantage of the BasicLookAndFeel, you'll have little (if anything) to do here. In the case of SliderUI, the BasicSliderUI.install( ) method does the following things:

- Enables the slider and makes it opaque
- Adds six listeners to the slider to track its state
- Retrieves resource defaults from the UIManager
- Installs the border, background, and foreground colors (from resource values) on the component
- Adds keyboard actions to the slider, allowing it to be adjusted with keys as well as with a mouse
- Defines a Timer used when scrolling
- Calculates the bounds of each region of the slider for use in painting

We list these items to give you an idea of the types of things typically done in installUI( ). In PlainSliderUI, we don't bother reimplementing this method, since the default does everything we need.

The uninstall( ) method should undo anything done by installUI( ). In particular, any listeners should be removed. BasicSliderUI.uninstall( ) does the following for us:

- Removes the border
- Stops the Timer
- Uninstalls the listeners
- Sets fields to null

Again, we chose not to override uninstallUI( ) in PlainSliderUI.

Define component size

Recall that the ComponentUI base class defines the three standard sizing methods: getMinimumSize( ), getMaximumSize( ), and getPreferredSize( ). Depending on the component, and on how much you are going to customize your L&F, you may or may not need to worry about implementing these methods. Also, some of the implementations of these methods are broken down into several additional methods.

In the case of BasicSliderUI, the preferred and minimum size methods are broken down into pairs, based on the orientation of the slider. The following four methods are used:

```
public Dimension getMinimumHorizontalSize( )
public Dimension getMinimumVerticalSize( )
public Dimension getPreferredHorizontalSize( )
public Dimension getPreferredVerticalSize( )
```

If you want to change the preferred or minimum size of the slider, these methods can be overridden. In PlainSliderUI, we do the following:

```
private static final Dimension PREF_HORIZ = new Dimension(250, 15);
private static final Dimension PREF_VERT = new Dimension(15, 250);
private static final Dimension MIN_HORIZ = new Dimension(25, 15);
private static final Dimension MIN_VERT = new Dimension(15, 25);

public Dimension getPreferredHorizontalSize() {
  return PREF_HORIZ;
}
public Dimension getPreferredVerticalSize() {
  return PREF_VERT;
}
public Dimension getMinimumHorizontalSize() {
  return MIN_HORIZ;
}
public Dimension getMinimumVerticalSize() {
  return MIN_VERT;
}
```

These are very simple size preferences; more complicated components need to calculate their preferred and minimum sizes based on the dynamic configuration of the pieces that make them up.

Override component-specific details

So far, we've laid most of the groundwork for creating the custom UI delegate. The next thing is to look for any little details the Basic delegate allows you to customize. This, of course, varies greatly from component to component. For sliders, the following two methods allow us to specify the size of certain parts of the slider. The values returned by these methods are used in various calculations.

```
protected Dimension getThumbSize()
protected int getTickLength()
```

In PlainSliderUI, we provide the following implementations of these methods:

```
// Define the size of the thumb.
protected Dimension getThumbSize() {
  Dimension size = new Dimension();

  if (slider.getOrientation() == JSlider.VERTICAL) {
    size.width = 10;
    size.height = 7; // Needs to be thick enough to be able to grab it
  }
  else {
    size.width = 7;  // Needs to be thick enough to be able to grab it
    size.height = 10;
  }
  return size;
}
```

```
// How big are major ticks?
protected int getTickLength( ) {
  return 6;
}
```

There are quite a few other methods that involve calculating sizes, but the defaults for these methods serve us well enough.

Paint the component

At last, the fun part! When all is said and done, the reason you create your own L&F is to be able to paint the components in your own special way. As you might guess, this is where the paint( ) method comes in. However, if you had to implement paint( ) from scratch, you'd have to deal with a lot of details that are the same for all L&Fs. Luckily, the Basic L&F has matured over time into a nice, clean framework with lots of hooks to allow you to customize certain aspects of the display, without worrying about every little detail.

Turning our attention to the slider delegate, we find that the BasicSliderUI's paint( ) method is broken down into five other methods:

public void paintFocus(Graphics g)
public void paintLabels(Graphics g)
public void paintThumb(Graphics g)
public void paintTicks(Graphics g)
public void paintTrack(Graphics g)
    These methods let us paint the specific pieces of the slider that we want to control, without having to deal with the things we don't want to change. In PlainSliderUI, we've chosen to implement only paintThumb( ) and paintTrack( ).

The paintFocus( ) method in BasicSliderUI paints a dashed rectangle around the slider when it has focus. This is reasonable default behavior for our L&F. The paintLabels( ) method takes care of painting the optional labels at the correct positions, and paintTicks( ) draws all the little tick marks. We have influenced how this method works by overriding the getTickLength( ) method. The BasicSliderUI. paintTicks( ) method uses this length for major ticks and cuts it in half for minor ticks. If we didn't like this strategy, we could override paintTicks( ). Better still, we could override the four methods it uses:

protected void paintMajorTickForHorizSlider(Graphics g, Rectangle tickBounds, int x)
protected void paintMajorTickForVertSlider(Graphics g, Rectangle tickBounds, int y)
protected void paintMinorTickForHorizSlider(Graphics g, Rectangle tickBounds, int x)
protected void paintMinorTickForVertSlider(Graphics g, Rectangle tickBounds, int y)
    These methods allow us to paint each tick any way we want, without having to do the calculations performed by paintTicks( ). It's important to look for methods like these in each UI delegate that you implement—they can be major time-savers.

Back to `PlainSliderUI`. As we said, we've chosen to implement only two of the methods `paint()` uses, making our `PlainSliderUI` as simple as possible. The first of these methods is `paintTrack()`. This is where we paint the line that the slider thumb slides along. In fancier L&Fs, this is made up of various lines and rectangles that create a nicely shaded track. Here's our much simpler implementation:

```
// Paint the track as a single solid line.
public void paintTrack(Graphics g) {
   int x = trackRect.x;
   int y = trackRect.y;
   int h = trackRect.height;
   int w = trackRect.width;

   g.setColor(slider.getForeground());

   if (slider.getOrientation() == JSlider.HORIZONTAL) {
      g.drawLine(x, y+h-1, x+w-1, y+h-1);
   }
   else {
      g.drawLine(x+w-1, y, x+w-1, y+h-1);
   }
}
```

We've chosen to draw a single line, using the slider's foreground color, along the bottom of the available bounds defined by `trackRect`. You're probably wondering where this `trackRect` variable came from. This is a protected field defined in `BasicSliderUI` that keeps track of the area in which the slider's track should be painted. There are all sorts of protected fields like this in the Basic L&F.

The next slider painting method we've implemented is `paintThumb()`. Given our simple painting strategy, it actually looks surprisingly like `paintTrack()`.

```
// Paint the thumb as a single solid line, centered in the thumb area.
public void paintThumb(Graphics g) {
   int x = thumbRect.x;
   int y = thumbRect.y;
   int h = thumbRect.height;
   int w = thumbRect.width;

   g.setColor(slider.getForeground());
   if (slider.getOrientation() == JSlider.HORIZONTAL) {
      g.drawLine(x+(w/2), y, x+(w/2), y+h-1);
   }
   else {
      g.drawLine(x, y+(h/2), x+w-1, y+(h/2));
   }
}
```

Here, we use another protected field called `thumbRect` to determine where we're supposed to paint the thumb. Recall from our `getThumbSize()` method that we set the thumb width (or height for horizontal sliders) to 7. However, we want to paint only a single short line, centered relative to the total width. This is why you see (w/2) and (h/2) as part of the calculations.

Don't Forget to Use It

The last step is to make sure our PlainLookAndFeel actually uses this nice new class. All we have to do is add a line to the array we've created in the initClassDefaults() method of PlainLookAndFeel. Since this is the only custom delegate we've created, our implementation of this method looks like this:

```
protected void initClassDefaults(UIDefaults table) {
    super.initClassDefaults(table); // Install the "basic" delegates.

    Object[] classes = {
        "SliderUI", PlainSliderUI.class.getName()
    };

    table.putDefaults(classes);
}
```

How's It Look?

That just about covers our PlainSliderUI. Let's take a look at a few "plain" sliders and see how it turned out. Figure 26-15 shows four sliders with different tick settings, labels, and orientations.

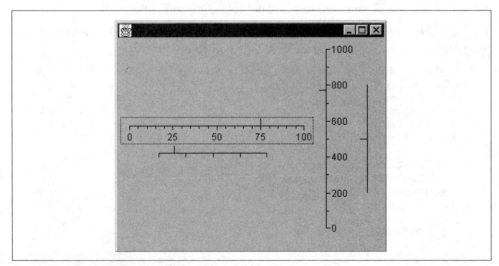

Figure 26-15. PlainSliderUI examples

One Down...

Creating a custom L&F is not a trivial task. As we've said, it's beyond the scope of this book to get into the details of every UI delegate. What we've tried to do instead is give you an idea of the general procedure for implementing component-specific delegates by extending the Basic L&F. The remaining steps can be described very loosely as "repeat until done." Some of the other components are easier to deal with than the slider, and some are more challenging. In any case, this section has introduced the core ideas you need to implement the rest of the UI delegates.

Swing Utilities

There are many tasks you run into that are common and not terribly difficult. Hence, they get rewritten several times in several small variations. Ideally, you would code the task up into a method or class, and keep it around for reuse later. There are several small classes and methods strewn about the javax.swing package that fall into this category. This chapter presents those bits and pieces and points out where you might be able to put them to use in your own code. They may not be as fundamental as the wheel, but anytime you don't have to rewrite something, you're doing your part to create better OO programs!

We've called this chapter "Swing Utilities," but in fact it covers a range of subjects. In order of presentation, we'll look at:

Swing utilities
    The SwingUtilities class and SwingConstants interface

Timers
    The Timer class

Tooltips
    The TooltipManager and JToolTip classes

Rendering
    The CellRendererPane, Renderer, and GrayFilter classes

Events
    The EventListenerList, KeyStroke, MouseInputAdapter, and SwingPropertyChangeSupport classes

Figure 27-1 shows the classes covered in this chapter.

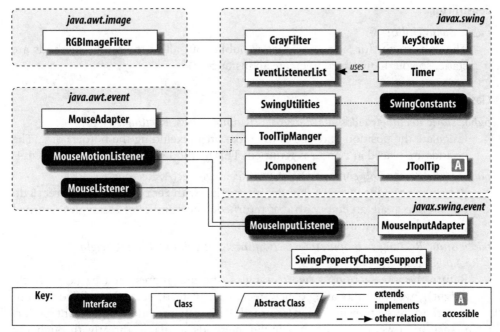

Figure 27-1. Class diagram for the utility classes

Utility Classes

The utilities presented here are meant to be used with any part of your application. The constants from SwingConstants and static methods of the SwingUtilities class are used throughout the Swing source code and will probably be useful to you as well. You'll find a lot of these utilities fairly straightforward, and maybe even easy to reproduce with your own code. But try to familiarize yourself with these APIs; they're meant to keep you from reinventing those wheels with each new application you write.

The SwingUtilities Class

This class serves as a collection point for several methods common in more advanced GUI development projects. You probably won't use all of the methods in any one application, but some of the methods will doubtless come in handy from time to time. While the purpose of many of these methods is obvious from their signatures, here's a brief description of the utility calls at your disposal. For a more detailed discussion of the invokeLater( ) and invokeAndWait( ) methods, check out Chapter 28.

Constructor

public SwingUtilities()

    The constructor for `SwingUtilities` is public, but all of the public methods are static, so you do not need to create an instance.

Class methods

public static Rectangle calculateInnerArea (JComponent c, Rectangle r)

    Calculate the position and size of the inner area (excluding the border) of c. The bounds are placed in r and r is returned. This method was introduced in SDK 1.4.

public static Rectangle[] computeDifference(Rectangle rectA, Rectangle rectB)

    Return the regions in `rectA` that do not overlap with `rectB`. If `rectA` and `rectB` do not overlap at all, an empty array is returned. The number of rectangles returned depends on the nature of the intersection.

public static Rectangle computeIntersection(int x, int y, int width, int height,
   Rectangle dest)

    Return the intersection of two rectangles (the first represented by (x, y, width, height)), without allocating a new rectangle. Instead, `dest` is modified to contain the intersection and then returned. This can provide a significant performance improvement over the similar methods available directly through the `Rectangle` class, if you need to do several such intersections.

public static int computeStringWidth(FontMetrics fm, String str)

    Given a particular font's metrics, this method returns the pixel length of the string `str`.

public static Rectangle computeUnion(int x, int y, int width, int height, Rectangle dest)

    Return the union of the rectangle represented by (x, y, width, height) and `dest`. As with `computeIntersection( )`, `dest` is modified and returned; no new `Rectangle` object is allocated.

public static MouseEvent convertMouseEvent(Component source,
   MouseEvent sourceEvent, Component destination)

    Return a new `MouseEvent`, based on `sourceEvent` with the (x, y) coordinates translated to `destination`'s coordinate system and the source of the event set as `destination`, provided `destination` is not `null`. If it is, `source` is set as the source for the new event. The actual translation of (x, y) is done with `convertPoint( )`.

public static Point convertPoint(Component source, Point aPoint,
   Component destination)
public static Point convertPoint(Component source, int x, int y,
   Component destination)

    Convert a point from the source coordinate system to the destination coordinate system. If either `source` or `destination` is `null`, the other component's root component coordinate system is used. If both are `null`, the point is returned untranslated.

public static void convertPointFromScreen(Point p, Component c)
Convert a point on the screen, p, to a coordinate relative to the upper-left corner of the component, c.

public static void convertPointToScreen(Point p, Component c)
Opposite of the previous method, this method takes a point, p, relative to the upper-left corner of the component, c, and converts it to a coordinate on the screen. Such a conversion makes light work of tiling popup windows.

public static Rectangle convertRectangle(Component source, Rectangle aRectangle, Component destination)
Translate aRectangle from the source coordinate system to the destination coordinate system, following the same rules as convertPoint( ).

public static Component findFocusOwner(Component c)
Return the component at or below c that has the keyboard focus, if any. Because of security restrictions, this may not work for non-Swing components in applets. Note that this method has been deprecated as of SDK 1.4.1.

public static Accessible getAccessibleAt(Component c, Point p)
Return the Accessible component at point p (relative to the component c). If no such component exists, null is returned.

public static Accessible getAccessibleChild(Component c, int i)
Return the ith accessible child of component c that implements the Accessible interface.

public static int getAccessibleChildrenCount(Component c)
Return the number of accessible children in component c that implement the Accessible interface.

public static int getAccessibleIndexInParent(Component c)
For a given component c, this method returns its index in its accessible parent. If the component does not have an accessible parent, -1 is returned.

public static AccessibleStateSet getAccessibleStateSet(Component c)
Return the set of accessible states active for the component c.

public static Container getAncestorNamed(String name, Component comp)
Return the first container named name that contains component comp. null is returned if name cannot be found.

public static Container getAncestorOfClass(Class c, Component comp)
Similar to getAncestorNamed( ), this method returns the first container that is an instance of class c that contains component comp.

public static Component getDeepestComponentAt(Component parent, int x, int y)
> Perform a recursive search through the component hierarchy starting at `parent`, and returns the last component containing the point (x, y). If `parent` is not a container, it is returned.

public static Rectangle getLocalBounds(Component aComponent)
> Return a rectangle containing `aComponent` relative to `aComponent`, i.e., (`0`, `0`, `width`, `height`).

public static Component getRoot(Component c)
> Return the parent `Window` component, or the last applet to contain `c` if it is in a browser environment.

public static JRootPane getRootPane(Component c)
> Find the root pane containing `c`. If no `JRootPane` is found containing `c`, `null` is returned.

public static void invokeAndWait(Runnable obj)
  throws InterruptedException, InvocationTargetException
public static void invokeLater(Runnable obj)
> These methods take `Runnable` arguments and place them on the event queue to be executed after all pending events have been dispatched. The `invokeLater()` method essentially just pushes this `Runnable` onto the event queue. The `invokeAndWait()` method pushes it onto the queue and blocks until it has been dispatched.
>
> `JComponent` is an example of a Swing component that uses this technique of delayed execution. It delays revalidation of any layout components until any other events pending have been handled by calling `invokeLater()`. Some events rely on the location of their source to function properly (like tooltips), and moving the components before the event has been properly dispatched could cause confusion.
>
> As mentioned earlier, Chapter 28 contains a more detailed discussion of these methods.

public static boolean isDescendingFrom(Component a, Component b)
> Return `true` if component a descends from b in the component hierarchy.

public static boolean isEventDispatchThread()
> Return `true` if the current thread is the event-dispatching thread.

public static boolean isLeftMouseButton(MouseEvent anEvent)
public static boolean isMiddleMouseButton(MouseEvent anEvent)
public static boolean isRightMouseButton(MouseEvent anEvent)
> These convenience methods return `true` if `anEvent` was performed with the left, middle, or right mouse button, respectively.

public static final boolean isRectangleContainingRectangle(Rectangle a, Rectangle b)
> Return `true` if rectangle a completely contains rectangle b.

public static String layoutCompoundLabel(FontMetrics fm, String text, Icon icon,
    int verticalAlignment, int horizontalAlignment, int verticalTextPosition,
    int horizontalTextPosition, Rectangle viewR, Rectangle iconR, Rectangle textR,
    int textIconGap)

> Lay out a label with text and an icon, using the font metrics, alignments, and text positions supplied relative to the viewR rectangle. If text cannot be contained in the label, it is truncated and "..." is appended. The resulting string is returned; textR and iconR are updated to contain the coordinates required to accomplish the desired layout.

public static void paintComponent(Graphics g, Component c, Container p, int x, int y,
    int w, int h)

public static void paintComponent(Graphics g, Component c, Container p, Rectangle r)

> Paint the component c in an arbitrary graphics object g, bounded by the given rectangle, r. The container p is set as the new parent of c to stop the propagation of any validate( ) or repaint( ) calls to c. This is an easy way to rubber-stamp a component's image on a graphics area. For example, you might want to use this method in a tree or table cell renderer to draw "read-only" versions of components such as sliders. The image would look like a slider, but would just be an image, not a real component.

public static void updateComponentTreeUI(Component c)

> Tell all components contained below c to update their current UI. This is useful if you allow the user to change the L&F of an application at runtime.

public static Window windowForComponent(Component aComponent)

> This convenience method returns the Window object containing aComponent. If no containing window is found, null is returned. This method can be very handy when you're writing your own generalized (and occasionally modal) dialogs.

The SwingConstants Interface

This interface defines the location constants (shown in Table 27-1) that are used throughout the Swing package. Quite often, this interface is implemented by a component so that the constants appear as regular parts of the class for ease of use. (The AbstractButton, JLabel, and SwingUtilities classes are examples of such classes.)

Table 27-1. SwingConstants constants

Constant	Data type	Description
BOTTOM	int	Bottom location for vertical placement
CENTER	int	Center location or justification
EAST	int	East (right-side) location
HORIZONTAL	int	Horizontal position or orientation

[1.4]since 1.4

Table 27-1. SwingConstants constants (continued)

Constant	Data type	Description
LEADING	int	Leading edge for left-to-right or right-to-left text
LEFT	int	Left location or justification
NEXT[1.4]	int	The next direction in a sequence
NORTH	int	North (top, center) location
NORTH_EAST	int	Northeast (upper-right) location
NORTH_WEST	int	Northwest (upper-left) location
PREVIOUS[1.4]	int	The previous direction in a sequence
RIGHT	int	Right location or justification
SOUTH	int	South (bottom, center) location
SOUTH_EAST	int	Southeast (lower-right) location
SOUTH_WEST	int	Southwest (lower-left) location
TOP	int	Top location for vertical placement
TRAILING	int	Trailing edge for left-to-right or right-to-left text
VERTICAL	int	Vertical orientation
WEST	int	West (left-side) location, typically centered vertically

[1.4]since 1.4

The Timer Class

The Timer class provides a mechanism to generate timed events. It has properties and events, and thus can be used in application builders that understand JavaBeans. It fires an ActionEvent at a given time. The timer can be set to repeat, and an optional initial delay can be set before the repeating event starts.

Properties

The Timer class properties give you access to the timer delays and nature of the event firing loops. They are listed in Table 27-2. The delay property dictates the length between repeated timer events (if repeats is true) and initialDelay determines how long to wait before starting the regular, repeating events. Both properties expect values in milliseconds. If your timer is not repeating, then the value of initialDelay determines when the timer fires its event. You can check to see if the timer is running with the running property. The coalesce property dictates whether or not the timer combines pending events into one single event (to help listeners keep up). For example, if the timer fires a tick every 10 milliseconds, but the application is busy and has not handled events for 100 milliseconds, 10 action events are queued up for delivery. If coalesce is false, all 10 of these are delivered in rapid succession. If coalesce is true (the default), only one event is fired. The `logTimers` property can be turned on to generate simple debugging information to the standard output stream each time an event is processed.

Table 27-2. Timer properties

Property	Data type	get	is	set	Default value
actionListeners[1.4]	ActionListener[]	•		•	Empty array
delay	int	•		•	From constructor
coalesce	boolean		•	•	true
initialDelay	int	•		•	this.delay
logTimers	boolean	•		•	false
repeats	boolean		•	•	true
running	boolean		•		false

[1.4]since 1.4

Events

A `Timer` generates an `ActionEvent` whenever it "goes off." You can listen for ActionEvents if you want to react to a timer tick.

public void addActionListener(ActionListener l)
public void removeActionListener(ActionListener l)
> Add or remove listeners interested in receiving action events from the timer.

public EventListener[] getListeners(Class listenerType)
> Retrieve all listeners of type `listenerType`. Used by `getActionListeners()` to return, well, action listeners.

The `Timer` class also contains its own `fireActionPerformed()` method to facilitate reporting events to listeners.

protected void fireActionPerformed(ActionEvent e)
> Send `ActionEvent` objects to any registered listeners.

Constructor

public Timer(int delay, ActionListener listener)
> Create a `Timer` object that notifies its `listener` every `delay` milliseconds. The listener argument can be `null`. The timer is not started right away; you must manually call the `start()` method.

Timer Control Methods

You also have a few methods to control the timer at runtime:

public void start( )
> Start the timer. The first event comes after initialDelay milliseconds, and if it's a repeating timer, every delay milliseconds after that.

public void restart( )
> Restart the timer. This method calls stop( ) and then start( ).

public void stop( )
> Stop the timer. Any timer events not yet fired are deleted.

Figure 27-2 shows a ClockLabel that updates itself every second, using events from a Timer. The code to produce our ticking label is remarkably short when we use a Timer.

```java
// ClockLabel.java
// An extension of the JLabel class that listens to events from a Timer object to
// update itself with the current date & time.
//
import java.util.Date;
import java.awt.event.*;
import javax.swing.*;

public class ClockLabel extends JLabel implements ActionListener {

  public ClockLabel( ) {
    super("" + new Date( ));
    Timer t = new Timer(1000, this);
    t.start( );
  }

  public void actionPerformed(ActionEvent ae) {
    setText((new Date( )).toString( ));
  }
}
```

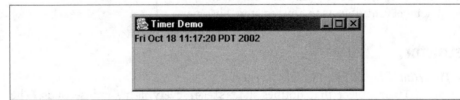

Figure 27-2. The Timer class in action with a ClockLabel

And here's the application that displays the ClockLabel object:

```java
// ClockTest.java
// A demonstration framework for the Timer driven ClockLabel class
//
```

```
import javax.swing.*;
import java.awt.*;

public class ClockTest extends JFrame {

  public ClockTest( ) {
    super("Timer Demo");
    setSize(300, 100);
    setDefaultCloseOperation(EXIT_ON_CLOSE);

    ClockLabel clock = new ClockLabel( );
    getContentPane( ).add(clock, BorderLayout.NORTH);
  }

  public static void main(String args[]) {
    ClockTest ct = new ClockTest( );
    ct.setVisible(true);
  }
}
```

Tooltips

You have probably already seen several examples of using basic tooltips with components such as JButton and JLabel. The following classes give you access to much more of the tooltip system in case you need to develop something beyond simple text tips.

The ToolTipManager Class

This class manages the tooltips for an application. Following the singleton pattern, any given virtual machine will have, at most, one ToolTipManager at any time—a new instance is created when the class is loaded. (Of course, you're already familiar with *Design Patterns* by Gamma et al., right?) You can retrieve the current manager using the ToolTipManager.sharedInstance( ) method.

Properties

The ToolTipManager properties shown in Table 27-3 give you control over the delays (in milliseconds) involved in showing tooltips and determines whether or not tooltips are even active. The enabled property determines whether or not tooltips are active. The dismissDelay property determines how long a tooltip remains on the screen if you don't do something to dismiss it manually (such as move the mouse outside the component's borders). The initialDelay property determines how long the mouse must rest inside a component before the tooltip pops up, and reshowDelay determines how long you must wait after leaving a component before the same tooltip shows up again when you reenter the component. (These properties are used by a timer whose delays are triggered by mouse events.) If the `lightWeightPopupEnabled` property is true, all-Java tooltips are used. A `false` value indicates native tooltips should be used.

Table 27-3. ToolTipManager properties

Property	Data type	get	is	set	Default value
dismissDelay	int	•		•	4000
enabled	boolean		•	•	true
initialDelay	int	•		•	750
lightWeightPopupEnabled	boolean		•	•	true
reshowDelay	int	•		•	500

Miscellaneous methods

If need be, you can manually register or unregister components with the manager. Normally this is done using the `JComponent.setToolTipText( )` method for the component itself. If you pass in a non-null tip string, the component is registered. If you pass in a `null` tip string, the component is unregistered. The VSX2 example in Chapter 17 shows off how to use these methods in detail, but the synopsis is:

```
ToolTipManager.sharedInstance( ).registerComponent(yourComponent);
```

public void registerComponent(JComponent component)
Register component with the `ToolTipManager` to make sure that its tips get shown after an appropriate mouse event occurs.

public static ToolTipManager sharedInstance( )
Return the `ToolTipManager` singleton. You use this to get access to the manager and change its delay properties. For example, you could cut the initial delay to 250 milliseconds like this:

```
ToolTipManager.sharedInstance( ).setInitialDelay(250);
```

public void unregisterComponent(JComponent component)
Unregister component from the `ToolTipManager`. Tooltips are no longer shown for this component.

The JToolTip Class

Of course, the whole purpose of having a tooltip manager is to manage tooltips. The tooltips themselves are simple popups containing a short, descriptive string that often shows up if you let your mouse cursor rest over a component. They are embodied here in the `JToolTip` class. `JToolTip` is a fairly simple class, thanks to the MVC architecture in place for Swing. All it really needs to know is what text to display and who to display it for. With SDK 1.4, `JToolTip` can take advantage of the same HTML formatting as the `JLabel` class. See Chapter 4 for all the details.

If you want to display something besides text, you can create your own subclass of JToolTip and render just about anything you want. (Recall that JToolTip extends from JComponent.) To make your custom tooltip available, you'll also need to subclass the component to which you want to add your tip and override the createToolTip() method to return an instance of your tip.

Properties

The properties that support the JToolTip class are shown in Table 27-4. The component property determines which component this tip applies to. The tipText property contains the text to display for the tip. Both of these properties are currently stored in package-private variables.

Table 27-4. JToolTip properties

Property	Data type	get	is	set	Default value
accessibleContext	AccessibleContext	•			JToolTip.AccessibleJToolTip()
component	Component	•		•	null
tipText	String	•		•	null
UI[b, o]	ToolTipUI	•		•	From L&F
UIClassID[o]	String	•			"ToolTipUI"

[b]bound, [o]overridden

Constructor

The JToolTip class has only one constructor:

public JToolTip()
    Create a new JToolTip object with no text or component association.

Rendering Odds and Ends

Both the JTree and JTable classes make use of cell renderers to display cells and cell editors to modify cell values. The following classes round out the utilities available for rendering information.

The CellRendererPane Class

This utility class was built to keep renderers from propagating repaint() and validate() calls to the components using renderer components such as JTree and JList. If you played around with creating your own renderers for any of the Swing components that use them, you'll recall that you did not use this class yourself. Normally this pane is wrapped around the renderer and the various paintComponent()

methods below are used to do the actual drawing. Developers do not normally need to worry about this class.

The Renderer Interface

The Swing package includes a `Renderer` interface (which does not appear to be used within Swing itself) with the following methods:

public Component getComponent()
> Return a `Component` you can use with something like the `SwingUtilities.paintComponent()` method to draw the value on the screen.

public void setValue(Object aValue, boolean isSelected)
> This method can initialize the rendering component to reflect the state of the object `aValue`.

This interface could be useful if you were to create a library of renderers for use with your own applications; however, it is not implemented anywhere in the Swing package as of SDK 1.4.1.

The GrayFilter Class

The `GrayFilter` class is an extension of the `java.awt.image.RGBImageFilter` class. This class contains a static method that returns a "disabled" version of an image passed in. The image is converted to a grayscale version, and some lighter parts of the image are amplified to ensure the image is recognizable. All of the components that can display images use this class to present a default disabled version of the image if an explicit disabled image is not provided.

If you want the gory details on image manipulation with Java 2, check out *Java 2D Graphics* by Jonathan Knudsen (O'Reilly & Associates).

Constructor

public GrayFilter(boolean brighter, int percent)
> Create an instance of the `GrayFilter` class that you can use to do your own filtering. (Normally you don't call this, but use `createDisabledImage()` instead.) Both the `brighter` and `percent` arguments are used to convert color pixels to appropriately shaded gray pixels.

Image methods

public static Image createDisabledImage(Image i)
> Use this method to retrieve a grayed-out version of the image i. This method creates an instance of the `GrayFilter` class with `brighter` turned on and a gray percent of 50.

public int filterRGB(int x, int y, int rgb)
>Override the `filterRGB()` method in `RGBImageFilter`, convert the `rgb` pixel to a gray pixel, and return that.

Event Utilities

If you extend one of the Swing components to add functionality, or indeed, build your own component from scratch, you need to handle event listeners for any events you might generate. The `EventListenerList` class (from the `javax.swing.event` package) is designed to aid in that task. This class is similar in many ways to the `AWTEventMulticaster`; however, it supports any type of listener and assumes you'll use only the appropriate listeners for a given event type.

The `KeyStroke` class can also help handle keyboard events. Rather than listening to every key that gets pressed and throwing out the things you don't care about, you can use the `KeyStroke` class to register specific actions with specific keys. The `MouseInputAdapter` can help deal with the other common low-level event generator: the mouse. And last but not least, this section also covers the `SwingPropertyChangeSupport` class to show you a fast way of generating property change events.

The EventListenerList Class

If your component generates events, it must contain methods to add and remove interested listeners. Following the JavaBeans design patterns, these are the `add`*Type*`Listener()` and `remove`*Type*`Listener()` methods. Typically you store the listeners in a collection, and then use the vector as a rollcall for who to send events to when the time comes. This is a very common task for components that generate events, and the `EventListenerList` can help lift some (but certainly not all) of the burden of coding the event firing.

The `EventListenerList` stores listeners as pairs of objects: one object to hold the listener's type and one to hold the listener itself. At any time, you can retrieve all of the current listeners as an array of `Object`s and use that array to fire off any events you need.

Here is a `SecretLabel` class that extends `JLabel` and fires `ActionEvent` messages when clicked. The label does not give any indication it has been clicked; that's why it's called secret. The code for this label demonstrates how an `EventListenerList` is typically used. Figure 27-3 shows the `SecretLabel` up and running.

We set up the standard `addActionListener()` and `removeActionListener()` methods, which delegate to the listener list, and pass in the type of listener we're attaching. (Recall that `EventListenerList` can store any type of listener.) When we actually fire an event, we search the listener list array, checking the even-numbered indices for a particular type of listener. If we find the right type (`ActionListener`, in this case) we use the

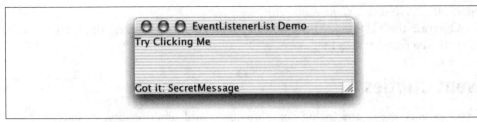

Figure 27-3. A JLabel that uses an EventListenerList to facilitate dispatching events

next entry in the list as an event recipient. You can find other such examples throughout the Swing package in such models as DefaultTreeModel, DefaultTableModel, and DefaultButtonModel.

The EventListenerList provides a generic dispatcher that works in just about every situation. However, it is not the only way to dispatch events. For a particular application you may find a more efficient means.

```java
// SecretLabel.java
// An extension of the JLabel class that listens to mouse clicks and converts
// them to ActionEvents, which in turn are reported via an EventListenersList object
//
import java.awt.*;
import java.awt.event.*;
import javax.swing.*;

public class SecretLabel extends JLabel {

  public SecretLabel(String msg) {
    super(msg);
    addMouseListener(new MouseAdapter() {
      public void mouseClicked(MouseEvent me) {
        fireActionPerformed(new ActionEvent(SecretLabel.this,
                                ActionEvent.ACTION_PERFORMED,
                                "SecretMessage"));
      }
    });
  }

  public void addActionListener(ActionListener l) {
    // We'll just use the listenerList we inherit from JComponent.
    listenerList.add(ActionListener.class, l);
  }

  public void removeActionListener(ActionListener l) {
    listenerList.remove(ActionListener.class, l);
  }

  protected void fireActionPerformed(ActionEvent ae) {
    Object[] listeners = listenerList.getListeners(ActionListener.class);
```

```
        for (int i = 0; i < listeners.length; i++) {
            ((ActionListener)listeners[i]).actionPerformed(ae);
        }
    }
}
```

Our addActionListener( ) and removeActionListener( ) methods just defer to a listener list to register and unregister listeners. We don't have to do anything special to
get an EventListenerList; we're extending JLabel and therefore inherit a
listenerList field from JComponent. fireActionPerformed( ) does the actual work; it
calls the actionPerformed( ) method of every action listener stored in the listener list.
Note that we walk through the array of listeners two at a time; as we'll see, the elements in this array alternate between Class objects that tell us what kind of listener
we have, and the actual listener objects themselves. Figure 27-4 shows how the array
is set up.

Here's the application that creates the SecretLabel and hooks it up to the reporting
label. We use the same addActionListener( ) that we would for things like buttons or
lists:

```
// SecretTest.java
// A demonstration framework for the EventListenerList-enabled SecretLabel class
//
import javax.swing.*;
import java.awt.event.*;
import java.awt.*;

public class SecretTest extends JFrame {

    public SecretTest( ) {
        super("EventListenerList Demo");
        setSize(200, 100);
        setDefaultCloseOperation(EXIT_ON_CLOSE);

        SecretLabel secret = new SecretLabel("Try Clicking Me");
        final JLabel reporter = new JLabel("Event reports will show here...");
        secret.addActionListener(new ActionListener( ) {
            public void actionPerformed(ActionEvent ae) {
                reporter.setText("Got it: " + ae.getActionCommand( ));
            }
        } );
        getContentPane( ).add(secret, BorderLayout.NORTH);
        getContentPane( ).add(reporter, BorderLayout.SOUTH);
    }

    public static void main(String args[]) {
        SecretTest st = new SecretTest( );
        st.setVisible(true);
    }
}
```

If you have set up your own event source components before, the EventListenerList class may not seem to provide much improvement. But, as the documentation points out, it provides a single access point for serializing your list of listeners.

Constructor

public EventListenerList( )
> Create a new listener list.

Listener methods

public void add(Class t, EventListener l)
> Add a new listener to the list.

public int getListenerCount( )
public int getListenerCount(Class t)
> Return a count of the listeners contained in the list. If a Class argument is provided, you get the number of listeners of that type in the list.

public Object[] getListenerList( )
> Return an array of objects organized as in Figure 27-4. The listener type entry is always a Class object. You typically work through this array in increments (or decrements) of 2.

0	Listener type
1	Listener
2	Listener type
3	Listener
...	...
n	Listener type
n+1	Listener

Figure 27-4. The EventListenerList object array structure

public EventListener[] getListeners(Class t)
> Added in the 1.3 release of the SDK, this method returns an array containing only listeners matching the requested class, t. This eliminates the tedium of looping through all the registered listeners when you only want a particular type. Many classes that use the EventListenerList helper class provide a pass through a version of this method so you can access the listeners directly. (See the Timer class earlier in this chapter.)

public remove(Class t, EventListener l)
> Remove a listener from the list.

The KeyStroke Class

Another convenient class for dealing with events is the KeyStroke class. This class allows you to associate actions with particular keys through the InputMap class. While not technically part of Swing, it plays an integral role in setting up the maps.

Properties

The KeyStroke class contains the properties shown in Table 27-5. The keyChar property is the character this keystroke represents, such as A or $. The keyCode property is the int value associated with a particular key on your keyboard. This might be the ASCII value of a letter, or some other value associated with a function key. The modifiers property contains information on whether or not any of the modifier keys (Control, Alt, Meta, Shift) are attached to this keystroke. The acceptable key codes come from the java.awt.event.KeyEvent class and are shown in Table 27-6. The onKeyRelease property determines when events associated with this keystroke should be triggered. A true value treats the keystroke as a keyTyped( ) event, while a false value behaves like a keyPressed( ) event.

Table 27-5. KeyStroke properties

Property	Data type	get	is	set	Default value
keyChar	char	•			'\0'
keyCode	int	•			0
modifiers	int	•			0
onKeyRelease	boolean		•		false

Table 27-6. Virtual key codes for KeyStroke

KeyEvent constant	Decimal value	Hexadecimal value	char equivalent
VK_0	48	0x30	'0'
VK_1	49	0x31	'1'
VK_2	50	0x32	'2'
VK_3	51	0x33	'3'
VK_4	52	0x34	'4'
VK_5	53	0x35	'5'
VK_6	54	0x36	'6'
VK_7	55	0x37	'7'
VK_8	56	0x38	'8'
VK_9	57	0x39	'9'
VK_A	65	0x41	'A'

[1.3]since 1.3, [1.4]since 1.4

*Pseudo-deprecated in favor of VK_SEPARATOR.

Table 27-6. Virtual key codes for KeyStroke (continued)

KeyEvent constant	Decimal value	Hexadecimal value	char equivalent
VK_B	66	0x42	'B'
VK_C	67	0x43	'C'
VK_D	68	0x44	'D'
VK_E	69	0x45	'E'
VK_F	70	0x46	'F'
VK_G	71	0x47	'G'
VK_H	72	0x48	'H'
VK_I	73	0x49	'I'
VK_J	74	0x4a	'J'
VK_K	75	0x4b	'K'
VK_L	76	0x4c	'L'
VK_M	77	0x4d	'M'
VK_N	78	0x4e	'N'
VK_O	79	0x4f	'O'
VK_P	80	0x50	'P'
VK_Q	81	0x51	'Q'
VK_R	82	0x52	'R'
VK_S	83	0x53	'S'
VK_T	84	0x54	'T'
VK_U	85	0x55	'U'
VK_V	86	0x56	'V'
VK_W	87	0x57	'W'
VK_X	88	0x58	'X'
VK_Y	89	0x59	'Y'
VK_Z	90	0x5a	'Z'
VK_ACCEPT	30	0x1e	
VK_ADD	107	0x6b	
VK_AGAIN	65481	0xffc9	
VK_ALL_CANDIDATES	256	0x0100	
VK_ALPHANUMERIC	240	0x00f0	
VK_ALT	18	0x12	
VK_ALT_GRAPH	65406	0xff7e	
VK_AMPERSAND	150	0x96	'&'
VK_ASTERISK	151	0x97	'*'

[1.3]since 1.3, [1.4]since 1.4

*Pseudo-deprecated in favor of VK_SEPARATOR.

Table 27-6. Virtual key codes for KeyStroke (continued)

KeyEvent constant	Decimal value	Hexadecimal value	char equivalent
VK_AT	512	0x0200	'@'
VK_BACK_QUOTE	192	0xc0	
VK_BACK_SLASH	92	0x5c	'\\'
VK_BACK_SPACE	8	0x08	'\b'
VK_BRACELEFT	161	0xa1	
VK_BRACERIGHT	162	0x12	
VK_CANCEL	3	0x03	
VK_CAPS_LOCK	20	0x14	
VK_CIRCUMFLEX	514	0x0202	
VK_CLEAR	12	0x0c	
VK_CLOSE_BRACKET	93	0x5d	']'
VK_CODE_INPUT	256	0x0100	
VK_COLON	513	0x0201	':'
VK_COMMA	44	0x2c	','
VK_COMPOSE	65312	0xff20	
VK_CONTROL	17	0x11	
VK_CONVERT	28	0x1c	
VK_COPY	65485	0xffcd	
VK_CUT	65489	0xffd1	
VK_DEAD_ABOVEDOT	134	0x86	
VK_DEAD_ABOVERING	136	0x88	
VK_DEAD_ACUTE	129	0x81	
VK_DEAD_BREVE	133	0x85	
VK_DEAD_CARON	138	0x90	
VK_DEAD_CEDILLA	139	0x91	
VK_DEAD_CIRCUMFLEX	130	0x82	
VK_DEAD_DIAERESIS	135	0x87	
VK_DEAD_DOUBLEACUTE	137	0x89	
VK_DEAD_GRAVE	128	0x80	
VK_DEAD_IOTA	141	0x93	
VK_DEAD_MACRON	132	0x84	
VK_DEAD_OGONEK	140	0x92	
VK_DEAD_SEMIVOICED_SOUND	143	0x95	
VK_DEAD_TILDE	131	0x83	

[1.3]since 1.3, [1.4]since 1.4

*Pseudo-deprecated in favor of VK_SEPARATOR.

Table 27-6. Virtual key codes for KeyStroke (continued)

KeyEvent constant	Decimal value	Hexadecimal value	char equivalent
VK_DEAD_VOICED_SOUND	142	0x94	
VK_DECIMAL	110	0x6e	
VK_DELETE	127	0x7f	
VK_DIVIDE	111	0x6f	
VK_DOLLAR	515	0x0203	'$'
VK_DOWN	40	0x28	
VK_END	35	0x23	
VK_ENTER	10	0x0a	'\n'
VK_EQUALS	61	0x3d	'='
VK_ESCAPE	27	0x1b	
VK_EURO_SIGN	516	0x0204	
VK_EXCLAMATION_MARK	517	0x0205	
VK_F1	112	0x70	
VK_F2	113	0x71	
VK_F3	114	0x72	
VK_F4	115	0x73	
VK_F5	116	0x74	
VK_F6	117	0x75	
VK_F7	118	0x76	
VK_F8	119	0x77	
VK_F9	120	0x78	
VK_F10	121	0x79	
VK_F11	122	0x7a	
VK_F12	123	0x7b	
VK_F13	61440	0xf000	
VK_F14	61441	0xf001	
VK_F15	61442	0xf002	
VK_F16	61443	0xf003	
VK_F17	61444	0xf004	
VK_F18	61445	0xf005	
VK_F19	61446	0xf006	
VK_F20	61447	0xf007	
VK_F21	61448	0xf008	
VK_F22	61449	0xf009	

[1.3]since 1.3, [1.4]since 1.4

*Pseudo-deprecated in favor of VK_SEPARATOR.

Table 27-6. Virtual key codes for KeyStroke (continued)

KeyEvent constant	Decimal value	Hexadecimal value	char equivalent
VK_F23	61450	0xf00a	
VK_F24	61451	0xf00b	
VK_FINAL	24	0x18	
VK_FIND	65488	0xffd0	
VK_FULL_WIDTH	243	0xf3	
VK_GREATER	160	0xa0	'>'
VK_HALF_WIDTH	244	0xf4	
VK_HELP	156	0x9c	
VK_HIRAGANA	242	0xf2	
VK_HOME	36	0x24	
VK_INPUT_METHOD_ON_OFF[1.3]	263	0x0107	
VK_INSERT	155	0x9b	
VK_INVERTED_EXCLAMATION_MARK	518	0x0206	
VK_JAPANESE_HIRAGANA	260	0x0104	
VK_JAPANESE_KATAKANA	259	0x0103	
VK_JAPANESE_ROMAN	261	0x0105	
VK_KANA	21	0x15	
VK_KANA_LOCK[1.3]	262	0x0106	
VK_KANJI	25	0x19	
VK_KATAKANA	241	0xf1	
VK_KP_DOWN	225	0xe1	
VK_KP_LEFT	226	0xe2	
VK_KP_RIGHT	227	0xe3	
VK_KP_UP	224	0xe0	
VK_LEFT	37	0x25	
VK_LEFT_PARENTHESIS	519	0x0207	'('
VK_LESS	153	0x99	'<'
VK_META	157	0x9d	
VK_MINUS	45	0x2d	'-'
VK_MODECHANGE	31	0x1f	
VK_MULTIPLY	106	0x6a	
VK_NONCONVERT	29	0x1d	
VK_NUMBER_SIGN	520	0x0208	'#'
VK_NUM_LOCK	144	0x90	

[1.3]since 1.3, [1.4]since 1.4

*Pseudo-deprecated in favor of VK_SEPARATOR.

Table 27-6. *Virtual key codes for KeyStroke (continued)*

KeyEvent constant	Decimal value	Hexadecimal value	char equivalent
VK_NUMPAD0	96	0x60	
VK_NUMPAD1	97	0x61	
VK_NUMPAD2	98	0x62	
VK_NUMPAD3	99	0x63	
VK_NUMPAD4	100	0x64	
VK_NUMPAD5	101	0x65	
VK_NUMPAD6	102	0x66	
VK_NUMPAD7	103	0x67	
VK_NUMPAD8	104	0x68	
VK_NUMPAD9	105	0x69	
VK_OPEN_BRACKET	91	0x5b	'['
VK_PAGE_DOWN	34	0x22	
VK_PAGE_UP	33	0x21	
VK_PASTE	65487	0xffcf	
VK_PAUSE	19	0x13	
VK_PERIOD	46	0x2e	'.'
VK_PLUS	521	0x0209	'+'
VK_PREVIOUS_CANDIDATE	257	0x0101	
VK_PRINTSCREEN	154	0x9a	
VK_PROPS	65482	0xffca	
VK_QUOTE	222	0xde	
VK_QUOTEDBL	152	0x98	'\"'
VK_RIGHT	39	0x27	
VK_RIGHT_PARENTHESIS	522	0x020a	')'
VK_ROMAN_CHARACTERS	245	0xf5	
VK_SCROLL_LOCK	145	0x91	
VK_SEMICOLON	59	0x3b	';'
VK_SEPARATER*	108	0x6c	
VK_SEPARATOR[1.4]	108	0x6c	
VK_SHIFT	16	0x10	
VK_SLASH	47	0x2f	'/'
VK_SPACE	32	0x20	' '
VK_STOP	65480	0ffc8	
VK_SUBTRACT	109	0x6d	

[1.3]since 1.3, [1.4]since 1.4

*Pseudo-deprecated in favor of VK_SEPARATOR.

Table 27-6. Virtual key codes for KeyStroke (continued)

KeyEvent constant	Decimal value	Hexadecimal value	char equivalent
VK_TAB	9	0x09	'\t'
VK_UNDEFINED	0	0x00	
VK_UNDERSCORE	523	0x020b	
VK_UNDO	65483	0xffcb	
VK_UP	38	0x26	

[1.3]since 1.3, [1.4]since 1.4

*Pseudo-deprecated in favor of VK_SEPARATOR.

Key codes

Just for your reference, Table 27-6 lists the key codes defined by the java.awt.event. KeyEvent class. You'll notice that many of the key code values correspond to the ASCII value of the character associated with the key. This facilitates coding for common keys. Of course, as a good programmer, you always use the constant, right? In fact, even though you can use, for example, 'R' rather than VK_R, if you try to use 'r', it won't work. This is a good argument for using the constant; if you make a capitalization error the compiler will tell you right away, and you won't have to wait for bug reports from your users. Note that in the table we left out character equivalents that were not conceptually related to the virtual keycode constant.

Factory methods

The KeyStroke class does not have a public (or even protected) constructor. All keystrokes are cached for you. You can use any of the static methods to retrieve the instance you're looking for.

public static KeyStroke getKeyStroke(char keyChar)
public static KeyStroke getKeyStroke(char keyChar, int modifiers)
public static KeyStroke getKeyStroke(char keyChar, boolean onKeyRelease)

> Return the KeyStroke that represents a character, such as a. The modifiers argument allows you to look for keystrokes like Ctrl-A. The onKeyRelease argument determines whether actions associated with this keystroke are triggered when the key is pressed (false) or when it is released (true).

public static KeyStroke getKeyStroke(int keyCode, int modifiers)
public static KeyStroke getKeyStroke(int keyCode, int modifiers,
  boolean onKeyRelease)

> Return the KeyStroke that represents a given key code (see Table 27-6) and modifier combination. As with the previous getKeyStroke( ) methods, the onKeyRelease argument determines when to fire associated actions.

public static KeyStroke getKeyStroke(String representation)

> Return a KeyStroke from the given representation of the keystroke. Sometimes it's easier to think about keystrokes this way. For example, to retrieve Ctrl-A as a keystroke, you could call this method with "control A" as the argument. To get one of the function keys, representation would be "pressed F12" or "control alt released INSERT".

> The syntax for a valid representation is shown in Figure 27-5. Note to Mac users: you'll need to use "alt" for the Option key and "meta" for the Command key when building keystrokes with this method.

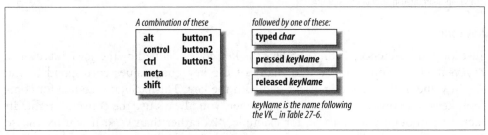

Figure 27-5. The valid construction of a keystroke by string representation

public static KeyStroke getKeyStrokeForEvent(KeyEvent anEvent)

> Extract a KeyStroke from anEvent.

The MouseInputAdapter Class

This simple implementation of the MouseInputListener interface (which is itself just a conglomeration of the MouseListener and MouseMotionListener interfaces) provides empty methods for each of the mouse event handlers. You can use this abstract convenience class like any other adapter, extending it and overriding only the methods that interest you. This class simply has the benefit of handling both mouse and mouse motion events.

Methods

public void mouseClicked(MouseEvent e)
public void mousePressed(MouseEvent e)
public void mouseReleased(MouseEvent e)
public void mouseEntered(MouseEvent e)
public void mouseExited(MouseEvent e)

> These methods come from the MouseListener interface. All have empty implementations.

public void mouseDragged(MouseEvent e)
public void mouseMoved(MouseEvent e)

> These methods come from the MouseMotionListener interface. Both have empty implementations.

The SwingPropertyChangeSupport Class

Many Swing components support bound properties as defined by the JavaBeans specification. In the java.beans package, a utility class called PropertyChangeSupport is defined to help you register property change listeners and fire property change events. The PropertyChangeSupport class does this work in a thread-safe manner that consumes a good bit of memory. The SwingPropertyChangeSupport class provides exactly the same set of features but does so without thread-safety to reduce memory usage and increase performance. If you're building your own components, you can use this class instead of PropertyChangeSupport.

Constructor

public SwingPropertyChangeSupport(Object sourceBean)
> This constructor creates a new SwingPropertyChangeSupport object with a reference to sourceBean kept for use in reporting events. The sourceBean is listed as the source for all property change events coming from this support object.

Methods

public void addPropertyChangeListener(PropertyChangeListener listener)
public void addPropertyChangeListener(String propertyName,
* PropertyChangeListener listener)*
public void removePropertyChangeListener(PropertyChangeListener listener)
public void removePropertyChangeListener(String propertyName,
* PropertyChangeListener listener)*
> Add or remove PropertyChangeListener objects interested in receiving property change events. If you give a propertyName, only changes to the specified property are reported.

public void firePropertyChange(String propertyName, Object oldValue,
* Object newValue)*
> Create a new PropertyChangeEvent object from propertyName, oldValue and newValue, then fire it to any registered listeners.

public void firePropertyChange(PropertyChangeEvent evt)
> Fire an existing PropertyChangeEvent, evt, to any registered listeners.

public boolean hasListeners(String propertyName)
> Return true if there are any listeners registered for the given propertyName. If a generic listener is present, this method returns true, regardless of whether or not any specific property listeners exist.

CHAPTER 28

Swing Under the Hood

While writing the first edition of this book, we sent mail to several Java newsgroups asking what topics developers would like to see explained in more detail. We received a tidal wave of responses, encompassing some rather arcane parts of Swing. Of those that were not covered elsewhere in the book, most of the replies concerned the same five areas:

- Understanding focus in Swing and altering the flow of focus over components
- Multithreading issues in Swing
- Mixing lightweight and heavyweight (Swing and AWT) components in Swing
- The Swing `RepaintManager`
- Creating your own Swing component

In response to your requests, we offer this collection of tips, tricks, and things that made us cry "Eureka!" at about two in the morning. Since many of these topics had little or no documentation when Swing was created, the authors had to dig through the Swing source code much more than normal to answer these questions. Hence, we called this chapter "Swing Under the Hood." As Swing has evolved, we've updated it to reflect today's realities and to incorporate new content.

Working with Focus

Prior to SDK 1.4, focus issues in Java were complicated and not adequately implemented. The problems were deeper than bugs in the code—of which there were certainly plenty, many due to inconsistencies between platforms. The design itself was fundamentally flawed.[*]

---

[*] For more details about the deficiencies and how they have been remedied, see Sun's article, "The AWT Focus Subsystem for Merlin" at *http://java.sun.com/products/jfc/tsc/articles/merlin/focus/*.

Because of these deep changes, the "right way" to do things now differs substantially from previous versions of Java. To avoid confusion, we discuss only the focus model introduced in 1.4. Developers who work with earlier releases should refer to the book's web site (*http://www.oreilly.com/catalog/jswing2*) for the first edition's version of this section.

Here are some highlights of changes in the focus system in 1.4:

- FocusManager has been deprecated and replaced by KeyboardFocusManager.
- It's now possible to learn which component currently has the focus.
- Lightweight children of Window (not just Frame or Dialog) are able to receive keyboard input.
- When focus changes, the component gaining focus can find out which one lost it, and vice versa.
- There is far less platform-dependent code; it has been replaced by a very extensible public API in AWT, with many levels where custom logic can be plugged in. Heavyweight and lightweight focus is much better integrated.
- Components can lose focus *temporarily* (e.g., to a scrollbar).
- It's a lot easier to work with.

The net result of all these changes is that the system tends to work the way you want it to, and even when you want to add fancy new features, doing so requires less effort and simpler code.

Overview

Focus specifies the component that receives keyboard events when the user presses keys on the keyboard. In managing focus, it is also important to define how and when focus transfers from one component to another, and the order in which components are traversed when focus moves forward or backward. These concepts are strongly linked: if a component can receive focus at all, then it participates in a focus traversal order, and vice versa.

In Swing, the KeyboardFocusManager keeps track of these relationships and interacts appropriately with components and the keyboard. It registers itself as a KeyEventDispatcher, monitoring the stream of keyboard events and deciding how to respond to them. (Your own classes can implement this interface if they need to watch, and potentially handle, all keyboard events regardless of focus.)

The KeyboardFocusManager uses a FocusTraversalPolicy to determine the traversal order as focus moves between components. A number of standard policy implementations are provided. If you don't explicitly request one, the LayoutFocusPolicy is installed by the standard layout managers and provides behavior that is backward-compatible with previous editions of Java. It examines the positions and sizes of the components within the container and provides traversal that is consistent with the

`ComponentOrientation` (for left-to-right containers, focus starts at the top left, moving along the top row until the right edge is reached, and then jumps to the left of the next row down). If you have special traversal needs, you can implement your own `FocusTraversalPolicy` and install it in a container, as we'll demonstrate later in this section.

Focus traversal

How does Swing know when it's time to move focus from one component to another? This almost always occurs in response to user actions. The most straightforward case involves the user clicking on a component with the mouse. If that component is enabled and focusable, it receives focus immediately. There are no tricky rules.

Focus traversal policies really come into play when users indicate, via the keyboard, that they're finished with the current component and are ready to move on to the next one. The specific keys used to signal such intentions are up to individual platforms and L&F implementations, but usually, Tab indicates a desire to move to the next component, while Shift-Tab requests a move back to the previous component. Because users enter substantial amounts of text into `TextArea` components and may want to insert a Tab character to indent a paragraph, Ctrl-Tab is commonly used to move focus forward out of a `TextArea`, and Ctrl-Shift-Tab is used to move backward. The `Component` class provides a set of properties to define and manipulate these focus traversal keys so that each component can define its own behavior. The fewer differences there are, of course, the more comfortable and productive the environment is for users.

The traversal policy is also consulted when a window is first shown to determine which component starts out with the focus (unless the application has already explicitly assigned focus). If the frame of an already visible window is clicked by the user, the component that previously had focus within that window generally gets it back, without intervention by any traversal policy.

There may be other times when your application wants to transfer focus. For example, if you have a serial-number entry dialog containing a series of small text fields, to visually separate each chunk of characters in the serial number, it would be friendly to automatically jump to the next field as each is filled. As you might expect, `KeyboardFocusManager` provides methods your code can invoke to move focus in any way that the user might request via the keyboard, and components can be explicitly given focus.

Validation

The focus traversal mechanism often interacts closely with application logic when it comes to validating user input. The point at which users are moving on from one of your entry fields is an excellent time to make sure that what they've entered is complete and valid. Listening for the FOCUS_LOST event provides just this capability. If your code finds an incorrect value, you display an error and set focus on the problem component or, less intrusively but perhaps more cryptically, simply beep and keep the focus from leaving by using a VetoableChangeListener. (There are some complexities involved in using this approach safely, though; you should study the relevant Javadoc carefully to avoid deadlocks and other pitfalls.) In fact, you no longer need to worry about these details: since SDK 1.3, Swing provides a convenient built-in facility for verifying user input when a component loses focus. The inputVerifier property of JComponent is discussed in Chapter 3, and the details of the mechanism are explained in Chapter 20.

Of course, this approach applies only to fields that can be validated on their own. There may also be important cross-field constraints that you'll validate only when the user has filled in an entire form and is trying to take action with it. Such code would not rely on the focus mechanism at all, being invoked in response to a button press or menu choice. At the opposite extreme, you may be able to validate some input on a key-by-key basis, screening out keystrokes that don't make sense, as in a numeric-only field.

Temporary focus changes

Swing makes a distinction between permanent and temporary focus changes. All of the discussion so far has been about permanent changes of focus, in which users have moved on to a different component and won't be coming back unless they want to (hence the appropriateness of validation). Sometimes, however, focus is expected to return to a component in a short amount of time, such as when a popup menu is shown or a scrollbar is dragged. In such cases, validation would be premature, as the user hasn't finished interacting with the component. The focus-related events provided by Swing allow your code to distinguish between these situations and react appropriately.

Focus cycles

As the user tabs between components, not every component on the screen gets focus. At the most obvious level, focus remains "trapped" within the top-level window in which it began (this also applies to JInternalFrames being used in a JDesktopPane) until the user or program explicitly moves it somewhere else. These containers are "focus cycle roots" because the components within them form a focus cycle, a group of components through which focus cycles without leaving. If you have a special situation in which you'd like to create a focus cycle root within another type of component, you can override the isFocusCycleRoot() method inherited from Component and return true. (As usual, you should have a good reason for doing this because it restricts the user's choices, probably in an unexpected way. There would need to be a strong visual cue about the relatedness of your enclosed components, to the exclusion of all others, in order for it to make sense.) Figure 28-1 shows the effect this property has on focus traversal.

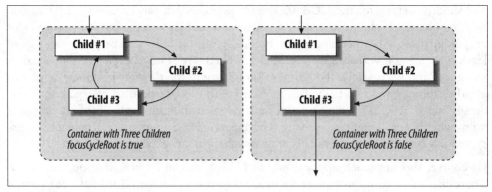

Figure 28-1. Focus cycle root behavior

In addition to the focus traversal keys, Swing lets components provide keys to enable the user to jump out of a focus cycle. Even though the support for these keys exists, and components may define them, none of the built-in components define any keys to perform these functions. Of course, there are also methods in KeyboardFocusManager that your application can use to request this kind of focus traversal.

Using Focus Properties

Here is an example that demonstrates some of the main focus properties:

```
// FocusExample.java
//
import java.awt.*;
import java.awt.event.*;

import javax.swing.*;
import javax.swing.border.*;

public class FocusExample extends JFrame {

    public FocusExample( ) {

        super("Focus Example");
        setDefaultCloseOperation(EXIT_ON_CLOSE);
        MyPanel mypanel = new MyPanel( );

        JButton  button1 = new JButton("One");
        JButton  button2 = new JButton("Two");
        JButton  button3 = new JButton("Three");
        JButton button4 = new JButton("Four");
        JButton button5 = new MyButton("Five*");
        JButton  button6 = new MyButton("Six*");
        JButton  button7 = new JButton("Seven");

        mypanel.add(button2);
        mypanel.add(button3);
```

```
JInternalFrame frame1 = new JInternalFrame("Internal Frame 1",
                                           true, true, true, true);

frame1.setBackground(Color.lightGray);
frame1.getContentPane( ).setLayout(new GridLayout(2, 3));
frame1.setSize(300, 200);

frame1.getContentPane( ).add(button1);
frame1.getContentPane( ).add(mypanel);
frame1.getContentPane( ).add(button4);
frame1.getContentPane( ).add(button5);
frame1.getContentPane( ).add(button6);
frame1.getContentPane( ).add(button7);

JDesktopPane desktop = new JDesktopPane( );
desktop.add(frame1, new Integer(1));
desktop.setOpaque(true);

// Now set up the user interface window.
Container contentPane = getContentPane( );
contentPane.add(desktop, BorderLayout.CENTER);
setSize(new Dimension(400, 300));
frame1.setVisible(true);
setVisible(true);
    }

    public static void main(String[] args) {
        new FocusExample( );
    }

    class MyButton extends JButton {
        public MyButton(String s) { super(s); }
        public boolean isFocusable( ) { return false; }
    }

    class MyPanel extends JPanel {
        public MyPanel( ) {
            super(true);
            java.util.Set upKeys = new java.util.HashSet(1);
            upKeys.add(AWTKeyStroke.getAWTKeyStroke(KeyEvent.VK_UP, 0));
            setFocusTraversalKeys(KeyboardFocusManager.UP_CYCLE_TRAVERSAL_KEYS,
                                  upKeys);
        }
        public boolean isFocusCycleRoot( ) { return true; }
    }
}
```

This program creates the seven buttons in the internal frame shown in Figure 28-2. The source shows several things worth noting. First, buttons Two and Three are contained in a special panel, called MyPanel, that has declared itself as the root of its own focus cycle. Hence, if you click on (or tab into) either of these two buttons and repeatedly press Tab, you'll see that the focus simply bounces back and forth between them. MyPanel also defines the up arrow key to move up out of the focus cycle root. (At press time, the released version of 1.4 seems to require you to hit the key twice before Tab takes you to a button outside the focus cycle; it's not clear why this would be desirable, and it may just be a bug that nobody's noticed because none of the standard components provide such keystrokes.)

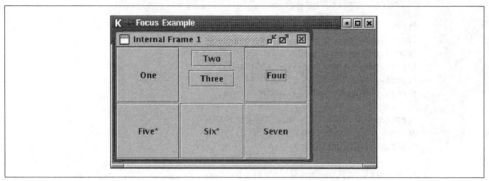

Figure 28-2. FocusExample in action

Buttons Five and Six are both of type MyButton, which sets the focusable property to false so they cannot receive focus (this is visually indicated in the example by the "*" after their names). Clicking on them leaves focus where it was, and pressing Tab when button Four has focus (as in the figure) jumps right to Seven.

The KeyboardFocusManager Class

The Swing keyboard focus manager is responsible for determining how the focus is transferred from one component to the next. It provides methods that allow your code to find out which component currently has focus, request a change in focus, and set up a different policy for focus traversal. In addition to asking about focus on an ad hoc basis, you can register a PropertyChangeListener to be notified about changes as they occur. The keyboard focus manager dispatches all FocusEvents, all WindowEvents that are related to focus, and all KeyEvents.

KeyboardFocusManager is an abstract class; Swing provides a default implementation, DefaultKeyboardFocusManager. Although it is possible to replace this default if you need to control focus at a very low level, doing so is extremely complicated and requires detailed knowledge of each platform's peer focus system. Luckily, this is almost never necessary because of the flexibility provided by FocusTraversalPolicy implementations, KeyEventDispatchers, VetoableChangeListeners, and the like, which enable you to manipulate focus on a higher level, where it relates to your immediate needs.

In addition to tracking which component is focused and receives KeyEvents, this class keeps track of the active and focused Windows (for a window to be focused means that it either contains, or is itself, the focus owner). Only a Frame or Dialog can be the focused window. A Window is active if it is focused, or if it is the first Frame or Dialog encountered while following the owner chain upward from the focused Window.

Although any given thread interacts only with a single KeyboardFocusManager, keep in mind that, in a web browser, applets from different code bases might be partitioned into separate, mutually inaccessible contexts. In such situations, each context has its own KeyboardFocusManager. Even in implementations with multiple focus managers, however, there is never more than one focused or active Window per ClassLoader.

Many of the methods in KeyboardFocusManager are intended to be used only by concrete implementations that need to access low-level internals in order to correctly manage the details of focus. As such, we'll omit discussion of them and cover the interface that is useful in more typical applications. In the unlikely event you are implementing your own manager, refer to the class Javadoc for the rest of the details. Since the new, pluggable focus architecture makes it possible to easily achieve most goals that used to require writing custom focus managers, few developers will face that task.

Constants

public static final int BACKWARD_TRAVERSAL_KEYS
public static final int DOWN_CYCLE_TRAVERSAL_KEYS
public static final int FORWARD_TRAVERSAL_KEYS
public static final int UP_CYCLE_TRAVERSAL_KEYS
> These constants are used in methods that manipulate the lists of keys with which the user can request changes of focus. They apply to both the defaultFocusTraversalKeys property of this class and the focusTraversalKeys property of the Component class.

Constructor

public KeyboardFocusManager( )
> Initialize the KeyboardFocusManager class. Since it's an abstract class, only subclasses can call this method directly. In any case, you're more likely to use the getCurrentKeyboardFocusManager( ) method in everyday coding.

Methods

public static KeyboardFocusManager getCurrentKeyboardFocusManager( )
> Retrieve the current focus manager for the context associated with the calling thread.

public static void setCurrentKeyboardFocusManager(FocusManager newManager)
> Establish a new focus manager for the calling thread's context.

public void clearGlobalFocusOwner( )

> Cause there to be no focus owner (both within Java and in the native window-ing environment). Upon completing this operation, all keyboard input from the user is discarded until the user or the application selects a new component to receive focus.

public void focusNextComponent( )

> Move focus to the component following the current focus owner according to the focus traversal policy.

public void focusPreviousComponent( )

> Move focus to the component preceding the current focus owner according to the focus traversal policy.

public void upFocusCycle( )

> Move focus up one focus cycle from the current focus owner.

public void downFocusCycle( )

> Move focus down one focus cycle from the current focus owner. Has no effect if the current focus owner is not a container that is a focus cycle root.

Properties

Several properties allow your application to learn about and manipulate the focus state. They are shown in Table 28-1. Since the class has been available only since SDK 1.4, all properties are new.

Table 28-1. KeyboardFocusManager properties

Property	Data type	get	set	Default value
activeWindow[c]	Window	•		
currentFocusCycleRoot[b, n]	Container	•		
defaultFocusTraversalKeys[b, i]	Set of AWTKeystrokes	•	•	See discussion in "Focus traversal"
defaultFocusTraversalPolicy[b]	FocusTraversalPolicy	•	•	LayoutFocusTraversalPol-icy
focusedWindow[c]	Window	•		
focusOwner[c]	Component	•		
permanentFocusOwner[c]	Component	•		

[b]bound, [c]constrained, [i]indexed (using the TRAVERSAL_KEYS constants), [n]not for general client use

The focusOwner property tracks the focus owner if there is one and if it belongs to the same context as the calling thread. Otherwise, the property is null. Similarly, the permanentFocusOwner property tracks the permanent focus owner, which is the same as the focusOwner unless a component (such as a pop up or scrollbar) has been tem-porarily given focus, in which case this property instead returns the component to which focus will shortly return.

The focusedWindow property tracks the Window that contains the focus owner if there is one and if it belongs to the same context as the calling thread. Similarly, the activeWindow property tracks the *active* Window, which is the same as the focused window unless it is not a Frame or a Dialog. If the focused window is some other class, the active window is the first Frame or Dialog that owns it, starting with the focused window and following the owner chain.

The defaultFocusTraversalPolicy property determines the focus traversal policy that is adopted by top-level components during initialization. Changing this affects future components; ones that have already been created retain their existing policies.

The defaultFocusTraversalKeys property determines the keys with which the user may, by default, request a specified focus traversal operation. The "index" for this property identifies the type of focus traversal that is of interest and must be one of the four constants listed above. The property value is a Set of AWTKeyStrokes to be used by all Windows that have not explicitly specified a different set and is inherited recursively by any child Component of these windows (again, unless that component has explicitly provided its own overriding set). (See "Using Focus Properties" for an example of manipulating these sets of keys.) The elements of the supplied Set must all be AWTKeyStrokes and must not represent any KEY_TYPED events. None of the keystrokes may already be in use by a different default focus traversal operation.

The currentFocusCycleRoot property is intended for internal use by classes implementing focus management and is listed here only because your listeners might receive property-change events about it since it's a bound property.

Listener lists

The keyboard focus manager provides several listener lists. Rather than detailing all the methods used to manipulate and query these lists (which are by now quite familiar), here is a high-level description of the purpose of each list:

PropertyChangeListener
> Allows clients to be notified of changes to any bound properties of the focus manager. Since all the properties are either bound or constrained, they all generate notifications.

VetoableChangeListener
> Allows clients to prevent impending changes to the constrained properties of the focus manager. It might seem strange to see properties in the table marked as constrained without any visible ability to "set" the properties. Even though there is no mutator method provided by this class to explicitly set, for example, the focused component, the focusNextComponent() method and its kin do affect these properties, and their operation can be vetoed. There is also a Component method to request focus, and listeners can veto that request. They can also veto changes in focus initiated by the user.

KeyEventDispatcher

Enables clients to access the stream of KeyEvents before they are processed. Each KeyEventDispatcher will be given a chance to examine the event (in the order in which the dispatchers were added) and may halt further processing of the event. Only if none of the registered dispatchers consume the event will the keyboard focus manager dispatch it to the focus owner in the normal way.

KeyEventPostProcessor

Enables clients to access the stream of KeyEvents after they have been handled by the focus owner. Each KeyEventPostProcessor is given a chance to examine the events (in the order in which they were added) and perform any desired post-processing. Each may also halt further post-processing of events.

The DefaultKeyboardFocusManager Class

The DefaultFocusManager class is a concrete implementation of the abstract KeyboardFocusManager class, performing the standard focus-related tasks for AWT and Swing applications. Because there are so many places you can plug in your own filters and behavior, you're far less likely to want to replace this class with your own than in previous Java releases. (In fact, readers who have access to the earlier edition of this book may want to compare the following example with the one starting on page 1125 in that edition, to see just how much simpler life has become! The new code is shorter, more focused, and more elegant, even though it has added support for recursively handling nested containers.)

The default keyboard focus manager handles all of the behavior described at the start of this section and any behavior expected of a Java program, including focus traversal keys, delivery of keystrokes to the focus owner, menu activation in response to keystrokes that were not otherwise consumed, and the like. By registering focus traversal policies and keystroke sets, property change listeners (often vetoable), and key event dispatchers and post-processors, you can achieve an unprecedented degree of control over focus behavior in an elegant, encapsulated way.

The FocusTraversalPolicy Class

The FocusTraversalPolicy class is abstract, providing a convenient framework for the implementation of arbitrary focus traversal policies. Five methods must be implemented:

public Component getFirstComponent(Container focusCycleRoot)
Return the first component in the traversal cycle for the specified container. This is the component given focus when traversal "wraps" past the end of the cycle.

public Component getLastComponent(Container focusCycleRoot)
Return the last component in the traversal cycle for the specified container.

public Component getDefaultComponent(Container focusCycleRoot)

> Return the default component to give focus. This is the component that is given focus when it first traverses down into the focus cycle root. It may be different from the first component in the cycle.

public Component getComponentAfter(Container focusCycleRoot,
> *Component aComponent)*

> Return the component that comes after the specified one in the traversal cycle. focusCycleRoot must be a focus cycle root of the component.

public Component getComponentBefore(Container focusCycleRoot,
> *Component aComponent)*

> Return the component that comes before the specified one in the traversal cycle. focusCycleRoot must be a focus cycle root of the component.

There is also one method you can override; the default definition is usually fine:

public Component getInitialComponent(Container focusCycleRoot)

> Return the component that should be given focus when the container is first made visible. The standard implementation calls getDefaultComponent( ).

A couple of focus traversal policies are provided. Swing applications with a standard L&F (or any other L&F that extends BasicLookAndFeel) use LayoutFocusTraversalPolicy as their default policy for all containers.

Writing Your Own Focus Traversal Policy

Here's a new focus traversal with distinctly different behavior than the default policy. Our focus manager moves the focus through a series of buttons in alphabetical order, according to the button labels. This is not a completely general example, as it won't transfer focus to or from components other than buttons, and you may think you'd *never* want a user interface like the example program that demonstrates it. Although you'd be completely right, notice that changing just a few details would give you something very much like an icon view of a directory, allowing you to tab through files in alphabetical order regardless of the icons' physical order.

```java
//  AlphaButtonPolicy.java
//
import java.awt.*;
import java.util.*;
import javax.swing.*;

public class AlphaButtonPolicy extends FocusTraversalPolicy {

    private SortedMap getSortedButtons(Container focusCycleRoot) {
        if (focusCycleRoot == null) {
            throw new IllegalArgumentException("focusCycleRoot can't be null");
        }
        SortedMap result = new TreeMap( );  // Will sort all buttons by text
        sortRecursive(result, focusCycleRoot);
```

```
        return result;
    }

    private void sortRecursive(Map buttons, Container container) {
        for (int i = 0; i < container.getComponentCount(); i++) {
            Component c = container.getComponent(i);
            if (c instanceof JButton) {   // Found another button to sort
                buttons.put(((JButton)c).getText(), c);
            }
            if (c instanceof Container) {   // Found a container to search
                sortRecursive(buttons, (Container)c);
            }
        }
    }

    // The rest of the code implements the FocusTraversalPolicy interface.

    public Component getFirstComponent(Container focusCycleRoot) {
        SortedMap buttons = getSortedButtons(focusCycleRoot);
        if (buttons.isEmpty()) { return null; }
        return (Component)buttons.get(buttons.firstKey());
    }

    public Component getLastComponent(Container focusCycleRoot) {
        SortedMap buttons = getSortedButtons(focusCycleRoot);
        if (buttons.isEmpty()) { return null; }
        return (Component)buttons.get(buttons.lastKey());
    }

    public Component getDefaultComponent(Container focusCycleRoot) {
        return getFirstComponent(focusCycleRoot);
    }

    public Component getComponentAfter(Container focusCycleRoot,
                                       Component aComponent) {
        if (!(aComponent instanceof JButton)) { return null; }
        SortedMap buttons = getSortedButtons(focusCycleRoot);
        // Find all buttons after the current one.
        String nextName = ((JButton)aComponent).getText() + "\0";
        SortedMap nextButtons = buttons.tailMap(nextName);
        if (nextButtons.isEmpty()) {   // Wrapped back to beginning
            if (!buttons.isEmpty()) {
                return (Component)buttons.get(buttons.firstKey());
            }
            return null;   // Degenerate case of no buttons
        }
        return (Component)nextButtons.get(nextButtons.firstKey());
    }

    public Component getComponentBefore(Container focusCycleRoot,
                                        Component aComponent) {
        if (!(aComponent instanceof JButton)) { return null; }
```

```
        SortedMap buttons = getSortedButtons(focusCycleRoot);
        SortedMap prevButtons =  // Find all buttons before this one.
            buttons.headMap(((JButton)aComponent).getText());
        if (prevButtons.isEmpty()) {  // Wrapped back to end
            if (!buttons.isEmpty()) {
                return (Component)buttons.get(buttons.lastKey());
            }
            return null;  // Degenerate case of no buttons
        }
        return (Component)prevButtons.get(prevButtons.lastKey());
    }
}
```

The first two methods in this class set up a SortedMap that contains all the buttons present in the container for which focus is being transferred, sorted by name. The first simply sets up context in which the second can perform a recursive descent through the container hierarchy, grabbing any buttons found. The rest of the class uses this map, and the wonderful power of the Java Collections framework, to implement the contract of the FocusTraversalPolicy with respect to alphabetically-sorted button labels.

If you plan to use such a policy with containers that held a large number of components, you may want to consider adding a cache to keep track of the sorted maps for each container the policy is asked to manage. This would save time during focus transfers, at the cost of complexity (the policy would have to listen for container events on each container it was managing so it would know when it needed to invalidate its cache entry).

Here is a simple program that demonstrates the new focus traversal policy:

```
//FocusTraversalExample.java
//
import java.awt.*;
import java.awt.event.*;
import javax.swing.*;

public class FocusTraversalExample extends JPanel {

    public FocusTraversalExample() {
        setLayout(new GridLayout(6, 1));
        JButton button1 = new JButton("Texas");
        JButton button2 = new JButton("Vermont");
        JButton button3 = new JButton("Florida");
        JButton button4 = new JButton("Alabama");
        JButton button5 = new JButton("Minnesota");
        JButton button6 = new JButton("California");

        setBackground(Color.lightGray);
        add(button1);
        add(button2);
        add(button3);
        add(button4);
```

```
        add(button5);
        add(button6);
    }

    public static void main(String[] args) {
        JFrame frame = new JFrame("Alphabetized Button Focus Traversal");
        frame.setFocusTraversalPolicy(new AlphaButtonPolicy());
        frame.setDefaultCloseOperation(JFrame.EXIT_ON_CLOSE);
        frame.setContentPane(new FocusTraversalExample());
        frame.setSize(400, 300);
        frame.setVisible(true);
    }
}
```

The example is quite straightforward. The call to setFocusTraversalPolicy() installs our new focus manager. Figure 28-3 shows what the program looks like.

Figure 28-3. JButtons using the alphabetized button focus manager

Multithreading Issues in Swing

As we mentioned at the beginning of the book, threading considerations play a very important role in Swing. This isn't too surprising if you think about the fact that Java is a highly multithreaded environment, but there is only a single display on which all components must render themselves in an organized, cooperative way. Some of the low-level code that interacts with peers in the native windowing system is not reentrant, which means that it can't be invoked safely while it's in the middle of doing something. Of course, that's exactly what might happen if different threads interact with it! Because of this fundamental limitation, there would have been no real benefit to undertaking the major effort of making the Java methods in the Swing components themselves thread-safe—and indeed, with few exceptions, they are not.

In order to address this issue, Swing requires that all activity that interacts with components take place on a single thread, known as the event dispatch thread. This also allows Swing to consolidate repaints and otherwise improve the efficiency of the drawing process.

This restriction actually takes effect only after a component is *realized*, meaning that it's been painted on-screen or is ready to be painted. A top-level component is realized when it is made visible or has its pack( ) method called. At that point, any components it contains are also realized, and any components added to it later are immediately realized. This does mean, though, that it's safe to set up your application's interface components in your main application thread, as long as the last thing your code does to them is realize them. This is the way our code examples are structured. It is similarly safe to set up an applet's interface objects in its init( ) method.

However, this does place a burden on you as a developer to be aware of the threads that might invoke your methods. If it's possible that an arbitrary application thread can call a method that would interact with Swing components, that activity needs to be separated and deferred to a method that runs on the event dispatch thread.

By confining updates of component visual state to the event dispatch thread, you keep changes in sync with the repainting requests of the RepaintManager and avoid potential race conditions.

It is always safe to call the repaint( ) and revalidate( ) methods defined in JComponent. These methods arrange for work to be performed later in the event dispatch thread, using the mechanisms described below. It's also always safe to add or remove event listeners, as this has no effect on an ongoing event dispatch.

When Is Thread Safety an Issue?

It's important to understand when you need to worry about this and when you do not. In many situations, you'll update the state of your user interface only in response to various user events (such as a mouse click). In this case, you can freely update your components since your event-handling methods (in your listeners) are automatically invoked by the event dispatch thread.

The only time you have to worry about updating the state of a Swing component is when the request for the update comes from some other thread. The simplest (and very common) example is when you want to display an asynchronous progress bar. Or suppose you want a display driven by some outside process responsible for notifying your application when the world changes, such as a sports score ticker that shows the scores of a collection of games as they are being played. A separate server process might push new scores to your client program. This program would have some sort of socket (or higher-level protocol) listener thread to handle the input from the server. This new data needs to be reflected in the user interface. At this point, you'd need to ensure that the updates were made in the event dispatch thread.

Another common scenario involves responding to a user request that may take a long time to be processed. Such requests might need to access a database, invoke a remote method on an RMI or CORBA object, load new Java classes, etc. In situations like these, the event-handling thread must not be held up while lengthy processing takes place. If it is, the user interface would become completely unresponsive until the call completes. The correct approach is to execute the lengthy call in a separate thread and update the user interface when the call eventually returns or as information becomes available. Once again, this update is no longer happening in the event dispatch thread, so we need to do something special to make it work.

One strategy for implementing this type of call is to use a special "worker" thread responsible for executing the lengthy call and then updating the user interface. The Swing team provides a sample implementation of this idea in a class called SwingWorker. This class, as well as a discussion of its purpose, can be found on the Swing Connection at *http://java.sun.com/products/jfc/tsc/articles/threads/threads2.html*. We include a slightly simpler (but less reusable) example of the worker concept in *InvokeExample.java* below.

Don't be fooled

You might think that you'd be safe calling the various fireXX( ) methods defined by certain Swing components and models. However, it's important to remember that while these methods do create Event objects and send them to registered listeners, this does *not* imply that these events are executed in the event dispatch thread. In fact, the methods called on the listeners are invoked just like all other Java method calls; the argument just happens to be an event object. So even if you're updating the user interface from another thread by firing some sort of event (perhaps to indicate that the model's state has changed), you still need to use the methods described below to ensure that the processing takes place in the event dispatch thread.

Updating Components from the Event Dispatch Thread

Swing provides two methods that allow you to execute code in the event-dispatch thread. These are static methods, defined by SwingUtilities, called invokeAndWait( ) and invokeLater( ). Both of these methods allow you to execute an arbitrary block of code in the event dispatch thread. The invokeAndWait( ) method blocks until the code has completed executing while invokeLater( ) just adds your code to the event queue and returns immediately. You should usually use invokeLater( ) rather than invokeAndWait( ).

You may be wondering how Swing manages to add arbitrary code to the event queue. Here's how it works. Both of the methods we just mentioned take a single Runnable as a parameter. This Runnable may be defined to do whatever you want. Typically, the Runnable's run( ) method performs some sort of update to the state of one or more components. When SwingUtilities receives the Runnable, it passes it to a class called SystemEventQueueUtilities, which wraps it in an instance of a special AWTEvent subclass (a private inner class called SystemEventQueueUtilities.RunnableEvent) and adds the new event to the system event queue. When the event thread gets around to running the special event, the processing of the event results in the Runnable's run() method being executed.

Figure 28-4 shows a more detailed breakdown of what's going on under the hood. Once the event is posted to the system event queue, the call to invokeLater() returns immediately. If this were an invokeAndWait() call, the calling thread would wait() until the event was executed, and then the processRunnableEvent() method would notify() the waiting thread that the Runnable had been executed. Only then would invokeAndWait() return. Note that SystemEventQueueUtilities and its inner classes RunnableEvent and RunnableTarget are non-public. We show them here only to give you an understanding of what's going on behind the scenes. The EventQueue class is part of java.awt.

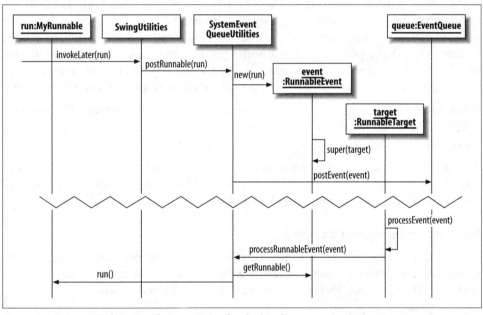

Figure 28-4. SwingUtilities.invokeLater() (under the hood)

Methods

Here are the method signatures for the SwingUtilities methods we just described. The rest of the SwingUtilities class was described in Chapter 27.

public static void invokeAndWait(Runnable doRun)
  throws InterruptedException, InvocationTargetException

> Place a special event onto the system event queue. When processed, this event simply executes doRun's run( ) method. The invokeAndWait( ) call does not return until the run( ) method finishes. If the run( ) method throws an exception, it is caught, and an InvocationTargetException is thrown by invokeAndWait( ). An InterruptedException is thrown if the execution of the Runnable's run( ) method is interrupted for any reason.

public static void invokeLater(Runnable doRun)

> Place a special event onto the system event queue. When processed, this event simply executes doRun's run( ) method. The invokeLater( ) call returns immediately after the event has been added to the queue. Note that any exceptions thrown by the Runnable's run( ) method are caught and ignored.

There are a number of caveats surrounding the use of invokeAndWait( ) that don't apply when using invokeLater( ), which is why Sun recommends you use the latter. Fundamentally, invokeAndWait( ) causes your thread to block for a potentially long time, so you need to be careful that it does not hold any locks that might be needed by other threads, or performance will suffer (in the worst case, deadlock might even cause your application to freeze). Also, if you try to call this method, and you happen to be running in the event dispatch thread, you'll be rewarded with an exception.

If you can't tell by inspecting your code whether a particular method will always (or never) be called by the event dispatch thread, you can check using SwingUtilities. isEventDispatchThread( ) and take the appropriate action at runtime.

For situations in which you want to update your user interface at scheduled or periodic intervals, you'll likely find the javax.swing.Timer class helpful. It manages all these threading issues for you, providing a nice programmatic interface.

Managing synchronization properly

Here is an example that shows three ways you might try to invoke a long-running method in response to a user-generated event. Only one of these strategies works correctly. The other two show the types of things you should avoid.

```
// InvokeExample.java
//
import javax.swing.*;
import java.awt.*;
import java.awt.event.*;

public class InvokeExample {
  private static JButton good = new JButton("Good");
  private static JButton bad = new JButton("Bad");
  private static JButton bad2 = new JButton("Bad2");
  private static JLabel resultLabel = new JLabel("Ready", JLabel.CENTER);
```

```java
public static void main(String[] args) {
  JFrame f = new JFrame( );
  f.setDefaultCloseOperation(JFrame.EXIT_ON_CLOSE);

  // Layout
  JPanel p = new JPanel( );
  p.setOpaque(true);
  p.setLayout(new FlowLayout( ));
  p.add(good);
  p.add(bad);
  p.add(bad2);

  Container c = f.getContentPane( );
  c.setLayout(new BorderLayout( ));
  c.add(p, BorderLayout.CENTER);
  c.add(resultLabel, BorderLayout.SOUTH);

  // Listeners
  good.addActionListener(new ActionListener( ) {
    public void actionPerformed(ActionEvent ev) {
      resultLabel.setText("Working...");
      setEnabled(false);

      // We're going to do something that takes a long time, so we spin off a
      // thread and update the display when we're done.
      Thread worker = new Thread( ) {
        public void run( ) {
          // Something that takes a long time. In real life, this might be a DB
          // query, remote method invocation, etc.
          try {
            Thread.sleep(5000);
          }
          catch (InterruptedException ex) {}

          // Report the result using invokeLater( ).
          SwingUtilities.invokeLater(new Runnable( ) {
            public void run( ) {
              resultLabel.setText("Ready");
              setEnabled(true);
            }
          });
        }
      };

      worker.start( ); // So we don't hold up the dispatch thread
    }
  });

  bad.addActionListener(new ActionListener( ) {
    public void actionPerformed(ActionEvent ev) {
      resultLabel.setText("Working . . .");
      setEnabled(false);
```

```
      // We're going to do the same thing, but not in a separate thread.
      try {
        Thread.sleep(5000); // The dispatch thread is starving!
      }
      catch (InterruptedException ex) {}

      // Report the result.
      resultLabel.setText("Ready");
      setEnabled(true);
    }
  });

  bad2.addActionListener(new ActionListener( ) {
    public void actionPerformed(ActionEvent ev) {
      resultLabel.setText("Working...");
      setEnabled(false);

      // The wrong way to use invokeLater( ). The runnable( ) shouldn't starve the
      // dispatch thread.
      SwingUtilities.invokeLater(new Runnable( ) {
        public void run( ) {
          try {
            Thread.sleep(5000); // The dispatch thread is starving!
          }
          catch (InterruptedException ex) {}

          resultLabel.setText("Ready");
          setEnabled(true);
        }
      });
    }
  });

  f.setSize(300, 100);
  f.setVisible(true);
}

// Allows us to turn the buttons on or off while we work
static void setEnabled(boolean b) {
  good.setEnabled(b);
  bad.setEnabled(b);
  bad2.setEnabled(b);
}
}
```

In the first listener ("Good"), we use a worker thread to execute our lengthy process.
In this thread's run( ) method, we execute our code (in this case, just a sleep( ) call)
and then use invokeLater( ) to update the display. This is the proper strategy.

In the next listener ("Bad"), we show what happens if we run this code directly in the
event listener. As you'd expect, any attempt to resize or repaint the display fails while
we have taken over the dispatch thread.

Finally, we show another incorrect attempt ("Bad2"). In this case, we use invokeLater( ), but we use it incorrectly. The problem here is that the run( ) method called by invokeLater( ) takes a long time to execute. It's just as bad to have a long-running method in an invokeLater( ) call as it is to perform it directly in your event listener code: they are both run in the event dispatch thread—the whole point of invokeLater( ) being to run your code on the event dispatch thread!

Figure 28-5 shows the display after clicking each of the three buttons and then covering part of the display with another window. In the first bad case, our label update and the disabling of the buttons doesn't even occur, since we never got back into the event queue to let those updates happen. In the second bad case, those things are able to occur before we put the dispatch thread to sleep, but we have still made a big mess of things by holding up the event queue.

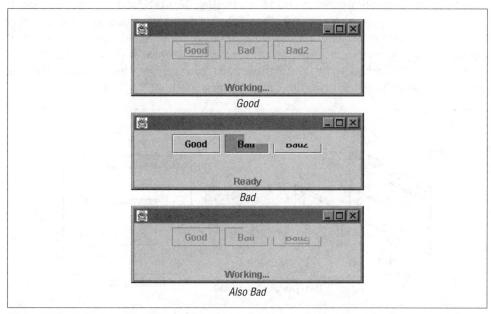

Figure 28-5. Correct and incorrect management of the event dispatch thread

When you run this example, try resizing the frame (or covering it with another window) to see how the different strategies perform. The key lesson here is that the system event queue uses a single thread to execute events, so any sort of long-running processing should be kept out of the event queue.

Lightweight Versus Heavyweight Components

The issue of lightweight versus heavyweight components has complicated Swing since its inception. The concept of lightweight components managed entirely by Java code is, of course, one of the major benefits introduced by Swing. What has confused the majority of programmers from the start is the issue of *z-order*, or layering, between Swing lightweight components and AWT heavyweight components.

Understanding the Z-Order

In Swing, it might help to think of a heavyweight component as an artist's easel. Top-level components in Swing (JWindow, JDialog, JApplet, and JFrame) are heavyweight, while everything else isn't. Lightweight components added to those top-level heavyweights can be thought of as drawings on the canvas of each easel. Therefore, if another heavyweight component (another easel) is moved in front of the original easel, or even attached to it, the lightweight paintings on the original easel are obscured. Figure 28-6 demonstrates this analogy.

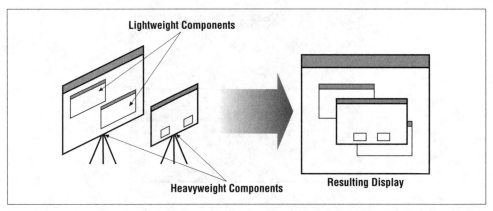

Figure 28-6. Consider heavyweight components as easels and lightweight components as drawings

The same is true for how Swing interprets the z-order of lightweight and heavyweight components, even in a container. If a heavyweight component is added to a container that has lightweight components, the heavyweight is always on top; the lightweight components must share the same z-order as the parent container. In addition, lightweight components cannot draw themselves outside the container (easel) they reside in, or they are clipped.

Mixing Swing and AWT

Our first bit of advice is: *don't do it*. If you can get around mixing the two (by solely using lightweight components), then you'll save yourself a mountain of testing grief. That being said, let's discuss some of the common problems that you're likely to run into if you decide, or are forced, to make the attempt.

Overlapping heavyweight and lightweight components

As we mentioned above, the heavyweight component always displays itself on top despite the intended z-order. The basic strategy is to ensure that lightweight components and heavyweight components in the same container do not overlap. On that note, Table 28-2 shows a list of layout managers and panes that can and cannot be used to mix lightweight and heavyweight components.

Table 28-2. Heavyweight-friendly Swing layout managers and panes

Layout manager	Can be used to mix heavyweight and lightweight?
BorderLayout	Yes
BoxLayout	Yes
CardLayout	Yes
FlowLayout	Yes
GridBagLayout	Yes
GridLayout	Yes
JLayeredPane	No
JScrollPane	No
JSplitPane	Yes
JTabbedPane	Yes*
OverlayLayout	No
SpringLayout	No

*In some cases, this layout manager may still fail.

Heavyweight components in front of lightweight menus

Heavyweight components are always drawn in front of lightweight menus. This creates another (somewhat comical) Swing and AWT problem. While the menu bar is usually not disturbed, any menus that are drawn are placed *behind* the component. Hence, a user may bring up a menu but be unable to select a specific menu item.

Figure 28-7 shows four heavyweight panels positioned in front of a lightweight Edit menu. While you can still select a menu, you can't see it—the repainting mechanism in Java redraws the heavyweight panels over the menus as they are activated. Because anchored menus are essentially combinations of buttons and pop-up menus, you will have the same problem if you attach a lightweight pop-up menu to a heavyweight component.

Figure 28-7. Lightweight menus obscured by heavyweight panels

Pop ups

Pop-up components are easy targets for these problems. Pop-up components include elements found in Swing menus, pop-up menus, and combo boxes. These components get into trouble because they may be called upon to display themselves outside the confines of their heavyweight top-level container. For example, if you activate a pop-up menu in a component near the bottom of a JFrame, the pop up might extend beyond the bottom of the frame when it is raised. If this is the case, then it cannot be rendered using a lightweight component; if it is, it is clipped against the container boundary.

Swing knows that if this is the case, it can use a heavyweight AWT Window to display the pop up instead. However, what if you need to include a heavyweight component inside a container in whi'ch pop ups are used? Fortunately, pop-up components in Swing contain a property that allows them to switch from lightweight to heavyweight to display themselves. Incidentally, this is a type of behavior that you may wish to mimic if you create your own pop-up components.

This single boolean property is called lightWeightPopupEnabled. It can be set to true or false, depending on how you want Swing to display the component. If lightWeightPopupEnabled is true, the component uses a lightweight component to display itself if it is wholly contained inside a top-level component, and uses a Panel otherwise. If lightWeightPopupEnabled is false, the component uses either a heavyweight AWT Panel or a Window to display itself, depending on where it is displayed. Table 28-3 shows which type of component Swing uses in various scenarios.

Table 28-3. The lightWeightPopupEnabled property

lightWeightPopupEnabled	Drawn inside the top-level container	Drawn outside the top-level container
true	Lightweight Popup	Heavyweight Window
false	Heavyweight Panel	Heavyweight Window

For example, you can get around the lightweight menu problem discussed earlier by setting the lightWeightPopupEnabled property to false on each of the pop-up portions of the menus:

```
JMenu menu = new JMenu("Edit");
menu.getPopupMenu( ).setLightWeightPopupEnabled(false);
```

Although there will be a noticeable flicker as the components struggle to repaint themselves, the menu should end up on the right side of the heavyweight component included in the container. If you plan to mix lightweight and heavyweight components, you should always set the lightWeightPopupEnabled property for any pop ups in the application to false, including menus.

Heavyweight components in JScrollPane

There really isn't a workaround to make heavyweight components work correctly in a JScrollPane. What invariably happens is that the component inside the JScrollPane object fails to clip properly when it is placed inside the pane, and visible artifacts are easy to pick up. Stay as far away from this as you possibly can. Figure 28-8 shows the problem of placing heavyweight components in a JScrollPane object.

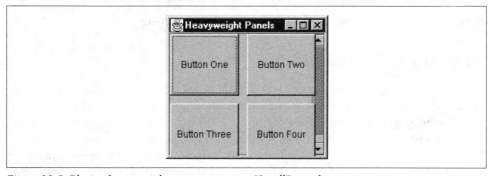

Figure 28-8. Placing heavyweight components in a JScrollPane object

Heavyweight components inside internal frames

Placing heavyweight components inside internal frames is also an inherently bad idea. The problem here is that internal frames can, by design, overlap. If an overlap occurs, and the internal frame with the heavyweight component is on the bottom, the component is still drawn on top of the overlapping internal frame. Figure 28-9 shows what happens when a heavyweight component in one internal frame overlaps another internal frame. Again, stay away from this scenario.

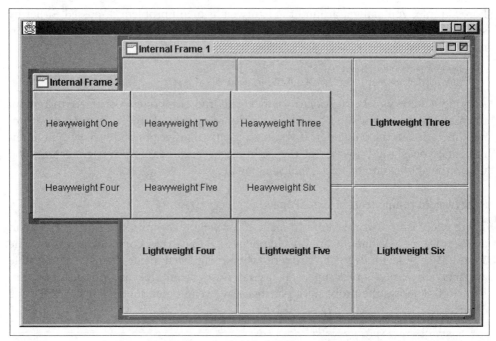

Figure 28-9. Using heavyweight components inside of an internal frame

Painting and Repainting

Repainting is a fundamental task for a graphical application, but one that is rarely explained in the detail you'd expect for something so central. This section is intended to give you a better feel for how painting and repainting via the repaint manager and JComponent work. You typically do not need to get involved with the RepaintManager class, and only the extremely brave override it. However, there are some instances in which a firm understanding of the repaint manager can help avoid confusion, and, starting with SDK 1.4, Swing provides a way for savvy code to take advantage of accelerated graphics hardware when it is available.

Swing Responsibilities

Recall that Swing uses lightweight components, which are drawn inside heavyweight top-level containers. Since the operating system has no knowledge of lightweight components (that's what makes them lightweight), it can't help coordinate their repainting. To continue the analogy first presented in the earlier lightweight and heavyweight discussion, Swing is responsible for painting and repainting everything inside its own easels. Swing delegates this duty to a RepaintManager class, which organizes and schedules repainting when told to do so.

The RepaintManager Class

The RepaintManager class is responsible for keeping track of the components (and the components' parts) that have become *dirty*, which means that they need to be repainted. Note that the "dirty region" does not necessarily include the entire region of affected components, but often only portions of them. The RepaintManager is also charged with the second responsibility of revalidating components that have been marked invalid. Both responsibilities ultimately result in the same thing: redrawing the component.

There is only one RepaintManager per thread group. Like the FocusManager class, you don't instantiate one directly. Instead, the static methods currentManager( ) and setCurrentManager( ) retrieve and set the current repaint manager, respectively. (Note that there is no RepaintManager.getCurrentManager( ) method.) Once a repaint manager is activated for a thread group, it remains active until it is replaced or that thread group is shut down.

You typically access the current manager as follows:

```
RepaintManager rm = RepaintManager.currentManager( );
```

At the heart of the RepaintManager are two data structures: a Hashtable of component references and their rectangular regions that need to be repainted, and a Vector of invalidated components. You can add component regions to the hashtable of dirty regions with the addDirtyRegion( ) method. Likewise, you can add a component to the invalidation vector with a call to addInvalidComponent( ). If you wish to remove a component from the invalidation vector, you can remove it with a call to removeInvalidComponent( ).

Here are some important rules for working with the repaint manager:

- If a component has a dirty region on the repaint queue, and another region from the same component is added, the repaint manager takes the rectangular union of the two sections. As a result, there is never more than one dirty region per component on the queue at any time.

- If a component has been invalidated with the addInvalidComponent( ) method, the RepaintManager invalidates the first ancestor of this component to return true for the isValidateRoot( ) method (typically a container). This has the desirable side effect of invalidating all the components below it.

- Repainting and revalidating are handled via *work requests*, which are Runnable objects sent to the system event queue. Since the work request repaints and revalidates any components that need it at the time it is processed, it doesn't make sense (and would be wasteful) to have more than one in the event queue for each top-level container. The SystemEventQueueUtilities class takes care of this optimization for the repaint manager.

You can get the current dirty region for each component by using the getDirtyRegion( ) method. If you want to mark the entire component as dirty, forcing a complete redraw on its next paint, use the markCompletelyDirty( ) method. You can check to see if an entire component's region is marked as dirty with the isCompletelyDirty( ) method if this will let your paint operation run more efficiently because it doesn't need to worry about optimizing or clipping its drawing operations. To remove a component's dirty region from the list, use the markCompletelyClean( ) method.

The RepaintManager class is equipped with a double-buffering mechanism, which it provides as a service to all JComponent objects. By default, it is enabled for all components that wish to take advantage of it, unless the operating system is already performing double-buffering natively (as Mac OS X does). Many built-in components use double-buffering effectively for smooth drawing. You can manually override the operation of this feature using the setDoubleBufferingEnabled( ) method, but there should be no reason to do this because its default value is optimized for the graphics environment. The maximum size of the double buffer is, by default, the size of the entire screen. If for some reason you need to, you can alter it by calling setDoubleBufferMaximumSize( ). To find out the current setting, use getDoubleBufferMaximumSize( ).

SDK 1.4 introduced a new VolatileImage class that allows components to take advantage of accelerated graphics hardware for extremely efficient double-buffering. Because using such hardware presents some special conditions that don't arise with normal Image buffers, components must explicitly request them via the getVolatileOffscreenBuffer( ) method. It's worth learning how to use this method (and the VolatileImage class) because of the potential performance boost it can give your components.

Key methods

The Swing repaint manager works closely with a few key methods in JComponent: paint( ), repaint( ), revalidate( ), and paintImmediately( ). A call to repaint( ) at the component level results in a region being added to the dirty list queue and, consequently, scheduled for repainting. This sets up a work request that is placed in the system event queue. Once the work request is processed, the current RepaintManager calls back the paintImmediately( ) method of the component. This method finally renders the dirty portion of the component (without delay, as it's running in the event dispatch thread).

The revalidate( ) method in JComponent adds the component to the RepaintManager invalidation queue. At that point, the revalidation of the component and its ancestors, if necessary, is sent as a work request to the system event queue. Once the request is dequeued, the method calls the validate( ) method of the appropriate container, recomputing its layout to account for the changes that prompted the revalidation request. Figure 28-10 shows the RepaintManager at work repainting dirty regions and revalidating invalid components.

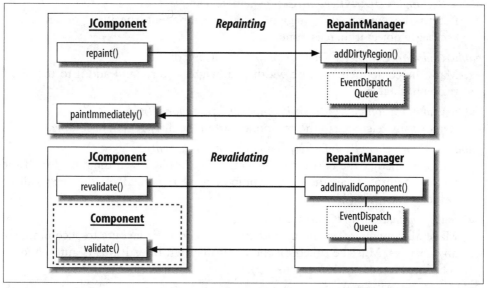

Figure 28-10. Repainting and revalidating with JComponent and the RepaintManager

Methods

public static RepaintManager currentManager(JComponent comp)
Return the current RepaintManager. If there isn't one available, Swing initializes one and sets it for this thread group.

public static void setCurrentManager(RepaintManager aRepaintManager)
Set the current RepaintManager for the invoker's thread group. It's unlikely you'll ever use this method.

public void addInvalidComponent(JComponent invalidComponent)
Add a component to the invalidation vector. The method searches for the first ancestor component that returns true for isValidateRoot( ) and queues a validation and repaint for that component, and consequently all components below it. Generally, JComponent's revalidate( ) method calls this for you.

public void removeInvalidComponent(JComponent component)
Remove a component from the invalidation vector.

public void addDirtyRegion(JComponent c, int x, int y, int w, int h)
Add a rectangular region for a specific component to the hashtable of dirty regions that need to be repainted. If a rectangular region for that component already exists in the hashtable, a rectangle that encompasses both regions is calculated and placed on the hashtable to represent that component. There is at

most one rectangular region for each component on the dirty-region hashtable at any time.

public Rectangle getDirtyRegion(JComponent aComponent)
Return the current dirty region for the component specified, or an empty `Rectangle` object if there is none.

public void markCompletelyDirty(JComponent aComponent)
Mark the component's entire width and height as dirty and add it to the dirty-region hashtable.

public void markCompletelyClean(JComponent aComponent)
Remove any reference to the component from the dirty-region hashtable.

public boolean isCompletelyDirty(JComponent aComponent)
Indicate whether the entire component has been placed on the dirty list. If the method returns `true`, the entire component is repainted on the next call to `paintDirtyRegions( )`.

public void validateInvalidComponents( )
Make all containers on the invalidation list redo their layouts to accommodate any changes. Must be called on the event dispatch thread; this is automatically scheduled by `addInvalidComponent( )`.

public void paintDirtyRegions( )
Make each of the dirty regions immediately repaint themselves. Must be called on the event dispatch thread; this is automatically scheduled by `addDirtyRegion( )`.

public String toString( )
Return a textual description of the state of the `RepaintManager` for debugging.

public Image getOffscreenBuffer(Component c, int proposedWidth, int proposedHeight)
Return an offscreen `Image` that can be used as a double buffer. The size of the double buffer is typically set to the proposed width and height passed in, unless it violates a preset maximum buffer size.

public Image getVolatileOffscreenBuffer(Component c, int proposedWidth,
  int proposedHeight)
Return an offscreen `VolatileImage` that can be used as a double buffer, taking advantage of accelerated graphics hardware. Components coded to handle the special requirements of working with `VolatileImage` (primarily, the occasional need to recreate the image if the operating system has stolen its resources while you were trying to use it) can get a performance boost by using this method. The size of the double buffer is typically set to the proposed width and height passed in, unless it violates a preset maximum buffer size.

public void setDoubleBufferMaximumSize(java.awt.Dimension d)
Set the maximum size of the `RepaintManager` object's offscreen drawing buffer.

public Dimension getDoubleBufferMaximumSize( )

Retrieve the maximum size of the `RepaintManager` object's offscreen drawing buffer.

public void setDoubleBufferingEnabled(boolean aFlag)

Activate or deactivate the double-buffering mechanism. You should generally leave this alone, as it is initialized to the right value for the system graphics environment.

public boolean isDoubleBufferingEnabled( )

Return a `boolean` indicating whether the double buffering mechanism is enabled for this `RepaintManager` object.

Creating Your Own Component

So you've been bitten by the bug. There isn't a component anywhere in the Swing library that fits your needs, and you've decided that it's time to write your own. Unfortunately, you're dreading the prospect of creating one. Maybe you've heard somewhere that it is a complex task, or your jaw is still bouncing on the floor after browsing through some of the Swing component source code.

This section should help dispel those fears. Creating your own component isn't hard—just extend the `JComponent` class with one of your own and away you go! On the other hand, getting it to behave or even display itself correctly can take a bit of patience and fine-tuning. So here is a step-by-step guide to steer you clear of the hidden "gotchas" that lurk in the task of creating a component.

When creating Swing components, it's always a good idea to adhere to the Java-Beans standards. Not only can such components be used programmatically, but they can also be plugged into one of the growing number of GUI-builder tools. Therefore, whenever possible, we try to highlight areas that you can work on to make your components more JavaBeans-friendly.

Getting Started

First things first. If you haven't already, you should read through the `JComponent` section of Chapter 3. This will help you get a feel for the kinds of features you can expect in a Swing component and which ones you might want to use (or even disable) in your own component. If you are creating a component that is intended as a container,* be sure to glance at the overview sections on focus policies and layout managers as well. Remember that you can use any layout manager with a Swing component.

---

* This is sort of confusing. Because of the class hierarchy of `JComponent`, all classes that extend it are capable of acting as containers. For example, it is legal to add a `JProgressBar` to a `JSlider`. Clearly, the slider is not meant to act as a container, but Swing will allow it nevertheless...with undefined results.

After you've done that, you're ready to start. Let's go through some steps that will help you flesh out that component idea into working Swing code.

You should have a model and a UI delegate

If you really want to develop your idea into a true Swing component, you should adhere to the MVC-based architecture of Swing. This means defining models and UI delegates for each component. Recall that the model is in charge of storing the state information for the component. Models typically implement their own model interface, which outlines the accessors and methods that the model must support. The UI delegate is responsible for painting the component and handling any input events that are generated. The UI-delegate object always extends the `ComponentUI` class, which is the base class for all UI-delegate objects. Finally, the component class itself extends the abstract `JComponent` and ties together the model and the delegate.

Figure 28-11 shows the key classes and interfaces involved in creating a Swing component. The shaded boxes indicate items that the programmer must provide. This includes the model, the basic UI delegate and its type class, and an implementation of the component to bundle the model and UI delegate pieces together. Finally, you may need to create your own model interface if a suitable one does not exist.

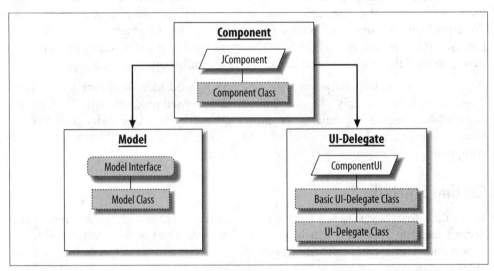

Figure 28-11. The three parts of a Swing component

If you wish to support multiple L&Fs with your component, you may consider breaking your UI-delegate class down into an abstract "skeleton," implementing functionality that is independent of L&F (such as those classes found in `javax.swing.plaf.basic`), as well as functionality specific to each L&F (such as those in the `javax.swing.plaf.metal` package or the `com.sun.java.swing.plaf.motif` package). Some common functionality that you might find in the former is the ability to handle various mouse or keyboard events, while painting and sizing the component is typically the domain of the latter. See Chapter 26 for more details on L&Fs.

So now that we know what we have to build, let's continue our discussion with a look at each piece, starting with the model.

Creating a Model

The model of the object is responsible for storing the state data of the component. Models are not hard to build, but they are not necessarily easy to get right either. Here are some important tips to think about when working with models.

Reuse or extend existing models whenever possible

Creating a data model from scratch looks trivial, but it typically takes more time and effort than most people think. Remember that good models are abstractions of component state and are often capable of representing more than one type of component. For example, the BoundedRangeModel serves the JSlider, JProgressBar, and JScrollBar components. In addition, models are responsible for storing event listeners, handling synchronization issues, and firing property change events to the components that use them. The ability to come up with useful, general models is one of the hallmarks of the experienced API designer.

A great deal of time was spent in creating the individual models for the Swing components. And because they are central to the functionality of the Swing components, you can be assured that they're well tested. For example, with the jog shuttle example (shown later in this chapter), we decided to reuse the BoundedRangeModel. This model does an excellent job with any component that contains a value within a closed range. Chances are that there might already be a model that meets your needs, and you can either reuse or extend it to your liking.

Table 28-4 summarizes the Swing component models that we cover in this book. This should give you a good feel for whether a certain data model can be reused or extended in your own component. For an example of a component built with an existing model, take a look at Chapter 16.

Table 28-4. Swing models

Model	Chapter	Description
ButtonModel	5	Holds the state of a button (like JButton), including its value and whether it is enabled, armed, selected, or pressed; supports "rollover" images
BoundedRangeModel	6	Holds an int value that can vary between fixed maximum and minimum limits; used for JSlider, JProgressBar, JScrollBar, and their relatives

Table 28-4. Swing models (continued)

Model	Chapter	Description
ComboBoxModel	7	Holds the elements of a list and a single selected element; used for JComboBox
Document	20	Holds the content (i.e., text) of a document that might be displayed in an editor; used by the text components
ListModel	7	Holds the elements of a list (as in a JList)
ListSelectionModel	7	Holds one or more elements selected from a list
SingleSelectionModel	14	Holds an index into an array of possible selections; used by JMenuBar and JPopupMenu
TableModel	15	Holds a two-dimensional array of data; the basis for JTable
TableColumnModel	15	Controls the manipulation of columns in a table
TreeModel	17	Holds items that can be displayed with branches; used by JTree
TreeSelectionModel	17	Holds one or more elements selected from a tree

Decide on properties and create the model interface

This is the fun part. You should decide which properties will be located in the model and how to access them. Properties can be read/write, read-only, or write-only. They can be any type of object or primitive data type. Also, according to the JavaBeans standard, properties can be indexed as well as bound or constrained. For an explanation of these qualifiers, see Table 28-5.

Table 28-5. Property types

Property type	Description
Bound	The property must send a PropertyChangeEvent to all registered listeners when it changes state.
Indexed	The property is an array of objects or values. Accessors must provide an index to determine which element they want to set or retrieve.
Constrained	The property must fire a VetoableChangeEvent to all registered listeners before it changes state. Any one listener is allowed to veto the state change, in which case the original property state is preserved.

As you are probably aware, there are three types of methods that you will commonly use to interact with object properties: "get," "set," and "is." You use the "get" accessor to retrieve an object or primitive property (for readability, boolean properties usually use "is" rather than "get") and the "set" mutator to alter the value. The JavaBeans standard states that property accessors should adhere to the method signatures shown in Table 28-6. The *PropertyType* in the table should reflect the object or primitive type of the property.

Table 28-6. Method signatures for property accessors

Type	"get" accessor	"set" mutator	"is" accessor
Standard	*PropertyType* getProperty( )	void setProperty(*PropertyType*)	boolean isProperty( )
Indexed	*PropertyType* getProperty(int)	void setProperty(int, *PropertyType*)	boolean isProperty(int)

The interface for the model should contain only the appropriate accessor methods for each of the properties you decide on. This ensures that the access rights are enforced in whatever implementation of the model is provided. You should also include methods to add, remove, and enumerate the relevant ChangeEvent or PropertyChangeEvent listeners from your model. It is *not* necessary to include a method to actually fire off a change event. Although this behavior is implicitly part of the implementing classes, it has no place in the interface itself. The easy way to provide it is discussed below.

Here is the interface for the SimpleModel class we develop later:

```
//  SimpleModelInteface.java
//
import javax.swing.*;
import javax.swing.event.*;

public interface SimpleModelInterface
{
    public int getValue( );
    public void setValue(int v);

    public boolean isActivated( );
    public void setActivated(boolean b);

    public void addChangeListener(ChangeListener l);
    public void removeChangeListener(ChangeListener l);
    public ChangeListener[] getChangeListeners( );
}
```

Send events when bound properties change

This is critical. Components and UI-delegate objects are intrinsically linked and must know immediately when any bound or constrained property in the model has changed state. For example, with the ButtonModel, if a button is disabled, the component needs to know immediately that the button cannot be pressed. In addition, the UI delegate needs to know immediately that the button should be grayed on the screen. Both objects can be notified by firing an event that describes the change in state of the bound model property.

Depending on how many changes you intend to send at any given time, you can use either a PropertyChangeEvent or a ChangeEvent to signal a change to a model property. PropertyChangeEvent is the more informative event that is used with JavaBeans components; it describes the source object of the change as well as the name of the property and its old and new state. ChangeEvent, on the other hand, merely flags that a change has taken place. The only data bundled with a ChangeEvent object is the source object. The former is more descriptive and does not require the listener to request the current property state from the model. The latter is more useful if many change events can be fired in a short amount of time and if the recipients typically need to look at the overall model state anyway. (It would be shortsighted to think that your code was more efficient because you saved the effort of building a detailed PropertyChangeEvent if each recipient of the event then had to look up that specific information!)

As we mentioned earlier, this means that you must also have addPropertyChange-Listener( ) and removePropertyChangeListener( ) methods or addChangeListener( ) and removeChangeListener( ) methods to maintain a list of event subscribers, depending on the type of change event you intend to support. These method signatures are typically given in the model interface. You'll also need a protected method that fires the change events to all registered listeners; this is provided in the model. For new models it makes sense to define the accessor method to return the list of registered listeners (getChangeListeners( ) in our example above) as part of the interface. This has not been done for existing Swing model interfaces because it would have broken backward compatibility with third-party implementations of those interfaces written before the accessors were recognized as a standard and useful part of the models.

Reuse the EventListenerList class

If you look closely through the otherwise mundane javax.swing.event package, you might find a surprise waiting for you: the EventListenerList class. This handy class allows you to maintain a list of generic event listeners that you can retrieve at any time. In order to use it, simply declare an EventListenerList object in your model and have each of your event subscription methods call methods associated with the EventListenerList:

```
EventListenerList theList = new EventListenerList( );

public void addChangeListener(ChangeListener l) {
    theList.add(ChangeListener.class, l);
}

public void removeChangeListener(ChangeListener l) {
    theList.remove(ChangeListener.class, l);
}
```

When you need to retrieve the listener list to fire a ChangeEvent, you can do so with the following code:

```
ChangeEvent theEvent;

protected void fireStateChanged( ) {
```

```
        Object[] list = theList.getListenerList();
        for (int index = list.length-2; index >= 0; index -= 2) {
            if (list[index]==ChangeListener.class) {
                if (theEvent == null)
                    theEvent = new ChangeEvent(this);
                ((ChangeListener)list[index+1]).stateChanged(theEvent);
            }
        }
    }
```

There are a couple curious features about this code worth explaining. `EventListenerList` is intended to store all listener registrations for a particular component. Because objects might be registered more than once as listeners for different kinds of events (through different interfaces), the list needs to keep track of both the interface under which the listener was registered and the reference to the listener itself. It does this by storing pairs of entries in the array. Even-numbered subscripts contain the interface under which a listener has been registered, and the following subscript contains the reference to the listener itself—hence, the loop that checks for the proper listener class before invoking the method on the associated listener. Because the even subscripts are known to contain specific interface references, a fast equality check (==) can be used instead of the more expensive `instanceof` operator.

Changing this method to handle the more robust `PropertyChangeEvent` is simply a matter of adding three parameters to the method signature, which are used in instantiating the event object.

Don't put component properties in the model

Model properties define the state data of a component type; component properties typically define unique characteristics of a specific component—including the display format. Be sure not to confuse the two. While accessors for model properties are available at the component level, they are delegated to corresponding methods in the model. Clients of the component can either call the component's accessors for model properties or use the model itself. Display properties, on the other hand, exist only at the component level. Hence, it is important that component properties stay in the component and don't creep into the model.

An example might better explain the differences. The `minimum`, `maximum`, and `value` properties apply to all bounded-range components, including `JScrollBar` and `JProgressBar`. Furthermore, these properties relate to data values, not display. For these reasons, they make sense as properties of the data model that all bounded-range components use. Major and minor tick marks, as well as labels, are specific to the `JSlider` object and how it displays itself. They serve better as component properties.

Implement the model

Finally, complete the model by implementing the model interface. This example shows a model that can be used as a reference. (We don't use this model for the JogShuttle component we develop later.)

```java
//  SimpleModel.java
//
import javax.swing.*;
import javax.swing.event.*;

public class SimpleModel implements SimpleModelInterface
{
    protected transient ChangeEvent changeEvent = null;
    protected EventListenerList listenerList = new EventListenerList();

    private int value = 0;
    private boolean activated = false;

    public SimpleModel() { }
    public SimpleModel(int v) { value = v; }
    public SimpleModel(boolean b) { activated = b; }
    public SimpleModel(int v, boolean b) {
        value = v;
        activated = b;
    }

    public int getValue() { return value; }

    public synchronized void setValue(int v) {
        if (v != value) {
            value = v;
            fireChange();
        }
    }

    public boolean isActivated() { return activated; }

    public synchronized void setActivated(boolean b) {
        if (b != activated) {
            activated = b;
            fireChange();
        }
    }

    public void addChangeListener(ChangeListener l) {
        listenerList.add(ChangeListener.class, l);
    }

    public void removeChangeListener(ChangeListener l) {
        listenerList.remove(ChangeListener.class, l);
    }
```

```
    public ChangeListener[] getChangeListeners( ) {
        return (ChangeListener[])listenerList.getListeners(ChangeListener.class);
    }

    protected void fireChange( )
    {
        Object[] listeners = listenerList.getListenerList();
        for (int i = listeners.length - 2; i >= 0; i -=2 ) {
            if (listeners[i] == ChangeListener.class) {
                if (changeEvent == null) {
                    changeEvent = new ChangeEvent(this);
                }
                ((ChangeListener)listeners[i+1]).stateChanged(changeEvent);
            }
        }
    }

    public String toString( )  {
        String modelString = "value=" + getValue( ) + ", " +
            "activated=" + isActivated( );
        return getClass( ).getName( ) + "[" + modelString + "]";
    }
}
```

The UI Delegate

Once you've found or created the right model, you need to create a UI delegate for
your component. Because your UI will likely be implemented by different classes in
different L&Fs, you first create a simple abstract superclass that defines the *type* of
the UI delegate. As noted below, this class is often empty.

Create an abstract type class

Start by creating an abstract superclass to be shared by all L&F implementations of
your new UI. This extends the abstract javax.swing.plaf.ComponentUI class. If there
are any new methods that should be provided by all implementations of the UI,
define them as abstract in this superclass. (This requires subclasses to implement
them.) In simple cases, there are no such methods needed; if you look at the Swing
source code, you'll see that many of the UI delegate superclasses are completely
empty. They extend ComponentUI and thus require subclasses to flesh out its abstract
methods, but add nothing else. The new class, even if empty, does define a new type
for use in parameter and variable declarations. Remember, Java's all about type
safety!

One good thing to put in the "empty" superclass is the string constant that identifies
this kind of UI for the UIManager: the UI class ID. This way, the programmers of components and delegates won't have to try to remember exactly how this string was
spelled or capitalized, reducing the opportunity for mistakes.

```
// JogShuttleUI.java
//
import javax.swing.plaf.*;

public abstract class JogShuttleUI extends ComponentUI {
    public static final String UI_CLASS_ID = "JogShuttleUI";
}
```

In our example, the standard implementation of the UI is placed in a file called *Basic-JogShuttleUI.java*.

You must implement a paint method

In the UI-delegate object (`BasicJogShuttleUI` in our example), the `paint( )` method is responsible for performing the actual rendering of the component. The `paint( )` method takes two parameters: a reference to the component needing to be drawn and a `Graphics` context with which it can draw the component:

```
public void paint(Graphics g, JComponent c)
```

You can use the `Graphics` object to access any drawing utilities needed to render the component. In addition, the reference to the `JComponent` object lets you obtain the current model and display properties as well as any other utility methods that `JComponent` (or your specific component type) provides.

Remember that in the `paint( )` method, you are working in component coordinate space and not in container coordinate space. This means that you will be interested in the `c.getHeight( )` and `c.getWidth( )` values, which are the maximum height and width of space that has been allocated to you by the container's layout manager. You will *not* be interested in the `c.getX( )` or `c.getY( )` values. The latter values give the position of the component in the *container's* coordinate space, not the component's. Within the component coordinate space, the upper-left corner of the drawing area that you will use is (0,0).

One more caveat: remember that Swing components can take borders or insets. The size of these, however, is included in the width and height reported by the component. It's always a good idea to subtract the border or insets from the total space before drawing a component. You can adjust your perspective by implementing the following code:

```
public void paint(Graphics g, JComponent c) {

    // We don't want to paint inside of the insets or borders, so subtract them.
    Insets insets = c.getInsets( );  // Takes border into account if needed
    g.translate(insets.left, insets.top);
    int width = c.getWidth( )-insets.left-insets.right;
    int height = c.getHeight( )-insets.top-insets.bottom;

    // Do our actual painting here...
```

```
    // Restore state for the rest of the objects that need painting.
    g.translate(-insets.left, -insets.top);
}
```

Be able to resize yourself

Your component should always be able to draw itself correctly, based on its current size as dictated by the layout manager minus any insets. Recall that when the component is validated in the container's layout manager, the manager attempts to retrieve the preferred or minimum size of the component. If nothing has been set by overriding getMinimumSize( ) or getPreferredSize( ), the layout manager assigns the component an arbitrary size, based on the constraints of the layout. (Of course, even if you report preferences, they might need to be ignored due to lack of available space.)

Drawing a component (or parts of it) using a static size is asking for trouble. You should not hardcode specific widths of shapes, unless they are always one or two pixels when the component is resized. Remember that the "left" size of the insets may be different than the "right," and the "top" different from the "bottom." Above all, you should be aware that components can sometimes be called upon to fit into seemingly impossible sizes, especially during application development. While the programmer will quickly understand that this is not what's intended, the more gracefully the component can handle this, the better.

As you are creating your component, place it in various layout managers and try resizing it. Try giving the component ridiculously low (or high) widths and heights. You may not be able to make it look pretty, but be sure not to throw any unnecessary runtime exceptions to derail your user's application!

Creating the Component Itself

There are three final steps to creating a fully functioning component: deciding on properties, registering your class as a listener for relevant events, and sending events when the component's properties change.

Deciding on properties

When creating the component, you need to decide which data properties you want to make available to the programmer. Public properties usually include several from the data model and others that can be used to configure the component's display. All of these properties need to have one or more public methods that programmers can use to obtain or alter their values. (See the previous discussion on model properties for details about creating properties and naming methods.)

There are several properties that you almost always want to provide, to fit well in the Swing MVC architecture. They are shown in Table 28-7.

Table 28-7. Commonly exported properties

Property	Description
model	Data model for the component
UI	UI delegate
UIClassID	Read-only class ID string of the UI delegate; used by the `UIManager`

Unless there is a really good reason, you should always try to keep the fields that store the properties of your components private to enforce the use of accessors—even for subclasses. To see why, we should take a look at Swing buttons and the `AbstractButton` class. With this class, there are a few restrictions that we should mention:

- Only buttons that are enabled can be armed. In this case, the mutator named `setArmed()` first checks the button's enabled property to see if it is true. If it isn't, the button cannot be armed.

- You can't press the button with the `setPressed()` method unless it is armed. Therefore, the `setPressed()` method checks the `isArmed()` method to see if it returns true. If not, the button cannot be pressed.

Both of these cases demonstrate examples of a conditional mutator. In other words, if you call a mutator to set a property, there are isolated cases in which it might not succeed. It also demonstrates why you should try to avoid properties that are protected. In this case, prerequisites were needed for the mutator method to succeed and the property to be set to a specific state. If a subclass is allowed, override the accessors and ignore any prerequisites on that property; the component state could become unsynchronized, and the results could be unpredictable. Even if you know right now that there are no such cases in your own component, you should buy some insurance and plan for the future with this more JavaBeans-friendly approach.

Listening to your models

The model is an essential part of any component. If it is sending events, you need to react. Essentially, this means that you should add your component as a listener for any events that the model fires (typically, `ChangeEvent` or `PropertyChangeEvent` objects). This can be done through the `addChangeListener()` or the `addPropertyChangeListener()` method of the model.

It's always a good idea to add your component class as a listener to the model in the `setModel()` method. When doing so, be sure to also unregister yourself with any previous model to which you might have been listening. Finally, make sure a call to `setModel()` happens during the initialization phase of your component to make sure that everything is set up correctly.

When a change in the model occurs, you should probably repaint your component to reflect the new state. If you are not interested in performing extra tasks when a change event is sent to you, nor in propagating model change events to outside objects, you can probably get away with just calling repaint(). In such cases, you may even choose not to listen to the event at all, letting the UI delegate handle it for you.

Sending events when bound properties change

Other components in the outside world may be interested in knowing when properties inside your component have changed. You should decide which of your properties make sense as bound or constrained.

You can use the firePropertyChangeEvent() method of JComponent to fire off PropertyChangeEvent objects to all registered listeners. The JComponent class contains overloaded versions of these methods for all primitive data types (int, long, boolean, etc.), as well as for the Object class, which pretty much covers everything else. JComponent also contains addPropertyChangeListener() and removePropertyChangeListener() methods, as well as a selection of getPropertyChangeListeners() methods. There is a similar set of methods for vetoable property changes (to support constrained properties). This all means you don't have to worry about maintaining your own event listener list; it's taken care of for you.

Some Final Questions

Finally, before writing that component and placing it in the Swing libraries, here are some questions that you can ask yourself while customizing your component. If the answer to any of these is "Yes," then follow the instructions provided.

Do you want the component to avoid getting focus at all, or through traversal?
  Focus traversal refers to the action of pressing Tab or Shift-Tab to cycle the focus onto a component. If you want your component to avoid accepting the focus at all, set its focusable property to false. If you want it to be skipped in the focus cycle, provide a custom focus traversal policy as described at the beginning of this chapter.

Do you want your component to maintain its own focus cycle?
  In order to do this, override the isFocusCycleRoot() method of JComponent and return true. This specifies that the component traverses repeatedly through itself and each of its children, but does not leave the component tree unless focus is explicitly moved up or down the tree.

```
public boolean isFocusCycleRoot() {return true;}
```

Do you want to prevent a border from being placed around your component?
  You can override the getBorder() method to return null:

```
public Border getBorder() {return null;}
```

Are you always opaque?

Your component should correctly report its opaqueness with the isOpaque( ) method. If your component always fills in every pixel of its assigned area, override this method and return true, as follows:

```
public boolean isOpaque( ) {return true;}
```

The Jog Shuttle: a Simple Swing Component

Here is an example of a component that mimics a *jog shuttle*, which is a control found on fancier VCRs and television remote controls, and on professional film and video editing equipment. It's a dial that can be turned through multiple revolutions; turning clockwise increases the dial's value, and turning counterclockwise decreases it. The shuttle has a fixed minimum and maximum value; the range (the difference between the minimum and maximum) may be more than a single turn of the dial, though it defaults to one turn. This sounds like a job for the BoundedRangeModel, and we reuse this model rather than develop our own. However, we have created our own delegate that handles mouse events and is capable of moving the jog shuttle when the mouse is dragged over it.

The component

Here is the code for the component portion, JogShuttle. This class extends JComponent, relying on another class, JogShuttleUI, to display itself. JogShuttle implements ChangeListener so it can receive ChangeEvent notifications from the model.

```
// JogShuttle.java
//
import java.awt.*;
import java.awt.event.*;

import javax.swing.*;
import javax.swing.event.*;
import javax.swing.border.*;

public class JogShuttle extends JComponent implements ChangeListener {

    private BoundedRangeModel model;

    // The dialInsets property tells how far the dial is inset from the sunken
    // border.
    private Insets dialInsets = new Insets(3, 3, 3, 3);

    // The valuePerRevolution property tells how many units the dial takes to make a
    // complete revolution.
    private int valuePerRevolution;

    // Constructors
    public JogShuttle( ) {
```

```
        init(new DefaultBoundedRangeModel( ));
    }

    public JogShuttle(BoundedRangeModel m) {
        init(m);
    }

    public JogShuttle(int min, int max, int value) {
        init(new DefaultBoundedRangeModel(value, 1, min, max));
    }

    protected void init(BoundedRangeModel m) {
        setModel(m);
        valuePerRevolution = m.getMaximum( ) - m.getMinimum( );
        setMinimumSize(new Dimension(80, 80));
        setPreferredSize(new Dimension(80, 80));
        updateUI( );
    }

    public void setUI(JogShuttleUI ui) {super.setUI(ui);}

    public void updateUI( ) {
      setUI((JogShuttleUI)UIManager.getUI(this));
      invalidate( );
    }

    public String getUIClassID( ) {
        return JogShuttleUI.UI_CLASS_ID;
    }

    public void setModel(BoundedRangeModel m) {
        BoundedRangeModel old = model;
        if (old != null)
            old.removeChangeListener(this);

        if (m == null)
            model = new DefaultBoundedRangeModel( );
        else
            model = m;
        model.addChangeListener(this);

        firePropertyChange("model", old, model);
    }

    public BoundedRangeModel getModel( ) {
        return model;
    }

    // Methods
    public void resetToMinimum( ) {model.setValue(model.getMinimum( ));}

    public void resetToMaximum( ) {model.setValue(model.getMaximum( ));}

    public void stateChanged(ChangeEvent e) {repaint( );}
```

```java
    // Accessors and mutators
    public int getMinimum( ) {return model.getMinimum( );}

    public void setMinimum(int m) {
        int old = getMinimum( );
        if (m != old) {
            model.setMinimum(m);
            firePropertyChange("minimum", old, m);
        }
    }

    public int getMaximum( ) {return model.getMaximum( );}

    public void setMaximum(int m) {
        int old = getMaximum( );
        if (m != old) {
            model.setMaximum(m);
            firePropertyChange("maximum", old, m);
        }
    }

    public int getValue( ) {return model.getValue( );}

    public void setValue(int v) {
        int old = getValue( );
        if (v != old) {
            model.setValue(v);
            firePropertyChange("value", old, v);
        }
    }


    // Display-specific properties
    public int getValuePerRevolution( ) {return valuePerRevolution;}

    public void setValuePerRevolution(int v) {
        int old = getValuePerRevolution( );
        if (v != old) {
            valuePerRevolution = v;
            firePropertyChange("valuePerRevolution", old, v);
        }
        repaint( );
    }

    public void setDialInsets(Insets i) {dialInsets = i;}

    public void setDialInsets(int top, int left, int bottom, int right) {
        dialInsets = new Insets(top, left, bottom, right);
    }

    public Insets getDialInsets( ) {return dialInsets;}
}
```

The component itself is very simple. It provides several constructors, offering the programmer different ways to set up the data model, which is an instance of BoundedRangeModel. You can set the minimum, maximum, and initial values for the jog shuttle in the constructor, or provide them afterwards using the mutator methods setMinimum( ), setMaximum( ), and setValue( ). Regardless of which constructor you call, most of the work is done by the init( ) method, which registers the JogShuttle as a listener for the model's ChangeEvent notifications, sets its minimum and preferred sizes, and calls updateUI( ) to install the appropriate user interface.

Most of the JogShuttle code consists of methods that support various properties. Accessors for the model properties, like getMinimum( ), simply delegate to the equivalent accessor in the model itself. Other properties, like valuePerRevolution, are display-specific and are maintained directly by the JogShuttle class. (The amount the value changes when the shuttle turns through one revolution has a lot to do with how you display the shuttle and how you interpret mouse events, but nothing to do with the actual data that the component represents.) The user interface object (which we'll discuss below) queries these properties to find out how to paint itself.

Of course, the JogShuttle needs to inform the outside world of changes to its state— a component that never tells anyone that something has changed isn't very useful. To keep the outside world informed, we have made several of our properties bound properties. The bound properties include minimum, maximum, and value, plus a few of the others. JComponent handles event-listener registration for us. The mutator methods for the bound properties fire PropertyChangeEvent notifications to any event listeners. Of course, if some undisciplined code makes changes to the model directly, these notifications won't occur, so that code had better be *listening* to the model directly, too. To resolve this issue would require adding code to JogShuttle to receive events from the model and pass them on to its own listeners; it wouldn't be enough to just eliminate public access to the getModel( ) method because there's a constructor that takes a model as input, and there is no way to prevent other code from keeping references to that model.

One other method worth looking at is stateChanged( ). This method is called whenever the model issues a ChangeEvent, meaning that one of the model properties has changed. All we do upon receiving this notification is call repaint( ), which lets the repaint manager schedule a call to the user interface's paint( ) method, redrawing the shuttle. This may seem roundabout. The UI delegate handles some mouse events, figures out how to change the shuttle's value, and informs the model of the change; in turn, the model generates a change event, and the component receives the event and calls the repaint manager to tell the component's UI delegate to redraw itself. It is important to notice that this roundabout path guarantees that everyone is properly informed of the component's state, that everyone can perform their assigned task, and furthermore, that the repaint operation is scheduled by the repaint manager, so it occurs on the right thread and won't interfere with other event processing.

The UI delegate

BasicJogShuttleUI is our "delegate" or "user interface" class, and therefore extends JogShuttleUI and consequently ComponentUI. It is responsible for painting the shuttle and interpreting the user's mouse actions, and so implements the MouseListener and MouseMotionListener interfaces. Although this requires a fair amount of code, it is a fundamentally simple class:

```
// BasicJogShuttleUI.java
//
import java.awt.*;
import java.awt.event.*;

import javax.swing.*;
import javax.swing.plaf.*;
import javax.swing.border.*;

public class BasicJogShuttleUI extends JogShuttleUI
    implements MouseListener, MouseMotionListener
{
    private static final int KNOB_DISPLACEMENT = 3;
    private static final int FINGER_SLOT_DISPLACEMENT = 15;

    private double lastAngle;  // Used to track mouse drags

    public static ComponentUI createUI(JComponent c) {
        return new BasicJogShuttleUI();
    }

    public void installUI(JComponent c) {
        JogShuttle shuttle = (JogShuttle)c;
        shuttle.addMouseListener(this);
        shuttle.addMouseMotionListener(this);
    }

    public void uninstallUI(JComponent c) {
        JogShuttle shuttle = (JogShuttle)c;
        shuttle.removeMouseListener(this);
        shuttle.removeMouseMotionListener(this);
    }

    public void paint(Graphics g, JComponent c) {
        // We don't want to paint inside the insets or borders.
        Insets insets = c.getInsets();
        g.translate(insets.left, insets.top);
        int width = c.getWidth() - insets.left - insets.right;
        int height = c.getHeight() - insets.top - insets.bottom;

        // Draw the outside circle.
        g.setColor(c.getForeground());
        g.fillOval(0, 0, width, height);
```

```
        Insets d = ((JogShuttle)c).getDialInsets();
        int value = ((JogShuttle)c).getValue();
        int valuePerRevolution = ((JogShuttle)c).getValuePerRevolution();

        // Draw the edge of the dial.
        g.setColor(Color.darkGray);
        g.fillOval(d.left, d.top, width-(d.right*2), height-(d.bottom*2));

        // Draw the inside of the dial.
        g.setColor(Color.gray);
        g.fillOval(d.left + KNOB_DISPLACEMENT,
                   d.top + KNOB_DISPLACEMENT,
                   width - (d.right + d.left) - KNOB_DISPLACEMENT * 2,
                   height - (d.bottom + d.top) - KNOB_DISPLACEMENT * 2);

        // Draw the finger slot.
        drawFingerSlot(g, c, value, width, height, valuePerRevolution,
                FINGER_SLOT_DISPLACEMENT - 1,
                (double)(width/2) - d.right - FINGER_SLOT_DISPLACEMENT,
                (double)(height/2) - d.bottom - FINGER_SLOT_DISPLACEMENT);

        g.translate(-insets.left, -insets.top);
    }

    private void drawFingerSlot(Graphics g, JComponent c, int value,
        int width, int height, int valuePerRevolution, int size,
        double xradius, double yradius) {

        int currentPosition = value % valuePerRevolution;

        // Obtain the current angle in radians.
        double angle = ((double)currentPosition / valuePerRevolution) *
                        java.lang.Math.PI * 2;

        // Obtain the x and y coordinates of the finger slot, with the minimum value
        // at twelve o'clock.
        angle -= (java.lang.Math.PI / 2);
        int xPosition = (int) (xradius * java.lang.Math.sin(angle));
        int yPosition = (int) (yradius * java.lang.Math.cos(angle));
        xPosition = (width / 2) - xPosition;
        yPosition = (height / 2) + yPosition;

        // Draw the finger slot with a crescent shadow on the top left.
        g.setColor(Color.darkGray);
        g.fillOval(xPosition-(size/2), yPosition-(size/2), size, size);
        g.setColor(Color.lightGray);
        g.fillOval(xPosition-(size/2) + 1, yPosition - (size/2) + 1,
                size - 1, size - 1);

    }

    // Figure out angle at which a mouse event occurred with respect to the
    // center of the component for intuitive dial dragging.
    protected double calculateAngle(MouseEvent e) {
```

```
        int x = e.getX() - ((JComponent)e.getSource()).getWidth() / 2;
        int y = -e.getY() + ((JComponent)e.getSource()).getHeight() / 2;
        if (x == 0) {  // Handle case where math would blow up.
            if (y == 0) {
                return lastAngle;   // Can't tell...
            }
            if (y > 0) {
                return Math.PI / 2;
            }
            return -Math.PI / 2;
        }
        return Math.atan((double)y / (double)x);
    }

    public void mousePressed(MouseEvent e) { lastAngle = calculateAngle(e); }
    public void mouseReleased(MouseEvent e) { }
    public void mouseClicked(MouseEvent e) { }
    public void mouseEntered(MouseEvent e) { }
    public void mouseExited(MouseEvent e) { }

    // Figure out the change in angle over which the user has dragged,
    // expressed as a fraction of a revolution.
    public double angleDragged(MouseEvent e) {
        double newAngle = calculateAngle(e);
        double change = (lastAngle - newAngle) / Math.PI;
        if (Math.abs(change) > 0.5) {   // Handle crossing origin.
            if (change < 0.0) {
                change += 1.0;
            } else {
                change -= 1.0;
            }
        }

        lastAngle = newAngle;
        return change;
    }

    public void mouseDragged(MouseEvent e) {
        JogShuttle theShuttle = (JogShuttle)e.getComponent();
        theShuttle.setValue(theShuttle.getValue() +
            (int)(angleDragged(e) * theShuttle.getValuePerRevolution()));
    }

    public void mouseMoved(MouseEvent e) { }
}
```

BasicJogShuttleUI starts by overriding several methods of ComponentUI. createUI() is a simple static method that returns a new instance of our UI object. installUI() registers our UI object as a listener for mouse events from its component (the JogShuttle). uninstallUI() does the opposite: it unregisters the UI as a listener for mouse events.

Most of the code is in the paint( ) method and its helper, drawFingerSlot( ), and the event handlers that translate mouse gestures into a sense of the angle through which the user has tried to turn the dial. paint( ) draws the jog shuttle on the screen. Its second argument, c, is the component that we're drawing—in this case, an instance of JogShuttle. The paint( ) method is careful to ask the shuttle for all the information it needs without making any assumptions about what it might find. (In turn, JogShuttle delegates many of these requests to the model.)

We handle input using mousePressed( ) to store the angle (relative to the center of the dial) at which a drag starts. Then mouseDragged( ) figures out the angle of the new mouse position and what fraction of a revolution this move represents. It then calls setValue( ) to inform the shuttle (and hence, the model) of its new value.

A Toy Using the Shuttle

Here is a short application that demonstrates the JogShuttle component. We've mimicked a simple toy that lets you doodle on the screen by manipulating two dials. This example also demonstrates how easy it is to work with JComponent.

```
//  Sketch.java
//
import java.awt.*;
import java.awt.event.*;
import java.beans.*;
import java.util.*;

import javax.swing.*;
import javax.swing.border.*;

public class Sketch extends JPanel
    implements PropertyChangeListener, ActionListener
{
    JogShuttle shuttle1;
    JogShuttle shuttle2;
    JPanel board;
    JButton clear;

    int lastX, lastY;  // Keep track of the last point we drew.

    public Sketch( ) {
        super(true);

        setLayout(new BorderLayout( ));
        board = new JPanel(true);
        board.setPreferredSize(new Dimension(300, 300));
        board.setBorder(new LineBorder(Color.black, 5));

        clear = new JButton("Clear Drawing Area");
        clear.addActionListener(this);

        shuttle1 = new JogShuttle(0, 300, 150);
        lastX = shuttle1.getValue( );
```

```
        shuttle2 = new JogShuttle(0, 300, 150);
        lastY = shuttle2.getValue();

        shuttle1.setValuePerRevolution(100);
        shuttle2.setValuePerRevolution(100);

        shuttle1.addPropertyChangeListener(this);
        shuttle2.addPropertyChangeListener(this);

        shuttle1.setBorder(new BevelBorder(BevelBorder.RAISED));
        shuttle2.setBorder(new BevelBorder(BevelBorder.RAISED));

        add(board, BorderLayout.NORTH);
        add(shuttle1, BorderLayout.WEST);
        add(clear, BorderLayout.CENTER);
        add(shuttle2, BorderLayout.EAST);
    }

    public void propertyChange(PropertyChangeEvent e) {
        if (e.getPropertyName() == "value") {
            Graphics g = board.getGraphics();
            g.setColor(getForeground());
            g.drawLine(lastX, lastY,
                        shuttle1.getValue(), shuttle2.getValue());
            lastX = shuttle1.getValue();
            lastY = shuttle2.getValue();
        }
    }

    public void actionPerformed(ActionEvent e) {
        // The button must have been pressed.
        Insets insets = board.getInsets();
        Graphics g = board.getGraphics();
        g.setColor(board.getBackground());
        g.fillRect(insets.left, insets.top,
                    board.getWidth()-insets.left-insets.right,
                    board.getHeight()-insets.top-insets.bottom);
    }

    public static void main(String[] args) {
        UIManager.put(JogShuttleUI.UI_CLASS_ID, "BasicJogShuttleUI");
        Sketch s = new Sketch();
        JFrame frame = new JFrame("Sample Sketch Application");
        frame.setDefaultCloseOperation(JFrame.EXIT_ON_CLOSE);
        frame.setContentPane(s);
        frame.pack();
        frame.setVisible(true);
    }
}
```

There's really nothing surprising (except that you might suddenly wish you had two
mice when you run the program). The main() method calls UIManager.put() to tell
the interface manager about the existence of our new user interface. Whenever a
component asks for a UI with a class ID "JogShuttleID", the UI manager looks for a

class named `BasicJogShuttleUI`, creates an instance of that class, and uses that class to provide the user interface. Having registered the `JogShuttleUI`, we can then create our shuttles, register ourselves as a property change listener, and place the shuttles in a `JPanel` with a `BorderLayout`. Our property change method simply checks which property changed; if the `value` property changed, we read the current value of both shuttles, interpret them as a pair of coordinates, and draw a line from the previous location to the new point. Figure 28-12 shows what our toy looks like.

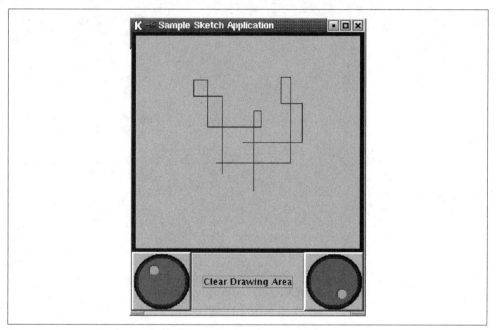

Figure 28-12. The Sketch application with two jog shuttles

Look-and-Feel Resources

Table A-1 shows a complete list of the component UI resources (with the resource name and its expected value type) defined by BasicLookAndFeel. Application-wide changes can be made to these properties using UIManager.put(). For example, the following line would cause all JButtons instantiated after this call to be created with a background color of black:

```
UIManager.put("Button.background", Color.black);
```

Alternately, a custom L&F typically defines values for many of these properties in its initComponentDefaults() method. In this case, most resource values should be tagged as UIResources. For more information, see Chapter 26.

Table A-1. Swing PLAF resources

Resource name	Type
AuditoryCues.cuelist	Array of cue names
AuditoryCues.allAuditoryCues	Array of cue names
AuditoryCues.noAuditoryCues	Array containing "mute"
AutitoryCues.playlist	null (override to give cues)
Button.background	Color
Button.border	Border
Button.darkShadow	Color
Button.font	Font
Button.focusInputMap	InputMap
Button.foreground	Color
Button.highlight	Color
Button.light	Color
Button.margin	Insets
Button.shadow	Color

Resource name	Type
Button.textIconGap	Integer
Button.textShiftOffset	Integer
CheckBox.background	Color
CheckBox.border	Border
CheckBox.focusInputmap	InputMap
CheckBox.font	Font
CheckBox.foreground	Color
CheckBox.icon	Icon
CheckBox.margin	Insets
CheckBox.textIconGap	Integer
CheckBox.textShiftOffset	Integer
CheckBoxMenuItem.acceleratorFont	Font
CheckBoxMenuItem.acceleratorForeground	Color
CheckBoxMenuItem.acceleratorSelectionForeground	Color
CheckBoxMenuItem.arrowIcon	Icon
CheckBoxMenuItem.background	Color
CheckBoxMenuItem.border	Border
CheckBoxMenuItem.borderPainted	Boolean
CheckBoxMenuItem.checkIcon	Icon
CheckBoxMenuItem.commandSound	null
CheckBoxMenuItem.disabledForeground	Color
CheckBoxMenuItem.font	Font
CheckBoxMenuItem.foreground	Color
CheckBoxMenuItem.margin	Insets
CheckBoxMenuItem.selectionBackground	Color
CheckBoxMenuItem.selectionForeground	Color
ColorChooser.background	Color
ColorChooser.font	Font
ColorChooser.foreground	Color
ColorChooser.rgbRedMnemonic	Integer
ColorChooser.rgbGreenMnemonic	Integer
ColorChooser.rgbBlueMnemonic	Integer
ColorChooser.selectedColorBorder	Border
ColorChooser.swatchesSwatchSize	Dimension
ColorChooser.swatchesRecentSwatchSize	Dimension
ColorChooser.swatchesDefaultRecentColor	Color

Table A-1. Swing PLAF resources (continued)

Resource name	Type
ComboBox.ancestorInputMap	InputMap
ComboBox.background	Color
ComboBox.buttonBackground	Color
ComboBox.buttonDarkShadow	Color
ComboBox.buttonHighlight	Color
ComboBox.buttonShadow	Color
ComboBox.disabledBackground	Color
ComboBox.disabledForeground	Color
ComboBox.font	Font
ComboBox.foreground	Color
ComboBox.selectionBackground	Color
ComboBox.selectionForeground	Color
Desktop.ancestorInputMap	InputMap
Desktop.background	Color
DesktopIcon.border	Border
EditorPane.background	Color
EditorPane.border	Border
EditorPane.caretBlinkRate	Integer
EditorPane.caretForeground	Color
EditorPane.font	Font
EditorPane.foreground	Color
EditorPane.inactiveForeground	Color
EditorPane.keyBindings	JTextComponent.KeyBinding[]
EditorPane.margin	Insets
EditorPane.selectionBackground	Color
EditorPane.selectionForeground	Color
FileChooser.ancestorInputMap	InputMap
FileChooser.cancelButtonMnemonic	Integer
FileChooser.detailsViewIcon	Icon
FileChooser.directoryOpenButtonMnemonic	Integer
FileChooser.helpButtonMnemonic	Integer
FileChooser.homeFolderIcon	Icon
FileChooser.listViewIcon	Icon
FileChooser.newFolderIcon	Icon
FileChooser.openButtonMnemonic	Integer
FileChooser.saveButtonMnemonic	Integer

Table A-1. Swing PLAF resources (continued)

Resource name	Type
FileChooser.upFolderIcon	Icon
FileChooser.updateButtonMnemonic	Integer
FileView.computerIcon	Icon
FileView.directoryIcon	Icon
FileView.fileIcon	Icon
FileView.floppyDriveIcon	Icon
FileView.hardDriveIcon	Icon
FormattedTextField.background	Color
FormattedTextField.border	Border
FormattedTextField.caretBlinkRate	Integer
FormattedTextField.caretForeground	Color
FormattedTextField.focusInputMap	InputMap
FormattedTextField.font	Font
FormattedTextField.foreground	Color
FormattedTextField.inactiveBackground	Color
FormattedTextField.inactiveForeground	Color
FormattedTextField.margin	Insets
FormattedTextField.selectionBackground	Color
FormattedTextField.selectionForeground	Color
InternalFrame.activeTitleBackground	Color
InternalFrame.activeTitleForeground	Color
InternalFrame.border	Border
InternalFrame.borderColor	Color
InternalFrame.borderDarkShadow	Color
InternalFrame.borderHighlight	Color
InternalFrame.borderLight	Color
InternalFrame.borderShadow	Color
InternalFrame.closeIcon	Icon
InternalFrame.closeSound	null
InternalFrame.icon	Icon
InternalFrame.iconifyIcon	Icon
InternalFrame.inactiveTitleBackground	Color
InternalFrame.inactiveTitleForeground	Color
InternalFrame.maximizeIcon	Icon
InternalFrame.maximizeSound	null
InternalFrame.minimizeIcon	Icon

Resource name	Type
InternalFrame.minimizeSound	null
InternalFrame.restoreDownSound	null
InternalFrame.restoreUpSound	null
InternalFrame.titleFont	Font
InternalFrame.windowBindings	Array of key bindings
Label.background	Color
Label.border	Border
Label.disabledForeground	Color
Label.disabledShadow	Color
Label.font	Font
Label.foreground	Color
List.background	Color
List.border	Border
List.cellRenderer	ListCellRenderer
List.focusCellHighlightBorder	Border
List.focusInputMap	InputMap
List.focusInputMap.RightToLeft	InputMap
List.font	Font
List.foreground	Color
List.selectionBackground	Color
List.selectionForeground	Color
Menu.acceleratorFont	Font
Menu.acceleratorForeground	Color
Menu.acceleratorSelectionForeground	Color
Menu.arrowIcon	Icon
Menu.background	Color
Menu.border	Border
Menu.borderPainted	Boolean
Menu.checkIcon	Icon
Menu.disabledForeground	Color
Menu.font	Font
Menu.foreground	Color
Menu.margin	Insets
Menu.menuPopupOffsetX	Integer
Menu.menuPopupOffsetY	Integer
Menu.selectionBackground	Color

Resource name	Type
Menu.selectionForeground	Color
Menu.shortcutKeys	Integer array of key masks
Menu.submenuPopupOffsetX	Integer
Menu.submenuPopupOffsetY	Integer
MenuBar.background	Color
MenuBar.border	Border
MenuBar.font	Font
MenuBar.foreground	Color
MenuBar.highlight	Color
MenuBar.shadow	Color
MenuBar.windowBindings	Array of key bindings
MenuItem.acceleratorDelimiter	String
MenuItem.acceleratorFont	Font
MenuItem.acceleratorForeground	Color
MenuItem.acceleratorSelectionForeground	Color
MenuItem.arrowIcon	Icon
MenuItem.background	Color
MenuItem.border	Border
MenuItem.borderPainted	Boolean
MenuItem.checkIcon	Icon
MenuItem.commandSound	null
MenuItem.disabledForeground	Color
MenuItem.font	Font
MenuItem.foreground	Color
MenuItem.margin	Insets
MenuItem.selectionBackground	Color
MenuItem.selectionForeground	Color
OptionPane.background	Color
OptionPane.border	Border
OptionPane.buttonAreaBorder	Border
OptionPane.buttonClickThreshold	Integer
OptionPane.errorIcon	Icon
OptionPane.errorSound	null
OptionPane.font	Font
OptionPane.foreground	Color
OptionPane.informationIcon	Icon

Resource name	Type
OptionPane.informationSound	null
OptionPane.messageAreaBorder	Border
OptionPane.messageForeground	Color
OptionPane.minimumSize	Dimension
OptionPane.questionIcon	Icon
OptionPane.questionSound	null
OptionPane.warningIcon	Icon
OptionPane.warningSound	null
OptionPane.windowbindings	Array of key bindings
Panel.background	Color
Panel.font	Font
Panel.foreground	Color
PasswordField.background	Color
PasswordField.border	Border
PasswordField.caretBlinkRate	Integer
PasswordField.caretForeground	Color
PasswordField.font	Font
PasswordField.foreground	Color
PasswordField.inactiveBackground	Color
PasswordField.inactiveForeground	Color
PasswordField.keyBindings	JTextComponent.KeyBinding[]
PasswordField.margin	Insets
PasswordField.selectionBackground	Color
PasswordField.selectionForeground	Color
PopupMenu.background	Color
PopupMenu.border	Border
PopupMenu.font	Font
PopupMenu.foreground	Color
PopupMenu.popupSound	null
PopupMenu.selectedWindowInputMapBindings	Array of key bindings
PopupMenu.selectedWindowInputMapBindings.RightToLeft	Array of key bindings
ProgressBar.background	Color
ProgressBar.border	Border
ProgressBar.cellLength	Integer
ProgressBar.cellSpacing	Integer
ProgressBar.cycleTime	Integer

Resource name	Type
ProgressBar.font	Font
ProgressBar.foreground	Color
ProgressBar.repaintInterval	Integer
ProgressBar.selectionBackground	Color
ProgressBar.selectionForeground	Color
RadioButton.background	Color
RadioButton.border	Border
RadioButton.darkShadow	Color
RadioButton.focusInputMap	InputMap
RadioButton.font	Font
RadioButton.foreground	Color
RadioButton.highlight	Color
RadioButton.icon	Icon
RadioButton.light	Color
RadioButton.margin	Insets
RadioButton.shadow	Color
RadioButton.textIconGap	Integer
RadioButton.textShiftOffset	Integer
RadioButtonMenuItem.acceleratorFont	Font
RadioButtonMenuItem.acceleratorForeground	Color
RadioButtonMenuItem.acceleratorSelectionForeground	Color
RadioButtonMenuItem.arrowIcon	Icon
RadioButtonMenuItem.background	Color
RadioButtonMenuItem.border	Border
RadioButtonMenuItem.borderPainted	Boolean
RadioButtonMenuItem.checkIcon	Icon
RadioButtonMenuItem.commandSound	null
RadioButtonMenuItem.disabledForeground	Color
RadioButtonMenuItem.font	Font
RadioButtonMenuItem.foreground	Color
RadioButtonMenuItem.margin	Insets
RadioButtonMenuItem.selectionBackground	Color
RadioButtonMenuItem.selectionForeground	Color
RootPane.defaultButtonWindowKeyBindings	Array of key bindings
ScrollBar.background	Color
ScrollBar.border	Border

Table A-1. Swing PLAF resources (continued)

Resource name	Type
ScrollBar.focusInputMap	InputMap
ScrollBar.focusInputMap.RightToLeft	InputMap
ScrollBar.foreground	Color
ScrollBar.maximumThumbSize	Dimension
ScrollBar.minimumThumbSize	Dimension
ScrollBar.thumb	Color
ScrollBar.thumbDarkShadow	Color
ScrollBar.thumbHighlight	Color
ScrollBar.thumbShadow	Color
ScrollBar.track	Color
ScrollBar.trackHighlight	Color
ScrollBar.width	Integer
ScrollPane.ancestorInputMap	InputMap
ScrollPane.background	Color
ScrollPane.border	Border
ScrollPane.font	Font
ScrollPane.foreground	Color
ScrollPane.viewportBorder	Border
Separator.background	Color
Separator.foreground	Color
Separator.highlight	Color
Separator.shadow	Color
Slider.background	Color
Slider.border	Border
Slider.focus	Color
Slider.focusInputMap	InputMap
Slider.focusInputMap.RightToLeft	InputMap
Slider.focusInsets	Insets
Slider.foreground	Color
Slider.highlight	Color
Slider.shadow	Color
Spinner.ancestorInputMap	InputMap
Spinner.arrowButtonSize	Dimension
Spinner.background	Color
Spinner.border	Border
Spinner.font	Font

Table A-1. Swing PLAF resources (continued)

Resource name	Type
Spinner.foreground	Color
SplitPane.ancestorInputMap	InputMap
SplitPane.background	Color
SplitPane.border	Border
SplitPane.darkShadow	Color
SplitPane.dividerSize	Integer
SplitPane.highlight	Color
SplitPane.shadow	Color
SplitPaneDivider.border	Border
TabbedPane.ancestorInputMap	InputMap
TabbedPane.background	Color
TabbedPane.contentBorderInsets	Insets
TabbedPane.darkShadow	Color
TabbedPane.focus	Color
TabbedPane.focusInputmap	InputMap
TabbedPane.font	Font
TabbedPane.foreground	Color
TabbedPane.highlight	Color
TabbedPane.light	Color
TabbedPane.selected	null
TabbedPane.selectedTabPadInsets	Insets
TabbedPane.shadow	Color
TabbedPane.tabAreaInsets	Insets
TabbedPane.tabInsets	Insets
TabbedPane.tabRunOverlay	Integer
TabbedPane.textIconGap	Integer
Table.ancestorInputMap	Inputmap
Table.ancestorInputMap.RightToLeft	Inputmap
Table.background	Color
Table.focusCellBackground	Color
Table.focusCellForeground	Color
Table.focusCellHighlightBorder	Border
Table.font	Font
Table.foreground	Color
Table.gridColor	Color
Table.scrollPaneBorder	Border

Table A-1. Swing PLAF resources (continued)

Resource name	Type
Table.selectionBackground	Color
Table.selectionForeground	Color
TableHeader.background	Color
TableHeader.cellBorder	Border
TableHeader.font	Font
TableHeader.foreground	Color
TextArea.background	Color
TextArea.border	Border
TextArea.caretBlinkRate	Integer
TextArea.caretForeground	Color
TextArea.font	Font
TextArea.foreground	Color
TextArea.inactiveForeground	Color
TextArea.keyBindings	JTextComponent.KeyBinding[]
TextArea.margin	Insets
TextArea.selectionBackground	Color
TextArea.selectionForeground	Color
TextField.background	Color
TextField.border	Border
TextField.caretBlinkRate	Integer
TextField.caretForeground	Color
TextField.darkShadow	Color
TextField.font	Font
TextField.foreground	Color
TextField.highlight	Color
TextField.inactiveBackground	Color
TextField.inactiveForeground	Color
TextField.keyBindings	JTextComponent.KeyBinding[]
TextField.light	Color
TextField.margin	Insets
TextField.selectionBackground	Color
TextField.selectionForeground	Color
TextField.shadow	Color
TextPane.background	Color
TextPane.border	Border
Textpane.caretBlinkRate	Integer

Table A-1. Swing PLAF resources (continued)

Resource name	Type
TextPane.caretForeground	Color
TextPane.font	Font
TextPane.foreground	Color
TextPane.inactiveForeground	Color
TextPane.keyBindings	JTextComponent.KeyBinding[]
TextPane.margin	Insets
TextPane.selectionBackground	Color
TextPane.selectionForeground	Color
TitledBorder.border	Border
TitledBorder.font	Font
TitledBorder.titleColor	Color
ToggleButton.background	Color
ToggleButton.border	Border
ToggleButton.darkShadow	Color
ToggleButton.focusInputMap	InputMap
ToggleButton.font	Font
ToggleButton.foreground	Color
ToggleButton.highlight	Color
ToggleButton.light	Color
ToggleButton.margin	Insets
ToggleButton.shadow	Color
ToggleButton.textIconGap	Integer
ToggleButton.textShiftOffset	Integer
Toolbar.ancestorInputMap	InputMap
ToolBar.background	Color
ToolBar.border	Border
ToolBar.darkShadow	Color
ToolBar.dockingBackground	Color
ToolBar.dockingForeground	Color
ToolBar.floatingBackground	Color
ToolBar.floatingForeground	Color
ToolBar.font	Font
ToolBar.foreground	Color
Toolbar.highlight	Color
Toolbar.light	Color
ToolBar.separatorSize	Dimension

Table A-1. Swing PLAF resources (continued)

Resource name	Type
ToolBar.shadow	Color
ToolTip.background	Color
ToolTip.border	Border
ToolTip.font	Font
ToolTip.foreground	Color
Tree.ancestorInputMap	InputMap
Tree.background	Color
Tree.changeSelectionWithFocus	Boolean
Tree.closedIcon	Icon
Tree.collapsedIcon	Icon
Tree.drawsFocusBorderAroundIcon	Boolean
Tree.editorBorder	Border
Tree.expandedIcon	Icon
Tree.focusInputMap	InputMap
Tree.focusInputMap.RightToLeft	InputMap
Tree.font	Font
Tree.foreground	Color
Tree.hash	Color
Tree.leafIcon	Icon
Tree.leftChildIndent	Integer
Tree.openIcon	Icon
Tree.rightChildIndent	Integer
Tree.rowHeight	Integer
Tree.scrollsOnExpand	Boolean
Tree.selectionBackground	Color
Tree.selectionBorderColor	Color
Tree.selectionForeground	Color
Tree.textbackground	Color
Tree.textForeground	Color
Viewport.background	Color
Viewport.font	Font
Viewport.foreground	Color

APPENDIX B

Component Actions

This appendix lists the various JComponent descendants and the Actions you can pull from their respective ActionMaps. If the action is bound to a keystroke via the component's InputMaps, those associations are listed for the Metal and Mac L&Fs. The Windows and Motif L&Fs are quite similar to the Metal L&F, but if you want the definitive list, you should also check out the API document on this topic (*<yourJavaDocDir>/api/javax/swing/doc-files/Key-Index.html* or the online copy of the docs (*http://java.sun.com/j2se/1.4/docs/*).

It's important to remember that there are three input maps associated with a component—one for each of three focus states. If you recall from Chapter 3, the possibilities are WHEN_FOCUSED, WHEN_ANCESTOR_OF_FOCUSED_COMPONENT, and WHEN_IN_FOCUSED_WINDOW. The titles of the tables indicate which state the table describes.

The information in this appendix is largely based on SDK 1.4, but the Mac L&F reflects the 1.3.1 release of the SDK on OS X. Some components did not exist until 1.4. Some actions are bound in 1.4 that are not bound in 1.3 (rarely vice versa, although some unbound actions did exist in 1.3 that are no longer part of 1.4). Because of this variability, we are including our Mapper application (*Mapper.java* in the utilities available on the book's web site). You can run the application, type in a class, choose the input map condition, and grab a current set of bound actions. You can also see the InputMap or the ActionMap without the associated binding if you prefer.

In Tables B-1 through B-45, you'll find key names with a -P or -R suffix, which stands for "pressed" or "released," respectively. Where you see the arrow keys (up, down, left, right), be aware that some keyboards have two sets of these keys. Either set should work with the bindings listed.

Finally, at the end of this appendix, we list the actions that were introduced as part of the auditory feedback mechanism introduced with SDK 1.4.

JButton

Table B-1. Bound JButton actions (when focused)

ActionMap entry	Metal L&F	Mac L&F
pressed	Space-P	Space-P
released	Space-R	Space-R

JCheckBox

Table B-2. Bound JCheckBox actions (when focused)

ActionMap entry	Metal L&F	Mac L&F
pressed	Space-P	Space-P
released	Space-R	Space-R

JCheckBoxMenuItem

Table B-3. Unbound JCheckBoxMenuItem action

doClick

JComboBox

Table B-4. Bound JComboBox actions (when ancestor of focused component)

ActionMap entry	Metal L&F	Mac L&F
endPassThrough	End-P	Not bound
enterPressed	Enter-P	Enter-P
hidePopup	Escape-P	Not bound
homePassThrough	Home-P	Not bound
pageDownPassThrough	Page Down-P	Not bound
pageUpPassThrough	Page Up-P	Not bound
selectNext	Down-P	Not bound
selectPrevious	Up-P	Not bound
spacePopup	Space-P	Not bound
togglePopup	Alt Down-P Alt Up-P	Not bound

JDesktopPane

Table B-5. Bound JDesktopPane actions (when ancestor of focused component)

ActionMap entry	Metal L&F	Mac L&F
close	Ctrl F4-P	Not bound
down	Down-P	Not bound
escape	Escape-P	Not bound
left	Left-P	Not bound
maximize	Ctrl F10-P	Not bound
minimize	Ctrl F9-P	Not bound
move	Ctrl F7-P	Not bound
navigateNext	Ctrl F12-P	Not bound
navigatePrevious	Ctrl+Shift F12-P	Not bound
resize	Ctrl F8-P	Not bound
restore	Ctrl F5-P	Not bound
right	Right-P	Not bound
selectNextFrame	Ctrl F6-P Ctrl+Alt F6-P Ctrl Tab-P	Not bound
selectPreviousFrame	Ctrl+Alt+Shift F6-P	Not bound
shrinkDown	Shift Down-P	Not bound
shrinkLeft	Shift Left-P	Not bound
shrinkRight	Shift Right-P	Not bound
shrinkUp	Shift Up-P	Not bound
up	Up-P	Not bound

JEditorPane

Table B-6. Bound JEditorPane actions (when focused)

ActionMap entry	Metal L&F	Mac L&F
caret-backward	Left-P	Left-P
caret-begin	Ctrl Home-P	Home-P Command Up-P
caret-begin-line	Home-P	Command Left-P
caret-begin-paragraph	Not bound	Option Up-P
caret-down	Down-P	Down-P

*This is actually stored as the ASCII DEL character (0x7F), the character sent when the Delete key is pressed.

Table B-6. Bound JEditorPane actions (when focused) (continued)

ActionMap entry	Metal L&F	Mac L&F
caret-end	Ctrl End-P	End-P Command Down-P
caret-end-line	End-P	Command Right-P
caret-end-paragraph	**Not bound**	Option Down-P
caret-forward	Right-P	Right-P
caret-next-word	Ctrl Right-P	Option Right-P
caret-previous-word	Ctrl Left-P	Option Left-P
caret-up	Up-P	Up-P
copy-to-clipboard	Ctrl C-P Copy-P	Command C-P
cut-to-clipboard	Ctrl X-P Cut-P	Command X-P
delete-next	Delete-P	Delete-P Shift Delete-P
delete-previous	Backspace*	Shift Backspace-P Backspace-P
insert-break	Enter-P	Enter-P
insert-tab	Tab-P	Tab-P
page-down	Page Down-P	Page Down-P
page-up	Page Up-P	Page Up-P
paste-from-clipboard	Ctrl V-P Paste-P	Command V-P
select-all	Ctrl A-P	Command A-P
selection-backward	Shift Left-P	Shift Left-P
selection-begin	Ctrl+Shift Home-P	Command+Shift Up-P Shift Home-P
selection-begin-line	Shift Home-P	Command Left-P Command+Shift Left-P
selection-begin-paragraph	**Not bound**	Option+Shift Up-P
selection-begin-word	**Not bound**	Option+Shift Left-P
selection-down	Shift Down-P	Shift Down-P
selection-end	Ctrl+Shift End-P	Shift End-P Command+Shift Down-P
selection-end-line	Shift End-P	Command+Shift Right-P Command Right-P

*This is actually stored as the ASCII DEL character (0x7F), the character sent when the Delete key is pressed.

Table B-6. Bound JEditorPane actions (when focused) (continued)

ActionMap entry	Metal L&F	Mac L&F
selection-end-paragraph	Not bound	Option+Shift Down-P
selection-end-word	Not bound	Option+Shift Right-P
selection-forward	Shift Right-P	Shift Right-P
selection-next-word	Ctrl+Shift Right-P	Not bound
selection-page-down	Shift Page Down-P	Shift Page Down-P
selection-page-left	Ctrl+Shift Page Up-P	Not bound
selection-page-right	Ctrl+Shift Page Down-P	Not bound
selection-page-up	Shift Page Up-P	Shift Page Up-P
selection-previous-word	Ctrl+Shift Left-P	Not bound
selection-up	Shift Up-P	Shift Up-P
toggle-componentOrientation	Ctrl+Shift O-P	Not bound
unselect	Ctrl \-P	Not bound

*This is actually stored as the ASCII DEL character (0x7F), the character sent when the Delete key is pressed.

Table B-7. JEditorPane bindings with no default actions (when focused)

ActionMap key	Metal L&F	Mac L&F
activate-link-action	Ctrl Space-P	Not present
next-link-action	Ctrl T-P	Not present
previous-link-action	Ctrl+Shift T-P	Not present

Table B-8. Unbound JEditorPane actions

beep	insert-tab
caret-begin-word	paste
caret-end-word	requestFocus
copy	select-line
cut	select-paragraph
default-typed	select-word
dump-model	set-read-only
insert-break	set-writable
insert-content	

JFormattedTextField

Table B-9. Bound JFormattedTextField actions (when focused)

ActionMap entry	Metal L&F	Mac L&F
caret-forward	Right-P	This component does not exist in the 1.3 release of the Java 2 SDK.
selection-begin-line	Shift Home-P	
cut-to-clipboard	Ctrl X-P Cut-P	
caret-backward	Left-P	
toggle-componentOrientation	Ctrl+Shift O-P	
caret-next-word	Ctrl Right-P	
delete-previous	Backspace*	
caret-previous-word	Ctrl Left-P	
unselect	Ctrl \-P	
delete-next	Delete-P	
select-all	Ctrl A-P	
selection-end-line	Shift End-P	
notify-field-accept	Enter-P	
reset-field-edit	Escape-P	
caret-end-line	End-P	
paste-from-clipboard	Ctrl V-P Paste-P	
selection-next-word	Ctrl+Shift Right-P	
caret-begin-line	Home-P	
selection-previous-word	Ctrl+Shift Left-P	
copy-to-clipboard	Copy-P Ctrl C-P	
selection-forward	Shift Right-P	
selection-backward	Shift Left-P	

*This is actually stored as the ASCII DEL character (0x7F), the character sent when the Delete key is pressed.

Table B-10. JFormattedTextField bindings with no default actions (when focused)

ActionMap Key	Metal L&F	Mac L&F
decrement	Down-P	This component does not exist in the 1.3 release of the Java 2 SDK.
increment	Up-P	

Table B-11. Unbound JFormattedTextField actions

beep	requestFocus
caret-begin	selection-begin
caret-begin-paragraph	selection-begin-paragraph
caret-begin-word	selection-begin-word
caret-down	selection-down
caret-end	selection-end
caret-end-paragraph	selection-end-paragraph
caret-end-word	selection-end-word
caret-up	selection-page-down
copy	selection-page-left
cut	selection-page-right
default-typed	selection-page-up
dump-model	selection-up
insert-break	select-line
insert-content	select-paragraph
insert-tab	select-word
page-down	set-read-only
page-up	set-writable
paste	

JInternalFrame

Table B-12. Unbound JInternalFrame actions

CheckBoxMenuItem.commandSound	InternalFrame.restoreDownSound
showSystemMenu	OptionPane.questionSound
OptionPane.errorSound	PopupMenu.popupSound
InternalFrame.maximizeSound	InternalFrame.closeSound
OptionPane.informationSound	OptionPane.warningSound
InternalFrame.restoreUpSound	RadioButtonMenuItem.commandSound
InternalFrame.minimizeSound	MenuItem.commandSound

JLabel

Nothing defined.

JList

ActionMap entry	Metal L&F	Mac L&F
clearSelection	Ctrl \-P	Not bound
copy	Copy-P Ctrl C-P	Not bound
cut	Ctrl X-P Cut-P	Not bound
paste	Ctrl V-P Paste-P	Not bound
scrollDown	Page Down-P	Page Down-P
scrollDownExtendSelection	Shift Page Down-P	Shift Page Down-P
scrollUp	Page Up-P	Page Up-P
scrollUpExtendSelection	Shift Page Up-P	Shift Page Up-P
selectAll	Ctrl /-P Ctrl A-P	Command A-P
selectFirstRow	Home-P	Home-P
selectFirstRowExtendSelection	Shift Home-P	Shift Home-P
selectLastRow	End-P	End-P
selectLastRowExtendSelection	Shift End-P	Shift End-P
selectNextColumn	Right-P	Not bound
selectNextColumnExtendSelection	Shift Right-P	Not bound
selectNextRow	Down-P	Down-P
selectNextRowExtendSelection	Shift Down-P	Shift Down-P
selectPreviousColumn	Left-P	Not bound
selectPreviousColumnExtendSelection	Shift Left-P	Not bound
selectPreviousRow	Up-P	Up-P
selectPreviousRowExtendSelection	Shift Up-P	Shift Up-P

JMenu

doClick   selectMenu

JMenuBar

Table B-15. Bound JMenuBar actions (when in focused window)

ActionMap entry	Metal L&F	Mac L&F
takeFocus	F10-P	Not bound

JMenuItem

Table B-16. Unbound JMenuItem action

doClick

JOptionPane

Table B-17. Bound JOptionPane actions (when in focused window)

ActionMap entry	Metal L&F	Mac L&F
close	Escape-P	Escape-P

JPasswordField

Table B-18. Bound JPasswordField actions (when focused)

ActionMap entry	Metal L&F	Mac L&F
caret-backward	Left-P	Left-P
caret-begin-line	Home-P	Up-P Command Left-P
caret-end-line	End-P	Down-P Command Right-P
caret-forward	Right-P	Right-P
caret-next-word	Ctrl Right-P	Option Right-P
caret-previous-word	Ctrl Left-P	Option Left-P
copy-to-clipboard	Ctrl C-P Copy-P	Command C-P
cut-to-clipboard	Cut-P Ctrl X-P	Command X-P
delete-next	Delete-P	Delete-P Shift Delete-P
delete-previous	Backspace*	Shift Backspace-P Backspace-P

*This is actually stored as the ASCII DEL character (0x7F), the character sent when the Delete key is pressed.

Table B-18. Bound JPasswordField actions (when focused) (continued)

ActionMap entry	Metal L&F	Mac L&F
notify-field-accept	Enter-P	Enter-P
paste-from-clipboard	Ctrl V-P Paste-P	Command V-P
select-all	Ctrl A-P	Command A-P
selection-backward	Shift Left-P	Shift Left-P
selection-begin-line	Shift Home-P	Shift Up-P
selection-begin-word	Not bound	Command Left-P Command+Shift Left-P
selection-end	Not bound	Option+Shift Left-P
selection-end-line	Shift End-P	Shift Down-P
selection-end-word	Not bound	Command+Shift Right-P Command Right-P
selection-forward	Shift Right-P	Option+Shift Right-P
selection-next-word	Ctrl+Shift Right-P	Not bound
selection-previous-word	Ctrl+Shift Left-P	Not bound
toggle-componentOrientation	Ctrl+Shift O-P	Not bound
unselect	Ctrl \-P	Not bound

*This is actually stored as the ASCII DEL character (0x7F), the character sent when the Delete key is pressed.

Table B-19. Unbound JPasswordField actions

beep	page-up
caret-begin	paste
caret-begin-paragraph	requestFocus
caret-begin-word	selection-begin
caret-down	selection-begin-paragraph
caret-end	selection-down
caret-end-paragraph	selection-end
caret-end-word	selection-end-paragraph
caret-up	selection-page-down
copy	selection-page-left
cut	selection-page-right
default-typed	selection-page-up
dump-model	selection-up
insert-break	select-line
insert-content	select-paragraph
insert-tab	select-word

notify-field-accept	set-read-only
page-down	set-writable

JPopupMenu

Nothing defined.

JProgressBar

Nothing defined.

JRadioButton

Table B-20. Bound JRadioButton actions (when focused)

ActionMap entry	Metal L&F	Mac L&F
pressed	Space-P	Space-P
released	Space-R	Space-R

JRadioButtonMenuItem

Table B-21. Unbound JRadioButtonMenuItem action

doClick

JRootPane

Table B-22 . Unbound JRootPane actions

press	release

JScrollBar

Table B-23. Bound JScrollBar actions (when focused)

ActionMap entry	Metal L&F	Mac L&F
positiveUnitIncrement	Down-P Right-P	Not bound
positiveBlockIncrement	Page Down-P	Not bound
negativeUnitIncrement	Left-P Up-P	Not bound

ActionMap entry	Metal L&F	Mac L&F
negativeBlockIncrement	Page Up-P	Not bound
minScroll	Home-P	Not bound
maxScroll	End-P	Not bound

JScrollPane

Table B-24. Bound JScrollPane actions (when ancestor of focused component)

ActionMap entry	Metal L&F	Mac L&F
scrollDown	Page Down-P	Page Down-P
scrollEnd	Ctrl End-P	End-P
scrollHome	Ctrl Home-P	Home-P
scrollLeft	Ctrl Page Up-P	Command Left-P
scrollRight	Ctrl Page Down-P	Command Right-P
scrollUp	Page Up-P	Page Up-P
unitScrollDown	Down-P	Down-P
unitScrollLeft	Left-P	Left-P
unitScrollRight	Right-P	Right-P
unitScrollUp	Up-P	Up-P

JSlider

Table B-25. Bound JSlider actions (when focused)

ActionMap entry	Metal L&F	Mac L&F
maxScroll	End-P	End-P
minScroll	Home-P	Home-P
negativeBlockIncrement	Ctrl Page Down-P Page Down-P	Page Down-P
negativeUnitIncrement	Down-P Left-P	Down-P Left-P
positiveBlockIncrement	Page Up-P Ctrl Page Up-P	Page Up-P
positiveUnitIncrement	Right-P Up-P	Right-P Up-P

JSpinner

Table B-26. Bound JSpinner actions (when ancestor of focused component)

ActionMap entry	Metal L&F	Mac L&F
decrement	Down-P	This component does not exist in the 1.3 release of the Java 2 SDK.
increment	Up-P	

JSplitPane

Table B-27. Bound JSplitPane actions (when ancestor of focused component)

ActionMap entry	Metal L&F	Mac L&F
negativeIncrement	Up-P Left-P	Up-P Left-P
positiveIncrement	Down-P Right-P	Down-P Right-P
selectMax	End-P	End-P
selectMin	Home-P	Home-P
startResize	F8-P	F8-P
toggleFocus	F6-P	F6-P

JTabbedPane

Table B-28. Bound JTabbedPane actions (when focused)

ActionMap entry	Metal L&F	Mac L&F
navigateDown	Down-P	Down-P
navigateLeft	Left-P	Left-P
navigateRight	Right-P	Right-P
navigateUp	Up-P	Up-P
requestFocusForVisibleComponent	Ctrl Down-P	Command Down-P

Table B-29. Bound JTabbedPane actions (when ancestor of focused component)

ActionMap entry	Metal L&F	Mac L&F
navigatePageDown	Ctrl Page Down-P	Command Page Down-P
navigatePageUp	Ctrl Page Up-P	Command Page Up-P
requestFocus	Ctrl Up-P	Command Up-P

Table B-30. Unbound JTabbedPane actions

navigateNext	scrollTabsForwardAction
navigatePrevious	setSelectedIndex
scrollTabsBackwardAction	

JTable

Table B-31. Bound JTable actions (when ancestor of focused component)

ActionMap entry	Metal L&F	Mac L&F
cancel	Escape-P	Escape-P
copy	Copy-P Ctrl C-P	**Not bound**
cut	Ctrl X-P Cut-P	**Not bound**
paste	Ctrl V-P Paste-P	**Not bound**
scrollDownChangeSelection	Page Down-P	Page Down-P
scrollDownExtendSelection	Shift Page Down-P	Shift Page Down-P
scrollLeftChangeSelection	Ctrl Page Up-P	Command Left-P
scrollLeftExtendSelection	Ctrl+Shift Page Down-P	Command+Shift Right-P
scrollRightChangeSelection	Ctrl Page Down-P	Command Right-P
scrollRightExtendSelection	Ctrl+Shift Page Up-P	Command+Shift Left-P
scrollUpChangeSelection	Page Up-P	Page Up-P
scrollUpExtendSelection	Shift Page Up-P	Shift Page Up-P
selectAll	Ctrl A-P	Command A-P
selectFirstColumn	Home-P	Home-P
selectFirstColumnExtendSelection	Shift Home-P	**Not bound**
selectFirstRow	Ctrl Home-P	Command Home-P
selectFirstRowExtendSelection	Ctrl+Shift Home-P	Shift Home-P
selectLastColumn	End-P	End-P
selectLastColumnExtendSelection	Shift End-P	**Not bound**
selectLastRow	Ctrl End-P	Command End-P
selectLastRowExtendSelection	Ctrl+Shift End-P	Shift End-P
selectNextColumn	Right-P	Right-P
selectNextColumnCell	Tab-P	Tab-P
selectNextColumnExtendSelection	Shift Right-P	Shift Right-P
selectNextRow	Down-P	Down-P
selectNextRowCell	Enter-P	Enter-P

ActionMap entry	Metal L&F	Mac L&F
selectNextRowExtendSelection	Shift Down-P	Shift Down-P
selectPreviousColumn	Left-P	Left-P
selectPreviousColumnCell	Shift Tab-P	Shift Tab-P
selectPreviousColumnExtendSelection	Shift Left-P	Shift Left-P
selectPreviousRow	Up-P	Up-P
selectPreviousRowCell	Shift Enter-P	Shift Enter-P
selectPreviousRowExtendSelection	Shift Up-P	Shift Up-P
startEditing	F2-P	F2-P

JTextArea

Table B-32. Bound JTextArea actions (when focused)

ActionMap entry	Metal L&F	Mac L&F
caret-backward	Left-P	Left-P
caret-begin	Ctrl Home-P	Home-P Command Up-P
caret-begin-line	Home-P	Command Left-P
caret-begin-paragraph	Not bound	Option Up-P
caret-down	Down-P	Down-P
caret-end	Ctrl End-P	End-P Command Down-P
caret-end-line	End-P	Command Right-P
caret-end-paragraph	**Not bound**	Option Down-P
caret-forward	Right-P	Right-P
caret-next-word	Ctrl Right-P	Option Right-P
caret-previous-word	Ctrl Left-P	Option Left-P
caret-up	Up-P	Up-P
copy-to-clipboard	Ctrl C-P Copy-P	Command C-P
cut-to-clipboard	Ctrl X-P Cut-P	Command X-P
delete-next	Delete-P	Delete-P Shift Delete-P
delete-previous	Backspace*	Shift Backspace-P Backspace-P
insert-break	Enter-P	Enter-P

*This is actually stored as the ASCII DEL character (0x7F), the character sent when the Delete key is pressed.

Table B-32. Bound JTextArea actions (when focused) (continued)

ActionMap entry	Metal L&F	Mac L&F
insert-tab	Tab-P	Tab-P
page-down	Page Down-P	Page Down-P
page-up	Page Up-P	Page Up-P
paste-from-clipboard	Ctrl V-P Paste-P	Command V-P
select-all	Ctrl A-P	Command A-P
selection-backward	Shift Left-P	Shift Left-P
selection-begin	Ctrl+Shift Home-P	Command+Shift Up-P Shift Home-P
selection-begin-line	Shift Home-P	Command Left-P Command+Shift Left-P
selection-begin-paragraph	Not bound	Option+Shift Up-P
selection-begin-word	Not bound	Option+Shift Left-P
selection-down	Shift Down-P	Shift Down-P
selection-end	Ctrl+Shift End-P	Shift End-P Command+Shift Down-P
selection-end-line	Shift End-P	Command+Shift Right-P Command Right-P
selection-end-paragraph	Not bound	Option+Shift Down-P
selection-end-word	Not bound	Option+Shift Right-P
selection-forward	Shift Right-P	Shift Right-P
selection-next-word	Ctrl+Shift Right-P	Not bound
selection-page-down	Shift Page Down-P	Shift Page Down-P
selection-page-left	Ctrl+Shift Page Up-P	Not bound
selection-page-right	Ctrl+Shift Page Down-P	Not bound
selection-page-up	Shift Page Up-P	Shift Page Up-P
selection-previous-word	Ctrl+Shift Left-P	Not bound
selection-up	Shift Up-P	Shift Up-P
toggle-componentOrientation	Ctrl+Shift O-P	Not bound
unselect	Ctrl \-P	Not bound

*This is actually stored as the ASCII DEL character (0x7F), the character sent when the Delete key is pressed.

Table B-33. JTextArea bindings with no default actions (when focused)

ActionMap key	Metal L&F	Mac L&F
activate-link-action	Ctrl Space-P	Not present
next-link-action	Ctrl T-P	Not present
previous-link-action	Ctrl+Shift T-P	Not present

Table B-34. Unbound JTextArea actions

beep	page-down
caret-begin-word	page-up
caret-end-word	paste
copy	requestFocus
cut	select-line
default-typed	select-paragraph
dump-model	select-word
insert-break	set-read-only
insert-content	set-writable
insert-tab	

JTextField

Table B-35. Bound JTextField actions (when focused)

ActionMap entry	Metal L&F	Mac L&F
caret-backward	Left-P	Left-P
caret-begin-line	Home-P	Up-P Command Left-P
caret-end-line	End-P	Down-P Command Right-P
caret-forward	Right-P	Right-P
caret-next-word	Ctrl Right-P	Option Right-P
caret-previous-word	Ctrl Left-P	Option Left-P
copy-to-clipboard	Ctrl C-P Copy-P	Command C-P
cut-to-clipboard	Cut-P Ctrl X-P	Command X-P
delete-next	Delete-P	Delete-P Shift Delete-P
delete-previous	Backspace*	Shift Backspace-P Backspace-P
notify-field-accept	Enter-P	Enter-P
paste-from-clipboard	Ctrl V-P Paste-P	Command V-P
select-all	Ctrl A-P	Command A-P
selection-backward	Shift Left-P	Shift Left-P
selection-begin	Not bound	Shift Up-P

*This is actually stored as the ASCII DEL character (0x7F), the character sent when the Delete key is pressed.

Table B-35. Bound JTextField actions (when focused) (continued)

ActionMap entry	Metal L&F	Mac L&F
selection-begin-line	Shift Home-P	Command Left-P Command+Shift Left-P
selection-begin-word	Not bound	Option+Shift Left-P
selection-end	Not bound	Shift Down-P
selection-end-line	Shift End-P	Command+Shift Right-P Command Right-P
selection-end-word	Not bound	Option+Shift Right-P
selection-forward	Shift Right-P	Shift Right-P
selection-next-word	Ctrl+Shift Right-P	Not bound
selection-previous-word	Ctrl+Shift Left-P	Not bound
toggle-componentOrientation	Ctrl+Shift O-P	Not bound
unselect	Ctrl \-P	Not bound

*This is actually stored as the ASCII DEL character (0x7F), the character sent when the Delete key is pressed.

Table B-36. Unbound JTextField actions

beep	page-down
caret-begin	page-up
caret-begin-paragraph	paste
caret-begin-word	requestFocus
caret-down	selection-begin-paragraph
caret-end	selection-down
caret-end-paragraph	selection-end-paragraph
caret-end-word	selection-page-down
caret-up	selection-page-left
copy	selection-page-right
cut	selection-page-up
default-typed	selection-up
dump-model	select-line
insert-break	select-paragraph
insert-content	select-word
insert-tab	set-read-only
notify-field-accept	set-writable

JTextPane

Table B-37. Bound JTextPane actions (when focused)

ActionMap entry	Metal L&F	Mac L&F
caret-backward	Left-P	Left-P
caret-begin	Ctrl Home-P	Home-P Command Up-P
caret-begin-line	Home-P	Command Left-P
caret-begin-paragraph	**Not bound**	Option Up-P
caret-down	Down-P	Down-P
caret-end	Ctrl End-P	End-P Command Down-P
caret-end-line	End-P	Command Right-P
caret-end-paragraph	**Not bound**	Option Down-P
caret-forward	Right-P	Right-P
caret-next-word	Ctrl Right-P	Option Right-P
caret-previous-word	Ctrl Left-P	Option Left-P
caret-up	Up-P	Up-P Up-P
copy-to-clipboard	Ctrl C-P Copy-P	Command C-P
cut-to-clipboard	Ctrl X-P Cut-P	Command X-P
delete-next	Delete-P	Delete-P Shift Delete-P
delete-previous	Backspace*	Shift Backspace-P Backspace-P
insert-break	Enter-P	Enter-P
insert-tab	Tab-P	Tab-P
page-down	Page Down-P	Page Down-P
page-up	Page Up-P	Page Up-P
paste-from-clipboard	Ctrl V-P Paste-P	Command V-P
select-all	Ctrl A-P	Command A-P
selection-backward	Shift Left-P	Shift Left-P
selection-begin	Ctrl+Shift Home-P	Command+Shift Up-P Shift Home-P
selection-begin-line	Shift Home-P	Command Left-P Command+Shift Left-P
selection-begin-paragraph	**Not bound**	Option+Shift Up-P

*This is actually stored as the ASCII DEL character (0x7F), the character sent when the Delete key is pressed.

Table B-37. Bound JTextPane actions (when focused) (continued)

ActionMap entry	Metal L&F	Mac L&F
selection-begin-word	Not bound	Option+Shift Left-P
selection-down	Shift Down-P	Shift Down-P
selection-end	Ctrl+Shift End-P	Shift End-P Command+Shift Down-P
selection-end-line	Shift End-P	Command+Shift Right-P Command Right-P
selection-end-paragraph	Not bound	Option+Shift Down-P
selection-end-word	Not bound	Option+Shift Right-P
selection-forward	Shift Right-P	Shift Right-P
selection-next-word	Ctrl+Shift Right-P	Not bound
selection-page-down	Shift Page Down-P	Shift Page Down-P
selection-page-left	Ctrl+Shift Page Up-P	Not bound
selection-page-right	Ctrl+Shift Page Down-P	Not bound
selection-page-up	Shift Page Up-P	Shift Page Up-P
selection-previous-word	Ctrl+Shift Left-P	Not bound
selection-up	Shift Up-P	Shift Up-P
toggle-componentOrientation	Ctrl+Shift O-P	Not bound
unselect	Ctrl \-P	Not bound

*This is actually stored as the ASCII DEL character (0x7F), the character sent when the Delete key is pressed.

Table B-38. JTextPane bindings with no default actions (when focused)

ActionMap key	Metal L&F	Mac L&F
activate-link-action	Ctrl Space-P	Not present
next-link-action	Ctrl T-P	Not present
previous-link-action	Ctrl+Shift T-P	Not present

Table B-39. Unbound JTextPane actions

beep	font-size-24
caret-begin-word	font-size-36
caret-end-word	font-size-48
center-justify	font-underline
copy	insert-break
cut	insert-content
default-typed	insert-tab
dump-model	left-justify
font-bold	page-down
font-family-Monospaced	page-up

Table B-39. Unbound JTextPane actions

font-family-SansSerif	paste
font-family-Serif	requestFocus
font-italic	right-justify
font-size-8	select-line
font-size-10	select-paragraph
font-size-12	select-word
font-size-14	set-read-only
font-size-16	set-writable
font-size-18	

JToggleButton

Table B-40. Bound JToggleButton actions (when focused)

ActionMap entry	Metal L&F	Mac L&F
pressed	Space-P	Space-P
released	Space-R	Space-R

JToolBar

Table B-41. Bound JToolBar actions (when ancestor of focused component)

ActionMap entry	Metal L&F	Mac L&F
navigateDown	Down-P	Down-P
navigateLeft	Left-P	Left-P
navigateRight	Right-P	Right-P
navigateUp	Up-P	Up-P

JToolTip

Nothing defined.

JTree

Table B-42. Bound JTree actions (when focused)

ActionMap entry	Metal L&F	Mac L&F
clearSelection	Ctrl \-P	Command \-P
copy	Copy-P Ctrl C-P	Not bound

ActionMap entry	Metal L&F	Mac L&F
cut	Ctrl X-P Cut-P	Not bound
extendSelection	Shift Space-P	Shift Space-P
paste	Ctrl V-P Paste-P	Not bound
scrollDownChangeLead	Ctrl Page Down-P	Command Page Down-P
scrollDownChangeSelection	Page Down-P	Page Down-P
scrollDownExtendSelection	Shift Page Down-P Ctrl+Shift Page Down-P	Shift Page Down-P Command+Shift Page Down-P
scrollLeft	Ctrl Left-P	Command Left-P
scrollRight	Ctrl Right-P	Command Right-P
scrollUpChangeLead	Ctrl Page Up-P	Command Page Up-P
scrollUpChangeSelection	Page Up-P	Page Up-P
scrollUpExtendSelection	Ctrl+Shift Page Up-P Shift Page Up-P	Command+Shift Page Up-P Shift Page Up-P
selectAll	Ctrl /-P Ctrl A-P	Command A-P
selectChild	Right-P	Right-P
selectFirst	Home-P	Home-P
selectFirstChangeLead	Ctrl Home-P	Command Home-P
selectFirstExtendSelection	Shift Home-P	Shift Home-P
selectLast	End-P	End-P
selectLastChangeLead	Ctrl End-P	Command End-P
selectLastExtendSelection	Shift End-P	Shift End-P
selectNext	Down-P	Down-P
selectNextChangeLead	Ctrl Down-P	Command Down-P
selectNextExtendSelection	Shift Down-P	Shift Down-P
selectParent	Left-P	Left-P
selectPrevious	Up-P	Up-P
selectPreviousChangeLead	Ctrl Up-P	Command Up-P
selectPreviousExtendSelection	Shift Up-P	Shift Up-P
startEditing	F2-P	F2-P
toggle	Not bound	Enter-P
toggleSelectionPreserveAnchor	Ctrl Space-P Space-P	Command Space-P Space-P

Table B-43. Bound JTree actions (when ancestor of focused component)

ActionMap entry	Metal L&F	Mac L&F
cancel	Escape-P	Escape-P

Table B-44. Unbound JTree actions

scrollLeftChangeLead	selectChildChangeLead
scrollLeftExtendSelection	selectParentChangeLead
scrollRightChangeLead	toggleSelection
scrollRightExtendSelection	

JViewport

Nothing defined.

Non-JComponent Containers

The top-level containers such as JDialog, JFrame, and JWindow—and JApplet, technically—are not descendants of JComponent. As such, they don't have their own input or action maps. Certainly, their contained components have those maps. They also all have an active JRootPane, which has a few unbound actions (see Table B-22).

This is not to say that there aren't keystrokes that affect these components—they are simply implemented using other mechanisms.

Auditory Feedback Actions

A general framework for providing auditory feedback in response to user interface actions was introduced in Version 1.4. BasicLookAndFeel (as described in Chapter 26) provides most of the support, and other L&Fs extend it in order to actually play appropriate sounds. As of SDK 1.4.1, none of the standard L&Fs turn on any sounds by default. Comments in the source code indicate that this has been delayed due to sound bugs.

The list of possible actions to which a sound can be assigned is contained in a special ActionMap managed by BasicLookAndFeel. It is protected since only subclasses are likely to need access to it. They can obtain (or create, if necessary) the map by calling getAudioActionMap( ). The keys in this map are shown in Table B-45. The values are Actions that produce appropriate sounds when they are performed. The standard L&Fs define inner AudioAction classes for this purpose.

Table B-45 . Audio actions defined by BasicLookAndFeel

CheckBoxMenuItem.commandSound	InternalFrame.closeSound
InternalFrame.maximizeSound	InternalFrame.minimizeSound
InternalFrame.restoreDownSound	InternalFrame.restoreUpSound
MenuItem.commandSound	OptionPane.errorSound
OptionPane.informationSound	OptionPane.questionSound
OptionPane.warningSound	PopupMenu.popupSound
RadioButtonMenuItem.commandSound	

Index

We'd like to hear your suggestions for improving our indexes. Send email to *index@oreilly.com*.

actionPerformed( ), 28, 30
  Action interface, 44
  AddFrameAction.java (example), 278
  AlignmentAction class, 874
  BeepAction class, 863
  BoldAction class, 874
  CopyAction class, 864
  CutAction class, 864
  DefaultKeyTypedAction class, 863
  DropTargetAutoScroller class, 966
  FontFamilyAction class, 873
  FontSizeAction class, 873
  ForegroundAction class, 873
  InsertBreakAction class, 864
  InsertContentAction class, 864
  InsertTabAction class, 864
  ItalicAction class, 874
  JComboBox class, 206
  JList class, 161
  PasteAction class, 864
  UnderlineAction class, 874
actions, 41–48, 861, 863
  AbstractAction class, 44–48
  AccessibleAction interface, 983
  Action interface, 42–44
  ActionListener interface, 28, 42
  AlignmentAction class, 873
  BeepAction class, 863
  BoldAction class, 874
  CopyAction class, 37, 864
  custom, creating, 909
  CutAction class, 864
  default, 870
  DefaultEditorKit and, 859–861
  DefaultKeyTypedAction class, 863
  disabling, 47
  examples of, 46–47, 277–284, 861,
    993–995
  FontFamilyAction class, 873
  FontSizeAction class, 873
  ForegoundAction class, 873
  for hyperlinks, 898
  InsertBreakAction class, 864
  InsertContentAction class, 864
  InsertTabAction class, 864
  ItalicAction class, 874
  JComponent class descendants
    and, 1170–1192
  for menu items/toolbars, creating, 45–47
  PasteAction class, 864
  StyledEditorKit and, 870

StyledTextAction class, 871
TextAction class, 857
UnderlineAction class, 874
actions property
  DefaultEditorKit class, 858
  EditorKit class, 855
  HTMLEditorKit class, 890
  JFormattedTextField class, 712
  JTextComponent class, 686
  JTextField class, 693
  StyledEditorKit class, 869
activateFrame( )
  DefaultDesktopManager class, 273
  DesktopManager interface, 272
active component (see focus)
active property (DropTarget), 921
ActiveValue interface, 1015, 1022
activeWindow property
    (KeyboardFocusManager), 1111
add( ), 41
  AccessibleStateSet class, 980
  ButtonGroup class, 128, 131
  DefaultMutableTreeNode class, 597
  EventListenerList class, 1092
  JComponent class, 55
  JFrame class, 247
  JLayeredPane class, 243
  JMenu class, 462, 464
  JMenuBar class, 439, 442
  JPopupMenu class, 453, 457
  JTabbedPane class, 337
  JToolBar class, 485
addAccessibleSelection( )
    (AccessibleSelection), 986
addActionForKeyStroke( ) (Keymap), 756
addActionListener( )
  AbstractButton class, 109
  ButtonModel interface, 104
  ComboBoxEditor interface, 198
  DefaultButtonModel class, 105
  JComboBox class, 204
  JFileChooser class, 376
  JTextField class, 694
  Timer class, 1083
addAdjustmentListener( ) (JScrollBar), 141
addAll( ) (AccessibleStateSet), 980
addAncestorListener( ) (Component), 76
addAttribute( )
  MutableAttributeSet interface, 770
  SimpleAttributeSet class, 773
  StyleContext class, 783

JViewport class, 330–332
  actions and, 1192
  properties table for, 331
JVM (Java virtual machine), 968–972,
  996–998
JWindow class, 251–254
  properties table for, 253
  Splash.java (example), 251

K

key bindings, 73
key selection manager, 206
keyboard
  DefaultKeyTypedAction class, 863
  functionality for, adding to
    components, 757–759
keyboard accelerators (shortcuts), 432
  JMenu objects and, 462
  menu items and, 87, 116–119, 444
  (see also keystrokes)
keyboard actions, 72, 73
  example of, 757–759
  online material for, xix
keyboard events, 48, 72–75, 755
  focus and, 70, 72
  MenuKeyEvent class, 452
  MenuKeyListener interface, 453
keyboard-driven selection, 182
KeyboardFocusManager class, 1108–1112
keyChar property
  KeyStroke class, 1093
  MenuKeyEvent class, 452
keyCode property
  KeyStroke class, 1093
  MenuKeyEvent class, 452
KeyEventDispatcher list, 1112
KeyEventPostprocessor list, 1112
Keymap interface, 734, 754–759
  properties table for, 755
keymap property (JTextComponent), 686
KeymapExample.java (example), 757
keymaps, 734, 754–759
  implementation for, 756
keys( )
  ActionMap class, 83
  InputMap class, 81
KeySelectionManager interface, 202
KeyStroke class, 444, 1093–1100
  properties table for, 1093

keystrokes, 72, 1093–1100
  mapping
    to item selections in combo
      boxes, 202
    to logical action names, 80
  (see also keyboard accelerators)
killed edits, 677

L

L&F (see look-and-feel)
label property (JPopupMenu), 456
labelFor property (JLabel), 86–87
labels, 84–94
  border around, 413
  ClockLabel.java (example), 1084
  content alignment and, 86, 88
  content position and, 87
  examples of, 87, 90, 1090
  images in, 90–92
  JLabel class, 84–94
  layered, 339
  SimpleJLabelExample.java (example), 85
  for sliders, 142, 145
labelTable property (JSlider), 145
LabelView class, 841
LAFState class, 1028
largeModel property (JTree), 585
last( ) (Segment), 825
lastDividerLocation property
  (JSplitPane), 317
lastEdit( ) (CompoundEdit), 647
lastElement( ) (DefaultListModel), 168
lastIndexOf( ) (DefaultListModel), 167
lastRow property (TableModelEvent), 515
lastVisibleIndex property (JList), 187
layer property (JInternalFrame), 264
layered labels, OverlayLayout class for
  creating, 339
layered pane, 229, 239–246
  JLayeredPane class, 239–246
  methods for, 265
LayeredHighlighter class, 751
LayeredHighlighter.LayerPainter class, 752
layeredPane property
  JApplet class, 257
  JFrame class, 247
  JInternalFrame class, 263
  JWindow class, 252

X

x property
    JComponent class, 58
    MenuDragMouseEvent class, 451
XML, custom tags and, 880
XML documents, tree displaying, 579–582

Y

y property
    JComponent class, 58
    MenuDragMouseEvent class, 451

Z

ZoneView class, 841
z-order, 17, 1124

About the Authors

Marc Loy is a senior programmer at Galileo Systems, LLC, but his day job seems to be teaching Java and Perl to various companies—including Sun Microsystems. He has played with Java since the alpha days and can't find his way back to C. In addition to teaching, he also develops Java applications of all sizes for various companies. He received his master's degree in computer science at the University of Wisconsin-Madison, and still lives in Madison with his partner, Ron Becker.

Robert Eckstein enjoys dabbling with just about anything related to computers. In fact, most of his friends agree that Robert spends far too much time in front of a computer screen. At O'Reilly, Robert mostly edits Java books, and in his spare time has been known to provide online coverage for popular conferences. Robert holds bachelor's degrees in computer science and communications from Trinity University in San Antonio, Texas. In the past, he has worked for the USAA insurance company and for Motorola's cellular software division. He now lives in Round Rock, Texas with his wife Michelle and their talking puppy, Ginger.

David Wood is a Java architect from Denver, Colorado. Formerly a member of the Sun Microsystems Java Center, Dave has spent the last several years at a number of small startup companies in the Denver area. His BS and MS degrees are in computer science from the University of Colorado. He has been involved in object-oriented design and development his entire career and has been obsessed with Java since its early days. When he's not in front of a keyboard, Dave enjoys taking advantage of the beautiful Colorado scenery while cycling, hiking, or golfing. He also enjoys spending time with his wife, Shannon (the "real" architect of the family), twin babies, Aidan and Ailie, three dogs, and two cats.

James Elliott is a senior software engineer at Berbee, with over 10 years of professional experience as a systems developer. He began cultivating his involvement and fascination with computers a decade before that, and started designing with objects well before his work environments made this convenient. He has a passion for building high-quality tools and frameworks to simplify the tasks of other developers, and loves how using Java effectively can help in that effort. After a globe-trotting childhood, Jim earned his bachelor's degree in computer science at Rensselaer Polytechnic in upstate New York and his master's at the University of Wisconsin-Madison, with some interesting stints at Bell Laboratories (in Murray Hill, birthplace of C and Unix). Although he succumbed to the allure of the real world shortly after completing his Ph.D. qualifying exams, he was happy to find interesting work in Madison, where he lives with his partner Joe Buberger and two challenging cats.

Brian Cole has been working with Java since its early days and has taught it at venues ranging from Sun Microsystems to public high school. Though his Java skills are always in high demand, he also enjoys programming in functional languages, such as Scheme. Lately, he has been doing a lot of work in XSLT. He earned a B.A. from Oberlin College and an M.S. from the University of Wisconsin-Madison. He plays the larger sizes of clarinet and saxophone in various community ensembles and hopes to find time to learn the trombone. He lives with his wife, Beth, and some smaller mammals in the suburbs of Washington, DC.

Colophon

Our look is the result of reader comments, our own experimentation, and feedback from distribution channels. Distinctive covers complement our distinctive approach to technical topics, breathing personality and life into potentially dry subjects.

The animal on the cover of *Java Swing*, Second Edition, is a spider monkey (*Ateles geoffroyi*). Most spider monkeys can be found in the forests of Central America from Southern Mexico to Panama. Almost all varieties of spider monkeys live exclusively in trees and maintain a diet of fruit and nuts.

What gives the spider monkey its name is its long limbs and tail (it sometimes resembles a spider as it moves). *A. geoffroyi*'s fur is black, brown, golden, or reddish.

Spider monkeys are social and can form groups of approximately 30 animals. They live in treetops and forage diurnally in troops often led by females, which have a more active role than males in the food-gathering process. Spider monkeys are often seen hanging by one branch or by their unusually long tails, which basically function as a fifth limb. They can even grasp objects with their tails.

When approached or threatened, spider monkeys will bark and flail wildly, which usually scares off intruders. If this tactic is unsuccessful, they will break away from their groups and retreat.

Matt Hutchinson was the production editor and copyeditor for *Java Swing*, Second Edition. Matt Hutchinson and Mary Brady proofread the book. Tatiana Apandi Diaz and Sarah Sherman provided quality control. Genevieve d'Entremont and Andrew Savikas provided production assistance. Brenda Miller updated the index from the first edition.

Hanna Dyer designed the cover of this book, based on a series design by Edie Freedman. The cover image is a 19th-century engraving from the Dover Pictorial Archive. Emma Colby produced the cover layout with QuarkXPress 4.1 using Adobe's ITC Garamond font.

David Futato designed the interior layout. The text font is Linotype Birka; the heading font is Adobe Myriad Condensed; and the code font is LucasFont's TheSans Mono Condensed. The illustrations that appear in the book were produced by Robert Romano and Jessamyn Read using Macromedia FreeHand 9 and Adobe Photoshop 6. The tip and warning icons were drawn by Christopher Bing. This colophon was written by Matt Hutchinson.

Related Titles Available from O'Reilly

Java

Ant: The Definitive Guide
Eclipse: A Java Developer's Guide
Enterprise JavaBeans, *3rd Edition*
Hardcore Java
Head First Java
Head First Servlets & JSP
Head First EJB
J2EE Design Patterns
Java and SOAP
Java & XML Data Binding
Java & XML
Java Cookbook
Java Data Objects
Java Database Best Practices
Java Enterprise Best Practices
Java Enterprise in a Nutshell, *2nd Edition*
Java Examples in a Nutshell, *3rd Edition*
Java Extreme Programming Cookbook
Java in a Nutshell, *4th Edition*
Java Management Extensions
Java Message Service
Java Network Programming, *2nd Edition*
Java NIO
Java Performance Tuning, *2nd Edition*
Java RMI
Java Security, *2nd Edition*
Java ServerPages, *2nd Edition*
Java Serlet & JSP Cookbook
Java Servlet Programming, *2nd Edition*
Java Web Services in a Nutshell
Learning Java, *2nd Edition*
Mac OS X for Java Geeks
NetBeans: The Definitive Guide
Programming Jakarta Struts
Tomcat: The Definitive Guide
WebLogic: The Definitive Guide

O'REILLY®

Our books are available at most retail and online bookstores.
To order direct: 1-800-998-9938 • *order@oreilly.com* • *www.oreilly.com*
Online editions of most O'Reilly titles are available by subscription at *safari.oreilly.com*

Keep in touch with O'Reilly

1. Download examples from our books

To find example files for a book, go to:

www.oreilly.com/catalog

select the book, and follow the "Examples" link.

2. Register your O'Reilly books

Register your book at *register.oreilly.com*

Why register your books?
Once you've registered your O'Reilly books you can:

- Win O'Reilly books, T-shirts or discount coupons in our monthly drawing.
- Get special offers available only to registered O'Reilly customers.
- Get catalogs announcing new books (US and UK only).
- Get email notification of new editions of the O'Reilly books you own.

3. Join our email lists

Sign up to get topic-specific email announcements of new books and conferences, special offers, and O'Reilly Network technology newsletters at:

elists.oreilly.com

It's easy to customize your free elists subscription so you'll get exactly the O'Reilly news you want.

4. Get the latest news, tips, and tools

www.oreilly.com

- "Top 100 Sites on the Web"—PC Magazine
- CIO Magazine's Web Business 50 Awards

Our web site contains a library of comprehensive product information (including book excerpts and tables of contents), downloadable software, background articles, interviews with technology leaders, links to relevant sites, book cover art, and more.

5. Work for O'Reilly

Check out our web site for current employment opportunities:

jobs.oreilly.com

6. Contact us

O'Reilly & Associates
1005 Gravenstein Hwy North
Sebastopol, CA 95472 USA

TEL: 707-827-7000 or 800-998-9938
(6am to 5pm PST)

FAX: 707-829-0104

order@oreilly.com
For answers to problems regarding your order or our products. To place a book order online, visit:

www.oreilly.com/order_new

catalog@oreilly.com
To request a copy of our latest catalog.

booktech@oreilly.com
For book content technical questions or corrections.

corporate@oreilly.com
For educational, library, government, and corporate sales.

proposals@oreilly.com
To submit new book proposals to our editors and product managers.

international@oreilly.com
For information about our international distributors or translation queries. For a list of our distributors outside of North America check out:

international.oreilly.com/distributors.html

adoption@oreilly.com
For information about academic use of O'Reilly books, visit:

academic.oreilly.com

POGUE PRESS™
O'REILLY®